CENSUS OF INDIA 1891

Owing to the antiquity and rarity of this book, certain pages are regrettably absent, and readability is compromised due to the blurring of the original text. If you possess any insights regarding the availability of these missing sections, kindly inform us. Your assistance is crucial in ensuring the completion of this significant work for the benefit of future generations.

CENSUS OF INDIA, 1891

BOOK-11: VOL. VI

Berar or the Hyderabad Assigned Districts

WARREN HASTINGS

GYAN

Published by

Gyan Publishing House
5, Ansari Road
Daryaganj, New Delhi-110002
Phone: 011-47034999, 9811692060
E-mail: books@gyanbooks.com

Distribution Network
gyanbooks.com
India, USA, Canada, UK, Australia

ISBN: 978-81-212-7129-5 (Set) 28 Vols. In 49 Bindings
978-81-212-6963-6 (PB) Book-11, Vol. VI

First Published, 1892

2nd Impression 2024

Printed at: Gyan Press, Delhi.

CENSUS OF INDIA 1891

CENSUS OF INDIA, 1891.

VOLUME VI.

BERAR,

OR THE

HYDERABAD ASSIGNED DISTRICTS.

BY

WARREN HASTINGS, *Captain, Indian Staff Corps,*

DEPUTY COMMISSIONER, HYDERABAD ASSIGNED DISTRICTS, AND
PROVINCIAL SUPERINTENDENT OF CENSUS OPERATIONS.

To be obtained from the Curator, Government Central Book Depôt, Akola, Berar.

CALCUTTA:
OFFICE OF THE SUPERINTENDENT OF GOVERNMENT PRINTING, INDIA.
1892.

CONTENTS.

CHAPTER VIII.

LANGUAGES.

CHAPTER IX.

BIRTHPLACE.

CHAPTER X.

CASTES.

CHAPTER XI.

OCCUPATIONS.

CHAPTER XII.

ADMINISTRATION OF THE CENSUS OPERATIONS.

TABLES.

TABLES—*continued.*

CENSUS OF INDIA, 1861.

VOLUME VI.

BERAR,

OR THE

HYDERABAD ASSIGNED DISTRICTS.

CHAPTER I.

GENERAL DESCRIPTION.

VERY few persons outside the province know where Berar is or what it is. This is not very surprising, as its existence as a separate entity dates only from 1853, and it has done nothing since to acquire any notoriety. It is essentially a rural area, a succession of fields of cotton or *jowari*, or of tracts of unculturable waste and jungle. Archæologically or historically it possesses nothing of much interest or importance; artistically or scientifically it is absolutely barren; in material and industrial concerns it is barbarous and rude. Its only claim to fame lies in the cotton market, where the name of Oomras or Oomrawattees refers in uncouth and archaic form to the chief product and the chief mart of the province. It may be as well then to explain that geographically Berar occupies a position which may be regarded as the navel of India, and that it is a slice off the northern portion of the territory of the Nizam of Hyderabad, assigned for certain specific purposes to the British Government under the Treaties of 1853 and 1861, whence is derived the official designation of the Hyderabad Assigned Districts.

The following general description is extracted from the *Berar Gazetteer*, published in 1870:—

Geographical and physical description.

Berar forms the northernmost portion of the Hyderabad State, running up from the south with a breadth gradually narrowing until an extreme point touches the Tapti river, half surrounded on the east, north, and north-west by the Central Provinces, and meeting the Khandesh district of the Bombay Presidency along a section of about 40 miles of its western border. The Gawilgarh hills, a range belonging to the Satpura mountains, form the geographical boundary of Berar on the north, with a deep indent made by the Melghat tract; on the east its frontier is marked accurately by the Wardha river down to its confluence with the Painganga, and on the south by the Painganga for about two-thirds of the frontier's length. On the west the border is merely an artificial line cutting across a broad valley from the Satpura mountains to the hills on which stands Ajanta, and proceeding southward over these hills until it turns eastward by a sharp angle near Jalna.

This Ajanta range intersects the whole province from west to east, and its steep ridge divides the interior geography into two systems. Setting aside the Melghat mountain tract as abnormal, we have two distinct sections of Berar, the *Payanghat*, or lowland country, bounded on the north by the Gawilgarh hills, and on the south by the outer scarps of the Ajanta range; and the *Balaghat* or upland country above the Ajanta ridge, sloping down southward beyond the ghâts or passes which lead up to it. So that the Payanghat is a wide valley running up eastward between this ridge and the Gawilgarh hills like a long backwater or deep bay, varying in breadth from 40 to 50 miles, and broader towards the end than at its mouth. The surface of this valley is not flat or even; it rises and descends by very long, low waves with their troughs cutting mostly north and south flowing up eastward to a point just beyond Amraoti; here this formation is broken up by a chain of low hills that run in a north-westerly direction across the plain. These hills mark a change in the country's watershed. Westward of them the main slope of the valley is towards the west, from the point where the Purna river makes almost a right angle by its sudden turn; but eastward of Amraoti the streams take an opposite direction, and their course is to the Wardha or some of its affluents.

The Payanghat valley contains all the best land in Berar; it is full of that deep rich black alluvial soil called *regar*, of almost inexhaustible fertility, and it undulates just enough to maintain a natural system of drainage, which is probably very favourable to the productive powers of the land. Here and there are barren tracts, where the hills spread out ample skirts far into the plain, covered with round stones and scrub jungles; or where a few outlying flat-topped hills, often with hummocks or humps looking like huge cairns on their crown, stand forward beyond the ranks to which they belong. But there is nothing picturesque about this broad strip of alluvial champaign country; it is very destitute of trees, except near the villages close under the hills; and besides the Purna it has hardly a perennial stream. In the early autumn it is one sheet of cultivation, and looks fresh enough, but from the beginning of the hot season, when the crops have been gathered, its generally monotonous plain is relieved by neither verdure, shade, nor water, and the landscape is desolate and depressing.

However, the aspect of the country above the passes which lead to the Balaghat is quite different. Here is the extreme northern limit of the tableland of the Deccan; the sides and summits of the outer hills are covered with low forest; from their crests the main slope of the land is southward; wide basalt downs follow each other in successive expanses of open fields sloping down to narrow channels, which carry off the water like gutters between two parts of a low roof. The trees are finer and the groves more frequent than in the valley below; water is more plentiful and nearer to the surface. This is the character of much of the Balaghat highlands in the west of Berar, where they fall southward toward the Nizam's country by gradual decline, and by a series of ridges or steppes. But the whole face of the Balaghat has no uniform feature; it stretches into downs and dales where it is most open; then it gets broken up into flat-topped hills and steep ravines; while in its eastern section the country is still more sharply accidented by a splitting up of the main hill range, which has caused a variety of low-lying plains, high plateaus, fertile bottoms, and rocky wastes.

The Melghat tract referred to here as abnormal consists of a rugged mountainous country, the hillsides and valleys forming extensive forests, and the tops stretching out into wide plateaus and open downs, the highest points of which are attained in a steep ridge on the south immediately facing the Payanghat plain. The old historic fort of Gawilgarh dominating the town of Ellichpur stands at an elevation of 3,500 feet. Behind it the plateau of Chikalda, the sanitarium of Berar, rises to some 200 feet higher; and further to the west the top of Bairat attains about 4,200. The Ajanta range on the south of Berar is of an entirely different character. The aspect is nowhere mountainous; the elevation at the highest point in the west towards Buldana does not probably exceed 2,000 feet; and, were there a good road, one might drive a team of horses from one end to the other without having to put on the break or to complain of the collar work.

The Payanghat valley itself stands at a considerable elevation above the sea, from about 800 feet on the west to 1,200 on the east, and this has to be remembered in considering the heights of the hill ranges.

Briefly, then, Berar consists of three distinct tracts—the mountainous forest region on the north, the wide plain stretching from west to east across the middle, and the more or less broken upland on the south. It will be seen in the following pages, in the consideration of the statistics furnished by the census, that the distinction between these three regions is not confined to their physical features. Between the inhabitants of the southern uplands and those of the central plain there is perhaps no very striking diversity, but the people of the Melghat differ from the rest in religion, in language, and in every aspect of social life.

Climatic conditions.

Among other influences which affect the economy of mankind, climatic conditions are not unimportant, and some description of these may be desirable. The rainfall has as yet been registered with any reliable accuracy in only a few places, and there are not sufficient data to generalise with certainty upon the character of its distribution. The following averages at the registering stations named have been furnished by the Meteorological Reporter to the Government of India:—

	Inches.
Chikalda	68·84
Makhla	72·19
Ellichpur	39·57
Amraoti	33·15
Akola	31·00
Buldana	33·81
Basim	38·62
Yeotmal	43·07
Wun	41·73

Of these stations, Chikalda has been already mentioned as occupying one of the highest plateaus of the Gawilgarh range. Makhla is another hill-top a few miles to the north-east of Chikalda. Ellichpur lies at the foot of the range. Amraoti and Akola are centrically situated between the two hill ranges towards the east and west respectively of the valley. Buldana stands on one of the most elevated plateaus of the Ajanta range at the west, and Basim is towards the centre and Yeotmal at the east of the same line of hills, at the foot of which, on the south-east, near the junction of the Wardha and Painganga rivers, lies the town of Wun. The figures quoted accordingly appear to indicate that in each of the three regions the heaviest rainfall is in the east. The rainy season of Berar is, however, that of the south-west monsoon, and it would be natural to expect that the heaviest fall, other things being equal, would be in the west. Chikalda, to the west of Makhla and at a higher elevation, should catch the heavier fall; Akola should have more than Amraoti; Buldana should have much more than Yeotmal, standing as it does at a much higher elevation and having the advantage of perhaps 125 miles in the distance from the sea; Wun, lastly, shut off by the uplands from the west and north-west, should have least of all. The explanation of this apparent contradiction may be in the possible fact that the east of Berar is more within the influence of cyclonic and other disturbances from the Bay of Bengal. Certain it is that a large proportion of the annual rainfall is frequently due to these causes. So far, however, as regards the three distinct tracts into which the province divides itself, the rainfall is consistent with what might be expected; the heaviest fall is in the Gawilgarh hills, and the lightest in the central plain. In other climatic conditions also the three tracts have marked distinctions. In the Gawilgarh hills, while the upper plateaus enjoy a moderate and equable temperature, the valleys suffer from extremes of heat in the day and of cold in the night, and are notoriously unhealthy except during the dry months of the hot season. In the plain at that season of the year the heat is excessive, and the temperatures registered at Amraoti and Akola in the months of March, April, and May are frequently the highest of the day in India. In the southern tract the temperature takes a middle place between that of the other two; it is not so hot as in the plain during the hot weather, and during the rest of the year it is not subject to the damp and the extremes of heat and cold of the valleys in the Melghat.

Area and population.

The area of Berar, according to the latest surveys, is 17,717·87 square miles. In the report of the census of 1881 it is given as 17,711, but the increase is due to corrections of measurement and not to any addition of territory.

The census was taken on the 26th February 1891, when the population was found to be 2,897,491. The census of 1881 was taken on the 17th February, and the increase of population in the interval of ten years and nine days has been 224,818, or 8·41 per cent.

Density.

The number of persons per square mile is 163; in 1881, the number was 151. Berar is more closely populated than either Scotland or Ireland. It is a little larger in area than both Denmark and Switzerland, and it is intermediate between the two in the density of its population. Of the British Colonies, Berar may be best compared with Ceylon, which is somewhat larger in area, but where the population is only a little more than three millions and the density 118. In extent of area Berar has no affinity to any other Indian province or state, but in population it is rather larger than Sindh, Kashmir, and Baroda, and somewhat smaller than Upper Burma. In density of population it cannot compare with Oudh, Bengal, the North-West Provinces, or Madras, but it approaches that of Mysore (176) and the Punjab (189). It is, however, more thickly populated than the State of Hyderabad (140) on the south, the Central Provinces (125) on the east, and the Khandesh district (134) of the Bombay Presidency on the west.

Administrative divisions.

The province is divided, for administrative purposes, into six districts and twenty-two taluks. Of the taluks, twelve comprise the central plain and nine the southern uplands, while the Melghat hill tract constitutes one in itself. Of the taluks of the plain, the four easternmost form the Amraoti district; two on the north, together with the Melghat, make up the district of Ellichpur; five in the centre and north-west compose the Akola district; the last, on the extreme west, Malkapur, belongs to the district of Buldana, which is completed by the two westernmost of the southern hill range; the three central taluks of these form the Basim district, and the remaining four in the south-east the district of Wun. The districts thus divide themselves into three northern—Amraoti, Akola, and Ellichpur; and three southern—Buldana, Basim, and Wun; and this distinction the statistics of the population will be found not infrequently to preserve.

Table I (page 2) shows the area, houses, and population of each district and of each taluk. The total population of the districts arranged in order of numbers is here reproduced. Amraoti, it will be seen, has more than twice the population of Ellichpur.

Amraoti	655,645
Akola	574,782
Buldana	481,021
Wun	471,613
Basim	398,181
Ellichpur	315,798

Arranged in order of area the districts come as follows. Wun largely exceeds all the other districts in size, while the difference between each of the latter is not very great.

	Sq. miles.
Wun	3,911·23
Basim	2,955·92
Buldana	2,808·81
Amraoti	2,759·20
Akola	2,659·39
Ellichpur	2,623·32

The density of the population in each district is shown in the adjoining statement, No. 1. Here the density in Amraoti is seen to be almost twice as great as in Ellichpur, but the average in the latter district is reduced by the abnormal Melghat taluk, which has an area of 1,649 square miles and a population of only 47,031. Eliminating the Melghat figures, the density for the remaining portion of the Ellichpur district is as high as 275.

Statement No. 1.

District.	Number of persons per square mile. 1891.	1881.	Variation since 1881.
Amraoti	237·6	208·5	+29·1
Akola	216·1	222·8	—6·7
Buldana	171·2	156·8	+14·4
Basim	134·3	121·3	+13·0
Wun	120·5	100·4	+20·1
Ellichpur	120·3	119·6	+·7

I.—Map illustrating the Density of the Population in Taluks.

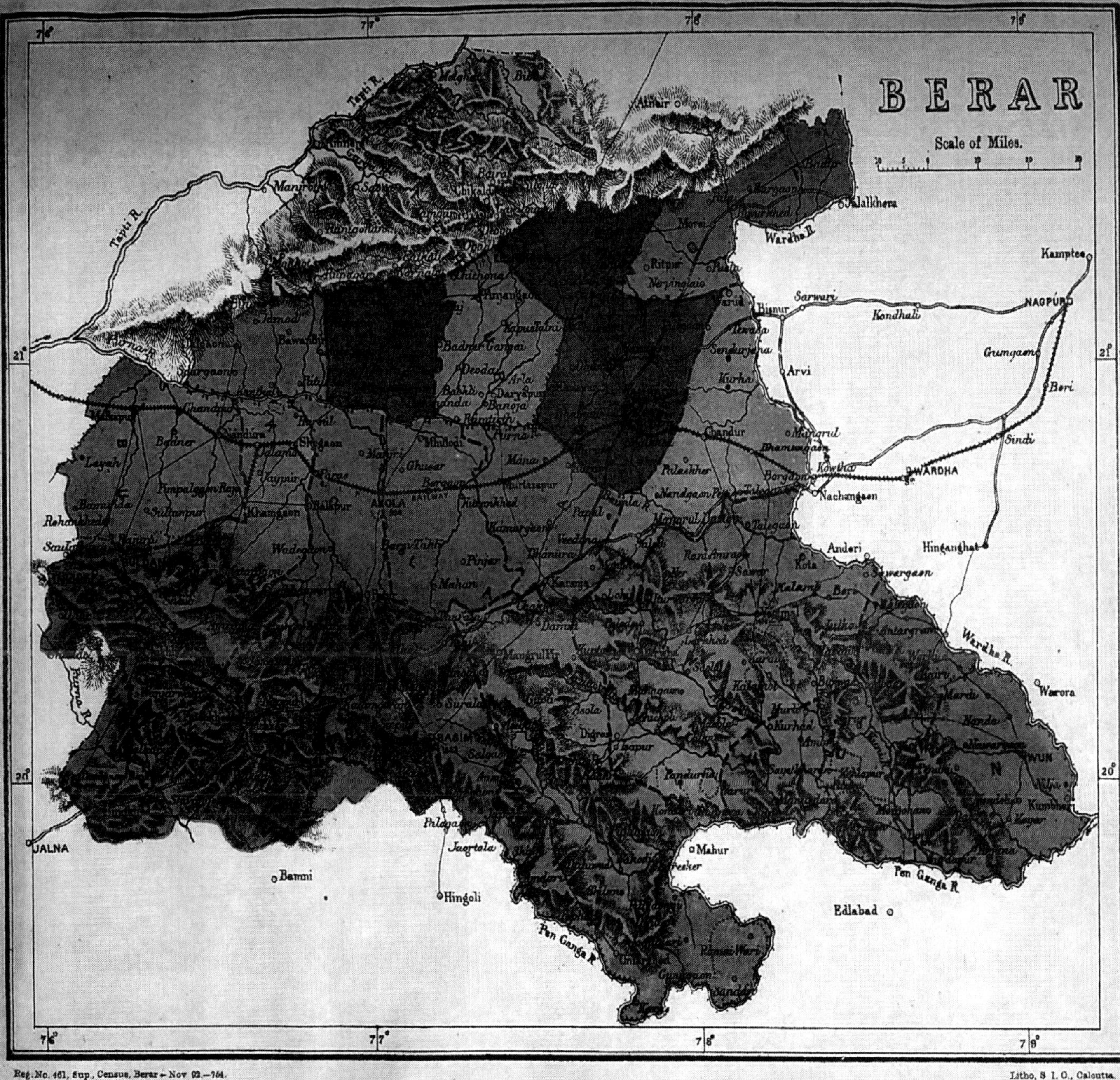

Reg. No. 461, Sup., Census, Berar.—Nov 02.—764.

Litho, S. I. O., Calcutta.

DIAGRAM No. 1 showing Variation in Density of Population in each Taluk from 1867 to 1891.

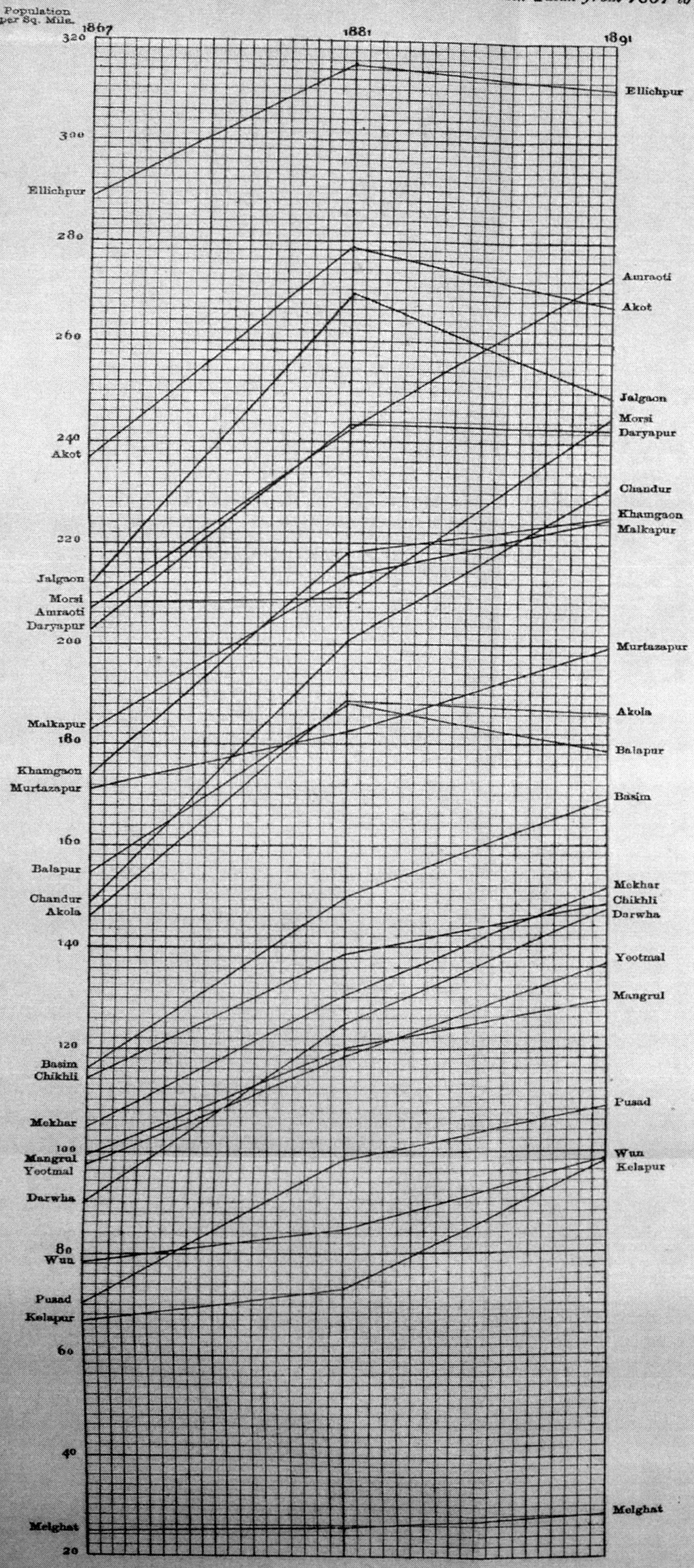

Reg. No. 461, Sup., Census. Berar — Nov 92 — 154.

Zinco. S. I. O., Calcutta.

It was observed in Mr. Kitt's Report on the Census of 1881 that the districts in Berar approximated closely in size to some of the English counties, Amraoti being three square miles smaller than Lincolnshire, and Akola and Ellichpur each rather larger than Devonshire. In density, however, Amraoti exceeds Lincolnshire, where there are only 171 persons to the square mile. Jamaica strikes the imagination as an island of considerable size, and it certainly possesses an imposing array of administrative officials; yet the area of Jamaica, 4,424 square miles, is not much larger than that of the Wun district, and its population, 585,582, is less than that of Amraoti. For Amraoti some ten or a dozen officers, European and Native, combine between them, with the aid of a sixth part of a Civil and Sessions Judge and of a Judicial Commissioner, to dispose of the entire judicial administration, civil and criminal, besides attending to multifarious other duties of an executive character, while the judicial requirements alone of Jamaica demand a Chief Justice and two Puisne Judges besides several District Judges and stipendiary Magistrates. Cyprus is smaller in area than the Wun district and has a population of considerably less than one-half, and there also the number of executive and judicial officials is comparatively very large. Unless the people of these islands are of a very much more litigious and unruly disposition than those of this province, it would seem that the Berar official is far more heavily worked than his brother of the Colonial services.

Taking now the taluks, Melghat, the hill tract on the north, is by far the largest in area, with 1,649 square miles. Then comes Pusad in the Balaghat range on the south with 1,274.6, and the next eight taluks in size all belong to this tract. Of the taluks of the Payanghat or plain region, the largest is Chandur with 854·97 square miles, and the remainder range down to Jalgaon, with 392·1. In population Chandur comes first with 198,106 and Melghat last with 47,031, and Mangrul last but one with 82,446. The adjoining statement No. 2 shows the density of population in each taluk with that in 1881 and in 1867. It illustrates very clearly the distinction between the three physical divisions of Berar described before. The first twelve taluks in order comprise the central plain, the next nine the upland or hilly region in the south, and the last the mountain tract on the north. The twelve taluks of the plain have an aggregate area of 7184.43 square miles, and an average density of population of 253. The nine taluks of the Balaghat contain an area of 8,884.44 square miles, with a density of 132.

Statement No. 2.

Taluk.	Population per square mile.			
	1891.	1881.	1867.	Variation since 1881.
1 Ellichpur	311·6	315·7	289·1	− 4·1
2. Amraoti	273·2	243·2	207·8	+ 30·0
3. Akot	266·4	278·5	236·8	− 12·1
4. Jalgaon	248·9	269·7	212·0	− 20·8
5. Morsi	244·8	208·5	208·0	+ 36·3
6. Daryapur	242·6	243·8	203·6	− 1·2
7. Chandur	231·7	200·7	149·3	+ 31·0
8. Khamgaon	225·2	218·1	174·0	+ 7·1
9. Malkapur	224·7	213·3	183·6	+ 11·4
10. Murtazapur	199·3	181·3	171·6	+ 18·0
11. Akola	186·7	188·7	148·4	− 2·0
12. Balapur	178·7	188·1	155·3	− 9·4
13. Basim	169·4	150·0	116·5	+ 19·4
14. Mehkar	151·8	130·6	105·0	+ 21·2
15. Chikhli	148·6	138·8	114·8	+ 9·8
16. Darwha	147·5	125·0	90·1	+ 22·5
17. Yeotmal	136·9	118·6	97·4	+ 18·3
18. Mangrul	129·7	120·1	99·6	+ 9·6
19. Pusad	108·6	98·2	71·5	+ 10·4
20. Wun	98·4	84·8	78·3	+ 13·6
21. Kelapur	97·9	73·0	67·0	+ 24·9
22. Melghat	28·5	25·9	24·7	+ 2·6

Map No. 1 illustrates the relative density of the different taluks at the present census, and diagram No. 1 the variation in the density since 1867. For the purpose of classification the taluks have been arranged, and shown on the map in five groups. The first three taluks, Ellichpur, Amraoti, and Akot, may be regarded as *densely* populated, the proportion ranging from 266 upwards. The next six, Jalgaon, Morsi, Daryapur, Chandur, Khamgaon, and Malkapur, form the second group or *fairly densely* populated, the rate ranging from 224 to 248. The third group consists of Murtazapur, Akola, Balapur, and Basim, and is *averagely densely* populated, the range being from 169 to 199.

Mehkar, Chikhli, Darwha, Yeotmal, and Mangrul form the fourth group, or *thinly* populated, with a range from 129 to 151. Pusad, Wun, and Kelapur make the last group, or *sparsely* populated, with a range from 97 to 108. Melghat comes by itself last of all as *very sparsely* populated.

				sq. miles.		
The first group	contains	an area	of	1,657·58	with a density of	282.
„ second	ditto	do.		3,609·05	ditto	235.
„ third	ditto	do.		2,963·72	ditto	182.
„ fourth	ditto	do.		4,622·55	ditto	144.
„ fifth	ditto	do.		3,215·97	ditto	102.

From the map it will be seen that, with the exception of Amraoti, the densest taluks are those which lie at the foot of the Gawilgarh range of mountains, and that the first two groups comprise the taluks of the plain, with the exception of three out of the four central ones of the southern half. It will also be observed that the six taluks whose density has decreased since 1881 comprise four of the densest and two of the contiguous central ones, while the three taluks whose density has increased in the same period in much greater proportion than the rest, that is Morsi, Chandur, and Amraoti, form the eastern portion of the Berar plain.

Turning to the diagram it will be seen that the taluks which have made the most rapid and regular increase in density since 1867 are Chandur and Amraoti in the plain and Darwha and Basim in the upland tract, while all the taluks of the latter region have made a considerable and more or less uniform advance. Of the rest it is curious to note that Morsi, which has the largest increase of all since 1881, was the only taluk which made no appreciable increase in the former period.

Agricultural statistics in relation to population.

The consideration of some agricultural statistics in relation to the population will be now proceeded with.

From the Revenue Report for 1890-91 it appears that the amount of culturable land available for occupation in each district was as follows:—

	Number of acres occupied.	Number of acres available but unoccupied.
Amraoti	1,496,175	10,885
Akola	1,458,316	37,055
Ellichpur (excluding Melghat)	560,141	1,747
Buldana	1,477,069	35,865
Wun	1,382,507	256,044
Basim	1,247,338	69,714

From these figures it is ascertained that for every 100 persons of the entire population, there are in the Ellichpur district (excluding Melghat) 208 acres of land in occupation; in Amraoti 228; in Akola 253; in Wun 293; in Buldana 307; and in Basim 313. The whole area under crop in the province is stated to be 6,697,281 acres, which gives 2·31 acres for each individual of the population. The average in Great Britain under crop and pasture is believed to be somewhat less than an acre per head.

Taking the whole culturable area, in occupation and unoccupied, the density of population per square mile is as follows:—

Ellichpur (excluding Melghat)	305·92
Amraoti	279·04
Akola	245·76
Buldana	203·52
Basim	189·44
Wun	184·32

Comparing these figures with those given in Statement No. 1, of the density proper, it is seen that the relative differences between the districts of the plain, the first three, and the districts of the upland region, the last three, are diminished; that is to say that in the cultivated area there is not so marked a distinction, but that yet even there the southern districts are less thickly populated, and it may be inferred that the lesser density of this region is due both to the larger proportion of unworkable jungle and barren soil, and also to the want of development of the land which is available for cultivation.

The same Report gives the following figures as the number of acres assigned in each district for free grazing :—

	Acres.
Amraoti	52,757
Akola	47,124
Ellichpur (excluding Melghat)	15,665
Buldana	77,288
Wun	357,043
Basim	173,912

and from these it appears that for every 10 acres of free grazing land there are in the Ellichpur district (exclusive of Melghat), 171 persons, in Amraoti 124, in Akola 123, in Buldana 62, in Basim 23, and in Wun 13. There is, therefore, more than thirteen times as much free grazing land to each individual in the Wun district as in Ellichpur.

The number of acres set apart for village purposes in each district are: Amraoti 10,894; Akola 12,903; Ellichpur (exclusive of Melghat) 3,293; Buldana 11,451; Wun 9,019, and Basim 8,294. The average acreage assigned to each inhabited village is, therefore, in Akola 13·2; in Buldana 12·7; in Amraoti 10·5; in Basim 9·9; in Wun 7·3; and in Ellichpur 7·1.

House accommodation.

Table I also shows the number of occupied houses in each district and taluk. Endeavour was made in the preliminary organisation to secure complete uniformity in the interpretation of the term "house," and the following definition was adopted :—

A dwelling place of one or more families with their respective servants, having a separate principal entrance from the common way.

This was not, however, everywhere rightly understood, as will be explained subsequently in the chapter upon the administration of the census operations (see page clix). It is sufficient to note the fact here that the definition was not strictly adhered to in some localities, and that therefore the deductions to be drawn from a comparison of the figures should be accepted with reserve. It will be understood also that the definition is necessarily somewhat artificial, and that a house from the census point of view is not always what the word commonly conveys. A building architecturally one house may consist of several census houses; for instance, the principal tenement of a holding may have attached to it several out-houses in the occupation of the servants of the owner or tenant, and the whole forming one set of premises would be commonly regarded as forming one house, but in the census operations each inhabited out-house would have been regarded as a separate house. The definition also was not confined to buildings, but included any temporary erection of sticks and leaves which was at the time of the census used as a habitation. Under these circumstances it may be open to question whether any value can be attached to the numbers of the houses returned, though no doubt the exceptional cases do not make a very appreciable difference in the aggregate results. This reservation, however, will not apply to the consideration of individual towns and villages, nor will it be safe to place much reliance upon a comparison of the figures of this and the last census, when the term house included "garhis," or village forts, and enclosures, each of which frequently consisted of a number of buildings which have been, or should have been, regarded on the present occasion as separate houses.

Statement No. 3 gives the number of persons per house in towns and villages for each taluk and also the number of houses per square mile. In towns the number of persons per house varies from 4.1 to 6, and in villages from 4.3 to 5.9. The density of the houses, as might be expected, approximates more or less with the density of the population, and there is a marked difference between the taluks of the plain and the remainder, Balapur, the lowest among the former, having 38.5 houses to the square mile, and Basim, the highest of the latter, having only 30. In Pusad, Melghat, Mehkar, and Basim, the house accommodation appears to be the least and the people most crowded, and in Akot and Jalgaon the most accommodation per individual.

Statement No. 3.

Taluk.	Number of persons per house.		Number of houses per square mile.
	In towns.	In villages.	
Ellichpur	4.3	4.7	68.5
Akot	4.1	4.3	61.8
Jalgaon	4.3	4.4	56.9
Amraoti	4.6	4.9	56.2
Daryapur	4.5	4.7	52.3
Morsi	4.6	4.8	51.7
Khamgaon	4.3	4.5	50.1
Chandur	4.8	4.8	48.4
Malkapur	4.6	4.7	47.9
Akola	4.2	4.5	41.9
Murtazapur	4.2	4.9	41.0
Balapur	4.5	4.7	38.5
Basim	5.3	5.6	30.2
Chikhli	4.8	4.9	29.9
Darwha	4.8	4.9	29.7
Yeotmal	4.4	4.9	27.8
Mehkar	6.0	5.6	26.8
Mangrul	4.9	5.1	25.6
Wun	...	5.2	18.9
Pusad	5.9	5.9	13.1
Kelapur	...	5.5	17.9
Melghat	...	5.7	5.0

Towns and villages.

Table I also gives the number of towns and villages in each district and taluk. Under the head of towns are included all municipalities and all places with 5,000 inhabitants; under the head of villages come all other inhabited places; unoccupied village sites are not shown. Ordinarily the villages correspond with the revenue areas known as such, but not entirely, as in some cases a town or village proper consists of two or more revenue villages. Altogether there are 39 towns and 5,785 villages in Berar. Of the towns, 14 lie in the Amraoti district, 10 in Akola, 5 in Ellichpur, 4 each in Buldana and Basim, and 2 in Wun. Table III (page 8) gives the number of towns and villages classified by population. Table IV (page 10) gives a list of the towns with their population compared with that of 1881. The last column of table III shows the population assembled at fairs and includes the inhabitants of some railway stations and premises. The people attending the fairs do not belong to the villages where they happened to be held, and to combine their numbers with those of the villages is to give the latter undue proportions and to vitiate the classification. In the same way railway stations frequently have no real connection with any village proper, and sometimes while situate on the lands of one revenue village will bear the name of another. Where the stations are within touch of a village no distinction has been made, but where they are absolutely apart and unconnected, the population has been shown separately and included in the miscellaneous element given in the last column of the table.

Statement No. 4 shows what is termed the "areality" of the towns and villages, that is to say, the average area available for each. The first column of figures includes both towns and villages; the second column towns only. The villages are closest together in the Ellichpur district, the Melghat taluk being eliminated, and are farthest apart in

Statement No. 4.

District.	Number of square miles per town and village.	Number of square miles per town only.
Ellichpur (without Melghat)	2.06	194.86
Amraoti	2.62	197.08
Akola	2.69	265.93
Buldana	3.11	702.20
Wun	3.16	1,955.61
Basim	3.51	738.98

Areality.

Statement No. 5.

Taluk.	Number of square miles per town and village.	Mean proximity in miles.
Daryapur	2·02	1·53
Ellichpur	2·11	1·56
Akot	2·24	1·61
Murtazapur	2·28	1·62
Jalgaon	2·39	1·66
Akola	2·51	1·70
Amraoti	2·54	1·71
Malkapur	2·65	1·75
Chandur	2·76	1·78
Morsi	2·92	1·84
Wun	2·98	1·85
Yeotmal	3·03	1·87
Mangrul	3·08	1·88
Mehkar	3·11	1·89
Darwha	3·17	1·91
Basim	3·23	1·93
Kamgaon	3·28	1·95
Balapur	3·36	1·97
Kelapur	3·44	1·99
Chikhli	3·60	2·04
Pusad	4·07	2·17
Melghat	4·98	2·40

Urban and rural proportions.

Statement No. 6.

Showing the percentage of Urban and Rural population in each District and Taluk.

District.		Taluk.	Urban.	Rural.
Amraoti—		Amraoti	33·04	66·96
Urban	19·02	Chandur	6·39	93·61
Rural	80·98	Morsi	24·26	75·74
		Murtazapur	11·87	88·13
Akola—		Akola	19·22	80·78
Urban	18·73	Akot	16·35	83·65
Rural	81·27	Balapur	21·91	78·09
		Jalgaon	9·53	90·47
		Khamgaon	27·08	72·92
Ellichpur—		Ellichpur	33·42	66·58
Urban	18·83	Daryapur	7·55	92·45
Rural	81·17	Melghat	...	100·
Buldana—		Chikhli	4·92	95·08
Urban	5·86	Malkapur	8·82	91·18
Rural	94·14	Mehkar	3·33	96·67
Wun—		Yeotmal	5·2	94·8
Urban	2·45	Darwha	3·25	96·75
Rural	97·55	Kelapur	...	100·
		Wun	...	100·
Basim—		Basim	6·99	93·01
Urban	7·33	Mungrul	6·36	93·64
Rural	92·67	Pusad	8·35	91·65

Basim. The towns are nearest in the Ellichpur and Amraoti districts and widest apart in Wun, where each of the towns feeds an area of nearly 2,000 square miles. The areality of towns and villages together can, however, be better appreciated by a consideration of each taluk as shown in Statement No. 5, which also shows the mean average distance between each village. The mean proximity of villages in the Daryapur taluk is a very little more than a mile and half, and it increases slightly in each taluk in the order given in the statement down to Melghat, where it is rather more than two miles and three furlongs.

Statement No. 6 shows the relative proportions of the urban and rural population. Of the districts, Amraoti, Ellichpur, and Akola come together with very similar proportions and with the highest urban population. Of the taluks Ellichpur, Amraoti, Khamgaon, Morsi, Balapur, Akola, and Akot have the highest proportions of urban population. In Melghat, Kelapur, and Wun there are no towns; and in Darwha, Mehkar, and Chikhli the proportion of urban population is less than 5 per cent.

Of large villages with population above 3,000 and less than 5,000, from which future towns may be evolved, there are altogether 53. Of these, 21 are in the Amraoti district, and as many as 7 in the Morsi taluk; in the Ellichpur and Buldana districts there are 9 each; in Akola 7, in Wun 4, and in Basim 3.

The largest number of small villages is in the Wun district, and in taluks in Melghat, where out of a total of 331 occupied villages 266 have less than 200 inhabitants each. The proportion of the population of each district residing in villages of this class and of the next lowest with less than 500 inhabitants is as follows:—

	Respectively.		
Amraoti	5·12	and	17·59
Akola	6·18	„	19·06
Ellichpur	13·40	„	20·68
Buldana	5·71	„	22·45
Wun	10·56	„	32·94
Basim	7·41	„	27·62

From this it is seen that in the Wun district 43·5 per cent of the population, or nearly one-half, reside in villages of less than 500 inhabitants; in the Amraoti district 22·71 per cent, or nearly one quarter; and in the other districts the proportions are intermediate between these two extremes.

The present census shows an increase of five towns on the number at the last: Balgaon Jagir, Pusla, and Nandgaon Peth, in the Amraoti district; Mehkar in the Buldana district; Yeotmal and Digras in the Wun district; and Mangrul Pir in the Basim district, have all risen to the dignity of towns since 1881. Three places shown as towns in 1881—Pathrot, in the Ellichpur district and Jamod and Sonala in the Akola district—have now less than 5,000 inhabitants, and are therefore omitted from the list of towns. Amraoti camp, although it has a population of only 4,709, of which a large proportion is purely rural and the rest suburban, is included in the list by virtue of its municipal character.

Amraoti.

The town of Amraoti, which was second on the list in 1881, now takes the first place, with a population of 28,946, being an increase of 5,396, or 22·91 per cent. This increase must, however, be regarded as only approximate, as the limits of the municipality have undergone considerable change, and it is not possible to ascertain the figures for the same actual area. In 1881 the figures for the town included those of the civil lines which now form part of the Camp municipality, the population of which is given separately; and, on the other hand, the Town municipal limits now include the hamlets of Rajapeth and Mahajanpura, which were shown as separate villages in 1881. The population of these hamlets in 1881 amounted, together, to 2,883, which is probably considerably in excess of the population of the civil lines, the actual figures for which are not available, as they are combined with those of the rest of the area comprising the Camp municipality; but it may be safely assumed that the population gained by the town of Amraoti by the extension of the municipal area is larger than that lost by the exclusion of the civil lines, and that, therefore, the actual increase of population in the town is not so great as it appears to be from Table IV. The increase, however, still remains considerable, and this is the more remarkable because in the period from 1867 to 1881 the population varied very inappreciably; it was surmised then that a great deal of trade had left the town, but it would seem now that this has largely returned and that the town has made a great advance in general development during the last decade. Twenty per cent of the population is now supported by commerce and the kindred occupations associated with the transport and storage of goods and material. Five hundred and thirteen persons or 18 in a thousand subsist upon banking and money-lending. (I may note here in passing that the figures given for occupations include both actual workers and those who are dependent upon them, as the numbers of the actual workers alone are not available.) Thirty five per cent are engaged in industrial pursuits described in the classification prescribed for occupations as the "preparation and supply of material substances." Nine per cent are employed in the supply of food and drink, and the same proportion in the preparation and supply of textile fabrics and dress. Cotton finds employment in some form or other for 1,173 persons; 2,127 persons, or 7 per cent, are engaged in the professions, learned or artistic, and this is a much larger proportion than is shown by any other town; 8 per cent are employed in personal and domestic service; and 2,809 persons, or 10 per cent, are engaged in agricultural pursuits. Of the latter, 116 persons are concerned in gardens, etc., and the majority of the remainder are probably the inhabitants of the hamlets which have been recently included within the municipal limits.

Ellichpur.

Ellichpur, which Sir Alfred Lyall stated in 1870 "had probably for five centuries been the most populous town in Berar," has now at last lost its pride of place. Its population shows a slight decrease since 1881, and it is possible that the population proper is even smaller than that given, as at the time of the final census there happened to be a gathering in the city of some hundreds of persons from outside to attend the funeral obsequies of a recently deceased rich Marwari. In the period from 1867 to 1881 there was a decrease in the population of the city of nearly 4 per cent, and it is probable that the downward movement has been going on for a considerable time and will continue. This is easily explained. The old military importance of the town has entirely gone. In former times, when depredatory hordes invaded the Deccan from Upper India, their road lay across the passes of the Satpuras, and the importance of Ellichpur as a stronghold, whence troops could issue to repel the advance and where refugees from the country-side could obtain protection, was strategically great; now the position is of no value, and although the suburb of Paratwada still remains a military cantonment, the garrison is small and the need for living within reach of its protection is no longer felt. On the other hand, trade and manufacture follow the railway, and as the line which passes through Berar is more than 30 miles distant, it is only to be expected that the old business of the city should leave it for places that are more conveniently situated in this respect. A branch line, which may come in the course of time, would probably go far towards restoring the importance of Ellichpur. The policy of the construction of such a line is another question. Having regard to the dense population of the area that the line would supply, there can be no question as to a sufficiency of traffic, and the pecuniary success of the undertaking might be very confidently anticipated. From a military point of view, also, if Ellichpur is to be continued as a cantonment, a line seems desirable; the strategic point has shifted from the hill passes to the main line of rail, and it certainly appears incongruous to keep the only troops in the province in an eccentric situation without railway communication. If that were the only consideration the obvious remedy would be to move the garrison, but as a railway to Ellichpur seems sooner or later inevitable, it might be expedient on this ground to accelerate its construction.

A very large proportion of the population of the town is engaged in industrial pursuits, 12,852 persons, or 48 per cent, being returned in this category; 5,537 persons are concerned with the preparation and supply of cotton as weavers, spinners, dyers, and manufacturers of dhurries; 5,610 persons, or 21 per cent, are agriculturists. Only 7 per cent belong to the commercial class, and 4 per cent to the professional.

Akola.

Next to Ellichpur in size comes Akola, with a population of 21,470. This town has been uniformly progressing in population for many years; in the period from 1867 to 1881 the increase amounted to nearly 14 per cent, and in the last decade it has reached to more than 29 per cent. Its convenient centrical position upon the main line of railway accounts for this growth, and will no doubt encourage its continuance in the future. Only 1,956 persons, or 9 per cent, of the population are engaged in agricultural pursuits, and of these 97 persons are gardeners and fruit-growers, etc., 36 per cent belong to the industrial class, of whom 1,365 persons, or more than one-sixth, are concerned with cotton, chiefly as cotton factory hands. The commercial class number 3,241, or 15 per cent, and the professional class 897 or 4 per cent; 1,918 persons, or 9 per cent, are employed in personal and domestic service.

Badnera.

Other towns which have largely increased since 1881 are Badnera, Karanja, and Khamgaon, the populations of which have risen respectively by 53, 32, and nearly 26 per cent. The increase in Badnera is chiefly due to its position as a railway depôt and shunting station, which brings together a number of railway servants and labourers, and also to the establishment of a large cotton mill which employs upwards of nine hundred hands. The industrial class altogether number 3,621 persons, or more than 36 per cent of the population; the commercial class number 1,236, or more than 12 per cent. One hundred and twenty-five persons are engaged in gardens, etc, and 3,215 persons, or 32 per cent, in agriculture proper.

Karanja.

The population of Karanja decreased in the period from 1867 to 1881, and its present recovery is to some extent due to its growing importance as a cotton depôt and the establishment of some cotton presses. Two steam presses and two ginning factories have been established during the decade. Karanja now takes the sixth place in the province in point of size, and in this respect has some claim to be included amongst the number of those which enjoy a municipal constitution. In the composition of its population also Karanja is distinctly more urban than some of the towns which rank as municipalities: 6,528 persons, or 45 per cent, belong to the industrial class, and of these 1,850 persons are concerned in the preparation of cotton as weavers, ginners, spinners, dyers, and factory hands. The commercial class number 2,398, or more than 16 per cent, a proportion which is only exceeded by Amraoti and Khamgaon. The agriculturists proper number 2,916, or 20 per cent.

Khamgaon.

Khamgaon is steadily developing as an important centre of the cotton trade, and has almost doubled its population since 1867: 2,104 persons, or 13 per cent of the population, are concerned in the preparation of cotton, and the whole industrial class number 6,826, or 44 per cent. To the commercial class belong 2,856 persons, or 18 per cent, and to the professional class 617 persons, or 4 per cent; of agriculturists proper, the proportion is only 11 per cent. In its non-agricultural composition Khamgaon ranks next to Akola and Amraoti, and in its commercial element to Amraoti only.

Shegaon.

Shegaon, which increased very rapidly in the former period, has not maintained its progress since 1881, the increase of population in the decade amounting only to 3 per cent. It has a large agricultural population, the proportion of this class being more than 47 per cent of the whole. The industrial class forms 23 per cent and the commercial class 14 per cent. In respect of the strength of the last element the town ranks fifth in the province.

Akot.

Akot, although the fourth town in the province in size, is very rural in the composition of its population, of whom 45 per cent are land occupants, cultivators, and field labourers; 30 per cent belong to the industrial class, and 7 per cent to the commercial. It, however, ranks next to Amraoti in its proportion of workers in metals.

Basim.

In Basim the proportion of the agricultural population is 22 per cent. The industrial class form 34 per cent, the proportion of those engaged upon buildings as artificers or suppliers of building material being higher than in any other town. To the commercial class belong 9 per cent, and to the professional 5 per cent, and in this last respect Basim comes next to Amraoti in the province, but at a considerable interval.

Anjangaon.

In Anjangaon the industrial population form 52 per cent of the whole, the highest proportion in the province; this is largely due to the number of cotton weavers, of whom there are more than in any town but Ellichpur. The proportion of cane and palm leaf workers is also comparatively high. Agriculturists form 29 per cent and the commercial class 6 per cent.

Balapur.

In Balapur the industrial element amounts to 45 per cent of the population, and a large proportion of these are concerned in the preparation of cotton as weavers and dhurrie makers. The agricultural class forms 22 per cent and the commercial nearly 8 per cent.

In the town of Patur in the Balapur taluk there has been an apparent large decrease, but this is due to the inclusion in the population of 1881 of the persons who attended the fair there at the time of the census; these numbered 1,226, so that the population proper of Patur in 1881 was 5,993 and the present return shows an actual increase of 163 persons.

Urban religions.

The proportion of the urban population which is Hindu is considerably less than that of the rural tracts, and the Animistic tribes are very barely represented in the towns. On the other hand, Mahomedans, Jains, Parsis, and Christians are met with in larger numbers in the towns than in the country. Of every 10,000 persons in the province 8,738 are Hindus and 717 are Mahomedans; but of the same number of the urban population, 7,657 are Hindus and 2,069 are Mahomedans. Of the Animistic tribes, out of a total of 137,108 for the province only 2,044 are found in the towns. The Parsis and Christians are almost entirely confined to the towns, the urban proportion of the total numbers under these denominations being 94·2 and 88·1 per cent respectively. Of the total 177 Sikhs (by religion) found in the province, 77 belong to the towns, and of these 49 were returned in Akola. 35·9 per cent of the total Mahomedans and 32·4 per cent of the Jains reside in the towns, while only 10·9 per cent of the Hindus are included in the urban population.

Mahomedan towns.

In sixteen towns the Mahomedan element exceeds 20 per cent of the population. The old town of Balapur, "the chief military station of the Moghal rulers of Berar after Ellichpur," heads the list with the large proportion of 43·2 per cent, though in actual numbers Ellichpur, Akola, and Amraoti exceed it. Mangrul Pir in the Basim district has a Mahomedan population amounting to 35·1 per cent; Malkapur comes next with 33·3 per cent; Patur next with 31·7 per cent; Barsi Takli next with 30·6 per cent; Paratwada, the cantonment, next with 29·7 per cent; then Akola with 28·6 per cent; Kholapur with 28·4 per cent; Ellichpur with 27·4 per cent; and Karanja with 24·8 per cent.

Jain.

Karanja possesses the largest Jain element, the numbers being 719 and the proportion 4·9 per cent. In Amraoti there are 651 Jains and in Balapur 475.

Parsi.

Of the Parsis 183 out of the urban total of 388 are found in Badnera; there are 68 in Akola, 38 in Shegaon, and 33 in Amraoti.

Christian.

The largest Christian population, 315, is found in Amraoti camp; Akola has 188, Badnera 187, and Paratwada 108.

CHAPTER II.

MOVEMENT OF THE POPULATION.

Variation since 1881.

TABLE II, page 5, shows the variation in the population since 1881. The actual increase in the province is, as has been stated, 224,818, or 8·41 per cent; the increase among males has been 111,334, or 8·06 per cent, and among females 113,484, or 8·78 per cent. The annual rate of increase has been 8·11 per mille. If the same rate of increase is maintained during the next decade, the population in 1901 will amount to 3,141,240; but the rate of increase during the period preceding the last census from 1867 was 8·50 per mille, and it, therefore, appears that the annual rate is diminishing. It seems probable that it will continue to diminish as the province gradually approaches its containing limit. The rate of increase at the present time implies a daily increment of about 64 persons, or upwards of 2,000 every month.

Nature of growth, vital statistics, and migration.

The increase is of course the net result of the sum of births minus deaths plus immigration minus emigration. From the Sanitary Commissioner's Report for 1890, it appears that the excess of the registered births over deaths during the period from 1881 to 1890 was 142,692. If these figures are reliable, it follows that the excess of immigration over emigration during the same period has been 82,126. From the Annual Administration Reports, it appears that the immigration locally recorded from time to time has amounted to 18,370 and the emigration to 7,598, but these statistics are clearly of no value whatever. The census returns, however, do not enable us to arrive at more than a rough approximation of the figures, as positive data are not available. The table of birthplaces, Table XI, page 174, shows that 450,915 persons were born outside the province, but this number includes those who immigrated before 1881. The return for the last census showed that 435,933 persons were then recorded as born outside the province, so that the actual increase of immigrants has been 14,982; but the number of persons immigrating during the decade must have been largely in excess of this number, as a considerable number of those returned in 1881 must have died since. There is, of course, no information as to the actual number of deaths, but an approximation may be made by applying the probable death rate. The question is what is the probable death rate applicable to this class of people. That recorded for the province, the mean of which for the ten years is 35 per mille, is most probably much too high, as an immigrant body does not carry with it a very appreciable proportion of sick, weakly, or infirm people, and is necessarily a stronger and more healthy class than the average of the general population. In the Wun district, where it will be seen a large proportion of the immigrants were enumerated, the mean rate of mortality has been 29 per mille, and allowing a higher rate for the indigenous population, it seems that 25 per mille may be assumed to be fairly applicable to the immigrant body, though that possibly is too high. At this rate, however, the survivors of the immigrants of 1881 number 347,107, and this gives the number of immigrants between 1881 and the census of 1891 as 103,808. Turning now to the emigrants, the number of persons born in Berar and enumerated elsewhere at the census of 1881 is given in the Report for India as 63,191; but of these not one is shown in the State of Hyderabad, which is obviously an error of considerable magnitude. It is absolutely impossible that in an adjoining state with which there is constant communication there should not have been enumerated a single individual of Berar birth, and the probability is that the number of emigrants to Hyderabad was very considerable; but as it is unknown we must represent the number of survivors by the symbol x in our calculation. For the rest, in the absence of any information, the same rate of mortality as was applied to the immigrants may be adopted, and at that rate the number of survivors is 50,315. With the exception of those found in Bengal, the number of whom I have not been able to ascertain, but which is probably comparatively small, the total number of persons born in Berar and enumerated elsewhere at the present census is 101,968. Deducting from this number the number of the survivors of the emigrants of 1881, we get $51,653-x$ as the number of persons who have emigrated between 1881 and 1891, and deducting this from the corresponding number of immigrants we get $52,155+x$ as the excess of immigration over emigration during the decade. If we now assume x to be about 30,000, and leave out of consideration the number of emigrants to Bengal, we arrive at the same result as that deduced above by the adoption of the vital statistics, and if the assumption of the value for x be at all approximate, it follows that the vital statistics are fairly accurate in general results also. As to what value should be given to x there is considerable doubt. The Census Superintendent, Hyderabad, has given me 30,674 as the number of persons born in Berar and enumerated in that state in 1891; but whether the number has increased or decreased, or remained fairly stationary since 1881, there is no means of ascertaining. Roughly, then, it may be estimated that the number of immigrants since 1881 has been about 100,000, and the number of emigrants about 20,000. A statement of the details of immigration and emigration will be found in Chapter IX, and I leave this topic for the present to consider the local variations.

Local variations.

From Table II it is seen that the largest actual increase of population has occurred in the taluk of Kelapur, where it amounts to 27,112. Chandur comes second with 26,495. Khamgaon shows the smallest increase, 3,606, and as the town of Khamgaon has increased by 3,208, the rest of the taluk shows a very inappreciable variation. The increase in the Melghat taluk, 4,376, is to a large extent accidental, as at the time of the census there happened to be a body of labourers numbering 2,133 at work on the construction of the Koha road, and it is believed that nearly all these were strangers to the taluk who were brought in by the contractors for the work and who would leave again at its conclusion. Some no doubt belonged to Akot and other taluks of the Akola district, but they were mostly up-country people. Of these labourers, 1,305 were males and 828 females. Six taluks show a decrease of population—Daryapur, Akola, Ellichpur, Balapur, Akot, and Jalgaon. In Daryapur the decrease is very slight, 557, but in Jalgaon it amounts to 8,123.

The result in the actual variation of each district is reproduced in the adjoining statement, which also shows the proportion per cent. Amraoti has the largest actual increase, but Wun runs it very close and has a much higher proportional increment. Buldana and Basim come next, but the proportion in Basim is higher than that in Buldana. The actual increase in Ellichpur is only 1,993, so that had it not been for the Koha road labourers this district would have shown a decrease as well as Akola. As it is, Akola stands alone as the only district in which there has been a fall-off in the population.

Statement No. 7.

District.	Variation.	
	Actual.	Per cent.
Wun	+79,511	+20·3
Amraoti	+80,317	+13·9
Basim	+39,298	+10·9
Buldana	+41,258	+9·4
Ellichpur	+1,993	+·6
Akola	−18,010	−3·0

Statement No. 8 shows the proportional variation in each taluk. This variation is also illustrated in map No. 2 and in diagram No. 2. From the map it will be seen that the increase above 15 per cent is almost exclusively confined to the eastern portion of the province, the exception being the Mehkar taluk. Kelapur, which has the largest actual increase, easily comes first with the highest proportion, which is indeed almost twice as large as that of Darwha, which comes second. The map also shows that the taluks which show a decrease are centrically situated and either confined to the interior of the province or bounded on their outer limits by mountainous country. It also to some extent shows a uniform progression in the scale of increase. A straight line from Daryapur to Wun shows a rise from below zero, or a decrease, to an increase of first more than 10 per cent, then to more than 15 per cent, and then to above 30 per cent, from which it drops again to the over 15 per cent grade; a curved line from Akola through Khamgaon and Chikhli to Mehkar shows a similar progression from below zero to an increase of less than 5 per cent, then to above 5 and less than 10 per cent, and then to above 15 per cent. It may be further observed that the decrease is confined to the taluks of the plain; and by comparing this map with map No. 1, it will be seen that of the six taluks in which a decrease has occurred, two are of those in which the population is most dense, two are of those of the second group or fairly dense, and two are of the third group, the averagely dense.

Statement No. 8.

Variation per cent in each taluk.

Kelapur	+ 34·39
Darwha	+ 17·92
Morsi	+ 17·49
Mehkar	+ 16·61
Wun	+ 16·54
Chandur	+ 15·44
Yeotmal	+ 15·38
Basim	+ 12·40
Amraoti	+ 12·27
Pusad	+ 10·74
Melghat	+ 10·26
Murtazapur	+ 10·02
Mangrul	+ 8·28
Chikhli	+ 7·20
Malkapur	+ 5·56
Khamgaon	+ 3·75
Daryapur	— ·45
Akola	— 1·03
Ellichpur	— 1·23
Akot	— 4·53
Balapur	— 5·15
Jalgaon	— 7·68

The diagram compares the proportional variation in the two periods from 1867 to 1881 and from 1881 to 1891. From this it may be seen that only five taluks— Kelapur, Wun, Murtazapur, Melghat, and Morsi—have increased their rate of progression, and these five were those which showed the smallest rate of increase in the earlier period. Mehkar, Yeotmal, and Amraoti are the only taluks which have maintained a fairly uniform rate of progression; but Darwha, Pusad, Chandur, and Basim, which showed very high rates of increase in the earlier period, have still maintained an advance above the average of the province.

Villages.

We may now come to a consideration of the changes which have taken place in each taluk in detail, and for this purpose must revert to Table III and review the variation in the village classification. In the Report upon the Census of 1881 it was shown that there were 5,551 inhabited villages, and there, therefore, now appears to be an increase of 234 inhabited villages, but the real increase is only 123. The explanation of the difference is that in 1881 certain villages which were regarded as lying so close together as to form one inhabited site were combined, and in several instances two or more villages were thus shown as one. Many of the towns in Berar are aggregations of different villages, but it is doubtful whether this principle of aggregation can be safely extended to smaller groupings. The towns are few and well known, and there is no difficulty in obtaining an authoritative decision as to what sites they comprise, but in the case of smaller aggregations of villages there is no record to show which of them should be regarded as separate villages and which as combined; each aggregation must be dealt with on its own merits, and the opinions of local officers may differ and cannot be accepted as authoritative. It is known that in some instances in 1881 villages were regarded as united which were in reality quite separate and distinct, and it has now therefore been deemed more prudent to treat them all as distinct.

DIAGRAM No. 2 Comparing Proportional Variation in the Period from 1867 to 1881 with that from 1881 to 1891.

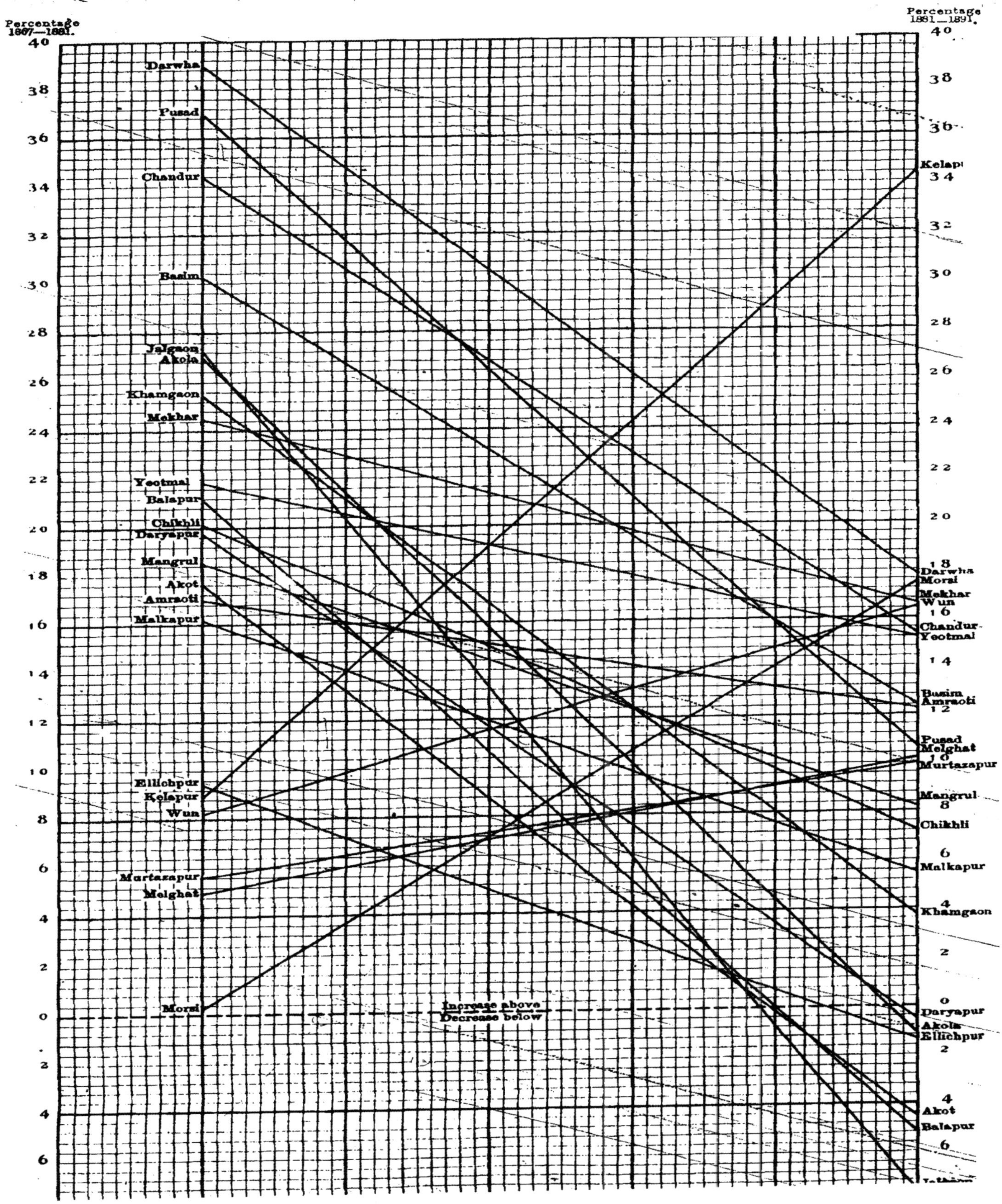

II.—Map illustrating Increase or Decrease of Population in Taluks since 1881.

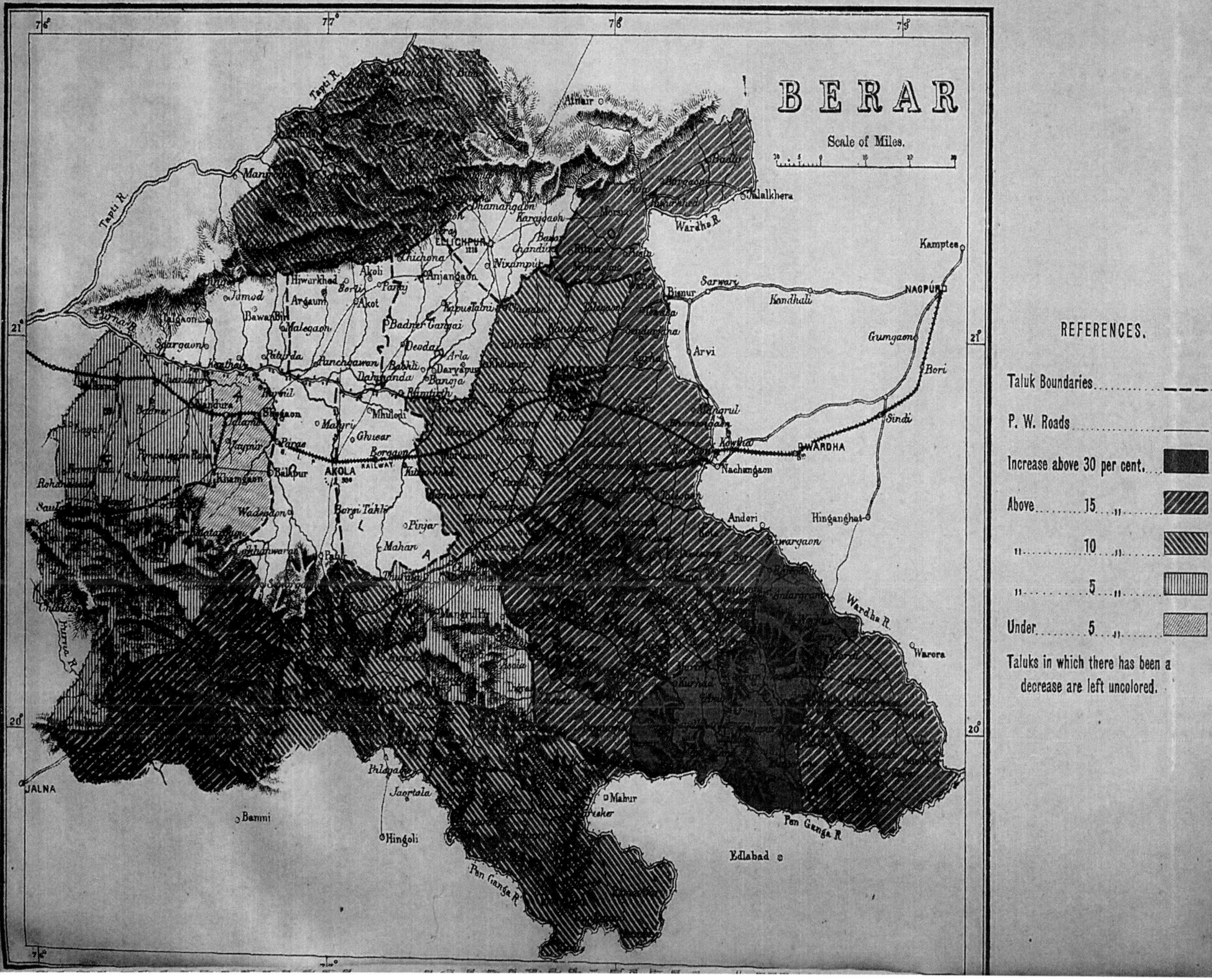

Statement No. 9.

Taluk.	Variation in number of villages since 1881.	Population of small villages. 1881.	Population of small villages. 1891.	Population of large villages. 1881.	Population of large villages. 1891.	Population of towns 1881.	Population of towns 1891.	Variation of population since 1881. Small villages.	Variation of population since 1881. Large villages.	Variation of population since 1881. Towns.
Amraoti	+2	67,472	69,064	59,512	58,273	36,462	55,931	+1,622	−1,249	+19,469
Chandur	+4	90,576	92,314	69,407	91,152	11,628	12,661	+1,738	+21,745	+1,033
Morsi	−3	62,821	58,710	39,523	56,207	27,344	36,973	−4,111	+16,684	+9,629
Murtazapur	+6	68,830	74,649	30,820	32,572	10,923	14,436	+5,819	+1,752	+3,513
Akola	*nil*	73,167	77,206	44,263	34,194	21,991	26,516	+4,039	−10,069	+4,525
Akot	*nil*	63,150	60,309	57,666	54,836	23,437	22,515	−2,781	−2,830	−922
Balapur	+1	46,861	48,254	35,780	29,658	24,559	22,278	+1,393	−6,122	−2,281
Jalgaon	−2	43,982	43,509	40,977	42,448	20,780	9,307	−473	+1,471	−11,473
Khamgaon	*nil*	46,778	46,686	25,932	26,014	23,469	27,020	−92	+82	+3,551
Ellichpur	−5	58,814	55,792	35,045	41,378	54,182	48,862	−3,022	+6,333	−5,320
Daryapur	+4	71,740	65,588	41,527	45,108	9,842	10,593	−6,152	+3,581	+751
Melghat	+19	42,655	43,835	...	1,063	...	...	+1,180	+1,063	...
Chikhli	+4	85,927	89,977	47,059	52,739	7,025	7,382	+4,050	+5,680	+357
Malkapur	−2	91,806	96,389	61,807	65,747	14,895	15,693	+4,583	+3,940	+798
Mehkar	+8	89,534	99,426	41,710	48,518	...	5,102	+9,892	+6,808	+5,102
Yeotmal	+18	77,914	86,584	29,932	31,381	...	6,464	+8,670	+1,449	+6,464
Darwha	+8	90,301	103,952	42,487	47,547	...	5,081	+13,651	+5,060	+5,081
Kelapur	+39	64,880	86,727	13,934	19,199	...	...	+21,847	+5,265	...
Wun	+22	59,860	69,415	12,794	15,263	...	...	+9,555	+2,469	...
Basim	*nil*	105,555	106,556	40,559	57,918	11,576	12,389	+1,001	+17,359	+813
Mangrul	−2	58,184	58,406	17,958	18,799	...	5,241	+222	+841	+5,241
Pusad	+2	87,133	91,577	26,912	35,239	11,006	11,558	+4,444	+8,327	+552

Statement No. 9 shows the variation since 1881 in the number of inhabited villages in each taluk, the population of small villages, of large villages, and of towns in 1881 and 1891, and the variation in the population of the three groups. As in 1881, those villages which have a population of less than 1,000 persons are treated as small villages, and those with from 1,000 to less than 5,000 as large villages; and for purposes of comparison the figures for 1881 have been adjusted to the same conditions as those for 1891 by the separation of the combinations referred to. In each taluk there have been some changes in the occupation of village sites, old sites being deserted and new sites inhabited, and the figures given in this statement are the net results. The greatest number of changes and the largest net results are shown in the Wun district. In the Kelapur taluk 48 new sites have been occupied and 9 old ones deserted; in the Wun taluk the numbers are 36 and 14 respectively; in the Yeotmal taluk 30 and 12; in Darwha 13 and 5. Elsewhere, except in the Melghat taluk, where the numbers are 65 and 49, the changes are comparatively few.

Taluks.

In the Amraoti taluk the increase of population appears to be almost entirely urban, but this is due to the inclusion in the urban figures of the populations of Balgaon Jagir and Nandgaon Peth, which together account for 11,344 persons; allowing for the deduction of this number, it will be seen that the population of the class of large villages has considerably increased. In Chandur a very large proportion of the increase is in this class. In the Morsi taluk the urban increase is high owing to the rise of Pusla from the large village to the town class, and although its population has now been deducted from the large village class, the increase in the latter is yet proportionally very high, while the population of the small village class has largely decreased. This means that the small villages have grown into big ones. In the Murtazapur taluk the chief increase has been among the small villages. In Akola the urban population has been increased by the growth of the town of Akola itself, and while the small village class has also increased the large village class has largely diminished. This does not mean that there has been an increase in the number of villages or that the growth of the small villages has been general, but that, owing to the diminution of the population of the large villages, several of the latter have been reduced to the lower class. In Akot the decrease has been general throughout the three classes. In Balapur the decrease has been in the urban and the large village class. In Jalgaon the decrease has been general, although the large village class shows an actual increase. The large urban decrease is due to the reduction of Jamod and Sonala from the town to the large village class, while the town of Jalgaon itself has also considerably decreased; Jamod now numbers 3,772 and Sonala 4,497; and as these are now added to the population of the large villages with the net result of an increase of only 1,471, it is seen that the large villages have also much diminished. In the Khamgaon taluk there has been no appreciable change, although the town of Khamgaon has increased. In the Ellichpur taluk the large urban decrease is almost entirely due to the reduction of Pathrot from the town class; it now numbers a population of 4,857, and allowing for their addition to the large village class the increase of the latter is reduced to 1,476; as this is less than the decrease in the small village class, it appears that the loss in the taluk population is chiefly among the latter. In Daryapur, also, the chief decrease appears to be in the small villages, though not to the extent that is actually shown in the statement, as the increase in the large village class shows that some of the decrease in the lower class is due to the growth of small villages into large ones. In the Melghat there were no large villages, but there is one now, which numbers 1,063 persons. In Chikhli, Malkapur, and Mehkar the increase has been general through the three classes and Mehkar itself now ranks as a town, which accounts for the apparently large urban increase in that taluk. In the same way the urban increase in the taluks of Yeotmal, Darwha, and Mangrul is explained by the promotion of Yeotmal, Digras, and Mangrul Pir. In all the taluks of the Wun district there has been a large increase in the small village class, which, taken in conjunction with the general increase in the population and in the number of inhabited villages, is what might be expected. In the Basim taluk the main increase is in the large village class, which shows the general growth of the small villages; and the same may be said of Mangrul when the deduction of the population of Mangrul Pir from the village class is allowed for. In Pusad there has been a large increase in both the village classes.

Districts.

Regarding the general movement by districts, it will be seen that in the Amraoti district the tendency has been towards the towns and large villages; in the Akola district, with the exception of the towns of Akola and Khamgaon, the main loss of population has been in the towns and large villages; in the Ellichpur district the tendency has been away from the small villages but not to the gain of the others; in the Buldana and Wun districts there has been no tendency in any particular direction, but a general growth throughout; and in the Basim district the large villages have exhibited the most gain.

Proportions of indigenous population.

It is necessary now to consider the movement of the population by the light thrown upon it by the table of birthplaces already referred to. From that table is obtained the information comprised in Statement No. 10, which shows for each taluk the proportion of its population born (1) within the district in which the taluk is situate, (2) elsewhere within the province, (3) in the Central Provinces, (4) in Hyderabad territory, (5) in the Bombay Presidency, (6) in the North-Western Provinces and Oudh, and (7) in Rajputana and Central India.

The number of persons born elsewhere than in these provinces and states is comparatively insignificant. Chandur has the smallest proportion of home-born people, and the largest proportion of foreigners to the province; and Yeotmal runs it very close in both respects. Balapur has the largest percentage of indigenous population, and next to it come Jalgaon and Akot. Besides these, Chikhli, Malkapur, Melghat, and Akola have all more than 80 per cent of indigenous inhabitants. The migration from other parts of the province is most conspicuous in Daryapur, and after that in Murtazapur, Mangrul, and Darwha.

Statement No. 10.

Showing percentage of population of each of taluk born in localities named in heading.

Taluk.	District to which taluk belongs.	Rest of Berar.	Central Provinces.	Hyderabad territory.	Bombay Presidency.	North-Western Provinces and Oudh.	Rajputana and Central India.
Amraoti	68·62	9·51	12·97	1·39	2·14	2·55	1·49
Chandur	64·11	4·71	27·55	·31	·86	1·29	1·14
Morsi	76·46	3·54	18·09	·20	·25	·67	·72
Murtazapur	71·56	16·36	4·46	1·84	2·92	1·54	1·17
Akola	80·17	9·15	2·03	2·37	3·11	1·41	1·58
Akot	86·63	6·65	1·61	·51	1·51	1·37	1·57
Balapur	91·31	4·22	·30	1·25	1·49	·57	·77
Jalgaon	87·27	6·39	1·22	·39	2·78	·62	1·28
Khamgaon	77·85	8·81	·74	2·96	5·41	1·37	2·69
Ellichpur	78·56	8·16	6·96	2·13	·59	1·88	1·53
Daryapur	75·30	18·55	2·76	·34	·56	1·49	·88
Melghat	80·93	1·84	14·13	·36	·40	1·74	·50
Chikhli	83·50	2·74	·27	10·44	2·22	·27	·47
Malkapur	82·16	7·16	·32	·88	8·08	·41	·87
Mehkar	76·95	9·25	·22	9·70	2·52	·22	1·05
Yeotmal	64·50	5·28	26·40	·94	·79	1·23	·69
Darwha	72·66	14·51	6·81	3·35	1·22	·78	·58
Kelapur	75·36	1·25	15·64	5·31	1·23	·39	·75
Wun	75·01	·20	17·20	7·06	·17	·17	·13
Basim	78·18	8·70	·33	9·18	1·89	·39	1·21
Mangrul	77·07	15·30	·67	3·72	2·07	·45	·66
Pusad	78·30	2·25	·35	16·90	1·06	·35	·63

Movement within the province seems confined to the inner portions, and Wun, Kelapur, Melghat, Pusad, Chikhli, and Morsi, all outlying taluks, have very small proportions of their inhabitants derived from other districts of Berar. In Daryapur in every 10,000 persons 1,855 have been born in parts of Berar beyond the Ellichpur district; in a similar number in the Wun taluk only 20 have come from other districts of the province.

Statement No. 11.

Showing the number of persons in each taluk born in other districts in Berar.

DISTRICT OF BIRTH.

Taluk of enumeration.	Amraoti.		Akola.		Ellichpur.		Buldana.		Wun.		Basim.		Taluk total.		District total.	
	Males.	Females.	Males.	Females.	Males.	Females.	Males.	Females.	Males.	Females.	Males.	Females.	Males.	Females.	Males.	Females.
Amraoti	...	...	1,116	1,486	5,242	7,474	302	239	582	640	199	187	7,441	10,026	...	...
Chandur	...	...	479	495	783	788	96	74	2,467	3,452	385	326	4,210	5,135	...	...
Morsi	...	...	148	217	1,851	2,864	30	36	92	85	45	32	2,166	3,234	...	...
Murtazapur	...	...	2,666	4,384	1,991	2,761	176	192	1,393	2,132	1,762	2,454	7,988	11,923	21,805	30,318
Akola	2,237	3,145	...	...	1,069	1,517	561	511	162	208	1,383	1,835	5,412	7,216	...	...
Akot	663	1,097	...	...	2,490	3,801	376	422	64	67	77	105	3.670	5,492	...	...
Balapur	178	189	...	...	192	222	1,048	1,323	17	22	480	623	1,915	2,379	...	...
Jalgaon	137	162	...	...	222	257	2,196	3,190	10	12	24	37	2,589	3,658	...	...
Khamgaon	183	328	...	...	144	122	3,004	4,784	16	17	77	121	3,424	5,372	17,010	24,117
Ellichpur	3,717	6,169	698	865	...	...	77	65	68	85	97	92	4,657	7,276	...	...
Daryapur	3,761	5,978	4,504	7,747	...	...	99	112	122	130	113	168	8,599	14,135	...	...
Melghat	55	37	252	161	...	...	175	158	3	7	4	17	489	380	13,745	21,791
Chikhli	91	94	1,602	1,760	67	47	...	...	32	37	173	233	1,965	2,171	...	...
Malkapur	112	161	4,502	7,668	74	91	...	...	5	10	52	70	4,745	8,000	...	...
Mehkar	174	203	3,207	3,382	50	38	...	...	90	94	2,828	4,092	6,349	7,809	13,059	17,980
Yeotmal	2,556	2,948	170	146	108	85	58	40	...	...	258	235	3,150	3,454	...	...
Darwha	5,641	6,277	570	631	234	205	187	155	...	...	4,255	4,566	10,887	11,834	...	...
Kelapur	343	311	67	74	33	26	20	20	...	...	227	207	690	638	...	...
Wun	48	39	18	19	11	4	9	10	...	...	13	6	99	78	14,826	16,004
Basim	430	503	2,733	2,678	89	73	3,326	4,857	327	438	...	...	6,905	8,549	...	...
Mangrul	1,930	2,601	1,382	1,698	87	102	240	253	1,826	2,493	...	...	5,465	7,147	...	...
Pusad	178	165	246	150	39	27	101	96	1,058	1,063	...	...	1,622	1,501	13,992	17,197
TOTAL	22,434	30,407	24,360	33,561	14,776	20,504	12,081	16,537	8,334	10,992	12,452	15,406	...	...	...	...

Inter-provincial migration.

Statement No. 11, which gives the actual numbers in each taluk of persons born in other districts, shows the movement within the province more clearly perhaps than do the proportional figures. This statement read horizontally shows the number from

SUMMARY OF STATEMENT No. 11.

District.	Contributed to other Districts.		Received from other Districts.		Balance.			
					Gain.		Loss.	
	Males.	Females.	Males.	Females.	Males.	Females.	Males.	Females.
Amraoti	22,434	30,407	21,805	30,318	...	...	629	89
Akola	24,360	33,561	17,010	24,117	...	...	7,350	9,444
Ellichpur	14,776	20,504	13,745	21,791	...	1,287	1,031	...
Buldana	12,081	16,537	13,059	17,980	978	1,443	...	...
Wun	8,334	10,992	14,826	16,004	6,492	5,012	...	...
Basim	12,452	15,406	13,992	17,107	1,540	1,791	...	...

each district found in the different taluks of other districts; read vertically it shows the total population that each district has contributed to the rest of the province. The summary of the statement shows for each district the total number received from and the total contributed to other districts, with the net gain or loss. Altogether 221,844 persons, or 7·6 per cent of the total population, have taken part in this inter-provincial movement. Of these numbers 94,437 are males, or 6·3 per cent of the total male population, and 127,407 are females, or 9·1 per cent of the total female population. For every thousand females who have thus shifted their homes there are only 741 males, or about four women to three men. Wun is the only district in which the proportion of males to females is considerably larger amongst those who have entered the district than amongst those who have left; in Basim it is slightly higher; and in all the other districts it is less. The movement shows the largest proportion to the population in Ellichpur, where 11·3 per cent of the total population of the district have come from other districts and 11·2 have gone, and in this district also is the largest proportion of females in both directions. In Wun for every thousand females who have entered the district there are 926 males; in Ellichpur there are only 631; amongst those who have left the highest sex proportion is in Basim, where it is 808 males to 1,000 females, and the lowest is in Ellichpur, 721. In Akola 10·1 per cent of the population of the district have left and 7·1 per cent have come in. Of those who have left their districts, the smallest proportion to the total population is in Wun where it is 4·1 per cent, and of those who have come into the districts the smallest proportion is in Buldana, where it is 6·4 per cent. Taking the sexes separately, the proportion of males who have left their own for other districts varies from 3·4 per cent on the total male population of the district in Wun to 9·1 per cent in Ellichpur; of those who have entered the district from other districts it varies from 5·3 in Buldana to 8·4 in Ellichpur; amongst females the proportion of those who have left their districts varies from 4·8 in Wun to 13·4 in Ellichpur, and of those who have come in from 6·9 in Wun to 14·2 in Ellichpur.

Coming to the taluks, the statement shows that Daryapur and Darwha have received very largely, and Wun a remarkably small number. Most of the movement disclosed is between adjacent districts and is to be largely accounted for, especially amongst the women, by marriages, but some must be attributed to genuine migration. Thus, the large numbers received by Daryapur come almost entirely from the Amraoti and Akola districts; Murtazapur, which is very centrically situated, has received largely from Akola, Ellichpur, Basim, and Wun. On the other hand, the Amraoti district has contributed to distant taluks in not inconsiderable numbers; Buldana has contributed to Amraoti, Murtazapur, Melghat, Darwha, and Mangrul; Wun has contributed to Akola. The summary shows that the Akola district has lost heavily in the exchange, and that the decrease in the population of that district is to a great extent due to migra-

III.—Map illustrating Immigration in Taluks.

Taluks in which the Immigrants exceed 5 per cent. of the population being colored—

From the Central Provinces

" the Hyderabad Dominions

" the Bombay Presidency

tion to other parts of the province. The Report for 1881 (Table 99) shows that in the previous period there was a loss of 8,591 persons in the provincial interchange, so that the apparent unpopularity of the Akola district is not of recent date. It is not to be expected that the Melghat taluk should attract many people from outside, as its physical and climatic conditions are calculated to repel the ordinary lowlander, but it is somewhat astonishing that more persons should not have been drawn to the taluks of Wun and Kelapur from within the province. The facts elicited suggest the reflection whether it might not be desirable and feasible to take measures to induce some migration to these taluks from the more congested parts of other districts. The statistics of land and cultivation reproduced in the first chapter from the Revenue Report show that there is a large amount of culturable land available for occupation in the Wun district and scarcely any in Ellichpur. Some of the rising generation of agriculturists in the Ellichpur district must emigrate or follow some other occupation, which it need scarcely be said they will be very slow to do, and their attention might well be drawn to the facilities offered in Wun. The very superior advantages of free grazing in the Wun district, mentioned in page vii, should alone be a great inducement, but it is doubtful if such facts are known to the people in Ellichpur, or anywhere beyond the district itself.

The adjoining Statement No. 12 compares the population at 1881 and 1891 in each district of those born in other districts of the province. This shows that the interprovincial movement during the decade has been in favour of the Amraoti, Basim, and Buldana districts, and that Akola, Ellichpur, and Wun have proved less attractive provincially than the rest. It also appears to show that with an increase of population there is a tendency to a still greater increase of movement.

Statement No. 12.

District.	Number of persons returned as born in other districts of Berar.		
	1881.	1891.	Increase.
Amraoti . .	41,735	52,123	10,388
Akola . .	39,157	41,127	1,970
Ellichpur . .	34,457	35,536	1,079
Buldana . .	23,316	31,039	7,723
Wun . .	28,693	30,830	2,137
Basim . .	22,287	31,189	8,902

Immigration.

Reverting to Statement No. 10, it will be seen that the taluks Chandur, Yeotmal, Wun, Kelapur, Amraoti, Morsi, and Pusad, have the largest proportions of foreigners. The chief immigration is from the Central Provinces, where were born 216,488 of the inhabitants of Berar. In every 10,000 inhabitants of Chandur, 2,755 were born in the Central Provinces; of Yeotmal 2,640; of Morsi 1,809; of Wun 1,720; of Kelapur 1,561; of Melghat 1,413; of Amraoti 1,297; of Ellichpur 696; and of Darwha 681. Of the population of the province, 110,905 persons were born in the territory of the Nizam of Hyderabad; the largest proportion is found in the Pusad taluk, where they number 1,690 in every 10,000; in Chikhli the proportion is 1,044; in Mehkar 970; in Basim 918; in Wun 706; and in Kelapur 531. Of persons born in the Bombay Presidency, there are 59,805 in Berar, where they are widely distributed; they are most conspicuous in Malkapur, where they number 808 in every 10,000, and in Khamgaon, where the proportion is 541. From the North-West Provinces and Oudh have come 28,359 persons, and from Rajputana and Central India 32,076; these people penetrate to nearly all parts, but are found in the largest numbers in the taluks of Amraoti (9,254), Ellichpur (5,000), Chandur (4,706), Akola (4,141), Akot (4,062), and Khamgaon (4,051).

The immigration from the Central Provinces, the Hyderabad dominions, and the Bombay Presidency is illustrated in map No. 3, on which are coloured all taluks in which the immigrants exceed 5 per cent. of the population. This shows that the main body of immigrants settle for the time in the border taluks in which they first arrive, though the people from the Central Provinces have penetrated farther into the interior than the rest. Kelapur and Wun being contiguous to both the Central Provinces and Hyderabad, have attracted immigrants from both. The railway has helped to carry some of the immigration beyond the border taluks, as it reaches Amraoti on the one side and Khamgaon on the other, but there is no special locality which attracts all foreigners alike irrespective of distance.

In the marginal Statement No. 13 are compared the numbers returned at the present and the last census of those born in the three adjacent provinces from which the chief immigration is derived. The number of immigrants from the Central Provinces have increased by 31,346, or 16.9 per cent of their former total. Those from the Nizam's dominions and the Bombay Presidency, on the other hand, have diminished by 19,600, or 15 per cent, and by 17,588, or 22·7 per cent, respectively. The numbers from Central India and Rajputana together have risen from 17,675 to 32,076 or 81·5 per cent, and of those from the North-West Provinces and Oudh from 22,936 to 28,359 or 23.6 per cent.

Statement No. 13.

Persons born in	1881.	1891.	Variation.
Central Provinces	185,142	216,488	+31,346
Hyderabad territory . .	130,505	110,905	—19,600
Bombay Presidency . .	77,393	59,805	—17,588

In the next Statement, No. 14, are compared the numbers of the immigrants from outside the province in each district in 1881 and 1891. The features in this statement which at once attract attention are the large influx into the Amraoti district, especially that from the Central Provinces, and the diminution in the Akola district of immigrants from Hyderabad territory and Bombay. Of this class of people alone Akola has lost 18,492 since the last census.

Statement No. 14.

	Total extra-provincial immigrants.		From Central Provinces.		From Hyderabad.		From Bombay.		From Central India and Rajputana.		From N.-W. Provinces and Oudh.	
	1881.	1891.	1881.	1891.	1881.	1891.	1881.	1891.	1881.	1891.	1881.	1891.
Amraoti .	114,938	147,017	86,368	111,377	7,714	5,713	9,403	9,556	3,510	9,234	7,459	10,146
Akola . .	62,821	48,000	6,692	7,245	17,149	8,595	25,953	16,015	6,215	9,063	5,900	6,410
Ellichpur .	38,014	35,059	22,305	20,201	4,731	3,713	3,333	1,731	2,524	3,575	4,649	5,397
Buldana .	63,246	60,723	1,520	1,311	32,775	32,081	25,005	21,568	2,436	3,884	1,243	1,467
Wun . .	95,541	103,399	66,736	74,662	20,314	18,024	4,449	4,343	1,284	2,720	2,730	3,310
Basim . .	61,373	56,444	1,521	1,622	47,822	42,744	9,250	6,532	1,706	3,576	955	1,562
TOTAL .	435,933	450,642	185,142	216,418	130,505	110,870	77,393	59,745	17,675	32,052	22,936	28,292

In this statement the numbers of the railway passengers, etc, at the present census are omitted.

The birthplace table will be subsequently dealt with more fully in its own appropriate chapter to which the reader who desires further detail is requested, to refer, but one more point in connection with the movement of the population may be illustrated here. In Statement No. 15 are compared the numbers of those returned in each district as born there at the last and the present census, and the variation per cent of the numbers thus shown to be indigenous is compared with the variation per cent of the total population.

The variation of the indigenous population may be regarded as that due to natural causes, though it may be reduced by emigration, as to which we have no detailed inform-

Decrease in Akola.

ation. Akola, which shows a decrease of 3 per cent. on its total population, has a decrease of only 1 per cent in its indigenous population, that is to say, the chief decrease has been amongst the foreign element. The vital statistics for this district show an excess of registered births over deaths of 11,385, and whether these figures are trustworthy or not, there is no reason to suppose that the deaths have exceeded the births, so that the inference from the decrease in the indigenous population is that there has been some considerable emigration of those born in the district. From Statement No. 14 we see that in the extra-provincial immigration, there has been a fall-off of 14,821; from Statement No. 15 a decrease of 5,159 in the indigenous population; and from Statement No. 12 an increase of 1,970 of immigrants from other districts of Berar; the net result accounts for the total decrease in the district, 18,010. It will be shown in Chapter XI that this decrease is chiefly among the agriculturists, and this conclusion receives some confirmation in the caste table, which shows a diminution among Kunbis, Munarwars, and Marathes (who were all described as Kunbis in 1881), amounting to 18,334, but for reasons which will be explained in the chapter upon castes, this difference is not to be entirely relied upon. It has been suggested that the decrease is due to the departure since 1881 of immigrants who came into the district during the famine of 1877, but there is nothing in the returns of 1881 to show that there was any special influx into the Akola district on this account; on the contrary, the percentage of immigrants during the period from 1867 to 1881 was smaller in the Akola district than in any other. On the other hand, the figures quoted in statement No. 14 go some way to confirm this theory. The famine immigrants would have come from the Hyderabad dominions and the Bombay Presidency, and it is precisely in this direction that the chief decrease in the district lies. Other districts show a diminution in the numbers of these classes, but none to so great an extent as Akola, and it is possible that most of the famine immigrants entering the province by rail from the west may have temporarily settled in the Akola district, although, if it had been so, it seems probable that the fact would have been brought to light in the census of 1881. This explanation, however, does not account for the decrease in the indigenous population, and having regard to all the circumstances it seems clear that there must be some deterrent influence in the agricultural conditions of the district. In Amraoti the percentage of increase of the indigenous population, although normal, is less than that of the total, and the rate of increase has been more rapid in the foreign element; the total increment is made up of an increase of 37,850 in the indigenous population, of 32,079 in the extra-provincial immigrants, and of 10,388 in the inter-provincial immigrants. In Ellichpur the low rate of increase in the indigenous population indicates emigration, and there has been an actual decrease of 1,876 persons amongst the immigrants. The comparatively high density of population in the taluks of Ellichpur and Daryapur is sufficient to explain this movement. In Buldana and Basim the increase in the indigenous population has been normal, and the decrease in the extra-provincial immigration has been more than counterbalanced by the increase in immigrants from within the province. In Wun, as in Amraoti, there has been an increase under all three heads, and the high rate of increase amongst the indigenous population points to an excellent state of the public health and an abundance of the means of livelihood.

Statement No. 15.

	Indigenous population.		Variation.		Variation per cent. of total population.
	1881.	1891.	Actual.	Per cent.	
Amraoti	418,655	456,505	+37,850	+9·0	+13·9
Akola	419,814	485,655	−5,159	−1·0	−3·0
Ellichpur	241,334	245,203	+3,869	+1·6	+·6
Buldana	253,201	389,259	+36,058	+10·2	+9·4
Wun	267,868	337,384	+69,516	+25·9	+20·3
Basim	275,223	310,548	+35,325	+12·8	+10·9

Increase in other districts.

In the consideration of the increase or decrease of the population, and of the causes which have led to these results, the history of the province during the decade, so far as it regards the health and welfare of the people, may be of some interest and utility; and some brief notes compiled from the Administration Reports for each year are accordingly appended.

Sketch of the history of the province since 1881.

The year 1881-82 was agriculturally prosperous; there was a seasonable monsoon, good harvests everywhere, and food-grains were cheap; but there was a higher rate of mortality than in the previous year, though that may have been more apparent than real owing to some improvement in the registration. The trade of the province expanded; the value of imports increased by 29 lakhs of rupees over that of the previous year; the value of exports increased by 131 lakhs. The revenue increased by nearly three lakhs, and the provincial expenditure by rather more.

The year 1882-83 was not so favourable to the agriculturist; the rainfall was somewhat deficient, and its distribution was unequal and unseasonable; the price of the staple food-grain, *jowari*, rose from 38⅛ seers for the rupee to 28⅛. The value of imports again increased by more than 61 lakhs, while that of exports remained much the same as in the previous year.

In 1883-84 the rainfall was excessive and abnormally distributed, and the year was said to be one of much sickness, of poor crops, except in the spring, and of depressed trade. The short harvest of the staple food grains tended to raise their price, and the price of food generally remained at more than the average figure throughout the year. There was a severe epidemic of small-pox and of cholera, and the death rate rose to the high proportion of 51·3 per mille of population; at the same time there was a diminution in the birth rate.

In 1884-85 the rainfall was again excessive and unseasonable, but the prices of food-grain fell, and the year was remarkably healthy. There was an increase in the quantity of imports and exports, but a decrease in the value, which is, however, said to be due to a change in the method of account. Revenue and expenditure also increased.

In 1885-86 the rainfall was unseasonable and the year, on the whole, unfavourable to the agriculturist. The prices of most food-grains advanced, but that of the staple, *jowari*, fell somewhat. The mortality was higher than in the previous year, but, on the other hand, the birth-rate also rose considerably. There was an increase in both the imports and exports, and a rise of 28 per cent in the total value of trade. The provincial revenue and expenditure also again increased.

The year 1886-87 was generally an unhealthy one; the rate of mortality increased, and the birth-rate was abnormally low. The rainfall was sufficient but somewhat unseasonable; some of the crops were very poor, and the prices of food-grains advanced. There was, however, a steady growth of the provincial trade, and both imports and exports showed an increase of more than 20 per cent. The public revenue and expenditure continued to rise.

The next year, 1887-88, was particularly unhealthy, and a high rate of mortality was induced by an epidemic of cholera and an unusually heavy rainfall. Owing to a poor harvest the price of jowari rose from 29 to 20 seers for the rupee. The total value of the provincial trade remained much the same, but the value of the exports diminished. The revenue and expenditure, however, maintained a steady advance.

In 1888-89 the rainfall was considerably below the average, but its distribution was on the whole favourable to agricultural operations. The price of *jowari*, however, continued to rise slightly. The year was also a healthy one and free from epidemic disease. The total value of the trade increased considerably, but the conditions of the previous year were reversed, the imports having diminished, while the exports were largely increased. Revenue and expenditure again advanced.

The year 1889-90 was a very unhealthy one compared with its predecessor, and a high rate of mortality was returned. The monsoon rainfall was sufficient and seasonable, but the ordinary winter rain failed completely; the autumn crops were consequently abundant and the spring crops suffered. The prices of grain generally advanced, but that of *jowari* fell. Both the import and export trade increased, and the revenue and expenditure continued to advance.

In 1890-91 the rainfall was seasonable and sufficient and favourable to both harvests. The price of *jowari* again fell, but those of other grains continued to rise slightly. The year was also healthy and comparatively free from epidemic disease. The total value of the trade increased to a small extent, but that of exports somewhat diminished. The provincial revenue and expenditure for the first time for many years shows a decrease upon the returns of the previous year.

Progress of the revenue.

During the decade the revenue rose from £901,265 to £1,022,863 in 1889-90; in the last year it amounted to £1,009,595. The expenditure in the same period has risen from £761,970 to £876,390, and in the last year to £859,272. The surplus has varied from £119,319 in 1882-83 to £194,250 in 1885-86, and has aggregated in the decade the sum of £1,571,561, while the amount paid to His Highness the Nizam of Hyderabad during the same period under Treaty has been £1,579,943. That the province has been able to make so large a payment without any return is a good indication of its capacities. Taking the amount of the revenue in 1890-91, which was not so favourable as that of the preceding year, the increase during the decade has been 12 per cent, so that the revenue has increased faster than the population. Taking the combined value of the imports and exports as the index to trade, there has been an increase of nearly 12 per cent in this direction also. The value in 1881-82 was R5,55,72,521 and in 1890-91 R6,21,73,929. The manufactures of the province also show considerable progress, although they are mostly confined to the manipulation of cotton. In 1881-82 there were 16 steam cotton presses; in 1890-91 the number had risen to 27. There have also been established during the decade a spinning and weaving mill at Badnera, an oil-mill at Amraoti, and 41 ginning factories in different parts. Of the cotton presses 12 are in the Amraoti district and 15 in the Akola district.

Increase of trade and manufactures.

Extension of road and public works.

The communications between different parts of the province have been largely extended. Of metalled roads, that between Ellichpur and Pili, which opens out the Melghat forest reserves, the connecting link between this road and Chikalda, the road from Yeotmal to Wun, which supplies the south-west corner of the province with direct communication with the railway, the road through Morsi to the north-east frontier, which affords communication with the Central Provinces, that which links Basim to Karanja, that from Murtazapur to Daryapur, and that from Nandura to Jalgaon, both of which are feeders to the railway, are among the most important of those which have been completed. The lattice girder bridge across the Purna at Assegaon has been built, and with that at Bhugaon recently finished completes the communication between Ellichpur and Amraoti. Other important public works have been the construction of tanks and the supply of water to the towns of Amraoti and Khamgaon and to Amraoti camp. How far these undertakings have affected the sanitary condition of the towns and influenced their popularity are questions of considerable interest.

CHAPTER III.

RELIGIONS.

IN the Census Report for 1881 Mr. Kitts has given an exhaustive account of the religions of the province, the characteristics of the different sects, and the social habits and customs which are closely interwoven with the religious life of the people. No attempt is therefore made to deal with these subjects again, and this chapter will be confined to a notice of the statistical facts which the tables present.

Table No. VI, page 18, gives the numbers by sexes of each religion returned in each district and taluk. Sects have been tabulated for no religion except the Christian, and these are given in Table A, Part I, page 374.

In the following statement are summarised the total of each religion with the percentage on the total population. A very large majority of the population is Hindu, though it is probable that the numbers returned are not precisely accurate. The difficulty of defining the limits of Hinduism was fully dwelt upon at the last census, and has been frequently remarked. On the present occasion, however, an attempt has been made to distinguish between the orthodox Hindus and the aboriginal or forest tribes whose religion, whatever it may be, is not really Hindu, and who have been classified as "Animistic," the theory of spirits being the main idea which runs through a variety of heterogeneous beliefs. At the last census the people of these tribes, who were not shown as Hindus or Mahomedans, were described as "aborigines," and it was believed that their numbers were very much understated. Thirty-seven thousand three hundred and eighty-eight (37,388) persons were shown as "aboriginal" by religion, but in a tribal statement showing aboriginals without distinction of religion 164,941 persons were entered; and commenting on these figures the Census Commissioner for India remarked that he questioned whether the provincial authorities acted rightly in showing so large a proportion of these aboriginals as Hindus. The numbers returned on the present occasion would seem to show the justice of this criticism. The instructions to the enumerators were to enter the religion which each person returned, and that in the case of forest tribes, those who did not profess to be Hindus or Mahomedans (or of any other specific religion), were to be entered under their tribal name only. Thus a Gond who asserted himself to be a Hindu was entered as Hindu, but if he was doubtful of what the name of his religion was or did not claim to be other than Gond he was shown as such. The idiosyncrasies of the enumerator were thus eliminated from the question, and the result has been that 137,108 persons have been returned as Animistic by religion against 37,388 shown as aboriginal in 1881. This is sufficient to account for the decrease in the proportion of the Hindus to the total population which was shown in 1881 to be 90·8 per cent., and which is now 87·38 per cent.

Statement No. 16.

Religion.	Total.	Percentage on total population.
Hindu . . .	2,531,791	87·38
Musalman . . .	207,681	7·17
Animistic . . .	137,108	4·73
Jain . . .	18,952	·65
Christian . . .	1,359	·046
Parsi . . .	412	·014
Sikh . . .	177	·006
Others . . .	11	·0003

Distinction between Hinduism and Animism.

The adjoining statement, No. 17, shows the proportion of Hindus to the total population in each taluk. With the exception of the Melghat, Kelapur, Yeotmal, Wun, and Ellichpur taluks the proportion in the remainder is above the average for the province, and varies from 87·61 in Darwha to 93·89 in Mehkar. In the Ellichpur taluk the proportion is reduced by the strength of the Mahomedan element in the city and cantonment. Eliminating the figures for these localities the proportion of Hindus in the taluk is 89·50. The Hindu element is strongest in the Basim and Buldana Districts, and is almost everywhere greater in the rural tracts than in the towns. Deducting the figures of the urban population and excepting the Wun district and the Melghat taluk of the Ellichpur district, the proportion of Hindus in the rest of the province is 93·33, and is very evenly distributed, varying from 91·14 in the Amraoti district to 94·85 in the Basim district.

Distribution of Hindus.

Statement No. 17.

Taluk.	Percentage of Hindus.
Amraoti	87·91
Chandur	91·09
Morsi	87·75
Murtazapur	89·33
Akola	89·93
Akot	89·32
Balapur	87·93
Jalgaon	92·13
Khamgaon	91·80
Ellichpur	84·85
Daryapur	91·06
Melghat	17·73
Chikhli	91·16
Malkapur	91·11
Mehkar	93·89
Yeotmal	75·29
Darwha	87·61
Kelapur	70·60
Wun	77·28
Basim	93·65
Mangrul	93·83
Pusad	92·57

The proportional variation since 1881 among Hindus in each taluk follow more or less closely upon that of the total population, allowing for the exclusion of the Animistic. Where there has been an increase of the total population the percentage of increase among Hindus is rather less than that of the total; and where there has been a decrease the percentage of decrease is rather more. In taluks affected by the Animistic the differences are greater. As owing to the different treatment of the Animistic the variation among Hindus cannot be accurately given for each taluk, a statement of variation is omitted, but it is not probable that there would be any thing special to remark in it.

The proportion of Mahomedans to the total population in each taluk is shown in Statement No. 18. It is highest in Ellichpur, Balapur, and Amraoti, and lowest in Wun, Kelapur, and Melghat. Seventy-four thousand six hundred and thirty-four (74,634) Mahomedans, or 35·9 per cent. of their total number, are found in the towns. Deducting the urban populations and excepting the Melghat, Kelapur, and Wun taluks, the Musalman element is very evenly distributed in the rural tracts, the proportion varifying from 4·37 per cent. in the Basim district to 7·29 in the Ellichpur district. In the Yeotmal and Darwha taluks combined it is nearly 5 per cent.; in the Amraoti district 5·14; in Akola 5·58; and in Buldana 6·20. The principal towns in which Mahomedans are found have been mentioned in Chapter I.

Distribution of Mahomedans.

Statement No. 18.

Taluk.	Percentage of Musalmans to total population.
Amraoti	10·02
Chandur	4·57
Morsi	6·05
Murtazapur	8·92
Akola	9·03
Akot	9·68
Balapur	11·15
Jalgaon	7·10
Khamgaon	7·25
Ellichpur	13·01
Daryapur	8·37
Melghat	2·90
Chikhli	7·90
Malkapur	8·09
Mehkar	5·33
Yeotmal	4·50
Darwha	6·26
Kelapur	2·88
Wun	2·70
Basim	5·25
Mangrul	5·72
Pusad	6·49

The Musalman population has increased by 20,126 or 10·73 per cent. since 1881. The increase in the preceding period was 21 per cent but although the present proportion of increment is not so large it is higher than the average rate for the province. The percentage of variation in each taluk is shown in Statement No. 19. It varies very considerably from + 27·1 in Kelapur to — 10·5 in Melghat, but in many instances bears a close relation to the proportional variation of the total population. Kelapur, Darwha, Morsi, and Mehkar, the first four taluks in extent of variation per cent. on the total population are those in which the variation per cent. of the Musalman population is highest; and three out of four in which there has been a decrease amongst Mahomedans are of those in which there has been a decrease in the total population. Jalgaon, which shows a decrease of 7·7 per cent in its total population shows a decrease of 7·8 per cent. in its Mahomedan population; Ellichpur shows decreases of 1·2 and 1·5 per cent respectively. Considering how small a proportion of the total population the Mahomedans form such coincidences are curious. Yet they are not universal; Akola, Akot, and Daryapur. which have decreased generally, have an increase amongst Mahomedans; and in the Melghat the reverse is the case. It is also somewhat remarkable that the variation is to a large extent in inverse proportion to the numbers of the community. Like to like is the ordinary rule, and it might have been thought that the larger Mahomedan communities would have attracted the higher proportional increments, but it has not been so. The Ellichpur taluk had a considerably larger number of Mahomedans than any other in 1881, and the numbers have diminished; Amraoti, Malkapur, Akot, and Balapur, which came next in order of numbers in 1881, are amongst the lowest in order of the proportional variation since; on the other hand those with an increment exceeding 20 per cent had either a comparatively moderate or a small Mahomedan population in 1881. The Melghat taluk is exceptional; the numbers there were very small, and they have still further diminished. The same feature is observable in the towns. In places like Akola, Karanja, and Khamgaon where the total population has largely increased, there is also naturally a large increase in the Mahomedan element, but in what may be called the Mahomedan towns the increase of the Musalman element has been comparatively small and in some, such as Balapur, Kholapur, and Ellichpur, the number of Mahomedans has actually decreased. From these facts it is perhaps permissible to draw the inference that during the last decade at least there has been little or no proselytism to the Mahomedan religion, and that the increase in its numbers is due entirely to natural growth and immigration.

Their variation.

Statement No. 19.

Taluk.	Percentage of variation amongst Mahomedans since 1881.		
	Both Sexes.	Males.	Females.
Amraoti	+9·3	+10·2	+8·2
Chandur	+21·1	+23·5	+18·5
Morsi	+23·3	+23·8	+22·9
Murtazapur	+16·3	+17·6	+14·9
Akola	+11·9	+14·4	+9·2
Akot	+3·4	+2·5	+4·2
Balapur	—·2	—2·1	+1·8
Jalgaon	—7·8	—4·1	—11·8
Kha maon	+12·8	+15·4	+9·9
Ellichpur	—1·5	—3·5	+·6
Daryapur	+8·3	+9·7	+6·8
Melghat	—1·05	—15·4	—3 2
Chikhli	+15·1	+15·2	+15·0
Malkapur	+8·1	+7·5	+8·7
Mehkar	+26·6	+28·9	+24·2
Yeotmal	+17·8	+16·9	+18·9
Darwha	+25·5	+26·2	+24·8
Kelapur	+27·1	+26·9	+27·2
Wun	+9·9	+10·5	+9·4
Basim	+18·0	+ 18·9	+17·1
Mangrul	+13·5	+15·4	+11·5
Pusad	+17·2	+15·3	+19·4

Regarding the variation by sexes it is to be noted that where there is an increase it is generally larger among males; but in Akot, Malkapur, Yeotmal, Kelapur, and Pusad, the female increment is proportionally greater, while, in Balapur and Ellichpur, a diminution amongst the males is accompanied with an increase amongst females. In Jalgaon the decrease amongst females is very high.

Jains.

The Jains number 18,952, and are found in all taluks, but there are only 2 in the Melghat and 48 in Wun. Their highest actual number is in Basim, where there are 1,864 which form 1·05 per cent of the total population; Murtazapur comes next with 1,791, but with the largest proportion, 1·47 per cent. In each taluk of the Amraoti and Buldana districts they exceed 1,000 in number, and in order of strength in proportion to the taluk populations after Murtazapur and Basim, come Balapur with ·90, Chikhli with ·89, Chandur with ·81, Malkapur with ·78, Khamgaon and Mehkar with ·76, Akola with ·70, Morsi with ·69, Amraoti with ·67, and Pusad with ·63. Like the Mahomedans the Jains largely affect the towns where are found 6,138 of their number or 32·4 per cent.

In 1881, the Jains numbered 20,020, and the present census, therefore, shows a decrease of 1,068 or 5·3 per cent. This is remarkable, as in the preceding period from 1867 they had more than doubled their number. Mr. Kitts attributed the increment mainly to immigration, and considering the class of people regarded it as a high tribute to the prosperity of the province. The present diminution must then, it is feared, be regarded as an adverse reflection on the state of the country. Those who flocked in to a land of promise have apparently been disappointed, and if they have not all left it again they have, it would seem, warned others from following their example and turned the current to the ebb.

Actual Jain variation.

Statement No. 20.

Taluk.	Both sexes.	Males.	Females.
Amraoti	−455	−248	−207
Chandur	− 4	+ 4	− 8
Morsi	+130	+ 27	+103
Murtazapur	−138	− 85	− 53
Akola	+ 67	+ 24	+ 43
Akot	− 80	− 24	− 56
Balapur	−363	−235	−128
Jalgaon	+ 51	+ 39	+ 12
Khamgaon	− 46	− 16	− 30
Ellichpur	+ 15	+ 1	+ 14
Daryapur	− 21	− 16	− 5
Melghat	− 5	− 3	− 2
Chikhli	+ 6	− 4	+ 10
Malkapur	+275	+107	+168
Mehkar	− 96	− 69	− 27
Yeotmal	+ 65	+ 43	+ 22
Darwha	−167	−110	− 57
Kelapur	+ 51	+ 39	+ 12
Wun	− 64	− 32	− 32
Basim	+ 34	+ 11	+ 23
Mangrul	−353	−177	−176
Pusad	+ 30	+ 15	+ 15

The variations of Jains in the different taluks as shown in the adjoining Statement No. 20 is curiously irregular. In 12 taluks there is a decrease and in 10 an increase. In Mangrul the diminution is more than one-half; in Balapur it amounts to 28·4 per cent, in Amraoti to 27·1 per cent and in Darwha to 18·9 per cent. Malkapur is the only taluk in which there is any substantial increase, and there it amounts to 24·6 per cent. Between the sexes the decrease is larger among males, the proportion being 6·6 per cent against 3.9 per cent. among females. The movements of the Jain population in the towns present very similar features to those in the taluks, although in the towns there is a net increase of 480 or 8·4 per cent., and the irregularity of the variation throughout appears to indicate a general restlessness in this community.

Christians.

The Christians number 1,359, of whom 1,197 are found in the towns. There are 34 fewer male Christians than there were in 1881 and 58 more females, while in the towns the males have increased by 52 and the females by 140; but the inclusion in the towns of Yeotmal, the head-quarters of a district with a consequent Eurasian population, accounts for much of the urban increase. In Amraoti taking the town and civil lines together as they were in 1881, the numbers have increased from 266 to 397, and in Badnera from 83 to 187; in Paratwada, the military cantonment of Ellichpur, there has been a decrease from 192 to 108, probably due to a change of troops; in Khamgaon a decrease from 87 to 52; and in Akola and Basim a slight diminution also. In Amraoti the increase is believed to be chiefly due to official changes involving the transfer of some Europeans and several Eurasians; and in Badnera it is probably due to an increase of the same classes in the service of the railway.

Christian sects and races.

In Table A, Parts I and II, pages 374—376, Christians are shown according to sect and race. The foreigners, or Europeans and Americans, etc, number 330 or 24·3 per cent., the Eurasians number 318 or 23·4 per cent, and the Native Christians number 711 or 52·3 per cent. Among the foreigners there are 13 males to 10 females; among the Eurasians the sexes are nearly equal; among the natives the proportion is 12 males to 10 females. Since 1881 the Native Christian element has increased very largely, their numbers then being 579 or 43 per cent. of the community; and the number of foreigners has increased by 116, while that of Eurasians has diminished by 224. These differences are probably more apparent than real as there is no known cause to account for any large increase of Europeans or decrease of Eurasians, and it is not improbable that persons who were classed as Eurasians in 1881 have in some cases claimed an European nationality on the present occasion. It is also not impossible that a similar explanation may be given for part at least of the increase among Native Christians, some of those who may be really Eurasians being classed by the enumerators as natives. Thus the numbers of the other two classes may have been unduly augmented at the cost of the Eurasian community.

Regarding sects, the Church of England has the largest number, 562 or 41.3 per cent. of the Christian population; the Roman Catholics number 541 or 39.8 per cent.; the Free Church or Church Mission or Mission Church, as it has been indifferently described, number 74 or 5.4 per cent; other sects have a few followers each, while 105 persons or nearly 8 per cent are shown as Unsectarian.

In 1881 the Church of England, or Episcopalians as they were then described, numbered 583, and they have therefore slightly diminished. Two hundred and twenty-eight (228) are Eurasians, 218 are foreigners, and 116 are natives. The Roman Catholics have decreased from 620 to 541; 416 of these are natives, 56 are foreigners, and 69 Eurasians; the number of natives of this persuasion has increased from 372 and of foreigners from 14, while the number of Eurasians has diminished by 166 or more than 70 per cent. The Free Church has increased from 18 to 74, all of whom are natives. The Presbyterians number 24, of whom 13 are foreigners and 11 natives; they have decreased largely since 1881 when there were 71 of this community. The Congregationalists, of whom there were 18 in 1881, now number 24, of whom 5 are foreigners and 19 natives. The Methodists number 11, of whom 7 are foreigners and 4 Eurasians; there were only 5 in 1881. The Baptists number 6, 1 foreigner and 5 natives; the Wesleyans are 5, all foreigners. Besides these there are 4 members of the Greek Church and 3 of the Church of Scotland. The Unsectarians comprise 19 foreigners, 16 Eurasians, and 70 natives. Of the foreigners nearly 66 per cent belong to the Church of England, 17 per cent are Roman Catholics and the remainder are distributed over all the other sects with the exception of the Free Church. Of the Eurasians nearly 72 per cent are members of the Church of England, and 21 per cent are Roman Catholics. The majority of the natives are Roman Catholics to whose Church belong nearly 59 per cent. of their number; only 16 per cent. belong to the Church of England; 10 per cent. belong to the Free Church; and almost the same number are Unsectarian. From these figures, especially those for the Free Church, it would appear that as proselytising agents the natives are the most successful.

The Parsis number 412, of whom 388 are found in the towns. Many of them are in the service of the railway and of mills and Badnera now possesses quite a colony numbering 183. In the town of Akola there are 68, in Shegaon 38, in Amraoti 33, and in Khamgaon 27. In 1881, there were only 242 in the province so that their numbers have nearly doubled; in Badnera they have been trebled. The sexes are unevenly balanced, the males being nearly twice as many as the females, and the fact implies that the majority are not settlers, but have come into the province in service or on business leaving their families elsewhere.

Parsis.

The Sikhs number 177 and have largely decreased since 1881 when there were 525. Very few probably are true Sikhs by religion and race. One hundred and fourteen (114) of those who have returned their religion as Sikh claim to be Sikhs by caste or race; on the other hand the Sikh religion has been claimed by a few who have been shown of ordinary Hindu castes such as Teli, Wani, and Khatri; and 202 persons described as Sikhs by race have given their religion as Hindu, so that it appears that the majority under the influence of their surroundings have returned to the fold which their forefathers left.

Sikhs.

Buddhism has been returned by a few Chinese in Akola; there are 2 Jews; and 3 Europeans have returned themselves, respectively as Deist, Agnostic, and Positivist.

Others.

The Animistic have been left to be treated last as presenting some interesting features. It has been remarked that the religion of the aboriginal tribes is being gradually assimilated to Hinduism, and it might have been instructive if a comparison could have been made between the numbers who adhered to their primitive faith in 1881 and now, and to see at what rate this process of absorption is going on, but unfortunately owing to the difference of treatment in the enumeration noticed before, no comparison can be made. At the same time it is by no means certain that a comparative statement would be of much value, as the information on which it must be based would after all be of a very doubtful character. It is known that the aboriginal tribes have adopted some of the gods, forms of worship, and beliefs of Hindus, and combined them with their own, and the question as to how far the process has gone can only be answered in such an emuneration as that of the census on the very questionable authority of each individual. Persons whose beliefs in no way differ from each other may have different opinions as to the character of their creed, or having no opinion at all, may describe it variously; and it is not to be accepted without reserve that all those who have now been shown as Hindus are more Hindu than their brethren, nor that all those who gave their tribal names to their religion are less Hindu than the remainder. There is, however, no universal and recognised test which can be applied to the question, and so the plan of allowing each individual to settle it for himself is probably the best and most feasible, and probably also furnishes fairly approximate results. In the following statement, No. 21, are shown the tribes whose tribal religion is Animistic with the number of persons in each returned as Animistic, Hindu, or Musalman, with the proportion per cent of those who profess to adhere to their primitive faith. Accepting these professions of faith for the moment for the purpose of the consideration of the statement, it is seen that more than half of the total aborigines still retain an Animistic belief. The Andhs have nearly all become Hindu, and the Gaolans and Lajjhars are largely Hindu. More than half the Bhils are Hindu, and nearly one-third are Mahomedan. On the other hand the Korkus

The Animistic.

are nearly all Animistic, and so are a very large majority of the Kolams, Gonds, Nihals, and Pardhans. Included in the Gonds are 121 persons who, while giving Gond as their religion, have described themselves as belongiug to Hindu castes, such as Teli, Lohar, Kalal, Bhat, Burud, Otari, Mahar, Mehtar, and Mang; they probably have no connection with these castes at all, but have adopted the names in consequence of their occupations. In the same way five persons have given their caste as Pardhi and their religion as Korku; they are probably Korkus who have adopted game-snaring as a profession, and possibly they have been admitted into a gang of Pardhis.

Statement No. 21.

Tribe.	Numbers of persons by Religion.			Percentage of Animistic to tribal total.
	Animistic.	Hindu.	Musalman.	
Andh	305	43,297	...	·7
Arakh	18	235	...	7·1
Balai	78	249	...	23·8
Basod	70	26	...	72·9
Bhil	783	3,483	1,928	12·6
Gaolan (gawari)	771	35,680	...	2·1
Gond	71,990	9,058	...	88·8
Gorwan	148	13	...	91·9
Koilabhute	10	...	...	100·
Kolam	16,460	954	...	94·5
Korku	34,607	379	...	98·9
Lajjhar	97	1,763	...	5·2
Moghe	217	2	...	99·1
Nihal	2,201	104	...	95·5
Pardhan	9,170	3,766	...	70·9
Thoti	18	43	...	80·9
TOTAL	1370,108	99,052	1,928	57·6

Their distribution.

The Animistic are mostly found in the Melghat and the border taluks on the east of the province, Morsi, Chandur, Yeotmal, Kelapur, and Wun, which with Darwha contain 95 per cent. of their total number. There are none in Malkapur, Mekhar or Basim, and very small numbers in Chikhli, Balapur, Khamgaon, and Mangrul. In the adjoining statement, No. 22, is shown the proportion which the Animistic bear to the total population in the taluks where they are found in any considerable numbers. It is noteworthy that there are not more of them in the hills and jungles of the Pusad taluk, but the aborigines there are mostly Andhs who have called themselves Hindus. Very few of the Animistic are found in the towns.

Statement No. 22.

Taluk.	Number of Animistic per 10,000 of population.
Melghat	7,935
Kelapur	2,628
Wun	1,997
Yeotmal	1,956
Darwha	567
Morsi	550
Chandur	351
Ellichpur	151
Amraoti	96
Jalgaon	60
Akot	57
Pusad	29

Incongruities.

It remains now to notice what may be called the curiosities of religions. As might be expected the enumeration schedules exhibit a number of various inconsistencies; some of these have been traced back to their originators and adjusted accordingly, but there still remain others which may or may not be mistakes, and which it is desirable to mention. One hundred and twenty (120) Banjaras have given their religion as Mahomedan; the Banjaras are low caste Hindus and it is quite possible that some of them may have been converted to Islam, but the numbers are somewhat remarkable. Twenty-nine (29) persons of the same caste have given their religion as Jain which is perhaps more remarkable still; perhaps the chief characteristic of the Jains is their respect for all forms of animal life, and it is difficult to credit a gipsy people like the Banjaras with such a sentiment. Seventeen (17) persons of the Teli caste, 11 Kulals, 11 Ghisadis, 9 Kolhatis, 9 Panchals, and 1 Otari have given their religion as Musalman. Thirty-six (36) Brahmans have been returned as Jains and under the same form of religion have been entered 13 persons of the Sutar caste, 13 Kunbis, 10 Malis, 9 Sugandhis, 6 Labhanis, 5 Jats, 5 Joshis, 3 Mhalis, 2 Sonars, and 1 Gaoli, Gurao, and Halwai. One (1) Chinaman has been shown as Hindu but this is probably a mistake on the part of the enumerator, as is certainly the entry of 5 Parsis under the same religion.

CHAPTER IV.

AGE AND SEX.

TABLE VII, Part A, page 22, shows the distribution of the total population by different age-periods, and the other parts of the table give the same information for the numbers of the different religions already specified. The sex distribution is shown in all the tables.

General considerations.

The subject of the relative proportions of the sexes and the causes which tend to produce them, is one of considerable interest and importance, and it would be a matter of great satisfaction if the facts elicited at the recent census could be utilised in the elucidation of a problem, the solution of which may have momentous consequences for mankind, but which still remains to be discovered. Unfortunately it is very doubtful whether the data supplied by the census in this province in respect to age and sex can be regarded as facts at all, and the results shown by the returns are of so abnormal a character, that probably the only safe deduction is that they are incorrect. I can therefore hope to arrive at very little more than rough generalities, and it is only with diffidence and hesitation that I would be understood to express any conclusions. Generally speaking the ordinary conditions of the civilised world under ordinary circumstances are that more male than female children are born, but that on the whole female life is so much better than male life that in the total population there are more females than males, and that in respect to age there is a gradual declension in numbers from childhood to the close of life. In Berar while the statistics furnished by the registration of births show an excess of male births over female, the census returns give more females than males under one year of age, many more males than females in the total population, and great irregularities of proportion in the sequence of ages.

Proportions of the sexes.

In the adjoining statement are compared the proportions of the sexes in a number of countries, and it will be seen at once how largely the position of Berar differs from nearly all. The population of Canada and of the whites of the United States are of course exceptional, and the balance of the sexes is largely influenced by the preponderance of males amongst their immigrants. The remaining countries where females are in excess are indeed all in Europe, and it may be that the difference in the conditions of life is sufficient to account for the diversity of the proportions, but even among Indian populations Berar takes a somewhat extreme place. In some respects, however, Berar may be regarded as in the exceptional position of a comparatively new country, as, although there are no old census records to refer to, there is little doubt that there has been very extensive immigration and settlement since 1853, when the province was assigned to British administration, and that therefore the normal conditions of a country settled for several centuries or even generations cannot be expected to apply.

Statement No. 23.

Country.	Number of females to 1,000 males.
Portugal	1,091
Scotland	1,076
Sweden	1,061
Norway	1,061
England and Wales	1,055
Austria	1,047
Spain	1,045
Ireland	1,043
Germany	1,043
Switzerland	1,041
Denmark	1,036
Hungary	1,030
Holland	1,023
France	1,005
Belgium	1,001
Italy	995
Japan	977
United States (Whites)	961
Berar	942
Canada	929

The present census shows an increase of 6 per 1,000 in the proportion of females to males above that at 1881, when the returns gave 936 females to 1,000 males. This difference cannot perhaps be regarded as indicating an increase among females relatively to males, but rather a fuller enumeration of the women. At the census of 1867 the female proportion was 935, so that it may be said that on this occasion we have made some advance towards overcoming the prejudice against, and other obstacles to, the complete enumeration of females, but their numbers even now are probably considerably understated. The balance of the sexes is no doubt partly disturbed by the numbers of the immigrants amongst whom the male element predominates, but of those who have been returned as born in Berar there are only 957 females to 1,000 males.

Urban conditions.

It is to be expected that the male element should be stronger in the towns than in the rural tracts owing to the greater variety of urban occupations that are followed by men whose families are resident elsewhere, and the larger the town and the less agricultural its inhabitants, the stronger the male element. In all the towns together the proportion of females is 919 to 1,000, and in the three towns which have a population of more than 20,000 it is only 878. Deducting the urban population, the proportion in the rest of the province is 945. In the different districts it is as follows:—

District conditions.

	Females to 1,000 males.		Females to 1,000 males.
Buldana	965	Ellichpur	938
Wun	951	Akola	935
Basim	944	Amraoti	927

In Buldana both the strictly urban population and the immigration from distant provinces is comparatively small, and consequently equilibrium between the sexes is more nearly approached; in Amraoti, on the contrary, the disturbing elements are in the greatest force, and the balance is most upset.

Taluk conditions.

The adjoining statement, No. 24, shows the proportion of the sexes in each taluk for both 1891 and 1881, and a comparison of the figures affords some measure of the improvement in the enumeration. In 16 of the 22 taluks the proportion of females has risen. In Malkapur the increase has been remarkable, and is due to the large influx of females from Khandesh. In Balapur the increase is even greater but the proportion attained is not nearly so high. In Akot also there has been a considerable rise, and in both these taluks the increments considered in the light of the decrease in the population point to the large emigration of males and to the possibility that, as they have left their women behind, these emigrants may return and restore the normal condition of a gradual growth. In Chandur the decrease in the proportion of females is attributable to the preponderance of males amongst the immigrants, the excess of male over female immigrants in this taluk being about 4,000; but this cause is not assignable for the fall in Morsi, Murtazapur, Jalgaon, and Mangrul; in the last-named taluk

Statement No. 24.

Taluk.	Number of Females to 1,000 Males.	
	1891.	1881.
Amraoti	921	915
Chandur	925	932
Morsi	942	948
Murtazapur	920	928
Akola	923	921
Akot	950	930
Balapur	957	923
Jalgaon	940	942
Khamgaon	905	902
Ellichpur	942	935
Daryapur	935	928
Melghat	930	920
Chikhli	961	956
Malkapur	972	948
Mehkar	961	954
Yeotmal	936	930
Darwha	939	939
Kelapur	967	961
Wun	977	966
Basim	943	933
Mangrul	927	931
Pusad	955	951

Age Periods.

DIAGRAM No. 3 showing the Number of Females to 1,000 Males at each Age Period.

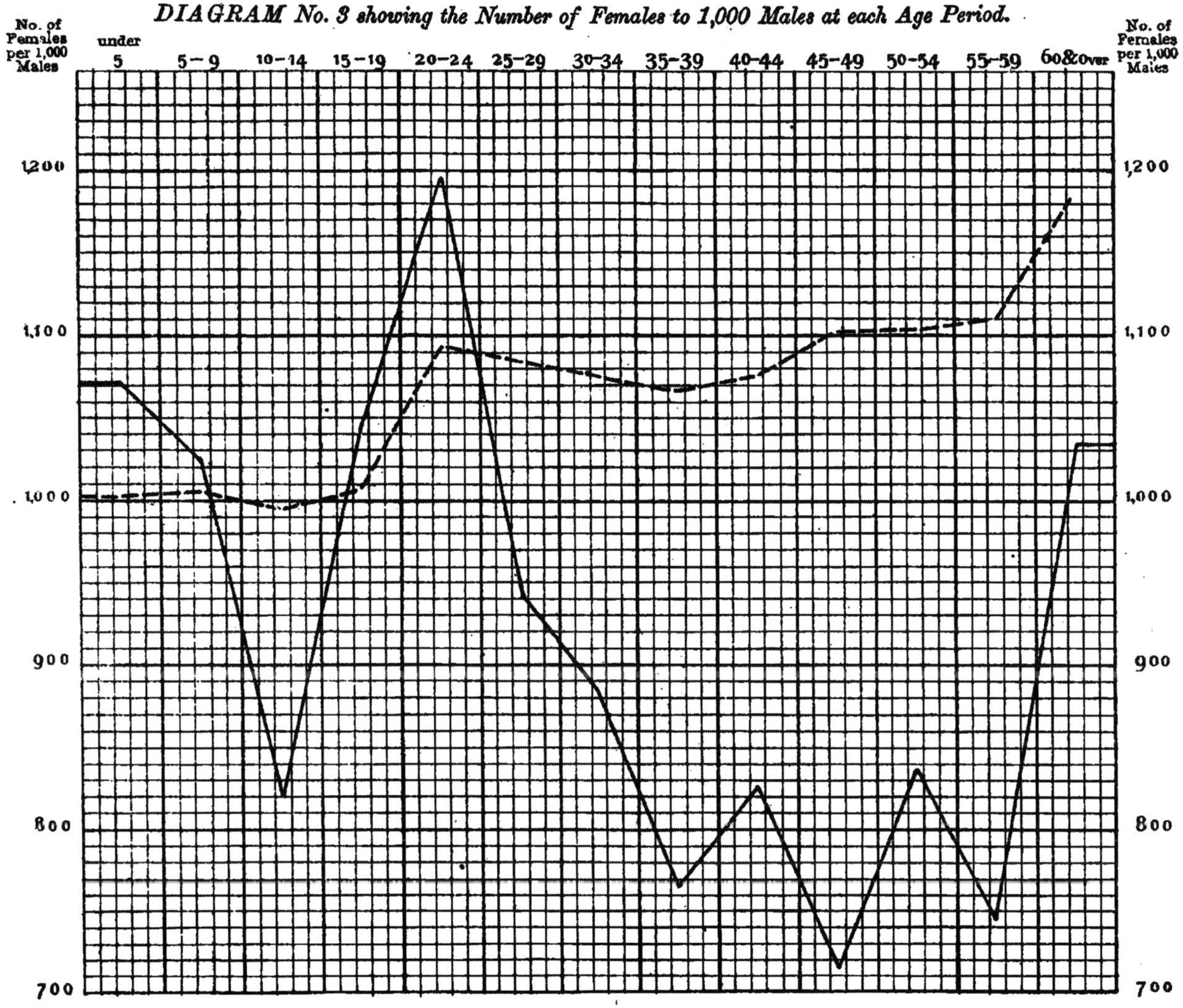

Berar, shown thus —————— England and Wales, shown thus — — — — — —

Age Periods.

DIAGRAM No. 4 showing Number of Females to 1,000 Males at each Age Period.

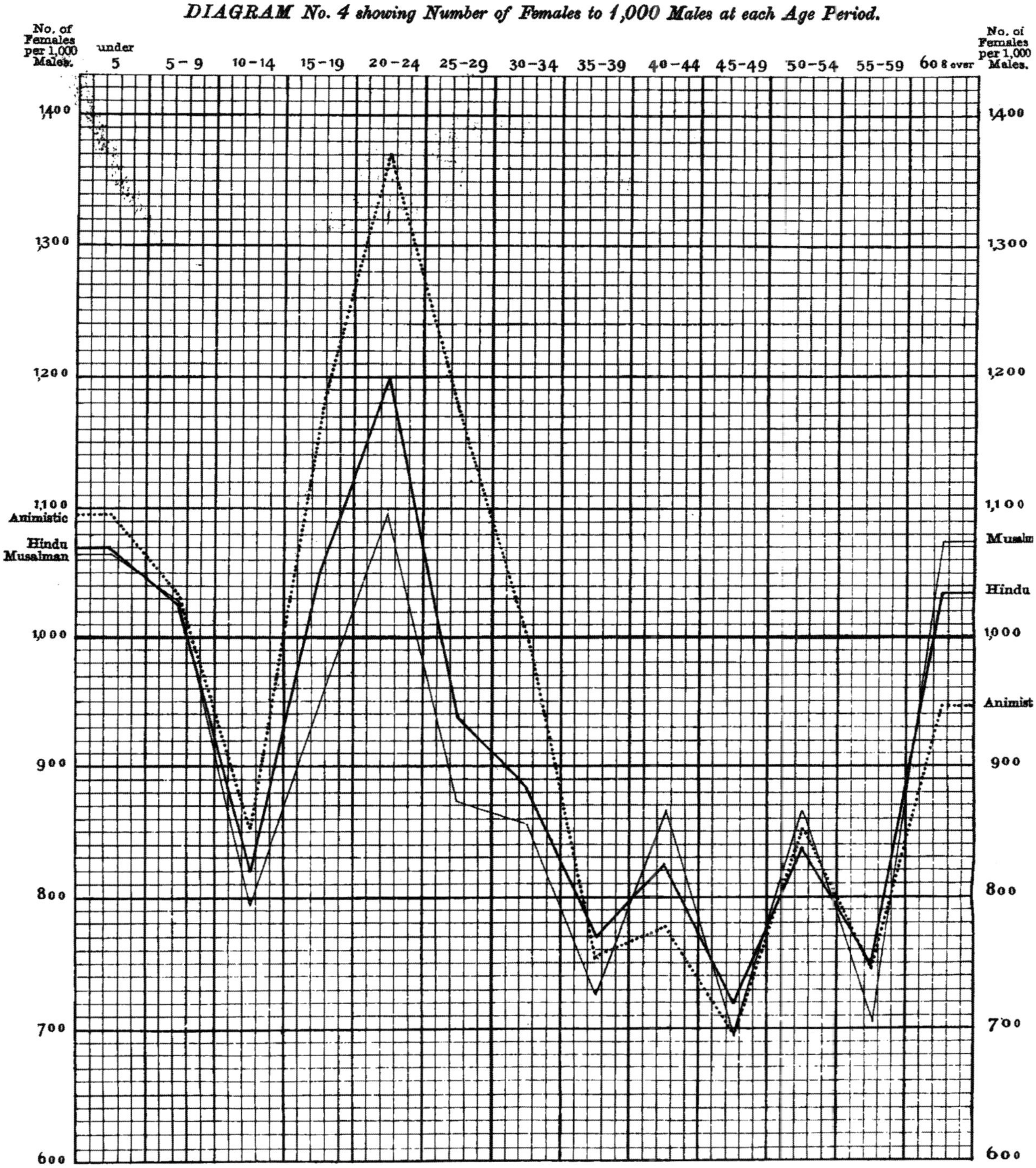

Hindu population, thus ————————

Musalman do. „ ————————

Animistic do. „ ················

Reg. No 461, Sup., Census, Berar.—Nov. 99 —754.

Litho, S. I. O., Calcu

indeed the number of female immigrants considerably exceeds that of the male. In Murtazapur and Mangrul the proportion is very low, and taking this fact in conjunction with that of a fall since 1881, and with the absence of any known disturbing influence, it seems probable that in these two taluks at least the numbers of the women have been largely understated. The largest proportion of females is found in Wun as it was in 1881 ; in Kelapur also the proportion is comparatively high, and the figures afford satisfactory indication of the permanent character of the immigration into these two taluks which, as has been shown, has been considerable. In Khamgaon the smallness of the proportion of females is extraordinary : it is no doubt to a great extent due to the disproportion of the sexes in the towns of Khamgaon and Shegaon, which are largely of a commercial character; in the town of Khamgaon the proportion of females is only 771 ; in Shegaon it is 892, and in the two towns combined, it is 825 ; but even when the urban population is eliminated, the proportion in the rest of the taluk rises only to 937. Were it not for the uniformity of the proportion (905) with that (902) at the census of 1881, the conclusion would be irresistable, in the absence of any other explanation, that the women have escaped enumeration in considerable numbers, but unless some systematic method of concealment was adopted on both occasions the parity of the proportions precludes the supposition. In Daryapur the disproportion of the sexes is also great considering the agricultural character of the taluk and also the fact that, amongst the immigrants, the females exceeded the males by more than 3,000. The inference is that there has been a large emigration of males, or that here too the enumeration of the females has been very incomplete.

Conditions in religious communities.

Coming now to the proportion of the sexes amongst the followers of the different religions, we find the following figures :—

	Females.		Males.
Among Hindus there are	942	to	1,000
" Mahomedans there are	922	"	1,000
" Animistic there are	991	"	1,000
" Jains there are	887	"	1,000
" Christians there are	84	"	100
" Parsis there are	52	"	100
" Sikhs there are	8	"	10

In 1881 the proportions for the principal religions were : Hindus, 937 ; Mahomedans, 929, Aboriginies, 993, and Jains 862. The rise among Hindus is almost analogous with that in the whole population of which they form so large a part. For the fall among Mahomedans there is no known cause, and it is more than probable that the numbers of their females are understated. Among the Animistic we have the nearest approach to equilibrium between the sexes, as was the case with the smaller class of aborigines in 1881. The rise in the proportion of females among the Jains, coupled with the decrease in their total numbers, points to the departure of a large proportion of single males, many of whom were probably amongst the immigrants in the period prior to 1881, and who, becoming subsequently dissatisfied with their prospects in the province, have emigrated again.

Proportions of the sexes at different ages.

We come now to a consideration of the proportions of the sexes at different age-periods. Statement No. 25 gives this information for the total population and for each district, and Statement No. 26, for each of the principal religions. Diagram No. 3 illustrates the proportions in the total population and compares them with those obtaining in England and Wales. Diagram No. 4 compares the proportions between Hindus, Mahomedans, and the Animistic tribes.

Statement No. 25.

Showing the number of females to 1,000 males at each age-period for the Province and each District.

	Under 1 year.	1 year.	2 years.	3.	4.	0—4.	5—9.	10—14.	15—19.	20—24.	25—29.	30—34.	35—39.	40—44.	45—49.	50—54.	55—59.	60 and over.
Province	1,011	1,073	1,091	1,142	1,043	1,071	1,024	820	1,047	1,196	941	886	766	825	715	838	744	1,033
DISTRICT.																		
Amraoti	999	1,036	1,061	1,146	1,021	1,053	1,047	825	1,016	1,178	983	882	741	782	673	802	719	979
Akola	1,006	1,084	1,078	1,142	1,064	1,070	1,028	819	1,037	1,144	912	856	772	846	749	858	766	1,032
Ellichpur	1,015	1,079	1,057	1,110	1,024	1,054	1,028	843	1,048	1,135	948	882	747	805	723	859	768	1,039
Buldana	1,023	1,103	1,125	1,173	1,057	1,094	1,029	856	1,075	1,253	869	879	806	915	783	850	714	1,077
Wun	1,015	1,047	1,116	1,125	1,032	1,069	1,016	793	1,034	1,252	1,032	943	774	790	669	849	782	1,022
Basim	1,014	1,102	1,109	1,141	1,057	1,084	989	784	1,094	1,229	910	883	766	830	697	831	732	1,103

Statement No. 26.

Showing the number of females to 1,000 males of each age-period for each Religion.

	Under 1 year.	1.	2.	3.	4.	0—4.	5—9.	10—42.	15—19.	20—24.	25—29.	30—34.	35—39.	40—44.	45—49.	50—54.	55—59.	60 and over.
Hindu	1,009	1,071	1,091	1,144	1,042	1,070	1,024	821	1,051	1,199	938	883	770	823	718	836	747	1,034
Musalman	998	1,066	1,083	1,130	1,056	1,064	1,025	795	949	1,096	872	856	728	865	693	861	706	1,072
Animistic	1,079	1,109	1,106	1,130	1,047	1,093	1,030	852	1,172	1,370	1,178	1,001	754	778	694	854	742	948
Jain	948	1,223	1,010	1,091	923	1,038	1,042	746	863	1,010	840	846	716	907	615	844	832	1,021

The most noticeable feature in these statements is the deficiency of females from 10 to 14 years of age, which is common to the whole population, regarded from the basis of locality or of religion, and which is compensated for by a corresponding excess of females through the period from 15 to 19 years up to that from 20 to 24, in which it is very high. Among the Jains and Mahomedans the excess is not reached until the latter of these two periods, but the proportion of total females to males among the followers of these religions is less than in the rest of the population. Other general features which are seen at a glance in the diagram are the large proportion of females amongst children, the relative decrease of females at the odd decennial periods from 35 to 55 years, and finally, the excess of females from 60 years of age. Generally, with the exception of the period from 10 to 14 years of age, the females are in excess of the males from infancy until the 25th year, and again in old age. The great deficiency from 10 to 14 years and the corresponding large excess in the next two periods is certainly unreal and due to a misrepresentation of age. The same peculiarity characterised the age returns of 1881, as the following comparison will show:—

		5 to 9	10 to 14	15 to 19	20 to 24
Females to 1,000 males	1881 . . .	1,008	814	1,059	1,229
	1891 . . .	1,024	820	1,047	1,196

Upon the figures for 1881 Mr. Kitts remarked:—"This (10—14) is the period of puberty, and hence even when the age is accurately known, prevarication, especially in the case of girls, is to be expected." This failing was not peculiar to Berar, but was common to all India, and here at least appears unfortunately to be as prevalent now as then. Whatever may be the object of the deception, there appears to be no doubt that the ages of a large proportion of girls of a marriageable age are systematically incorrectly stated. Judging from the returns, it would appear that a small proportion are understated, but that the great majority are exaggerated. Those which are understated are probably the unmarried, parents being possibly loath to admit the existence of an unmarried daughter of marriageable age, but why 5 years or more should be added to the age of a married girl is not easily explicable. It is possible that the true explanation is that the large numbers in the period from 20 to 24 is due to understatement of women of more advanced ages, which, judging from the habits of ladies elsewhere, may be regarded as a sexual foible, and that the deficiency from 10 to 14 is due to actual concealment. The total numbers of the sexes, coupled with the increase of females relatively to males since 1881, point to some deficiency in the enumeration of females then and in 1891, but the coincidence in the proportions at these ages then and now, and above all the compensating character of the fall and rise, seem to weaken the supposition that that is the whole explanation. More probably each of these causes has contributed to the final result: some actual concealment of women, especially in the period from 10 to 14; some understatement of age of those of these ages who are unmarried; some overstatement of age of those of these ages who are married; and some understatement of age of those above 25 years of age.

Examining the figures in further detail the following points are noticeable.

District conditions.

In the Amraoti district the male infants are just in excess of the female; and there, as elsewhere, the proportion of females rises from infancy until the 4th year of life when the number of girls to 1,000 boys varies from 1,110 in Ellichpur, to 1,173 in Buldana. In the 5th year male life begins relatively to improve, but except in the Basim district the number of females is still in excess from the 6th to the 10th year. The big drop in the next period is succeeded throughout by an excess in the one after, and this is largely increased in the period from 20 to 24, the extreme being reached in the Buldana and Wun districts. From 25 to 29 years comes another big drop, although in the Wun district the females are still in excess; and from this age until the last period female life is relatively bad, and males are largly in excess.

Among religions.

Turning to the religious divisions, it is seen that the general characteristics apply to the Hindus. Among Mahomedans male infants are slightly in excess, and, as has been before noticed, the males are in excess in the period from 15 to 19 years, but to a very much less extent than in the previous period. Among the Animistic the females are in excess up to the 35th year with the exception of the 10 to 14 period, and the males are in excess for the rest of life. In the period from 20 to 24 the women attain the large proportion of 1,370 to 1,000 men, a feature which is brought markedly to notice in the diagram. Among the Jains while the male infants outnumber the female, there is a remarkable excess of females in the second year of life, which, if accurate, points to a very heavy mortality among Jain males relatively to females at that age. The males are in excess in the 5th year, and after the 9th year the females are only in excess during the period from 20 to 24 years and from 60 years.

Comparison with England and Wales.

In Statement No. 27 are compared the proportions of the sexes at the different age-periods in this province and in England and Wales. It is to be noted that the period of from 10 to 14 years, so apparently fatal to girls in India marks a decrease in female life in England also, although to a small extent only. It is to be observed also that the period of from 20 to 24 years is characterised by a large increase of females in both countries, but from thence onwards while males preponderate in Berar until the last period, females are in excess in England throughout. This difference is to some extent to be explained by the preponderance of male immigrants in Berar on the one hand and the emigration or foreign service of male adults from England on the other; but the chief inference to be gathered from this statement is the comparatively exaggerated, and therefore probably unreliable, character of the Berar figures. This exaggeration is most conspicuous among the Animistic and Mahomedans, as may be seen on reference to the diagram No. 4.

Statement No. 27.

Number of Females to 1,000 Males.

Age.	England, and Wales.	Berar.
Under 1 year	998	1,011
1 year	1,004	1,073
2 years	1,003	1,091
3 "	1,006	1,142
4 "	1,004	1,043
TOTAL UNDER FIVE YEARS	1,003	1,071
5—9 years	1,006	1 024
10—14 "	997	820
15—19 "	1,008	1,047
20—24 "	1,093	1,196
25—29 "	1,087	941
30—34 "	1,077	886
35—39 "	1,069	766
40—44 "	1,079	825
45—49 "	1,103	715
50—54 "	1,104	838
55—59 "	1,111	744
60 and over	1,187	1,033

Generalising on the whole subject, and allowing for concealment of women and misrepresentation of age, it seems probable that the females are in excess from shortly after birth and remain moderately so until about the 20th year, and that then males predominate until old age is reached, when the numbers more or less coincide.

Excess of female children.

The preponderance of females among infants is a point that demands further examination in view of the fact that the birth statistics of the province invariably show an excess of male over female births. In commenting upon the returns of the last census which presented very similar features, Mr. Kitts, while admitting that an excess of male over female births is always expected, came to the conclusion that the age returns for the first five years of life "unmistakably" proved the contrary, and remarked "that if the mortality in both sexes was uniform from the date of birth to the taking of the census, the ratio of the births is 103 females to 100 males." It is possible, however, that the mortality is not uniform, and the subject has to be considered on that hypothesis. The registration of births is admittedly incomplete, but it may be assumed that any shortcomings would apply equally to either sex. It has been argued that the registration of females is more commonly omitted owing to the comparative unimportance attaching to that sex in the native mind, but this is only a supposition and not a demonstrated fact, and it is as plausible to presume that where registration is omitted it is the fact of the birth itself, irrespective of sex, which escapes notice either through defective arrangements of the registering authority, or through ignorance or indifference on the part of the parents. On this assumption the incompleteness of the birth statistics may be disregarded in a consideration of the proportion of the sexes. In the Report of the Sanitary Commissioner for 1890, the proportion of the sexes in the births registered during the year is shown to be 1,066 males to 1,000 females. Approximately speaking those individuals returned at the census in February 1891 as under one year of age may be taken as the survivors of those born in 1890, the births in January and February of one year, a comparatively small number, being set off against those born in the same period of the other. Among the survivors, however, we find the position reversed, and instead of a preponderance of males, it is seen that there are 1,011 females a 1,000 males. Taking the details for each district, we get the following comparative statement:—

Statement No. 28.

Number of Males to 1,000 Females.

District.	Born in 1890	Enumerated in 1891.	Diminution per cent.
Amraoti	1,070	1,001	6·4
Akola	1,063	994	6·5
Ellichpur (excluding Melghat)	1,071	1,007	6·0
Buldana	1,045	978	6·4
Wun	1,111	985	11·3
Basim	1,048	986	5·9

The figures in the first column are derived from the birth statistics given in the Sanitary Commissioner's Report, and the figures in the second column are obtained from the census returns. On the assumption that the proportions of the sexes in the statistics of birth are only approximately accurate, this statement shows very clearly the diminution of males relatively to females during the interval between birth and census; and as females cannot have increased in number, the only inference is that mortality is much higher among male infants than among female. In the Wun district it is seen to have been much higher than elsewhere, and in the remaining districts it was of more or less uniform proportions. Turning now to the numbers of deaths of children under one year registered in 1890, we find some correspondence between the results, the registered male deaths in the province being 16 per cent higher than the female. The district details certainly do not tally; Wun does not show a larger proportion than the rest; but they all agree in showing an excess male mortality which varies from 13 to 19 per cent. The evidence, therefore, being in favour of relatively high male mortality, there is no reason to doubt the assertion that male births exceed female notwithstanding the preponderance of female infants at the census.

Measure of error in the vital statistics.

Before leaving the subject of the registration of births and deaths, it may be as well to show here to what extent the censns returns afford a measure of the incompleteness of registration. Again treating the numbers enumerated at the census as under one year of age as the survivors of those born in 1890, we have the following equation: that the total births in 1890 equal the total infant deaths in 1890, *plus* the survivors in 1891. Now, the registered births in 1890 were 111,450, and if x represents the unregistered births, the total births $= x + 111{,}450$. The registered deaths of infants numbered 23,843, and if y represents the unregistered deaths, the total infant deaths $= y + 23{,}843$. The survivors we see from the census table numbered 93,148. Thus we get $x + 111{,}450 = y + 23{,}843 + 93{,}148$, or $x = y + 5{,}541$; that is to say the unregistered births exceed the unregistered infant deaths by 5,541. If now we may assume that the chance of a birth or a death escaping registration is equal, and there is, *primâ facie*, no reason why deaths of infants should be more accurately registered than births, or *vice versa*, the ratio of unregistered births to registered births equals the ratio of unregistered deaths to registered deaths, or $\frac{x}{111{,}450} = \frac{y}{23{,}843}$, and from these two equations it will be found that x, the number of unregistered births, is 7,049, and y the number of unregistered infant deaths, is 1,508; and consequently that the total number of births in 1890 was 118,499, and the total number of infant deaths was 25,351. This gives 40·9 per mille as the birth rate for the province in 1890. It is probable, however, as will be shewn later on, that the census return of children under one year of age, that is, the "survivors" in the equation, is somewhat overstated and the error in the registration is therefore probably something less than that arrived at.

Age distribution of each sex.

We pass now to a consideration of the age returns for each sex independently of their relative proportions to each other. Statement No. 29 shows the distribution of 10,000 persons of each sex in the province at the different age-periods, and compares them with the corresponding figures for 1881 as well as for England and Wales and for Jamaica. Jamaica has been selected for comparison as a fertile tropical island whose climatic conditions are not entirely dissimilar, and which is occupied by a negro population whose education and intelligence is probably much on a par with that of the native of Berar. The diagrams, No. 5 to No. 9, illustrate the details given in this table. Statement No. 30 gives similar information for each district; Statement No. 31 for each taluk; and Statement No. 32 for each of the main religions.

Statement No. 29.

Age distribution of 10,000 persons of each sex.

Age.	Berar, 1891.		Berar, 1881.		England and Wales.		Jamaica.	
	Males.	Females.	Males.	Females.	Males.	Females	Males.	Females.
Under 1 year	310	333	305	337	298	282	225	214
1 year	177	201	266	296	270	257	256	241
2 years	283	328	283	325	278	255	257	244
3 ,,	276	334	276	325	273	260	282	280
4 ,,	264	292	260	284	272	258	329	315
Total under five years.	1,310	1,488	1,390	1,567	1,391	1,322	1,349	1,294
5-9 years.	1,319	1,434	1,242	1,338	1,241	1,184	1,333	1,297
10-14 ,,	1,105	962	1,087	945	1,109	1,048	1,287	1,213
15-19 ,,	626	695	624	706	1,003	959	973	976
20-24 ,,	694	881	712	935	880	912	1,017	1,036
25-29 ,,	911	911	969	945	776	800	861	908
30-34 ,,	950	893	1,007	900	665	679	705	708
35-39 ,,	670	545	645	491	589	597	566	570
40-44 ,,	763	668	739	673	533	545	488	467
45-49 ,,	380	288	319	263	433	453	350	354
50-54 ,,	539	480	541	512	385	402	277	291
55-59 ,,	155	122	142	119	302	319	173	186
60 and over	578	633	583	606	693	780	621	700

BERAR.—Males, 1891 and 1881.

DIAGRAM No. 6 showing Distribution by Age of 10,000 Males in 1891 and 1881.

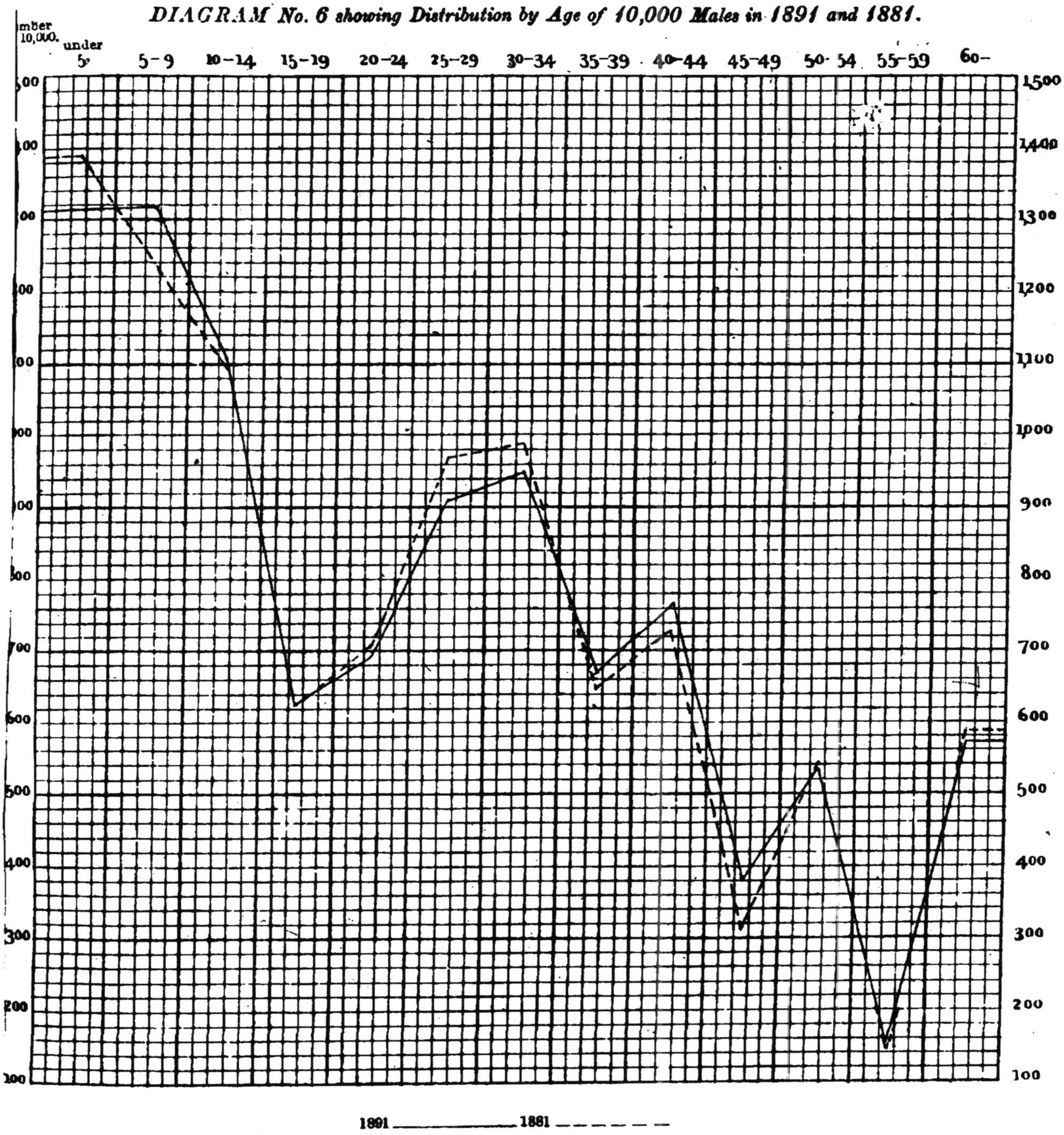

Reg No. 461 Sup. Census, Berar—Nov 93—156.

Zinco. S. I. O., Calcutta.

Females.

DIAGRAM No. 9 Comparing Distribution by Age of 10,000 Females in Berar, England, and Jamaica.

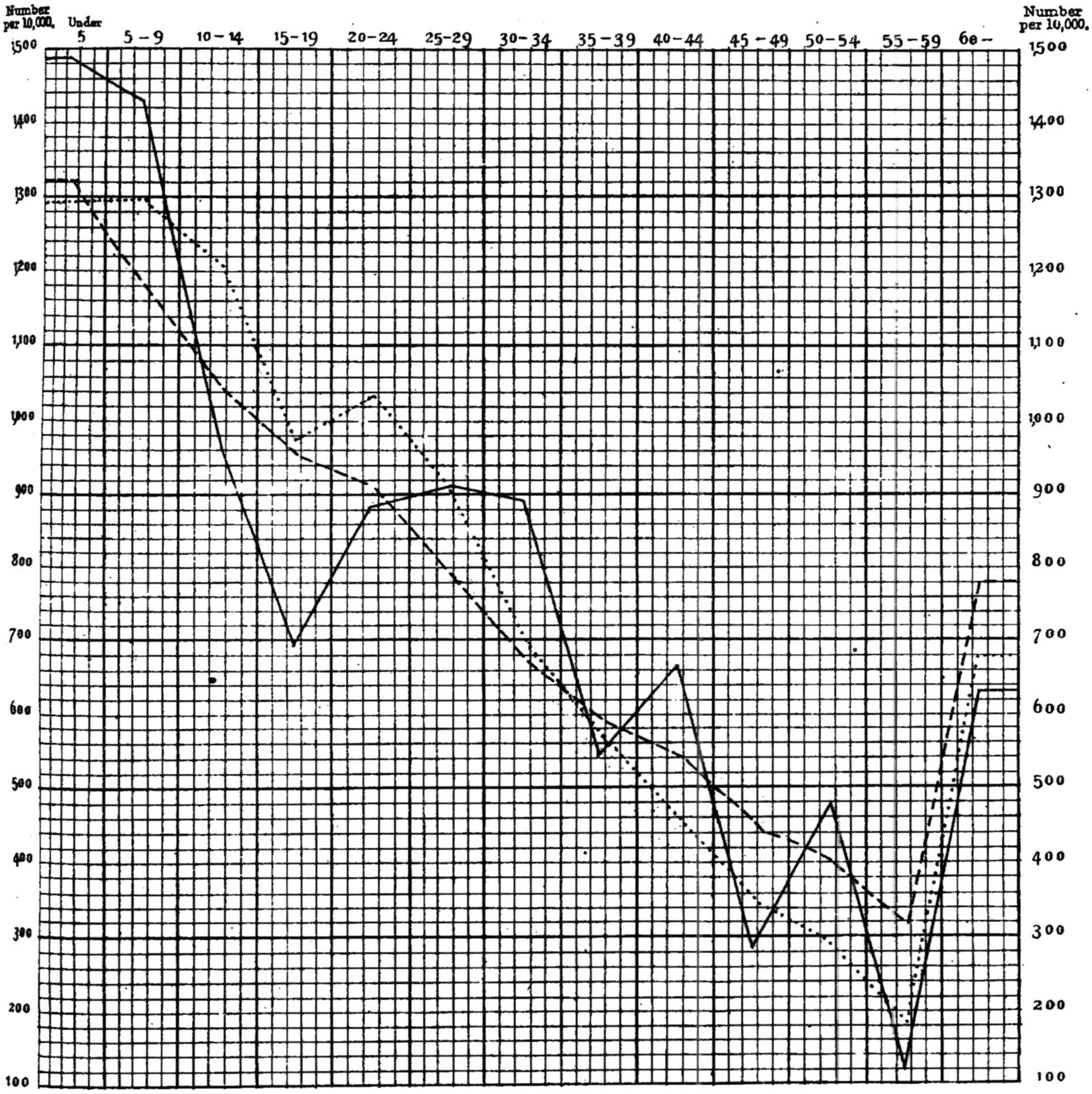

Berar ————— England — — — — — Jamaica ....

Reg. No. 461, Sup., Census, Berar – Nov 93 – 754.

Zinco. B. I. O., Calcutta.

Statement No. 30.

Showing the numbers in each age-period of 10,000 persons of each sex in each District.

District.	Under 1 year.		1		2		3		4		0–4		5–9		10–14		15–19	
	Males.	Females.	Males.	Females.	Males.	Females.	Males.	Females.	Males.	Females	Males.	Females.	Males.	Females.	Males.	Females.	Males.	Females.
Amraoti	298	321	161	180	276	316	258	319	237	261	1,230	1,397	1,233	1,392	1,063	946	622	682
Akola	332	357	156	180	252	291	260	317	226	257	1,226	1,402	1,233	1,356	1,077	943	655	726
Ellichpur	315	341	151	174	266	300	266	316	238	259	1,236	1,390	1,244	1,363	1,074	965	649	725
Buldana	320	340	191	219	277	323	282	343	280	306	1,350	1,531	1,379	1,471	1,155	1,025	668	744
Wun	289	308	199	219	308	361	295	349	309	336	1,400	1,573	1,446	1,546	1,166	973	589	640
Basim	312	335	210	246	330	388	307	371	311	348	1,470	1,688	1,424	1,491	1,109	921	564	653

District.	20–24		25–29		30–34		35–39		40–44		45–49		50–54		55–59		60 and over.	
	Males.	Females.	Males.	Females.	Males.	Females.	Males.	Females.	Males.	Females.	Males.	Females.	Males.	Females.	Males.	Females.	Males.	Females.
Amraoti	697	885	866	919	966	919	722	577	818	690	410	298	571	494	165	128	637	673
Akola	732	896	943	920	955	874	723	597	751	680	415	333	547	501	174	143	569	629
Ellichpur	743	900	882	892	958	902	694	553	788	676	404	312	540	495	161	132	627	695
Buldana	693	900	985	887	930	848	617	516	686	650	356	288	503	443	156	115	522	582
Wun	631	830	839	910	920	912	629	512	779	647	358	252	528	472	137	112	578	621
Basim	671	874	960	925	965	903	600	486	746	656	318	235	531	467	124	96	518	605

Statement No 31.

Showing the number in each age-period of 10,000 persons of each sex in each Taluk.

Taluk.	Under 1 year.		1		2		3		4		0—4		5—9		10—14		15—19	
	Males.	Females.	Males.	Females.	Males.	Females.	Males.	Females.	Males.	Females.	Males.	Females.	Males.	Females.	Males.	Females.	Males.	Females.
Amraoti	283	300	166	192	263	297	248	303	226	256	1,186	1,347	1,177	1,347	1,044	939	642	698
Chandur	303	333	158	172	290	323	261	304	240	269	1,252	1,400	1,280	1,434	1,104	1,000	619	676
Morsi	316	330	149	162	281	330	271	345	239	260	1,256	1,427	1,270	1,403	1,045	926	612	659
Murtazapur	288	318	172	200	269	318	253	335	247	258	1,229	1,429	1,205	1,377	1,048	906	611	697
Akola	316	356	146	176	246	282	256	324	220	258	1,184	1,396	1,246	1,373	1,031	902	638	701
Akot	338	362	159	178	244	278	247	292	210	232	1,198	1,342	1,158	1,291	1,068	946	654	732
Balapur	332	339	162	174	270	316	276	346	259	289	1,299	1,464	1,360	1,453	1,095	918	653	707
Jalgaon	342	361	155	191	257	288	261	308	219	249	1,234	1,397	1,228	1,351	1,131	1,019	675	743
Khamgaon	337	367	158	185	249	297	264	322	228	264	1,236	1,435	1,196	1,328	1,081	947	662	757
Ellichpur	297	322	143	165	268	304	251	303	216	239	1,175	1,333	1,185	1,320	1,064	920	668	694
Daryapur	354	365	154	167	254	285	250	290	225	241	1,237	1,348	1,196	1,307	1,039	969	645	744
Melghat	269	337	172	220	289	327	356	423	338	371	1,424	1,678	1,549	1,643	1,193	1,094	595	773
Chikhli	285	312	175	214	270	308	273	335	285	293	1,288	1,472	1,421	1,496	1,196	1,046	670	722
Malkapur	365	385	181	198	272	305	290	346	262	304	1,370	1,538	1,334	1,407	1,141	1,003	685	776
Mehkar	302	373	219	248	291	348	283	349	295	323	1,390	1,581	1,389	1,520	1,132	1,030	646	728
Yeotmal	301	311	189	209	281	337	273	322	282	302	1,326	1,481	1,355	1,473	1,150	986	584	663
Darwha	316	352	174	204	312	364	291	357	294	325	1,387	1,602	1,437	1,551	1,116	919	576	690
Kelapur	234	243	242	263	325	367	317	370	334	371	1,452	1,613	1,507	1,597	1,179	973	592	626
Wun	285	307	207	207	319	384	308	346	350	359	1,469	1,603	1,525	1,577	1,270	1,051	615	607
Basim	299	330	224	262	301	347	301	373	302	324	1,427	1,635	1,376	1,458	1,084	917	570	664
Mangrul	290	295	203	239	315	369	292	358	290	336	1,390	1,597	1,414	1,522	1,112	909	528	644
Pusad	341	364	198	230	376	451	323	376	336	386	1,574	1,807	1,492	1,516	1,140	932	577	645

Statement No. 31—continued.

Showing the numbers in each age-period of 10,000 persons of each sex in each Taluk—continued.

Taluk.	20—24		25—29		30—34		35—39		40—44		45—49		50—54		55—59		60 and over.	
	Males.	Females	Males.	Females.	Males.	Females.	Males.	Females.	Males.	Females.	Males.	Females.	Males.	Females.	Males.	Females.	Males.	Females.
Amraoti	748	915	873	922	997	929	715	570	821	722	399	298	590	506	158	122	650	695
Chandur	665	843	839	887	916	920	717	600	820	670	433	312	562	470	172	132	621	696
Morsi	665	875	843	932	959	935	736	571	810	675	404	294	567	511	164	137	669	665
Murtazapur	708	920	926	918	1,010	882	722	559	819	720	395	279	559	495	164	120	604	678
Akola	741	897	943	943	977	895	751	602	773	682	410	318	554	507	165	138	587	646
Akot	725	913	928	923	990	894	744	606	786	701	433	342	563	513	184	152	569	645
Balapur	691	881	882	897	897	880	694	564	717	680	399	304	552	491	162	126	599	635
Jalgaon	747	871	966	893	959	835	702	603	729	652	413	371	516	505	180	153	520	607
Khamgaon	755	910	1,002	935	939	851	708	605	731	677	416	330	538	484	181	144	565	597
Ellichpur	740	892	877	883	917	888	676	562	825	726	415	327	575	534	171	147	712	784
Daryapur	753	917	900	883	973	901	715	582	770	688	425	324	555	505	170	134	622	698
Melghat	730	881	856	945	1,047	948	696	450	718	593	313	229	395	345	106	81	378	420
Chikhli	666	885	982	897	953	880	614	530	704	652	346	272	511	466	148	108	501	574
Malkapur	698	860	943	868	861	793	652	552	643	625	404	348	483	439	200	150	586	641
Mehkar	711	960	1,038	900	986	880	579	459	718	678	310	235	520	446	113	82	468	581
Yeotmal	640	849	846	979	938	934	656	528	798	663	388	276	561	473	148	112	610	633
Darwha	641	842	851	899	895	885	664	542	777	654	388	261	541	453	146	117	581	625
Kelapur	601	832	836	929	952	971	621	472	798	630	326	225	494	464	122	94	520	574
Wun	635	779	807	881	902	896	536	485	730	632	299	235	497	512	119	128	596	654
Basim	688	904	971	956	1,015	890	616	486	738	661	316	250	538	462	129	99	532	618
Mangrul	652	834	919	899	938	895	627	535	749	663	372	268	557	470	155	112	587	652
Pusad	660	859	970	902	919	924	560	456	756	646	289	198	507	472	99	82	457	562

Statement No. 32.

Showing the numbers in each age period of 10,000 persons of each sex for each Religion.

		Under 1 year.	1	2	3	4	0–4.	5–9.	10–14.	15–19.	20–24.	25–29.	30–34.	35–39.	40–44.	45–49.	50–54.	55–59.	60 and over.
HINDU	Males	313	176	283	274	259	1,305	1,311	1,102	625	690	915	950	677	763	386	540	158	578
	Females	336	200	327	333	287	1,483	1,425	962	697	879	911	891	553	667	295	479	125	634
MUSALMAN	Males	296	168	261	255	259	1,239	1,276	1,095	666	786	942	964	610	766	335	567	138	616
	Females	320	195	307	322	296	1,430	1,418	944	686	933	891	896	481	718	252	530	105	716
ANIMISTIC	Males	282	205	333	352	370	1,542	1,574	1,177	562	595	771	915	637	774	328	488	120	517
	Females	307	229	371	401	391	1,699	1,636	1,012	664	823	915	924	485	608	230	420	90	494
JAIN	Males	302	138	230	219	207	1,096	1,079	1,113	793	811	982	915	699	732	432	543	190	615
	Females	322	191	285	269	216	1,283	1,268	936	771	923	930	873	565	749	300	516	178	708

Statement No. 33.

Showing the number of persons actually returned of each year of age in a specific population numbering 36,131 males and 34,191 females.

Age.	Males.	Females.	Age.	Males.	Females.	Age.	Males.	Females.	Age.	Males.	Females.
			Years.			Years.			Years.		
Under 1 year	1,171	1,136	26	195	157	52	72	35	78	1	1
1 year	584	655	27	184	116	53	14	9	79	1	...
2 years	948	1,091	28	311	236	54	11	10	80	142	158
3 „	932	1,107	29	70	91	55	520	386	81	2	3
4 „	862	960	30	2,864	2,744	56	20	19	82	1	1
5 „	1,149	1,194	31	57	37	57	13	6	83	...	...
6 „	807	854	32	423	294	58	37	12	84	1	1
7 „	1,082	1,108	33	77	64	59	13	12	85	7	17
8 „	755	725	34	52	41	60	1,256	1,285	86	1	...
9 „	777	847	35	2,095	1,650	61	18	20	87	1	...
10 „	1,398	1,231	36	131	85	62	31	19	88	...	...
11 „	388	412	37	41	40	63	3	6	89	1	...
12 „	1,405	1,007	38	87	98	64	9	6	90	19	27
13 „	273	250	39	58	56	65	227	194	91	...	...
14 „	413	370	40	2,643	2,163	66	8	14	92	...	...
15 „	724	675	41	35	30	67	5	5	93	...	...
16 „	698	741	42	140	93	68	9	3	94	...	...
17 „	188	171	43	25	17	69	3	5	95	2	8
18 „	577	665	44	31	15	70	527	369	96	...	...
19 „	125	149	45	1,181	873	71	5	4	97	...	...
20 „	1,612	2,109	46	46	27	72	8	6	98	...	1
21 „	116	105	47	31	26	73	1	...	99	...	...
22 „	575	452	48	61	49	74	1	2	100	1	1
23 „	119	102	49	37	28	75	88	82			
24 „	160	129	50	1,905	1,618	76	5	2			
25 „	2,589	2,577	51	39	15	77	1	2			

Before examining these statements, however, I wish to direct attention to Statement No. 33 which gives the actual numbers returned at each year of age in a number of blocks selected indifferently from various parts of the province but avoiding the localities inhabited by the Animistic or any specially uneducated class, so as to procure a return representative of the average intelligence of the province. It will be observed that there is a very large decrease in the second year of life, and that thereafter there is a distinct prominence in the numbers recorded for the ages of 5, 7, 10, 12, 15, 16, 18, 20, 22, 25, 30, 35, 40, 45, 50, 55, 60, 65, 70, 75, 80, and 90, and that of these from and after 30 the even multiplies of five are more popular than the odd. The comparatively small number of the age of one year was also a feature in the returns for 1881, and the explanation offered was based upon the consequences of the previous immigration from the famine districts in 1877 and 1878. The repetition of the feature at this census shows that the true explanation must be sought in some more constant factor. A very simple cause, which is probably responsible for much of the discrepancy, is to be found in the wording of the enumerator's instructions ; instead of recording a child as "under one year," he was directed to write "infant", and he would naturally include in the same category all those whom their mothers described as such ; but a mother would probably describe her child as an infant so long as it was not weaned, and as some children of one year of age are not weaned, they would be entered as infants instead of as of one year of age. Thus the number of infants is probably exaggerated, while those of one year of age are unduly diminished. The vital statistics, so far as they can be relied upon, lend force to this explanation. The numbers against the age of 5 no doubt include some of 4 and some of 6 years of age, and those of 7 include some of 6 and some of 8, the numbers 5 and 7 being apparently more popular with the ignorant and uneducated. "Ten or twelve" is a common way of expressing the age of a child there or thereabouts, while 11 and 13 are comparatively rarely given. "Fifteen or sixteen" is again a common expression for adolescence, and 18 seems to be popular, but 17 or 19 are very infrequently heard. 20 marks the commencement of adult life, and 21 is rare; 22 seems to be a comparatively favourite number, but why I do not know. 25 represents the attainment of full maturity, and thence-after life moves on in stages of 5 or 10 years at a time, and only pedants note the intermediate steps. Such appear to be the conceptions of the ordinary native of Berar; and with a population who only deal with round figures or a few popular numbers, and whose notions of years are extremely vague, it is impossible to obtain statistics of age which can be of much value.

Taking them, however, for what they are worth, and referring to Statement No. 29 and the diagrams, we find among males a very fair proportion of boys under 10 years of age, but a very large proportion of girls in comparison with the other countries described. There are more boys also between 5 and 9 than under 5, which is contrary to expectation and opposed to the conditions in the other countries. From 10 to 14 there is a declension among the boys which brings their number down to that in England and much below that in Jamaica. Among girls the decrease is sufficient to bring their number considerably below that of both countries. In the next quinquennial period there is a particularly sharp decline among the boys, and the numbers of both sexes are considerably below that of the other countries, which approximate closely to each other. In the next period the numbers of both sexes rise, the females more rapidly than the males, and the rise is continued, but at reversed rates, in the period from 25 to 29, when the number of males is larger than in the other countries, and the females, though more numerous than in England, are almost identical in number with those in Jamaica. From 30 to 34 the males again increase, and both sexes are in excess of what we may regard as normal. No doubt the large proportion of the population of both sexes between the ages of 20 and 34 is attributable to the presence of immigrants, the majority of whom may be expected to belong to that period of life; but while the great decrease of girls between the ages of 10 and 19 is susceptible of some explanation and possible modification on the grounds of concealment or misstatement of age, no apparent cause can be shown for the equally large decrease among boys of the same age. From 35 years, or rather, practically, from 30—as comparatively very few give any intermediate age—until 60 years, the numbers vary so irregularly, as the zigzag course of the lines in the diagrams exemplifies, that no comparison is possible beyond this that the differences are more sharply accentuated among females than among males, that is to say, in other words, among the most illiterate section of the people. Taking a mean, however, between the variations, the number of males is somewhat higher than in England, and the number of females somewhat lower, whilst the numbers of both sexes exceed those of the negro population. Coming to the period of old age both sexes show smaller numbers than either England or Jamaica, and all three countries exemplify the condition of more old women than old men.

Comparing 1891 with 1881 there is not much to remark upon, but it is to be observed, and is a matter for congratulation so far as it goes, that the extremes of variation in both sexes are less accentuated now than they were ten years ago, the reason for which may, it is to be hoped, be found in the growth of education and intelligence, and in the propagation, slow though it may be, of a tendency to make some approach to accuracy.

Among religions.

Coming now to the religious divisions of the population, we find that the extremes of variation beyond the period 30—34 are most conspicuous amongst the Animistic, which is also the most illiterate class, and most moderate among the Jains who are the best educated, and more marked among Mahomedans than among Hindus. The Animistic have a very high proportion of children of both sexes both under 5 years of age and from 5 to 9. The Hindus have more children than the Mahomedans, and the Jains have an unusually small number. In the period from 10—14 the Jain males show the exceptional condition of an increase in numbers and the decrease in the number of females of these people is proportionately less than amongst the rest. The Animistic have a higher proportion than the rest in the first 34 years of life, especially of females, and amongst all there are more females than males in this section of life, notwithstanding that there are more females than males over 60 years of age except only amongst the Animistic. The women of the Animistic tribes lead a life of labour which may be the cause of their earlier decease, and the large proportion of the young shows that both sexes are comparatively short-lived. They live for the most part in the jungles out of reach of even the most elementary medical assistance, and their food supplies are probably also much more limited in variety if not in extent, and inferior in quality to those procurable by the ordinary population located nearer the centers of civilisation.

Among local divisions.

Turning to the details of the local divisions of the province (Statements Nos. 30 and 31), we find a considerable range of variation, but if we except the middle periods of life from 15 to 34 years, we see a marked tendency towards a distinction between the statistics for the three districts of the plains, Amraoti, Akola, and Ellichpur (especially if the Melghat taluk is eliminated), and those of the southern hilly region. There is a larger proportion of children in the southern districts than in the northern, and a smaller proportion of the middle-aged and elderly. The smallest proportion of children is in Akola; the largest in Basim. The greatest decline in the period from 10 to 14 years is also in the Basim district, and the least in Ellichpur. The most old men are in Amraoti, the most old women in Ellichpur; the fewest old men in Basim and the fewest old women in Buldana. Pursuing the enquiry into taluks, we find that of male children under 5 years of age there are less than 1,200 per 10,000 in Ellichpur, Akola, Amraoti, and Akot, and on the other hand as many as 1,574 in Pusad and more than 1,400 in Wun, Kelapur, Basim, and Melghat. Of girls of this period the smallest numbers are in Khamgaon, Amraoti, and Daryapur, and the largest in Pusad, Melghat, and Basim, the numbers in Pusad attaining the high proportion of 1,807. The greater decline among females in the period from 10 to 14 years is found in all the taluks of the Wun and Basim Districts, and in Mehkar and Melghat. The most conspicuous extremes of variation are in Pusad, Basim, Kelapur, and Mehkar. Of persons over 60 years of age, the Ellichpur taluk has a markedly higher number of each sex, and Melghat an equally marked lower number than any other. Amraoti, Morsi, and Daryapur have also comparatively large numbers of old people, and Mehkar, Pusad, Chikhli, and Kelapur, are conspicuous for their small numbers. If we take longevity of life as a criterion of health, the north-eastern portion of the province shows a marked superiority, while Melghat with its mountainous jungles is as distinctly the most insalubrious. Of the rest the least healthy would appear to be Pusad, Kelapur, and Mehkar, of which the two former are next to Melghat the most prominent for more or less hill and jungle.

Proportion of the working population.

The relative proportion of the working population to that supported by it is a question of some interest, and some light can be thrown upon it by the statistics of age, although of course only to an approximate degree. Taking the working age of males as from 18 to 59, inclusive, and that of females as from 15 to 44, inclusive, and deducing the proportion from the figures given in Statement No. 33, which deals with about a fortieth part of the total population, we find that in 10,000 males there are 5.366 workers, and in 10,000 females 4,643 workers, or combining the sexes there are 5,005 workers to 4,995 non-workers, that is to say, the productive population is just more than half the total. The population dealt with in the statement is, however, not representative of the whole, as it does not include such classes as the Animistic nor many urban residents, and a different result might be arrived at in deducing the proportion for the whole population, but this I am not in a position to calculate, as the numbers of the ages of 18 and 19 years for the whole population have not been separately tabulated. Many males, however, commence to be productive before the age of 18, and many cease to be workers before the age of 60, and I think that a fair approximation of the productive population may be arrived at by taking the males from 15 to 54, inclusive, and the females as before from 15 to 44. On this basis are obtained the results given in the marginal Statement No. 34, which shows the proportions for the whole population and for each district. It will be observed that the districts divide themselves again into the two classes of north and south, Amraoti, Akola, and Ellichpur having a majority of the workers and the southern districts a majority of non-workers. It may be of some advantage to compare the proportions for Berar with those for some countries of Europe and elsewhere, and the latter are therefore shown in the adjoining Statement No. 35. These calculations are, however, based upon the assumption of the age of the productive class being from 20 to 59, which is considered as more appropriate to the different conditions of life in the countries named than the earlier period adopted for this province. The proportion for Berar calculated upon the same basis would be 4,925 workers to 5,075 non-workers. France has, or rather had in 1886, a considerable majority of workers, but with that exception in all the countries mentioned the non-workers predominate.

Statement No. 34.

	Workers.	Non-workers.
Province	5,063	4,937
Amraoti	5,172	4,828
Akola	5,207	4,793
Ellichpur	5,153	4,847
Buldana	4,992	5,008
Wun	4,862	5,138
Basim	4,926	5,074

Statement No. 35.

Country.	Workers.	Non-workers.
France, 1886	5,239	4,761
Italy, 1881	4,960	5,040
Austria, 1880	4,898	5,102
Sweden, 1880	4,811	5,189
Holland, 1879	4,709	5,291
Germany, 1885	4,703	5,297
England, 1881	4,635	5,365
Scotland, 1881	4,548	5,452
Jamaica	4,479	5,521
Canada	4,370	5,630
Ireland, 1881	4,352	5,648

Mean age.

The last point to be dealt with is that of the mean age, and this can be only approximately calculated from the quinquennial age-periods by taking the averages of each period. On this basis the mean age for the total population in Berar is 25·30 years. In 1881, it was shown to be 25·25, and the increase would imply an improvement of life during the last 10 years, but that very little reliance can be placed on such inaccurate data as the age returns. Taking the population whose ages are given in statement No. 33, which gives the numbers for each year of life, and which therefore enables us to ascertain the exact mean for the numbers dealt with, we find that the mean age of the males is 25·10 years and of the females 23·94. There is, however, probably little doubt that the true mean is higher than this. Among the old, whose ages should raise the average, there is a general tendency to understatement, although in a few individual instances the reverse may be the case even to exaggeration. A person of 60 years of age will frequently according to his or her own view remain 60 for an indefinite period, and a very large majority of those actually between 60 and 70 will give 60 only. On the other hand, a person who possibly has attained 80 years will probably claim 100, but the numbers of these are of course comparatively few, and the excess due to exaggeration does very little to counteract the deficiency due to the understatement of the others.

CHAPTER V.

CIVIL CONDITION.

THE different parts of Table VIII (pages 58 to 125) show the distribution of the population for the whole province and for each religion under the three conditions of unmarried, married, and widowed.

Social aspect of marriage.

The marriage institution in this country is not so strictly defined as it is in Europe. Many women are maintained under conditions which, while perfectly moral and socially recognised, do not amount to more than concubinage; and although every endeavour was made at the enumeration to confine the description of married to those subject to a legal tie according to the law applicable in each case, yet it is possible that some misrepresentations may have been made. There is, however, nothing in the returns to indicate the existence of any error of this description, but it is desirable that such a possible source of inaccuracy should not be overlooked. Marriage in India also is not what it frequently is in Europe, an index or measure of prosperity. Wife and children here too are no "hostages to fortune," for they are fellow-workers and assistants rather than "impediments to enterprise." Poor people may indeed be temporarily deterred from marriage by the initial expenditure attendant upon the ceremony, which is frequently of a recklessly improvident character, but sooner or later the necessary funds are raised, and even the very poorest can marry. But notwithstanding the absence from the statistics of marriage of some of the elements of interest found in Europe, they are among the most instructive which the census returns supply, and throw considerable light upon the customs of the people and the social problems of the day which zealous reformers are eager to solve. In dealing with the subject it will unfortunately be necessary to introduce a number of tabular statements, seldom objects of attraction to the reader, but I have endeavoured to limit them to what is essential for the illustration of the different points of interest, and I think that they will repay attention.

The actual numbers of the population in each condition are as follows:—

	Males.	Females.
Unmarried	572,594	370,446
Married	833,575	810,883
Widowed	85,657	224,336

Proportion of both sexes in each condition.

Taking the males alone, 38 per cent are unmarried, 56 per cent are married, and 6 per cent are widowed. Of the females 26 per cent are unmarried, 58 per cent are married, and 16 per cent are widowed. At the census of 1881 it was found that Berar contained the most married population in India, and although the proportion has now slightly decreased, the situation is probably still maintained. The proportions at the two enumerations are here given—

	Males.		Females.	
	1881.	1891.	1881.	1891.
Unmarried	38·4	38·4	25·9	26·3
Married	56·2	55·9	58·5	57·7
Widowed	5·4	5·7	15·6	16·0

Amongst males the proportion of unmarried is the same, and consequently that of those who have married, but the proportion of widowers has increased; amongst females the proportion of widows has also increased, and so has that of the unmarried. Regarding the latter fact in conjunction with that of the increase of females relatively to males noted in the previous chapter, it seems probable that the difference is due to a fuller enumeration of the unmarried females on this occasion. In the adjoining statement, No. 36, are compared the proportions in Berar with those for all India in 1881, and with those for some countries in Europe. The proportions of the married are very much higher in India than in Europe, as might be expected, and in Berar much higher than in India generally. The high proportion of widows in India is also remarkable, but in this respect Berar shows a smaller number. With regard to widowers, the variations are not so extreme; in all the countries the proportion of widows is much higher than that of widowers, and in both France and Italy the number of widowers relatively to the number of married men is higher than in Berar.

Statement No. 36.

Showing distribution of 10,000 persons of each sex.

	Unmarried.		Married.		Widowed.	
	Males.	Females.	Males.	Females.	Males.	Females.
Berar	3,838	2,635	5,588	5,769	574	1,596
India, 1881	4,841	3,232	4,670	4,895	489	1,873
England	6,193	5,928	3,463	3,314	344	758
France	5,513	5,041	3,954	3,934	533	1,025
Italy	5,989	5,397	3,610	3,672	401	931

Comparison with other countries.

Statement No. 37.

Showing distribution of 10,000 persons of each sex by civil condition.

	Unmarried.		Married.		Widowed.	
	Males.	Females.	Males.	Females.	Males.	Females.
Province	3,838	2,635	5,588	5,769	574	1,596
Amraoti District	3,906	2,682	5,461	5,645	633	1,673
Akola "	3,506	2,259	5,873	6,079	621	1,662
Ellichpur "	4,005	5,790	5,364	5,519	631	1,691
Buldana "	3,743	2,497	5,773	5,983	484	1,520
Wun "	4,089	2,969	5,404	5,571	507	1,460
Basim "	3,895	2,750	5,554	5,696	651	1,554
Amraoti Taluk	3,930	2,668	5,451	5,610	619	1,722
Chandur "	3,998	2,763	5,386	5,605	616	1,632
Morsi "	3,927	2,730	5,437	5,628	636	1,642
Murtazapur "	3,698	2,511	5,623	5,782	679	1,707
Akola "	3,594	2,368	5,794	5,961	612	1,671
Akot "	3,514	2,254	5,819	5,989	667	1,757
Balapur "	3,571	2,320	5,851	6,105	578	1,575
Jalgaon "	3,437	2,211	5,924	6,106	639	1,683
Khamgaon "	3,372	2,098	6,030	6,317	598	1,585
Ellichpur "	3,927	2,603	5,375	5,519	698	1,878
Daryapur "	3,643	2,355	5,711	5,892	646	1,753
Melghat "	5,188	4,511	4,425	4,545	387	944
Chikhli "	3,864	2,550	5,668	5,853	468	1,597
Malkapur "	3,623	2,386	5,881	6,110	496	1,504
Mehkar "	3,764	2,575	5,753	3,960	483	1,465
Yeotmal "	4,195	3,041	5,273	5,459	532	1,500
Darwha "	4,113	2,994	5,294	5,515	593	1,491
Kelapur "	4,236	3,160	5,355	5,407	409	1,433
Wun "	3,696	2,581	5,872	6,039	432	1,380
Basim "	3,664	2,580	5,777	5,903	559	1,517
Mangrul "	3,782	2,624	5,578	5,783	640	1,593
Pusad "	4,261	3,041	5,253	5,382	486	1,577

Statement No. 37 gives the proportions for each district and each taluk in the province, and Statement No. 38, for each of the main religions. It will be seen that the proportions of the married are much higher in the Akola and Buldana districts than elsewhere. Khamgaon has an exceptionally high proportion in both sexes, and it will be remembered that it was in this taluk that an exceptionally small proportion of females to males was found. In Jalgaon, Balapur and Akot, all of the Akola district, and in Malkapur and the Wun taluk the proportions are high. In Melghat the conditions are entirely different from the rest of the province, and approximate to what may be described as a European standard. Excluding this taluk the smallest proportions of married are to be found in Pusad, Yeotmal, Darwha, and Kelapur. The difference between Wun and the other taluks of the Wun District is very marked. So is that, but in the reversed condition, between Pusad and the other taluks of the Basim district. The widowed are most conspicuous in Ellichpur, Daryapur, Akot, Murtazapur, and Amraoti, the widows in Ellichpur attaining the high proportion of 19 per cent of the female population. In the Wun taluk in particular, and in the Wun district generally, the proportion of widowed is comparatively small. Coming to the religions it will be seen that the highest proportion of married is shown by the Hindus, and the lowest by the Mahomedans. The Jains have a much larger proportion of married women than men, and a very high proportion of widows. The Animistic have a very small proportion of widowers, and a comparatively small proportion of widows. Among Mahomedans the number of widows relatively to married women is very high.

Statement No. 38.

Showing distribution of 10,000 persons in each condition for each religion.

	Unmarried.		Married.		Widowed.	
	Males.	Females.	Males.	Females.	Males.	Females.
Hindu	3,683	2,472	5,729	5,922	588	1,606
Musalman	4,990	3,629	4,502	4,558	508	1,813
Animistic	4,930	4,143	4,687	4,805	383	1,052
Jain	4,016	2,293	5,240	5,656	744	2,051

Proportions in local divisions.

Among religions.

From these general conditions we proceed to examine the marriage statistics in connection with the age returns, which reveal several important features. Statement No. 39 shows the distribution of the population by civil condition at each age period, and statement No. 40, the distribution by age in each condition. In No. 39 the distinctive element is the age, and in No. 40 the civil condition, in both the figures should be read horizontally. Thus, in No. 39, it will be seen that out of 10,000 males under five years of age 9,901 are unmarried, 95 are married, and 4 are widowed, and from No. 40 out of 10,000

Statement No. 39.

Showing distribution by condition of 10,000 persons of each sex at each age period.

Yaars.	Sexes.	Unmarried.	Married.	Widowed.
0—4	Males	9,901	95	4
	Females	9,678	314	8
5—9	Males	9,381	595	24
	Females	6,389	3,539	72
10—14	Males	6,640	3,262	98
	Females	2,150	7,637	213
15—19	Males	3,598	6,245	157
	Females	384	9,383	233
20—24	Males	1,886	7,865	249
	Females	144	9,519	337
25—29	Males	905	8,714	381
	Females	102	9,283	615
30—34	Males	522	8,910	568
	Females	85	8,731	1,184
35—39	Males	360	8,897	743
	Females	79	8,001	1,920
40—44	Males	301	8,718	981
	Females	72	6,696	3,232
45—49	Males	238	8,596	1,166
	Females	55	5,680	4,265
50—54	Males	225	8,241	1,534
	Females	47	3,955	5,998
55—59	Males	202	7,947	1,851
	Females	40	3,563	6,397
60—	Males	189	6,981	2,830
	Females	38	1,332	8,630

Statement No. 40.

Showing distribution by age of 10,000 persons of each sex in each condition.

		0—4	5—9	10—14	15—19	20—24	25—29	30—34	35—39	40—44	45—49	50—54	55—59	60 and over.
Unmarried	Males	3,379	3,223	1,912	586	341	215	129	63	60	24	32	8	28
	Females	5,466	3,476	785	101	48	35	29	16	18	6	9	2	9
Married	Males	22	140	645	699	977	1,425	1,514	1,067	1,191	584	794	220	722
	Females	81	880	1,273	1,130	1,453	1,465	1,351	756	776	284	329	76	146
Widowed	Males	9	56	189	171	301	604	939	867	1,305	773	1,440	500	2,846
	Females	7	64	128	102	186	351	663	656	1,353	771	1,803	490	3,426

unmarried females 5,466 are under five years of age, 3,476 are between the ages of five and nine, and so on. The proportions given in statement No. 39 are also given in a graphic form in diagram No. 10. The most noticeable general features are that the females marry at a much earlier age than the males, and become widowed very much sooner. The statements, however, show that of the males a considerable number do marry at very early ages, and the numbers of married rapidly increase at each age period until about the 25th year, by which time more than four-fifths of the sex have entered matrimony. Thenceforward, the numbers continue to increase, but with gradually diminishing strength until the close of life. Less than 2 per cent of those over 60 years of age remain unmarried. There are widowers of all ages, but their numbers begin to acquire an appreciable importance about the 20th year, after which they increase with each period until in the last they amount to more than 28 per cent of the numbers of the sex of 60 years or more. Nearly 98 per cent of the unmarried males are under 35 years of age, and in an average group of 1,000 bachelors there would not be more than 3 who could be described as old men. Fifteen per cent of the married males are under 20 years of age, and nearly 69 per cent of the widowers are of 40 years or more, while more than 4 per cent are under 20. Turning to the other sex, 3 per cent of the girls under five years of age are married; of those between the ages of 10 and 14 years three out of every four are married, and including those who have already lost their husbands 8 out of every 10 have been married. Only one woman in a hundred attains to about the 25th year unmarried. With infant marriages there are infant widows, and their numbers assume importance from the age of 10 and gradually increase until about the 25th year, after which they advance with great and growing rapidity until amongst those of 60 years of age or more they amount to the large proportion of 86 per cent. Out of 100 unmarried females 55 are under 5 years of age, 89 are under 10, and 97 are under 15; there are two between 15 and 30, and one of more than 30. Old maids are very scarce; out of 1,000 unmarried women there are only 6 above the age of 34, and only 2 of 50 years or more. Of 1,000 married females 8 are under 5 years of age, 96 are under 10, and 223 are under 15; only 83 are more than 44 years old. Of 1,000 widows one will be less than 5 years of age, seven will be under 10, 20 under 15, 30 under 20, and 49 under 25. If we take 30 as the age up to which a widow might hope to remarry, if there were no social impediments in the way, and it is not probable that many would possess sufficient attractions at a later age, the chance of remarriage could only come to 8 in every hundred widows. More than three-fourths of them are over 40 years of age.

Distribution by condition at each age-period, and by each age in each condition.

It is to be observed that in both sexes there is a diminution in the numbers of the unmarried in each successive age period from the first to the last, and this might be regarded as indicating that in each age period there are a certain number who marry. If there were no marriage at advanced ages, and the death-rate of the unmarried

Gradual diminution in numbers of unmarried at each age.

were the same as among the rest of the community, the proportion of unmarried would remain constant, and its steady diminution implies either marriage at all ages up to 60 or a more rapid mortality among the unmarried. Marriage at advanced ages is not uncommon amongst men, although it is probable that it is more often widowers who remarry than old bachelors who take to themselves wives, but amonst women it seems highly improbable that any elderly spinster should marry, and in their case at least, even if it does not apply to both sexes, we are forced to the conclusion that the unmarried have comparatively shorter lives.

Statement No. 41.

Showing 10,000 persons of each sex and condition by age.

		0—14.		15—24.		25—39.		40—49.		50 and over.	
		Males.	Females.	Males.	Females.	Males.	Females.	Males.	Females.	Males.	Females.
Berar	Unmarried	8,514	9,727	927	149	407	80	84	24	68	20
India, 1881	Unmarried	7,646	9,487	1,622	377	568	89	88	24	76	23
France	Unmarried	4,937	5,301	2,985	2,756	1,294	1,004	350	365	434	574
Berar	Married	807	2,234	1,676	2,583	4,006	3,572	1,775	1,060	1,736	551
India, 1881	Married	534	1,454	1,696	2,984	4,221	3,840	1,814	1,095	1,734	627
France	Married	Nil	Nil.	305	1,045	3,379	3,636	2,429	2,235	3,887	3,084
Berar	Widowed	254	199	472	288	2,410	1,670	2,078	2,124	4,786	5,719
India, 1881	Widowed	176	137	690	543	2,516	2,271	1,975	2,243	4,643	4,806
France	Widowed	Nil	Nil	72	139	884	976	1,299	395	7,745	7,490

Comparison with India and Europe.

A comparison of the conditions in Berar with those maintaining in India generally in 1881, and in one European country, is given in Statement No. 41. France has been selected as the details of all the age periods for England are not available to me. It is seen here that in Berar both sexes marry at a much earlier age than in India generally, and the proportion of the widowed young is consequently greater also. It is curious that in all India and in Berar of the widowed persons under 15 years of age the males exceed the females. If the number of infant widows is due to the marriage of young girls with old men, it would seem from these figures that young boys are married to still older women. The true interpretation, probably, is that boy bridegrooms are wedded to baby brides, of whom a large proportion die in infancy. The proportion of widowers is indeed in excess up to 39 years of age, and this is probably to be accounted for by the greater mortality of women during the child-bearing age. This is not the case in France nor in Europe generally, and the inference is that in Europe female mortality relatively to male at this period of life is not so great as in India, or in other words, that women in child-birth are better cared for in Europe. Of the widowed of 50 years of age and over, the proportion in Berar in both sexes is higher than the all-India figures, which points to better life in Berar than the average for India, or to less remarriage, and the greater disparity between the sexes of the elderly widowed which distinguishes Berar would seem to imply a greater disparity of age between husbands and wives than is usual in India generally. Comparing the figures for Berar with those for France, the main feature is the much later age for marriage in the latter country, and the consequent postponement of the period of widowhood. Three-fourths of the widowed in France are 50 or more years of age, whereas in Berar about one-half are of this age; in other words, the widowed in Berar under 50 years of age are about twice as numerous proportionally as in France.

Mean age in each condition.

It may be of interest to consider here the mean ages of the population in each condition, which are as follows:—

	Males.	Females.
Unmarried	9·45 years	5·71 years
Married	35·05 "	26·51 "
Widowed	47·17 "	50·08 "

These figures are the averages of the combined ages of the people of each sex in each condition, and being spread over wide variations are not of much value except for comparison between the two sexes and for a few very general deductions. Husbands are on the average 8⅛ years older than their wives; but when it is remembered that there are a large number of males married as children between whom and their wives there cannot be anything like this difference, it will be realised that in the marriages which take place in the later life of the males there must be a very considerable discrepancy between the ages of husbands and wives. The married life of the man lasts, it appears, some four or five years longer than that of the woman, who spends half her life in widowhood.

Statement No. 42.

Showing the percentage of those who have married (married and widowed) to total number of sex at each age period.

Taluk.	Males.					Females.				
	0—4.	5—9.	10—14.	15—19.	20—24.	0—4.	5—9.	10—14.	15—19.	20—24.
Amraoti	.94	2.90	21.23	54.20	76.21	1.89	24.25	74.42	95.96	98.30
Chandur	.72	3.20	23.24	55.26	76.85	1.85	26.17	72.98	96.27	98.83
Morsi	1.53	4.97	25.61	52.95	76.88	3.31	29.24	73.59	95.22	97.80
Murtazapur	1.05	5.15	31.91	63.52	80.12	2.74	35.71	80.49	96.85	98.77
Akola	.86	5.27	34.67	66.81	81.45	2.93	40.63	84.64	97.16	98.87
Akot	.77	5.75	36.83	69.63	82.19	2.30	43.21	84.82	97.31	98.68
Balapur	1.05	8.45	45.70	73.09	85.40	4.28	50.60	84.93	97.16	98.84
Jalgaon	.77	6.12	43.69	76.08	87.95	2.38	48.26	89.05	98.35	99.39
Khamgaon	.84	9.03	46.98	74.06	85.26	4.91	55.50	89.62	98.22	99.03
Ellichpur	.71	3.17	21.92	54.23	75.19	1.67	26.21	74.49	95.84	98.56
Daryapur	.75	3.96	30.01	69.14	84.15	1.88	35.22	86.19	97.98	99.17
Melghat	1.04	1.64	5.23	24.74	55.18	1.18	2.39	19.64	70.59	92.14
Chikhli	1.04	6.48	33.00	68.25	84.63	3.95	37.95	85.39	97.54	99.08
Malkapur	.70	5.55	43.00	77.33	89.67	2.31	47.29	90.49	98.37	98.82
Mehkar	1.34	8.92	41.70	69.63	85.65	4.69	44.34	84.32	96.96	98.90
Yeotmal	.61	2.87	20.21	52.34	76.75	1.47	22.01	64.41	94.16	98.24
Darwha	.72	6.45	31.21	57.37	77.39	2.86	29.89	69.68	95.21	98.51
Kelapur	1.02	5.43	29.64	58.00	79.25	2.96	26.18	66.14	93.31	98.29
Wun	1.54	15.91	51.39	71.13	87.32	8.02	47.46	78.40	96.26	99.26
Basim	1.38	10.02	46.02	73.52	85.33	4.93	44.27	83.58	97.11	98.56
Mangrul	1.26	8.99	41.80	69.54	81.41	5.00	43.20	80.43	96.71	98.70
Pusad	1.15	7.55	34.65	62.12	80.12	3.98	34.02	76.52	95.78	98.06

Characteristics of local divisions.

Coming to the territorial divisions of the province, I think it is scarcely worth while to show the proportions for each condition and each age period for every taluk; the time occupied in the calculation would be great and the examination of the result would be wearisome to the reader; but I give the most important features in statement No. 42, which shows for each taluk the proportion under each age period up to from 20 to 24 years of those who have married, not distinguishing those who have become widowed. The statement exhibits some marked variations between the different localities. In the Wun taluk very early marriages are more common than elsewhere, 8 per cent of the girls under 5 years of age having been married. Mangrul comes next with 5 per cent, and Basim, Khamgaon, Mehkar, Balapur, Pusad, and Chikhli have all a high proportion. Morsi has a high proportion among boys and above the average also for girls. In the next period Khamgaon, Balapur, Jalgaon, Wun, and Malkapur are the most prominent among females, and Wun, Basim, Khamgaon, Mangrul, Mehkar, and Balapur among males. In Khamgaon as many as 55·50 per cent of the females between 5 and 9 have been married and in Wun 15·91 per cent of the males, a very markedly high proportion. In the next period from 10 to 14 Malkapur comes first among the females with 90·49 per cent, and Wun is again first among the males with 51·39 per cent. In the next two periods the numbers begin to close up, especially for the females, and there is not so much variation. Khamgaon, Jalgaon, Malkapur, and Wun have the most prominent figures. Amongst the females between 20 and 24 the proportion exceeds 99 per cent in no less than five taluks, Jalgaon, Wun, Daryapur, Chikhli, and Khamgaon. Altogether taking both sexes the highest proportions are shown in Wun, Khamgaon, Jalgaon, and Malkapur, and the lowest proportions (always excepting Melghat) in Yeotmal, Amraoti, Ellichpur, Kelapur, Morsi, Darwha, and Chandur. It will be seen here how the customs in respect of the marriage age run by locality; excepting Wun, which stands by itself in marked contrast to the rest of the district of that name and to the greater part of the province, the ages for marriage are earliest in the western and latest in the eastern taluks. In the Melghat the circumstances are entirely distinct. Males do not marry in any numbers before the sixteenth year, and at about the twenty-third year only one man in two is married. Very few girls are married before the eleventh year, and the majority do not marry until after the sixteenth.

Statement No. 43.

Showing the percentage of those who have been married to total of sex at each age-period.

	Males.					Females.				
	0—4.	5—9.	10—14.	15—19.	20—24.	0—4.	5—9.	10—14.	15—19.	20—24.
Hindu	·98	6·85	37·49	69·74	85·35	3·48	40·62	84·94	97·76	99·00
Musalman	·72	1·17	4·61	18·05	45·82	1·21	4·56	31·64	86·45	96·13
Animistic	1·49	2·61	8·86	32·71	64·59	1·79	6·12	32·27	81·14	94·62
Jain	·64	2·49	22·81	51·38	74·33	1·93	32·48	84·53	98·40	99·76

Among religious communities.

Statement No. 43 gives similar information to the last for the main religions. The Animistic have the highest proportion of married males under five years of age, but with this exception the Hindus marry much earlier than the rest. Among females above 10 years of age, the proportion of the Jains and Hindus are much the same, the Jains attaining the very high rate of 99·76 per cent in the period from 20 to 24. The Hindu proportion is obtained from a very much larger range of numbers, but the actual figures for the Jains are remarkable; out of 822 females of ages from 20 to 24, only two are unmarried. The Animistic males appear to marry about five years later than the Hindu, and among the Mahomedan males there is not much early marriage comparatively, and even in the period from 20 to 24 years of age less than half the men have been married. Among females the Mahomedan and Animistic proportions do not greatly differ, and the large majority of marriages would seem to take place after the sixteenth year.

The next aspect from which the marriage statistics may be viewed is that of the comparison of the sexes. Taking the whole population there are to each thousand males in each condition respectively, 647 spinsters, 973 wives, and 2,619 widows. In the adjoining Statement No. 44 are given the proportions for each taluk, and in Statement No. 45 the proportions for each religion. The small proportion of unmarried females and the large proportion of widows we have been prepared to expect from what has gone before, but the excess of husbands to wives is certainly remarkable. The reverse might well have been looked for, as married men will leave their homes and their wives for purposes of trade or labour, while wives very rarely go without their husbands. The situation is to be partially accounted for by the influx of married men from other provinces, which is not counteracted by the emigration from Berar, but it is improbable that this cause is alone sufficient to explain the whole difference, and having regard to the irregular proportions of the sexes in the total population, I think it may be accepted that some of the married women have escaped enumeration. In two taluks only—Malkapur and Wun—do the wives outnumber the husbands; in Balapur the numbers are almost equal, and in Mehkar and Chikhli the excess of husbands is not very large. The low proportion of wives in Amraoti, Khamgaon, and Akola, is no doubt largely attributable to trade and the consequent influx of married men, but it is not so apparent why the lowest proportion of all should be in Murtazapur, which is not so important a trade center. Among the Animistic wives are in excess, which is probably due to some polygamy. Among Mahomedans the husbands largely outnumber the wives, and as these are the people who are said to be most prone to throw obstacles in the way of any disclosures affecting their women, the fact tends to confirm the theory of the omission of women in the enumeration. The Jains have a small proportion of wives, but they are not a settled community in Berar, as a whole that is, and numbers of them are no doubt married traders whose homes are beyond the province. The Jains have a very small proportion of spinsters to bachelors, and the Mahomedans a very large proportion of widows to widowers. Musalman widowers largely re-marry, and even old men on the loss of their wives at once take steps to replace them. The Animistic have a comparatively large number of spinsters, and their bachelors should have no trouble in suiting themselves. A glance down the first column of Statement No. 44 will show the nature of the competition for wives in the different localities. In Khamgaon it must be particularly keen, and in Jalgaon, Daryapur, Akola, and Akot, the supply of spinsters to bachelors is comparatively small. Excepting the Melghat, the most favourable taluks are those

Relative conditions of the sexes.

Statement No. 44.

Showing number of females to 1,000 males in each condition.

	Unmarried.	Married.	Widowed.
Province	647	973	2,619
Amraoti	625	948	2,564
Chandur	640	963	2,451
Morsi	655	975	2,431
Murtazapur	625	946	2,313
Akola	608	950	2,520
Akot	609	978	2,503
Balapur	622	999	2,609
Jalgaon	604	968	2,478
Khamgaon	563	948	2,398
Ellichpur	625	968	2,537
Daryapur	604	965	2,539
Melghat	808	955	2,270
Chikhli	634	992	3,277
Malkapur	640	1,010	2,944
Mehkar	657	996	2,913
Yeotmal	678	969	2,638
Darwha	683	978	2,362
Kelapur	721	977	3,393
Wun	682	1,005	3,123
Basim	664	964	2,559
Mangrul	643	962	2,310
Pusad	682	979	3,101

Statement No. 45.

Showing the percentage of females to males.

	Unmarried.	Married.	Widowed.
Hindu	63·2	97·4	257·0
Musalman	67·1	93·4	328·8
Animistic	83·3	101·6	272·4
Jain	50·6	95·7	244·6

of the Wun district and Pusad. The widowers seem to take advantage of these circumstances to re-marry, judging by the high proportion of widows to widowers in some of these taluks.

Relative conditions of the sexes at different ages.

I now proceed to examine the proportions of the sexes at the different ages in each condition which are shown in Statement No. 46.

Statement No. 46.

Showing number of females to 100 males in each age-period for each condition.

	0—4	5—9	10—14	15—19	20—24	25—29	30—34	35—39	40—44	45—49	50—54	55—59	60
Unmarried	105	70	27	11	9	11	14	17	20	16	17	15	21
Married	355	610	192	157	145	100	87	69	63	47	40	33	20
Widowed	216	302	178	156	162	152	185	198	271	261	328	257	315

This statement illustrates much of what has been already said, but in another form; how the unmarried males outnumber the unmarried females, how the young wives outnumber the young husbands, how towards the 28th year or thereabouts the number of husbands and wives is equalised, how thereafter the balance is turned, and in each succeeding period the excess of husbands over wives increases, and how at all periods of life the widows outnumber the widowers. But it brings into striking prominence the extraordinary paucity of spinsters in proportion to bachelors at all ages except in infancy and early childhood, and suggests the difficulty attendant on the search of a wife of any but tender years. What this difficulty may actually and practically amount to is shown in the following imaginary statement by a Hindu, resident in a village with a population of 1,000 persons of the same community:—

"Yes, Saheb, my wife is dead and I wish to marry again, but I do not want a child-wife. I have my work to do, and I want a wife old enough to look after my house and my children, but it is difficult. A large village? It is true there are a thousand inhabitants, but of these, 515 are males and only 485 are females. Of the females 287 are married, 78 are widows, and 120 are unmarried. Of the unmarried females, 111 are under 10 years of age and 7 are between the ages of 10 and 14. I wish to marry a girl of from 15 to 20 years of age, or so, but there is only one such in the village unmarried, and for her there are many competitors. Of the men of the village, 295 are married, 30 are widowers, of whom I am one, and 190 are unmarried. Of the widowers, there are 20 over 19 and under 60 years of age—19 besides myself; and of unmarried men between the same ages there are 14. All these men wish to marry and want a wife who is not a child, so that for the one girl of suitable age in our village I have to compete with 33 other men; 33 of us must therefore look elsewhere. If we stretch a point and marry the girls between the ages of 10 and 14, 26 of us will still remain unprovided for and must therefore marry children under 10 years of age, or remain single. Even if the widows might remarry, it would not make much difference to us. There are only 5 widows above 14 and under 30 years of age and only 1 between 10 and 14. It is true that there are 10 widows between 30 and 40 years of age, but they are too old to please most of us, and even if we married all these there would still remain 10 of us—10 out of the original 34 unmarried. So you see, as there is the same competition on the average in every other Hindu village, more than two-thirds of the men must marry children if they do not marry widows, and even if there were no restriction on the remarriage of widows, still more than one-third must marry children if they marry at all."

Local differences.

To examine the bearing on this subject of the circumstances of different localities reference may be made to Statement No. 47, which gives for

Statement No. 47.

Showing number of females to 1,000 males of the unmarried population.

	0—4	5—9	10—14	15—19	20—24
Amraoti	1,036	822	269	88	81
Chandur	1,023	794	295	84	59
Morsi	1,052	776	293	103	117
Murtazapur	1,051	713	228	90	74
Akola	1,065	638	190	87	68
Akot	1,048	638	202	94	89
Balapur	1,044	552	223	109	97
Jalgaon	1,046	570	165	71	55
Khamgaon	1,008	492	155	51	72
Ellichpur	1,059	800	266	89	66
Daryapur	1,007	689	172	70	59
Melghat	1,095	979	723	472	197
Chikhli	1,066	671	183	80	76
Malkapur	1,073	572	142	79	136
Mehkar	1,056	642	235	108	99
Yeotmal	1,030	817	358	130	94
Darwha	1,061	759	341	119	81
Kelapur	1,054	800	384	163	110
Wun	96	632	359	125	69
Basim	1,042	619	243	120	121
Mangrul	1,025	623	255	122	83
Pusad	1,065	692	281	119	121

each taluk the proportion of females to males of the unmarried population in each age-period up to 24 years. It will be seen how small are the proportions between 10 and 24 in Khamgaon, Jalgaon, Daryapur, Chikhli, Akola, and Malkapur.

Statement No. 48.

Showing number of persons in 1,000 of each age-period who are or have been married.

Castes.	Males.			Females.		
	All ages.	0—9.	10—14.	All ages.	0—9.	10—14.
Mali	717	70	664	823	367	966
Sutar	688	31	366	784	238	920
Teli	680	36	455	799	285	950
Kunbi	677	50	467	797	292	940
Simpi (Jain)	668	26	382	775	228	942
Kumbhar	668	31	303	749	172	824
Wanjari	666	80	552	786	328	931
Mhali	664	36	404	788	256	917
Simpi (Hindu)	662	18	297	786	206	938
Dhangar	661	52	482	772	264	937
Koshti	644	29	233	774	166	796
Lohar	637	35	246	750	171	837
Chambhar	635	49	409	746	211	872
Warthi	633	28	324	758	158	886
Sonar	624	24	291	774	202	915
Koli	601	21	238	732	165	866
Kalal	600	13	181	736	121	734
Gaoli	598	21	217	682	109	621
Wani (Hindu)	595	28	229	753	142	761
Wani (Jain)	595	15	208	773	159	815
Brahman	586	13	129	770	91	873
Mahar	581	32	327	688	154	779
Rajput	574	14	138	751	108	753
Mang	572	35	329	682	147	790
Gond (Hindu)	554	18	92	646	46	398
Gond (Animistic)	543	26	116	636	56	419
Bhoi	537	27	141	637	71	504
Andh (Hindu)	536	35	279	634	111	713
Pardhan (Hindu)	506	15	100	598	42	426
Shekh	504	8	48	636	27	321
Bhil	503	12	95	621	58	443
Pardhan (Animistic)	501	21	128	590	43	483
Pathan	497	11	39	646	29	323
Korku	459	13	43	529	16	177
Banjari	442	13	96	560	48	371

Relative conditions among certain castes.

The last point to be considered is the relative conditions of the different castes, the details of the most important of which, in point of numbers, are given in Table E, page 438.

The proportions of those who have married, including therein the widowed, are given in Statement No 48. The proportions of widows to total females are shown in Statement No. 49. It will be seen that the Malis marry more and earlier than any other caste. Next to the Malis, the Sutars among males, and the Telis and Kunbis in both sexes are conspicuous for the high proportion of married persons. The Wanjaris marry early, and so do the Dhangars, Kunbis, and Telis; the Chambhars and Malis are also conspicuous for early marriage among males, and the Jain Simpis among females. The difference between the conditions of the Wanjaris and Banjaris is somewhat remarkable; the two castes are said to be of the same stock, but the Wanjaris have settled down to a quiet life of domestication, while their brethren retain their old nomadic habits; and while a large proportion of the former marry, of the latter less than half the men and only a little more than half the women do so. Of the Simpis and Wanis the Jain castes in the female sex marry more and earlier than the Hindu; of the two divisions of the Gonds and the Pardhans the Hindu has a larger proportion of married in both sexes than the Animistic. In the Mahomedan tribes, Shekh and Pathan, the proportion of married is far below the average, and early marriage is comparatively uncommon. The Korkus are distinguished by the smallest proportion of married women, and especially of young married women, child-marriage in either sex being apparently quite exceptional. It is perhaps chiefly on this account that the Korkus exhibit the smallest proportion of widows, a ratio which, for an Indian community, appears to be remarkably low. The Brahmans, Rajputs, and Wanis, on the other hand, have a very high proportion of widows. Of the Brahmans the number of widows is only just less than half that of wives, and exceeds that of unmarried females. A state of society in which the widows out-number the spinsters and yet are prohibited from remarriage, presents conditions which are quite beyond the conception of the European mind; the imagination can scarcely picture the existence of such circumstances in the Western world or realise the social and moral consequences that would ensue were they to arise. The Brahman widows number 7,575; of these 15 are under 10 years of age, 93 are under 15, and 2,257 are under 40 years of age; that is to say nearly one-third are possible mothers, and probably one-fourth would marry again if they were permitted to do so. The effects of the prohibition of remarriage generally are clearly seen in the statement of the proportion of widows (No. 49). The order in which the castes appear might almost be taken as the order of social precedence. The higher castes who follow the Brahmans in the prohibition of remarriage have a large proportion of widows and come at the top, and the low castes and aboriginal tribes who repudiate the doctrine have a small proportion of widows, and come at the bottom. The number of widows is of course also affected by the relative ages of husbands and wives. Amongst the Pathans there are 52 wives to 10 husbands under 15 years of age; amongst the Brahmans and Rajputs there are 51; amongst the Shekhs 49. A high proportion of young wives points to considerable discrepancy of age between the married, and consequently to a tendency to greater widowhood, and to this cause is probably due the high proportion of widows in

Statement No. 49.

Showing for each caste the number of widows in 1,000 females.

Caste	Widows	Caste	Widows
Brahman	255	Mali	159
Rajput	231	Kumbhar	155
Wani (Hindu)	220	Koli	152
Wani (Jain)	206	Dhangar	150
Sonar	188	Wanjari	148
Simpi (Jain)	188	Bhoi	143
Pathan	185	Gaoli	136
Koshti	183	Bhil	134
Kalal	183	Gond	129
Shekh	182	Chambhar	129
Mhali	176	Mahar	127
Simpi (Hindu)	175	Mang	125
Kunbi	166	Andh	123
Lohar	165	Banjari	118
Warthi	165	Pardhan (Hindu)	116
Teli	163	Pardhan (Animistic)	101
Sutar	161	Korku	81

the Musalman tribes and in the low caste of Kalals who do not prohibit widow remarriage, but who have 42 young wives to 10 young husbands.

The postponement of the age of marriage among females, and the removal of the restriction against the remarriage of widows, are two most pressing questions in the Hindu social economy of the day, and are receiving some attention from the enlightened members of the community. The circumstances brought to light by the marriage statistics show what immense difficulties there are in the way of the first, and what assistance towards it the second would afford. Where almost every man is desirous of marrying no one will be willing to prejudice the fulfilment of his hopes by deferring the opportunity, and in a population in which, practically, the only marriageable females are girls of tender age, it is apparent that, unless heroic measures are adopted, no improvement can be looked for within any reasonable period of time; but were the widows permitted to remarry, although the numbers who may be regarded as of a marriageable age are comparatively small, there are enough of them in early womanhood to give very sensible relief to the congestion in the marriage market.

CHAPTER VI.

INFIRMITIES.

General considerations.

TABLES XII to XVA (pages 178 to 203) give the numbers of the population enumerated respectively as Insane, Deaf-mute, Blind, and Leper. No definition of insanity was attempted, nor was any distinction made between lunatics and idiots. The entry of deaf-mutes was to be confined to those born deaf and dumb, of the blind to those entirely blind, and of lepers to those suffering from corrosive leprosy, no record being made of those affected with mere discoloration of the skin only. With what degree of accuracy the instructions were carried out can only be a matter of surmise; the diagnosis in each case rested with the parents or friends of the afflicted person or with the enumerator, all equally unskilled, and in the absence of any scientific opinion, it is very probable that some mistakes were made. With regard to the blind and deaf-mutes there was not much room for doubt, but in the case of persons in whom leprosy was beginning to develop, there would be some question; and as to the insane, those at least who are lunatic at intervals only and monomaniacs of a harmless character would probably be omitted, and a more careful enquiry than was possible to the enumerator is necessary to obtain an accurate return. I have heard also that the enumerator sometimes complicated matters, but narrowed the enquiry, by extending the words "from birth," which qualified the deaf-mutes to the insane and the leprous, but how far this may be true I cannot say. Again, in the abstraction of the schedule entries there is considerable room for error, as there is no possible check on the work, except that of repeated abstraction, which, unfortunately, often leads only to different results on each occasion or by each manipulator. Complete reliance cannot, therefore, be placed on the results produced, but there is no normal standard that I am aware of by which they can be tested.

Actual numbers.

The actual numbers returned for each infirmity are as follows:—

	Males.	Females.
Insane	280	198
Deaf-mutes	317	213
Blind	3,380	3,388
Lepers	2,886	812
TOTAL AFFLICTED	6,863	4,611

Comparison with 1881.

The numbers returned at the census of 1881 were—

	Males.	Females.
Insane	499	333
Deaf-mutes	1,412	1,044
Blind	4,563	5,198
Lepers	2,971	777
TOTAL AFFLICTED	9,475	7,352

The proportional figures are compared in the following abstract:—
In 100,000 persons of each sex there were—

	In 1881.		In 1891.	
	Males.	Females.	Males.	Females.
Insane	36	26	19	14
Deaf-mutes	104	81	1	15
Blind	330	402	226	241
Lepers	215	60	193	58

The numbers of the lepers at the two years are the only figures that approximate. Whether the differences are due to over-statement in 1881 or to under-statement in 1891, or to an actual decrease of infirmities, cannot be positively asserted; possibly all three causes have combined to affect the results. With regard to the deaf-mutes, however, it is remarked in the Census Report for 1881 that the numbers then recorded included cases which were not congenital, and pains were taken on this occasion to avoid this mistake, so that the variation now shown does not of itself throw doubt upon the present returns. It would be interesting if the statistics collected in the Medical Department could be used to throw any light upon the question; but the Sanitary Commisssioner, to whom the tables have been referred, was unfortunately not in a position to examine them from a professional standpoint.

Statement No. 50.

Showing number of persons afflicted in 10,000 of each sex.

	Insane.		Deaf-mute.		Blind.		Leper.	
	Males.	Females.	Males.	Females.	Males.	Females.	Males.	Females.
Berar	2	1	2	2	23	24	19	6
India, 1881	5	3	11	7	23	25	9	3
England and Wales	31	33	6	5	9	8	...	...
Scotland	38	39	3	2	9	8	...	...
Ireland	38	34	8	7	11	12	...	...
Italy	8	6	6	5	8	7	...	...
Austria	22	19	15	11	10	8	...	...
Ceylon	13	9	2	1	24	18	...	...

Comparison with other countries.

Statement No. 50 compares the figures for Berar with those for India in 1881 and for Ceylon and some countries in Europe. The figures for the insane in Berar are remarkably small; those for India are small in comparison with the European figures, and those for Berar are less than half those for India. The proportion of deaf-mutes is almost identical with that in Ceylon and Scotland, but is considerably less than in India generally and in the other countries given. The numbers of the blind are almost the same as those for India in 1881, and approximate to those in Ceylon, but are much higher than those for the European countries, which, as was pointed out in the Census Report for 1881, is what might be expected; heat, glare, dust, insects, and the pungent smoke of cowdung fuel are among other influences affecting the eyes and sight to which the natives of this country are constantly subject, and in a walk through an ordinary village so many children with sore-eyes may be seen that, considering what small opportunity the people enjoy of efficient medical care and attention, it need not be a matter of surprise that there should be so many who are blind. The proportion of lepers in Berar compared with India generally is very high. In 1881 it was more than double that of any other province in India, except Bengal, which it still exceeded very largely, and the present returns, so far as the comparison is to be relied upon, show but a small improvement. The subject of leprosy has, however, lately been engaging the attention of a special commission of experts, and the circumstances of this province have no doubt received their consideration, so that there will be no advantage in attempting to discuss the topic here.

Distribution by age.

The next statements deal with the infirmities in relation to age. Statement No. 51 shows the distribution of the infirm by age, that is to say the proportion of the total infirm of each sex who are found at each period. Statement No. 52 gives the ratio of the infirm of each age period to the total population of each sex of the same age. Among the insane under 15 years of age, the proportion of girls is greater than boys; from 15 to 34 the proportion of males is much higher; and from 45 years upwards the females predominate. In a hundred insane males 20 are under 15, 47 between 15 and 34, and 15 of 45 and over; in the same number of insane females 21 are under 15, 39 between 15 and 34, and 23 above 44. The number of insane males rises in each period up to from 30 to 34 and then declines;

among the females there is an irregular rise and fall throughout. In 100,000 males between the ages of 30 and 34, 37 are insane, almost double the proportion to the same number of all ages. The largest proportion of insane females is between the ages of 45 and 49, and 55 and 59, the ratio at each age period being more than double the average on all ages. Among the deaf-mutes under 15 years of age also, the proportion of girls is higher than boys, and the proportion of children is much greater than among the insane. From 15 to 34 the males predominate, and from 40 and over, the females. In a hundred deaf-mutes of each sex 28 of the males and 29 of the females are under 15 years of age; and 21 of the males and 25 of the females are over 44. The proportion of those who reach the age of 60 is almost twice as great as among the insane. Among males the numbers rise until the period from 15 to 19, and then decline; among females, as in the case of the insane, the progression of the numbers is irregular. Among the blind there is a general, though irregular, increase in the numbers of both sexes from infancy to old age; from 40 years they begin to increase rapidly, and a very large proportion are 60 and over. Among the young blind the males predominate; in one thousand blind persons of each sex 198 males and 137 females are under 15 years of age, and 387 males and 278 females are under 30; on the other hand, while there are 481 males of 40 years or more, there are 589 females, and of these 241 of the males and 314 of the females are 60 or more years of age. In ten thousand children of each sex under 5 years of age there are 10 boys and 7 girls who are blind, and most of these are probably born so; but blindness is principally incident to old age, for not only are a large proportion of the blind over 60 years old, but a considerable number of the persons who attain the age of 60 are blind; of a thousand persons of each sex of that age, 9 men and 12 women are blind, while the average among persons of all ages is 3 men and 4 women. Very few children are lepers; the disease begins apparently to develop after the 10th year, and the numbers increase until the period from 40 to 44. Of a hundred lepers of each sex 5 males and 11 females are under 20 years of age, 55 males and 58 females are between 20 and 44, and 40 males and 31 females are 45 years old or more; and of these latter 12 males and 11 females attain the age of 60. Relatively to the total population, the lepers are in the greatest proportion at the period from 50 to 54 among males, and from 55 to 59 among females; but they diminish considerably in the last period. Comparing the effects of the different infirmities, it is seen that while blindness is little or no obstacle to longevity, but rather an accompaniment, comparatively few of those afflicted with any of the other infirmities attain the age of 60. Lepers begin to die off after 45 or 50; the insane after 35, and the deaf-mutes still earlier, although those of the deaf mutes who survive their youth have a better life than the insane, and more of them reach old age.

Statement No. 51.

Showing the percentage of infirm of each sex in each age-period.

	Insane.		Deaf-mute.		Blind.		Lepers.	
	Males.	Females.	Males.	Females.	Males.	Females.	Males.	Females.
0-4 . . .	1·07	1·52	3·47	5·63	5·71	4·10	·07	·37
5-9 . . .	7·14	7·07	13·25	12·21	7·78	4·96	·35	...
10-14 . . .	11·78	12·63	11·36	11·74	6·27	4·63	1·94	4·93
15-19 . . .	7·50	7·07	11·67	7·04	5·21	3·78	2·95	5·30
20-24 . . .	8·93	11·11	8·20	8·92	5·83	4·60	5·75	7·88
25-29 . . .	12·50	7·07	10·09	10·33	7·87	5·70	7·59	8·99
30-34 . . .	18·57	12·12	10·41	9·39	7·57	7·35	13·03	14·41
35-39 . . .	6·79	9·09	6·31	4·23	5·65	5·96	12·09	11·08
40-44 . .	10·36	9·09	4·73	5·16	7·31	8·29	16·49	15·64
45-49 . . .	2·86	6·06	3·79	5·16	4·62	4·84	9·88	7·02
50-54 . . .	6·43	7·07	4·73	4·70	9·05	10·51	14·69	10·10
55-59 . . .	·71	2·52	1·58	·94	3.05	3·87	3·53	3·69
60— . . .	5·36	7·58	10·41	14·55	24·08	31·41	11·64	10·59

Statement No. 52.

Showing the percentage of infirm of each sex in each age-period.

	Insane.		Deaf-mute.		Blind.		Lepers.	
	Males.	Females.	Males.	Females.	Males.	Females.	Males.	Females.
0-4	·0015	·0014	·0056	·0057	·0988	·0664	·0010	·0014
5-9	·0102	·0069	·0213	·0129	·1337	·0834	·0050	...
10-14	·0200	·0185	·0218	·0185	·1286	·1161	·0340	·0296
15-19	·0225	·143	·0396	·0153	·1886	·1310	·0911	·0440
20-24	·0241	·0178	·0251	·0153	·1903	·1260	·1603	·0517
25-29	·0257	·0109	·0235	·0172	·1956	·1508	·1611	·0570
30-34	·0367	·0191	·0233	·0159	·1807	·1984	·2654	·0932
35-39	·0190	·0235	·0200	·0117	·1910	·2637	·3491	·1175
40-44	·0254	·0191	·0132	·0117	·2168	·2991	·4179	·1352
45-49	·0141	·0296	·0211	·0271	·2749	·4044	·5022	·1406
50-54	·0224	·0208	·0186	·0148	·3804	·5279	·5271	·1216
55-59	·0087	·0291	·0216	·0116	·4460	·7619	·4417	·1745
60.	·0174	·0168	·0383	·0348	·9445	1·1948	·3899	·0966

Relative proportions of the sexes.

The relative proportions of the sexes at different ages among the different infirmities are given in Statement No. 53. Taking the whole number or all ages there are to a thousand males 707 females among the insane, 598 among deaf-mutes, 1,002 among the blind, and 281 among lepers. Leprosy, it is seen, attacks nearly four males for every female, and there is considerable disparity between the sexes among the insane and the deaf-mutes. If we accept the results as fairly accurate, the causes which tend to produce them form an interesting subject of enquiry, but one which requires scientific treatment and which I therefore refrain from approaching. The proportions of the sexes at the different age-periods exhibit great diversity, and permit of few general deductions. Among the blind the males predominate until about the 35th year, and after that the females are in excess to the close of life. Among lepers the disparity between the sexes is least among the young and then increases almost uniformly until the period from 50 to 54 years of age, after which it diminishes again to a small extent.

Statement No. 53.

Showing number of females to 100 males.

	Insane.	Deaf-mute.	Blind.	Lepers.
0—4	100	109	72	150
5—9	70	62	64	...
10—14	76	69	74	71
15—19	67	40	73	51
20—24	88	73	79	38
25—29	40	69	72	33
30—34	46	61	97	31
35—39	95	45	106	26
40—44	62	73	114	27
45—49	150	92	105	20
50—54	78	67	116	19
55—59	250	40	127	29
60	100	94	131	26
All ages	71	60	100	28

Local conditions.

I now proceed to examine the subject in relation to the local divisions of the province. Statement No. 54 gives the percentage of the infirm on the total population of each sex for each district and taluk. Of insane males the Ellichpur, Melghat, and Jalgaon taluks have the largest proportions, and Melghat, Amraoti, and Mangrul of the females. Kelapur, Wun, and Mangrul have the smallest proportions among males and Mehkar, Wun, and Chikhli among females. Taking the sexes together, the proportion is highest in Melghat with ·029 per cent, Ellichpur with ·025, and Amraoti with ·021, and lowest in Wun and Mehkar with ·009, and Kelapur with ·010. The actual numbers are, however, in no case very large; Ellichpur heads the males with 24, and Amraoti the females with 20. In Kelapur there are only three insane males, and in Wun four of each sex. Taking the districts the proportions for both sexes range from ·013 per cent in Wun to ·023 in Ellichpur. In actual numbers Akola heads the list with 107 insane and Amraoti comes next with 102. Wun has only 60.

Statement No. 54.

Showing percentages of the infirm on the total population for each sex.

District.	Insane.		Deaf-mute.		Blind.		Lepers.		Total afflicted.	
	Males.	Females.	Males.	Females.	Males.	Females.	Males.	Females.	Males.	Females.
Amraoti	·017	·014	·020	·017	·224	·212	·218	·060	·479	·304
Akola	·023	·014	·026	·016	·235	·259	·234	·077	·519	·366
Ellichpur	·028	·017	·035	·025	·266	·252	·255	·071	·584	·366
Buldana	·015	·012	·012	·009	·256	·280	·245	·075	·529	·377
Wun	·013	·012	·017	·013	·167	·200	·118	·040	·316	·265
Basim	·018	·017	·020	·011	·221	·254	·071	·015	·331	·297
Taluk.										
Amraoti	·019	·023	·018	·018	·235	·198	·178	·042	·450	·281
Chandur	·014	·011	·016	·017	·200	·202	·183	·051	·413	·281
Morsi	·022	·011	·024	·009	·238	·233	·297	·086	·581	·339
Murtazapur	·013	·010	·025	·027	·229	·226	·239	·067	·507	·331
Akola	·022	·017	·021	·019	·222	·205	·219	·065	·484	·306
Akot	·024	·010	·034	·018	·224	·258	·221	·073	·503	·359
Balapur	·019	·014	·023	·012	·248	·247	·289	·096	·579	·369
Jalgaon	·028	·013	·018	·008	·270	·311	·240	·093	·556	·425
Khamgaon	·023	·015	·034	·023	·221	·295	·214	·063	·493	·396
Ellichpur	·032	·018	·013	·013	·275	·224	·247	·082	·567	·337
Daryapur	·024	·010	·063	·045	·294	·279	·287	·067	·668	·402
Melghat	·029	·031	·033	·013	·164	·273	·193	·048	·418	·366
Chikhli	·014	·009	·004	·009	·272	·306	·274	·088	·564	·413
Malkapur	·019	·017	·028	·012	·273	·262	·325	·105	·645	·397
Mehkar	·011	·008	·001	·005	·223	·276	·125	·028	·361	·317
Yeotmal	·015	·013	·019	·017	·182	·203	·165	·053	·381	·286
Darwha	·018	·010	·015	·013	·198	·223	·131	·039	·363	·286
Kelapur	·005	·015	·015	·006	·113	·142	·076	·027	·209	·190
Wun	·009	·009	·023	·017	·156	·227	·075	·038	·264	·291
Basim	·019	·015	·014	·013	·265	·313	·066	·016	·365	·357
Mangrul	·009	·023	·016	·018	·159	·219	·093	·023	·278	·282
Pusad	·022	·016	·029	·004	·202	·199	·065	·010	·319	·230

Of deaf-mutes Daryapur has a very much larger proportion than any other taluk, and almost twice as many as Khamgaon, which comes next; Akot has the same proportion among males as Khamgaon, and among females Murtazapur has a higher percentage; but taking the sexes together, while Daryapur has ·055 per cent Khamgaon has only ·029, and Akot and Murtazapur ·026. In Mehkar and Chikhli in both sexes, and in Kelapur and Pusad among females, the proportions are the smallest. In actual numbers Mehkar has only 1 male and 4 females, Chikhli 3 males and 7 females, Pusad, Kelapur, and Melghat 3 females each, and Jaigaon 4 females. In Pusad, however, there are 21 males, and the disparity between the sexes is remarkable. Of the districts, Ellichpur has the largest proportion, ·031 per cent for both sexes, and Buldana the least, ·011. In actual numbers Amraoti and Akola have 124 each, and Buldana only 51.

Of the blind the highest proportions are in Daryapur, Ellichpur, Malkapur, Chikhli, and Jalgaon, among males, and in Basim, Jalgaon, Chikhli, and Khamgaon, among females. In Kelapur the proportions in both sexes are considerably smaller than anywhere else; Wun and Mangrul have the next lowest among males, and Amraoti and Pusad among females. Taking the proportions for both sexes combined, Jalgaon with ·289 per cent, Chikhli and Basim with ·288, and Daryapur with ·286 form a distinct group at the head of the taluks, the next highest proportion being ·268 in Malkapur, and after that ·256 in Khamgaon. In Kelapur the proportion is ·127, and the next lowest are Mangrul with ·188, Wun with ·191, and Yeotmal with ·192. Taking the districts, Buldana with ·268 has the highest proportion, and Wun with ·183 the lowest. The proportion

... Illustrating Relative Prevalence of Blindness and Leprosy in Taluks.

Taluks in which the prevalence is markedly high are colored—

For Leprosy ....

For Blindness ....

The figures in red show the number afflicted in 100,000 of the population, or that ratio.

of males varies from ·266 in Ellichpur to ·167 in Wun, and that of females from ·280 in Buldana to ·200 in Wun.

For leprosy Malkapur takes a markedly prominent place in the taluks; in actual numbers there are 385 of both sexes, and in no other taluk are there as many as 300; and the proportion among the males is as high as ·325 per cent. Morsi, Balapur, and Daryapur come next for males, and Balapur again, Jalgaon, and Chikhli for females. For both sexes together Malkapur has a proportion of ·216 per cent, Morsi and Balapur have each ·195, Chikhli, ·183, and Daryapur ·181. The smallest amount of leprosy is found in Pusad, Basim, Kelapur, Wun, and Mangrul, the proportional figures for both sexes being Pusad ·038 per cent, Basim ·042, Kelapur ·052, Wun ·057, and Mangrul ·059. Of the districts, Ellichpur has the percentage of ·166 for both sexes, Buldana ·162, Akola ·158, Amraoti ·142, and then there comes a drop to ·79 in Wun and ·44 in Basim. In the Basim district the comparative freedom from leprosy is remarkable: there are there 176 lepers altogether, less than one-twentieth of the number in the province, and of female lepers there are only 30.

From this summary, it may be seen that Daryapur, Malkapur, Balapur, and Jalgaon, with, perhaps, Ellichpur and Morsi, are the most conspicuons taluks for the prevalence of infirmities generally, while Kelapur, Wun, Pusad, and Mangrul enjoy the greatest exemption; but beyond these distinctions there seems to be no particular relation in the extent of prevalence between the different infirmities, and no special topographical characteristics of distribution. If we take the districts and note them in order of prevalence for both sexes together, and for each sex separately for each infirmity, and total the serial numbers of all the lists, we shall arrive at a resultant order of prevalence as follows: Ellichpur, Akola, Buldana, Amraoti, Basim, Wun,—from which the very general deduction may be drawn that the south and east is freer from infirmity than the north and west. To some extent there is some relation between the prevalence of infirmities and the density of the population, Ellichpur, Daryapur, Khamgaon, Jalgaon, and Akot being conspicuous among the taluks for both high densities of population and large prevalence of infirmities, and, on the other hand, Kelapur, Wun, Mangrul, Darwha, Yeotmal, and Pusad are amongst those with the lowest densities and the smallest proportions of the infirm; but the correspondence is not sufficiently universal to warrant a precise rule. The topographical prevalence of blindness and leprosy is illustrated in map No. 4. Those taluks in which these infirmities are most conspicuous are coloured pink and blue, respectively, and the ratio of the number afflicted to 100,000 persons is given for each.

Relative proportions among castes.

The last point to be dealt with is the relation of the infirmities to the different castes.

The principal proportions are given in the next four statements Nos. 55 to 58; but before examining them I have to point out that the figures in the tables for the tribe of Musalman are untrustworthy. Most Mahomedans have given specific tribal names, and for a small number only does "Musalman" appear as the tribal or caste designation, and the proportions to this small number of the numbers entered in the tables of infirmities by caste are so very much larger than any other section of the population, that it seems clear that they are erroneous, especially as a very simple explanation of the mistake offers itself. The probability is that the abstractors of the infirmity details have in some instances confused the column for religion in the schedule with that for caste, and have recorded some entries of infirmities under the designation of "Musalman" instead of under that of Shekh, Syed, or other specific tribal name. I have not unfortunately discovered the mistake in time to rectify it. There was nothing in the actual numbers to attract attention at the time of abstraction or compilation, and the error has only come to light on analysing the tables at a time when the Abstraction Office has been closed and the establishment discharged. Under the circumstances, all that I can do is to acknowledge the mistake and regret it.

Statement No. 55.

	Percentage of Insane in Castes most affected.	
	Males.	Females.
Bhoi	·042	...
Brahman	·024	·017
Gaoli, etc.	·030	...
Korku	·028	·035
Kunbi	·017	·011
Mahar	·022	·012
Mali	·017	·014
Rajput	·011	·025
Shekh	·029	·018
Sonar	·053	...
Teli	·024	·010
Wani (Hindu)	·018	·022

Statement No. 56.

	Percentage of Deaf-mutes in Castes most affected.	
	Males.	Females.
Andh	·041	·027
Chambhar	·046	...
Dhangar	·022	·028
Gaoli, etc.	·035	
Kunbi	·015	·013
Mahar	·029	·015
Mali	·024	·012
Mana	·019	·019
Rajput	·033	·033
Shekh	·008	·020
Sutar	·046	...
Wani (Hindu)	·033	...

Statement No. 57.

	Percentage of Blind in Castes most affected.	
	Males.	Females.
Bari	·311	·181
Beldar	·259	·198
Bhoi	·140	·259
Dhangar	·250	·365
Gosawi	·435	·304
Gurao	·301	·284
Kasar	·396	·269
Koshti	·298	·351
Kumbhar	·226	·215
Kunbi	·265	·269
Lohar	·263	·185
Mahar	·216	·213
Mali	·285	·273
Maratha	·209	·316
Rajput	·272	·253
Sali	·293	·205
Simpi	·187	·255
Sonar	·258	·255
Sutar	·252	·233
Teli	·242	·255
Vidur	·244	·316
Wanjari	·214	·382
Wani (H)	·240	·267
Warthi	·221	·247

Statement No. 58.

	Percentage of Lepers in Castes most affected.	
	Males.	Females.
Andh	·114	·027
Bari	·371	·063
Bhoi	·147	·099
Chambhar	·211	·043
Gaoli, etc.	·206	·075
Gosawi	·421	·171
Gurao	·365	·175
Kasar	·371	·134
Korku	·197	·046
Koshti	·246	·042
Kumbhar	·169	·072
Kunbi	·220	·054
Lohar	·239	·093
Mahar	·152	·052
Mali	·305	·101
Mhali	·208	·076
Pardhan	·292	·078
Rajput	·220	·083
Sali	·366	·051
Sutar	·218	...
Teli	·275	·115
Vidur	·320	...
Wanjari	·147	·078
Warthi	·238	·150

Glancing at the tables, the numbers of the infirm among the Kunbis, Mahars, and Malis at once catch the eye, but these are the most common castes in the province and the proportions of the infirm among them are not remarkable. Of the insane, the highest proportions are among Sonars, Bhois, and Gaolis, for the males, and among the Korkus and Rajputs for the females. Chambhars, Sutars, and Andhs among males, and Rajputs, Dhangars, and Andhs among females, have the highest proportions of deaf-mutes. Of the blind, the Gosawis have the high ratio of ·435 among males, and ·304 among females; the Kasars and Baris have also high proportions among males and Wanjaris, Dhangars, and Koshtis among females. The Gosawis have also a very high proportion of lepers of both sexes; the proportions among the Guraos and Malis for both sexes among the Baris, Kasars, Salis, and Vidurs for males, and among the Warthis, Telis, and Bhois for females, are the most conspicuous of the rest; but it is to be noted that in nearly all the castes included in the statements the proportions in one sex or the other are above the average for the province.

CHAPTER VII.

EDUCATION.

TABLE IX shows the distribution of the population, as a whole and for each religion, under the three categories of learning, literate, and illiterate. The first comprises the number of those who, at the time of the census, were under instruction of some sort either at home or at school; the second, those who were able to read and write and were no longer under instruction; and the third, those unable both to read and write. Table D gives the same information for each caste, tribe, or race with the addition of the numbers of the "literate" who have some knowledge of English. No attempt has been made to show the degree of education of the "learning" and "literate," and such details scarcely fall within the scope of a general census; but the tables afford a clear indication of the attitude of the people and of their separate sections towards education generally.

Proportions.

In 10,000 males of the general popualtion there are 258 under instruction, 584 who have been under instruction, and 9,158 absolutely illiterate. Of the same number of females, the proportions are 7 pupils, 12 instructed, and 9,981 illiterate. Nothing marks the social distinction between the sexes better than these figures.

Illiteracy of Berar.

The returns for the census of 1881 showed that Berar was then one of the most illiterate provinces of India; and although the present enumeration points to some improvement, considerable further progress will be necessary before even the average for all India is attained. The marginal Statement No. 59 compares the proportions of the illiterate of both sexes in Berar with those for India in 1881 and some other countries. It will be at once apparent from these figures how vastly the European standard differs from that of this country. Even in Ceylon the condition of education is far in advance of that of Berar and of India generally. In 1881 the proportions for Berar were 938 for males and 999 for females, so that there has been a substantial diminution of illiteracy in the decade amongst the males. As to the females it can at least be said that they have made a beginning. Now one man in 12 and one woman in 521 know or are learning how to read and write.

Comparison with other countries.

Statement No. 59.

Showing number of illiterate in 1,000 persons of each sex.

	Males.	Females.
Berar, 1891	916	998
India, 1881	909	996
Ireland	446	499
Italy	623	764
Austria	479	533
Hungary	592	717
Portugal	750	892
Ceylon	731	971

Under-statement of those "learning."

Before going further, I have to draw attention to an error which the returns of the Education Department bring to light. It is stated in the Administration Report that on the 31st March 1891 there were 48,578 male and 1,764 female scholars in all the recognised schools of all classes in the province, whereas the numbers returned at the census as "learning" were 38,502 males and 976 females. The latter figures are palpably wrong, as, with the exception of the comparatively few new pupils who may have joined the schools between the 26th February and the 31st March, all those at least who were on the books of the Education Department as scholars should have been shown at the census as "learning," the numbers of which might be expected to include also some who were under instruction at home or in small schools not within the cognizance of the department. The explanation of the discrepancy probably is that a large number of pupils were returned as "literate" owing to miscomprehension of the instructions by parents or enumerators. To a man who can just read and write while his son at school is very much farther advanced, a by-no-means uncommon coincidence, it does not seem clearly intelligible why he should return himself as "instructed" and his son as only "learning." Doubts upon this point were sometimes expressed by the enumeration staff, and judging by the result, I am inclined to think that they were very commonly entertained. On the other hand, the distinction between "learning" and "illiterate" is clearly defined; the literal meaning of the vernacular expressions used is "is learning" and "not taught," and there does not appear to be much room for doubt between them. Thus while it appears that the numbers of the learning are largely understated and little value can be attached to any deductions drawn from their numbers alone, I think there is no reason to question the approximate accuracy of the numbers of "learning" and "literate" combined, and consequently of the "illiterate," and that the proportions and comparisons deduced from these figures may be safely accepted. I, however, give the separate proportions in some cases for what they may be worth.

Proportions according to religion.

The adjoining statement No. 60 shows the distribution of the population according to religion in all three categories. It will be seen that the Animistic tribes are supremely illiterate; out of 10,000 males only 19 ever have learnt or are learning to read and write, and of the women, numbering, it should be remembered, more than 68,000, there is not a single individual who has received any instruction at all. Of the Hindus 823 in 10,000 males have received some education, but only 13 in the same number of females. The Mahomedans show a better condition than the Hindus, 1,158 males and 56 females in 10,000 of each sex being included among the learning or the literate. The Jains are very much more advanced as regards the males, and show a smaller proportion of illiteracy than several countries of Europe, but the condition of the females is the same as that among the Mahomedans, and exhibits a remarkable contrast with that of the other sex. Among the Jains almost every other man has received some education; among the Mahomedans one man in 9; among the Hindus one man in 12; and among the Animistic one in 538. Of the women there is one in 178 among Jains; one in 179 among Mahomedans; and one in 744 among Hindus. The Christians and Parsis exhibit a very high percentage of instruction, but their populations are not properly typical; the proportions among Christians are largely influenced by the numbers of the Europeans and true Eurasians who, with the exception of young children, are practically all educated, and the numbers of the Parsis are not representative of all classes and ages of that community. Of the natives of the country, however, the Christians are less illiterate than the rest, and they do not neglect the education of the female sex. In 100 Native Christians of each sex only 41 of the males and 67 of the females are illiterate. Of a similar number of Eurasians there are 23 illiterate males and 25 females.

Statement No. 60.

Showing percentage of each condition on total of sex for each religion.

Religion.	Learning.		Literate.		Illiterate.	
	Males.	Females.	Males.	Females.	Males.	Females.
Hindu	2·53	·05	5·70	·08	91·77	99·87
Musalman	3·99	·24	7·59	·32	88·42	99·44
Animistic	·10	*Nil.*	·09	*Nil.*	99·81	*All*
Jain	10·08	·28	38·20	·28	51·72	99·44
Christian	10·30	9·16	60·03	48·31	29·67	42·51
Parsi	13·65	9·93	70·11	49·64	16·24	40·43

The attitude of the people as regards education may, however, be more accurately appreciated by a consideration of the proportions in what may be termed the school-going age, 5 to 14. The tables show the actual numbers from 0 to 14, but it may be assumed that a very small number of the learning and certainly none of the literate are under 5 years of age, and therefore if we deduct the numbers of those under 5 from the total and from the number of illiterate, we get a fair approximation of the proportion of those of school-going age who are either learning or have been taught to read and write. The next statement, No. 61, shows the percentages for the whole population and each religion in the three age periods 5—14, 15—24, and 25 and over. From this we see that in 100 Hindu boys who might be or have been at school, there are only 10 who have fulfilled that condition, of the Mahomedans there are 16, of the Jains there are 50, of the Christians 83, and of the Parsis 80. Of the Animistic there are only 3 in 1,000 boys. Of the girls there are among Hindus only 26 in 10,000, while Mahomedans have 115, and Jains 163. Of the Christians there are 72 girls in 100, and of the Parsis 83. Put in other words the meaning of these figures as regards Hindu girls is this, that in a number of villages aggregating a total population of between 8,000 and 9,000 souls, of whom 1,000 are girls of school-going age, two or perhaps three of these individuals are or have been at school. It is, however, to be noted that in the province there are 28 Hindu women between the ages of 15 and 24, and 25 of 25 years or more, who are stated to be still under instruction. The statement also shows that among all classes, excepting of course the Animistic females, the proportion of illiterate is higher in the last period than in the first two, which indicates the increased spread of education in the rising generation, and a comparison of the figures affords some measure of the rate of progress in the different communities. Among Mahomedans education is spreading more rapidly than among Hindus, and among the Jains faster than in any other class of natives.

Proportions in school-going age.

Statement No. 61.

Showing the percentage of educated at each age-period.

	Males.						Females.					
	5—14		15—24		25 and over.		5—14		15—24		25 and over.	
	Learning or literate.	Illiterate.	Learning or literate.	Illiterate.	Learning or literate.	Illiterate.	Learning or literate.	Illiterate.	Learning or literate.	Illiterate.	Learning or literate.	Illiterate.
Province	10·43	89·57	13·39	86·61	8·34	91·66	·36	99·64	·29	99·71	·13	99·87
Hindu	10·25	89·75	13·06	86·94	8·14	91·86	·26	99·74	·20	99·80	·09	99·91
Musalman	16·20	83·80	17·38	82·62	10·56	89·44	1·15	98·85	·81	99·19	·33	99·67
Animistic	·32	99·68	·31	99·69	·13	99·87	...	100	...	100	...	100
Jain	50·45	49·55	65·90	34·10	52·18	47·82	1·63	98·37	·46	99·54	·26	99·74
Christian	82·76	17·24	80·17	19·83	79·90	20·10	71·83	28·17	72·14	27·86	62·86	37·14
Parsi	80·49	19·51	96·36	3·64	94·63	5·37	82·76	17·24	87·10	12·90	57·89	42·11

I now proceed to examine the conditions in the different local divisions of the province. The proportions of the learning, literate, and illiterate in each district is given in the

Local conditions.

following statement, No. 62. Wun and Basim are the most illiterate districts and Akola the least. In Akola one male in 9 and one female in 343 can or are learning to read and write; in Amraoti one man in 10 and one woman in 371; in Ellichpur one man in 10 and one woman in 577; in Buldana one man in 12 and one woman in 722; in Basim one man in 17 and one woman in 1,007; and in Wun one man in 19 and one woman in 931.

Statement No. 62.

Showing the percentage in each condition on total of sex in each district.

	Males.			Females.		
	Learning.	Literate	Illiterate.	Learning.	Literate.	Illiterate.
Amraoti	2·83	6·75	90·42	·08	·19	99·73
Akola	3·51	7·40	89·09	·13	·16	99·71
Ellichpur	3·05	6·67	90·28	·05	·12	99·83
Buldana	2·59	5·59	91·82	·05	·09	99·86
Wun	1·56	3·61	94·83	·04	·07	99·89
Basim	1·65	4·31	94·04	·04	·06	99·90

Taking only the numbers of the school-going age, calculated as before, the proportion of those in 10,000 persons of each sex who can or are learning to read and write is—

in Akola . . . . . . 1,452 boys and 67 girls;
in Ellichpur . . . . . . 1,238 „ „ 28 „
in Amraoti . . . . . . 1,209 „ „ 44 „
in Buldana . . . . . . 1,022 „ „ 24 „
in Basim . . . . . . 673 „ „ 17 „
in Wun . . . . . . 600 „ „ 19 „

Coming to the taluks, the proportions in the same category are as follows:—

1. Akot . . . . . . 1,619 boys and 65 girls.
2. Amraoti . . . . . . 1,587 „ „ 105 „
3. Ellichpur . . . . . . 1,525 „ „ 45 „
4. Khamgaon . . . . . . 1,483 „ „ 56 „
5. Malkapur . . . . . . 1,473 „ „ 33 „
6. Akola . . . . . . 1,445 „ „ 97 „
7. Daryapur . . . . . . 1,442 „ „ 21 „
8. Jalgaon . . . . . . 1,389 „ „ 32 „
9. Balapur . . . . . . 1,288 „ „ 76 „
10. Chandur . . . . . . 1,130 „ „ 16 „
11. Murtazapur . . . . . . 1,024 „ „ 48 „
12. Morsi . . . . . . 1,021 „ „ 7 „
13. Yeotmal . . . . . . 841 „ „ 23 „
14. Chikhli . . . . . . 826 „ „ 30 „
15. Basim . . . . . . 712 „ „ 19 „
16. Mehkar . . . . . . 710 „ „ 9 „
17. Mangrul . . . . . . 699 „ „ 32 „
18. Darwha . . . . . . 637 „ „ 19 „
19. Pusad . . . . . . 610 „ „ 7 „
20. Kelapur . . . . . . 438 „ „ 6 „
21. Wun . . . . . . 406 „ „ 30 „
22. Melghat . . . . . . 70 „ „ 5 „

These figures demonstrate what great differences in the progress of education there are between the several taluks, and also how much room there is for improvement. If in Akot there are 1,619 boys in 10,000 of school-going age who are or have been at school, it follows that there are 8,381 who have not enjoyed that advantage. In other words, for every boy in Akot sent to school there are 5 more who might be but are not; and omitting Melghat, the numbers in the different taluks vary from this to 24 in Wun. In the Melghat 143 boys of school-going age are not taught for one who is. Female education is most advanced in Amraoti and Akola, and, besides Melghat, is very backward in Kelapur, Pusad, Morsi, and Mehkar.

Taking the total number of learning and literate without regard to age, the taluks do not observe quite the same order of strength, as may be seen from

Statement No. 63, which shows these proportions for each sex and compares them with the conditions existent in 1881. In every taluk there has been a substantial increase in the proportion of the educated of the male sex, notably in Melghat, Chikhli, Mangrul, Khamgaon, and Akola. Among females the increase has been considerable in Amraoti, Akot, Balapur, Darwha, Mangrul, and Wun; but in Chikhli and Mehkar, there has been some diminution, and in Melghat the proportions remain the same. There has been no regularity of variation in the extent of female education, and it appears to bear little or no relation to that among males, except that it is larger in the taluks in which the most important towns are situate. In Amraoti the proportion of females instructed or under instruction is conspicuously higher than elsewhere, but it has no doubt been largely influenced by the presence of Europeans and Eurasians; and the same applies in a lesser degree to most of the taluks in which district head-quarters are situated.

Statement No. 63.

Showing number of persons in 10,000 of each sex instructed or under instruction.

Taluk.	Males.		Females.		Number of persons among whom one is instructed or under instruction.	
	1891.	1881.	1891.	1881.	Males.	Females.
Amraoti	1,291	956	66	18	8	151
Ellichpur	1,240	909	27	14	8	366
Khamgaon	1,149	748	26	21	9	385
Akola	1,145	774	46	23	9	218
Akot	1,129	860	29	5	9	339
Malkapur	1,056	766	16	13	9	631
Jalgaon	1,052	841	13	5	10	763
Daryapur	949	683	10	4	11	971
Balapur	944	660	25	5	11	404
Murtazapur	857	675	20	11	12	503
Chandur	835	569	10	3	12	1,024
Morsi	796	563	9	7	13	1,212
Chikhli	744	461	18	20	13	566
Yeotmal	664	457	13	7	15	752
Basim	644	478	17	5	16	775
Mehkar	615	459	8	9	16	1,293
Darwha	562	428	10	2	18	948
Mangrul	559	356	13	2	18	793
Pusad	556	408	5	1	18	2,183
Kelapur	387	318	6	3	26	1,736
Wun	375	266	14	1	27	734
Melghat	207	122	4	4	48	2,266

Increase of schools.

In connection with the comparison of the educated population at the two enumerations, it may be of interest to note the increase in the number of schools and of scholars during the decade as recorded in the Administration Reports. Without distinguishing between the different classes of schools there were, in March 1882, 884 schools, on the books of which were enrolled 35,422 boys, and in March 1891, 1,235 schools and 48,578 male scholars; in 1882 there were 12 girls' schools with 469 girls, and in 1891, 49 schools with 1,764 female scholars.

To the comparative figures in the last statement are appended two columns showing the number of persons among whom is found one who can read and write or is under instruction, and these figures serve to compare very clearly the extent of education in each taluk. In Amraoti one male in every 8 is literate or learning; in Melghat one male in every 48. The condition of Amraoti considered alone is poor, and that of Melghat is very poor indeed; yet, bad as it is, the latter is three times better than that of the females in the most advanced taluk of the province.

Relative conditions among castes.

Turning now to Table D, we obtain the conditions of education in the different castes and races of which the population is composed. Omitting Europeans, Eurasians, and Native Christians, whose numbers have been examined under the denomination of Christians, and also those whose representatives in this province are few, the groups of castes and races take the order given in the subjoined list, which shows the number in 1,000 males who are learning or know how to read and write :—

1 Group	5,	Priests	629
2 ,,	9,	Writers	503
3 ,,	14,	Traders	488
4 ,,	21,	Brass and copper smiths	256
5 ,,	17,	Goldsmiths	246
6 ,,	22,	Tailors	229
7 ,,	7,	Temple servants	227
8 ,,	45,	Miscellaneous	178
9 ,,	22b,	Perfumers	174
10 ,,	36,	Distillers	173
11 ,,	22a,	Confectioners	148
12 ,,	23,	Weavers	140
13 ,,	8,	Genealogists	127
14 ,,	6,	Devotees	125
15 ,,	48,	Non-Indian Asiatics	119
16 ,,	44,	Hunters	82
17 ,,	20,	Carpenters, etc.	74
18 ,,	27,	Oil-pressers	66
19 ,,	2a,	Cultivators	63
20 ,,	19,	Blacksmiths	53
21 ,,	18,	Barbers	45
22 ,,	10,	Astrologers	44
23 ,,	25,	Cotton-cleaners	41
24 ,,	11,	Musicians	40
25 ,,	15,	Pedlars	33
26 ,,	35,	Fishermen, etc.	23
27 ,,	43,	Mat-makers, etc.	21
28 ,,	28,	Potters	20
29 ,,	24,	Washermen	19
30 ,,	2b,	Graziers, etc.	17
31 ,,	37,	Butchers	16
32 ,,	26,	Shepherds, etc.	15
33 ,,	40,	Stone-quarriers, etc.	12
	41,	Earth-workers, etc.	
35 ,,	16,	Carriers	10
	38,	Leather-workers	
37 ,,	38a,	Village watchmen, etc	9
38 ,,	46,	Acrobats	8
39 ,,	39,	Scavengers	6
	47,	Jugglers, etc.	
41 ,,	4,	Forest and hill tribes	2

The priestly group are pre-eminently first, and then come the writing and the trading castes, whose hereditary avocations demand some knowledge of reading and writing; these three groups exhibit a high proportion of literate and learning. After them there is a distinct drop to some of the groups of skilled artisans, and after these and the temple servants, who are only represented by the Gurabs, there is another drop to the perfumers and distillers and others. The forest and hill tribes are at the bottom of the list; they possess only 24 in 10,000 able or learning to read and write. The hunters take a comparatively high place considering the nature of their calling; but in the case of the Bedars, Berads, and Mutrasis, whose numbers raise the proportion of educated, it is probable that the hereditary occupation has been abandoned. The astrologers might be expected to take a higher place than they do, but the science of their profession is apparently not due to book-lore.

Proceeding from the groups to the individual castes which compose them, we find the Parbhus first with a percentage of 76 males who are literate or learning; the Goanese next with 71 per cent.; then the Boharis with 69 per cent, then the Brahmans and Kachhis with 64 per cent, and then the Jain Gujarathis with 63 per cent. With the exception of the Brahmans the actual numbers of all these castes are small; of the large castes the Brahmans are conspicuously the most educated. The position of the least educated is enjoyed by the Nihals and some of the other smaller forest and hill tribes, who are all illiterate. The Kolams have 999 entirely illiterate in every 1,000 males, and in the whole tribe there is only one literate and one under instruction. The Korkus have the

Statement No. 64.

Percentage of males of each caste in each condition.

Caste.	Illiterate.	Pupil.	Literate.
Bari	97·2	1·3	1·5
Gujar	82·6	5·9	11·5
Jat	92·5	2·0	5·5
Kunbi	93·7	2·6	3·7
Lodhi	96·1	1·0	2·9
Mali	96·3	1·6	2·1
Munarwar	98·1	·8	1·1
Pahad	94·5	3·0	2·5
Rajput	81·9	5·6	12·5
Velama	90·2	5·3	4·5
Gaoli (H)	98·3	·6	1·1
Kanadi	93·1	2·3	4·6
Andh (H)	99·7	·13	·12
Bhil	99·4	·1	·5
Gond (H)	99·3	·3	·4
Do. (An)	99·7	·16	·12
Kolam	99·9	·01	·01
Korku	99·9	·04	·05
Lajjhad	99·7	·2	·1
Pardhan	99·8	·1	·1
Brahman	36·2	14·2	49·6
Jangam	72·5	6·3	21·2
Beragi	81·7	2·8	15·5
Bharadi	99·1	·1	·8
Fakir	94·0	2·3	3·7
Gosawi	87·6	3·1	9·3
Panchal	94·5	1·1	4·4
Gaondi	91·0	4·2	4·8
Sutar	92·7	2·8	4·5
Kasar (H)	69·2	9·1	21·7
Otari	95·3	1·3	3·4
Tambatkar	82·6	6·2	11·2
Simpi (H)	79·7	5·8	14·5
Do. (J)	62·3	9·5	28·2
Bharadbhunja	88·6	3·4	8·0
Halwai	75·0	5·7	19·3
Tamboli	83·8	3·9	12·3
Halbi	94·3	1·3	4·4
Hatgar	93·8	2·0	4·2
Khatri	69·5	7·2	23·3
Koshti	90·8	3·0	6·2
Momin	87·0	4·3	8·7
Patwi	84·7	5·0	10·3
Rangari (H)	73·6	7·5	18·9
Do. (J)	70·0	11·3	18·7
Sali	87·0	3·8	9·2
Warthi	98·1	1·0	·9
Pinjari (M)	95·6	1·3	3·1
Dhangar	98·5	·75	·75
Teli	93·4	2·6	4·0
Kumbhar	98·0	1·1	·9
Kachar	88·0	4·9	7·1
Moghal	87·2	4·2	8·6
Pathari	88·8	4·2	7·0
Shekh	88·5	3·9	7·6
Syed	84·9	5·0	10·1

Caste.	Illiterate.	Pupil.	Literate.
Jogi	96·7	1·4	1·9
Manbhao	63·6	6·8	29·6
Nath	92·9	2·1	5·0
Gurao	77·3	6·8	15·9
Bhat	81·8	4·0	14·2
Thakur	90·5	2·6	6·9
Kast	44·3	9·2	46·5
Kayet	65·5	6·8	27·7
Parbhu	23·6	29·8	46·6
Garpagari	93·9	2·7	3·4
Gondhali	96·1	1·3	2·6
Bohari	30·8	13·7	55·5
Kachhi	36·4	2·6	61·0
Komti	65·1	6·5	28·4
Lad (H)	41·6	12·7	45·7
Do. (J)	50·2	12·7	37·1
Wani (H)	52·0	8·9	39·1
Do. (J)	47·9	10·4	41·7
Perki	97·5	1·2	1·3
Banjari	99·7	·1	·2
Labhani	99·8	...	·2
Wanjari	97·5	1·1	1·4
Sonar	75·3	7·5	17·2
Mhali	95·4	2·1	2·5
Jirayet	83·1	6·9	10·0
Lohar	94·6	1·9	3·5
Lonari	96·3	2·0	1·7
Bhoi	99·3	·3	·4
Kahar	87·5	2·2	10·3
Koli	96·5	1·7	1·8
Kalal (H)	82·3	4·0	13·7
Pasi	93·1	1·6	5·3
Kasai (H)	98·4	·9	·7
Chambhar	99·2	·4	·4
Dohor	99·6	·1	·3
Zingar	89·4	3·8	6·8
Mahar	99·1	·4	·5
Bhangi	97·4	·3	2·3
Mang	99·5	·2	·3
Takankar	98·8	·5	·7
Beldar	98·7	·6	·7
Burud	94·8	1·3	3·9
Bedar	77·2	6·4	16·4
Pardhi	99·1	·4	·5
Bhamti	97·7	1·1	1·2
Gujrathi (H)	73·2	7·0	19·8
Do. (J)	37·4	12·3	50·3
Marathe	90·2	3·4	6·4
Pardeshi	85·7	3·9	10·4
Telanga	94·7	·9	4·4
Vidur	63·2	10·3	26·5
Kolhati	96·6	1·4	2·0
Goanese	29·1	17·1	53·8
Native Christian	46·5	10·2	43·3

same proportion of illiterate in a 1,000, but they have 9 in 10,000 who are either pupils or literate. The Labhanis are the next worse with 998 illiterate in 1,000 males; and besides the forest tribes of Andhs, Gonds, and Bhils, the Banjaris, Dohors, Mangs, Bhois, Chambhars, Mahars, and Pardhis have all more than 990 per mille illiterate. The proportions among males of the principal castes are given in Statement No. 64. Among females the Parbhus have 16 per cent literate or learning, the Boharis 15 per cent, the Manbhaos 9 per cent, and the Brahmans 2 per cent; among Mahommedans the Syeds have 1 per cent, but in no other caste is the proportion noticeable.

Knowledge of English.

The last feature illustrated in Table D is that of the numbers of the educated population who have some knowledge of the English language. There are altogether in the province 2,493 males and 225 females who are so returned. Nearly all the literate Europeans and Eurasians know English, and it is rather remarkable that the numbers of these are not larger than they are. Some of the Europeans, French and others, may not know English, but it is not easily explicable how it is that among the literate Eurasians there are 27 males and 14 females who are not returned as knowing English; possibly these are so-called half-caste Portuguese, the distinction between whom and the Eurasian proper is not always observed, especially when they describe themselves. The Christian converts, whose education is largely due to the Mission schools, have a fair proportion with a knowledge of English, there being so returned 97 out of 183 literate males and 27 out of 85 literate females. The Parsis also largely cultivate the language, and have 129 who know English out of 195 male literates, or 66 per cent of the latter, and 5 out of 70 literate females. Deducting these four small classes, Europeans, Eurasians, Christian converts, and Parsis, there remain 2,043 males and 5 females who know English, which gives a percentage of ·14 on the total remaining male population, or 14 in 10,000, and of 2·4 on the remaining male literates, or 24 in 1,000 of that class. The Parbhus have 53 out of 164 literates or 32 per cent; the Brahmans 1,219 out of 20,704 or 6 per cent; the Malis 85 out of 2,213 or 4 per cent; the Rajputs 59 out of 3,355 or 18 per mille; the Shekhs 81 out of 4,856 or 17 per mille; the Kunbis 127 out 15,751 or 8 per mille; and the Wanis 59 out of 13,620 or 4 per mille. These are the most conspicuous numbers tabulated; a few other castes have proportions as high or higher than some of these, such as the Kasts, Kayets, Hindu Lads, Boharis, Bedars, Khatris, Pathans, and Syeds, but their actual numbers are small.

CHAPTER VIII.

LANGUAGES.

Statement No. 65.

Showing classification of the languages and dialects shown in the schedules, with the number of persons returned against each.

	Both sexes.	Males.	Females.
Indian Languages.			
A.—ARYAN FAMILY—			
I.—ERANIC GROUP—			
Pashtu dialects :—			
1. Afghani (Amiramrayan)	46	40	6
2. Pashtu	918	781	137
3. Rohili or Kabuli	90	84	6
TOTAL ERANIC GROUP	1,054	905	149
II.—INDIC GROUP—			
1. Kashmiri	1	1	...
2. Punjabi dialects—			
1. Gurumukhi	3	3	...
2. Multani	40	20	20
3. Punjabi	312	208	104
4. Sikhi	14	6	8
Total Punjabi	369	237	132
3. Sindhi	5	4	1
4. Hindi dialects—			
1. Braj	795	465	330
2. Jaipuri	161	79	82
3. Jharichi (or Jharpi)	75	41	34
4. Kanoji	40	25	15
5. Kawaiya	4	2	2
6. Kiradhi	459	236	223
7. Lodhi	153	80	73
8. Shekhawati (Hingi or Balgadki)	6	3	3
9. Mathuri	347	209	138
10. Moghe	85	49	36
11. Nagri	278	187	91
12. Nevi	70	33	37
13. Rajputi	718	367	351
14. Rathodi	22	13	9
15. Udiyani	1	1	...
Rangadi Hindi—			
1. Rangadi	37	19	18
2. Malvi	36	19	17
3. Chatarpuri	181	98	83
4. Chokari	9	6	3
5. Danguri	6	4	2
6. Dolachi	67	36	31
Total Rangadi Hindi	336	182	154

Statement No. 65—*continued.*

Showing classification of the languages and dialects shown in the schedules, with the number of persons returned against each—continued.

	Both sexes.	Males.	Females.
Indian Languages—*contd.*			
A.—ARYAN FAMILY—*contd.*			
II.—INDIC GROUP—*contd.*			
Nimadi Hindi—			
Nimadi	2,404	1,205	1,199
Bagri Hindi—			
Bikaneri	6	5	1
Marwadi Hindi—			
1. Agarwali . . .	1	1	...
2. Ajmiri . . .	3	2	1
3. Jodhpuri . . .	2	1	1
4. Marwadi . . .	36,602	23,170	13,432
Total Marwadi Hindi .	36,608	23,174	13,434
Urdu—			
1. Hindustani . . .	68,152	43,158	24,994
2. Urdu Musalmani . . } 3. Urdu Farsi . . .	205,950	106,725	99,225
Total Urdu .	274,102	149,883	124,219
Hindi-mixed Dravidian or Gipsy dialects—			
1. Banjari	35,905	19,221	16,684
2. Beldari (Lunia or Nunia)	1,473	763	710
3. Charani . . .	91	49	42
4. Ghisadi . . .	174	84	90
5. Kaikadi . . .	1,033	492	541
6. Kangedi . . .	34	16	18
7. Kangari . . .	1	...	1
8. Kolhati . . .	488	249	239
9. Labhani . . .	33,256	17,410	15,846
10. Ladi	13	6	7
11. Ladsi	420	210	210
12. Pardhi	763	403	360
13. Takankari (or Takari) .	326	179	147
14. Tirguli . . .	270	140	130
15. Wadari . . .	536	270	266
16. Waghri . . .	48	27	21
Total Gipsy dialects .	74,831	39,519	35,312
Hindi-mixed Kolarian—			
1. Bhili (Khandeshi, Naikadi, Tatia) . . .	461	222	239
2. Halbi	315	156	159
3. Nihali	394	210	184
Total mixed Kolarian .	1,170	588	582
Total Hindi .	392,671	216,346	176,325
5. Gujarathi dialects—			
1. Gujar	18	16	2
2. Gujarathi . . .	20,704	11,300	9,404
3. Shrawaki . . .	15	7	8

Statement No. 65—*continued.*

Showing classification of the languages and dialects shown in the schedules, with the number of persons returned against each—continued.

	Both sexes.	Males.	Females.
Indian Languages—*contd.*			
A.—ARYAN FAMILY—*concld.*			
II.—INDIC GROUP—*concld.*			
Kachhi Gujarathi—			
Kachhi . . .	344	267	77
Patnuli Gujarathi—			
1. Khadi or Khad . .	43	33	10
2. Khatri . . .	174	101	73
Total Gujarathi .	21,298	11,724	9,574
6. Marathi dialects—			
1. Marathi . . . (Maharashtra, Waradi, Malbati, Kunbi, Bawane, Bangi, Bharadi.)	2,300,349	1,170,689	1,129,660
2. Ahirni . . .	165	83	82
3. Chitrakathi . . .	2	1	1
4. Dakhani . . .	74	41	33
5. Gadhavo . . .	1	1	...
6. Koshti . . .	278	150	128
7. Kosri . . .	420	207	213
8. Kumbhari . . .	58	28	30
9. Machandar . . .	1	1	...
10. Mankari . . .	274	140	134
11. Panchali . . .	35	12	23
12. Panguli . . .	6	5	1
13. Rangari . . .	19	17	2
14. Wanjari . . .	906	492	414
Konkani Marathi—			
Konkani (or Konkiamin) .	100	55	45
Gomantaki Marathi—			
1. Goanese . . .	50	37	13
2. Portuguese . . .	85	53	32
Total Gomantaki .	135	90	45
Total Marathi .	2,302,823	1,172,012	1,130,811
7. Bengali	14	8	6
8. Sanskrit—Girwan . .	2	2	
TOTAL INDIC GROUP .	2,717,183	1,400,334	1,316,849
TOTAL ARYAN FAMILY .	2,718,237	1,401,239	1,316,998
B.—DRAVIDIAN—			
I.—SOUTHERN—			
1. Tamil dialects—			
1. Arvi . . .	52	27	25
2. Dravidi . . .	91	44	47
3. Tamil . . .	296	155	141
Total Tamil .	439	226	213

Statement No. 65—*continued.*

Showing classification of the languages and dialects shown in the schedules, with the number of persons returned against each—continued.

	Both sexes.	Males.	Females.
Indian Languages—*contd.*			
B.—DRAVIDIAN—*contd.*			
I.—SOUTHERN—*contd.*			
2. Telugu dialects—			
1. Komti	179	62	117
2. Telugu	42,982	21,568	21,414
Total Telugu	43,161	21,630	21,531
3.—Kanarese—			
Kanadi	1,088	655	433
4.—Malayalum—			
Malayali	3	3	...
TOTAL SOUTHERN DRAVIDIAN	44,691	22,514	22,177
II.—NORTHERN—			
1. Gond dialects—			
1. Balai	66	39	27
2. Gowari	116	73	43
3. Gondi	79,004	39,919	39,085
4. Kolami	15,539	7,858	7,681
5. Ladhadi (or Lajhari or Lajhad)	1,231	586	645
6. Mannè	3	2	1
7. Maràl	16	9	7
8. Pardhani	138	67	71
9. Portipali	4	1	3
10. Uikapali	1	1	...
Total Gond	96,118	48,555	47,563
TOTAL DRAVIDIAN	140,809	71,069	69,740
C.—KOLARIAN—			
Korku or Kur dialects—			
1. Gaulani	105	59	46
2. Korku	37,021	18,708	18,313
TOTAL KOLARIAN	37,126	18,767	18,359
Languages foreign to India.			
A.—ARYAN FAMILY—			
ERANIC GROUP—			
1. Armenian	1	1	...
2. Persian	428	259	169
TOTAL ERANIC	429	260	169
GREEK	4	4	...
ITALIC—			
French	14	1	13

Statement No. 65—*concluded*.

***Showing classification of the languages and dialects shown in the schedules, with the number of persons returned against each*—concluded.**

	Both sexes.	Males.	Females.
Languages foreign to India—*contd.*			
A.—ARYAN FAMILY—*contd.*			
TEUTONIC—			
1. German	5	4	1
2. English	653	364	289
TOTAL TEUTONIC .	658	368	290
TOTAL ARYAN .	1,105	633	472
B.—SEMITIC FAMILY—			
Arabic	201	109	92
C.—MONGOLIAN FAMILY—			
Chinese	8	5	3
LANGUAGE UNSPECIFIED .	5	4	1

Table X, page 164, shows the distribution of the population according to the parent tongue, and the languages and dialects enumerated with the number of persons returning them are shown in a classified form in Statement No. 65.

General considerations.

That a population of less than three millions occupying an area of about $\frac{1}{78}$rd of the extent of the Indian peninsula should enjoy the possession of more than one hundred different languages and dialects is an indication of the wide diversity and Babel-like complexity of constitution of an Indian community. To what extent these dialects really differ, and how far they merit the distinction of separate nomenclature, are questions which must be left to philologists to discuss, but it may be assumed that in a great number of cases the names of places or of castes have been given, in the absence of any clear understanding on the part of the person enumerated or on that of the enumerator, as to what was the proper name of the mother tongue. For instance, among Hindi dialects the names of Ajmeri, Jaipuri, and Jodhpuri, suggest that the persons returning them were natives of those places and gave their mother tongue as the language of Ajmere, and so on, without intending to claim any special distinction. It is to be remembered that a vast majority of the people are ignorant of what their language is or wherein it differs from any other. To the enumerator's enquiry the ordinary reply took some such form as this: "My language is what I speak; how do I know what language it is?" If the enumerator recognised the tongue he would enter it accordingly, but if not, he would consider the caste and the birth-place and arrive at some solution from the general results. However, the names have been tabulated as they were entered, but where they were clearly synonomous, they have been grouped together. Marathi, for instance, which is the general language of the province, appears under a variety of names, which have been shown in the list in brackets, and these, it may be assumed, were intended to indicate one and the same language. Only one of the names used, Madrasi, has been omitted from the list, and the reason for this is that it seems probable that it was used incorrectly. Madrasi is properly, it is understood, a Tamil dialect, but there was reason to believe that the persons who returned it spoke Telugu and not Tamil at all, and so the numbers have been included under the head of Telugu; and as Madrasi would be out of its place in the classification as a Telugu dialect, it has been omitted altogether.

Principal tongues.

Marathi in some form or other, and according to the Gazetteer "with much provincial accent and idiom," is spoken by 2,302,823 persons, or 79·5 per cent of the population of the province. Urdu, more or less corrupt, by 274,102 or 9·5 per cent. Marwari by 36,608, or 1·3 per cent. Other forms of Hindi by 81,961, or 2·8 per cent. Gondi and cognate dialects by 96,118, or 3·3 per cent. Telugu by 43,161, or 1·5 per cent. Korku by 37,126, or 1·3 per cent. Gujarathi by 21,298, or ·7 per cent.

Variations since 1881.

Considering the doubtful character of many of the returns, it may be open to question whether any value is to be attached to a comparison of the numbers shown against the principal languages or groups with those given at the last census, but the variations may be taken for what they are worth. The numbers speaking Marathi have increased by 95,233, or 4·3 per cent. of their former total. The Urdu-speaking have increased by 50,342, or 22·5 per cent. The Marwari by 14,921, or 68·8 per cent. Other Hindi dialects by 21,205, or 34·9 per cent. Gujarati by 5,975, or 38·9 per cent. Gondi by 23,774, or 32·9 per cent. Korku, by 8,445, or 29·4 per cent. Telugu by 3,830, or 9·7 per cent.

Pashtu and Punjabi.

The Pashtu and Punjabi dialects have been returned chiefly by itinerant traders from the north-west frontier. They penetrate to all parts of the province, but they happened to be enumerated in the largest numbers near the railway. Nearly all those speaking Afghani were found in Akola; 128 males and 38 females of those speaking Pashtu were found in Malkapur, but a large number of the latter, 86 males and 64 females, were enumerated in the Pusad taluk. Those speaking Rohili and Punjabi were much scattered, but 24 of the former were found in Kelapur, and 43 of the latter in Akot. The birth-place table shows that 765 men and 26 women were returned as born in Afghanistan, and these would account for most of the dialects included in the Eranic group, the remainder being probably attributable to some of those born in the Punjab. Combining the figures there are 1,142 men and 281 women returned as speaking a Pashtu or Punjabi dialect, and there are 1,460 men and 236 women returned as born in Afghanistan and the Punjab. It is probable that the excess males under the birth-place category gave their mother tongue as Persian or some form of Hindi, and it is possible that the excess females in the language return were born in India; but in the case of the women, as the returns were furnished by the men, it is probable that the birth-place figures would be the more accurate of the two and the mother tongue assumed.

Marwari.

Marwari is the language of traders from Marwar, who have more or less settled in the province, and the increase in the numbers, from 21,687 in 1881 to 36,602 now, affords some measure of the extent of trade development. The numbers exceed those who are returned as born in Central India and Rajputana, but there is no inconsistency in this, as many of them would have been born in Berar, the children of settlers. They are found throughout the province, though the numbers in the Wun and Melghat taluks are very small; they are strongest in Amraoti, Khamgaon, Basim, and Ellichpur, all convenient trade centers.

Hindustani.

Hindustani or Urdu, as it is indifferently termed, is here mainly the language of the Mahomedans, but not sufficiently so to furnish even an approximate index to the amount of the Musalman element. The immigrants from the North-West Provinces and Oudh help to swell the numbers of the Urdu-speaking people; but even including all these, there still remains a considerable excess who are probably to be accounted for amongst the immigrants from the Nizam's Dominions. The language is now the mother tongue of nearly one-tenth of the population, and is moreover, as Sir A. Lyall observed in the Gazetteer,—" understood and even spoken imperfectly throughout the province." Before the assignment to the British it was the official language of the courts, and it seems almost a pity that we have not endeavoured to encourage and improve it. Even corrupt Hindustani would probably go further and be more useful than bad Marathi of purely local appreciation.

Gipsy dialects.

Of the other Hindi dialects the mixed gipsy forms of speech are returned in the largest numbers, Banjari and Labhani, which are more or less akin and spoken by the Banjaras, being shown for 69,161 persons. Of these nearly 19,000 are found in Darwha, and more than 14,000 in Pusad; Mangrul, Basim, and Mehkar also show large numbers.

Bhili.

It has long been known that the Bhils of Berar have lost their tribal language, and although there is an increase in the number now returning it upon that at the last census, it is insignificant in comparison with the number of the tribe. Of those who have retained it the majority are found in the Pusad taluk and the remainder in Chikhli and Mehkar. The rest of the tribe have given Marathi or Urdu.

Gujarathi.

Gujarathi, more or less mixed, is spoken by several castes, but the numbers returning it are chiefly attributable to immigrants from the Western Presidency. In its purest form it is probably found among the Parsis, but their numbers are comparatively very small.

Portuguese.

The Goanese and Portuguese are bastard dialects in which Marathi is probably the principal element, although the persons who speak them are wont to claim a pure European descent. Their numbers are small and are confined chiefly to the towns.

Girwan or Sanskrit.

A Sanyasi or ascetic and an up-country Brahman have given Girwan as their mother tongue, but as this is a dead language the correctness of the return is open to doubt. It is probably an affectation assumed in support of an unworldly character.

Tamil.

The Tamil dialects are returned in small numbers, and are chiefly attributable to immigrants from Southern India; the persons speaking them are mostly found in the towns of Amraoti, Akola, Ellichpur, and Khamgaon.

Telugu.

Of those who speak Telugu, or the kindred Komti, there are 43,161 persons some of whom are found in all parts of the province, but more than half of them are located in the Kelapur and Wun taluks. The increase in the numbers since the last census is not more than that due to natural growth, and there seems to have been no influx of this race as in the case of the rest of those whose language may be regarded as foreign.

Gondi.

Gondi and the Gond dialects are almost confined to the Wun district, the Chandur and Morsi taluks of the Amraoti district, and the Melghat, that is to say, to the hilly country and to that part of the province in which the immigration from the Central Provinces is most conspicuous. Kelapur, a tract of hill and forest, has the largest share in the actual numbers and a very large share in proportion to its population.

Korku.

The Korku language is peculiar to the Melghat, where are found nine-tenths of those who return it as their mother-tongue. It is found, however, much more scattered through the province than in 1881, when only 257 persons speaking it were enumerated outside the Ellichpur district, against 2,106 at the present census. The primitive hill-men are beginning to find their way into the world, and as they do so their language will probably merge into that of the province. Nihali is an instance of a tribal tongue which is disappearing; it is akin to Korku, but is classified as Hindi-mixed Kolarian. In the Gazetteer of 1870 it was remarked that their original tongue might still be lingering among the Nihals, and in 1881 it was returned as the mother-tongue of 774 persons; now only half as many persons claim it; ten years ago 31 per cent of the tribe were included in the number, and now only 17 per cent. are shown.

Nihali.

The Sikh language has been returned by only 14 persons, although there are 316 persons of the Sikh caste or race, of whom 114 profess the Sikh religion. The others have given Punjabi or Urdu.

The returns under the head Nimadi are probably doubtful. It is not characteristic of any caste or tribe, but has been returned for persons of many and various castes in the Melghat taluk.

Local characteristics.

Regarding the subject of languages from a territorial point of view, the adjoining Statement No. 66 shows the principal languages and dialects returned in the different taluks and the number of persons in every thousand whose parent tongue they are. From this it will be seen that Marathi, including all its dialects, is spoken most in Chikhli, where it is the parent tongue of 875 persons in every thousand, and the other three taluks which form the western border of the province, Jalgaon, Malkapur, and Mehkar, come next; with the exception of the Melghat taluk, it is spoken least in the four taluks of the Wun district, so that, generally speaking, it is more characteristic of the west than of the east of the province. In the Kelapur taluk only every other man speaks Marathi, and in the Melghat it is quite a foreign language and not so widely known as Urdu. The latter is most spoken in Ellichpur and Amraoti, and its strength is probably due to the larger urban population; it is least spoken in Kelapur and Wun. Marwari is strongest in Khamgaon, and Gujarathi in Malkapur. The main distribution of Gondi has been already mentioned. In the Melghat 719 persons in every thousand speak Korku. Kolami is well represented in the Wun district, and Labhani and Banjari throughout the southern taluks of the province.

Statement No. 66.

Showing for principal languages the number of representatives per 1,000 of population in each taluk.

Taluk.	Marathi.	Urdu.	Marwari.	Gujarathi.	Gondi.	Korku.	Kolami.	Labhani.	Banjari.	Telugu.	Lajjhar.	Nimadi.
Amraoti	779	154	21	11	9	1	...	...	2	11	...	...
Chandur	859	76	11	2	39	...	...	4	3	3	...	...
Morsi	839	87	9	...	56	2	...	...	...	2	5	...
Murtazapur	828	116	14	14	6	...	...	8	2	5	...	...
Akola	821	116	18	14	3	...	...	7	3	12	...	...
Akot	826	128	18	12	4	5	...	...	2	1	...	...
Balapur	850	112	11	13	2	...	...	2	2	3	...	...
Jalgaon	866	87	17	15	3	8	...	...	...	...	...	...
Khamgaon	847	93	33	12	...	...	...	...	...	9	...	...
Ellichpur	759	179	19	5	10	8	...	...	1	7	2	...
Daryapur	851	116	11	17	3	...	...	...	...	...	...	...
Melghat	71	94	...	1	53	719	...	...	...	3	2	47
Chikhli	875	99	7	2	...	...	...	...	1	7	...	...
Malkapur	862	97	11	22	...	...	...	...	...	2	...	...
Mehkar	861	69	16	2	...	...	...	31	8	8	...	...
Yeotmal	673	67	7	2	124	...	63	19	17	18	...	...
Darwha	718	73	4	2	48	...	5	34	86	24	...	...
Kelapur	528	34	2	1	205	1	40	27	22	135	...	...
Wun	699	34	1	...	129	1	31	5	1	96	...	...
Basim	859	64	20	2	...	...	...	33	8	9	...	...
Mangrul	841	66	7	...	1	...	...	37	37	5	...	...
Pusad	795	71	6	...	2	...	...	36	69	12	...	...

CHAPTER IX.
BIRTH-PLACE.

Statement No. 67.

Summary of Table XI.

District.	Total Population.			Classification by Birth Place.																	
	Total.	Males.	Females.	A.—Born in district where enumerated.			B.—Born in district immediately contiguous to that where enumerated.			C.—Born in remote districts of the same province.			D.—Born in remote parts of India.			E.—Born in other countries of Asia.			F.—In other continents.		
				Total.	Males.	Females.	Total.	Males.	Females.	Total.	Males.	Females.	Total.	Males.	Females.	Total.	Males.	Females.	Total.	Males.	Females.
Amraoti	655,645	340,235	315,410	456,505	238,650	217,855	72,091	31,139	40,952	1,145	604	541	125,678	69,648	56,030	173	165	8	53	29	24
Akola	574,782	297,011	277,771	485,655	250,444	235,211	46,131	19,512	26,619	595	269	326	42,207	26,605	15,602	167	157	10	27	24	3
Ellichpur	315,798	162,969	152,829	245,203	128,237	116,966	38,201	15,240	22,961	1,592	758	834	30,697	18,644	12,053	86	80	6	19	10	9
Buldana	481,021	244,799	236,222	389,259	202,501	186,758	65,614	27,729	37,885	1,470	695	775	24,451	13,650	10,801	223	220	3	4	4	...
Wun	471,613	241,688	229,925	337,384	173,286	164,098	61,170	29,637	31,533	2,900	1,485	1,415	69,990	37,116	32,874	164	160	4	5	4	1
Basim	398,181	204,798	193,383	310,548	162,497	148,051	52,940	23,786	29,154	417	215	202	34,181	18,219	15,962	89	78	11	6	3	3
Railway passengers, etc.	451	326	125	178	115	63	...	...	...	...	...	...	259	203	56	2	2	...	12	6	6
Total	2,897,491	1,491,826	1,405,665	2,224,732	1,155,730	1,069,002	336,147	147,043	189,104	8,119	4,026	4,093	327,463	184,085	143,378	904	862	42	126	80	46

THE subject matter of this chapter has been to a considerable extent anticipated in the consideration of the movement of the population in chapter II. Table XI shows the distribution of the population according to birth-place, and the adjoining statement No. 67 is a summary of this table and classifies the population in six groups: those born in the district where they were enumerated, those born in districts immediately contiguous, which include the border districts of neighbouring provinces, those born in the remaining districts of the province, those born in other parts of India, those born in Asia beyond India, and those born in other continents. Statement No. 68 gives the same information in proportional form.

Birth-place classified.

It will be observed that it is only in the second and third groups that the females exceed the males, while among those born in remote parts, whether of India or elsewhere, the males largely preponderate. In the first group, of the home-born population, there are 1,081 males to 1,000 females. Of those born in remote parts of India, there are 1,284 males to 1,000 females. Of those born in other countries of Asia, there are 205 males to every 10 females. Of those born in other continents there are 17 males to every 10 females. On the other hand, of those born in contiguous districts, there are only 777 males to 1,000 females; and of those in other parts of the province, not contiguous to the district of enumeration, there are 984 males to 1,000 females. The explanation of these differences is, that the men not uncommonly take their wives from adjoining districts, and that the immigrants from a distance either leave their women behind them or settle and marry in the province. The greater the distance the fewer the women, appears to be a rule to which the only exception is in the case of the last group, which consists almost entirely of Europeans. Some actual figures will illustrate this rule very clearly. In the Amraoti taluk, of those who were born in the Ellichpur district, 5,242 are males and 7,474 are females; of those who come from the Central Provinces, 12,165 are males and 11,633 are females; of those from the Bombay Presidency, 2,246 are males and 1,681 are females; of those from Rajputana and Central India, 3,070 are males and 1,497 are females; of those from the North-Western Provinces and Oudh, 3,636 are males and 1,051 are females; of those from the Punjab, 71 are males and 26 are females; of those from Bengal 78 are males and 10 are females; and from Afghanistan, there are 58 males and only 1 female.

Relative proportions of sexes.

Taking the figures for the province, inclusive of the railway passengers, there are born in the—

Foreign element.

Central Provinces . . .	109,495	males and	106,993	females.
Hyderabad territory . .	53,264	,,	57,641	,,
Bombay Presidency . .	31,376	,,	28,429	,,
Rajputana and Central India .	22,169	,,	9,907	,,
North-West Provinces and Oudh .	22,818	,,	5,541	,,
Punjab	695	,,	210	,,
Madras Presidency . . .	473	,,	350	,,
Bengal	343	,,	76	,,
Afghanistan	777	,,	26	,,

Hyderabad territory is the only foreign quarter from which the majority of immigrants is female; and if the figures for the purely indigenous population are examined, it is seen that the average preponderance of males in the province has been somewhat raised by the foreign element. Of those born in Berar, there are 1,250,167 males and 1,196,409 females, and the proportion of males to females is 1,045 to 1,000, while for the total population it is 1,061.

Statement No. 68.

Showing the percentage on the total population, and on the total of each sex, of the groups given in Statement No. 67.

	Group A.			Group B.			Group C.			Group D.			Group E.			Group F.		
	Total.	Males.	Females.	Total.	Males.	Females.	Total.	Males.	Females.	Total.	Males.	Females.	Total.	Males.	Females.	Total.	Males.	Females.
Province	76·78	77·47	76·05	11·60	9·86	13·45	·28	·27	·29	11·30	12·34	10·20	·03	·06	·003	·004	·005	·003
Districts.																		
Amraoti	69·63	70·14	69·07	10·99	9·15	12·98	·17	·18	·17	19·17	20·47	17·76	·03	·05	·002	·008	·008	·008
Akola	84·49	84·32	84·68	8·03	6·57	9·58	·10	·09	·12	7·34	8·96	5·62	·03	·05	·004	·005	·008	·001
Ellichpur	77·64	78·69	76·53	12·10	9·35	15·02	·50	·46	·55	9·72	11·44	7·89	·03	·05	·004	·006	·006	·006
Buldana	80·92	82·72	79·06	13·64	11·33	16·04	·30	·28	·33	5·08	5·58	4·57	·04	·09	·001	·001	·002	—
Wun	71·54	71·70	71·37	12·97	12·26	13·71	·61	·61	·61	14·84	15·36	14·30	·03	·07	·002	·001	·002	·0004
Basim	77·99	79·34	76·56	13·29	11·61	15·08	·10	·10	·10	8·58	8·90	8·25	·02	·04	·01	·001	·001	·001

Indigenous population.

The total indigenous population is 2,446,576, which is 84·44 per cent of the total population of the province. In 1881 the number born within the province formed 83·69 per cent of the whole. The actual increase of this class amounts to 209,836 and the rate of increase to 9·38 per cent, which is somewhat higher than the rate for the province. This is only another way of viewing the fact that the indigenous population has, as a whole, increased faster than the foreign element.

Preponderance of females in inter-provincial migration.

Of natives of Berar who were enumerated in districts other than that of their birth there are 94,437 males and 127,407 females, or 741 males to 1,000 females, which shows how much more largely the women take part in the inter-provincial movement. This is slightly more marked in the movement between adjoining districts. Of natives of Berar born in districts contiguous to that of their enumeration, there are 90,526 males and 123,377 females, or 734 males to 1,000 females. Of those who have come from contiguous districts beyond the border into the adjoining districts of the province, there are 56,632 males and 65,790 females, and the proportion is 861 males to 1,000 females. So that in the movement between contiguous districts, whether within or without the province, while the female element predominates throughout, it is greater in the inter-provincial migration than in the immigration from outside, from which it may be inferred that while there is considerable intermarriage between contiguous districts, yet in the selection of wives preference is given on the whole to the native women. This may be as much due to the want of facilities of communication across the border for a great part of its length as to the superior charms of the ladies of Berar.

Immigration from contiguous districts.

The numbers contributed by each district of the province to the different taluks have been given in statement No. 11 in Chapter II. The following statement, No. 69, shows the most conspicuous contributions from the contiguous districts of the adjoining provinces :—

Statement No. 69.

Province and District of Birth.		Taluk where enumerated.	Males.	Females.	Total.
Central Provinces	Wardha	Chandur	5,620	6,350	11,970
"	"	Morsi	1,283	1,571	2,854
"	"	Yeotmal	6,587	6,748	13,335
"	"	Kelapur	4,174	4,196	8,370
"	Chanda	Wun	3,916	4,309	8,225
"	Betul	Morsi	2,255	2,282	4,537
"	"	Melghat	1,405	1,269	2,674
Hyderabad territory	Aurangabad	Chikhli	5,408	6,964	12,372
"	"	Mehkar	2,777	3,297	6,074
"	Parbhani	"	1,147	1,424	2,571
"	"	Basim	4,654	6,144	10,798
"	"	Pusad	4,768	5,462	10,230
"	Nander	"	3,576	5,392	8,968
Bombay	Khandesh	Malkapur	4,622	7,589	12,211

The preponderance of females from Khandesh in the Malkapur taluk is very striking. It is to be noted also that the taluks of enumeration shown in this statement are all on the borders of the province. Taking the total contributions from these districts across the border to all parts of Berar, we find that 40,272 come from Wardha, of whom 20,915 are females and 19,357 males; 26,654 come from Parbhani, of whom 14,425 are females and 12,229 males; 25,088 come from Aurangabad, of whom 13,461 are females and 11,627 males; 22,821 come from Khandesh, of whom 12,850 are females and 9,971 males; 10,640 come from Chanda, of whom 5,404 are females and 5,236 males; 10,271 come from Nander, of whom 6,019 are females and 4,252 males; and 9,037 come from Betul, and of these 4,601 are males and 4,436 females. With the exception of the last, the numbers of the females predominate in all. The number of immigrants from these seven districts form 31·4 per cent of the total immigrant population.

Referring to the proportional statement No. 68, we find that of the persons born in the districts in which they were enumerated, the proportion of females is greater that that of males in the Akola district only; that is to say, that relatively to the other sex there are more home-born women in Akola than in any other district. This does not mean that they are more stay-at-home or in lesser demand in the matrimonial market, as in fact Akola contributes more women to the rest of the province than any other district; but it means that fewer women are brought into the district, and this fact with that of Akola having lost largely in the inter-provincial exchange are to some extent mutually explanatory of each other. From the proportional figures for the second group, those born in districts contiguous to that of enumeration, the analogous fact is illustrated that Akola has received comparatively the smallest contribution, especially of the male sex. The third group is unimportant. The fourth group shows that the Buldana district has received the smallest proportional contribution from remote parts of India, that is from all districts not immediately contiguous. All districts show in this group a higher proportion of the male sex, and the disparity is most marked in Akola and Ellichpur, the two districts from which there has been comparatively considerable emigration. Regarding only the actual numbers of the immigrants in Akola and Ellichpur, it might be considered that there was a distinct movement tending to compensate for the loss by emigration; but this would probably be an erroneous conclusion, and it would be safer to infer that where the male element largely predominates in the immigration, the people only come temporarily and not to settle. Groups E and F are comparatively insignificant, but it is somewhat curious that there should be as many as 803 persons from Afghanistan in the province. These are traders from the border lands beyond the Punjab who find their way down every year and generally go away again as the hot weather comes on.

Classes of immigrants.

The immigrants from the Central Provinces, the Nizam's Dominions, and the Bombay Presidency, are for the most part settlers drawn to the province by either trade or agriculture. Those from Rajputana and Central India, and from the North-West Provinces and Oudh, are mostly labourers who come here for the season or take temporary service. Like the up-country traders, they generally go to their homes in the hot weather, when work becomes scarce, but though not settlers they are very regular visitors.

Comparison of immigration and emigration with that of 1881.

In the next two statements, Nos. 70 and 71, are given the details of the principal immigration and emigration for both 1881 and 1891, the chief features in which have been

Statement No. 70.

Of principal immigrants or persons enumerated in Berar and born elsewhere.

Birth-place.	1891.		1881.		Variation since 1881.	
	Males.	Females.	Males.	Females.	Males.	Females.
Bombay	31,376	28,429	41,285	36,196	−9,909	−7,767
Central Provinces	109,495	106,993	95,798	89,344	+13,697	+17,649
Hyderabad territory	53,264	57,641	67,192	63,313	−13,928	−5,672
Central India	3,469	1,833	1,382	777	+2,087	+1,056
Rajputana	18,700	8,074	10,567	4,949	+8,133	+3,125
North-West Provinces }	19,826	4,834	16,564	6,372	+6,254	−831
Oudh }	2,992	707				
Punjab	695	210	337	120	+358	+90
Madras	473	350	503	315	−30	+35
Bengal	343	76	452	170	−109	−94
Afghanistan	777	26	74	16	+703	+10

Statement No. 71.

Of principal emigrants, or persons born in Berar and enumerated elsewhere.

Province where enumerated.	1891.		1881.		Variation since 1881.	
	Males.	Females.	Males.	Females.	Males.	Females.
Bombay	7,874	10,288	4,538	5,018	+3,336	+5,270
Central Provinces	21,655	30,862	23,287	29,024	—1,632	+1,838
North-West Provinces and Oudh	196	196	37	38	+159	+158
Hyderabad	14,231	16,443	?	?	?	?
Madras	49	20	8	6	+41	+14
Punjab	25	36	14	11	+11	+25
Baroda	50	40	208	197	—158	—157
Bengal	?	?	381	412	?	?

already noticed either in this chapter or in chapter II, but it remains to observe that in the interchange with the Bombay Presidency since 1881 the province has suffered a net loss of 13,245 males and 13,037 females, and in that with the Central Provinces it has acquired a net gain of 15,329 males and 15,811 females. The variation in the relations with Hyderabad territory cannot be ascertained for want of the figures of the emigrants in 1881.

CHAPTER X.
CASTES.

Introductory.

THE distribution of the population according to its component castes, tribes, and races, is shown in table XVI, page 206. In an appendix to this chapter is given an alphabetical index to all the classes detailed in the table, together with a complete list of all the subdivisions of each caste, which have been returned in the enumeration schedules. In the schedule there was a prescribed column for the caste and another for the subdivision, but there was not infrequently some confusion as to the distinction, and the columns were thus sometimes transposed; the spelling, too, and the use of synonyms led to a good deal of variation, and the number of different names for caste and subdivision that were actually recorded was very large indeed. Where, however, the mistakes were obvious the entries were corrected, and the Caste Index, which still contains more than 300 main castes and more than 3,000 subdivisions of castes, represents the result. This list might no doubt be considerably revised, but that is a matter for separate consideration. It may, perhaps, be doubted whether the advantage of an enquiry into all the existing castes and sub-castes is commensurate with the expenditure of time and labour it entails. The subject is full of complications and of seemingly unlimited range. A large proportion of the people have very indefinite ideas as to the nomenclature of their caste, and comparatively few possess fixed notions as to the subdivision to which they belong. It is open to any one to manufacture an appellation to his own liking, and the names of places and of occupations are in this way largely introduced. At the same time the social distinctions, customs and habits which characterise each caste and subdivision tend to vary and increase with each new formation, so that to ascertain the peculiarities of each would involve a very elaborate investigation and at the same time would lead to no finality. At the last census a very full enquiry was made with respect to the principal castes, and nothing further in this direction has been now attempted; the changes that have since taken place and the local distribution of the different castes and tribes are alone dealt with here, and, as in the case of the religions, reference should be made to Mr. Kitts' interesting report for 1881 for details of their characteristic features. In the table the castes have been classified, under the instructions of the Census Commissioner for India, according to the general hereditary occupation of each and the groups have been arranged "more or less in accordance with the position generally assigned to each in the social scale." Following this arrangement, I shall proceed to take the castes as they come in the order of the table, and treat of those which, from their numerical importance or special characteristics, seem to be worthy of attention.

Baris.

The first group, the Military and Dominant, calls for no comment: the Sikhs, of whom it is mostly composed, have been already noticed under the head of religion. The next group is that of the "cultivators," of whom the Baris are the first to claim attention. They number 25,920 and have increased by 2,230, or 9·4 per cent, since 1881. They are now, as then, found in much larger numbers in Jalgaon than elsewhere, and in that taluk they comprise more than 5 per cent of the total population; they are also found in considerable numbers in Ellichpur, Morsi, Amraoti, Akot, Daryapur, Chandur, Darwha, and to a lesser extent Pusad. Their speciality is, Mr. Kitts says, to keep *pan* gardens.

Gujars.

The Gujars, who come from the Punjab and the North-West Provinces, number 990; there were 967 in 1881, and they have therefore done little more than maintain their position since; nearly three-fourths of them are to be found in Amraoti, Morsi and Akot. In 1881 their numbers were relatively strong in Akola, but they seem to have now deserted that taluk for Akot; in Khamgaon there has been some diminution also, and in Amraoti a large increase. A few in the Balapur taluk have been returned as Jains.

Kapuwars.

The Gurud Kapuwars, the Kapuwaru, and the Reddi Kapuwars are probably the same people and are a Telugu caste who are found in the Kelapur and Wun taluks only, with the exception of a few individuals in Morsi; they number now 592 against 340 in 1881, so that they have increased largely.

Jats.

Jats number 527 and are found chiefly in Mehkar, Amraoti and Murtazapur. In 1881 only 89 persons were returned as of this caste, but 639 were shown as belonging to the Jat subdivision of Rajputs, and judging from the localities affected by them then they appear to be the same people who are now shown as Jats, but no comparison of numbers can be made, as it is not known how many of them may have adhered to the description of Rajput. This is an instance of the confusion of name; whether these people are Jats or Rajputs or Rajput Jats, probably very few of them have any notion.

Kunbis.

The Kunbis, who in point of numbers in all India are second only to the Brahmans, are numerically by far the most important element of the population of this province; but owing to their numerous subdivisions and to some mixed nomenclature, it is somewhat difficult to ascertain their actual numbers or their variation since 1881. All subdivisions develop a tendency to cleavage from the parent stem and to subsequent independent growth, and in this way the Marathe and Munarwars at least, who only appeared as subdivisions in 1881, have now achieved a separate entity. In 1881 the Maratha Kunbis numbered 125,210, and those who have now discarded the Kunbi and described themselves as Marathe only number 19,038, so that it would seem that the latter do not represent more than about one-sixth of the original subdivision. On the other hand, the number of Munarwars now is out of all proportion to the number of the subdivision in 1881; there were then shown to be 206, of whom 199 were in the Kelapur taluk; there now appear to be 2,120, of whom more than half belong to the same taluk and the greater portion of the remainder to the same district. The name of Munarwar is, I believe, unknown outside Berar, so that the increment is not due to immigration, and as it cannot be due to natural growth, it seems that either there was some misdescription in 1881 or that there has been since what may perhaps be called conversion. Both Marathe and Munarwars may probably be properly regarded as Kunbis, but the list of subdivisions returned at this census numbering more than 160 suggests that the caste name has been adopted by people of other castes as a general appellation indicating possibly the possession of land. A Teli Kunbi means probably a Kunbi who follows the occupation of an oil-presser, and a Mhali Kunbi a Kunbi barber, but a Manbhao Kunbi, for instance, seems an absurdity, unless it is taken to mean a Manbhao landholder or cultivator. Those, however, who have returned themselves as Kunbis number 834,432, and if the Marathe and Munarwars are added, the aggregate amounts to 855,590, which is nearly 30 per cent of the total population, and which shows an increase of 21,416, or 2·6 per cent, over the number in 1881. This increment is small, but as it is impossible to say what numbers should be eliminated from the totals recorded for either 1881 or 1891, no accurate comparison of the numbers of the Kunbi proper can be arrived at. Taking only those described under the caste name, they are found in large numbers in every taluk except the Melghat, and bear a proportion to the total population varying from nearly 41 per cent in Chikhli to 18 per cent in Darwha. In Wun they form 39 per cent, in Khamgaon 38 per cent, in Malkapur 37 per cent, in Basim 36 per cent, and in Akot 34 per cent; and generally, with the exception of Wun, the proportions in the western taluks are higher than those in the eastern, which points to their western origin and connection with the Kunbis of Khandesh and the Deccan.

Lodhis.

The Lodhis number 1,920 and have increased by 147, or 8·3 per cent, since 1881. They probably come from the North-West or the Central Provinces, and more than half of them are found in the Ellichpur, Chandur and Amraoti taluks. They used to be comparatively strong in Daryapur, but their numbers there have diminished from 232 to 136. A few of them in Akot have returned their religion as Musalman.

Malis.

The Malis are numerically the third most important caste in Berar, the Mahars ranking second to the Kunbis. The numbers of the Malis are 202,498, which amounts to nearly 7 per cent of the total population. In 1881 they numbered 195,981, and the increase is only a little more than 3 per cent, less than half the rate for the province. They are most numerous in Morsi, Chandur, Ellichpur and Malkapur; in Morsi they form nearly 15 per cent of the population, in Ellichpur 12 per cent, in Chandur 9, and in Malkapur 8 per cent; but they are found in considerable numbers in every taluk except the Melghat, and in Wun the numbers are small in comparison with the rest. They have decreased in several taluks, notably in Akot, where their numbers have fallen from 12,996 to 11,607, or nearly 11 per cent.

Manas.

The Manas come from the Central Provinces, and are found chiefly in Kelapur, Wun and Chandur. They number only 217, but as there were none recorded in Berar in 1881, they are interesting as marking the immigration of a new caste.

Munarwars.

The Munarwars are a Telugu caste from Hyderabad territory who are nearly all found in the Wun district; their numbers have fallen from 3,230 to 2,120, a very large diminution which points to a retrograde movement. In Kelapur their numbers have risen from 743 to 1,175, but in Wun they have fallen from 1,535 to 539, and in Pusad from 808 to 49, which is wholesale desertion. The variation, however, may be entirely attributable to the adoption of the name of Kunbi.

Pahads.

The Pahads are probably the same as the Paharis, who, Mr. Kitts says, are also known as Keotis. They number 836 against 1,164 in 1881, and therefore show a diminution of 28 per cent, which probably means some emigration.

Phanadis.

The Phanadis, who number 102, and who, with the exception of a few individuals in Balapur, are only found in Pusad, are noticeable as a small caste peculiar to this province. At the last census they numbered 117.

Rajputs.

The Rajputs number 50,930 and have increased by 6,797, or more than 15 per cent, since 1881. The list of subdivisions, amounting to nearly 200, suggests, however, that many of those who call themselves Rajputs do not belong to the caste at all. Taking them as returned, they comprise 1·76 per cent of the total population, and are found in all parts of the province, but more than one-third of their number were enumerated in Malkapur, Chikhli and Chandur. Fourteen in the Akola taluk gave their religion as Sikh.

Tirmalis.

The Tirmalis, or Tirumalis, who mostly affect Darwha, Chandur and Morsi, have diminished from 494 to 449, the decrease being almost entirely among males. The colony in Murtazapur is new.

Yelamas.

The Yelamas are a Telugu caste who are apparently pushing their way up the country from Southern India through Hyderabad territory; they numbered 295 in Berar at the last census and have now added 200 more. They are confined to the Kelapur, Pusad and Wun taluks, the south-eastern corner of the province.

Gaolis.

The Gaolis, including the synonymous Ahir, Gahlan, and Gawari, number 37,268 and form 1·29 per cent of the total population; they have increased since 1881 by 7,109, or nearly 24 per cent. They are found in every taluk, but two-thirds of their number were enumerated in the Wun and Amraoti districts, and they are especially numerous in the Yeotmal and Chandur taluks, which suggests that many of them have come in with the immigration from the Central Provinces. The number in the Melghat amounts to 5·7 per cent of the population of that taluk. Naturally a Hindu caste, 771 of them have relapsed into Animism, 815 have become converts to Islam, and 1 has returned himself as Jain.

Golkars.

The Golkars, or Golawaru, are a pastoral Telugu caste who are helping to colonise the Kelapur and Wun taluks. They now number 2,454 and have increased by 688, or nearly 39 per cent, since 1881. In Kelapur their numbers have risen from 1,204 to 1,931, but in Wun they have somewhat diminished.

Kanadis.

The Kanadis are another pastoral caste, who come presumably from Kanara. At the last census they numbered, all told, 1,963, of whom 1,324 were enumerated in the Bombay Presidency and 639 in Berar. They now number 1,447 in Berar alone, so it would seem that there has been considerable immigration of these people since 1881. They are strongest in Basim and Murtazapur, and there are a fair number in Mangrul, Amraoti and Akot. In 1881 more than half their number were found in Basim, so they may be regarded as having established their head-quarters there and to have pushed out a line of communication to the north-east, with several detached posts. Yeotmal and Darwha, where a good proportion were found in 1881, they now seem to have almost deserted.

We now come to the forest and hill tribes, who constitute numerically an important element of the populution of the province.

Andhs.

The Andhs number 43,602 and have increased by 6,592, or nearly 18 per cent, since 1881. They are strongest in Pusad, Darwha, Basim and Mangrul, but are foand in considerable numbers also in Mehkar, Yeotmal, Balapur and Akola. In Balapur, however, they have diminished by 309, or more than 11 per cent, since the last census. Very little seems to be known about these people, but they are said to be cultivators and peculiar to Berar and the neighbouring Hyderabad territory. Mr. Kitts refers to them as "completely Hinduised," but a small number, 305 altogether, in the Yeotmal and Pusad taluks still adhere to the primitive form of religion.

Arakhs.

The Arakhs seem to be disappearing from Berar. There were 371 in 1881 and only 253 at the present census, of whom the greater number were found in the Morsi and Amraoti taluks.

Bhils.

The Hindu and Animistic Bhils classed together number 4,266 and show the slight increase of 83, a little less than 2 per cent, since 1881. The Mahomedan Bhils, on the other hand, have increased from 1,125 to 1,928, or more than 71 per cent. A large proportion of the Hindu Bhils are found in Pusad, and there are considerable numbers in Darwha, Chikhli and Malkapur; the Animistic Bhils were mostly enumerated in Darwha; and the Mahomedans in Jalgaon and Melghat. The Gazetteer of 1870 refers to the Bhils of the western extremity of the Gawilgarh range as all Mahomedans, and quotes the tradition of their chiefs having been—

"all forcibly converted by Aurangzeb, who then entrusted to them the watch and ward of the forts and passes of the Satpuras."

This clan have since spread into the taluks at the foot of the hills, and are probably quite distinct from the Bhils of the Balaghat.

Bopchis.

The Bopchis are sometimes said to be a class of Korkus, and their numbers were presumably included with the Korkus at the last census. On the present occasion 613 were enumerated, who were nearly all in the Morsi taluk.

Gonds.

The Gonds number 80,927 and form 2·79 per cent of the population of the province. A large majority are found in the Wun district, and in Kelapur they are especially numerous and form 20 per cent of the taluk population. In Morsi and Chandur their numbers are also large, and in the Melghat they are not inconsiderable, but they are not so numerous in the latter taluk as might be expected from their history. If the Gazetteer may be accepted as an accurate authority of its time, there have been great changes in the habitat of the Gonds during the last twenty years. They are there described as inhabiting the Melghat and a strip of wild country along the Wardha river. A small proportion only are now found in the Melghat, and those who live near the Wardha occupy much more than a strip of country, and that no longer wild. The religion of the tribe is animistic, but 9,058 persons, or rather more than 11 per cent, have become Hindus; these converts are most conspicuous in the taluks of the plain.

Gorwans.

The Gorwans number 161, of whom 13 are Hindus and the remainder Animistic. With the exception of 6 individuals in Kelapur, they were enumerated in the Melghat taluk, and as there is no mention of them in the records of the last census and I can discover no trace of them outside Berar, I am disposed to think that the name must be a corruption of Gaolán, the aboriginal herdsmen of the Gawilgarh hills.

Kolams.

The Kolams number 17,419, of whom 954 are Hindus. They have increased by 5,256 or 43 per cent since 1881. They were then and now nearly all enumerated in the Wun district, but there is a not inconsiderable number in the Melghat, where none were shown at the last census, and as they are sometimes regarded as a division of the Gond tribe, the Melghat people may have been so described on that occasion. 373 of those enumerated in the Melghat returned their parent-tongue as Korku. The large increase in the Wun district is probably due to immigration from the Central Provinces.

Korkus.

The Korkus number 34,981, of whom 379 are Hindus; their numbers since 1881 have increased by 6,531, or 23 per cent; 31,611 are found in the Melghat taluk, where they form 67 per cent of the population, and where their numbers have increased by 4,830 or 18 per cent. Some of them are, it seems, beginning to make their way into the plains, and there are considerable numbers in Ellichpur, Akot and Jalgaon, and not a few in Morsi, Amraoti, and Chandur; there are now close upon 10 per cent of their number found outside Melghat against only 6 per cent in 1881, and none in 1870 *pace* the Gazetteer, but this increase may very possibly be due not to a descent from the hills of Berar but to immigration from the Central Provinces, where the numbers of the tribe are large. The total increment points with a certainty to some immigration; but whether this movement has been through the hills into Melghat or across the plains from the east, or in both ways, must remain a matter of conjecture.

Koyela Bhute.

The Koyela Bhute is sometimes held to be a Gond clan. In 1881 there were 43 in the Melghat, but these have entirely disappeared, and the tribe or clan is now represented in Berar by only 10 individuals in the Yeotmal taluk.

Lajjhads.

The Lajjhads or Lajars, described in the Gazetteer as "mostly hewers of wood on the fringes of the Satpura hills," have now spread in small numbers over the country, but a large majority are still located in Morsi. They number 1,860, which is an increase of only 36 over their numbers in 1881. They are mostly Hindus.

Marals.

The Marals, numbering 410, are new to Berar. They are firewood sellers who have immigrated from the Central Provinces and were mostly enumerated in Wun.

Moghes.

The Moghes are fast disappearing. In 1881 there were 344 and now there are only 218. They inhabit the Melghat, but one adventurer was found in Amraoti.

Nihals.

The Nihals also have lost some of their number; there are now 2,305 against 2,483 in 1881. They are said to be the "village drudges" of the Korkus or Gonds of the Melghat, but they are gradually leaving the hills, 245 having been enumerated in the plains against 97 in 1881. Their language is fast disappearing, as has been already remarked.

Pardhans.

The Pardhans number 12,936, and have increased by 1,908, or 17 per cent, since 1881. Originally they were a Gond division and they are described as the hereditary priests of the tribe "but of very low social status." A large proportion of them are now Hindus. They are most numerous in Kelapur and the Wun district generally, where 88 per cent were enumerated, but there are a considerable number in Chandur and Akot, and others elsewhere.

The next group is that of the priests, which is composed of Brahmans, Jangams, a few Jatis and Pirzade and one Mulla.

Brahmans.

The Brahmans number 71,308 and form 2·46 per cent of the population of the province. Since 1881 their numbers have increased by 5,554 or 8·4 per cent. They are found in every taluk, but there are only a small number in Melghat, and in Kelapur, Wun, Darwha and Mangrul their numbers are much below the average. In the Amraoti taluk they are much stronger than elsewhere and number 7,584 or 4·1 per cent of the population of the taluk. Since 1881 there has been considerable movement amongst this caste in the province; in Amraoti their numbers have increased by 29 per cent, in Khamgaon by 25 per cent, in Ellichpur by 17 per cent, and in Akola by 15 per cent; and on the other hand, there has been a decrease in Akot of 14 per cent, in Jalgaon and Daryapur of 8 per cent, and in Balapur of 5 per cent. There is a very great disparity between the sexes of the Brahmans, there being only 706 females to 1,000 males. 36 Jains have been returned as Brahmans, but these are, I imagine, not really Brahmans by caste. It seems rather that they have adopted the caste name to signify their occupation or character as priests of the Jains. The same may be said of some of the subdivisions of the caste that were returned, such as the Marwari; by a Marwari Brahman is probably meant a Marwari priest, and not a Brahman from Marwar. In this way the strength of the actual caste has possibly been overstated.

Jangams.

The Jangams are the priestly class of the Hindu Wanis. They number 1,882 and have decreased by 634 or 25 per cent since the last census. They are found, however, in every taluk except Melghat.

Beragis.

The next group are the devotees, of whom the Beragis number 1,436; they have decreased by 93 or 6 per cent, the most marked diminution being in the Akot taluk, where the numbers have fallen from 127 to 47. The Beragis are found in every taluk.

Bharadis.

The Bharadis have increased from 1,314 to 1,452, of whom nearly half are in the Amraoti district and but a few individuals in Basim. They have shifted their quarters very considerably everywhere.

Fakirs.

The Fakirs number 7,190, more than double what they were in 1881. They are found in every taluk, and are particularly strong in Akot.

Gosawis.

The Gosawis number 12,152, and show a decrease of 861 or nearly 7 per cent. They are strongest in Chandur and Basim, but are found in every taluk. The greatest decrease is in the Akola district, where their numbers have diminished by 400, or 15 per cent.

Jogis.

The Jogis number 2,177, or 30 more than they did in 1881. They are mostly found in the southern districts, Buldana, Basim, and Wun, and are strongest in the Basim and Mangrul taluks.

Manbhaos.

The Manbhaos number 3,559 against 4,111 in 1881, the decrease being 11 per cent. They are scattered all over the province with the exception of Wun, and there are very few in Kelapur and only 1 in Melghat. They are strong in Morsi and Ellichpur, which is explained by the existence of the chief institution of the Manbhao sect at Ritpur (or Ridhpur) in the Morsi taluk.

Naths.

The Naths number 2,973, which is more than double the number shown in the returns for 1881. Of the Nath sect there were, however, over 9,000, and it seems probable that there was some confusion between sect and caste, and a comparison is therefore not very reliable. A large proportion are found in the Akola district, especially in the Akola, Balapur, and Akot taluks; there are considerable numbers also in Mehkar and Amraoti.

Wasudeos.

The number of the Wasudeos has also been doubled. There are 314, of whom a large majority are in the Pusad taluk. Most of these devotee castes are also religious sects, and a full account of their characteristics is given in the Census Report for 1881.

Guraos.

The Guraos number 9,230, within 4 of their number in 1881. They are temple servants and to some extent mendicants of a semi-religious character, but they do not wander, and therefore their local distribution does not differ much from what it was in 1881. Now, as then, a large proportion are found in the Chandur and Amraoti taluks.

Bhats.

The group of genealogists comprises the Bhats and Thakurs. They are said to be almost identical, both castes following the calling of village bard and combining it not infrequently with mendicancy. The Bhats number 3,157, which shows the large increase of 25 per cent upon their number in 1881. They have decreased in the Akola and Ellichpur districts, but increased elsewhere. They are strongest in the Amraoti, Morsi, and Chandur taluks. In the last-named there are 47 who have been returned as Animistic by religion, which, with 45 Mahomedans, is somewhat curious, and instances the influence of Hinduism upon the whole social fabric of the province.

Thakurs.

The Thakurs number 5,099, or 45 more than they did. They are found in every taluk, and are most numerous in Basim, Akola, Darwha, Malkapur, and Akot.

Borals and Golaks.

The representatives of the writer castes in Berar are few. As may be seen from Table D, the few there are have comparatively a large proportion of literates and pupils. The numbers of the Borals (25) and Golaks (146) are doubtful; they numbered 163 and 356 respectively at the last census, and as they are illegitimate people, they may be disposed to repudiate their origin.

Kasts.

The Kasts have decreased from 379 to 259, nearly one-third of whom are in the Murtazapur taluk.

Kayets.

The Kayets have decreased from 1,066 to 974, the chief diminution being in the Ellichpur taluk. They are scattered in small numbers throughout the province.

Parbhus.

The Parbhus have increased from 477 to 632, of whom a large proportion are found in the Amraoti taluk.

Purbhaye.

The numbers of the Purbhaye have fallen from 262 to 94, of whom 40 were enumerated in Chikhli. From the Amraoti district, where there were 144, they have almost entirely disappeared.

Garpagaris.

The group of astrologers comprises the Garpagari, Joshi, and Sarode castes. The Garpagaris, or hail-averters, number 3,041, and have lost 1,164 or nearly 28 per cent of their strength; but this decrease and the corresponding increase among Naths, noted above, are probably due to the same cause and show differences more apparent than real; the Garpagaris belong to the Nath sect, and it is probable that some of them returned the name of the sect for that of the caste. The aggregate of both castes, Nath and Garpagari, is 6,014 for 1891 against 5,632 in 1881.

Joshis and Sarodes.

The Joshis number 424. They were not separately tabulated at the last census, but were treated as synonymous with the Sarodes, of whom there were 1,180. The Sarodes alone now number 1,330, and the two together aggregate 1,754, which shows an increase of 574 or nearly half as many again. The Joshis are mostly found in the Basim and Buldana districts, and especially in the Basim taluk; the Sarodes in the Wun district.

Gondhalis.

Of the group of musicians the Gondhalis are the most numerous, but their numbers have fallen from 3,212 to 3,033. The chief decrease is in the Akola district, but a large proportion of the caste still remain there.

Boharas.

Coming to the trading castes, we find that the Boharas have increased from 202 to 479. They are mostly found in the Amraoti, Khamgaon, and Akola taluks, and presumably their head-quarters are in the principal towns where their business takes them. Some, however, are said to have taken to agriculture, and this may account for the 37 enumerated in the Melghat. The male sex very largely predominates, and this indicates that the caste is not settled in the province; most of them come temporarily for trade, and the increase of trade explains the increase of Boharas.

Kachhis.

The Musalman Kachhis have increased from 37 to 175, of whom nearly one-third were enumerated in the Amraoti taluk. They should not be confounded with the Hindu caste of the same name, who are agriculturists from the North-West Provinces. The Khojas are new to Berar, and those enumerated in the Wun district, 27 in number, were probably wandering pedlars.

Khojas.

The Komtis have apparently largely decreased, their numbers having fallen from 5,430 to 2,750, but as they sometimes describe themselves as members of the Komti division of the Wani caste, it is probable that some of them have been entered as Wanis; but of those enumerated a very large proportion were returned, as in 1881, in the Wun district, and a large roportion of the remainder in the Basim district.

Komtis.

The Lads (or Lars) have increased from 2,520 to 2,825, or by 12 per cent. Rather more than half are Jains; a large proportion of the Hindu Lads are found in the Mehkar and Chikhli taluks, and more than half the Jain Lads in the Basim taluk.

Lads.

The Wanis, taken altogether, Hindu, Jain, and Sikh, are a large caste, numbering 63,533, or 2·19 per cent of the population of the province. The Hindu Wanis number 50,270, but an accurate comparison with the numbers in 1881 cannot be made, as on that occasion they included some of those who are now shown as separate castes. Excluding the Bhattia, Jangam, Komti, and Lar castes from the Hindu Wanis of 1881, there were 50,191, but the Gujarathis complicate the question, and possibly some of the smaller subdivisions also. There does not, however, appear to have been more than a small increase any way. The Hindu Wanis are strongest in the taluks of Amraoti, Pusad, and Basim. The Jain Wanis have more than doubled their number, the figures having risen from 6,329 to 13,260; they are most conspicuous in Murtazapur and Chandur, and in the Amraoti district generally.

Wanis.

The Perkis are a Telugu caste, and the chief representatives of the Pedlar group, but it is not probable that they follow their hereditary calling in Berar. They number 1,499, and have increased by nearly 18 per cent. As in 1881, they are almost entirely confined to the Wun district, and two-thirds of them are found in the Kelapur taluk, where seemingly many of those formerly enumerated in the neighbouring taluk of Wun have now moved on.

Perkis.

Of the carrier castes the Banjaras number 52,619 and the Labhanas 25,587, and together they aggregate 78,206. In 1881 the Labhanas were treated as a division of Banjaras, and their numbers were not shown separately, but the total amounted to 60,511. The increase has therefore been 17,695 or nearly 23 per cent. This large increment shows that the immigration of these people from Hyderabad territory, which has been going on for the last quarter of a century at least, if not longer, has been fully maintained. Since 1867 they have increased by more than 50 per cent. In the Berar Gazetteer Sir A. Lyall expressed the opinion that "neither their trade nor their tribal system can survive another generation of English predominance," but the prediction has only been partly verified. The tribal system is still flourishing, but their trade is diminishing and is confined to the south-west portion of the province which lies between the railway and the Nizam's dominions. Although they are Hindu castes, both the Banjari and the Labhani have a few followers of the Musalman and Jain creeds. Banjaras are found in every taluk, but they are especially strong in Darwha, where one-third of their number were enumerated and where they formed 11 per cent of the whole population. They are also very strong in Pusad, where they form more than 7 per cent of the population. In Mangrul, Yeotmal, Kelapur, Mehkar, and Basim, there are also considerable numbers. The Musalman Banjaras were found in

Banjaras and Labhanas.

Darwha, Kelapur, and Mangrul, and the Jains in Yeotmal. The Labhanas are strongest in Basim, Pusad, and Mehkar. Taking Labhanas and Banjaras together, they form 12·5 per cent of the population of Darwha, 10·7 per cent in Pusad, 8·9 in Mangrul, 5·3 in Kelapur, 5·0 per cent in Basim, 4·9 per cent in Mehkar, and 3·7 per cent in Yeotmal. In 1881 these were the favourite taluks, but the percentages in each case were somewhat less than they are now, so that the increase among these people has been greater than among the rest of the population in these localities. The increase among males has been slightly greater than among females.

Wanjaras.

The Wanjaras number 31,802 and have increased by 4,307, or nearly 16 per cent. The distinction between these people and the Banjaras is rather a nice point. Mr. Kitts says that to confound them with the Banjaras gives them great offence, but the names are practically identical, although different derivations may be attributed to them, and it seems probable that they are of the same stock, the difference between them being, as has been remarked in an earlier chapter, that the Wanjaras are Banjaras who have given up a nomadic existence and have settled down to a civilised life. More than two-fifths of them are found in Mehkar, where they form nearly 9 per cent of the population. Their numbers are very large also in Basim and Chikhli, that is to say, their principal location is in the south-west corner of the province, and the Banjaras carry on the line across the south to the east.

Sonars.

The Sonar is the chief of the artisan castes. It numbers 29,219 members and shows an increase of 6 per cent. The Sonars are very generally distributed through the province with the exception of the Melghat, where there are very few. In Akot, Balapur, Jalgaon, and Daryapur their numbers have diminished, the decrease in Jalgaon amounting to nearly 15 per cent of their former strength.

Mhalis.

The Mhalis or barbers number 35,245, of whom 17 are Mahomedans and 3 are Jains. They have increased by only 5 per cent, and while the principal increase has taken place in Kelapur and Wun and the Balaghat generally, in most of the plain taluks, Murtazapur, Ellichpur, and Daryapur, and all those of the Akola district, there has been a decrease.

Dangare.

Of the Blacksmiths the Dangare, who are found mostly in Chandur, have diminished in number, though it is possible that some of them may have been included among the Kunbis, of whom they are sometimes regarded as a subdivision.

Ghisadis.

The Ghisadis have increased from 534 to 719. They affect the southern taluks from Chikhli to Pusad.

Jirayets.

The Jirayets number 312, slightly more than they did in 1881. They are mostly found in the Akola and Buldana districts, a fourth of them being in the Jalgaon taluk.

Lohars.

The Lohars number 15,907, and have increased more than 14 per cent. They are found everywhere, but are most numerous in Chandur and the taluks of the Wun districts; in Kelapur their numbers have risen from 680 to 1,111, and in Wun from 887 to 1,240.

Panchals.

The Panchals, who are vagrant blacksmiths, number 1,885 and have increased from 1,431, or by nearly 32 per cent. They are scattered over the province and were enumerated in every taluk but the Melghat; they are most numerous in Wun and Kelapur. A small party in Yeotmal are Mahomedans.

Gaondis.

Of the carpenters, turners, and masons, there are only a few castes. The Gaondis, or Raj, are masons and number 639, of whom a large proportion belong to the Pusad taluk. They have increased by nearly 20 per cent, and in Pusad have more than doubled their number.

Gosangi.

A few masons in Jalgaon gave their castes as Gosangi. They are believed to be a Telugu caste.

Sutars.

The Sutars number 32,491 and have increased by 7 per cent. They are most numerous in Chandur, Morsi and Amraoti; their numbers have largely increased in the two former while they have diminished in the latter, and also in Akot and Jalgaon and in the taluks of the Ellichpur district.

Kasars.

The Kasars, Otaris and Tambatkars are the brass and coppersmith castes. "The Kasars take their name from the bell-metal (kanse) in which they work," and rank high among artisans. They number 7,754, of whom 196 are Jains; the increase is 90 only, or rather more than 1 per cent. They are found in every taluk but their numbers exhibit a great deal of variation since 1881. In Mehkar and Chandur there have been the largest increments and in Malkapur, Wun, and Balapur the greatest diminution; in Wun the numbers have dropped from 103 to 17; but now, as formerly, the greatest strength is in Basim.

Otaris.

The Otaris have increased in number from 1,348 to 1,484, or by 10 per cent. They are found in all taluks except Kelapur, but are most numerous in Akot and Jalgaon, where, contrary to the general fashion, their numbers have considerably increased. In Basim one man returned himself as Mahomedan and a few in Darwha are Animistic.

Tambatkars.

The Tambatkars number only 590, or nearly one-third less than they did in 1881. They are chiefly found in Akola and Ellichpur, although their numbers in the latter taluk have been reduced by nearly one-half.

Simpis.

The Simpis (or Darzis) are the only tailor caste. They number 16,365, of whom 2,626, or 16 per cent, are Jains. The increase since 1881 has been 856, or more than 5 per cent. They are found in every taluk, but are most numerous in Jalgaon and Malkapur, although their numbers have somewhat diminished in the former.

Bharadbhunjas.

The Bharadbhunjas (or Bharbhunjas) are gram-parchers, whose numbers have risen from 396 to 601, much of the increase being no doubt due to immigration from the North-West Provinces. A large proportion were enumerated in the Ellichpur taluk, as was the case at the previous census. The disparity between the sexes is remarkable, there being 413 males and only 188 females, or a proportion of 100 to 45·5; the same feature is noticeable in the figures for 1881, when the proportion was 100 to 49.

Halwais.

The Halwais, or confectioners, number 238, of whom one woman has been returned as a Jain. The increase has been 46, mostly in the Amraoti district. They are most numerous in Chikhli.

Gandhis.

The Gandhis, or perfumers, have increased from 56 to 101, of whom 38 were enumerated in the Ellichpur taluk. A few are Jains.

Tambolis.

The numbers of the Tambolis, or betel-leaf sellers, have risen from 637 to 765, or 20 per cent. A large proportion are found in Pusad, and Ellichpur and Amraoti exhibit conspicuous numbers. In Ellichpur, however, they have fallen considerably, as they have also in Daryapur, whereas they have increased largely in the Amraoti taluk and district generally.

In the next group of the weavers, calenderers, and dyers, there are several castes, of which not a few are recent introductions into Berar. These are the Alkori, who are dyers probably from Madras, the Bunkars, weavers from the Central Provinces or North-West Provinces, the Chenwars, who are probably the same as the Chanwars, weavers of Hyderabad, the Inkars, of whom nothing is known, the Katiars, weavers from the Central Provinces, the Momins, who are the same as the Julahas of Upper India, and the Patuals, weavers from Gujarat. Of these the Bunkars number 99, of whom the majority are found in Ellichpur; the Chenwars number 203, who are all found in Pusad, in which taluk the Inkars also were enumerated; the Katias occur in Morsi; the Momins number 290, of whom a large majority were enumerated in Malkapur; and the Patuals, of whom there are 20, are found in Akot.

Bunkars. Chenwars. Inkars. Katias. Momins. Patuals.

The Ataris are dyers, who are mostly found in Amraoti, Murtazapur, and Basim; their numbers are small but have risen from 75 to 92, of whom two-thirds are Mahomedans.

Ataris.

One single individual in the Melghat represents the Chhipa or cloth-stamping caste.

The Halbis, who are weavers, number 2,841, and have increased by 636, or nearly 29 per cent. This increase is remarkable because the Halbi caste is peculiar to Berar; the name at least, I believe, is not to be found in the returns of other provinces for the Census of 1881, and yet so large an increase cannot be entirely due to natural growth from within. The explanation possibly lies in the fact that some of them sometimes describe themselves as Kunbis, although in the returns for 1881 only a dozen are so shown, but there may have been others who adopted other appellations. This case illustrates the absolutely indefinite character of a good deal of the caste nomenclature. The chief increase is in the Ellichpur taluk, where nearly one-half of the caste is found.

Halbis.

The numbers of the Hatgars exhibit great variation from those recorded in 1881, and as this is probably due to the inclusion of some of their number among Dhangars, the consideration of the Hatgar caste is deferred till the latter are reached.

Hatgars.

The Khatris are weavers, whose numbers have fallen; there are now 1,714 against 2,015 in 1881, the decrease amounting to nearly 15 per cent. The chief diminution is in the Amraoti taluk, where the numbers have fallen from 678 to 441, but they are still more numerous there than in any other taluk. In Ellichpur and Darwha there has been a considerable decrease, and from Mehkar and Yeotmal, though their numbers before were not large, they have almost disappeared. In Akot on the other hand, where they were unknown, there are now 111, of whom 4 were returned as of the Sikh religion.

Khatris.

The Koris have largely increased and now number 435. In 1881 there were only 68, who were nearly all in the Ellichpur district; now there are 143 in the Amraoti taluk alone, 64 in the Melghat, and small numbers scattered over most of the rest of the province.

Koris.

The Koshtis are the largest of the weaving castes; they number 14,818, which is very little more than their total in 1881. They are most numerous in Morsi and Ellichpur,

Koshtis.

although in the latter taluk there has been some diminution. In Daryapur, Darwha, and Chandur their numbers are also considerable. In the Amraoti taluk the numbers have fallen from 1,140 to 832. Some of these people are Jains.

Patwis.

The numbers of the Patwis have decreased from 747 to 524, the chief loss being in the taluks of Ellichpur, Daryapur, and Amraoti, and throughout the Akola district. They are still most numerous in Ellichpur, Amraoti, and Chikhli.

Rangaris.

The Rangaris also exhibit a decrease, their numbers having fallen from 12,471 to 12,190. The loss has been distributed over several taluks, but is most marked in the Akola district. The chief numbers are in Malkapur, Darwha, and Ellichpur.

Salis, etc.

The Salewar, Salve, and Sali are probably all of one caste, the first being the Telugu name adopted by those enumerated in Kelapur and Wun. They are weavers from Southern India, and number 9,105 or 21 less than their total in 1881. The local distribution does not show much variation, and Chikhli and Ellichpur are, as before, the favourite taluks.

Warthis.

The Warthi, otherwise known as Dhobi and Parit, is a large caste, numbering 23,084, which shows an increase of 7 per cent on the number in 1881. As the washermen of the country they are found in every taluk, but not, as might be hoped, in every village; in the Melghat there are only 24, all told, but the Korkus possibly do their washing at home. The caste is most numerous in Amraoti, Akola, Ellichpur, Chandur, and Malkapur. In Kelapur and Wun there has been a considerable increase.

Pinjaris.

The Pinjaris show a very large increase. In 1881, there appear to have been only 149, all Mahomedans; there are now 1,085 Mahomedans and 67 Hindus. They are most numerous in the Amraoti taluk and the Wun district; elsewhere they are scarce.

Dhangars.

The Dhangars, or Shepherds, who are also sometimes blanket-weavers, are one of the largest castes in Berar. The Hatgars are sometimes regarded as a subdivision of Dhangars, and although they have been tabulated as separate castes both on this occasion and in 1881, it appears, from the figures for the Pusad and Darwha taluks at least, that the names have been indiscriminately applied. The Pusad taluk and the north bank of the Painganga river has been the home of the Hatgars since about 1600 A.D., when, according to the Ain-i-Akbari, they were driven westward across the Wardha by the Gonds, and in 1881 the number of this caste enumerated there was 5,013; on the present occasion the returns show only 733. On the other hand, the Dhangars numbered 4,747 in 1881 and as many as 9,713 in 1891. So in Darwha, while the returns show a rise among Hatgars from 59 to 1,155, they exhibit a fall among Dhangars from 4,934, to 4,253. How far the error extends it is impossible to say, and the only comparisons that can be safely made are those of the combined figures for both castes. For the whole province these amount to 87,626 or 3 per cent of the total population; for 1881, they were 83,164, and the increase is 4,462 or 5·4 per cent. Of the total 10,446, or nearly 12 per cent, are found in the Pusad taluk, where they form 7·5 per cent of the population. In Malkapur they number 5,991, in Darwha 5,308, and in Chandur 5,279. In Kelapur there has been a comparatively large increase, the numbers having risen from 1,610 to 2,213, or more than 37 per cent. In Morsi, Wun, Malkapur, Murtazapur and Chikhli, there have also been considerable increments; in Pusad it amounts to 786 or 8 per cent. In Daryapur, Akola, Jalgaon, Khamgaon, Ellichpur, and Akot, there has been some diminution.

The Telis, or oil-pressers, are another of the large castes of Berar and number 82,095 or 2·8 per cent of the total population. In 1881 they numbered 75,552, and the increase has been 6,543, or 8·7 per cent. There has been considerable variation in the local distribution. In Kelapur the numbers have risen from 1,752 to 2,604, or by 48·6 per cent; in Darwha from 4,446 to 5,541, or by 24·6 per cent; in Chandur from 9,943 to 12,187, or by 22·6 per cent; in Morsi from 3,704 to 4,494, or by 21·3 per cent; in Yeotmal from 5,195 to 6,021, or by 15·9 per cent; and in Amraoti from 6,769 to 7,829, or by 15·7 per cent. On the other hand, they have fallen in Jalgaon from 2,832 to 2,272, or by 19·8 per cent; in Akot from 3,244 to 2,865, or by 11·7 per cent; and in Ellichpur from 4,062 to 3,825, or by 5·8 per cent. The caste is most numerous in Chandur, where it forms rather more than 6 per cent of the whole population; in Yeotmal it forms 4·8 per cent; in Amraoti 4·3 per cent; and in Darwha 3·4 per cent. It thus appears that the chief strength of the caste lies in the eastern taluks, where also the largest increments have taken place, and it may be deduced from these results that the Teli caste have formed no inconsiderable item in the immigration from the Central Provinces.

Telis.

The Kumbhars are potters who number 22,465, and have increased by 2,399, or nearly 12 per cent. They are most numerous in Amraoti and Chandur, in which two taluks nearly one-fifth of their number were enumerated. In Chandur the numbers exhibit a remarkable increase, having risen from 1,294 to 2,046 or 58 per cent. There have been considerable increments in the other taluks of the Amraoti district also, in the Wun district, and in Basim and Mehkar. In Balapur and Akot there has been a diminution.

Kumbhars.

The Kachars, or Kanchari, are glass-workers, whose numbers have risen from 436 to 564, or 29 per cent. They are most numerous in Chikhli, Darwha, Balapur and Chandur. In the Ellichpur district their numbers have dropped from 104 to 34. This caste are the makers of glass bangles. The Lakharis are the makers of bangles in lac; they number 126 against 99 in 1891, and nearly half of them are found in the Amraoti taluk.

Kachars.

Lakharis.

The Lonaris, or salt-workers, have increased from 888 to 1,096, or 23·4 per cent. They are most numerous in Akot, Jalgaon, Khamgaon, and Balapur; and in these taluks also the increment has been very large.

Sonaris.

The Bhois, or fishermen, number 27,415, and have increased by more than 19 per cent. The increase is most marked in Chandur, Kelapur and Wun, but is very general; Ellichpur and Daryapur are the only taluks which show a diminution. "The Bhois still cleave to their hereditary caste occupations much more closely than is the case with many castes," and they are consequently to be found where rivers or tanks supply them with fishing. They are most numerous in Chandur, Kelapur, Amraoti, Ellichpur and Wun, and least so in Mangrul, Mehkar, and Basim.

Bhois.

The Injhwar are a caste of fishermen who come from the Central Provinces and number 221. They are new to Berar, and are mostly found in Ellichpur.

Injhwars.

The Kahars are represented in small numbers only, but they have risen from 247 to 359. Of these, 76 belong to Malkapur, 70 to Melghat, and 61 to Amraoti.

Kahars.

Kevati.

The Kevati, or probably Kewats, are new to Berar. They are a fishing caste well known in Bengal and the Central Provinces. Although they number only 76 and are apparently recent immigrants, they seem to have scattered themselves throughout most of the taluks.

Kolis.

The Kolis number 32,628, which shows an increase of 2,230, or rather more than 7 per cent. The largest increase is in Basim, where the numbers have risen from 849 to 1,503, but the caste is most numerous in Malkapur, where there are 5,812, or 18 per cent of their total; in Amraoti, where there are 15 per cent, and in Akot, where there are 11 per cent. In Jalgaon they have decreased from 2,512 to 2,269, and there has been considerable diminution in Khamgaon, Wun and Mangrul. The Kolis are classed as fishermen, but the hereditary occupation has fallen into disuse in Berar. In the Gazetteer they are referred to as having acted in former times as a sort of militia to guard the hill passes on both sides of the Berar plain, but they have practically disappeared now from the Northern hills, and comparatively few are found on the Ajanta range.

Kalals.

The Kalals have increased from 14,943 to 16,234, or by 8·6 per cent. In Chandur there has been a remarkable increase, the numbers having risen from 1,348 to 2,500; in the Akola district there has been a decrease of 13 per cent, chiefly in Akot and Jalgaon, and in the Ellichpur district a decrease of 10 per cent. The caste is now most numerous in the eastern taluks, Chandur, Yeotmal, Amraoti, Darwha, Kelapur and Morsi, which contain between them more than half its numbers.

Pasis.

The Pasis, the tari-drawers of Bengal and the North-West Provinces, have increased from 256 to 467. They are most numerous in Amraoti, Murtazapur and Ellichpur, though in the last named their numbers have fallen from 100 to 65.

Kasais and Khatiks.

The Hindu Kasais, or Khatiks, number 4,959, and show an increase of 472 or more than 10 per cent. The Musalman Kasais have increased from 20 to 384. Of the former, nearly one-half are found in the Amraoti district, and nearly one-half of these in the Amraoti taluk; they occur in considerable numbers also in Ellichpur and Daryapur. Of the latter, a large proportion are in the Buldana district, and especially in the Chikhli taluk.

Chambhar.

Of the leather-workers, the chief caste is the Chambhar, who number 29,174; they have increased by 7·5 per cent. In Mehkar the numbers have increased from 1,106 to 1,605 and in Malkapur from 2,502 to 2,892; in Akot, Balapur, and Daryapur, there has been a diminution, but the Akola district still contains the greatest number. They are, however, much more numerous in Malkapur than in any other taluk.

Dabgars.

The Dabgars, or tanners, are disappearing; in 1881 there were 105 and now there are but 56, who are all located in the Balapur taluk.

Dohors.

The Dohors number 5,082, which shows an increase of 605, or more than 13 per cent. The chief increment is in Mehkar, where the numbers have risen from 641 to 1,005; from Yeotmal, where there were 60, they have all but one disappeared. The caste is most numerous in Mehkar, Chikhli, and Ellichpur, where are found more than half its number.

Madhgis.

The Madgis, or Madhige, are a Telugu caste of leather-workers, who have increased largely since 1881, their numbers having risen from 1,595 to 2,677, or by nearly 68 per cent. With the exception of one individual, they are all found in the Wun district, and they are most numerous in the Kelapur taluk.

Zingars.

The numbers of the Zingars have fallen from 1,503, to 1,313, or nearly 13 per cent. The chief decrease is in Chikhli and Ellichpur, which were among the most favourite taluks in 1881. They are now most numerous in Akot.

Mahars.

We now come to the group of village servants, watchmen and menials, of whom the Mahars, or Dhers, are the most important. Next to the Kunbis the Mahars are the largest caste in Berar; they number 355,005 and form 12·25 per cent of the total population. Since 1881 they have increased by 47,011, or more than 15 per cent. There is now very little disparity between the sexes, the proportion being 998 females to 1,000 males; in 1881 the proportion of females was 986, so that in this caste the present census may be taken as indicating less concealment of females. The chief increments have been as follows:—in Kelapur 1,959 or 44 per cent; in Morsi 4,840 or 34 per cent; in Mehkar 4,183 or 29 per cent; in Chandur 6,771 or 28 per cent; in Darwha 3,577 or 25 per cent; in Amraoti 6,093 or 24 per cent; in Basim 4,427 or 23 per cent, and in Murtazapur 3,489 or 22 per cent. In the Akola and Ellichpur districts the increase has been very small, but Ellichpur is the only taluk in which there has been a decrease. The caste is now most numerous in Amraoti, where they form 17·1 per cent of the population of the taluk; in Chandur they form 15·8 per cent; in Murtazapur 15·7 per cent; in Akola 15·0 per cent; in Mangrul 14·8 per cent; and in Basim 13·4 per cent. In the Melghat, Kelapur, and Wun, the numbers are comparatively small.

Balahis.

The Balahis hold a position among the hill tribes analogous to that of the Mahars, but their numbers are small and they seem to be fast disappearing; at the last census there were 803, but there are now only 327, who were all enumerated in the Melghat taluk.

Bhangis.

The Bhangis are the Hindu scavenger caste: the paucity of their numbers has long been observed, but a considerable increase has taken place since 1881, the numbers having risen from 691 to 1,303. Besides these 180 have been returned as Mahomedans, but they are probably not of the Bhangi caste, but Mehtars, who have adopted the name from their occupation. The Hindu Bhangis are most numerous in the Amraoti taluk, and at some distance in Khamgaon, Akola and Akot.

Mangs.

The Mangs are the lowest of all castes in Berar. They number 52,151 and have increased by 5,785 or 12·7 per cent. This caste shows the exceptional condition of an excess of the female sex, the proportion being 1,008 females to 1,000 males. The chief increments have been—in Mehkar 26·9 per cent; in Morsi 23·8 per cent; in Basim 23·6 per cent; in Chandur 21·8 per cent; in Malkapur 18·2 per cent; and in Mangrul 18·0 per cent. In Akola, Jalgaon, Ellichpur, Melghat, and Wun, there has been some diminution. The caste is far more numerous in the Basim taluk than in any other, and they form there 3·8 per cent of the population.

Mang-Garodis.

The Mang-Garodis, who are a wandering tribe, have decreased from 218 to 161, all enumerated in Kelapur and Wun.

Tagwale.

The Tagwale, numbering 113, are new to Berar under that name; they are believed to be connected with Mangs. These people were enumerated in Chikhli and Mehkar.

Gotefods and Pathrats.

The Gotefods and Pathrats are stone-dressers; the numbers of the former are small and have diminished; those of the latter have risen from 783 to 877; they are most numerous in Balapur, Murtazapur, Darwha, and Chikhli. There seems to have been a good deal of movement among these people; in 1881 there were six individuals in Murtazapur and now there are 137; and in Malkapur, where there were 100, there are only 11.

Takankars.

The Takankars, whose hereditary occupation is that of repairing stone hand-mills, articles of universal use, number 5,414, and have increased by 1,067 or 24·5 per cent. In Balapur, where none were returned in 1881, there are now 260, and besides this there have been considerable increments in Murtazapur, Chandur, and Amraoti; in Mangrul there has been a large diminution. The caste is now most numerous in Akot, Amraoti, Akola, Murtazapur, and Daryapur.

Beldars.

The numbers of the Beldars, or earth-workers, have risen from 11,494 to 12,228, or by 6·4 per cent. There has been a considerable increase in Khamgaon, Mehkar, and Basim, and a decrease in Ellichpur, Yeotmal, and Wun, but a large proportion of the caste is found now as in 1881 in Darwha and Chandur.

Gochki.

The next four names in this group, the Gochki, Manewad, Sagur and Silawat, are new to Berar as caste appellations. The Gochki were found in the Wun taluk and are probably immigrants from the east or south; they are earth-workers.

Manewads.

Manewad is probably a corruption of Mannu Waddar, the name in use by the Waddars of Mysore.

Sagurs.

The Sagurs are earth-workers, mostly enumerated in Mehkar and a few in Morsi.

Silawats.

The Silawats are a small caste of stone-workers, who at the last census were found in Ajmere and the Central Provinces. The few now returned were enumerated in Malkapur and have possibly come from Ajmere.

Waddars.

The Waddars show a large decrease, their numbers being fallen from 7,596 to 6,116; and their local distribution exhibits the extreme of variation from that of 1881. Little importance, however, attaches to either fact, as these people are earth-workers from Southern India, whose movements depend upon the demand for labour for roads and other public works, and it is probable that they are continually shifting their quarters.

Basods and Bansfod.

The Basods and Bansfod are sometimes said to be synonymous; both castes are bamboo-splitters and workers. The numbers of the Basods have increased from 107 to 261; they are are mostly found in Morsi and the Melghat, where their occupation finds scope and the increase in their numbers points to immigration from the Central Provinces.

Borekars.

The Borekars seem to be new. They are mat-makers, found mostly in the Akola district, but scattered in small numbers.

Buruds.

The Buruds are bamboo-workers, whose numbers have risen from 1,201 to 1,269. There has been some variation in their local distribution, but they are still, as before, most numerous in the Ellichpur taluk; Amraoti, Chandur, Khamgaon, and Kelapur all contain more than 100.

Kekadis.

The Kekadis, or Kaikaris, have largely decreased, their numbers having fallen from 3,103 to 2,024. They are a vagrant people, ostensibly basket and broom makers, but of a loose and sometimes troublesome character, and the diminution in their numbers is not a matter for regret. They are most numerous in Chikhli and Mehkar.

Thotis.

The Thotis are a small Telugu caste found in the Wun district, and have not varied much in numbers or distribution. Their classification is doubtful. Mr. Kitts describes them as scavengers.

Bedars. Of the group of hunters and fowlers the Pardhis and Bedars are the most numerous. The Bedars have increased very largely, their numbers having risen from 1,273 to 3,041, nearly half of whom are found in the Akola taluk alone.

Berads. The Berads, who are sometimes said to be of the same caste, are mostly found in the Darwha taluk, where there are no Bedars; their numbers are small and have diminished.

Pardhis. The numbers of the Pardhis have risen from 5,834 to 6,899, or by nearly 12 per cent. They are a wandering people ostensibly occupied in snaring game, and not much importance attaches to their distribution at the time of the census. Malkapur, however, seems to be a favourite taluk with them, as a large proportion of their number were enumerated there both in 1881 and in 1891; in Amraoti and Daryapur there are also considerable numbers. Wild country and jungle they evidently avoid, as there are none in the Melghat and but a few individuals in Pusad, and it is not improbable that their predatory habits find play in the haunts of man as well as in those of the beast and the bird.

Aridra and Balsanto. The Aridra and Balsanto are Telugu mendicant castes, of whom a few individuals were enumerated in Kelapur; they are new to Berar.

Bhamtis. The Bhamtis number 1,774, which shows an increase of less than 5 per cent. They are mostly found in Yeotmal, Balapur, and Chandur, and they appear to have settled in the two first named, as their numbers there were much the same in 1881.

Dangats. The Dangats are a small caste of mendicants, but their numbers have risen from 271 to 486, and this is noteworthy, as in 1881 but 440 were enumerated in all India. They are mostly found in Malkapur, where their numbers have risen from 25 to 345.

Gujarathis. The people who call themselves Gujarathi number 1,445, of whom 347 are Jains. They are most numerous in Balapur, Daryapur, Chikhli, Akola, and Amraoti. No useful comparison can be made with the numbers in 1881, as the name merely desigates a country and is indiscriminately used in some cases to indicate a caste subdivision.

Marathe. Pardeshis. Telanga. The same may be said of the Marathe, who number 19,038, and of the Pardeshis, who number 639. The Telanga have increased from 2,002 to 2,081, a large majority of whom are found in the Wun district; there has been a very decided movement of these people from the Kelapur to the Wun taluk, as the number in Kelapur has fallen from 1,373 to 421, while in Wun it has risen from 239 to 1,044.

Vidurs. The Vidurs or Krishnapakshis, a hybrid caste, number 10,695, which shows a decrease of 1,052 or 9 per cent. They are found everywhere, but are most numerous in Chandur, Amraoti, and Morsi.

Gopals. The Gopals are by hereditary vocation acrobats, but frequently mendicants and rascals generally in practice. Their numbers have increased from 3,076 to 3,419, or by 11 per cent. A large proportion are found in Basim and Mehkar, and as this was also the case in 1881, it is possible that they may be settling down to useful occupations.

Panguls. The Panguls are sometimes described as a division of the Gopals. They number 2,085 and have increased by 14 per cent. Two-thirds of them are found in Darwha and Basim.

Kolhatis. The Kolhatis have somewhat decreased and now number 1,257, of whom more than half are found in the Akola district, but they are most numerous in the Malkapur taluk.

Chitrakathis. The numbers of the Chitrakathi have risen from 1,554 to 1,612, or nearly 4 per cent; a very large proportion were enumerated in Murtazapur, as was the case, but not to the same extent, in 1881; in Akola, Chandur, and Yeotmal, the numbers are also conspicuous.

Shekhs. Pathans. Syeds. Moghals. Of the Mahomedan tribes which are represented in the returns, the Shekhs are the most numerous and number 124,232, or nearly 60 per cent of the total number of this community; the Pathans number 48,393, or 23 per cent; the Syeds number 15,107, or a little more than 7 per cent, and the Moghals number 4,437, or 2 per cent. The remaining 8 per cent are made up of 1,992 who have returned themselves indefinitely as Musalman, and of the various items scattered through a number of different castes, tribes and races. Omitting these miscellaneous components, the Musalman tribes taken together are most numerous in the Ellichpur taluk, where they amount to 18,194 and form 12·4 per cent of the whole population; in actual numbers Amraoti with 17,163, Malkapur with 13,562, Akot with 12,186, Akola with 11,863, and Balapur with 11,027 come next in order, but in proportion to the total population Balapur comes second with 10·8, and Amraoti third with 9·4 per cent. In the Melghat there are only 606, or 1·3 per cent; in Wun the proportion is 2·5 per cent, and in Kelapur 2·6.

Taluk components. Having examined the local distribution of the principal castes the subject may be considered from the opposite direction and the composition of each taluk reviewed. This is provided for in the following lists, in which is given for each taluk all castes whose numbers amount to 1 per cent or more of the taluk population. Under the designation of "Musalman tribes" are included only the Shekhs, Pathans, Syeds, Moghals and Musalmans indefinite; it does not refer to all who may be Musalman by religion.

Amraoti Taluk.

	Caste	Per cent.
1.	Kunbi	20·7
2.	Mahar	17·1
3.	Musalman tribes	9·4
4.	Mali	6·7
5.	Teli	4·3
6.	Brahman	4·1
7.	Wani	3·1
8.	Koli	2·6
9.	Rajput	2·2
10.	Dhangar	2·1
11.	Mang	1·9
12.	Gaoli	1·6
13.	Bari	1·5
14.	Gond	1·3
15.	Mhali	1·3
16.	Bhoi	1·2
17.	Sutar	
18.	Kumbhar	
19.	Chambhar	1·1
20.	Sonar	
21.	Others	14·3

Chandur Taluk.

	Caste	Per cent.
1.	Kunbi	25·4
2.	Mahar	15·8
3.	Mali	9·2
4.	Teli	6·2
5.	Musalman tribes	4·3
6.	Gond	3·8
7.	Gaoli	2·6
8.	Dhangar	
9.	Rajput	2·5
10.	Brahman	2·2
11.	Wani	1·8
12.	Bhoi	1·5
13.	Sutar	
14.	Mang	
15.	Mhali	1·3
16.	Kalal	
17.	Maratha	1·2
18.	Bari	1·1
19.	Sonar	
20.	Kumbhar	1·0
21.	Others	12·1

MORSI TALUK.

	Caste	Per cent
1.	Kunbi	28·1
2.	Mali	14·6
3.	Mahar	12·5
4.	Musalman tribes	5·8
5.	Gond	5·3
6.	Teli	2·9
7.	Dhangar	2·1
8.	Gaoli	2·0
9.	Bari	}
10.	Brahman	} 1·9
11.	Koshti	}
12.	Wani	1·8
13.	Sutar	1·5
14.	Rajput	1·4
15.	Mhali	1·3
16.	Sonar	} 1·2
17.	Bhoi	}
18.	Mang	1·0
19.	Others	11·6

MURTAZAPUR TALUK.

	Caste	Per cent
1.	Kunbi	29·6
2.	Mahar	15·7
3.	Musalman tribes	7·9
4.	Mali	6·9
5.	Brahman	3·0
6.	Wani	} 2·9
7.	Dhangar	}
8.	Teli	2·8
9.	Mang	1·9
10.	Rajput	} 1·3
11.	Sonar	}
12.	Mhali	1·2
13.	Banjari	}
14.	Sutar	} 1·1
15.	Bhoi	}
16.	Chambhar	}
17.	Gaoli	} 1·0
18.	Kumbhar	}
19.	Others	16·2

AKOLA TALUK.

	Caste	Per cent
1.	Kunbi	31·4
2.	Mahar	15·0
3.	Musalman tribes	8·6
4.	Mali	5·3
5.	Brahman	3·3
6.	Dhangar	3·0
7.	Wani	} 2·3
8.	Teli	}
9.	Koli	} 2·1
10.	Mang	}
11.	Rajput	1·8
12.	Mhali	} 1·4
13.	Chambhar	}
14.	Wanjari	1·3
15.	Gaoli	}
16.	Sutar	} 1·1
17.	Warthi	}
18.	Bedar	}
19.	Sonar	1·0
20.	Others	13·3

AKOT TALUK.

	Caste	Per cent.
1.	Kunbi	34·0
2.	Mahar	10·4
3.	Musalman tribes	8·8
4.	Mali	8·4
5.	Brahman	3·6
6.	Dhangar	2·7
7.	Koli	2·6
8.	Wani	2·4
9.	Teli	2·1
10.	Bari	1·9
11.	Mang	1·8
12.	Rajput	1·7
13.	Sonar	1·5
14.	Mhali	1·4
15.	Chambhar	1·3
16.	Bhoi	} 1·1
17.	Sutar	}
18.	Warthi	} 1·0
19.	Kumbhar	}
20.	Others	11·2

BALAPUR TALUK.

	Caste	Per cent
1.	Kunbi	29·8
2.	Mahar	12·9
3.	Musalman tribes	10·8
4.	Mali	10·5
5.	Dhangar	3·6
6.	Andh	2·4
7.	Brahman	2·3
8.	Teli	2·2
9.	Wani	2·1
10.	Rajput	1·8
11.	Mang	1·5
12.	Mhali	1·3
13.	Sutar	} 1·2
14.	Warthi	}
15.	Chambhar	1·1
16.	Bhoi	1·0
17.	Others	14·3

JALGAON TALUK.

	Caste	Per cent
1.	Kunbi	29·7
2.	Mali	11·8
3.	Mahar	9·4
4.	Musalman tribes	6·1
5.	Bari	5·3
6.	Dhangar	3·3
7.	Brahman	3·2
8.	Rajput	3·0
9.	Teli	} 2·3
10.	Koli	}
11.	Wani	2·2
12.	Simpi	2·0
13.	Chambhar	1·6
14.	Mang	1·4
15.	Mhali	1·3
16.	Bhoi	1·1
17.	Rangari	}
18.	Sutar	} 1·0
19.	Sonar	}
20.	Others	11·1

KHAMGAON TALUK.

	Caste	Per cent.
1.	Kunbi	37·6
2.	Mahar	11·2
3.	Mali	9·7
4.	Musalman tribes	7·0
5.	Brahman	3·8
6.	Wani	3·3
7.	Dhangar }	3·1
8.	Rajput }	
9.	Teli	2·1
10.	Chambhar	1·6
11.	Mang	1·5
12.	Mhali	1·3
13.	Sonar	1·2
14.	Sutar	1·1
15.	Koli	1·0
16.	Others	11·4

ELLICHPUR TALUK.

	Caste	Per cent.
1.	Kunbi	24·4
2.	Musalman tribes	12·4
3.	Mahar	12·1
4.	Mali	12·0
5.	Brahman	3·3
6.	Teli	2·6
7.	Bari	2·2
8.	Rajput }	1·9
9.	Wani }	
10.	Koshti }	1·6
11.	Dhangar }	
12.	Bhoi	1·5
13.	Mang	1·4
14.	Mhali }	1·3
15.	Sonar }	
16.	Gaoli	1·2
17.	Gond }	1·1
18.	Sutar }	
19.	Warthi }	
20.	Chambhar }	1·0
21.	Halbi }	
22.	Others	12·0

DARYAPUR TALUK.

	Caste	Per cent.
1.	Kunbi	32·2
2.	Mahar	14·2
3.	Musalman tribes	7·9
4.	Mali	7·7
5.	Dhangar	3·4
6.	Brahman	2·3
7.	Mang	2·2
8.	Koli }	2·1
9.	Teli }	
10.	Bari	2·0
11.	Wani	1·7
12.	Rajput	1·4
13.	Koshti }	1·3
14.	Sonar }	
15.	Mhali }	
16.	Chambhar }	

DARYAPUR TALUK—*contd.*

	Caste	Per cent.
17.	Warthi	1·2
18.	Kumbhar }	1·1
19.	Sutar }	
20.	Bhoi	1·0
21.	Others	11·2

MELGHAT TALUK.

	Caste	Per cent.
1.	Korku	67·2
2.	Gaoli	5·7
3.	Gond	4·9
4.	Nihal	4·4
5.	Mahar	2·4
6.	Rajput	1·6
7.	Bhil	1·5
8.	Musalman tribes	1·3
9.	Kolam	1·0
10.	Others	10·0

CHIKHLI TALUK.

	Caste	Per cent.
1.	Kunbi	40·6
2.	Mahar	12·3
3.	Musalman tribes	7·3
4.	Rajput	4·0
5.	Mali	3·7
6.	Brahman	2·9
7.	Wanjari	2·5
8.	Mang }	2·2
9.	Teli }	
10.	Dhangar	2·1
11.	Wani	1·9
12.	Koli	1·2
13.	Mhali }	1·1
14.	Sonar }	
15.	Sutar	1·0
16.	Others	13·9

MALKAPUR TALUK.

	Caste	Per cent.
1.	Kunbi	37·0
2.	Mahar	10·7
3.	Mali	8·4
4.	Musalman tribes	7·6
5.	Rajput	3·7
6.	Koli	3·3
7.	Dhangar	3·1
8.	Teli	2·7
9.	Brahman	2·2
10.	Wani	1·9
11.	Chambhar }	1·6
12.	Mang }	
13.	Mhali	1·3
14.	Rangari }	1·1
15.	Sonar }	
16.	Sutar }	
17.	Simpi	1·0
18.	Others	10·6

Mehkar Taluk.

Caste	Per cent.
1. Kunbi	33·0
2. Mahar	12·1
3. Wanjari	8·7
4. Mali	6·7
5. Musalman tribes	5·1
6. Labhani	2·8
7. Wani	2·6
8. Mang	2·5
9. Dhangar	2·4
10. Brahman	2·3
11. Andh	2·2
12. Banjari	2·1
13. Teli	1·7
14. Maratha	1·2
15. Chambhar 16. Mhali	1·0
17. Others	12·6

Yeotmal Taluk.

Caste	Per cent.
1. Kunbi	19·8
2. Gond	11·7
3. Mahar	9·5
4. Kolam	6·9
5. Mali	5·3
6. Gaoli	5·0
7. Teli	4·8
8. Musalman tribes	4·2
9. Banjari	2·9
10. Dhangar	2·5
11. Andh	2·2
12. Brahman 13. Pardhan	1·8
14. Wani	1·6
15. Bhoi	1·4
16. Kalal 17. Sutar	1·2
18. Maratha 19. Mhali	1·1
20. Mang	1·0
21. Others	13·0

Darwha Taluk.

Caste	Per cent.
1. Kunbi	18·0
2. Mahar	11·4
3. Banjari	11·3
4. Andh	6·2
5. Musalman tribes	5·9
6. Mali	5·3
7. Gond	5·2
8. Teli	3·4
9. Dhangar	2·7
10. Mang 11. Wani	2·3
12. Brahman	1·4
13. Bari 14. Labhani	1·2
15. Rajput	1·1
16. Gaoli 17. Mhali 18. Beldar	1·0
19. Others	18·1

Kelapur Taluk.

Caste	Per cent.
1. Gond	20·3
2. Kunbi	19·1
3. Mahar	6·0
4. Kolam	4·4
5. Pardhan	4·1
6. Mali	3·3
7. Banjari	3·2
8. Gaoli	3·0
9. Musalman tribes	2·6
10. Teli	2·5
11. Bhoi 12. Labhani	2·1
13. Golkar	1·8
14. Dhangar	1·6
15. Madgi	1·4
16. Mhali 17. Sutar 18. Wani	1·2
19. Munarwar	1·1
20. Brahman 21. Kalal 22. Lohar 23. Warthi	1·0
24. Others	13·8

Wun Taluk.

Caste	Per cent.
1. Kunbi	39·4
2. Gond	12·7
3. Mahar	6·1
4. Pardhan	4·5
5. Kolam	3·2
6. Dhangar	3·0
7. Bhoi 8. Musalman tribes	2·5
9. Sutar	1·6
10. Lohar 11. Mhali 12. Teli	1·5
13. Mali	1·4
14. Brahman 15. Warthi	1·3
16. Telanga	1·2
17. Gaoli 18. Madgi	1·1
19. Others	12·6

Basim Taluk.

Caste	Per cent.
1. Kunbi	36·3
2. Mahar	13·4
3. Musalman tribes	5·0
4. Andh 5. Mang	3·8
6. Mali	3·4
7. Labhani	3·2
8. Wanjari	3·0
9. Wani	2·5
10. Dhangar	2·4
11. Brahman	2·2
12. Teli	2·1

BASIM TALUK—*contd.*

	Per cent.
13. Banjari	1·9
14. Mhali } 15. Sutar	1·1
16. Chambhar } 17. Rajput	1·0
18. Others	12·8

MANGRUL TALUK.

	Per cent.
1. Kunbi	31·5
2. Mahar	14·8
3. Banjari	6·2
4. Andh	6·1
5. Musalman tribes	5·2
6. Mali	4·6
7. Dhangar	3·9
8. Teli	2·8
9. Labhani	2·7
10. Mang	2·4
11. Wani	2·1
12. Brahman	1·4
13. Mhali	1·2
14. Sutar	1·1

MANGRUL TALUK—*contd.*

	Per cent.
15. Chambhar } 16. Rajput	1·0
17. Others	12·0

PUSAD TALUK.

	Per cent.
1. Kunbi	22·2
2. Mahar	12·0
3. Andh	8·3
4. Banjari	7·6
5. Dhangar	7·0
6. Musalman tribes	6·3
7. Wani	3·6
8. Labhani	3·2
9. Mang	2·4
10. Mali } 11. Teli	2·3
12. Gaoli	2·1
13. Brahman	2·0
14. Bhil	1·3
15. Chambhar } 16. Koli } 17. Mhali	1·0
18. Others	14·4

CASTE INDEX, BERAR.

The names returned as main Castes are printed in Antique type and serially numbered, and the Sub-divisions mentioned for each follow in Roman type. The figures refer to the full strength of the Caste.

Caste	Religion	Strength
1. Afridi	**Musalmán**	4
2. Aghori	**Hindu**	10
3. Ahir	**Hindu**	(*See* Gaoli.)
Ahir	**Musalmán**	(*See* Gaoli.)
Bharadhiá	Hindu.	
Dawarbansi	Do.	
Dhidore	Do.	
Dhendkar	Do.	
Dher	Do.	
Gálbansi	Do.	
Gaoli	Do.	
Gármale	Do.	
Gaurbans	Do.	
Gawál	Do.	
Gole	Do.	
Gond	Do.	
Govhál	Do.	
Jadubansi	Do.	
Karmaryá	Do.	
Khadore	Do.	
Krishna-awatári	Do.	
Nand	Do.	
Nandwanshi	Do.	
Nimbar	Do.	
Pardeshi	Do.	
Pardeshi Hindu-stáni.	Do.	
Somawanshi	Do.	
4. Alkari	**Hindu**	7
Alkari Kachawá	Do.	
5. Andh	**Hindu**	43,297
Andh	**Animistic**	305
Abdure	Hindu.	
Agundare	Do.	
Bhand	Do.	
Bharkáde	Do.	
Bhope	Do.	
Bhote	Do.	
Bramhál	Do.	
Dakhore	Do.	
Dhengale	Do.	
Duber	Do.	
Girátkár	Do.	
Gire	Do.	
Holkar	Do.	
Ingale	Do.	
Jániá	Do.	
Kalambe	Do.	
Kawáne	Do.	
Khule	Do.	
Kshatri	Do.	
Kurkuti	Do.	
Machhang	Do.	
Maráthe	Do.	
Mendalci	Do.	
Mohare	Do.	
Mushari	Do.	
Minde	Do.	
Nibhor	Do.	
Pardhi	Do.	
Patáre	Do.	
Rile	Do.	
Saune	Do.	
Shelki	Do.	
Shikári	Do.	
Sinde	Do.	
Sontake	Do.	
Tálcare	Do.	
Táyade	Do.	
Thete	Do.	
Ughade	Do.	
Valgare	Do.	
Wághamáre	Do.	
Wahise	Do.	
Wákale	Do.	
Wále	Do.	
Wanjári	Do.	
6. Arab	**Musalmán**	84
Sháfari	Do.	
7. Arakh	**Hindu**	235
Arakh	**Animistic**	18
Bal	Hindu.	
Banmurat	Do.	
Gond	Do.	
Haral	Do.	
Mána	Do.	
8. Aridra	**Hindu**	4
9. Armenian	**Christian**	1
Persian	Do.	
10. Arvi	**Hindu**	11
11. Atári	**Hindu**	32
Atári	**Musalmán**	60
Chándani	Hindu.	
12. Aughad	**Hindu**	5
13. Ayáwár	**Hindu**	132
Cháran	Do.	
Ságán	Do.	
Sátal	Do.	
Sátáne	Do.	
14. Badhai	**Hindu**	(*See* Sutar.)
Gahumár Jháde	Do.	
Ginkár	Do.	
Hindustáni	Do.	
Jháde	Do.	
Kokas	Do.	
Láde	Do.	
Magdiyá	Do.	
Makará	Do.	
Mánusmár	Do.	
Pardeshi	Do.	
Wagankar	Do.	
15. Bágari	**Hindu**	1
Barbadyá	Do.	
16. Bagwán	**Musalmán**	124
17. Baheliyá	**Hindu**	61
18. Bahurupi (Rái-rang).	Do.	157
Bahurupi	**Musalmán**	6
Ráyrand	Hindu	
19. Bairági	**Hindu**	1,436
Agarji	Do.	
Agarwálá	Do.	
Bhandár Bairági	Do.	
Bisanswami	Do.	
Brámhan	Do.	
Brámhan Dudhai	Do.	
Chaturbhuji	Do.	
Chaturbhuwá	Do.	
Dátuarthi	Do.	
Gaud	Do.	
Gharbári	Do.	
Hárbihansi	Do.	
Hurávhá	Do.	
Jamáwat	Do.	
Kháki	Do.	
Májun	Do.	
Márwádi	Do.	
Nimáth	Do.	
Nimawant	Do.	
Nirádhári	Do.	
Prasádáipásane	Do.	
Rádhábanshi	Do.	
Rám	Do.	
Rámánandi	Do.	
Rámánuj	Do.	
Rámáwant	Do.	
Rámáwár	Do.	
Rámkabir	Do.	
Rámpratápi	Do.	
Rátasjogi	Do.	
Sankarái	Do.	
Satnámi	Do.	
Shribás	Do.	
Shrisampadá	Do.	
Udási	Do.	
Vaishnao	Do.	
Vishnu	Do.	
20. Bakarkasai	**Musalmán**	(*See* Kasai.)
Syed	Do.	
21. Balhái (or Balái)	**Hindu**	249
Balhái	**Animistic**	78
Dhehere	Hindu.	
Nemádyá	Do.	
22. Balsanto	**Hindu**	4
23. Baniyá	**Hindu**	(*See* Wáni.
Baniyá	**Jain**	(Do.)
Agarwálá	Do.	
Agrahári	Hindu.	
Amasdár	Do.	
Dángá	Do.	
Dasá	Do.	
Dilliwálá	Do.	
Ekráháti	Do.	
Gawai	Do.	
Kesarban	Do.	
Lakháte	Do.	
Mahesari	Do.	
Pancham	Do.	
Posar	Do.	
Purwár	Do.	
Shráwak	Do.	
24. Banjári	**Hindu**	52,470
Banjári	**Musalmán**	120
Banjári	**Jain**	29
Ajmerá	Hindu.	
Anyá	Do.	
Bálnáth	Do.	
Bayanáth	Do.	
Bhát	Do.	
Bhukyá	Do.	
Bhulyá	Do.	
Birját	Do.	
Cháran	Do.	
Chobhe	Do.	
Dályá	Do.	
Dewraj	Do.	
Dhádi	Do. and Musalmán.	
Gáse	Hindu.	
Gautam	Do.	
Gokaran	Do.	
Jenáwat	Do.	
Jharbak	Do.	
Kelwant	Do.	
Khok	Do.	
Kodár	Do.	
Kudadekar	Do.	
Kurá	Do.	
Kushá	Do.	
Labhári	Do.	
Lád	Do.	
Lákháwat	Do.	
Lawadiyá	Do.	
Mháli	Do.	
Majure	Do.	
Máli	Do.	
Máng Dhole	Do.	
Mathuriyá	Do.	
Meghwádi	Do.	
Megháwant	Do.	
Mud	Do.	
Nimawant	Do.	
Páotyá	Do.	
Pawár	Do.	
Potráte	Do.	
Rajput	Do.	
Rámáwat	Do.	
Ráobhil	Do.	
Ráthod	Do.	
Ráthod Rajput	Do.	
Sirghade	Do.	
Sonár	Do.	
Suratwanshi	Do.	
Udtyá	Do.	
Udyá	Do.	
Wadwá	Do.	
Wárik	Do.	
25. Bankar	**Hindu**	1
26. Bánsfod	**Hindu**	26
27. Baral	**Hindu**	142
Goláit	Do.	
28. Bári	**Hindu**	25,920
Dáud	Do.	
Goláit	Do.	
Jhádpe	Do.	
Kumbhárdom	Do.	
Kunam	Do.	
Lingáit	Do.	
Pánbári	Do.	
Pardeshi	Do.	
Sáteli	Do.	
Siripanthi	Do.	

Caste	Religion	Number
28. **Bári**—*contd.*		
Surase	Hindu.	
Suryawanshi	Do.	
29. **Basod**	**Hindu**	191
Basod	**Animistic**	70
Basod Gond	Hindu.	
Gondi Basod	Animistic.	
Károd	Hindu.	
Mandká	Do.	
Mang Basod	Do.	
Párakh Basod	Do.	
Pardeshi	Do.	
30. **Bedar**	**Hindu**	3,041
Ban Bedar	Do.	
Beral	Do.	
Gathagi	Do.	
Govingwád	Do.	
Japábun	Do.	
Jawháre	Do.	
Kalál	Do.	
Kánadi	Do.	
Ládwan	Do.	
Lagadbhát	Do.	
Lingáit	Do.	
Maherawi	Do.	
Munwár	Do.	
Náyar	Do.	
Somas	Do.	
Surya	Do.	
Telangi	Do.	
31. **Beldár**	**Hindu**	12,217
Beldár	**Musalmán**	11
Bamubáke	Hindu.	
Bhoyar	Do.	
Chhetri	Do.	
Chirade	Do.	
Dagadfod	Do.	
Desáli	Do.	
Gaondi	Do.	
Gurud Kapuwár	Do.	
Hindustáni	Do.	
Jane	Do.	
Jhele	Do.	
Julepe	Do.	
Kantále	Do.	
Káse	Do.	
Kátekar	Do.	
Kawhále	Do.	
Kene	Do.	
Lodhi	Do.	
Loni	Do.	
Luniyá	Do.	
Mahege	Do.	
Máti	Do.	
Mujiyá	Do.	
Munarwár	Do.	
Nuniyá	Do.	
Pardeshi	Do.	
Parwár	Do.	
Rajput	Do.	
Rao Panchware	Do.	
Rátalai	Do.	
Rudár	Do.	
Sagun	Do.	
Sárase	Do.	
Sultáni	Do.	
Telangá	Do.	
Ude	Do.	
Wade	Do.	
Wádhi	Do.	
Wás	Do.	
Yelgawaye	Do.	
32. **Berad**	**Hindu**	163
Ghâre Berad	Do.	
Maráthi	Do.	
Somási	Do.	
33. **Bhámti**	**Hindu**	1,774
Chokar	Do.	
Maráthi	Do.	
Pardeshi	Do.	
Patil Maráthi	Do.	
Ráne Rajput	Do.	
Ráut	Do.	
Ráut Bhámti	Dc.	
Tátpattiwále	Do.	
34. **Bhanári**	**Hindu**	21
35. **Bhánd**	**Musalmán**	2
Shekh	Do.	
36. **Bhandári**	**Hindu**	2
37. **Bhangi (Halálkhor, Khákrob and Mehtar).**	**Hindu**	1,303
Bhangi	**Musalmán**	180
Badaráwále	Hindu.	
37. **Bhangi**—*contd.*		
Dumár	Hindu.	
Hem	Do.	
Kunbi	Do.	
Lálbegi	Do.	
Márwádi	Do.	
Mhésari	Do.	
Sunni	Musalmán.	
38. **Bharadbhunjá**	**Hindu**	601
Bhunjawá	Do.	
Bhunjawá Pardeshi.	Do.	
Godele	Do.	
Gurdáshi	Do.	
Kanoje	Do.	
Rátod	Do.	
Satiyá	Do.	
39. **Bharádi**	**Hindu**	1,452
Chándak	Do.	
Damaru	Do.	
Damaru Wájavináre.	Do.	
Deore	Do.	
Gorakh	Do.	
Kánfáde	Do.	
Marathe	Do.	
Maráthe Bharádi	Do.	
Medh	Do.	
Sawaranáth	Do.	
40. **Bhát**	**Hindu**	3,065
Bhát	**Animistic**	47
Bhát	**Musalmán**	45
Bágorá	Hindu.	
Bramha Bhát	Do.	
Bramhan	Do.	
Chawhán	Do.	
Dewiputra	Do.	
Gaud	Do.	
Ghod Bhát	Do.	
Ghod Thakur	Do.	
Hindustáni	Do.	
Kánnav	Do.	
Kayare	Do.	
Kshatri	Do.	
Kumbhuyá	Do.	
Lálche	Do.	
Máháputra	Do.	
Málvi	Do.	
Maráthi	Do.	
Márwádi	Do.	
Panjatani	Musalmán.	
Pardesbi	Hindu.	
Raganáwant	Musalmán.	
Rája Bhát	Hindu.	
Rajput	Do.	
Solankhi	Do.	
Thákare Bhát	Do.	
Thákur	Do.	
Tumbadiwále	Do.	
41. **Bhátiá**	**Hindu**	104
Bhátiá	**Jain**	55
Asá Aráwel	Do.	
Kerasati	Hindu.	
Lawháne	Do.	
Nanakbanshi	Do.	
Wáni	Jain.	
42. **Bhattáwád**	**Hindu**	8
Telangi	Do.	
43. **Bhatyári**	**Musalmán**	2
44. **Bhil**	**Hindu**	3,483
Bhil	**Animistic**	783
Bhil	**Musalmán**	1,928
Dháme	Hindu.	
Káone	Do.	
Kátewane	Do.	
Kátonyá	Do.	
Kothári	Do.	
Matkari	Do.	
Náikadá	Do.	
Pawár	Do.	
Sunni	Musalmán.	
Tadwi	Hindu.	
Tirkámte	Do.	
45. **Bhisti**	**Musalmán**	5
46. **Bhoi (Windhewár).**	**Hindu**	27,378
Baidár	Hindu.	
Banarase	Do.	
Báone	Do.	
Bátwád	Do.	
Bedurá	Do.	
Beliwar	Do.	
46. **Bhoi**—*contd.*		
Beshram	Hindu.	
Beturá	Do.	
Bhanore	Do.	
Bhokare	Do.	
Bundhale	Do.	
Burad	Do.	
Darwár	Do.	
Dhangar	Do.	
Dhip	Do.	
Dhíwar	Do.	
Dhulayá Káhár	Do.	
Dhuryá	Do.	
Dukare	Do.	
Gádhawe	Do.	
Gaose	Do.	
Gáoti	Do.	
Gaotiyá	Do.	
Goriyá	Do.	
Gothiyá	Do.	
Járpe	Do.	
Jháde	Do.	
Jhadiwále	Do.	
Jingare	Do.	
Káhár	Do.	
Kále	Do.	
Kánade	Do.	
Keot	Do.	
Lonáre	Do.	
Machhandar	Do.	
Maláh	Do.	
Maniyár	Do.	
Marát	Do.	
Maráthe Bhoi	Do.	
Márte	Do.	
Mharwar	Do.	
Mhayesad	Do.	
Náik	Do.	
Nánakbanshi	Do.	
Navghaná	Do.	
Pachare	Do.	
Pálewár	Do.	
Pálkhiwále	Do.	
Pánbude	Do.	
Pardeshi	Do.	
Parkirwád	Do.	
Pathamá	Do.	
Pawár	Do.	
Pratikwár	Do.	
Pujári	Do.	
Purbhaye	Do.	
Ráj Bhoi	Do.	
Ráni Bhoi	Do.	
Raotimá	Do.	
Rotyá	Do.	
Shikár	Do.	
Sodhiyá	Do.	
Somuyá	Do.	
Sonár	Do.	
Sudip	Do.	
Sutayá Bhoi	Do.	
Tákare	Do.	
Talbá	Do.	
Telangá	Do.	
Wághamáre	Do.	
47. **Bhoyer**	**Hindu**	30
Deshmukh	Do.	
Dholewár	Do.	
Pawár	Do.	
48. **Bhumak**	**Hindu**	11
Maráthe	Do.	
49. **Bhute**	**Hindu**	1
50. **Bhuwaish**	**Hindu**	6
51. **Bijhad**	**Hindu**	5
52. **Bohari**	**Musalmán**	479
Tuba	Do.	
53. **Bopchi**	**Hindu**	613
Gond Bopchi	Do.	
Korku	Do.	
54. **Boral**	**Hindu**	25
Bele	Do.	
55. **Borekar**	**Hindu**	120
Gopál	Do.	
Kovari	Do.	
56. **Bráhman**	**Hindu**	71,272
Bráhman	**Jain**	36
Abhir	Hindu.	
Adgand	Do.	
Antgol	Do.	
Apastambh	Do.	
Ashruráj	Do.	
Ashwaláyen	Do.	
Atigand	Do.	
Avasthi	Do.	
Awdak	Do.	
Bágad Brahman	Do.	

No.	Caste	Religion	Number
56.	**Bráhman**—*contd.*		
	Bajági	Hindu.	
	Banwáshi	Do.	
	Bhágwat	Do.	
	Bhárgao	Do.	
	Bhikshuk	Do.	
	Bhivad	Do.	
	Bramhachári	Do.	
	Bundelkhandi	Do.	
	Chhagáni	Do.	
	Charakh	Do.	
	Chaube	Do.	
	Chitpáwan	Do.	
	Dakhane	Do.	
	Dámte	Do.	
	Dáyamá	Do.	
	Deorukhe	Do.	
	Deshasth	Do.	
	Dikshit	Do.	
	Drávid	Do.	
	Dube	Do.	
	Dube Pardeshi	Do.	
	Gárga	Do.	
	Gargye	Do.	
	Gaud	Do.	
	Gautam	Do.	
	Gokul	Do.	
	Golak	Do.	
	Golápuri	Do.	
	Gowardhan	Do.	
	Gujráthi	Do.	
	Gurjar	Do.	
	Hindustáni	Do.	
	Hiranyekashya	Do.	
	Hishande	Do.	
	Jayjati	Do.	
	Jhurjhurtiyá	Do.	
	Kánade	Do.	
	Kannao	Do.	
	Kankubja	Do.	
	Kanoje	Do.	
	Karhåde	Do.	
	Karnátaki	Do.	
	Karyá	Do.	
	Kást	Do.	
	Kátewádi	Do.	
	Kátyáyani	Do.	
	Káyast	Do.	
	Khandalwál	Do.	
	Khandewál	Do.	
	Kokanastha	Do.	
	Kosaripámisar	Do.	
	Kshatri	Do.	
	Mádhyanjan	Do.	
	Madrási	Do.	
	Máhájan	Do.	
	Mahárashtra	Do.	
	Máhát	Do.	
	Maithil	Do.	
	Málwi	Do.	
	Márwádi	Do.	
	Márwádi-dad-Mháli	Do.	
	Márwádidátyá	Do.	
	Mathuni Tiwár	Do.	
	Misar	Do.	
	Misrok	Do.	
	Mule	Do.	
	Nágari	Do.	
	Nagarwále Joshi	Do.	
	Nandwád	Do.	
	Narandeo	Do.	
	Nárbad	Do.	
	Nijoti	Do.	
	Nishedh	Do.	
	Padariye	Do.	
	Pálibándewásu	Do.	
	Paliwál	Do.	
	Palliwálá	Do.	
	Panchdrávid	Do.	
	Panchgaud	Do.	
	Pánde	Do.	
	Panjábi	Do.	
	Paráshari	Do.	
	Pardeshi	Do.	
	Párigh Márwádi	Do.	
	Párikh	Do.	
	Párik Parwat	Do.	
	Pariwád	Do.	
	Parot	Do.	
	Páthak	Do.	
	Patriwál	Do.	
	Pawár	Do.	
	Pokal	Do.	
	Pokarne	Do.	
	Pránpárik	Do.	
	Prathamshákhi	Do.	
	Punad	Do.	
	Purohit	Do.	
	Pushkarni	Do.	
	Rajáwandí	Do.	
	Rájgand	Do.	
	Rámanándi	Do.	
	Rámanáthi	Do.	
	Rudragand	Do.	
	Rugvedi	Do.	
	Sajoti	Do.	
	Sakaldini	Do.	
	Sanád	Do.	
56.	**Bráhman**—*concld.*		
	Sanáwad	Hindu.	
	Sanáwat	Do.	
	Sankhya	Do.	
	Sanodiyá	Do.	
	Sanyáshi	Do.	
	Sáraswat	Do.	
	Sárdhá	Do.	
	Sarotyá	Do.	
	Sarwariyá	Do.	
	Seniwát	Do.	
	Shewak	Do.	
	Shrimáli	Do.	
	Shriwadpanthi	Do.	
	Shukla	Do.	
	Sikwál	Do.	
	Smárth	Do.	
	Sukal	Do.	
	Sukul	Do.	
	Támil	Do.	
	Táyede	Do.	
	Telangá	Do.	
	Telang Drávid	Do.	
	Tirmale	Do.	
	Tiwári	Do.	
	Trifale	Do.	
	Upádhyá	Do.	
	Upamanyu	Do.	
	Vishnu	Do.	
	Wájashani	Do.	
	Wajhyá	Do.	
	Wallabhácharya	Do.	
	Warádi	Do.	
	Warmaliyá	Do.	
	Watet	Do.	
	Yajurvedi	Do.	
57.	**Bunkar**	**Hindu**	99
	Ghewár	Do.	
	Kochar	Do.	
58.	**Burud**	**Hindu**	1,247
	Burud	**Animistic**	22
	Dukare	Hindu.	
	Gondi Burud	Animistic.	
	Kásawe	Hindu.	
	Lingáit	Do.	
	Marála	Do.	
	Maráthe	Do.	
	Telang	Do.	
	Tháte	Do.	
59.	**Chámbhár (Mochi and Mochewála.)**	**Hindu**	29,174
	Ahirao	Do.	
	Bangaliwále	Do.	
	Barátbhakta	Do.	
	Bhatkar	Do.	
	Budelgir	Do.	
	Chandalkore	Do.	
	Dhábal	Do.	
	Dhále	Do.	
	Gaoli	Do.	
	Gavhále	Do.	
	Ghátole	Do.	
	Hágare	Do.	
	Hárále	Do.	
	Hokalá	Do.	
	Hokhan	Do.	
	Jagad	Do.	
	Kathai	Do.	
	Katipardeshi	Do.	
	Khandále	Do.	
	Khanjare	Do.	
	Lákyá	Do.	
	Lodhe	Do.	
	Mádagi	Do.	
	Malhá	Do.	
	Málvi	Do.	
	Mánkar	Do.	
	Maráthe	Do.	
	Márwádi	Do.	
	Mháli	Do.	
	Mochi	Do.	
	Molode	Do.	
	Ojhale	Do.	
	Oswál	Do.	
	Paose	Do.	
	Pardeshi	Do.	
	Párale	Do.	
	Párave	Do.	
	Pustake	Do.	
	Putáde	Do.	
	Rápi—Chámbhár	Do.	
	Rohidás	Do.	
	Romo	Do.	
	Sadhu	Do.	
	Sálank	Do.	
	Sarnári	Do.	
	Sáwarkád	Do.	
	Shewále	Do.	
	Wánare	Do.	
60.	**Chenwár**	**Hindu**	203
61.	**Chhipá**	**Hindu**	1
	Pardeshi	Do.	
62.	**Chinese**	**Hindu**	1
	Chinese	**Buddhist**	4
63.	**Chitári**	**Hindu**	76
	Madalsá	Do.	
	Mevajavi	Do.	
64.	**Chitarkathi**	**Hindu**	1,612
	Bhikmágnáre	Do.	
	Gangápor	Do.	
	Haradás	Do.	
	Kalsutre	Do.	
	Khandeshi	Do.	
	Nirále	Do.	
	Rasankute	Do.	
65.	**Dabgar**	**Hindu**	56
	Maráthe	Do.	
66.	**Dakalwád**	**Hindu**	30
	Warádi	Do.	
67.	**Dáliye**	**Hindu**	1
	Liwe Dáliye	Do.	
68.	**Dandigán**	**Hindu**	184
	Maráthe	Do.	
	Sasáne	Do.	
69.	**Dángre**	**Hindu**	188
	Maisari	Do.	
	Maráthe	Do.	
	Rajput	Do.	
70.	**Dángat**	**Hindu**	486
	Bhoi	Do.	
	Dakhane	Do.	
71.	**Darzi**	**Hindu**	(*See* Simpi.)
	Darzi	**Musalmán**	
	Vaishnav	Hindu.	
72.	**Dásari**	**Hindu**	64
	Ahiwár	Do.	
	Koriwar	Do.	
73.	**Devalwár**	**Hindu**	103
74.	**Dhádi**	**Musalmán**	5
75.	**Dhangar**	**Hindu**	81 02
	Adhod	Do.	
	Ahir	Do.	
	Ahiran	Do.	
	Ahirão	Do.	
	Aughad	Do.	
	Bajáde	Do.	
	Baldeodand	Do.	
	Bande	Do.	
	Bangi	Do.	
	Bansod	Do.	
	Básti	Do.	
	Bedár	Do.	
	Bhore	Do.	
	Chavare	Do.	
	Dhangao	Do.	
	Dhankar	Do.	
	Dháve	Do.	
	Dhende	Do.	
	Digar	Do.	
	Gadariyá	Do.	
	Galimán	Do.	
	Gaoli	Do.	
	Gaoli Dhangar	Do.	
	Gaoni	Do.	
	Garályá	Do.	
	Gávande	Do.	
	Ghongá	Do.	
	Ghongadi Winanár	Do.	
	Hate Kamáni	Do.	
	Hatkar	Do.	
	Hendre	Do.	
	Hindustáni	Do.	
	Holkar	Do.	
	Jádibansi	Do.	
	Jakhade	Do.	
	Jhåde	Do.	
	Kátade	Do.	
	Khadkar	Do.	
	Khekar	Do.	
	Khutáfale	Do.	
	Kurile	Do.	
	Lingáit	Do.	
	Máhore	Do.	
	Málve Dhangar	Do.	
	Maráthe	Do.	
	Mendke	Do.	
	Mogare	Do.	
	Nikhal	Do.	
	Nikhar	Do.	

No.	Caste	Religion	Strength
75.	**Dhangar**—*contd.*		
	Pádanchivde	Hindu	
	Pardeshi	Do.	
	Pradhán	Do.	
	Rátol	Do.	
	Ráut	Do.	
	Shekote	Do.	
	Táyale	Do.	
	Tirke	Do.	
	Tunkar	Do.	
	Vidur	Do.	
	Waitkár	Do.	
	Waráde	Do.	
76.	**Dher**	Hindu	(*See* Mahar.)
	Agaryán	Do.	
	Bhawnyá	Do.	
	Karimidá	Do.	
	Maráthe	Do.	
	Nikar	Do.	
	Somas	Do.	
	Telange	Do.	
77.	**Dhobi**	Musalmán	(*See* Warthi.)
78.	**Dohor**	Hindu	5,082
	Bhát	Do.	
	Budelkhandi	Do.	
	Bundele	Do.	
	Burad	Do.	
	Dhálewár	Do.	
	Gánge	Do.	
	Gáse	Do.	
	Jorwar	Do.	
	Kalále	Do.	
	Kánade	Do.	
	Kankál	Do.	
	Katái	Do.	
	Kataryá	Do.	
	Katve	Do.	
	Khandalyá	Do.	
	Látki	Do.	
	Madrási	Do.	
	Makte	Do.	
	Nehálkar	Do.	
	Páhári	Do.	
	Pardeshi	Do.	
	Pibel	Do.	
	Sinde	Do.	
	Telangi	Do.	
	Tikare	Do.	
	Wánse	Do.	
	Yarwár	Do.	
	Yekarban	Do.	
79	**Dusádh**	Hindu	5
	Paraswán	Do.	
80.	**Eurasian (Anglo-Indian, East Indian and Indo-Briton).**	Christian.	318
81.	**European (American).**	Christian	329
	European (American).	Others	4
82.	**Fakir**	Musalmán	7,190
	Aleshâni	Do.	
	Ali	Do.	
	Alkhurásh	Do.	
	Ashkán	Do.	
	Ashkari	Do.	
	Bágwále	Do.	
	Bángi	Do.	
	Bánvá	Do.	
	Chishti	Do.	
	Chishtyá	Do.	
	Diwangán	Do.	
	Gavali Ashkán	Do.	
	Imámshâhi	Do.	
	Jámdár	Do.	
	Jogi	Do.	
	Kádari	Do.	
	Kárván	Do.	
	Khojá	Do.	
	Madári	Do.	
	Malang	Do.	
	Mogláni	Do.	
	Nakáli	Do.	
	Nandshá	Do.	
	Nawáli	Do.	
	Nishándá	Do.	
	Rafáik	Do.	
	Ramái	Do.	
	Sháhá Madári	Do.	
	Sháhá Madár	Do.	
	Tabkát	Do.	
	Warádi	Do.	
83.	**Fatarfod**	Hindu	(*See* Gotefod.)
	Maráthe	Do.	
84.	**Fulári**	Hindu	29
	Lingáyat	Do.	
85.	**Gadariyá**	Hindu	49
	Chendan	Do.	
	Dhengar	Do.	
	Jikhar	Do.	
	Pankhar	Do.	
	Pardeshi	Do.	
86.	**Gahlán**	Hindu	1
87.	**Gandhi (Sugandhi).**	Hindu	92
	Gandhi (Sugandhi).	Jain	9
	Gujráthe	Hindu.	
	Jaswál	Jain.	
	Jawal	Do.	
	Naswálá	Hindu.	
88.	**Gaoli (Ahir, Gaulán and Gawári.)**	Hindu	35,680
	Gaoli	Jain	1
	Gaoli (Ahir and Gawári).	Musalmán	815
	Ahare	Hindu.	
	Bás	Do.	
	Bhákare	Do.	
	Bhohur	Do.	
	Bhokar	Do.	
	Bhokar Akarmáse	Do.	
	Bhor	Do.	
	Chale Gaoli	Do.	
	Deo	Do.	
	Dudh	Do.	
	Gawálwanshi	Do.	
	Gawarbandh	Do.	
	Gáya	Do.	
	Ghádhe	Do.	
	Ghuwár	Do.	
	Hekali	Do.	
	Hindustáni	Do.	
	Hydarábádi	Musalmán.	
	Jadubansi	Hindu.	
	Janose	Do.	
	Lingáit	Do.	
	Lodhi	Do.	
	Mol	Do.	
	Nagarkar	Do.	
	Nand	Do.	
	Nandbansi	Do.	
	Nandbhokar	Do.	
	Pángul	Do.	
	Pardeshi	Do.	
	Pathán	Musalmán.	
	Potyá	Hindu.	
	Rále	Do.	
	Shekh	Musalmán.	
	Taráne	Hindu.	
	Yawalyá	Do.	
89.	**Gárpagári**	Hindu	3,041
	Andh	Do.	
	Babu	Do.	
	Gorakh	Do.	
	Gorakhnáth	Do.	
	Gosáwi	Do.	
	Jogi	Do.	
	Khápare	Do.	
	Megh	Do.	
	Náth	Do.	
	Ráthái Nágari	Do.	
	Ráoi	Do.	
	Ráojogi	Do.	
	Rául	Do.	
	Ráut	Do.	
	Ráyadási	Do.	
	Ráyan	Do.	
	Satnáth	Do.	
	Suryanási	Do.	
	Tarwadebávi	Do.	
	Wáyajare	Do.	
90.	**Gaulán**	Hindu	(*See* Gaoli.)
	Gaulán (Gawári)	Animistic	771
	Dhade	Hindu.	
	Ghás Gaoli	Do.	
	Karámache	Do.	
	Medkar	Do.	
	Melgháte	Do.	
	Rájanpan	Do.	
	Warmá	Do.	
	Wárwe	Do.	
91.	**Gaondi (Ráj)**	Hindu	639
	Bhandárwan	Do.	
	Dhagu	Do.	
	Hawan	Do.	
	Jadabhári	Do.	
	Lawagat	Do.	
	Ráj Gaondi	Do.	
	Sagarbás	Do.	
92.	**Gawári**	Hindu	(*See* Gaoli.)
	Gawári	Musalmán	(*See* Gaoli.)
	Gawári	Animistic	(*See* Gaulán.)
	Ambádayariá	Hindu.	
	Bude	Do.	
	Dáut	Do.	
	Dhári	Do.	
	Dhorwád	Do.	
	Dudh	Do.	
	Eját	Do.	
	Ejáre	Do.	
	Gálákari	Do.	
	Gond Gawári	Do.	
	Ijhwar	Do.	
	Inátwár	Do.	
	Jhádpi	Do.	
	Kunbi	Do.	
	Nágpure	Do.	
	Ráut	Do.	
	Rekwár	Do.	
	Sáhriá	Do.	
	Simpwár	Do.	
	Wágáliá	Do.	
93.	**Gázulábalijá**	Hindu	2
	Náidu	Do.	
94.	**Ghisádi**	Hindu	708
	Ghisadi	Musalmán	11
	Chavhán	Hindu.	
	Maráthe	Do.	
	Panchál	Do.	
	Pawár	Do.	
95.	**Goánese**	Christian	172
	Goá	Do.	
	Portuguese	Do.	
96.	**Gochki**	Hindu	94
97.	**Golak**	Hindu	146
	Máhvi	Do.	
	Rand Golak	Do.	
98.	**Golkar**	Hindu	2,454
	Erangulwár	Do.	
	Telangá	Do.	
99.	**Gond**	Hindu	9,058
	Gond	Animistic	71,869
	Adayá	Hindu.	
	Andh	Do.	
	Arakh	Do.	
	Arav	Animistic.	
	Ardaksil	Hindu.	
	Batká	Do.	
	Bhute	Do.	
	Budhe	Do.	
	Burad	Do.	
	Chandiá	Do.	
	Dhadiá	Do.	
	Dhadve	Do.	
	Dhruv	Do.	
	Dudhe	Do.	
	Gakar	Do.	
	Gawári	Do.	
	Ghatiá	Do.	
	Girdhá	Do.	
	Gond Gawári	Do.	
	Gondi Waddar	Do.	
	Gondráj	Animistic.	
	Kangoli	Hindu.	
	Khándeshi	Do.	
	Kharphánde	Do.	
	Khatule	Do.	
	Korám	Do.	
	Korku	Do.	
	Mesrám	Do.	
	Nábu	Do.	
	Padale Gond	Do.	
	Pardhán	Do.	
	Pardhán Gond	Do.	
	Partigi	Do.	
	Ráj Devi	Do.	
	Ráj Gond	Do.	
	Rujhe	Do.	
	Ruse	Do.	
	Ságarwáshi	Do.	
	Sáhádeo	Do.	
	Sátbais	Do.	
	Sayám	Do.	
	Serám	Do.	
	Thákare	Do.	
	Tháte	Do.	
	Uiká	Do.	
	Ulke	Do.	
	Wajhe	Do.	
	Wuchle	Do.	
100.	**Gondhali**	Hindu	3,033
	Bharádi	Do.	
	Bhond	Do.	
	Ekrái	Do.	

Caste	Religion	Number
100. **Gondhali**—*contd.*		
Gosáwi	Hindu.	
Gurao	Do.	
Kabna Maráthi	Do.	
Kadam Maráthi	Do.	
Kadam Gondhali	Do.	
Kadam Rái	Do.	
Kálmukhe	Do.	
Káte	Do.	
Maráthe	Do.	
Máya Mukhi Gurao.	Do.	
Rájake	Do.	
Renurái	Do.	
Sambal Gondhali	Do.	
Supalkár	Do.	
Táyade	Do.	
Waráde	Do.	
Wapunrái	Do.	
101. **Gopál**	Hindu	3,419
Bangi Dhangar	Do.	
Borekár	Do.	
Dhangar	Do.	
Dhole	Do.	
Elu Gopál	Do.	
Gavháne	Do.	
Guruwáre	Do.	
Hatkar	Do.	
Indra	Do.	
Ira	Do.	
Kálpáde	Do.	
Khutáfale	Do.	
Koshti	Do.	
Maráthe	Do.	
Naughare	Do.	
Pahelwán	Do.	
Susáne	Do.	
Wáni	Do.	
102. **Gorwán**	Hindu	13
Gorwán	Animistic	148
103. **Gosangi**	Hindu	6
104. **Gosáwi**	Hindu	12,152
Anandsár	Do.	
Anandwári	Do.	
Aparnáth	Do.	
Bais	Do.	
Bálápure	Do.	
Bán	Do.	
Bánganikar	Do.	
Begam	Do.	
Bhárthi	Do.	
Bhovarwár	Do.	
Dashnámi	Do.	
Dudh Bamhan	Do.	
Dudhádhári	Do.	
Ghanwati	Do.	
Ghátole	Do.	
Ghuri	Do.	
Gindi	Do.	
Giri	Do.	
Girinámá	Do.	
Hindustáni	Do.	
Jati	Do.	
Jong	Do.	
Kannáke	Do.	
Kánari	Do.	
Kánfáde	Do.	
Karinámá	Do.	
Kheli	Do.	
Koli	Do.	
Kunbi Tilole	Do.	
Lavange	Do.	
Malat	Do.	
Maráthe	Do.	
Medhil	Do.	
Meghanáth	Do.	
Mokasi	Do.	
Nand	Do.	
Parbat	Do.	
Pardeshi	Do.	
Pargat	Do.	
Parhans	Do.	
Puri	Do.	
Rajput	Do.	
Rámánandi	Do.	
Rukhar	Do.	
Saodágiri	Do.	
Saraswate	Do.	
Sarode	Do.	
Shivgarji	Do.	
Singhi	Do.	
Sipnáth	Do.	
Tirmalá	Do.	
Udási	Do.	
105. **Gotefod (Fatar-fod)**	Hindu	132
Maráthe Gotefod	Do.	
106. **Gujar**	Hindu	981
Gujar	Jain	9
Badháná	Hindu.	
Bánde	Do.	
Bend Gujar	Do.	
Chaiti	Do.	
Dále	Do.	
Doi	Do.	
Gaoli	Do.	
Kumáwant	Do.	
Kumáyant	Do.	
Lebe	Do.	
Sup	Do.	
Tiwári	Do.	
107. **Gujráthi**	Hindu	1,098
Gujráthi	Jain	347
Ajnáth	Hindu.	
Badháná	Do.	
Band	Do.	
Bhiwadi	Do.	
Daliye	Do.	
Hisálád	Do.	
Junarvedi	Do.	
Lewe	Do.	
Mansárá	Do.	
Mode	Do.	
Nima	Do.	
Raghuvire	Do.	
Sawdágar	Do.	
108. **Gurao**	Hindu	9,229
Gurao	Jain	1
Akshwati	Hindu	
Barni	Do.	
Daliyá	Do.	
Dángat	Do.	
Dáve	Do.	
Devibhakta	Do.	
Fulkari	Do.	
Ganáchári	Do.	
Gárpáthi	Do.	
Gawaye	Do.	
Gáoráni	Do.	
Jadewár	Do.	
Kálmukh	Do.	
Kánámukh	Do.	
Mairál	Do.	
Málvi	Do.	
Maráthe	Do.	
Patrále	Do.	
Pujári	Do.	
Rámdási	Do.	
Renur	Do.	
Shende	Do.	
Shete	Do.	
Shév Gurao	Do.	
Shiv Pujári	Do.	
Wáindeshe	Do.	
Wájantri	Do.	
Wájwináre	Do.	
Waráde	Do.	
Wasu Gurao	Do.	
109. **Gurudkápuwar**	Hindu	501
110. **Hajjám**	Hindu	(*See* Mhali.)
Hajjám	Musalmán	(*See* Mhali.)
Ambunkár	Hindu	
Banbaheru	Do.	
Bangore Khawás	Do.	
Báone	Do.	
Doi	Do.	
Hindustáni	Do.	
Lingáit	Do.	
Márwádi	Do.	
Oswál	Do.	
Pardeshi	Do.	
Ráut	Do.	
Sejabhagat	Do.	
Sirbastán	Do.	
Somawanshi	Do.	
Táyade	Do.	
Telangi	Do.	
Waráde	Do.	
Wárik	Do.	
Yakhande	Do.	
111. **Halálkhor**	Hindu	(*See* Bhangi.)
Halálkhor	Musalmán	(*See* Bhangi.)
Hale	Hindu.	
112. **Halbi**	Hindu	2,841
Bhoyar	Do.	
Dadoli	Do.	
Gáwal	Do.	
Nand Nambar	Do.	
Narai	Do.	
Pobekarnár	Do.	
Pohokonde	Do.	
Saráte	Do.	
Surusbanshi	Do.	
Tákur	Do.	
Wátghar	Do.	
113. **Halwái**	Hindu	237
Halwái	Jain	1
Hindustáni	Hindu	
Kanoje	Do.	
114. **Hamál**	Hindu	99
115. **Hátgar**	Hindu	6,599
Badge	Do.	
Dewang	Do.	
Dewat Hátgar	Do.	
Ghadanálpat	Do.	
Gond	Do.	
Hawgan	Do.	
Jhádyáwále	Do.	
Kánade	Do.	
Lingáit	Do.	
Nukud	Do.	
Patnáwalkondi	Do.	
116. **Hindustáni**	Hindu	32
Banojá	Do.	
117. **Hirmushti**	Hindu	4
Telangi	Do.	
118. **Injhwar**	Hindu	258
Chándewár	Do.	
Gadhewár Injhwar.	Do.	
Sábare	Do.	
119. **Inkar**	Hindu	5
Ládwan	Do.	
120. **Isabzai**	Musalmán	12
121. **Jangam**	Hindu	1,882
Charati	Do.	
Dháwari	Do.	
Ganácharya	Do.	
Gharbári	Do.	
Ghatulkar	Do.	
Kalamkor	Do.	
Khasnámi	Do.	
Mathpati	Do.	
Mitmati	Do.	
Nurwarga	Do.	
Padolbangi	Do.	
Pancham	Do.	
Peshima	Do.	
Somawant	Do.	
Stháwar	Do.	
Telangi	Do.	
Thawartik	Do.	
Virshaiva	Do.	
122. **Ját**	Hindu	513
Ját	Musalmán	2
Ját	Sikh	7
Ját	Jain	5
Acherá	Hindu.	
Barák	Do.	
Chawdhari	Do.	
Dhilan	Sikh.	
Dhiwán	Hindu.	
Golan	Do.	
Labyál	Do.	
Márwádi	Do.	
Oswál	Do.	
Sáraj	Do.	
Tilan	Musalmán.	
123. **Jati**	Jain	17
Jati	Hindu	6
124. **Jew**	Jew	2
Native	Do.	
125. **Jhárekari**	Musalmán	1
126. **Jhingá Bhoi**	Hindu	75
Khár Bhoi	Do.	
127. **Jingar**	Hindu	1,313
Chári	Do.	
Chhatri	Do.	
Chitrekarnár	Do.	
Igate	Do.	
Jiráit	Do.	
Kshatriya	Do.	
Ládwan	Do.	
Maráthe	Do.	
Sonkshatri	Do.	
Suransi	Do.	
Takári	Do.	
Wanapi	Do.	
Wánkhede	Do.	

Caste	Religion	Number
128. **Jiráyat**	Hindu	312
Chitári	Do.	
Gujráthi	Do.	
Karachkar	Do.	
Panchál	Do.	
129. **Jogi**	Hindu	2,177
Ajnáth	Do.	
Bharáde	Do.	
Gáo Jogi	Do.	
Kadam	Do.	
Kingri Wájwinár	Do.	
Madjogi	Do.	
Navnáth Jogi	Do.	
Ráwal	Do.	
Sárangiwále	Do.	
130. **Johari**	Hindu	161
Chaván	Do.	
Jogi Johari	Do.	
Kshetri	Do.	
Pardeshi	Do.	
131. **Joshi**	Hindu	419
Joshi	Jain	5
Firaste	Hindu.	
Kápadi	Do.	
Madhange	Do.	
Medhagar	Do.	
Meldange	Do.	
Ráj Guru	Do.	
132. **Kabir**	Hindu	5
Pardeshi	Do.	
133. **Kachár**	Hindu	564
Chángale	Do.	
Lingáyet	Do.	
Manári	Do.	
Telangi	Do.	
134. **Kachhi**	Musalmán	175
Almá	Do.	
Kámel Kachhi	Do.	
Murái	Do.	
Syed Baheján	Do.	
135. **Kachhwáhá**	Hindu	1
Pardeshi	Do.	
136. **Káchi**	Hindu	28
Kánav	Do.	
Máli	Do.	
137. **Káhár**	Hindu	359
Badmiyá	Do.	
Begar	Do.	
Bhoi	Do.	
Dhiwar	Do.	
Dhuryá	Do.	
Duryá	Do.	
Gharuk	Do.	
Gudiyá	Do.	
Gunhe Káhár	Do.	
Jain	Do.	
Kituriyá	Do.	
Máhule	Do.	
Pardeshi	Do.	
Rawáni Káhár	Do.	
Sanwiyá	Do.	
Sutayá	Do.	
Tagar	Do.	
Turdyá	Do.	
138. **Kaikádi**	Hindu	2,024
Aghori	Do.	
Dát	Do.	
Gayamáwád	Do.	
Jádhare	Do.	
Kaikádi Maráthe	Do.	
Kuchiwále	Do.	
Mánke	Do.	
Máne	Do.	
Maráthe	Do.	
Maráthe Jadhao	Do.	
Nyáhálimasar	Do.	
Tumbiwále	Do.	
139. **Kakar**	Hindu	102
Jain	Do.	
Jetwár	Do.	
Kapsewár	Do.	
Kosar	Do.	
Kosari Kakar	Do.	
Pardeshi	Do.	
Sáwji Dhwád	Do.	
140. **Kákizai**	Musalmán	1
Panjábi	Do.	
141. **Kalál**	Jain	186
Kalál	Hindu	16,035
Kalál	Animistic	2
Kalál	Musalmán	11
Akarmáse	Hindu.	
Bharatwál	Do.	
Bhattiwále	Do.	
Dongare	Do.	
Gond Kalál	Do.	
Jain	Do.	
Jawápuri	Do.	
Jayawár	Do.	
Jestakar	Do.	
Jeswár	Do.	
Jháre	Do.	
Káchare	Do.	
Kásodari	Do.	
Ládse	Do.	
Machadi	Do.	
Machariyá Kalál	Do.	
Mádari	Do.	
Málwe	Do.	
Maráthe	Do.	
Máte	Do.	
More	Do.	
Motkariyá	Do.	
Nerbási	Do.	
Oswál	Do.	
Pardeshi	Do.	
Purbhaye	Do.	
Sáo	Do.	
Sáoji	Do.	
Seduryá	Do.	
Seriyá Kalál	Do.	
Shribás	Do.	
Siware	Do.	
Telang	Do.	
142. **Kalsutri**	Hindu	1
Maráthe	Do.	
143. **Kalwant**	Hindu	94
Maráthe	Do.	
Rám-upásani	Do.	
144. **Kalwár**	Hindu	49
145. **Kámáthi**	Hindu	22
Telangá	Do.	
146. **Kánadi**	Hindu	1,447
Gámnit	Do.	
Kumáyat	Do.	
Lingáyat	Do.	
Patnáre	Do.	
Tikholi	Do.	
147. **Kángar**	Hindu	35
Kángar	Musalmán	2
Maráthe	Hindu.	
148. **Kanjhar**	Hindu	1
149. **Kápuwáru**	Hindu	82
150. **Kasai (Bakar Kasai and Khátik).**	Hindu	4,959
Kasai	Musalmán	384
Dhangar	Hindu.	
Sunni	Musalmán.	
Warádi	Hindu.	
151. **Kásár**	Hindu	7,558
Kásár	Jain	196
Agar	Hindu.	
Ahev	Do.	
Akarmáse	Do.	
Bagarál	Do.	
Bágárwál	Do.	
Bangdiwálá	Do.	
Begalkar	Do.	
Begar	Do.	
Begár	Do.	
Belgar	Do.	
Bhándekar	Do.	
Bhoyál	Do.	
Bhupál	Do.	
Dakhane	Do.	
Deshasta	Do.	
Deshur	Do.	
Dewan Bhagat	Do.	
Devikar	Do.	
Dikar	Do.	
Gogar	Do.	
Jhádekásár	Do.	
Kasbi	Do.	
Kshatri	Do.	
Lagar	Do.	
Maráthe	Do.	
Mhashikár	Do.	
Násaki	Do.	
Pahurkar	Do.	
Panchál	Do.	
Pardeshi	Do.	
Peshkar	Do.	
151. **Kásár**—*contd.*		
Ráo	Hindu.	
Rokade	Do.	
Sadegháte	Do.	
Shráogi	Do.	
Somawanshi	Do.	
Tagar	Do.	
Tirge	Do.	
Waráde	Do.	
Wéshnav	Do.	
152. **Kasban (Kasbi)**	Hindu	14
Kasban (Kasbi and Naikan).	Musalmán	15
Shekh	Musalmán.	
153. **Kásid**	Hindu	12
154. **Kást**	Hindu	259
Kátyáyani	Do.	
Upáyani	Do.	
155. **Kátekar**	Hindu	1
Pardeshi	Do.	
156. **Kathilkar**	Hindu	20
Mere Sonár	Do.	
157. **Katiá**	Hindu	2
158. **Káyet**	Hindu	974
Bhangir	Do.	
Chakshetri	Do.	
Khade	Do.	
Khair Shriwás	Do.	
Pukad Dhamán	Do.	
Saksáni	Do.	
Sawáseni	Do.	
Shribarnám	Do.	
Shribasam	Do.	
Shribástám	Do.	
Shrite	Do.	
Shriwásudeo	Do.	
159. **Keoti**	Hindu	76
Haribin	Do.	
Nawáp	Do.	
160. **Khákrob**	Hindu	(*See* Bhangi.)
Khákrob	Musalmán	(*See* Bhangi.)
Nanak	Hindu.	
161. **Khán**	Musalmán	11
Gáe Kasáb	Do.	
162. **Khangar**	Hindu	229
Pardeshi	Do.	
Ráo	Do.	
Thákur	Do.	
163. **Khánzádá**	Musalmán	1
164. **Kháti**	Hindu	(*See* Lohár.)
Ahir	Do.	
Asale	Do.	
Chandalkár	Do.	
Dápu	Do.	
Ját	Do.	
Jhále Ráut	Do.	
Jhám	Do.	
Kásalimak	Do.	
Kothare	Do.	
Lingáit	Do.	
Maju	Do.	
Manumate	Do.	
Márwádi	Do.	
Rátiwále	Do.	
Rosiwál	Do.	
Sankhuwáti	Do.	
Siliwár	Do.	
165. **Khátik**	Hindu	(*See* Kasai.)
Khátik	Musalmán	(*See* Kasai.)
Bakále	Hindu.	
Kurekar	Do.	
Lád	Do.	
Malanchi	Do.	
Maráthe	Do.	
Winkar	Do.	
166. **Khatri**	Hindu	1,710
Khatri	Sikh	4
Aráde	Hindu.	
Arakh	Do.	
Arjun	Do.	
Beruwar	Do.	
Bhangad	Do.	
Bise	Do.	
Dase	Do.	
Gháse	Do.	
Kapure	Do.	
Kawte	Do.	

No.	Caste and Sub-caste	Religion	Number
166.	**Khatri**—*contd.*		
	Ogar	Hindu.	
	Pandobás	Do.	
	Panjábi	Do.	
	Patvi	Do.	
	Sábarjan	Do.	
	Sahasra Arjun	Do.	
	Sálankhe	Do.	
	Sharwan	Do.	
	Surjanwáni	Do.	
	Thákur	Do.	
	Vihále	Do.	
167.	**Khawás**	Hindu	8
168.	**Khichar**	Hindu	1
	Pardeshi	Do.	
169.	**Khojá**	Musalmán	27
170.	**Khorásáni**	Musalmán	5
171.	**Kol**	Hindu	11
172.	**Kolám**	Hindu	954
	Kolám	Animistic	16,460
	Atrám	Hindu and Animistic.	
	Bhil	Hindu.	
	Bhil Kolám	Do.	
	Dadamyá	Do.	
	Edaskár	Do.	
	Ekám Kolám	Do.	
	Kásár	Animistic.	
	Kudmetá	Hindu.	
	Meshrám	Animistic.	
	Mesrám Kolám	Do.	
	Pesrám	Do.	
	Pilwán	Hindu.	
	Rewade	Animistic.	
	Sapkár	Do.	
	Tumkánde	Do.	
	Wágde	Do.	
173.	**Kolháti**	Hindu	1,248
	Kolháti	Musalmán	9
	Bore	Hindu.	
	Dánd Kolháti	Do.	
	Dukare	Do.	
	Kabirpanthi	Do.	
	Khám Kolháti	Do.	
	Munarwád	Do.	
	Maráthe	Do.	
	Pánd Kolháti	Do.	
	Telangá	Do.	
174.	**Koli**	Hindu	32,628
	Agarkar	Do.	
	Báre	Do.	
	Báwsir	Do.	
	Bhikoli	Do.	
	Biyán	Do.	
	Dhimál	Do.	
	Dhiwar	Do.	
	Diwál	Do.	
	Gatlawi	Do.	
	Gawálbanshi	Do.	
	Ghote	Do.	
	Gotebháde	Do.	
	Gujráthi	Do.	
	Kabirpanthi	Do.	
	Káháre	Do.	
	Kánadá	Do.	
	Kanoje	Do.	
	Khárkoli	Do.	
	Khatri	Do.	
	Khubar	Do.	
	Koli Kuthár	Do.	
	Kshatri	Do.	
	Kunbi Koli	Do.	
	Malhári	Do.	
	Mudrás	Do.	
	Mutráj	Do.	
	Mutrási	Do.	
	Pánbhare	Do.	
	Pánbharekoli	Do.	
	Pánde	Do.	
	Pardeshi	Do.	
	Rámánandi	Do.	
	Rámoshi	Do.	
	Ránmir	Do.	
	Shikáre	Do.	
	Sol	Do.	
	Sononi	Do.	
	Takári	Do.	
	Táyade	Do.	
	Telangá	Do.	
	Thamál	Do.	
	Wághmáre	Do.	
	Walhe Koli	Do.	
175.	**Komti**	Hindu	2,750
	Ayarwádi	Do.	
	Egin	Do.	
	Hegin	Do.	
	Hindu Wáni	Do.	
	Parampáwál	Do.	
	Srivishnu	Do.	
	Telangi	Do.	
	Unchi	Do.	
	Vaishnav	Do.	
	Vaishya	Do.	
176.	**Kori**	Hindu	435
	Bajodhiyá	Do.	
	Bayarási	Do.	
	Bhágatá	Do.	
	Dahare Kori	Do.	
	Dhamál	Do.	
	Dijáng	Do.	
	Hindustáni	Do.	
	Jeswár	Do.	
	Kothár	Do.	
	Maháre	Do.	
	Pardeshi	Do.	
	Rohidás	Do.	
	Sanváni	Do.	
177.	**Korku**	Hindu	379
	Korku	Animistic	34,602
	Abu	Do.	
	Adale Kuran	Hindu.	
	Aswá	Do.	
	Bais	Animistic.	
	Baláí	Hindu.	
	Bhoyete	Do.	
	Bote	Animistic.	
	Busum	Hindu.	
	Chekati	Do.	
	Chiláti	Do.	
	Dhársiyá	Do.	
	Dhi	Do.	
	Dhikár	Animistic.	
	Kásadá	Hindu.	
	Máwshi	Do.	
	Melgháte	Do.	
	Moghe	Do.	
	Nán	Animistic.	
	Nihál	Do.	
	Puthár	Hindu.	
	Rukhá	Do.	
	Rumá	Do.	
	Sákum	Animistic.	
	Sewti	Do.	
	Táhiyá	Hindu.	
	Toghá	Do.	
	Wachhad	Do.	
178.	**Koshti**	Hindu	14,549
	Koshti	Jain	269
	Ahir	Hindu.	
	Bahiben	Jain.	
	Baldi	Hindu.	
	Bendare	Do.	
	Bhil Koshti	Do.	
	Dakhane	Do.	
	Dewágan	Do.	
	Dháne	Do.	
	Dhanmán Koshti	Do.	
	Dhawshá	Do.	
	Dhope	Do.	
	Dhotre	Jain.	
	Dika Koshti	Hindu.	
	Ekali	Jain.	
	Ekain	Hindu.	
	Gadewálá	Do.	
	Gangatri	Do.	
	Halbi	Do.	
	Halde	Do.	
	Halwái	Do.	
	Hatgare	Do.	
	Hindustáni	Do.	
	Jain	Do.	
	Jeswár	Do.	
	Jiwhári	Do.	
	Kabirdás	Do.	
	Kabirpanthi	Do.	
	Kalmál	Do.	
	Kánare	Do.	
	Kapade Wiknár	Do.	
	Lád	Do.	
	Lád Koshti	Do.	
	Lingáit	Do.	
	Maliná	Do.	
	Niráli	Do.	
	Nirdali	Jain.	
	Padamsali	Hindu.	
	Parbhu Koshti	Do.	
	Pardeshi	Do.	
	Ráojiwáte	Do.	
	Sái	Do.	
	Sáki	Do.	
	Sankwár	Do.	
	Sáwal	Do.	
	Shiware	Do.	
	Takuriyá	Do.	
	Vinkar	Do.	
179.	**Kotwál**	Hindu	(*See* Mahár.)
	Deryá	Do.	
	Gupte	Do.	
	Korku	Do.	
	Pardeshi	Do.	
180.	**Koyelábhuti**	Animistic	10
181.	**Krishna Pakshi**	Hindu	(*See* Vidur.)
	Bráhman	Do.	
	Gurkiyá	Do.	
	Kunbi	Do.	
	Maháráshtra	Do.	
	Pisát	Do.	
	Pursál	Do.	
	Wányáchá	Do.	
182.	**Kumbhár**	Hindu	22,465
	Babare	Do.	
	Báldyá	Do.	
	Bardiyá	Do.	
	Barukyá	Do.	
	Bhágwat	Do.	
	Bhándekar	Do.	
	Bideshi	Do.	
	Bipdyá	Do.	
	Chaikbais	Do.	
	Chamábes	Do.	
	Gádhav Kumbhár	Do.	
	Gadhiyá	Do.	
	Gorá	Do.	
	Hirge	Do.	
	Kanoje	Do.	
	Kanojiyá	Do.	
	Kat	Do.	
	Kobnyá	Do.	
	Kumál	Do.	
	Lád	Do.	
	Ládne	Do.	
	Lingáit	Do.	
	Made	Do.	
	Máli	Do.	
	Maráthe	Do.	
	Máru	Do.	
	Márwádi	Do.	
	Mhasiyá	Do.	
	Nirnyá	Do.	
	Pardeshi	Do.	
	Pardeshi Rajput	Do.	
	Patyá	Do.	
	Ráje Kumbhár	Do.	
	Ráne	Do.	
	Sakal	Do.	
	Sháliwáhán	Do.	
	Shiwáchári	Do.	
	Shiwasádari	Do.	
	Sojáde	Do.	
	Tányá	Do.	
	Telangá	Do.	
183.	**Kunbi**	Hindu	834,419
	Kunbi	Jain	13
	Adhán	Hindu.	
	Ahir	Do.	
	Akarmáse	Do.	
	Athariyá	Do.	
	Bádar	Do.	
	Bádhekár	Do.	
	Bahárgayá	Do.	
	Bangrase	Do.	
	Bardiyá	Do.	
	Bármáse	Do.	
	Báwne	Do.	
	Begar	Do.	
	Bhárathi	Do.	
	Bhátերáo	Do.	
	Bhiwarthade	Do.	
	Bhosale	Do.	
	Bhoyar	Do.	
	Chandaniyá	Do.	
	Chandnan	Do.	
	Chandol	Do.	
	Chandran	Do.	
	Chánu	Do.	
	Chanu Pardeshi	Do.	
	Chapariyá	Do.	
	Chatariyá	Do.	
	Chawdhari	Do.	
	Chawhán	Do.	
	Chawre	Do.	
	Chedu	Do.	
	Chendan	Do.	
	Chendre	Do.	
	Chenwár	Do.	
	Chohor	Do.	
	Chorbane	Do.	
	Dakhane	Do.	
	Desálu	Do.	
	Dhanjode	Do.	
	Dhanoje	Do.	
	Dhanwate	Do.	
	Dhanwin	Do.	
	Dhoryá	Do.	
	Dhotre	Do.	
	Dikshiwant	Do.	
	Dongare	Do.	
	Dowáne	Do.	

No.	Caste and sub-caste	Religion	Number
183.	**Kunbi**—*contd.*		
	Drávid	Hindu.	
	Gangápuri	Do.	
	Gangthadi	Do.	
	Gáwad	Do.	
	Gawári	Do.	
	Gharbári	Do.	
	Ghátole	Do.	
	Giri	Do.	
	Gorti	Do.	
	Gosáwi	Do.	
	Gumáni	Do.	
	Gurudwád	Do.	
	Halde	Do.	
	Hatkar	Do.	
	Hendre	Do.	
	Hindustáni	Do.	
	Ingale	Do.	
	Jadhav	Do.	
	Jángde	Do.	
	Jarote	Do.	
	Jayshán	Do.	
	Jeswál	Do.	
	Jháde	Do.	
	Jhádiwále	Do.	
	Juniyá	Do.	
	Kadam Maráthe	Do.	
	Kagarját	Do.	
	Kákade	Do.	
	Kanhere	Do.	
	Kanojá	Do.	
	Kanoti	Do.	
	Kápse	Do.	
	Karál	Do.	
	Kháltáte	Do.	
	Khandále	Do.	
	Khándan	Do.	
	Khándeshe	Do.	
	Kharchak	Do.	
	Karchi	Do.	
	Khátekar	Do.	
	Khayare	Do.	
	Khiràle	Do.	
	Khirságar	Do.	
	Koralkár	Do.	
	Kotháne	Do.	
	Kurande	Do.	
	Langote	Do.	
	Lawáne	Do.	
	Lewe	Do.	
	Lonáre	Do.	
	Madrási	Do.	
	Máháráshtra	Do.	
	Mánbháo	Do.	
	Máne	Do.	
	Maráthe	Do.	
	Maregal	Do.	
	Márwádi	Do.	
	Meghásan	Do.	
	Mháli	Do.	
	Mhasne	Do.	
	Mhátármáre	Do.	
	Mohole	Do.	
	More	Do.	
	Munarwád	Do.	
	Nágpure	Do.	
	Náikade	Do.	
	Naose	Do.	
	Pájne	Do.	
	Pandharpure	Do.	
	Pardeshi	Do.	
	Pátále	Do.	
	Pátálpure	Do.	
	Pátalwanshi	Do.	
	Pátanbás	Do.	
	Patariá	Do.	
	Patkár	Do.	
	Pawár	Do.	
	Punekar	Do.	
	Rajane	Do.	
	Rajput	Do.	
	Ráut	Do.	
	Ráo-Maráthe	Do.	
	Rede	Do.	
	Rewate	Do.	
	Rewe	Do.	
	Sádhu	Do.	
	Sagarwanshi	Do.	
	Sagráu	Do.	
	Sáhádeo	Do.	
	Sajod	Do.	
	Sálkare	Do.	
	Sálu	Do.	
	Sangrul	Do.	
	Sarwariyá	Do.	
	Sengar	Do.	
	Shekar	Do.	
	Shengalá	Do.	
	Shewe	Do.	
	Sinde	Do.	
	Singrár	Do.	
	Singrul	Do.	
	Sirchá	Do.	
	Solanki	Do.	
	Sukáre	Do.	
	Talagháte	Do.	
	Tángad Teke	Do.	
	Telang	Do.	
183.	**Kunbi**—*contd.*		
	Telangá	Hindu.	
	Thákur	Do.	
	Tharchan	Do.	
	Tilole	Do.	
	Tipile	Do.	
	Tirolá	Do.	
	Tiwári	Do.	
	Ujechhá	Do.	
	Wajhari	Do.	
	Wanjári	Do.	
	Wáyandeshi	Do.	
	Vidur	Do.	
	Yádaw	Do.	
184.	**Kunjdá**	**Musalmán**	1
185.	**Kuramwár**	**Hindu**	3
186.	**Labháni**	**Hindu**	25,525
	Labháni	**Musalmán**	56
	Labháni	**Jain**	6
	Akarmáse	Hindu.	
	Alwant	Do.	
	Bálnáth	Do.	
	Banjári Bhuke	Do.	
	Banmet	Do.	
	Bhuke	Do.	
	Bhuliwat	Do.	
	Chámbhár	Do.	
	Cháran	Hindu and Jain.	
	Chawhán	Hindu.	
	Chitran	Do.	
	Dewáwat	Do.	
	Dewsábá	Do.	
	Dhádi	Hindu and Musalmán.	
	Dhalyá	Hindu.	
	Dhánáwant	Do.	
	Dharamsáde	Do.	
	Gautam	Do.	
	Hádke	Do.	
	Isakwant	Do.	
	Jhirpalá	Do.	
	Jotár	Do.	
	Kawdiyá	Do.	
	Korá	Do.	
	Mathurá	Do.	
	Mathure Chámbhár	Do.	
	Megháwant	Do.	
	Mháli	Do.	
	Misláwant	Do.	
	Mud	Do.	
	Padam	Do.	
	Pálthe	Do.	
	Parwá	Do.	
	Pawár	Do.	
	Ragalá	Do.	
	Rámáwat	Do.	
	Ráthod	Do.	
	Thákur	Do.	
	Tihile	Do.	
	Udtyá	Do.	
	Wádtyá	Do.	
187.	**Lád**	**Hindu**	1,371
	Lád	**Jain**	1,454
	Bangarwál	Hindu.	
	Chipliwár	Do.	
	Dendu	Do.	
	Dendu Lád	Do.	
	Dhákad	Do.	
	Dhákad Lád	Do.	
	Gaoli	Do.	
	Jawre	Do.	
	Krishnapakshi	Do.	
	Oswál	Do.	
	Pitámbari	Do.	
	Shráwak	Do.	
	Shráogi	Do.	
	Shrimán	Do.	
	Wálale	Do.	
188.	**Lajjhad**	**Hindu**	1,763
	Lajjhad	**Animistic**	97
	Jhádpe	Hindu.	
	Pardeshi	Do.	
189.	**Lakhári**	**Hindu**	126
	Bangadi	Hindu.	
	Chudewále	Do.	
	Márwádi	Do.	
190.	**Lodhi**	**Hindu**	1,915
	Lodhi	**Musalmán**	5
	Badhawá	Hindu.	
	Rahus	Do.	
	Bathamba	Do.	
	Bhát	Do.	
	Chandelá	Do.	
190.	**Lodhi**—*contd.*		
	Chandrenyu	Hindu.	
	Hindustáni	Do.	
	Jángade	Do.	
	Jangade	Musalmán.	
	Jangale	Hindu.	
	Jatyá	Do.	
	Jeriyá	Do.	
	Jesiyá	Do.	
	Jetiyá	Do.	
	Jheriyá	Do.	
	Jime	Do.	
	Kahás	Do.	
	Kharaswár	Do.	
	Máhá Lodhi	Do.	
	Muli	Do.	
	Narse	Do.	
	Nirá	Do.	
	Pathán	Musalmán.	
	Pardeshi	Hindu.	
	Rajput	Do.	
	Singrol	Do.	
	Takári	Musalmán.	
191.	**Lohár (Kháti)**	**Hindu**	15,889
	Lohár (Kháti)	**Animistic**	18
	Akarmáse	Hindu.	
	Bans	Do.	
	Bepári	Do.	
	Biskarmá	Do.	
	Dhuriá	Do.	
	Fulmáole	Do.	
	Ghisádi	Do.	
	Gondi	Animistic.	
	Gond Lohár	Hindu.	
	Jhádiwále	Do.	
	Jiráit	Do.	
	Káranjkar	Do.	
	Lád	Do.	
	Lingáyat	Do.	
	Máhure	Do.	
	Malvi	Do.	
	Manopanchál	Do.	
	Manu	Do.	
	Manwári	Do.	
	Mathariá	Do.	
	Mohalbanch	Do.	
	Panchál	Do.	
	Pardeshi	Do.	
	Purbhayá	Do.	
	Rekal	Do.	
	Shade	Do.	
	Shiságure	Do.	
	Surajse	Do.	
	Telangi	Do.	
	Umarjhare	Do.	
	Wádhi	Do.	
	Wásudeo	Do.	
	Yáhudbans	Do.	
192.	**Lonári (or Luniyá)**	**Hindu**	1,096
	Barsáte	Hindu.	
	Chawhán	Do.	
	Gawhád	Do.	
	Kálesar	Do.	
	Maráthe	Do.	
	Phul	Do.	
193.	**Londhári**	**Hindu**	23
	Ahir	Do.	
	Maráthe	Do.	
194.	**Lugáwár**	**Hindu**	5
	Maráthe	Do.	
195.	**Mádgi**	**Hindu**	2,670
	Mádgi	**Animistic**	7
	Cheratwál	Hindu.	
	Karanwar	Do.	
	Kárpadve	Do.	
	Kodkar	Do.	
	Telangá	Do.	
196.	**Madrási**	**Hindu**	16
197.	**Mahár (Dhed and Kotwál.)**	**Hindu**	354,997
	Mahár	**Animistic**	8
	Andhawan	Hindu	
	Badse	Do.	
	Balái	Do.	
	Banawá	Do.	
	Banjári	Do.	
	Bansod	Do.	
	Báone	Do.	
	Bárke	Do.	
	Bate	Do.	
	Báwanghade	Do.	
	Bedar	Do.	
	Beldár	Do.	
	Belkhede	Do.	
	Bhagat	Do.	
	Bhálerao	Do.	

No.	Caste	Religion	Number
197.	**Mahár**—*contd.*		
	Bhát	Hindu.	
	Bhojande	Do.	
	Bunkar Ládsi	Do.	
	Chopde	Do.	
	Dakhane	Do.	
	Deheriá	Do.	
	Deoman	Do.	
	Dhámdhari	Do.	
	Dohari	Do.	
	Fadebandhanár	Do.	
	Gangotre	Do.	
	Ghátole	Do.	
	Gond Mahár	Do.	
	Hajjam	Do.	
	Hálte	Do.	
	Holar	Do.	
	Ingole	Do.	
	Jhádiwále	Do.	
	Jhádpe	Do.	
	Kalwant	Do.	
	Kánadi	Do.	
	Karmankar	Do.	
	Kasture	Do.	
	Káte Ládvan	Do.	
	Khadse	Do.	
	Kochare	Do.	
	Kosare	Do.	
	Kotwál Daheriá	Do.	
	Ládwan	Do.	
	Lokhande	Do.	
	Lonáre	Do.	
	Málvi	Do.	
	Mánike	Do.	
	Manore	Do.	
	Maráthe	Do.	
	Mháli	Do.	
	Moghe	Do.	
	Narkas	Do.	
	Nemádi	Do.	
	Nikade	Do.	
	Panchál	Do.	
	Pardhán	Do.	
	Do.	Animistic.	
	Sándane	Hindu.	
	Sarkache	Do.	
	Singáde	Do.	
	Sojane	Do.	
	Somas	Do.	
	Somase	Do.	
	Somawanshi	Do.	
	Tarfade	Do.	
	Telangi	Do.	
	Tháriyá	Do.	
	Tidyá	Do.	
	Wánkhede	Do.	
198.	**Máli**	**Hindu**	**202,488**
	Máli	**Jain**	**10**
	Akarmáse	Hindu	
	Al	Do.	
	Bánkar	Do.	
	Bardiyá	Do.	
	Bhandekar	Do.	
	Bhuriyá	Do.	
	Dashesahasra	Do.	
	Fal	Do.	
	Fulmáli	Do.	
	Gangotre	Do.	
	Gáse	Do.	
	Gási Kadu	Do.	
	Ghási Máli	Do.	
	Gujráthi	Do.	
	Hálde	Do.	
	Hárdiyá	Do.	
	Hindustáni	Do.	
	Jáb	Do.	
	Jambu	Do.	
	Jiri Máli	Do.	
	Kachawá	Do.	
	Kachhi	Do.	
	Káchi Máli	Do.	
	Kalwant	Do.	
	Kánadi	Do.	
	Kanoje	Do.	
	Kás	Do.	
	Kote	Do.	
	Káti	Do.	
	Kedári	Do.	
	Khupale	Do.	
	Kod	Do.	
	Kori	Do.	
	Kosare	Do.	
	Lád	Do.	
	Lonári	Do.	
	Márwádi	Do.	
	Matyá	Do.	
	Mukari Máli	Do.	
	Murái	Do.	
	Pahád	Do.	
	Pardeshi	Do.	
	Rajput	Do.	
	Rán Máli	Do.	
	Sagar Máli	Do.	
	Simore	Do.	
	Telange	Do.	
198.	**Máli**—*contd.*		
	Tirmale	Hindu.	
	Wan Máli	Do.	
199.	**Mallá**	**Hindu**	**4**
200.	**Máná**	**Hindu**	**217**
	Badaváik	Do.	
	Badván	Do.	
201.	**Mánbháo**	**Hindu**	**3,559**
	Bairági	Do.	
	Bálbramhachári	Do.	
	Bhápe	Do.	
	Bhiksheshwari	Do.	
	Bhodin	Do.	
	Bhowave	Do.	
	Bhoyál	Do.	
	Bidhar	Do.	
	Dhobi	Do.	
	Dikshiwant	Do.	
	Ghangás	Do.	
	Gharbári	Do.	
	Hansrupi	Do.	
	Jamesin	Do.	
	Káranjkar	Do.	
	Kavishwar	Do.	
	Keshri	Do.	
	Khándeshi	Do.	
	Lád	Do.	
	Lahang	Do.	
	Machol	Do.	
	Mane	Do.	
	Maráthe	Do.	
	Mathpati	Do.	
	Mudit	Do.	
	Ráinand	Do.	
	Sáraswat	Do.	
	Serági	Do.	
	Sheole	Do.	
	Udarbhare	Do.	
	Vishnu	Do.	
	Vishvawanshi	Do.	
	Wáindeshkar	Do.	
	Wairágya	Do.	
	Waitági	Do.	
	Warádi	Do.	
202.	**Máng**	**Hindu**	**52,150**
	Máng	**Animistic**	**1**
	Alsarwár	Hindu.	
	Azgare	Do.	
	Babubanji	Do.	
	Badve	Do.	
	Bangir	Do.	
	Banjári	Do.	
	Bánsphod	Do.	
	Bende	Do.	
	Bhádále	Do.	
	Borekari	Do.	
	Borkar	Do.	
	Burad	Do.	
	Chapne	Do.	
	Chawghade	Do.	
	Dafadewále	Do.	
	Dakalwár	Do.	
	Dakhane	Do.	
	Dandewán	Do.	
	Desáli	Do.	
	Dháliyá	Do.	
	Dheriyá	Do.	
	Dhole	Do.	
	Dotonde	Do.	
	Fadebandhanár	Do.	
	Fadewále	Do.	
	Gádiwále	Do.	
	Gáekwád	Do.	
	Gáodhále	Do.	
	Gaoli	Do.	
	Gárodi	Do.	
	Ghádke	Do.	
	Ghatade	Do.	
	Ghatole	Do.	
	Ghode	Do.	
	Gofane	Do.	
	Gondhali	Do.	
	Gorle	Do.	
	Hiwle	Do.	
	Huble	Do.	
	Ingole	Do.	
	Jádhao	Do.	
	Jogdand	Do.	
	Kágle	Do.	
	Kákade	Do.	
	Kákare	Do.	
	Kámbale	Do.	
	Kámbe	Do.	
	Kanade Máng	Do.	
	Kánore	Do.	
	Khadse	Do.	
	Khandáre	Do.	
	Kharáre	Do.	
	Kokare	Do.	
	Ládjin	Do.	
	Mánkodiyá	Do.	
	Maráthe	Do.	
	Mochi	Do.	
202.	**Máng**—*contd.*		
	Nágarkar	Hindu.	
	Nágpuriya	Do.	
	Náwkar	Do.	
	Nikálne	Do.	
	Panále	Do.	
	Pendhári	Do.	
	Rámoshi	Do.	
	Ranbaole	Do.	
	Rángade	Do.	
	Ráut	Do.	
	Sáble	Do.	
	Sákre	Do.	
	Sasáne	Do.	
	Sáte	Do.	
	Sáwle	Do.	
	Senwále	Do.	
	Shikári	Do.	
	Surse	Do.	
	Telangi	Do.	
	Teng	Do.	
	Tewele	Do.	
	Thele	Do.	
	Umake	Do.	
	Wájantri	Do.	
	Wángade	Do.	
	Waráde	Do.	
	Waráde Akar-máse	Do.	
	Wayabas	Do.	
203.	**Máng Gárodi**	**Hindu**	**161**
204.	**Manihár**	**Musalmán**	**15**
205.	**Mantri**	**Hindu**	**1**
206.	**Marál**	**Hindu**	**410**
	Bhor	Do.	
	Kosare Máli	Do.	
207.	**Maráthe**	**Hindu**	**19,038**
	Bhiwarthade	Do.	
	Bhosale	Do.	
	Bhoyar	Do.	
	Chhapan Kuliche	Do.	
	Daburkár	Do.	
	Dakhane	Do.	
	Deshkar	Do.	
	Dhage	Do.	
	Dhole	Do.	
	Gáikwád	Do.	
	Gangthade	Do.	
	Gáonde	Do.	
	Gavháne	Do.	
	Ghatiyá	Do.	
	Ghátmáthe	Do.	
	Gonwár	Do.	
	Jánve	Do.	
	Javáre	Do.	
	Jog	Do.	
	Kadam	Do.	
	Khándeshi	Do.	
	Kháse	Do.	
	Kshirságar	Do.	
	Lashkari	Do.	
	Mahárle	Do.	
	Pone	Do.	
	Reve	Do.	
	Sháhánaukuli	Do.	
	Shinde	Do.	
	Surse	Do.	
	Wáindeshi	Do.	
208.	**Márwádi**	**Hindu**	(*See* Wáni.)
	Márwádi	**Jain**	(*See* Wáni.)
	Adhval	Hindu.	
	Bábliá	Do.	
	Bodelwálá	Do.	
	Bahak	Do.	
	Berán	Do.	
	Bhattad	Do.	
	Bhatkar	Do.	
	Bhatod	Do.	
	Bijawári	Do.	
	Dádupanthi	Do.	
	Dargad	Do.	
	Dáymá	Do.	
	Dhámae	Do.	
	Durandá	Do.	
	Gulche	Do.	
	Jhawár	Do.	
	Kábará	Do.	
	Kánale	Do.	
	Kawi	Do.	
	Khargbári	Do.	
	Kochar	Do.	
	Kotkar	Do.	
	Mal	Do.	
	Med	Do.	
	Mukhadá	Do.	
	Nisari	Do.	
	Párth	Do.	
	Sheval	Do.	
	Untawále	Do.	
	Vishnu	Do.	

No.	Caste and sub-caste	Religion	Number
208.	Márwádi—*contd.*		
	Wádesá	Hindu.	
	Waradwad	Do.	
	Ware	Do.	
209.	Máwhár	Hindu	1
	Dhuryá Mawhár	Do.	
210.	Mehtar	Hindu	(*See* Bhangi.)
	Mehtar	Musalmán	(Do.)
	Mehtar	Sikh	32
	Mehtar	Animistic	2
	Dumár	Hindu.	
	Hele	Do.	
	Lálbeg	Musalmán.	
	Lálbegi	Hindu and Sikh.	
	Makhiár	Animistic.	
211.	Meman	Musalmán	7
	Alábáni	Do.	
	Kachhi	Do.	
212.	Mháli (Hajjam, Nhávi and Wárik).	Hindu	35,225
	Mháli	Musalmán	17
	Mháli (Hajjam)	Jain	3
	Abulkár	Do.	
	Abuse	Do.	
	Banáit	Do.	
	Banjári	Do.	
	Chámbhár Mháli	Do.	
	Dakhane	Hindu.	
	Dakshasar	Do.	
	Deváne	Do.	
	Gádhade	Do.	
	Gangáner	Do.	
	Gangone	Do.	
	Gangotri	Do.	
	Gaoli	Do.	
	Hajjám	Do.	
	Hendre	Do.	
	Hidshámi	Do.	
	Hindustáni	Do.	
	Hinoyá	Do.	
	Holkar	Do.	
	Kádkar	Do.	
	Kádmágan	Do.	
	Lád Wáni	Do.	
	Lingáyat	Do.	
	Mahár Mháli	Do.	
	Makháyá	Do.	
	Maráthe	Do.	
	Máru	Do.	
	Márwádi	Do.	
	Nánderkar	Do.	
	Nhávi	Do.	
	Nibaráne	Do.	
	Oswál	Do.	
	Pardeshi	Do.	
	Purbhaye	Do.	
	Rájoriá	Do.	
	Ranmá	Do.	
	Shribástar	Do.	
	Shribisan	Do.	
	Solankhe	Do.	
	Surose	Do.	
	Táede	Do.	
	Telange	Do.	
	Wánkhede	Do.	
	Waráde	Do.	
	Wárik	Do.	
213.	Miná	Hindu	12
214.	Mirási	Hindu	5
	Gurunám	Do.	
215.	Mochi	Hindu	(*See* Chámbhár.)
	Duhsiá	Do.	
	Durin	Do.	
	Durlebas	Do.	
	Kori	Do.	
	Kuril	Do.	
	Pardeshi	Do.	
	Rohidás	Do.	
	Shisodá	Do.	
	Telangi	Do.	
216.	Moghal	Musalmán	4,437
	Badámi	Do.	
	Chektái	Do.	
	Chokh	Do.	
	Mirzá	Do.	
	Osmániganí	Do.	
	Yesliá	Do.	
217.	Moghe	Hindu	2
	Do.	Animistic	217
	Gondi	Hindu.	
218.	Momin	Musalmán	290
219.	Mudliár	Hindu	66
220.	Muliá	Musalmán	1
221.	Multáni	Do.	9
222.	Munarwár	Hindu	2,120
223.	Munewádi or Manewád.	Hindu	54
	Ibitdár	Do.	
	Telangi	Do.	
224.	Muráde	Hindu	1
	Bhaktiá	Do.	
225.	Murái	Hindu	119
	Munarwád	Do.	
	Pardeshi	Do.	
	Phulmáli	Do.	
226.	Musalmán	Musalmán	1,992
	Hindustáni	Do.	
227.	Mutrájlu or Mutrási.	Hindu	29
228.	Naghát	Hindu	5
229.	Náidu	Hindu	52
230.	Náikan	Musalmán	(*See* Kasban.)
231.	Nálband	Hindu	13
232.	Náumuslim	Musalmán	1
233.	Nánakshábi	Hindu	22
	Mehet	Do.	
	Udási	Do.	
234.	Náth	Hindu	2,973
	Adináth	Do.	
	Anand	Do.	
	Bharádi	Do.	
	Dári	Do.	
	Dhanjogi	Do.	
	Dokri	Do.	
	Dori	Do.	
	Gorakh	Do.	
	Gorakhnáth	Do.	
	Jogindra	Do.	
	Kánphade	Do.	
	Machhindar	Do.	
	Mandjogi	Do.	
	Ráthor	Do.	
	Rául	Do.	
	Sadnáth Balhe	Do.	
	Sanjogi	Do.	
	Sárisatnáth	Do.	
	Sarsing	Do.	
	Satnámi	Do.	
	Satnáth	Do.	
	Shivnáth	Do.	
	Shridatt	Do.	
	Sirsat	Do.	
	Tihile	Do.	
235.	Native Christian.	Christian	533
	Goánese	Do.	
	Máng	Do.	
	Madrasi	Do.	
236.	Náyer	Hindu	14
237.	Nhávi	Hindu	(*See* Mháli.)
	Nhávi	Musalmán	(Do.)
238.	Nihál	Animistic	2,201
	Nihál	Hindu	104
	Bote	Animistic.	
	Dársiá	Do.	
	Dhi	Do.	
	Jábu	Do.	
	Nágwále	Do.	
	Otári	Hindu.	
	Do.	Do.	
	Rumá	Animistic.	
239.	Niráli	Hindu	61
240.	Otári (Watankár).	Hindu	1,477
	Otári	Musalmán	1
	Otári	Animistic	6
	Bharái	Hindu.	
	Bharan Otári	Do.	
	Chaholiyá	Do.	
	Kásár	Do.	
	Máne	Do.	
	Maráthe	Do.	
	Panchál	Do.	
	Penám	Do.	
	Toshti	Do.	
	Wághore	Do.	
	Waráde	Do.	
	Wativkár	Do.	
241.	Pádhar	Musalmán	9
	Kasbi	Do.	
242.	Pahád	Hindu	836
	Bodre	Do.	
	Deskar	Do.	
	Mákne	Do.	
	Nerpahád	Do.	
	Sutshekhar	Do.	
	Wanmáli	Do.	
	Wasot	Do.	
243.	Pahelwán	Hindu	3
	Pratikwár	Do.	
244.	Pakháli	Hindu	99
245.	Panchál (Panchál Lohár).	Hindu.	1,876
	Panchál (Do.)	Musalmán	9
	Bháte	Hindu.	
	Chavhán	Do.	
	Dakhane	Do.	
	Firaste	Do.	
	Gadhe	Do.	
	Ghisáde	Do.	
	Kánade	Do.	
	Mánbháo	Do.	
	Manu	Do.	
	Maráthe	Do.	
	Páthrat	Do.	
246.	Panchál Lohár	Hindu	(*See* Panchál.)
247.	Pángul	Hindu	2,085
	Bedre	Do.	
	Gaoli	Do.	
	Maráthe	Do.	
	Pálmágawine	Do.	
248.	Panká	Hindu	1
	Maráthe	Do.	
249.	Parbhu	Hindu	62
	Chándrasháeni	Do.	
	Kátyáeni	Do.	
	Kayesth Chándrasháeni.	Do.	
	Káyasth Chándrawanshi.	Do.	
	Kaysth Parbhu	Do.	
	Mháharashtra	Do.	
	Maráthe	Do.	
	Pátáne	Do.	
250.	Pardeshi	Hindu	639
	Angal	Do.	
	Dhol Pánde	Do.	
	Gáde	Do.	
	Gaul	Do.	
	Hágle-Pánde	Do.	
	Mutrái	Do.	
	Serábahiyá	Do.	
251.	Pardhán	Hindu	3,766
	Pardhán	Animistic	9,170
	Atrám	Hindu.	
	Bused	Do.	
	Dewar	Do.	
	Dewás	Do.	
	Dhurve	Do.	
	Gond	Do.	
	Gondi Bhát	Do.	
	Heliyá	Do.	
	Kadam	Do.	
	Kanám	Do.	
	Káre	Do.	
	Karewatá	Do.	
	Káte Pardhán	Do.	
	Kumariá	Do.	
	Mázghare	Do.	
	Medáwi	Do.	
	Mesrám	Do.	
	Padrám	Do.	
	Pángomási-Bhoi	Do.	
	Ráj Pardhán	Do.	
	Sidám	Do.	

No.	Caste / Sub-caste	Religion	Number
251.	**Pardhán**—*contd.*		
	Surpán	Hindu.	
	Thákur	Do.	
	Ulakmedáwi	Do.	
252.	**Párdhi**	**Hindu**	6,894
	Párdhi	**Animistic**	5
	Báori	Hindu.	
	Gan	Do.	
	Ghosle	Do.	
	Gujráthi	Do.	
	Haran Párdhi	Hindu and Animistic.	
	Kále	Hindu.	
	Kalyá	Do.	
	Kuresi	Do.	
	Langote	Do.	
	Máháráshtra	Do.	
	Maráthe	Do.	
	Moghe	Do.	
	Páhále	Do.	
	Pál	Do.	
	Pawár	Do.	
	Phus	Do.	
	Ráj	Do.	
	Ráo	Do.	
	Reochik	Do.	
	Sálankhe	Do.	
	Sángli	Do.	
	Shikári Párdhi	Animistic.	
	Sirkoli	Hindu.	
	Solankhi	Do.	
	Udiál	Do.	
	Wághari	Do.	
	Wárdhe	Do.	
253.	**Parit**	**Hindu**	(*See* Warthi.)
	Báone	Do.	
	Modhokár	Do.	
	Nandkár	Do.	
	Rajak	Do.	
254.	**Pársi**	**Pársi**	417
	Behdin	Do.	
	Mobed	Do.	
255.	**Pási**	**Hindu**	467
	Barási	Do.	
	Bárpesi	Do.	
	Báyefási	Do.	
	Bes Pási	Do.	
	Buriyá	Do.	
	Deo Káriyá	Do.	
	Dukar Pási	Do.	
	Káyagawál	Do.	
	Káyathwá	Do.	
	Parasharám	Do.	
256.	**Patáliyá**	**Hindu**	2
257.	**Pathán**	**Musalmán**	48,393
	Bahelwi	Do.	
	Bájero	Do.	
	Ballucbi	Do.	
	Banodari	Do.	
	Barakzai	Do.	
	Bhurákhatel	Do.	
	Dastátur	Do.	
	Gadezai	Do.	
	Galni	Do.	
	Giliyáni	Do.	
	Giyáni	Do.	
	Gori	Do.	
	Huseni	Do.	
	Irákhzai	Do.	
	Jángad	Do.	
	Kábuli	Do.	
	Káemkháni	Do.	
	Káemsáenu	Do.	
	Kikad	Do.	
	Kikade	Do.	
	Khákar or Kikar	Do.	
	Khákbinwáli	Do.	
	Lawangi	Do.	
	Lawháni	Do.	
	Lodhi	Do.	
	Lohani	Do.	
	Madan	Do.	
	Mahamadzai	Do.	
	Miyán	Do.	
	Ninási	Do.	
	Shábmáni	Do.	
	Sulemáni	Do.	
	Surikhá	Do.	
	Turájne	Do.	
	Yusafzai	Do.	
258.	**Páthar**	**Hindu**	(*See* Páthrat.)
259.	**Pátharkár**	**Hindu**	(Do.)
	Khed	Do.	
260.	**Páthrat (Páthar and Páthar-kár).**	**Hindu**	877
	Kasbi	Do.	
	Panchál	Do.	
	Pawár	Do.	
	Sálkar	Do.	
261.	**Patnál**	**Hindu**	20
262.	**Patwekar**	**Hindu**	(*See* Patwi.)
	Deobansi	Do.	
	Visámoli	Do.	
263.	**Patwi (Patwe-kar).**	**Hindu**	466
	Patwi	**Jain**	58
	Gujráthi	Hindu.	
	Khambáitwále	Do.	
	Maráthe	Do.	
	Palewár	Do.	
	Sahasrárjun	Do.	
	Sárjanal	Do.	
	Wáni	Do.	
264.	**Perki**	**Hindu**	1,499
	Agyáwád	Do.	
	Barbaw-wad	Do.	
	Bedaknid	Do.	
	Bhurewád	Do.	
	Chitakunwád	Do.	
	Dáreräjwád	Do.	
	Godliwád	Do.	
	Golwád	Do.	
	Jiriwál	Do.	
	Kunbi Perki	Do.	
	Pálewád	Do.	
	Ráthe	Do.	
	Sheti	Do.	
	Sheti Kolám Te-langi.	Do.	
265.	**Phanádi**	**Hindu**	102
	Duke	Do.	
	Maráthi	Do.	
	Pawár	Do.	
266.	**Pinjári**	**Hindu**	67
	Pinjári	**Musalmán**	1,085
	Bháb	Hindu.	
	Jhádiwále	Do.	
	Waradi	Do.	
	Do.	Musalmán.	
267.	**Pirzáde**	**Musalmán**	6
	Khandelwál	Do.	
268.	**Pube**	**Hindu**	2
269.	**Purbhaiye**	**Hindu**	94
	Chaner	Do.	
	Patekár	Do.	
270.	**Ráerang**	**Hindu**	(*See* Bahu-rupi.)
271.	**Ráj**	**Hindu**	(*See* Ga-ondi.)
	Desli	Hindu.	
	Sagar	Do.	
	Ságarwáshi	Do.	
	Sikár Ráj	Do.	
	Somwanshi	Do.	
272.	**Rajput**	**Hindu**	50,916
	Rajput	**Sikh**	14
	Abeshiyá	Hindu.	
	Abhetiyá	Do.	
	Ahir	Do.	
	Alkári	Do.	
	Alkhánde	Do.	
	Ameriá	Do.	
	Ametiyá	Do.	
	Anand	Do.	
	Arekár	Do.	
	Aryá	Do.	
	Askhod	Do.	
	Baderá Thákur	Do.	
	Badoriá	Do.	
	Baghel	Do.	
	Baghne	Do.	
	Bagle	Do.	
	Bahál	Do.	
	Baheliyá	Do.	
	Baherá Thákur	Do.	
	Bahtiyá	Do.	
	Bairági	Do.	
	Bais	Do.	
	Banáfar	Do.	
	Bangi	Do.	
	Banjárá	Do.	
	Banore	Do.	
272.	**Rajput**—*contd.*		
	Barak	Hindu.	
	Bárok	Do.	
	Báse	Do.	
	Báyeki	Do.	
	Beliá	Do.	
	Bhadariyá	Do.	
	Bhadawár Thá-kur.	Do.	
	Bhádekar	Do.	
	Bhadrim	Do.	
	Bhagli	Do.	
	Bhále Sultán	Do.	
	Bháradwáj	Do.	
	Bijápuri	Do.	
	Bisle	Do.	
	Bisen	Do.	
	Bisyen	Do.	
	Bople	Do.	
	Bramha Khatri	Do.	
	Bundelá	Do.	
	Bundelkhandi	Do.	
	Chabli Gaoli	Do.	
	Chadoki	Do.	
	Chakar Gawár	Do.	
	Chamal Gankar	Do.	
	Chamargán	Do.	
	Chámar Gaud	Do.	
	Chandan Thákur	Do.	
	Chandrabanchhi	Do.	
	Chandrawanshi	Do.	
	Chanle Thákur	Do.	
	Chauhán	Do.	
	Chawkas	Do.	
	Chhatri	Do.	
	Chembargor	Do.	
	Chepadá	Do.	
	Chiture	Do.	
	Dánge	Do.	
	Dawad	Do.	
	Deshmukh	Do.	
	Dhákarwár	Do.	
	Dhákre	Do.	
	Dhanáwat	Do.	
	Dhárwár	Do.	
	Dikshiwant	Do.	
	Dudhe	Do.	
	Dusar Baniyá	Do.	
	Gaharwár	Do.	
	Gadariyá	Do.	
	Garewál	Do.	
	Gaud	Do.	
	Gaud Bansi	Do.	
	Gautam	Do.	
	Gáyekne	Do.	
	Gáyelat	Do.	
	Goharwár	Do.	
	Goikad	Do.	
	Gokulbansi	Do.	
	Gond	Do.	
	Gopál	Do.	
	Gujar	Do.	
	Guru	Do.	
	Hádbháde	Do.	
	Hádke	Do.	
	Hárdaniyá	Do.	
	Hendre	Do.	
	Ingle	Do.	
	Jádná	Do.	
	Jadubansi	Do.	
	Jagdeo	Do.	
	Janglá	Do.	
	Jaswár	Do.	
	Ját	Do.	
	Kabir	Do.	
	Kabne	Do.	
	Kachhwá	Do.	
	Kachhwá Thákur	Do.	
	Kaherwál	Do.	
	Kámbhoj	Do.	
	Kanoje	Do.	
	Kánpuriyá	Do.	
	Kante	Do.	
	Kapod	Do.	
	Kargoth	Do.	
	Karkhádwant	Do.	
	Káshiryá	Do.	
	Katoriyá	Do.	
	Katyár	Do.	
	Kekád	Do.	
	Keote	Do.	
	Khangál	Do.	
	Khariwár	Do.	
	Khist	Do.	
	Kinhipátumar	Do.	
	Kirád	Do.	
	Komti	Do.	
	Kshatrya	Do.	
	Kshatrya	Sikh.	
	Kumásh	Hindu.	
	Kumáwant	Do.	
	Kunbi	Do.	
	Kuwár	Do.	
	Labhán	Do.	
	Láhányá	Do.	
	Lahariyá	Do.	
	Láthod	Do.	
	Lodhi	Do.	

No.	Caste and sub-caste	Religion	Number
272.	**Rajput**—*concld.*		
	Maisri	Hindu.	
	Málwi	Do.	
	Márod	Do.	
	Mehekari	Do.	
	Melátre	Do.	
	Miniyár	Do.	
	Mohodam	Do.	
	Mokál	Do.	
	Mokan	Do.	
	Motwa	Do.	
	Nágarchál	Do.	
	Nandbansi	Do.	
	Nikumbh	Do.	
	Pandobás	Do.	
	Paniyár	Do.	
	Panjábi	Do.	
	Parihár	Do.	
	Parihári	Do.	
	Parwár	Do.	
	Páthak	Do.	
	Pawár	Do.	
	Pawarbanchhi	Do.	
	Pragatiyá	Do.	
	Raghubansi	Do.	
	Rájá	Do.	
	Raj Kumár	Do.	
	Rajput Dube	Do.	
	Ráj Thákur	Do.	
	Rámdási	Do.	
	Ráne	Do.	
	Ráthod	Do.	
	Rekwár	Do.	
	Sahasrárjun	Do.	
	Sájol	Do.	
	Sáni	Do.	
	Sárwajun	Do.	
	Savehali	Do.	
	Segar	Do.	
	Seti	Do.	
	Shakarvir	Do.	
	Shakáwat	Do.	
	Shángar	Do.	
	Shejáriyá	Do.	
	Shekáyat	Do.	
	Shikarwár	Do.	
	Shiobansi	Do.	
	Sikh	Do.	
	Silare	Do.	
	Single	Do.	
	Sipor	Do.	
	Solanke	Do.	
	Somawanshi	Do.	
	Sonak	Do.	
	Sulki	Do.	
	Suryawanshi	Do.	
	Tágwále	Do.	
	Thákur	Do.	
	Thanan	Do.	
	Tilokchandi	Do.	
	Tiwári	Do.	
	Udási Nának-panthi.	Do.	
	Uwári	Do.	
	Varangátri	Do.	
	Vaishya	Do.	
273.	**Rámjáni**	Hindu	4
274.	**Rámoshi**	Hindu	91
	Borde	Do.	
	Dakhane	Do.	
	Kothár	Do.	
275.	**Rangári**	Hindu	11,865
	Rangári	Jain	325
	Adhore	Hindu.	
	Bárse	Do.	
	Bháosár	Do.	
	Chhikhár	Do.	
	Chhiyá	Do.	
	Gáosar	Do.	
	Hárak	Do.	
	Jimánandi	Do.	
	Lád	Do.	
	Málve	Do.	
	Maráthe	Do.	
	Mehesri Bháosár	Do.	
	Nemádi	Do.	
	Pardeshi	Do.	
	Phul	Do.	
	Sadáwashe	Do.	
	Telangá	Do.	
276.	**Reddi**	Hindu	1
277.	**Reddi Kápuwár**	Hindu.	9
	Chárgavat	Do.	
278.	**Rohilá**	Musalmán	174
	Afghán	Do.	
	Pathán	Do.	
279.	**Sádhu**	Hindu	27
	Bairági	Do.	
	Harinám	Do.	
	Piábansi	Do.	
280.	**Sagur**	Hindu	63
281.	**Sálewár**	Hindu	1,103
	Argotuwád	Do.	
	Mahnowád	Do.	
	Padamsálewár	Do.	
	Padamsáli	Do.	
	Patel Sálewár	Do.	
	Telangi	Do.	
	Trimál	Do.	
282.	**Sáli**	Hindu	7,985
	Sáli	Jain	12
	Dakhane	Hindu	
	Dhuriyá	Do.	
	Dikshiwant	Do.	
	Káwadche	Do.	
	Máháráshtra	Do.	
	Padam Sáli	Do.	
	Sakun	Do.	
	Sarákshit	Do.	
	Shudha Sáli	Do.	
	Shukla Sáli	Do.	
	Sut	Do.	
	Telange	Do.	
	Tikán	Do.	
283.	**Sálve**	Hindu	5
	Dakhane	Do.	
284.	**Sanyáshi**	Hindu	28
	Anand	Do.	
	Sampradáye	Do.	
	Sáraswat	Do.	
	Surat Kshatri	Do.	
285.	**Sárlan**	Hindu	2
286.	**Sarode**	Hindu	1,330
	Alaspure	Do.	
	Dákáp	Do.	
	Diwáne	Do.	
	Gáoráne	Do.	
	Maráthe	Do.	
	Márwádi	Do.	
	Medhe	Do.	
287.	**Shekdáu**	Hindu	1
288.	**Shekh**	Musalmán	124,232
	Ahelefaresh	Do.	
	Alinur	Do.	
	Bágwále	Do.	
	Deshi Shekh	Do.	
	Din Mahamadi	Do.	
	Farodi	Do.	
	Guldáoni	Do.	
	Huseni	Do.	
	Hydrábádi	Do.	
	Ichni	Do.	
	Kureshání	Do.	
	Kureshi	Do.	
	Londhári	Do.	
	Máne Kasáb	Do.	
	Mukeri	Do.	
	Sidhik-khuráshá	Do.	
	Turwáne	Do.	
	Warádi	Do.	
289.	**Shelki**	Hindu	1
290.	**Shikharpáni-wále.**	Hindu	3
	Rewáwár	Do.	
291.	**Simpi (Darzi)**	Hindu	13,725
	Simpi	Jain	2,626
	Simpi (Darzi)	Musalmán	14
	Ahir	Hindu.	
	Bárse	Do.	
	Bhusánewár	Do.	
	Deonáth	Do.	
	Depábali	Do.	
	Dnyandeo	Do.	
	Gand	Do.	
	Hindustáni	Do.	
	Jain	Jain	
	Jot	Hindu	
	Káoliyá	Do.	
	Lataswe	Do.	
	Lingáyat	Do.	
	Mahes	Do.	
	Mahesri	Do.	
	Málsure	Do.	
	Márá	Do.	
	Maráthe	Do.	
	Márwádi	Do.	
	Mirgi	Do.	
	Námdeo	Do.	
	Párináth	Do.	
	Rákhechá	Do.	
	Ráyat Simpi	Do.	
	Rode	Do.	
	Shráoki	Do.	
291.	**Simpi**—*contd.*		
	Telangi	Hindu.	
	Vishnu	Do.	
	Vishnu Bhakta	Do.	
292.	**Sikh**	Sikh	114
	Sikh	Hindu	202
	Govindi	Do.	
	Do.	Sikh.	
	Jumedár	Hindu.	
293.	**Sikligar**	Hindu	36
	Sikligar	Musalmán	37
294.	**Siláwat**	Hindu	6
	Máháráshtra	Do.	
295.	**Singhálese**	Christian	5
296.	**Soliá**	Hindu	1
	Bhaktiá Gotri	Do.	
297.	**Sonár**	Hindu	29,217
	Sonár	Jain	2
	Bakwári	Hindu.	
	Bárki	Do.	
	Bháti	Do.	
	Bramhasiyá	Do.	
	Chárwe	Do.	
	Dále	Do.	
	Dáywábáne	Do.	
	Deogan	Do.	
	Deokaran	Do.	
	Deonyá	Do.	
	Deorán Panchál	Do.	
	Deshi	Do.	
	Devadnye	Do.	
	Gangákhede	Do.	
	Hadke	Do.	
	Hármatkar	Do.	
	Hebjhi	Do.	
	Jháde	Do.	
	Jhádpe	Do.	
	Kharkár	Do.	
	Kshatri	Do.	
	Lád	Do.	
	Ládsi	Do.	
	Láthal	Do.	
	Madsonár	Do.	
	Mahesri	Do.	
	Málvi	Do.	
	Maráthe	Do.	
	Márwádi	Do.	
	Máyel	Do.	
	Mendh	Do.	
	Paithankar	Do.	
	Panchál	Do.	
	Pátkar	Do.	
	Shrigandmáli	Do.	
	Shrigul Málvi	Do.	
	Shri Máli	Do.	
	Shirsi Málvi	Do.	
	Telangi	Do.	
	Tiláye	Do.	
	Ujinyá	Do.	
	Vaishya	Do.	
	Vishwa Karma	Do.	
	Wanjári	Do.	
298.	**Sugandhi**	Hindu	(*See* Gandhi.)
	Gujráthi	Do.	
299.	**Sutár (Badhái and Wádhi).**	Hindu	32,478
	Sutár	Jain	13
	Báone	Hindu.	
	Barekare	Do.	
	Burge	Do.	
	Gawári	Do.	
	Hendre	Do.	
	Hindustáni	Do.	
	Ingle	Do.	
	Jángde	Do.	
	Jháde	Do.	
	Jogi	Do.	
	Khadási	Do.	
	Kháti	Do.	
	Khátwádhi	Do.	
	Kukás	Do.	
	Kukásband	Do.	
	Kukásbási	Do.	
	Ládekar	Do.	
	Lekrá	Do.	
	Lingáyat	Do.	
	Madalbás	Do.	
	Máhure	Do.	
	Máhure Panchál	Do.	
	Maráthe	Do.	
	Márwádi	Do.	
	Do.	Jain.	
	Máyá	Hindu.	
	Mohre	Do.	
	Nemádi	Do.	

No.	Caste	Religion	Number
299.	**Sutár**—*contd.*		
	Oswál	Hindu.	
	Panchál	Do.	
	Pási Panchál	Do.	
	Purbhaiye	Do.	
	Rájas	Do.	
	Rájotikhá	Do.	
	Rákhudi	Do.	
	Sád	Do.	
	Sájune	Do.	
	Sángatkar	Do.	
	Shribans	Do.	
	Wádhi	Do.	
300.	**Swámi**	**Hindu**	3
	Nimawat	Do.	
301.	**Syed**	**Musalmán**	15,107
	Afridi	Do.	
	Ahelekuresh	Do.	
	Bahurupi	Do.	
	Báriwángám	Do.	
	Birbi	Do.	
	Hálfi	Do.	
	Huseni	Do.	
	Kágdi	Do.	
	Kureshi	Do.	
	Náimáwádi	Do.	
	Saodágar	Do.	
	Sidki	Do.	
302.	**Tágwále**	**Hindu**	113
	Fadewiknár	Do.	
	Kewat	Do.	
	Pardeshi	Do.	
	Tág Karnár	Do.	
303.	**Tákankár (Takári).**	**Hindu**	5,414
	Báori	Do.	
	Chhatrapati	Do.	
	Dábhe	Do.	
	Dábiráo	Do.	
	Gawári	Do.	
	Ghádfod	Do.	
	Gujar	Do.	
	Hongare	Do.	
	Kaikádi	Do.	
	Khudikán	Do.	
	Kutwád	Do.	
	Maráthe	Do.	
	Pawár	Do.	
	Ráj	Do.	
	Rám	Do.	
	Ráone	Do.	
	Ráthode	Do.	
	Sálanki	Do.	
	Sanbiyás	Do.	
	Siri	Do.	
	Sisob	Do.	
304.	**Takári**	**Hindu** (*See* Tákankár.)	
	Gujráthe	Do.	
	Shikári	Do.	
305.	**Tálkute**	**Hindu**	18
	Kápdi	Do.	
306.	**Támbatkár**	**Hindu**	590
	Beswe	Do.	
	Bhukiá	Do.	
	Deogan	Do.	
	Jiráit	Do.	
	Hásne	Do.	
	Nemádkar	Do.	
	Panchlam	Do.	
	Sák	Do.	
	Tavashtik	Do.	
307.	**Támboli**	**Hindu**	754
	Támboli	**Musalmán**	11
	Cháresi	Hindu.	
	Maráthe	Do.	
	Mitkari	Do.	
	Shekh	Musalmán.	
	Suryawanshi	Hindu.	
308.	**Tarkihár**	**Hindu**	1
309.	**Telangá**	**Hindu**	2,081
	Boche	Do.	
	Shripadsár	Do.	
	Támilwár	Do.	
310.	**Teli**	**Hindu**	82,069
	Teli	**Musalmán**	17
	Teli	**Sikh**	1
	Teli	**Animistic**	8
	Andelá	Hindu.	
	Ardal	Do.	
310.	**Teli**—*contd.*		
	Ardiwále	Hindu.	
	Balyáhut	Do.	
	Banárase	Do.	
	Bankari	Do.	
	Banjári	Do.	
	Baone	Do.	
	Bardale	Do.	
	Bayán	Do.	
	Bhagat	Do.	
	Bhokne	Do.	
	Bhusáre	Do.	
	Bile	Do.	
	Chhatarpure	Do.	
	Chokhámelá	Do.	
	Dáble	Do.	
	Dakhane	Do.	
	Dhánar	Do.	
	Dhopre	Do.	
	Dikshiwant	Do.	
	Dubaile	Do.	
	Ekbaili	Do.	
	Erande	Do.	
	Gaoli	Do.	
	Gatafane	Do.	
	Ghánáde	Do.	
	Gharbári	Do.	
	Godel Teli	Do.	
	Gujráthi Sugandhi.	Do.	
	Gulále	Do.	
	Gulháni	Do.	
	Gulod	Do.	
	Hátgháne	Do.	
	Jaunpuri	Do.	
	Jaysinge	Do.	
	Jeswár	Do.	
	Jhadiwále	Do.	
	Jhádpe	Do.	
	Kabir	Do.	
	Kadál	Do.	
	Kalál	Do.	
	Kanted	Do.	
	Káode	Do.	
	Káple	Do.	
	Kane	Do.	
	Lád	Do.	
	Ládhodi	Do.	
	Láthod	Do.	
	Lavel	Do.	
	Lingáyet	Do.	
	Lokhande	Do.	
	Mádle	Do.	
	Máhákál	Do.	
	Máne	Do.	
	Mánsote	Do.	
	Maráthe	Do.	
	Marchi	Do.	
	Math	Do.	
	Mathir Pardeshi	Do.	
	Meháre	Do.	
	More Sugandhi	Do.	
	Nágpure	Do.	
	Nimkáthe	Do.	
	Nirápure	Do.	
	Pardeshi	Do.	
	Pund	Do.	
	Rále	Do.	
	Ráne	Do.	
	Rangde	Do.	
	Ráoji	Do.	
	Ráo Ráthod	Do.	
	Ráthod	Do.	
	Ráya Ráthod	Do.	
	Sáoji	Do.	
	Serde	Do.	
	Sheti	Do.	
	Shrinagar	Do.	
	Sipá Pardeshi	Do.	
	Sipni	Do.	
	Sitbháte	Do.	
	Sivalkar	Do.	
	Sugandhi	Do.	
	Taráne	Do.	
	Taráte	Do.	
	Telangi	Do.	
	Tilwan	Do.	
	Ugháde	Do.	
	Vasankár	Do.	
	Váshe	Do.	
	Vishe	Do.	
	Vyawáháre	Do.	
	Wánkhede	Do.	
311.	**Thaenak**	**Hindu**	1
	Rájguru	Do.	
312.	**Thákur**	**Hindu**	5,099
	Arakh	Do.	
	Badiyá	Do.	
	Bais	Do.	
	Bardiyá	Do.	
	Basgod	Do.	
	Báwangoti	Do.	
	Beher	Do.	
	Beján	Do.	
	Bhádgalgopi	Do.	
	Bhásle	Do.	
	Bhátariyá	Do.	
312.	**Thákur**—*contd.*		
	Bhopál	Hindu.	
	Bichi	Do.	
	Bramha Bhát	Do.	
	Budhe Bhát	Do.	
	Budhel	Do.	
	Chamle	Do.	
	Chandan Thákur	Do.	
	Davheno	Do.	
	Deviputra	Do.	
	Disot	Do.	
	Durasband	Do.	
	Gáo Thákur	Do.	
	Gautam	Do.	
	Gopál	Do.	
	Gor	Do.	
	Gosávi	Do.	
	Jháde	Do.	
	Katariyá	Do.	
	Kshatri	Do.	
	Madáse	Do.	
	Nemáde	Do.	
	Pardeshi	Do.	
	Pawár	Do.	
	Rajayáni	Do.	
	Rajput	Do.	
	Rajwat	Do.	
	Rán Thákur	Do.	
	Sanak	Do.	
	Sáonak	Do.	
	Segar	Do.	
	Shekpál	Do.	
	Sheluk	Do.	
	Singrol	Do.	
	Somwansi	Do.	
	Táodi	Do.	
	Tilokchandi	Do.	
	Wánkhede	Do.	
313.	**Thoti**	**Hindu**	43
	Thoti	**Animistic**	183
	Burud Thoti	Do.	
314.	**Tirmale**	**Hindu**	449
	Akarmáse	Do.	
	Páras	Do.	
	Phule	Do.	
315.	**Udási**	**Hindu**	109
	Udási	**Sikh**	2
	Abnási	Hindu.	
	Bárghane	Do.	
	Bramhacháriya	Do.	
	Dhorode	Do.	
	Gharbári	Do.	
	Gurunának	Do.	
	Kshatri	Do.	
	Mále-Khali	Do.	
	Nánakshábi	Do.	
	Panáwar	Do.	
	Sangat Sobat	Do.	
	Satnámi	Do.	
316.	**Vellálár**	**Hindu**	17
	Sanjá Vellálár	Do.	
317.	**Vidur (Krishnapakshi).**	**Hindu**	10,691
	Vidur	**Jain**	4
	Boral	Hindu	
	Komtiyáche	Do.	
	Kshatriyache	Do.	
	Mádhejan	Do.	
	Raghuwanshi	Do.	
	Simpiyáche	Do.	
318.	**Virbhadra**	**Hindu**	44
	Maráthe	Do.	
319.	**Waddar**	**Hindu**	6,116
	Bengar	Do.	
	Dukar	Do.	
	Firaste	Do.	
	Gádi Waddar	Do.	
	Ganjál	Do.	
	Gaud	Do.	
	Girhe	Do.	
	Jádho	Do.	
	Jápal	Do.	
	Játekarnár	Do.	
	Kojar	Do.	
	Máli	Do.	
	Máti Waddar	Do.	
	Mhaski	Do.	
	Mohore	Do.	
	Pendhári	Do.	
	Powár	Do.	
	Rán Waddar	Do.	
	Ságare	Do.	
	Siple	Do.	
320.	**Wádhi**	**Hindu** (*See* Sutár).	

No.	Caste	Religion	Number
321.	**Wághade**	Hindu	2
	Játekar	Do.	
322.	**Wághe**	Hindu	47
	Akarmáse	Do.	
323.	**Walher**	Hindu	4
	Maráthe	Do.	
324.	**Wáni (Baniyá and Márwádi)**	Hindu	50,270
	Wáni (Do.)	Jain	13,260
	Wáni	Sikh	3
	Agarwálá	Hindu.	
	Akarmáse	Do.	
	Badnure	Do.	
	Bagde	Do.	
	Do.	Jain.	
	Bangarwál	Do.	
	Batwá Lingait	Hindu.	
	Benore	Do.	
	Bháttiyá	Do.	
	Boral	Do.	
	Bráhmanjai	Do.	
	Chándak	Do.	
	Chhatarpure	Do.	
	Cháwde	Do.	
	Chilwant	Do.	
	Chitode	Do.	
	Chopde	Do.	
	Dasewesadar	Do.	
	Dendu Lád	Do.	
	Dikshit	Do.	
	Dikshiwant	Do.	
	Dusar Wáni	Do.	
	Gangarwál	Jain.	
	Gavaye	Hindu.	
	Gaoli	Do.	
	Ghuskar	Do.	
	Gujrathi	Do.	
	Guleehá	Do.	
	Harset	Do.	
	Hátgar	Do.	
	Káju	Do.	
	Kákariyá	Do.	
	Kánadi	Do.	
	Káthar	Do.	
	Kesar Wáni	Do.	
	Kesheo Nand	Do.	
	Kewne	Do.	
	Khadewál	Do.	
	Khandalwál	Do.	
	Khariyá	Do.	
	Kombare	Do.	
	Komti	Do.	
	Kulwant	Do.	
	Lád	Do.	
	Lakhári	Do.	
	Lingáit	Do.	
	Márwádi	Do.	
	Mathpati	Do.	
	Meghal	Do.	
	Mahesri	Do.	
	Mitkari	Do.	
324.	**Wáni**—*contd.*		
	Mol	Hindu.	
	Mor	Do.	
	Mudadá	Do.	
	Nevi	Jain.	
	Oswál	Hindu.	
	Do.	Jain.	
	Pancham	Hindu.	
	Pitámbari	Do.	
	Popat	Do.	
	Porwád	Do.	
	Punam	Do.	
	Purád	Do.	
	Purwár	Do.	
	Rásod	Do.	
	Rásot	Do.	
	Ráthi	Do.	
	Sadáwarte	Do.	
	Saitwál	Do.	
	Sarásak	Do.	
	Sekati	Do.	
	Shekháwati	Do.	
	Shráwak	Do.	
	Shráwgi	Jain.	
	Tákalekar	Do.	
	Tákarkár	Do.	
	Tengráj	Do.	
	Tirale	Do.	
	Ukársare	Do.	
	Umar	Do.	
	Ume	Do.	
	Vidur	Do.	
	Warbad	Do.	
	Vayál	Do.	
	Virshaiva	Do.	
325.	**Wanjári**	Hindu	31,802
	Akarmáse	Do.	
	Bago	Do.	
	Bhákre	Do.	
	Bhardi	Do.	
	Bhosárni	Do.	
	Dakhane	Do.	
	Gautam	Do.	
	Ghátole	Do.	
	Ghune	Do.	
	Gojil	Do.	
	Hendre	Do.	
	Kachute	Do.	
	Kájin	Do.	
	Karále	Do.	
	Káse	Do.	
	Kelukh	Do.	
	Korá	Do.	
	Kunbi	Do.	
	Lád	Do.	
	Láderao	Do.	
	Ládjen	Do.	
	Ládjin	Do.	
	Ládvan	Do.	
	Málwe	Do.	
	Maráthe	Do.	
	Márgil	Do.	
	Mul	Do.	
	Nángre	Do.	
	Paole	Do.	
	Patáre	Do.	
	Pawár	Do.	
	Rájin	Do.	
325.	**Wanjári**—*contd.*		
	Ráo	Hindu.	
	Ráojin	Do.	
	Ráone	Do.	
	Ráonit	Do.	
	Sheole	Do.	
	Takar Wanjári	Do.	
	Tilole	Do.	
	Udtyá	Do.	
	Wadibhare	Do.	
326.	**Wárik**	Hindu	(*See* Mháli.)
327.	**Warthi (Dhobi and Parit).**	Hindu	23,075
	Warthi (Do.)	Musalmán	6
	Badhyá	Hindu.	
	Banwár	Do.	
	Báone	Do.	
	Bhátao	Do.	
	Bhoyar	Do.	
	Bundhale	Do.	
	Gadewálá	Do.	
	Gangápanthe	Do.	
	Ghongde	Do.	
	Gosákhe	Do.	
	Hindustáni	Do.	
	Lonárkar	Do.	
	Maháráshtra	Do.	
	Márwádi Dhobi	Do.	
	Nemádi	Do.	
	Pardeshi	Do.	
	Purbhaye	Do.	
	Ráut	Do.	
	Sheoni	Do.	
	Shráogi	Do.	
	Singáre	Do.	
	Telangi	Do.	
	Waráde	Do.	
328.	**Wásudeo**	Hindu	314
	Kolán	Do.	
	Maráthe	Do.	
	Ráj Gurao	Do.	
	Topiwále	Do.	
	Wághe	Do.	
	Wándeo	Do.	
329.	**Watankár**	Hindu	(*See* Otári.)
	Watankár	Animistic	(*See* Otári.)
	Máne	Hindu.	
	Do.	Animistic.	
330.	**Windhewár**	Hindu	(*See* Bhoi.)
331.	**Yelamá**	Hindu	495
	Akarmáse	Do.	
	Padmanáth	Do.	
	Vidur	Do.	
332.	**Unrecognizable**	Hindu	140
	Do.	Musalmán	11
	Do.	Unspecified.	1

CHAPTER XI.

OCCUPATIONS.

THE distribution of the population by occupation, or more correctly by their means of livelihood, is shown in the three parts of Table XVII. Part A gives the details by sex and certain age-periods for the whole province and for the urban and rural populations respectively; Part B shows the distribution by districts; and Part C shows the numbers and occupations of those who combine agriculture with other undertakings.

The occupations have been classified according to the scheme given below, which has been framed with the object of embracing the general distribution in India. There are first 7 main classes, to one or other of which all occupations may be assorted. These general heads comprise 24 orders which the Census Commissioner has described as follows :—

The first few explain themselves. As regards the seventh, eighth, ninth, tenth, and eleventh, the object the article or service is intended for is placed more prominently than the material dealt with. On the other hand from the twelfth to the seventeenth, the latter is regarded as more characteristic of the occupation than the object for which the prepared article is intended. The distribution is, of course, conventional only and not economic, as in both orders the makers and the sellers of an article are combined, and it is only in the eighteenth order that special mention is made of those who return themselves as exclusively engaged in distribution.

The orders are divided into 77 sub-orders, some of which are further subdivided into groups, and to the sub-orders or groups are appropriated the typical descriptions, upwards of 500 in number, which apply to the individual occupations returned.

GENERAL SCHEME OF CLASSIFICATION OF MEANS OF LIVELIHOOD.

Class.	Order.	Sub-order and group, where any.	
A. GOVERNMENT	I. ADMINISTRATION	1. Service of the Imperial and Provincial Governments.	
		2. Service of Local and Municipal Bodies.	
		3. Village service.	
	II. DEFENCE	4. Army.	
		5. Navy and Marine.	
	III. FOREIGN AND FEUDATORY STATE SERVICE.	6. Administrative service.	
		7. Military and other service.	
B. PASTURE AND AGRICULTURE.	IV. PROVISION AND CARE OF CATTLE.	8. Stock breeding and dealing.	(a) *Horses and horned cattle.*
			(b) *Other draught animals.*
			(c) *Small cattle.*
		9. Subsidiary services in connection with animals.	(a) *Training and care of cattle.*
			(b) *Vermin destroying.*
	V. AGRICULTURE	10. Interest in land.	
		11. Agricultural labour.	
		12. Growth of special produce, of trees, etc.	
		13. Agricultural training and supervision.	
C. PERSONAL SERVICES.	VI. PERSONAL, HOUSEHOLD, AND SANITARY SERVICES.	14. Personal and domestic services.	
		15. Non-domestic entertainment.	
		16. Sanitation.	

Class.	Order.	Sub-order and group, where any.
D. PREPARATION AND SUPPLY OF MATERIAL SUBSTANCES.	VII. FOOD AND DRINK, ETC.	17. Animal food.
		18. Vegetable food.
		19. Drinks, condiments, and narcotics.
	VIII. LIGHT, FIRING, AND FORAGE.	20. Lighting.
		21. Fuel and forage.
	IX. BUILDINGS . .	22. Building materials.
		23. Artificers in building.
	X. VEHICLES AND VESSELS.	24. Railway plant.
		25. Carts, carriages, etc.
		26. Ships and boats.
	XI. SUPPLEMENTARY REQUIREMENTS.	27. Paper.
		28. Books and prints.
		29. Watches, clocks, and scientific instruments.
		30. Carving and engraving.
		31. Toys and curiosities.
		32. Music and musical instruments.
		33. Necklaces, garlands, sacred threads, bracelets, and beads, etc.
		34. Furniture.
		35. Harness.
		36. Tools and Machinery.
		37. Arms and Ammunition.
	XII. TEXTILE FABRICS AND DRESS.	38. Wool and Fur.
		39. Silk.
		40. Cotton.
		41. Hemp, flax and coir, etc.
		42. Dress.
	XIII. METALS AND PRECIOUS STONES.	43. Gold, silver, and precious stones.
		44. Brass, copper, and bell metal.
		45. Tin, zinc, quicksilver, and lead.
		46. Iron and steel.
	XIV. GLASS, POTTERY, AND STONEWARE.	47. Glass and China ware.
		48. Earthen and stoneware.
	XV. WOOD, CANE AND LEAVES, ETC.	49. Wood and Bamboos.
		50. Cane, matting, and leaves, etc.
	XVI. DRUGS, DYES, GUMS, ETC.	51. Gums, Resins and similar Forest produce.
		52. Drugs, dyes, pigments, etc.
	XVII. LEATHER . .	53. Leather, horns, bones, and grease.
E. COMMERCE, TRANSPORT, AND STORAGE.	XVIII. COMMERCE . .	54. Money and Securities.
		55. General merchandise.
		56. Dealing unspecified.
		57. Middlemen . (*a*) *Brokers, agents.*
		(*b*) *Contractors, Farmers.*
	XIX. TRANSPORT AND STORAGE.	58. Railway . (*a*) *Administration.*
		(*b*) *Working staff.*
		59. Road . . (*a*) *Carts, carriages, trams, etc.*
		(*b*) *Pack animals.*
		60. Water . (*a*) *Vessel owners, Agents, etc.*
		(*b*) *Working staff.*
		61. Messages . (*a*) *Postal and other messengers.*
		(*b*) *Telegraph and Telephone.*
		62. Storage and weighing.
F. PROFESSIONS.	XX. LEARNED AND ARTISTIC PROFESSIONS.	63. Religion . (*a*) *Priests, ministers, etc.*
		(*b*) *Subsidiary religious services.*
		64. Education.
		65. Literature.
		66. Law.
		67. Medicine . (*a*) *Practitioners.*
		(*b*) *Subsidiary medical services.*
		68. Engineering and Survey. (*a*) *Engineers and surveyors.*
		(*b*) *Subsidiary staff.*
		69. Other sciences (*Astronomy and natural sciences.*
		(*b*) *Minor sciences.*
		70. Pictorial art, sculpture, etc.
		71. Music, acting, and dancing.

Class.	Order.	Sub-order and group, where any,	
F. PROFESSIONS —*concld.*	XXI. Sport and Amusements.	72. Sport.	(a) *Catching, training, and exhibiting animals.*
		73. Exhibitions and games.	(b) *Conjuring, fortune-telling, and similar exhibitions.*
			(c) *Acrobatic and athletic exhibitions.*
			(d) *Service of places of entertainment.*
G. INDEFINITE AND INDEPENDENT.	XXII. Complex Occupations.	. . . .	(*To be subdivided provincially.*)
	XXIII. Indefinite.	74. Unskilled labour.	(a) *Earthwork and special branches of labour.*
			(b) *General unskilled labour.*
		75. Undefined and disreputable means of livelihood.	
	XXIV. Independent of work.	76. Property and Alms.	(a) *Property and allowances.*
			(b) *Charity and endowments.*
		77. At the Public charge.	(a) *Pensions.*
			(b) *Prisoners, etc.*

As the people described their occupations in their own words it may be conceived that the variety of expressions used was very large, and as a fact more than 4,000 different designations were abstracted. A considerable proportion of these were synonymous terms, but when these were eliminated, there still remained a large number with some definite distinction between them. For the purpose of classification, however, these distinctions have not been preserved beyond the typical heads which have been adopted.

Explanatory.

To some extent the expression " occupation " is misleading. The enumerators' instructions were to enter the exact occupations or means of livelihood of all those who worked or lived on private property, etc., and, in the case of women or children who did not support themselves, the occupations of those upon whom they were dependent. In the tables no distinction has been made between the workers and the dependents, and the figures, therefore, do not represent the actual numbers of those employed in the different occupations, but of those who are supported by them. Thus in the first sub-order, 265 persons are shown against the occupation of " officers, " which does not mean that there are actually 265 officers, but that the officers with their families and dependents number so many. Under these circumstances the age-periods in Part A do not seem to be of much value. Were the actual workers shown separately, it would be of some interest to know the numbers of those under 15 years of age who were engaged in any particular calling, or of those above 15 years of age who were still dependent on others, but as matters stand I am not aware what information is derivable from the age distribution. Certainly the numbers of those under 5 years of age may be regarded as all dependents and non-workers, but it cannot be assumed that all those between 5 and 14 are non-workers, or that all those of 15 years of age and over are workers. The same may be said of the distribution by sex. The tables do not show the numbers of each sex who are actually employed, and although it may be presumed that nearly all the adult males are actively engaged, for adult females only very general deductions can be arrived at. We know that more males than females have been enumerated, and therefore if more females than males are shown for any occupation it may be deduced that some independent females are actually employed in it, besides the numbers of those who are dependent on the males returned ; in the same way if the number of males is largely in excess, it may be presumed that the females are not actual workers. With these remarks I may proceed to examine the figures, and it will be understood that unless the contrary is expressly stated the numbers quoted will have reference to the aggregates of workers and dependents and not to the actual workers only.

Class proportions.

The proportions of the population supported in each class are given in the following statement. To Class B, that of pasture and agriculture, belong nearly three-fourths of the population. Class D, that of the preparation and supply of material substances, claims nearly one-seventh. The Government of the province provides for 3 per cent, which is a little more than the proportion supported by commerce and the distribution of material. Personal service comes next, and the professions, learned or otherwise, come last, the class of indefinite or independent occupations accounting for a larger proportion than any but the first two. In the agricultural and indefinite classes the proportions of the females are greater than those of the males.

Statement No. 72,

Showing Percentage in each Class.

	Total.	Male.	Female.
Class A . . .	3·05	3·61	2·47
„ B . . .	69·76	68·43	71·18
„ C . . .	2·50	2·60	2·38
„ D . . .	13·88	14·34	13·39
„ E . . .	2·84	3·31	2·34
„ F . . .	1·38	1·64	1·10
„ G . . .	6·59	6·07	7·14

District characteristics.

The proportions for each class in the different districts are shown in the adjoining Statement No. 73. In the class of Government the percentage on the total population varies from 3·76 in Ellichpur to 2·42 in Amraoti; as Amraoti is in most respects the first district in importance, it is curious that it should come last in the proportions of this class; the high proportion in Ellichpur is due to the presence of troops. Among males the percentage varies from 4·52 in Ellichpur to 2·91 in Wun; and among females from 3·05 in Buldana to 1·86 in Amraoti. In the second or agricultural class Wun has the highest, and Ellichpur the lowest proportions for each and both sexes. In the personal service class the proportion varies from 2·86 per cent in Ellichpur to 2·08 in Basim; Wun has the highest proportion among females, and in both Buldana and Basim the proportion of females is higher than that of males. In the class for material substances Ellichpur is first with a markedly high proportion, and Basim is last. In the commercial class Amraoti comes first closely followed by Akola where the percentage among males is highest; the proportion in Wun is distinctly below the rest. In the professional class Amraoti again comes first and Wun also the last; Ellichpur takes a slight lead of Akola, and Buldana of Basim. In the indefinite class the proportions in Buldana and Basim are very high, especially amongst females. The general features then are, that the Ellichpur District is distinguished by the numbers supported by the preparation and supply of material substances and of those engaged in Government and personal service, Amraoti by the commercial and professional classes, and Wun by the predominance of agriculture.

Statement No. 73,

Showing percentage in each class of occupation for each district.

		Amraoti.	Akola.	Ellichpur.	Buldana.	Wun.	Basim.
Class A	Total	2·42	3·15	3·76	3·70	2·49	3·26
	Males	2·95	3·72	4·52	4·34	2·91	3·74
	Females . . .	1·86	2·54	2·94	3·05	2·06	2·74
Class B	Total	70·12	68·34	64·63	68·90	74·83	70·41
	Males	67·99	66·90	63·38	68·32	73·55	69·00
	Females . . .	72·41	69·88	65·97	69·50	76·17	71·27
Class C	Total	2·52	2·61	2·86	2·20	2·73	2·08
	Males	2·66	2·93	3·13	2·07	2·87	1·94
	Females . . .	2·37	2·27	2·57	2·33	2·58	2·22

Statement No. 73—*contd.*

Showing percentage in each class of occupation for each district—contd.

		Amraoti.	Akola.	Ellichpur.	Buldana.	Wun.	Basim.
Class D	Total	14·59	14·38	19·30	12·56	12·30	11·16
	Males	15·39	14·56	19·35	12·79	13·12	11·58
	Females	13·72	14·19	19·26	12·31	11·44	10·73
Class E	Total	3·47	3·44	2·49	2·62	1·51	3·03
	Males	4·01	4·13	2·88	3·03	1·68	3·52
	Females	2·38	2·69	2·07	2·20	1·33	2 51
Class F	Total	1·75	1·43	1·46	1·26	1·04	1·17
	Males	2·09	1·69	1·71	1·49	1·26	1·36
	Females	1·39	1·15	1·18	1 01	·80	·97
Class G	Total	5·13	6·65	5·50	8·76	5·10	8·89
	Males	4·91	6·07	5·03	7·96	4·61	8·26
	Females	5·37	7·28	6·01	9·60	5·62	9·56

Urban and rural features.

The urban and rural populations are distributed in the following proportions :—

	Urban.	Rural.
Class A	5·48	2·71
,, B	35·66	74·61
,, C	4·86	2·16
,, D	32·20	11·28
Class E	8·95	1·97
,, F	3·55	1·07
,, G	9·30	6·20

Three-fourths of the rural population it is seen are entirely supported by agriculture, and it is to be noted that this number does not include those who combine agriculture with some other occupation. The proportion of the urban population dependent upon agriculture is also high, but many of the smaller towns are merely overgrown villages of a distinctly rural character. In every other class the proportion in the urban population is much higher than in the rural.

No satisfactory comparison can be made with the general divisions returned in 1881, as a different method of classification has been adopted, and also because while the tables for 1881 do show the numbers of the actual workers of each sex, they do not show the numbers dependent upon the various means of livelihood, but in some cases the details of the occupations, which will now be examined in the order of their occurrence, will yield to some approximate comparison.

Order 1, Administration.—This includes those who are engaged in the service of the Provincial Government, of Local and Municipal bodies, and of village administration, but does not include those employed in the special functions of the State, such as Education, Sanitation, Medical practice, Engineering, the Postal Department, etc, which are separately shown under their appropriate designations. The order contains 86,464 persons or 2·98 per cent of the total population. Sub-order 1, the service of the Provincial Government, contains 20,594 persons or ·71 per cent; a large majority are messengers and menials, whose families comprise about two-fifths of the whole number; the Police rank and file with their families account for one-fourth. The second sub-order, the service of Local and Municipal bodies, numbers 1,559 or ·05 per cent; they are mostly menials. Sub-order 3, Village service, numbers 64,311 or 2·22 per cent, and includes patels, not being agriculturists, patwaris, and jaglias. It is probable that comparatively few of the hereditary village menials are comprised,

Sub-order 1.

Sub-order 2.

Sub-order 3.

as unless they were specifically described as in village service they would be classed under the general designation, and as they often have other occupations to which their village offices are secondary, the latter would not, under the rules (see page cxc), be enumerated at all. It seems probable also that the number of non-agricultural village headmen or patels is incorrect; patels if not actually cultivators have generally some landed interest in their villages, and all such should have returned their agricultural connection and have been included in Order V.

It is in this sub-order and under the head of "Watchmen and other menials" that the explanation is to be found of the small proportion of Class A in the Amraoti District which was remarked above. The proportions in each district of "Watchmen, etc," (and their dependents) is as follows: Buldana 299 in 10,000 of the district population; Basim 249; Ellichpur 230; Akola 224; Wun 191; and Amraoti 165. For each inhabited village there are in Buldana 16, in Akola 13, in Basim 12, in Amraoti 10, in Ellichpur 9, and in Wun 7. Whether there are such actual differences in the village service is a question which can if necessary be better solved by direct enquiry.

Order II and Sub-order 4.

Order II, Defence, which is confined to Sub-order 4, Army, contains 1,959 persons of whom less than 900 are shown as males over 15 years of age, being officers and rank and file. They were mostly enumerated in the Ellichpur District, where Paratwada, the only military cantonment, is situated. Seven persons in 10,000 of the Province are dependent upon the Army for their support.

Order III.

Order III, Foreign and Feudatory State Service, contains but a few individuals who chanced to be in the province at the time of the enumeration. These three orders comprise Class A.

Order IV. Stock breeding and dealing.

Class B, pasture and agriculture, consists of Orders IV and V. Order IV Live-stock, contains 35,078 persons, or 1·21 per cent of the population, who are dependent upon stock-breeding and dealing or subsidiary services to stock. A very large proportion of these are herdsmen or shepherds. The numbers returned as cattle or buffalo breeders and dealers afford no indication of the extent of these occupations, as they are in general subsidiary to agriculture or any other occupation; every Berari owns a cow or a buffalo as every Irishman keeps a pig. Pig-breeding here, as a means of livelihood, has very few followers, and there are not many who depend upon horses or camels. Only 20 males over 15 years of age are returned as farriers, and 18 of these belong to the towns chiefly of the Akola and Ellichpur Districts; these figures point to the very small use made of the horse, but a horse as distinct from a pony is rarely met with and the smaller equine animal generally goes unshod. The occupation of herdsman is most largely followed in the Wun District, the grazing facilities of which have been previously noticed; those who are dependent upon this source of livelihood number 8,176 or 173 in 10,000 of the population; in Ellichpur there are 114 in 10,000, a large proportion of whom presumably belong to the Melghat; in Amraoti the proportion is 74, in Basim 65, in Buldana 61, and in Akola 59. In Buldana the number of shepherds and sheep breeders is conspicuous as it was in 1881; ass and mule-breeding find more followers in Ellichpur than any where and the only pig breeders are in Amraoti.

Order V.

Order V, agriculture, relates to the main occupation of the province. It consists of four sub-orders, those who have an interest in land, agricultural labourers, growers of special products and trees, and those engaged in agricultural training and supervision, which last is statistically of no importance. The order contains 1,986,265 persons or 68·55 per cent of the total population. In addition to these Part C shows that 23,121 persons are concerned in agriculture in combination with some other occupation, so that 2,009,386 persons or 69·35 per cent of the population are more or less dependent for their livelihood upon agriculture apart from the breeding of stock.

Sub-order 10.

Sub-order 10, of those with some interest in land, contains 997,602 persons or 34·43 per cent of the population. Of these 10,967 or ·38 per cent are non-cultivating land occupants; 642,689 or 22·18 per cent are cultivating occupants, and 343,895 or 11·87 per cent are cultivating tenants or sharers. The proportion of non-cultivating occupants is seen to be comparatively very small, and this is a satisfactory indication that the land is not passing into the hands of money-lenders to any great extent, as it has in some other parts of the Deccan. The sharers in Berar are practically occupants and are not therefore properly classed with tenants, but there is no provision in the table for distinguishing between them. Taking the figures as they stand, it is seen that the occupants are to the tenants as about two to one, and allowing for the transfer of sharers from the one category to the other the proportion is greater still; in 1881 the actual numbers for the two classes were 157,146 occupants to 103,821 sharers and tenants, or about three to two, so that the proportion of occupants to sharers and tenants has largely increased, which is another satisfactory indication of the stability of the agricultural class.

Non-cultivating land occupants.

Sharers.

Proportion of occupants to tenants.

Sub-order 11. Agricultural labourers.

Sub-order 11, agricultural labourers, contains 986,644 persons or 34·05 per cent, which is almost identical with the number of the previous sub-order, or nearly a labourer for every land occupant or tenant. There is, however, considerable difference in the sexes of the two categories; in 10,000 persons of each sex 3,609 males and 3,267 females have an interest in land, whereas 3,042 males and 3,790 females are agricultural labourers; in other words, while probably but a few females have an interest in land independently of the males of their families, a number of females are actual and independent labourers; in fact, it may be assumed that nearly all the females as well as the males of 15 years and over shown in sub-order 11 are actual workers, and in addition many of those under 15. The sub-order has been divided into farm servants and field labourers, etc, but it is doubtful whether the distinction is of much value here as the designations were very indifferently adopted at the enumeration. The adults of both classes aggregate 624,874, and of the land occupants and cultivators as well as of the labourers (that is sub-orders 10 and 11 combined or the agriculturists proper) they number 1,219,253 of both sexes. The corresponding class of actual occupants and workers in 1881 numbered 1,142,168, but many of these were boys and girls under 15 years of age. The Report says that of all the children under 15 years of age four-fifths of the boys and seventeen-twentieths of the girls were unemployed, and of the remainder more than four-fifths were engaged in some form of agricultural pursuit. Working out the processes here indicated it will be ascertained that the number of children so engaged was (about) 141, 841, and deducting these from the total gives 1,000,327 as the number of adult working agriculturists in 1881. The increment in the number now shown is therefore 218,926 on the supposition that all the adults, male and female, are actually employed. This is, of course, not the case, but allowing for the old and infirm and for a number of women of the richer class of occupants who do not work in the fields, it will be apparent that there has a been considerable increase. As there has been no corresponding increment in the extent of cultivation, it follows that the land has to support more people than it did ten years ago.

Numbers of agriculturists compared with those in 1881.

Statement No. 74.

Showing percentage of agricultural population on total of each district.

		Amraoti.	Akola.	Ellichpur.	Buldana.	Wun.	Basim.
ORDER V	Total	69·09	67·45	63·26	67·71	72·79	69·51
	Males	66·35	65·53	61·33	66 58	70·52	68·21
	Females	72·06	69·50	65·33	68·87	75·17	70 88
SUB-ORDER 10	Total	27·27	36·10	30 09	42·62	30·05	42·59
	Males	28·59	37·27	31·01	43·86	33·67	44·49
	Females	25·84	34·85	29·09	41 33	26·24	40·57
" 11	Total	41·72	31·28	33·10	25·03	42·69	26·88
	Males	37·66	28·17	30·22	22·65	36·79	23·67
	Females	46·10	34·61	36·18	27·50	48·90	30·27
NON-CULTIVATING OCCUPANTS (37).	Total	·61	·41	·43	·10	·43	·19
	Males	·56	·40	·46	·10	·47	·20
	Females	·66	·42	·39	·10	·38	·19
CULTIVATING OCCUPANTS (38).	Total	20·27	25·25	21·65	26·95	15·91	23·00
	Males	20·68	25·51	21·64	27·58	16·98	23·78
	Females	19·83	24·97	21·65	26·30	14·79	22·17
TENANTS, ETC. (41)	Total	6·38	10·44	8·01	15 57	13·71	19·40
	Males	7·34	11·36	8·91	16·18	16·22	20·51
	Females	5·34	9·46	7·05	14 93	11·07	18·21

Composition of district conditions.

The district conditions are compared in Statement No. 74. Buldana has a very small proportion of non-cultivating land occupants and Basim has considerably less than Akola, Ellichpur and Wun, where the proportions are very similar; Amraoti has a far higher proportion than the rest, and the fact is possibly due to a number of khatidars (or registered land occupants) finding employment in the professional or commercial business of the town. Of those who have an interest in land the proportions in Buldana and Basim are much above the average and in Amraoti much below. Buldana and Akola have the largest proportions of cultivating occupants and Wun a markedly smaller proportion than any other district, but of tenants and sharers Basim, Buldana, and Wun have the most; the difference between Basim and Amraoti in this category is striking. On the other hand Wun and Amraoti have a considerably larger proportion of agricultural labourers than the rest, and Basim and Buldana show the smallest. In the former districts the agricultural labourers largely outnumber the land occupants and tenants, while in the latter the reverse is the case, and the conditions are similarly contrasted, but to a much smaller extent in Ellichpur and Akola. These facts considered in the light of the immigration suggest that the immigrants from the Central Provinces are mostly agricultural labourers, and it is open to doubt whether they can be regarded as a permanent factor in the population; the census was taken at a time when agricultural operations were in full force, and it is possible that a large number of the immigrants in the Amraoti and Wun Districts were merely temporary visitors who returned to their homes after the crops were harvested. In 1881 also the proportion of agricultural labourers was highest in Wun and Amraoti, but there was not so much difference between these and the other districts as on this occasion. The influence of the influx of agricultural labourers upon the proportions of the agricultural population is suggested also by the comparisons shown in the following Statement No. 75, in which the distribution of the purely agricultural population is given, that is, of

Distribution of the agricultural population.

Statement No. 75,

Showing distribution by districts of the agricultural population.

	1881.	1891.
Amraoti	21·17	22·79
Akola	20·68	19·52
Ellichpur	10·70	10·06
Buldana	17·71	16·40
Wun	15·50	17.29
Basim	14·24	13·94

land occupants, tenants, and labourers, or sub-orders 10 and 11, which together represent the same class as the agriculturist category sub-order 1 in the tables of 1881 with the exception of the herdsmen whose numbers have been excluded from the comparison.

I will now attempt a comparison of the agricultural figures for each district in 1881 and 1891, but as the age-periods are not shown in the district table (Part B) I must adopt another method of procedure than that used above for obtaining a comparison between the figures for the province. In another place in the report for 1881 it is said that—

"Of field employés (males) about one quarter are boys—of those who work in fields belonging to the head of their house one-sixth of the males are boys—and of field labourers more than one-sixth of the males are boys."

For the purposes of this calculation I will, therefore, assume that one-fifth of the total agricultural males are boys in actual employment, which is possibly over the mark. Those under 5 years of age may be rejected as non-workers, and the numbers of those between 5 and 14 amount to 25 per cent of the whole, and this leaves only 5 per cent of the boys between those ages unemployed. The adults form sixty-one per cent of the whole and of these 9 per cent or 5 per cent of the whole are over 60 years of age, the majority of whom are probably past work. 61 *plus* 20 *minus* 5 gives 76, and as this is possibly too high a percentage, it may be calculated that the number of working male agriculturists is between 70 and 75 per cent of the whole number shown in the Table. On this basis the figures for 1891 work out as shown in the following statement, No. 76, where they are compared with the actuals for 1881. Although the results here obtained are based on a somewhat circuitous calculation which may be more or less faulty, and therefore cannot be accepted as positive facts, yet their value for purposes of comparison between the different districts is not affected as the error is common to all; and if they are at all approximately correct, they serve to indicate very clearly the source of the decrease in the total population of Akola and of the meagreness of the increase in Ellichpur. The Annual Administration Reports show that land in both districts has gone out of cultivation since 1881, and the agricultural population have gone with it. Whether the land has been voluntarily abandoned, or whether the agriculturists have moved elsewhere because the land has not been available, is a question which can only be answered by the Revenue authorities.

Decrease in Akola.

Statement No. 76.

Male Agricultural Workers.

District.	1881.	1891.		Difference.		Mean variation per cent.
		At 70 per cent.	At 75 per cent.	At 70 per cent.	At 75 per cent.	
Amraoti	145,025	157,774	169,043	+12,749	+24,018	+12·7
Akola	147,509	136,054	145,772	—11,455	— 1,737	— 4·5
Ellichpur	71,776	69,851	74,847	— 1,925	+ 3,071	+ 1·6
Buldana	110,988	113,992	122,134	+ 3,004	+11,146	+ 6·4
Wun	93,957	119,194	127,708	+25,237	+33,751	+31·4
Basim	90,981	97,717	104,697	+ 6,736	+13,716	+11·2

The number of persons returned as combining agriculture with some other occupation is 23,121 or 25 in 1,000 of the population not solely agricultural. Of these, 16,437 are land occupants, 3,435 tenants, and 3,249 farm servants or field-labourers. This number does not include patels who have been presumed to be agriculturists as a rule, and have been shown independently as patels in sub-order 3 when

Agriculture combined with other occupations.

not agriculturists. Of those who have returned dual occupations 20 per cent are money-lenders, 10 per cent are patwaris and village menials, 8 per cent belong to the sub-order of personal and domestic service, 6 per cent to that of cotton and to that of property and alms, 5 per cent are concerned in timber and wood, and also in drink and condiments, 4 per cent in religion and the same proportion in the supply of fuel and forage, and 3 per cent in oil-pressing, in the supply of dress materials, and in gold and silver work.

Of the whole number of money-lenders, 24 per cent are connected with agriculture, the greater number being returned as owners or occupants; four individuals have been shown as farm servants and field-labourers, and as money-lenders therefore they may be presumed not to operate on an extensive scale. Of those who are dependent upon house-rent or other property not land, 20 per cent are also concerned in agriculture. Of patwaris there are 17 per cent; of wood-cutters 12 per cent; of dealers in raw cotton, of priests and of pensioners, there are 9 per cent each; of sheep dealers 6 per cent; of barbers, oil-pressers, and general merchants, 5 per cent each; and of brass and copper smiths, grindstone menders, and religious mendicants, 4 per cent each; who are engaged in agriculture in combination with their other occupations.

Of the religious mendicants, 568 are returned as land occupants and 122 as tenants, and of ordinary beggars, 738 are occupants and 96 are tenants. These figures throw some light upon the curious ethics of begging in this country.

As field-labourers 18 midwives find additional employment; so also 111 shoe-makers and 233 tailors. Others who thus supplement their means of livelihood in any numbers are village menials, herdsmen, washermen and indoor servants, fishermen, firewood-gatherers and grass-cutters, cotton-cleaners and spinners, wood-cutters, bullock-drivers, and village musicians.

Sub-order 12.
Gardeners, etc.

The next sub-order 12, growers of special products and trees, numbers only 2,017 persons or ·07 per cent of the population. They comprise gardeners, fruit-growers, betel-vine and areca nut growers, and the employés in Government forests. Betel-vine, etc, growers are most numerous in the Amraoti District; fruit-growers in Buldana and Akola; and gardeners in Amraoti and Akola.

Order VI.

Class C, and Order VI, personal and household services, contain 72,301 persons or 2·50 per cent of the population. 2·60 per cent of the males and 2·38 of the females belong to this class and order, which comprises three sub-orders. Sub-order 14, personal and domestic services, contains 70,118 persons, of whom a large majority are indoor servants, barbers, and washermen. The male barbers number 13,233 and the females 8,050, and the latter are presumably all non-workers. Among washermen and indoor servants on the contrary females predominate. The sub-order is most numerous in Amraoti and least in Basim. The next sub-order, that of non-domestic establishments, contains only a few persons connected with lodging-houses, serais, etc. Sub-order 16 refers to sanitation and contains 2,088 persons who are mostly sweepers and scavengers, of whom nearly two-thirds belong to the towns.

Sub-order 14.
Barbers.

Sub-order 15.

Sub-order 16.

Order VII.

Class D, the preparation and supply of material substances, comprises 11 orders and 37 sub-orders. Order VII, food and drink, contains 84,002 persons or 2·90 per cent of the population; of the males there are 3·10 per cent and of the females 2·68 per cent. Sub-order 17 relates to animal food, and contains 25,295 persons, of whom more than half are fishermen, one-fourth are butchers, and more

Sub-order 17.
Fishermen, Butchers, and Dairymen.

than one-sixth are milk and buttermen. The dairymen are most numerous in Amraoti and Ellichpur; butchers in Akola and Amraoti; and fishermen in Wun and Amraoti. Among cow-keepers and milk-sellers the females predominate.

Sub-order 18. Grain dealers.

Sub-order 18 relates to vegetable food, and contains 19,692 persons, of whom 8,920 are grain dealers who are most numerous in Akola and Amraoti; grain parchers number 2,959, and more than one-third of these are found in Akola; pulse and flour sellers number 1,513 and are most numerous in Amraoti; bakers number only 116 and are almost confined to the urban population of Akola and Amraoti; vegetable sellers number 2,256 and are most numerous in Akola; fruit and sugarcane sellers number 1,387 and are most numerous in Ellichpur; in Wun their number is merely nominal; confectioners number 2,327, of whom a half are found in the towns and a large proportion in Amraoti and Akola. Wun and Basim are much below the average in the numbers of the sub-order generally.

Bakers. Vegetable sellers. Confectioners.

Sub-order 19. Country spirits.

Sub-order 19 deals with drink, condiments, and narcotics, and contains 39,015 persons. Country spirit distillers and sellers number 6,160, of whom 3,739 are males, and 2,421 are females. A large majority are found in the country, and they are most numerous in Wun and Amraoti; 844 persons are concerned in the tapping and drawing of toddy (tari), and of these the males are to the females as two to one; a large proportion are found in Amraoti and Basim, while in Akola, Ellichpur, and Buldana the numbers are nominal. The makers and sellers of jaggery and gur number 1,410 and are much more numerous in Wun than elsewhere, while in Basim there are very few. Dealers in salt number 615 who are distributed in much the same way. Asafœtida claims 238 persons, of whom 138 are in Wun where highly flavoured articles are apparently in good demand. Of pickle makers there are but a few in Amraoti and Basim, and they present the unusual feature of being all females. General grocers naturally form a large proportion of this sub-order; they number 19,852 and are found everywhere, but in conspicuously smaller numbers in Ellichpur than elsewhere. Of betel-leaf and areca-nut sellers there are 6,285, of whom nearly two-thirds are females; of adult males there are 1,417, and of adult females 3,073, and it is evident that this is specially a feminine occupation, more particularly in the towns; they are most numerous in Amraoti and fewest in Basim. Upon the manufacture and sale of tobacco and snuff are dependent 2,626 persons, of whom the largest numbers are found in Akola, Amraoti, and Wun. Opium dealers number 886, of whom one half are adult males, and females are seemingly not much concerned in the preparation or sale of the drug; they are most numerous in Wun where are also found 22 out of 26 concerned in the manufacture of ganja, etc., and these 22 are, it is curious to note, all females. The taste for highly flavoured condiments in Wun is apparently accompanied with a partiality for strong drinks and narcotics, and judging from the numbers of those whose livelihood depends upon the supply of these articles, this district is the most indulgent in the province as Buldana is the most abstemious.

Tari. Grocers. Betel-leaf sellers. Tobacconists.

Order VIII. Sub-order 20.

Order VIII, light, fuel and forage, contains 44,691 persons, or 1·54 per cent of the population. Sub-order 20, lighting, is almost confined to oil-pressers and sellers who number 16,311. There are 169 dealers in kerosine oil, and 104 persons, of whom 89 are males, are shown as match makers and sellers, but it is probable that they are sellers only and not makers.

Sub-order 21.
Firewood and grass sellers.

In sub-order 21 come the firewood and grass gatherers and sellers and firewood contractors and dealers between whom there is probably not much difference; the former number 19,903 and the latter 2,400, and in both categories the females largely outnumber the males. Of charcoal burners there are only 505, of whom 212 are adult males. There are 1,118 cow-dung fuel preparers, and of these 541 or nearly one half are adult females; 4,144 persons are shown as hay or grass contractors and dealers, and of these a considerable majority are females. Taking the grass-cutters and dealers and firewood and cow-dung sellers together there are 10 adult females to 7 adult males, and we find here therefore some distinctly female occupations.

Oil-pressers.

The oil-pressers are very generally distributed through the province with a larger proportion in Amraoti than elsewhere. Of the firewood and grass gatherers, contractors, and dealers, a conspicuously large proportion belong to Ellichpur owing no doubt to the Melghat forests. The charcoal burners are most numerous in Ellichpur and Akola; in Wun and Basim there is one individual each, which is remarkable having regard to the extent of forest lands in those districts. Of the yay and grass contractors, etc, Amraoti has a very large share.

Brick and tile burners.
Sub-order 22.
Order IX.

The next order, IX, buildings, contains 18,101 persons or ·62 per cent of the population. Sub-order 22 deals with building material. Of brick and tile burners there are 5,709, of whom three-fifths are adult males. Lime burners, etc, number 898 and thatchers only 67, of whom 27 are adult males; in 1881, 22 males were shown as actual workers in thatching, and as such small numbers as these could not possibly meet the requirements of the province, it seems that the occupation is generally combined with some other.

Sub-order 23.
Masons.

Sub-order 23 relates to artificers in buildings. Of masons there are 5,839, of whom the males largely outnumber the females; the number of adult males is 2,286, and most of these are probably actual workers. In 1881 the number was 1,266 males and 55 females, and the increase points to growth in the demand for brick-built houses in lieu of the common structure of mud. The number of mud-wall builders is 4,702, and, as constructions of mud are infinitely more numerous than those of brick or stone, the fact that there are a smaller number of mud-wall builders than of masons suggests that the people to a large extent build for themselves; the mass of the population are no doubt content with the very rudest of shelter. Stone-workers, that is, cutters and dressers, number 476, of whom 149 are adult males; 263 persons, of whom 111 are adult males, have been returned as builders and joiners, and 116 as plasterers and house painters. A large proportion of the lime burners, thatchers, masons, builders, and plasterers are found in the towns and the mud-wall builders belong mostly to the country. It is to be noted that there are no plumbers and glaziers and no tilers, work of the nature indicated by these callings being no doubt carried out, when requisite, by those included under the designations of builders and masons.

Mud-wall builders.

Of the brick burners nearly one-half are found in the Amraoti District; in Buldana and Basim the numbers are small, but there the mud-wall builders are most numerous. Lime burners are most numerous in Akola and Amraoti.

Order X.
Cart makers.

Order X, vehicles and vessels, contains only 292 persons of whom 151 are adult males; 101 of the adult males are cart makers, and they are nearly all found in the country and in the Amraoti district. The common country cart is apparently an article of home construction elsewhere in the province. Of boat builders, etc, there are none.

Order XI.
Sub-order 27.

Order XI, supplementary requirements of a miscellaneous character, contains 10,183 persons or ·35 per cent of the population. Sub-order 27, which relates to paper, etc, is represented by 111 paper makers and sellers, and 125 stationers, most of whom belong to the towns. The paper makers and sellers are nearly all found in Akola.

Sub-order 28.

Sub-order 28, books and prints, contains 314 persons; of the adult males 49 are returned as book-sellers, 35 as printers, 22 as print and picture dealers, and 17 as book-binders. Three adult males are shown as newspaper proprietors and managers. A large proportion of the book-sellers and print dealers are found in the country, and half the book-sellers in the Ellichpur District. The three southern districts are very barely represented in this sub-order. The next sub-order, No. 29, that relating to watches, clocks, and scientific instruments, contains but 33 persons, who with the exception of one individual in Buldana, who calls himself a scale maker, are all watch makers and sellers and are almost all found in Amraoti. It is curious that such a large town as that of Ellichpur with its neighbouring cantonment should not possess a single watch maker; possibly such work as cleaning and repairing of watches and clocks is there done by some of those who have been returned as gold and silver workers.

Sub-order 29.

Sub-order 30.

Sub-order 30, carving, engraving, etc, contains 160 persons, of whom 99 are turners and 52 granite stone workers. Wood carvers are represented by 6 persons and mica, flint, and talc workers by 3. There are no engravers. The turners are most numerous in Wun and Amraoti.

Sub-order 31.

Sub-order 31, toys, curiosities, etc, claims 379 persons, who are nearly all makers of kites and of little earthen dolls. The numbers of the females preponderate in this occupation. The majority belong to Akola and Amraoti.

Sub-order 32.

Sub-order 32 relating to musical instruments is almost as slenderly represented as that of watches. There are 27 dealers in music and musical instruments and 11 drum makers; 23 out of the 38 belong to Amraoti; there are none in Wun or Basim.

Sub-order 33.
Bangle makers, etc.

Sub-order 33 comprises bangle makers, beads and garland makers, and the makers and sellers of imitation jewellery. In the supply of such articles as these the numbers are comparatively strong. Of bangle makers in general and fitters, there are 6,358; of these, 674 are returned as working in lac, 22 in wood and bone, and 586 in glass, and it is probable that the majority who have not specified the material deal in bangles of clay. The fitters number 305 and a large majority of these are females. Makers and sellers of imitation jewellery number 498, among whom the males predominate. Of bead makers there are only 26 who are mostly male, and of rosary and necklace makers there are 8 who are all females. Flower garland makers number 464, among the adults of whom females are slightly in excess. A few spangle makers and dealers in sacred thread complete the numbers of the sub-order. These occupations are fairly distributed between town and country and between all districts with the exception of Wun where their numbers are small.

Sub-order 34.

In the next sub-order, No. 34, the numbers are very small. There are 19 furniture makers and five frame makers. The requirements of the country in these respects are very limited.

Sub-order 35.

Sub-order 35 relates to harness, and contains 484 persons, the majority of whom belong to the towns; a large proportion are found in Akola.

Sub-order 36.

Sub-order 36, relating to tools and machinery, numbers 875 persons; knife and tool makers and sellers number 66, and grinders 470; 77 adult males are returned as agricultural implement makers and 62 are shown indefinitely as mechanics. In the sub-order generally males largely predominate, and three-fifths of the total are found in Akola and Amraoti.

Sub-order 37.

Sub-order 37, arms and ammunition, contains 250 persons, of whom more than half are concerned in the manufacture and sale of gunpowder; 42 are gun sellers and menders, and the same number make fireworks. The Amraoti district claims a large proportion of the total number. This concludes Order XI.

Order XII. Sub-order 38. Blanket weavers.

Order XII relates to textile fabrics and dress, and contains 112,142 persons or 3·87 per cent of the population. In sub-order 38, wool and fur, there are 5,287 persons, of whom 4,827 are blanket weavers; 65 are woollen cloth manufacturers, and 272 are woollen yarn spinners; of the last named nearly all are females. 112 persons have been returned as fur dealers, but I think that this must be a mistake; the climate of Berar is not calculated to foster any local demand for furs. A large proportion of this sub-order belong to the country and to the Buldana district; in Basim also they are numerous, and in Ellichpur conspicuously few.

Sub-order 39.

Sub-order 39, silk, contains 1,891 persons, of whom 1,387 are spinners and 481 weavers. Among the spinners females predominate, and among the weavers males. These are apparently urban occupations, as two-thirds of the number are found in the towns. More than one-third belong to Amraoti.

Sub-order 40. Cotton-weavers. Ginners, etc.

The next sub-order, 40, relates to cotton, the staple commodity of the province; it numbers 71,905 persons, or 248 in every 10,000 of the population; 27,212 are cotton-weavers, among whom the adult males are to the adult females in the proportion of 10 to 7; 14,103 are cleaners and ginners, etc, and among these the conditions are more than reversed, the adult females being three times more numerous than the males. Spinners and sizers number 8,342 and among these the preponderance of females is greater still, the proportion of adult females to males being nearly 11 to 1. Of dealers in raw cotton there are 7,731, and 3,102 are adult males; 7,424 persons are cotton dyers among whom the males are but slightly in excess, but they preponderate again among the undefined cotton factory hands who number 4,883. Cotton carpet and rug (dhurrie) makers number 1,900, of whom 737 are adult males. Of calenderers and cotton printers there are but a nominal number. The Amraoti district claims the largest number of cotton cleaners and ginners, of dealers in raw cotton, of spinners, and of factory hands; Akola also has a considerable proportion in the same categories; Ellichpur has the largest number of weavers, and Buldana of dyers.

Cotton dealers. Dyers.

Sub-order 41.

Sub-order 41, jute, flax, coir, etc, contains 2,485 persons Makers of hemp-rope number 851, and are most numerous in Amraoti and Wun where the females also predominate, although they are not in excess among the total number, 1,587 persons are returned as makers of sacking, tarpaulin, and gunny; they are the makers and menders of the wonderful patchwork material in which the cotton is packed for market; a large majority are males, and it seems probable that women do not actively engage in this occupation. They are most numerous in Amraoti, and while there are considerable numbers in Basim, Akola, and Buldana, there are remarkably few in Ellichpur.

Sub-order 42.
Tailors.

Sub-order 42 is related with dress, and contains 30,574 persons; 12,139 are shown as tailors and darners and of these the female adults are slightly in excess of the male; 1,914 are out-fitters, among whom the males predominate and who mostly belong to the towns. They are conspicuously numerous in Ellichpur Embroiderers number 482 who are almost all females; even amongst children the proportion is very large, and it would seem that girls are employed in this occupation from a very early age; they are found in all districts. 15,973 persons are shown as piece-goods dealers; they are the ordinary cloth sellers found in all bazars and markets; of the adults 6,693 are males and only 3,864 females. A considerable proportion belong to the towns, but they are also very evenly distributed throughout the districts.

Cloth dealers.

Order XIII.
Sub-order 43.
Goldsmiths, etc.

Order XIII, metals and precious stones, contains 38,129 persons, or 1·32 per cent of the population. Of these, 21,260 belong to sub-order 43 which relates to gold, silver, and precious stones; 20,180 persons are returned as gold and silver workers; they are found in considerable numbers in both town and country and throughout all districts, but are most numerous in Amraoti and Akola. Gold and silver dealers number 394, of whom 170 are adult males; one-third of the number belong to Amraoti. There are a few electro-platers, nearly all adult males, who with one exception in Basim all belong to Amraoti. Of wire-drawers and plated-ware dealers the numbers are small and they are mostly adult males of whom a considerable proportion are found in Wun where they would not ordinarily be expected. Of pearl and precious stone dealers there are 326, of whom nearly a half belong to Amraoti. There were a few coral dealers returned in Wun who were probably travellers.

Sub-order 44.
Brass workers.

Sub-order 44, brass, copper, and bell-metal, numbers 3,099 persons. Of these 1,622 are brass and copper dealers among whom the adult males are twice as numerous as the adult females, the disparity being even more marked in the rural portion, especially in Akola where they are strongest. Brass pot makers are most numerous in Akola, and workers in bell-metal in Basim and Wun.

Sub-order 45.
Tin, etc.

The next sub-order contains 946 persons, of whom 849 are workers in tin; they are most numerous in Amraoti, but a considerable number belong to Wun. A few workers in zinc are found in the towns of the Amraoti and Akola Districts; 79 general workers in tin, lead and zinc have been returned in Wun.

Sub-order 46.
Blacksmiths.

Sub-order 46, iron and steel, contains 12,824 persons who are nearly all shown as blacksmiths. They are most numerous in Wun and Amraoti.

Order XIV.

Order XIV relates to glass, pottery, and stone-ware, and contains 18,884 persons or ·65 per cent of the population. Only 30 of these belong to the sub-order of glass and china-ware, and they are dealers. There are no glass-blowers or makers, and in this respect there is, I think, an opening in Berar which should be taken advantage of. Close to the town, or rather village, of Wun there is a considerable area covered with sand of an exquisite fineness and most delicate shades of colour. This is at present entirely unworked, and, although I am unable to speak with any special knowledge on the subject, I think it right to call attention here to this deposit which seems to me to consist of material admirably adapted to the manufacture of a very superior glass.

Sub-order 48. Potters.

Sub-order 48, earthen and stone-ware, numbers 18,854 persons. Of potters there are 15,921; of stone hand mill makers and menders 2,890; and of stone idol-makers and sellers 43. The potters are most numerous in Amraoti and fewest in Ellichpur; their workmanship is of the most inferior character. Of the stone mill makers a large proportion belong to Akola and considerable numbers to Buldana and Basim.

Order XV. Sub-order 49. Carpenters.

Order XV, relating to wood, cane, and leaves, etc, contains 48,149 persons or 1·66 per cent of the population. Sub-order 49, timber and wood, numbers 34,365, of whom 28,942 are shown as carpenters, and of these the adult males are nearly twice as numerous as the adult females. They are found in all parts but are most numerous in Amraoti and in considerably less numbers in Ellichpur than elsewhere. Their handiwork like that of the potters is of a very low standard. Timber and bamboo dealers number 2,819, and among them also the adult males largely predominate; more than three-fifths of the number are found in the Ellichpur district, and a considerable number in Akola; in Buldana, Wun, and Basim there are remarkably few. Of wood-cutters and sawers there are 2,531; the adult males number 1,302 and are more than three times as numerous as the females; a good proportion belong to the towns, and the numbers in Amraoti and Akola are much larger than elsewhere. Of coopers and box-makers there are a few who are mostly adult males and belong chiefly to Basim.

Sub-order 50.

Sub-order 50, cane-work, etc, claims 13,784 persons. Bamboo splitters and workers number 889 among whom females preponderate; basket-weavers number 6,573, the sexes being evenly balanced; of mat-makers there are 917 and the females are slightly in excess; broom makers and sellers number 4,795 among whom there are 4 adult females to 3 adult males. In all these categories the women actively engage in the occupations. Among leaf-plate makers who number 452, females are in a minority. Besides these there are a few brush-makers and tooth stick sellers who are mostly females. Bamboo-workers, basket-makers, and mat-makers are most numerous in Akola; most of the leaf-plate makers belong to Wun, and of the brush-makers to Ellichpur; Buldana has a large proportion of the broom-makers. The sub-order generally is principally represented in Akola and Buldana. Neither the soil nor the climate of the province is congenial to the growth of the bamboo, and except in the Melghat forests it is rarely met with; the number of bamboo-workers is consequently small and most of the people occupied in the production of baskets, mats, and brooms, etc, work with the leaf of the palm.

Broom-makers.

Order XVI. Sub-order 51.

Order XVI relates to drugs, gums, dyes, etc, and contains 3,745 persons or ·13 per cent of the population. Sub-order 51 numbers 668, of whom the great majority are collectors of wax, honey, and minor forest produce, and these are mostly found in Basim and Buldana. In Wun there are a few females engaged in the collection of camphor and gum. Sub-order 52 contains 3,077 persons, of whom 1,356 are concerned in the preparation and sale of the red powder known as "kanku," a material used in personal adornment by Hindu married women; females engage in this occupation and their numbers are in excess. There are 772 chemists and druggists and 672 perfume preparers and sellers. The representatives of all three categories are most numerous in Amraoti where are also found 73 out of 99 workers in alum and soda. Workers in indigo, madder, and logwood and kusumb dye, and ink-makers are mostly found in Ellichpur.

Sub-order 52.

Order XVII, in which there is but one sub-order relating to leather, hides, etc, contains 23,883 persons, or ·82 per cent of the population. Shoe-makers number 20,839, among whom there is a considerable predominance of males; of the adults there are five males to three females. Hide, horns, and bone dealers number 1,113, and among these there are two adult males to one female. Leather dyers number 986, bucket-makers 679, tanners 228, and catgut preparers 38. Buldana is conspicuous for its numbers in this order.

Order XVII.

Shoe-makers.

This concludes Class D. In the report for 1881 it was observed that the industrial class had largely increased since 1867, and it would be of interest to ascertain if this progress has been continued. The industrial class of 1881 more or less corresponds with the present Class D, the preparation and supply of material substances, and eliminating the figures for the occupations now otherwise classed and adding the numbers for those now included, I find that the corresponding occupations compare thus:

Comparison of industrial class in 1881 and 1891.

	Males.		Females.
1881	118,281	and	85,395
1891	142,013	,,	117,644

The numbers for 1891 are those of the adults who are (in this class) probably in some excess of the actual workers especially amongst females, but allowing for this over statement the margin of difference is sufficient to warrant the assumption of an increase proportionately not less at least than that of the total population and possibly much greater.

I now pass to class E, of which the first order (No. XVIII) relates to commerce and contains 52,671 persons or 2·84 per cent of the population. Sub-order 54, dealers in money and securities, numbers 20,351 of whom 19,282 are money-lenders and pawn-brokers, and 1,041 are money-changers. The number of males above 14 years of age in the sub-order generally is 8,360, and it may be assumed perhaps that the number actually employed is less than 8,000. In 1881 the number of males actually working as bankers, that is to say, bankers and money-lenders, was 5,325 and of money-changers 809, so the number of dealers in money generally would seem to have considerably increased. They are most numerous in Akola and Amraoti; Buldana also shows a considerable number who probably belong for the most part to Malkapur.

Order XVIII.

Sub-order 54.

Money-lenders.

Sub-order 55, general merchandise, numbers 5,164 persons of whom 1,618 are returned as general merchants and 3,546 as their assistants, clerks, etc. Among the former females are in excess, but in the latter they are in a considerable minority; Akola and Amraoti again show the largest numbers.

Sub-order 55.

Sub-order 56 relates to dealing unspecified, and contains 21,211 persons; 624 are returned as shop-keepers' clerks, salesmen, etc; 12,910 as shop-keepers' and money-lenders' servants; 5,764 as shop-keepers unspecified; and 1,913 as pedlars. Among the general unspecified shop-keepers females are in excess, but in the other categories the males largely predominate. A large proportion of the sub-order generally belongs to Amraoti, but the unspecified shop-keepers are most numerous in Basim and Buldana, which is no doubt to be accounted for by the greater specialisation of trades in the larger towns. It is to be noted that the number of money-lenders' servants is smaller than that of the money-lenders; the designation refers only to business assistants and not to domestics, and it may be inferred that a large number of the money-lenders operate on a very small scale.

Sub-order 56.

Sub-order 57.

Sub-order 57 relates to middlemen, etc, and numbers 5,945 persons, of whom 2,910 are shown as brokers and agents; 1,134 as farmers of liquor and opium; 1,667 as general contractors, and the remainder as auctioneers, farmers of tolls, lessees of markets and contractors for labour. Among the general contractors the females are largely in excess, and of 16 adult auctioneers 13 are women, but I think it is improbable that women actually engage in these occupations. Nearly half the brokers belong to Amraoti and a large proportion of the remainder to Akola; the number of general contractors is very conspicuous in Wun where also the preponderance of females is very abnormal.

Order XIX. Sub-order 58. Railway employés. Carriers.

Order XIX is concerned with transport and storage and contains 29,687 persons, or 1·02 per cent of the population. Sub-order 58 relates to the railway whose employés number 3,410. Sub-order 59 relates to transport by road and contains 17,023 persons, of whom 14,738 are cart-owners and drivers who follow the occupation of carrier, and 1,917 are carriers by pack-bullocks. A large proportion of the cart owners belong to the towns, and they are most numerous in Basim where they no doubt find occupation on the high road connecting Hyderabad territory with the railway at Akola; the pack-bullock drivers are probably all Banjaras who are engaged in the same way in carrying grain from Hyderabad territory to the railway, and they are found mostly in Basim and Buldana. Within the province where roads are good and transport by carts is more convenient and economical the services of carriers by animals are not required, and as railways increase and communications improve the old trade of the Banjaras must die out.

Sub-order 60.

Sub-order 60 relating to transport by water is blank but for a few boatmen in Wun and some divers in Amraoti. The latter possibly were temporary visitors, as unless they dived down wells it would be difficult for them to exercise their calling in that district.

Sub-order 61.

Sub-order 61 relates to the postal and telegraph services, and contains 3,734 persons, of whom however 2,725, who are shown as messengers unspecified, have nothing to do with either one or the other but are private servants employed as peons.

Sub-order 62.

Sub-order 62, storage and weighing, numbers 5,508, of whom 4,094 are common porters, 786 are weighmen and measurers 180 are watchmen, and 436 are engaged in warehouse services. In these categories, as might be expected, the males predominate, and nearly nine-tenths of their number belong to Akola and Amraoti.

Order XX. Sub-order 63.

We now come to class F., of which Order XX relates to learned and artistic professions, and contains 36,438 persons or 1·26 per cent of the population. Sub-order 63, religion, numbers 18,850 persons, or more than half of the order. Of these 15,077 are religious mendicants, etc; the males largely predominate, and as there are 6,771 adutl males to 3,728 adult females it seems that celibacy is practised to some extent among the men, but the existence of 1,552 children under five years of age shows that it must be the exception among the women. A large proportion are found in the Amraoti district. There are 2,504 priests, etc, of all religions and denominations, and of these 954 are adult males, so that the actual number of "workers" in this profession is probably not more than 900, as it is unlikely that the women or any of those under 15 years of age are actively employed. Of catechists, etc, there are 179, of whom 97 are adult males; this category is confined to Christians and is very indifferently represented in the Wun district where there is but one

Religious mendicants.

Priests, etc.

individual. Exorcists, hail-averters, etc, number 155, more than half of whom belong to Amraoti. Of miscellaneous subsidiary religious servants there are 935, of whom 424 are male adults. Taking the whole sub-order together there are 65 persons whose means of livelihood are dependent upon some religious function in every 10,000 of the population.

Sub-order 64.

Sub-order 64, education, contains 4,967 persons who are concerned in the administration, inspection, and conduct of schools and other educational institutions. The number of males above 14 years of age shown as teachers is 2,306, and as the returns of the Education Department give 1,275 as the number of existing public institutions, it seems probable that they absorb most of the available teachers, and that there is not any appreciable provision for private instruction. In 1881, 1,451 males and 2 females were returned as actual school principals and teachers.

School teachers.

Sub-order 65.

Sub-order 65, literature, contains 529 persons, of whom a large majority are clerks whose specific employment has not been described. The adult males shown under the head of authors, editors, journalists, and ballad-makers, are 14 in number. These do not include newspaper proprietors and managers who have been shown in sub-order 28.

Sub-order 66.

Pleaders, etc.

Sub-order 66, law, numbers 1,903 persons or about one in 1,500 of the total population. Of the males above 14 years of age among barristers and pleaders there are 229, but, as actual employment in this profession is not attained at so early an age the number of practitioners is probably considerably less; it must, however, have increased very largely since 1881 when there were only 102; 186 adult males are shown as stamp vendors and 182 as petition writers. Pleaders and petition writers are most numerous in Amraoti and stamp vendors in Akola. In Wun there is a large proportion of kazis, but of other dependents on law there are not many.

Sub-order 67.

Medical practitioners.

Sub-order 67 relates to medicine and contains 2,753 persons, more than half of whom are practitioners without diploma. The number of males above 14 years of age shown as practitioners by diploma is 60, and allowing for some youths and dependents among these there are probably between 40 and 50 certificated practitioners; in the same way the actual number of unqualified practitioners may be estimated at about 500. There appear to be therefore in round numbers about 1 diplomaed practitioner and 10 undiplomaed to 50,000 inhabitants which cannot be regarded as a very adequate supply of medical assistance, but there has been some improvement since 1881, if an increase in the number of unqualified practitioners may be so regarded, as there were then but 337 of these or 1 to nearly 8,000 inhabitants. The diplomaed practitioners are believed to be mostly Government servants. 869 persons are shown as dependent on midwifery, but the actual number of midwives will be found among the adult females who number 653; in 1881 there were 591 and there are probably now not many more. In a previous chapter it was calculated that the number of births in 1890 was 118,499, and if we take the number of midwives actually practising at 600, we find that for each midwife there are 197 births, a proportion which shows that a large number of births must take place without any professional assistance whatever. A large proportion of the practitioners without diploma and of midwives are found in the Amraoti District; in Basim the numbers are very small.

Midwives.

Sub-order 68.

Sub-order 68, engineering and surveying, contains 458 persons, of whom the adult males number 197; the actual workers are probably mostly in Government service.

Sub-order 69.

In sub-order 69, other sciences, a few persons are shown as astrologers and genealogists; and in the next sub-order, pictorial art and sculpture, 49 persons are returned as painters and 17 as photographers.

Sub-order 71.

Sub-order 71, music, acting, and dancing, contains 6,878 persons; 5,669 are players of instruments the actual performance of which is probably confined to the adult males who number 2,579, and a third of these are found in the towns, while a large proportion belong to Amraoti. Actors, singers and dancers number 1,203.

Order XXI.
Sub-order 72.
Shikaris.

Order XXI relates to sport and amusements, and contains 3,490 persons or 12 in ten thousand of the population; 1,366 belong to sub-order 72, sport, and are returned as shikaris and birdcatchers; nearly two-thirds of the number were found in Wun, and none in Ellichpur. This occupation is, however, certainly understated, and there is probably some objection to confess to it. The Pardhis alone number nearly 7,000 and they are instinctive snarers of deer and game birds, but as they are also regarded, not without reason, as rogues and vagabonds, they probably assumed at the enumeration various occupations of a less suspicious character.

Sub-order 73.

Sub-order 73, exhibitions and games, contains 2,124 persons. Exhibitors of bears, monkeys, etc, number 474, of whom 174 are adult males; they were most numerous in Wun, but are probably from the nature of their calling but temporary residents anywhere. 263 are shown as story and ballad reciters, and among these the males largely predominate; 491 are exhibitors of puppets and pictures, and here the adult males are to the adult females in the proportion of six to one, and 839 persons, of whom 319 are adult males, are acrobats. Taking the adult males of these categories there are 918 against 568 similarly described in 1881, and as it is probable that most of the adult males are actual performers, the increase is very large and indicates the encouragement which the people give to these entertainments and the prosperity which enables them to pose as patrons. It is curious too that the rural districts, Wun, Buldana, and Basim, are the most popular with the entertaining class; in Amraoti and Akola there are considerable numbers, but in Ellichpur there are very few.

Increase of exhibitors.

The first order in Class G, that of complex occupations, is shown blank. There is no known regular combination in this province and the instruction to the enumerators to record only the principal of two or more occupations, except in the case of agriculture, prevented all but exceptional representation of dual occupations, and in these instances there was nothing in either the nature of the occupations or of the numbers returning them to indicate any special combinations.

Order XXIII.
Sub-order 74.
General labour.

Order XXIII, indefinite occupations, contains 138,794 persons, or 4·79 per cent of the population. 132,632 belong to sub-order 74, unskilled labour, and of these 103,383 are shown under the head of general labour; the females largely preponderate and among the adults are in the proportion of 3 to 2 males. In 1881 the numbers of actual general labourers were 30,588 males and 36,807 females, but these probably included large numbers under 15 years of age, so that no satisfactory comparison can be made. In the present return they are most numerous in Buldana, Basim, and Akola. 17,035 are shown as road and railway labourers, and among these males predominate; their distribution is of small importance as it was dependent upon the works that chanced to be in progress at the time of the census, and is of a temporary character. 3,888 are quarrymen and stone-splitters, and among these also the males predominate; they were most numerous in Basim, Buldana, and Amraoti. 8,130 persons are shown as rice-pounders; this is a specially feminine occupation, and the adult females number 5,870, which may be compared with 7,860 returned as grain-pounders in 1881. The latter is the more correct designation in this province, as grain, and not rice, is the staple food. Not much weight, however, attaches to the comparison as the occupation is commonly carried on by the women of the poorer classes for their own domestic purposes, and has merely not been distinguished in the case of some of those shown as "dependents."

Sub-order 75.

In sub-order 75 there are 6,162 persons whose means of livelihood are shown as dependent, disreputable, or undefined. The first category is confined to those who have been returned as dependent upon others whose occupations have not been mentioned, such as "house work"; they number 1,242 and the females predominate. 2,347 have been returned as of disreputable livelihood; of these, 1,644 are adult females who are prostitutes or connected with prostitution; at the last census there were 1,582; now as then they are most numerous in Akola and Amraoti; nearly one-half are found in the towns. One noticeable feature in the distribution is with respect to the children; to 765 female adults in the towns there are 216 children of both sexes under 15 years of age, and to 879 female adults in the country there are 336 children; of the children under 5 years of age there are 122 in the country to 62 in the towns. The adult males shown in this category are attendants and professional servants.

The undefined number 2,573; this is less than 1 in 1,000 and as it comprises indefinite and unrecognizable terms as well as blank returns, the proportion is perhaps as small as can be expected.

Order XXIV.
Sub-order 76.
Beggars.

The last order relates to those whose means of livelihood are independent of work, and contains 52,123 persons or 1·80 per cent of the population. Sub-order 76, property and alms, numbers 49,286 persons, of whom 46,927 persons are ordinary beggars. Males predominate but a large number of the women and of the children take an active share in this occupation. In 1881 the ordinary beggars and the religious mendicants were classed together and numbered 30,072 males and 9,139 females. Combining the number now returned there are 36,812 males and 25,192 females. Allowing for the inclusion in the latter figures of young children who are dependents and not actually beggars it appears probable that the male beggars have decreased in number, while the females have either increased largely or are to a large extent not beggars themselves but the dependents of beggars. It has been remarked above in connection with the consideration of the occupations combined with agriculture that no inconsiderable number both of religious mendicants and of ordinary beggars are land occupants and tenants. Begging in this country by no means implies proverty; in the case of the religious mendicant it is another term for levying fees for consideration given, though the consideration may be of an unsubstantial character; the ordinary beggar is generally old, or crippled, or afflicted with some infirmity, and claims the right to tax his neighbours on the ground of his physical disability.

2,069 persons are shown as supported by house-rent and shares and other private property, not land. A few have scholarships or allowances from relatives, etc; and in connection with these the number of children is curious; the children themselves are not the recipients of these means, but are the dependents of those who are themselves thus dependant. It has, however, been noticed before that in this country want of means is but a temporary bar to marriage.

Sub-order 77.

Prisoners.

Sub-order 77 relates to those who are supported at the public charge. 1,943 persons are shown as pensioners and of these the adult males number 702, and the actual recipients of pensions are probably included in this and considerably less. 74 persons are returned as prisoners under trial, 5 as prisoners for debt, and 815 as convicts. The great majority of these are adult males, but the numbers include 24 adult females and a few children who have accompanied their mothers to jail. In 1881 the number of convicts was 1,323 males and 58 females. The present numbers show a large and presumably satisfactory reduction; but the causes therefor can be more appropriately and efficiently enquired into by the judicial authorities than in these pages.

Economic distribution and district characteristics.

This concludes the list which is summarised in the following Statement, No. 77, which shows for each district the distribution of 1,000 persons among the different occupations or groups of kindred occupations. The proportions given illustrate the economic distribution of the population generally, and mark the main distinctions which characterise the different districts:—

Statement No. 77.

Showing distribution of 1,000 persons of each district.

AMRAOTI DISTRICT.

Agricultural labourers	417
Land occupants and cultivators	273
Unskilled labour	32
Workers and dealers in cotton	30
Personal and domestic service	24
Commerce (including 8 money dealers)	22
Village service	17
Supply of drink, condiments, and narcotics	15
Ordinary beggars	15
Workers and dealers in timber and wood	12
Supply of dress	11
Supply of fuel and forage	9
Religious services	9
Goldsmiths and jewellers, etc.	8
Service of Provincial Government	7
Herdsmen	7
Supply of vegetable food	7
Fishermen	6
Oil-pressers	6
Potters and stoneware workers	6
Leather-workers, etc.	6
Workers, etc, in iron and steel	5
Carriers by cart	5
Supply of building materials	4
Artificers in building	4
Storage and weighing	4
Butchers	3
Cane and palm-leaf workers	3
Music and dancing	3
Breeding and care of sheep	2
Cow-keepers and milkmen	2

Statement No. 77.

Showing distribution of 1,000 persons of each district—continued.

Amraoti District—*continued.*

Supply of bangles, trinkets, etc.	2
Railway service	2
Messengers, including postal and telegraph service	2
Education	2
Grower of special products	1
Blanket-weaver	1
Worker in brass, copper, etc.	1
Worker — silk	1
Law	1
Medicine	1
Disreputable	1
House-rent	1
Supported at the public charge	1
Others, in the aggregate	9

Akola District.

Land occupants and cultivators	361
Agricultural labourers	313
Unskilled labour	46
Workers and dealers in cotton	25
Personal and domestic service	25
Village service	22
Commerce (including 9 money dealers)	21
Ordinary beggars	16
Supply of drink, condiments, and narcotics	12
Workers and dealers in timber and wood	12
Supply of dress	11
Supply of vegetable food	10
Supply of fuel and forage	9
Leather-workers, etc.	9
Service of Provincial Government	8
Goldsmiths and jewellers, etc.	8
Potters and stoneware-workers	8
Cane and palm-leaf-workers	8
Religious services	7
Herdsmen	6
Carriers by cart	5
Oil-pressers	4
Artificers in building	4
Workers, etc, in iron and steel	4
Storage and weighing	4
Breeding and care of sheep	3
Butchers	3
Fishermen	3
Supply of bangles, trinkets, etc	3
Supply of building materials	2
Railway service	2
Messengers, including postal and telegraph service	2
Education	2

Statement No. 77.

Showing distribution of 1,000 persons of each district—continued.

Akola District—*continued.*

Music and dancing	2
Supported at the public charge	2
Scavenger	1
Cow-keeper and milkman	1
Blanket-weaver	1
Worker in brass, copper, etc.	1
Law	1
Medicine	1
Disreputable	1
Others, in the aggregate	11

Ellichpur District.

Agricultural labourers	331
Land occupants and cultivators	301
Workers and dealers in cotton	44
Unskilled labour	36
Supply of fuel and forage	31
Personal and domestic service	27
Village service	23
Commerce (including 7 money dealers)	17
Workers and dealers in timber and wood	15
Supply of dress	14
Ordinary beggars	14
Supply of drink, condiments, and narcotics	13
Herdsmen	11
Supply of vegetable food	9
Service of Provincial Government	8
Oil-pressers	8
Goldsmiths and jewellers, etc.	8
Leather-workers, etc.	8
Religious services	8
Fishermen	6
Potters and stoneware-workers	6
Army	5
Carriers by cart	5
Supply of building materials	4
Workers, etc, in iron and steel	4
Cane and palm-leaf workers	4
Cow-keepers and milkmen	3
Butchers	3
Supply of bangles, trinkets, etc.	3
Breeding and care of sheep	2
Artificers in building	2
Messengers, including postal and telegraph service	2
Education	2
Music and dancing	2
Supported at the public charge	2
Scavenger	1
Silk-worker	1

Statement No. 77.

Showing distribution of 1,000 persons of each district—continued.

ELLICHPUR DISTRICT—*continued.*

Worker in brass, copper, etc.	1
Medicine	1
Disreputable	1
Others, in the aggregate	14

BULDANA DISTRICT.

Land occupants and cultivators	426
Agricultural labourers	250
Unskilled labour	66
Village service	30
Personal and domestic service	21
Commerce (including 9 money dealers)	18
Workers and dealers in cotton	18
Ordinary beggars	17
Supply of drink, condiments, and narcotics	12
Workers and dealers in timber and wood	11
Leather-workers, etc.	11
Supply of dress	9
Service of Provincial Government	7
Goldsmiths and jewellers, etc.	7
Potters and stoneware-dealers	7
Cane and palm-leaf workers	7
Herdsmen	6
Supply of vegetable food	6
Oil-pressers	6
Artificers in building	6
Religious services	6
Breeding and care of sheep	5
Supply of fuel and forage	5
Blanket-weavers	4
Workers, etc., in iron and steel	4
Carriers by cart	4
Supply of bangles, trinkets, etc.	3
Butchers	2
Education	2
Music and dancing	2
Fisherman	1
Supply of building materials	1
Railway service	1
Carrier by bullock	1
Medicine	1
House-rent	1
Amusement	1
Others, in the aggregate	15

WUN DISTRICT.

Agricultural labourers	427
Land occupants and cultivators	300
Unskilled labour	32

Statement No. 77.

Showing distribution of 1,000 persons of each District—contd.

WUN DISTRICT—*continued.*

Personal and domestic service	27
Workers and dealers in cotton	20
Village service	19
Herdsmen	17
Ordinary beggars	17
Supply of drink, condiments, and narcotics	15
Commerce (including 3 money dealers)	12
Workers and dealers in timber and wood	11
Fishermen	10
Supply of dress	9
Leather-workers, etc.	8
Service of Provincial Government	6
Oil-pressers	6
Supply of fuel and forage	6
Goldsmiths and jewellers, etc.	6
Workers, etc., in iron and steel	6
Potters and stoneware-workers	5
Supply of vegetable food	4
Religious services	4
Breeding and care of sheep	3
Artificers in building	3
Cow-keepers and milkmen	2
Supply of building materials	2
Cane and palm-leaf workers	2
Carriers by cart	2
Shikaris	2
Butcher	1
Supply of bangles, trinkets, etc.	1
Blanket-weaver	1
Education	1
Music and dancing	1
Amusement	1
Others, in the aggregate	11

BASIM DISTRICT.

Land occupants and cultivators	426
Agricultural labourers	269
Unskilled labour	68
Village service	25
Personal and domestic service	21
Ordinary beggars	18
Commerce (including 6 money dealers)	16
Supply of drink, condiments, and narcotics	14
Workers and dealers in { cotton	14
Workers and dealers in { timber and wood	11
Carriers by cart	10
Supply of dress	8
Leather-workers, etc.	8
Service of the Provincial Government	7

Statement No. 77.

Showing distribution of 1,000 persons of each district—continued.

BASIM DISTRICT—*continued.*

Herdsmen	7
Potters and stoneware-workers	7
Goldsmiths and jewellers, etc.	6
Supply of { vegetable food	5
Supply of { fuel and forage	5
Oil-pressers	5
Artificers in buildings	5
Cane and palm-leaf workers	5
Religious services	5
Workers, etc., in iron and steel	4
Supply of bangles, trinkets, etc.	3
Carriers by bullock	3
Music and dancing	3
Breeding and care of sheep	2
Blanket-weavers	2
Butcher	1
Fisherman	1
Supply of building materials	1
Worker in brass, copper, etc.	1
Education	1
Amusement	1
Others, in the aggregate	12

CHAPTER XII.

ADMINISTRATION OF THE CENSUS OPERATIONS.

THE results of the census having been analysed and explained, it remains to give an account of the measures adopted for making the enumeration, and for the treatment of the material obtained. The arrangements for the census of 1881 were made by the Commissioner, Hyderabad Assigned Districts, but on the present occasion it was decided to entrust the work to an officer deputed for the purpose, and towards the end of April 1890 I received instructions to undertake the operations. I was at the time holding the office of Deputy Commissioner of Amraoti, and I was not relieved of that duty until the middle of September, so that for the first five months or so the time at my disposal for census purposes was very limited. It is necessary that this should be mentioned, as it is a contingency which, in my opinion, it will be very desirable on a future occasion to avoid. Unless the Superintendent is an expert—and the circumstances of Indian service hardly permit of that—there is a great deal for him to learn, and it would certainly facilitate the progress and efficiency of the work if he is allowed sufficient leisure at the beginning to thoroughly study the subject and mature his plans. The due preparation for the taking of a census may be compared to the building of a house, the construction of which has to be completed by a fixed date. Proper plans must be prepared before a sod can be turned; foundations must be dug before the walls can be built; and the walls must be raised before the roof can be laid on. Each step in the census operations is a preliminary to another, and delay or scamped work in the earlier proceedings can only lead to jerry building and bad results.

Superintendence.

I had intended to have made an endeavour to give here a complete narrative of the operations with an accurate record of what was done and of what was omitted, so as to furnish as useful a guide as possible for a future occasion, and with this view Deputy Commissioners were asked to supply full reports upon all points connected with the arrangements in their respective districts (see Circular No. 11, page cxciv). The reports received, however, were generally somewhat meagre in detail, and I must content myself with a less complete account than I hoped to give. The Deputy Commissioner of Akola (Mr. Nicholetts) went so far as to remark that he made his report as brief as possible at my request. His words are—

"This report has been made as short as possible at the request of the Census Superintendent in his Circular No. 11, dated 10th February last."

The circular speaks for itself, and I can only suppose that this observation was intended as a satire upon the voluminous character of its requirements, but the jest was unfortunately no compensation for the omission of the particulars that I wanted.

The instructions for the preliminary organisation, and the different operations up to the final enumeration were detailed in a series of circulars, the most important of which are reproduced in an appendix to this chapter. The first circular upon the subject of the preliminary organisation was addressed to Deputy Commissioners on the 10th May. The taluk being the administrative area under a Tehsildar, Deputy Commissioners were requested to divide these areas into *Charges*,

Organisation.

the Charges into *Circles*, and the Circles into *Blocks*. The Block became the unit of area and was to comprise generally from 40 to 50 houses, with a maximum limit of 60; at the same time each village with its prescribed lands was to form an integral Block or number of Blocks. As the entire area of a taluk is divided into definite and demarcated Revenue village areas, the arrangement provided that each such village area should form a Census unit or combination of units, and thus that every inch of territory should be included in a separate Census area. The only exception to this was the railway, the lands and premises of which were separately organised. The number of houses in a Block would under the arrangement necessarily vary very considerably. Where a village contained not more than 60 houses, it constituted one Block, however small the number of houses might be. In larger villages and in towns the size of the Block would vary according to the convenience of the locality and the density of the population. The Block was to constitute the area, the population of which one man—the enumerator—would record, but where they were small an enumerator was entrusted with two or more. There was one misconception in connection with this subject which I may mention here. It was sometimes supposed that the size of the Block was regulated only by a consideration of the area, the population of which it was possible for one man to enumerate in one evening, and there was a tendency in many places to increase the size of the Block when the houses were closely and conveniently situated. But this was not the only consideration; when the enumerator has done his work, the results have to be abstracted item by item, and one large Block presents far more difficulties to the Abstractor than two small ones; this question must, however, be dealt with later on when considering the subject of Abstraction.

The Block.

The Circle was to consist generally of from 400 to 500 houses, or of about on the average ten Blocks, and each Circle was to constitute the charge of a supervisor. A group of Circles was to form a charge at the head of which was a Charge Superintendent. The Charges were to make up the taluk, the supervision of which was to rest with the Tehsildar, under the Deputy Commissioner, who was responsible for all the arrangements in his district.

The Circle.

The Charge.

The first thing to be done was to prepare a rough map of the taluk and to demarcate upon it the boundaries of the Charges and Circles, and then to nominate provisional Charge Superintendents and Supervisors. These officers had then to test the maps for their respective areas upon the ground and to report the names of villages the condition of which, as inhabited or not, was incorrectly entered; and the Supervisors had to split up their Circles into Blocks, and submit reports showing the number of villages in their Circles, the number of houses in each village, and the proposed divisions of Blocks. Upon the receipt of these reports Deputy Commissioners were required to examine the entire organisation for their respective districts, to correct the maps, and to check, and, where necessary, revise the general distribution. This having been done, it remained to embody the results in the subdivisional register of each taluk (see Appendix page clxxxiv). This register was to form the basis for the calculation of the subsequent requirements, the supply of schedules and of various forms, and the numbers of the enumerators it would be necessary to engage; it was also to serve as a taluk index in the Census office when the returns came to be dealt with. The next step was the preparation of the indents for schedules, which it was desirable to furnish to the Press by the first week in September. Then the houses had to be numbered and the lists of men for appointment as Enumerators to be prepared. The Supervisors then had to prepare village lists showing the names of

General plan.

villages in their circles, the serial numbers of the blocks in each village, the serial numbers of the houses in each block collectively, and the names of the proposed Enumerators. This form was necessary as a guide to the composition of each circle and of its staff. Then they had to prepare block lists, showing the details of each block, the serial number of each house, the description of the buildings, and the names of the principal occupants. This form was the Enumerator's guide. After this, the enumeration books had to be distributed and the Enumerators to be instructed and practised in their duties before the 15th January, when the preliminary enumeration was to commence. This was calculated to occupy about a fortnight, and while it was being carried out, and during the subsequent interval before the final census on the 26th February, the preliminary record was to be everywhere thoroughly examined and tested.

In order that the Enumerators should have time to learn their instructions and to be practised in filling up schedules, it was necessary tha t the enumeration books should be in their hands by the 1st December. A Deputy Commissioner observed at the time that this date seemed full early; he thought a week was ample time for a man to learn the work thoroughly. No doubt this might have been the case if we had had to deal only with small numbers and competent instructors; but when it is remembered that the Enumerators were numbered by thousands, that each Supervisor had to instruct some ten or a dozen Enumerators, that both Supervisors and Enumerators had other occupations to follow and could noly give a portion of their time to this instruction, that the Enumerators were scattered in different villages, and that the Supervisors had to go from place to place to teach them, that the Supervisors themselves required instruction, and that the superior officers competent to give this instruction had to travel over a large area for the purpose, it will be admitted that six weeks was not too long a period to allow. As a matter of fact in the end they did not get six weeks or anything like it, and the result was in many places inefficient instruction and bad enumeration. However, in order that the books might reach the Enumerators by the 1st December, it was necessary that the Supervisors should have them by the 15th November, as they had to copy the block lists into them before their distribution. To enable this to be done it was necessary that the Tehsildars should have their full supplies by the beginning of November, and to that end it was desirable that the indent should reach the Press by the beginning of September, two months not being too much time to allow for the printing, binding, and despatch of the books. As the taluk indents were certain to require careful checking and revision, and as they could not be prepared without the information embodied in the subdivisional register, and as that register itself would also require careful examination, and probably also revision necessitating some correspondence, and, therefore, delay, it will be seen that the end of June was not too early a date to fix for the submission of the register, and that in order that this might be done, it was necessary for Deputy Commissioners to take immediate action on the receipt of the first circular. Again, the Supervisors could not prepare the enumeration books for distribution until their village and blocks lists had been approved, and these could not be prepared and submitted for consideration until the houses had been numbered, and the numbering of the houses could not be undertaken until the constitution of the blocks had been definitively settled. Thus, it will be seen how each succeeding step depended upon the one before, and how necessary it was that each proceeding should be undertaken in sufficient time for its careful consideration and possible revision before the time for the next arrived. The situation, however, was not grasped, and it soon became a continual effort to make up for lost time, and at the same moment to pick up the dropped threads. two processes which do not well admit of combination.

The above outline indicates the general scheme of operations; the different points which call for further remark will now be dealt with in detail.

Preliminary counting of houses.

The instructions given in the first circular contemplated as one of the earliest proceedings to be undertaken the counting of the houses in each village, as, without counting, the reports referred to in paragraph 13 of the circular could not be properly prepared.

This duty should have been carried out everywhere by the Supervisors, but unfortunately many of the Tehsildars contented themselves either with the numbers at the last census or some other vague calculations. This did not transpire at the time, and the result was an incorrect return, which vitiated the subsequent indents for schedules and all the calculations based upon the subdivisional register, and when the houses came to be numbered, necessitated a revision of the Blocks and correction of registers, which caused much trouble and loss of time. Had the instructions been carried out, the labour would have been slight and the subsequent steps very much facilitated. All that was required was that each Supervisor should have been directed to go round the villages in his Circle and count the houses; as the average number of houses per Circle was less than 500, this duty could have been done generally in a few hours, and at the most, where the houses were scattered, the information could have been obtained in two or three days. I lay stress upon this point, as I am sure that for a future census organisation it is of the first importance to start with a fairly correct approximation of the number of houses in each village or town, and this can only be obtained by actual counting. Some officers confused counting with numbering, but it is scarcely necessary to observe here that the two operations are distinct. Perfect accuracy is not essential for the preliminary basis; it would make no difference to the organisation whether there were 50 or 52 houses in a village, but it would make a material difference whether there were 40 or 70; and where the figures of a previous census are relied upon, such differences might well arise. In the course of ten years there are great changes in small areas, and the old numbers are no guide on which to base a calculation that can be trustowrthy. On the present occasion this was more especially the case as the definition of a house had been somewhat narrowed.

Definition of a house.

In 1881 the definition of a house included 'garhis' and enclosures, and was said to be—

"the dwelling-place of one or more persons or families with their servants, having a separate principal entrance from the public way."

As garhis and enclosures may contain several houses in entirely distinct and separate occupation, which, for census purposes, should be regarded as different buildings, the definition was modified by the substitution of the word "common" way for "public" way. The roadway inside an enclosure is not a public way, but it is a way common to the residents of the different houses within the enclosure. In the first circular the revised definition, which was framed at the Agra Conference in 1889, was given without comment, but it was unfortunately misunderstood in some parts, and notably in the districts of Akola and Buldana, and this involved serious errors in the subdivisional registers and a second numbering of the houses. As it came to my notice that the definition was not everywhere correctly comprehended (though the extent of the error was not then discovered), the definition was repeated in the manual of instructions issued early in September (*see* Appendix page clxxxvi) and further explained by the following remark :—

"The common way is not necessarily a public way; thus the servants' quarters attached to a bungalow have not generally a separate entrance giving on to the public way, but as they have separate entrances from the common way, that is, the way common to each, it follows that each is a distinct house."

On this subject the Deputy Commissioner, Akola, writes—

"The definition was first understood to include any number of connected houses or rooms having one entrance on to a general road, The definition was afterwards interpreted by the Superintendent of Census to mean each house or room with a separate entrance."

The Deputy Commissioner, Buldana, also writes—

"First the numbering of houses was done according to the definition of house given in paragraph 12 (2) of the Census Circular No. 1. This numbering had, however, to be changed to make it conformable to the definition of house in its widened (*sic*) signification under paragraph 2 of the Census Manual received afterwards."

These officers misunderstood the definition, but it may be doubted if they were justified in attributing the error to the wording of the definition, instead of to their comprehension of it. Fortunately the mistake was not universal. The Deputy Commissioner of Wun writes—

"The definition of 'house' as given in Circular No. 1, and repeated with explanation in the Census Manual, was generally understood by the Officers of the Census Operations."

The Deputy Commissioner of Ellichpur says—

"The definition of house is given in the Census Circular No. 1 and is also explained in the Manual. Though the definition is very clear, there was at first some misunderstanding in some places in the Ellichpur taluk."

From what came under my own observation, I am disposed to believe that the misunderstanding, where it occurred, was due to careless adherence to the old definition of 1881 and failure to recognise the change in the instructions on the present occasion.

The application of the definition of a house was in many instances a matter of some difficulty. In the following diagram four houses are represented, and it will be seen that they are separate and distinct houses, each having a separate principal entrance—A, B, C, D—on to the public and common way. Subsidiary entrances are omitted.

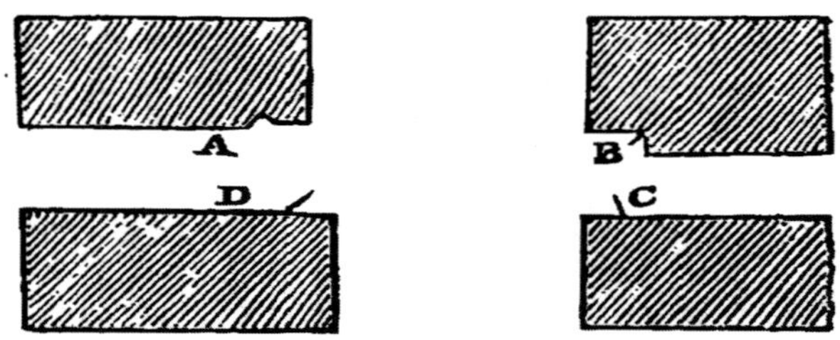

Fig: 1.

If now the outer walls be joined, an illustration of an enclosure is given with an entrance E to the public way, but a separate principal entrance—A, B, C, D— in each house to the common way as before.

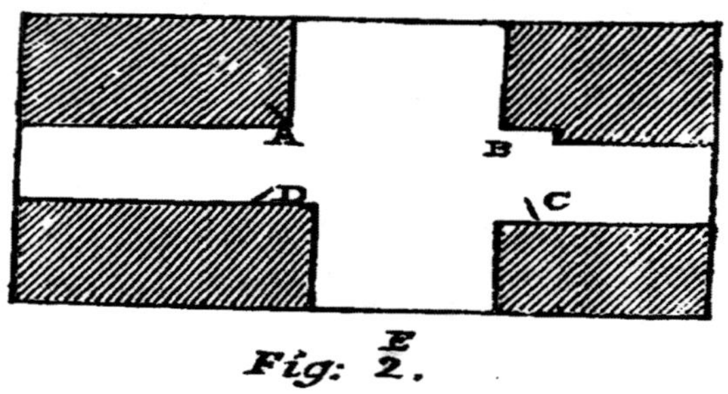

Fig: 2.

Now let other houses be built in the vacant intervals, and we have the following:—

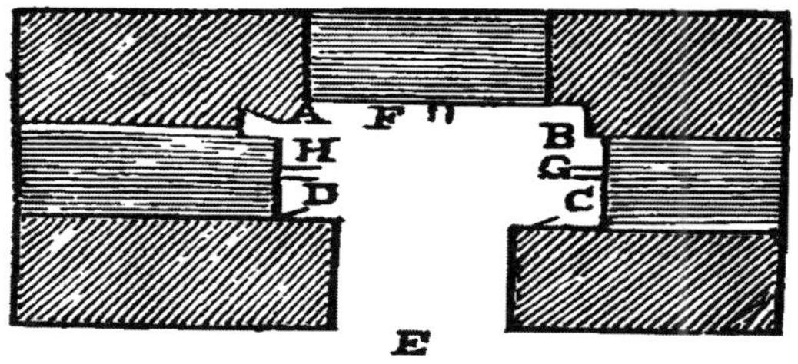

Fig: 3.

Here there are seven houses having separate principal entrances—A, B, C, D, F, G, H—to the common way, and although there may be a large gate at E that leads to the public way, they still remain with separate principal entrances on the common way, and therefore, according to the definition, distinct houses. But now we come to the following, which may be taken as not an uncommon type of a town-house, a building with seven rooms of which the inner ones open on to a court-yard.

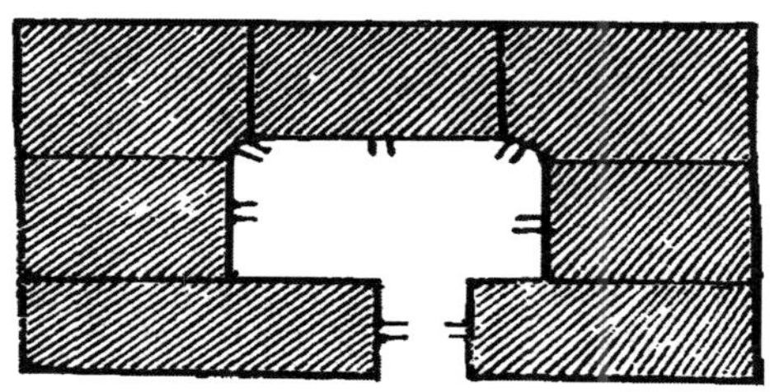

Fig: 4.

So long as this is in the occupation of one family, there is no difficulty in accepting it as one house, but if the partitions between the rooms are blocked up and the separate rooms let out to different lodgers, is it still to be regarded as one house, or as seven houses? And if as one house, where is the difference between this building and that in figure 3, which shows seven houses? The difference really is architectural, but it is difficult so to express the definition that every Supervisor should be able to apply it in every case with uniformity, and it is of course impracticable for every doubtful case to be referred to the central authority for decision. The object of a definition is not only to secure uniformity but also to ensure the enumeration of all the inmates of the house. The Enumerator obtains his information from the head of the house, but if the house in figure 4 is divided and let to different tenants, there are seven heads of houses whom the Enumerator must interrogate; and if he regards it as one house, there is danger of his omitting one or more of the separate tenants. Perhaps the best definition of a house for census purposes in this province would be the tenement in the occupation of one family of one or more persons using the same *chulha*, and of their resident servants.

Statement No. 78.

Census Areas.

Taluk.	Area in square miles.	No. of charges.	No. of circles.	No. of blocks.	No. of occupied houses	Average houses per block.	Average area of charges.	Average area of circles.
District Amraoti—							Sq. miles.	Sq. miles.
Amraoti	671·60	10	65	920	37,728	41	67·16	10·33
Chandur	854·97	8	75	953	41,378	43	106·87	11·40
Morsi	622·38	4	51	707	32,185	45	155·59	12·20
Murtazapur	610·25	4	45	618	25,037	40	152·56	13·56
Fairs, etc.	...	1	1	17	...	...	...	...
Total	2,759·20	27	237	3,215	136,328			
District Akola—								
Akola	738·80	8	57	780	30,954	40	92·35	12·96
Akot	516·81	7	75	732	31,954	44	73·83	6·89
Balapur	568·75	8	43	567	21,881	39	71·09	13·23
Jalgaon	392·10	4	51	506	22,322	44	98·02	7·69
Khamgaon	442·93	8	44	486	22,222	46	55·37	10·07
Fairs, etc.	...	3	8	30	...	...	...	..
Total	2,659·39	38	278	3,101	129,333			
District Ellichpur—								
Ellichpur	469·17	13	60	657	32,122	49	36·09	7·82
Daryapur	505·15	7	53	692	26,416	38	72·16	9·53
Melghat	1,649·00	5	16	369	8,277	22	329·80	103·06
Fairs, etc.	...	1	1	9	...	...	...	...
Total	2,623·32	26	130	1,727	66,815			
District Buldana—								
Chikhli	1,009·44	12	67	699	30,188	43	84·12	15·07
Malkapur	791·52	9	83	893	37,955	42	87·95	9·54
Mehkar	1,007·85	12	70	663	27,055	41	83·99	14·40
Total	2,808·81	33	220	2,255	95,198			
District Wun—								
Yeotmal	908·31	6	49	613	25,170	41	151·38	18·54
Darwha	1,061·55	7	61	788	31,539	40	151·65	17·40
Kelapur	1,081·19	8	44	500	19,370	39	135·15	24·57
Wun	860·18	5	39	453	16,227	36	172·04	22·06
Total	3,911·23	26	193	2,354	92,306			
District Basim—								
Basim	1,045·92	12	65	758	31,609	42	87·16	16·09
Mangrul	635·40	5	32	404	16,304	40	127·08	19·86
Pusad	1,274·60	8	51	593	23,115	39	159·32	24·99
Fairs, etc.	...	1	1	7	...	...	...	...
Total	2,955·92	26	149	1,762	71,028			
GRAND TOTAL	17,717·87	176	1,207	14,414	591,008			
Grand Total, excluding fairs	...	170	1,196	14,351	...			

Statement No. 78 shows the number of census areas as finally constituted.

Areas constituted.

The areas given for "fairs, etc," were not adopted for the preliminary organisation, but were arranged as circumstances demanded for the night of the final census; they include all special areas, such as large markets or bazars, and some roads for which separate arrangements were made. Excluding these the regular organisation consisted of 170 Charges, 1,196 Circles, and 14,351 Blocks. Excluding the Melghat taluk the average number of houses in each block varied from 38 in Daryapur to 49 in Ellichpur; in Melghat it was 22. The average area of the Charges, again excluding Melghat, varied from 36 square miles in Ellichpur to 172 in Wun; and of Circles, from nearly 7 square miles in Akot to 25 in Pusad. The size of a Charge is not a matter of very great importance, and indeed in a future organisation I think the Charges might be omitted with advantage, as they do not much more than form a fifth wheel to the coach. In the case of Circles it is important that the area should not be greater than the Supervisor can cover in a day's work, but the number of men available for this office is a factor in the question which has to be taken into consideration, and in such a district as Wun, for example, especially in the Wun and Kelapur taluks, there is considerable difficulty in procuring the services of suitable men not only for the post of Supervisor but for that of Enumerator also. If at the next census the Charges are abolished, there will be more men of superior intelligence and education available for the post of Supervisor; two or three officers might be selected to assist the Tehsildar and would do all that the Charge Superintendents were required to do on this occasion. If, however, they are retained, it will be desirable to carefully revise the areas of some of the Charges and Circles; on the present occasion the reports of the arrangements made were received much too late to admit of proper revision; but if the existing maps and records are preserved and forthcoming, the opportunity might be taken to adjust the areas at the beginning of the operations. In the Buldana district most of the Charges were too small and many of the Circles too large; in the original scheme for this district, and for Basim also, one Charge consisted of one Circle only, but there *was* time to revise that arrangement. In Wun and Basim many of the Circles were too large, and in the taluks of Ellichpur, Daryapur, Akot, Balapur and Khamgaon, some of the Charges were too small.

Charge Superintendents and Supervisors.

The appointment of Charge Superintendents and Supervisors was an important matter. The duties of the former consisted chiefly of inspection; but the brunt of the heavy work fell upon the Supervisors, who had to arrange the blocks, number the houses, prepare the village and block lists, and actively supervise and often assist in the actual enumeration. The Charge Superintendents belonged for the most part to the Police and Revenue Departments; whilst patwaris, schoolmasters, and ex-perganah officers formed a large majority of the Supervisors; the services of several private individuals were also secured. As, with a few exceptions, the appointments were honorary, these men deserve great credit for their work, which was almost everywhere carried out with great zeal and good will. Statements Nos. 79 and 80 show the classes from which these officers were respectively drawn. In connection with these posts it may be noted that

Statement No. 79.

Showing classes from which Charge Superintendents were drawn in each district.

Ordinary occupation.	Amraoti.	Akola.	Ellichpur.	Buldana.	Wun.	Basim.	TOTAL.
1. Revenue Department	13	10	2	4	10	16	55
2. Police "	7	7	9	10	6	4	43
3. Registration "	...	...	3	...	1	1	5
4. Educational "	2	1	4	1	2	...	10
5. Medical "	...	1	...	...	...	...	1
6. Forest "	...	1	1	...	...	1	3
7. Local Fund Officer	...	...	...	...	1	...	1
8. Government servant undefined	1	...	...	...	...	...	1
9. Village Officers	1	11	...	7	3	1	23
10. Ex-perganah Officers	...	2	5	8	1	1	17
11. Special Magistrates	...	1	...	...	...	1	2
12. Pensioners	...	1	1	...	...	...	2
13. Pleaders	1	1	...	...	...	...	2
14. Editor	1	...	...	...	...	...	1
15. Kazi	...	1	...	...	...	...	1
16. Contractor	...	1	...	...	...	...	1
17. Sahucar	...	...	...	1	...	...	1
18. Others	1	...	1	2	2	1	7
TOTAL	27	38	26	33	26	26	176

during the eight or nine months prior to the final census there were a large number of changes in the census staff; some men were transferred in the course of their ordinary duty, police or other, from one district or taluk to another, some went away on leave of absence, some fell sick, and others resigned from various causes. Where such changes can be obviated it would be desirable to do so; transfers in some cases might be postponed, and persons who are known to be about to take leave of absence need not be appointed.

Statement No. 80.

Showing classes from which Supervisors were drawn.

Ordinary occupation.	Amraoti.	Akola.	Ellichpur.	Buldana.	Wun.	Basim.	TOTAL.
1. Revenue Department	...	1	6	7	26	...	40
2. Police "	1	1	2	...	11	...	15
3. Educational "	21	24	21	70	42	18	196
4. Forest "	...	...	3	1	...	2	6
5. Registration "	...	1	4	...	4	...	9
6. Public Works "	...	...	1	...	...	...	1
7. Vaccination "	...	...	1	1	...	...	2
8. Local Board Officials	1	...	...	...	...	1	2
9. Municipal Officials	1	9	...	...	...	2	12
10. Government servants undefined	17	19	...	...	...	3	39
11. Village Officers	138	202	74	66	44	110	634
12. Ex-perganah Officers	38	8	4	37	17	5	109
13. Pensioners	...	3	...	1	...	...	4
14. Pleaders	...	3	1	...	...	1	5
15. Petition Writers	...	...	...	9	...	...	9
16. Sahucars	1	1	1	4	...	...	7
17. Jagirdars and Izaradars	...	4	...	1	1	...	6
18. Pleaders	...	...	...	...	22	...	22
19. Agriculturists	...	...	...	...	18	...	18
20. Private Schoolmasters	...	...	...	...	2	...	2
21. Others undefined	19	2	12	23	6	7	69
TOTAL	237	278	130	220	193	149	1,207

Subdivisional register.

After the selection of these officers and the submission of their preliminary reports came the preparation of the subdivisional register. The importance of this document was hardly anywhere properly appreciated; it was not only submitted very unpunctually, as has been already remarked, but it was in many cases prepared with a want of care and precision and of attention to instructions which gave much trouble at the time, and the consequences of which have been felt throughout the preliminary operations and up to the very preparation of the census tables. This register should not only furnish information for the calculation of the requisite numbers of schedules and forms and enumeration staff, but should be an accurate index of the taluk according to which the enumeration books should be docketed and with which they can be subsequently compared and checked. The following are some of the errors which led to confusion. Inaccuracy of the revenue numbers of a village; the names of villages only are insufficient for identification as some of them are common to several places. Some registers did not show the villages which were supposed to be uninhabited, and as some of these were found to be inhabited at the census it was a difficult matter to locate them; all villages should have been shown. Many villages have offshoots, known as 'mazras,' which are adjuncts to the main village and are situated on the lands included in the same revenue number, but some of the mazras were shown as distinct villages, thereby apparently increasing the number of villages. Most towns and big villages consist of aggregations of 'khels' or quarters, formerly separate villages and mazras, bearing different names and revenue numbers; in some cases the register showed only the name of the town while the enumeration books bore the names of the khels. For instance, the town of Jalgaon consists of 12 khels with different names and numbers, but while the town of Jalgaon alone appeared in the register the names of the khels only were entered on the enumeration books, from which it was difficult to know whether they belonged to distinct villages or, if not, to what other village or town; there was nothing to show either on the books or in the register that they belonged to Jalgaon. The preparation of Table III especially was much hindered by such mistakes as these.

House numbering.

The instructions for the numbering of houses were contained in a manual issued early in September (see Appendix, page clxxxvi), and the 15th October was prescribed as the date by which the operation should be completed. In some taluks this date was not exceeded, and in most, except where renumbering was necessary, the work was completed by the end of October. In the Melghat taluk it was not finished till the end of November. In the Akola district numbering was commenced without orders in July, and consequently when the instructions were issued it was found necessary to do the work over again. The material generally used was charcoal and oil, coal-tar, or red ochre (garu). The most efficient mode of numbering was to put a patch of white chunam upon the house wall beside the principal entrance and to paint the number in bold figures upon the white ground. In Wun and one or two other places the work was made the occasion for considerable artistic display, and appeared to afford much amusement to the village children. In some places, on the other hand, the Supervisor's object seems to have been to make it a puzzle to ascertain where and what the number was, the situation being screened, and the figures microscopic. In some of the towns of the Ellichpur district tin plates bearing painted numbers were affixed to the houses, the cost being met by local subscription, which the Deputy Commissioner states was given willingly. The cost of the ordinary numbering was generally very small, though it seems to have varied considerably; figures for the districts of Ellichpur and Basim are not forthcoming; of the rest, the cost in Wun was R10, in Buldana and Amraoti between R40 and R50, and in Akola a little more than R121. Whether the variation was actual or nominal and due to a matter of account is not known, but no doubt the renumbering in Akola and Buldana accounts to some extent for the higher cost in those districts. Taking the figures as they stand, the average cost in Wun for every thousand houses was less than two annas, in Amraoti between five and six annas, in Buldana seven annas and a half, and in Akola nearly fifteen annas; and for the aggregate of the four districts a little less than eight annas.

Indents for schedules.

In Circular No. 4 Deputy Commissioners were asked to submit their indents for enumeration books before the end of August, and with one exception the date was observed; but the indents received were found upon examination to be so irregular and apparently unreliable that it was necessary to entirely revise them upon the data supplied by the subdivisional registers, which at that time there was no reason to mistrust. These indents had been prepared for each taluk by Tehsildars, and seemed to have been framed on mere guess-work and to have been passed on by Deputy Commissioners without any scrutiny. The books, it had been mentioned, were to be bound in four standards, containing respectively 10, 30, 50, and 70 schedules. Yet one indent contained a demand for books of 20 schedules; in the same indent was a demand for 647 books of the lowest standard for one taluk, while for a larger taluk in the same district the demand was for 100 only; in another district the demands for two taluks were 28 and 402 respectively; and so on. The revision necessitated correspondence and occasioned delay, so that a precise indent for the province was not ready until the 21st October; a provisional indent was, however, despatched to the press on the 19th September, and this met the subsequently ascertained requirements with fair approximation.

The books were printed and bound at the Government Central Press, Bombay, and were despatched to their several destinations at the end of October and the beginning of November; and I may here record my sense of obligation to the Superintendent of the Press for the promptitude with which these indents and other printing requirements were dealt with; the work turned out by the Press was also excellent, the printing was good, the binding, with a few exceptions, was accurate and strong, and the cost extremely moderate; 18,389 books were supplied at a cost of R1,668, or less than an anna and a half each. The preparation of indents is an important matter. A sufficient supply of books is essential, and to ensure this some reserve is necessary to meet damage, waste, and unforeseen demands; but on the other hand a superfluity involves unnecessary expense. If the preliminary organisation is carried out with care, there is no reason why the requirements of each taluk should not be calculated to a nicety. On the present occasion 15,915 books were actually used for enumeration, and there was an additional expenditure of 784 books, presumably damaged, which was nearly 5 per cent. of the actual requirements. There remained unused a balance of 1,606 books, which have been since sold for R19-13-9. These figures do not quite make up the number charged for by the Press, but the latter included a small supply to some of the Contingent stations in the Hyderabad dominions, and an accurate account of the receipt and expenditure of books is perhaps not to be expected, although it is desirable; there are so many demands in the last few days for a supplemental book here or a few extra schedules there, which involve transfers from one area to another, and the tearing up of books for the distribution of the loose sheets, that it is intelligible that there may be some difficulty in keeping a check upon the receipts and issues, especially when the responsible officers have other duties independent of the census demanding their attention at the same time. The following Statement No. 81 shows the expenditure of each standard of books as reported by Deputy Commissioners, but these figures are possibly not quite accurate, and in some taluks a few manuscript books were used.

Statement No. 81.

Showing number of enumeration books reported as used.

District.	Books of 10 schedules.	Books of 30 schedules.	Books of 50 schedules.	Books of 70 schedules.	Total.	Balance unused.
Amraoti	248	260	975	1,976	3,459	358
Akola	354	320	1,108	1,756	3,537	268
Ellichpur	257	302	550	887	1,996	189
Buldana	440	201	767	1,226	2,674	273
Wun	283	399	845	1,097	2,624	241
Basim	626	290	687	806	2,409	277
TOTAL	2,208	1,772	4,932	7,787	16,699	1,606

Standards of books.

The different standards of enumeration books were adopted for purposes of economy. Each book was primarily intended to suffice for one block, each house having a separate page or schedule; and as the sizes of the block varied, there would have been a considerable waste of schedules if only one standard had been adopted. The books of 10 schedules were intended chiefly for supplemental purposes in cases where for any reason the original book was found insufficient; those of 30 schedules were for blocks of less than 26 houses; those of 50 schedules for blocks of from 26 to 45 houses; and those of 70 schedules for the larger blocks. I think that the margin allowed was not quite sufficient, and that each standard except the lowest might have been with advantage a little larger. Each schedule contained space for the enumeration of eight persons, which would suffice for the majority of households, but in the interval between the preliminary and final enumeration there may be changes which necessitate the use of a second schedule, and if there are not sufficient spare pages, a supplemental book is necessary, and this for the subsequent purpose of abstraction it is better to avoid as far as possible. For the 14,414 blocks (irrespective of the Railway) there were used, as has been said, 15,915 books, or about one supplemental book in every ten blocks. The number of supplemental books and those damaged or otherwise expended amounted together to 15 per cent. on the number of blocks.

Enumeration book.

The enumeration book contained first the general instructions to the Enumerators for both the preliminary and the final records; then rules in detail for filling up each column of the schedule; a sample schedule with the entries completed; a series of standard questions that the Enumerators might put to householders to obtain the requisite information for filling up each column; a form of abstract to show the number of occupied houses and the number of persons of each sex enumerated, to be filled in after the final census; then the block list, which has been already described; and finally the schedules for the enumeration. On the cover was a form of docket for the description of the block to which the book belonged.

Enumerators.

When the block list had been completed the books were distributed to the Enumerators, the numbers of whom, with the classes from which they were drawn in each district, are given in Statement No. 82. A large number of patels and patwaris, ex-pergannah

Statement No. 82.

Showing the classes from which the Enumerators were drawn.

Ordinary occupation.	Amraoti.	Akola.	Ellichpur.	Buldana.	Wun.	Basim.	Total.
1. Revenue Department	11	...	59	21	34	50	175
2. Police "	...	...	13	11	21	16	61
3. Educational "	39	...	132	121	44	60	396
4. Public Works "	...	...	2	1	...	...	3
5. Registration "	...	...	1	...	2	...	3
6. Forest "	...	...	36	1	3	7	47
7. Vaccination "	...	...	2	...	...	...	2
8. Medical "	...	...	1	...	4	...	5
9. Jail "	...	...	...	...	1	1	2
10. Government clerks, servants, etc., undefined.	267	1,002	1	...	6	8	1,284
11. Local Board or Fund Officers	...	...	3	...	1	...	4
12. Municipal Officers and servants	2	...	3	...	...	...	5
13. Village Officers	753	...	308	718	458	280	2,517
14. Ex-pergannah Officers	214	77	18	112	79	66	566
15. Pensioners	...	13	...	1	...	1	15
16. Government and other office candidates.	...	...	19	...	18	55	92
17. Petition writers	9	36	...	14	3	8	70
18. Stamp-vendors	...	19	2	17	13	32	83
19. Jagirdars, Inamdars and Izaradars	2	2	...	2	43	...	49
20. Agriculturists	381	1,119	556	...	576	277	2,909
21. Sahucars and their employés	114	111	35	46	...	95	401
22. Private Schoolmasters	...	...	28	48	35	50	161
23. Students	30	58	1	...	26	12	127
24. Priests and mendicants	...	69	5	...	...	79	153
25. Private servants	28	410	138	...	158	109	843
26. Traders and others	1,442	193	67	1,243	415	543	3,903
27. Paid enumerators	...	...	24	...	...	...	24
Total	3,292	3,109	1,454	2,356	1,940	1,749	13,900

officers, village school-masters, and clerks and other subordinates of various Government offices were employed, but the majority were private persons whose services with a few exceptions were obtained gratuitously. For the Melghat taluk the Deputy Commissioner found it necessary to depute 24 men specially for the purpose from Ellichpur or elsewhere, and they were paid R12 each to cover their travelling and living expenses while so employed. In the Wun district a number of men were paid small sums to meet the actual cost of travelling; this was necessary, as in many villages, especially in the Wun and Kelapur taluks, there were no residents qualified to act as Enumerators, and those who did the work had in some cases to make long journeys for the purpose: the whole expenditure on this account was R168. In Amraoti there were a few small payments, amounting to R3-8, on the final night for the enumeration of road travellers, voluntary agency at the last moment being wanting. The average numbers of persons recorded by each Enumerator was 211.

Instruction of the Agency.

For the general guidance of all officers a manual of instructions was issued, and a copy in Marathi was supplied to every Charge Superintendent and Supervisor. This pamphlet contained most of the instructions requisite for those officials and for Enumerators also, so that the former could learn from it what they had to do themselves and what they had to teach others to do. With the instructions were included several miscellaneous examples of schedule entries and lists of some of the principal sects of religion and subdivisions of caste that are met with in Berar. The enumeration book also, as has been described, contained the Enumerators' instructions and afforded three lights to guide him in any particular difficulty in filling a schedule: first, a suitable question or questions calculated to elicit the information required, secondly, a specific rule applicable to each column of entry, and thirdly, an example. Personal instruction was also given. I made a tour of the province from October to January, and in each taluk held a meeting of as many Charge Superintendents and Supervisors as could be got together. The meetings were generally very well attended, though very unpunctually, as might be expected from the Berari; the instructions and rules were successively read and explained, and any difficulties that were propounded were discussed and disposed of; some of the men were then practised in filling up the enumeration schedules by recording entries for others of the persons present, and the mode of proceeding and the mistakes to be guarded against were thus practically illustrated. Tehsildars, Charge Superintendents and Supervisors were enjoined to hold similar meetings of Enumerators, so that every one of the staff might have some instruction, and the Deputy Commissioners report that such meetings were held, but they give no details as to the number of meetings or who attended them, and judging from the results, I am of opinion that this duty was very insufficiently performed The best work in this respect that came under my own observation was in the Daryapur taluk, which I did not reach till late in my tour, and where I found that the Tehsildar, Mr. Shapurji Virji, had very efficiently anticipated me, and that his subordinates were fully instructed. There appears to have been no reason, however, why this duty should have been left to the Tehsildars only. Deputy Commissioners and their Assistants might have done much good work in this respect in their tours, and it was prescribed in paragraph 14 of the Manual, but it does not appear that they did anything at all. Granting that there was some delay, Enumerators were appointed in most places before the 1st of December, and between that date and the 15th of January each District Officer might have held one or two meetings every week in different parts of the districts, and every Enumerator might thus have had the benefit of superior instruction. The work turned out shows that it was very much needed.

Preliminary record.

The preliminary record was commenced on the 15th January, and in most places occupied about a fortnight. In the *Chikhli* taluk it was completed in five days; in some taluks it was not finished until the middle of February, and in the Pusad taluk, owing to an insufficient supply of books, not until the 23rd of that month. The advantage that should have been taken (see paragraph 15 of the Manual) in the interval before the final cen-

Checking.

sus of checking the preliminary record was, judging again from results, very much neglected. The Deputy Commissioners all report in general terms that the work was thoroughly examined, but they do not state what measures were adopted for the purpose, nor give any details. The most common form of error was the blank return, the omission to fill in one or more of the columns of the schedule, a defect which could have been detected at a glance. The following are a few examples of the errors of commission. In column 8, for the civil condition, a person was entered as "married and widowed;" whether this meant that he had been married and had become widowed, or that he had been widowed and had married again can only be guessed; an "unmarried widow" is a little less doubtful. In column 9 for "parent-tongue" two languages were entered, one for each parent possibly. The sex in column 6 was often opposed to the sex of the name and of the adjectival terminations in the other columns; a man's name would be coupled with the condition of "widow." Sometimes both sexes were given, as "stri-purush" or "purush-stri." The parent-tongue of an infant was given as "cannot talk," or left blank for presumably the same reason. In the case of infants also the civil condition and education was often regarded as sufficiently accounted for by the repetition of the word "infant;" the education might certainly be deduced, although in one case an infant was entered as "literate;" but as infants may be not only married, but widowed, the civil condition was left in doubt. Caste and religion were intermixed in every conceivable way; one man's religion was entered as "Marathi;" another's was given as Hindu, but his sect, caste, and subdivision of caste were stated to be "Musalman;" one whose name was "John" was entered as "Christian," sect "Mission Church," and caste "Israelite." Some Chinese in Akola were stated to be Hindus of the Smarth sect and Sutar caste, although they were born in Canton and spoke Chinese; another Chinaman was entered as a Hindu of the Chinese caste. About the most extraordinary jumble was the entry of a woman as of the Hindu religion, Jain caste, and Gond sub-caste. These are some of the most striking, but mistakes of some kind or other were not exceptional; some of the books teemed with errors, and the general record cannot be pronounced anything but bad. In the taluks of the Wun and Akola districts and in some others the preliminary record was made in rough, with the intention that after revision fair copies should be made in the enumeration books; this would have been an excellent plan if the copies had been always completed, but unfortunately in many instances they were not; for example, in one book eight persons were entered on one schedule and the first four columns completed, but the rest left blank, as if the writer had been interrupted in his work and had forgotten to finish it afterwards. Some errors were to be expected, especially in connection with sect and caste, but the great mass of mistakes were of such an obvious character that the only conclusion can be that the books were not properly examined. In the Abstraction Office it was attempted to rectify the mistakes by a local enquiry in each case, and several hundred queries were sent out with this object, but the plan had to be abandoned, as it was found that the abstraction work was impeded by the necessity of putting aside the books pending the receipt of replies.

Examples of bad enumeration.

The final census on the night of the 26th February was taken without much difficulty. The weather was fine, and there was a bright moon. The work consisted only of bringing up to date the enumeration already recorded by cancelling the entries for persons no longer present and adding fresh entries for the new-comers. It was commenced generally about an hour after sunset, and was completed in most places before midnight. There was a fair at Bhiltek in the Amraoti district, at Ooperai in the Ellichpur dis-

Final round.

Fairs.

trict, at Pathur, Malsoor, and Dhanora in the Akola district, and at Pardi, Asra, and another at Dhanora in the Basim district, and for the enumeration of the people assembled a special staff was appointed; it would have been interesting to know what arrangements were made for this enumeration, but beyond the general fact that they were 'special' no information has been furnished to me.

Travellers by road.

The enumeration of travellers on the roads was taken either by the ordinary local staff assisted by village mahars who watched the roads, or, where the traffic was heavy, by additional Enumerators. The travellers after enumeration were provided with tickets to prevent their being counted again, and the number of tickets thus issued in each district was as follows:—

Amraoti, 4,246; Ellichpur, 3,201; Akola, 2,777; Buldana, 3,355; Wun, 1,893; and Basim, 1,202—total 16,674. The largest demand for these tickets was in Malkapur, from where it appears a number of the people were starting on the census night for a fair in Khandesh. The total number with the number of railway passengers represents the travelling population of the province, though probably roughly only, as tickets may have been issued to persons who were not *bonâ fide* travellers. They amount to 59 persons in every 10,000 of the population.

Officers in camp.

In paragraph 9 of the manual officers in camp had been instructed to enumerate the parties attached to them, but in some cases they prepared their private schedules only and left their servants and followers to be enumerated by the local staff. This was a troublesome mistake, as the local Enumerators had no alternative but to include these persons as new-comers in their blocks and they thus augmented their village returns. As these persons properly belonged not to the village where they happened to be enumerated, but to the same locality as their masters, it was necessary to eliminate them subsequently from the village returns, and it was a matter of difficulty to distinguish them accurately.

Householders' schedules.

For the enumeration of Europeans and Eurasians loose sheets called "householders' schedules" were issued, and the head of each house was required to fill them up and return them the next day. The intention of these schedules was merely to facilitate the work, it being thought that a native Enumerator would be likely to make mistakes in the translation or transliteration of the details. It is doubtful, however, whether the advantage is not more than counterbalanced by the trouble which the loose sheets give afterwards, as they are very liable to be torn and misplaced. The use of them should at least be strictly circumscribed, and the idea that any privilege is conferred by the use of a private schedule should be discouraged. One native officer who was given a private schedule filled it up in the vernacular, and as he was apparently unable to read the instructions which were printed in English, he inserted sixteen persons on one page, which was intended for eight only, and the entries were confusing. There was no reason why this officer and his family should not have been enumerated in the ordinary manner. There is a danger also in the use of a private schedule of a double enumeration; at least it would seem so, as the Deputy Commissioner of Buldana was enumerated twice, on his own householder's schedule and in the Enumerator's block book, but how such a mistake could occur it is not easy to see. In connection with the returns of European officers, it may be noted that many of those having military rank entered their occupations wrongly; 'Colonel,' 'Surgeon-major,' etc, are ranks, not occupations, and the entry of such terms does not show whether the officers are in the administrative or army service. As directly the schedule is abstracted the identity of the individual is lost, it is a matter of some difficulty to trace the returns back to the schedules and correct the mistakes subsequently, but this had to be done, as the original results showed several more military officers than the troops in the province justified and the apparent absence of several of the higher administrative officials.

Day census.

A day-census was taken on the morning of the 27th February in the Melghat taluk and in parts of the Yeotmal, Wun, and Kelapur taluks. This was necessitated by the jungly or hilly character of the localities which prevented the movement of the census staff by night, but the enumeration was made synchronous with that of the 26th by referring the enquiries to the facts of the previous night and not to those of that morning. The people in these tracts were requested to facilitate the work by not leaving their houses until they had been visited by the Enumerator, and this arrangement, it is believed, was cheerfully concurred in. In the Wun district the enumeration was completed before noon and in the Melghat by 2 P. M.

Abstracts.

On the 27th February the enumerators were required to prepare abstracts showing the total number of occupied houses and of males and females in their respective blocks. This information was transmitted by the Supervisors to the Charge Superintendents, and by them to Tehsildars, who in their turn reported the totals for their taluks to Deputy Commissioners. From these returns district summaries were prepared and the results were telegraphed to the Census Commissioner for India at Simla on the following dates: Buldana, 3rd March; Basim, 4th; Amraoti, 5th; Akola and Wun, 9th; and Ellichpur, 16th. The Ellichpur summary was delayed by the Melghat return. These summaries showed a total population for the province of 2,896, 681, which was short of the total as finally ascertained in the Census Office by 810, an error of ·028 per cent of the whole.

Census on the railway.

The census of the railway population, which included passengers and all railway employés who either resided or were on the census night on duty within the railway premises, was taken by the railway authorities. Extracts from the instructions issued are given in the Appendix (page cxciv). In one respect the railway census organisation was unsatisfactory in that it was departmental instead of territorial, as it was in 1881 and as it was originally intended to be for this census. The consequence is that the majority of the railway population, that is to say, the passengers, permanent-way employés, and some others cannot be allocated to certain districts as was done before, but have to be treated as a whole for the province, and they are shown in the different tables under a separate heading accordingly. Where possible however, as in the case of residents at stations, the numbers have been included in the district returns.

The enumeration in municipalities and the cantonment of Paratwada calls for no comment. The organisation was similar to that for the rest of the province, and no circumstances requiring special treatment have been brought to notice.

Attitude of the people.

On the general question of the census I believe there was no public feeling whatever. The Deputy Commissioner of Buldana writes :—

"No difficulty was experienced in realizing the necessary information from the people at the time of filling in of the schedules. Tahsildar, Malkapur (*sic*), observes that even the Rohillas gave the necessary information readily."

This seems to have been the general experience. The Deputy Commissioner of Akola alone mentions any opposition ; he says :—

"The object of Government in taking census is not yet thoroughly understood by the people, especially by the ignorant and superstitious, who make it a point to refrain from giving information on some plea or other, such as the Musalman who dislikes the idea of the names and ages of the female relatives being known by another. These difficulties existed at places where there are large communities of Mussulmans, Rajputs, Maratha Deshmuks and others, there the Act and its provisions was really a help. Such difficulties were removed by the engagement of the opponents' co-religionists as Supervisors and enumerators, and by making known the provisions of the Act through them."

This language is somewhat general and the Deputy Commissioner mentions no facts to illustrate it, and he says further on :—

"The attitude of people was on the whole favourable omitting a few instances in which the opposition did not last long";

so that it may probably be accepted that the experience in the Akola district was much the same as elsewhere. There will probably always be some individuals who object to the inquisition of the Enumerator, but the census is now no novelty and I venture to hazard the opinion that so far as the attitude of the people is concerned no population in the world could have been enumerated with less trouble than that of Berar. As to the objection to give the names of females, it was of no importance, the entries in such cases being "wife, daughter, etc, of so and so." There were no prosecutions under the Census Act, and the only provision which there would have been any occasion to put in force was that empowering punishment to a Census Officer for refusing to act as such, but as a matter of fact the Census Act was of no practical utility in Berar, as it was not brought into force until it was too late to take any steps under it. The Act was passed on the 16th October 1890, but it was not until the 23rd January that its extension to Berar was notified in the *Gazette of India*, and it was of course some days later before the text of the Act and the intimation of its extension reached the Deputy Commissioners. Earlier in the operations several complaints were made of persons refusing to act as Enumerators, and in some places there was some difficulty in arranging for the performance of the duty. The difficulties were got over, but they were none the less real, and a single prosecution for recusancy at the beginning, had the Act been in operation, would have had useful effect.

The Census Act.

When the census was over the enumeration books of each taluk were collected and despatched by the Tehsildars to the Census Office. It has been said that no time was allowed for checking the work after the census, as in 1881, but it was intended that the main portion of it, that is, the preliminary record, should have been checked before the final census, after which it would only have remained to check the additions (entered in red ink for facility of reference), and this would not have occupied long. The instructions of the Census Commissioner for India to commence abstraction as early as possible did not, however, admit of the grant of further time for checking purposes; but, except in a few instances, the despatch of the books was not so prompt as to prevent some further examination. The books of the Murtazapur taluk were the first to arrive and were received on the 2nd March, as early a date as was possible; those for Amraoti, Balapur, Akola and Morsi came in on the 5th and 6th; between the 10th and 14th, seven more batches arrived; then there was a lapse of nine days before any more came in, and the rest were received on different dates up to the 2nd of April, with the exception of the books of the Chikhli taluk, which did not arrive until the 18th April, an altogether unnecessary delay, which was made the subject of a communication to the Commissioner, Hyderabad Assigned Districts, at the time. It is well to mention here that in some cases the books were very badly packed and were found to be perforated and torn by the nails with which the boxes had been fastened; this might have been avoided with ordinary care, and should not be allowed to happen again. As in the course of abstraction each book passes through many hands, one that starts in a ragged condition has small chance of surviving to the end.

Collection and despatch of books.

The Census Office.

The first thing to be done in the Census Office was to see that the dockets of the books were properly and legibly filled in and that the full complement of books for each taluk was received, and then to register and arrange them for subsequent distribution. This required the supervision of a capable ministerial officer, and the services of a clerk in the office of the Deputy Commissioner of Amraoti, who had been selected as Record-keeper, had been promised from the 1st March, but there was very unfortunately some delay in relieving him, and he did not report himself at the Census Office until the 11th. Meanwhile, a large number of books had arrived and there had been no one to dispose of them, and when the Record-keeper found what was before him he was so appalled that he fell sick. The circumstances were undoubtedly most trying; masses of books to be examined, sorted, registered and arranged; invoices to be compared with the packages and receipts to be given, and at the same time demands from the Abstraction Office for books to work upon, such demands necessitating further registration and compliance with the rules framed for their issue and return. The situation required a cool head and a clear brain, and it is not to be wondered at that the Record-keeper was not equal to the occasion. It was accordingly a long time before this branch of the Office settled down into proper working order, and one serious consequence was some neglect in registration, which resulted in the issue of the same books for abstraction several times over, and thus caused a waste of time and labour. I have gone into this circumstance at length, as it seems desirable to show the absolute necessity of the requisite staff being at their posts beforehand ready to dispose of the material as it arrives. With the books of each taluk, except the Melghat, came a Munserim or Karkun, whose business it was on arrival to deliver his books to the Record-keeper in good order. It was soon found, however, that the dockets of many of the books were incomplete. These dockets were very important; without a docket the contents of a book were all but valueless, as it was all that identified the book with the locality to which it related; and until the docket was complete with the name of the taluk and village and the number of the Block, Circle and Charge to which it belonged, it could not be received for abstraction. This should have been done before the census, and Tehsildars and their subordinate Census staff were particularly enjoined to be careful on this point; the matter would have been a simple one if dealt with at the right time and there was no excuse for its neglect. It was, however, not so simple a matter to make good the omissions afterwards, and many of the Munserims were engaged for days and even weeks in putting their books into order. The services of most of them were not therefore available for assistance in the abstraction office until long after the work had commenced.

Meanwhile a number of clerks had been engaged, and on the 11th March 163 men were set to work to learn how to abstract the contents of the enumeration books on to working sheets, and on the 14th the work began in real earnest. Other men were taken on from day to day, and by the end of the month the sanctioned establishment of 225 men had been entertained; there were, however, many more than this upon the books in the course of the month, as some men were dismissed from time to time for incapacity; others resigned their employment, and new candidates were taken on as vacancies arose. Yet the number of men actually at work was always below the sanctioned establishment, owing to the daily absence of some or other of them for various reasons. Those present also were not all available for abstraction work, as it was found necessary to draft several as assistants to the Record-keeper and for other miscellaneous duties. To assist in the control and management of this establishment I was afforded the services of Mr. Ardesir Dinshaji Chinoy, Extra Assistant Commissioner, Mr. Sobarayaloo Naidoo, Tehsildar, the clerk of the Deputy Commissioner's office already mentioned, and the Munserims, who, as has been explained, were not available at the beginning. The petty officers, or squad inspectors, were therefore at first selected from amongst the Abstractors themselves, and thus the number of men available for actual abstraction was further reduced. The abstraction was for the most part completed early in July in 90 working days, during which there was an average of 188 Abstractors at work each day. After that most of the men were drafted to testing work, while a few small squads carried on the remaining abstraction. The testing was very troublesome work, and was not finished until early in October. Meanwhile, in the last week of July a commencement was made with the tabulation, and this proceeded until the 10th March 1892; but in October, when the abstraction and testing was completed, the number of men was largely reduced owing to their incapacity to work at tabulation, and during the last few months there were many resignations and desertions as the men saw their temporary occupation coming to an end, and took any opportunities that arose of obtaining other employment. The average daily number of Tabulators was 11 from the 25th July until the 10th August, 25 from that date till the end of the month, then 43 until the 16th September, 57 from that date until the 5th October, and 84 thence onward until the 7th March. As the tabulation of the different registers was completed, the compilation was taken in hand, and the compilation sheets for the Tables from I to XIV A were completed by the end of October; copies or summaries of these, styled "compilation slips," were supplied to the Census Commissioner for India to enable him to fill up the tables and compare results as the work progressed. The preparation of the tables was then taken in hand, and on the 12th November the first table was sent to press, and was followed by others from day to day until the 16th December, by which date all the tables up to XV A, inclusive, had been despatched. Some of the remainder occupied much time, and the last was not completed until the 31st March 1892.

Difficulties experienced.

The chief difficulty in the abstraction office was that of obtaining good material to work with. Berar, as has been already remarked, holds a backward place in education, and good writers or computators are not to be obtained in large numbers unless high salaries are offered, and possibly not then. The Census Commissioner's estimates of work upon which the strength of the office was based were common for all India, but a Bengali Babu will work very much faster and far more accurately than a Berari, and if the work in Berar is required to keep pace with that in other provinces, a proportionately larger number of men must be employed and higher salaries must be given. In respect of the rates of pay and of the number of the establishment, it is very desirable that the hands of the Superintendent should not be tied, that is to say if it is considered of importance to bring the work to an early conclusion; if he is limited to a sanctioned establishment and a fixed rate of pay, and cannot at his discretion modify the one or the other, he must be hampered; he cannot foresee all his requirements, and I think it should be considered sufficient if he keeps within the total expenditure provided on a fairly liberal estimate. This consideration leads to another point which I may mention here, though it has no connection with abstraction. At the beginning of the operations it was suggested by the Census Commissioner that the Provincial Superintendents should for facility of reference be regarded as occupying positions of the character of Under-Secretaries to Government. For Berar especially, separated as it is from the head of its administration, I think the adoption of some such plan would have much facilitated progress. The ordinary channel of communication is too slow to admit of the disposal of most of the questions arising in the census administration, which, if not dealt with at once, possibly cannot be dealt with at all. Another of the difficulties in the abstraction office was that of combining quality with quantity of work, speed with accuracy. It was attempted to adjust rewards and fines for the work turned out, but the plan was not successful. Some men would work fast and show a large outturn, and until the quality could be tested would seem to be doing well; on the other hand, others whose outturn seemed comparatively very poor did their work more carefully, with more satisfactory results in the end. Until, therefore, the quality could be tested no adjustment of fine or reward could be made, but in order that the system may have any beneficial effect it is necessary that the notification of fine or reward should closely follow the work. This cannot be done unless the testing is undertaken as the work proceeds, but it was found impracticable to carry on the testing, owing to the mistakes in the schedules which it was at first attempted to rectify by local enquiry, pending which the books had to be set aside. For instance, a book was abstracted on sheet I which dealt with the sex, age, religion, and civil condition; then it was given out for abstraction on sheet II, which dealt with education, when it was found that column 12 of the schedule was blank or improperly filled in; this required correction, and until it could be made further abstraction of the book could not be proceeded with; but in order to test the work the book must be first abstracted on all the different working sheets, and if the abstraction on some sheets is stopped for any cause those sheets which have been abstracted before the stoppage cannot be tested until after some delay. If the schedules are all properly filled in, or if only such mistakes occur as can be at once corrected under general rules, the abstraction of one book on the different sheets can proceed in regular sequence, but even then the work will require careful adjustment as some sheets are worked off quicker than others and the differing capacities of the abstractors have also to be taken into consideration. Theoretically the system appears good, but I doubt if it is a practicable one when starting a new office with raw material of unknown quality.

Successful abstraction depended a good deal upon the size of the blocks, and I found that generally a population of 200 was the maximum that could be satisfactorily worked. Where this number was exceeded mistakes invariably occurred, especially in the more complicated sheets which dealt with age-periods. The ruling of some of the working sheets was bad. This is an important matter, as bad ruling leads to incorrect totalling.

The tabulation registers were in my opinion too small; each page contained space for the entries for ten blocks, and the page totals had of course to be carried on; if each page had been ruled for twenty or twenty-five blocks the amount of page totalling and 'carrying over' would have been much reduced.

Suggestions.

As regards the schedule, I think that for a future census the requirements might be curtailed with much advantage. Sect of religion and subdivision of caste might be omitted; the distinctions between sect and religion, except in the case of Christians, and between caste and subdivision are not generally understood; the returns are largely incorrect and probably of very little value. Parent-tongue would perhaps not be required again, and the information given under this head is often of doubtful accuracy. The occupation return is to some extent unreliable and the detail probably entirely incommensurate in value with the cost of obtaining it. With regard to education, I concur with the opinion expressed at the Conference at Simla, which I was unfortunately for myself unable to attend, that the enquiry should be confined to literate and illiterate.

If, however, it is possible at the next census to limit the enquiry to a few simple heads, I would advocate the system of individual cards in place of schedule books. For each person enumerated there would be a separate card, on which would be recorded the information now set down in a book. The advantage of cards is the simplification in the abstraction of the contents. To merely count the cards is to arrive at the total population; to divide them into two packets and to count these gives the numbers of each sex; to deal each of these again into three heaps is to separate the married, unmarried, and widowed; to ascertain the education it is only necessary to divide these again and sum up the results; and so on. With a little practice the cards can be dealt with rapidity and accuracy, and it is easier to count the number of cards in a pack than to total up the same number of strokes on a sheet of paper. The only objection to the system is, I believe, the danger of cards being lost, but under proper precautions this might be guarded against.

Assuming, however, that the present system is again adopted, I would recommend that there should be no haste in commencing abstraction. A month or so spent at the commencement in putting the books into proper order and in teaching, examining, and finally selecting the men would be more than made up within the year. When the books are collected at the tehsili they should be thoroughly examined there and all omissions and mistakes rectified by the Supervisors and Enumerators concerned, who might be required to attend pending the inspection of their books. The Tehsildars, or other specially deputed officers, should be personally responsible for the proper performance of this duty, and should send in the books to the abstraction office with a statement showing the revenue number and name of each village, the number of the Charge (if Charges are retained), of the Circle and of the Block or Blocks which the village comprises, the number of books used for each Block, and the numbers of the males and females and of the houses recorded. The last three items would be obtained from the abstracts and would afford a useful check in the Census Office. A fortnight might be allowed for this work and another week for the despatch and carriage of the books, so that within three weeks from the census the whole of the books should be at the Census office; the dockets being complete, they could be at once registered and sorted, and by another week they would all be arranged and ready for issue. Meanwhile candidates for employment should be taught the work of abstraction in small squads, and for this purpose copies of the preliminary record of some blocks should be provided; after a few days' practice the candidates should be examined by requiring them to abstract specific books and noting the time occupied and testing the results. Those who give satisfaction would be retained and the rest dismissed, and thus by the time the books are ready to be dealt with an establishment of qualified men would be prepared to cope with them.

These recommendations have reference of course to the treatment of the census returns in a local office, but I venture to suggest that the most efficient and economical plan for the preparation and publication of census statistics would be the establishment of a permanent Census Office for all India. Much of the time and, therefore, money, spent upon the preparation of the tables under the present system is due to the inexperience of the working establishment, which entails a slow rate of work with inaccurate results and the consequent necessity of doing it over again. Remarkable rapidity and accuracy can be attained after some training and practice, but in a temporary office the work is completed by the time these qualities are acquired. In a permanent office a comparatively small number of men would work with more expedition and precision and would turn out the results from time to time with the regularity of a machine. Such an office would not be suitable for dealing with the returns of a decennial synchronous census, but there seems no necessity for any further simultaneous enumeration, and different portions of the empire could be dealt with in turns, so that the census of each would be taken at least once in ten years. The cost under this plan would not only be probably less than it is now, but it would be spread over a much longer period.

Cost of the undertaking.

It now only remains to state the cost of the undertaking and a detailed account of the expenditure is furnished on the next page. The expenditure shown for the current year is approximate only and subject to revision, but it includes all that has been incurred up to the time of writing together with some small estimated sums which may be expended before the date of closing the work; the only important item that remains to be added is the cost of the publication of this report against which must be set off the proceeds of its sale. The total expenditure has been R45,315, of which R3,586 have been incurred on account of the enumeration and the abstraction and tabulation of the records of Secunderabad, the Hyderabad Residency bazars, the stations of the Hyderabad Contingent, and the railway population within the Nizam's dominions. The total expenditure for Berar has been R41,728, of which nearly R494 has been contributed from municipal funds. Against this sum must be set off R351 recovered by the sale of unused schedules, furniture, and waste paper. The net cost has, therefore been R41,377, but as this sum includes an item of R484 on account of the purchase of an arithmometer, which is now to be made over to the Commissioner, Hyderabad Assigned Districts, I may take credit on paper for the odd R377 for this transaction, and this reduces the expenditure to R41,000, which amounts to a very little more than R14 per thousand of population. The cost of the actual enumeration was only R4,454 or R1-8 per thousand.

On the services rendered by the officers in the abstraction office, I have already addressed the Commissioner, Hyderabad Assigned Districts, but I may here in conclusion repeat my sense of indebtedness to Mr. Ardesir D. Chinoy for his able and indefatigable assistance.

Statement of Account.

	Main Head.	Sub-head.	1890-91. Revised estimate.	1890-91. Actual expenditure.	1891-92. Revised estimate.	1891-92. Actual expenditure.	1892-93. Estimate.	1892-93. Actual expenditure.	Total expenditure 1890 to 1893.	Amount incurred on account of stations in Hyderabad dominions.	Total expenditure for Berar.
			R	R a. p.	R a. p.	R a. p.	R	R a. p.	R a. p.	R a. p.	R a. p.
PART A.—ENUMERATION.	I.—District Charges.	1. District office establishment	...	...	...	...	...	...	...	...	...
		2. Contingent charges of establishment	...	735 3 9	...	44 0 0	...	...	779 3 9	...	779 3 9
		3. House-numbering	...	219 1 8	...	15 2 3	...	...	234 3 11	...	234 3 11
		4. Lights, ink, etc.	...	205 10 9	...	32 14 0	...	...	238 8 9	...	238 8 9
		5. Remuneration of census officers	...	...	...	459 8 0	...	...	459 8 0	...	459 8 0
		6. Special travelling allowances	...	135 10 6	...	113 5 6	...	...	249 0 0	...	249 0 0
		7. Freight of schedules, etc., from stations and landing places	...	126 15 6	...	89 0 0	...	...	215 15 6	...	215 15 6
		Total I.—District Charges	3,650	1,422 10 2	1,133 0 9	753 13 9	...	...	2,176 7 11	...	2,176 7 11
	II.—Enumeration Printing.	8. Paper for schedules, etc., at press			...	...	...	...			
		9. Printing and binding	...	2,313 11 3	...	...	...	...	2,313 11 3	270 15 0	2,277 6 10
		10. Despatching from press	...	234 10 7	...	...	...	...	234 10 7		
		Total II.—Paper and Printing	2,250	2,548 5 10	...	...	...	...	2,548 5 10	270 15 0	2,277 6 10
		A.—Total Enumeration	5,900	3,971 0 0	1,133 0 9	753 13 9	...	...	4,724 13 9	270 15 0	4,453 14 9
PART B.—ABSTRACTION AND COMPILATION.	III.—Tabulation Office.	11. Office rent		35 0 0			140				
		12. Office furniture and repairs, etc.	1,800	742 1 0	1,300 0 0	1,303 4 8	...	...	2,080 5 8	110 0 0	1,970 5 8
		13. Record establishment	...	...	...	...	...	...	...	...	...
		14. Correspondence and account establishment		...	900 0 0	780 0 10	260	140 0 0	920 0 10	43 0 0	877 0 10
		15. Menial establishment	100	...	730 0 0	792 2 6	200	135 0 0	927 2 6	44 0 0	883 2 6
		16. Working staff, including superintendence officials		...	4,000 0 0	3,472 9 0	430	...	3,472 9 0	2,393 15 3	22,065 0 0
		17. Working staff clerks specially entertained		...	21,500 0 0	20,986 6 3	900	...	20,986 6 3		
		18. Travelling allowance to and from Census office	800	61 6 0	150 0 0	125 13 0	150	...	187 3 0	...	187 3 0
		19. Freight of schedules, etc., to office	70	...	...	...	...	...	...	...	...
		20. Petty stationery and contingencies	50	225 1 11	850 0 0	626 13 9	100	...	851 15 8	48 0 0	808 15 8
		Total III.—Tabulation Office	2,820	1,063 8 11	29,430 0 0	28,087 2 0	2,180	275 0 0	29,425 10 11	2,638 15 3	26,786 11 8
	IV.—Tabulation Printing.	21. Paper for sheets, registers and tables at press			350 0 0	240 10 0		...			
		22. Printing of forms, tables and report	1,400	1,202 9 5	500 0 0	...	5,000	310 3 4	1,969 9 3	105 0 0	1,864 9 3
		23. Freight of sheets, etc., to office			150 0 0	...		216 2 6			
		Total IV.—Paper and Printing	1,400	1,202 9 5	1,000 0 0	240 10 0	5,000	526 5 10	1,969 9 3	105 0 0	1,864 9 3
		Total Compilation	4,220	2,266 2 4	30,430 0 0	28,327 12 0	7,180	801 5 10	31,395 4 2	2,743 15 3	28,651 4 11

Berar. PART C.—SUPERINTENDENCE.	V.—SUPERINTENDENCE.	24. Provincial Superintendent's deputation allowance	2,200	2,200 0 0	2,400 0 0	2,004 4 10	668	750 0 0	4,954 4 10	...	4,954 4 10
		25. Pay of substitute of Superintendent	1,500	...	...	...	...	...	...	...	...
		26. Travelling allowance of Superintendent	1,200	1,088 2 0	500 0 0	...	...	...	1,088 2 0	...	1,088 2 0
		TOTAL V.—Superintendent's personal charges	4,900	3,288 2 0	2,900 0 0	2,004 4 10	668	750 0 0	6,042 6 10	...	6,042 6 10
	VI.—SUPERINTENDENT'S OFFICE.	27. Superintendent's office establishment	1,310 (27 and 28)	1,241 7 0	650 0 0	596 10 8	200	225 0 0	2,063 1 8	571 4 2	1,491 13 6
		28. Travelling allowance for ditto		71 2 0	...	...	...	...	71 2 0	...	71 2 0
		29. Office contingencies for ditto	520	520 0 0	600 0 0	448 4 0	150	50 0 0	1,018 4 0	...	1,018 4 0
		30. Rent of Superintendent's office establishment	...	...	...	...	...	...	...	...	...
		TOTAL VI.—Superintendence Establishment	1,830	1,832 9 0	1,250 0 0	1,044 14 8	350	275 0 0	3,152 7 8	571 4 2	2,581 3 6
		TOTAL SUPERINTENDENCE	6,730	5,120 11 0	4,150 0 0	3,039 3 6	1,018	1,025 0 0	9,194 14 6	571 4 2	8,623 10 4
		GRAND TOTAL	16,850	11,357 13 4	35,713 0 9	32,130 13 3	8,198	1,826 5 10	45,315 0 5	3,586 2 5	41,728 14 0
										Recoveries	351 12 3
										Net cost	41,377 1 9

APPENDIX.

SELECTIONS FROM GENERAL INSTRUCTIONS ISSUED TO DEPUTY COMMISSIONERS.

Circular No. 1.

Under the instructions of the Census Commissioner for India I have the honour to request that you will be so good as to take in hand at once the administrative arrangements of your district for the ensuing Census, which will be taken on the night of the 26th February 1891.

2. The operations will be based on the lines of those for the Census of 1881, and I beg to invite your attention to Mr. Kitts's Report upon that undertaking.

3. As in 1881, the Taluk will be the basis of area upon which the scheme is to be framed. Each Taluk should be divided into a number of *Charges;* each *Charge* into a number of *Circles;* and each *Circle* into a number of *Blocks.*

4. The Taluk arrangements will be in charge of the Tehsildar under your immediate control. Each *Charge* will be placed in charge of a *Charge-Superintendent;* each *Circle* in charge of a *Supervisor;* and each *Block* in charge of an *Enumerator.*

5. The Charges and Circles should be generally the same as those adopted in 1881, the record of which it is presumed is in your office. Some of them may, however, require re-adjustment, especially in the case of towns where there has been any large variation of population.

6. Should you have no record of the arrangements for the last Census it will be necessary for you to form the divisions afresh. In this case you should be guided (1) by the Police subdivisions of the Taluk, a Police Station range forming a convenient area for one or more complete Charges, and (2) by the average number of houses to a Circle adopted at the last Census, which you will find detailed in Table No. 1, page 1, of the Census Report.

7. Having formed Charges and Circles, it will be necessary to demarcate them on a map. If the maps in use for the last Census are forthcoming, they will, with some correction perhaps, serve again; if not, a map should be prepared for each Taluk on a scale of one inch to a mile, and on these the outlines of the Charges should be traced in thick lines and outlines of the Circles in dotted lines, in red ink. Each Charge should be given a serial number in the Taluk, and each Circle a serial number in the Charge, and the number should be marked upon the map, also in red ink, Roman figures being used to distinguish the Charges.

8. Having put the preparation of these maps in hand, you should proceed to appoint the Charge Superintendents and Supervisors. For these the same agency should be used as in 1881. Tables 2 and 4, pages 2 and 3 of the Census Report, show the classes from which these officials were drawn on that occasion. It is desirable that the Supervisors should, if possible, be selected from residents in the Circles to which they are appointed. The Charge-Superintendents should generally be Government Officers whose activity and intelligence can be thoroughly relied upon.

9. When the appointments are made each Charge-Superintendent should be given a copy of the map showing the extent of his Charge and a list of the villages in it; and each Supervisor should be given a list of the villages in his Circle, or where in the case of a town or large village a portion is only allotted to him, a description of the area entrusted to him.

10. It will then be the duty of each Charge-Superintendent to go over his Charge with the Supervisors of the respective Circles and test the map on the ground, and to make a report of all villages marked on it which have ceased to be inhabited and of all new villages which have been omitted. The Taluk maps should then be corrected by these reports, and a tracing of the corrected maps be supplied to this office.

11. Meanwhile it will be the duty of the Supervisors under the general direction of the Charge-Superintendents to split up their Circles into Blocks.

12. In the formation of Blocks the Supervisors should be guided by the following rules:—

(1) Each Block should contain from about 40 to 50 houses. If necessary, the number may be increased to 60, but should not exceed that limit.

(2) By the term "a house" is meant "a dwelling-place of one or more families with their resident servants, having a separate principal entrance from the common way."

(3) Stables, sheds, out-houses, etc., which are not ordinarily used as dwellings are not to be reckoned as separate houses.

(4) In forming Blocks villages must not be mixed up; that is, two villages or parts of two villages, however small, must not be thrown into the same Block.

13. When the Blocks have been formed, the Supervisor should submit a report showing the number of houses in each village, or where he has only a portion of a village the number in the area, the number of Blocks in the Circle, a brief description of the area of the Block sufficient to identify it, and the number of houses in each block.

14. Upon the receipt of these reports you will be in a position to check the general distribution.

15. The above scheme refers to your district generally. Where Municipalities exist similar arrangements should be made, but their area should be excluded from that of the Taluk for administrative purposes, and the Municipal Committee should represent the controlling authority immediately subordinate to yourself.

16. These preliminary arrangements should be completed with as little delay as possible.

Dated the 10th May 1890.

Circular No. 3.

I have the honour to request that you will furnish me before the end of this month with a statement in the accompanying form, which is described as the *Subdivisional Register*, for each Taluk in your District.

The names and figures entered upon the form are given as examples of the way in which it should be filled up.

The entries in column 4 should be checked with the Tehsilwar Register so as to ensure that no villages have been omitted.

Dated the 10th June 1890.

TALUK AMRAOTI—CONSISTING OF 4 CHARGES.

SUB-DIVISIONAL REGISTER.

Charge No. 2 under Charge-Superintendent Ram Rao, Inspector of Police, consisting of 8 Circles.

1	2	3	4	5	6	7	8	9
Serial No. of Circle.	Name, occupation, and residence of Supervisor.	Names of villages in the Circle.	No. of village in Tehsilwar Register.	No. of houses in each village.	Description of limits of Circle when it does not include the whole village.	No. of Blocks in each village.	No. of Blocks in each Circle.	REMARKS.
1	Govind Rao, Deshpandya, Ramapur	Ramapur Wadali Ashti	5 23 14	220 150 80	... ...	5 3 2	10	
2	Ramchandra, Putwari, Bulgaon	Bulgaon	65	1,025	All north of main Bazar Road	22	10	
3	Kishen Singh, Sub-Registrar, Bulgaon	Ditto	,,	,,	All south of main Bazar Road	,,	12	
4								

Circular No. 4.

I have the honour to request you to furnish me with an indent for the supply of Schedules that you will require for your District.

2. Each house will require a separate Schedule, and each Schedule will contain space for the enumeration of eight persons only, so that it will be necessary to have two or more Schedules for each house containing more than eight persons. It is believed, however, that there will not be many instances of such large households if the definition of a house given in Circular No. 1 has been strictly applied in the preparation of Blocks.

3. The Schedules will be bound in books, and there will be a separate book, or books, for each Block.

4. It is proposed to bind the books in numbers of 10, 30, 50 and 70 Schedules. The first size of 10 Schedules is intended for those villages which contain only a nominal number of houses, and also for the supply of subsidiary Schedules where such may be required owing to spoilage and waste. The other sizes are intended for Blocks containing, respectively, from 10 to 25 houses, from 26 to 45 houses, and from 46 to 60 houses. In each case a margin has been allowed for supplementary requirements.

5. You will also require a certain number of separate *Householder's Schedules*. These are prepared in English only and are intended for the use of Europeans and Eurasians and such native gentlemen of position as know English and will undertake to fill them up.

6. In this connection I have to add the following instructions on the preliminary organisation.

7. All jails, hospitals, Police barracks, religious institutions, and other establishments where there are a large number of residents, should be made into separate Blocks, and a note of all such Blocks should be made in the column of remarks in the Sub-divisional Register.

8. In the case of officers' bungalows, etc., where servants reside in separate and detached houses, each such house will be reckoned separately, and the Householder's Schedule will be provided for the principal occupier of the premises and those actually resident under his own roof only.

9. Railway premises and any houses upon them are not to be included in the arrangements for the Taluk.

10. The indent you are now asked to prepare should show in tabular form how many of each class of Schedule Book and how many Householder's Schedules you will require, with full instructions as to where and how you desire them to be despatched. It should be furnished as soon as practicable and at latest by the end of August, and I have to request your particular attention to its punctual transmission.

Dated the 24th July 1890.

Circular No. 5.

I have the honour to inform you that the sum of R is allotted to your District on account of contingencies in connection with the Census. This amount is intended to meet all expenditure necessarily incurred on account of the Census, such as the preparation of maps, house numbering, lights, red ink for the final record, and petty stationery for the use of the non-official staff.

Amraoti	475
Akola	500
Ellichpur	300
Buldana	450
Wun	425
Basim	400
TOTAL	2,550

2. The expenditure should be carefully regulated, as while the items will be small individually the numbers will be large.

3. There need be little or no expenditure for lighting. On the final Census night there will be moonlight, and each householder should provide a light for the enumerator to read and write by at his visit. At the last Census the expenditure on this account was excessive while in only one other province in India was any incurred at all.

4. The expenditure should be included in your ordinary district contingent bills debited to Census, and an account should be transmitted to this office at the close of each month showing the total expenditure under each head.

5. No fixed allotment can be made to meet the cost of carriage and distribution of Schedule books, etc., but any expenditure on this account that is actually necessary may be incurred and debited in the same way.

6. No expenditure on account of payment of enumerators may be incurred without special sanction.

7. In Municipalities the expenditure should be met from municipal funds, and should not be included in the district charges.

Dated the 3rd September 1890.

Circular No. 6.

I have the honour to advise the despatch to you under another cover of copies of a Census Manual in English, and to request that you will be good enough to acknowledge their receipt.

2. The Manual is intended to cover general instructions for all officers up to the taking of the Census.

3. The present copies are for distribution to all District Gazetted Officers who know English, and to Municipal Committees.

4. Copies in Marathi are in course of preparation and will be forwarded as soon as they are ready. These are for distribution to all Charge-Superintendents and Supervisors and to such Gazetted officers as do not know English.

5. Forms of certificates of appointment for Supervisors and Enumerators will be supplied to you.

Dated the 5th September 1890.

Census Manual for Berar.

1. The following is a sketch of the general scheme of operations. Each Taluk and Municipality having been divided into Charges, Circles, and Blocks, and Charge-Superintendents and Supervisors having been appointed, the next steps to be taken will be the numbering of the houses and the preparation of lists of men for appointment as Enumerators. When this has been done, Village lists will be prepared in a prescribed form. The Schedule books will then be distributed and the Block lists prepared and entered in the books. On the 15th January the Enumerators will commence the first round or preliminary record, going from house to house and filling up the Schedules in accordance with their instructions. This will be completed by the 1st February, and during this period and the interval before the final Census night, the Enumerator's work will be checked. On the night of the 26th February they will go round their entire Blocks, correcting to date the record they will have already made. In certain special tracts of the country this will be done on the next day. After the second round the Schedules will be finally tested and the records collected.

2. House numbering will be taken in hand at once on receipt of these instructions and should be completed by the 15th October at latest.

It will be the duty of the Supervisors to number the houses. It will be done with such material (inexpensive) as Deputy Commissioners may direct. A mixture of charcoal and lamp-oil makes a good pigment; there need be no attempt at permanency, as it is only requisite that the numbers should last until the 31st March, before which their removal is forbidden under the Census Act.

A separate number must be given to every house which is used or intended for human habitation. A house has already been defined to be the "dwelling-place of one or more families with their resident servants having a separate principal entrance from the common way." The "common way" is not necessarily a public way: thus the servants' quarters attached to a bungalow have not generally a separate entrance giving on to the public way, but as they have separate entrances from the common way, that is, the way common to each, it follows that each is a distinct house. Separate numbers will not be given to stables, out-houses, etc., which are not used as dwellings. Ruined houses may be omitted, but houses in course of construction and likely to be completed before the Census night should be numbered.

If there is any difficulty in painting the number, as in the case perhaps of a grass chupper or of a house under construction, it can be written on a piece of paper, or painted on a large stone, or a board, etc., and given to the occupier to keep or to attach to the house.

The numbers must be serial for the whole village and consecutive for each Block; and the numbering of one Block must be completed before that of the next is commenced. Ordinarily the last number of the last Block will show the total number of houses in a village; thus in a village of 150 houses consisting of three Blocks of 50 houses each, the first Block will be numbered from 1 to 50 the second from 51 to 100, and the third from 101 to 150. In the case of large villages and towns consisting of two or more Circles the numbering of the first Circle must be completed before that of the next is commenced. In Municipalities divided into wards the numbers may be serial for each ward. In these cases the Charge-Superintendents will direct the process and see that there is no delay in continuing the numbering from one Circle to the next.

Supervisors must be very careful in carrying out this work. Before painting the numbers they should make a preliminary round and roughly number the houses with dry charcoal or chalk or some substance which will easily rub off; and then having carefully checked them and corrected any mistakes they should proceed to paint the numbers finally.

If, subsequently to this process, it is found that a house has been omitted, or a new house not calculated for constructed, it should be given the number next to it with a letter attached; thus a house omitted between No. 46 and No. 47 would be numbered 46 A. Such houses must not be forgotten in the abstraction; *vide* paragraph 13.

3. Having completed the house-numbering Supervisors will give a serial number to each Block in their Circles and prepare their Village Lists showing the serial numbers of the Blocks, the serial numbers of the houses in each Block, and the names of the proposed Enumerators. Where the Blocks are very small and two or more are so close together that one man can visit all the houses in them in one evening, a separate Enumerator need not be appointed to each. Jails, hospitals, and other institutions which have been treated as separate Blocks will be enumerated by the Officer or other person in charge. Such buildings will not be numbered. The Village Lists on completion should be sent in to the Deputy Commissioner without delay, and at latest by the 20th of October.

4. Supervisors will then prepare their Block Lists, putting down each house as it is numbered with its description and the name of the principal occupant. At the foot of the list they will enter any mango-topes, encamping grounds, etc., within the Block where travellers halt and may be found on the Census night. No numbers will be given to these places. They will also note in the column for remarks the houses where private or Householder's Schedules are to be left.

5. When the Village Lists have been finally approved by Deputy Commissioners, and Enumerators appointed, the Schedule books will be distributed. The distribution should be arranged so

that the books may reach the Supervisors by the 15th November. Tehsildars will keep an account of all books issued to each Charge-Superintendent and see that they are returned after the Census. Similarly Charge-Superintendents and Supervisors will keep an account of their receipts and issues. The most careful attention must be given to this duty. Each officer in turn will fill up the entries in the Docket on the cover of the books, so far as is applicable, as they pass through his hands.

6. On receipt of the Schedule books Supervisors will enter in them on the page provided a copy of the Block Lists they will have already prepared, and deliver the books to the Enumerators by the 1st December. The Block Lists will be a guide to the Enumerators of the houses and places they have to visit. Supervisors will direct them to go round their Blocks and satisfy themselves that the lists are complete and that no houses have been omitted; if there are any mistakes or if any alterations take place before the 26th February, it will be their duty to bring them to the notice of the Supervisors and to have their lists corrected accordingly. During the interval before the 15th January the Enumerators will be expected to learn the Instructions printed in the Schedule Books and take care to ascertain thoroughly what they have to do and how to do it. They will also be required to practise enumeration by filling up rough forms of Schedules on plain paper which the Supervisors will examine and subsequently destroy. If there are any doubtful points not provided for in the Instructions they should ask about them at once. Supervisors will convey the above directions to the Enumerators.

7. On the 15th January the preliminary record will be commenced, and Supervisors should arrange to accompany each Enumerator to a few houses and to see him fill in the entries in the Schedules, on that or the next day.

8. During the week before the 26th February the Householder's Schedules will be distributed, through the Enumerators, to such houses as Deputy Commissioners may direct.

9. Officers in camp will be required to enumerate the entire party with them, and for this purpose will obtain beforehand the requisite Schedules from the Deputy Commissioner direct, and return them completed the next day to the Supervisor of the area in which the camp is situated, taking a receipt.

10. If any fairs are being held on the 26th February, Deputy Commissioners will make special arrangements for their enumeration, treating them as separate areas the returns of which are to be kept apart from those of the ordinary residents of the locality.

11. If any troops are on the march, Deputy Commissioners will arrange for their enumeration as in the case of Officers in camp.

Final Census.

12. On the night of the 26th February Enumerators will go their final rounds in accordance with their detailed instructions. Supervisors will be expected to visit every Block in their Circles and ascertain that Enumerators are doing, or have done, their duty. Charge-Superintendents will assist Supervisors in this respect as far as possible.

Supervisors will see before hand that each Enumerator is provided with red ink for this occasion, They should also warn all householders to have lights ready at their houses to enable the Enumerators to do their work.

If at the first round any difficulty is experienced by a Hindu Enumerator in the case of Mahomedan families, or if any such difficulty is anticipated on the final night, the Supervisor should arrange for an influential Mahomedan to accompany the Enumerator to such houses.

13. Testing.

On the morning of the 27th February Enumerators will fill up their Abstracts, and join their Supervisor at a time and place to be named by him. The Supervisor will then cause each Enumerator's book or books to be separately abstracted by two other Enumerators, one after the other. Any mistakes found will then be enquired into and corrected. When they have all been tested and corrected the Supervisor will sign the certificate at foot of the Abstract and fastening all the books together take them in to the Charge-Superintendent. He in turn will check the number of books, sign the dockets, and from the Abstracts in each book compile a similar Abstract for his Charge, and then take all on again to the Tehsildar.

Further instructions on this head may be issued hereafter.

14. General instruction.

Deputy Commissioners and their Assistants and Tehsildars should hold meetings of Census Officials and go through the Instructions and Rules clause by clause, so that there may be no misunderstanding. Practical experience will be gained by filling up the Schedule entries in a rough form for any of the persons present.

15. Checking.

Many opportunities will occur to Officers of all Departments and all grades when moving in camp in the cold season to assist in the very necessary and important duty of checking the work of the Census Staff. Deputy Commissioners should give their Assistants special instructions in this respect.

*In the preliminary stages it can be seen whether houses have been properly numbered or whether there are any omissions; Village and Block Lists can be examined; Supervisors and Enumerators questioned. From the 15th January when the enumeration commences the work should be everywhere daily examined, by Supervisors, Charge-Superintendents, Tehsildars, Taluk Officers, Police Officers, Deputy Commissioners, and any others who can; and it should be seen that the entries in the Schedules are strictly in accordance with the instructions. Obvious errors should be at once explained and corrected, and doubtful points referred.

16. Changes.

Any changes made in the Census Staff should be entered in the lists and Registers and duly reported to offices concerned.

A reserve list should be kept of men available for any of the posts which may become vacant before the Census night. Supervisors especially should have one or two men ready at hand on the Census night in case any Enumerator should fail at the last moment.

17. Certificates of appointment will be given to all Charge-Superintendents, Supervisors, and Enumerators. Those who are not so supplied should apply for them.

18. Appended is a copy of the Instructions to Enumerators, which should be carefully perused by all Superintending Officers.

Also a specimen schedule showing a variety of entries which will serve as guide in doubtful cases.

Also lists* of the chief sects of religion and subdivisions of castes to be found in Berar.

* Omitted.

APPENDIX I.

Instructions to Enumerators.

A.—The first Round. (Preliminary record.)

1. Beginning from the 15th of January 1891, you will visit every house in your block to which a separate number has been affixed, in the order in which they are entered in the list in your book, and enter in the schedules in that book every person residing in those houses in the manner prescribed below.

2. You must use black ink, and write very clearly in the character you know best; and write between the ruled lines.

3. You must take a fresh page for each house. If there are more than eight persons in a house you should continue the entries for that house on the next page, repeating at the top of that page the number of the house in question, with the word "continued" after it in brackets. You must never begin the entries for a fresh house in the middle of a page, but should leave the unused lines blank.

4. If the entry for any person in any of the columns of the Schedule be the same as that for the person entered on the line above, you must repeat the entry and never write the word "ditto" or make dots.

5. If one of the houses on the list be found unoccupied, you should write the word "empty" after the number of that house on the top of the form.

6. You are to enter all persons who ordinarily live and take their meals from the house, even though any of them may be, at the time of your visit, absent for a short time at the bazar, town, watching crops, fishery, or even for a few days at a wedding, or on a pilgrimage, provided they are to be back at the house before the 26th February. After the residents you should enter the visitors, if any, stopping in the house, but not such as are only there for a day or two, as for a wedding, etc., and will not remain there till the 26th February. In dharmshalas, serais, or temples, you should enter on this occasion only those who usually live there and not travellers, etc., stopping only a day or a night or so in the building.

7. Before beginning to make these entries you must read carefully the rules for filling up each column which are printed on the next page and also the specimen schedule on the page opposite those rules. Read also the standard questions printed at the back of the specimen schedule. These questions indicate the main points on which enquiries are to be made, but if the answers given do not contain the information required according to the Rules additional questions must be asked.

8. You should point out to the Supervisor entries about which you are in doubt and receive his instructions. You must have completed all the entries in your block by the 1st of February 1891.

B.—The Second Round. (Final record.)

9. At nightfall on the 26th February 1891, you will take this book as already filled in and again visit every house in your block in order, taking red ink with you.

10. You must summon the chief member of each family residing in the house, and read over to him the entries made for his family in the schedule. You will strike out the entries for persons who are not present, and fill up the form for any person now in the house who was not there when the first visit was made, such as guests, infants newly born, and others. You are to consider as present all living in or taking their meals from the house, even though any of them may be out fishing or watching in the fields or at a shop, etc., for the night.

11. If there be no room left on the schedule for the fresh entries above mentioned, you must take a fresh page at the end of your book, and enter on it the house number with the word "continued" after it, as prescribed in paragraph 3 above.

12. Before you start on your round you must see that you are yourself enumerated in the house where you are stopping.

13. You must make no alteration whatever in any entry against the name of any person unless you have to strike out the entries altogether because he or she is no longer present. When you strike out a person, you must draw the line completely through all the entries following that person's name and not merely through column 1.

14. You must use only red ink for entries and erasures made on the round on the 26th February.

15. Whilst going on this round you must visit every house marked "empty" in your book to see whether any person is now living there, and if you find any you must enumerate them.

16. After visiting as above all the dwelling houses, you must go to the dharmshalas, serais, encampments and landing places, where travellers rest for the night, and enter all particulars in the schedules for the way-farers, boatmen, pilgrims, etc., you may find there, and strike out the entries already made against persons who are not now persent. You should ascertain from the village watchmen if any wandering gang, etc,, has come to pitch in your block, and if there be any such you should go and enumerate it as above prescribed for other persons.

17. After your book has been inspected by the Supervisor you will prepare the short abstract printed on the back of the specimen schedule in it, as directed by the Supervisor, and he will not take charge of your book until he has certified it to be correct.

18. According to the Census Act every person is legally bound to furnish you with such information as is necessary for filling up the schedule; but you are forbidden to ask for any information not required for the purposes of the Census. Any Enumerator detected in extorting money on any pretext connected with the Census renders himself liable to punishment under the Census Act or the Penal Code.

C.—Rules for filling up the Schedule.

RULE 1.—Column 1 (*Serial number and name*).—Enter first the chief resident member of the family, whether male or female, then the other members of the family and their resident servants, if any, and lastly, visitors or temporary residents. If there be any objection made to giving the name of a female, write the word "female" in this column (with her relationship to some member of the household).

If an infant has not yet been named, enter the word "infant." The serial number must not be added till the final record.

RULE 2.—Column 2 (*Religion*).—Enter here the religion which each person returns:—As Hindu, Mussalman, Jain, Christian, Parsi. Forest tribes who are not Hindus, Mussalmans, etc., should have the name of their tribe entered in this column, as Bhil, Gond, Korku, etc.

RULE 3.—Column 3 (*Sect of religion*).—Enter the sect of religion followed by each person as they return it:—As Smarth, Vaishnav, Manbhao, Nath, Bairagi, Lingaiat, etc., for Hindus; Sunni Shiah, etc., for Mussalmans; and for Christians enter whether Church of England, Roman Catholic, Presbyterian, Lutheran, Baptist, etc. If the sect cannot be stated, enter "not returned" in this column, but do not leave it blank.

RULE 4.—Column 4 (*Caste, etc.*).——Enter the caste of Hindus and Jains, and the tribes of those who have not castes, and the races of Christians, Buddhists, etc,:—As Brahman, Rajput, Bania, Kunbi, for Hindus; Pathan, Moghal, etc., for Mussalmans; Eurasian or Native Christian for Christians. Do not enter vague terms, such as Hindustani, Marwari, Marathi, Panjabi, etc.

RULE 5.—Column 5 (*Subdivision of Caste, etc.*).—If the caste has been entered in column 4, enter here the subdivision, as Maharastra, Kanujia or Nagar of Brahmans, Osval of Banias, etc. If tribe, enter the clan; such as Tadwi, Pawada, etc., for Bhils; if race, enter the tribe or nationality, as English for European.

Some races or castes may not return subdivisions, and in their case the entry in column 4 should be repeated, but this column must not be left blank. Native Christians, for instance, may be returned as Portuguese, East Indian, Madrasi, or by their caste, if recognized.

RULE 6.—Column 6 (*Male or Female*).—Enter here each person as either male or female, even though you have written the word "female" in column 1 already.

RULE 7.—Column 7 (*Age*).—Enter the number of years each person has completed. For infants less than one year old, enter the word "infant."

If a person cannot state his or her age exactly, the enumerator should ask the relations, or if the person be present, make a guess at the age from the appearance. He must never insist on seeing any female who is not voluntarily produced before him.

RULE 8.— Column 8 (*Marriage, etc*).—Enter each person, whether infant, child, or grown up, as either married, unmarried, or widowed. This column must not be left blank for any one of whatever age.

Children who have been married should be entered as married, even though they may not have begun to actually live with their wives or husbands. Persons who have been married, but have no wife or husband living, should be entered as widowed.

RULE 9.— Column 9 (*Parent-tongue*).—Enter the language which each person returns as ordinarily spoken in the household of his parents.

RULE 10.—Column 10 (*Birth-place*).—Enter the district in which each person was born, and if the person be not born in Berar add the name of the province or state to the district of birth.

If the person be born out of India, enter the country, as China, Kabul, Ceylon, etc. The names of villages, tehsils, etc., are not to be given.

RULE 11.—Column 11 (*Occupation or means of subsistence*) [*Read this rule very carefully and ask the Supervisor about all cases which seem doubtful to you.*]—Enter here the exact occupation or means of livelihood of all males or females who do work or live on private property, such as house-rent, pension, etc. In the case of children and women who do no work, enter the occupation of the head of their family or of the person who supports them, adding the word "dependent." but do not leave this column unfilled for anyone, even an infant. If a person have two or more occupations, enter only the chief one, except when a person owns or cultivates land in addition to another occupation, when both should be entered.

No vague terms should be used, such as "service," "Government service," "shop-keeping," "writing," or "labour," etc.; but the exact service, the goods sold, the class of writing or labour must be stated. When a person's occupation is connected with agriculture it should be stated whether the land is cultivated in person or all let to tenants; if he be an agricultural labourer, it should be stated whether he be engaged by the month or year, or is a daily field-labourer. Women who earn money by occupations independent of their husbands, such as selling firewood, cow-dung cakes, grass, or by rice-pounding, weaving or doing house-work for wages, should be shown under those occupations. If a person makes the articles he sells, he should be entered as "maker and seller" of them. If a person lives on alms, it should be stated whether he is a religious mendicant or an ordinary beggar. When a person is in Government, Railway, or Municipal service, the special service should be entered first, and the word Government or Municipal, etc., after, as clerk-Government, sweeper-Municipal, labourer-Railway.

If a person be temporarily out of employ, enter the last or ordinary occupation.

RULE 12.—Column 12 (*Instruction*).—Enter in this column against each person, whether grown up, child, or infant, either learning, literate, or illiterate. Enter all those as learning who are under instruction either at home or at school or college. Enter as literate those who are able to both read and write any language, but are not under instruction as above. Enter as illiterate those who are not under instruction, and who do not know how to both read and write, or who can read, but not write, or can sign their own name but not read.

RULE 13.—Column 13 (*Language known by literate*).—Enter here the language which those shown as literate in column 12 can both read and write, and if a person knows how to read and write English, as well as a Vernacular, enter "English" also.

This column is to be left blank for those shown in column 12 as learning or literate, and except when English is known, only one language, that best known, should be entered.

RULE 14.—Column 14 (*Infirmities*).—If any person be blind of both eyes, or deaf and dumb from birth, or insane or suffering from corrosive leprosy, enter the name of the infirmity in this column.

Do not enter those blind of one eye only, or who have become deaf and dumb after birth, or who are suffering from white leprosy only.

APPENDIX II.

Specimen Schedule Entries.

Serial number and name.	Religion.	Sect of religion. (See Rule 3).	Caste of Hindus and Jains. Tribe or race of others. (See Rule 4.)	Subdivision of caste, etc. (See Rule 5.)	Male or Female.	Age.	Married, unmarried or widowed.	Parent-tongue.	Birth district or province. (See Rule 10.)	Occupation, or means of subsistence. (See Rule 11.)	Learning, literate, or illiterate.	Language known by literate. (See Rule 13.)	If any person be insane, deaf mute from birth, totally blind or a leper, enter that person as such below.
1	2	3	4	5	6	7	8	9	10	11	12	13	14
1. Nago	Korku	Not returned	Korku	Korku	Male	23	Unmarried	Korku	Wun	Monthly field labourer	Illiterate.		
2. Ramsing	Sikh	Khuka	Jat	Dhillon	Male	45	Married	Panjabi	Amritsar (Punjab)	Peon, Government	Illiterate.		
3. Laxuman	Hindu	Not returned	Mahar	Mahar	Male	52	Widowed	Marathi	Buldana	Village servant	Illiterate.		
4. Goma	Hindu	Not returned	Chambhar	Chambhar	Male	33	Married	Marathi	Nasik (Bombay)	Maker and seller of shoes	Illiterate.		
5. George Brown	Christian	Presbyterian	Eurasian	Eurasian	Male	25	Unmarried	English	Poona (Bombay)	Clerk, Municipal	Literate	English.	
6. Samuel	Christian	Roman Catholic	Native	Madrasi	Male	30	Widowed	Telugu	Madras	Domestic servant	Illiterate.		
7. D'Souza	Christian	Roman Catholic	Native	Portuguese	Male	40	Married	Goanese	Goa	Cook	Illiterate.		
8. Mookoondrao	Jain	Digambari	Wani	Gangarwal	Male	35	Married	Marathi	Akola	Sub-Registrar	Literate	English and Marathi.	
9. Sakoobai	Hindu	Not returned	Rajput	Chanhan	Female	25	Widow	Hindustani	Ellichpur	Butter-milk seller	Illiterate.		
10. Tanoo	Gond	Not returned	Gond	Gond	Male	32	Married	Gondi	Ellichpur	Timber wood seller and agriculturist Batailar	Illiterate.		
11. Venketswami	Hindu	Vaishnav	Mudelliyer	Mudelliyer	Male	18	Unmarried	Tamil	Bangalore (Madras)	Mason	Illiterate.		
12. Noorkhan	Mussulman	Sunni	Pathan	Afridi	Male	40	Married	Pushto	Afghanistan	Fruit seller	Illiterate.		
13. Goolabshah	Mussulman	Sunni	Shekh	Madari	Male	50	Widowed	Urdu	Akola	Ordinary beggar	Illiterate.		Deaf-mute.
14. Goolam Hoosen	Mussulman	Shiah	Bohra	Sulaimani	Male	30	Married	Guzrathi	Ajmere (Rajputana)	Cloth merchant, khatedar—lessor	Literate	Guzrathi.	
15. Koolsoombi	Mussulman	Mehdvi	Shekh	Shekh	Female	Infant.	Unmarried	Urdu	Amraoti	Peon, Government, 'dependent'	Illiterate.		
16. Golabkhan	Mussulman	Not returned	Bhil	Tadvi	Male	48	Widowed	Urdu	Nemar (Central Provinces.)	Wood and bamboo seller	Illiterate.		

Circular No. 7.

I have the honour to forward by copies of the forms of Village List and Block List referred to in paragraphs 3 and 4 of the Census Manual, for distribution to all Supervisors in your District.

2. The Village List will show the constitution of the Circle and its personnel, and will be a guide to any Inspecting Officer and to any one appointed to replace a Supervisor on an emergency. Columns 1 and 2 of this form should be filled up in your Office from the Subdivisional Register before distribution. The Supervisors will fill in columns 3 and 4 and submit the lists to you for approval, and on approval they should be returned to the Supervisors.

3. The Block List will give a detailed description of each Block. It should be prepared by the Supervisors and be submitted to such approval as you think fit.

4. Specimen copies showing how the forms should be filled up are enclosed herewith.

Dated the 7th September 1890.

VILLAGE LIST.

Vide *Section 3 of the Berar Census Manual for 1891.*

TALUKA—AMRAOTI; CHARGE NO. 2; CIRCLE NO. 1.

Supervisor—Luxman Turerao, Deshmukh of Murtazapur.

Names of villages or description of Circle as given in column 6 of the Subdivisional Register.	Serial number of Block in the Circle.	Serial numbers of the houses in each Block.	Name, occupation, and residence of the Enumerator.	REMARKS.
1	2	3	4	5
Ramapur . .	1	1 to 40	Krishnarao, Patwari of Ramapur.	
	2	41 to 89	Ram Chandra, Schoolmaster, Ramapur.	
	3	90 to 134	Tukaram, Stamp-vendor of Ramapur.	
	4	135 to 177	Sadashiv, Gumasta of Ramapur.	
	5	178 to 220	Chandrabhan wd. Punjaji, Agriculturist of Ramapur.	
Wadali . . .	6	1 to 47	Bakaram, Patel of Wadali.	
	7	48 to 101	Kisan, Compounder, Amraoti Camp.	
	8	102 to 150	Narayan, Petition-writer, Amraoti.	
Ashti . . .	9	1 to 40	Daryaji, Gumasta-Patwari of Ashti.	
	10	41 to 80	Balmukund, Shroff of Ashti.	

NOTE.—In this suppositious Circle there are three villages containing respectively 5, 3, and 2 Blocks. From columns 3 and 7 of the Subdivisional Register, columns 1 and 2 of this list can be filled up. It should be noted that the number of Blocks is serial for the whole Circle, but the numbers of the houses serial for each village. When house numbering is completed the Supervisor can fill in column 3.

BLOCK LIST.

VILLAGE OR QUARTER—WADALI, BLOCK NO. 6; BOOK NO. 1; CIRCLE 1.

Description of the Block, *e.g.*, village, pura, road, etc.	HOUSES.		FAMILIES IN EACH HOUSE.		REMARKS.
	Serial No.	Description, *i.e.*, whether a dwelling-house, shop, serai, etc.	Serial No.	The name of the head of every family.	
	1	Dwelling-house . . .	1	Kishen Patel.	
	2	Ditto . . .	1	...	
	3	Shop	1	...	
	4	Temple	1	...	
	5	Lodging house . . .	1	...	
	...	. . . .	2	...	
	...	. . . .	3	...	
	6	Serai	1	...	
		etc., throughout the Block.			

NOTE.—The Block number above will correspond with that given in column 2 of the Village List and the Circle number will be that of the Circle in the Subdivisional Register.

Circular No. 9.

In continuation of para. 13 of the Census Manual, I have the honour to issue the following further instructions.

2. When the Supervisors reach the Charge-Superintendent with their Enumeration books they should at once prepare from the Enumerator's Abstracts a summary of the items for their respective Circles, and the Charge-Superintendent should then cause each Circle summary to be separately totalled by a second Supervisor. When the summaries have thus been tested and, if necessary corrected, the Charge-Superintendent will prepare a summary for his Charge in the following form :—

DISTRICT. TALUK. CHARGE NO.

Circle.	Occupied houses.	Population.			Remarks.
		Male.	Female.	Total.	
1	2	3	4	5	6
Charge No. Total					

Tested and submitted to the Tehsildar on the ______ of ______ 1891.

(Signed) ______

Charge Superintendent.

3. On receipt of the Charge Abstracts and books the Tehsildar should prepare a summary for the Taluk in a similar form putting Taluk for Charge and Charge for Circle, and transmit it at once to you.

4. Officers in charge of the enumeration in Municipalities should submit to you similar summaries for those areas.

5. You should then prepare a District Summary in the same form showing the totals for Taluks, Municipalities, Railway Circles (which will be communicated by the Railway authorities), troops on the march, camps of officers on tour (which are to be considered as forming part of the head quarters of the District and should not be entered in the Charge Summaries), fairs, and any other special areas not included in the Taluk returns.

6. When the totals are complete you should telegraph the results to the Census Commissioner at Simla and to the Provincial Superintendent in the following concise form :—" *Houses*——. *Males* - ——. *Females*——. *Total*"——. You should also transmit by post to the above officers detailed summaries showing totals for Municipalities (Cantonments) and Rural areas, and grand total.

7. It is hoped that you will be good enough to see that no delay occurs in the preparation and submission of these summaries; I would also ask your special attention to (*a*) the testing of the original addition by the enumerators, and (*b*) the inclusion of the miscellaneous schedules such as those for camps, etc., which may be overlooked.

Dated 30th October 1890.

Circular No. 10.

With reference to your letter No. , dated , I have the honour to convey the following remarks and instructions regarding the Census of travellers.

2. The arrangements already prescribed provide for the Census (1) of persons who on the night of the 26th February will be found at their homes and of their visitors, (2) of those who are temporarily absent in the fields, etc., (3) of those who as travellers halt for the night at recognised camping grounds, etc., and (4) of those who travel by railway. It remains only to provide for those who may travel by road through the night or who may halt temporarily at unknown places.

3. It appears that it may be regarded as certain that travellers on the village roads between sunset and sunrise will be only those who shortly after sunset are returning home or who shortly before sunrise are starting on a journey. Both of these classes will be found at their homes during the night and should be enumerated there. Travellers on the village roads may therefore be disregarded.

4. On the main trunk roads however through travellers will be found. Every portion of these roads lies within the boundaries of some village, and the village authorities should be directed to post

men an hour or so after sunset at one or more spots, as may be necessary, on the road with instructions to put to all passers by the following questions :—

First.—Have you been enumerated to-night? (The preliminary enumeration, it must be remembered, is not sufficient.)

Second —If not, do you intend to travel through the night?

Third.—If not, where do you intend to halt?

Those persons who answer the first question in the affirmative will be allowed to proceed. Those who answer the second question in the affirmative will be directed to stop where they are until they have been enumerated, and the Enumerator will be called. Those who answer the first two questions in the negative and reply to the third will be allowed to proceed to their destination and the village authorities of that place will arrange for their enumeration.

5. At the entrances to towns the municipal or other local authorities will make similar arrangements.

6. For the tracts where the final Census will be taken in the day-time on the 27th an Enumerator should be posted from sunrise for the day on the road at the boundary or limit of the tract and enumerate travellers passing *out* of the tract if they have not been already enumerated.

7. It may be necessary in some cases to appoint special Enumerators for the Census of travellers.

8. Every person who is thus enumerated on the road should be given a ticket which he can show if again questioned; and I shall be glad if you will inform me at an early date of the number of tickets that you will require.

Dated the January 1891.

Circular No. 11.

I have the honour to request that you will be good enough to furnish me before the 1st April next with a full report upon the Census Operations in your District.

2. The object of this report is to obtain for future guidance an accurate record of all the steps taken and the difficulties met with, and I would ask you therefore to favour me with a chronological narrative of the entire undertaking and to state in complete detail the action taken, with the dates in each case, upon the instructions issued from this office, the points upon which those instructions were departed from with the grounds therefor, and the difficulties experienced from time to time with your suggestions for their future avoidance.

3. I append an outline of some of the subjects to be dealt with, and it will be convenient if you will treat them in the order mentioned. You will understand that the list is not intended to be exhaustive, and I shall be glad if you will touch upon every point which requires attention.

1.—Organisation :—formation of Census areas, Maps, Sub-Divisional Register, Number of Charges, Circles, and Blocks as finally revised, average number of houses per Block in towns and villages.

2.—Agency :—number of Charge-Superintendents, Supervisors and Enumerators, and classes from which drawn.

3.—House numbering :—definition of "house", how applied, mode of numbering, dates of commencement and completion, how checked. Village and Block lists.

4.—Schedules :—supply, indents how prepared, receipts, distribution. Form of Schedules, standard of books.

5.—Instruction of Agency :—mode of and extent, Manual and Circulars.

6.—Preliminary record :—time occupied in taking, extent of checking and testing, degree of accuracy of the work done.

7.—Final Census :—time occupied, extent of supervision, strength of staff, special Enumerators and reserve, traffic on road (Cir. 10), fairs and markets, marriages and festivals. Preparation of abstracts, collection of books and schedules.

8.—Special areas, municipalities, cantonments, troops on the march, tracts requiring a day Census.

9.—Legislation :—need of Census Act, and action taken under it, attitude of people.

10.—Correctness of record, opinion and reasons.

11.—Expenditure.

Dated the 10th February 1891.

EXTRACTS FROM THE INSTRUCTIONS ISSUED BY RAILWAY AUTHORITIES.

GREAT INDIAN PENINSULA RAILWAY.

Circular No. 54.

Census on the night of Thursday, the twenty-sixth of February 1891.

All concerned are advised, with reference to the instructions given in the third clause of para. two, and in the eighth para. of the Agent's Circular No. 10 of the twenty-seventh of October 1890, and the last clause of para. five of the joint Circular No. 278, of the seventeenth of December 1890, as to the enumeration of Passengers and the Company's Staff who may be travelling upon this Railway on the night appointed for taking the Census, that the following instructions should be adhered to, namely :—

First.—All persons who take tickets after twelve o'clock (noon) on the twenty-sixth of February, to travel by any Train, throughout the whole line (except as hereinafter mentioned) to such places as will involve their being in the Train after twenty hours on that evening, should, as far as is practicable, be enumerated when they take their Tickets, and a Census Check Ticket should be given to each one when so enumerated.

Second.—All persons alighting from any Train throughout the whole line (except as hereinafter mentioned) after twenty hours on the night of the twenty-sixth of February, should be enumerated as they alight, provided that they have no Census Check Ticket in their possession.

Third.—Census Check Tickets should be given to each person at the time of the enumeration, except to those who are enumerated when they alight from any Train *after* six hours on the twenty-seventh of February. But a Census Check Ticket should be given to, or should be in the possession of, each one who alights *before* that time.

* * * * *

Fifth.—As far as may be possible, additional Guards and Enumerators should travel with the Trains, especially those which run for long distances, and should ride in the carriages, having with them a supply of blank returns and Check Tickets. At every convenient opportunity, that is, at the stoppages at Stations, etc., these special Enumerators should record the names, etc., of Passengers not previously enumerated, and who have no Check Ticket, and they should give a Check Ticket to each one so enumerated. By this process the numbers to be enumerated as they alight will be greatly reduced.

* * * * *

2. The following detailed instructions should be carried out in regard to passengers in the Trains that are mentioned, who may have taken their Tickets before the times named in para. one of these instructions, or who are travelling to places which they will not reach until after the time named herein, namely :—

First.—No. 33 Down Nagpur Passenger Train leaving Bombay at 7-30 o'clock on the 26th of February. Passengers booked by this train *from* stations between Bombay and Bhusawal inclusive, *to* stations between Bhusawal and Nagpur inclusive of Nagpur, but not inclusive of Bhusawal, and to stations on the Bengal-Nagpur Railway, should be enumerated at the stations at which they take their Tickets, and a Check Ticket given to each one. And they should be checked at their destinations when they alight. Any who, when they alight at their destinations, may not have the Check Ticket should then be enumerated. Passengers booked at stations between Bhusawal and Nagpur both inclusive, should, if not already enumerated, be enumerated at those stations on taking their tickets. All passengers to Nagpur, or to stations on the Bengal-Nagpur Railway, alighting from Great Indian Peninsula Trains at Nagpur, and who have not been previously enumerated, should be enumerated at Nagpur.

* * * * *

Twelfth.—No. 211 Down Nagpur Passenger Train leaving Bhusawal at 9-20 o'clock on the 26th February. Passengers booked by this train from stations between Bombay and Sindi inclusive, to stations between Sindi and Nagpur inclusive, should be enumerated at the Booking stations, and they should also be checked at their destinations when they alight, and any not enumerated should be enumerated before they leave the station. Passengers booked locally between Sindi and Nagpur should be enumerated at the time of booking, but passengers holding through tickets for the Bengal-Nagpur Railway need not be enumerated on this line.

* * * * *

Seventeenth.—No. 41 Down Tranship Goods train, which carries Passengers leaving Bhusawal at 16-40 o'clock on the 26th of February. Passengers booked by this train from Stations between Bhusawal and Malkapur inclusive, to Stations between Malkapur and Nagpur inclusive, should be enumerated at the starting Stations, and they should be checked when they alight at their destinations. Passengers booked by this Train from Stations between Biswa and Nagpur, not inclusive of the latter Station, should, if not already enumerated, be enumerated at those Stations, and it should be seen that all who are in the train when it arrives at Nagpur have been enumerated.

* * * * *

Twenty-eighth.—No. 86 Up Tranship Goods train which carries passengers, leaving Nagpur at 22-5 o'clock on the 26th of February. As this train will start from Nagpur within the hours when the Census will be in operation, it is likely that many of the passengers joining the train at Nagpur and at Stations up to and inclusive of Chandur, will have been enumerated, but notwithstanding this, passengers must be asked both at the Station where they join the Train up to and inclusive of Chandur, and also when they alight, if they alight at stations between Nagpur and Sheogaon. At Sheogaon the train halts for some time, and all alighting there or remaining in the train should then be enumerated on the arrival of the train.

Twenty-ninth.—All the Company's staff of all Departments who are travelling by, or are in charge of, Goods Trains, or Ballast Trains, or Light Engines, or are working on Shunting Engines between 20 o'clock on the 26th of February and 6 o'clock on the 27th, should be enumerated when they join their Train or Engine, and a Check Ticket given to them if they have not been previously enumerated, and they should be checked when they leave their Trains or Engines or at the first station at which they stop, after 6 o'clock on the 27th, and if not previously enumerated they should be enumerated then.

3. Passengers and the Company's Staff who travel by or are in charge of the following Trains, which will leave their respective starting stations and arrive at their respective destinations between 20 o'clock on the night of the 26th and 6 o'clock in the morning on the 27th February, should be enumerated before they enter the train, and should be carefully checked at their destinations, and any found not to have been previously enumerated should be enumerated before they leave the station. Except that, in the case of the Local Trains running between Bombay and Kalyan, only passengers who hold *single journey tickets* need be enumerated. Those who hold return or Periodical Tickets should not be enumerated by the Railway Staff. It should be seen that all passengers, with the foregoing exceptions, are enumerated at the destinations of these trains :—

Number and description of trains.	Station from	Time of Departure.	Station to	Time of arrival.
265 Mixed	Jalamb	4·30	Kamgaon	5·15
273 do.	Badnera	2·30	Amraoti	2·50
270 do.	Khamgaon	21·10	Jalamb	21·55
280 do.	Amraoti	23·55	Badnera	0·15

* * * * *

Bombay, the 11th of February 1891.

GREAT INDIAN PENINSULA RAILWAY.

Circular No. 62.

Census on the night of Thursday, the 26th of February 1891.

All concerned are advised, with reference to the instructions given in Circular No. 54 of the 11th of February 1891, as to the enumeration of Passengers and the Company's Staff who may be travelling upon this Railway on the night appointed for the taking of the Census, that the following additional instsuctions should be carried out, namely :—

* * * * *

Second.—No. 84 Up Nagpur Passenger Train, leaving Nagpur at 20 o'clock on Thursday, the 26th of February. As this train will start from Nagpur within the hours when the Census will be in operation, it is likely that many of the passengers joining the Train at Nagpur and at stations up to Bhusawal, will have been enumerated. But notwithstanding this Passengers must be asked both at the stations were they join the train, and also when they alight, if they alight at stations between Nagpur and Bhusawal, and, if not already enumerated, they should be enumerated when they alight, and it should be seen that all have been enumerated before they leave Bhusawal Station.

* * * * *

Bombay, the 17th of February 1891.

TABLE I.

Area, Houses, and Population.

TABLE I.—Area, Houses, and Population.

District and Taluk.		Area in square miles.	Number of Towns.	Number of Villages.	Occupied Houses. Total.	Occupied Houses. Towns.	Occupied Houses. Villages.	Population. Total. Total.	Population. Total. Towns.	Population. Total. Villages.	Population. Males. Total.	Population. Males. Towns.	Population. Males. Villages.	Population. Females. Total.	Population. Females. Towns.	Population. Females. Villages.
1		2	3	4	5	6	7	8	9	10	11	12	13	14	15	16
District Amraoti		2,759.20	14	1,039	136,328	27,174	1,09,154	655,645	124,710	530,935	340,235	65,604	274,631	315,410	59,106	256,304
" Akola		2,659.39	10	981	129,333	25,102	1,04,231	574,782	107,636	467,146	297,011	56,520	240,491	277,771	51,116	226,655
" Ellichpur		2,623.32	5	796	66,815	13,874	52,941	315,798	59,455	256,343	162,969	30,404	132,565	152,829	29,051	123,778
" Buldana		2,808.81	4	898	95,198	5,749	89,449	481,021	28,177	452,844	244,799	14,274	230,525	236,222	13,903	222,319
" Wún		3,911.23	2	1,233	92,306	2,532	89,774	471,613	11,545	460,068	241,688	6,225	235,463	229,925	5,320	224,605
" Basim		2,955.92	4	838	71,028	5,374	65,654	398,181	29,188	368,993	204,798	14,938	189,860	193,383	14,250	179,133
Railway Passengers, etc.		...	...	...	...	...	...	451	...	...	326	...	...	125	...	...
Total		17,717.87	39	5,785	591,008	79,805	511,203	2,897,491	360,711	2,536,329	1,491,826	187,965	1,303,535	1,405,665	172,746	1,232,794
Amraoti District	Taluk Amraoti	671.60	6	258	37,728	13,038	24,690	183,508	60,640	122,868	95,536	32,565	62,971	87,972	28,075	59,897
	" Chandur	854.97	2	307	41,378	2,663	38,715	198,106	12,661	185,445	102,885	6,496	96,389	95,221	6,165	89,056
	" Morsi	622.38	5	208	32,185	8,041	24,144	152,374	36,973	115,401	78,451	18,931	59,520	73,923	18,042	55,881
	" Murtazapur	610.25	1	266	25,037	3,432	21,605	121,657	14,436	107,221	63,363	7,612	55,751	58,294	6,824	51,470
Akola District	Taluk Akola	738.80	2	292	30,954	6,341	24,613	137,988	26,516	111,472	71,744	14,367	57,377	66,244	12,149	54,095
	" Akot	516.81	2	228	31,954	5,457	26,497	137,720	22,515	115,205	70,630	11,643	58,987	67,090	10,872	56,218
	" Balapur	568.75	3	166	21,881	4,953	16,928	101,673	22,278	79,395	51,941	11,000	40,941	49,732	11,278	38,454
	" Jalgaon	392.10	1	163	22,322	2,146	20,176	97,616	9,307	88,309	50,323	4,705	45,618	47,293	4,602	42,691
	" Khamgaon	442.93	2	132	22,222	6,205	16,017	99,785	27,020	72,765	52,373	14,805	37,568	47,412	12,215	35,197
Ellichpur District	Taluk Ellichpur	469.17	4	218	32,122	11,462	20,660	146,215	48,862	97,353	75,271	24,973	50,298	70,944	23,889	47,055
	" Daryapur	505.15	1	247	26,416	2,412	24,004	122,552	10,593	111,959	63,329	5,431	57,898	59,223	5,162	54,061
	" Melghát	1,649.00	...	331	8,277	...	8,277	47,031	...	47,031	24,369	...	24,369	22,662	...	22,662
Buldana District	Taluk Chikhli	1,009.44	1	279	30,188	1,524	28,664	150,098	7,382	142,716	76,540	3,649	72,891	73,558	3,733	69,825
	" Malkapur	791.52	2	296	37,955	3,378	34,577	177,877	15,693	162,184	90,215	8,027	82,188	87,662	7,666	79,996
	" Mehkar	1,007.85	1	323	27,055	847	26,208	153,046	5,102	147,944	78,044	2,598	75,446	75,002	2,504	72,498
Wún District	Taluk Yeotmal	908.31	1	298	25,170	1,472	23,698	124,429	6,464	117,965	64,275	3,548	60,727	60,154	2,916	57,238
	" Darwha	1,061.55	1	333	31,539	1,060	30,479	156,580	5,081	151,499	80,746	2,677	78,069	75,834	2,404	73,430
	" Kelapur	1,081.19	...	311	19,370	...	19,370	105,926	...	105,926	53,845	...	53,845	52,081	...	52,081
	" Wún	860.18	...	288	16,227	...	16,227	84,678	...	84,678	42,822	...	42,822	41,856	...	41,856
Basim District	Taluk Basim	1,045.92	1	322	31,609	2,350	29,259	177,250	12,389	164,861	91,200	6,434	84,766	86,050	5,955	80,095
	" Mangrul	635.40	1	205	16,304	1,065	15,239	82,446	5,241	77,205	42,773	2,646	40,127	39,673	2,595	37,078
	" Pusad	1,274.60	2	311	23,115	1,959	21,156	138,485	11,558	126,927	70,825	5,858	64,967	67,660	5,700	61,960

TABLE II.

Variation in the enumerated Population since last Census.

NOTE.—In the Census of 1881 Railway travellers were included in the District Returns.

TABLE II.—Showing the Variation in the enumerated Population since last Census.

District and Taluk.	Total. 1891.	Total. 1881.	Total. Variation.	Males. 1891.	Males. 1881.	Males. Variation.	Females. 1891.	Females. 1881.	Females. Variation.
1	2	3	4	5	6	7	8	9	10
District Amraoti	655,645	575,328	+ 80,317	340,235	298,051	+ 42,184	315,410	277,277	+ 38,133
" Akola	574,782	592,792	− 18,010	297,011	308,046	− 11,035	277,771	284,746	− 6,975
" Ellichpur	315,798	313,805	+ 1,993	162,969	162,590	+ 379	152,829	151,215	+ 1,614
" Buldana	481,021	439,763	+ 41,258	244,799	225,243	+ 19,556	236,222	214,520	+ 21,702
" Wún	471,613	392,102	+ 79,511	241,688	201,491	+ 40,197	229,925	190,611	+ 39,314
" Basim	398,181	358,883	+ 39,298	204,798	185,071	+ 19,727	193,383	173,812	+ 19,571
Railway Passengers, etc.	451	...	+ 451	326	...	+ 326	125	...	+ 125
Total	**2,897,491**	**2,672,673**	**+ 224,818**	**1,491,826**	**1,380,492**	**+ 111,334**	**1,405,665**	**1,292,181**	**+ 113,484**
Amraoti District. Taluk Amraoti	183,508	163,456	+ 20,052	95,536	85,333	+ 10,203	87,972	78,123	+ 9,849
" Chandur	198,106	171,611	+ 26,495	102,885	88,813	+ 14,072	95,221	82,798	+ 12,423
" Morsi	152,374	129,688	+ 22,686	78,451	66,563	+ 11,888	73,923	63,125	+ 10,798
" Murtazapur	121,657	110,573	+ 11,084	63,363	57,342	+ 6,021	58,294	53,231	+ 5,063
Akola District. Taluk Akola	137,988	139,421	− 1,433	71,744	72,560	− 816	66,244	66,861	− 617
" Akot	137,720	144,253	− 6,533	70,630	74,755	− 4,125	67,090	69,498	− 2,408
" Balapur	101,673	107,200	− 5,527	51,941	55,739	− 3,798	49,732	51,461	− 1,729
" Jalgaon	97,616	105,739	− 8,123	50,323	54,434	− 4,111	47,293	51,305	− 4,012
" Khamgaon	99,785	96,179	+ 3,606	52,373	50,558	+ 1,815	47,412	45,621	+ 1,791
Ellichpur District. Taluk Ellichpur	146,215	148,041	− 1,826	75,271	76,514	− 1,243	70,944	71,527	− 583
" Daryapur	122,552	123,109	− 557	63,329	63,859	− 530	59,223	59,250	− 27
" Melghát	47,031	42,655	+ 4,376	24,369	22,217	+ 2,152	22,662	20,438	+ 2,224
Buldana District. Taluk Chikhli	150,098	140,011	+ 10,087	76,540	71,595	+ 4,945	73,558	68,416	+ 5,142
" Malkapur	177,877	168,508	+ 9,369	90,215	86,478	+ 3,737	87,6 2	82,030	+ 5,632
" Mehkar	153,046	131,244	+ 21,802	78,044	67,170	+ 10,874	75,002	64,074	+ 10,928
Wún District. Taluk Yeotmal	124,429	107,846	+ 16,583	64,275	55,877	+ 8,398	60,154	51,969	+ 8,185
" Darwha	156,580	132,788	+ 23,792	80,746	68,468	+ 12,278	75,834	64,320	+ 11,514
" Kelapur	105,926	78,814	+ 27,112	53,845	40,194	+ 13,651	52,081	38,620	+ 13,461
" Wún	84,678	72,654	+ 12,024	42,822	36,952	+ 5,870	41,856	35,702	+ 6,154
Basim District. Taluk Basim	177,250	157,690	+ 19,560	91,200	81,565	+ 9,635	86,050	76,125	+ 9,925
" Mangrul	82,446	76,142	+ 6,304	42,773	39,426	+ 3,347	39,673	36,716	+ 2,957
" Pusad	138,485	125,051	+ 13,434	70,825	64,080	+ 6,745	67,660	60,971	+ 6,689

TABLE III.

Towns and Villages classified by Population.

TABLE III.—Towns and Villages classified by Population.

District and Taluk.	Total number of Towns and Villages.	Total Population.	1–199		200–499		500–999		1,000–1,999		2,000–2,999		3,000–4,999		5,000–9,999		10,000–14,999		15,000–19,999		20,000–49,999		Fairs, special encampments, etc.	
			No.	Population.	No.	Population.	No.	Population.	No.	Population.	No.	Population.	No.	Population.	No.	Population.	No.	Population.	No.	Population.	No.	Population.	No.	Population.
1	2	3	4	5	6	7	8	9	10	11	12	13	14	15	16	17	18	19	20	21	22	23	24	25
District Amraoti	1,053	655,645	350	33,573	352	115,356	212	145,808	84	110,204	21	50,154	21	77,846	10	66,576	2	24,479	...	...	1	28,946	...	2,703
" Akola	991	574,782	359	35,548	329	109,557	187	130,919	81	113,963	18	46,362	7	26,825	5	32,901	2	21,672	2	31,593	1	21,470	...	3,972
" Ellichpur	801	315,798	462	42,334	208	65,327	82	57,554	30	40,270	5	11,769	9	35,510	3	22,225	1	10,593	...	...	1	26,637	...	3,579
" Buldana	902	481,021	267	27,485	323	108,023	210	150,935	78	104,516	11	27,403	9	34,434	4	28,177	...	...	...	...	...	...	...	48
" Wún	1,235	471,613	480	49,822	474	155,359	210	141,497	57	77,108	8	18,773	4	17,509	2	11,545	...	...	...	...	...	...	...	...
" Basim	842	398,181	261	29,532	333	109,997	168	117,229	70	91,135	3	8,166	3	12,436	3	16,799	1	12,389	...	...	...	...	...	498
Railway Passengers, etc.	...	451	...	...	...	...	...	...	...	...	...	...	...	...	...	...	...	...	...	...	...	...	...	451
Total	5,824	2,897,491	2,179	218,294	2,019	663,619	1,069	743,942	400	537,196	66	162,627	53	204,560	27	178,223	6	69,133	2	31,593	3	77,053	...	11,251
Amraoti District. Taluk Amraoti	264	183,508	90	8,484	95	29,785	44	30,795	18	23,321	8	19,197	4	15,755	4	26,985	...	...	...	...	1	28,946	...	240
" Chandur	309	198,106	82	7,804	102	34,085	74	50,425	35	47,005	6	14,617	8	29,530	2	12,661	...	...	...	...	...	...	...	1,979
" Morsi	213	152,374	69	6,324	60	19,758	49	32,628	22	29,413	1	2,039	7	24,755	4	26,930	1	10,043	...	...	...	...	...	484
" Murtazapur	267	121,657	109	10,961	95	31,728	45	31,960	9	10,465	6	14,301	2	7,806	...	...	1	14,436	...	...	...	...	...	...
Akola District. Taluk Akola	293	137,988	127	11,899	98	32,215	48	33,092	15	21,936	3	8,398	1	3,860	1	5,046	...	...	...	...	1	21,470	...	72
" Akot	230	137,720	81	8,271	81	28,217	36	23,881	21	30,726	7	17,304	2	6,806	1	6,520	...	...	1	15,995	...	...	...	...
" Balapur	169	101,673	59	5,876	52	16,412	36	25,966	15	19,663	4	9,995	...	...	2	12,028	1	10,250	...	...	...	...	...	1,483
" Jalgaon	165	97,616	59	5,992	56	18,926	27	18,591	16	23,486	1	2,803	4	16,159	1	9,307	...	...	...	...	...	...	...	2,352
" Khamgaon	134	99,785	33	3,510	42	13,787	40	29,389	14	18,152	3	7,862	...	...	...	...	1	11,422	1	15,598	...	...	...	65
Ellichpur District. Taluk Ellichpur	222	146,215	94	8,977	72	23,276	32	23,339	14	19,492	2	4,169	4	17,717	3	22,225	...	...	...	...	1	26,637	...	183
" Daryapur	248	122,552	102	10,133	78	25,478	44	29,977	15	19,715	3	7,600	5	17,793	...	...	1	10,593	...	...	...	...	...	1,263
" Melghát	331	47,031	266	23,224	58	16,573	6	4,038	1	1,063	...	...	...	...	...	...	...	...	...	...	...	...	...	2,133
Buldana District. Taluk Chikhli	279	150,098	80	7,780	110	37,791	59	45,551	24	32,707	3	7,056	3	11,831	1	7,382	...	...	...	...	...	...	...	...
" Malkapur	298	177,877	93	9,843	75	25,434	87	61,112	35	46,933	4	11,051	2	7,763	2	15,693	...	...	...	...	...	...	...	48
" Mehkar	325	153,046	94	9,862	138	44,798	64	44,272	19	24,876	4	9,296	4	14,840	1	5,102	...	...	...	...	...	...	...	...
Wún District. Taluk Yeotmal	299	124,429	108	11,597	117	38,442	53	36,545	16	20,567	3	7,133	1	3,681	1	6,464	...	...	...	...	...	...	...	...
" Darwha	334	156,580	96	10,725	139	46,699	70	46,528	24	33,844	2	4,731	2	8,972	1	5,081	...	...	...	...	...	...	...	...
" Kelapur	314	105,926	124	13,535	129	40,625	49	32,567	9	12,290	3	6,909	...	...	...	...	...	...	...	...	...	...	...	...
" Wún	288	84,678	152	13,965	89	29,593	38	25,857	8	10,407	...	...	1	4,856	...	...	...	...	...	...	...	...	...	...
Basim District. Taluk Basim	323	177,250	75	9,241	134	44,505	76	52,810	34	46,483	1	2,286	2	9,149	...	...	1	12,389	...	...	...	...	...	387
" Mángrul	206	82,446	78	8,921	76	24,909	36	24,576	15	18,799	...	...	...	...	1	5,241	...	...	...	...	...	...	...	...
" Pusad	313	138,485	108	11,370	123	40,583	56	39,843	21	25,853	2	5,880	1	3,287	2	11,558	...	...	...	...	...	...	...	111

TABLE IV.

Towns according to Population, compared with the preceding Census.

Table IV.—Towns according to Population, compared with the preceding Census.

Town.	District.	Municipality, Suburbs or Cantonments.	Total Population. 1891.	Total Population. 1881.	Total Population. Variation.	Males. 1891.	Males. 1881.	Males. Variation.	Females. 1891.	Females. 1881.	Females. Variation.
1	2	3	4	5	6	7	8	9	10	11	12
Amraoti	Amraoti	Municipality	28,946	23,550	+5,396	15,833	12,859	+2,974	13,113	10,691	+2,422
Ellichpur	Ellichpur	Municipality	26,637	26,728	—91	13,389	13,346	+43	13,248	13,382	—134
Akola	Akola	Municipality	21,470	16,614	+4,856	11,814	8,834	+2,980	9,656	7,780	+1,876
Akot	...	Municipality	15,995	16,137	—142	8,417	8,278	+139	7,578	7,859	—281
Khamgaon	...	Municipality	15,598	12,390	+3,208	8,769	6,718	+2,051	6,829	5,672	+1,157
Karanja	Amraoti	...	14,436	10,923	+3,513	7,612	5,631	+1,981	6,824	5,292	+1,532
Basim	Basim	Municipality and Civil Station	12,389	11,576	+813	6,434	6,015	+419	5,955	5,561	+394
Shegaon	Akola	Municipality	11,422	11,079	+343	6,036	5,753	+283	5,386	5,326	+60
Anjangaon	Ellichpur	...	10,593	9,842	+751	5,431	5,060	+371	5,162	4,782	+380
Balapur	Akola	...	10,250	11,244	—994	4,970	5,542	—572	5,280	5,702	—422
Shendurjana	Amraoti	...	10,043	8,501	+1,542	5,090	4,242	+848	4,953	4,259	+694
Badnera	...	...	9,916	6,460	+3,456	5,260	3,291	+1,969	4,656	3,169	+1,487
Paratwada	Ellichpur	Cantonment and Civil Station	9,603	9,445	+158	5,352	5,155	+197	4,251	4,290	—39
Jalgaon	Akola	...	9,307	10,392	—1,085	4,705	5,267	—562	4,602	5,125	—523
Malkapur	Buldana	...	9,222	8,152	+1,070	4,773	4,108	+665	4,449	4,044	+405
Deulgaon Raja	...	...	7,382	7,025	+357	3,649	3,467	+182	3,733	3,558	+175
Warud	Amraoti	...	7,291	6,607	+684	3,709	3,314	+395	3,582	3,293	+289
Morsi	...	...	7,104	5,592	+1,512	3,653	2,822	+831	3,451	2,770	+681
Ner Pinglai	...	...	6,848	6,644	+204	3,607	3,574	+33	3,241	3,070	+171
Karasgaon	Ellichpur	...	6,846	7,330	—484	3,397	3,771	—374	3,449	3,559	—110
Hiwarkhed	Akola	...	6,520	7,300	—780	3,226	3,723	—497	3,294	3,577	—283
Nandura	Buldana	...	6,471	6,743	—272	3,254	3,488	—234	3,217	3,255	—38
Yeotmal	Wun	...	6,464	4,445	+2,019	3,548	2,400	+1,148	2,916	2,045	+871
Talegaon—Dashasahasra	Amraoti	...	6,440	5,506	+934	3,284	2,862	+422	3,156	2,644	+512
Umarkhed	Basim	...	6,414	5,959	+455	3,231	3,029	+202	3,183	2,930	+253
Mangrul Dastagir	Amraoti	...	6,221	6,122	+99	3,212	3,163	+49	3,009	2,959	+50
Patur	Akola	...	6,156	7,219	—1,063	3,108	4,171	—1,063	3,048	3,048	...
Balgaon Jagir	Amraoti	...	5,939	4,905	+1,034	3,168	2,553	+615	2,771	2,352	+419
Wadegaon	Akola	...	5,872	6,096	—224	2,922	3,064	—142	2,950	3,032	—82
Sirasgaon	Ellichpur	...	5,776	5,408	+368	2,835	2,757	+78	2,941	2,651	+290
Kholapur	Amraoti	...	5,725	6,452	—727	2,837	3,261	—424	2,888	3,191	—303
Pusla	...	...	5,687	4,611	+1,076	2,872	2,323	+549	2,815	2,288	+527
Nandgaon Peth	...	...	5,405	4,418	+987	2,796	2,347	+449	2,609	2,071	+538
Mangrul Pir	Basim	...	5,241	4,900	+341	2,646	2,481	+165	2,595	2,419	+176
Pusad	...	...	5,144	5,047	+97	2,627	2,641	—14	2,517	2,406	+111
Mehkar	Buldana	...	5,102	4,374	+728	2,598	2,281	+317	2,504	2,093	+411
Digras	Wun	...	5,081	4,235	+846	2,677	2,136	+541	2,404	2,099	+305
Barsi Takli	Akola	...	5,046	5,377	—331	2,553	2,697	—144	2,493	2,680	—187
Amraoti Camp	Amraoti	Municipality and Civil Station	4,709	unknown	...	2,671	...	...	2,038	...	...

TABLE V.

Towns arranged territorially, with Population by Religion.

NOTE.—The heading "Others" includes—

Buddhist . .	2 males	2 females.
Jew . . .	2 ,,	
Deist . . .	1 ,,	
Positivist . .	1 ,,	
Agnostic . .	1 ,,	
Unspecified . .	1 ,,	
TOTAL .	8	2

TABLE V.—Towns arranged territorially, with Population by Religion.

District.	Town.	Total Population. Total.	Total Population. Males.	Total Population. Females.	Hindu. Total.	Hindu. Males.	Hindu. Females.	Musalman. Total.	Musalman. Males.	Musalman. Females.	Animistic. Total.	Animistic. Males.	Animistic. Females.	Jain. Total.	Jain. Males.	Jain. Females.	Sikh. Total.	Sikh. Males.	Sikh. Females.	Christian. Total.	Christian. Males.	Christian. Females.	Parsi. Total.	Parsi. Males.	Parsi. Females.	Others. Total.	Others. Males.	Others. Females.
1	2	3	4	5	6	7	8	9	10	11	12	13	14	15	16	17	18	19	20	21	22	23	24	25	26	27	28	29
Amraoti	Amraoti Municipality	28,946	15,833	13,113	22,810	12,529	10,281	5,312	2,820	2,492	57	29	28	651	387	264	...	...	...	82	49	33	33	18	15	1	1	...
	Karanja	14,436	7,612	6,824	10,083	5,377	4,706	3,584	1,833	1,751	30	14	16	719	374	345	4	...	4	12	10	2	4	4	...	...	...	...
	Shendurjana	10,043	5,090	4,953	8,831	4,499	4,332	928	449	479	43	22	21	241	120	121	...	...	...	...	...	...	...	...	...	...	...	...
	Badnera	9,916	5,260	4,656	7,454	3,962	3,492	1,868	988	880	65	40	25	159	81	78	...	...	...	187	90	97	183	99	84	...	...	...
	Warud	7,291	3,709	3,582	6,391	3,275	3,116	794	382	412	12	7	5	93	44	49	...	...	...	...	...	...	1	1	...	...	...	...
	Morsi	7,104	3,653	3,451	5,849	3,008	2,841	1,067	538	529	186	105	81	1	1	...	...	...	...	1	1	...	...	...	...	...	...	...
	Ner Pinglai	6,848	3,607	3,241	5,896	3,101	2,795	699	382	317	56	46	50	157	78	79	...	...	...	...	...	...	...	...	...	...	...	...
	Talegaon-Dashasahasra	6,440	3,284	3,156	5,214	2,663	2,551	935	478	457	280	136	144	11	7	4	...	...	...	...	...	...	...	...	...	...	...	...
	Mangrul Dastagir	6,221	3,212	3,009	5,633	2,917	2,716	509	257	252	79	38	41	...	...	...	...	...	...	...	...	...	...	...	...		...	...
	Balgaon Jagir	5,939	3,168	2,771	5,155	2,719	2,436	702	409	293	43	19	24	32	20	12	...	...	...	7	1	6	...	...	...	...	...	...
	Kholapur	5,725	2,837	2,888	4,003	2,013	1,990	1,624	774	850	3	1	2	95	49	46		...	...	...	...	...	...	...	...	...	...	...
	Pusla	5,687	2,872	2,815	5,161	2,621	2,540	316	145	171	156	82	74	54	24	30	...	...	...	...	...	...	...	...	...	...	...	...
	Nandgaon Peth	5,405	2,796	2,609	4,183	2,163	2,020	1,132	585	547	28	12	16	62	36	26	...	...	...	...	...	...	...	...	...	...	...	...
	Amraoti Camp	4,709	2,671	2,038	3,593	2,040	1,553	735	450	285	39	26	13	22	8	14	2	1	1	315	144	71	3	2	1	...	...	...
Akola	Akola	21,470	11,814	9,656	14,660	8,242	6,418	6,150	3,173	2,977	98	58	40	252	162	90	49	29	20	188	101	87	68	46	22	5	3	2
	Akot	15,995	8,417	7,578	12,060	6,434	5,626	3,794	1,895	1,899	...	...	...	127	78	49	...	...	...	6	5	1	8	5	3	...	...	...
	Khamgaon	15,598	8,769	6,829	11,922	6,721	5,201	3,257	1,768	1,489	7	6	1	330	212	118	1	1	...	52	36	16	27	23	4	2	2	...
	Shegaon	11,422	6,036	5,386	10,084	5,300	4,784	1,152	619	533	...	...	...	99	53	46	6	3	3	43	28	15	38	33	5	...	...	...
	Balapur	10,250	4,970	5,280	5,340	2,621	2,719	4,433	2,124	2,309	...	...	...	475	223	252	...	...	...	...	...	...	2	2	...	...	...	...
	Jalgaon	9,307	4,705	4,602	7,789	3,965	3,824	1,497	730	767	...	...	...	17	8	9	4	2	2	...	...	...	...	...	...	...	...	...
	Hiwarkhed	6,520	3,226	3,294	5,430	2,692	2,738	963	468	495	32	16	16	95	50	45	...	...	...	...	...	...	...	...	...	...	...	...
	Patur	6,156	3,108	3,048	4,128	2,105	2,023	1,954	965	989	...	...	...	67	34	33	...	...	...	7	4	3	...	...	...	...	...	...
	Wadegaon	5,872	2,922	2,950	5,388	2,697	2,691	484	225	259	...	...	...	...	...	...	...	...	...	...	...	...	...	...	...	...	...	...
	Barsi Takli	5,046	2,553	2,493	3,454	1,744	1,710	1,547	790	757	...	...	...	45	19	26	...	...	...	...	...	...	...	...	...	...	...	...
Ellichpur	Ellichpur	26,637	13,389	13,248	19,042	9,831	9,211	7,301	3,406	3,895	41	22	19	250	127	123	...	...	...	...	...	...	3	3	...	...	...	...
	Anjangaon	10,593	5,431	5,162	8,186	4,202	3,984	2,187	1,119	1,068	...	...	...	219	109	110	...	...	...	...	...	...	1	1	...	...	...	...
	Paratwada	9,603	5,352	4,251	6,593	3,725	2,868	2,853	1,537	1,316	11	5	6	29	17	12	...	...	...	108	50	49	8	8	...	1	1	...
	Karasgaon	6,846	3,397	3,449	5,953	2,980	2,973	801	370	431	15	9	6	77	38	39	...	...	...	...	...	...	...	...	...	...	...	...
	Sirasgaon	5,776	2,835	2,941	4,799	2,373	2,426	880	412	468	27	16	11	70	34	36	...	...	...	...	...	...	...	...	...	...	...	...
Buldana	Malkapur	9,222	4,773	4,449	5,900	3,043	2,857	3,075	1,595	1,480	...	...	...	232	126	106	...	...	...	11	6	5	4	3	1	...	...	...
	Deulgaon Raja	7,382	3,649	3,733	5,872	2,927	2,945	1,072	500	572	...	...	...	430	218	212	...	...	...	8	4	4	...	...	...	...	...	...
	Nandura	6,471	3,254	3,217	5,154	2,609	2,545	1,085	540	545	...	...	...	224	101	123	...	...	...	8	4	4	...	...	...	...	...	...
	Mehkár	5,102	2,598	2,504	3,994	2,057	1,937	1,096	535	561	...	...	...	6	4	2	...	...	...	6	2	4	...	...	...	...	...	...
Wún	Yeotmal	6,464	3,548	2,916	5,134	2,801	2,333	874	501	373	328	177	151	37	19	18	1	1	...	85	45	40	5	4	1	...	...	...
	Digras	5,081	2,677	2,404	3,553	1,888	1,665	1,076	561	515	368	183	185	84	45	39	...	...	...	...	...	...	...	...	...	...	...	...
Basim	Basim	12,389	6,434	5,955	9,362	4,909	4,453	2,656	1,339	1,317	...	...	...	300	151	149	...	...	...	70	34	36	...	...	...	1	1	...
	Umarkhed	6,414	3,231	3,183	4,880	2,440	2,440	1,423	735	688	...	...	...	111	56	55	...	...	...	...	...	...	...	...	...	...	...	...
	Mangrul Pir	5,241	2,646	2,595	3,295	1,694	1,601	1,841	897	944	...	...	...	104	54	50	...	...	...	1	1	...	...	...	...	...	...	...
	Pusad	5,144	2,627	2,517	3,595	2,080	1,915	978	465	513	...	...	...	161	76	85	10	6	4	...	...	...	...	...	...	...	...	...

TABLE VI.

Religions.

RELIGIONS :—

Hindu.	Sikh.
Musalman.	Christian.
Animistic.	Parsi.
Jain.	Others.

NOTE :—The "Others" comprise the following :—

Buddhist	2 males	2 females.
Jew	2 ,,	
Deist	1 ,,	
Positivist	1 ,,	
Agnostic	1 ,,	
Unspecified	2 ,,	
TOTAL .	9	2

TABLE VI.—Religions.

District and Taluk.		Total Population.			Hindu.			Musalman.			Animistic.		
		Total.	Males.	Females.	Total.	Males.	Females.	Total.	Males.	Females.	Total.	Males.	Females.
1		2	3	4	5	6	7	8	9	10	11	12	13
District Amraoti		655,645	340,235	315,410	584,178	303,130	281,048	47,522	24,931	22,591	17,391	8,727	8,664
" Akola		574,782	297,011	277,771	518,046	267,316	250,730	51,302	26,717	24,585	1,545	813	732
" Ellichpur		315,798	162,969	152,829	243,992	126,423	117,569	30,645	15,671	14,974	39,745	20,101	19,644
" Buldana		481,021	244,799	236,222	442,588	225,016	217,572	34,405	17,679	16,726	7	4	3
" Wún		471,613	241,688	229,925	371,084	190,766	180,318	20,727	10,932	9,795	77,968	38,977	38,991
" Basim		398,181	204,798	193,383	371,537	190,873	180,664	23,020	12,053	10,967	449	225	224
Railway Passengers, etc.		451	326	125	366	261	105	60	52	8	3	...	3
Total		2,897,491	1,491,826	1,405,665	2,581,791	1,308,785	1,228,006	207,681	108,085	99,646	137,108	68,847	68,261
Amraoti District.	Taluk Amraoti	183,508	95,536	87,972	161,331	83,853	77,478	18,384	9,712	8,672	1,756	870	886
	" Chandur	198,106	102,885	95,221	180,463	93,700	86,763	9,060	4,794	4,266	6,954	3,507	3,447
	" Morsi	152,374	78,451	73,923	133,708	69,017	64,691	9,225	4,729	4,496	8,383	4,190	4,193
	" Murtazapur	121,657	63,363	58,294	108,676	56,560	52,116	10,853	5,696	5,157	298	160	138
Akola District.	Taluk Akola	137,988	71,744	66,244	124,098	64,430	59,668	12,463	6,545	5,918	143	80	63
	" Akot	137,720	70,630	67,090	123,010	63,087	59,923	13,330	6,804	6,526	785	415	370
	" Balapur	101,673	51,941	49,732	89,399	45,726	43,673	11,340	5,722	5,618	8	3	5
	" Jalgaon	97,616	50,323	47,293	89,937	46,177	43,760	6,933	3,742	3,191	589	299	290
	" Khamgaon	99,785	52,373	47,412	91,602	47,896	43,706	7,236	3,904	3,332	20	16	4
Ellichpur District.	Taluk Ellichpur	146,215	75,271	70,944	124,059	64,174	59,885	19,020	9,464	9,556	2,213	1,133	1,080
	" Daryapur	122,552	63,329	59,223	111,595	57,515	54,080	10,263	5,439	4,824	214	110	104
	" Melghát	47,031	24,369	22,662	8,338	4,734	3,604	1,362	768	594	37,318	18,858	18,460
Buldana District.	Taluk Chikhli	150,098	76,540	73,558	136,828	69,694	67,134	11,853	6,112	5,741	7	4	3
	" Malkapur	177,877	90,215	87,662	162,064	82,146	79,918	14,395	7,334	7,061	...	...	...
	" Mehkar	153,046	78,044	75,002	143,696	73,176	70,520	8,157	4,233	3,924	...	...	...
Wún District.	Taluk Yeotmal	124,429	64,275	60,154	93,683	48,599	45,084	5,595	3,006	2,589	24,334	12,223	12,111
	" Darwha	156,580	80,746	75,834	137,182	70,651	66,531	9,797	5,219	4,578	8,887	4,482	4,405
	" Kelapur	105,926	53,845	52,081	74,783	38,276	36,507	3,052	1,564	1,488	27,836	13,861	13,975
	" Wún	84,678	42,822	41,856	65,436	33,240	32,196	2,283	1,143	1,140	16,911	8,411	8,500
Basim District.	Taluk Basim	177,250	91,200	86,050	165,987	85,247	80,740	9,313	4,936	4,377	...	...	...
	" Mangrul	82,446	42,773	39,673	77,356	40,129	37,227	4,718	2,450	2,268	39	17	22
	" Pusad	138,485	70,825	67,660	128,194	65,497	62,697	8,089	4,667	4,322	410	208	202

Table VI.—Religions.

District and Taluk.	Jain. Total.	Jain. Males.	Jain. Females.	Sikh. Total.	Sikh. Males.	Sikh. Females.	Christian. Total.	Christian. Males.	Christian. Females.	Parsi. Total.	Parsi. Males.	Parsi. Females.	Others. Total.	Others. Males.	Others. Females.
	14	15	16	17	18	19	20	21	22	23	24	25	26	27	28
District Amraoti	5,660	2,984	2,676	29	13	16	629	317	312	235	132	103	1	1	...
" Akola	3,365	1,825	1,540	67	41	26	305	183	122	145	111	34	7	5	2
" Ellichpur	1,269	684	585	1	1	...	123	68	55	22	20	2	1	1	...
" Buldana	3,883	2,023	1,860	30	13	17	103	60	43	5	4	1	...	...	...
" Wún	1,702	937	765	38	23	15	89	49	40	5	4	1	...	...	...
" Basim	3,073	1,590	1,483	12	7	5	88	48	40	...	...	...	2	2	...
Railway Passengers, etc.	...	...	...	...	...	...	22	13	9	...	...	...	...	...	...
Total	18,952	10,043	8,909	177	98	79	1,859	788	621	412	271	141	11	9	2
Amraoti District. Taluk Amraoti	1,222	692	530	2	1	1	592	287	305	220	120	100	1	1	...
" Chandur	1,596	861	735	18	10	8	15	13	2	...	...	...	...	...	...
" Morsi	1,051	509	542	...	...	...	5	4	1	2	2	...	...	...	...
" Murtazapur	1,791	922	869	9	2	7	17	13	4	13	10	3	...	...	...
Akola District. Taluk Akola	971	507	464	49	29	20	191	104	87	68	46	22	5	3	2
" Akot	574	308	266	7	6	1	6	5	1	8	5	3	...	...	...
" Balapur	914	481	433	..	...	...	8	5	3	4	4	...	...	...	...
" Jalgaon	151	101	50	4	2	2	2	2	...	...	...	...	...	...	...
" Khamgaon	755	428	327	7	4	3	98	67	31	65	56	9	2	2	...
Ellichpur District. Taluk Ellichpur	800	427	373	...	...	...	111	61	50	11	11	...	1	1	...
" Daryapur	467	255	212	1	1	...	1	...	1	11	9	2	...	...	...
" Melghát	2	2	...	...	...	...	11	7	4	...	...	...	...	...	...
Buldana District. Taluk Chikhli	1,331	682	649	1	...	1	77	47	30	1	1	...	..	...	...
" Malkapur	1,304	721	673	...	...	...	20	11	9	4	3	1	...	...	...
" Mehkar	1,158	620	538	29	13	16	6	2	4	...	..	...	...	..	...
Wún District. Taluk Yeotmal	722	393	329	1	1	...	89	49	40	5	4	1	...	...	...
" Darwha	713	393	320	1	1	...	...	...	...	...	...	...	...	...	...
" Kelapur	219	123	96	36	21	15	...	...	...	...	...	...	...	...	...
" Wún	48	28	20	...	...	...	...	...	...	...	...	...	...	...	...
Basim District. Taluk Basim	1,864	970	894	...	...	...	85	46	39	...	...	...	1	1	...
" Mangrul	332	176	156	...	...	...	1	1	...	...	...	...	...	...	...
" Pusad	877	444	433	12	7	5	2	1	1	...	...	...	1	1	...

TABLE VII.

Ages by Religions.—Part A.—TOTAL POPULATION.

TABLE VII.—Ages by Religions.—Part A—TOTAL POPULATION.

District and Taluk.	Total Population: Total.	Total Population: Males.	Total Population: Females.	Under 1 year: Males.	Under 1 year: Females.	1 year: Males.	1 year: Females.	2 years: Males.	2 years: Females.	3 years: Males.	3 years: Females.	4 years: Males.	4 years: Females.	Total 0–4: Males.	Total 0–4: Females.	5–9: Males.	5–9: Females.	10–14: Males.	10–14: Females.
1	2	3	4	5	6	7	8	9	10	11	12	13	14	15	16	17	18	19	20
District Amraoti	655,645	340,235	315,410	10,119	10,112	5,475	5,675	9,404	9,978	8,782	10,062	8,070	8,237	41,850	44,064	41,950	43,911	36,175	29,843
" Akola	574,782	297,011	277,771	9,859	9,922	4,621	5,008	7,489	8,073	7,714	8,809	6,703	7,134	36,386	38,946	36,621	37,665	31,983	26,205
" Ellichpur	315,798	162,969	152,829	5,136	5,212	2,464	2,658	4,334	4,582	4,343	4,822	3,872	3,967	20,149	21,241	20,267	20,830	17,497	14,747
" Buldana	481,021	244,799	236,222	7,842	8,019	4,679	5,162	6,782	7,633	6,912	8,111	6,846	7,237	33,061	36,162	33,758	34,739	28,277	24,212
" Wún	471,613	241,688	229,925	6,976	7,053	4,807	5,035	7,441	8,307	7,133	8,026	7,480	7,718	33,837	36,169	34,962	35,538	28,189	22,368
" Basim	398,181	204,798	193,383	6,385	6,476	4,310	4,751	6,759	7,496	6,286	7,171	6,373	6,738	30,113	32,632	29,163	28,833	22,717	17,806
Railway Passengers, etc.	451	326	125	2	5	3	7	2	4	4	7	1	4	12	27	19	12	15	18
Total	2,897,491	1,491,826	1,405,665	46,319	46,829	26,359	28,296	42,211	46,073	41,174	47,008	39,845	41,035	195,408	209,241	196,740	201,528	164,853	135,199
Amraoti District. Taluk Amraoti	183,508	95,536	87,972	2,701	2,640	1,589	1,684	2,512	2,611	2,369	2,661	2,161	2,256	11,332	11,852	11,244	11,854	9,971	8,266
" Chandur	198,106	102,885	95,221	3,115	3,176	1,624	1,628	2,986	3,077	2,686	2,897	2,472	2,557	12,883	13,335	13,114	13,655	11,361	9,525
" Morsi	152,374	78,451	73,923	2,477	2,443	1,171	1,195	2,203	2,437	2,125	2,549	1,872	1,923	9,848	10,547	9,960	10,376	8,203	6,769
" Murtazapur	121,657	63,363	58,294	1,826	1,853	1,091	1,168	1,703	1,853	1,602	1,955	1,565	1,501	7,787	8,330	7,632	8,026	6,640	5,283
Akola District. Taluk Akola	137,988	71,744	66,244	2,268	2,361	1,045	1,163	1,765	1,867	1,839	2,146	1,580	1,710	8,497	9,247	8,936	9,093	7,398	5,978
" Akot	137,720	70,630	67,090	2,380	2,427	1,130	1,195	1,720	1,864	1,748	1,959	1,481	1,558	8,459	9,003	8,177	8,661	7,542	6,350
" Balapur	101,673	51,941	49,732	1,727	1,686	839	868	1,403	1,571	1,432	1,720	1,345	1,438	6,746	7,283	7,064	7,224	5,689	4,566
" Jalgaon	97,616	50,323	47,293	1,720	1,706	781	906	1,294	1,362	1,314	1,456	1,104	1,178	6,213	6,608	6,178	6,390	5,690	4,820
" Khamgaon	99,785	52,373	47,412	1,764	1,742	826	876	1,307	1,409	1,381	1,528	1,193	1,250	6,471	6,805	6,266	6,297	5,664	4,491
Ellichpur District. Taluk Ellichpur	146,215	75,271	70,944	2,235	2,285	1,072	1,171	2,019	2,153	1,892	2,148	1,626	1,697	8,844	9,454	8,917	9,366	8,011	6,527
" Daryapur	122,552	63,329	59,223	2,245	2,164	974	989	1,611	1,687	1,584	1,715	1,422	1,429	7,836	7,984	7,575	7,741	6,578	5,740
" Melghát	47,031	24,369	22,662	656	763	418	498	704	742	867	959	824	841	3,469	3,803	3,775	3,723	2,908	2,480
Buldana District. Taluk Chikhli	150,098	76,540	73,558	2,185	2,297	1,339	1,576	2,063	2,342	2,000	2,462	2,179	2,151	9,856	10,828	10,874	11,006	9,154	7,695
" Malkapur	177,877	90,215	87,662	3,297	3,376	1,628	1,733	2,450	2,678	2,617	3,030	2,363	2,661	12,355	13,478	12,039	12,332	10,290	8,794
" Mehkar	153,046	78,044	75,002	2,360	2,346	1,712	1,853	2,269	2,613	2,205	2,619	2,304	2,425	10,850	11,856	10,845	11,401	8,833	7,723
Wún District. Taluk Yeotmal	124,429	64,275	60,154	1,938	1,867	1,214	1,258	1,804	2,027	1,758	1,940	1,812	1,817	8,526	8,909	8,711	8,861	7,391	5,932
" Darwha	156,580	80,746	75,834	2,555	2,668	1,403	1,546	2,524	2,758	2,350	2,711	2,371	2,466	11,203	12,149	11,605	11,758	9,011	6,969
" Kelapur	105,926	53,845	52,081	1,262	1,264	1,304	1,365	1,748	1,914	1,708	1,927	1,797	1,933	7,819	8,403	8,117	8,317	6,350	5,070
" Wún	84,678	42,822	41,856	1,221	1,284	886	866	1,305	1,608	1,317	1,448	1,500	1,502	6,289	6,708	6,529	6,602	5,437	4,397
Basim District. Taluk Basim	177,250	91,200	86,050	2,728	2,844	2,041	2,247	2,748	2,985	2,750	3,207	2,751	2,790	13,018	14,073	12,549	12,546	9,887	7,893
" Mangrul	82,446	42,773	39,673	1,240	1,172	868	947	1,349	1,462	1,247	1,421	1,241	1,333	5,945	6,335	6,050	6,039	4,758	3,607
" Pusad	138,485	70,825	67,660	2,417	2,460	1,401	1,557	2,662	3,049	2,289	2,543	2,381	2,615	11,150	12,224	10,504	10,248	8,072	6,306

District and Taluk.	Age Periods. 15—19 Males.	15—19 Females.	20—24 Males.	20—24 Females.	25—29 Males.	25—29 Females.	30—34 Males.	30—34 Females.	35—39 Males.	35—39 Females.	40—44 Males.	40—44 Females.	45—49 Males.	45—49 Females.	50—54 Males.	50—54 Females.	55—59 Males.	55—59 Females.	60 and over Males.	60 and over Females.
	21	22	23	24	25	26	27	28	29	30	31	32	33	34	35	36	37	38	39	40
District Amraoti	21,173	21,509	23,694	27,908	29,465	28,979	32,871	28,986	24,568	18,204	27,824	21,764	13,944	9,389	19,422	15,582	5,612	4,038	21,687	21,233
" Akola	19,456	20,176	21,739	24,879	28,011	25,551	28,356	24,278	21,486	16,583	22,320	18,893	12,326	9,238	16,231	13,928	5,181	3,969	16,915	17,460
" Ellichpur	10,569	11,078	12,115	13,758	14,381	13,635	15,619	13,784	11,310	8,455	12,836	10,336	6,578	4,758	8,802	7,564	2,626	2,018	10,220	10,625
" Buldana	16,347	17,576	16,957	21,249	24,120	20,954	22,759	20,023	15,106	12,177	16,796	15,362	8,706	6,816	12,323	10,476	3,819	2,727	12,770	13,749
" Wún	14,227	14,717	15,247	19,086	20,268	20,928	22,243	20,971	15,211	11,781	18,822	14,873	8,658	5,797	12,758	10,840	3,303	2,584	13,963	14,273
" Basim	11,545	12,628	13,741	16,894	19,655	17,891	19,773	17,464	12,265	9,395	15,286	12,694	6,519	4,547	10,878	9,038	2,538	1,858	10,605	11,703
Railway Passengers, etc.	14	6	28	5	52	12	58	12	30	5	26	9	13	5	27	9	14	...	18	5
Total	98,831	97,690	103,521	123,779	135,952	127,950	141,679	125,518	99,976	76,600	118,910	93,931	56,744	40,550	80,441	67,437	28,093	17,194	86,178	89,048
Amraoti District. Taluk Amraoti	6,129	6,138	7,142	8,051	8,342	8,115	9,525	8,171	6,834	5,012	7,842	6,262	3,809	2,619	5,641	4,448	1,514	1,069	6,211	6,115
" Chandur	6,370	6,434	6,851	8,027	8,642	8,450	9,423	8,758	7,386	5,708	8,437	6,381	4,456	2,973	5,791	4,469	1,772	1,258	6,399	6,248
" Morsi	4,803	4,874	5,215	6,465	6,612	6,889	7,521	6,914	5,773	4,222	6,357	4,989	3,174	2,171	4,447	3,778	1,288	1,011	5,250	4,918
" Murtazapur	3,871	4,063	4,486	5,365	5,869	5,525	6,402	5,143	4,575	3,262	5,188	4,132	2,505	1,626	3,543	2,887	1,038	700	3,827	3,952
Akola District. Taluk Akola	4,580	4,641	5,316	5,941	6,765	6,246	7,011	5,928	5,385	3,989	5,546	4,516	2,939	2,110	3,974	3,361	1,185	915	4,212	4,279
" Akot	4,623	4,914	5,121	6,125	6,552	6,192	6,995	5,995	5,258	4,065	5,553	4,701	3,057	2,295	3,975	3,442	1,299	1,021	4,019	4,326
" Balapur	3,393	3,516	3,589	4,381	4,580	4,460	4,661	4,374	3,602	2,806	3,724	3,381	2,072	1,513	2,867	2,443	843	629	3,111	3,156
" Jalgaon	3,395	3,514	3,759	4,117	4,864	4,222	4,825	3,949	3,534	2,854	3,668	3,084	2,078	1,754	2,558	2,387	905	724	2,616	2,870
" Khamgaon	3,465	3,591	3,954	4,315	5,250	4,431	4,864	4,032	3,707	2,869	3,829	3,211	2,180	1,566	2,817	2,295	949	680	2,557	2,829
Ellichpur District. Taluk Ellichpur	5,032	4,923	5,567	6,328	6,598	6,263	6,905	6,299	5,088	3,990	6,212	5,078	3,126	2,317	4,325	3,789	1,287	1,045	5,359	5,565
" Daryapur	4,086	4,404	4,770	5,433	5,697	5,230	6,163	5,337	4,525	3,445	4,874	4,074	2,690	1,922	3,514	2,993	1,080	790	3,941	4,130
" Melghát	1,451	1,751	1,778	1,997	2,086	2,142	2,551	2,148	1,697	1,020	1,750	1,184	762	519	963	782	259	183	920	930
Buldana District. Taluk Chikhli	5,131	5,313	5,100	6,510	7,516	6,595	7,293	6,470	4,700	3,898	5,391	4,793	2,646	2,003	3,915	3,432	1,132	793	3,832	4,222
" Malkapur	6,175	6,806	6,309	7,541	8,503	7,608	7,770	6,952	5,884	4,837	5,803	5,481	3,645	3,051	4,354	3,850	1,801	1,316	5,287	5,616
" Mehkar	5,041	5,457	5,548	7,198	8,101	6,751	7,696	6,601	4,522	3,442	5,602	5,088	2,415	1,762	4,054	3,194	886	618	3,651	3,911
Wún District. Taluk Yeotmal	3,756	3,990	4,111	5,108	5,435	5,586	6,032	5,620	4,213	3,177	5,131	3,988	2,492	1,658	3,605	2,847	949	672	3,523	3,806
" Darwha	4,649	4,927	5,178	6,388	6,875	6,814	7,223	6,714	5,358	4,113	6,271	4,961	3,133	1,980	4,368	3,432	1,182	887	4,690	4,742
" Kelapur	3,186	3,259	3,238	4,331	4,502	4,840	5,127	5,056	3,344	2,459	4,294	3,279	1,754	1,174	2,658	2,417	659	488	2,757	2,988
" Wún	2,636	2,541	2,720	3,259	3,456	3,688	3,861	3,581	2,296	2,032	3,126	2,645	1,279	985	2,127	2,144	513	537	2,553	2,737
Basim District. Taluk Basim	5,197	5,712	6,277	7,775	8,857	8,222	9,252	7,660	5,615	4,185	6,730	5,691	2,880	2,146	4,907	3,979	1,177	854	4,854	5,314
" Mangrul	2,259	2,554	2,787	3,310	3,930	3,564	4,013	3,551	2,683	2,123	3,204	2,631	1,591	1,062	2,381	1,863	660	446	2,512	2,588
" Pusad	4,089	4,362	4,677	5,809	6,868	6,105	6,508	6,253	3,967	3,087	5,352	4,372	2,048	1,339	3,590	3,196	701	558	3,239	3,801

TABLE VII.

Ages by Religions.—Part B.—HINDU.

TABLE VII.—Ages by Religions.—Part B.—HINDU.

District and Taluk.	TOTAL HINDU.			AGE PERIODS.															
				Under 1 year.		1 year.		2 years.		3 years.		4 years.		Total 0–4		5–9		10–14	
	Total.	Males.	Females.	Males.	Females.	Males.	Females.	Males.	Females.	Males.	Females.	Males.	Females.	Males.	Females.	Males.	Females.	Males.	Females.
1	2	3	4	5	6	7	8	9	10	11	12	13	14	15	16	17	18	19	20
District Amraoti	584,178	303,130	281,048	9,068	9,100	4,923	5,060	8,421	8,941	7,813	8,977	7,176	7,335	37,401	39,413	37,383	39,077	32,126	26,540
" Akola	518,046	267,316	250,730	8,949	8,976	4,124	4,529	6,799	7,318	6,979	7,999	5,977	6,366	32,828	35,188	33,094	33,895	28,841	23,626
" Ellichpur	243,992	126,423	117,569	4,075	4,033	1,897	1,932	3,316	3,502	3,170	3,520	2,735	2,796	15,153	15,783	14,997	15,622	13,241	11,135
" Buldana	442,588	225,016	217,572	7,239	7,397	4,316	4,767	6,219	7,016	6,347	7,522	6,275	6,639	30,396	33,341	31,058	32,013	26,061	22,404
" Wún	371,084	190,766	180,318	5,576	5,622	3,667	3,840	5,728	6,371	5,527	6,127	5,635	5,756	26,133	27,716	27,116	27,412	22,256	17,640
" Basim	371,537	190,873	180,664	5,933	6,095	4,089	4,477	6,353	7,043	5,907	6,742	5,971	6,302	28,253	30,659	27,258	26,955	21,191	16,611
Railway Passengers, etc.	366	261	105	2	5	3	6	1	4	3	6	1	3	10	24	16	9	10	13
Total	2,631,791	1,308,785	1,228,006	40,842	41,228	22,979	24,611	36,887	40,195	35,746	40,893	33,770	35,197	170,174	182,124	170,922	174,983	143,726	117,969
Amraoti District. Taluk Amraoti	161,331	83,853	77,478	2,418	2,352	1,400	1,497	2,222	2,343	2,080	2,359	1,902	1,991	10,022	10,542	9,875	10,429	8,697	7,270
" Chandur	180,463	93,700	86,763	2,854	2,915	1,499	1,487	2,743	2,805	2,431	2,645	2,272	2,348	11,799	12,200	11,966	12,469	10,348	8,685
" Morsi	133,708	69,017	64,691	2,185	2,164	1,057	1,042	1,955	2,150	1,850	2,239	1,615	1,684	8,662	9,279	8,726	9,022	7,164	5,860
" Murtazapur	108,676	56,560	52,116	1,611	1,669	967	1,034	1,501	1,643	1,452	1,734	1,387	1,312	6,918	7,392	6,816	7,157	5,917	4,725
Akola District. Taluk Akola	124,098	64,430	59,668	2,049	2,119	914	1,032	1,606	1,674	1,655	1,956	1,420	1,537	7,644	8,318	8,037	8,203	6,674	5,417
" Akot	123,010	63,087	59,923	2,117	2,180	1,002	1,074	1,439	1,672	1,561	1,753	1,284	1,355	7,503	8,034	7,287	7,677	6,718	5,631
" Balapur	89,399	45,726	43,673	1,538	1,506	730	765	1,250	1,408	1,272	1,525	1,151	1,254	5,941	6,458	6,245	6,306	4,968	3,975
" Jalgaon	89,937	46,177	43,760	1,586	1,574	724	849	1,194	1,249	1,204	1,345	1,019	1,071	5,727	6,088	5,695	5,891	5,245	4,477
" Khamgaon	91,602	47,856	43,706	1,659	1,597	764	809	1,210	1,315	1,287	1,420	1,103	1,149	6,013	6,290	5,830	5,818	5,236	4,126
Ellichpur District. Taluk Ellichpur	124,059	64,174	59,885	1,930	1,961	983	988	1,729	1,833	1,591	1,807	1,376	1,386	7,549	7,975	7,521	7,922	6,777	5,513
" Daryapur	111,595	57,515	54,080	2,065	1,970	885	887	1,485	1,563	1,467	1,590	1,264	1,298	7,166	7,308	6,898	7,101	5,981	5,244
" Melghát	8,338	4,734	3,604	80	102	49	57	102	106	112	123	95	112	438	500	578	599	483	378
Buldana District. Taluk Chikhli	136,828	69,694	67,134	2,012	2,091	1,221	1,436	1,846	2,132	1,882	2,267	1,976	1,962	8,937	9,688	9,968	10,038	8,369	7,071
" Malkapur	162,064	82,146	79,918	3,005	3,100	1,487	1,576	2,235	2,426	2,411	2,775	2,138	2,409	11,276	12,286	10,867	11,198	9,403	8,074
" Mehkar	143,696	73,176	70,520	2,222	2,206	1,608	1,755	2,038	2,458	2,054	2,480	2,161	2,268	10,183	11,167	10,223	10,777	8,289	7,259
Wún District. Taluk Yeotmal	93,683	48,599	45,084	1,472	1,389	883	890	1,304	1,485	1,280	1,394	1,319	1,267	6,258	6,425	6,466	6,507	5,569	4,513
" Darwha	137,182	70,651	66,531	2,256	2,367	1,294	1,334	2,216	2,409	2,080	2,380	2,067	2,162	9,823	10,652	10,171	10,484	7,842	6,129
" Kelapur	74,783	38,276	36,507	500	875	502	940	1,175	1,254	1,161	1,294	1,151	1,223	5,289	5,586	5,578	5,653	4,549	3,602
" Wún	65,436	33,240	32,196	948	991	678	676	1,033	1,223	1,006	1,059	1,098	1,104	4,763	5,053	4,501	4,968	4,296	3,396
Basim District. Taluk Basim	165,987	85,247	80,740	2,548	2,693	1,932	2,121	2,586	2,824	2,591	3,027	2,587	2,622	12,244	13,287	11,763	11,783	9,246	7,378
" Mangrul	77,356	40,129	37,227	1,166	1,103	829	910	1,278	1,369	1,183	1,342	1,167	1,264	5,623	5,988	5,686	5,678	4,465	3,371
" Pusad	128,194	65,497	62,697	2,219	2,299	1,328	1,446	2,489	2,850	2,133	2,373	2,217	2,416	10,386	11,384	9,809	9,494	7,480	5,862

Table VII.—Ages by Religions.

District and Taluk.	Age Periods. 15—19 Males.	15—19 Females.	20—24 Males.	20—24 Females.	25—29 Males.	25—29 Females.	30—34 Males.	30—34 Females.	35—39 Males.	35—39 Females.	40—44 Males.	40—44 Females.	45—49 Males.	45—49 Females.	50—54 Males.	50—54 Females.	55—59 Males.	55—59 Females.	60 and over. Males.	60 and over. Females.
	21	22	23	24	25	26	27	28	29	30	1	32	33	34	35	36	37	38	39	40
District Amraoti	18,759	19,272	20,930	24,677	26,232	25,894	29,232	25,765	22,136	16,348	24,757	19,248	12,535	8,465	17,202	13,792	5,070	3,654	9,367	18,903
" Akola	17,402	18,229	19,266	22,327	25,183	23,119	25,493	21 910	19,495	15,317	20,137	16,885	11,318	8,501	14,517	12,522	4,708	3,670	15,034	15,541
" Ellichpur	8,258	8,457	9,316	10,572	11,216	10,467	12,152	10,548	8,978	6,824	10,139	8,162	5,368	3,886	7,083	5,929	2,172	1,675	8,320	8,507
" Buldana	15,010	16,235	15,510	19,536	22,208	19,302	20,976	18,398	13,991	11,279	15,354	14,063	8,038	6,345	11,301	9,597	3,518	2,507	11,595	12,552
" Wún	11,279	11,599	12,247	15,048	16,143	16,409	17,654	16,493	12,129	9,375	14,814	11,751	6,986	4,710	10,179	8,537	2,708	2,123	11,122	11,505
" Basim	10,692	11,764	12,705	15,775	18,326	16,707	18,372	16,313	11,459	8,788	14,258	11,807	6,074	4,269	10,061	8,410	2,386	1,739	9,838	10,867
Railway Passengers, etc.	10	5	21	5	47	10	42	11	24	5	22	5	12	5	22	8	11	...	14	5
Total	81,410	85,561	89,995	107,940	119,855	111,908	128,921	109,438	88,212	67,936	99,481	81,921	50,861	36,183	70,865	58,795	20,573	15,368	75,290	77,880
Amraoti District. Taluk Amraoti	5,363	5,441	6,176	7,018	7,298	7,155	8,385	7,164	6,090	4,444	6,879	5,478	3,364	2,341	4,896	3,886	1,335	950	5,473	5,360
" Chandur	5,772	5,894	6,204	7,270	7,835	7,684	8,553	7,955	6,765	5,246	7,668	5,764	4,076	2,713	5,252	4,058	1,626	1,148	5,836	5,677
" Morsi	4,223	4,201	4,562	5,659	5,864	6,089	6,574	6,065	5,138	3,691	5,590	4,298	2,830	1,924	3,881	3,298	1,162	908	4,641	4,307
" Murtazapur	3,401	3,646	3,988	4,730	5,235	4,966	5,720	4,581	4,143	2,967	4,620	3,708	2,265	1,487	3,173	2,550	947	648	3,417	3,559
Akola District. Taluk Akola	4,098	4,191	4,705	5,309	6,082	5,614	6,301	5,367	4,858	3,644	5,003	4,030	2,666	1,937	3,560	3,052	1,064	825	3,738	3,761
" Akot	4,093	4,409	4,500	5,426	5,877	5,562	6,266	5,384	4,743	3,721	4,994	4,186	2,809	2,112	3,566	3,044	1,193	928	3,538	3,809
" Balapur	2,925	3,078	3,107	3,818	4,081	3,942	4,109	3,827	3,233	2,548	3,319	2,935	1,852	1,355	2,459	2,113	735	579	2,672	2,739
" Jalgaon	3,132	3,236	3,420	3,816	4,427	3,882	4,398	3,641	3,239	2,691	3,348	2,837	1,931	1,642	2,374	2,201	838	690	2,403	2,668
" Khamgaon	3,154	3,315	3,534	3,958	4,716	4,119	4,419	3,691	3,422	2,713	3,473	2,897	2,020	1,455	2,518	2,112	878	648	2,683	2,564
Ellichpur District. Taluk Ellichpur	4,268	4,194	4,689	5,353	5,596	5,305	5,919	5,318	4,439	3,424	5,324	4,236	2,724	2,041	3,652	3,097	1,133	923	4,583	4,584
" Daryapur	3,685	4,019	4,264	4,886	5,115	4,778	5,587	4,684	4,162	3,222	4,402	3,710	2,488	1,773	3,209	2,673	590	728	3,568	3,754
" Melghát	305	244	363	333	505	384	646	346	377	178	413	216	186	74	222	159	49	24	169	169
Buldana District. Taluk Chikhli	4,703	4,878	4,575	5,952	6,888	5,999	6,657	5,907	4,310	3,537	4,850	4,362	2,415	1,832	3,546	3,118	1,030	718	3,446	3,834
" Malkapur	5,597	6,230	5,716	6,823	7,740	6,930	7,090	6,309	5,428	4,484	5,256	4,947	3,391	2,848	3,959	3,498	1,659	1,207	4,764	5,084
" Mehkar	4,710	5,127	5,219	6,761	7,580	6,373	7,229	6,182	4,253	3,258	5,248	4,754	2,232	1,665	3,796	2,981	829	582	3,385	3,634
Wún District. Taluk Yeotmal	2,865	2,984	3,196	3,821	4,164	4,198	4,613	4,280	3,197	2,402	3,868	3,033	1,933	1,289	2,745	2,131	743	537	2,982	2,964
" Darwha	4,021	4,337	4,480	5,617	6,009	5,949	6,307	5,867	4,742	3,594	5,463	4,342	2,782	1,769	3,829	3,025	1,064	784	4,118	4,182
" Kelapur	2,312	2,308	2,370	3,087	3,262	3,420	3,744	3,593	2,403	1,797	3,091	2,346	1,270	861	1,940	1,718	471	368	1,577	2,168
" Wún	2,081	1,970	2,181	2,523	2,708	2,842	2,990	2,753	1,787	1,582	2,392	2,030	1,001	791	1,665	1,663	430	434	2,045	2,191
Basim District. Taluk Basim	4,812	5,340	5,807	7,325	8,297	7,727	8,642	7,187	5,256	3,917	6,315	5,315	2,677	2,040	4,559	3,702	1,116	801	4,513	4,938
" Mangrul	2,111	2,386	2,577	3,098	3,695	3,314	3,742	3,329	2,537	2,019	2,979	2,444	1,513	1,015	2,218	1,740	618	422	2,365	2,423
" Pusad	3,769	4,038	4,321	5,352	6,334	5,666	5,988	5,797	3,666	2,852	4,964	4,048	1,884	1,214	3,284	2,968	652	516	2,560	3,506

TABLE VII.

Ages by Religions.—Part C.—MUSALMAN.

TABLE VII.—Ages by Religions.—Part C.—MUSALMAN.

District and Taluk.	Total Musalman.			Age Periods.															
	Total.	Males.	Females.	Under 1 year.		1 year.		2 years.		3 years.		4 years.		Total 0–4		5–9		10–14	
				Males.	Females.	Males.	Females.	Males.	Females.	Males.	Females.	Males.	Females.	Males.	Females.	Males.	Females.	Males.	Females.
1	2	3	4	5	6	7	8	9	10	11	12	13	14	15	16	17	18	19	20
District Amraoti	47,522	24,931	22,591	715	682	390	416	664	691	630	727	607	609	3,006	3,125	3,128	3,235	2,750	2,104
" Akola	51,302	26,717	24,585	835	839	457	432	629	673	661	725	655	699	3,237	3,368	3,203	3,435	2,847	2,351
" Ellichpur	30,645	15,671	14,974	442	482	224	273	371	404	375	429	362	407	1,774	1,995	1,869	1,900	1,696	1,370
" Buldana	34,405	17,679	16,726	531	562	336	363	510	549	511	536	525	559	2,413	2,569	2,476	2,456	1,984	1,618
" Wún	20,727	10,932	9,795	296	294	215	212	281	348	250	321	301	283	1,343	1,458	1,469	1,481	1,245	934
" Basim	23,020	12,053	10,967	377	330	197	244	369	393	326	374	348	397	1,617	1,738	1,641	1,625	1,305	1,029
Railway Passengers, etc.	60	52	8	...	...	...	...	...	...	...	...	...	...	...	...	3	1	4	2
Total	207,881	108,035	99,646	8,196	3,189	1,819	1,940	2,824	3,058	2,758	3,112	2,798	2,954	13,390	14,253	13,789	14,133	11,881	9,408
Amraoti District. Taluk Amraoti	18,384	9,712	8,672	246	229	169	162	244	222	249	241	219	229	1,127	1,083	1,173	1,205	1,069	795
" Chandur	9,060	4,794	4,266	139	152	65	74	123	151	132	142	115	105	574	624	632	610	545	418
" Morsi	9,225	4,729	4,496	154	141	48	65	128	141	120	155	115	115	565	617	625	658	533	420
" Murtazapur	10,853	5,696	5,157	176	160	108	115	169	177	129	189	158	160	740	801	698	753	603	471
Akola District. Taluk Akola	12,463	6,545	5,918	203	218	119	112	142	176	173	166	144	155	781	827	830	803	654	510
" Akot	13,330	6,804	6,526	243	215	119	112	163	173	162	177	177	182	864	859	793	881	738	651
" Balapur	11,340	5,722	5,618	175	160	100	96	147	151	150	188	177	177	749	772	766	858	674	555
" Jalgaon	6,933	3,742	3,191	122	115	54	52	88	89	97	95	72	91	433	442	422	448	405	311
" Khamgaon	7,236	3,904	3,332	92	131	65	60	89	84	79	99	85	94	410	468	392	445	376	324
Ellichpur District. Taluk Ellichpur	19,020	9,464	9,556	253	273	134	168	244	267	243	294	205	271	1,079	1,273	1,155	1,220	1,065	837
" Daryapur	10,263	5,439	4,824	169	176	84	97	118	119	110	120	149	125	630	637	632	604	558	473
" Melghát	1,362	768	594	20	33	6	8	9	18	22	15	8	11	65	85	82	76	73	60
Buldana District. Taluk Chikhli	11,853	6,112	5,741	153	183	106	130	192	185	191	179	188	178	830	855	836	863	694	563
" Malkapur	14,395	7,334	7,061	262	253	134	145	200	230	188	233	206	238	990	1,099	1,087	1,037	818	645
" Mehkar	8,157	4,233	3,924	116	126	96	88	118	134	132	124	131	143	593	615	553	556	472	410
Wún District. Taluk Yeotmal	5,595	3,006	2,589	76	84	62	56	81	95	60	78	72	67	351	380	386	352	315	256
" Darwha	9,797	5,219	4,578	152	143	101	105	116	171	127	152	145	135	641	706	701	721	607	434
" Kelapur	3,052	1,564	1,488	36	35	37	34	44	51	37	54	49	41	203	215	218	229	182	145
" Wún	2,283	1,143	1,140	32	32	15	17	40	31	26	37	35	40	148	157	164	179	141	99
Basim District. Taluk Basim	9,313	4,936	4,377	146	123	97	105	141	133	130	159	129	149	643	669	648	634	526	425
" Mangrul	4,718	2,450	2,268	67	61	35	36	69	90	58	71	72	68	301	326	335	331	272	224
" Pusad	8,989	4,667	4,322	164	146	65	103	159	170	138	144	147	180	673	743	658	660	507	380

District and Taluk.	15—19 Males.	15—19 Females.	20—24 Males.	20—24 Females.	25—29 Males.	25—29 Females.	30—34 Males.	30—34 Females.	35—39 Males.	35—39 Females.	40—44 Males.	40—44 Females.	45—49 Males.	45—49 Females.	50—54 Males.	50—54 Females.	55—59 Males.	55—59 Females.	60 and over. Males.	60 and over. Females.
	21	22	23	24	25	26	27	28	29	30	31	32	33	34	35	36	37	38	39	40
District Amraoti	1,645	1,507	1,965	2,179	2,261	1,955	2,423	2,057	1,521	1,139	1,989	1,672	863	573	1,487	1,185	337	227	1,556	1,633
" Akola	1,823	1,759	2,198	2,336	2,521	2,186	2,582	2,168	1,763	1,140	1,950	1,840	888	666	1,543	1,293	417	268	1,745	1,775
" Ellichpur	1,101	1,047	1,335	1,420	1,489	1,303	1,517	1,314	930	710	1,235	1,105	539	401	888	949	221	167	1,077	1,293
" Buldana	1,173	1,200	1,290	1,509	1,696	1,493	1,592	1,482	992	771	1,282	1,163	561	408	918	792	261	187	1,041	1,078
" Wún	718	594	796	862	1,054	926	1,042	894	691	529	901	623	390	235	570	502	127	109	586	648
" Basim	733	725	896	991	1,150	1,014	1,247	1,006	688	507	915	751	376	224	719	559	119	90	647	708
Railway Passengers, etc.	3	1	5	...	4	1	14	...	4	...	4	3	1	...	4	...	2	...	4	...
Total	7,196	6,833	8,485	9,297	10,175	8,878	10,417	8,921	6,589	4,796	8,276	7,157	3,618	2,507	6,129	5,280	1,484	1,048	6,656	7,135
Amraoti District. Taluk Amraoti	644	577	800	869	877	765	933	792	586	460	763	655	337	224	645	482	136	96	622	669
" Chandur	324	279	376	381	436	369	451	383	290	216	386	298	176	132	264	190	73	48	267	309
" Morsi	302	310	368	397	399	359	480	411	292	240	361	360	152	105	272	240	56	46	324	333
" Murtazapur	375	341	421	532	549	462	559	471	353	223	479	359	198	112	306	273	72	37	343	322
Akola District. Taluk Akola	425	400	536	558	594	560	630	513	454	317	499	439	236	158	375	284	104	83	427	466
" Akot	480	472	565	651	622	576	662	554	462	309	482	408	221	169	366	370	97	82	452	484
" Balapur	406	397	438	538	462	464	518	504	342	236	365	415	159	145	332	300	97	43	414	391
" Jalgaon	239	248	310	280	389	303	388	283	260	143	258	235		98	205	177	62	31	200	192
" Khamgaon	273	242	349	309	454	283	384	314	245	135	306	283		96	265	162	57	29	252	242
Ellichpur District. Taluk Ellichpur	671	645	777	852	875	814	854	827	542	479	725	738	326	247	567	619	131	104	697	901
" Daryapur	384	361	483	512	542	427	548	420	334	201	438	334	179	143	283	298	79	59	349	355
" Melghát	46	41	75	56	72	62	115	67	54	30	72	33	34	11	38	32	11	4	31	37
Buldana District. Taluk Chikhli	369	387	465	486	558	543	575	509	343	312	489	389	200	144	331	277	87	65	335	348
" Malkapur	513	525	544	649	692	623	616	595	414	305	489	492	218	183	359	327	124	92	470	489
" Mehkar	291	288	281	374	446	327	401	378	235	154	304	282	143	81	228	188	50	30	236	241
Wún District. Taluk Yeotmal	187	165	221	227	277	250	302	238	204	134	250	157	121	76	181	154	34	24	177	176
" Darwha	359	272	402	405	498	430	470	392	301	275	419	295	181	103	278	209	69	50	293	286
" Kelapur	99	89	101	130	168	127	149	158	112	67	138	109	51	42	65	65	16	19	62	93
" Wún	73	68	72	100	111	119	121	106	74	53	94	62	37	14	46	74	8	16	54	93
Basim District. Taluk Basim	318	295	385	390	458	398	534	397	288	207	354	305	163	78	295	239	47	34	277	306
" Mangrul	134	157	200	201	219	232	255	199	134	96	212	170	72	41	146	118	36	22	134	151
" Pusad	281	273	311	400	473	384	458	410	266	204	349	276	141	105	278	202	36	34	236	251

TABLE VII.

Ages by Religions.—Part D.—ANIMISTIC.

Table VII.—Ages by Religions.

TABLE VII.—Ages by Religions.—Part D—ANIMISTIC.

District and Taluk.	Total Animistic.			Age Periods.															
				Under 1 year.		1 year.		2 years.		3 years.		4 years.		Total 0—4		5—9		10—14	
	Total.	Males.	Females.	Males.	Females.	Males.	Females.	Males.	Females.	Males.	Females.	Males.	Females.	Males.	Females.	Males.	Females.	Males.	Females.
1	2	3	4	5	6	7	8	9	10	11	12	13	14	15	16	17	18	19	20
District Amraoti	17,391	8,727	8,664	236	237	116	135	222	265	261	259	225	227	1,060	1,123	1,097	1,221	950	912
" Akola	1,545	813	732	26	35	6	13	24	35	30	44	26	28	112	155	125	126	84	67
" Ellichpur	39,745	20,101	19,644	593	674	372	444	631	660	780	860	759	750	3,135	3,388	3,311	3,242	2,484	2,186
" Buldana	7	4	3	...	...	...	...	...	...	2	...	...	...	2	...	1	...	...	...
" Wún	77,968	38,977	38,991	1,079	1,146	911	964	1,410	1,558	1,343	1,562	1,532	1,658	6,275	6,888	6,267	6,543	4,558	3,718
" Basim	449	225	224	8	4	3	5	5	16	7	12	7	6	30	43	38	36	28	25
Railway Passengers, etc.	3	...	3	...	...	...	...	...	...	...	...	...	1	...	1	...	1	...	...
Total	137,108	68,847	68,261	1,942	2,096	1,408	1,561	2,292	2,534	2,428	2,737	2,549	2,670	10,614	11,598	10,839	11,169	8,104	6,908
Amraoti District. Taluk Amraoti	1,756	870	886	12	30	11	8	17	24	20	27	17	18	77	107	92	117	106	106
" Chandur	6,954	3,507	3,447	98	85	49	50	102	102	102	90	74	93	425	420	443	463	373	357
" Morsi	8,383	4,190	4,193	122	118	54	75	101	133	135	135	133	113	545	574	544	622	448	437
" Murtazapur	298	160	138	4	4	2	2	2	6	4	7	1	3	13	22	18	19	23	12
Akola District. Taluk Akola	143	80	63	2	1	1	2	1	1	1	5	1	1	6	10	3	10	4	2
" Akot	785	415	370	12	17	2	7	11	12	17	23	13	12	55	71	66	69	46	40
" Balapur	8	3	5	1	1	...	...	...	...	...	1	...	...	1	2	...	...	...	...
" Jalgaon	589	299	290	10	16	3	4	11	22	12	15	11	15	47	72	55	47	33	25
" Khamgaon	20	16	4	1	...	...	...	1	...	...	...	1	...	3	...	1	...	1	...
Ellichpur District. Taluk Ellichpur	2,213	1,133	1,080	36	36	9	9	36	41	45	37	34	31	160	154	184	178	124	137
" Daryapur	214	110	104	1	10	...	2	2	1	2	2	4	1	9	16	13	16	10	8
" Melghát	37,318	18,858	18,460	556	628	363	433	593	618	733	821	721	718	2,966	3,218	3,114	3,048	2,350	2,041
Buldana District. Taluk Chikhli	7	4	3	...	...	...	...	...	...	2	...	...	...	2	...	1	...	...	...
" Malkapur	...	...	...	...	...	...	...	...	...	...	...	...	...	...	...	...	...	...	...
" Mehkar	...	...	...	...	...	...	...	...	...	...	...	...	...	...	...	...	...	...	...
Wún District. Taluk Yeotmal	24,334	12,223	12,111	378	383	261	302	410	431	414	459	413	473	1,876	2,048	1,806	1,951	1,448	1,133
" Darwha	8,887	4,482	4,405	140	152	94	102	184	169	137	175	155	161	710	759	696	718	512	370
" Kelapur	27,836	13,861	13,975	322	350	363	387	525	606	508	576	597	669	2,315	2,588	2,303	2,421	1,600	1,313
" Wún	16,911	8,411	8,500	239	261	193	173	291	352	284	352	367	355	1,374	1,493	1,462	1,453	998	902
Basim District. Taluk Basim	...	...	...	...	...	...	...	...	...	...	...	...	...	...	...	...	...	...	...
" Mangrul	39	17	22	...	1	...	...	...	1	1	...	1	...	2	2	2	5	...	3
" Pusad	410	208	202	8	3	3	5	5	15	6	12	6	6	28	41	36	31	28	22

Table VII.—Ages by Religions.

District and Taluk.	15—19 Males.	15—19 Females.	20—24 Males.	20—24 Females.	25—29 Males.	25—29 Females.	30—34 Males.	30—34 Females.	35—39 Males.	35—39 Females.	40—44 Males.	40—44 Females.	45—49 Males.	45—49 Females.	50—54 Males.	50—54 Females.	55—59 Males.	55—59 Females.	60 and over. Males.	60 and over. Females.
	22	23	24	25	26	27	28	29	30	31	32	33	34	35	36	37	38	39	40	41
District Amraoti	493	497	514	739	656	853	865	864	643	534	806	642	389	261	562	430	147	103	545	485
" Akola	47	42	49	46	57	71	76	61	65	46	81	44	32	16	49	23	8	6	28	29
" Ellichpur	1,159	1,526	1,403	1,705	1,594	1,799	1,883	1,859	1,347	887	1,405	1,016	602	451	785	643	216	162	777	780
" Buldana	...	...	...	1	...	...	...	...	...	...	...	1	1	...	...	1	...	...	...	...
" Wún	2,154	2,451	2,120	3,097	2,977	3,517	3,450	3,501	2,315	1,834	3,024	2,433	1,234	836	1,954	1,764	449	339	2,200	2,070
" Basim	14	16	14	28	22	11	24	21	14	7	13	12	4	5	9	6	5	2	10	12
Railway Passengers, etc.	...	...	...	...	...	...	...	...	...	...	...	...	...	...	...	1	...	...	...	...
Total	3,867	4,532	4,100	5,616	5,306	6,251	6,298	6,306	4,384	3,308	5,829	4,148	2,262	1,569	3,859	2,868	825	612	3,560	3,376
Amraoti District. Taluk Amraoti	39	44	50	65	66	105	100	125	73	45	107	69	40	22	55	39	17	6	48	36
" Chandur	194	200	205	305	278	338	335	345	251	213	312	270	167	107	224	178	61	48	239	203
" Morsi	249	239	252	355	300	394	410	385	306	269	369	295	176	126	274	207	66	49	251	241
" Murtazapur	11	14	7	14	12	16	20	9	13	7	18	8	6	6	9	6	3	...	7	5
Akola District. Taluk Akola	3	5	7	4	6	9	11	5	11	4	9	7	7	...	7	1	3	...	3	6
" Akot	23	13	26	24	23	32	39	32	27	23	53	28	13	5	29	13	2	3	13	17
" Balapur	...	...	...	...	...	...	1	1	...	...	...	...	...	...	1	2	...	...	...	...
" Jalgaon	20	24	15	17	25	29	23	21	27	19	16	9	12	11	12	7	2	3	12	6
" Khamgaon	1	...	1	1	3	1	2	2	...	...	3	...	...	...	...	...	1	...	...	...
Ellichpur District. Taluk Ellichpur	54	59	62	86	76	100	84	107	73	69	124	71	55	15	72	46	13	6	52	52
" Daryapur	5	1	2	11	10	4	9	17	11	8	17	10	5	2	10	6	4	1	5	4
" Melghát	1,100	1,466	1,339	1,608	1,508	1,695	1,790	1,735	1,263	810	1,264	935	542	434	703	591	199	155	720	724
Buldana District. Taluk Chikhli	...	...	...	1	...	...	...	...	...	...	...	1	1	...	...	1	...	...	...	...
" Malkapur	...	...	...	...	...	...	...	...	...	...	...	...	...	...	...	...	...	...	...	...
" Mehkar	...	...	...	...	...	...	...	...	...	...	...	...	...	...	...	...	...	...	...	...
Wún District. Taluk Yeotmal	665	810	661	1,018	951	1,104	1,074	1,066	779	621	980	769	420	287	659	545	165	108	739	651
" Darwha	243	287	255	343	337	405	409	424	284	228	352	295	152	102	235	183	43	43	254	248
" Kelapur	766	852	739	1,104	1,057	1,282	1,221	1,291	819	589	1,053	817	423	267	646	629	166	101	753	721
" Wún	480	502	465	632	632	726	746	720	433	396	639	552	239	180	414	407	75	87	454	450
Basim District. Taluk Basim	...	...	...	...	...	...	...	...	...	...	...	...	...	...	...	...	...	...	...	...
" Mangrul	...	...	2	3	...	...	4	4	3	...	...	...	...	3	2	...	1	...	1	2
" Pusad	14	16	12	25	22	11	20	17	11	7	13	12	4	2	7	6	4	2	9	10

TABLE VII.

Ages by Religions.—Part E.—JAIN.

TABLE VII.—Ages by Religions.—Part E.—JAIN.

District and Taluk.	Total Jain: Total.	Total Jain: Males.	Total Jain: Females.	Under 1 year: Males.	Under 1 year: Females.	1 year: Males.	1 year: Females.	2 years: Males.	2 years: Females.	3 years: Males.	3 years: Females.	4 years: Males.	4 years: Females.	Total 0—4: Males.	Total 0—4: Females.	5—9: Males.	5—9: Females.	10—14: Males.	10—14: Females.
1	2	3	4	5	6	7	8	9	10	11	12	13	14	15	16	17	18	19	20
District Amraoti	5,660	2,084	2,676	84	76	39	55	86	70	64	80	54	55	327	336	292	323	319	240
" Akola	3,365	1,825	1,540	45	67	29	32	30	40	37	40	38	36	179	215	172	186	187	149
" Ellichpur	1,269	684	585	21	20	11	9	12	13	15	12	15	13	74	67	84	60	72	51
" Buldana	3,883	2,023	1,860	72	58	25	32	51	63	49	52	45	37	242	242	214	258	226	184
" Wún	1,702	937	765	21	20	14	18	20	28	11	14	11	20	77	100	102	95	122	73
" Basim	3,073	1,590	1,483	60	46	21	24	32	40	44	42	45	31	202	183	220	208	192	137
Total	18,952	10,043	8,909	303	287	139	170	231	254	220	240	208	192	1,101	1,143	1,084	1,130	1,118	834
Amraoti District. — Taluk Amraoti	1,222	692	530	10	12	3	9	19	12	8	15	16	7	56	55	58	52	72	51
" Chandur	1,596	861	735	24	24	11	16	17	19	20	20	11	11	83	90	72	101	93	64
" Morsi	1,051	509	542	16	20	11	13	19	13	20	20	9	11	75	77	64	74	58	52
" Murtazapur	1,791	922	869	34	20	14	17	31	26	16	25	18	26	113	114	98	96	96	73
Akola District. — Taluk Akola	971	507	464	12	19	9	15	11	12	7	18	10	12	40	76	49	60	48	39
" Akot	574	308	266	8	15	6	2	6	6	7	6	7	9	34	38	31	34	38	28
" Balapur	914	481	433	13	19	9	7	6	12	9	6	17	7	54	51	53	59	45	36
" Jalgaon	151	101	50	2	1	...	1	1	2	1	1	2	1	6	6	6	4	7	7
" Khamgaon	755	428	327	10	13	5	7	6	8	13	9	2	7	36	44	33	29	49	39
Ellichpur District. — Taluk Ellichpur	800	427	373	11	12	6	6	6	9	10	9	10	8	43	44	52	41	43	36
" Daryapur	467	255	212	10	8	5	3	6	4	5	3	5	5	31	23	32	19	29	15
" Melghát	2	2	...	...	...	...	...	...	...	...	...	...	...	...	...	...	...	...	...
Buldana District. — Taluk Chikhli	1,331	682	649	20	21	10	10	23	23	12	16	14	9	79	79	65	99	88	59
" Malkapur	1,394	721	673	30	23	7	12	15	20	18	21	19	14	89	90	82	95	69	74
" Mehkar	1,158	620	538	22	14	8	10	13	20	19	15	12	14	74	73	67	64	69	51
Wún District. — Taluk Yeotmal	722	393	329	10	10	8	10	8	14	3	7	7	9	36	50	49	47	54	27
" Darwha	713	393	320	7	6	4	5	8	9	6	4	4	8	29	32	37	35	50	36
" Kelapur	219	123	96	2	4	2	3	3	3	1	3	...	...	8	13	14	11	16	10
" Wún	48	28	20	2	...	...	...	1	2	1	...	...	3	4	5	2	2	2	...
Basim District. — Taluk Basim	1,864	970	894	28	27	12	20	21	24	27	20	33	18	121	109	133	120	115	87
" Mangrul	332	176	156	7	7	4	1	2	2	5	8	1	1	19	19	27	25	21	9
" Pusad	877	444	433	25	12	5	3	9	14	12	14	11	12	62	55	60	63	56	41

Table VII.—Ages by Religions.

District and Taluk.	15–19 Males.	15–19 Females.	20–24 Males.	20–24 Females.	25–29 Males.	25–29 Females.	30–34 Males.	30–34 Females.	35–39 Males.	35–39 Females.	40–44 Males.	40–44 Females.	45–49 Males.	45–49 Females.	50–54 Males.	50–54 Females.	55–59 Males.	55–59 Females.	60 and over. Males.	60 and over. Females.
	21	22	23	24	25	26	27	28	29	30	31	32	33	34	35	36	37	38	39	40
District Amraoti	245	195	234	266	271	233	310	266	226	153	234	183	123	77	160	156	48	49	195	199
" Akola	162	129	178	137	204	155	156	123	141	70	133	116	72	49	107	82	42	23	92	106
" Ellichpur	47	44	53	55	68	56	56	56	48	30	47	52	36	16	40	41	16	14	43	43
" Buldana	162	139	151	195	208	156	183	136	118	122	151	132	102	61	100	84	39	33	127	118
" Wún	74	64	79	73	85	71	92	76	70	39	73	62	38	15	53	35	19	13	53	49
" Basim	106	116	119	96	150	157	122	121	99	89	97	122	63	49	85	62	27	27	108	116
Total	796	687	814	822	986	828	919	778	702	503	785	667	434	267	545	460	191	159	618	631
Amraoti District. Taluk Amraoti	55	39	70	53	64	49	70	58	47	34	60	43	37	21	36	24	18	13	49	38
" Chandur	78	61	62	71	90	58	83	74	79	33	70	48	34	21	50	42	11	14	56	58
" Morsi	29	34	33	54	48	46	56	53	36	22	37	36	16	16	20	33	3	8	34	37
" Murtazapur	83	61	69	88	69	80	101	81	64	64	67	56	36	19	54	57	16	14	56	66
Akola District. Taluk Akola	42	31	50	50	60	50	46	31	47	14	27	36	20	12	25	21	10	5	34	39
" Akot	25	19	28	24	29	21	24	24	26	12	23	19	14	9	13	14	7	8	16	16
" Balapur	62	40	42	25	36	53	33	42	26	22	39	31	20	13	35	28	11	7	25	26
" Jalgaon	4	6	13	4	22	8	16	4	7	1	5	3	4	3	7	1	3	...	1	3
" Khamgaon	29	33	45	34	57	23	37	22	35	21	39	27	14	12	27	18	11	3	16	22
Ellichpur District. Taluk Ellichpur	35	21	32	32	41	35	37	41	31	16	32	32	19	12	28	25	9	12	25	26
" Daryapur	12	23	20	23	27	21	19	15	16	14	15	20	17	4	12	16	7	2	18	17
" Melghát	...	...	1	...	...	...	...	...	1	...	...	...	...	...	...	...	...	...	...	...
Buldana District. Taluk Chikhli	58	46	57	67	67	51	56	50	43	46	45	40	27	27	37	35	14	10	46	40
" Malkapur	65	51	47	68	68	54	62	46	41	48	57	42	36	20	34	25	18	17	53	43
" Mehkar	39	42	47	60	73	51	65	40	34	28	49	50	39	14	29	24	7	6	28	35
Wún District. Taluk Yeotmal	38	25	28	37	37	32	39	32	28	16	24	26	12	5	18	15	7	3	23	14
" Darwha	26	31	41	23	31	30	37	31	31	16	37	29	17	6	26	15	6	10	25	26
" Kelapur	8	7	8	9	12	8	12	11	9	6	11	6	7	4	7	5	6	...	5	6
" Wún	2	1	2	4	5	1	4	2	2	1	1	1	2	...	2	...	...	...	...	3
Basim District. Taluk Basim	67	70	80	56	95	95	70	74	66	59	58	69	38	28	51	38	13	19	63	70
" Mangrul	14	11	8	8	16	18	11	19	9	8	13	17	6	3	15	5	5	2	12	12
" Pusad	25	35	31	32	39	44	41	28	24	22	26	36	19	18	19	19	9	6	33	34

TABLE VII.

Ages by Religions.—Part F.—SIKH.

TABLE VII.—Ages by Religions.—Part F.—SIKH.

DISTRICT AND TALUK.	TOTAL SIKH.			AGE PERIODS.																
				UNDER 1 YEAR.		1 YEAR.		2 YEARS.		3 YEARS.		4 YEARS.		Total 0–4		5–9		10–14	
	TOTAL.	Males.	Females.	Males.	Females.	Males.	Females.	Males.	Females.	Males.	Females.	Males.	Females.	Males.	Females.	Males.	Females.	Males.	Females.
1	2	3	4	5	6	7	8	9	10	11	12	13	14	15	16	17	18	19	20
DISTRICT AMRAOTI	29	13	16	...	...	...	1	1	1	1	...	...	...	2	2	1	3	2	3
" AKOLA	67	41	26	...	...	...	...	...	1	...	...	2	...	2	1	2	3	4	1
" ELLICHPUR	1	1	...	...	...	...	...	...	...	...	...	...	...	...	...	...	...	...	...
" BULDANA	30	13	17	...	...	...	...	...	...	...	...	...	...	...	...	2	4	3	3
" WÚN	38	23	15	2	...	...	1	1	...	1	...	...	...	4	1	4	3	3	...
" BASIM	12	7	5	1	...	...	...	...	...	...	...	...	1	1	1	1	...	1	1
Total	177	98	79	3	...	...	2	2	2	2	...	2	1	9	5	10	13	18	8
AMRAOTI DISTRICT. Taluk Amraoti	2	1	1	...	...	...	...	...	...	...	...	...	...	...	...	...	...	...	...
" Chandur	18	10	8	...	...	...	1	1	...	1	...	...	...	2	1	1	2	2	1
" Morsi	...	...	...	...	...	...	...	...	...	...	...	...	...	...	...	...	...	...	...
" Murtazapur	9	2	7	...	...	...	...	...	1	...	...	...	...	...	1	...	1	...	2
AKOLA DISTRICT. Taluk Akola	49	29	20	...	...	...	...	...	1	...	...	1	...	1	1	2	3	1	1
" Akot	7	6	1	...	...	...	...	...	...	...	...	...	...	...	...	...	...	2	...
" Balapur	...	...	...	...	...	...	...	...	...	...	...	...	...	...	...	...	...	...	...
" Jalgaon	4	2	2	...	...	...	...	...	...	...	...	...	...	...	...	...	...	...	...
" Khamgaon	7	4	3	...	...	...	...	...	...	...	...	1	...	1	...	...	...	1	...
ELLICHPUR DISTRICT. Taluk Ellichpur	...	...	...	...	...	...	...	...	...	...	...	...	...	...	...	...	...	...	...
" Daryapur	1	1	...	...	...	...	...	...	...	...	...	...	...	...	...	...	...	...	...
" Melghát	...	...	...	...	...	...	...	...	...	...	...	...	...	...	...	...	...	...	...
BULDANA DISTRICT. Taluk Chikhli	1	...	1	...	...	...	...	...	...	...	...	...	...	...	...	...	...	...	...
" Malkapur	...	...	...	...	...	...	...	...	...	...	...	...	...	...	...	...	...	...	...
" Mehkar	29	13	16	...	...	...	...	...	...	...	...	...	...	...	...	2	4	3	3
WÚN DISTRICT. Taluk Yeotmal	1	1	...	...	...	...	...	...	...	...	...	...	...	...	...	...	...	...	...
" Darwha	1	1	...	...	...	...	...	...	...	...	...	...	...	...	...	...	...	...	...
" Kelapur	36	21	15	2	...	...	1	1	...	1	...	...	...	4	1	4	3	3	...
" Wún	...	...	...	...	...	...	...	...	...	...	...	...	...	...	...	...	...	...	...
BASIM DISTRICT. Taluk Basim	...	...	...	...	...	...	...	...	...	...	...	...	...	...	...	...	...	...	...
" Mangrul	...	...	...	...	...	...	...	...	...	...	...	...	...	...	...	...	...	...	...
" Pusad	12	7	5	1	...	...	...	...	...	...	...	...	1	1	1	1	...	1	1

Table VII.—Ages by Religions.

District and Taluk.	Age Periods. 15—19 Males.	15—19 Females.	20—24 Males.	20—24 Females.	25—29 Males.	25—29 Females.	30—34 Males.	30—34 Females.	35—39 Males.	35—39 Females.	40—44 Males.	40—44 Females.	45—49 Males.	45—49 Females.	50—54 Males.	50—54 Females.	55—59 Males.	55—59 Females.	60 and over. Males.	60 and over. Females.
	21	22	23	24	25	26	27	28	29	30	31	32	33	34	35	36	37	38	39	40
District Amraoti	2	...	...	...	1	...	...	2	...	1	1	1	...	...	1	2	1	...	2	2
" Akola	1	...	3	3	6	5	6	1	4	3	3	...	1	3	4	4	3	...	2	2
" Ellichpur	...	...	...	...	...	...	...	...	...	...	...	...	...	...	...	...	...	...	1	...
" Buldana	1	...	1	3	2	...	...	1	...	2	1	1	1	2	...	1	...	...	2	...
" Wún	1	3	...	1	3	3	1	3	1	...	1	1	5	...	...	...	...	...	...	...
" Basim	...	...	2	...	...	...	...	...	...	2	...	...	...	...	1	1	...	...	1	...
Total	5	3	6	7	12	8	7	7	5	8	6	3	7	5	6	8	4	...	8	4
Amraoti District. — Taluk Amraoti	...	...	...	...	...	...	...	...	...	...	...	...	...	...	...	...	...	...	1	1
" Chandur	1	...	...	...	1	...	...	1	...	...	...	1	...	...	1	1	1	...	1	1
" Morsi	...	...	...	...	...	...	...	...	...	...	...	...	...	...	...	...	...	...	...	...
" Murtazapur	1	...	...	...	...	...	...	1	...	1	1	...	...	...	...	1	...	...	...	...
Akola District. — Taluk Akola	...	...	1	2	4	5	6	1	4	3	2	...	1	2	3	1	2	...	2	1
" Akot	1	...	1	...	1	...	...	...	...	...	1	...	...	...	...	1	...	...	...	...
" Balapur	...	...	...	...	...	...	...	...	...	...	...	...	...	...	...	...	...	...	...	...
" Jalgaon	...	...	1	...	1	...	...	...	...	...	...	...	...	...	...	1	...	...	...	1
" Khamgaon	...	...	...	1	...	...	...	...	...	...	...	...	...	1	1	1	1	...	...	...
Ellichpur District. — Taluk Ellichpur	...	...	...	...	...	...	...	...	...	...	...	...	...	...	...	...	...	...	...	...
" Daryapur	...	...	...	...	...	...	...	...	...	...	...	...	...	...	...	...	...	...	1	...
" Melghát	...	...	...	...	...	...	...	...	...	...	...	...	...	...	...	...	...	...	...	...
Buldana District. — Taluk Chikhli	...	...	...	1	...	...	...	...	...	...	...	...	...	...	...	...	...	...	...	...
" Malkapur	...	...	...	...	...	...	...	...	...	...	...	...	...	...	...	...	...	...	...	...
" Mehkar	1	...	1	2	2	...	...	1	...	2	1	1	1	2	...	1	...	...	2	...
Wún District. — Taluk Yeotmal	...	...	...	...	...	...	...	...	...	...	...	...	1	...	...	...	...	...	...	...
" Darwha	...	...	...	...	...	...	...	...	...	...	...	...	1	...	...	...	...	...	...	...
" Kelapur	1	3	...	1	3	3	1	3	1	...	1	1	3	...	...	...	...	...	...	...
" Wún	...	...	...	...	...	...	...	...	...	...	...	...	...	...	...	...	...	...	...	...
Basim District. — Taluk Basim	...	...	...	...	...	...	...	...	...	...	...	...	...	...	...	...	...	...	...	...
" Mangrul	...	...	...	...	...	...	...	...	...	...	...	...	...	...	...	...	...	...	...	...
" Pusad	...	...	2	...	...	...	...	...	...	2	...	...	...	...	1	1	...	...	1	...

TABLE—VII.

Ages by Religions.—Part G.—CHRISTIAN.

TABLE VII.—Ages by Religions.—Part G.—CHRISTIAN.

DISTRICT AND TALUK.	TOTAL CHRISTIAN.			AGE PERIODS.															
				UNDER 1 YEAR.		1 YEAR.		2 YEARS.		3 YEARS.		4 YEARS.		Total 0–4		5–9		10–14	
	TOTAL.	MALES.	FEMALES.	Males.	Females.	Males.	Females.	Males.	Females.	Males.	Females.	Males.	Females.	Males.	Females.	Males.	Females.	Males.	Females.
1	2	3	4	5	6	7	8	9	10	11	12	13	14	15	16	17	18	19	20
DISTRICT AMRAOTI	629	317	312	8	15	5	7	7	6	10	12	7	6	37	46	31	40	17	33
„ AKOLA	305	183	122	3	5	3	1	5	3	3	1	4	4	18	14	15	16	18	9
„ ELLICHPUR	123	68	55	5	3	...	...	4	3	3	1	1	1	13	8	6	5	4	5
„ BULDANA	103	60	43	...	2	2	...	2	5	3	1	1	2	8	10	7	8	3	3
„ WÚN	89	40	40	2	1	...	...	1	2	1	2	1	1	5	6	4	4	5	3
„ BASIM	88	48	40	6	1	...	1	...	4	2	1	2	1	10	8	5	9	...	3
Railway Passengers, etc.	22	13	9	...	...	...	1	1	...	1	1	...	...	2	2	...	1	1	3
Total	1,359	738	621	24	27	10	10	20	23	23	19	16	15	93	94	68	83	48	59
AMRAOTI DISTRICT. Taluk Amraoti	592	287	305	8	15	4	7	7	6	9	12	6	6	34	46	28	39	17	33
„ Chandur	15	13	2	...	...	...	...	...	...	...	...	...	...	...	...	...	1	...	...
„ Morsi	5	4	1	...	...	1	...	...	...	...	...	...	...	1	...	1	...	...	...
„ Murtazapur	17	13	4	...	...	...	...	...	...	1	...	1	...	2	...	2	...	...	...
AKOLA DISTRICT. Taluk Akola	191	104	87	1	4	2	1	4	2	...	1	4	4	11	12	9	11	16	7
„ Akot	6	5	1	...	...	...	...	...	...	...	...	...	...	...	...	...	...	...	...
„ Balapur	8	5	3	...	...	...	...	...	...	1	...	...	...	1	...	...	1	2	...
„ Jalgaon	2	2	...	...	...	...	...	...	...	...	...	...	...	...	...	...	...	...	...
„ Khamgaon	98	67	31	2	1	1	...	1	1	2	...	...	...	6	2	6	4	...	2
ELLICHPUR DISTRICT. Taluk Ellichpur	111	61	50	5	3	...	...	4	3	3	1	1	1	13	8	5	5	2	4
„ Daryapur	1	...	1	...	...	...	...	...	...	...	...	...	...	...	...	...	...	...	...
„ Melghát	11	7	4	...	...	...	...	...	...	...	...	...	...	...	...	1	...	2	1
BULDANA DISTRICT. Taluk Chikhli	77	47	30	...	2	2	...	2	2	3	...	1	2	8	6	4	6	3	2
„ Malkapur	20	11	9	...	...	...	...	...	2	...	1	...	...	...	3	3	2	...	1
„ Mehkar	6	2	4	...	...	...	...	...	1	...	...	...	...	...	1	...	...	...	...
WÚN DISTRICT. Taluk Yeotmal	89	49	40	2	1	...	...	1	2	1	2	1	1	5	6	4	4	5	3
„ Darwha	...	...	...	...	...	...	...	...	...	...	...	...	...	...	...	...	...	...	...
„ Kelapur	...	...	...	...	...	...	...	...	...	...	...	...	...	...	...	...	...	...	...
„ Wún	...	...	...	...	...	...	...	...	...	...	...	...	...	...	...	...	...	...	...
BASIM DISTRICT. Taluk Basim	85	46	39	6	1	...	1	...	4	2	1	2	1	10	8	5	9	...	3
„ Mangrul	1	1	...	...	...	...	...	...	...	...	...	...	...	...	...	...	...	...	...
„ Pusad	2	1	1	...	...	...	...	...	...	...	...	...	...	...	...	...	...	...	...

Table VII.—Ages by Religions.

DISTRICT AND TALUK.	AGE PERIODS. 15—19 Males.	15—19 Females.	20—24 Males.	20—24 Females.	25—29 Males.	25—29 Females.	30—34 Males.	30—34 Females.	35—39 Males.	35—39 Females.	40—44 Males.	40—44 Females.	45—49 Males.	45—49 Females.	50—54 Males.	50—54 Females.	55—59 Males.	55—59 Females.	60 AND OVER. Males.	60 AND OVER. Females.
	21	22	23	24	25	26	27	28	29	30	31	32	33	34	35	36	37	38	39	40
DISTRICT AMRAOTI	23	31	32	33	27	34	28	26	31	23	28	14	30	8	10	13	6	3	17	8
" AKOLA	18	14	22	25	17	11	25	9	12	5	12	7	9	3	7	3	3	2	7	4
" ELLICHPUR	4	4	3	5	8	10	8	7	5	4	8	1	1	2	5	2	1	...	2	2
" BULDANA	1	2	5	4	6	3	7	6	5	3	7	2	3	...	3	1	1	...	4	1
" WÚN	1	6	4	5	6	2	4	4	5	3	8	3	4	1	1	2	...	...	2	1
" BASIM	...	7	5	4	7	2	6	3	5	2	3	2	2	...	3	...	1	...	1	...
Railway Passengers, etc.	1	...	2	...	1	1	2	1	2	...	...	1	...	...	1	...	1	...	...	...
Total	48	64	73	76	72	63	80	56	65	40	66	30	49	14	30	21	18	5	33	16
DISTRICT AMRAOTI: Taluk Amraoti	22	30	28	33	23	31	25	26	28	23	25	13	27	7	9	13	6	3	15	8
" Chandur	1	...	4	...	2	1	1	...	1	...	1	...	3	...	...	...	...	...	...	...
" Morsi	...	...	...	...	1	1	...	...	1	...	...	...	...	...	...	...	...	...	...	...
" Murtazapur	...	1	...	...	1	1	2	...	1	...	2	1	...	1	1	...	...	...	2	...
DISTRICT AKOLA: Taluk Akola	12	12	10	15	11	8	10	6	8	5	5	4	6	1	3	1	2	2	1	3
" Akot	1	...	1	...	...	...	2	1	...	...	...	...	...	...	1	...	...	...	...	...
" Balapur	...	1	1	...	...	1	...	...	...	...	1	...	...	...	...	...	...	...	...	...
" Jalgaon	...	...	...	...	...	...	...	...	1	...	1	...	...	...	...	...	...	...	...	...
" Khamgaon	5	1	10	10	6	2	13	2	3	...	5	3	3	2	3	2	1	...	6	1
DISTRICT ELLICHPUR: Taluk Ellichpur	4	4	3	5	7	9	8	6	3	2	7	1	1	2	5	2	1	...	2	2
" Daryapur	...	...	...	...	...	...	...	1	...	...	...	...	...	...	...	...	...	...	...	...
" Melghát	...	...	...	...	1	1	...	...	2	2	1	...	...	...	...	...	...	...	...	...
DISTRICT BULDANA: Taluk Chikhli	1	2	3	3	3	2	5	4	4	3	7	1	3	...	1	1	1	...	4	...
" Malkapur	...	...	2	...	3	1	1	2	1	...	...	...	...	...	1	...	...	...	...	...
" Mehkar	...	...	...	1	...	...	1	...	...	...	...	1	...	...	1	...	...	...	...	1
DISTRICT WÚN: Taluk Yeotmal	1	6	4	5	6	2	4	4	5	3	8	3	4	1	1	2	...	...	2	1
" Darwha	...	...	...	...	...	...	...	...	...	...	...	...	...	...	...	...	...	...	...	...
" Kelapur	...	...	...	...	...	...	...	...	...	...	...	...	...	...	...	...	...	...	...	...
" Wún	...	...	...	...	...	...	...	...	...	...	...	...	...	...	...	...	...	...	...	...
DISTRICT BASIM: Taluk Basim	...	7	5	4	7	2	5	2	5	2	3	2	2	...	2	...	1	...	1	...
" Mangrul	...	...	...	...	...	...	1	...	...	...	...	...	...	...	...	...	...	...	...	...
" Pusad	...	...	...	...	...	...	...	1	...	...	...	...	...	...	1	...	...	...	...	...

TABLE VII.

Ages by Religions.—Part H.—PARSI.

TABLE VII.—Ages by Religions.—Part H.—PARSI.

District and Taluk.		Total Parsi. Total.	Total Parsi. Males.	Total Parsi. Females.	Under 1 year. Males.	Under 1 year. Females.	1 year. Males.	1 year. Females.	2 years. Males.	2 years. Females.	3 years. Males.	3 years. Females.	4 years. Males.	4 years. Females.	Total 0—4 Males.	Total 0—4 Females.	5—9 Males.	5—9 Females.	10—14 Males.	10—14 Females.
1		2	3	4	5	6	7	8	9	10	11	12	13	14	15	16	17	18	19	20
District Amraoti		235	132	103	8	2	2	1	3	4	3	7	1	5	17	19	18	12	11	11
" Akola		145	111	34	1	...	2	1	2	3	3	...	1	1	9	5	10	3	2	2
" Ellichpur		22	20	2	...	...	...	...	...	...	...	...	...	...	...	...	...	1	...	...
" Buldana		5	4	1	...	...	...	...	...	...	...	...	...	...	...	...	...	...	...	...
" Wún		5	4	1	...	...	...	...	...	...	...	...	...	...	...	...	...	...	...	...
" Basim		...	...	...	...	...	...	...	...	...	...	...	...	...	...	...	...	...	...	...
Total		412	271	141	9	2	4	2	5	7	6	7	2	6	26	24	28	16	13	13
Amraoti District.	Taluk Amraoti	220	120	100	7	2	2	1	3	4	3	7	1	5	16	19	18	12	10	11
	" Chandur	...	...	...	...	...	...	...	...	...	...	...	...	...	...	...	...	...	...	...
	" Morsi	2	2	...	...	...	...	...	...	...	...	...	...	...	...	...	...	...	...	...
	" Murtazapur	13	10	3	1	...	...	...	...	...	...	...	...	...	1	...	...	...	1	...
Akola District.	Taluk Akola	68	46	22	1	...	...	1	1	1	2	...	...	1	4	3	6	2	1	2
	" Akot	8	5	3	...	...	1	...	1	1	1	...	...	...	3	1	...	...	...	...
	" Balapur	4	4	...	...	...	...	...	...	...	...	...	...	...	...	...	...	...	...	...
	" Jalgaon	...	...	...	...	...	...	...	...	...	...	...	...	...	...	...	...	...	...	...
	" Khamgaon	65	56	9	...	...	1	...	...	1	...	...	1	...	2	1	4	1	1	...
Ellichpur District.	Taluk Ellichpur	11	11	...	...	...	...	...	...	...	...	...	...	...	...	...	...	...	...	...
	" Daryapur	11	9	2	...	...	...	...	...	...	...	...	...	...	...	...	...	1	...	...
	" Melghát	...	...	...	...	...	...	...	...	...	...	...	...	...	...	...	...	...	...	...
Buldana District.	Taluk Chikhli	1	1	...	...	...	...	...	...	...	...	...	...	...	...	...	...	...	...	...
	" Malkapur	4	3	1	...	...	...	...	...	...	...	...	...	...	...	...	...	...	...	...
	" Mehkar	...	...	...	...	...	...	...	...	...	...	...	...	...	...	...	...	...	...	...
Wún District.	Taluk Yeotmal	5	4	1	...	...	...	...	...	...	...	...	...	...	...	...	...	...	...	...
	" Darwha	...	...	...	...	...	...	...	...	...	...	...	...	...	...	...	...	...	...	...
	" Kelapur	...	...	...	...	...	...	...	...	...	...	...	...	...	...	...	...	...	...	...
	" Wún	...	...	...	...	...	...	...	...	...	...	...	...	...	...	...	...	...	...	...
Basim District.	Taluk Basim	...	...	...	...	...	...	...	...	...	...	...	...	...	...	...	...	...	...	...
	" Mangrul	...	...	...	...	...	...	...	...	...	...	...	...	...	...	...	...	...	...	...
	" Pusad	...	...	...	...	...	...	...	...	...	...	...	...	...	...	...	...	...	...	...

DISTRICT AND TALUK.	AGE PERIODS. 15—19 Males.	Females.	20—24 Males.	Females.	25—29 Males.	Females.	30—34 Males.	Females.	35—39 Males.	Females.	40—44 Males.	Females.	45—49 Males.	Females.	50—54 Males.	Females.	55—59 Males.	Females.	60 and over. Males.	Females.
	21	22	23	24	25	26	27	28	29	30	31	32	33	34	35	36	37	38	39	40
DISTRICT AMRAOTI	6	7	19	14	16	10	13	6	11	6	9	4	4	5	...	4	3	2	5	3
" AKOLA	3	3	21	5	23	4	17	6	6	1	4	1	5	...	4	1	...	...	7	3
" ELLICHPUR	...	...	5	1	5	...	3	...	2	...	2	...	2	...	1	...	...	...	...	...
" BULDANA	...	...	...	1	...	...	1	...	...	...	1	...	...	...	1	...	...	...	1	...
" WÚN	...	...	1	...	...	...	...	...	...	1	1	...	1	...	1	...	...	...	...	...
" BASIM	...	...	...	...	...	...	...	...	...	...	...	...	...	...	...	...	...	...	...	...
Total	9	10	46	21	44	14	34	12	19	8	17	5	12	5	7	5	3	2	13	6
AMRAOTI DISTRICT. Taluk Amraoti	6	7	18	13	13	10	12	6	10	6	8	4	4	4	...	4	2	1	3	3
" Chandur	...	...	...	...	...	...	...	...	...	...	...	...	...	...	...	...	...	...	...	...
" Morsi	...	...	...	...	...	...	1	...	...	...	...	...	...	...	...	...	1	...	...	...
" Murtazapur	...	...	1	1	3	...	...	...	1	...	1	...	...	1	...	...	...	1	2	...
AKOLA DISTRICT. Taluk Akola	...	2	6	3	8	...	7	5	3	1	1	...	2	...	1	1	...	...	7	3
" Akot	...	1	...	...	...	1	2	...	...	...	...	...	...	...	...	...	...	...	...	...
" Balapur	...	...	1	...	1	...	...	...	1	...	...	...	1	...	...	...	...	...	...	...
" Jalgaon	...	...	...	...	...	...	...	...	...	...	...	...	...	...	...	...	...	...	...	...
" Khamgaon	3	...	14	2	14	3	8	1	2	...	3	1	2	...	3	...	...	...	...	...
ELLICHPUR DISTRICT. Taluk Ellichpur	...	...	4	...	2	...	3	...	...	...	...	...	1	...	1	...	...	...	...	...
" Daryapur	...	...	1	1	3	...	...	...	2	...	2	...	1	...	...	...	...	...	...	...
" Melghát	...	...	...	...	...	...	...	...	...	...	...	...	...	...	...	...	...	...	...	...
BULDANA DISTRICT. Taluk Chikhli	...	...	...	...	...	...	...	...	...	...	...	...	...	...	...	...	...	...	1	...
" Malkapur	...	...	...	1	...	...	1	...	...	...	1	...	...	...	1	...	...	...	...	...
" Mehkar	...	...	...	...	...	...	...	...	...	...	...	...	...	...	...	...	...	...	...	...
WÚN DISTRICT Taluk Yeotmal	...	...	1	...	...	...	...	...	...	1	1	...	1	...	1	...	...	...	...	...
" Darwha	...	...	...	...	...	...	...	...	...	...	...	...	...	...	...	...	...	...	...	...
" Kelapur	...	...	...	...	...	...	...	...	...	...	...	...	...	...	...	...	...	...	...	...
" Wún	...	...	...	...	...	...	...	...	...	...	...	...	...	...	...	...	...	...	...	...
BASIM DISTRICT. Taluk Basim	...	...	...	...	...	...	...	...	...	...	...	...	...	...	...	...	...	...	...	...
" Mangrul	...	...	...	...	...	...	...	...	...	...	...	...	...	...	...	...	...	...	...	...
" Pusad	...	...	...	...	...	...	...	...	...	...	...	...	...	...	...	...	...	...	...	...

TABLE VII.

Ages by Religions.—Part I.—Others.

TABLE VII.—Ages by Religions.—Part I.—OTHERS.

DISTRICT AND TALUK.	TOTAL OTHERS.			AGE PERIODS.															
				UNDER 1 YEAR.		1 YEAR.		2 YEARS.		3 YEARS.		4 YEARS.		Total 0–4		5–9		10–14	
	Total.	Males.	Females.	Males.	Females.	Males.	Females.	Males.	Females.	Males.	Females.	Males.	Females.	Males.	Females.	Males.	Females.	Males.	Females.
1	2	3	4	5	6	7	8	9	10	11	12	13	14	15	16	17	18	19	20
District Amraoti	1	1	...	...	...	...	...	...	...	...	...	...	...	...	...	...	...	...	...
" Akola	7	5	2	...	...	...	...	...	...	1	...	...	...	1	...	...	1	...	...
" Ellichpur	1	1	...	...	...	...	...	...	...	...	...	...	...	...	...	...	...	...	...
" Buldana	...	...	...	...	...	...	...	...	...	...	...	...	...	...	...	...	...	...	...
" Wún	...	...	...	...	...	...	...	...	...	...	...	...	...	...	...	...	...	...	...
" Basim	2	2	...	...	...	...	...	...	...	...	...	...	...	...	...	...	...	...	...
Total	11	9	2	...	...	...	...	...	...	1	...	...	...	1	...	...	1	...	...
Amraoti District — Taluk Amraoti	1	1	...	...	...	...	...	...	...	...	...	...	...	...	...	...	...	...	...
" Chandur	...	...	...	...	...	...	...	...	...	...	...	...	...	...	...	...	...	...	...
" Morsi	...	...	...	...	...	...	...	...	...	...	...	...	...	...	...	...	...	...	...
" Murtazapur	...	...	...	...	...	...	...	...	...	...	...	...	...	...	...	...	...	...	...
Akola District — Taluk Akola	5	3	2	...	...	...	...	...	...	1 Buddhist	...	...	...	1 Buddhist	...	...	1 Buddhist	...	...
" Akot	...	...	...	...	...	...	...	...	...	...	...	...	...	...	...	...	...	...	...
" Balapur	...	...	...	...	...	...	...	...	...	...	...	...	...	...	...	...	...	...	...
" Jalgaon	...	...	...	...	...	...	...	...	...	...	...	...	...	...	...	...	...	...	...
" Khamgaon	2	2	...	...	...	...	...	...	...	...	...	...	...	...	...	...	...	...	...
Ellichpur District — Taluk Ellichpur	1	1	...	...	...	...	...	...	...	...	...	...	...	...	...	...	...	...	...
" Daryapur	...	...	...	...	...	...	...	...	...	...	...	...	...	...	...	...	...	...	...
" Melghat	...	...	...	...	...	...	...	...	...	...	...	...	...	...	...	...	...	...	...
Buldana District — Taluk Chikhli	...	...	...	...	...	...	...	...	...	...	...	...	...	...	...	...	...	...	...
" Malkapur	...	...	...	...	...	...	...	...	...	...	...	...	...	...	...	...	...	...	...
" Mehkar	...	...	...	...	...	...	...	...	...	...	...	...	...	...	...	...	...	...	...
Wún District — Taluk Yeotmal	...	...	...	...	...	...	...	...	...	...	...	...	...	...	...	...	...	...	...
" Darwha	...	...	...	...	...	...	...	...	...	...	...	...	...	...	...	...	...	...	...
" Kelapur	...	...	...	...	...	...	...	...	...	...	...	...	...	...	...	...	...	...	...
" Wún	...	...	...	...	...	...	...	...	...	...	...	...	...	...	...	...	...	...	...
Basim District — Taluk Basim	1	1	...	...	...	...	...	...	...	...	...	...	...	...	...	...	...	...	...
" Mangrul	...	...	...	...	...	...	...	...	...	...	...	...	...	...	...	...	...	...	...
" Pusad	1	1	...	...	...	...	...	...	...	...	...	...	...	...	...	...	...	...	...

TABLE VII.—Age by Religions.

DISTRICT AND TALUK.	AGE PERIODS. 15—19 Males.	15—19 Females.	20—24 Males.	20—24 Females.	25—29 Males.	25—29 Females.	30—34 Males.	30—34 Females.	35—39 Males.	35—39 Females.	40—44 Males.	40—44 Females.	45—49 Males.	45—49 Females.	50—54 Males.	50—54 Females.	55—59 Males.	55—59 Females.	60 and over. Males.	60 and over. Females.
	21	22	23	24	25	26	27	28	29	30	31	32	33	34	35	36	37	38	39	40
DISTRICT AMRAOTI	...	...	...	...	1	...	...	...	...	...	...	...	...	...	...	...	...	...	...	...
" AKOLA	...	...	2	...	...	...	1	...	...	1	...	...	1	...	...	...	...	...	...	...
" ELLICHPUR	...	...	...	...	1	...	...	...	...	...	...	...	...	...	...	...	...	...	...	...
" BULDANA	...	...	...	...	...	...	...	...	...	...	...	...	...	...	...	...	...	...	...	...
" WÚN	...	...	...	...	...	...	...	...	...	...	...	...	...	...	...	...	...	...	...	...
" BASIM	...	...	...	...	...	...	2	...	...	...	...	...	...	...	...	...	...	...	...	...
Total	...	...	2	...	2	...	3	...	...	1	...	...	1	...	...	...	...	...	...	...
AMRAOTI DISTRICT — Taluk Amraoti	...	...	...	...	1 Jew	...	...	...	...	...	...	...	...	...	...	...	...	...	...	...
" Chandur	...	...	...	...	...	...	...	...	...	...	...	...	...	...	...	...	...	...	...	...
" Morsi	...	...	...	...	...	...	...	...	...	...	...	...	...	...	...	...	...	...	...	...
" Murtazapur	...	...	...	...	...	...	...	...	...	...	...	...	...	...	...	...	...	...	...	...
AKOLA DISTRICT — Taluk Akola	...	...	1 Buddhist	...	...	...	...	...	...	1 Buddhist	...	...	1 Positivist	...	...	...	...	...	...	...
" Akot	...	...	...	...	...	...	...	...	...	...	...	...	...	...	...	...	...	...	...	...
" Balapur	...	...	...	...	...	...	...	...	...	...	...	...	...	...	...	...	...	...	...	...
" Jalgaon	...	...	...	...	...	...	...	...	...	...	...	...	...	...	...	...	...	...	...	...
" Khamgaon	...	...	1 Jew	...	...	...	1 Unspecified	...	...	...	...	...	...	...	...	...	...	...	...	...
ELLICHPUR DISTRICT — Taluk Ellichpur	...	...	...	...	1 Deist	...	...	...	...	...	...	...	...	...	...	...	...	...	...	...
" Daryapur	...	...	...	...	...	...	...	...	...	...	...	...	...	...	...	...	...	...	...	...
" Melghat	...	...	...	...	...	...	...	...	...	...	...	...	...	...	...	...	...	...	...	...
BULDANA DISTRICT — Taluk Chikhli	...	...	...	...	...	...	...	...	...	...	...	...	...	...	...	...	...	...	...	...
" Malkapur	...	...	...	...	...	...	...	...	...	...	...	...	...	...	...	...	...	...	...	...
" Mehkar	...	...	...	...	...	...	...	...	...	...	...	...	...	...	...	...	...	...	...	...
WÚN DISTRICT — Taluk Yeotmal	...	...	...	...	...	...	...	...	...	...	...	...	...	...	...	...	...	...	...	...
" Darwha	...	...	...	...	...	...	...	...	...	...	...	...	...	...	...	...	...	...	...	...
" Kelapur	...	...	...	...	...	...	...	...	...	...	...	...	...	...	...	...	...	...	...	...
" Wún	...	...	...	...	...	...	...	...	...	...	...	...	...	...	...	...	...	...	...	...
BASIM DISTRICT — Taluk Basim	...	...	...	...	...	...	1 Agnostic	...	...	...	...	...	...	...	...	...	...	...	...	...
" Mangrul	...	...	...	...	...	...	...	...	...	...	...	...	...	...	...	...	...	...	...	...
" Pusad	...	...	...	...	...	...	1 Unspecified	...	...	...	...	...	...	...	...	...	...	...	...	...

TABLE VIII.

Civil Condition by Religion and Age.— Part A.—TOTAL POPULATION.

TABLE VIII.—Civil Condition by Religion and Age.—Part A.—TOTAL POPULATION.

DISTRICT AND TALUK.		(1) UNMARRIED.												
		Total unmarried.			Age Periods.									
					0–4		5–9		10–14		15–19		20–24	
		Total.	Males.	Females.	Males.	Females.	Males.	Females.	Males.	Females.	Males.	Females.	Males.	Females.
1		2	3	4	5	6	7	8	9	10	11	12	13	14
District Amraoti		217,518	132,914	84,604	41,417	43,016	40,316	31,563	27,198	7,507	9,329	849	5,383	439
„ Akola		166,863	104,117	62,746	36,075	37,665	34,139	19,995	18,893	3,564	5,548	468	3,458	266
„ Ellichpur		107,906	65,273	42,633	19,991	20,888	19,622	15,560	13,615	4,451	4,056	809	2,934	293
„ Buldana		150,618	91,634	58,984	32,728	34,867	31,417	19,675	17,148	3,171	4,560	408	2,232	228
„ Wún		167,066	98,813	68,253	33,527	34,904	32,483	24,764	19,207	6,891	5,871	782	3,114	283
„ Basim		132,947	79,765	53,182	29,731	31,135	26,504	17,184	13,381	3,483	3,613	433	2,309	268
Railway Passengers, etc.		122	78	44	12	27	19	11	12	6	6	...	6	...
Total		943,040	572,594	370,446	193,481	202,502	184,560	128,752	109,454	29,073	33,583	3,749	19,526	1,777
Amraoti District	Taluk Amraoti	61,017	37,549	23,468	11,225	11,628	10,918	8,980	7,854	2,114	2,807	248	1,609	137
	„ Chandur	67,447	41,131	26,316	12,790	13,088	12,694	10,081	8,721	2,574	2,850	240	1,586	94
	„ Morsi	50,989	30,805	20,184	9,697	10,198	9,465	7,342	6,102	1,788	2,260	233	1,206	142
	„ Murtazapur	38,065	23,429	14,636	7,705	8,102	7,239	5,160	4,521	1,031	1,412	128	892	66
Akola District	Taluk Akola	41,472	25,788	15,684	8,424	8,976	8,465	5,399	4,833	918	1,520	132	986	67
	„ Akot	39,945	24,822	15,123	8,394	8,796	7,707	4,919	4,704	964	1,404	132	912	81
	„ Balapur	30,084	18,549	11,535	6,675	6,971	6,467	3,569	3,089	688	913	100	524	51
	„ Jalgaon	27,754	17 297	10,457	6,165	6,451	5,800	3,306	3,204	528	812	58	453	25
	„ Khamgaon	27,608	17,661	9,947	6,417	6,471	5,700	2,802	3,003	466	899	46	583	42
Ellichpur District	Taluk Ellichpur	48,021	29,556	18,465	8,781	9,296	8,634	6,911	6,255	1,665	2,303	205	1,381	91
	„ Daryapur	37,018	23,073	13,945	7,777	7,834	7,275	5,015	4,604	793	1,261	89	756	45
	„ Melghat	22,867	12,644	10,223	3,433	3,758	3,713	3,634	2,756	1,993	1,092	515	797	157
Buldana District	Taluk Chikhli	48,335	29,576	18,759	9,754	10,400	10,169	6,829	6,133	1,124	1,629	131	784	60
	„ Malkapur	53,601	32,686	20,915	12,269	13,167	11,371	6,500	5,865	836	1,400	111	652	89
	„ Mehkar	48,682	29,372	19,310	10,705	11,300	9,877	6,346	5,150	1,211	1,531	166	796	79
Wún District	Taluk Yeotmál	45,257	26,962	18,295	8,474	8,778	8,461	6,911	5,897	2,111	1,790	233	956	90
	„ Darwha	55,911	33,211	22,700	11,122	11,802	10,856	8,244	6,199	2,113	1,982	236	1,171	95
	„ Kelapur	39,268	22,811	16,457	7,739	8,154	7,676	6,140	4,468	1,717	1,338	218	672	74
	„ Wún	26,630	15,829	10,801	6,192	6,170	5,490	3,469	2,643	950	761	95	345	24
Basim District	Taluk Basim	55,608	33,411	22,197	12,839	13,380	11,292	6,992	5,337	1,296	1,376	165	921	112
	„ Mangrul	26,585	16,177	10,408	5,870	6,018	5,506	3,430	2,769	706	688	84	518	43
	„ Pusad	50,754	30,177	20,577	11,022	11,737	9,766	6,762	5,275	1,481	1,549	184	930	113

DISTRICT AND TALUK.	(1) UNMARRIED. Age Periods. 25—29 Males.	25—29 Females.	30—34 Males.	30—34 Females.	35—39 Males.	35—39 Females.	40—44 Males.	40—44 Females.	45—49 Males.	45—49 Females.	50—54 Males.	50—54 Females.	55—59 Males.	55—59 Females.	60 and over. Males.	60 and over. Females.
	15	16	17	18	19	20	21	22	23	24	25	26	27	28	29	30
District Amraoti	3,329	330	2,202	272	1,105	188	1,051	171	415	62	511	96	149	25	509	86
" Akola	2,230	208	1,347	157	722	106	651	128	273	45	365	64	96	14	320	66
" Ellichpur	1,725	189	988	140	546	77	480	92	197	29	231	48	60	6	228	51
" Buldana	1,502	183	777	147	343	76	340	95	153	31	203	35	47	10	184	58
" Wún	1,881	198	1,085	165	476	76	479	85	158	31	255	34	54	4	193	36
" Basim	1,628	198	995	181	405	79	423	107	155	25	247	39	59	9	195	41
Railway Passengers, etc.	10	...	7	...	2	...	1	...	1	...	...	...	2	...	...	...
Total	12,305	1,306	7,401	1,062	3,599	602	3,425	678	1,352	223	1,812	316	467	68	1,629	338
Amraoti District — Taluk Amraoti	1,046	103	760	84	360	51	334	54	136	14	169	24	48	2	193	29
" Chandur	954	60	571	62	287	35	287	26	105	13	134	20	34	8	118	15
" Morsi	712	125	456	100	241	80	257	67	115	26	130	40	34	14	130	29
" Murtazapur	617	42	415	26	217	22	173	24	59	9	78	12	33	1	68	13
Akola District — Taluk Akola	622	46	335	38	186	29	158	32	60	9	89	15	22	3	88	20
" Akot	550	62	398	47	204	30	200	38	80	14	99	18	26	2	84	20
" Balapur	322	40	190	27	112	28	88	22	39	10	62	12	9	6	59	11
" Jalgaon	325	32	198	16	98	7	92	12	44	5	48	8	19	2	39	7
" Khamgaon	411	28	226	29	122	12	113	24	50	7	67	11	20	1	50	8
Ellichpur District — Taluk Ellichpur	818	85	474	56	262	39	251	47	103	11	143	26	31	5	120	28
" Daryapur	487	43	209	38	194	24	160	26	71	8	74	16	27	...	88	14
" Melghat	420	61	215	46	90	14	69	19	23	10	14	6	2	1	20	9
Buldana District — Taluk Chikhli	470	61	243	42	111	38	119	27	42	15	59	10	11	2	53	20
" Malkapur	454	49	223	57	99	20	111	32	62	11	69	13	26	7	85	23
" Mehkar	578	73	311	48	133	18	110	36	49	5	75	12	10	1	47	15
Wún District — Taluk Yeotmal	567	54	333	46	147	17	149	23	41	9	77	15	18	1	52	7
" Darwha	731	76	450	52	204	27	205	24	74	8	107	9	19	2	91	12
" Kelapur	410	47	204	38	86	21	91	19	32	9	50	8	10	...	35	12
" Wun	173	21	98	29	39	11	34	19	11	5	21	2	7	1	15	5
Basim District — Taluk Basim	639	80	389	64	183	30	168	40	68	9	101	10	20	2	78	17
" Mangrul	322	33	209	42	78	14	90	21	30	4	47	5	14	3	36	5
" Pusad	667	85	397	75	144	35	165	46	57	12	99	24	25	4	81	19

TABLE VIII.—Civil Condition by Religion and Age.—Part A—TOTAL POPULATION.

DISTRICT AND TALUK.		Total married.			(2) Married. Age Periods. 0–4		5–9		10–14		15–19		20–24	
		Total.	Males.	Females.	Males.	Females.	Males.	Females.	Males.	Females.	Males.	Females.	Males.	Females.
1		2	3	4	5	6	7	8	9	10	11	12	13	14
District Amraoti		363,810	185,780	178,030	405	1,000	1,570	12,105	8,744	21,760	11,505	20,128	17,782	26,472
" Akola		343,299	174,442	168,857	309	1,272	2,408	17,394	12,787	21,986	13,567	19,265	17,687	23,814
" Ellichpur		171,758	87,411	84,347	153	346	632	5,203	3,807	10,062	5,819	10,018	8,002	12,960
" Buldana		282,658	141,333	141,325	325	1,273	2,252	14,788	10,804	20,551	11,498	16,749	14,341	20,302
" Wún		258,717	130,617	128,100	299	1,241	2,378	10,498	8,704	14,992	8,175	13,627	11,725	18,251
" Basim		223,908	113,755	110,153	362	1,447	2,462	11,342	8,934	13,885	7,623	11,871	10,957	16,021
Railway Passengers, etc.		308	237	71	...	...	...	1	3	12	8	6	21	5
Total		1,644,458	833,575	810,883	1,858	6,579	11,702	71,331	53,783	103,248	58,285	91,664	81,415	117,825
Amraoti District	Taluk Amraoti	101,433	52,079	49,354	90	209	313	2,821	2,076	6,013	3,264	5,741	5,285	7,618
	" Chandur	108,784	55,416	53,368	92	240	407	3,520	2,579	6,770	3,444	6,024	5,120	7,653
	" Morsi	84,253	42,653	41,600	143	332	471	2,954	2,038	4,870	2,481	4,545	3,903	6,083
	" Murtazapur	69,340	35,632	33,708	80	219	379	2,810	2,051	4,107	2,406	3,818	3,474	5,118
Akola District	Taluk Akola	81,055	41,564	39,491	71	269	458	3,628	2,406	4,925	2,093	4,411	4,200	5,681
	" Akot	81,276	41,098	40,178	65	205	461	3,686	2,729	5,212	3,146	4,659	4,069	5,865
	" Balapur	60,752	30,389	30,363	71	308	578	3,591	2,532	3,772	2,424	3,342	2,960	4,195
	" Jalgaon	58,688	29,813	28,875	48	157	363	3,041	2,438	4,169	2,509	3,382	3,198	3,969
	" Khamgaon	61,528	31,578	29,950	54	333	548	3,448	2,592	3,908	2,495	3,471	3,251	4,104
Ellichpur District	Taluk Ellichpur	79,613	40,461	39,152	60	154	277	2,415	1,716	4,747	2,689	4,606	4,563	5,974
	" Daryapur	71,061	36,167	34,894	58	148	294	2,702	1,943	4,835	2,776	4,211	3,885	5,186
	" Melghat	21,084	10,783	10,301	35	44	61	86	148	480	354	1,201	954	1,800
Buldana District	Taluk Chikhli	86,434	43,380	43,054	101	420	683	4,082	2,935	6,386	3,412	5,030	4,208	6,213
	" Malkapur	106,618	53,052	53,566	84	306	654	5,750	4,329	7,809	4,675	6,567	5,529	7,239
	" Mehkar	89,606	44,901	44,705	140	547	915	4,956	3,540	6,356	3,411	5,152	4,604	6,850
Wún District	Taluk Yeotmal	66,729	33,893	32,836	52	129	245	1,909	1,443	3,698	1,926	3,681	3,063	4,876
	" Darwha	84,570	42,746	41,824	78	339	705	3,418	2,604	4,688	2,583	4,572	3,832	6,087
	" Kelapur	56,998	28,835	28,163	74	243	424	2,118	1,840	3,263	1,822	2,972	2,517	4,121
	" Wún	50,420	25,143	25,277	95	530	1,004	3,053	2,727	3,343	1,844	2,402	2,313	3,167
Basim District	Taluk Basim	103,486	52,688	50,798	172	679	1,104	5,409	4,352	6,416	3,675	5,400	5,156	7,388
	" Mangrul	46,804	23,860	22,944	68	302	516	2,536	1,806	2,792	1,514	2,414	2,169	3,153
	" Pusad	73,618	37,207	36,411	122	466	752	3,397	2,686	4,677	2,434	4,057	3,632	5,480

Table VIII.—Civil condition by Religion and Age.

(2) MARRIED.

DISTRICT AND TALUK.	Age Periods. 25—29 Males.	25—29 Females.	30—34 Males.	30—34 Females.	35—39 Males.	35—39 Females.	40—44 Males.	40—44 Females.	45—49 Males.	45—49 Females.	50—54 Males.	50—54 Females.	55—59 Males.	55—59 Females.	60 and over. Males.	60 and over. Females.
	15	16	17	18	19	20	21	22	23	24	25	26	27	28	29	30
DISTRICT AMRAOTI	25,027	26,743	28,737	25,135	21,485	14,392	23,870	14,601	11,786	5,251	15,680	6,181	4,339	1,384	14,760	2,878
" AKOLA	24,489	23,825	25,179	21,394	19,013	13,341	19,346	12,531	10,521	5,215	13,349	5,343	4,150	1,353	11,637	2,124
" ELLICHPUR	12,121	12,514	13,650	11,931	9,862	6,717	10,917	6,808	5,536	2,654	7,048	2,958	2,002	739	6,962	1,437
" BULDANA	21,821	19,482	20,915	17,448	13,842	9,682	15,012	10,242	7,682	3,927	10,493	4,043	3,181	1,019	9,167	1,819
" WÚN	17,727	19,638	20,037	18,560	13,749	9,672	16,719	10,368	7,628	3,436	10,713	4,711	2,672	1,000	10,091	2,106
" BASIM	17,244	16,560	17,665	15,108	10,971	7,478	13,416	8,341	5,609	2,544	8,982	3,428	1,999	631	7,531	1,497
Railway Passengers, etc.	41	11	51	12	28	5	24	7	12	5	26	6	8	...	15	1
Total	118,470	118,773	126,234	109,588	88,950	61,287	99,804	62,898	48,774	23,032	66,291	26,670	18,351	6,126	60,613	11,862
AMRAOTI DISTRICT. Taluk Amraoti	7,013	7,424	8,211	7,017	5,948	3,906	6,732	4,081	3,219	1,496	4,565	1,744	1,172	379	4,191	905
" Chandur	7,346	7,828	8,299	7,662	6,519	4,579	7,300	4,359	3,789	1,683	4,719	1,830	1,372	430	4,430	790
" Morsi	5,673	6,387	6,654	5,969	5,066	3,331	5,455	3,414	2,685	1,217	3,543	1,528	998	339	3,543	631
" Murtazapur	4,995	5,104	5,573	4,487	3,952	2,576	4,383	2,747	2,093	855	2,853	1,079	797	236	2,596	552
AKOLA DISTRICT. Taluk Akola	5,858	5,844	6,259	5,216	4,762	3,208	4,807	3,004	2,537	1,161	3,242	1,329	945	311	2,936	504
" Akot	5,694	5,715	6,080	5,265	4,599	3,213	4,715	3,058	2,573	1,238	3,222	1,230	1,027	331	2,718	501
" Balapur	4,058	4,181	4,187	3,897	3,238	2,295	3,287	2,312	1,799	893	2,418	962	704	217	2,124	398
" Jalgaon	4,294	3,955	4,289	3,484	3,132	2,283	3,174	1,979	1,742	992	2,109	884	722	224	1,705	356
" Khamgaon	4,585	4,130	4,364	3,532	3,282	2,342	3,363	2,178	1,870	931	2,358	938	752	270	2,064	365
ELLICHPUR DISTRICT. Taluk Ellichpur	5,547	5,709	5,988	5,371	4,381	3,114	5,212	3,252	2,590	1,259	3,402	1,424	954	376	3,582	751
" Daryapur	4,979	4,832	5,451	4,612	3,966	2,712	4,164	2,687	2,291	1,047	2,828	1,156	826	271	2,696	495
" Melghat	1,595	1,973	2,211	1,948	1,515	891	1,541	869	655	348	818	378	212	92	684	191
BULDANA DISTRICT. Taluk Chikhli	6,806	6,066	6,709	5,567	4,322	3,021	4,819	3,134	2,340	1,112	3,351	1,240	958	291	3,736	492
" Malkapur	7,780	7,178	7,177	6,135	5,413	3,942	5,211	3,792	3,224	1,855	3,694	1,625	1,408	517	3,784	851
" Mehkar	7,235	6,238	7,029	5,746	4,107	2,719	4,982	3,316	2,118	960	3,448	1,178	725	211	2,647	476
WÚN DISTRICT. Taluk Yeotmal	4,708	5,243	5,415	4,990	3,796	2,583	4,509	2,789	2,187	968	3,019	1,217	768	251	2,762	502
" Darwha	5,850	6,348	6,313	5,927	4,753	3,338	5,427	3,498	2,707	1,122	3,569	1,470	923	317	3,312	700
" Kelapur	3,974	4,552	4,708	4,430	3,063	2,019	3,808	2,187	1,571	670	2,274	1,011	556	164	2,114	413
" Wún	3,195	3,495	3,601	3,213	2,137	1,732	2,885	1,894	1,163	676	1,851	1,013	425	268	1,903	491
BASIM DISTRICT. Taluk Basim	7,854	7,641	8,338	6,682	5,013	3,378	5,924	3,875	2,492	1,246	4,104	1,631	944	317	3,470	736
" Mangrul	3,419	3,301	3,530	3,094	2,397	1,733	2,789	1,763	1,339	602	1,948	728	515	150	1,760	376
" Pusad	5,971	5,618	5,797	5,332	3,561	2,367	4,703	2,703	1,778	696	2,930	1,069	540	164	2,301	385

TABLE VIII.—Civil Condition by Religion and Age.—Part A.—TOTAL POPULATION.

DISTRICT AND TALUK.		(3) WIDOWED.												
		Total Widowed.			Age Periods.									
					0–4		5–9		10–14		15–19		20–24	
		Total.	Males.	Females.	Males.	Females.	Males.	Females.	Males.	Females.	Males.	Females.	Males.	Females.
1		2	3	4	5	6	7	8	9	10	11	12	13	14
District Amraoti		74,317	21,541	52,776	28	48	64	243	233	576	249	532	529	997
„ Akola		64,620	18,452	46,168	2	9	74	276	303	655	341	443	594	799
„ Ellichpur		36,134	10,285	25,849	5	7	13	67	75	234	94	251	279	505
„ Buldana		47,745	11,832	35,913	8	22	89	276	325	490	289	419	384	719
„ Wun		45,830	12,258	33,572	11	24	101	276	278	485	181	308	378	552
„ Basim		41,326	11,278	30,048	20	50	137	307	402	438	309	324	415	605
Railway Passengers, etc.		21	11	10	...	...	...	...	...	...	...	...	1	...
Total		309,993	85,657	224,336	74	160	478	1,445	1,616	2,878	1,463	2,277	2,580	4,177
Amraoti District	Taluk Amraoti	21,058	5,908	15,150	17	15	13	53	41	139	58	149	158	296
	„ Chandur	21,875	6,338	15,537	1	7	13	54	61	181	76	170	145	280
	„ Morsi	17,132	4,993	12,139	8	17	24	80	63	111	62	96	106	240
	„ Murtazapur	14,252	4,302	9,950	2	9	14	56	68	145	53	117	120	181
Akola District	Taluk Akola	15,461	4,392	11,069	2	2	13	66	69	135	67	98	130	193
	„ Akot	16,499	4,710	11,789	...	2	9	56	49	174	73	123	140	179
	„ Balapur	10,837	3,003	7,834	...	4	19	64	68	106	56	74	96	135
	„ Jalgaon	11,174	3,213	7,961	...	...	15	43	48	123	74	74	108	123
	„ Khamgaon	10,649	3,134	7,515	...	1	18	47	69	117	71	74	120	169
Ellichpur District	Taluk Ellichpur	18,581	5,254	13,327	3	4	6	40	40	115	40	112	123	263
	„ Daryapur	14,473	4,089	10,384	1	2	6	24	31	112	49	104	129	202
	„ Melghat	3,080	942	2,138	1	1	1	3	4	7	5	35	27	40
Buldana District	Taluk Chikhli	15,329	3,584	11,745	1	8	22	95	86	185	90	152	108	237
	„ Malkapur	17,658	4,477	13,181	2	5	14	82	96	149	100	128	128	213
	„ Mehkar	14,758	3,771	10,987	5	9	53	99	143	156	99	139	148	269
Wún District	Taluk Yeotmal	12,443	3,420	9,023	...	2	5	41	51	123	40	76	92	142
	„ Darwha	16,099	4,789	11,310	3	8	44	96	118	168	84	119	175	206
	„ Kelapur	9,660	2,199	7,461	6	6	17	59	42	90	26	69	49	136
	„ Wún	7,628	1,850	5,778	2	8	35	80	67	104	31	44	62	68
Basim District	Taluk Basim	18,156	5,101	13,055	7	14	63	145	198	181	146	147	200	275
	„ Mangrul	9,057	2,736	6,321	7	15	28	73	93	109	57	56	100	114
	„ Pusad	14,113	3,441	10,672	6	21	46	89	111	148	106	121	115	216

Table VIII.—Civil condition by Religion and Age.

(3)—WIDOWED.

DISTRICT AND TALUK.	Age Periods. 25—29 Males.	25—29 Females.	30—34 Males.	30—34 Females.	35—39 Males.	35—39 Females.	40—44 Males.	40—44 Females.	45—49 Males.	45—49 Females.	50—54 Males.	50—54 Females.	55—59 Males.	55—59 Females.	60 and over Males.	60 and over Females.
	15	16	17	18	19	20	21	22	23	24	25	26	27	28	29	30
District Amraoti	1,109	1,906	1,932	3,579	1,978	3,624	2,903	6,992	1,743	4,076	3,231	9,305	1,124	2,629	6,418	18,269
" Akola	1,292	1,518	1,830	2,727	1,751	3,136	2,323	6,234	1,532	3,978	2,517	8,521	935	2,602	4,958	15,270
" Ellichpur	535	932	981	1,713	902	1,661	1,439	3,436	845	2,075	1,523	4,558	564	1,273	3,030	9,137
" Buldana	797	1,289	1,067	2,428	921	2,419	1,444	5,025	871	2,858	1,627	6,398	591	1,698	3,419	11,872
" Wún	660	1,092	1,121	2,246	986	2,033	1,624	4,420	872	2,330	1,790	6,095	577	1,580	3,679	12,131
" Basim	783	1,133	1,113	2,175	889	1,838	1,447	4,246	755	1,978	1,649	5,571	480	1,218	2,879	10,165
Railway Passengers, etc.	1	1	...	...	...	...	1	2	...	...	1	3	4	...	3	4
Total	5,177	7,871	8,044	14,868	7,427	14,711	11,181	30,355	0,618	17,295	12,338	40,451	4,275	11,000	24,386	76,848
Amraoti District. Taluk Amraoti	283	588	554	1,070	526	1,055	776	2,127	454	1,109	907	2,680	294	688	1,827	5,181
" Chandur	342	562	553	1,034	580	1,094	850	1,996	562	1,277	938	2,619	366	820	1,851	5,443
" Morsi	227	377	411	845	466	811	645	1,508	374	928	774	2,210	256	658	1,577	4,258
" Murtazapur	257	379	414	630	406	664	632	1,361	353	762	612	1,796	208	463	1,163	3,387
Akola District. Taluk Akola	285	356	417	674	437	752	581	1,480	342	940	643	2,017	218	601	1,188	3,755
" Akot	308	415	517	683	455	822	638	1,605	404	1,043	654	2,194	246	688	1,217	3,805
" Balapur	200	239	284	450	252	483	349	1,047	234	610	387	1,469	130	406	928	2,747
" Jalgaon	245	235	338	449	304	564	402	1,093	292	757	441	1,495	164	498	782	2,507
" Khamgaon	254	273	274	471	303	515	353	1,009	260	628	392	1,346	177	409	843	2,456
Ellichpur District. Taluk Ellichpur	233	469	443	872	445	837	749	1,779	433	1,047	780	2,339	302	664	1,657	4,786
" Daryapur	231	355	413	687	305	709	550	1,361	328	867	612	1,821	217	519	1,157	3,621
" Melghat	71	108	125	154	92	115	140	296	84	161	131	398	45	90	216	730
Buldana District. Taluk Chikhli	240	468	341	861	267	839	453	1,632	264	876	505	2,182	163	500	1,044	3,710
" Malkapur	269	381	370	760	372	875	481	1,657	359	1,185	591	2,212	277	792	1,418	4,742
" Mehkar	283	440	356	807	282	705	510	1,736	248	797	531	2,004	151	406	957	3,420
Wún District. Taluk Yeotmal	160	289	284	584	270	577	473	1,176	264	681	509	1,615	163	420	1,109	3,297
" Darwha	204	390	460	735	401	748	639	1,439	352	850	692	1,953	240	568	1,287	4,030
" Kelapur	118	241	215	588	195	419	305	1,073	151	495	334	1,398	93	324	648	2,563
" Wún	88	172	162	339	120	289	207	732	105	304	255	1,129	81	268	635	2,241
Basim District. Taluk Basim	364	501	525	914	419	777	638	1,776	320	891	702	2,338	213	535	1,306	4,561
" Mangrul	189	230	274	415	208	376	325	847	222	456	386	1,130	131	293	716	2,207
" Pusad	230	402	314	846	262	685	484	1,623	213	631	561	2,103	136	390	857	3,397

TABLE VIII.

Civil Condition by Religion and Age.— Part B—HINDU.

TABLE VIII.—Civil Condition by Religion and Age.—Part B.—HINDU.

DISTRICT AND TALUK.	(1)—UNMARRIED.												
	Total Unmarried.			Age Periods.									
				0—4		5—9		10—14		15—19		20—24	
	Total.	Males.	Females.	Males.	Females.	Males.	Females.	Males.	Females.	Males.	Females.	Males.	Females.
1	2	3	4	5	6	7	8	9	10	11	12	13	14
District Amraoti	187,539	115,143	72,396	37,089	38,507	35,876	27,094	23,457	5,312	7,457	482	3,899	262
" Akola	143,111	89,910	53,201	32,527	33,936	30,641	16,421	15,914	1,888	3,898	228	2,221	164
" Ellichpur	74,658	46,409	28,249	15,040	15,490	14,424	10,502	9,549	1,643	2,835	185	1,539	98
" Buldana	133,923	81,677	52,246	30,087	32,098	28,766	17,149	15,078	2,085	3,531	273	1,526	165
" Wún	122,918	74,061	48,857	25,864	26,535	24,795	17,229	13,838	4,050	3,928	432	2,126	177
" Basim	121,454	72,879	48,575	27,891	29,198	24,696	15,499	12,004	2,783	2,987	314	1,870	218
Railway Passengers, etc.	89	55	34	10	24	16	8	7	2	2	...	2	...
Total	788,692	480,134	303,558	168,508	175,788	159,214	103,902	89,847	17,763	24,638	1,914	13,183	1,084
Amraoti District. Taluk Amraoti	51,858	31,988	19,870	9,933	10,335	9,565	7,615	6,642	1,429	2,181	150	1,181	93
" Chandur	60,205	36,802	23,403	11,712	11,962	11,556	8,969	7,772	2,041	2,408	153	1,244	75
" Morsi	42,885	26,187	16,698	8,598	9,035	8,326	6,146	5,193	1,170	1,817	107	848	53
" Murtazapur	32,591	20,166	12,425	6,846	7,175	6,429	4,364	3,850	672	1,051	72	626	41
Akola District. Taluk Akola	35,718	22,286	13,432	7,575	8,057	7,576	4,557	4,147	551	1,131	76	668	43
" Akot	33,633	21,105	12,528	7,441	7,832	6,825	3,983	3,969	454	969	58	573	49
" Balapur	24,753	15,413	9,340	5,872	6,153	5,654	2,697	2,415	299	532	41	285	28
" Jalgaon	24,513	15,346	9,167	5,679	5,935	5,318	2,821	2,773	309	594	25	297	18
" Khamgaon	24,494	15,760	8,734	5,960	5,959	5,268	2,363	2,610	275	672	28	398	26
Ellichpur District. Taluk Ellichpur	38,625	23,986	14,639	7,497	7,832	7,252	5,514	5,073	962	1,689	102	876	49
" Daryapur	32,463	20,256	12,207	7,110	7,161	6,604	4,414	4,039	436	928	40	485	33
" Melghat	3,570	2,167	1,403	433	497	568	574	437	245	218	43	178	16
Buldana District. Taluk Chikhli	42,547	26,128	16,419	8,842	9,472	9,277	5,928	5,386	729	1,291	88	514	47
" Malkapur	46,784	28,640	18,144	11,204	12,008	10,226	5,453	5,048	431	973	60	378	50
" Mehkar	44,592	26,909	17,683	10,041	10,618	9,263	5,768	4,644	925	1,267	125	634	68
Wún District. Taluk Yeotmal	32,032	19,509	12,523	6,217	6,309	6,239	4,703	4,187	1,210	1,180	130	650	56
" Darwha	47,522	28,277	19,245	9,749	10,324	9,460	6,891	5,136	1,629	1,540	175	865	67
" Kelapur	25,314	15,175	10,139	5,225	5,366	5,186	3,691	2,882	846	795	102	415	41
" Wún	18,050	11,100	6,950	4,673	4,536	3,910	1,944	1,633	365	413	25	196	13
Basim District. Taluk Basim	50,878	30,534	20,344	12,073	12,601	10,521	6,309	4,758	1,017	1,103	120	704	91
" Mangrul	24,381	14,858	9,523	5,549	5,681	5,147	3,093	2,494	545	578	56	406	36
" Pusad	46,195	27,487	18,708	10,269	10,916	9,028	6,097	4,752	1,221	1,306	138	760	91

Table VIII.—Civil Condition by Religion and Age.

DISTRICT AND TALUK.	UNMARRIED. Age Periods. 25–29 Males.	25–29 Females.	30–34 Males.	30–34 Females.	35–39 Males.	35–39 Females.	40–44 Males.	40–44 Females.	45–49 Males.	45–49 Females.	50–54 Males.	50–54 Females.	55–59 Males.	55–59 Females.	60 and over. Males.	60 and over. Females.
	15	16	17	18	19	20	21	22	23	24	25	26	27	28	29	30
District Amraoti	2,577	205	1,774	166	894	99	844	99	326	39	425	58	110	14	415	59
" Akola	1,630	155	1,056	115	609	83	543	85	239	27	293	44	79	12	260	43
" Ellichpur	1,029	84	680	77	413	49	338	53	167	17	165	26	49	...	181	25
" Buldana	1,055	139	626	114	268	57	271	72	124	25	162	22	38	8	145	39
" Wún	1,352	130	859	123	362	58	383	58	134	18	214	21	49	4	157	22
" Basim	1,311	165	826	155	357	64	354	93	138	23	214	25	53	8	178	30
Railway Passengers, etc.	9	...	5	...	...	...	1	...	1	...	...	...	2	...	...	...
Total	8,963	878	5,826	750	2,903	410	2,734	460	1,129	149	1,473	196	380	46	1,336	218
Amraoti District. Taluk Amraoti	826	72	615	57	306	31	280	39	114	9	146	18	39	2	160	20
" Chandur	766	53	490	53	255	31	251	17	95	13	119	16	28	7	106	13
" Morsi	502	50	318	38	158	21	167	28	65	10	92	17	14	5	89	18
" Murtazapur	483	30	351	18	175	16	146	15	52	7	68	7	29	...	60	8
Akola District. Taluk Akola	446	36	260	32	146	22	123	23	50	6	74	14	17	3	73	12
" Akot	414	44	321	31	180	25	173	25	72	7	80	7	20	...	68	13
" Balapur	216	33	137	21	97	20	70	16	35	7	51	10	6	6	43	9
" Jalgaon	242	20	155	13	80	7	81	6	39	2	35	5	18	2	35	4
" Khamgaon	312	22	183	18	106	9	96	15	43	5	53	8	18	1	41	5
Ellichpur District. Taluk Ellichpur	546	49	344	35	208	27	185	32	95	8	100	15	25	...	96	14
" Daryapur	348	28	243	32	161	18	120	19	59	7	61	10	23	...	75	9
" Melghat	135	7	93	10	44	4	33	2	13	2	4	1	1	...	10	2
Buldana District. Taluk Chikhli	309	45	197	32	88	28	94	19	35	13	48	7	9	1	38	10
" Malkapur	301	31	159	40	76	13	86	22	53	7	51	6	19	6	66	17
" Mehkar	445	63	270	42	104	16	91	31	36	5	63	9	10	1	41	12
Wún District. Taluk Yeotmal	402	36	246	33	108	14	117	13	35	6	66	9	17	1	45	3
" Darwha	573	55	376	42	162	20	174	21	63	6	88	4	18	2	73	9
" Kelapur	279	27	162	24	60	15	65	12	28	3	44	6	7	...	27	6
" Wún	98	12	75	24	32	9	27	12	8	3	16	2	7	1	12	4
Basim District. Taluk Basim	508	68	331	54	164	22	137	35	60	8	85	6	18	1	72	12
" Mangrul	266	28	166	37	66	13	75	20	28	4	40	4	12	3	31	3
" Pusad	537	69	329	64	127	29	142	38	50	11	89	15	23	4	75	15

TABLE VIII.—Civil Condition by Religion and Age.—Part B—HINDU—*contd.*

District and Taluk.	(2) Married. Total Married. Total.	Total Married. Males.	Total Married. Females.	Age Periods. 0–4. Males.	0–4. Females.	5–9. Males.	5–9. Females.	10–14. Males.	10–14. Females.	15–19. Males.	15–19. Females.	20–24. Males.	20–24. Females.
1	2	3	4	5	6	7	8	9	10	11	12	13	14
District Amraoti	330,346	168,611	161,735	201	867	1,450	11,764	8,452	20,679	11,070	18,300	16,551	23,540
„ Akola	316,811	160,610	156,201	209	1,245	2,379	17,205	12,627	21,099	13,175	17,585	16,492	21,456
„ Ellichpur	139,822	71,345	68,477	110	288	561	5,058	3,625	9,276	5,339	8,070	7,546	10,085
„ Buldana	264,788	132,346	132,442	302	1,222	2,204	14,593	10,662	19,847	11,192	15,563	13,616	18,718
„ Wún	210,430	106,403	104,027	261	1,159	2,227	9,929	8,151	13,159	7,189	10,913	9,795	14,423
„ Basim	211,722	107,405	104,317	347	1,422	2,431	11,158	8,792	13,401	7,408	11,155	10,430	15,013
Railway Passengers, etc.	260	196	64	...	...	...	1	3	11	8	5	18	5
Total	1,474,179	746,916	727,263	1,610	6,203	11,252	69,708	52,812	97,472	55,881	81,591	74,454	103,240
Amraoti District — Taluk Amraoti	90,942	46,632	44,310	78	197	300	2,773	2,018	5,709	3,130	5,160	4,852	6,664
„ Chandur	100,366	51,123	49,243	86	231	397	3,447	2,518	6,476	3,294	5,585	4,831	6,946
„ Morsi	75,741	38,354	37,387	56	230	380	2,803	1,912	4,580	2,348	4,091	3,616	5,395
„ Murtazapur	63,297	32,502	30,795	71	209	373	2,741	2,004	3,914	2,298	3,464	3,252	4,535
Akola District — Taluk Akola	74,528	38,154	36,374	67	259	448	3,583	2,458	4,734	2,004	4,020	3,919	5,096
„ Akot	74,615	37,696	36,919	62	201	453	3,640	2,701	5,006	3,054	4,238	3,798	5,216
„ Balapur	55,212	27,670	27,542	69	302	572	3,546	2,487	3,572	2,341	2,969	2,732	3,671
„ Jalgaon	55,092	27,845	27,247	48	153	362	3,027	2,424	4,047	2,465	3,141	3,020	3,688
„ Khamgaon	57,364	29,245	28,119	53	330	544	3,409	2,557	3,740	2,411	3,217	3,023	3,785
Ellichpur District — Taluk Ellichpur	69,930	35,616	34,314	51	140	263	2,370	1,665	4,445	2,541	3,994	3,707	5,102
„ Daryapur	65,992	33,495	32,497	55	145	289	2,664	1,915	4,699	2,711	3,885	3,658	4,676
„ Melghat	3,900	2,234	1,666	4	3	9	24	45	132	87	191	181	307
Buldana District — Taluk Chikhli	80,300	40,277	40,023	95	408	670	4,018	2,807	6,165	3,323	4,645	3,959	5,688
„ Malkapur	99,181	49,356	49,825	70	274	627	5,664	4,261	7,501	4,525	6,050	5,217	6,585
„ Mehkar	85,307	42,713	42,594	137	540	907	4,911	3,504	6,181	3,344	4,868	4,440	6,445
Wún District — Taluk Yeotmal	51,665	26,319	25,346	41	114	222	1,767	1,333	3,189	1,650	2,793	2,466	3,647
„ Darwha	75,425	38,092	37,333	73	322	671	2,305	2,591	4,352	2,405	4,058	3,457	5,370
„ Kelapur	42,125	21,405	20,720	50	214	377	1,909	1,629	2,680	1,404	2,152	1,938	2,945
„ Wún	41,215	20,587	20,628	88	509	957	2,948	2,598	2,938	1,640	1,910	1,934	2,461
Basim District — Taluk Basim	98,232	49,899	48,333	164	672	1,179	5,331	4,292	6,184	3,569	5,084	4,010	6,990
„ Mangrul	44,498	22,671	21,827	67	293	513	2,513	1,879	2,720	1,477	2,277	2,072	2,954
„ Pusad	68,992	34,835	34,157	116	457	739	3,314	2,621	4,497	2,362	3,794	3,454	5,069

Table VIII.—Civil Condition by Religion and Age.

District and Taluk.	(2) Married. Age Periods. 25—29 Males.		30—34 Males.		35—39 Males.		40—44 Males.		45—49 Males.		50—54 Males.		55—59 Males.		60 and over. Males.	
	Males.	Females.	Males.	Females.	Males.	Females.	Males.	Females.	Males.	Females.	Males.	Females.	Males.	Females.	Males.	Females.
	15	16	17	18	19	20	21	22	23	24	25	26	27	28	29	30
District Amraoti	22,669	23,981	25,737	22,427	19,434	13,004	21,285	12,998	10,627	4,779	13,892	5,541	3,934	1,260	13,219	2,595
" Akola	22,359	21,638	22,765	19,404	17,257	12,385	17,488	11,282	9,669	4,840	11,071	4,864	3,782	1,270	10,347	1,928
" Ellichpur	9,750	9,650	10,641	9,114	7,701	5,376	8,605	5,367	4,513	2,141	5,643	2,339	1,637	604	5,584	1,109
" Buldana	20,400	17,981	19,355	16,063	12,861	9,013	13,752	9,402	7,107	3,671	9,641	3,761	2,936	949	8,318	1,659
" Wun	14,220	15,394	15,860	14,541	10,920	7,620	13,073	8,073	6,109	2,759	8,469	3,607	2,172	800	7,957	1,650
" Basim	16,268	15,507	16,498	14,167	10,258	7,027	12,540	7,811	5,227	2,414	8,320	3,221	1,883	601	6,991	1,420
Railway Passengers, etc.	37	10	37	11	24	5	20	4	11	5	21	6	6	...	11	1
Total	105,703	104,161	110,898	95,727	78,545	54,430	86,769	54,937	48,268	20,609	57,957	23,339	16,350	5,484	52,427	10,362
Amraoti District. Taluk Amraoti	6,236	6,562	7,276	6,151	5,313	3,483	5,003	3,579	2,841	1,346	3,050	1,543	1,029	338	3,697	805
" Chandur	6,757	7,114	7,572	6,976	5,981	4,213	6,649	3,937	3,460	1,549	4,277	1,657	1,255	389	4,046	723
" Morsi	5,157	5,709	5,001	5,298	4,547	2,958	4,840	2,984	2,430	1,096	3,101	1,363	921	315	3,145	565
" Murtazapur	4,519	4,596	4,088	4,002	3,593	2,350	3,893	2,498	1,896	788	2,555	978	729	218	2,331	502
Akola District. Taluk Akola	5,371	5,263	5,662	4,736	4,301	2,945	4,347	2,701	2,306	1,077	2,005	1,222	856	286	2,610	452
" Akot	5,180	5,153	5,460	4,767	4,147	2,948	4,220	2,744	2,363	1,135	2,003	1,118	946	305	2,400	448
" Balapur	3,684	3,709	3,727	3,415	2,005	2,115	2,953	2,023	1,643	817	2,115	843	617	206	1,825	354
" Jalgaon	3,952	3,653	3,933	3,233	2,875	2,158	2,904	1,839	1,621	939	1,030	818	660	212	1,042	339
" Khamgaon	4,172	3,860	3,083	3,253	3,029	2,219	3,055	1,975	1,736	872	2,118	863	694	261	1,870	335
Ellichpur District. Taluk Ellichpur	4,850	4,881	5,179	4,578	3,839	2,690	4,506	2,772	2,247	1,125	2,885	1,234	838	345	3,045	638
" Daryapur	4,559	4,429	4,057	4,246	3,664	2,547	3,775	2,469	2,129	978	2,588	1,050	766	252	2,429	457
" Melghat	341	340	505	290	288	139	324	126	137	38	170	55	33	7	110	14
Buldana District. Taluk Chikhli	6,350	5,524	6,152	5,081	3,073	2,758	4,342	2,864	2,139	1,022	3,042	1,133	872	267	2,463	450
" Malkapur	7,187	6,564	6,575	5,589	5,002	3,676	4,732	3,423	3,000	1,738	3,308	1,509	1,338	484	3,404	768
" Mehkar	6,863	5,893	6,628	5,393	3,886	2,579	4,678	3,115	1,968	911	3,231	1,119	676	198	2,451	441
Wún District. Taluk Yeotmal	3,626	3,934	4,129	3,765	2,858	1,909	3,368	2,079	1,681	729	2,271	867	597	188	2,077	365
" Darwha	5,163	5,562	5,529	5,186	4,225	2,918	4,729	3,052	2,404	1,013	3,122	1,296	826	288	2,807	611
" Kelapur	2,891	3,208	3,419	3,122	2,181	1,455	2,786	1,505	1,125	478	1,638	661	391	117	1,477	274
" Wún	2,540	2,690	2,783	2,468	1,656	1,338	2,190	1,437	899	539	1,438	783	358	207	1,506	400
Basim District. Taluk Basim	7,446	7,208	7,817	6,293	4,692	3,186	5,570	3,642	2,324	1,200	3,815	1,532	808	308	3,223	703
" Mangrul	3,243	3,076	3,320	2,909	2,271	1,651	2,595	1,660	1,270	579	1,817	690	483	145	1,664	360
" Pusad	5,579	5,223	5,361	4,965	3,295	2,190	4,381	2,509	1,633	635	2,688	999	502	148	2,104	357

TABLE VIII.—Civil Condition by Religion and Age—Part B.—HINDU—*contd.*

DISTRICT AND TALUK.	(3) WIDOWED. Total Widowed. Total.	Total Widowed. Males.	Total Widowed. Females.	Age Periods. 0–4 Males.	0–4 Females.	5–9 Males.	5–9 Females.	10–14 Males.	10–14 Females.	15–19 Males.	15–19 Females.	20–24 Males.	20–24 Females.
1	2	3	4	5	6	7	8	9	10	11	12	13	14
District Amraoti	66,293	19,376	46,917	21	39	57	219	217	549	232	490	480	875
" Akola	58,124	16,796	41,328	2	7	74	269	300	639	329	416	553	707
" Ellichpur	29,512	8,669	20,843	3	5	12	62	67	216	84	202	231	389
" Buldana	43,877	10,993	32,884	7	21	88	271	321	472	287	399	368	653
" Wún	37,736	10,302	27,434	8	22	94	254	267	431	162	254	326	448
" Basim	38,361	10,589	27,772	15	39	131	298	395	427	297	295	399	544
Railway Passengers, etc.	17	10	7	...	...	...	...	...	...	...	...	1	...
Total	273,920	76,735	197,185	56	133	456	1,373	1,567	2,734	1,891	2,056	2,3 58	3,616
Amraoti District — Taluk Amraoti	18,531	5,233	13,298	11	10	10	41	37	132	52	131	143	261
" Chandur	19,892	5,775	14,117	1	7	13	53	58	168	70	156	129	249
" Morsi	15,082	4,476	10,606	8	14	20	73	59	110	58	93	98	211
" Murtazapur	12,788	3,892	8,896	1	8	14	52	63	139	52	110	110	154
Akola District — Taluk Akola	13,852	3,990	9,862	2	2	13	63	69	132	63	95	118	170
" Akot	14,762	4,286	10,476	...	1	9	54	48	171	70	113	129	161
" Balapur	9,434	2,643	6,791	...	3	19	63	66	104	52	68	90	119
" Jalgaon	10,332	2,086	7,346	...	...	15	43	48	121	73	70	103	110
" Khamgaon	9,744	2,891	6,853	...	1	18	46	69	111	71	70	113	147
Ellichpur District — Taluk Ellichpur	15,504	4,572	10,932	1	3	6	38	39	106	38	98	106	202
" Daryapur	13,140	3,764	9,376	1	2	5	23	27	109	46	94	121	177
" Melghat	868	333	535	1	...	1	1	1	1	...	10	4	10
Buldana District — Taluk Chikhli	13,981	3,289	10,692	...	8	21	92	86	177	89	145	102	217
" Malkapur	16,099	4,150	11,949	2	4	14	81	94	142	99	120	121	188
" Mehkar	13,797	3,554	10,243	5	9	53	98	141	153	99	134	145	248
Wún District — Taluk Yeotmal	9,986	2,771	7,215	...	2	5	37	49	114	35	61	80	118
" Darwha	14,235	4,282	9,953	1	6	40	88	115	148	76	104	158	180
" Kelapur	7,344	1,696	5,648	5	6	15	53	38	76	23	54	37	101
" Wún	6,171	1,553	4,618	2	8	34	76	65	93	28	35	51	49
Basim District — Taluk Basim	16,877	4,814	12,063	7	14	63	143	196	177	140	136	193	244
" Mangrul	8,477	2,600	5,877	7	14	26	72	92	106	56	53	99	108
" Pusad	13,007	3,175	9,832	1	11	42	83	107	144	101	106	107	192

(3) WIDOWED.

DISTRICT AND TALUK.	25—29 Males.	25—29 Females.	30—34 Males.	30—34 Females.	35—39 Males.	35—39 Females.	40—44 Males.	40—44 Females.	45—49 Males.	45—49 Females.	50—54 Males.	50—54 Females.	55—59 Males.	55—59 Females.	60 and over. Males.	60 and over. Females.
	15	16	17	18	19	20	21	22	23	24	25	26	27	28	29	30
District Amraoti	986	1,708	1,721	3,172	1,808	3,245	2,628	6,151	1,582	3,647	2,885	8,193	1,026	2,380	5,733	16,249
,, Akola	1,194	1,326	1,672	2,391	1,629	2,849	2,106	5,518	1,410	3,634	2,253	7,614	847	2,388	4,427	13,570
,, Ellichpur	437	733	831	1,357	774	1,399	1,196	2,742	718	1,730	1,275	3,564	486	1,071	2,555	7,373
,, Buldana	753	1,182	995	2,221	862	2,209	1,331	4,589	807	2,649	1,498	5,814	544	1,550	3,132	10,854
,, Wún	571	885	935	1,829	847	1,697	1,358	3,620	743	1,933	1,496	4,909	487	1,319	3,008	9,833
,, Basim	747	1,035	1,048	1,991	844	1,697	1,358	3,903	709	1,832	1,527	5,164	450	1,130	2,669	9,417
Railway Passengers, etc.	1	...	...	...	...	...	1	1	...	...	1	2	3	...	3	4
Total	4,689	6,869	7,202	12,961	6,764	13,096	9,978	26,524	5,969	15,425	1,035	35,260	3,843	9,838	21,527	67,300
Amraoti District. Taluk Amraoti	236	521	494	956	471	930	696	1,860	409	986	791	2,325	267	610	1,616	4,535
,, Chandur	312	517	491	926	529	1,002	768	1,810	521	1,151	856	2,385	343	752	1,684	4,941
,, Morsi	205	330	355	729	433	712	583	1,286	335	818	688	1,918	227	588	1,407	3,724
,, Murtazapur	233	340	381	561	375	601	581	1,195	317	692	550	1,565	189	430	1,026	3,049
Akola District. Taluk Akola	265	315	379	599	411	677	533	1,306	310	854	581	1,816	191	536	1,055	3,297
,, Akot	283	365	485	586	416	748	592	1,417	374	970	583	1,919	227	623	1,070	3,348
,, Balapur	181	200	245	391	231	413	206	896	214	531	333	1,260	112	367	804	2,376
,, Jalgaon	233	209	310	395	284	526	363	992	271	701	409	1,378	151	476	726	2,325
,, Khamgaon	232	237	253	420	287	485	322	907	241	578	347	1,241	166	386	772	2,224
Ellichpur District. Taluk Ellichpur	200	375	396	705	392	707	633	1,432	382	908	667	1,848	270	578	1,442	3,932
,, Daryapur	208	321	387	606	337	657	507	1,222	300	788	560	1,613	201	476	1,064	3,288
,, Melghat	29	37	48	46	45	35	56	88	36	34	48	103	15	17	49	153
Buldana District. Taluk Chikhli	229	430	308	794	249	751	414	1,479	241	797	456	1,978	149	450	945	3,374
,, Malkapur	252	335	356	680	350	795	438	1,502	338	1,103	540	1,983	252	717	1,294	4,299
,, Mehkar	272	417	331	747	263	663	479	1,608	228	749	502	1,853	143	383	893	3,181
Wún District. Taluk Yeotmal	136	228	238	482	231	479	383	941	217	554	408	1,255	129	348	860	2,596
,, Darwha	273	332	402	639	355	656	560	1,269	315	750	619	1,725	220	494	1,148	3,562
,, Kelapur	92	185	163	447	162	327	240	829	117	380	258	1,051	73	251	473	1,888
,, Wún	70	140	132	261	99	235	175	581	94	249	211	878	65	226	527	1,787
Basein District. Taluk Basim	343	451	494	840	400	709	608	1,638	293	832	659	2,164	200	492	1,218	4,223
,, Mungrul	186	210	256	383	200	355	309	764	215	432	361	1,046	123	274	670	2,060
,, Pusad	218	374	298	768	244	633	441	1,501	201	568	507	1,954	127	364	781	3,134

TABLE VIII.

Civil Condition by Religion and Age.— Part C—MUSALMAN.

TABLE VIII.—Civil Condition by Religion

(1) UN

DISTRICT AND TALUK.	TOTAL UNMARRIED.			AGE									
				0—4		5—9		10—14		15—19		20—24	
	Total.	Males.	Females.	Males.	Females.	Males.	Females.	Males.	Females.	Males.	Females.	Males.	Females.
1	2	3	4	5	6	7	8	9	10	11	12	13	14
District Amraoti	20,613	12,402	8,211	2,974	3,089	3,096	3,107	2,630	1,493	1,359	242	1,127	82
„ Akola	21,702	12,929	8,773	3,228	3,342	3,178	3,306	2,728	1,593	1,508	223	1,144	92
„ Ellichpur	12,898	7,789	5,109	1,762	1,980	1,853	1,835	1,633	979	984	125	759	42
„ Buldana	15,295	9,053	6,242	2,390	2,521	2,433	2,325	1,885	1,049	953	130	661	62
„ Wun	9,251	5,590	3,661	1,342	1,439	1,446	1,392	1,186	649	590	93	431	34
„ Basim	10,295	6,124	4,171	1,598	1,709	1,619	1,523	1,220	667	580	113	473	48
Railway Passengers, etc.	19	17	2	...	...	3	1	4	1	3	...	2	...
Total	90,073	58,904	36,169	13,294	14,080	13,628	13,489	11,286	6,431	5,897	926	4,597	360
Amraoti District. Taluk Amraoti	7,653	4,689	2,964	1,110	1,067	1,159	1,160	1,015	557	533	60	426	30
„ Chandur	4,068	2,455	1,613	570	617	626	598	528	293	261	68	219	15
„ Morsi	4,086	2,434	1,652	562	611	616	631	508	299	252	59	231	12
„ Murtazapur	4,806	2,824	1,982	732	794	695	718	579	344	313	55	251	25
Akola District. Taluk Akola	5,268	3,205	2,063	778	819	821	780	626	353	357	48	300	20
„ Akot	5,741	3,381	2,360	861	854	788	849	718	475	405	72	318	31
„ Balapur	4,992	2,905	2,087	747	766	760	825	636	383	338	58	222	23
„ Jalgaon	2,886	1,754	1,132	433	438	421	434	392	199	202	28	148	7
„ Khamgaon	2,815	1,684	1,131	409	465	388	418	356	183	206	17	156	11
Ellichpur District. Taluk Ellichpur	7,989	4,760	3,229	1,071	1,263	1,145	1,183	1,024	579	543	73	448	31
„ Daryapur	4,337	2,673	1,664	627	634	627	577	538	349	325	48	267	11
„ Melghat	572	356	216	64	83	81	75	71	51	36	4	44	...
Buldana District. Taluk Chikhli	5,289	3,130	2,159	824	844	824	820	668	383	310	41	254	13
„ Malkapur	6,336	3,744	2,592	976	1,068	1,062	976	767	393	404	49	259	38
„ Mehkar	3,670	2,179	1,491	590	609	547	529	450	273	239	40	148	11
Wun District. Taluk Yeotmal	2,403	1,483	920	351	375	384	328	302	174	152	19	119	11
„ Darwha	4,505	2,716	1,789	640	697	686	688	583	310	294	44	225	19
„ Kelapur	1,364	815	549	203	212	212	210	169	98	84	19	54	3
„ Wun	979	576	403	148	155	164	166	132	67	60	11	33	1
Basim District. Taluk Basim	4,093	2,458	1,635	635	663	639	600	488	265	250	42	200	21
„ Mangrul	2,090	1,248	842	300	318	332	318	261	157	107	28	110	7
„ Pusad	4,112	2,418	1,694	663	728	648	605	471	245	223	43	163	20

and Age.—Part C—MUSALMAN.

MARRIED.																
PERIOD.																
25—29		30—34		35—39		40—44		45—49		50—54		55 59		60 and over.		DISTRICT AND TALUK.
Males.	Females.	Males.	Females.	Males.	Females.	Males.	Females.	Males.	Females.	Males.	Females.	Males.	Females.	Males.	Females.	
15	16	17	18	19	20	21	22	23	24	25	26	27	28	29	30	31
543	42	280	41	119	31	119	35	38	7	46	19	15	3	56	20	DISTRICT AMRAOTI.
537	50	252	41	97	22	93	41	27	18	66	20	16	2	55	23	" AKOLA.
390	43	187	24	81	19	103	20	19	4	53	17	11	4	34	17	" ELLICHPUR.
390	44	129	30	58	19	54	23	25	6	36	12	8	2	31	19	" BULDANA.
272	21	128	12	69	3	55	6	17	1	26	6	2	...	26	5	" WUN.
299	33	163	23	41	14	68	13	12	2	32	14	5	1	14	11	" BASIM.
1	...	2	...	2	...	...	...	...	...	...	...	...	...	...	..	Railway Passengers, etc.
2,482	233	1,141	171	467	108	492	138	188	38	259	88	57	12	216	95	Total.
181	20	111	21	41	15	44	15	16	4	19	6	4	...	30	9	Taluk Amraoti (AMRAOTI DISTRICT.)
131	4	53	7	18	3	21	3	4	...	10	3	6	1	8	1	" Chandur
113	8	62	5	23	7	32	8	12	1	10	5	1	1	12	5	" Morsi
118	10	54	8	37	6	22	9	6	2	7	5	4	1	6	5	" Murtazapur
155	10	66	6	33	6	31	9	7	3	13	1	5	...	13	8	Taluk Akola (AKOLA DISTRICT.)
127	18	70	16	23	5	24	13	8	7	18	11	6	2	15	7	" Akot
97	7	44	6	13	8	17	4	3	3	11	2	3	...	14	2	" Balapur
75	9	40	2	15	...	8	6	5	3	11	3	...	...	4	3	" Jalgaon
83	6	32	11	13	3	13	9	4	2	13	3	2	...	9	3	" Khamgaon
238	28	113	17	43	12	60	13	7	3	39	11	6	4	23	12	Taluk Ellichpur (ELLICHPUR DISTRICT.)
131	15	53	6	30	6	38	6	11	1	11	6	4	...	11	5	" Daryapur
21	...	21	1	8	1	5	1	1	...	3	...	1	...	...	...	" Melghat
145	16	37	8	19	10	19	8	6	2	11	3	2	1	11	10	Taluk Chikhli (BULDANA DISTRICT.)
133	18	59	16	18	7	22	10	8	4	15	6	6	1	15	6	" Malkapur
112	10	33	6	21	2	13	5	11	...	10	3	...	...	5	3	" Mehkar
73	6	45	2	23	...	18	1	3	...	6	3	1	...	6	1	Taluk Yeotmal (WUN DISTRICT.)
132	14	57	6	28	3	26	2	11	1	18	3	1	...	15	2	" Darwha
47	...	17	4	14	...	8	2	2	...	1	...	...	...	4	1	" Kelapur
20	1	9	...	4	...	3	1	1	...	1	...	...	...	1	1	" Wun
119	12	57	9	12	7	31	5	5	1	15	4	2	1	5	5	Taluk Basim (BASIM DISTRICT.)
55	5	41	4	12	1	15	1	2	...	7	1	2	...	4	2	" Mangrul
125	16	65	10	17	6	22	7	5	1	10	9	1	...	5	4	" Pusad

TABLE VIII.—Civil Condition by Religion

(a) MAR

DISTRICT AND TALUK.	Total Married.			Age 0—4		5—9		10—14		15—19		20—24		25—29	
	Total.	Males.	Females.	Males.	Females.	Males.	Females.	Males.	Females.	Males.	Females.	Males.	Females.	Males.	Females.
1	2	3	4	5	6	7	8	9	10	11	12	13	14	15	16
District Amraoti	21,475	11,144	10,331	25	27	26	108	110	594	277	1,238	804	2,031	1,635	1,772
" Akola	23,669	12,321	11,348	9	24	25	123	116	744	305	1,514	1,025	2,160	1,901	1,965
" Ellichpur	13,624	6,976	6,648	10	15	15	63	60	380	192	899	552	1,304	1,051	1,142
" Buldana	15,721	7,933	7,788	23	47	43	128	96	557	218	1,054	618	1,393	1,271	1,358
" Wun	9,257	4,849	4,408	1	18	22	87	59	279	126	485	357	794	754	834
" Basim	10,268	5,380	4,888	14	20	19	93	80	355	146	587	413	892	824	907
Railway Passengers, etc.	38	34	4	...	...	...	...	...	1	...	1	3	...	3	...
Total	94,052	48,637	45,415	82	151	150	602	521	2,910	1,264	5,778	3,772	8,574	7,439	7,978
Amraoti District. Taluk Amraoti	8,583	4,474	4,109	11	11	11	33	50	232	106	503	359	817	660	688
" Chandur	3,969	2,084	1,885	4	7	6	20	16	119	62	206	147	357	293	338
" Morsi	4,044	2,042	2,002	3	3	6	23	22	120	48	248	134	371	270	325
" Murtazapur	4,879	2,544	2,335	7	6	3	32	22	123	61	281	164	486	412	421
Akola District. Taluk Akola	5,741	2,984	2,757	3	8	9	21	28	154	64	349	228	517	421	516
" Akot	5,964	3,033	2,931	3	4	5	30	19	173	72	391	238	604	473	510
" Balapur	5,086	2,502	2,584	2	5	6	32	36	171	66	337	211	500	350	425
" Jalgaon	3,259	1,783	1,476	...	4	1	14	13	110	36	216	158	260	302	270
" Khamgaon	3,619	2,019	1,600	1	3	4	26	20	136	67	221	190	279	355	244
Ellichpur District. Taluk Ellichpur	8,298	4,135	4,163	6	10	10	36	41	250	126	560	315	772	610	703
" Daryapur	4,680	2,470	2,210	3	3	4	26	17	121	56	305	209	479	391	381
" Melghat	646	371	275	1	2	1	1	2	9	10	34	28	53	50	58
Buldana District. Taluk Chikhli	5,381	2,735	2,646	6	11	12	41	26	174	58	340	206	457	403	494
" Malkapur	6,660	3,312	3,348	14	30	25	60	49	248	108	468	279	591	545	566
" Mehkar	3,680	1,886	1,794	3	6	6	27	21	135	52	246	133	345	323	298
Wun District. Taluk Yeotmal	2,578	1,376	1,202	...	5	2	24	13	79	35	139	101	210	196	229
" Darwha	4,299	2,244	2,055	1	8	14	31	24	122	63	224	170	371	352	380
" Kelapur	1,332	695	637	...	3	6	19	13	46	15	66	47	118	117	114
" Wun	1,048	534	514	...	2	...	13	9	32	13	56	39	95	89	111
Basim District. Taluk Basim	4,226	2,265	1,961	8	6	9	32	36	158	65	245	180	345	325	349
" Mangrul	2,105	1,082	1,023	1	8	3	12	11	65	27	126	89	188	161	212
" Pusad	3,937	2,033	1,904	5	6	7	49	33	132	54	216	144	359	338	346

and Age—Part C—MUSALMAN—*contd.*

RIED. — PERIOD. — 30—34 Males.	30—34 Females.	35—39 Males.	35—39 Females.	40—44 Males.	40—44 Females.	45—49 Males.	45—49 Females.	50—54 Males.	50—54 Females.	55—59 Males.	55—59 Females.	60 and over. Males.	60 and over. Females.	DISTRICT AND TALUK.
17	18	19	20	21	22	23	24	25	26	27	28	29	30	31
2,007	1,747	1,300	836	1,701	1,052	735	274	1,213	391	265	70	1,046	191	DISTRICT AMRAOTI.
2,190	1,812	1,565	845	1,661	1,131	752	337	1,245	438	326	74	1,201	181	„ AKOLA.
1,259	1,054	779	517	994	630	452	185	686	271	171	46	755	142	„ ELLICHPUR.
1,409	1,267	886	569	1,134	753	486	212	768	252	216	58	765	140	„ BULDANA.
859	744	591	397	776	401	328	112	464	158	101	29	411	70	„ WUN.
1,027	824	615	377	772	448	327	102	584	190	93	25	466	68	„ BASIM.
12	...	2	...	4	2	1	...	4	...	1	...	4	...	Railway Passengers, etc.
8,768	7,448	5,738	3,541	7,042	4,417	3,081	1,222	4,964	1,700	1,178	302	4,648	792	Total.
774	675	500	339	655	417	290	121	528	164	115	28	415	81	Taluk Amraoti (AMRAOTI DISTRICT.)
368	327	252	155	326	262	155	52	217	59	54	13	184	30	„ Chandur (AMRAOTI DISTRICT.)
389	339	253	169	307	221	125	48	221	83	40	15	224	37	„ Morsi (AMRAOTI DISTRICT.)
476	406	295	173	413	212	165	53	247	85	56	14	223	43	„ Murtazapur (AMRAOTI DISTRICT.)
532	437	399	239	422	270	201	77	307	99	75	24	295	46	Taluk Akola (AKOLA DISTRICT.)
564	445	405	230	416	276	185	92	283	104	74	23	296	49	„ Akot (AKOLA DISTRICT.)
438	448	313	163	300	270	139	70	276	110	80	10	285	43	„ Balapur (AKOLA DISTRICT.)
324	229	228	107	254	133	107	46	165	62	49	9	146	16	„ Jalgaon. (AKOLA DISTRICT.)
332	253	220	106	269	182	120	52	214	63	48	8	179	27	„ Khamgaon. (AKOLA DISTRICT.)
700	661	457	348	571	414	277	115	437	164	102	26	483	104	Taluk Ellichpur (ELLICHPUR DISTRICT.)
472	338	277	147	363	198	145	65	223	95	60	18	250	34	„ Daryapur (ELLICHPUR DISTRICT.)
87	55	45	22	60	18	30	5	26	12	9	2	22	4	„ Melghat (ELLICHPUR DISTRICT.)
508	444	311	225	439	239	175	70	277	95	74	20	240	36	Taluk Chikhli (BULDANA DISTRICT.)
549	502	378	228	428	342	192	103	297	105	97	29	351	76	„ Malkapur (BULDANA DISTRICT.)
352	321	197	116	267	172	119	39	194	52	45	9	174	28	„ Mehkar (BULDANA DISTRICT.)
243	201	173	101	217	97	100	44	148	47	27	8	121	18	Taluk Yeotmal (WUN DISTRICT.)
385	335	258	215	351	198	146	50	222	71	53	12	205	38	„ Darwha (WUN DISTRICT.)
124	120	94	44	120	68	47	12	55	18	14	3	43	6	„ Kelapur (WUN DISTRICT.)
107	88	66	37	88	38	35	6	39	22	7	6	42	8	„ Wun (WUN DISTRICT.)
451	328	264	154	302	190	137	33	248	89	38	5	202	27	Taluk Basim (BASIM DISTRICT.)
197	167	116	75	182	93	64	18	117	38	27	5	87	16	„ Mangrul (BASIM DISTRICT.)
379	329	235	148	288	165	126	51	219	63	28	15	177	25	„ Pusad (BASIM DISTRICT.)

TABLE VIII.—Civil Condition by Religion

(3) WI

District and Taluk.	Total Widowed. Total.	Total Widowed. Males.	Total Widowed. Females.	Age 0—4 Males.	0—4 Females.	5—9 Males.	5—9 Females.	10—14 Males.	10—14 Females.	15—19 Males.	15—19 Females.	20—24 Males.	20—24 Females.	25—29 Males.	25—29 Females.
1	2	3	4	5	6	7	8	9	10	11	12	13	14	15	16
District Amraoti	5,434	1,385	4,049	7	9	6	20	10	17	9	27	34	66	83	141
" Akola	5,931	1,467	4,464	...	2	...	6	3	14	10	22	29	84	83	171
" Ellichpur	4,123	906	3,217	2	...	1	2	3	11	5	23	24	74	48	118
" Buldana	3,389	693	2,696	...	1	...	3	3	12	2	16	11	54	35	91
" Wun	2,219	493	1,726	...	1	1	2	...	6	2	16	8	34	28	71
" Basim	2,457	549	1,908	5	9	3	9	5	7	7	25	10	51	27	74
Railway Passengers, etc.	3	1	2	...	...	...	...	...	...	...	...	...	...	...	1
Total	28,556	5,494	18,062	14	22	11	42	24	67	35	129	116	363	304	667
Amraoti District. Taluk Amraoti	2,148	549	1,599	6	5	3	12	4	6	5	14	15	22	36	37
" Chandur	1,023	255	768	...	...	...	1	1	6	1	5	10	9	12	27
" Morsi	1,095	253	842	...	3	3	4	3	1	2	3	3	14	16	26
" Murtazapur	1,168	328	840	1	1	...	3	2	4	1	5	6	21	19	31
Akola District. Taluk Akola	1,454	356	1,098	...	...	...	2	...	3	4	3	8	21	18	34
" Akot	1,625	390	1,235	...	1	...	2	1	3	3	9	9	16	22	48
" Balapur	1,262	315	947	...	1	...	1	2	1	2	2	5	15	15	32
" Jalgaon	788	205	583	...	...	...	...	...	2	1	4	4	13	12	24
" Khamgaon	802	201	601	...	...	...	1	...	5	...	4	3	19	16	33
Ellichpur District. Taluk Ellichpur	2,733	569	2,164	2	...	...	1	...	8	2	12	14	49	27	83
" Daryapur	1,246	296	950	...	...	1	1	3	3	3	8	7	22	20	31
" Melghat	144	41	103	...	...	...	...	..	...	...	3	3	3	1	4
Buldana District. Taluk Chikhli	1,183	247	936	...	...	..	2	...	6	1	6	5	16	10	33
" Malkapur	1,399	278	1,121	...	1	...	1	2	4	1	8	6	20	14	39
" Mehkar	807	168	639	...	...	...	...	1	2	...	2	...	18	11	19
Wun District. Taluk Yeotmal	614	147	467	...	...	...	...	...	3	...	7	1	6	8	15
" Darwha	993	259	734	...	1	1	2	...	2	2	4	7	15	14	36
" Kelapur	356	54	302	...	...	...	...	...	1	...	4	...	9	4	13
" Wun	256	33	223	...	...	...	...	...	...	...	1	...	4	2	7
Basim District. Taluk Basim	994	213	781	...	...	...	2	2	2	3	8	5	24	14	37
" Mangrul	523	120	403	...	...	...	1	...	2	...	3	1	6	3	15
" Pusad	940	216	724	5	9	3	6	3	3	4	14	4	21	10	22

and Age.—Part C—MUSALMAN—*concld.*

DOWED. PERIOD. 30—34 Males.	30—34 Females.	35—39 Males.	35—39 Females.	40—44 Males.	40—44 Females.	45—49 Males.	45—49 Females.	50—54 Males.	50—54 Females.	55—59 Males.	55—59 Females.	60 and over. Males.	60 and over. Females.	DISTRICT AND TALUK.	
17	18	19	20	21	22	23	24	25	26	27	28	29	30	31	
136	269	102	272	169	585	90	292	228	775	57	154	454	1,422	DISTRICT AMRAOTI.	
140	315	101	273	196	668	109	311	232	835	75	192	489	1,571	,, AKOLA.	
71	236	70	174	138	455	68	212	149	661	39	117	288	1,134	,, ELLICHPUR.	
54	185	48	183	94	387	50	190	114	528	37	127	245	919	,, BULDANA.	
55	138	31	129	70	216	45	122	80	338	24	80	149	573	,, WUN.	
57	159	32	116	75	290	37	120	103	355	21	64	167	629	,, BASIM.	
...	...	...	...	...	1	...	...	...	...	1	...	...	...	Railway Passengers, etc.	
513	1,302	384	1,147	742	2,602	399	1,247	906	3,492	254	734	1,792	6,248	Total.	
48	96	45	106	64	223	31	99	98	312	17	68	177	579	Taluk Amraoti .	AMRAOTI DISTRICT.
30	49	20	58	39	93	17	80	37	128	13	34	75	278	,, Chandur .	
29	67	16	64	22	131	15	56	41	152	15	30	88	291	,, Morsi .	
29	57	21	44	44	138	27	57	52	183	12	22	114	274	,, Murtazapur .	
32	70	22	72	46	160	28	78	55	184	24	59	119	412	Taluk Akola .	AKOLA DISTRICT.
28	93	34	74	42	179	28	70	65	255	17	57	141	428	,, Akot .	
36	50	16	65	48	141	17	72	45	188	14	33	115	346	,, Balapur .	
24	52	17	36	36	96	19	49	29	112	13	22	50	173	,, Jalgaon .	
20	50	12	26	24	92	17	42	38	96	7	21	64	212	,, Khamgaon .	
41	149	42	119	94	311	42	129	91	444	23	74	191	785	Taluk Ellichpur .	ELLICHPUR DISTRICT.
23	76	27	48	37	130	23	77	49	197	15	41	88	316	,, Daryapur .	
7	11	1	7	7	14	3	6	9	20	1	2	9	33	,, Melghat .	
30	57	13	77	31	142	19	72	43	179	11	44	84	302	Taluk Chikhli .	BULDANA DISTRICT.
8	77	18	70	39	140	18	76	47	216	21	62	104	407	,, Malkapur .	
16	51	17	36	24	105	13	42	24	133	5	21	57	210	,, Mehkar .	
14	35	8	33	15	59	18	32	27	104	6	16	50	157	Taluk Yeotmal .	WUN DISTRICT.
28	51	15	57	42	95	24	52	38	135	15	38	73	246	,, Darwha .	
8	34	4	23	10	39	2	30	9	47	2	16	15	86	,, Kelapur .	
5	18	4	16	3	23	1	8	6	52	1	10	11	84	,, Wun .	
26	60	12	46	21	110	21	44	32	146	7	28	70	274	Taluk Basim .	BASIM DISTRICT.
17	28	6	20	15	76	6	23	22	79	7	17	43	133	,, Mangrul .	
14	71	14	50	39	104	10	53	49	130	7	19	54	222	,, Pusad .	

TABLE VIII.

Civil Condition by Religion and Age.—Part D—ANIMISTIC.

TABLE VIII.—Civil Condition by Religion

(1) UN.

DISTRICT AND TALUK.	TOTAL UNMARRIED.			AGE 0—4		5—9		10—14		15—19		20—24	
	Total.	Males.	Females.	Males.	Females.	Males.	Females.	Males.	Females.	Males.	Females.	Males.	Females.
1	2	3	4	5	6	7	8	9	10	11	12	13	14
District Amraoti	7,162	3,962	3,200	974	1,023	1,008	1,092	837	628	359	100	257	86
" Akola	747	405	342	112	155	124	123	82	53	35	8	19	1
" Ellichpur	19,895	10,761	9,134	3,104	3,346	3,257	3,176	2,376	1,815	891	496	617	150
" Buldana	1	1	...	1	...	...	...	...	...	...	...	...	...
" Wun	34,230	18,717	15,513	6,235	6,825	6,135	6,064	4,071	2,169	1,310	249	555	69
" Basim	185	95	90	30	41	32	30	20	14	7	2	4	2
Railway Passengers, etc.	2	...	2	...	1	...	1	...	...	...	...	...	...
Total	**62,222**	**33,941**	**28,281**	**10,456**	**11,391**	**10,556**	**10,486**	**7,386**	**4,679**	**2,602**	**855**	**1,452**	**308**
AMRAOTI DISTRICT. Taluk Amraoti	699	375	324	77	107	92	113	104	78	31	15	32	6
" Chandur	2,674	1,545	1,129	433	419	439	447	354	226	142	19	98	4
" Morsi	3,677	1,977	1,700	461	476	459	513	358	317	179	66	124	76
" Murtazapur	112	65	47	13	21	18	19	21	7	7	...	3	...
AKOLA DISTRICT. Taluk Akola	46	24	22	6	10	3	10	4	1	2	1	2	...
" Akot	383	210	173	55	71	65	66	45	33	18	2	13	1
" Balapur	3	1	2	1	2	...	...	...	...	...	...	...	...
" Jalgaon	305	160	145	47	72	55	47	32	19	14	5	3	...
" Khamgaon	10	10	...	3	...	1	...	1	...	1	...	1	...
ELLICHPUR DISTRICT. Taluk Ellichpur	1,086	598	488	159	152	181	175	121	111	48	27	41	8
" Daryapur	90	47	43	9	16	13	16	9	8	5	1	2	1
" Melghat	18,719	10,116	8,603	2,936	3,178	3,063	2,985	2,246	1,696	838	468	574	141
BULDANA DISTRICT. Taluk Chikhli	1	1	...	1	...	...	...	...	...	...	...	...	...
" Malkapur	...	...	...	...	...	...	...	...	...	...	...	...	...
" Mehkar	...	...	...	...	...	...	...	...	...	...	...	...	...
WUN DISTRICT. Taluk Yeotmal	10,484	5,756	4,728	1,865	2,038	1,786	1,835	1,354	717	437	77	172	20
" Darwha	3,671	2,067	1,604	704	751	675	644	443	164	133	17	67	9
" Kelapur	12,493	6,753	5,740	2,299	2,562	2,260	2,228	1,398	770	453	96	201	30
" Wun	7,582	4,141	3,441	1,367	1,474	1,414	1,357	876	518	287	59	115	10
BASIM DISTRICT. Taluk Basim	...	...	...	...	...	...	...	...	...	...	...	...	...
" Mangrul	12	5	7	2	2	2	4	...	1	...	...	1	...
" Pusad	173	90	83	28	39	30	26	20	13	7	2	3	2

and Age.—Part D—ANIMISTIC.

MARRIED.																	
PERIOD																	
25—29		30—14		35—39		40—44		45—49		50—54		55—59		60 and over.		DISTRICT AND TALUK.	
Males.	Females.	Males.	Females.	Males.	Females.	Males.	Females.	Males.	Females.	Males.	Females.	Males.	Females.	Males.	Females.		
15	16	7	18	19	20	21	22	23	24	25	26	27	28	29	30	31	
149	72	112	60	71	52	69	37	42	16	30	19	21	8	33	7	District Amraoti.	
13	2	12	...	6	...	1	...	1	...	...	...	...	...	...	...	„ Akola.	
288	61	115	39	47	9	35	19	10	8	10	5	...	1	11	9	„ Ellichpur.	
...	...	...	...	...	...	...	...	...	...	...	...	...	...	...	...	„ Buldana.	
230	45	82	29	36	14	33	21	6	12	14	7	2	...	8	9	„ Wun.	
1	...	1	1	...	...	...	...	...	...	...	...	...	...	...	...	„ Basim.	
...	...	...	...	...	...	...	...	...	...	...	...	...	...	...	...	Railway Passengers, etc.	
681	180	822	129	160	75	188	77	59	36	54	31	28	9	52	25	Total.	
13	3	16	1	3	...	2	...	1	1	1	...	2	...	1	...	Taluk Amraoti	Amraoti District.
42	3	22	2	8	1	9	6	3	...	2	1	...	...	3	1	„ Chandur	
94	66	72	57	59	51	58	31	38	15	27	18	19	8	29	6	„ Morsi	
...	...	2	...	1	...	...	...	...	...	...	...	...	...	...	...	„ Murtazapur	
1	...	2	...	3	...	...	...	1	...	...	...	...	...	...	..	Taluk Akola	Akola District.
6	...	7	...	1	...	...	...	...	..	...	...	...	..	...	...	„ Akot	
...	...	...	...	...	...	...	...	...	...	...	...	...	...	...	...	„ Balapur	
5	2	1	...	2	...	1	...	...	...	...	...	...	...	...	...	„ Jalgaon	
1	...	2	...	...	...	...	...	...	...	...	...	...	...	...	...	„ Khamgaon	
20	7	12	4	8	...	3	2	1	...	3	...	...	...	1	2	Taluk Ellichpur	Ellichpur District.
4	...	2	...	2	...	1	1	...	...	...	...	...	...	...	...	„ Daryapur	
264	54	101	35	37	9	31	16	9	8	7	5	...	1	10	7	„ Melghat	
...	...	...	...	...	...	...	...	...	..	...	...	...	...	...	...	Taluk Chikhli	Buldana District.
...	...	...	...	...	...	...	...	...	...	...	...	...	...	...	...	„ Malkapur	
...	...	...	...	...	...	...	...	...	...	...	...	...	...	...	...	„ Mehkar	
78	10	33	10	14	3	10	9	2	3	4	3	...	...	1	3	Taluk Yeotmal	Wun District.
19	7	12	4	8	3	3	1	...	1	1	2	...	...	2	1	„ Darwha	
79	20	24	10	11	6	16	5	2	6	5	2	2	...	3	5	„ Kelapur	
54	8	13	5	3	2	4	6	2	2	4	...	...	...	2	...	„ Wun	
...	...	...	...	...	...	...	...	...	...	...	...	...	...	...	...	Taluk Basim	Basim District.
...	...	...	...	...	...	...	...	...	...	...	...	...	...	...	...	„ Mangrul	
1	...	1	1	...	...	...	...	...	...	...	...	...	...	...	...	„ Pusad.	

TABLE VIII.—Civil Condition by Religion

(2)

DISTRICT AND TALUK.	TOTAL MARRIED.			AGE 0—4		5—9		10—14		15—19		20—24	
	TOTAL.	Males.	Females.	Males.	Females.	Males.	Females.	Males.	Females.	Males.	Females.	Males.	Females.
1	2	3	4	5	6	7	8	9	10	11	12	13	14
DISTRICT AMRAOTI	8,519	4,236	4,283	86	100	88	129	113	281	128	388	250	619
" AKOLA	695	370	325	...	...	1	3	2	14	12	33	28	43
" ELLICHPUR	17,544	8,679	8,865	31	41	54	63	104	365	263	1,007	764	1,521
" BULDANA	3	1	2	...	...	...	...	..	...	...	...	...	1
" WUN	38,088	18,870	19,218	37	62	126	459	476	1,502	829	2,169	1,526	2,960
" BASIM	220	114	106	...	2	6	6	8	10	6	14	9	26
Total	65,069	32,270	32,799	154	205	275	660	708	2,172	1,238	3,611	2,577	5,170
AMRAOTI DISTRICT. Taluk Amraoti	899	436	463	...	...	...	4	2	27	8	26	18	55
" Chandur	3,583	1,745	1,838	2	1	4	16	19	129	47	175	104	284
" Morsi	3,879	1,974	1,905	84	98	84	109	90	120	69	173	124	266
" Murtazapur	158	81	77	...	1	...	...	2	5	4	14	4	14
AKOLA DISTRICT. Taluk Akola	83	49	34	...	...	...	...	...	1	1	4	4	4
" Akot	352	192	160	...	...	1	3	1	7	5	10	12	21
" Balapur	3	1	2	...	...	...	...	...	...	...	...	...	...
" Jalgaon	249	124	125	...	...	...	...	1	6	6	19	12	17
" Khamgaon	8	4	4	...	...	...	...	...	...	...	...	...	1
ELLICHPUR DISTRICT. Taluk Ellichpur	915	455	460	1	2	3	2	3	26	6	31	19	72
" Daryapur	98	50	48	...	...	...	...	...	...	...	...	...	9
" Melghat	16,531	8,174	8,357	30	39	51	61	101	339	257	976	745	1,440
BULDANA DISTRICT. Taluk Chikhli	3	1	2	...	...	...	...	...	...	...	...	...	1
" Malkapur	...	...	...	...	...	...	...	...	...	...	...	...	...
" Mehkar	...	...	...		...	...	...	...	...	...	...	...	...
WUN DISTRICT. Taluk Yeotmal	12,080	5,989	6,091	11	10	20	112	92	410	225	727	480	980
" Darwha	4,457	2,206	2,251	4	7	18	68	66	189	104	261	181	324
" Kelapur	13,419	6,669	6,750	15	26	41	187	198	530	310	746	526	1,049
" Wun	8,132	4,006	4,126	7	19	47	92	120	373	190	435	339	607
BASIM DISTRICT. Taluk Basim	...	...	...	...	...	...	...	...	...	...	...	...	...
" Mangrul	22	10	12	...	...	...	1	...	2	...	...	1	3
" Pusad	198	104	94	...	2	6	5	8	8	6	14	8	23

and Age.—Part D—ANIMISTIC—*contd.*

MARRIED. PERIOD. 25—29		30—34		35—39		40—44		45—49		50—54		55—59		60 and over		DISTRICT AND TALUK.	
Males.	Females.	Males.	Females.	Males.	Females.	Males.	Females.	Males.	Females.	Males.	Females.	Males.	Females.	Males.	Females.		
15	16	17	18	19	20	21	22	23	24	25	26	27	28	29	30	31	
483	743	692	714	524	421	659	436	304	157	452	193	105	33	352	69	DISTRICT AMRAOTI.	
43	67	57	58	54	44	75	33	29	12	44	8	6	5	19	5	" AKOLA.	
1,262	1,667	1,693	1,706	1,244	795	1,270	781	538	317	681	333	181	87	594	182	" ELLICHPUR.	
...	...	...	...	...	...	...	1	1	...	...	...	...	...	...	...	" BULDANA.	
2,688	3,340	3,244	3,209	2,177	1,625	2,808	1,847	1,149	558	1,735	933	386	169	1,689	385	" WUN.	
19	9	22	17	11	7	12	6	3	4	8	3	4	1	6	1	" BASIM.	
4,495	5,826	5,708	5,704	4,010	2,892	4,824	3,104	2,024	1,048	2,920	1,470	682	295	2,660	642	Total.	
47	96	77	115	61	42	97	47	33	14	46	23	12	2	35	12	Taluk Amraoti	AMRAOTI DISTRICT.
223	320	286	302	221	186	272	195	148	73	194	100	56	23	169	34	" Chandur	
202	311	312	289	234	187	275	188	118	65	204	68	34	8	144	23	" Morsi	
11	16	17	8	8	6	15	6	5	5	8	2	3	...	4	...	" Murtazapur	
5	8	5	5	8	4	9	6	5	...	6	...	3	...	3	2	Taluk Akola	AKOLA DISTRICT.
16	32	32	30	23	23	52	22	13	5	26	3	1	2	10	2	" Akot.	
...	...	...	1	...	...	...	...	...	...	1	1	...	...	...	...	" Balapur	
20	26	20	20	23	17	12	5	11	7	11	4	2	3	6	1	" Jalgaon	
2	1	...	2	...	...	2	...	...	...	...	...	...	...	...	...	" Khamgaon	
53	89	70	89	56	60	102	49	47	10	50	19	8	3	37	8	Taluk Ellichpur	ELLICHPUR DISTRICT.
6	4	4	14	8	7	12	7	3	2	9	3	3	1	5	1	" Daryapur	
1,203	1,574	1,619	1,603	1,180	728	1,156	725	488	305	622	311	170	83	552	173	" Melghat	
...	...	...	...	...	...	...	1	1	...	...	...	...	...	...	...	Taluk Chikhli	BULDANA DISTRICT.
...	...	...	...	...	...	...	...	...	...	...	...	...	...	...	...	" Malkapur	
...	...	...	...	...	...	...	...	...	...	...	...	...	...	...	...	" Mehkar	
858	1,048	1,012	993	734	557	898	595	390	191	583	296	139	53	547	119	Taluk Yeotmal	WUN DISTRICT.
312	379	370	382	250	193	321	226	142	57	204	97	39	17	195	51	" Darwha	
956	1,220	1,154	1,179	780	518	983	608	390	179	576	332	148	44	592	132	" Kelapur	
562	693	708	655	413	357	606	418	227	131	372	208	60	55	355	83	" Wun	
...	...	...	...	...	...	...	...	...	...	...	...	...	...	...	...	Taluk Basim	BASIM DISTRICT.
...	...	4	3	1	...	...	...	...	3	2	...	1	...	1	...	" Mangrul	
19	9	18	14	10	7	12	6	3	1	6	3	3	1	5	1	" Pusad	

TABLE VIII.—Civil Condition by Religion

(a) Wi…

DISTRICT AND TALUK.	TOTAL WIDOWED.			Age—									
				0—4		5—9		10—14		15—19		20—24	
	Total.	Males.	Females.	Males.	Females.	Males.	Females.	Males.	Females.	Males.	Females.	Males.	Females.
1	2	3	4	5	6	7	8	9	10	11	12	13	14
DISTRICT AMRAOTI	1,710	529	1,181	...	...	1	..	...	3	6	9	7	34
" AKOLA	103	38	65	...	...	...	...	...	...	...	1	2	2
" ELLICHPUR	2,306	661	1,645	...	1	...	3	4	6	5	23	22	34
" BULDANA	3	2	1	1	...	1	...	...	...	...	...	...	...
" WUN	5,650	1,390	4,260	3	1	6	20	11	47	15	33	39	68
" BASIM	44	16	28	...	...	...	...	...	1	1	...	1	...
Railway Passengers, etc.	1	..	1	...	...	...	...	...	..	...	...	...	...
Total	9,817	2,686	7,181	4	2	8	23	15	57	27	66	71	138
AMRAOTI DISTRICT. Taluk Amraoti	158	59	99	...	...	...	...	...	1	...	3	...	4
" Chandur	697	217	480	...	...	...	...	...	2	5	6	3	17
" Morsi	827	239	588	...	...	1	...	...	...	1	...	4	13
" Murtazapur	28	14	14	...	...	...	...	...	...	...	...	...	...
AKOLA DISTRICT. Taluk Akola	14	7	7	...	...	...	...	...	...	...	...	1	...
" Akot	50	13	37	...	...	...	...	...	...	...	1	1	2
" Balapur	2	1	1	...	...	...	...	...	...	...	...	...	...
" Jalgaon	35	15	20	...	...	...	...	...	...	...	...	...	...
" Khamgaon	2	2	...	...	...	...	...	...	...	...	...	...	...
ELLICHPUR DISTRICT. Taluk Ellichpur	212	80	132	...	...	...	1	...	...	...	1	2	6
" Daryapur	26	13	13	...	...		...	1	...	...	...	...	1
" Melghat	2,068	568	1,500	...	1	...	2	3	6	5	22	20	27
BULDANA DISTRICT. Taluk Chikhli	3	2	1	1	...	1	...	...	...	...	...	..	...
" Malkapur	...	...	...	...	...	...	...	...	...	...	...	...	...
" Mehkar	...	...	...	...	...	...	...	...	...	...	...	...	...
WUN DISTRICT. Taluk Yeotmal	1,770	478	1,292	...	...	...	4	2	6	3	6	9	18
" Darwha	759	209	550	2	1	3	6	3	17	6	9	7	10
" Kelapur	1,924	439	1,485	1	...	2	6	4	13	3	10	12	25
" Wun	1,197	264	933	...	...	1	4	2	11	3	8	11	15
BASIM DISTRICT. Taluk Basim	...	...	...	...	...	...	...	...	...	...	...	...	...
" Mangrul	5	2	3	...	...	...	...	...	...	...	...	...	...
" Pusad	39	14	25	...	...	...	...	...	1	1	...	1	...

and Age.—Part D—ANIMISTIC—*concld.*

DOWED.																
PERIOD.																
25—29		30—34		35—39		40—44		45—49		50—54		55—59		60 and over.		DISTRICT AND TALUK.
Males.	Females.	Males.	Females.	Males.	Females.	Males.	Females.	Males.	Females.	Males.	Females.	Males.	Females.	Males.	Females.	
15	16	17	18	19	20	21	22	23	24	25	26	27	28	29	30	31
24	38	61	90	48	61	78	69	43	88	80	218	21	62	160	409	DISTRICT AMRAOTI.
1	2	7	3	5	2	5	11	2	4	5	15	2	1	9	24	„ AKOLA.
44	71	75	114	56	83	100	216	54	126	94	305	35	74	172	589	„ ELLICHPUR.
...	...	...	...	...	...	...	...	...	...	...	1	...	...	...	...	„ BULDANA.
59	132	124	263	102	195	183	565	79	266	205	824	61	170	503	1,676	„ WUN.
2	2	1	3	3	...	1	6	1	1	1	3	1	1	4	11	„ BASIM.
...	...	...	...	...	...	...	...	...	...	...	1	...	...	...	...	Railway Passengers, etc.
180	245	268	473	214	341	867	967	179	485	385	1,367	120	308	848	2,709	Total.
6	6	7	9	9	3	8	22	6	7	8	16	3	4	12	24	Taluk Amraoti (AMRAOTI DISTRICT.)
13	15	27	41	22	26	31	69	16	34	28	77	5	25	67	168	„ Chandur
4	17	26	39	13	31	36	76	20	46	43	121	13	33	78	212	„ Morsi
1	...	1	1	4	1	3	2	1	1	1	4	...	...	3	5	„ Murtazapur
...	1	4	...	...	...	...	1	1	...	1	1	...	...	...	4	Taluk Akola (AKOLA DISTRICT.)
1	...	...	2	3	...	1	6	...	...	3	10	1	1	3	15	„ Akot
...	...	1	...	...	...	...	...	...	...	...	1	...	...	...	...	„ Balapur
...	1	2	1	2	2	3	4	1	4	1	3	...	...	6	5	„ Jalgaon
...	..	...	...	...	...	1	...	...	...	...	...	1	...	...	...	„ Khamgaon
3	4	2	14	9	9	19	20	7	5	19	27	5	3	14	42	Taluk Ellichpur (ELLICHPUR DISTRICT.)
...	...	3	3	1	1	4	2	2	...	1	3	1	...	...	3	„ Daryapur
41	67	70	97	46	73	77	194	45	121	74	275	29	71	158	544	„ Melghat
...	...	...	...	...	...	...	...	...	...	...	1	...	...	...	...	Taluk Chikhli (BULDANA DISTRICT.)
...	...	...	...	...	...	...	...	...	...	...	...	...	...	...	...	„ Malkapur
...	...	...	...	...	...	...	...	...	...	...	...	...	...	...	...	„ Mehkar
15	4[illegible]	29	63	31	61	72	165	28	93	72	246	26	55	191	529	Taluk Yeotmal (WUN DISTRICT.)
6	19	27	38	26	32	28	68	10	44	30	84	4	26	57	196	„ Darwha
22	42	43	102	28	65	54	204	31	82	65	295	16	57	158	584	„ Kelapur
16	25	25	60	17	37	29	128	10	47	38	199	15	32	97	367	„ Wun
...	...	...	...	...	...	...	...	...	...	...	...	...	...	...	...	Taluk Basim (BASIM DISTRICT.)
...	...	...	1	2	...	...	...	...	...	...	...	...	...	...	2	„ Mangrul
2	2	1	2	1	...	1	6	1	1	1	3	1	1	4	9	„ Pusad

TABLE VIII.

Civil Condition by Religion and Age.—
Part E—JAIN.

TABLE VIII.—Civil Condition by Religion

(1) UN

DISTRICT AND TALUK.	TOTAL UNMARRIED.			AGE									
				0—4		5—9		10—14		15—19		20—24	
	Total.	Males.	Females.	Males.	Females.	Males.	Females.	Males.	Females.	Males.	Females.	Males.	Females.
1	2	3	4	5	6	7	8	9	10	11	12	13	14
District Amraoti	*1,752*	1,164	588	324	331	287	216	245	34	125	3	62	1
" Akola	*1,050*	694	356	178	212	169	122	145	18	86	...	44	...
" Ellichpur	*383*	263	115	72	64	82	41	53	9	22	...	14	...
" Buldana	*1,333*	866	467	242	238	209	189	180	32	74	4	42	1
" Wun	*597*	403	194	77	98	99	72	104	20	41	2	28	...
" Basim	*961*	638	323	201	178	211	123	136	16	39	2	19	...
Total	*6,076*	4,033	2,043	1,094	1,121	1,057	763	863	129	387	11	209	2
Amraoti District. Taluk Amraoti	*390*	284	106	55	54	57	41	67	10	35	1	26	...
" Chandur	*485*	318	167	83	89	72	64	65	14	37	...	22	...
" Morsi	*338*	204	134	75	76	63	52	4	2	12	1	3	1
" Murtazapur	*539*	358	181	111	112	95	59	70	8	41	1	11	...
Akola District. Taluk Akola	*288*	176	112	48	74	48	35	38	3	19	...	6	...
" Akot	*178*	117	61	34	38	29	21	30	2	10	...	6	...
" Balapur	*328*	224	104	54	50	53	46	36	6	43	...	15	...
" Jalgaon	*48*	35	13	6	6	6	4	7	1	2	...	5	...
" Khamgaon	*208*	142	66	36	44	33	16	34	6	12	...	12	...
Ellichpur District. Taluk Ellichpur	*257*	172	85	41	41	51	34	35	9	19	...	11	...
" Daryapur	*125*	95	30	31	23	31	7	18	...	3	...	2	...
" Melghat	*1*	1	...	...	...	...	...	...	...	...	...	1	...
Buldana District. Taluk Chikhli	*455*	290	165	79	78	64	75	76	10	27	1	14	...
" Malkapur	*470*	297	173	89	88	80	69	50	11	23	2	14	1
" Mehkar	*408*	279	129	74	72	65	45	54	11	24	1	14	...
Wun District. Taluk Yeotmal	*286*	185	101	36	50	48	41	49	7	20	2	11	...
" Darwha	*213*	151	62	29	30	35	21	37	10	15	...	14	...
" Kelapur	*79*	55	24	8	13	14	8	16	3	5	...	2	...
" Wun	*19*	12	7	4	5	2	2	2	...	1	...	1	...
Basim District. Taluk Basim	*591*	395	196	121	108	127	74	91	11	23	1	15	...
" Mangrul	*101*	65	36	19	17	25	15	14	3	3	...	1	...
" Pusad	*269*	178	91	61	53	59	34	31	2	13	1	3	...

and Age—Part E—JAIN.

MARRIED.																
PERIOD.																
25—29		30—34		35—39		40—44		45—49		50—54		55—59		60 and over.		DISTRICT AND TALUK.
Males.	Females.	Males.	Females.	Males.	Females.	Males.	Females.	Males.	Females.	Males.	Females.	Males.	Females.	Males.	Females.	
15	16	17	18	19	20	21	22	23	24	25	26	27	28	29	30	31
47	2	27	...	13	1	14	...	6	...	9	...	1	...	4	...	DISTRICT AMRAOTI.
27	1	15	1	9	...	7	2	3	...	5	...	1	...	5	...	" AKOLA.
10	...	3	...	4	...	3	...	1	...	3	...	...	1	1	...	" ELLICHPUR.
53	...	19	2	17	...	13	...	4	...	5	1	1	...	7	...	" BULDNA.
22	1	13	...	9	1	6	...	...	...	1	...	1	...	2	...	" WUN.
15	...	3	2	4	1	1	1	4	...	1	...	1	...	3	...	" BASIM.
174	4	80	5	56	3	44	3	18	...	24	1	5	1	22	...	Total.
17	...	11	...	4	...	5	...	2	...	3	...	1	...	1	...	Taluk Amraoti (AMRAOTI DISTRICT.)
14	...	6	...	6	...	6	...	3	...	3	...	...	...	1	...	" Chandur
8	1	3	...	1	1	...	...	...	...	1	...	...	...	...	...	" Morsi
13	1	7	...	2	...	3	...	1	...	2	...	...	...	2	...	" Murtazapur
7	...	2	...	4	...	...	...	1	...	1	...	...	...	2	...	Taluk Akola (AKOLA DISTRICT.)
3	...	...	...	...	...	3	...	...	...	1	...	...	...	1	...	" Akot
8	...	9	...	2	...	1	2	1	...	...	...	...	...	2	...	" Balapur
2	1	2	1	1	...	1	...	...	...	2	...	1	...	...	...	" Jalgaon
7	...	2	...	2	...	2	...	1	...	1	...	...	...	...	...	" Khamgaon
7	...	2	...	3	...	2	...	...	...	1	...	...	1	...	...	Taluk Ellichpur (ELLICHPUR DISTRICT.)
8	...	1	...	1	...	1	...	1	...	2	...	...	...	1	...	" Daryapur
...	...	...	...	...	...	...	...	...	...	...	...	...	...	...	...	" Melghat
13	...	6	1	4	...	4	...	1	...	...	...	...	...	2	...	Taluk Chikhli (BULDANA DISTRICT.)
19	...	5	1	5	...	3	...	1	...	3	1	1	...	4	...	" Malkapur
21	...	8	...	8	...	6	...	2	...	2	...	...	...	1	...	" Mehkar
10	1	6	...	2	...	2	...	...	...	1	...	...	...	...	...	Taluk Yeotmal (WUN DISTRICT.)
7	...	5	...	6	1	2	...	...	...	...	...	...	...	1	...	" Darwha
4	...	1	...	1	...	2	...	...	...	...	...	1	...	1	...	" Kelapur
1	...	1	...	...	...	...	...	...	...	...	...	...	...	...	...	" Wun
10	...	...	1	4	1	...	...	2	...	1	...	...	...	1	...	Tatuk Basim (BASIM. DISTRICT.)
1	...	1	1	...	...	...	...	...	...	...	...	...	...	1	...	" Mangrul
4	...	2	...	...	...	1	1	2	...	...	...	1	...	1	...	" Pusad

TABLE VIII.—Civil Condition by Religion

(2) MAR

District and Taluk.	Total Married.			Age 0—4		5—9		10—14		15—19		20—24	
	Total.	Males.	Females.	Males.	Females.	Males.	Females.	Males.	Females.	Males.	Females.	Males.	Females.
1	2	3	4	5	6	7	8	9	10	11	12	13	14
District Amraoti	3,085	1,585	1,500	3	5	5	103	68	200	118	186	164	244
" Akola	1,888	995	893	1	3	3	63	42	129	74	125	128	133
" Ellichpur	701	368	333	2	2	2	19	18	41	25	41	37	48
" Buldana	2,085	1,018	1,067	...	4	5	67	45	146	88	132	104	183
" Wun	888	466	422	...	2	3	23	18	52	31	57	47	71
" Basim	1,655	831	824	1	3	6	85	54	118	63	110	95	88
Total	10,802	5,263	5,039	7	19	24	360	245	686	399	651	575	767
Amraoti District. — Taluk Amraoti	661	356	305	1	1	1	11	5	41	19	37	44	45
" Chandur	852	453	399	...	1	...	37	26	46	41	58	37	66
" Morsi	585	280	305	...	1	1	19	14	50	16	33	29	51
" Murtazapur	987	496	491	2	2	3	36	23	63	42	58	54	81
Akola District. — Taluk Akola	560	297	263	1	2	1	24	10	36	23	31	42	49
" Akot	336	171	165	...	...	2	13	8	26	15	19	21	24
" Balapur	447	213	234	...	1	...	13	9	29	17	36	26	24
" Jalgaon	87	60	27	...	...	...	...	...	6	2	6	8	4
" Khamgaon	458	254	204	...	...	...	13	15	32	17	33	31	32
Ellichpur District. — Taluk Ellichpur	419	223	196	2	2	1	7	7	26	16	20	20	27
" Daryapur	281	144	137	...	...	1	12	11	15	9	21	17	21
" Melghat	1	1	...	...	...	...	...	...	...	...	...	...	...
Buldana District. — Taluk Chikhli	720	349	371	...	1	1	23	12	47	31	45	42	64
" Malkapur	765	376	389	...	2	2	26	19	60	42	49	32	62
" Mehkar	600	293	307	...	1	2	18	14	39	15	38	30	57
Wun District. — Taluk Yeotmal	369	188	181	...	...	1	6	5	20	16	21	16	37
" Darwha	389	204	185	...	2	2	14	13	25	11	29	24	22
" Kelapur	105	58	47	...	...	...	3	...	7	3	6	6	8
" Wun	25	16	9	...	...	...	...	...	...	1	1	1	4
Basim District. — Taluk Basim	994	504	490	...	1	6	46	24	74	41	66	63	51
" Mangrul	179	97	82	...	1	...	10	6	5	10	11	7	8
" Pusad	482	230	252	1	1	...	29	24	39	12	33	25	29

and Age.—Part E—JAIN—*contd.*

RIED.																	
PERIOD.																	
25—29		30—34		35—39		40—44		45—49		50—54		55—59		60 and over.		DISTRICT AND TALUK.	
Males.	Females.	Males.	Females.	Males.	Females.	Males.	Females.	Males.	Females.	Males.	Females.	Males.	Females.	Males.	Females.		
15	16	17	18	19	20	21	22	23	24	25	26	27	28	29	30	31	
209	212	270	221	194	110	193	102	92	33	114	47	29	19	126	18	DISTRICT AMRAOTI.	
166	138	131	104	116	60	111	78	59	20	77	29	31	4	56	7	„ AKOLA.	
52	47	49	50	42	25	39	29	30	11	32	14	13	2	27	4	„ ELLICHPUR.	
146	140	146	113	90	95	120	83	84	42	81	30	28	12	81	20	„ BULDANA.	
61	66	72	60	55	26	56	44	35	6	43	12	13	2	32	1	„ WUN.	
128	135	112	97	85	64	84	74	51	24	66	14	19	4	67	8	„ BASIM.	
762	738	780	645	582	380	603	410	851	136	418	146	183	43	889	58	**Total.**	
43	45	55	51	43	22	48	27	30	8	24	5	11	10	32	2	Taluk Amraoti . .	AMRAOTI DISTRICT.
71	55	72	56	64	25	52	24	23	9	30	14	7	5	30	3	„ Chandur . .	
43	41	52	43	31	17	33	21	12	8	17	14	2	1	30	6	„ Morsi . .	
52	71	91	71	56	46	60	30	27	8	43	14	9	3	34	7	„ Murtazapur .	
51	46	43	26	39	13	25	23	16	4	19	6	8	1	19	2	Taluk Akola . .	AKOLA DISTRICT.
24	19	20	22	24	12	17	16	12	6	10	5	6	1	12	2	„ Akot . .	
24	46	22	33	19	17	33	19	16	6	26	8	7	1	14	1	„ Balapur . .	
20	6	12	2	5	1	4	2	3	...	3	...	2	...	1	...	„ Jalgaon . .	
47	21	34	21	29	17	32	18	12	4	19	10	8	1	10	2	„ Khamgaon .	
31	29	31	37	26	14	72	16	17	9	24	6	6	2	15	1	Taluk Ellichpur . .	ELLICHPUR DISTRICT.
21	18	18	13	15	11	12	13	13	2	8	8	7	...	12	3	„ Daryapur . .	
...	...	...	...	1	...	...	...	...	...	...	...	...	...	...	...	„ Melghat . .	
53	46	47	39	34	35	34	29	22	20	31	12	11	4	31	6	Taluk Chikhli . .	BULDANA DISTRICT.
46	47	51	42	32	38	50	27	32	14	28	11	13	4	29	7	„ Malkapur . .	
47	47	48	32	24	22	36	27	30	8	22	7	4	4	21	7	„ Mehkar . .	
26	31	30	28	26	12	21	15	12	3	15	6	5	2	15	...	Taluk Yeotmal . .	WUN DISTRICT.
23	27	29	24	20	12	26	22	15	2	21	6	5	...	15	...	„ Darwha . .	
8	7	10	6	7	2	8	6	6	1	5	...	3	...	2	1	„ Kelapur . .	
4	1	3	2	2	...	1	1	2	...	2	...	...	...	...	...	„ Wun . .	
78	82	65	59	55	37	50	41	30	13	39	10	8	4	45	6	Taluk Basim . .	BASIM DISTRICT.
15	13	9	15	9	7	12	10	5	2	12	...	4	...	8	...	„ Mangrul . .	
35	40	38	23	21	20	22	23	16	9	15	4	7	...	14	2	„ Pusad . .	

TABLE VIII.—Civil Condition by Religion

DISTRICT AND TALUK.	TOTAL WIDOWED.			(1) Wi									
				Age									
				0—4		5—9		10—14		15—19		20—24	
	Total.	Males.	Females.	Males.	Females.	Males.	Females.	Males.	Females.	Males.	Females.	Males.	Females.
1	2	3	4	5	6	7	8	9	10	11	12	13	14
District Amraoti	823	235	588	...	...	...	4	6	6	2	6	8	11
„ Akola	427	136	291	...	...	...	1	...	2	2	4	6	4
„ Ellichpur	185	48	137	...	1	...	...	1	1	...	3	2	7
„ Buldana	465	139	326	...	...	...	2	1	6	...	3	5	11
„ Wun	217	68	149	...	...	...	...	...	1	2	5	4	2
„ Basim	457	121	336	...	2	3	...	2	3	4	4	5	8
Total	2,574	747	1,827	...	3	8	7	10	19	10	25	80	53
Amraoti District. Taluk Amraoti	171	52	119	...	...	...	...	...	...	1	1	...	8
„ Chandur	259	90	169	...	...	...	...	2	4	...	3	3	5
„ Morsi	128	25	103	...	...	...	3	1	...	1	...	1	2
„ Murtazapur	265	68	197	...	...	...	1	3	2	...	2	4	6
Akola District. Taluk Akola	123	34	89	...	...	...	1	...	...	...	...	2	1
„ Akot	60	20	40	...	...	...	...	...	...	...	...	1	...
„ Balapur	139	44	95	...	...	...	...	...	1	2	4	1	1
„ Jalgaon	16	6	10	...	...	...	...	...	...	...	...	...	...
„ Khamgaon	89	32	57	...	...	...	...	...	1	...	...	2	2
Ellichpur District. Taluk Ellichpur	124	32	92	...	1	...	...	1	1	...	1	1	5
„ Daryapur	61	16	45	...	...	...	...	...	...	...	2	1	2
„ Melghat	...	...	...	...	...	...	...	...	...	...	...	...	...
Buldana District. Taluk Chikhli	156	43	113	...	...	...	1	...	2	...	...	1	3
„ Malkapur	159	48	111	...	...	...	...	...	3	...	...	1	5
„ Mehkar	150	48	102	...	...	...	1	1	1	...	3	3	3
Wun District. Taluk Yeotmal	67	20	47	...	...	...	...	...	...	2	2	1	...
„ Darwha	111	38	73	...	...	...	...	...	1	...	2	3	1
„ Kelapur	35	10	25	...	...	...	...	...	...	...	1	...	1
„ Wun	4	...	4	...	...	...	...	...	...	...	...	...	...
Basim District. Taluk Basim	279	71	208	...	...	...	...	...	2	3	3	2	5
„ Mangrul	52	14	38	...	1	2	...	1	1	1	...	...	...
„ Pusad	126	36	90	...	1	1	...	1	...	...	1	3	3

and Age.—Part E—JAIN—*concld.*

DOWED. PERIOD. 25–29		30–34		35–39		40–44		45–49		50–54		55–59		60 and over.		DISTRICT AND TALUK.	
Males.	Females.	Males.	Females.	Males.	Females.	Males.	Females.	Males.	Females.	Males.	Females.	Males.	Females.	Males.	Females.		
15	16	17	18	19	20	21	22	23	24	25	26	27	28	29	30	31	
15	19	13	45	19	42	27	81	25	44	37	109	18	30	65	181	District Amraoti.	
11	16	10	18	16	10	15	36	10	29	25	53	10	19	31	99	" Akola.	
6	9	4	6	2	5	5	23	5	5	5	27	3	11	15	39	" Ellichpur.	
9	16	18	21	11	27	18	49	14	19	14	53	10	21	39	98	" Buldana.	
2	4	7	16	6	12	11	18	3	9	9	23	5	11	19	48	" Wun.	
7	22	7	22	10	24	12	47	8	25	18	48	7	23	38	108	" Basim.	
50	86	59	128	64	120	88	254	65	13	108	313	58	115	207	573	**Total.**	
4	4	4	7	...	12	7	16	5	13	9	19	6	3	16	36	Taluk Amraoti .	Amraoti District.
5	3	5	18	9	8	12	24	8	12	17	28	4	9	25	55	" Chandur .	
2	4	1	10	4	4	4	15	4	8	2	19	1	7	4	31	" Morsi . .	
4	8	3	10	6	18	4	26	8	11	9	43	7	11	20	59	" Murtazapur .	
2	4	1	5	4	1	2	13	3	8	5	15	2	4	13	37	Taluk Akola . .	Akola District.
2	2	4	2	2	...	3	3	2	3	2	9	1	7	3	14	" Akot . .	
4	7	2	9	5	5	5	10	3	7	9	20	4	6	9	25	" Balapur .	
...	1	2	1	1	...	..	1	1	3	2	1	...	...	...	3	" Jalgaon .	
3	2	1	1	4	4	5	9	1	8	7	8	3	2	6	20	" Khamgaon .	
3	6	4	4	2	2	3	16	2	3	3	19	3	9	10	25	Taluk Ellichpur .	Ellichpur District.
3	3	...	2	...	3	2	7	3	2	2	8	...	2	5	14	" Daryapur .	
...	...	...	...	...	...	...	...	...	...	...	...	...	...	...	...	" Melghat .	
1	5	3	10	5	11	7	11	4	7	6	23	3	6	13	34	Taluk Chikhli .	Buldana District.
3	7	6	3	4	10	4	15	3	6	3	13	4	13	20	36	" Malkapur .	
5	4	9	8	2	6	7	23	7	6	5	17	3	2	6	28	" Mehkar .	
1	...	3	4	...	4	1	11	...	2	2	9	2	1	8	14	Taluk Yeotmal .	Wun District.
1	3	3	7	5	3	9	7	2	4	5	9	1	10	9	26	" Darwha .	
...	1	1	5	1	4	1	...	1	3	2	5	2	...	2	5	" Kelapur .	
...	...	...	...	...	1	...	...	...	...	...	...	...	...	...	3	" Wun . .	
7	13	5	14	7	21	8	28	6	15	11	28	5	15	17	64	Taluk Basim . .	Basim District.
...	5	1	3	...	1	1	7	1	1	3	5	1	2	3	12	" Mangrul .	
...	4	1	5	3	2	3	12	1	9	4	15	1	6	18	32	" Pusad . .	

TABLE VIII.

Civil Condition by Religion and Age.—
Part F—SIKH.

TABLE VIII.—Civil Condition by Religion

DISTRICT AND TALUK.	(1) UNMAR[RIED] Total Unmarried.			Age 0—4		5—9		10—14		15—19		20—24	
	Total.	Males.	Females.	Males.	Females.	Males.	Females.	Males.	Females.	Males.	Females.	Males.	Females.
1	2	3	4	5	6	7	8	9	10	11	12	13	14
District Amraoti	9	6	3	2	1	1	2	2	...	1	...	...	...
" Akola	22	17	5	2	1	2	3	4	1	1	...	2	...
" Ellichpur	1	1	...	...	...	...	...	...	...	...	...	...	...
" Buldana	11	5	6	...	...	2	4	2	2	1	...	...	...
" Wun	19	14	5	4	1	4	3	3	...	1	1	...	...
" Basim	5	4	1	1	1	1	...	1	...	...	...	1	...
Total	67	47	20	9	4	10	12	12	3	4	1	8	...
Amraoti District. Taluk Amraoti	...	...	...	...	...	...	...	...	...	...	...	...	...
" Chandur	9	6	3	2	1	1	2	2	...	1	...	...	...
" Morsi	...	...	...	...	...	...	...	...	...	...	...	...	...
" Murtazapur	...	...	...	...	...	...	...	...	...	...	...	...	...
Akola District. Taluk Akola	15	10	5	1	1	2	3	1	1	...	...	1	...
" Akot	4	4	...	...	...	...	...	2	...	1	...	1	...
" Balapur	...	...	...	...	...	...	...	...	...	...	...	...	...
" Jalgaon	1	1	...	...	...	...	...	...	...	...	...	...	...
" Khamgaon	2	2	...	1	...	...	...	1	...	...	...	...	...
Ellichpur District. Taluk Ellichpur	...	...	...	...	...	...	...	...	...	...	...	...	...
" Daryapur	1	1	...	...	...	...	...	...	...	...	...	...	...
" Melghat	...	...	...	...	...	...	...	...	...	...	...	...	...
Buldana District. Taluk Chikhli	...	...	...	...	...	...	...	...	...	...	...	...	...
" Malkapur	...	...	...	...	...	...	...	...	...	...	...	...	...
" Mehkar	11	5	6	...	...	2	4	2	2	1	...	...	...
Wun District. Taluk Yeotmal	1	1	...	...	...	...	...	...	...	...	...	...	...
" Darwha	...	...	...	...	...	...	...	...	...	...	...	...	...
" Kelapur	18	13	5	4	1	4	3	3	...	1	1	...	...
" Wun	...	...	...	...	...	...	...	...	...	...	...	...	...
Basim District. Taluk Basim	...	...	...	...	...	...	...	...	...	...	...	...	...
" Mangrul	...	...	...	...	...	...	...	...	...	...	...	...	...
" Pusad	5	4	1	1	1	1	...	1	...	...	...	1	...

and Age.—Part F—SIKH.

RIED.																
PERIOD.																
25—29		30—34		35—39		40—44		45—49		50—54		55—59		60 AND OVER.		DISTRICT AND TALUK.
Males.	Females.	Males.	Females.	Males.	Females.	Males.	Females.	Males.	Females.	Males.	Females.	Males.	Females.	Males.	Females.	
15	16	17	18	19	20	21	22	23	24	25	26	27	28	29	30	31
...	...	...	...	...	...	...	...	...	...	...	...	...	...	...	...	DISTRICT AMRAOTI.
3	...	1	...	...	...	1	...	...	...	1	...	...	...	...	...	" AKOLA.
...	...	...	...	...	...	...	...	...	...	...	...	...	...	1	...	" ELLICHPUR.
...	...	...	...	...	...	...	...	...	...	...	...	...	...	...	...	" BULDANA.
1	...	...	...	...	...	...	...	1	...	...	...	...	...	...	...	" WUN.
...	...	...	...	...	...	...	...	...	...	...	...	...	...	...	...	" BASIM.
4	...	1	...	...	...	1	...	1	...	1	...	...	...	1	...	**Total.**
...	...	...	...	...	...	...	...	...	...	...	...	...	...	...	...	Taluk Amraoti (AMRAOTI DISTRICT.)
...	...	...	...	...	...	...	...	...	...	...	...	...	...	...	...	" Chandur
...	...	...	...	...	...	...	...	...	...	...	...	...	...	...	...	" Morsi
...	...	...	...	...	...	...	...	...	...	...	...	...	...	...	...	" Murtazapur
2	...	1	...	...	...	1	...	...	...	1	...	...	...	...	...	Taluk Akola (AKOLA DISTRICT.)
...	...	...	...	...	...	...	...	...	...	...	...	...	...	...	...	" Akot
...	...	...	...	...	...	...	...	...	...	...	...	...	...	...	...	" Balapur
1	...	...	...	...	...	...	...	...	...	...	...	...	...	...	...	" Jalgaon
...	...	...	...	...	...	...	...	...	...	...	...	...	...	...	...	" Khamgaon
...	...	...	...	...	...	...	...	...	...	...	...	...	...	...	...	Taluk Ellichpur (ELLICHPUR DISTRICT.)
...	...	...	...	...	...	...	...	...	...	...	...	...	...	1	...	" Daryapur
...	...	...	...	...	...	...	...	...	...	...	...	...	...	...	...	" Melghat
...	...	...	...	...	...	...	...	...	...	...	...	...	...	...	...	Taluk Chikhli (BULDANA DISTRICT.)
...	...	...	...	...	...	...	...	...	...	...	...	...	...	...	...	" Malkapur
...	...	...	...	...	...	...	...	...	...	...	...	...	...	...	...	" Mehkar
...	...	...	...	...	...	...	...	1	...	...	...	...	...	...	...	Taluk Yeotmal (WUN DISTRICT.)
...	...	...	...	...	...	...	...	...	...	...	...	...	...	...	...	" Darwha
1	...	...	...	...	...	...	...	...	...	...	...	...	...	...	...	" Kelapur
...	...	...	...	...	...	...	...	...	...	...	...	...	...	...	...	" Wun
...	...	...	...	...	...	...	...	...	...	...	...	...	...	...	...	Taluk Basim (BASIM DISTRICT.)
...	...	...	...	...	...	...	...	...	...	...	...	...	...	...	...	" Mangrul
...	...	...	...	...	...	...	...	...	...	...	...	...	...	...	...	" Pusad

TABLE VIII.—Civil Condition by Religion

DISTRICT AND TALUK.	(2) MAR												
	TOTAL MARRIED.			AGE									
				0—4		5—9		10—14		15—19		20—24	
	TOTAL.	Males.	Females.	Males.	Females.	Males.	Females.	Males.	Females.	Males.	Females.	Males.	Females.
1	2	3	4	5	6	7	8	9	10	11	12	13	14
DISTRICT AMRAOTI	14	6	8	...	1	...	1	...	2	1	...	...	...
" AKOLA	36	21	15	...	...	...	...	...	...	...	...	...	3
" ELLICHPUR	...	...	...	...	...	...	...	...	...	...	...	...	...
" BULDANA	15	7	8	...	...	...	...	1	1	...	...	1	2
" WUN	17	8	9	...	...	...	...	...	...	...	2	...	1
" BASIM	6	3	3	...	...	...	...	...	1	...	...	1	...
Total	88	45	43	...	1	...	1	1	4	1	2	2	6
AMRAOTI DISTRICT — Taluk Amraoti	2	1	1	...	...	...	...	...	...	...	...	...	...
" Chandur	5	3	2	...	...	...	...	...	...	...	...	...	...
" Morsi	...	...	...	...	...	...	...	...	...	...	...	...	...
" Murtazapur	7	2	5	...	1	...	1	...	2	1	...	...	...
AKOLA DISTRICT — Taluk Akola	29	17	12	...	...	...	...	...	...	...	...	...	2
" Akot	2	2	...	...	...	...	...	...	...	...	...	...	...
" Balapur	...	...	...	...	...	...	...	...	...	...	...	...	...
" Jalgaon	...	...	...	...	...	...	...	...	...	...	...	...	...
" Khamgaon	5	2	3	...	...	...	...	...	...	...	...	...	1
ELLICHPUR DISTRICT — Taluk Ellichpur	...	...	...	...	...	...	...	...	...	...	...	...	...
" Daryapur	...	...	...	...	...	...	...	...	...	...	...	...	...
" Melghat	...	...	...	...	...	...	...	...	...	...	...	...	...
BULDANA DISTRICT — Taluk Chikhli	...	...	...	...	...	...	...	...	...	...	...	...	...
" Malkapur	...	...	...	...	...	...	...	...	...	...	...	...	...
" Mehkar	15	7	8	...	...	...	...	1	1	...	...	1	2
WUN DISTRICT — Taluk Yeotmal	...	...	...	...	...	...	...	...	...	...	...	...	...
" Darwha	...	...	...	...	...	...	...	...	...	...	...	...	...
" Kelapur	17	8	9	...	...	...	...	...	...	...	2	...	1
" Wun	...	...	...	...	...	...	...	...	...	...	...	...	...
BASIM DISTRICT — Taluk Basim	...	...	...	...	...	...	...	...	...	...	...	...	...
" Mangrul	...	...	...	...	...	...	...	...	...	...	...	...	...
" Pusad	6	3	3	...	...	...	...	...	1	...	...	1	...

and Age.—Part F—SIKH.

RIED. PERIOD. 25—29 Males.	25—29 Females.	30—34 Males.	30—34 Females.	35—39 Males.	35—39 Females.	40—44 Males.	40—44 Females.	45—49 Males.	45—49 Females.	50—54 Males.	50—54 Females.	55—59 Males.	55—59 Females.	60 AND OVER. Males.	60 AND OVER. Females.	DISTRICT AND TALUK.
15	16	17	18	19	20	21	22	23	24	25	26	27	28	29	30	31
1	...	...	1	...	1	1	1	...	...	1	...	...	...	2	1	DISTRICT AMRAOTI.
3	4	5	1	4	2	2	...	1	3	2	2	2	...	2	...	„ AKOLA.
...	...	...	...	...	...	...	...	...	...	...	...	...	...	...	...	„ ELLICHPUR.
2	...	...	...	...	2	1	1	1	2	...	...	...	...	1	...	„ BULDANA.
2	3	1	3	1	...	1	...	3	...	...	...	...	...	...	...	„ WUN.
...	...	...	...	...	2	...	...	...	...	1	...	...	...	1	...	„ BASIM.
8	7	6	5	5	7	5	2	5	5	4	2	2	...	6	1	Total.
...	...	...	...	...	...	...	...	...	...	...	...	...	...	1	1	Taluk Amraoti . . } AMRAOTI DISTRICT.
1	...	...	1	...	...	...	1	...	...	1	...	...	...	1	...	„ Chandur . .
...	...	...	...	...	...	...	...	...	...	...	...	...	...	...	...	„ Morsi . .
...	...	...	...	...	1	1	...	...	...	...	...	...	...	...	...	„ Murtazapur .
2	4	5	1	4	2	1	...	1	2	1	1	1	...	2	...	Taluk Akola . . } AKOLA DISTRICT.
1	...	...	...	...	...	1	...	...	...	...	...	...	...	...	...	„ Akot . .
...	...	...	...	...	...	...	...	...	...	...	...	...	...	...	...	„ Balapur . .
...	...	...	...	...	...	...	...	...	...	...	...	...	...	...	...	„ Jalgaon . .
...	...	...	...	...	...	...	...	...	1	1	1	1	...	...	...	„ Khamgaon .
...	...	...	...	...	...	...	...	...	...	...	...	...	...	...	...	Taluk Ellichpur . . } ELLICHPUR DISTRICT.
...	...	...	...	...	...	...	...	...	...	...	...	...	...	...	...	„ Daryapur . .
...	...	...	...	...	...	...	...	...	...	...	...	...	..	...	...	„ Melghat . .
...	...	...	...	...	...	...	...	...	...	...	...	...	...	...	...	Taluk Chikhli . . } BULDANA DISTRICT.
...	...	...	...	...	...	...	...	...	...	...	...	...	...	...	...	„ Malkapur . .
2	...	...	...	..	2	1	1	1	2	...	...	...	...	1	...	„ Mehkar . .
...	...	...	..	...	...	...	...	...	...	...	...	...	...	...	...	Taluk Yeotmal . . } WUN DISTRICT.
...	...	...	...	...	...	...	...	...	...	...	...	...	...	...	...	„ Darwha . .
2	3	1	3	1	...	1	...	3	...	...	...	...	...	...	...	„ Kelapur . .
...	...	...	...	...	...	...	...	...	...	...	...	...	...	...	...	„ Wun . .
...	...	...	...	...	...	...	...	...	...	...	...	...	...	...	...	Taluk Basim . . } BASIM DISTRICT.
...	...	...	...	...	...	...	...	...	...	...	...	...	...	...	...	„ Mangrul . .
...	...	...	...	...	2	...	...	...	...	1	...	...	...	1	...	„ Pusad . .

TABLE VIII.—Civil Condition by Religion

DISTRICT AND TALUK.	(3) Wi...													
	TOTAL WIDOWED.			Age...										
				0—4		5—9		10—14		15—19		20—24		
	Total.	Males.	Females.	Males.	Females.	Males.	Females.	Males.	Females.	Males.	Females.	Males.	Females.	
1	2	3	4	5	6	7	8	9	10	11	12	13	14	
District Amraoti	6	1	5	...	...	...	...	...	1	...	...	...	...	
" Akola	9	3	6	...	...	...	...	...	...	...	...	1	...	
" Ellichpur	...	...	...	...	...	...	...	...	...	...	...	...	...	
" Buldana	4	1	3	...	...	...	...	...	...	...	...	...	1	
" Wun	2	1	1	...	...	...	...	...	...	...	...	...	...	
" Basim	1	...	1	...	...	...	...	...	...	...	...	...	...	
Total	22	6	16	...	...	...	...	...	1	...	...	1	1	
Amraoti District — Taluk Amraoti	...	...	...	...	...	...	...	...	...	...	...	...	...	
" Chandur	4	1	3	...	...	...	...	...	1	...	...	...	...	
" Morsi	...	...	...	...	...	...	...	...	...	...	...	...	...	
" Murtazapur	2	..	2	...	...	...	...	...	...	...	...	...	...	
Akola District — Taluk Akola	5	2	3	...	...	...	...	...	...	...	...	...	...	
" Akot	1	...	1	...	...	...	...	...	...	...	...	...	...	
" Balapur	...	...	...	...	...	...	...	...	...	...	...	...	...	
" Jalgaon	3	1	2	...	...	...	...	...	...	...	...	1	...	
" Khamgaon	...	...	...	...	...	...	...	...	...	...	...	...	...	
Ellichpur District — Taluk Ellichpur	...	...	...	...	...	...	...	...	...	...	...	...	...	
" Daryapur	...	...	...	...	...	...	...	...	...	...	...	...	...	
" Melghat	...	...	...	...	...	...	...	...	...	...	...	...	...	
Buldana District — Taluk Chikhli	1	...	1	...	...	...	...	...	...	...	...	...	1	
" Malkapur	...	...	...	...	...	...	...	...	...	...	...	...	...	
" Mehkar	3	1	2	...	...	...	...	...	...	...	...	...	...	
Wun District — Taluk Yeotmal	...	...	...	...	...	...	...	...	...	...	...	...	...	
" Darwha	1	1	...	...	...	...	...	...	...	...	...	...	...	
" Kelapur	1	...	1	...	...	...	...	...	...	...	...	...	...	
" Wun	...	...	...	...	...	...	...	...	...	...	...	...	...	
Basim District — Taluk Basim	...	...	...	...	...	...	...	...	...	...	...	...	...	
" Mangrul	...	...	...	...	...	...	...	...	...	...	...	...	...	
" Pusad	1	...	1	...	...	...	...	...	...	...	...	...	...	

and Age.—Part F—SIKH.

DOWED																
PERIOD.																
25—29		30—34		35—39		40—44		45—49		50—54		55—59		60 AND OVER.		DISTRICT AND TALUK.
Males.	Females.	Males.	Females.	Males.	Females.	Males.	Females.	Males.	Females.	Males.	Females.	Males.	Females.	Males.	Females.	
15	16	17	18	19	20	21	22	23	24	25	26	27	28	29	30	31
...	...	...	1	...	...	...	...	...	...	...	2	1	...	...	1	DISTRICT AMRAOTI.
...	1	...	...	...	1	...	...	...	...	1	2	1	...	...	2	„ AKOLA.
...	...	...	...	...	...	...	...	...	...	...	...	...	...	...	...	„ ELLICHPUR.
...	...	...	1	...	...	...	...	...	...	...	1	...	...	1	...	„ BULDANA.
...	...	...	...	...	...	...	1	1	...	...	...	...	...	...	...	„ WUN.
...	...	...	...	...	...	...	...	...	...	...	1	...	...	...	...	„ BASIM.
...	1	...	2	...	1	...	1	1	...	1	6	2	...	1	3	**Total.**
...	...	...	...	...	...	...	...	...	...	...	...	...	...	...	...	Taluk Amraoti (AMRAOTI DISTRICT.)
...	...	...	...	...	...	...	...	...	...	...	1	1	...	...	1	„ Chandur (AMRAOTI DISTRICT.)
...	...	...	...	...	...	...	...	...	...	...	...	...	...	...	...	„ Morsi (AMRAOTI DISTRICT.)
...	...	...	1	...	...	...	...	...	...	...	1	...	...	...	...	„ Murtazapur (AMRAOTI DISTRICT.)
...	1	...	...	...	1	...	...	...	...	1	...	1	...	...	1	Taluk Akola (AKOLA DISTRICT.)
...	...	...	...	...	...	...	...	...	...	...	1	...	...	...	...	„ Akot (AKOLA DISTRICT.)
...	...	...	...	...	...	...	...	...	...	...	...	...	...	...	...	„ Balapur (AKOLA DISTRICT.)
...	...	...	...	...	...	...	...	...	...	...	1	...	...	...	1	„ Jalgaon (AKOLA DISTRICT.)
...	...	...	...	...	...	...	...	...	...	...	...	...	...	...	...	„ Khamgaon (AKOLA DISTRICT.)
...	...	...	...	...	...	...	...	...	...	...	...	...	...	...	...	Taluk Ellichpur (ELLICHPUR DISTRICT.)
...	...	...	...	...	...	...	...	...	...	...	...	...	...	...	...	„ Daryapur (ELLICHPUR DISTRICT.)
...	...	...	...	...	...	...	...	...	...	...	...	...	...	...	...	„ Melghat (ELLICHPUR DISTRICT.)
...	...	...	...	...	...	...	...	...	...	...	...	...	...	...	...	Taluk Chikhli (BULDANA DISTRICT.)
...	...	...	...	...	...	...	...	...	...	...	...	...	...	...	...	„ Malkapur (BULDANA DISTRICT.)
...	...	...	1	...	...	...	...	...	...	...	1	...	...	1	...	„ Mehkar (BULDANA DISTRICT.)
...	...	...	...	...	...	...	...	...	...	...	...	...	...	...	...	Taluk Yeotmal (WUN DISTRICT.)
...	...	...	...	...	...	...	...	1	...	...	...	...	...	...	...	„ Darwha (WUN DISTRICT.)
...	...	...	...	...	...	...	1	...	...	...	...	...	...	...	...	„ Kelapur (WUN DISTRICT.)
...	...	...	...	...	...	...	...	...	...	...	...	...	...	...	...	„ Wun (WUN DISTRICT.)
...	...	...	...	...	...	...	...	...	...	...	...	...	...	...	...	Taluk Basim (BASIM DISTRICT.)
...	...	...	...	...	...	...	...	...	...	...	...	...	...	...	...	„ Mangrul (BASIM DISTRICT.)
...	...	...	...	...	...	...	...	...	...	...	1	...	...	...	...	„ Pusad (BASIM DISTRICT.)

TABLE VIII.

Civil Condition by Religion and Age.—
Part G—CHRISTIAN.

TABLE VIII.—Civil Condition by Religion and Age.—

DISTRICT AND TALUK.	(1) UNMAR[RIED]												
	TOTAL UNMARRIED.			AGE									
				0—4		5—9		10—14		15—19		20—24	
	Total.	Males.	Females.	Males.	Females.	Males.	Females.	Males.	Females.	Males.	Females.	Males.	Females.
1	2	3	4	5	6	7	8	9	10	11	12	13	14
DISTRICT AMRAOTI	330	167	163	37	46	30	40	16	30	22	20	27	8
,, AKOLA	168	111	57	18	14	15	16	18	9	17	8	14	9
,, ELLICHPUR	65	40	25	13	8	6	5	4	5	4	3	3	3
,, BULDANA	55	32	23	8	10	7	8	3	3	1	1	3	...
,, WUN	51	28	23	5	6	4	4	5	3	1	5	4	3
,, BASIM	46	24	22	10	8	5	9	...	3	...	2	2	...
Railway Passengers, etc.	12	6	6	2	2	...	1	1	3	1	...	2	...
Total	727	408	319	93	94	67	83	47	56	6	39	55	23
AMRAOTI DISTRICT. Taluk Amraoti	311	150	161	34	46	27	39	16	30	21	20	24	8
,, Chandur	6	5	1	...	...	...	1	...	...	1	...	3	...
,, Morsi	2	2	...	1	...	1	...	...	...	...	...	...	...
,, Murtazapur	11	10	1	2	...	2	...	...	...	...	...	...	...
AKOLA DISTRICT. Taluk Akola	108	67	41	11	12	9	11	16	7	11	6	5	4
,, Akot	2	2	...	...	...	...	...	...	...	1	...	1	...
,, Balapur	6	4	2	1	...	...	1	2	...	...	1	1	...
,, Jalgaon	1	1	...	...	...	...	...	...	...	...	...	...	...
,, Khamgaon	51	37	14	6	2	6	4	...	2	5	1	7	5
ELLICHPUR DISTRICT. Taluk Ellichpur	60	36	24	13	8	5	5	2	4	4	3	3	3
,, Daryapur	...	...	...	...	...	...	...	...	...	...	...	...	...
,, Melghat	5	4	1	...	...	1	...	2	1	...	...	...	...
BULDANA DISTRICT. Taluk Chikhli	43	27	16	8	6	4	6	3	2	1	1	2	...
,, Malkapur	11	5	6	...	3	3	2	...	1	...	...	1	...
,, Mehkar	1	...	1	...	1	...	...	...	...	...	...	...	...
WUN DISTRICT. Taluk Yeotmal	51	28	23	5	6	4	4	5	3	1	5	4	3
,, Darwha	...	...	...	...	...	...	...	...	...	...	...	...	...
,, Kelapur	...	...	...	...	...	...	...	...	...	...	...	...	...
,, Wun	...	...	...	...	...	...	...	...	...	...	...	...	...
BASIM DISTRICT. Taluk Basim	45	23	22	10	8	5	9	...	3	...	2	2	...
,, Mangrul	1	1	...	...	...	...	...	...	...	...	...	...	...
,, Pusad	...	...	...	...	...	...	...	...	...	...	...	...	...

Part G—CHRISTIAN.

RIED.																
PERIOD.																
25—29		30—34		35—39		40—44		45—49		50—54		55—59		60 AND OVER.		DISTRICT AND TALUK.
Males.	Females.	Males.	Females.	Males.	Females.	Males.	Females.	Males.	Females.	Males.	Females.	Males.	Females.	Males.	Females.	
15	16	17	18	19	20	21	22	23	24	25	26	27	28	29	30	31
9	9	8	5	6	5	5	...	8	...	1	...	2	...	1	...	DISTRICT AMRAOTI.
13	...	8	...	1	1	5	...	2	...	...	...	...	...	...	...	„ AKOLA.
5	1	3	...	1	...	1	...	...	...	...	...	...	...	...	...	„ ELLICHPUR.
4	...	3	1	...	...	2	...	...	...	...	...	...	...	1	...	„ BULDANA.
4	1	3	1	...	...	2	...	...	...	...	...	...	...	...	...	„ WUN.
2	...	1	...	3	...	...	...	1	...	...	...	...	...	...	...	„ BASIM.
...	...	...	...	...	...	...	...	...	...	...	...	...	...	...	...	Railway Passengers, etc.
37	11	26	7	11	6	15	...	6	...	1	...	2	...	2	...	**Total.**
7	8	7	5	5	5	3	...	3	...	...	...	2	...	1	...	Taluk Amraoti . (AMRAOTI DISTRICT.)
1	...	...	...	...	...	...	...	...	...	...	...	...	...	...	...	„ Chandur . (AMRAOTI DISTRICT.)
...	...	...	...	...	...	...	...	...	...	...	...	...	...	...	...	„ Morsi . (AMRAOTI DISTRICT.)
1	1	1	...	1	...	2	...	...	...	1	...	...	...	...	...	„ Murtazapur . (AMRAOTI DISTRICT.)
8	...	3	...	...	1	3	...	1	...	...	...	...	...	...	...	Taluk Akola . (AKOLA DISTRICT.)
...	...	...	...	...	...	...	...	...	...	...	...	...	...	...	...	„ Akot . (AKOLA DISTRICT.)
...	...	...	...	...	...	...	...	...	...	...	...	...	...	...	...	„ Balapur . (AKOLA DISTRICT.)
...	...	...	...	...	...	1	...	...	...	...	...	...	...	...	...	„ Jalgaon . (AKOLA DISTRICT.)
5	...	5	...	1	...	1	...	1	...	...	...	...	...	...	...	„ Khamgaon . (AKOLA DISTRICT.)
5	1	3	...	...	...	1	...	...	...	...	...	...	...	...	...	Taluk Ellichpur . (ELLICHPUR DISTRICT.)
...	...	...	...	...	...	...	...	...	...	...	...	...	...	...	...	„ Daryapur . (ELLICHPUR DISTRICT.)
...	...	...	...	1	...	...	...	...	...	...	...	...	...	...	...	„ Melghat . (ELLICHPUR DISTRICT.)
3	...	3	1	...	...	2	...	...	...	...	...	...	...	1	...	Taluk Chikhli . (BULDANA DISTRICT.)
1	...	...	...	...	...	...	...	...	...	...	...	...	...	...	...	„ Malkapur . (BULDANA DISTRICT.)
...	...	...	...	...	...	...	...	...	...	...	...	...	...	...	...	„ Mehkar . (BULDANA DISTRICT.)
4	1	3	1	...	...	2	...	...	...	...	...	...	...	...	...	Taluk Yeotmal . (WUN DISTRICT.)
...	...	...	...	...	...	...	...	...	...	...	...	...	...	...	...	„ Darwha . (WUN DISTRICT.)
...	...	...	...	...	...	...	...	...	...	...	...	...	...	...	...	„ Kelapur . (WUN DISTRICT.)
...	...	...	...	...	...	...	...	...	...	...	...	...	...	...	...	„ Wun . (WUN DISTRICT.)
2	...	...	...	3	...	...	...	1	...	...	...	...	...	...	...	Taluk Basim . (BASIM DISTRICT.)
...	...	1	...	...	...	...	...	...	...	...	...	...	...	...	...	„ Mangrul . (BASIM DISTRICT.)
...	...	...	...	...	...	...	...	...	...	...	...	...	...	...	...	„ Pusad . (BASIM DISTRICT.)

TABLE VIII.—Civil Condition by Religion and Age—

DISTRICT AND TALUK.	TOTAL MARRIED.			(2) MAR AGE 0—4		5—9		10—14		15—19		20—24	
	TOTAL.	Males.	Females.	Males.	Females.	Males.	Females.	Males.	Females.	Males.	Females.	Males.	Females.
1	2	3	4	5	6	7	8	9	10	11	12	13	14
DISTRICT AMRAOTI	259	139	120	...	..	1	...	1	3	1	11	5	24
" AKOLA	120	67	53	...	...	...	...	...	...	1	6	7	14
" ELLICHPUR	50	27	23	...	...	...	...	...	...		1	...	1
" BULDANA	42	25	17	...	...	...	...	...	...	...	...	2	4
" WUN	33	18	15	...	...	...	...	...	...	...	1	...	2
" BASIM	36	21	15	...	...	...	...	...	...	...	5	3	2
Railway Passengers, etc.	10	7	3	...	...	...	...	...	...	...	...	...	...
Total	550	804	246	...	...	1	...	1	3	2	24	17	47
AMRAOTI DISTRICT — Taluk Amraoti	241	126	115	...	...	1	...	1	3	1	10	4	24
" Chandur	9	8	1	...	...	...	...	...	...	...	...	1	...
" Morsi	3	2	1	...	...	...	...	...	...	...	...	...	...
" Murtazapur	6	3	3	...	...	...	...	...	...	...	1	...	...
AKOLA DISTRICT — Taluk Akola	74	36	38	...	...	..	...	...	...	1	6	4	10
" Akot	3	2	1	...	..	...	...	...	...	...	...	...	...
" Balapur	2	1	1	...	...	...	...	...			...	...	...
" Jalgaon	1	1	...	...	...	...	...	...	...	...	...	...	...
" Khamgaon	40	27	13	...	...	...	...	...	...	...	...	3	4
ELLICHPUR DISTRICT — Taluk Ellichpur	43	24	19	...	..	...	...	...	...	...	1	...	1
" Daryapur	1	...	1	.	...	...	...	...	...	...	...	...	...
" Melghat	6	3	3	...	..	...	...	...	...	...	...	...	...
BULDANA DISTRICT — Taluk Chikhli	29	17	12	...	. .	...	...	...	...	...	...	1	3
" Malkapur	9	6	3	...	...	...	...	...	...	...	...	1	...
" Mehkar	4	2	2	...	...	...	...	...	...	...	...	...	1
WUN DISTRICT — Taluk Yeotmal	33	18	15	...	...	...	...	...	...	...	1	...	2
" Darwha	...	...	...	...	...	...	...	...	...	...	...	...	...
" Kelapur	...	...	...	...	...	...	...	...	...	...	...	...	...
" Wun	...	...	...	...	...	...	...	...	...	...	...	...	...
BASIM DISTRICT — Taluk Basim	34	20	14	...	...	...	...	...	...	...	5	3	2
" Mangrul	...	...	...	...	...	...	...	...	...	...	...	...	...
" Pusad	2	1	1	...	...	...	...	...	...	...	...	...	...

Part G—CHRISTIAN.

RIED.																
PERIOD.																
25—29		30—34		35—39		40—44		45—49		50—54		55—59		60 AND OVER.		DISTRICT AND TALUK.
Males.	Females.	Males.	Females.	Males.	Females.	Males.	Females.	Males.	Females.	Males.	Females.	Males.	Females.	Males.	Females.	
15	16	17	18	19	20	21	22	23	24	25	26	27	28	29	30	31
17	25	20	19	25	14	22	8	24	6	8	8	4	..	11	2	DISTRICT AMRAOTI.
4	9	17	9	11	3	6	6	6	3	6	1	3	...	6	2	" AKOLA.
3	8	5	7	4	4	7	1	1	...	5	1	...	...	2	...	" ELLICHPUR.
2	3	4	5	5	3	4	2	3	...	3	..	1	...	1	...	" BULDANA.
2	1	1	3	5	3	4	3	3	1	1	1	...	...	2	...	" WUN.
5	2	5	3	2	1	2	2	1	...	3	...	...	...	...	...	" BASIM.
1	1	2	1	2	...	...	1	...	...	1	...	1	...	...	...	Railway Passengers, etc.
4	49	54	47	54	28	5	23	38	10	27	11	9	...	22	4	**Total.**
15	23	18	19	23	14	21	7	21	5	8	8	4	...	9	2	Taluk Amraoti . . } AMRAOTI DISTRICT.
1	1	1	...	1	...	1	...	3	...	...	...	...	...	...	...	" Chandur . . } AMRAOTI DISTRICT.
1	1	...	...	1	...	...	...	...	...	...	...	...	...	...	...	" Morsi . . } AMRAOTI DISTRICT.
...	...	1	...	...	...	...	1	...	1	...	...	...	...	2	...	" Murtazapur . } AMRAOTI DISTRICT.
3	7	7	6	8	3	2	4	5	1	3	...	2	...	1	1	Taluk Akola . . } AKOLA DISTRICT.
...	..	2	1	...	...	...	...	...	...	...	...	...	...	...	...	" Akot . . } AKOLA DISTRICT.
...	1	...	...	...	...	1	...	...	...	...	...	...	...	...	...	" Balapur . . } AKOLA DISTRICT.
...	...	...	...	1	...	..	...	...	...	...	...	...	...	...	...	" Jalgaon . . } AKOLA DISTRICT.
1	1	8	2	2	...	3	2	1	2	3	1	1	...	5	1	" Khamgaon . } AKOLA DISTRICT.
2	7	5	6	3	2	6	1	1	...	5	1	...	...	2	...	Taluk Ellichpur . } ELLICHPUR DISTRICT.
...	...	...	1	...	...	..	...	...	...	...	...	...	...	...	...	" Daryapur . } ELLICHPUR DISTRICT.
1	1	...	...	1	2	1	...	...	...	...	...	...	...	...	...	" Melghat . . } ELLICHPUR DISTRICT.
...	2	2	3	4	3	4	1	3	...	1	...	1	...	1	...	Taluk Chikhli . . } BULDANA DISTRICT.
2	1	1	2	1	...	...	...	...	...	1	...	...	..	.	...	" Malkapur . } BULDANA DISTRICT.
...	...	1	...	...	...	...	1	...	...	1	...	...	...	...	...	" Mehkar . . } BULDANA DISTRICT.
2	1	1	3	5	3	4	3	3	1	1	1	...	...	2	...	Taluk Yeotmal . . } WUN DISTRICT.
...	...	...	...	...	...	...	...	...	...	...	...	...	...	...	...	" Darwha . . } WUN DISTRICT.
...	...	...	...	...	...	...	...	...	...	...	...	...	...	...	...	" Kelapur . . } WUN DISTRICT.
...	...	..	...	...	...	...	...	...	...	..	...	...	...	...	...	" Wun . . } WUN DISTRICT.
5	2	5	2	2	1	2	2	1	...	2	...	...	...	...	...	Taluk Basim . . } BASIM DISTRICT.
...	...	...	...	...	...	...	...	...	...	...	...	...	...	...	...	" Mangrul . } BASIM DISTRICT.
...	...	...	1	...	..	...	...	...	...	1	...	...	...	...	...	" Pusad . . } BASIM DISTRICT.

TABLE VIII.—Civil Condition by Religion and

DISTRICT AND TALUK.	Total Widowed.			(3) WIDOW Age 0—4		5—9		10—14		15—19		20—24	
	Total.	Males.	Females.	Males.	Females.	Males.	Females.	Males.	Females.	Males.	Females.	Males.	Females.
1	2	3	4	5	6	7	8	9	10	11	12	13	14
District Amraoti	40	11	29	...	...	...	...	...	...	...	...	...	1
,, Akola	17	5	12	...	...	...	...	...	...	...	...	1	2
,, Ellichpur	8	1	7	...	...	...	...	...	...	...	...	...	1
,, Buldana	6	3	3	...	...	...	...	...	...	...	1	...	...
,, Wun	5	3	2	...	...	...	...	...	...	...	...	...	...
,, Basim	6	3	3	...	...	...	...	...	...	...	...	...	2
Total	**82**	**26**	**56**	...	...	...	...	...	...	...	**1**	**1**	**6**
Amraoti District. Taluk Amraoti	40	11	29	...	...	...	...	...	...	...	...	...	1
,, Chandur	...	...	...	...	...	...	...	...	...	...	...	...	...
,, Morsi	...	...	...	...	...	...	...	...	...	...	...	...	...
,, Murtazapur	...	...	...	...	...	...	...	...	...	...	...	...	...
Akola District. Taluk Akola	9	1	8	...	...	...	...	...	...	...	...	1	1
,, Akot	1	1	...	...	...	...	...	...	...	...	...	...	...
,, Balapur	...	..	...	...	...	...	...	...	...	...	...	...	...
,, Jalgaon	...	...	...	...	...	...	...	...	...	...	...	...	...
,, Khamgaon	7	3	4	...	...	...	...	...	...	...	...	...	1
Ellichpur District. Taluk Ellichpur	8	1	7	...	...	...	...	...	...	...	...	...	1
,, Daryapur	...	...	...	...	...	...	...	...	...	...	...	...	...
,, Melghat	...	...	...	...	...	...	...	...	..	...	...	...	...
Buldana District. Taluk Chikhli	5	3	2	...	...	...	...	...	...	...	1	...	...
,, Malkapur	...	...	...	...	...	...	...	...	...	...	...	...	...
,, Mehkar	1	...	1	...	...	...	...	...	...	...	...	...	...
Wun District. Taluk Yeotmal	5	3	2	...	...	...	...	...	...	...	...	...	...
,, Darwha	...	...	...	...	...	...	...	...	...	...	...	...	...
,, Kelapur	...	...	...	...	...	...	...	...	...	...	...	...	...
,, Wun	...	...	...	...	...	...	...	...	...	...	...	...	...
Basim District. Taluk Basim	6	3	3	...	...	...	...	...	...	...	...	...	2
,, Mangrul	...	...	...	...	...	...	...	...	...	...	...	...	...
,, Pusad	...	...	...	...	...	...	...	...	...	...	...	...	...

Age.—Part G—CHRISTIAN.

ED.																
PERIOD.																
25—29		30—34		35—39		40—44		45—49		50—54		55—59		60 AND OVER.		DISTRICT AND TALUK.
Males.	Females.	Males.	Females.	Males.	Females.	Males.	Females.	Males.	Females.	Males.	Females.	Males.	Females.	Males.	Females.	
15	16	17	18	19	20	21	22	23	24	25	26	27	28	29	30	31
1	...	...	2	...	4	1	6	3	2	1	5	...	3	5	6	DISTRICT AMRAOTI.
...	2	...	...	...	1	1	1	1	...	1	2	...	2	1	2	„ AKOLA.
...	1	...	...	...	...	...	...	...	2	...	1	1	...	...	2	„ ELLICHPUR.
...	...	...	...	...	...	1	...	...	...	...	1	...	...	2	1	„ BULDANA.
...	...	...	...	...	...	2	...	1	...	...	1	...	...	...	1	„ WUN.
...	...	...	...	...	1	1	...	...	...	...	...	1	...	1	...	„ BASIM.
1	**3**	...	**2**	...	**6**	**6**	**7**	**5**	**4**	**2**	**10**	**2**	**5**	**9**	**12**	**Total.**
1	...	...	2	...	4	1	6	3	2	1	5	...	3	5	6	Taluk Amraoti (AMRAOTI DISTRICT.)
...	...	...	...	...	...	...	...	...	...	...	...	...	...	...	...	„ Chandur
...	...	...	...	...	...	...	...	...	...	...	...	...	...	...	...	„ Morsi
...	...	...	...	...	...	...	...	...	...	...	...	...	...	...	...	„ Murtazapur
...	1	...	...	...	1	...	...	...	...	...	1	...	2	...	2	Taluk Akola (AKOLA DISTRICT.)
...	...	...	...	...	...	...	...	...	...	1	...	...	...	...	...	„ Akot
...	...	...	...	...	...	...	...	...	...	...	...	...	...	...	...	„ Balapur
...	...	...	...	...	...	...	...	...	...	...	...	...	...	...	...	„ Jalgaon
...	1	...	...	...	...	1	1	1	...	...	1	...	...	1	...	„ Khamgaon
...	1	...	...	...	...	...	...	...	2	...	1	1	...	...	2	Taluk Ellichpur (ELLICHPUR DISTRICT.)
...	...	...	...	...	...	...	...	...	...	...	...	...	...	...	...	„ Daryapur
...	...	...	...	...	...	...	...	...	...	...	...	...	...	...	...	„ Melghat
...	...	...	...	...	...	1	...	...	...	...	1	...	...	2	...	Taluk Chikhli (BULDANA DISTRICT.)
...	...	...	...	...	...	...	...	...	...	...	...	...	...	...	...	„ Malkapur
...	...	...	...	...	...	...	...	...	...	...	...	...	...	...	1	„ Mehkar
...	...	...	...	...	...	2	...	1	...	...	1	...	...	...	1	Taluk Yeotmal (WUN DISTRICT.)
...	...	...	...	...	...	...	...	...	...	...	...	...	...	...	...	„ Darwha
...	...	...	...	...	...	...	...	...	...	...	...	...	...	...	...	„ Kelapur
...	...	...	...	...	...	...	...	...	...	...	...	...	...	...	...	„ Wun
...	...	...	...	...	1	1	...	...	...	...	...	1	...	1	...	Taluk Basim (BASIM DISTRICT.)
...	...	...	...	...	...	...	...	...	...	...	...	...	...	...	...	„ Mangrul
...	...	...	...	...	...	...	...	...	...	...	...	...	...	...	...	„ Pusad

TABLE VIII.

Civil Condition by Religion and Age.—
Part H.—PARSI.

TABLE VIII.—Civil Condition by Religion and Age.—

DISTRICT AND TALUK.	(1) UNMAR												
	TOTAL UNMARRIED.			AGE									
				0—4		5—9		10—14		15—19		20—24	
	Total.	Males.	Females.	Males.	Females.	Males.	Females.	Males.	Females.	Males.	Females.	Males.	Females.
1	2	3	4	5	6	7	8	9	10	11	12	13	14
District Amraoti	112	69	43	17	19	18	12	11	10	6	2	11	...
,, Akola	59	48	11	9	5	10	3	2	2	3	1	13	...
,, Ellichpur	5	4	1	...	...	...	1	...	...	...	...	2	...
,, Buldana	...	...	...	...	...	...	...	...	...	...	...	...	...
,, Wun	...	...	...	...	...	...	...	...	...	...	...	...	...
,, Basim	...	...	...	...	...	...	...	...	...	...	...	...	...
Total	176	121	55	26	24	28	16	18	12	9	3	26	...
Amraoti District — Taluk Amraoti	105	62	43	16	19	18	12	10	10	6	2	10	...
,, Chandur	...	...	...	...	...	...	...	...	...	...	...	...	...
,, Morsi	1	1	...	...	...	...	...	...	...	...	...	...	...
,, Murtazapur	6	6	...	1	...	...	...	1	...	...	...	1	...
Akola District — Taluk Akola	27	19	8	4	3	6	2	1	2	...	1	4	...
,, Akot	4	3	1	3	1	...	...	...	...	...	...	...	...
,, Balapur	2	2	...	...	...	...	...	...	...	...	...	1	...
,, Jalgaon	...	...	...	...	...	...	...	...	...	...	...	...	...
,, Khamgaon	26	24	2	2	1	4	1	1	...	3	...	8	...
Ellichpur District — Taluk Ellichpur	3	3	...	...	...	...	...	...	...	...	...	2	...
,, Daryapur	2	1	1	...	...	...	1	...	...	...	...	...	...
,, Melghat	...	...	...	...	...	...	...	...	...	...	...	...	...
Buldana District — Taluk Chikhli	...	...	...	...	...	...	...	...	...	...	...	...	...
,, Malkapur	...	...	...	...	...	...	...	...	...	...	...	...	...
,, Mehkar	...	...	...	...	...	...	...	...	...	...	...	...	...
Wun District — Taluk Yeotmal	...	...	...	...	...	...	...	...	...	...	...	...	...
,, Darwha	...	...	...	...	...	...	...	...	...	...	...	...	...
,, Kelapur	...	...	...	...	...	...	...	...	...	...	...	...	...
,, Wun	...	...	...	...	...	...	...	...	...	...	...	...	...
Basim District — Taluk Basim	...	...	...	...	...	...	...	...	...	...	...	...	...
,, Mangrul	...	...	...	...	...	...	...	...	...	...	...	...	...
,, Pusad	...	...	...	...	...	...	...	...	...	...	...	...	...

Part H—PARSI.

RIED.

PERIOD.

25—29		30—34		35—39		40—44		45—49		50—54		55—59		60 AND OVER.		DISTRICT AND TALUK.
Males.	Females.	Males.	Females.	Males.	Females.	Males.	Females.	Males.	Females.	Males.	Females.	Males.	Females.	Males.	Females.	
15	16	17	18	19	20	21	22	23	24	25	26	27	28	29	30	31
3	...	1	...	2	...	...	...	...	...	...	...	...	...	...	...	DISTRICT AMRAOTI.
7	...	2	...	...	...	1	...	1	...	...	...	...	...	...	...	" AKOLA.
2	...	...	...	...	...	...	...	...	...	...	...	...	...	...	...	" ELLICHPUR.
...	...	...	...	...	...	...	...	...	...	...	...	...	...	...	...	" BULDANA.
...	...	...	...	...	...	...	...	...	...	...	...	...	...	...	...	" WUN.
...	...	...	...	...	...	...	...	...	...	...	...	...	...	...	...	" BASIM.
12	...	3	...	2	...	1	...	1	...	...	...	...	...	...	...	**Total.**
1	...	...	...	1	...	...	...	...	...	...	...	...	...	...	...	Taluk Amraoti (AMRAOTI DISTRICT.)
...	...	...	...	...	...	...	...	...	...	...	...	...	...	...	...	" Chandur
...	...	1	...	...	...	...	...	...	...	...	...	...	...	...	...	" Morsi
2	...	...	...	1	...	...	...	...	...	...	...	...	...	...	...	" Murtazapur
3	...	1	...	...	...	...	...	...	...	...	...	...	...	...	...	Taluk Akola (AKOLA DISTRICT.)
...	...	...	...	...	...	...	...	...	...	...	...	...	...	...	...	" Akot
1	...	...	...	...	...	...	...	...	...	...	...	...	...	...	...	" Balapur
...	...	...	...	...	...	...	...	...	...	...	...	...	...	...	...	" Jalgaon
3	...	1	...	...	...	1	...	1	...	...	...	...	...	...	...	" Khamgaon
1	...	...	...	...	...	...	...	...	...	...	...	...	...	...	...	Taluk Ellichpur (ELLICHPUR DISTRICT.)
1	...	...	...	...	...	...	...	...	...	...	...	...	...	...	...	" Daryapur
...	...	...	...	...	...	...	...	...	...	...	...	...	...	...	...	" Melghat
...	...	...	...	...	...	...	...	...	...	...	...	...	...	...	...	Taluk Chikhli (BULDANA DISTRICT.)
...	...	...	...	...	...	...	...	...	...	...	...	...	...	...	...	" Malkapur
...	...	...	...	...	...	...	...	...	...	...	...	...	...	...	...	" Mehkar
...	...	...	...	...	...	...	...	...	...	...	...	...	...	...	...	Taluk Yeotmal (WUN DISTRICT.)
...	...	...	...	...	...	...	...	...	...	...	...	...	...	...	...	" Darwha
...	...	...	...	...	...	...	...	...	...	...	...	...	...	...	...	" Kelapur
...	...	...	...	...	...	...	...	...	...	...	...	...	...	...	...	" Wun
...	...	...	...	...	...	...	...	...	...	...	...	...	...	...	...	Taluk Basim (BASIM DISTRICT.)
...	...	...	...	...	...	...	...	...	...	...	...	...	...	...	...	" Mangrul
...	...	...	...	...	...	...	...	...	...	...	...	...	...	...	...	" Pusad

TABLE VIII.—Civil Condition by

DISTRICT AND TALUK.	(2) MAR			AGE										
	TOTAL MARRIED.			0—4		5—9		10—14		15—19		20—24	
	TOTAL.	Males.	Females.	Males.	Females.	Males.	Females.	Males.	Females.	Males.	Females.	Males.	Females.
1	2	3	4	5	6	7	8	9	10	11	12	13	14
DISTRICT AMRAOTI	112	59	53	...	...	...	...	...	1	...	5	8	14
„ AKOLA	77	56	21	...	...	...	...	...	...	...	2	6	5
„ ELLICHPUR	17	16	1	...	...	...	...	...	...	...	...	3	1
„ BULDANA	4	3	1	...	...	...	...	...	...	...	...	...	1
„ WUN	4	3	1	...	...	...	...	...	...	...	...	...	...
„ BASIM	...	...	...	...		...	...	...	...	...	...	...	...
Total	214	87	77	...	...	...	...	...	1	...	7	17	21
AMRAOTI DISTRICT. Taluk Amraoti	105	54	51	...	...	...	...	...	1	...	5	8	13
„ Chandur	...	...	...	...	...	...	...	...	...	...	...	...	...
„ Morsi	1	1	...	...	...	...	...	...	...	...	...	...	...
„ Murtazapur	6	4	2	...	...	...	...	...	...	...	...	...	1
AKOLA DISTRICT. Taluk Akola	37	25	12	...	...	...	...	...	...	...	1	2	3
„ Akot	4	2	2	...	...	...	...	...	...	...	1	...	...
„ Balapur	2	2	...	...	...	...	...	...	...	...	...	...	...
„ Jalgaon	...	...		...	...	...	...	...	...	...	...	...	...
„ Khamgaon	34	27	7	...	...	...	...	...	...	...	...	4	1
ELLICHPUR DISTRICT. Taluk Ellichpur	8	8	...	...	...	...	...	...	...	...	...	2	...
„ Daryapur	9	8	1	...	...	...	...	...	...	...	...	1	1
„ Melghat	...	...	...	...	...	...	...	...	...	...	...	...	...
BULDANA DISTRICT. Taluk Chikhli	1	1	...	...	...	...	...	...	...	...	...	...	...
„ Malkapur	3	2	1	...	...	...	...	...	...	...	...	...	1
„ Mehkar	...	...	...	...	...	...	...	...	...	...	...	...	...
WUN DISTRICT. Taluk Yeotmal	4	3	1	...	...	...	...	...	...	...	...	...	...
„ Darwha	...	...	...	...	...	...	...	...	...	...	...	...	...
„ Kelapur	...	...	...	...	...	...	...	...	...	...	...	...	...
„ Wun	...	...	...	...	...	...	...	...	...	...	...	...	...
BASIM DISTRICT. Taluk Basim	...	...	...	...	...	...	...	...	...	...	...	...	...
„ Mangrul	...	...	...	...	...	...	...	...	...	...	...	...	...
„ Pusad	...	...	...	...	...	...	...	...	...	...	...	...	...

Religion and Age.—Part H—PARSI.

RIED.																
PERIOD.																
25—29		30—34		35—39		40—44		45—49		50—54		55—59		60 AND OVER.		DISTRICT AND TALUK.
Males.	Females.	Males.	Females.	Males.	Females.	Males.	Females.	Males.	Females.	Males.	Females.	Males.	Females.	Males.	Females.	
15	16	17	18	19	20	21	22	23	24	25	26	27	28	29	30	31
13	10	11	6	8	6	9	4	4	2	...	1	2	2	4	2	DISTRICT AMRAOTI.
13	4	14	6	6	1	3	1	4	...	4	1	...	...	6	1	„ AKOLA.
3	...	3	...	2	...	2	...	2	...	1	...	...	...	...	...	„ ELLICHPUR.
...	...	1	...	...	...	1	...	...	...	...	...	...	...	1	...	„ BULDANA.
...	...	...	...	...	1	1	...	1	...	1	...	...	...	...	...	„ WUN.
...	...	...	...	...	...	...	...	...	...	...	...	...	...	...	...	„ BASIM.
29	**14**	**29**	**12**	**16**	**8**	**16**	**5**	**11**	**2**	**6**	**2**	**2**	**2**	**11**	**3**	**Total.**
12	10	11	6	8	6	8	4	4	2	...	1	1	1	2	2	Taluk Amraoti . . } AMRAOTI DISTRICT.
...	...	...	...	...	...	...	...	...	...	...	...	...	...	...	...	„ Chandur . .
...	...	...	...	...	...	...	...	...	...	...	...	1	...	...	...	„ Morsi . .
1	...	...	...	...	...	1	...	...	...	...	...	...	1	2	...	„ Murtazapur . .
5	...	5	5	3	1	1	...	2	...	1	1	...	...	6	1	Taluk Akola . . } AKOLA DISTRICT.
...	1	2	...	...	...	...	...	...	...	...	...	...	...	...	...	„ Akot . .
...	...	...	...	1	...	...	...	1	...	...	...	...	...	...	...	„ Balapur . .
...	...	...	...	...	...	...	...	...	...	...	...	...	...	...	...	„ Jalgaon . .
8	3	7	1	2	...	2	1	1	...	3	...	...	...	...	...	„ Khamgaon . .
1	...	3	...	...	...	...	...	1	...	1	.	...	...	...	...	Taluk Ellichpur . . } ELLICHPUR DISTRICT.
2	...	...	...	2	...	2	...	1	...	...	...	...	...	...	...	„ Daryapur . .
...	...	...	...	...	...	...	...	...	...	...	...	...	...	...	...	„ Melghat . .
...	...	...	...	...	...	...	...	...	...	...	...	...	...	1	...	Taluk Chikhli . . } BULDANA DISTRICT.
...	...	1	...	...	...	1	...	...	...	...	...	...	...	...	...	„ Malkapur . .
...	...	...	...	...	...	...	...	...	...	...	...	...	...	...	...	„ Mehkar . .
...	...	...	...	...	1	1	...	1	...	1	...	...	...	...	...	Taluk Yeotmal . . } WUN DISTRICT.
...	...	...	...	...	...	...	...	...	...	...	...	...	...	...	...	„ Darwha . .
...	...	...	...	...	...	...	...	...	...	...	...	...	...	...	...	„ Kelapur . .
...	...	...	...	...	...	...	...	...	...	...	...	...	...	...	...	„ Wun . .
...	...	...	...	...	...	...	...	...	...	...	...	...	...	...	...	Taluk Basim . . } BASIM DISTRICT.
...	...	...	...	...	...	...	...	...	...	...	...	...	...	...	...	„ Mangrul . .
...	...	...	...	...	...	...	...	...	...	...	...	...	...	...	...	„ Pusad . .

Table VIII.—Civil Condition by Religion and Age.

TABLE VIII.—Civil Condition by Religion

(3) Wi

DISTRICT AND TALUK.	TOTAL WIDOWED.			Age 0—4		5—9		10—14		15—19		20—24	
	Total.	Males.	Females.	Males.	Females.	Males.	Females.	Males.	Females.	Males.	Females.	Males.	Females.
1	2	3	4	5	6	7	8	9	10	11	12	13	14
District Amraoti	11	4	7	...	...	...	...	...	...	...	...	...	...
" Akola	9	7	2	...	...	...	...	...	...	...	...	2	...
" Ellichpur	...	...	...	...	...	...	...	...	...	...	...	...	...
" Buldana	1	1	...	...	...	...	...	...	...	...	...	...	...
" Wun	1	1	...	...	...	...	...	...	...	...	...	1	...
" Basim	...	...	...	...	...	...	...	...	...	...	...	...	...
Total	22	13	9	...	...	...	...	...	...	...	...	3	...
Amraoti District — Taluk Amraoti	10	4	6	...	...	...	...	...	...	...	...	...	...
" Chandur	...	...	...	...	...	...	...	...	...	...	...	...	...
" Morsi	...	...	...	...	...	...	...	...	...	...	...	...	...
" Murtazapur	1	...	1	...	...	...	...	...	...	...	...	...	...
Akola District — Taluk Akola	4	2	2	...	...	...	...	...	...	...	...	...	...
" Akot	...	...	...	...	...	...	...	...	...	...	...	...	...
" Balapur	...	...	...	...	...	...	...	...	...	...	...	...	...
" Jalgaon	...	...	...	...	...	...	...	...	...	...	...	...	...
" Khamgaon	5	5	...	...	...	...	...	...	...	...	...	2	...
Ellichpur District — Taluk Ellichpur	...	...	...	...	...	...	...	...	...	...	...	...	...
" Daryapur	...	...	...	...	...	...	...	...	...	...	...	...	...
" Melghat	...	...	...	...	...	...	...	...	...	...	...	...	...
Buldana District — Taluk Chikhli	...	...	...	...	...	...	...	...	...	...	...	...	...
" Malkapur	1	1	...	...	...	...	...	...	...	...	...	...	...
" Mehkar	...	...	...	...	...	...	...	...	...	...	...	...	...
Wun District — Taluk Yeotmal	1	1	...	...	...	...	...	...	...	...	...	1	...
" Darwha	...	...	...	...	...	...	...	...	...	...	...	...	...
" Kelapur	...	...	...	...	...	...	...	...	...	...	...	...	...
" Wun	...	...	...	...	...	...	...	...	...	...	...	...	...
Basim District — " Basim	...	...	...	...	...	...	...	...	...	...	...	...	...
" Mangrul	...	...	...	...	...	...	...	...	...	...	...	...	...
" Pusad	...	...	...	...	...	...	...	...	...	...	...	...	...

and Age.—Part H—PARSI.

[WI]DOWED.																
PERIOD.																
25—29		30—34		35—39		40—44		45—49		50—54		55—59		60 AND OVER.		DISTRICT AND TALUK.
Males.	Females.	Males.	Females.	Males.	Females.	Males.	Females.	Males.	Females.	Males.	Females.	Males.	Females.	Males.	Females.	
15	16	17	18	19	20	21	22	23	24	25	26	27	28	29	30	31
...	...	1	...	1	...	...	...	...	3	...	3	1	...	1	1	DISTRICT AMRAOTI.
3	...	1	...	...	...	...	...	...	...	...	...	...	...	1	2	" AKOLA.
...	...	...	...	...	...	...	...	...	...	...	...	...	...	...	...	" ELLICHPUR.
...	...	...	...	...	...	...	...	...	...	1	...	...	...	...	...	" BULDANA.
...	...	...	...	...	...	...	...	...	...	...	...	...	...	...	...	" WUN.
...	...	...	...	...	...	...	...	...	...	...	...	...	...	...	...	" BASIM.
3	...	**2**	...	**1**	...	...	...	...	**3**	**1**	**3**	**1**	...	**2**	**3**	**Total.**
...	...	1	...	1	...	...	...	...	2	...	3	1	...	1	1	Taluk Amraoti (AMRAOTI DISTRICT.)
...	...	...	...	...	...	...	...	...	...	...	...	...	...	...	...	" Chandur
...	...	...	...	...	...	...	...	...	...	...	...	...	...	...	...	" Morsi
...	...	...	...	...	...	...	...	...	1	...	...	...	...	...	...	" Murtazapur
...	...	1	...	...	...	...	...	...	...	...	...	...	...	1	2	Taluk Akola (AKOLA DISTRICT.)
...	...	...	...	...	...	...	...	...	...	...	...	...	...	...	...	" Akot
...	...	...	...	...	...	...	...	...	...	...	...	...	...	...	...	" Balapur
...	...	...	...	...	...	...	...	...	...	...	...	...	...	...	...	" Jalgaon
3	...	...	...	...	...	...	...	...	...	...	...	...	...	...	...	" Khamgaon
...	...	...	...	...	...	...	...	...	...	...	...	...	...	...	...	Taluk Ellichpur (ELLICHPUR DISTRICT.)
...	...	...	...	...	...	...	...	...	...	...	...	...	...	...	...	" Daryapur
...	...	...	...	...	...	...	...	...	...	...	...	...	...	...	...	" Melghat
...	...	...	...	...	...	...	...	...	...	...	...	...	...	...	...	Taluk Chikhli (BULDANA DISTRICT.)
...	...	...	...	...	...	...	...	...	...	1	...	...	...	...	...	" Malkapur
...	...	...	...	...	...	...	...	...	...	...	...	...	...	...	...	" Mehkar
...	...	...	...	...	...	...	...	...	...	...	...	...	...	...	...	Taluk Yeotmal (WUN DISTRICT.)
...	...	...	...	...	...	...	...	...	...	...	...	...	...	...	...	" Darwha
...	...	...	...	...	...	...	...	...	...	...	...	...	...	...	...	" Kelapur
...	...	...	...	...	...	...	...	...	...	...	...	...	...	...	...	" Wun
...	...	...	...	...	...	...	...	...	...	...	...	...	...	...	...	Taluk Basim (BASIM DISTRICT.)
...	...	...	...	...	...	...	...	...	...	...	...	...	...	...	...	" Mangrul
...	...	...	...	...	...	...	...	...	...	...	...	...	...	...	...	" Pusad

TABLE VIII.

Civil Condition by Religion and Age.—
Part I—OTHERS.

NOTE.—There are no widowed "Others."

TABLE VIII.—Civil Condition by Religion

DISTRICT AND TALUK.	(1) UNMAR												
	TOTAL UNMARRIED.			AGE									
				0—4		5—9		10—14		15—19		20—24	
	TOTAL.	Males.	Females.	Males.	Females.	Males.	Females.	Males.	Females.	Males.	Females.	Males.	Females.
1	2	3	4	5	6	7	8	9	10	11	12	13	14
DISTRICT AMRAOTI	1	1	...	...	...	...	...	...	...	...	...	...	...
„ AKOLA	4	3	1	1	...	...	1	...	...	...	...	1	...
„ ELLICHPUR	1	1	...	...	...	...	...	...	...	...	...	...	...
„ BULDANA	...	...	...	...	...	...	...	...	...	...	...	...	...
„ WUN	...	...	...	...	...	...	...	...	...	...	...	...	...
„ BASIM	1	1	...	...	...	...	...	...	...	...	...	...	...
Total	7	6	1	1	...	...	1	...	...	...	...	1	...
AMRAOTI DISTRICT. Taluk Amraoti	1	1	...	...	...	...	...	...	...	...	...	...	...
„ Chandur	...	...	...	...	...	...	...	...	...	...	...	...	...
„ Morsi	...	...	...	...	...	...	...	...	...	...	...	...	...
„ Murtazapur	...	...	...	...	...	...	...	...	...	...	...	...	...
AKOLA DISTRICT. Taluk Akola	2	1	1	1 Buddhist	...	...	1 Buddhist	...	...	...	...	...	...
„ Akot	...	...	...	...	...	...	...	...	...	...	...	...	...
„ Balapur	...	...	...	...	...	...	...	...	...	...	...	...	...
„ Jalgaon	...	...	...	...	...	...	...	...	...	...	...	...	...
„ Khamgaon	2	2	...	...	...	...	...	...	...	...	...	1 Jew	...
ELLICHPUR DISTRICT. Taluk Ellichpur	1	1	...	...	...	...	...	...	...	...	...	...	...
„ Daryapur	...	...	...	...	...	...	...	...	...	...	...	...	...
„ Melghat	...	...	...	...	...	...	...	...	...	...	...	...	...
BULDANA DISTRICT. Taluk Chikhli	...	...	...	...	...	...	...	...	...	...	...	...	...
„ Malkapur	...	...	...	...	...	...	...	...	...	...	...	...	...
„ Mehkar	...	...	...	...	...	...	...	...	...	...	...	...	...
WUN DISTRICT. Taluk Yeotmal	...	...	...	...	...	...	...	...	...	...	...	...	...
„ Darwha	...	...	...	...	...	...	...	...	...	...	...	...	...
„ Kelapur	...	...	...	...	...	...	...	...	...	...	...	...	...
„ Wun	...	...	...	...	...	...	...	...	...	...	...	...	...
BASIM DISTRICT. Taluk Basim	1	1	...	...	...	...	...	...	...	...	...	...	...
„ Mangrul	...	...	...	...	...	...	...	...	...	...	...	...	...
„ Pusad	...	...	...	...	...	...	...	...	...	...	...	...	...

and Age.—Part I—OTHERS.

RIED.																
PERIOD.																
25—29		30—34		35—39		40—44		45—49		50—54		55—59		60 AND OVER.		DISTRICT AND TALUK.
Males.	Females.	Males.	Females.	Males.	Females.	Males.	Females.	Males.	Females.	Males.	Females.	Males.	Females.	Males.	Females.	
15	16	17	18	19	20	21	22	23	24	25	26	27	28	29	30	31
1	...	...	...	...	...	...	...	...	...	...	...	...	...	...	...	DISTRICT AMRAOTI.
...	...	1	...	...	...	...	...	...	...	...	...	...	...	...	...	" AKOLA.
1	...	...	...	...	...	...	...	...	...	...	...	...	...	...	...	" ELLICHPUR.
...	...	...	...	...	...	...	...	...	...	...	...	...	...	...	...	" BULDANA.
...	...	...	...	...	...	...	...	...	...	...	...	...	...	...	...	" WUN.
...	...	1	...	...	...	...	...	...	...	...	...	...	...	...	...	" BASIM.
2	...	**2**	...	...	...	...	...	...	...	...	...	...	...	...	...	**Total.**
1 Jew.	...	...	...	...	...	...	...	...	...	...	...	...	...	...	...	Taluk Amraoti (AMRAOTI DISTRICT.)
...	...	...	...	...	...	...	...	...	...	...	...	...	...	...	...	" Chandur (AMRAOTI DISTRICT.)
...	...	...	...	...	...	...	...	...	...	...	...	...	...	...	...	" Morsi (AMRAOTI DISTRICT.)
...	...	...	...	...	...	...	...	...	...	...	...	...	...	...	...	" Murtazapur (AMRAOTI DISTRICT.)
...	...	...	...	...	...	...	...	...	...	...	...	...	...	...	...	Taluk Akola (AKOLA DISTRICT.)
...	...	...	...	...	...	...	...	...	...	...	...	...	...	...	...	" Akot (AKOLA DISTRICT.)
...	...	...	...	...	...	...	...	...	...	...	...	...	...	...	...	" Balapur (AKOLA DISTRICT.)
...	...	...	...	...	...	...	...	...	...	...	...	...	...	...	...	" Jalgaon (AKOLA DISTRICT.)
...	...	1 Unspecified.	...	...	...	...	...	...	...	...	...	...	...	...	...	" Khamgaon (AKOLA DISTRICT.)
1 Deist	...	...	...	...	...	...	...	...	...	...	...	...	...	...	...	Taluk Ellichpur (ELLICHPUR DISTRICT.)
...	...	...	...	...	...	...	...	...	...	...	...	...	...	...	...	" Daryapur (ELLICHPUR DISTRICT.)
...	...	...	...	...	...	...	...	...	...	...	...	...	...	...	...	" Melghat (ELLICHPUR DISTRICT.)
...	...	...	...	...	...	...	...	...	...	...	...	...	...	...	...	Taluk Chikhli (BULDANA DISTRICT.)
...	...	...	...	...	...	...	...	...	...	...	...	...	...	...	...	" Malkapur (BULDANA DISTRICT.)
...	...	...	...	...	...	...	...	...	...	...	...	...	...	...	...	" Mehkar (BULDANA DISTRICT.)
...	...	...	...	...	...	...	...	...	...	...	...	...	...	...	...	Taluk Yeotmal (WUN DISTRICT.)
...	...	...	...	...	...	...	...	...	...	...	...	...	...	...	...	" Darwha (WUN DISTRICT.)
...	...	...	...	...	...	...	...	...	...	...	...	...	...	...	...	" Kelapur (WUN DISTRICT.)
...	...	...	...	...	...	...	...	...	...	...	...	...	...	...	...	" Wun (WUN DISTRICT.)
...	...	1 Agnostic.	...	...	...	...	...	...	...	...	...	...	...	...	...	Taluk Basim (BASIM DISTRICT.)
...	...	...	...	...	...	...	...	...	...	...	...	...	...	...	...	" Mangrul (BASIM DISTRICT.)
...	...	...	...	...	...	...	...	...	...	...	...	...	...	...	...	" Pusad (BASIM DISTRICT.)

TABLE VIII.—Civil Condition by Religion

DISTRICT AND TALUK.	(2) MAR…												
	TOTAL MARRIED.			AGE…									
				0—4		5—9		10—14		15—19		20—24	
	TOTAL.	Males.	Females.	Males.	Females.	Males.	Females.	Males.	Females.	Males.	Females.	Males.	Females.
1	2	3	4	5	6	7	8	9	10	11	12	13	14
DISTRICT AMRAOTI	...	...	...	...	...	...	...	...	...	...	...	...	...
" AKOLA	3	2	1	...	...	...	...	...	...	...	...	1	...
" ELLICHPUR	...	...	...	...	...	...	...	...	...	...	...	...	...
" BULDANA	...	...	...	...	...	...	...	...	...	...	...	...	...
" WUN	...	...	...	...	...	...	...	...	...	...	...	...	...
" BASIM	1	1	...	...	...	...	...	...	...	...	...	...	...
Total	4	3	1	...	...	...	...	...	...	...	...	1	...
AMRAOTI DISTRICT — Taluk Amraoti	...	...	...	...	...	...	...	...	...	...	...	...	...
" Chandur	...	...	...	...	...	...	...	...	...	...	...	...	...
" Morsi	...	...	...	...	...	...	...	...	...	...	...	...	...
" Murtazapur	...	...	...	...	...	...	...	...	...	...	...	...	...
AKOLA DISTRICT — Taluk Akola	3	2	1	...	...	...	...	...	...	...	...	1 Buddhist.	...
" Akot	...	...	...	...	...	...	...	...	...	...	...	...	...
" Balapur	...	...	...	...	...	...	...	...	...	...	...	...	...
" Jalgaon	...	...	...	...	...	...	...	...	...	...	...	...	...
" Khamgaon	...	...	...	...	...	...	...	...	...	...	...	...	...
ELLICHPUR DISTRICT — Taluk Ellichpur	...	...	...	...	...	...	...	...	...	...	...	...	...
" Daryapur	...	...	...	...	...	...	...	...	...	...	...	...	...
" Melghat	...	...	...	...	...	...	...	...	...	...	...	...	...
BULDANA DISTRICT — Taluk Chikhli	...	...	...	...	...	...	...	...	...	...	...	...	...
" Malkapur	...	...	...	...	...	...	...	...	...	...	...	...	...
" Mehkar	...	...	...	...	...	...	...	...	...	...	...	...	...
WUN DISTRICT — Taluk Yeotmal	...	...	...	...	...	...	...	...	...	...	...	...	...
" Darwha	...	...	...	...	...	...	...	...	...	...	...	...	...
" Kelapur	...	...	...	...	...	...	...	...	...	...	...	...	...
" Wun	...	...	...	...	...	...	...	...	...	...	...	...	...
BASIM DISTRICT — Taluk Basim	...	...	...	...	...	...	...	...	...	...	...	...	...
" Mangrul	...	...	...	...	...	...	...	...	...	...	...	...	...
" Pusad	1	1	...	...	...	...	...	...	...	...	...	...	...

and Age.—Part I—OTHERS—*contd.*

RIED.																
PERIOD.																
25—29		30—34		35—39		40—44		45—49		50—54		55—59		60 AND OVER.		DISTRICT AND TALUK.
Males.	Females.	Males.	Females.	Males.	Females.	Males.	Females.	Males.	Females.	Males.	Females.	Males.	Females.	Males.	Females.	
15	16	17	18	19	20	21	22	23	24	25	26	27	28	29	30	31
...	...	...	...	...	...	...	...	...	...	...	...	...	...	...	...	DISTRICT AMRAOTI.
...	...	...	...	...	1	...	...	1	...	...	...	...	...	...	...	" AKOLA.
...	...	...	...	...	...	...	...	...	...	...	...	...	...	...	...	" ELLICHPUR.
...	...	...	...	...	...	...	...	...	...	...	...	...	...	...	...	" BULDANA.
...	...	...	...	...	...	...	...	...	...	...	...	...	...	...	...	" WUN.
...	...	1	...	...	...	...	...	...	...	...	...	...	...	...	...	" BASIM.
...	...	1	...	...	1	...	...	1	...	...	...	...	...	...	...	**Total.**
...	...	...	...	...	...	...	...	...	...	...	...	...	...	...	...	Taluk Amraoti (AMRAOTI DISTRICT.)
...	...	...	...	...	...	...	...	...	...	...	...	...	...	...	...	" Chandur
...	...	...	...	...	...	...	...	...	...	...	...	...	...	...	...	" Morsi
...	...	...	...	...	...	...	...	...	...	...	...	...	...	...	...	" Murtazapur
...	...	...	...	...	1 Buddhist.	...	...	1 Positivist	...	...	...	...	...	...	...	Taluk Akola (AKOLA DISTRICT.)
...	...	...	...	...	...	...	...	...	...	...	...	...	...	...	...	" Akot
...	...	...	...	...	...	...	...	...	...	...	...	...	...	...	...	" Balapur
...	...	...	...	...	...	...	...	...	...	...	...	...	...	...	...	" Jalgaon
...	...	...	...	...	...	...	...	...	...	...	...	...	...	...	...	" Khamgaon
...	...	...	...	...	...	...	...	...	...	...	...	...	...	...	...	Taluk Ellichpur (ELLICHPUR DISTRICT.)
...	...	...	...	...	...	...	...	...	...	...	...	...	...	...	...	" Daryapur
...	...	...	...	...	...	...	...	...	...	...	...	...	...	...	...	" Melghat
...	...	...	...	...	...	...	...	...	...	...	...	...	...	...	...	Taluk Chikhli (BULDANA DISTRICT.)
...	...	...	...	...	...	...	...	...	...	...	...	...	...	...	...	" Malkapur
...	...	...	...	...	...	...	...	...	...	...	...	...	...	...	...	" Mehkar
...	...	...	...	...	...	...	...	...	...	...	...	...	...	...	...	Taluk Yeotmal (WUN DISTRICT.)
...	...	...	...	...	...	...	...	...	...	...	...	...	...	...	...	" Darwha
...	...	...	...	...	...	...	...	...	...	...	...	...	...	...	...	" Kelapur
...	...	...	...	...	...	...	...	...	...	...	...	...	...	...	...	" Wun
...	...	...	...	...	...	...	...	...	...	...	...	...	...	...	...	Taluk Basim (BASIM DISTRICT.)
...	...	...	...	...	...	...	...	...	...	...	...	...	...	...	...	" Mangrul
...	...	1 Unspecified.	...	...	...	...	...	...	...	...	...	...	...	...	...	" Pusad

TABLE IX.

Education by Religion and Age.—Part A —TOTAL POPULATION.

TABLE IX.—Education by Religion and Age.—Part A—TOTAL POPULATION.

DISTRICT AND TALUK.	TOTAL POPULATION.			TOTAL BY EDUCATION.						AGE PERIODS. 0–14							
				Learning.		Literate.		Illiterate.		Total.		Learning.		Literate.		Illiterate.	
	Total.	Males.	Females.	Males.	Females.	Males.	Females.	Males.	Females.	Males.	Females.	Males.	Females.	Males.	Females.	Males.	Females.
1	2	3	4	5	6	7	8	9	10	11	12	13	14	15	16	17	18
District Amraoti	655,645	340,235	315,410	9,627	240	22,976	611	307,632	314,559	119,975	117 818	8,306	213	1,143	114	110,526	117,491
„ Akola	574,782	297,011	277,771	10,414	365	21,984	445	264,613	276,961	104,990	102,816	9,003	348	873	82	95,024	102,386
„ Ellichpur	315,798	162,969	152,829	4,976	80	10,866	185	147,127	152,564	57,913	56,818	4,316	76	360	26	53,237	56,716
„ Buldana	481,021	244,799	236,222	6,347	127	13,673	200	224,779	235,895	95,066	95,113	5,718	121	623	24	88,755	94,968
„ Wun	471,613	241,688	229,925	3,762	93	8,732	154	229,194	229,678	96,988	94,075	3,378	82	408	28	93,202	93,965
„ Basim	398,181	204,798	193,383	3,370	71	8,829	121	192,599	193,191	81,993	79,271	3,020	65	472	16	78,501	79,190
Railway Passengers, etc.	451	326	125	6	...	68	6	252	119	46	57	6	...	2	3	38	54
Total	2,897,491	1,491,826	1,405,665	38,502	976	87,128	1,722	1,366,196	1,402,967	557,001	545,968	33,837	905	8,881	293	519,283	544,770
Amraoti District. Taluk Amraoti	183,508	95,536	87,972	3,604	150	8,729	431	83,203	87,391	32,547	31,972	2,982	131	384	81	29,181	31,760
„ Chandur	198,106	102,885	95,221	2,681	31	5,912	62	94,292	95,128	37,358	36,515	2,389	28	376	10	34,593	36,477
„ Morsi	152,374	78,451	73,923	1,878	13	4,367	48	72,206	73,862	28,011	27,692	1,657	10	199	3	26,155	27,679
„ Murtazapur	121,657	63,363	58,294	1,464	46	3,968	70	57,931	58,178	22,059	21,639	1,278	44	184	20	20,597	21,575
Akola District. Taluk Akola	137,988	71,744	66,244	2,674	127	5,539	177	63,531	65,940	24,831	24,318	2,162	116	197	30	22,472	24,172
„ Akot	137,720	70,630	67,090	2,643	81	5,331	117	62,656	66,892	24,178	24,014	2,349	80	196	17	21,633	23,917
„ Balapur	101,673	51,941	49,732	1,604	77	3,297	46	47,040	49,609	19,499	19,073	1,443	75	201	15	17,855	18,983
„ Jalgaon	97,616	50,323	47,293	1,701	29	3,592	33	45,030	47,231	18,081	17,818	1,532	28	117	8	16,432	17,782
„ Khamgaon	99,785	52,373	47,412	1,792	51	4,225	72	46,356	47,289	18,401	17,593	1,607	49	162	12	16,632	17,532
Ellichpur District. Taluk Ellichpur	146,215	75,271	70,944	2,807	53	6,523	141	65,941	70,750	25,772	25,347	2,360	50	222	21	23,190	25,276
„ Daryapur	122,552	63,329	59,223	2,132	25	3,876	36	57,321	59,162	21,989	21,465	1,924	24	118	4	19,947	21,437
„ Melghat	47,031	24,369	22,662	37	2	467	8	23,865	22,652	10,152	10,006	32	2	20	1	10,100	10,003
Buldana District. Taluk Chikhli	150,098	76,540	73,558	1,678	53	4,014	77	70,848	73,428	29,884	29,529	1,483	48	173	9	28,228	29,472
„ Malkapur	177,877	90,215	87,662	3,285	61	6,241	78	80,689	87,523	34,684	34,604	2,996	60	292	10	31,396	34,534
„ Mehkar	153,046	78,044	75,002	1,384	13	3,418	45	73,242	74,944	30,528	30,980	1,239	13	158	5	29,131	30,962
Wun District. Taluk Yeotmal	124,429	64,275	60,154	1,3 6	26	2,029	54	60,010	60,074	24,628	23,702	1,209	26	145	8	23,274	23,668
„ Darwha	156,580	80,746	75,834	1,329	39	3,210	41	76,207	75,754	31,819	30,876	1,185	29	128	6	30,506	30,841
„ Kelapur	105,926	53,845	52,081	613	3	1,472	27	51,760	52,051	22,286	21,790	558	3	75	5	21,653	21,782
„ Wun	84,678	42,822	41,856	484	25	1,121	32	41,217	41,799	18,255	17,707	426	24	60	9	17,709	17,674
Basim District. Taluk Basim	177,250	91,200	86,050	1,542	31	4,331	80	85,327	85,939	35,454	34,512	1,374	28	224	11	33,856	34,473
„ Mangrul	82,446	42,773	39,673	730	29	1,658	21	40,385	39,623	16,753	15,981	665	27	91	4	15,097	15,950
„ Pusad	138,485	70,825	67,660	1,008	11	2,840	20	66,887	67,629	29,786	28,778	981	10	157	1	28,648	28,767

Table IX.—Education by Religion and Age.

DISTRICT AND TALUK.	AGE PERIODS. 15–24 Total. Males.	Total. Females.	Learning. Males.	Learning. Females.	Literate. Males.	Literate. Females.	Illiterate. Males.	Illiterate. Females.	25 AND OVER. Total. Males.	Total. Females.	Learning. Males.	Learning. Females.	Literate. Males.	Literate. Females.	Illiterate. Males.	Illiterate. Females.
19	20	21	22	23	24	25	26	27	28	29	30	31	32	33	34	35
District Amraoti	44,867	49,417	1,225	14	5,822	199	37,820	49,204	175,393	148,175	96	13	16,011	298	159,286	147,864
" Akola	41,195	45,055	1,255	12	5,787	165	34,153	44,878	150,826	129,900	66	5	15,324	198	135,436	129,697
" Ellichpur	22,684	24,836	601	4	2,749	62	19,334	24,770	82,372	71,175	59	...	7,757	97	74,556	71,078
" Buldana	33,304	38,825	596	3	3,326	68	29,382	38,754	116,399	102,284	33	3	9,724	108	106,642	102,173
" Wun	29,474	33,803	363	7	2,216	56	26,895	33,740	115,226	102,047	21	4	6,108	70	109,097	101,973
" Basim	25,286	29,522	315	4	2,084	53	22,887	29,465	97,519	84,590	35	2	6,273	52	91,211	84,536
Railway Passengers, etc.	42	11	...	...	16	...	26	11	238	57	...	...	50	3	188	54
Total	196,852	221,469	4,355	44	22,000	603	170,497	220,822	787,978	638,228	810	27	61,247	826	676,416	637,375
Amraoti District. Taluk Amraoti	13,271	14,189	585	9	2,201	155	10,485	14,025	49,718	41,811	37	10	6,144	195	43,537	41,606
" Chandur	13,221	14,461	269	2	1,634	13	11,318	14,446	52,306	44,245	23	1	3,902	39	48,381	44,205
" Morsi	10,018	11,339	203	1	1,034	16	8,781	11,322	40,422	34,892	18	2	3,134	29	37,270	34,861
" Murtazapur	8,357	9,428	168	2	953	15	7,236	9,411	32,947	27,227	18	...	2,831	35	30,098	27,192
Akola District. Taluk Akola	9,896	10,582	497	6	1,434	66	7,965	10,510	37,017	31,344	15	5	3,908	81	33,094	31,258
" Akot	9,744	11,039	272	1	1,435	43	8,037	10,995	36,708	32,037	22	...	3,700	57	32,986	31,980
" Balapur	6,982	7,897	153	2	877	13	5,952	7,882	25,460	22,762	8	...	2,219	18	23,233	22,744
" Jalgaon	7,154	7,631	163	1	927	14	6,064	7,616	25,088	21,844	6	...	2,548	11	22,534	21,833
" Khamgaon	7,419	7,906	170	2	1,114	29	6,135	7,875	26,553	21,913	15	...	2,949	31	23,589	21,882
Ellichpur District. Taluk Ellichpur	10,599	11,251	393	3	1,608	46	8,598	11,202	38,900	34,346	54	...	4,693	74	34,153	34,272
" Daryapur	8,856	9,837	204	1	1,038	12	7,614	9,824	32,484	27,921	4	...	2,720	20	29,760	27,901
" Melghat	3,229	3,748	4	...	103	4	3,122	3,744	10,988	8,908	1	...	344	3	10,643	8,905
Buldana District. Taluk Chikhli	10,231	11,823	186	2	924	28	9,121	11,793	36,425	32,206	9	3	2,017	40	33,499	32,163
" Malkapur	12,484	14,347	274	1	1,584	25	10,626	14,321	43,047	38,711	15	...	4,365	43	38,667	38,668
" Mehkar	10,589	12,655	136	...	818	15	9,635	12,640	36,927	31,367	9	...	2,442	25	34,476	31,342
Wun District. Taluk Yeotmal	7,867	9,098	121	...	757	22	6,989	9,076	31,780	27,354	6	...	2,027	24	29,747	27,330
" Darwha	9,827	11,315	132	7	796	15	8,899	11,293	39,100	33,643	12	3	2,286	20	36,802	33,620
" Kelapur	6,424	7,590	52	...	363	8	6,009	7,582	25,135	22,701	3	...	1,034	14	24,098	22,687
" Wun	5,356	5,800	58	...	300	11	4,998	5,789	19,211	18,349	...	1	761	12	18,450	18,336
Basim District. Taluk Basim	11,474	13,487	149	3	1,056	36	10,269	13,448	44,272	38,051	19	...	3,051	33	41,202	38,018
" Mangrul	5,046	5,864	58	1	394	7	4,594	5,856	20,974	17,828	7	1	1,173	10	19,794	17,817
" Pusad	8,766	10,171	108	...	634	10	8,024	10,161	32,273	28,711	9	1	2,049	9	30,215	28,701

TABLE IX.

Education by Religion and Age.—
Part B—HINDU.

TABLE IX.—Education by Religion and Age.—Part B—HINDU.

DISTRICT AND TALUK.	TOTAL HINDU.			TOTAL BY EDUCATION.						AGE PERIODS. 0–14							
				Learning.		Literate.		Illiterate.		Total.		Learning.		Literate.		Illiterate.	
	Total.	Males.	Females.	Males.	Females.	Males.	Females.	Males.	Females.	Males.	Females.	Males.	Females.	Males.	Females.	Males.	Females.
1	2	3	4	5	6	7	8	9	10	11	12	13	14	15	16	17	18
District Amraoti	584,178	303,130	281,048	8,258	133	19,658	295	275,214	280,620	106,910	105,030	7,136	113	935	55	98,839	104,862
" Akola	518,046	267,316	250,730	9,117	272	18,773	301	239,426	250,157	94,763	92,709	7,985	259	705	63	86,073	92,387
" Ellichpur	243,992	126,423	117,569	4,255	43	9,289	106	112,879	117,420	43,301	42,540	3,725	43	208	15	39,368	42,482
" Buldana	442,588	225,016	217,572	5,391	95	11,658	144	207,967	217,333	87,515	87,758	4,872	90	514	17	82,129	87,651
" Wun	371,084	190,766	180,318	3,178	75	7,455	99	180,133	180,144	75,505	72,768	2,858	64	327	19	72,320	72,685
" Basim	371,537	190,873	180,664	2,796	25	7,491	62	180,586	180,577	76,702	74,225	2,507	21	394	9	73,801	74,195
Railway Passengers, etc.	366	261	105	4	...	46	...	211	105	36	46	4	...	...	...	32	46
Total	2,531,791	1,303,785	1,228,006	32,999	643	74,370	1,007	1,196,416	1,226,356	484,822	475,076	29,087	590	3,178	178	452,562	474,308
Amraoti District. Taluk Amraoti	161,331	83,853	77,478	3,019	79	7,318	173	73,516	77,226	28,594	28,241	2,492	65	204	32	25,808	28,144
" Chandur	180,463	93,700	86,763	2,399	24	5,179	48	86,122	86,691	34,113	33,354	2,148	22	323	8	31,642	33,324
" Morsi	133,708	69,017	64,691	1,631	9	3,890	32	63,496	64,650	24,552	24,161	1,439	6	171	2	22,942	24,153
" Murtazapur	108,676	56,560	52,116	1,209	21	3,271	42	52,080	52,053	19,651	19,274	1,057	20	147	13	18,447	19,241
Akola District. Taluk Akola	124,098	64,430	59,668	2,252	97	4,588	101	57,590	59,470	22,355	21,938	1,822	88	160	25	20,373	21,825
" Akot	123,010	63,087	59,923	2,371	56	4,696	103	56,020	59,764	21,508	21,342	2,106	55	167	15	19,235	21,272
" Balapur	89,399	45,726	43,673	1,295	63	2,676	24	41,755	43,586	17,154	16,739	1,177	62	145	6	15,832	16,671
" Jalgaon	89,937	46,177	43,760	1,600	26	3,279	29	41,298	43,705	16,667	16,456	1,442	25	104	7	15,121	16,424
" Khamgaon	91,602	47,896	43,706	1,599	30	3,534	44	42,763	43,632	17,079	16,234	1,438	29	129	10	15,512	16,195
Ellichpur District. Taluk Ellichpur	124,059	64,174	59,885	2,351	24	5,491	74	56,332	59,787	21,847	21,410	1,998	24	179	13	19,670	21,373
" Daryapur	111,595	57,515	54,080	1,881	19	3,426	31	52,208	54,030	20,045	19,653	1,706	19	105	2	18,234	19,632
" Melghat	8,338	4,734	3,604	23	...	372	1	4,339	3,603	1,499	1,477	21	...	14	...	1,464	1,477
Buldana District. Taluk Chikhli	136,828	69,694	67,134	1,368	42	3,352	62	64,974	67,030	27,274	26,997	1,205	38	142	8	25,927	26,951
" Malkapur	162,064	82,146	79,918	2,875	43	5,393	46	73,878	79,829	31,546	31,558	2,643	42	249	5	28,654	31,511
" Mehkar	143,696	73,176	70,520	1,148	10	2,913	36	69,115	70,474	28,695	29,203	1,024	10	123	4	27,548	29,189
Wun District. Taluk Yeotmal	93,683	48,599	45,084	1,144	23	2,441	29	45,014	45,032	18,293	17,445	1,038	23	105	4	17,150	17,418
" Darwha	137,182	70,651	66,531	1,101	28	2,689	22	66,861	66,481	27,836	27,065	983	18	104	4	26,749	27,043
" Kelapur	74,783	38,276	36,507	524	2	1,313	21	36,439	36,484	15,416	14,841	478	2	62	5	14,876	14,834
" Wun	65,436	33,240	32,196	409	22	1,012	27	31,819	32,147	13,960	13,417	359	21	56	6	13,545	13,390
Basim District. Taluk Basim	165,987	85,247	80,740	1,268	13	3,590	38	80,389	80,689	33,253	32,448	1,130	12	191	5	31,932	32,431
" Mangrul	77,356	40,129	37,227	603	5	1,433	14	38,093	37,208	15,774	15,037	553	3	69	3	15,152	15,031
" Pusad	128,194	65,497	62,697	925	7	2,488	10	62,104	62,680	27,675	26,740	824	6	134	1	26,717	26,733

Table IX.—Education by Religion and Age.

AGE PERIODS—*contd.*

DISTRICT AND TALUK.	15—24 Total. Males.	15—24 Total. Females.	15—24 Learning. Males.	15—24 Learning. Females.	15—24 Literate. Males.	15—24 Literate. Females.	15—24 Illiterate. Males.	15—24 Illiterate. Females.	25 and over. Total. Males.	25 and over. Total. Females.	25 and over. Learning. Males.	25 and over. Learning. Females.	25 and over. Literate. Males.	25 and over. Literate. Females.	25 and over. Illiterate. Males.	25 and over. Illiterate. Females.
19	20	21	22	23	24	25	26	27	28	29	30	31	32	33	34	35
District Amraoti	39,689	43,949	1,045	8	5,008	105	33,636	43,836	156,531	132,069	77	12	13,715	135	142,739	131,922
" Akola	36,668	40,556	1,080	8	4,934	101	30,654	40,447	135,885	117,465	52	5	13,134	137	122,699	117,323
" Ellichpur	17,574	19,029	492	...	2,335	34	14,747	18,995	65,458	56,000	38	...	6,656	57	58,764	55,943
" Buldana	30,520	35,771	406	3	2,811	52	27,213	35,716	106,981	94,043	23	2	8,333	75	98,625	93,966
" Wun	23,526	26,647	304	7	1,887	37	21,335	26,603	91,735	80,903	16	4	5,241	43	86,478	80,856
" Basim	23,397	27,539	264	2	1,724	23	21,409	27,514	90,774	78,900	25	2	5,373	30	85,376	78,868
Railway Passengers, etc.	31	10	...	...	10	...	21	10	194	49	...	...	36	...	158	49
Total	171,405	193,501	8,681	28	18,709	352	149,015	193,121	647,558	559,429	231	25	52,488	477	594,839	558,927
Amraoti District. Taluk Amraoti	11,539	12,459	501	5	1,859	75	9,179	12,379	43,720	36,778	26	9	5,165	66	38,529	36,703
" Chandur	11,976	13,164	231	1	1,433	12	10,312	13,151	47,611	40,245	20	1	3,423	28	44,168	40,216
" Morsi	8,785	9,950	175	1	917	9	7,693	9,940	35,680	30,580	17	2	2,802	21	32,861	30,557
" Murtazapur	7,389	8,376	138	1	799	9	6,452	8,366	29,520	24,466	14	...	2,325	20	27,181	24,446
Akola District. Taluk Akola	8,803	9,500	420	4	1,193	29	7,190	9,467	33,272	28,230	10	5	3,235	47	30,027	28,178
" Akot	8,593	9,835	245	1	1,252	39	7,096	9,795	32,986	28,746	20	...	3,277	49	29,689	28,697
" Balapur	6,032	6,896	112	1	714	6	5,206	6,889	22,540	20,038	6	...	1,817	12	20,717	20,026
" Jalgaon	6,552	7,052	156	1	851	12	5,545	7,039	22,958	20,252	2	...	2,324	10	20,632	20,242
" Khamgaon	6,688	7,273	147	1	924	15	5,617	7,257	24,129	20,199	14	...	2,481	19	21,634	20,180
Ellichpur District. Taluk Ellichpur	8,957	9,547	317	...	1,340	22	7,300	9,525	33,370	28,928	36	...	3,972	39	29,362	28,889
" Daryapur	7,9 9	8,905	173	...	909	11	6,867	8,894	29,521	25,522	2	...	2,412	18	27,107	25,504
" Melghat	668	577	2	...	86	1	580	576	2,567	1,550	...	...	272	...	2,295	1,550
Buldana District. Taluk Chikhli	9,278	10,830	158	2	738	23	8,382	10,805	33,142	29,307	5	2	2,472	31	30,665	29,274
" Malkapur	11,313	13,053	221	1	1,377	16	9,715	13,036	39,287	35,307	11	...	3,767	25	35,509	35,282
" Mehkar	9,929	11,888	117	...	696	13	9,116	11,875	34,552	29,429	7	...	2,094	19	32,451	29,410
Wun District. Taluk Yeotmal	6,061	6,805	103	...	633	13	5,325	6,792	24,245	20,834	3	...	1,703	12	22,539	20,822
" Darwha	8,501	9,954	107	7	650	8	7,744	9,939	34,314	29,512	11	3	1,935	10	32,368	29,499
" Kelapur	4,702	5,395	44	...	327	6	4,331	5,389	18,158	16,271	2	...	924	10	17,232	16,261
" Wun	4,262	4,493	50	...	277	10	3,935	4,483	15,018	14,286	...	1	679	11	14,339	14,274
Basim District. Taluk Basim	10,619	12,665	123	1	848	16	9,648	12,648	41,375	35,627	15	...	2,551	17	38,809	35,610
" Mangrul	4,688	5,484	46	1	342	6	4,300	5,477	19,667	16,706	4	1	1,022	5	18,641	16,700
" Pusad	8,090	9,390	95	...	534	1	7,461	9,389	29,732	26,567	6	1	1,800	8	27,926	26,558

TABLE IX.

Education by Religion and Age.—
Part C—MUSALMAN.

TABLE IX.—Education by Religion and Age.—Part C—MUSALMAN.

DISTRICT AND TALUK.	TOTAL MUSALMAN.			TOTAL BY EDUCATION.						AGE PERIODS. 0—14							
				Learning.		Literate.		Illiterate.		Total.		Learning.		Literate.		Illiterate.	
	Total.	Males.	Females.	Males.	Females.	Males.	Females.	Males.	Females.	Males.	Females.	Males.	Females.	Males.	Females.	Males.	Females.
1	2	3	4	5	6	7	8	9	10	11	12	13	14	15	16	17	18
District Amraoti	47,522	24,931	22,591	1,036	64	1,943	100	21,952	22,427	8,884	8,464	881	60	135	16	7,868	8,388
„ Akola	51,302	26,717	24,585	1,073	54	2,184	70	23,460	24,461	9,287	9,154	914	52	116	15	8,257	9,087
„ Ellichpur	30,645	15,671	14,974	637	34	1,280	43	13,754	14,897	5,339	5,265	511	30	51	7	4,777	5,228
„ Buldana	34,405	17,679	16,726	710	26	1,161	41	15,808	16,659	6,873	6,643	623	25	68	5	6,182	6,613
„ Wun	20,727	10,932	9,795	459	16	838	31	9,635	9,748	4,057	3,873	406	16	44	3	3,607	3,854
„ Basim	23,020	12,053	10,967	387	43	787	33	10,879	10,891	4,563	4,392	340	41	58	2	4,165	4,349
Railway Passengers, etc.	60	52	8	2	...	11	...	39	8	7	3	2	...	1	...	4	3
Total	207,681	108,035	99,646	4,304	237	8,204	318	95,527	99,091	39,010	37,794	8,677	224	478	48	34,860	37,522
Amraoti District: Taluk Amraoti	18,384	9,712	8,672	461	29	840	56	8,411	8,587	3,369	3,083	383	27	65	8	2,921	3,048
„ Chandur	9,060	4,794	4,266	222	7	373	11	4,199	4,248	1,751	1,661	190	6	25	1	1,536	1,654
„ Morsi	9,225	4,729	4,496	203	4	337	13	4,189	4,479	1,723	1,695	176	4	17	...	1,530	1,691
„ Murtazapur	10,853	5,696	5,157	150	24	393	20	5,153	5,113	2,041	2,025	132	23	28	7	1,881	1,995
Akola District: Taluk Akola	12,463	6,545	5,918	335	8	648	29	5,562	5,881	2,265	2,140	265	8	25	3	1,975	2,129
„ Akot	13,330	6,804	6,526	246	24	523	10	6,035	6,492	2,395	2,391	217	24	23	1	2,155	2,366
„ Balapur	11,340	5,722	5,618	256	6	368	19	5,098	5,593	2,189	2,185	225	5	38	8	1,926	2,172
„ Jalgaon	6,933	3,742	3,191	98	3	247	4	3,397	3,184	1,260	1,201	87	3	9	1	1,164	1,197
„ Khamgaon	7,236	3,904	3,332	138	13	398	8	3,368	3,311	1,178	1,237	120	12	21	2	1,037	1,223
Ellichpur District: Taluk Ellichpur	19,020	9,464	9,556	409	26	851	36	8,204	9,494	3,299	3,330	317	23	38	5	2,944	3,302
„ Daryapur	10,263	5,439	4,824	220	6	351	3	4,868	4,815	1,820	1,714	187	5	10	2	1,623	1,707
„ Melghat	1,362	768	594	8	2	78	4	682	588	220	221	7	2	3	...	210	219
Buldana District: Taluk Chikhli	11,853	6,112	5,741	234	8	380	6	5,498	5,727	2,360	2,281	210	7	15	...	2,135	2,274
„ Malkapur	14,395	7,334	7,061	323	15	535	27	6,476	7,019	2,895	2,781	277	15	32	4	2,586	2,762
„ Mehkar	8,157	4,233	3,924	153	3	246	8	3,834	3,913	1,618	1,581	136	3	21	1	1,461	1,577
Wun District: Taluk Yeotmal	5,595	3,006	2,589	137	3	269	4	2,600	2,582	1,052	988	123	3	18	...	911	985
„ Darwha	9,797	5,219	4,578	191	9	365	16	4,663	4,553	1,949	1,861	166	9	14	...	1,769	1,852
„ Kelapur	3,052	1,564	1,488	63	1	115	6	1,386	1,481	603	589	56	1	8	...	539	588
„ Wun	2,283	1,143	1,140	68	3	89	5	986	1,132	453	435	61	3	4	3	388	429
Basim District: Taluk Basim	9,313	4,036	4,377	155	15	367	17	4,414	4,345	1,817	1,728	132	13	19	1	1,666	1,714
„ Mangrul	4,718	2,450	2,268	103	24	184	7	2,163	2,237	908	881	91	24	21	1	796	856
„ Pusad	8,989	4,667	4,322	120		236	9	4,302	4,309	1,838	1,783	117	4	18	...	1,703	1,779

DISTRICT AND TALUK.	AGE PERIODS. 15—24 TOTAL.		LEARNING.		LITERATE.		ILLITERATE.		25 AND OVER. TOTAL.		LEARNING.		LITERATE.		ILLITERATE.	
	Males.	Females.	Males.	Females.	Males.	Females.	Males.	Females.	Males.	Females.	Males.	Females.	Males.	Females.	Males.	Females.
19	20	21	22	23	24	25	26	27	28	29	30	31	32	33	34	35
District Amraoti	3,610	3,686	140	3	487	31	2,083	3,652	12,437	10,441	15	1	1,321	53	11,101	10,387
" Akola	4,021	4,095	146	2	573	26	3,302	4,067	13,409	11,336	13	...	1,495	29	11,901	11,307
" Ellichpur	2,436	2,467	106	4	350	20	1,980	2,443	7,816	7,242	20	...	879	16	6,997	7,226
" Buldana	2,463	2,709	78	...	316	14	2,069	2,695	8,343	7,374	9	1	777	22	7,557	7,351
" Wun	1,514	1,456	51	...	220	11	1,243	1,445	5,361	4,466	2	...	574	17	4,785	4,449
" Basim	1,629	1,716	40	2	215	18	1,374	1,696	5,861	4,859	7	...	514	13	5,340	4,846
Railway Passengers, etc.	8	1	...	...	3	...	5	1	37	4	...	...	7	..	30	4
Total	15,681	16,130	561	11	2,164	120	12,956	15,999	58,344	45,722	66	2	5,567	150	47,711	45,570
Amraoti District — Taluk Amraoti	1,444	1,446	70	1	206	20	1,168	1,425	4,899	4,143	8	1	569	28	4,322	4,114
" Chandur	700	660	30	1	105	1	565	658	2,343	1,945	2	...	243	9	2,098	1,936
" Morsi	670	707	26	...	92	6	552	701	2,336	2,094	1	...	228	7	2,107	2,087
" Murtazapur	796	873	14	1	84	4	698	868	2,859	2,259	4	...	281	9	2,574	2,250
Akola District — Taluk Akola	961	958	66	...	165	13	730	945	3,319	2,820	4	...	458	13	2,857	2,807
" Akot	1,045	1,123	27	...	148	3	870	1,120	3,364	3,012	2	...	352	6	3,010	3,006
" Balapur	844	935	29	1	86	6	729	928	2,689	2,498	2	...	244	5	2,443	2,493
" Jalgaon	549	528	7	...	65	2	477	526	1,933	1,462	4	...	173	1	1,756	1,461
" Khamgaon	622	551	17	1	109	2	496	548	2,104	1,544	1	...	268	4	1,835	1,540
Ellichpur District — Taluk Ellichpur	1,448	1,497	74	3	228	17	1,146	1,477	4,717	4,729	18	...	585	14	4,114	4,715
" Daryapur	867	873	31	1	106	...	730	872	2,752	2,237	2	...	235	1	2,515	2,236
" Melghat	121	97	1	...	16	3	104	94	427	276	...	...	59	1	368	275
Buldana District — Taluk Chikhli	834	873	20	...	109	4	705	869	2,918	2,587	4	1	256	2	2,658	2,584
" Malkapur	1,057	1,174	43	...	139	8	875	1,166	3,382	3,106	3	...	364	15	3,015	3,091
" Mehkar	572	662	15	...	68	2	489	660	2,043	1,681	2	...	157	5	1,884	1,676
Wun District — Taluk Yeotmal	408	392	13	...	70	1	325	391	1,546	1,209	1	...	181	3	1,364	1,206
" Darwha	761	677	24	...	105	7	632	670	2,509	2,040	1	...	246	9	2,262	2,031
" Kelapur	200	219	7	...	27	2	166	217	761	680	...	...	80	4	681	676
" Wun	145	168	7	...	18	1	120	167	545	537	...	...	67	1	478	536
Basim District — Taluk Basim	703	685	20	2	110	8	573	675	2,416	1,964	3	...	238	8	2,175	1,956
" Mangrul	334	358	10	...	45	1	279	357	1,208	1,029	2	...	118	5	1,088	1,024
" Pusad	592	673	10	...	60	9	522	664	2,237	1,866	2	...	158	...	2,077	1,866

TABLE IX.

Education by Religion and Age.—Part D—ANIMISTIC.

TABLE IX.—Education by Religion and Age.—Part D—ANIMISTIC.

DISTRICT AND TALUK.	TOATL ANIMISTIC.			TOTAL BY EDUCATION.						AGE PERIODS.							
				Learning.		Literate.		Illiterate.		0–14							
										Total.		Learning.		Literate.		Illiterate.	
	Total.	Males.	Females.	Males.	Females.	Males.	Females.	Males.	Females.	Males.	Females.	Males.	Females.	Males.	Females.	Males.	Females.
1	2	3	4	5	6	7	8	9	10	11	12	13	14	15	16	17	18
District Amraoti	17,391	8,727	8,664	21	...	10	...	8,696	8,664	3,107	3,256	15	...	2	...	3,090	3,256
" Akola	1,545	813	732	2	...	...	...	811	732	321	348	1	...	...	...	320	348
" Ellichpur	39,745	20,101	19,644	7	...	11	...	20,083	19,644	8,930	8,816	5	...	1	...	8,924	8,816
" Buldana	7	4	3	...	...	...	...	4	3	3	...	...	...	...	...	3	...
" Wun	77,968	38,977	38,991	38	...	39	...	38,900	38,991	17,100	17,149	33	...	4	...	17,063	17,149
" Basim	449	225	224	...	...	...	...	225	224	96	104	...	...	...	...	96	104
Railway Passengers, etc.	3	...	3	...	...	...	...	...	3	...	2	...	...	...	...	...	2
Total	137,108	68,847	68,261	68	...	60	...	68,719	68,261	29,557	29,675	54	...	7	...	29,496	29,675
Amraoti District — Taluk Amraoti	1,756	870	886	9	...	...	...	861	886	275	330	5	...	...	...	270	330
" Chandur	6,954	3,507	3,447	3	...	4	...	3,500	3,447	1,241	1,240	2	...	1	...	1,238	1,240
" Morsi	8,383	4,190	4,193	8	...	6	...	4,176	4,193	1,537	1,633	7	...	1	...	1,529	1,633
" Murtazapur	298	160	138	1	...	...	...	159	138	54	53	1	...	...	...	53	53
Akola District — Taluk Akola	143	80	63	2	...	...	...	78	63	13	22	1	...	...	...	12	22
" Akot	785	415	370	...	...	...	...	415	370	167	180	...	...	...	...	167	180
" Balapur	8	3	5	...	...	...	...	3	5	1	2	...	...	...	...	1	2
" Jalgaon	589	299	290	...	...	...	...	299	290	135	144	...	...	...	...	135	144
" Khamgaon	20	16	4	...	...	...	...	16	4	5	...	...	...	...	...	5	...
Ellichpur District — Taluk Ellichpur	2,213	1,133	1,080	1	...	...	...	1,132	1,080	468	469	1	...	...	...	467	469
" Daryapur	214	110	104	...	...	...	...	110	104	32	40	...	...	...	...	32	40
" Melghat	37,318	18,858	18,460	6	...	11	...	18,841	18,460	8,430	8,307	4	...	1	...	8,425	8,307
Buldana District — Taluk Chikhli	7	4	3	...	...	...	...	4	3	3	...	...	...	...	...	3	...
" Malkapur	...	...	...	...	...	...	...	...	...	...	...	...	...	...	...	...	...
" Mehkar	...	...	...	...	...	...	...	...	...	...	...	...	...	...	...	...	...
Wun District — Taluk Yeotmal	24,334	12,223	12,111	17	...	18	...	12,188	12,111	5,130	5,132	15	...	1	...	5,114	5,132
" Darwha	8,887	4,482	4,405	1	...	7	...	4,474	4,405	1,918	1,847	1	...	2	...	1,915	1,847
" Kelapur	27,836	13,861	13,975	15	...	7	...	13,839	13,975	6,218	6,322	13	...	1	...	6,204	6,322
" Wun	16,911	8,411	8,500	5	...	7	...	8,399	8,500	3,834	3,848	4	...	...	...	3,830	3,848
Basim District — Taluk Basim	...	...	...	...	...	...	...	...	...	...	...	...	...	...	...	...	...
" Mangrul	39	17	22	...	...	...	...	17	22	4	10	...	...	...	...	4	10
" Pusad	410	208	202	...	...	...	...	208	202	92	94	...	...	...	...	92	94

Table IX.—Education by Religion and Age.

DISTRICT AND TALUK.	AGE PERIODS—*contd.* 15–24 TOTAL. Males.	Females.	LEARNING. Males.	Females.	LITERATE. Males.	Females.	ILLITERATE. Males.	Females.	25 AND OVER. TOTAL. Males.	Females.	LEARNING. Males.	Females.	LITERATE. Males.	Females.	ILLITERATE. Males.	Females.
19	20	21	22	23	24	25	26	27	28	29	30	31	32	33	34	35
DISTRICT AMRAOTI	1,007	1,236	4	...	1	...	1,002	1,236	4,613	4,172	2	...	7	...	4,604	4,172
" AKOLA	96	88	1	...	...	...	95	88	396	296	...	...	...	...	396	296
" ELLICHPUR	2,562	3,231	1	..	1	...	2,560	3,231	8,609	7,597	1	...	9	...	8,599	7,597
" BULDANA	...	1	...	...	...	...	...	1	1	2	...	...	...	...	1	2
" WUN	4,274	5,548	4	...	13	...	4,257	5,548	17,603	16,294	1	...	22	...	17,580	16,294
" BASIM	28	44	...	...	...	...	28	44	101	76	...	...	...	...	101	76
Railway Passengers, etc.	...	...	...	...	...	...	...	...	..	1	...	...	...	...	..	1
Total	7,967	10,148	10	...	15	...	7,942	10,148	31,828	28,438	4	...	88	...	31,281	28,438
AMRAOTI DISTRICT — Taluk Amraoti	89	109	2	...	...	...	87	109	506	447	2	...	...	...	504	447
" Chandur	399	505	1	...	1	...	397	505	1,867	1,702	...	...	2	...	1,865	1,702
" Morsi	501	594	1	...	...	...	500	594	2,152	1,966	...	...	5	...	2,147	1,966
" Murtazapur	18	28	...	...	...	...	18	28	88	57	...	...	...	...	88	57
AKOLA DISTRICT — Taluk Akola	10	9	1	...	...	...	9	9	57	32	...	...	...	...	57	32
" Akot	49	37	...	...	...	...	49	37	199	153	...	...	...	...	199	153
" Balapur	...	...	...	...	...	...	...	...	2	3	...	...	...	...	2	3
" Jalgaon	35	41	...	...	...	.	35	41	129	105	...	...	...	...	129	105
" Khamgaon	2	1	...	...	...	...	2	1	9	3	...	...	...	...	9	3
ELLICHPUR DISTRICT — Taluk Ellichpur	116	145	...	...	...	...	116	145	549	466	...	...	...	...	549	466
" Daryapur	7	12	...	..	...	...	7	12	71	52	...	...	...	...	71	52
" Melghat	2,439	3,074	1	...	1	...	2,437	3,074	7,989	7,079	1	...	9	...	7,979	7,079
BULDANA DISTRICT — Taluk Chikhli	...	1	...	...	...	...	...	1	1	2	...	...	...	...	1	2
" Malkapur	...	...	...	...	...	...	...	...	...	...	..	...	...	...	...	...
" Mehkar	...	...	...	...	...	...	...	...	...	...	...	...	...	...	...	...
WUN DISTRICT — Taluk Yeotmal	1,326	1,828	2	...	8	...	1,316	1,828	5,767	5,151	...	...	9	...	5,758	5,151
" Darwha	498	630	...	...	2	...	496	630	2,066	1,928	...	...	3	...	2,063	1,928
" Kelapur	1,505	1,956	1	...	2	...	1,502	1,956	6,138	5,697	1	...	4	...	6,133	5,697
" Wun	945	1,134	1	...	1	...	943	1,134	3,632	3,518	...	...	6	...	3,626	3,518
BASIM DISTRICT — Taluk Basim	...	...	...	...	...	...	...	...	...	...	...	...	...	...	...	...
" Mangrul	2	3	...	...	...	...	2	3	11	9	...	...	...	...	11	9
" Pusad	26	41	...	...	...	...	26	41	90	67	...	...	...	...	90	67

TABLE IX.

Education by Religion and Age.—
Part E—JAIN.

Table IX.—Education by Religion and Age.

TABLE IX.—Education by Religion and Age.—Part E—JAIN.

District and Taluk.	Total Jain.			Total by Education.						Age Periods. 0–14							
				Learning.		Literate.		Illiterate.		Total.		Learning.		Literate.		Illiterate.	
	Total.	Males.	Females.	Males.	Females.	Males.	Females.	Males.	Females.	Males.	Females.	Males.	Females.	Males.	Females.	Males.	Females.
1	2	3	4	5	6	7	8	9	10	11	12	13	14	15	16	17	18
District Amraoti	5,660	2,084	2,676	254	3	1,084	10	1,646	2,663	938	899	220	3	59	3	659	893
" Akola	3,365	1,825	1,540	176	17	828	2	821	1,521	538	550	154	17	47	1	337	532
" Ellichpur	1,269	684	585	75	1	221	3	388	581	230	178	73	1	6	...	151	177
" Buldana	3,883	2,023	1,860	240	2	821	2	962	1,856	682	684	217	2	40	1	425	681
" Wun	1,702	937	765	83	2	363	4	491	759	301	268	77	2	29	2	195	264
" Basim	3,073	1,590	1,433	184	...	520	4	886	1,479	614	528	170	...	19	...	425	528
Total	18,952	10,043	8,909	1,012	25	3,837	25	5,194	8,859	3,303	3,107	911	25	200	7	2,192	3,075
Amraoti District: Taluk Amraoti	1,222	692	530	62	2	322	4	308	524	186	158	52	2	13	1	121	155
" Chandur	1,596	861	735	55	...	346	3	460	732	248	255	48	...	27	1	173	254
" Morsi	1,051	509	542	6	...	131	2	342	540	197	203	35	...	10	1	152	202
" Murtazapur	1,791	922	869	101	1	285	1	536	867	307	283	85	1	9	...	213	282
Akola District: Taluk Akola	971	507	464	56	2	204	...	247	462	146	175	48	2	9	...	89	173
" Akot	574	308	266	25	1	104	1	179	264	103	100	25	1	5	1	73	98
" Balapur	914	481	433	51	8	247	...	183	425	152	146	39	8	18	...	95	138
" Jalgaon	151	101	50	3	...	64	...	34	50	19	17	3	...	4	...	12	17
" Khamgaon	755	428	327	41	6	209	1	178	320	118	112	39	6	11	...	68	106
Ellichpur District: Taluk Ellichpur	800	427	373	44	1	130	3	253	369	138	121	42	1	3	...	93	120
" Daryapur	467	255	212	31	...	90	...	134	212	92	57	31	...	3	...	58	57
" Melghat	2	2	...	...	...	1	...	1	...	...	...	...	...	...	...	...	...
Buldana District: Taluk Chikhli	1,331	682	649	72	...	259	...	351	649	232	237	64	...	15	...	153	237
" Malkapur	1,394	721	673	85	2	305	1	331	670	240	259	74	2	11	1	155	256
" Mehkar	1,158	620	538	83	...	257	1	280	537	210	188	79	...	14	...	117	188
Wun District: Taluk Yeotmal	722	393	329	34	...	164	1	195	328	139	124	29	...	17	...	93	124
" Darwha	713	393	320	36	2	149	3	208	315	116	103	35	2	8	2	73	99
" Kelapur	219	123	96	11	...	37	...	75	96	38	34	11	...	4	...	23	34
" Wun	48	28	20	2	...	13	...	13	20	8	7	2	...	...	...	6	7
Basim District: Taluk Basim	1,864	970	894	118	...	347	3	505	891	369	316	111	...	13	...	245	316
" Mangrul	332	176	156	24	...	40	...	112	156	67	53	21	...	1	...	45	53
" Pusad	877	444	433	42	...	133	1	269	432	278	159	38	...	5	...	135	159

Table IX.—Education by Religion and Age.

DISTRICT AND TALUK.	AGE PERIODS—*contd.*															
	15—24								25 AND OVER.							
	TOTAL.		LEARNING.		LITERATE.		ILLITERATE.		TOTAL.		LEARNING.		LITERATE.		ILLITERATE.	
	Males.	Females.	Males.	Females.	Males.	Females.	Males.	Females.	Males.	Females.	Males.	Females.	Males.	Females.	Males.	Females.
19	20	21	22	23	24	25	26	27	28	29	30	31	32	33	34	35
DISTRICT AMRAOTI	479	461	32	...	262	3	185	458	1,567	1,316	2	...	763	4	802	1,312
" AKOLA	340	266	21	...	229	1	90	265	947	724	1	...	552	...	394	724
" ELLICHPUR	100	99	2	...	52	1	46	98	354	308	...	...	163	2	191	306
" BULDANA	313	334	22	...	196	...	95	334	1,028	842	1	...	585	1	442	841
" WUN	153	137	4	...	92	...	57	137	483	360	2	...	242	2	239	358
" BASIN	225	212	11	...	138	2	76	210	751	743	3	...	303	2	385	741
Total	1,610	1,509	92	...	969	7	549	1,502	5,180	4,293	9	...	2,668	11	2,453	4,282
AMRAOTI DISTRICT. Taluk Amraoti	125	92	9	...	78	2	38	90	381	280	1	...	231	1	149	279
" Chandur	140	132	6	..	91	...	43	132	473	348	1	...	228	2	244	346
" Morsi	62	88	1	...	25	1	36	87	250	251	...	...	96	...	154	251
" Murtazapur	152	149	16	...	68	...	68	149	403	437	...	...	208	1	255	436
AKOLA DISTRICT. Taluk Akola	92	81	7	...	53	...	32	81	269	208	1	...	142	...	126	208
" Akot	53	43	...	...	34	...	19	43	152	123	...	...	65	...	87	123
" Balapur	104	65	12	...	75	...	17	65	225	222	...	...	154	...	71	222
" Jalgaon	17	10	...	...	10	...	7	10	65	23	..	...	50	...	15	23
" Khamgaon	74	67	2	...	57	1	15	66	236	148	...	...	141	...	95	148
ELLICHPUR DISTRICT. Taluk Ellichpur	67	53	2	...	30	1	35	52	222	199	...	...	97	2	125	197
" Daryapur	32	46	...	...	22	...	10	46	131	109	...	...	65	...	66	109
" Melghat	1	...	...	...	...	...	1	...	1	...	...	...	1	...	...	...
BULDANA DISTRICT. Taluk Chikhli	115	113	8	...	74	...	33	113	335	299	...	...	170	...	165	299
" Malkapur	112	119	10	...	68	...	34	119	309	295	1	...	226	...	142	295
" Mehkar	86	102	4	...	54	...	28	102	324	248	...	...	189	1	135	247
WUN DISTRICT. Taluk Yeotmal	66	62	3	...	42	...	21	62	188	143	2	...	105	1	81	142
" Darwha	67	54	1	...	39	..	27	54	210	163	...	...	102	1	108	162
" Kelapur	16	16	...	...	7	...	9	16	69	46	...	...	26	...	43	46
" Wun	4	5	...	...	4	...	...	5	16	8	...	...	9	...	7	8
BASIM DISTRICT. Taluk Basim	147	126	6		93	2	48	124	454	452	1	...	241	1	212	451
" Mangrul	22	19	2	...	7	...	13	19	87	84	1	...	32	...	54	84
" Pusad	56	67	3	...	38	...	15	67	210	207	1	...	90	1	119	206

TABLE IX.

Education by Religion and Age.—
Part F—SIKH.

TABLE IX.—Education by Religion

DISTRICT AND TALUK.	TOTAL SIKH.			TOTAL BY EDUCATION.						AGE 0—14							
				Learning.		Literate.		Illiterate.		Total.		Learning.		Literate.		Illiterate.	
	Total.	Males.	Females.	Males.	Females.	Males.	Females.	Males.	Females.	Males.	Females.	Males.	Females.	Males.	Females.	Males.	Females.
1	2	3	4	5	6	7	8	9	10	11	12	13	14	15	16	17	18
District Amraoti	29	13	16	1	...	2	...	10	16	5	8	1	..	...	...	4	8
,, Akola	67	41	26	3	...	13	2	25	24	8	5	3	...	1	...	4	5
,, Ellichpur	1	1	...	...	...	...	...	1	...	...	..	...	...	...	...	...	...
,, Buldana	30	13	17	...	...	2	...	11	17	5	7	...	...	...	...	5	7
,, Wun	38	23	15	...	...	...	...	23	15	11	4	...	...	...	...	11	4
,, Basim	12	7	5	2	...	3	...	2	5	3	2	2	...	...	...	1	2
Total	177	98	79	6	...	20	2	72	77	82	26	6	...	1	...	25	26
Amraoti District. Taluk Amraoti	2	1	1	...	...	...	...	1	1	...	...	...	...	...	...	...	...
,, Chandur	18	10	8	1	...	...	...	9	8	5	4	1	...	...	...	4	4
,, Morsi	...	...	...	...	...	...	...	...	...	...	...	...	...	...	...	...	...
,, Murtazapur	9	2	7	...	...	2	...	...	7	...	4	...	...	...	...	...	4
Akola District. Taluk Akola	49	29	20	2	...	9	1	18	19	4	5	2	...	...	...	2	5
,, Akot	7	6	1	1	...	3	...	2	1	2	...	1	...	1	...	...	...
,, Balapur	...	...	...	..	...	...	...	...	...	...	...	...	...	...	...	...	...
,, Jalgaon	4	2	2	...	...	1	...	1	2	...	...	...	...	...	...	...	...
,, Khamgaon	7	4	3	...	...	..	1	4	2	2	...	...	...	...	...	2	...
Ellichpur District. Taluk Ellichpur	...	...	...	...	...	...	...	...	...	...	...	...	...	...	...	...	...
,, Daryapur	1	1	...	...	...	...	...	1	...	...	...	...	...	...	...	...	...
,, Melghat	...	...	...	...	...	...	...	...	...	...	...	..	...	...	...	...	...
Buldana District. Taluk Chikhli	1	...	1	...	...	...	...	...	1	...	...	...	...	...	...	...	...
,, Malkapur	...	...	...	...	...	...	...	...	...	...	...	...	...	...	...	...	...
,, Mehkar	29	13	16	...	...	2	..	11	16	5	7	...	...	...	...	5	7
Wun District. Taluk Yeotmal	1	1	...	...	...	...	...	1	...	...	...	...	...	...	...	...	...
,, Darwha	1	1		...	...	...	...	1	...	...	..	...	...	...	..	...	...
,, Kelapur	36	21	15	...	...	...	..	21	15	11	4	...	...	...	...	11	4
,, Wun	...	...	...	...	...	...	...	...	...	...	...	...	...	...	...	...	...
Basim District. Taluk Basim	...	...	...	...	...	...	...	...	...	...	...	...	...	...	...	...	...
,, Mangrul	...	...	...	...	...	...	...	..	...	...	...	...	...	..	...	...	...
,, Pusad	12	7	5	2	...	3	..	2	5	3	2	2	...	...	...	1	2

and Age.—Part F.—SIKH.

PERIODS. 15—24 Total Males	15—24 Total Females	15—24 Learning Males	15—24 Learning Females	15—24 Literate Males	15—24 Literate Females	15—24 Illiterate Males	15—24 Illiterate Females	25 and over Total Males	25 and over Total Females	25 and over Learning Males	25 and over Learning Females	25 and over Literate Males	25 and over Literate Females	25 and over Illiterate Males	25 and over Illiterate Females	District and Taluk.
19	20	21	22	23	24	25	26	27	28	29	30	31	32	33	34	35
2	...	...	...	1	...	1	...	6	8	...	...	1	...	5	8	District Amraoti.
4	3	...	...	1	1	3	2	29	18	...	...	11	1	18	17	" Akola.
...	...	...	...	...	...	...	...	1	...	...	...	...	...	1	...	" Ellichpur.
2	3	...	...	...	...	2	3	6	7	...	...	2	...	4	7	" Buldana.
1	4	...	...	...	...	1	4	11	7	...	...	...	...	11	7	" Wun.
2	...	...	...	2	...	...	...	2	3	...	...	1	...	1	3	" Basim.
11	10	...	...	4	1	7	9	55	43	...	...	15	1	40	42	**Total.**
...	...	...	...	...	...	...	...	1	1	...	...	...	...	1	1	Taluk Amraoti (Amraoti District)
1	...	...	...	...	...	1	...	4	4	...	...	...	...	4	4	" Chandur (Amraoti District)
...	...	...	...	...	...	...	...	...	...	...	...	...	...	...	...	" Morsi (Amraoti District)
1	...	...	...	1	...	...	...	1	3	...	...	1	...	...	3	" Murtazapur (Amraoti District)
1	2	...	...	...	...	1	2	24	13	...	...	9	1	15	12	Taluk Akola (Akola District)
2	...	...	...	...	...	2	...	2	1	...	...	2	...	...	1	" Akot (Akola District)
...	...	...	...	...	...	...	...	...	...	...	...	...	...	...	...	" Balapur (Akola District)
1	...	...	...	1	...	...	...	1	2	...	...	...	...	1	2	" Jalgaon (Akola District)
...	1	...	...	...	1	...	...	2	2	...	...	...	...	2	2	" Khamgaon (Akola District)
...	...	...	...	...	...	...	...	...	...	...	...	...	...	...	...	Taluk Ellichpur (Ellichpur District)
...	...	...	...	...	...	...	...	1	...	...	...	...	...	1	...	" Daryapur (Ellichpur District)
...	...	...	...	...	...	...	...	...	...	...	...	...	...	...	...	" Melghat (Ellichpur District)
...	1	...	...	...	...	...	1	...	...	...	...	...	...	...	...	Taluk Chikhli (Buldana District)
...	...	...	...	...	...	...	...	...	...	...	...	...	...	...	...	" Malkapur (Buldana District)
2	2	...	...	...	...	2	2	6	7	...	...	2	...	4	7	" Mehkar (Buldana District)
...	...	...	...	...	...	...	...	1	...	...	...	...	...	1	...	Taluk Yeotmal (Wun District)
...	...	...	...	...	...	...	...	1	...	...	...	...	...	1	...	" Darwha (Wun District)
1	4	...	...	...	...	1	4	9	7	...	...	...	...	9	7	" Kelapur (Wun District)
...	...	...	...	...	...	...	...	...	...	...	...	...	...	...	...	" Wun (Wun District)
...	...	...	...	...	...	...	...	...	...	...	...	...	...	...	...	Taluk Basim (Basim District)
...	...	...	...	...	...	...	...	...	...	...	...	...	...	...	...	" Mangrul (Basim District)
[illegible]	...	...	...	2	...	...	...	2	3	...	...	1	...	1	3	" Pusad (Basim District)

TABLE IX.

Education by Religion and Age.—
Part G—CHRISTIAN.

TABLE IX.—Education by Religion and Age.—Part G—CHRISTIAN.

DISTRICT AND TALUK.	TOTAL CHRISTIAN.			TOTAL BY EDUCATION.						AGE PERIODS. 0—14							
				Learning.		Literate.		Illiterate.		Total.		Learning.		Literate.		Illiterate.	
	Total.	Males.	Females.	Males.	Females.	Males.	Females.	Males.	Females.	Males.	Females.	Males.	Females.	Males.	Females.	Males.	Females.
1	2	3	4	5	6	7	8	9	10	11	12	13	14	15	16	17	18
District Amraoti	629	317	312	33	31	201	155	83	126	85	119	32	29	11	29	42	61
" Akola	305	183	122	30	17	100	53	53	52	51	39	26	15	3	3	22	21
" Ellichpur	123	68	55	2	2	44	32	22	21	23	18	2	2	4	4	17	12
" Buldana	103	60	43	6	4	27	12	27	27	18	21	6	4	1	1	11	16
" Wun	89	49	40	4	...	33	20	12	20	14	13	4	...	4	4	6	9
" Basim	88	48	40	1	3	27	22	20	15	15	20	1	3	1	5	13	12
Railway passengers, etc.	22	13	9	...	...	11	6	2	3	3	6	...	...	1	3	2	3
Total	1,359	738	621	76	57	443	300	219	264	209	236	71	53	25	49	118	134
Amraoti District: Taluk Amraoti	592	287	305	30	31	180	150	77	124	79	118	30	29	11	29	38	60
" Chandur	15	13	2	1	...	10	...	2	2	...	1	...	...	...	...	...	1
" Morsi	5	4	1	...	...	2	1	2	...	2	...	...	...	...	...	2	...
" Murtazapur	17	13	4	2	...	9	4	2	...	4	...	2	...	...	...	2	...
Akola District: Taluk Akola	191	104	87	20	16	58	36	26	35	36	30	18	14	3	2	15	14
" Akot	6	5	1	...	...	3	1	2	...	...	...	...	...	...	...	...	...
" Balapur	8	5	3	2	...	2	3	1	...	3	1	2	...	...	1	1	...
" Jalgaon	2	2	...	...	...	1	...	1	...	...	...	...	...	...	...	...	...
" Khamgaon	98	67	31	8	1	36	13	23	17	12	8	6	1	...	...	6	7
Ellichpur District: Taluk Ellichpur	111	61	50	2	2	39	28	20	20	20	17	2	2	2	3	16	12
" Daryapur	1	...	1	...	...	...	1	...	...	...	...	...	...	...	...	...	...
" Melghat	11	7	4	...	...	5	3	2	1	3	1	...	...	2	1	1	...
Buldana District: Taluk Chikhli	77	47	30	4	3	22	9	21	18	15	14	4	3	1	1	10	10
" Malkapur	20	11	9	2	1	5	3	4	5	3	6	2	1	...	...	1	5
" Mehkar	6	2	4	...	.	...	...	2	4	...	1	...	...	...	...	...	1
Wun District: Taluk Yeotmal	89	49	40	4	...	33	20	12	20	14	13	4	...	4	4	6	9
" Darwha	...	...	...	...	...	...	...	...	...	...	...	...	...	...	...	...	...
" Kelapur	...	...	...	...	...	...	...	...	...	...	...	...	...	...	...	...	...
" Wun	...	...	...	...	...	...	...	...	...	...	...	...	...	...	...	...	...
Basim District: Taluk Basim	85	46	39	1	3	26	22	19	14	15	20	1	3	1	5	13	12
" Mangrul	1	1	...	...	...	1	...	...	...	...	...	...	...	...	...	...	...
" Pusad	2	1	1	...	...	...	...	1	1	...	...	...	...	...	...	...	...

Table IX.—Education by Religion and Age.

DISTRICT AND TALUK.	AGE PERIODS—contd. 15—24 Total. Males.	Total. Females.	Learning. Males.	Learning. Females.	Literate. Males.	Literate. Females.	Illiterate. Males.	Illiterate. Females.	25 AND OVER. Total. Males.	Total. Females.	Learning. Males.	Learning. Females.	Literate. Males.	Literate. Females.	Illiterate. Males.	Illiterate. Females.
19	20	21	22	23	24	25	26	27	28	29	30	31	32	33	34	35
District Amraoti	55	64	1	2	43	44	11	18	177	129	...	...	147	82	30	47
" Akola	40	39	4	2	29	28	7	9	92	44	...	...	68	22	24	22
" Ellichpur	7	9	...	...	6	6	1	3	38	28	...	...	34	22	4	6
" Buldana	6	6	...	...	3	1	3	5	36	16	...	...	23	10	13	6
" Wun	5	11	...	...	3	8	2	3	30	16	...	...	26	8	4	8
" Basim	5	11	...	...	5	10	...	1	28	9	...	...	21	7	7	2
Railway Passengers, etc.	3	...	...	...	3	...	...	...	7	3	...	...	7	3	...	...
Total	121	140	5	4	92	97	24	39	408	245	...	...	326	154	82	91
Amraoti District — Taluk Amraoti	50	63	...	2	39	43	11	18	158	124	...	...	130	78	28	46
" Chandur	5	...	1	...	4	...	...	...	8	1	...	...	6	...	2	1
" Morsi	...	...	...	...	...	...	...	...	2	1	...	...	2	1	...	...
" Murtazapur	...	1	...	...	...	1	...	...	9	3	...	...	9	3	...	...
Akola District — Taluk Akola	22	27	2	2	18	19	2	6	46	30	...	...	37	15	9	15
" Akot	2	...	...	...	1	...	1	...	3	1	...	...	2	1	1	...
" Balapur	1	1	...	...	1	1	..	...	1	1	...	...	1	1	...	...
" Jalgaon	...	...	...	...	...	...	...	...	2	...	...	...	1	...	1	...
" Khamgaon	15	11	2	...	9	8	4	3	40	12	...	...	27	5	13	7
Ellichpur District — Taluk Ellichpur	7	9	...	...	6	6	1	3	34	24	...	...	31	19	3	5
" Daryapur	...	...	...	...	...	...	...	...	...	1	...	...	...	1	...	...
" Melghat	...	...	...	...	...	...	...	...	4	3	...	...	3	2	1	1
Buldana District — Taluk Chikhli	4	5	...	...	3	1	1	4	28	11	...	...	18	7	10	4
" Malkapur	2	...	...	...	...	...	2	...	6	3	...	...	5	3	1	...
" Mehkar	..	1	...	...	...	...	...	1	2	2	...	...	...	...	2	2
Wun District — Taluk Yeotmal	5	11	...	...	3	8	2	3	30	16	...	...	26	8	4	8
" Darwha	...	...	...	...	...	...	...	...	...	...	...	...	...	...	...	...
" Kelapur	...	...	...	...	...	...	...	...	...	...	...	...	...	...	...	...
" Wun	...	...	...	...	...	...	...	...	...	...	...	...	...	...	...	...
Basim District — Taluk Basim	5	11	...	...	5	10	...	1	26	8	...	...	20	7	6	1
" Mangrul	...	...	...	...	...	...	...	...	1	...	...	...	1	...	...	...
" Pusad	...	...	...	...	...	...	...	...	1	1	...	...	...	...	1	1

TABLE IX.

Education by Religion and Age.—
Part H—PARSI.

TABLE IX.—Education by Religion

DISTRICT AND TALUK.	TOTAL PARSI.			TOTAL BY EDUCATION.						AGE 0—14							
				LEARNING.		LITERATE.		ILLITERATE.		TOTAL.		LEARNING.		LITERATE.		ILLITERATE.	
	Total.	Males.	Females.	Males.	Females.	Males.	Females.	Males.	Females.	Males.	Females.	Males.	Females.	Males.	Females.	Males.	Females.
1	2	3	4	5	6	7	8	9	10	11	12	13	14	15	16	17	18
District Amraoti	235	132	103	24	9	78	51	30	43	46	42	21	8	1	11	24	23
„ Akola	145	111	34	13	5	84	17	14	12	21	10	10	5	1	...	10	5
„ Ellichpur	22	20	2	..	...	20	1	...	1	...	1	...	...	...	...	...	1
„ Buldana	5	4	1	...	...	4	1	...	...	...	...	...	...	...	...	...	...
„ Wun	5	4	1	...	...	4	...	...	1	...	...	...	...	...	...	...	...
„ Basim	...	...	...	...	...	...	...	...	...	...	...	...	...	...	...	...	...
Total	412	271	141	37	14	190	70	44	57	67	53	31	13	2	11	34	29
Amraoti District. Taluk Amraoti	220	120	100	23	9	69	48	28	43	44	42	20	8	1	11	23	23
„ Chandur	...	...	...	...	...	...	...	...	...	...	...	...	...	...	...	...	...
„ Morsi	2	2	...	...	...	1	...	1	...	...	...	...	...	...	...	...	...
„ Murtazapur	13	10	3	1	...	8	3	1	...	2	...	1	...	...	...	1	...
Akola District. Taluk Akola	68	46	22	7	4	31	10	8	8	11	7	6	4	...	...	5	3
„ Akot	8	5	3	...	...	2	2	3	1	3	1	...	...	...	...	3	1
„ Balapur	4	4	...	...	...	4	...	...	...	...	...	...	...	...	...	...	...
„ Jalgaon	...	...	...	..	...	...	...	...	...	...	...	...	...	...	...	...	...
„ Khamgaon	65	56	9	6	1	47	5	3	3	7	2	4	1	1	...	2	1
Ellichpur District. Taluk Ellichpur	11	11	...	...	...	11	...	...	...	...	...	...	...	...	...	...	...
„ Daryapur	11	9	2	...	...	9	1	...	1	...	1	...	...	...	...	...	1
„ Melghat	...	...	..	...	...	...	...	...	...	...	...	...	...	...	...	...	...
Buldana District. Taluk Chikhli	1	1	...	...	...	1	...	...	...	...	...	...	...	...	...	...	...
„ Malkapur	4	3	1	...	...	3	1	...	...	...	...	...	...	...	...	...	...
„ Mehkar	...	...	...	...	...	...	...	...	...	...	...	...	...	...	...	...	...
Wun District. Taluk Yeotmal	5	4	1	...	...	4	...	...	1	...	...	...	...	...	...	...	...
„ Darwha	...	...	...	...	...	...	...	...	...	...	...	...	...	...	...	...	...
„ Kelapur	...	...	...	...	...	...	...	...	...	...	...	...	...	...	...	...	...
„ Wun	...	...	...	...	...	...	...	...	...	...	...	...	...	...	...	...	...
Basim District. Taluk Basim	...	...	...	...	...	...	...	...	...	...	...	...	...	...	...	...	...
„ Mangrul	...	...	...	...	...	...	...	...	...	...	...	...	...	...	...	...	...
„ Pusad	...	...	...	...	...	...	...	...	...	...	...	...	...	...	...	...	...

and Age.—Part H—PARSI.

PERIODS. 15—24. Total. Males.	Females.	Learning. Males.	Females.	Literate. Males.	Females.	Illiterate. Males.	Females.	25 and over. Total. Males.	Females.	Learning. Males.	Females.	Literate. Males.	Females.	Illiterate. Males.	Females.	DISTRICT AND TALUK.
19	20	21	22	23	24	25	26	27	28	29	30	31	32	33	34	35
25	21	3	1	20	16	2	4	61	40	...	...	57	24	4	16	District Amraoti.
24	8	3	...	21	8	...	...	66	16	...	...	62	9	4	7	" Akola.
5	1	...	...	5	1	...	...	15	...	...	...	15	...	...	...	" Ellichpur.
...	1	...	...	...	1	...	...	4	...	...	...	4	...	...	...	" Buldana.
1	...	...	...	1	...	...	...	3	1	...	...	3	...	...	1	" Wun.
...	...	...	...	...	...	...	...	...	...	...	...	...	...	...	...	" Basim.
55	31	6	1	47	26	2	4	19	157	...	...	141	33	8	24	**Total.**
24	20	3	1	19	15	2	4	52	38	...	...	49	22	3	16	Taluk Amraoti (Amraoti District)
...	...	...	...	...	...	...	...	...	...	...	...	...	...	...	...	" Chandur (Amraoti District)
...	...	...	...	...	...	...	...	2	...	...	...	1	...	1	...	" Morsi (Amraoti District)
1	1	...	...	1	1	...	...	7	2	...	...	7	2	...	...	" Murtazapur (Amraoti District)
6	5	1	...	5	5	...	...	29	10	...	...	26	5	3	5	Taluk Akola (Akola District)
...	1	...	...	...	1	...	...	2	1	...	...	2	1	...	...	" Akot (Akola District)
1	...	...	...	1	...	...	...	3	...	...	...	3	...	...	...	" Balapur (Akola District)
...	...	...	...	...	...	...	...	...	...	...	...	...	...	...	...	" Jalgaon (Akola District)
17	2	2	...	15	2	...	...	32	5	...	...	31	3	1	2	" Khamgaon (Akola District)
4	...	...	...	4	...	...	...	7	...	...	...	7	...	...	...	Taluk Ellichpur (Ellichpur District)
1	1	...	...	1	1	...	...	8	...	...	...	8	...	...	...	" Daryapur (Ellichpur District)
...	...	...	...	...	...	...	...	...	...	...	...	...	...	...	...	" Melghat (Ellichpur District)
...	...	...	...	...	...	...	...	1	...	...	...	1	...	...	...	Taluk Chikhli (Buldana District)
...	1	...	...	...	1	...	...	3	...	...	...	3	...	...	...	" Malkapur (Buldana District)
...	...	...	...	...	...	...	...	...	...	...	...	...	...	...	...	" Mehkar (Buldana District)
1	...	...	...	1	...	...	...	3	1	...	...	3	...	...	1	Taluk Yeotmal (Wun District)
...	...	...	...	...	...	...	...	...	...	...	...	...	...	...	...	" Darwha (Wun District)
...	...	...	...	...	...	...	...	...	...	...	...	...	...	...	...	" Kelapur (Wun District)
...	...	...	...	...	...	...	...	...	...	...	...	...	...	...	...	" Wun (Wun District)
...	...	...	...	...	...	...	...	...	...	...	...	...	...	...	...	Taluk Basim (Basim District)
...	...	...	...	...	...	...	...	...	...	...	...	...	...	...	...	" Mangrul (Basim District)
...	...	...	...	...	...	...	...	...	...	...	...	...	...	...	...	" Pusad (Basim District)

TABLE IX.

Education by Religion and Age.— Part I—OTHERS.

TABLE IX.—Education by Religion and

DISTRICT AND TALUK.	TOTAL OTHERS.			TOTAL BY EDUCATION.						AGE 0—14							
				Learning.		Literate.		Illiterate.		Total.		Learning.		Literate.		Illiterate.	
	Total.	Males.	Females.	Males.	Females.	Males.	Females.	Males.	Females.	Males.	Females.	Males.	Females.	Males.	Females.	Males.	Females.
1	2	3	4	5	6	7	8	9	10	11	12	13	14	15	16	17	18
District Amraoti	1	1	...	...	...	...	...	1	...	...	...	...	...	...	...	...	...
" Akola	7	5	2	...	...	2	...	3	2	1	1	...	...	...	...	1	1
" Ellichpur	1	1	...	...	...	1	...	...	...	...	...	...	...	...	...	...	...
" Buldana	...	...	...	...	...	...	...	...	...	...	...	...	...	...	...	...	...
" Wun	...	...	...	...	...	...	...	...	...	...	...	...	...	...	...	...	...
" Basim	2	2	...	...	...	1	...	1	...	...	...	...	...	...	...	...	...
Total	11	9	2	...	...	4	...	5	2	1	1	...	...	...	...	1	1
Amraoti District. Taluk Amraoti	1	1	...	...	...	...	...	1	...	...	...	...	...	...	...	...	...
" Chandur	...	...	...	...	...	...	...	...	...	...	...	...	...	...	...	...	...
" Morsi	...	...	...	...	...	...	...	...	...	...	...	...	...	...	...	...	...
" Murtazapur	...	...	...	...	...	...	...	...	...	...	...	...	...	...	...	...	...
Akola District. Taluk Akola	5	3	2	...	...	1	...	2	2	1	1	...	...	...	...	1 Buddhist.	1 Buddhist.
" Akot	...	...	...	...	...	...	...	...	...	...	...	...	...	...	...	...	...
" Balapur	...	...	...	...	...	...	...	...	...	...	...	...	...	...	...	...	...
" Jalgaon	...	...	...	...	...	...	...	...	...	...	...	...	...	...	...	...	...
" Khamgaon	2	2	...	...	...	1	...	1	...	...	...	...	...	...	...	...	...
Ellichpur District. Taluk Ellichpur	1	1	...	...	...	1	...	...	...	...	...	...	...	...	...	...	...
" Daryapur	...	...	...	...	...	...	...	...	...	...	...	...	...	...	...	...	...
" Melghat	...	...	...	...	...	...	...	...	...	...	...	...	...	...	...	...	...
Buldana District. Taluk Chikhli	...	...	...	...	...	...	...	...	...	...	...	...	...	...	...	...	...
" Malkapur	...	...	...	...	...	...	...	...	...	...	...	...	...	...	...	...	...
" Mehkar	...	...	...	...	...	...	...	...	...	...	...	...	...	...	...	...	...
Wun District. Taluk Yeotmal	...	...	...	...	...	...	...	...	...	...	...	...	...	...	...	...	...
" Darwha	...	...	...	...	...	...	...	...	...	...	...	...	...	...	...	...	...
" Kelapur	...	...	...	...	...	...	...	...	...	...	...	...	...	...	...	...	...
" Wun	...	...	...	...	...	...	...	...	...	...	...	...	...	...	...	...	...
Basim District. Taluk Basim	1	1	...	...	...	1	...	...	...	...	...	...	...	...	...	...	...
" Mangrul	...	...	...	...	...	...	...	...	...	...	...	...	...	...	...	...	...
" Pusad	1	1	...	...	...	...	...	1	...	...	...	...	...	...	...	...	...

and Age, Part I.—OTHERS.

PERIODS.																
15—24								25 AND OVER.								DISTRICT AND TALUK.
TOTAL.		LEARNING.		LITERATE.		ILLITERATE.		TOTAL.		LEARNING.		LITERATE.		ILLITERATE.		
Males.	Females.	Males.	Females.	Males.	Females.	Males.	Females.	Males.	Females.	Males.	Females.	Males.	Females.	Males.	Females.	
19	20	21	22	23	24	25	26	27	28	29	30	31	32	33	34	35
...	...	...	...	...	...	...	...	1	...	...	...	...	...	1	...	DISTRICT AMRAOTI.
2	...	...	...	...	...	2	...	2	1	...	...	2	...	...	1	" AKOLA.
...	...	...	...	...	...	...	...	1	...	...	...	1	...	...	...	" ELLICHPUR.
...	...	...	...	...	...	...	...	...	...	...	...	...	...	...	...	" BULDANA.
...	...	...	...	...	...	...	...	...	...	...	...	...	...	...	...	" WUN.
...	...	...	...	...	...	...	...	2	...	...	...	1	...	1	...	" BASIM.
2	...	...	...	...	...	2	...	6	1	...	...	4	...	2	1	**Total.**
...	...	...	...	...	...	...	...	1	...	...	...	...	...	1 Jew.	...	Taluk Amraoti . (AMRAOTI DISTRICT.)
...	...	...	...	...	...	...	...	...	...	...	...	...	...	...	...	" Chandur . (AMRAOTI DISTRICT.)
...	...	...	...	...	...	...	...	...	...	...	...	...	...	...	...	" Morsi . (AMRAOTI DISTRICT.)
...	...	...	...	...	...	...	...	...	...	...	...	...	...	...	...	" Murtazapur . (AMRAOTI DISTRICT.)
1	...	...	...	...	...	Buddhist 1	...	1	1	...	...	Positivist. 1	...	...	Buddhist 1	Taluk Akola . (AKOLA DISTRICT.)
...	...	...	...	...	...	...	...	...	...	...	...	...	...	...	...	" Akot . (AKOLA DISTRICT.)
...	...	...	...	...	...	...	...	...	...	...	...	...	...	...	...	" Balapur . (AKOLA DISTRICT.)
...	...	...	...	...	...	...	...	...	...	...	...	...	...	...	...	" Jalgaon . (AKOLA DISTRICT.)
1	...	...	...	...	...	Jew. 1	...	1	...	...	...	Unspecified. 1	...	...	...	" Khamgaon . (AKOLA DISTRICT.)
...	...	...	...	...	...	...	...	1	...	...	...	1 Deist.	...	...	...	Taluk Ellichpur . (ELLICHPUR DISTRICT.)
...	...	...	...	...	...	...	...	...	...	...	...	...	...	...	...	" Daryapur . (ELLICHPUR DISTRICT.)
...	...	...	...	...	...	...	...	...	...	...	...	...	...	...	...	" Melghat . (ELLICHPUR DISTRICT.)
...	...	...	...	...	...	...	...	...	...	...	...	...	...	...	...	Taluk Chikhli . (BULDANA DISTRICT.)
...	...	...	...	...	...	...	...	...	...	...	...	...	...	...	...	" Malkapur . (BULDANA DISTRICT.)
...	...	...	...	...	...	...	...	...	...	...	...	...	...	...	...	" Mehkar . (BULDANA DISTRICT.)
...	...	...	...	...	...	...	...	...	...	...	...	...	...	...	...	Taluk Yeotmal . (WUN DISTRICT.)
...	...	...	...	...	...	...	...	...	...	...	...	...	...	...	...	" Darwha . (WUN DISTRICT.)
...	...	...	...	...	...	...	...	...	...	...	...	...	...	...	...	" Kelapur . (WUN DISTRICT.)
...	...	...	...	...	...	...	...	...	...	...	...	...	...	...	...	" Wun . (WUN DISTRICT.)
...	...	...	...	...	...	...	...	1	...	...	...	Agnostic. 1	...	...	...	Taluk Basim . (BASIM DISTRICT.)
...	...	...	...	...	...	...	...	...	...	...	...	...	...	...	...	" Mangrul . (BASIM DISTRICT.)
...	...	...	...	...	...	...	...	1	...	...	...	...	...	Unspecified. 1	...	" Pusad . (BASIM DISTRICT.)

TABLE—X.

Parent-tongue.

TABLE X.—

DISTRICT AND TALUK.	TOTAL POPULATION.			VERNACULARS					
				MARATHI.			URDU.		
	TOTAL.	Males.	Females.	TOTAL.	Males.	Females.	TOTAL.	Males.	Females.
1	2	3	4	5	6	7	8	9	10
DISTRICT AMRAOTI	655,645	*340,235*	315,410	541,623	*276,777*	264,846	70,704	*40,043*	30,661
„ AKOLA	574,782	*297,011*	277,771	482,440	*245,386*	237,054	62,832	*34,258*	28,574
„ ELLICHPUR	315,798	*162,969*	152,829	218,584	*111,083*	107,501	44,764	*24,515*	20,249
„ BULDANA	481,021	*244,799*	236,222	416,645	*210,817*	205,828	42,695	*22,120*	20,575
„ WUN	471,613	*241,688*	229,925	311,426	*158,773*	152,653	26,256	*14,531*	11,725
„ BASIM	398,181	*204,798*	193,383	331,627	*168,873*	162,754	26,703	*14,291*	12,412
Railway Passengers, &c.	451	*326*	125	243	*158*	85	148	*125*	23
Total	**2,897,491**	***1,491,826***	**1,405,665**	**2,302,588**	***1,171,867***	**1,130,721**	**274,102**	***149,883***	**124,219**
DISTRICT AMRAOTI. Taluk Amraoti	183,508	*95,536*	87,972	142,823	*72,599*	70,224	28,260	*16,069*	12,191
„ Chandur	198,106	*102,885*	95,221	170,197	*87,056*	83,141	14,989	*8,844*	6,145
„ Morsi	152,374	*78,451*	73,923	127,882	*65,496*	62,386	13,273	*7,173*	6,100
„ Murtazapur	121,657	*63,363*	58,294	100,721	*51,626*	49,095	14,182	*7,957*	6,225
DISTRICT AKOLA. Taluk Akola	137,988	*71,744*	66,244	113,239	*57,890*	55,349	16,066	*8,693*	7,373
„ Akot	137,720	*70,630*	67,090	113,711	*57,221*	56,490	17,630	*9,611*	8,019
„ Balapur	101,673	*51,941*	49,732	86,427	*43,769*	42,658	11,361	*5,979*	5,382
„ Jalgaon	97,616	*50,323*	47,293	84,529	*43,076*	41,453	8,478	*4,686*	3,792
„ Khamgaon	99,785	*52,373*	47,412	84,534	*43,430*	41,104	9,297	*5,289*	4,008
DISTRICT ELLICHPUR. Taluk Ellichpur	146,215	*75,271*	70,944	110,934	*56,331*	54,603	26,131	*13,781*	12,350
„ Daryapur	122,552	*63,329*	59,223	104,330	*52,954*	51,376	14,221	*8,080*	6,141
„ Melghat	47,031	*24,369*	22,662	3,320	*1,798*	1,522	4,412	*2,654*	1,758
DISTRICT BULDANA. Taluk Chikhli	150,098	*76,540*	73,558	131,374	*66,618*	64,756	14,857	*7,774*	7,083
„ Malkapur	177,877	*90,215*	87,662	153,421	*77,397*	76,024	17,277	*8,952*	8,325
„ Mehkar	153,046	*78,044*	75,002	131,850	*66,802*	65,048	10,561	*5,394*	5,167
DISTRICT WUN. Taluk Yeotmal	124,429	*64,275*	60,154	83,809	*42,841*	40,968	8,342	*4,778*	3,564
„ Darwha	156,580	*80,746*	75,834	112,502	*57,286*	55,216	11,438	*6,332*	5,106
„ Kelapur	105,926	*53,845*	52,081	55,899	*28,552*	27,347	3,620	*1,993*	1,627
„ Wun	84,678	*42,822*	41,856	59,216	*30,094*	29,122	2,856	*1,428*	1,428
DISTRICT BASIM. Taluk Basim	177,250	*91,200*	86,050	152,228	*77,671*	74,557	11,380	*6,179*	5,201
„ Mangrul	82,446	*42,773*	39,673	69,327	*35,633*	33,694	5,422	*2,906*	2,516
„ Pusad	138,485	*70,825*	67,660	110,072	*55,569*	54,503	9,901	*5,206*	4,695

Parent-tongue.

OF INDIA.

Marwadi. Total.	Marwadi. Males.	Marwadi. Females.	Gipsy Dialects. Total.	Gipsy Dialects. Males.	Gipsy Dialects. Females.	Other Hindi Dialects. Total.	Other Hindi Dialects. Males.	Other Hindi Dialects. Females.	Konkani. Total.	Konkani. Males.	Konkani. Females.	District and Taluk.
11	12	13	14	15	16	17	18	19	20	21	22	23
9,131	5,632	3,499	4,687	2,467	2,220	966	532	434	2	...	2	District Amraoti.
11,019	7,183	3,836	2,760	1,602	1,158	681	369	312	11	3	8	„ Akola
4,165	2,726	1,439	590	310	280	3,409	1,769	1,640	...	...	...	„ Ellichpur.
5,407	3,376	2,031	7,661	3,981	3,680	491	277	214	...	...	...	„ Buldana.
1,879	1,170	709	30,264	15,923	14,341	189	108	81	87	52	35	„ Wun.
5,002	3,082	1,920	28,869	15,236	13,633	224	127	97	...	...	...	„ Basim.
5	5	...	...	...	...	...	...	...	...	...	...	Railway Passengers, &c.
36,608	23,174	13,434	74,831	39,519	35,312	5,960	3,182	2,778	100	55	45	Total.
3,909	2,387	1,522	1,045	526	519	242	139	103	2	...	2	Taluk Amraoti (Amraoti District.)
2,194	1,391	803	1,582	857	725	340	187	153	...	...	...	„ Chandur (Amraoti District.)
1,363	816	547	557	281	276	102	60	42	...	...	...	„ Morsi (Amraoti District.)
1,665	1,038	627	1,503	803	700	282	146	136	...	...	...	„ Murtazapur (Amraoti District.)
2,482	1,689	793	1,517	882	635	189	112	77	...	...	...	Taluk Akola (Akola District.)
2,445	1,620	825	475	278	197	209	115	94	11	3	8	„ Akot (Akola District.)
1,132	711	421	548	324	224	220	116	104	...	...	...	„ Balapur (Akola District.)
1,641	1,024	617	85	46	39	60	25	35	...	...	...	„ Jalgaon (Akola District.)
3,319	2,139	1,180	135	72	63	3	1	2	...	...	...	„ Khamgaon (Akola District.)
2,831	1,825	1,006	437	231	206	1,026	565	461	...	...	...	Taluk Ellichpur (Ellichpur District.)
1,297	874	423	74	36	38	8	6	2	...	...	...	„ Daryapur (Ellichpur District.)
37	27	10	79	43	36	2,375	1,198	1,177	...	...	...	„ Melghat (Ellichpur District.)
1,031	628	403	955	541	414	95	60	35	...	...	...	Taluk Chikhli (Buldana District.)
1,932	1,189	743	374	188	186	313	168	145	...	...	...	„ Malkapur (Buldana District.)
2,444	1,559	885	6,332	3,252	3,080	83	49	34	...	...	...	„ Mehkar (Buldana District.)
826	518	308	5,179	2,758	2,421	95	51	44	...	...	...	Taluk Yeotmal (Wun District.)
717	435	282	19,127	10,125	9,002	30	19	11	...	...	...	„ Darwha (Wun District.)
254	165	89	5,368	2,718	2,650	49	30	19	38	27	11	„ Kelapur (Wun District.)
82	52	30	590	322	268	15	8	7	49	25	24	„ Wun (Wun District.)
3,596	2,183	1,413	7,799	3,902	3,897	9	4	5	...	...	...	Taluk Basim (Basim District.)
567	347	220	6,234	3,347	2,887	141	77	64	...	...	...	„ Mangrul (Basim District.)
839	552	287	14,836	7,987	6,849	74	46	28	...	...	...	„ Pusad (Basim District.)

TABLE X.—

DISTRICT AND TALUK.	VERNACULARS OF											
	GOND DIALECTS.			KORKU.			BHIL DIALECTS.			GUJARATHI DIALECTS.		
	TOTAL.	Males.	Females.	TOTAL.	Males.	Females.	TOTAL.	Males.	Females.	TOTAL.	Males.	Females.
26	27	28	29	30	31	32	33	34	35	36	37	38
DISTRICT AMRAOTI	18,622	9,417	9,205	480	241	239	27	16	11	4,454	2,454	2,000
" AKOLA	1,442	776	666	1,434	731	703	152	78	74	7,671	4,284	3,387
" ELLICHPUR	4,427	2,285	2,142	35,010	17,687	17,323	252	141	111	2,953	1,563	1,390
" BULDANA	81	38	43	23	12	11	82	47	35	4,635	2,361	2,274
" WUN	71,094	35,798	35,296	179	96	83	286	139	147	752	467	285
" BASIM	448	240	208	...	...	...	371	167	204	476	315	161
Railway Passengers, &c.	4	1	3	...	...	...	...	...	...	13	13	...
Total	96,118	48,555	47,563	37,126	18,767	18,359	1,170	588	582	20,954	11,457	9,497
AMRAOTI DISTRICT. Taluk Amraoti	1,713	892	821	218	104	114	...	...	...	2,256	1,244	1,012
" Chandur	7,665	3,889	3,776	5	3	2	10	5	5	386	240	146
" Morsi	8,481	4,232	4,249	257	134	123	17	11	6	145	83	62
" Murtazapur	763	404	359	...	...	...	...	...	...	1,667	887	780
AKOLA DISTRICT. Taluk Akola	387	203	184	1	1	...	8	8	...	1,993	1,183	810
" Akot	522	278	244	674	349	325	...	...	...	1,669	930	739
" Balapur	162	82	80	...	...	...	...	...	...	1,346	687	659
" Jalgaon	334	185	149	759	381	378	142	69	73	1,498	767	731
" Khamgaon	37	28	9	...	...	...	2	1	1	1,165	717	448
ELLICHPUR DISTRICT. Taluk Ellichpur	1,560	782	778	1,197	654	543	5	2	3	745	402	343
" Daryapur	349	171	178	8	6	2	...	...	...	2,116	1,099	1,017
" Melghat	2,518	1,332	1,186	33,805	17,027	16,778	247	139	108	92	62	30
BULDANA DISTRICT. Taluk Chikhli	22	9	13	23	12	11	54	31	23	373	198	175
" Malkapur	9	4	5	...	...	...	...	...	...	3,886	1,915	1,971
" Mehkar	50	25	25	...	...	...	28	16	12	376	248	128
WUN DISTRICT. Taluk Yeotmal	23,279	11,758	11,521	...	...	...	169	86	83	228	157	71
" Darwha	8,268	4,221	4,047	...	...	...	107	49	58	376	223	153
" Kelapur	25,944	13,049	12,895	103	50	53	10	4	6	127	71	56
" Wun	13,603	6,770	6,833	76	46	30	...	...	...	21	16	5
BASIM DISTRICT. Taluk Basim	29	18	11	...	...	...	...	...	...	322	191	131
" Mangrul	94	51	43	...	...	...	...	...	...	45	36	9
" Pusad	325	171	154	...	...	...	371	167	204	109	88	21

Parent-tongue.

INDIA—*contd.*

Kachhi. Total.	Males.	Females.	Kanari. Total.	Males.	Females.	Telugu. Total.	Males.	Females.	Tamil. Total.	Males.	Females.	District and Taluk.	
35	36	37	38	39	40	41	42	43	44	45	46	47	
52	40	12	296	183	113	3,593	1,834	1,759	194	93	101	District Amraoti.	
185	149	36	275	147	128	3,170	1,535	1,635	131	70	61	" Akola.	
27	25	2	62	33	29	1,225	615	610	58	30	28	" Ellichpur.	
12	11	1	159	82	77	2,753	1,392	1,361	9	5	4	" Buldana.	
51	27	24	57	39	18	28,641	14,242	14,399	34	19	15	" Wun.	
17	15	2	239	171	68	3,761	2,001	1,760	13	9	4	" Basim.	
...	...	...	...	...	...	18	11	7	...	...	...	Railway Passengers, &c.	
344	267	77	1,088	655	433	43,161	21,630	21,531	439	226	213	Total.	
31	25	6	202	121	81	2,077	1,034	1,043	170	79	91	Taluk Amraoti	Amraoti District.
10	7	3	15	12	3	593	311	282	9	5	4	" Chandur	
...	...	...	12	7	5	254	136	118	7	5	2	" Morsi	
11	8	3	67	43	24	669	353	316	8	4	4	" Murtazapur	
13	11	2	113	56	57	1,680	815	865	74	40	34	Taluk Akola	Akola District.
8	8	...	47	25	22	173	83	90	1	1	...	" Akot	
10	10	...	83	48	35	323	164	159	1	1	...	" Balapur	
7	4	3	19	11	8	45	35	10	2	1	1	" Jalgaon	
147	116	31	13	7	6	949	438	511	53	27	26	" Khamgaon	
7	7	...	58	29	29	1,026	506	520	45	21	24	Taluk Ellichpur	Ellichpur District.
20	18	2	3	3	...	67	31	36	11	7	4	" Daryapur	
...	...	...	1	1	...	132	78	54	2	2	...	" Melghat	
2	2	...	90	49	41	1,132	551	581	1	1	...	Taluk Chikhli	Buldana District.
10	9	1	29	13	16	405	216	189	8	4	4	" Malkapur	
...	...	...	40	20	20	1,216	625	591	...	...	...	" Mehkar	
7	5	2	5	3	2	2,308	1,194	1,114	25	16	9	Taluk Yeotmal	Wun District.
19	15	4	37	29	8	3,826	1,914	1,912	2	1	1	" Darwha	
...	...	...	2	2	...	14,404	7,102	7,302	1	1	...	" Kelapur	
25	7	18	13	5	8	8,103	4,032	4,071	6	1	5	" Wun	
9	7	2	98	57	41	1,595	869	726	8	5	3	Taluk Basim	Basim District.
...	...	...	99	82	17	455	252	203	...	...	...	" Mangrul	
8	8	...	42	32	10	1,711	880	831	5	4	1	" Pusad	

TABLE X.—

DISTRICT AND TALUK.	VERNACULARS OF INDIA—*contd.*											
	MALAYALUM.			GOMANTAKI.			PUNJABI DIALECTS.			SINDHI.		
	TOTAL.	Males.	Females.	TOTAL.	Males.	Females.	TOTAL.	Males.	Females.	TOTAL.	Males.	Females.
46	47	48	49	50	51	52	53	54	55	56	57	58
DISTRICT AMRAOTI	2	2	...	69	47	22	63	40	28	...	...	...
" AKOLA	...	...	...	38	28	10	94	72	22	...	...	...
" ELLICHPUR	1	1	...	6	3	3	53	29	24	...	...	...
" BULDANA	...	...	...	2	2	...	40	24	16	...	...	...
" WUN	...	...	...	11	7	4	64	38	26	5	4	1
" BASIM	...	...	...	8	2	6	50	34	16	...	...	...
Railway Passengers, etc.	...	...	...	1	1	...	...	...	...	...	...	...
Total	3	3	...	135	90	45	369	237	132	5	4	1
AMRAOTI DISTRICT. Taluk Amraoti	2	2	...	65	44	21	16	12	4	...	...	...
" Chandur	...	...	...	...	...	...	39	21	18	...	...	...
" Morsi	...	...	...	...	...	...	2	...	2	...	...	...
" Murtazapur	...	...	...	4	3	1	11	7	4	...	...	...
AKOLA DISTRICT. Taluk Akola	...	...	...	15	8	7	27	17	10	...	...	...
" Akot	...	...	...	...	...	...	54	43	11	...	...	...
" Balapur	...	...	...	...	...	...	4	4	...	...	...	...
" Jalgaon	...	...	...	...	...	...	4	3	1	...	...	...
" Khamgaon	...	...	...	23	20	3	5	5	...	...	...	...
ELLICHPUR DISTRICT. Taluk Ellichpur	...	...	...	6	3	3	45	24	21	...	...	...
" Daryapur	...	...	...	...	...	...	6	3	3	...	...	...
" Melghat	1	1	...	...	...	...	2	2	...	...	...	...
BULDANA DISTRICT. Taluk Chikhli	...	...	...	2	2	...	13	10	3	...	...	...
" Malkapur	...	...	...	...	...	...	11	5	6	...	...	...
" Mehkar	...	...	...	...	...	...	16	9	7	...	...	...
WUN DISTRICT. Taluk Yeotmal	...	...	...	11	7	4	21	13	8	3	2	1
" Darwha	...	...	...	...	...	...	...	...	...	2	2	...
" Kelapur	...	...	...	...	...	...	42	24	18	...	...	...
" Wun	...	...	...	...	...	...	1	1	...	...	...	...
BASIM DISTRICT. Taluk Basim	...	...	...	7	1	6	23	16	7	...	...	...
" Mangrul	...	...	...	1	1	...	1	1	...	...	...	...
" Pusad	...	...	...	...	...	...	26	17	9	...	...	...

Parent-tongue.

Bengali. Total.	Males.	Females.	Sanskrit. Total.	Males.	Females.	Kashmiri. Total.	Males.	Females.	Pashtu dialects. Total.	Males.	Females.	DISTRICT AND TALUK.
			VERNACULARS OF ASIATIC COUNTRIES BEYOND INDIA.									
59	60	61	62	63	64	65	66	67	68	69	70	71
6	3	3	2	2	...	...	...	...	134	132	2	District Amraoti.
7	4	3	...	...	...	...	...	...	205	191	14	" Akola.
1	1	...	...	...	...	...	...	...	77	77	...	" Ellichpur.
...	...	...	...	...	...	...	...	...	232	194	38	" Buldana.
...	...	...	...	...	...	...	...	...	192	171	21	" Wun.
...	...	...	...	...	...	1	1	...	213	139	74	" Basim.
...	...	...	...	...	...	...	...	...	1	1	...	Railway Passengers, etc..
14	8	6	2	2	...	1	1	...	1,054	906	149	Total.
6	3	3	2	2	...	...	...	...	49	48	1	Taluk Amraoti (Amraoti District.)
...	...	...	...	...	...	...	...	...	31	31	...	" Chandur
...	...	...	...	...	...	...	...	...	11	11	...	" Morsi
...	...	...	...	...	...	...	...	...	43	42	1	" Murtazapur
6	3	3	...	...	...	...	...	...	70	65	5	Taluk Akola (Akola District.)
1	1	...	...	...	...	...	...	...	39	37	2	" Akot
...	...	...	...	...	...	...	...	...	38	36	2	" Balapur
...	...	...	...	...	...	...	...	...	6	6	...	" Jalgaon
...	...	...	...	...	...	...	...	...	52	47	5	" Khamgaon
...	...	...	...	...	...	...	...	...	51	51	...	Taluk Ellichpur (Ellichpur District.)
...	...	...	...	...	...	...	...	...	26	26	...	" Daryapur
1	1	...	...	...	...	...	...	...	...	...	...	" Melghat
...	...	...	...	...	...	...	...	...	26	26	...	Taluk Chikhli (Buldana District.)
...	...	...	...	...	...	...	...	...	166	128	38	" Malkapur
...	...	...	...	...	...	...	...	...	40	40	...	" Mehkar
...	...	...	...	...	...	...	...	...	60	56	4	Taluk Yeotmal (Wun District.)
...	...	...	...	...	...	...	...	...	87	72	15	" Darwha
...	...	...	...	...	...	...	...	...	45	43	2	" Kelapur
...	...	...	...	...	...	...	...	...	...	...	...	" Wun
...	...	...	...	...	...	1	1	...	30	30	...	Taluk Basim (Basim District.)
...	...	...	...	...	...	...	...	...	30	20	10	" Mangrul
...	...	...	...	...	...	...	...	...	153	89	64	" Pusad

TABLE X.—

DISTRICT AND TALUK.	VERNACULARS OF ASIATIC COUNTRIES BEYOND INDIA—*contd.*											
	ARABIC.			PERSIAN.			ARMENIAN.			CHINESE.		
	TOTAL.	Males.	Females.	TOTAL.	Males.	Females.	TOTAL.	Males.	Females.	TOTAL.	Males.	Females.
72	73	74	75	76	77	78	79	80	81	82	83	84
DISTRICT AMRAOTI	87	41	46	107	64	43	...	...	...	1	1	...
" AKOLA	26	20	6	74	39	35	1	1	...	7	4	3
" ELLICHPUR	16	6	10	49	30	19	...	...	...	...	...	...
" BULDANA	12	9	3	45	33	12	...	...	...	...	...	...
" WUN	14	11	3	72	42	30	...	...	...	...	...	...
" BASIM	46	22	24	81	51	30	...	...	...	...	...	...
Railway Passengers, etc.	...	...	...	...	...	...	...	...	...	...	...	...
Total	201	109	92	428	259	169	1	1	...	8	5	3
AMRAOTI DISTRICT — Taluk Amraoti	57	21	36	47	28	19	...	...	...	1	1	...
" Chandur	8	5	3	27	15	12	...	...	...	...	...	...
" Morsi	...	...	...	10	5	5	...	...	...	...	...	...
" Murtazapur	22	15	7	23	16	7	...	...	...	...	...	...
AKOLA DISTRICT — Taluk Akola	17	15	2	10	6	4	1	1	...	7	4	3
" Akot	4	3	1	42	20	22	...	...	...	...	...	...
" Balapur	1	1	...	16	8	8	...	...	...	...	...	...
" Jalgaon	4	1	3	1	1	...	...	...	...	...	...	...
" Khamgaon	...	...	...	5	4	1	...	...	...	...	...	...
ELLICHPUR DISTRICT — Taluk Ellichpur	14	5	9	35	16	19	...	...	...	...	...	...
" Daryapur	2	1	1	14	14	...	...	...	...	...	...	...
" Melghat	...	...	...	...	...	...	...	...	...	...	...	...
BULDANA DISTRICT — Taluk Chikhli	7	5	2	9	7	2	...	...	...	...	...	...
" Malkapur	3	3	...	28	22	6	...	...	...	...	...	...
" Mehkar	2	1	1	8	4	4	...	...	...	...	...	...
WUN DISTRICT — Taluk Yeotmal	...	...	...	2	1	1	...	...	...	...	...	...
" Darwha	7	5	2	35	18	17	...	...	...	...	...	...
" Kelapur	6	5	1	14	9	5	...	...	...	...	...	...
" Wun	1	1	...	21	14	7	...	...	...	...	...	...
BASIM DISTRICT — Taluk Basim	45	21	24	39	23	16	...	...	...	...	...	...
" Mangrul	1	1	...	29	19	10	...	...	...	...	...	...
" Pusad	...	...	...	13	9	4	...	...	...	...	...	...

Parent-tongue.

European Languages. English. Total.	Males.	Females.	French. Total.	Males.	Females.	German. Total.	Males.	Females.	Greek. Total.	Males.	Females.	Unspecified. Total.	Males.	Females.	District and Taluk.
85	86	87	88	89	90	91	92	93	94	95	96	97	98	99	100
314	165	149	14	1	13	4	3	1	1	1	...	5	4	1	District Amraoti.
124	78	46	...	...	...	1	1	...	2	2	...	...	...	...	" Akola.
69	40	29	...	...	...	...	...	...	...	...	...	...	...	...	" Ellichpur.
36	17	19	...	...	...	...	...	...	1	1	...	...	...	...	" Buldana.
60	31	29	...	...	...	...	...	...	...	...	...	...	...	...	" Wun.
32	22	10	...	...	...	...	...	...	...	...	...	...	...	...	" Basim.
18	11	7	...	...	...	...	...	...	...	...	...	...	...	...	Railway Passengers, &c.
653	**364**	**289**	**14**	**7**	**13**	**5**	**4**	**1**	**4**	**4**	...	**5**	**4**	**1**	**Total.**
[illegible]	147	144	14	1	13	4	3	1	1	1	...	5	4	1	Taluk Amraoti — Amraoti District.
6	6	...	...	...	...	...	...	...	...	...	...	...	...	...	" Chandur — Amraoti District.
1	1	...	...	...	...	...	...	...	...	...	...	...	...	...	" Morsi — Amraoti District.
16	11	5	...	...	...	...	...	...	...	...	...	...	...	...	" Murtazapur — Amraoti District.
73	42	31	...	...	...	...	...	...	...	...	...	...	...	...	Taluk Akola — Akola District.
5	4	1	...	...	...	...	...	...	...	...	...	...	...	...	" Akot — Akola District.
1	1	...	...	...	...	...	...	...	...	...	...	...	...	...	" Balapur — Akola District.
2	2	...	...	...	...	...	...	...	...	...	...	...	...	...	" Jalgaon — Akola District.
43	29	14	...	...	...	1	1	...	2	2	...	...	...	...	" Khamgaon — Akola District.
62	36	26	...	...	...	...	...	...	...	...	...	...	...	...	Taluk Ellichpur — Ellichpur District.
...	...	...	...	...	...	...	...	...	...	...	...	...	...	...	" Daryapur — Ellichpur District.
7	4	3	...	...	...	...	...	...	...	...	...	...	...	...	" Melghat — Ellichpur District.
31	15	16	...	...	...	...	...	...	1	1	...	...	...	...	Taluk Chikhli — Buldana District.
5	2	3	...	...	...	...	...	...	...	...	...	...	...	...	" Malkapur — Buldana District.
...	...	...	...	...	...	...	...	...	...	...	...	...	...	...	" Mehkar — Buldana District.
60	31	29	...	...	...	...	...	...	...	...	...	...	...	...	Taluk Yeotmal — Wun District.
...	...	...	...	...	...	...	...	...	...	...	...	...	...	...	" Darwha — Wun District.
...	...	...	...	...	...	...	...	...	...	...	...	...	...	...	" Kelapur — Wun District.
...	...	...	...	...	...	...	...	...	...	...	...	...	...	...	" Wun — Wun District.
32	22	10	...	...	...	...	...	...	...	...	...	...	...	...	Taluk Basim — Basim District.
...	...	...	...	...	...	...	...	...	...	...	...	...	...	...	" Mangrul — Basim District.
...	...	...	...	...	...	...	...	...	...	...	...	...	...	...	" Pusad — Basim District.

TABLE XI.

Birth-place.

Table XI.—Birth-place.

TABLE XI.—Birth-place.

DISTRICT, STATE, PROVINCE, OR COUNTRY OF BIRTH.	TOTAL OF PROVINCE.			DISTRICT. AMRAOTI.			AKOLA.			ELLICHPUR.			BULDANA.			WUN.			BASIM.			Railway Passengers, &c.		
	Total.	Males.	Females.	Total.	Males.	Females.	Total.	Males.	Females.	Total.	Males.	Females.	Total.	Males.	Females.	Total.	Males.	Females.	Total.	Males.	Females.	Total.	Males.	Females.
1	2	3	4	5	6	7	8	9	10	11	12	13	14	15	16	17	18	19	20	21	22	23	24	25
A.—Districts within the Province—																								
Amraoti	509,425	261,138	248,287	456,505	238,650	217,855	8,319	3,398	4,921	19,717	7,533	12,184	835	377	458	18,163	8,588	9,575	5,807	2,538	3,269	79	54	25
Akola	543,632	274,835	268,797	10,991	4,409	6,582	485,655	250,444	235,211	14,227	5,454	8,773	22,121	9,311	12,810	1,695	825	870	8,887	4,361	4,526	56	31	25
Ellichpur	280,489	143,016	137,473	23,754	9,867	13,887	10,036	4,117	5,919	245,203	128,237	116,966	367	191	176	706	386	320	417	215	202	6	3	3
Buldana	417,906	214,605	203,301	1,145	604	541	17,415	7,185	10,230	686	351	335	389,259	202,501	186,758	499	274	225	8,873	3,667	5,206	29	23	6
Wun	356,718	181,624	175,094	10,843	4,534	6,309	595	269	326	415	193	222	263	127	141	337,384	173,286	164,098	7,205	3,211	3,994	8	4	4
Basim	338,406	174,949	163,457	5,390	2,391	2,999	4,762	2,041	2,721	491	214	277	7,448	3,053	4,395	9,767	4,753	5,014	310,548	162,497	148,051	...	...	...
Total	2,446,576	1,250,167	1,196,409	508,628	260,455	248,173	526,782	267,454	259,328	280,739	141,982	138,757	420,298	215,560	204,738	368,214	188,112	180,102	341,737	176,489	165,248	178	115	63
B.—Provinces or States in India beyond the Province—																								
Bombay	59,805	31,376	28,429	9,556	5,595	3,961	16,015	8,852	7,163	1,731	1,040	691	21,568	9,588	11,980	4,343	2,512	1,831	6,532	3,742	2,790	60	47	13
Central Provinces	216,488	109,495	106,993	111,377	55,640	55,737	7,245	3,960	3,285	20,201	10,573	9,628	1,311	632	679	74,662	37,708	36,954	1,622	933	689	70	49	21
Hyderabad Territory	110,905	53,264	57,641	5,713	3,171	2,542	8,595	4,689	3,906	3,713	2,088	1,625	32,081	14,789	17,292	18,024	8,868	9,156	42,744	19,633	23,111	35	26	9
Central India	5,302	3,469	1,833	2,211	1,487	724	818	551	267	365	265	100	388	281	107	936	548	388	569	324	245	15	13	2
Rajputana	26,774	18,700	8,074	7,023	4,952	2,071	8,245	5,765	2,480	3,210	2,273	937	3,496	2,405	1,091	1,784	1,169	615	3,007	2,127	880	9	9	...
Baroda	3	2	1	...	...	...	3	2	1	...	...	...	...	...	...	...	...	...	...	...	...	...	...	...
North-West Provinces	24,660	19,826	4,834	8,824	7,153	1,671	5,692	4,615	1,077	4,748	3,876	872	1,145	908	237	2,814	2,130	684	1,382	1,098	284	55	46	9
Oudh	3,699	2,992	707	1,322	1,053	269	718	606	112	649	558	91	322	270	52	496	359	137	180	136	44	12	10	2
Punjab	905	695	210	213	167	46	187	141	46	176	131	45	100	72	28	74	57	17	153	125	28	2	2	...
Patiala	22	16	6	...	...	...	1	1	...	...	...	...	...	...	...	...	...	...	21	15	6	...	...	...
Madras	823	473	350	332	177	155	192	118	74	117	59	58	35	27	8	56	35	21	91	57	34	...	...	...
Goa	37	35	2	25	23	2	6	6	...	...	...	...	3	3	...	2	2	...	1	1	...	...	...	...
Mysore	43	31	12	14	12	2	3	1	2	...	...	...	8	4	4	16	13	3	2	1	1	...	...	...
Bengal	419	343	76	181	156	25	86	69	17	44	34	10	39	36	3	23	11	12	45	36	9	1	1	...
Andaman Islands	4	1	3	...	...	...	...	...	...	4	1	3	...	...	...	...	...	...	...	...	...	...	...	...
Burma	4	4	...	...	...	...	...	...	...	...	...	...	...	...	...	4	4	...	...	...	...	...	...	...
Kashmir	1	1	...	...	...	...	...	...	...	...	...	...	...	...	...	1	1	...	...	...	...	...	...	...
Total	449,894	240,723	209,171	146,791	79,586	67,205	47,806	29,376	18,430	34,958	20,898	14,060	60,496	29,015	31,481	108,235	58,417	49,818	56,349	28,228	28,121	259	203	56

DISTRICT, STATE, PROVINCE, OR COUNTRY OF BIRTH.	Total of Province.			District. Amraoti.			Akola.			Ellichpur.			Buldana.			Wun.			Basim.			Railway Passengers, etc.		
	Total.	Males.	Females.	Total.	Males.	Females.	Total.	Males.	Females.	Total.	Males.	Females.	Total.	Males.	Females.	Total.	Males.	Females.	Total.	Males.	Females.	Total.	Males.	Females.
1	2	3	4	5	6	7	8	9	10	11	12	13	14	15	16	17	18	19	20	21	22	23	24	25
C.—Countries in Asia beyond India—																								
Nepal	14	8	6	4	2	2	1	...	1	5	2	3	2	2	...	...	...	...	2	2	...	...	...	...
Afghanistan	803	777	26	153	151	2	144	136	8	74	74	...	207	205	2	143	139	4	81	71	10	1	1	...
Beluchistan	34	34	...	...	...	...	11	11	...	1	1	...	2	2	...	15	15	...	4	4	...	1	1	...
Ceylon	8	7	1	1	1	...	1	1	...	...	...	...	4	3	1	1	1	..	1	1	...	...	...	...
Arabia	23	20	3	11	9	2	5	5	...	2	2	...	4	4	...	...	...	...	1	...	1	...	...	...
Syria	1	...	1	1	...	1	...	...	...	...	...	...	...	...	...	...	...	...	...	...	...	...	...	...
Persia	5	5	...	...	...	...	2	2	...	...	...	...	3	3	...	...	...	...	...	...	...	...	...	...
China	6	4	2	3	2	1	2	1	1	...	...	...	1	1	...	..	...	...	...	...	...	...	...	...
Turkey	1	1	...	...	...	...	1	1	...	...	...	...	...	...	...	...	...	...	...		...	...	...	...
Total	895	856	39	173	165	8	167	157	10	82	79	3	223	220	3	159	155	4	89	78	11	2	2	...
D.—Countries in Europe—																								
England and Wales	72	45	27	23	14	9	11	10	1	16	8	8	2	2	...	4	3	1	4	2	2	12	6	6
Scotland	13	11	2	5	4	1	7	6	1	1	1	...	...	...	...	...	...	...	...	...	...	...	...	...
Ireland	8	8	...	5	5	...	3	3	...	...	...	...	...	...	...	..	...	...	...	...	...	...	...	...
Guernsey	1	1	...	1	1	...	...	...	...	...	...	...	...	...	...	...	...	...	...	...	...	...	...	...
France	13	1	12	13	1	12	...	...	...	...	...	...	...	...	...	...	...	...	..	...	...	...	...	...
Belgium	1	1	...	...		...	...	...	...	...	...	...	1	1	...	...	...	...	...	...	...	...	...	...
Germany	4	3	1	4	3	1	...	...	...	...	...	...	...	...	...	...	...	...	...	...	...	...	...	...
Switzerland	1	...	1	1	...	1	...	...	...	...	...	...	...	...	...	...	...	...	...	...	...	...	...	...
Greece	2	2	...	...	...	...	1	1	...	...	...	...	1	1	...	...	...	..	...	...	...	..	...	...
Europe (undefined)	1	1	...	...	...	...	1	1	...	...	...	...	...	...	...	...	...	...	...	...	...	...	...	...
Total	116	73	43	52	28	24	23	21	2	17	9	8	4	4	...	4	3	1	4	2	2	12	6	6
F.—Countries in Africa—																								
Egypt	1	1	...	1	1	...	...	...	...	...	...	...	...	...	...	...	...	...	...	...	...	...	...	...
Africa (undefined)	2	2	...	...	...	...	1	1	...	...	...	...	...	...	...	1	1	...	...	...	...	...	...	...
Total	3	3	...	1	1	...	1	1	...	...	...	...	...	...	...	1	1	...	..	...	...	...	...	...
—Countries in America—																								
America (undefined)	7	4	3	...	...	...	3	2	1	2	1	1	...	...	...	...	...	...	2	1	1	...	...	...
Total Population	2,897,491	1,491,826	1,405,665	655,645	340,235	315,410	574,782	297,011	277,771	315,798	162,969	152,829	481,021	244,799	236,222	471,613	241,688	229,925	398,181	204,798	193,383	451	326	125

TABLE XII.

Persons of Unsound Mind by Age.

TABLE XII.—Persons of Unsound Mind by Age.

District and Taluk.	Total Afflicted.			Distribution by Age.																									
	Total.	Males.	Females.	0—4		5—9		10—14		15—19		20—24		25—29		30—34		35—39		40—44		45—49		50—54		55—59		60 and over.	
				Males.	Females.	Males.	Females.	Males.	Females.	Males.	Females.	Males.	Females.	Males.	Females.	Males.	Females.	Males.	Females.	Males.	Females.	Males.	Females.	Males.	Females.	Males.	Females.	Males.	Females.
1	2	3	4	5	6	7	8	9	10	11	12	13	14	15	16	17	18	19	20	21	22	23	24	25	26	27	28	29	30
District Amraoti	102	57	45	...	1	3	2	5	3	4	3	9	2	6	4	10	7	7	5	6	4	1	5	4	2	...	3	2	4
" Akola	107	69	38	1	...	4	4	7	5	3	3	7	7	10	1	15	2	1	4	10	5	2	3	4	2	1	1	4	1
" Ellichpur	72	46	26	1	1	5	1	5	1	7	2	5	6	5	...	8	2	2	3	3	2	2	1	1	4	...	...	2	3
" Buldana	66	38	28	...	...	3	2	4	6	3	3	2	3	7	3	7	2	2	2	2	2	1	1	4	1	...	1	3	2
" Wun	60	32	28	.	...	3	2	6	8	2	3	...	1	2	2	8	4	3	1	2	1	...	1	3	3	1	...	2	2
" Basim	71	38	33	1	1	2	3	6	2	2	...	2	3	5	4	4	7	4	3	6	4	2	1	2	2	...	...	2	3
Total	478	280	198	3	3	20	14	33	25	21	14	25	22	35	14	52	24	19	18	29	18	8	12	18	14	2	5	15	15
Amraoti District: Taluk Amraoti	38	18	20	...	1	1	...	1	1	...	1	4	1	2	3	4	5	2	1	2	2	...	3	2	...	...	1	...	1
" Chandur	25	14	11	...	...	...	2	2	1	1	1	2	...	...	1	...	1	3	2	2	...	1	1	1	1	...	1	2	...
" Morsi	25	17	8	...	...	2	...	2	...	1	...	1	1	3	...	5	1	...	1	2	2	...	1	1	1	...	...	...	1
" Murtazapur	14	8	6	...	...	...	...	...	1	2	1	2	...	1	...	1	...	2	1	...	...	...	...	...	...	...	1	...	2
Akola District: Taluk Akola	27	16	11	...	..	1	3	2	1	...	1	1	...	4	...	3	1	...	1	3	2	...	...	1	1	1	1	...	...
" Akot	24	17	7	1	...	...	...	4	1	...	...	1	1	...	1	3	1	1	1	2	...	...	1	3	1	...	...	2	...
" Balapur	17	10	7	...	.	2	...	1	1	...	1	...	3	1	...	4	...	...	...	1	...	1	1	...	...	...	...	...	1
" Jalgaon	20	14	6	...	...	1	1	...	2	2	1	2	1	3	...	3	...	...	...	2	1	1	...	...	...	...	...	...	...
" Khamgaon	19	12	7	...	...	...	...	...	...	1	...	3	2	2	...	2	...	...	2	2	2	...	1	...	...	...	...	2	...
Ellichpur District: Taluk Ellichpur	37	24	13	...	...	3	...	3	1	5	1	3	3	3	...	3	2	...	...	1	2	2	...	1	4	...	...	...	...
" Daryapur	21	15	6	...	...	1	...	...	...	2	...	1	2	2	...	3	...	2	2	2	...	...	1	...	...	...	...	2	1
" Melghat	14	7	7	1	1	1	1	2	...	...	1	1	1	...	...	2	...	...	1	...	...	...	...	...	...	...	...	...	2
Buldana District: Taluk Chikhli	18	11	7	...	...	...	1	1	2	...	1	...	...	3	1	3	...	1	...	...	1	...	...	1	...	...	...	2	1
" Malkapur	33	18	15	...	...	2	.	1	3	1	2	1	2	4	1	3	1	1	2	2	1	1	1	1	1	...	1	1	...
" Mehkar	15	9	6	...	...	1	1	2	1	2	...	1	1	...	1	1	1	...	...	...	...	...	...	2	...	...	...	...	1
Wun District: Taluk Yeotmal	18	10	8	...	...	...	...	2	...	1	2	...	...	1	1	4	1	...	1	...	1	...	...	1	2	...	...	1	...
" Darwha	23	15	8	...	...	2	2	3	2	1	1	...	1	1	...	2	...	2	...	2	...	...	1	1	...	...	...	1	1
" Kelapur	11	3	8	...	...	1	...	...	5	...	...	...	...	...	1	2	2	...	...	...	...	...	...	...	...	...	...	...	...
" Wun	8	4	4	...	...	...	...	1	1	...	...	...	...	...	...	...	1	1	...	...	...	...	...	1	1	1	...	...	1
Basim District: Taluk Basim	31	18	13	1	1	1	...	2	1	2	...	2	1	...	1	3	3	2	1	2	3	1	...	1	2	...	...	1	...
" Mangrul	13	4	9	...	...	1	2	...	...	...	...	...	1	1	...	...	2	1	2	...	...	...	1	1	...	...	...	...	1
" Pusad	27	16	11	...	...	...	1	4	1	...	...	...	1	4	3	1	2	1	...	4	1	1	...	...	...	...	...	1	2

TABLE XIIA.

Persons of Unsound Mind by Caste, Tribe, or Race.

TABLE XIIA.—Persons of Unsoun

CASTE, TRIBE, OR RACE.	TOTAL.			DISTRIBUTIO																			
				District Amraoti.								District Akola.										D	
				Taluk Amraoti.		Taluk Chandur.		Taluk Morsi.		Taluk Murtazapur.		Taluk Akola.		Taluk Akot.		Taluk Balapur.		Taluk Jalgaon.		Taluk Khamgaon		Taluk Ellichpur.	
	Total.	Males.	Females.	Males.	Females.	Males.	Females.	Males.	Females.	Males.	Females.	Males.	Females.	Males.	Females.	Males.	Females.	Males.	Females.	Males.	Females.	Males.	Females.
1	2	3	4	5	6	7	8	9	10	11	12	13	14	15	16	17	18	19	20	21	22	23	24
1. Andh	6	2	4	...	...	...	...	...	...	...	...	...	...	...	...	...	...	...	...	...	...	...	...
2. Bairági	1	...	1	...	...	...	...	...	...	...	...	...	...	...	...	...	...	...	...	...	...	...	...
3. Banjári	5	4	1	...	...	...	...	...	...	...	...	...	...	...	...	...	...	...	...	...	...	...	...
4. Beldár	2	2	...	...	...	...	...	...	...	...	...	1	...	...	...	...	...	...	...	...	...	...	...
5. Bhámti	1	1	...	...	...	...	...	...	...	...	...	...	...	...	...	...	...	...	...	...	...	...	...
6. Bhát	2	2	...	...	...	...	...	1	...	...	...	...	...	...	...	...	...	...	...	...	...	...	...
7. Bhoi	7	6	1	...	1	...	...	1	...	...	...	...	...	2	...	...	...	...	...	...	...	...	...
8. Bráhman	15	10	5	1	1	1	...	...	1	...	...	...	1	1	...	1	...	...	1	1	...	2	...
9. Burad	1	...	1	...	1	...	...	...	...	...	...	...	...	...	...	...	...	...	...	...	...	...	...
10. Dhangar	8	4	4	...	...	...	...	...	...	...	...	...	...	...	...	...	...	...	2	...	...	...	...
11. Fakir	2	1	1	...	...	...	...	...	...	...	1	...	...	...	...	...	...	...	...	...	...	1	...
12. Gaoli	7	6	1	1	...	3	1	...	...	...	...	...	...	...	...	...	...	...	...	...	...	...	...
13. Gárpagári	1	1	...	...	...	...	...	...	...	...	...	...	...	...	...	...	...	...	...	...	...	...	...
14. Gawári	1	...	1	...	...	...	...	...	...	...	...	...	...	...	...	...	...	...	...	...	...	...	...
15. Golkar	1	...	1	...	...	...	...	...	...	...	...	...	...	...	...	...	...	...	...	...	...	...	...
16. Gond	7	2	5	...	...	...	1	...	1	...	...	...	...	...	...	...	...	...	...	...	...	1	...
17. Gosávi	2	1	1	...	...	...	...	...	...	...	...	...	...	...	...	...	1	...	...	...	...	...	...
18. Gurao	4	1	3	...	...	...	1	...	1	...	...	...	...	...	...	...	1	...	...	...	...	...	...
19. Halbi	2	2	...	...	...	...	...	1	...	...	...	...	...	...	...	...	...	...	...	...	...	1	...
20. Jogi	1	1	...	...	...	...	...	...	...	1	...	...	...	...	...	...	...	...	...	...	...	...	...
21. Kalál	2	...	2	...	...	...	...	...	...	...	...	...	...	...	...	...	...	...	...	...	...	...	1
22. Kásár	2	2	...	...	...	...	...	...	...	...	...	...	...	...	...	...	...	...	...	...	...	1	...
23. Khátik	3	...	3	...	3	...	...	...	...	...	...	...	...	...	...	...	...	...	...	...	...	...	...
24. Kolám	3	...	3	...	...	...	...	...	...	...	...	...	...	...	...	...	...	...	...	...	...	...	...
25. Koli	4	3	1	1	1	...	...	...	...	...	...	1	...	...	...	...	...	...	...	...	...	...	...
26. Komti	1	...	1	...	...	...	...	...	...	...	...	...	...	...	...	...	...	...	...	...	...	...	...
27. Korku	11	5	6	...	...	...	...	...	...	...	...	...	...	...	...	...	...	...	...	...	...	...	1
28. Koshti	5	4	1	...	...	...	...	1	...	...	...	...	...	...	...	...	...	...	...	...	...	2	...
29. Kumbhár	2	...	2	...	...	...	...	...	...	...	...	...	1	...	...	...	...	...	...	...	...	...	...
30. Kunbi	119	74	45	5	4	3	3	3	1	...	1	5	2	4	4	1	...	6	1	4	4	4	3
31. Labháni	2	...	2	...	...	...	...	...	...	...	...	...	1	...	...	...	...	...	...	...	...	...	...
32. Lajjhar	1	...	1	...	...	...	1	...	...	...	...	...	...	...	...	...	...	...	...	...	...	...	...
33. Lohár	5	4	1	1	1	...	...	1	...	...	...	...	...	...	...	...	...	...	...	...	...	1	...
34. Mahár	61	40	21	1	1	3	1	1	...	1	1	6	2	4	1	2	2	1	...	5	1	3	1
35 Máli	32	18	14	...	3	...	...	4	2	2	1	...	1	1	1	2	1	3	1	...	1	1	...
36. Mháli	6	1	5	...	...	...	...	...	1	...	...	...	...	...	...	...	...	...	...	...	...	...	...
37. Mánbháo	5	4	1	...	...	1	...	1	...	...	...	...	...	...	...	1	...	...	...	...	...	1	...
38. Máng	6	2	4	...	...	...	...	...	...	...	...	...	...	...	...	...	...	...	...	...	...	...	...
39. Maráthá	3	3	...	...	...	1	...	...	...	...	...	...	...	...	...	...	...	...	...	...	...	...	...
40. Márwári	1	...	1	...	...	...	...	...	...	...	...	...	...	...	...	...	...	...	...	...	...	...	...
41. Mehtar (Sikh)	1	1	...	...	...	...	...	...	...	...	...	1	...	...	...	...	...	...	...	...	...	...	...
42. Munarwár	1	...	1	...	...	...	...	...	...	...	...	...	...	...	...	...	...	...	...	...	...	...	...
43. Musalmán	11	5	6	...	2	...	...	...	...	...	...	...	...	1	1	1	...	...	...	...	...	...	...
44. Nihál	1	...	1	...	...	...	...	...	...	...	...	...	...	...	...	...	...	...	...	...	...	...	...
45. Pardhán	2	2	...	...	...	...	...	...	...	...	...	...	...	...	...	...	...	...	...	...	...	...	...
46. Párdhi	5	3	2	2	...	...	...	...	...	...	...	...	...	...	...	...	...	...	...	...	...	...	...
47. Patháu	8	4	4	...	...	...	...	...	...	...	1	1	...	...	...	...	...	...	...	...	...	...	1
48. Purbhayá	1	1	...	...	...	...	...	...	...	...	...	...	...	...	...	...	...	...	...	...	...	...	...
49. Rajput	9	3	6	...	...	...	...	...	...	...	1	...	...	1	...	...	2	...	...	...	...	...	...
50. Rangári	2	1	1	1	...	...	...	...	...	...	...	...	...	...	...	...	...	...	...	...	...	...	1
51. Sáli	1	...	1	...	...	...	...	...	...	...	...	...	...	...	...	...	...	...	1	...	...	...	...
52. Shekh	30	19	11	3	...	...	...	...	...	2	...	...	2	2	...	...	...	2	...	...	...	4	4
53. Simpi	4	3	1	...	...	...	...	...	...	...	...	...	...	...	...	1	...	...	...	...	...	...	...
54. Sonár	9	8	1	1	...	2	...	...	...	...	...	...	...	...	...	...	...	2	...	...	...	...	1
55. Sutár	4	1	3	...	1	...	1	...	...	...	...	...	...	...	...	...	...	...	...	...	...	...	...
56. Syed	1	...	1	...	...	...	...	...	...	...	...	...	...	...	...	...	...	...	...	...	...	...	...
57. Tákankár	1	1	...	...	...	...	...	...	...	...	...	...	...	...	...	...	...	...	...	...	...	...	...
58. Teli	14	10	4	1	1	...	...	...	...	2	...	...	...	1	...	...	...	...	...	1	1	1	...
59. Thákur	2	1	1	...	...	...	1	1	...	...	...	...	...	...	...	...	...	...	...	...	...	...	...
60. Vidur	2	1	1	...	...	...	1	1	...	...	...	...	...	...	...	...	...	...	...	...	...	...	...
61. Waddar	2	1	1	...	...	...	...	...	...	...	...	...	...	...	...	...	...	...	...	...	...	...	...
62. Wanjári	3	...	3	...	...	...	...	...	...	...	...	...	...	...	...	...	...	...	...	...	...	...	...
63. Wáni (Hindu)	10	5	5	...	...	...	...	...	1	...	...	1	1	...	...	...	...	...	...	...	...	1	...
64. Wáni (Jain)	2	2	...	...	...	...	...	1	...	...	...	...	...	...	...	...	...	...	...	...	...	...	...
65. Warthi	2	2	...	...	...	...	...	...	...	...	...	...	...	...	...	1	...	...	...	1	...	...	...
Total	478	280	158	18	20	14	11	17	8	8	6	16	11	17	7	10	7	14	6	12	7	24	13

Mind by Caste, Tribe, or Race.

BY DISTRICTS.

[Dis]trict Ellichpur.				District Buldana.						District Wun.								District Basim.						
Taluk Daryapur.		Taluk Melghat.		Taluk Chikhli.		Taluk Malkapur.		Taluk Mehkar.		Taluk Yeotmal.		Taluk Darwha.		Taluk Kelapur.		Taluk Wun.		Taluk Basim.		Taluk Mangrul.		Taluk Pusad.		CASTE, TRIBE, or RACE
Males.	Females.	Males.	Females.	Males.	Females.	Males.	Females.	Males.	Females.	Males.	Females.	Males.	Females.	Males.	Females.	Males.	Females.	Males.	Females.	Males.	Females.	Males.	Females.	
25	26	27	28	29	30	31	32	33	34	35	36	37	38	39	40	41	42	43	44	45	46	47	48	49
...	...	...	...	...	...	...	...	...	...	...	...	...	...	...	...	...	...	1	...	...	4	1	...	1. Andh.
...	1	...	...	...	...	...	...	...	...	...	...	...	...	...	...	...	...	...	...	...	...	...	...	2. Baiárgi.
...	...	...	...	...	...	...	...	...	...	...	...	4	...	...	...	...	...	...	...	...	...	...	1	3. Banjári.
...	...	...	...	...	...	...	...	...	...	...	...	...	...	1	...	...	...	...	...	...	...	...	...	4. Beldár.
...	...	...	...	...	...	...	...	...	...	1	...	...	...	...	...	...	...	...	...	...	...	...	...	5. Bhámti.
1	...	...	...	...	...	...	...	...	...	...	...	...	...	...	...	...	...	...	...	...	...	...	...	6. Bhát.
...	...	1	...	...	...	...	...	...	...	...	...	...	...	...	...	2	...	...	...	...	...	...	...	7. Bhoi.
...	...	...	...	...	...	1	1	1	...	1	...	...	...	...	...	...	...	...	...	...	...	...	...	8. Bráhman.
...	...	...	...	...	...	...	...	...	...	...	...	...	...	...	...	...	...	...	...	...	...	...	...	9. Burad.
2	1	...	...	...	...	...	1	...	...	...	...	...	...	...	...	...	...	1	...	...	...	1	...	10. Dhangar.
...	...	...	...	...	...	...	...	...	...	...	...	...	...	...	...	...	...	...	...	...	...	...	...	11. Fakir.
...	...	1	...	...	...	...	...	...	...	...	...	...	...	...	...	...	...	...	...	...	...	1	...	12. Gaoli.
...	...	...	...	...	...	...	...	...	...	1	...	...	...	...	...	...	...	...	...	...	...	...	...	13. Gárpagári.
...	...	...	...	...	...	...	...	...	...	...	...	...	...	...	1	...	...	...	...	...	...	...	...	14. Gawári.
...	...	...	...	...	...	...	...	...	...	...	...	...	...	...	1	...	...	...	...	...	...	...	...	15. Golkar.
...	...	...	...	...	...	...	...	...	...	1	1	...	...	...	1	...	1	...	...	...	...	...	...	16. Gond.
...	...	...	...	...	...	...	...	...	...	...	...	...	...	...	...	...	...	1	...	...	...	...	...	17. Gosávi.
...	...	...	...	...	...	...	...	...	...	...	...	1	...	...	...	...	...	...	...	...	...	...	...	18. Gurao.
...	...	...	...	...	...	...	...	...	...	...	...	...	...	...	...	...	...	...	...	...	...	...	...	19. Halbi.
...	...	...	...	...	...	...	...	...	...	...	...	...	...	...	...	...	...	...	...	...	...	...	...	20. Jogi.
...	...	...	...	...	...	...	...	...	...	...	...	...	...	...	...	...	...	...	...	...	...	...	1	21. Kalál.
...	...	...	...	...	...	...	...	...	...	...	...	1	...	...	...	...	...	...	...	...	...	...	...	22. Kásár.
...	...	...	...	...	...	...	...	...	...	...	...	...	...	...	...	...	...	...	...	...	...	...	...	23. Khátik.
...	...	...	...	...	...	...	...	...	...	...	1	...	...	...	2	...	...	...	...	...	...	...	...	24. Kolám.
...	...	...	...	...	...	...	...	...	...	...	...	...	...	...	...	...	...	...	...	1	...	...	...	25. Koli.
...	...	...	...	...	...	...	...	...	...	...	...	...	...	...	...	...	1	...	...	...	...	...	...	26. Komti.
...	...	5	5	...	...	...	...	...	...	...	...	...	...	...	...	...	...	...	...	...	...	...	...	27. Korku.
...	...	...	...	...	1	...	...	...	...	...	...	1	...	...	...	...	...	...	...	...	...	...	...	28. Kushti.
...	...	...	...	...	...	...	1	...	...	...	...	...	...	...	...	...	...	...	...	...	...	...	...	29. Kumbhár.
5	1	...	...	6	1	5	2	4	1	1	1	4	1	...	...	...	2	8	8	1	2	5	3	30. Kunbi.
...	...	...	...	...	...	...	...	...	...	...	...	...	...	...	...	...	...	...	1	...	...	...	...	31. Labháni.
...	...	...	...	...	...	...	...	...	...	...	...	...	...	...	...	...	...	...	...	...	...	...	...	32. Lajjhar.
...	...	...	...	...	...	...	...	...	...	...	...	...	...	...	...	...	...	1	...	...	...	...	...	33. Lohár.
3	2	...	...	2	...	...	2	...	3	2	2	1	1	...	...	1	...	1	...	1	...	2	1	34. Mahár.
...	...	...	...	...	...	1	1	1	...	2	...	...	1	...	...	...	...	...	...	1	1	...	...	35 Máli.
...	...	...	...	...	...	...	...	1	...	...	...	...	...	...	...	...	...	...	2	...	1	...	1	36. Mháli.
...	...	...	...	...	...	...	1	...	...	...	...	...	...	...	...	...	...	...	...	...	...	...	...	37. Mánbháo.
...	...	...	...	...	...	...	1	...	...	...	2	...	...	...	...	...	...	1	...	...	...	1	1	38. Máng.
...	...	...	...	...	...	1	...	...	...	...	...	...	...	...	...	...	...	...	...	...	...	1	...	39. Maráthá.
...	...	...	...	...	...	...	1	...	...	...	...	...	...	...	...	...	...	...	...	...	...	...	...	40. Márwári.
...	...	...	...	...	...	...	...	...	...	...	...	...	...	...	...	...	...	...	...	...	...	...	...	41. Mehtar (Sikh).
...	...	...	...	...	...	...	...	...	...	...	...	...	...	...	1	...	...	...	...	...	...	...	...	42. Munarwár.
...	1	...	...	...	...	1	...	1	...	...	...	...	...	...	...	...	...	...	1	...	...	1	1	43. Musalmán.
...	...	...	1	...	...	...	...	...	...	...	...	...	...	...	...	...	...	...	...	...	...	...	...	44. Nihál.
...	...	...	...	...	...	...	...	...	...	1	...	...	...	1	...	...	...	...	...	...	...	...	...	45. Pardhán.
...	...	...	...	...	...	...	...	...	...	...	...	1	2	...	...	...	...	...	...	...	...	...	...	46. Párdhi.
...	...	...	...	...	1	3	...	...	...	...	...	...	...	...	...	...	...	...	...	...	...	...	1	47. Pathán.
...	...	...	...	1	...	...	...	...	...	...	...	...	...	...	...	...	...	...	...	...	...	...	...	48 Purbhayá.
...	...	...	1	1	1	1	...	...	...	...	...	...	...	...	1	...	...	...	...	...	...	...	...	49. Rajput.
...	...	...	...	...	...	...	...	...	...	...	...	...	...	...	...	...	...	...	...	...	...	...	...	50. Rangári.
...	...	...	...	...	...	...	...	...	...	...	...	...	...	...	...	...	...	...	...	...	...	...	...	51. Sáli.
...	...	...	...	...	...	4	2	...	...	...	...	1	2	...	...	...	...	1	...	...	1	...	...	52. Shekh.
2	...	...	...	...	...	...	1	...	...	...	...	...	...	...	...	...	...	...	...	...	...	...	...	53. Simpi.
1	...	...	...	...	...	...	...	1	...	...	...	...	...	1	...	...	...	...	...	...	...	...	...	54. Sonár.
...	...	...	...	1	...	...	...	...	...	...	...	...	1	...	...	...	...	...	...	...	...	...	...	55 Sutár.
...	...	...	...	...	1	...	...	...	...	...	...	...	...	...	...	...	...	...	...	...	...	...	...	56. Syed.
...	...	...	...	...	...	...	...	...	...	...	...	1	...	...	...	...	...	...	...	...	...	...	...	57. Tákankár.
1	...	...	...	...	...	...	...	...	...	...	1	...	...	...	...	1	...	2	1	...	...	...	...	58. Teli.
...	...	...	...	...	...	...	...	...	...	...	...	...	...	...	...	...	...	...	...	...	...	...	...	59. Thákur.
...	...	...	...	...	...	...	...	...	...	...	...	...	...	...	...	...	...	...	...	...	...	...	...	60. Vidur.
...	...	...	...	...	...	...	...	...	1	...	...	...	...	...	...	...	...	...	...	...	...	1	...	61. Waddar.
...	...	...	...	...	1	...	...	...	1	...	...	...	...	...	1	...	...	...	...	...	...	...	...	62. Wanjári.
...	...	...	...	...	1	1	1	...	...	...	...	...	...	...	...	...	...	...	...	...	...	2	1	63. Wáni (Hindu).
...	...	...	...	...	...	...	...	...	...	...	...	...	...	...	...	...	...	1	...	...	...	...	...	64. Wáni (Jain).
...	...	...	...	...	...	...	...	...	...	...	...	...	...	...	...	...	...	...	...	...	...	...	...	95. Warthi.
15	6	7	7	11	7	18	15	9	6	10	8	15	8	3	8	4	4	18	13	4	9	16	11	Total.

TABLE XIII.

Deaf-mutes by Age.

TABLE XIII.—Deaf-mutes by Age.

DISTRICT AND TALUK.	TOTAL AFFLICTED.			DISTRIBUTION BY AGE.																									
				0–4		5–9		10–14		15–19		20–24		25–29		30–34		35–39		40–44		45–49		50–54		55–59		60 AND OVER.	
	Total.	Males.	Females.	Males.	Females.	Males.	Females.	Males.	Females.	Males.	Females.	Males.	Females.	Males.	Females.	Males.	Females.	Males.	Females.	Males.	Females.	Males.	Females.	Males.	Females.	Males.	Females.	Males.	Females.
1	2	3	4	5	6	7	8	9	10	11	12	13	14	15	16	17	18	19	20	21	22	23	24	25	26	27	28	29	30
District Amraoti	124	69	55	4	6	12	8	8	6	8	4	7	5	8	4	5	6	7	2	...	2	2	3	1	...	1	...	6	9
" Akola	124	78	46	1	3	9	4	6	4	8	4	6	4	6	7	10	3	4	2	8	4	3	5	6	1	1	...	10	5
" Ellichpur	97	58	39	...	1	4	3	6	4	6	2	5	5	6	2	8	5	5	2	2	2	2	...	2	3	2	1	10	9
" Buldana	51	29	22	1	1	4	4	4	5	8	2	3	1	3	1	2	1	...	1	1	1	2	2	...	1	...	...	1	2
" Wun	72	42	30	2	1	6	1	7	3	6	3	2	3	3	5	5	3	3	2	1	1	2	...	2	4	1	1	2	3
" Basim	62	41	21	3	...	7	6	5	3	1	...	3	1	6	3	3	2	1	...	3	1	1	1	4	1	...	...	4	3
Total	530	317	213	11	12	42	26	36	25	37	15	26	19	32	22	33	20	20	9	15	11	12	11	15	10	5	2	33	31
Amraoti District. Taluk Amraoti	33	17	16	...	...	4	3	2	4	3	1	1	2	1	1	1	2	2	1	...	...	1	...	1	...	...	...	1	2
" Chandur	33	17	16	...	2	3	2	2	...	1	3	2	1	3	1	1	...	3	1	...	1	...	3	...	...	...	...	2	2
" Morsi	26	19	7	2	2	4	1	3	...	2	...	2	1	..	...	...	1	2	...	...	1	1	...	...	...	1	...	2	1
" Murtazapur	32	16	16	2	2	1	2	1	2	2	...	2	1	4	2	3	3	...	...	...	...	...	...	...	...	...	...	1	4
Akola District. Taluk Akola	28	15	13	...	1	1	...	...	1	4	4	...	1	...	1	5	1	1	1	2	1	1	2	...	...	...	...	1	...
" Akot	36	24	12	...	1	2	1	1	1	1	...	2	...	1	3	1	1	2	...	2	1	2	1	4	...	...	...	6	3
" Balapur	18	12	6	...	1	3	1	1	...	2	...	...	2	1	1	3	...	...	...	1	1	...	...	...	...	...	...	1	...
" Jalgaon	13	9	4	...	...	...	1	2	...	1	...	2	...	2	2	1	...	3	...	...	...	...	...	...	...	...	...	...	1
" Khamgaon	29	18	11	1	...	3	1	2	2	...	...	2	1	2	...	...	1	...	1	3	1	...	2	2	1	1	...	2	1
Ellichpur District. Taluk Ellichpur	19	10	9	...	...	...	...	...	2	1	...	2	3	1	...	1	...	...	1	1	...	1	...	...	1	1	1	2	1
" Daryapur	67	40	27	...	1	4	3	2	1	5	1	3	2	5	2	5	4	5	1	1	2	1	...	...	2	1	...	8	8
" Melghat	11	8	3	...	...	...	...	4	1	...	1	...	...	...	...	2	1	...	...	...	...	...	...	2	...	...	...	...	...
Buldana District. Taluk Chikhli	10	3	7	...	...	1	1	...	3	1	...	...	1	...	...	...	1	...	...	...	...	...	...	...	...	...	...	1	1
" Malkapur	36	25	11	1	1	2	1	4	2	7	1	3	...	3	1	2	...	...	...	1	1	2	2	...	1	...	...	...	1
" Mehkar	5	1	4	...	...	1	2	...	...	...	1	...	...	...	...	...	...	...	1	...	...	...	...	...	...	...	...	...	...
Wun District. Taluk Yeotmal	22	12	10	...	...	...	...	3	...	3	2	...	2	...	1	2	1	1	1	...	...	1	...	...	2	...	...	2	1
" Darwha	22	12	10	1	1	2	1	3	...	1	...	...	...	1	2	2	1	...	1	...	1	1	...	1	2	...	1	...	...
" Kelapar	11	8	3	1	...	2	...	...	...	1	...	1	1	1	1	...	...	1	...	1	...	...	...	...	...	...	...	...	1
" Wun	17	10	7	...	...	2	...	1	3	1	1	1	...	1	1	1	1	1	...	...	...	...	...	1	...	1	...	...	1
Basim District. Taluk Basim	24	13	11	...	...	2	2	1	3	...	...	3	1	2	2	...	...	...	...	2	1	...	1	1	1	...	...	2	...
" Mangrul	14	7	7	3	...	1	2	1	...	...	...	...	...	...	1	1	2	...	...	1	...	...	...	...	...	...	...	...	2
" Pusad	24	21	3	...	...	4	2	3	...	1	...	...	...	4	...	2	...	1	...	...	...	1	...	3	...	...	...	2	1

TABLE XIII A.

Deaf-Mutes, by Caste, Tribe, or Race.

TABLE XIII A.—Deaf-Mutes,

CASTE, TRIBE, OR RACE.	TOTAL.			DISTRIBUTION																			
				District Amraoti.								District Akola.										District	
				Taluk Amraoti.		Taluk Chandur.		Taluk Morsi.		Taluk Murtaza-pur.		Taluk Akola.		Taluk Akot.		Taluk Balapur.		Taluk Jalgaon.		Taluk Kham-gaon.		Taluk Ellichpur.	
	Total.	Males.	Females.	Males.	Females.	Males.	Females.	Males.	Females.	Males.	Females.	Males.	Females.	Males.	Females.	Males.	Females.	Males.	Females.	Males.	Females.	Males.	Females.
1	2	3	4	5	6	7	8	9	10	11	12	13	14	15	16	17	18	19	20	21	22	23	24
1. Andh	15	9	6	...	...	...	...	...	...	...	...	...	...	...	...	...	1	...	...	...	...	...	...
2. Bairági	1	1	...	...	...	...	...	...	...	...	...	...	...	...	...	1	...	...	...	...	...	...	...
3. Banjári	6	5	1	...	1	...	...	...	...	...	...	1	...	...	...	...	...	...	...	...	...	...	...
4. Bári	3	1	2	1	1	...	...	...	...	...	...	...	...	...	...	...	...	...	...	...	...	...	...
5. Beldár	1	1	...	...	...	...	...	...	...	...	...	...	...	...	...	...	...	...	...	...	...	...	...
6. Bhil	1	1	...	...	...	...	...	...	...	...	...	...	...	...	...	...	...	...	...	...	...	...	...
7. Bhoi	4	3	1	...	...	...	...	...	...	...	...	...	...	...	...	...	...	...	...	1	...	...	...
8. Bráhman	11	7	4	...	...	...	...	...	...	...	...	...	...	2	...	2	1	...	...	1	...	...	...
9. Chámbhár	9	7	2	...	...	...	...	...	...	...	...	...	...	...	...	1	...	...	...	...	1	1	...
10. Dhangar	20	9	11	...	1	...	...	...	...	...	...	1	1	1	...	1	...	...	...	1	...	...	...
11. Gaoli	7	4	3	...	...	...	...	...	...	...	...	2	1	...	...	1	...	...	...	...	...	...	...
12. Gárpagári	2	2	...	...	...	...	...	...	...	...	...	...	...	...	...	...	...	...	...	...	...	...	...
13. Gawári	4	3	1	1	...	1	...	1	...	...	...	...	...	...	...	...	...	...	...	...	...	...	...
14. Gond	14	8	6	...	1	...	...	...	...	...	...	1	...	...	...	...	...	...	...	...	...	...	...
15. Gopál	2	2	...	...	...	...	...	...	...	...	...	1	...	...	...	...	...	...	...	...	...	...	...
16. Gosávi	7	3	4	...	...	...	...	...	...	...	1	...	...	1	1	...	...	...	...	...	...	...	...
17. Gujráthi	1	...	1	...	...	...	...	...	...	...	...	...	...	...	...	...	...	...	...	...	...	...	...
18. Gurao	2	2	...	...	...	...	...	1	...	...	...	...	...	...	...	...	...	...	...	...	...	...	...
19. Hatgar	2	2	...	...	...	...	...	...	...	...	...	...	...	...	...	1	...	...	...	...	...	...	...
20. Jingar	1	...	1	...	...	...	1	...	...	...	...	...	...	...	...	...	...	...	...	...	...	...	...
21. Jiráyat	2	1	1	...	...	...	...	...	...	...	...	...	...	1	1	...	...	...	...	...	...	...	...
22. Kahár	1	...	1	...	...	...	...	...	...	...	...	...	...	...	...	...	...	...	...	...	...	...	...
23. Kalál	2	1	1	...	...	...	...	...	...	...	...	...	...	...	...	...	...	...	...	...	...	...	...
24. Kánari	1	...	1	...	...	...	...	...	...	...	...	...	...	...	1	...	...	...	...	...	...	...	...
25. Kásth	2	1	1	...	...	...	...	...	...	1	...	...	1	...	...	...	...	...	...	...	...	...	...
26. Khátik	2	2	...	1	...	...	...	...	...	1	...	...	...	...	...	...	...	...	...	...	...	...	...
27. Kolám	4	2	2	...	...	...	...	...	...	...	...	...	...	...	...	...	...	...	...	...	...	...	...
28. Kolháti	1	1	...	...	...	...	...	...	...	...	...	...	...	...	...	...	...	...	...	...	...	...	...
29. Koli	3	2	1	...	...	...	...	...	...	...	...	...	1	...	...	...	...	1	...	...	...	...	...
30. Komti	2	1	1	...	...	...	...	...	...	...	...	...	...	...	...	...	1	...	...	...	...	...	...
31. Korku	7	5	2	1	...	...	...	...	...	...	...	...	...	...	...	...	...	...	...	...	...	...	...
32. Koshti	4	3	1	...	...	...	...	2	1	...	...	...	...	...	...	...	...	...	...	...	...	...	...
33. Kumbhár	4	1	3	...	...	...	...	...	...	...	...	...	1	...	...	...	...	...	...	...	...	...	...
34. Kunbi	119	66	53	3	3	6	3	6	3	4	5	...	2	5	5	3	...	1	2	6	4	6	4
35. Lohár	6	1	5	...	...	...	...	...	1	...	3	...	...	...	...	...	...	...	...	...	...	...	...
36. Mahár	78	52	26	2	3	4	5	3	1	3	3	5	2	7	...	1	...	1	2	1	1	1	1
37. Máli	37	25	12	3	...	2	2	5	...	1	...	...	1	1	1	1	...	1	...	2	1	...	1
38. Máng	10	5	5	...	1	...	...	...	...	1	...	1	1	1	...	...	...	...	...	...	...	...	...
39. Maráthá	3	1	2	...	...	...	1	...	...	1	...	...	...	...	...	...	...	...	...	...	...	...	...
40. Mháli	5	3	2	...	...	...	...	...	...	...	...	...	...	3	1	...	...	...	...	...	...	...	...
41. Munárwár	1	1	...	...	...	...	...	...	...	...	...	...	...	...	...	...	...	...	...	...	...	...	...
42. Musalmán	10	5	5	...	...	...	...	...	...	...	...	...	...	...	1	...	...	...	...	1	...	...	...
43. Náth	1	1	...	...	...	...	...	...	...	1	...	...	...	...	...	...	...	...	...	...	...	...	...
44. Native Christian	1	1	...	...	...	...	...	...	...	...	...	1	...	...	...	...	...	...	...	...	...	...	...
45. Nihál	2	2	...	...	...	...	...	...	...	...	...	...	...	...	...	...	...	...	...	...	...	...	...
46. Otári	1	...	1	...	...	...	...	...	1	...	...	...	...	...	...	...	...	...	...	...	...	...	...
47. Pakháli	2	2	...	...	...	...	...	...	...	...	...	...	...	...	...	...	...	...	...	...	...	...	...
48. Pángul	1	1	...	...	...	...	...	...	...	...	...	...	...	...	...	...	...	...	...	...	...	...	...
49. Pardhán	5	3	2	...	...	...	1	...	...	...	...	...	...	...	...	...	...	...	...	...	...	...	...
50. Pathán	4	2	2	...	...	...	...	...	...	...	...	...	...	1	...	...	...	...	...	...	1	1	...
51. Rajput	17	9	8	1	1	...	1	...	...	...	2	1	1	...	...	...	...	...	...	...	1	...	...
52. Rangári	1	...	1	...	...	...	...	...	...	...	...	...	...	...	...	...	...	...	...	...	...	...	...
53. Sáli	2	2	...	1	...	1	...	...	...	...	...	...	...	...	...	...	...	...	...	...	...	...	...
54. Sheke	17	5	12	1	3	...	...	...	...	...	2	...	...	1	1	...	2	1	...	1	1	...	1
55. Simpi (Hindu)	4	1	3	...	...	...	1	...	...	...	...	...	...	...	...	...	...	1	...	...	1	...	1
56. Simpi (Jain)	1	1	...	...	...	...	...	...	...	...	...	...	...	...	...	...	...	...	...	...	...	...	...
57. Sonár	5	4	1	1	...	...	...	...	...	...	...	...	...	...	...	...	...	...	...	1	...	...	...
58. Sutár	8	8	...	...	...	1	...	1	...	1	...	...	...	...	...	...	...	...	...	...	...	...	...
59. Syed	2	2	...	...	...	...	...	...	...	1	...	...	...	...	...	...	...	...	...	...	...	...	...
60. Tákankár	2	2	...	...	...	...	...	...	...	1	...	...	...	...	...	...	...	1	...	...	...	...	...
61. Teli	8	4	4	1	1	...	1	...	...	...	...	1	...	...	...	...	...	1	...	...	...	...	...
62. Thákur	3	2	1	...	...	...	...	...	...	...	...	...	...	...	...	...	...	...	...	...	...	...	...
63. Vidur	1	1	...	...	...	1	...	...	...	...	...	...	...	...	...	...	...	...	...	...	...	...	...
64. Waddar	1	...	1	...	...	...	...	...	...	...	...	...	1	...	...	...	...	...	...	...	...	...	...
65. Wáni (Hindu)	12	9	3	...	...	1	...	...	...	...	...	...	...	...	...	...	...	1	...	2	...	1	...
66. Wáni (Jain)	1	...	1	...	...	...	...	...	...	...	...	...	...	...	...	...	...	...	...	...	...	...	...
67. Wanjári	5	4	1	...	...	...	...	...	...	...	...	...	...	...	...	...	1	...	...	1	...	...	...
68. Warthi	5	2	3	...	...	...	...	...	...	...	...	...	...	...	...	...	...	...	...	...	...	...	1
Unspecified	1	...	1	...	...	...	...	...	...	...	...	...	...	...	...	...	...	...	...	...	...	...	...
Total	530	317	213	17	16	17	16	19	7	16	16	15	13	24	12	12	6	9	4	18	11	10	9

by Caste, Tribe, or Race.

BY DISTRICTS.

Ellichpur.				District Buldana.						District Wun.								District Basim.						
Taluk Daryapur.		Taluk Melghat.		Taluk Chikhli.		Taluk Malkapur.		Taluk Mehkar.		Taluk Yeotmal.		Taluk Darwha.		Taluk Kelapur.		Taluk Wun.		Taluk Basim.		Taluk Mangrul.		Taluk Pusad.		CASTE, TRIBE, OR RACE.
Males.	Females.	Males.	Females.	Males.	Females.	Males.	Females.	Males.	Females.	Males.	Females.	Males.	Females.	Males.	Females.	Males.	Females.	Males.	Females.	Males.	Females.	Males.	Females.	
25	26	27	28	29	30	31	32	33	34	35	36	37	38	39	40	41	42	43	44	45	46	47	48	49
...	...	...	...	...	...	...	...	...	...	...	...	...	2	...	...	...	...	3	2	1	...	5	1	1. Andh.
...	...	...	...	...	...	...	...	...	...	...	...	...	...	...	...	...	...	...	...	...	...	...	...	2. Bairági.
...	...	...	...	...	...	...	...	...	...	...	...	4	...	...	...	...	...	...	...	...	...	...	...	3. Banjári.
...	...	...	...	...	...	...	...	...	...	...	...	...	1	...	...	...	...	...	...	...	...	...	...	4. Bári.
...	...	...	...	...	...	...	...	...	...	...	...	...	...	...	...	1	...	...	...	...	...	...	...	5. Beldár.
...	...	...	...	...	...	...	...	...	...	...	...	1	...	...	...	...	...	...	...	...	...	...	...	6. Bhil.
2	1	...	...	...	...	...	...	...	...	...	...	...	...	...	...	...	...	...	...	...	...	...	...	7. Bhoi.
...	1	...	...	...	...	1	...	...	...	...	...	...	...	...	...	...	...	1	1	...	...	...	1	8. Bráhman.
3	...	...	...	...	...	1	...	...	...	...	...	1	1	...	...	...	...	...	...	...	...	...	...	9. Chámbhár.
1	1	...	...	...	...	2	3	...	...	...	1	...	2	...	...	...	...	...	1	...	1	2	...	10. Dhangar.
...	...	...	...	...	...	...	1	...	...	...	...	...	...	...	...	...	...	1	1	...	...	...	...	11. Gaoli.
2	...	...	...	...	...	...	...	...	...	...	...	...	...	...	...	...	...	...	...	...	...	...	...	12. Gárpagári.
...	...	...	...	...	...	...	...	...	...	...	1	...	...	...	...	...	...	...	...	...	...	...	...	13. Gawári.
...	...	1	...	...	...	...	...	...	...	1	2	...	1	3	1	2	1	...	...	...	...	...	...	14. Gond.
...	...	...	...	...	...	...	...	...	...	...	...	...	...	...	...	...	...	...	...	...	...	1	...	15. Gopál.
...	1	...	...	...	...	...	...	...	...	1	...	...	...	...	...	...	1	...	...	...	...	1	...	16. Gosávi.
...	1	...	...	...	...	...	...	...	...	...	...	...	...	...	...	...	...	...	...	...	...	...	...	17. Gujráthi.
...	...	...	...	...	...	...	...	...	...	...	...	...	...	...	...	1	...	...	...	...	...	...	...	18. Gurao.
...	...	...	...	...	...	...	...	...	...	...	...	...	...	...	...	...	...	...	...	...	...	1	...	19. Hatgar.
...	...	...	...	...	...	...	...	...	...	...	...	...	...	...	...	...	...	...	...	...	...	...	...	20. Jingar.
...	...	...	...	...	...	...	...	...	...	...	...	...	...	...	...	...	...	...	...	...	...	...	...	21. Jirávat.
...	...	...	...	...	...	...	1	...	...	...	...	...	...	...	...	...	...	...	...	...	...	...	...	22. Kahár.
...	...	...	...	...	...	1	...	...	...	...	...	...	1	...	...	...	...	...	...	...	...	...	...	23. Kalál.
...	...	...	...	...	...	...	...	...	...	...	...	...	...	...	...	...	...	...	...	...	...	...	...	24. Kánari.
...	...	...	...	...	...	...	...	...	...	...	...	...	...	...	...	...	...	...	...	...	...	...	...	25. Kásth.
...	...	...	...	...	...	...	...	...	...	...	...	...	...	...	...	...	...	...	...	...	...	...	...	26. Khátik.
...	...	...	1	...	...	...	...	...	...	2	1	...	...	...	...	...	...	...	...	...	...	...	...	27. Kolám.
...	...	...	...	...	...	1	...	...	...	...	...	...	...	...	...	...	...	...	...	...	...	...	...	28. Kolháti.
...	...	...	...	...	...	...	...	...	...	...	...	...	...	...	...	...	...	...	...	...	...	1	...	29. Koli.
1	...	...	...	...	...	...	...	...	...	...	...	...	...	...	...	...	...	...	...	...	...	...	...	30. Komti.
...	...	4	2	...	...	...	...	...	...	...	...	...	...	...	...	...	...	...	...	...	...	...	...	31. Korku.
...	...	...	...	...	...	...	...	...	...	...	...	...	...	...	...	...	...	...	...	...	...	1	...	32. Koshti.
...	...	...	...	...	...	...	...	...	...	...	...	...	...	...	...	...	1	1	...	...	...	...	1	33. Kumbhár.
11	4	...	...	1	5	6	...		2	2	1	1	...	1	1	1	2	2	4	1	3	...	...	34. Kunbi.
...	...	...	...	...	...	...	...	...	...	1	...	...	...	...	...	...	1	...	...	...	...	...	...	35. Lohár.
7	4	1	...	...	1	4	1	...	...	1	...	1	1	...	...	1	...	1	..	4	1	4	...	36. Mahár.
2	4	...	...		...	2	1	1	1	1	...	...	...	1	...	...	...	2	...	...	...	...	...	37. Máli.
1	...	...	...	...	1	...	1	...	...	1	...	...	...	...	...	...	...	...	...	...	1	...	...	38. Máng.
...	...	...	...	...	...	...	...	...	...	...	...	...	...	...	1	...	...	...	...	...	...	...	...	39. Maráthá.
...	...	...	...	...	...	...	...	...	...	...	...	...	...	...	...	...	...	...	1	...	...	...	...	40. Mháli.
...	...	...	...	...	...	...	...	...	...	...	...	...	...	...	...	1	...	...	...	...	...	...	...	41. Munárwár.
2	2	...	...	...	...	...	...	...	...	...	1	...	...	...	...	...	...	1	1	...	...	1	...	42. Musalmán.
...	...	...	...	...	...	...	...	...	...	...	...	...	...	...	...	...	...	...	...	...	...	...	...	43. Náth.
...	...	...	...	...	...	...	...	...	...	...	...	...	...	...	...	...	...	...	...	...	...	...	...	44. Native Christian.
...	...	2	...	...	...	...	...	...	...	...	...	...	...	...	...	...	...	...	...	...	...	...	...	45. Nihál.
...	...	...	...	...	...	...	...	...	...	...	...	...	...	...	...	...	...	...	...	...	...	...	...	46. Otári.
2	...	...	...	...	...	...	...	...	...	...	...	...	...	...	...	...	...	...	...	...	...	...	...	47. Pakháli.
...	...	...	...	...	...	...	...	...	...	...	...	1	...	...	...	...	...	...	...	...	...	...	...	48. Pángul.
...	...	...	...	...	...	...	...	...	...	...	...	...	...	1	.	2	1	...	...	...	...	...	...	49. Pardhán.
...	...	...	...	...	...	...	...	...	1	...	...	...	...	...	...	...	...	...	...	...	...	...	...	50. Pathán.
2	...	...	...	1	...	4	2	...	...	...	...	...	...	...	...	...	...	...	...	...	...	...	...	51. Rajput.
...	1	...	...	...	...	...	...	...	...	...	...	...	...	...	...	...	...	...	...	...	...	...	...	52. Rangári.
...	...	...	...	...	...	...	...	...	...	...	...	...	...	...	...	...	...	...	...	...	...	...	...	53. Sáli.
...	2	...	...	...	...	...	...	...	...	...	...	...	...	1	...	...	...	...	...	...	...	...	...	54. Shekh.
...	...	...	...	...	...	...	...	...	...	...	...	...	...	...	...	...	...	...	...	...	...	...	...	55. Simpi (Hindu).
1	...	...	...	...	...	...	...	...	...	...	...	...	...	...	...	...	...	...	...	...	...	...	...	56. Simpi (Jain).
...	...	...	...	...	...	2	...	...	...	...	...	...	1	...	...	...	...	...	...	...	...	...	...	57. Sonár.
3	...	...	...	...	...	...	...	...	...	1	...	...	...	...	...	1	...	...	...	...	...	...	...	58. Sutár.
...	...	...	...	...	...	...	...	...	...	1	...	...	...	...	...	...	...	...	...	...	...	...	...	59. Syed.
...	...	...	...	...	...	...	...	...	...	...	...	...	...	...	...	...	...	...	...	...	...	...	...	60. Tákankár.
...	1	...	...	...	...	...	1	...	...	...	...	...	...	1	...	...	...	...	...	...	...	...	...	61. Teli.
...	...	...	...	...	...	...	...	...	...	...	...	...	...	...	...	...	...	...	...	1	1	1	...	62. Thákur.
...	...	...	...	...	...	...	...	...	...	...	...	...	...	...	...	...	...	...	...	...	...	...	...	63. Vidur.
...	...	...	...	...	...	...	...	...	...	...	...	...	...	...	...	...	...	...	...	...	...	...	...	64. Waddar.
...	2	...	...	1	...	...	...	...	...	...	1	3	...	...	...	...	...	...	...	...	...	...	...	65. Wáni (Hindu).
...	1	...	...	...	...	...	...	...	...	...	...	...	...	...	...	...	...	...	...	...	...	...	...	66. Wáni (Jain).
...	...	...	...	...	...	...	...	...	...	...	...	...	...	...	...	...	...	1	...	...	...	2	...	67. Wanjári.
...	1	...	...	...	...	1	...	...	...	...	1	...	...	...	...	...	...	...	...	...	...	1	...	68. Warthi.
...	...	...	...	...	...	...	...	...	...	...	1	...	...	...	...	...	...	...	...	...	...	...	...	Unspecified.
40	27	8	3	3	7	26	11	1	4	12	10	12	10	8	3	10	7	13	11	7	7	21	3	Total.

TABLE XIV.

Blind Persons, by Age.

TABLE XIV.—Blind Persons, by Age.

District and Taluk.		Total Afflicted.			Distribution by Age.																									
					0–4		5–9		10–14		15–19		20–24		25–29		30–34		35–39		40–44		45–49		50–54		55–59		60 and over.	
		Total.	Males.	Females.	Males.	Females.	Males.	Females.	Males.	Females.	Males.	Females.	Males.	Females.	Males.	Females.	Males.	Females.	Males.	Females.	Males.	Females.	Males.	Females.	Males.	Females.	Males.	Females.	Males.	Females.
1		2	3	4	5	6	7	8	9	10	11	12	13	14	15	16	17	18	19	20	21	22	23	24	25	26	27	28	29	30
District Amraoti		1,433	763	670	33	18	56	28	46	30	39	22	44	23	48	40	65	35	36	46	51	48	42	31	80	85	24	26	193	238
" Akola		1,417	698	719	37	26	51	37	40	24	40	26	48	38	58	38	47	51	46	39	41	67	28	46	61	67	19	31	182	229
" Ellichpur		819	433	386	22	11	28	17	19	14	14	16	19	6	37	15	28	20	26	15	29	38	27	22	32	52	18	16	134	144
" Buldana		1,290	628	662	49	39	47	34	54	39	37	26	35	38	59	48	49	73	36	41	48	46	28	26	51	57	14	12	121	183
" Wun		865	405	460	12	11	36	21	19	16	23	16	24	27	30	22	35	39	29	31	28	37	16	21	32	45	18	24	03	150
" Basim		944	453	491	40	34	45	31	34	34	23	22	27	24	34	30	32	31	18	30	50	45	15	18	50	50	10	22	175	120
Total		6,768	3,880	3,388	193	139	263	168	212	157	176	128	197	156	266	193	256	249	191	202	247	281	156	164	806	356	108	131	814	1,064
Amraoti District.	Taluk Amraoti	399	225	174	8	7	17	5	13	8	13	4	12	4	8	13	23	11	11	11	12	13	14	...	25	20	11	9	58	69
	" Chandur	398	206	192	10	2	21	13	14	10	11	9	16	10	14	13	19	11	9	18	16	9	9	18	24	20	4	5	39	54
	" Morsi	359	187	172	6	4	14	4	12	8	10	5	13	5	14	9	8	7	6	9	13	14	8	5	17	29	5	9	61	64
	" Murtazapur	277	145	132	9	5	4	6	7	4	5	4	3	4	12	5	15	6	10	8	10	12	11	8	14	16	4	3	41	51
Akola District.	Taluk Akola	295	159	136	8	1	11	11	6	7	7	5	12	4	15	7	12	6	13	8	8	14	6	13	15	11	3	4	43	45
	" Akot	331	158	173	8	7	6	5	7	3	9	4	14	12	10	10	11	13	11	6	10	16	7	13	15	14	8	8	42	62
	" Balapur	252	129	123	5	6	12	9	8	3	6	3	10	8	10	10	9	10	6	6	8	9	8	7	9	13	2	6	36	33
	" Jalgaon	283	136	147	8	3	8	7	10	5	8	8	7	6	11	4	8	15	4	9	12	12	2	6	15	13	2	10	41	49
	" Khamgaon	256	116	140	8	9	14	5	9	6	10	6	5	8	12	7	7	7	12	10	3	16	5	7	7	16	4	3	20	40
Ellichpur District.	Taluk Ellichpur	366	207	159	6	3	14	4	10	5	4	3	8	3	18	3	14	9	8	9	10	15	4	11	22	20	6	7	83	67
	" Daryapur	351	186	165	15	6	8	10	6	5	8	8	7	3	13	7	11	6	15	5	16	17	21	9	10	23	9	5	47	61
	" Melghat	102	40	62	1	2	6	3	3	4	2	5	4	...	6	5	3	5	3	1	3	6	2	2	...	9	3	4	4	16
Buldana District.	Taluk Chikhli	433	208	225	14	12	17	13	18	11	12	10	15	16	6	17	16	29	13	12	19	16	10	5	20	26	5	6	43	52
	" Malkapur	476	246	230	21	14	18	8	19	12	14	9	14	10	29	14	20	23	12	17	16	17	11	13	16	19	8	3	48	71
	" Mehkar	381	174	207	14	13	12	13	17	16	11	7	6	12	24	17	13	21	11	12	13	13	7	8	15	12	1	3	30	60
Wun District.	Taluk Yeotmal	239	117	122	3	4	14	8	6	3	7	6	4	8	11	3	7	7	8	8	10	12	5	6	10	14	7	5	25	38
	" Darwha	329	160	169	5	5	15	4	7	9	15	8	9	7	10	14	13	18	9	10	13	16	7	8	13	12	6	10	38	48
	" Kelapur	135	61	74	3	1	4	5	2	3	1	2	8	6	4	2	8	4	6	6	2	4	1	2	5	7	5	2	12	30
	" Wun	162	67	95	1	1	3	4	4	1	...	...	3	6	5	3	7	10	6	7	3	5	3	5	4	12	...	7	28	34
Basim District.	Taluk Basim	511	242	269	22	20	23	10	20	19	8	8	13	14	20	18	14	16	10	17	23	31	10	14	27	25	6	15	46	62
	" Mangrul	155	68	87	3	3	9	5	4	6	5	4	3	3	3	4	4	7	2	3	8	7	1	3	7	7	1	2	18	33
	" Pusad	278	143	135	15	11	13	16	10	9	10	10	11	7	11	8	14	8	6	10	19	7	4	1	16	18	3	5	11	25

TABLE XIV A.

Blind, by Caste, Tribe, or Race.

TABLE XIVA.—Blind, by Caste,

CASTE, TRIBE, OR RACE.	TOTAL.			DISTRIBUTION BY																			
				District Amraoti.								District Akola.										District	
				Taluk Amraoti.		Taluk Chandur.		Taluk Morsi.		Taluk Murtazapur.		Taluk Akola.		Taluk Akot.		Taluk Balapur.		Taluk Jalgaon.		Taluk Khamgaon.		Taluk Ellichpur.	
	Total.	Males.	Females.	Males.	Females.	Males.	Females.	Males.	Females.	Males.	Females.	Males.	Females.	Males.	Females.	Males.	Females.	Males.	Females.	Males.	Females.	Males.	Females.
1	2	3	4	5	6	7	8	9	10	11	12	13	14	15	16	17	18	19	20	21	22	23	24
1. Andh	58	28	30	...	...	...	...	...	...	...	...	1	...	...	...	3	1	...	...	...	...	...	...
2. Bairági	6	5	1	2	...	...	...	1	...	...	...	...	...	...	...	...	...	...	...	1	...	1	...
3. Banjári	43	21	22	...	1	1	...	1	...	...	...	...	...	...	...	...	...	...	...	...	...	...	...
4. Bári	68	45	23	8	3	3	...	6	...	...	...	...	1	5	2	2	...	2	7	...	2	6	1
5. Basod	2	2	...	...	...	...	...	...	...	...	...	...	...	...	...	...	...	...	...	...	...	...	...
6. Bedar	7	1	6	...	...	...	...	...	...	...	...	...	4	...	...	...	...	1	...	...	2	...	...
7. Beldár	28	16	12	3	1	1	2	...	...	...	1	1	2	...	1	1	1	1	...	1	...	...	...
8. Bhámti	5	2	3	...	...	...	...	...	...	...	...	1	...	...	...	1	...	...	...	...	...	...	...
9. Bhangi	3	2	1	...	...	...	...	...	...	...	...	...	...	...	1	...	...	1	...	...	...	...	...
10. Bharádi	2	...	2	...	...	...	...	...	...	...	...	...	...	...	...	...	...	...	...	...	...	...	...
11. Bhát	6	4	2	...	...	1	...	...	1	...	...	...	...	...	...	...	...	...	...	...	...	...	...
12. Bhil	5	3	2	...	...	...	...	...	...	...	...	...	...	...	...	...	...	...	...	...	...	...	...
13. Bhoi	54	20	34	5	7	4	5	...	1	1	1	1	1	3	2	...	1	1	1	...	...	1	2
14. Bráhman	143	75	68	7	5	1	4	1	1	3	1	7	3	9	2	4	3	2	5	5	6	3	4
15. Bunkar	1	1	...	...	...	...	...	...	...	...	...	...	...	...	...	...	...	...	...	...	...	1	...
16. Burad	3	3	...	...	...	1	...	...	...	...	...	...	...	...	...	1	...	...	...	...	...	1	...
17. Chámbhár	56	26	30	1	1	2	...	...	2	...	3	1	...	1	2	1	3	3	2	1	1	...	...
18. Chhipá	1	...	1	...	...	...	...	...	1	...	...	...	...	...	...	...	...	...	...	...	...	...	...
19. Chitári	1	1	...	...	...	...	...	...	...	...	...	...	...	...	...	...	...	1	...	...	...	...	...
20. Chitrakathi	1	...	1	...	...	...	...	...	...	...	1	...	...	...	...	...	...	...	...	...	...	...	...
21. Dángat	2	2	...	...	...	...	...	...	...	...	...	...	...	...	...	...	...	...	...	...	...	...	...
22. Dhangar	248	104	144	5	5	8	8	3	8	2	7	2	2	1	9	3	10	4	12	4	7	7	4
23. Dohor	15	8	7	...	...	1	...	...	...	1	...	...	...	...	...	2	1	...	...	...	...	2	...
24. Elamá	1	1	...	...	...	...	...	...	...	...	...	...	...	...	...	...	...	...	...	...	...	...	...
25. Eurasian	*1	1	...	...	...	...	...	...	...	...	...	...	...	...	...	...	...	...	...	...	...	...	...
26. Fakir	12	7	5	...	1	...	...	...	...	...	...	...	...	2	...	1	...	...	...	...	...	2	..
27. Gaulán	2	...	2	...	...	...	...	...	...	...	...	...	...	...	...	...	...	...	...	...	...	...	...
28. Gaoli	30	20	10	...	...	2	...	6	1	...	...	1	4	2	...	...	1	...	...	...	...	1	1
29. Gaondi	3	1	2	...	...	...	...	...	...	...	...	...	...	...	...	...	...	...	...	...	...	...	...
30. Gárpagári	10	4	6	...	1	1	...	...	1	2	...	...	...	1	...	...	...	...	...	...	...	...	2
31. Gawári	18	9	9	2	...	1	2	1	1	...	...	...	...	...	...	...	...	...	...	...	...	...	...
32. Ghisádi	1	1	...	...	...	...	...	...	...	...	...	...	...	...	...	...	...	...	...	...	...	...	...
33. Golak	1	1	...	...	...	...	...	...	...	...	...	...	...	...	...	...	...	...	...	...	...	...	...
34. Golkar	2	1	1	...	...	...	...	...	...	...	...	...	...	...	...	...	...	...	...	...	...	...	...
35. Gond	137	56	81	3	2	6	5	11	8	...	2	...	...	...	1	...	...	...	...	...	...	...	2
36. Gondhali	7	1	6	...	3	...	1	...	...	...	...	...	...	...	...	...	...	...	...	1	...	...	...
37. Gopál	8	6	2	...	...	1	...	...	...	...	...	...	...	1	...	...	...	...	...	...	...	...	...
38. Gosáwi	46	30	16	3	...	1	1	1	...	2	1	2	3	1	...	1	1	...	...	2	...	1	1
39. Gujar	2	2	..	1	...	1	...	...	...	...	...	...	...	...	...	...	...	...	...	...	...	...	...
40. Gujráthi	3	2	1	...	...	...	...	...	...	...	...		...	...	...	1	...	...	...	...	...	...	...
41. Gurud Kápuwár	1	1	...	..	...	...	...	...	...	...	...	...	...	...	...	...	...	...	...	...	...	...	...
42. Gurao	27	14	13	2	2	2	2	2	1	...	...	...	1	...	2	...	...	...	...	1	...	...	...
43. Halbi	4	2	2	...	...	...	...	...	...	...	...	...	...	...	...	..	...	...	...	...	...	2	2
44. Hamál	1	...	1	...	...	...	...	...	...	...	...	...	...	...	...	...	...	...	...	...	...	...	1
45. Hatgar	12	9	3	...	...	...	...	...	...	...	...	1	1	...	...	...	...	...	...	...	...	...	...
46. Injhwar	1	...	1	...	...	...	...	...	...	...	...	...	...	...	...	...	...	...	...	...	...	...	...
47. Ját	1	1	...	...	...	...	...	...	...	...	...	...	...	...	...	...	...	...	...	1	...	...	...
48. Jogi	4	1	3	...	...	...	...	...	...	...	...	...	...	...	...	...	...	...	...	...	...	...	...
49. Kaikádi	2	1	1	1	...	...	...	...	1	...	...	...	...	...	...	...	...	...	...	...	...	...	...
50. Kalál	31	14	17	1	3	1	...	1	...	1	4	2	...	1	...	...	1	...	...	...	1	1	1
51. Kalsutri	1	...	1	...	...	...	...	...	...	...	...	...	...	...	...	...	...	...	...	...	...	...	...
52. Kalwant	1	...	1	...	...	...	...	...	...	...	...	...	...	...	...	...	...	...	...	...	...	...	...
53. Kánari	5	2	3	...	...	...	...	...	...	...	...	...	...	...	...	...	...	...	...	...	...	...	...
54. Kásár	26	16	10	...	...	2	...	...	...	1	1	...	...	3	...	...	...	2	...	1	...	...	1
55. Kásth	1	...	1	...	...	...	...	...	...	...	...	...	...	...	1	...	...	...	...	...	...	...	...
56. Káyet	1	1	...	...	...	...	...	...	...	...	...	...	...	...	...	...	...	...	...	...	...	1	...
57. Khátik	10	6	4	2	...	...	1	...	...	...	...	...	...	...	1	...	...	...	...	...	...	1	1
58. Khatri	2	...	2	...	...	...	1	...	...	...	...	...	...	...	...	...	...	...	...	...	...	...	...
59. Kolám	21	6	15	...	...	...	...	...	...	...	...	...	...	...	...	...	...	...	...	...	...	...	...
60. Kolhati	1	1	...	1	...	...	...	...	...	...	...	...	...	...	...	...	...	...	...	...	...	...	...
61. Koli	71	30	41	5	5	...	...	...	...	1	2	2	5	4	2	1	1	2	5	1	1	...	...
62. Komti	7	4	3	...	2	...	...	...	...	...	...	...	...	...	...	...	...	...	...	...	...	...	...
63. Korku	87	39	48	...	2	...	...	...	...	...	...	...	...	...	1	...	...	3	...	...	...	4	1
64. Koshti	48	23	25	2	...	4	4	1	5	...	...	...	...	1	...	...	...	...	...	...	...	5	5
65. Kumbhár	49	28	21	1	2	1	1	1	1	...	...	2	...	2	...	1	1	2	1	3	...	3	2
66. Kunbi	2,227	1,131	1,096	45	41	53	55	56	47	58	42	60	51	54	70	48	30	46	50	42	52	56	30
67. Labháni	20	11	9	...	...	1	...	...	...	...	...	1	...	...	...	...	...	...	...	...	...	...	...
68. Lajjhar	3	2	1	...	...	1	...	1	1	...	...	...	...	...	...	...	...	...	...	...	...	...	...
69. Lodh	4	2	2	...	...	1	...	...	...	...	...	...	...	...	1	...	...	...	...	...	...	1	...

DISTRICTS.																								
Ellichpur.				District Buldana.						District Wun.								District Basim.						
Taluk Daryapur		Taluk Melghat.		Taluk Chikhli.		Taluk Malkapur		Taluk Mehkar.		Taluk Yeotmal.		Taluk Darwha.		Taluk Kelapur		Taluk Wun.		Taluk Basim.		Taluk Mangrul.		Taluk Pusad.		CASTE, TRIBE, OR RACE.
Males.	Females.	Males.	Females.	Males.	Females.	Males.	Females.	Males.	Females.	Males.	Females.	Males.	Females.	Males.	Females.	Males.	Females.	Males.	Females.	Males.	Females.	Males.	Females.	
25	26	27	28	29	30	31	32	33	34	35	36	37	38	39	40	41	42	43	44	45	46	47	48	
...	...	...	...	...	1	...	...	4	1	1	...	8	11	...	...	...	...	4	5	2	6	5	5	1. Andh.
...	...	...	...	...	...	...	1	...	...	...	...	...	...	...	...	...	...	...	...	...	...	...	...	2. Bairági.
...	...	...	...	...	...	...	...	...	...	2	2	8	10	3	2	...	...	2	1	...	6	4	...	3. Banjári.
3	5	...	...	3	...	...	...	1	...	...	...	3	1	...	...	...	...	...	...	...	...	3	1	4. Bári.
...	...	2	...	...	...	...	...	...	...	...	...	...	...	...	...	...	...	...	...	...	...	...	...	5. Basod.
...	...	...	...	...	...	...	...	...	...	...	...	...	...	...	...	...	...	...	...	...	...	...	...	6. Bedar.
...	...	...	...	...	...	...	...	1	...	4	...	1	1	...	...	...	...	2	3	...	...	...	...	7. Beldár.
...	...	...	...	...	1	...	...	...	...	...	2	...	...	...	...	...	...	...	...	...	...	...	...	8. Bhámti.
...	...	...	...	...	...	...	...	...	...	1	...	...	...	...	...	...	...	...	...	...	...	...	...	9. Bhangi.
...	...	...	...	...	...	...	...	...	1	...	1	...	...	...	...	...	...	...	...	...	...	...	...	10. Bharádi.
2	...	...	...	...	...	1	...	...	...	...	...	...	1	...	...	...	...	...	...	...	...	...	...	11. Bhát.
...	...	...	...	...	...	...	...	...	...	...	1	1	...	...	...	...	...	...	...	1	...	1	1	12. Bhil.
...	4	...	...	...	...	...	...	...	...	1	2	2	2	1	1	...	4	...	...	...	...	...	...	13. Bhoi.
4	5	...	1	7	8	4	3	6	3	2	3	2	3	...	...	...	...	6	7	1	...	1	1	14. Bráhman.
...	...	...	...	...	...	...	...	...	...	...	...	...	...	...	...	...	...	...	...	...	...	...	...	15. Bunkar.
...	...	...	...	...	...	...	...	...	...	...	...	...	...	...	...	...	...	...	...	...	...	...	...	16. Burad.
...	2	...	...	...	1	6	2	1	4	1	...	2	3	1	...	1	2	3	...	...	...	1	2	17. Chámbhár.
...	...	...	...	...	...	...	...	...	...	...	...	...	...	...	...	...	...	...	...	...	...	...	...	18. Chhipá.
...	...	...	...	...	...	...	...	...	...	...	...	...	...	...	...	...	...	...	...	...	...	...	...	19. Chitari.
...	...	...	...	...	...	...	...	...	...	...	...	...	...	...	...	...	...	...	...	...	...	...	...	20. Chitrakathi.
...	...	...	...	...	...	2	...	...	...	...	...	...	...	...	...	...	...	...	...	...	...	...	...	21. Dángat.
10	7	...	...	3	13	14	16	6	3	4	5	4	5	...	...	3	6	7	5	1	2	13	10	22. Dhangar.
...	...	...	...	...	2	...	1	2	3	...	...	...	...	...	...	...	...	...	...	...	...	...	...	23. Dohor.
...	...	...	...	...	...	...	...	...	...	...	...	...	...	1	...	...	...	...	...	...	...	...	...	24. Elamá.
...	...	...	...	...	...	...	...	...	...	1	...	...	...	...	...	...	...	...	...	...	...	...	...	25. Eurasian.
1	...	...	...	...	1	...	...	...	...	1	1	...	1	...	...	...	...	...	1	...	...	...	...	26. Fakir.
...	...	...	1	...	...	...	...	...	...	...	...	...	...	...	...	...	...	...	...	...	1	...	...	27. Gaulán.
...	...	...	2	...	...	...	...	...	...	1	1	1	...	...	...	...	...	...	...	...	...	6	...	28. Gaoli.
...	...	...	...	1	1	...	...	...	...	...	...	...	...	...	...	...	...	...	...	...	1	...	...	29. Gaondi.
...	1	...	...	...	1	...	...	...	...	...	...	...	...	...	...	...	...	...	...	...	...	...	...	30. Garpagári.
1	...	...	...	...	...	...	...	...	...	2	4	...	...	2	1	...	1	...	...	...	...	...	...	31. Gawári.
...	...	...	...	1	...	...	...	...	...	...	...	...	...	...	...	...	...	...	...	...	...	...	...	32. Ghisádi.
...	...	...	...	1	...	...	...	...	...	...	...	...	...	...	...	...	...	...	...	...	...	...	...	33. Golak.
...	...	...	...	...	...	...	...	...	...	...	...	...	...	1	1	...	...	...	...	...	...	...	...	34. Golkar.
...	...	1	5	...	...	...	...	1	...	15	19	5	7	12	12	2	17	...	...	...	1	...	...	35. Gond.
...	...	...	...	...	1	...	...	...	...	...	...	...	1	...	...	...	...	...	...	...	...	...	...	36. Gondhali.
...	...	...	...	1	...	...	...	1	2	...	...	...	...	...	...	...	...	2	...	...	...	...	...	37. Gopál.
3	1	...	...	...	...	2	...	3	...	1	...	...	1	...	...	1	...	4	4	...	1	2	2	38. Gosáwi.
...	...	...	...	...	...	...	...	...	...	...	...	...	...	...	...	...	...	...	...	...	...	...	...	39. Gujar.
1	1	...	...	...	...	...	...	...	...	...	...	...	...	...	...	...	...	...	...	...	...	...	...	40. Gujráthi.
...	...	...	...	...	...	...	...	...	...	...	...	...	...	1	...	...	...	...	...	...	...	...	...	41. Gurud Kápuwár.
1	...	...	...	2	...	...	1	...	...	1	...	1	1	...	...	...	1	2	2	...	...	...	...	42. Gurao.
...	...	...	...	...	...	...	...	...	...	...	...	...	...	...	...	...	...	...	...	...	...	...	...	43. Halbi.
...	...	...	...	...	...	...	...	...	...	...	...	...	...	...	...	...	...	...	...	...	...	...	...	44. Hamál.
1	1	...	...	...	...	3	...	...	1	1	...	1	...	...	...	...	...	2	...	...	...	...	...	45. Hatgar.
...	1	...	...	...	...	...	...	...	...	...	...	...	...	...	...	...	...	...	...	...	...	...	...	46. Injhwar.
...	...	...	...	...	...	...	...	...	...	...	...	...	...	...	...	...	...	...	...	...	...	...	...	47. Ját.
...	...	...	...	...	...	...	...	...	...	...	...	...	...	1	...	...	...	...	3	...	...	...	...	48. Jogi.
...	...	...	...	...	...	...	...	...	...	...	...	...	...	...	...	...	...	...	...	...	...	...	...	49. Kaikádi.
1	...	...	...	...	...	...	2	...	1	1	...	3	2	...	1	...	1	...	...	...	...	1	...	50. Kalál.
...	...	...	...	...	...	...	1	...	...	...	...	...	...	...	...	...	...	...	...	...	...	...	...	51. Kalsutri.
...	...	...	...	...	...	...	...	...	...	...	...	...	...	...	...	...	...	...	...	...	...	...	1	52. Kalwant.
...	...	...	...	...	...	...	...	...	...	...	...	...	...	...	...	...	...	...	2	2	1	...	...	53. Kánari.
1	1	...	...	...	2	1	2	...	...	...	...	2	1	...	...	...	...	3	1	...	...	...	1	54. Kásár.
...	...	...	...	...	...	...	...	...	...	...	...	...	...	...	...	...	...	...	...	...	...	...	...	55. Kásth.
...	...	...	...	...	...	...	...	...	...	...	...	...	...	...	...	...	...	...	...	...	...	...	...	56. Káyet.
2	...	...	...	...	...	1	...	...	...	...	1	...	...	...	...	...	...	...	...	...	...	...	...	57. Khátik.
...	1	...	...	...	...	...	...	...	...	...	...	...	...	...	...	...	...	...	...	...	...	...	...	58. Khatri.
...	...	...	3	...	...	...	...	...	...	5	8	...	...	1	4	...	...	...	...	...	...	...	...	59. Kolám.
...	...	...	...	...	...	...	...	...	...	...	...	...	...	...	...	...	...	...	...	...	...	...	...	60. Kolháti.
6	4	...	...	1	3	4	5	...	...	1	...	...	1	...	...	...	...	...	5	...	...	2	2	61. Koli.
...	...	...	...	...	...	...	...	...	...	2	...	...	...	2	1	...	...	...	...	...	...	...	...	62. Komti.
...	...	32	44	...	...	...	...	...	...	...	...	...	...	...	...	...	...	...	...	...	...	...	...	63. Korku.
2	2	...	...	...	3	1	1	...	...	1	...	2	4	...	1	...	...	2	...	...	...	2	...	64. Koshti.
3	1	...	...	1	1	...	1	1	1	2	1	1	2	...	...	...	...	4	2	...	2	...	2	65. Kumbhár.
60	49	...	...	117	95	82	80	81	84	21	18	41	39	13	26	36	36	101	129	21	30	40	42	66. Kunbi.
...	...	...	...	...	...	1	...	2	2	1	1	...	1	...	2	...	...	2	2	1	1	2	...	67. Labháni.
...	...	...	...	...	...	...	...	...	...	...	...	...	...	...	...	...	...	...	...	...	...	...	...	68. Lajjhar.
...	...	...	...	...	...	...	...	...	...	...	...	...	...	...	...	...	1	...	...	...	...	...	...	69. Lodhi.

TABLE XIV A.—Blind, by Caste,

CASTE, TRIBE, OR RACE.	TOTAL: Total.	TOTAL: Males.	TOTAL: Females.	DISTRIBUTION — District Amraoti — Taluk Amraoti: Males.	Taluk Amraoti: Females.	Taluk Chandur: Males.	Taluk Chandur: Females.	Taluk Morsi: Males.	Taluk Morsi: Females.	Taluk Murtazapur: Males.	Taluk Murtazapur: Females.	District Akola — Taluk Akola: Males.	Taluk Akola: Females.	Taluk Akot: Males.	Taluk Akot: Females.	Taluk Balapur: Males.	Taluk Balapur: Females.	Taluk Jalgaon: Males.	Taluk Jalgaon: Females.	Taluk Khamgaon: Males.	Taluk Khamgaon: Females.	Dis[trict …] — Taluk Ellichpur: Males.	Taluk Ellichpur: Females.
1	2	3	4	5	6	7	8	9	10	11	12	13	14	15	16	17	18	19	20	21	22	23	24
70. Lohár	36	22	14	1	...	1	1	2	1	1	2	1	...	1	...	...	2	3	1	...	...	1	...
71. Lonári	2	...	2	...	...	...	...	...	...	...	...	...	...	...	...	...	...	...	1	...	...	...	...
72. Luniá	1	1	...	...	...	...	...	...	...	...	...	...	...	...	...	...	...	1	...	...	...	...	...
73. Mádgi	5	2	3	...	...	...	...	...	...	...	...	...	...	...	...	...	...	...	...	...	...	...	...
74. Mahár	762	384	378	32	26	28	27	25	25	24	15	24	17	10	19	10	13	15	11	8	11	27	29
75. Máli	565	293	272	24	15	19	19	42	37	12	15	10	8	19	14	14	14	16	12	14	10	22	27
76. Máná	1	...	1	...	...	...	...	...	...	...	...	...	...	...	...	...	...	...	...	...	...	...	...
77. Mánbháo	12	2	10	...	1	...	1	1	2	...	...	...	1	...	1	...	...	...	...	...	1	1	1
78. Máng	107	50	57	10	3	...	4	...	41	5	...	2	2	1	3	2	1	1	4	...	1	2	...
79. Mantár	1	...	1	...	...	...	...	...	...	...	...	...	...	...	...	...	...	...	...	...	...	...	...
80. Marál	2	1	1	...	...	...	...	...	...	...	...	...	...	...	...	...	...	...	...	...	...	1	...
81. Maráthá	50	20	30	2	2	3	5	2	1	2	1	...	...	...	1	1	3	1	...	...	...	...	...
82. Márwári	16	11	5	1	...	1	1	...	1	...	...	...	1	...	...	...	...	...	...	...	...	...	...
83. Mháli	79	41	38	2	2	2	2	...	1	...	1	3	1	3	4	1	4	2	2	3	2	6	1
84. Moghul	5	3	2	...	...	...	...	...	...	...	...	...	...	2	...	...	...	...	...	...	...	...	1
85. Mudliyár	1	...	1	...	...	...	...	...	...	...	...	...	1	...	...	...	...	...	...	...	...	...	...
86. Munarwár	4	1	3	...	...	...	...	...	...	...	...	...	...	...	...	...	...	...	...	...	...	...	...
87. Musalmán	90	41	49	...	1	...	...	...	...	...	...	4	5	5	...	2	6	4	2	...	4	...	...
88. Náth	4	...	4	...	...	...	...	...	...	...	...	...	...	...	1	...	1	...	...	...	...	...	...
89. Native Christian	1	1	...	...	...	...	...	...	...	...	...	1	...	...	...	...	...	...	...	...	...	...	...
90. Nihál	12	10	2	...	...	...	...	...	...	7	...	...	...	...	...	...	...	...	...	...	...	...	...
91. Otári	3	1	2	...	...	...	...	...	...	...	...	...	...	...	...	...	...	...	...	...	...	...	...
92. Pahád	3	1	2	1	...	...	...	...	...	...	1	...	...	...	...	...	...	...	...	...	...	...	...
93. Panchál	2	2	...	...	...	...	...	...	...	...	...	...	...	...	...	1	...	...	...	...	...	...	...
94. Pángul	6	1	5	...	...	...	...	...	...	1	...	...	...	...	1	...	...	...	...	...	...	...	...
95. Parbhu	1	1	...	...	...	...	...	...	...	...	...	...	...	...	...	...	...	...	...	...	...	...	...
96. Pardesi	1	...	1	...	...	...	...	...	...	...	...	...	...	...	...	...	...	...	...	...	...	...	...
97. Pardhán	26	12	14	...	...	...	2	...	...	...	...	...	...	...	1	...	...	...	...	...	...	...	...
98. Párdhi	19	11	8	2	1	...	...	...	...	1	1	1	...	...	...	...	...	2	...	1	1	2	...
99. Pársi	1	1	...	...	...	...	...	...	...	...	...	1	...	...	...	...	...	...	...	...	...	...	...
100. Pathán	79	42	37	5	2	2	3	1	...	...	3	2	1	3	2	4	...	2	2	2	14	4	1
101. Páthrat or Páthar	3	2	1	...	...	...	...	...	...	...	...	1	...	...	...	...	1	...	...	...	...	...	...
102. Patwi	2	...	2	...	...	...	...	...	...	...	...	...	...	...	...	...	...	...	...	...	...	...	1
103. Perki	2	1	1	...	...	...	...	...	...	...	...	...	...	...	...	...	...	...	...	...	...	...	...
104. Rajput	134	73	61	14	4	9	4	1	3	...	...	2	2	3	3	3	1	2	8	6	2	2	2
105. Rangári	24	12	12	...	...	...	...	...	...	...	1	1	1	...	...	1	...	...	2	...	...	1	2
106. Sáli	20	12	8	...	...	...	...	...	...	2	...	...	...	...	1	...	...	...	...	...	...	2	2
107. Sarode	2	...	2	...	1	...	...	...	...	...	...	...	...	...	...	...	...	...	...	...	...	...	...
108. Shekh	191	90	101	5	7	2	2	6	6	7	3	2	2	2	10	7	9	4	1	5	9	17	13
109. Sikalgar	1	1	...	...	...	...	...	...	...	...	...	...	...	...	...	...	...	...	...	...	...	...	...
110. Simpi	36	16	20	1	...	1	2	...	...	...	...	...	1	1	2	1	...	1	2	1	2	1	...
111. Sonár	75	39	36	1	1	3	2	...	3	2	...	3	3	2	3	4	2	2	...	2	...	2	1
112. Sugandhi	1	1	...	...	...	...	...	...	...	...	...	...	...	...	...	1	...	...	...	...	...	...	...
113. Sutár	79	44	35	4	1	3	4	2	2	1	2	3	...	2	1	2	2	2	5	2	2	2	2
114. Syed	26	11	15	3	1	...	4	...	...	...	...	...	2	1	1	...	...	2	1	...	1	1	2
115. Tákankár	9	3	6	...	...	...	1	...	...	...	2	1	...	1	1	...	...	...	...	...	...	1	1
116. Támbatkár	4	3	1	...	...	...	...	...	...	...	...	...	...	...	...	...	...	...	...	1	...	2	1
117. Támboli	4	2	2	1	...	...	...	...	...	...	...	...	...	...	...	...	...	...	...	...	...	1	...
118. Teli	204	102	102	6	10	18	9	3	3	3	9	4	...	4	1	1	2	4	7	5	2	3	6
119. Thákur	10	5	5	...	...	...	1	...	...	...	...	...	...	...	...	...	...	...	1	...	1	...	...
120. Udási	1	1	...	...	...	...	...	...	...	...	...	...	...	...	...	...	...	...	...	...	...	...	...
121. Vidur	30	13	17	1	3	3	2	3	2	...	1	1	1	...	...	...	2	...	...	...	3	...	1
122. Waddar	2	1	1	...	...	...	...	...	...	...	...	...	...	...	...	...	...	...	...	...	...	...	...
123. Wáni (Hindu)	127	66	61	5	4	8	2	3	2	2	9	3	2	1	3	1	2	1	1	1	...	5	2
124. Wáni (Jain)	24	9	15	1	...	...	...	1	1	...	...	1	...	2	...	...	1	...	...	1	...	...	...
125. Wanjári	94	35	59	...	...	...	...	...	...	2	...	2	4	2	...	...	1	...	...	...	2	...	...
126. Warthi	54	26	28	3	2	1	2	2	...	1	...	1	3	2	2	2	1	...	1	...	...	1	2
127. Wásudeo	1	...	1	...	...	...	...	...	...	...	...	...	...	...	...	...	...	...	...	...	...	...	...
Total	6,768	3,880	3,388	225	174	206	192	187	172	145	132	159	136	158	173	129	123	186	147	116	140	207	159

Tribe, or Race—*concld.*

BY DISTRICTS.

District Ellichpur.				District Buldana.						District Wun.								District Basim.						CASTE, TRIBE, OR RACE.
Taluk Daryapur.		Taluk Melghat.		Taluk Chikhli.		Taluk Malkapur.		Taluk Mehkar.		Taluk Yeotmal.		Taluk Darwha.		Taluk Kelapur.		Taluk Wun.		Taluk Basim.		Taluk Mangrul.		Taluk Pusad.		
Males.	Females.	Males.	Females.	Males.	Females.	Males.	Females.	Males.	Females.	Males.	Females.	Males.	Females.	Males.	Females.	Males.	Females.	Males.	Females.	Males.	Females.	Males.	Females.	
25	26	27	28	29	30	31	32	33	34	35	36	37	38	39	40	41	42	43	44	45	46	47	48	
1	...	...	...	...	...	...	...	...	...	...	3	1	2	...	1	7	...	2	...	...	...	...	1	70. Lohár.
...	...	...	...	...	...	...	1	...	...	...	...	...	...	...	...	...	...	...	...	...	...	...	...	71. Lonári.
...	...	...	...	...	...	...	...	...	...	...	...	...	...	...	...	...	...	...	...	...	...	...	...	72. Luniá.
...	...	...	...	...	...	...	...	...	...	...	...	...	...	1	2	1	1	...	...	...	...	...	...	73. Mádgi.
23	25	1	2	23	22	29	32	14	17	8	12	15	13	4	...	7	6	28	25	11	11	18	20	74. Mahár.
17	20	...	...	9	8	17	11	13	23	12	9	12	7	2	4	...	2	7	7	9	7	3	3	75. Máli.
...	...	...	...	...	...	...	...	...	...	...	...	...	...	...	...	...	1	...	...	...	...	...	...	76. Máná.
...	...	...	...	...	...	...	1	...	...	...	...	...	...	...	...	...	...	...	1	...	...	...	...	77. Mánbháo.
3	1	...	...	3	9	4	6	2	6	...	...	2	3	...	...	...	...	10	8	...	...	3	5	78. Máng.
...	...	...	...	...	...	...	1	...	...	...	...	...	...	...	...	...	...	...	...	...	...	...	...	79. Manyár.
...	...	...	...	...	...	...	...	...	...	...	...	...	...	...	...	...	1	...	...	...	...	...	...	80. Marál.
2	1	...	...	...	1	2	2	1	2	...	1	...	2	1	...	...	...	2	4	...	2	1	2	81. Maráthá.
...	...	...	...	1	...	4	1	1	...	...	...	...	...	...	...	...	...	1	1	1	...	1	...	82. Márwári.
6	2	...	...	...	3	2	2	2	1	1	1	1	3	1	1	...	4	1	1	3	...	2	...	83. Mháli.
...	...	...	...	...	...	1	...	...	...	...	...	...	...	...	...	...	...	...	...	...	1	...	...	84. Moghul.
...	...	...	...	...	...	...	...	...	...	...	...	...	...	...	...	...	...	...	...	...	...	...	...	85. Mudliyár.
...	...	...	...	...	...	...	...	...	...	...	...	...	1	...	2	1	...	...	...	...	...	...	...	86. Munarwár.
4	5	1	...	10	3	5	3	1	6	...	...	...	...	1	1	...	2	...	8	...	2	4	1	87. Musalmán.
...	...	...	...	...	...	...	...	...	1	...	...	...	...	...	...	...	...	...	1	...	...	...	...	88. Náth.
...	...	...	...	...	...	...	...	...	...	...	...	...	...	...	...	...	...	...	...	...	...	...	...	89. Native Christian.
...	...	3	2	...	...	...	...	...	...	...	...	...	...	...	...	...	...	...	...	...	...	...	...	90. Nihál.
...	1	...	...	...	1	...	...	...	...	...	...	...	...	...	...	...	...	...	...	...	...	1	...	91. Otári.
...	...	...	...	...	...	...	...	...	...	...	1	...	...	...	...	...	...	...	...	...	...	...	...	92. Pahád.
...	...	...	...	...	...	...	...	...	...	...	...	...	...	...	...	1	...	...	...	...	...	...	...	93. Panchál.
...	...	...	...	...	...	...	...	...	...	...	...	...	3	...	...	...	...	...	...	...	...	...	1	94. Pángul.
...	...	...	...	...	...	...	...	...	...	...	...	...	...	...	...	1	...	...	...	...	...	...	...	95. Parbhu.
...	...	...	...	...	...	...	1	...	...	...	...	...	...	...	...	...	...	...	...	...	...	...	...	96. Pardesi.
...	...	...	...	...	...	...	...	...	...	3	2	2	3	4	3	2	3	...	...	...	...	1	...	97. Pardhán.
1	2	...	...	...	1	...	1	...	...	1	1	...	...	...	...	...	...	...	...	...	...	...	...	98. Párdhi.
...	...	...	...	...	...	...	...	...	...	...	...	...	...	...	...	...	...	...	...	...	...	...	...	99. Pársi.
...	1	...	...	1	2	8	3	...	...	1	1	6	...	...	...	...	...	...	...	1	1	...	1	100. Pathán.
...	...	...	...	...	...	...	...	...	...	...	...	...	...	...	...	...	...	1	...	...	...	...	...	101. Páthrat or Páthar.
...	...	...	...	...	1	...	...	...	...	...	...	...	...	...	...	...	...	...	...	...	...	...	...	102. Patwi.
...	...	...	...	...	...	...	...	...	...	...	...	...	...	1	1	...	...	...	...	...	...	...	...	103. Perki.
3	1	...	2	9	10	8	9	...	2	2	2	1	3	2	...	...	...	3	1	1	...	2	2	104. Rajput.
...	...	...	...	1	...	3	3	...	...	...	...	2	3	...	...	...	...	1	...	...	...	2	...	105. Rangári.
1	3	...	...	...	1	1	...	1	...	...	...	1	...	1	...	...	...	3	...	...	...	...	1	106. Sáli.
...	...	...	...	...	...	...	...	...	...	...	1	...	...	...	...	...	...	...	...	...	...	...	...	107. Sarode.
6	...	...	...	2	7	13	11	2	3	1	4	3	6	...	...	...	4	5	...	...	1	1	3	108. Shekh.
...	...	...	...	...	...	...	...	...	...	...	...	...	...	...	...	...	...	...	...	1	...	...	...	109. Sikalgar.
1	2	...	...	...	1	3	3	...	...	1	1	3	1	...	1	...	...	1	2	...	...	...	...	110. Simpi.
1	4	...	...	2	2	3	1	3	3	1	2	1	2	1	3	...	...	4	2	...	1	2	1	111. Sonár.
...	...	...	...	...	...	...	...	...	...	...	...	...	...	...	...	...	...	...	...	...	...	...	...	112. Su andhi.
6	1	...	...	...	1	2	3	4	1	3	2	2	...	...	1	1	1	1	2	...	1	2	1	113. Sutár.
...	...	...	...	...	...	2	2	1	...	...	...	1	1	...	...	...	...	...	...	...	...	...	...	114. Syed.
...	...	...	...	...	...	...	...	...	...	...	...	...	...	...	...	...	...	...	...	...	...	...	...	115. Tákankár.
...	1	...	...	...	...	...	...	...	...	...	...	...	...	...	...	...	...	...	...	...	...	...	...	116. Támbatkár.
...	...	...	...	...	...	...	...	...	...	...	...	...	...	...	...	...	...	...	...	...	...	...	2	117. Támboli.
3	4	...	...	2	7	7	8	5	4	5	5	7	5	2	1	2	1	8	10	4	3	6	5	118. Teli.
1	...	...	...	1	...	...	...	...	...	...	...	2	...	...	...	...	...	1	...	...	2	...	...	119. Thákur.
...	...	...	...	...	...	1	...	...	...	...	...	...	...	...	...	...	...	...	...	...	...	...	...	120. Udási.
...	1	...	...	...	...	...	...	1	1	1	...	1	...	...	...	...	...	1	...	...	...	1	...	121. Vidur.
...	...	...	...	...	1	1	...	...	...	...	...	...	...	...	...	...	...	...	...	...	...	...	...	122. Waddar.
2	1	...	...	2	2	5	3	4	9	2	3	6	5	...	1	1	...	4	2	2	3	8	5	123. Wáni (Hindu).
1	...	...	...	1	1	...	...	...	1	...	...	...	...	...	...	...	...	1	11	...	...	...	...	124. Wáni (Jain).
...	...	...	...	2	7	...	3	8	19	...	...	3	3	...	...	...	...	10	10	6	...	...	10	125. Wanjári.
2	3	...	...	1	...	3	3	1	2	2	1	...	5	1	...	...	...	1	1	...	...	2	...	126. Warthi.
...	...	...	...	...	...	...	...	...	...	...	...	...	...	...	...	...	...	...	...	...	...	...	1	127. Wásudeo.
186	165	40	62	208	225	246	230	174	207	117	122	160	169	61	74	67	95	242	269	68	87	148	135	Total

TABLE XV.

Lepers, by Age.

TABLE XV.—Lepers, by Age.

District and Taluk.	Total Afflicted.			Distribution by Age.																									
				0—4		5—9		10—14		15—19		20—24		25—29		30—34		35—39		40—44		45—49		50—54		55—59		60 and over.	
	Total.	Males.	Females.	Males.	Females.	Males.	Females.	Males.	Females.	Males.	Females.	Males.	Females.	Males.	Females.	Males.	Females.	Males.	Females.	Males.	Females.	Males.	Females.	Males.	Females.	Males.	Females.	Males.	Females.
1	2	3	4	5	6	7	8	9	10	11	12	13	14	15	16	17	18	19	20	21	22	23	24	25	26	27	28	29	30
District Amraoti	932	743	189	...	...	5	...	15	10	19	10	41	10	52	16	101	31	90	20	126	36	66	9	108	22	22	9	98	16
„ Akola	910	696	214	1	1	4	...	20	12	18	11	45	21	54	15	101	34	94	20	104	34	79	17	85	20	24	6	67	23
„ Ellichpur	524	415	109	...	...	...	...	4	6	11	4	20	9	28	13	60	14	44	12	68	15	41	10	66	11	18	4	55	11
„ Buldana	779	601	178	1	2	1	...	8	9	23	12	43	14	56	21	75	28	70	18	109	26	61	5	77	14	20	7	57	22
„ Wun	377	285	92	...	...	...	...	6	1	9	6	11	5	22	6	28	7	35	16	42	13	24	10	59	13	15	4	34	11
„ Basim	176	146	30	...	...	...	...	3	2	5	...	6	5	7	2	11	3	16	4	27	3	14	6	29	2	3	...	25	3
Total	3,698	2,886	812	2	3	10	...	56	40	85	43	166	64	219	73	376	117	349	90	476	127	285	57	424	82	102	30	336	86
Amraoti District. — Taluk Amraoti	207	170	37	...	...	...	...	5	1	...	2	10	1	10	4	25	8	19	2	32	8	13	2	32	5	5	2	19	2
„ Chandur	237	188	49	...	...	2	...	1	3	1	4	6	3	12	3	24	6	22	7	29	6	22	4	30	3	8	4	31	6
„ Morsi	297	233	64	...	...	3	...	2	3	13	2	20	5	18	7	32	10	27	6	33	11	21	...	29	13	4	3	31	4
„ Murtazapur	191	152	39	...	...	...	...	7	3	5	2	5	1	12	2	20	7	22	5	32	11	10	3	17	1	5	...	17	4
Akola District. — Taluk Akola	200	157	43	...	...	2	...	4	3	2	1	7	6	8	3	18	6	15	6	23	9	25	1	31	3	4	1	18	4
„ Akot	205	156	49	...	1	...	...	1	3	7	1	6	5	12	4	22	8	23	5	31	5	14	3	19	5	7	2	14	7
„ Balapur	198	150	48	...	...	...	...	2	3	3	2	16	3	13	4	25	7	19	3	25	7	11	4	13	6	3	1	20	8
„ Jalgaon	165	121	44	1	...	2	...	6	2	5	6	8	4	13	1	19	5	18	5	13	8	12	4	14	4	6	2	4	3
„ Khamgaon	142	112	30	...	...	...	...	7	1	1	1	8	3	8	3	17	8	19	1	12	5	17	5	8	2	4	...	11	1
Ellichpur District. — Taluk Ellichpur	244	186	58	...	...	...	...	1	1	4	...	7	5	13	9	24	8	11	6	40	8	17	6	32	4	10	4	27	7
„ Daryapur	222	182	40	...	...	...	...	3	4	6	3	10	3	14	3	27	6	23	5	22	4	19	4	29	5	5	...	24	3
„ Melghat	58	47	11	...	...	...	...	...	1	1	1	3	1	1	1	9	...	10	1	6	3	5	...	5	2	3	...	4	1
Buldana District. — Taluk Chikhli	275	210	65	1	2	...	...	2	5	7	7	19	4	20	10	30	13	21	3	45	8	16	1	30	5	5	1	14	6
„ Malkapur	385	293	92	...	...	1	...	5	3	15	5	21	8	29	9	39	15	37	9	42	15	31	4	32	6	13	6	28	12
„ Mehkar	119	98	21	...	...	...	...	1	1	1	...	3	2	7	2	6	...	12	6	22	3	14	...	15	3	2	...	15	4
Wun District. — Taluk Yeotmal	138	106	32	...	...	...	...	1	...	4	1	5	1	9	2	10	3	12	7	17	4	8	3	22	5	2	...	16	6
„ Darwha	136	106	30	...	...	...	...	4	1	3	1	3	1	9	1	13	2	17	5	11	4	7	3	24	6	5	2	10	4
„ Kelapur	55	41	14	...	...	...	...	1	...	1	1	2	...	2	1	2	2	3	1	7	3	6	3	9	1	4	2	4	...
„ Wun	48	32	16	...	...	...	...	...	...	1	3	1	3	2	2	3	...	3	3	7	2	3	1	4	1	4	...	4	1
Basim District. — Taluk Basim	74	60	14	...	...	...	...	...	1	2	...	4	2	3	1	5	1	6	4	13	1	4	2	16	1	...	...	10	1
„ Mangrul	49	40	9	...	...	...	...	1	1	...	...	2	...	2	1	2	2	5	...	7	...	3	3	4	...	1	...	10	2
„ Pusad	53	46	7	...	...	...	...	2	...	3	...	...	3	2	...	4	...	5	...	7	2	7	1	9	1	2	...	5	...

TABLE XVA.

Lepers, by Caste, Tribe, or Race.

TABLE XVA.—Lepers, by

CASTE, TRIBE, OR RACE.	TOTAL.			DISTRIBUTION																			
				District Amraoti.								District Akola.										Dis	
				Taluk Amraoti.		Taluk Chandur.		Taluk Morsi.		Taluk Murtazapur.		Taluk Akola.		Taluk Akot.		Taluk Balapur.		Taluk Jalgaon.		Taluk Khamgaon.		Taluk Ellichpur.	
	Total.	Males.	Females.	Males.	Females.	Males.	Females.	Males.	Females.	Males.	Females.	Males.	Females.	Males.	Females.	Males.	Females.	Males.	Females.	Males.	Females.	Males.	Females.
1	2	3	4	5	6	7	8	9	10	11	12	13	14	15	16	17	18	19	20	21	22	23	24
1. Ahir	2	2	...	1	...	...	...	...	...	...	...	1	...	...	...	...	...	...	...	...	...	...	...
2. Andh	31	25	6	...	...	...	...	...	...	...	...	1	...	...	...	2	...	...	...	...	...	...	...
3. Bairági	1	1	...	...	...	...	...	...	...	...		...	...	...	...	...	...	...	...	...	...	1	...
4. Balái	1	1	...	...	...	...	...	...	...	...	...	...	...	...	...	...	...	...	...	...	...	...	...
5. Banjári	7	6	1	...	...	...	...	1	...	2	...	...	...	...	...	...	...	...	...	...	...	...	...
6. Bári	57	49	8	8	...	8	1	8	1	...	...	2	...	4	...	...	...	9	1	...	...	4	1
7. Bedar	3	2	1	...	...	...	...	...	...	...	...	1	...	...	...	...	...	...	...	...	1	...	...
8. Beldár	7	6	1	...	...	2	1	...	...	...	...	2	...	...	...	...	...	...	...	...	...	...	...
9. Bhámti	3	2	1	...	...	...	...	...	...	...	...	1	...	...	...	...	...	...	...	...	...	1	1
10. Bhangi	2	1	1	...	...	...	...	...	...	...	...	...	...	...	...	...	...	...	...	...	...	1	...
11. Bharádi	1	1	...	...	...	...	...	...	...	...	...	...	...	...	...	...	...	...	...	...	...	...	...
12. Bhát	3	2	1	...	...	...	...	2	...	...	...	...	...	...	1	...	...	...	...	...	...	...	...
13. Bhil	2	1	1	...	...	...	...	...	...	...	...	...	...	...	...	...	...	...	...	...	...	...	...
14. Bhil (Musalman)	1	1	...	...	...	...	...	...	...	...	...	...	...	...	...	...	...	1	...	...	...	...	...
15. Bhoi	34	21	13	1	2	...	1	1	...	1	1	...	1	3	...	...	1	2	...	...	...	2	2
16. Bopchi	3	2	1	...	...	...	...	2	1	...	...	...	...	...	...	...	...	...	...	...	...	...	...
17. Bráhman	63	50	13	7	2	3	1	...	...	6	2	1	...	2	...	4	...	1	...	1	...	2	...
18. Chámbhár	38	32	6	5	...	1	...	5	...	...	1	1	...	1	...	...	...	1	...	3	...	...	...
19. Chitrakathi	1	1	...	...	...	...	...	...	...	1	...	...	...	...	...	...	...	...	...	...	...	...	...
20. Dángat	1	1	...	...	...	...	...	...	...	...	...	...	...	...	...	...	...	...	...	...	...	...	...
21. Dángur	2	1	1	...	...	...	1	1	...	...	...	...	...	...	...	...	...	...	...	...	...	...	...
22. Dhangar	73	57	16	3	1	6	2	2	1	7	1	6	...	2	...	5	...	3	2	2	2	...	1
23. Dohor	12	7	5	1	...	1	1	2	...	...	1	...	...	1	...	...	...	...	...	...	...	1	1
24. Fakir	7	5	2	...	...	...	...	...	...	...	...	...	...	1	1	...	...	...	...	...	...	1	...
25. Gaoli	23	16	7	1	...	1	...	2	...	...	...	2	...	...	...	2	...	...	...	1	2	...	3
26. Gaulán	1	1	...	...	...	...	...	...	...	...	...	...	...	...	...	...	...	...	...	...	...	1	...
27. Gárpagári	6	6	...	...	...	...	...	3	...	...	...	1	...	1	...	...	...	...	...	...	...	...	...
28. Gawári	30	24	6	1	...	3	...	1	...	2	...	...	...	1	...	...	...	...	...	...	...	...	...
29. Ghisádi	1	1	...	...	...	...	...	...	...	...	...	...	...	...	...	...	...	...	...	...	...	...	...
30. Gond	77	57	20	4	...	3	3	6	3	2	...	2	...	...	...	1	...	2	1	...	...	3	...
31. Gondhali	6	6	...	...	...	...	...	...	...	...	...	1	...	...	...	2	...	...	...	...	...	1	...
32. Gosáwi	38	29	9	2	1	2	1	...	1	5	...	2	...	6	...	2	3	...	...	...	...	2	1
33. Gujar	1	1	...	...	...	...	...	...	...	...	...	...	...	1	...	...	...	...	...	...	...	...	...
34. Gujráthi	2	2	...	...	...	...	...	...	...	1	...	...	...	...	...	...	...	...	...	...	...	...	...
35. Gurao	25	17	8	3	1	3	1	1	2	...	...	1	1	...	...	...	...	...	1	1	...	1	...
36. Halbi	8	7	1	...	...	...	...	3	1	...	...	...	...	...	...	...	...	...	...	...	...	2	...
37. Jangam	2	1	1	1	...	...	...	...	...	...	...	...	...	...	...	...	1	...	...	...	...	...	...
38. Ját	2	1	1	1	1	...	...	...	...	...	...	...	...	...	...	...	...	...	...	...	...	...	...
39. Jingar	1	...	1	...	...	...	...	...	...	...	...	...	1	...	...	...	...	...	...	...	...	...	...
40. Jogi	1	...	1	...	...	...	...	...	...	...	...	...	...	...	...	...	...	...	...	...	...	...	...
41. Kahár	2	1	1	...	...	...	...	...	...	...	...	...	...	...	...	...	...	...	...	...	...	...	...
42. Kakar	1	1	...	...	...	...	...	...	...	...	...	...	...	...	...	...	...	...	...	...	...	...	...
43. Kalál	17	12	5	...	1	1	...	2	...	1	...	1	1	...	1	1	...	1	...	...	...	1	...
44. Kánari	4	4	...	2	...	...	...	...	...	...	...	...	...	...	...	...	...	...	...	...	...	...	...
45. Kángar	1	1	...	1	...	...	...	...	...	...	...	...	...	...	...	...	...	...	...	...	...	...	...
46. Kasái (Musalman)	1	1	...	...	...	...	...	...	...	...	...	1	...	...	...	...	...	...	...	...	...	...	...
47. Kásár	20	15	5	...	1	2	1	2	...	1	...	1	...	2	...	1	...	1	...	...	...	...	...
48. Khátik	8	8	...	2	...	...	...	...	...	...	...	...	...	...	...	...	...	...	...	...	...	4	...
49. Khatri	1	1	...	...	...	1	...	...	...	...	...	...	...	...	...	...	...	...	...	...	...	...	...
50. Kolám	9	8	1	...	...	...	...	...	...	...	...	...	...	...	...	...	...	...	...	...	...	...	...
51. Kolháti	2	2	...	...	...	...	...	...	...	...	...	...	...	...	...	...	...	...	...	...	...	...	...
52. Koli	37	28	9	...	...	...	...	...	...	2	...	3	...	3	2	...	1	4	2	...	1	...	...
53. Komti	1	1	...	...	...	...	...	...	...	...	...	...	...	...	...	...	...	...	...	...	...	...	...
54. Korku	43	35	8	...	...	...	...	...	...	...	...	...	...	...	...	...	...	...	...	...	...	1	1
55. Koshti	22	19	3	2	...	2	...	3	...	...	...	...	1	...	...	...	...	...	...	...	...	3	...
56. Kumbhár	28	21	7	...	...	3	...	1	1	1	1	2	1	2	1	1	...	1	...	...	...	3	...
57. Kunbi	1,159	938	221	45	6	61	11	67	23	51	15	48	7	70	20	51	9	37	11	43	10	60	11
58. Labháni	4	4	...	...	...	...	...	...	...	...	...	1	...	...	...	...	...	...	...	...	...	...	...
59. Lajjhar	3	2	1	...	...	...	...	1	1	...	...	...	...	...	...	...	...	...	...	...	...	1	...
60. Lád	4	4	...	1	...	...	...	...	...	...	...	...	...	...	...	...	...	...	...	...	...	...	...
61. Lodhi	6	5	1	...	...	1	...	...	...	...	...	...	...	...	...	...	...	...	...	...	...	3	1
62. Lohár	27	20	7	...	...	4	2	5	...	2	...	...	...	...	...	1	...	1	1	1	...	1	...
63. Lonári	1	1	...	...	...	...	...	...	...	...	...	...	...	...	...	1	...	...	...	...	...	...	...
64. Mahár	363	270	93	19	13	13	6	18	4	13	6	22	5	9	5	12	6	11	1	12	2	11	11
65. Máli	414	313	101	15	2	20	4	48	13	13	3	10	5	20	5	28	10	19	16	27	6	26	8
66. Mánbháo	8	7	1	...	...	1	...	2	...	...	...	...	...	...	...	1	...	...	...	...	...	1	...
67. Máng	52	41	11	2	...	2	...	3	2	2	...	4	1	...	1	3	1	1	1	1	...	1	...
68. Maráthá	18	12	6	...	...	2	...	2	1	...	...	2	...	1	...	...	...	1	...	...	...	...	...
69. Márwári	7	6	1	...	...	...	...	...	1	...	...	...	...	...	...	2	...	...	...	...	...	3	...
70. Mháli	51	38	13	2	...	3	1	2	2	2	...	2	2	3	...	1	2	2	...	2	1	6	...

Caste, Tribe or Race.

BY DISTRICTS.

District Ellichpur.				District Buldana.						District Wun.								District Basim.						
Taluk Daryapur.		Taluk Melghat.		Taluk Chikhli.		Taluk Malkapur.		Taluk Mehkar.		Taluk Yeotmal.		Taluk Darwha.		Taluk Kelapur.		Taluk Wun.		Taluk Basim.		Taluk Mangrul.		Taluk Pusad.		Caste, Tribe, or Race.
Males.	Females.	Males.	Females.	Males.	Females.	Males.	Females.	Males.	Females.	Males.	Females.	Males.	Females.	Males.	Females.	Males.	Females.	Males.	Females.	Males.	Females.	Males.	Females.	
25	26	27	28	29	30	31	32	33	34	35	36	37	38	39	40	41	42	43	44	45	46	47	48	49
...	...	...	...	...	...	...	...	...	...	...	...	...	...	...	...	...	...	...	...	...	...	...	...	1. Ahir.
...	...	...	...	2	...	...	...	7	1	3	1	2	4	...	...	...	...	2	...	2	...	4	...	2. Andh.
...	...	...	...	...	...	...	...	...	...	...	...	...	...	...	...	...	...	...	...	...	...	...	...	3. Bairági.
...	...	1	...	...	...	...	...	...	...	...	...	...	...	...	...	...	...	...	...	...	...	...	...	4. Balái.
...	...	...	...	...	...	...	...	...	...	...	...	...	...	...	...	...	...	...	1	...	...	3	...	5. Banjári.
2	...	...	...	...	1	3	1	...	...	...	...	1	1	...	...	...	1	...	...	...	...	...	...	6. Bári.
...	...	...	...	...	...	...	...	1	...	...	...	...	...	...	...	...	...	...	...	...	...	...	...	7. Bedar.
1	...	...	...	...	...	...	...	...	...	...	...	...	...	...	...	...	...	1	...	...	...	...	...	8. Beldár.
...	...	...	...	...	...	...	...	...	...	...	...	...	...	...	...	...	...	...	...	...	...	...	...	9. Bhámti.
...	...	...	...	...	...	...	...	...	...	...	...	...	...	...	1	...	...	...	...	...	...	...	...	10. Bhangi.
...	...	...	...	...	...	1	...	...	...	...	...	...	...	...	...	...	...	...	...	...	...	...	...	11. Bharádi.
...	...	...	...	...	...	...	...	...	...	...	...	...	...	...	...	...	...	...	...	...	...	...	...	12. Bhát.
...	...	...	...	...	...	...	1	...	...	...	...	...	...	...	...	...	...	...	...	...	...	1	...	13. Bhil (Hindu).
...	...	...	...	...	...	...	...	...	...	...	...	...	...	...	...	...	...	...	...	...	...	...	...	14. Bhil (Musalman).
3	...	...	...	1	1	...	2	...	...	1	...	1	1	1	1	4	...	...	...	...	...	...	...	15. Bhoi.
...	...	...	...	...	...	...	...	...	...	...	...	...	...	...	...	...	...	...	...	...	...	...	...	16. Bopchi.
4	...	...	...	2	4	2	1	3	...	2	2	3	...	1	...	1	1	1	...	1	...	3	...	17. Bráhman
4	...	...	...	1	1	5	2	1	...	2	...	...	...	...	...	...	...	1	1	1	1	...	...	18. Chámbhár.
...	...	...	...	...	...	...	...	...	...	...	...	...	...	...	...	...	...	...	...	...	...	...	...	19. Chitrakathi.
...	...	...	...	...	...	...	...	...	...	...	...	...	...	...	...	...	...	1	...	...	...	...	...	20. Dángat.
...	...	...	...	...	...	...	...	...	...	...	...	...	...	...	...	...	...	...	...	...	...	...	...	21. Dangur.
3	...	...	...	4	...	5	2	3	...	...	1	1	...	2	...	...	1	1	...	1	2	1	...	22. Dhangar.
...	...	...	...	1	2	...	...	...	...	...	...	...	...	...	...	...	...	...	...	...	...	...	...	23. Dohor.
...	1	...	...	1	...	1	...	...	...	...	...	...	...	...	...	...	...	...	...	...	...	1	...	24. Fakir.
2	...	3	...	...	2	...	...	...	...	...	...	...	...	...	...	1	...	...	...	...	...	1	...	25. Gaoli.
...	...	...	...	...	...	...	...	...	...	...	...	...	...	...	...	...	...	...	...	...	...	...	...	26. Gaulán.
...	...	...	...	...	...	1	...	...	...	...	...	...	...	...	...	...	...	...	...	...	...	...	...	27. Gárpagári.
1	...	...	...	...	...	...	...	...	...	12	3	1	1	2	2	...	...	...	...	...	...	...	...	28. Gawári.
...	...	...	...	1	...	...	...	...	...	...	...	...	...	...	...	...	...	...	...	...	...	...	...	29. Ghisádi.
...	1	2	...	...	1	...	...	1	...	14	5	5	3	7	2	5	1	...	...	...	...	...	...	30. Gond.
1	...	...	...	...	...	...	...	...	...	...	...	...	...	...	...	...	...	1	...	...	...	...	...	31. Gondhali.
...	...	...	...	1	...	4	...	...	...	...	1	2	...	...	...	...	1	1	...	...	...	...	...	32. Gosáwi.
...	...	...	...	...	...	...	...	...	...	...	...	...	...	...	...	...	...	...	...	...	...	...	...	33. Gujar.
1	...	...	...	...	...	...	...	...	...	...	...	...	...	...	...	...	...	...	...	...	...	...	...	34. Gujráthi.
...	...	...	...	...	...	4	1	...	...	...	...	1	...	...	...	2	...	...	1	...	...	...	...	35. Gurao.
...	...	...	...	...	...	...	...	...	...	...	...	2	...	...	...	...	...	...	...	...	...	...	...	36. Halbi.
...	...	...	...	...	...	...	...	...	...	...	...	...	...	...	...	...	...	...	...	...	...	...	...	37. Jangam.
...	...	...	...	...	...	...	...	...	...	...	...	...	...	...	...	...	...	...	...	...	...	...	...	38. Ját.
...	...	...	...	...	...	...	...	...	...	...	...	...	...	...	...	...	...	...	...	...	...	...	...	39. Jingar.
...	...	...	...	...	...	...	...	...	...	...	...	...	1	...	...	...	...	...	...	...	...	...	...	40. Jogi.
...	...	...	...	...	...	...	1	...	...	...	...	...	...	...	...	1	...	...	...	...	...	...	...	41. Kahár.
...	...	...	...	...	...	...	...	...	...	1	...	...	...	...	...	...	...	...	...	...	...	...	...	42. Kakar.
...	1	...	...	1	...	...	1	...	...	2	...	1	...	...	...	...	...	...	...	...	...	...	...	43. Kalál.
...	...	...	...	...	...	...	...	...	...	...	...	...	...	...	...	...	...	1	...	1	...	...	...	44. Kánari.
...	...	...	...	...	...	...	...	...	...	...	...	...	...	...	...	...	...	...	...	...	...	...	...	45. Kángar.
...	...	...	...	...	...	...	...	...	...	...	...	...	...	...	...	...	...	...	...	...	...	...	...	46. Kasái (Musalman).
1	...	...	...	...	...	1	3	1	...	...	...	...	...	2	...	...	...	...	...	...	...	...	...	47. Kásár.
1	...	...	...	...	...	...	...	...	...	1	...	...	...	...	...	...	...	...	...	...	...	...	...	48. Khátik.
...	...	...	...	...	...	...	...	...	...	...	...	...	...	...	...	...	...	...	...	...	...	...	...	49. Khatri.
...	...	3	...	...	...	...	...	...	...	2	1	...	...	3	...	...	...	...	...	...	...	...	...	50. Kolám.
...	...	...	...	...	...	2	...	...	...	...	...	...	...	...	...	...	...	...	...	...	...	...	...	51. Kolháti.
3	...	...	...	1	1	10	2	1	...	1	...	...	...	...	...	...	...	...	...	...	...	...	...	52. Koli.
...	...	...	...	...	...	...	...	...	...	1	...	...	...	...	...	...	...	...	...	...	...	...	...	53. Komti.
...	...	31	7	...	...	...	...	...	...	...	...	...	...	...	...	...	...	...	...	...	...	...	...	54. Korku.
...	...	...	...	3	...	1	...	...	...	...	1	5	1	...	...	...	...	...	...	...	...	...	...	55. Koshti.
3	...	...	1	...	...	...	...	1	...	1	...	1	1	...	1	...	...	...	...	1	...	...	...	56. Kumbhár.
66	16	...	1	56	23	114	34	31	7	16	...	30	5	8	2	8	6	18	3	10	1	8	...	57. Kunbi.
...	...	...	...	...	...	...	...	1	...	...	...	1	...	...	...	...	...	...	...	1	...	...	...	58. Labháni.
...	...	...	...	...	...	1	...	...	...	...	...	...	...	...	...	...	...	...	...	...	...	...	...	59. Lajjhar.
...	...	...	...	...	...	...	...	...	...	...	...	...	...	...	...	...	...	...	...	...	...	2	...	60. Lád.
...	...	...	...	...	...	1	...	...	...	...	...	...	...	...	...	...	...	...	...	...	...	...	...	61. Lodhi.
1	...	...	...	1	1	...	...	1	...	...	2	2	...	...	...	...	...	...	...	...	...	...	1	62. Lohár.
...	...	...	...	...	...	...	...	...	...	...	...	...	...	...	...	...	...	...	...	...	...	...	...	63. Lonári.
28	4	...	...	22	4	24	9	13	2	11	2	6	1	1	3	2	2	9	3	4	1	10	3	64. Mahár.
11	2	...	...	1	2	34	10	9	3	11	1	6	6	4	...	...	...	5	2	4	1	2	2	65. Máli.
2	...	...	...	...	...	...	1	...	...	...	...	...	...	...	...	...	...	...	...	...	...	...	...	66. Mánbháo.
2	1	...	...	10	2	4	...	...	...	1	...	...	1	...	...	...	...	3	1	1	...	1	...	67. Máng.
...	...	...	...	...	1	...	1	2	1	2	2	...	...	...	...	...	...	...	...	...	...	...	...	68. Maráthá.
...	...	...	...	...	...	1	...	...	...	...	...	...	...	...	...	...	...	...	...	...	...	...	...	69. Márwári.
4	1	...	...	1	...	3	2	1	...	...	1	1	1	...	...	...	...	1	...	...	...	2	...	70. Mháli.

TABLE XVA.—Lepers, by

Caste, Tribe, or Race.	Total			Distribution: District Amraoti. Taluk Amraoti.		Taluk Chandur.		Taluk Morsi.		Taluk Murtazapur.		District Akola. Taluk Akola.		Taluk Akot.		Taluk Balapur.		Taluk Jalgaon.		Taluk Khamgaon.		District … Taluk Ellichpur.	
	Total.	Males.	Females.	Males.	Females.	Males.	Females.	Males.	Females.	Males.	Females.	Males.	Females.	Males.	Females.	Males.	Females.	Males.	Females.	Males.	Females.	Males.	Females.
1	2	3	4	5	6	7	8	9	10	11	12	13	14	15	16	17	18	19	20	21	22	23	24
71. Moghul	5	4	1	...	...	1	...	...	...	...	...	...	...	...	1	...	...	...	...	...	...	...	...
72. Munarwár	2	2	...	...	...	...	...	...	...	...	...	...	...	...	...	...	...	...	...	...	...	...	...
73. Musalmán	48	37	11	1	...	...	...	...	...	...	...	...	...	2	...	3	1	1	...	...	2	...	...
74. Náth	1	1	...	...	...	...	...	...	...	...	...	1	...	...	...	...	...	...	...	...	...	...	...
75. Nihál	3	3	...	...	...	...	...	...	...	...	...	...	...	...	...	...	...	...	...	...	...	...	...
76. Otári	2	2	...	...	...	...	...	...	...	...	...	...	...	...	...	...	...	...	...	...	...	...	...
77. Pángul	2	2	...	...	...	...	...	...	...	...	...	...	...	...	...	...	...	...	...	...	...	...	...
78. Pardhán	24	19	5	...	...	...	...	1	...	...	...	...	...	1	...	...	...	...	...	...	...	...	...
79. Párdhi	9	8	1	...	...	...	...	...	...	...	...	1	...	...	...	...	...	...	...	1	...	1	...
80. Pathán	48	41	7	1	...	...	1	4	...	1	1	3	...	4	1	3	2	1	...	3	...	5	2
81. Páthrat	1	...	1	...	...	...	...	...	...	...	...	...	...	...	...	...	1	...	...	...	...	...	...
82. Patwi	1	1	...	...	...	...	...	...	...	...	...	...	...	...	...	...	...	...	...	...	...	...	...
83. Perki	2	2	...	...	...	...	...	...	...	...	...	...	...	...	...	...	...	...	...	...	...	...	...
84. Pinjári	1	1	...	...	...	...	...	...	...	...	...	...	...	...	...	...	...	...	...	...	...	1	...
85. Rajput	79	59	20	3	...	7	2	5	1	2	...	2	1	2	1	2	...	3	...	3	...	3	2
86. Rangári	14	10	4	...	...	...	...	1	...	...	...	1	...	...	...	1	2	...	...	...	...	...	...
87. Sáli	17	15	2	...	...	...	...	...	...	2	...	...	...	...	...	...	...	...	...	...	...	1	...
88. Shekh	105	87	18	12	1	1	...	7	...	7	3	5	2	4	1	6	1	...	...	...	1	15	3
89. Simpi	17	13	4	2	...	...	...	1	...	1	...	1	1	...	1	...	...	3	1	1	...	...	...
90. Sonár	31	25	6	1	...	1	1	...	...	...	...	1	1	1	1	1	...	...	1	1	...	2	...
91. Sutár	44	38	6	4	...	3	...	...	...	2	...	3	1	1	...	2	...	2	...	...	...	3	3
92. Syed	13	10	3	2	1	1	...	...	...	...	...	1	...	...	...	1	2	3	...	1	...	...	...
93. Tákankár	15	10	5	...	...	1	...	...	...	3	...	3	4	1	...	...	...	...	...	...	...	1	...
94. Támbatkár	1	1	...	...	...	...	...	...	...	...	...	1	...	...	...	...	...	...	...	...	...	...	...
95. Teli	162	116	46	10	3	16	5	8	3	12	4	5	4	2	1	4	2	8	4	2	...	6	4
96. Thákur	8	4	4	...	...	...	...	...	...	1	...	1	...	...	...	...	...	1	1	...	1	...	...
97. Tirmale	1	1	...	...	...	1	...	...	...	...	...	...	...	...	...	...	...	...	...	...	...	...	...
98. Vidur	20	17	3	2	1	3	1	2	...	1	...	...	...	1	...	...	...	...	...	3	...	...	...
99. Waddar	1	1	...	1	...	...	...	...	...	...	...	...	...	...	...	...	...	...	...	...	...	...	...
100. Wanjári	36	24	12	...	...	...	...	...	...	...	...	3	...	...	3	2	2	...	...	1	...	...	...
101. Wáni (Hindu)	39	32	7	...	...	1	...	5	...	5	...	...	2	2	1	2	...	...	...	...	...	...	...
102. Wáni (Jain)	8	7	1	...	...	...	...	...	...	...	...	2	...	...	...	...	...	...	...	...	...	...	...
103. Warthi	45	28	17	1	...	3	1	3	2	...	...	1	1	2	1	2	1	1	...	2	1	...	2
Total	3,698	2,886	812	170	37	188	49	238	64	152	39	157	43	156	49	150	48	121	44	112	30	186	58

Caste, Tribe or Race—*contd.*

BY DISTRICTS.																								
ELLICHPUR.				DISTRICT BULDANA.						DISTRICT WUN.								DISTRICT BASIM.						CASTE, TRIBE, OR RACE.
Taluk Daryapur.		Taluk Melghat.		Taluk Chikhli.		Taluk Malkapur.		Taluk Mehkar.		Taluk Yeotmal.		Taluk Darwha.		Taluk Kelapur.		Taluk Wun.		Taluk Basim.		Taluk Mangrul.		Taluk Pusad.		
Males.	Females.	Males.	Females.	Males.	Females.	Males.	Females.	Males.	Females.	Males.	Females.	Males.	Females.	Males.	Females.	Males.	Females.	Males.	Females.	Males.	Females.	Males.	Females.	
25	26	27	28	29	30	31	32	33	34	35	36	37	38	39	40	41	42	43	44	45	46	47	48	49
1	...	...	...	...	...	...	...	...	...	...	...	...	...	...	...	...	...	...	...	1	...	1	...	71. MOGHUL.
...	...	...	...	...	...	...	...	...	...	...	...	...	...	1	...	1	...	...	...	...	...	...	...	72. MUNARWÁR.
8	2	...	...	9	6	4	...	2	...	1	...	...	...	...	...	...	...	4	...	2	...	...	...	73. MUSALMÁN.
...	...	...	...	...	...	...	...	...	...	...	...	...	...	...	...	...	...	...	...	...	...	...	...	74. NÁTH.
...	...	3	...	...	...	...	...	...	...	...	...	...	...	...	...	...	...	...	...	...	...	...	...	75. NIHÁL.
...	...	...	...	1	...	...	...	...	...	...	...	...	...	...	...	...	...	1	...	...	...	...	...	76. OTÁRI.
...	...	...	...	...	...	...	...	...	...	...	...	2	...	...	...	...	...	...	...	...	...	...	...	77. PÁNGUL.
...	...	1	...	...	...	...	...	...	...	4	2	2	...	5	2	4	1	...	...	...	...	1	...	78. PARDHÁN.
1	1	...	...	...	...	4	...	...	...	...	...	...	...	...	...	...	...	...	...	...	...	...	...	79. PÁRDHI.
...	...	...	...	1	...	9	...	1	...	1	...	2	...	...	...	...	...	...	...	1	...	1	...	80. PATHÁN.
...	...	...	...	...	...	...	...	...	...	...	...	...	...	...	...	...	...	...	...	...	...	...	...	81. PÁTHRAT.
1	...	...	...	...	...	...	...	...	...	...	...	...	...	...	...	...	...	...	...	...	...	...	...	82. PATWI.
...	...	...	...	...	...	...	...	...	...	...	...	...	...	2	...	...	...	...	...	...	...	...	...	83. PERKI.
...	...	...	...	...	...	...	...	...	...	...	...	...	...	...	...	...	...	...	...	...	...	...	...	84. PINJÁRI.
3	4	...	1	8	3	10	1	...	3	3	...	1	...	...	...	...	...	1	1	1	...	...	...	85. RAJPUT.
...	1	...	1	...	...	1	...	...	...	...	...	4	...	...	...	...	...	1	...	...	...	1	...	86. RANGÁRI.
...	...	...	...	9	2	...	...	1	...	2	...	...	...	...	...	...	...	...	...	...	...	...	...	87. SÁLI.
1	1	...	...	10	...	10	3	1	...	...	...	7	1	...	...	...	...	...	1	1	...	...	...	88. SHEKH.
1	...	...	...	...	...	1	...	...	...	2	1	...	...	...	...	...	...	...	...	...	...	...	...	89. SIMPI.
5	...	...	...	4	...	1	1	1	...	3	1	1	...	...	...	...	...	...	...	2	...	...	...	90. SONÁR.
6	1	...	...	...	...	2	...	2	...	1	...	2	...	...	...	1	1	2	...	1	...	1	...	91. SUTÁR.
1	...	...	...	...	...	...	...	...	...	...	...	...	...	...	...	...	...	...	...	...	...	...	...	92. SYED.
...	...	...	...	...	...	1	...	...	...	...	...	...	...	...	...	...	...	...	...	...	1	...	...	93. TÁKANKÁR.
...	...	...	...	...	...	...	...	...	...	...	...	...	...	...	...	...	...	...	...	...	...	...	...	94. TÁMBATKÁR.
4	1	...	...	10	3	12	6	1	...	3	2	7	2	1	...	...	1	1	...	2	1	2	...	95. TELI.
...	...	...	...	...	1	1	1	...	...	...	...	...	...	...	...	...	...	...	...	...	...	...	...	96. THÁKUR.
...	...	...	...	...	...	...	...	...	...	...	...	...	...	...	...	...	...	...	...	...	...	...	...	97. TIRMALE.
...	...	...	...	...	...	1	...	...	1	...	...	1	...	1	...	1	...	...	...	1	...	...	...	98. VIDUR.
...	...	...	...	...	...	...	...	...	...	...	...	...	...	...	...	...	...	...	...	...	...	...	...	99. WADDAR.
...	...	...	...	3	4	4	1	9	2	...	...	1	...	...	...	...	...	1	...	...	...	...	...	100. WANJÁRI.
1	...	...	...	3	...	8	1	...	...	...	2	4	...	...	...	...	...	1	...	...	1	...	...	101. WÁNI (HINDU).
2	...	...	...	1	...	...	...	...	...	...	...	...	...	...	...	...	...	2	...	...	...	...	1	102. WÁNI (JAIN).
3	2	...	...	1	...	2	4	3	1	2	1	...	...	...	...	1	...	...	...	1	...	...	...	103. WARTHI.
182	40	47	11	210	65	298	92	98	21	106	32	106	30	41	54	82	16	60	14	40	9	46	7	TOTAL.

Berar.

TABLE XVI.

Castes, Tribes, and Races, by Nationality or Traditional Occupation.

TABLE XVI.—Castes, Tribes, and Races, by

Name and Classification.				Provincial Total.	Distribution	
					Amraoti.	Akola.
Class.	Group.	Caste.	Religion.	Total, Males, and Females.	Total, Males, and Females.	Total, Males, and Females.
1	2	3	4	5	6	7
A.—AGRICULTURAL.	1.—Military and Dominant.	Multáni	Musalman	T. 9 M. 4 F. 5	... ...	... ...
		Sikh	Hindu	T. 202 M. 105 F. 97	T. 50 M. 24 F. 26	T. 14 M. 9 F. 5
		Do.	Sikh	T. 114 M. 60 F. 54	T. 27 M. 12 F. 15	T. 13 M. 9 F. 4
			Total Group 1	*T. 325* *M. 169* *F. 156*	*T. 77* *M. 36* *F. 41*	*T. 27* *M. 18* *F. 9*
	2.—Other Agricultural— (a) Cultivators.	Ayáwár	Hindu	T. 132 M. 65 F. 67	T. 3 M. 2 F. 1	... ...
		Bágwán	Musalman	T. 124 M. 58 F. 66	... ...	... ...
		Barai	Hindu	T. 142 M. 66 F. 76	... ...	T. 5 M. 4 F. 1
		Bári	Do.	T. 25,928 M. 13,190 F. 12,738	T. 7,839 M. 3,947 F. 3,892	T. 8,532 M. 4,375 F. 4,157
		Bhanári	Do.	T. 21 M. 9 F. 12	... ...	... ...
		Bhoyer	Do.	T. 30 M. 26 F. 4	T. 24 M. 21 F. 3	... ...
		Bhute	Do.	T. 1 M. 1 ...	... ...	... ...
		Bhuvésh	Do.	T. 6 M. 2 F. 4	... ...	... ...
		Gujar	Do.	T. 981 M. 522 F. 459	T. 580 M. 310 F. 270	T. 280 M. 144 F. 136
		Do.	Jain	T. 9 M. 4 F. 5	... ...	T. 9 M. 4 F. 5
		Gurud Kápuwár	Hindu	T. 501 M. 241 F. 260	... ...	... ...
		Ját	Do.	T. 513 M. 292 F. 221	T. 235 M. 117 F. 118	T. 56 M. 36 F. 20
		Do.	Musalman	T. 2 M. 1 F. 1	... ...	... ...
		Do.	Jain	T. 5 M. 3 F. 2	T. 2 M. 1 F. 1	... ...
		Do.	Sikh	T. 7 M. 5 F. 2	... ...	... ...
		Kachhwárá	Hindu	T. 1 M. 1 ...	T. 1 M. 1 ...	... ...
		Káchi	Do.	T. 28 M. 22 F. 6	T. 16 M. 11 F. 5	T. 4 M. 4 ...

Nationality or traditional Occupation.

By District.				Railway Passengers, Etc.	District Amraoti.			
Ellichpur.	Buldana.	Wun.	Basim.		Amraoti.	Chandur.	Morsi.	Murtazapur.
Total, Males, and Females.	Total, Males, and Females.	Total, Males, and Females.	Total, Males, and Females.	Total, Males, and Females.	Total, Males, and Females.	Total, Males, and Females.	Total, Males, and Females.	Total, Males, and Females.
8	9	10	11	12	13	14	15	16
T. 7	...	...	T. 2	...	...	...	...	...
M. 3	...	...	M. 1	...	...	...	...	...
F. 4	...	...	F. 1	...	...	...	...	...
T. 11	T. 77	T. 23	T. 27	...	T. 8	T. 23	...	T. 19
M. 5	M. 43	M. 10	M. 14	...	M. 3	M. 11	...	M. 10
F. 6	F. 34	F. 13	F. 13	...	F. 5	F. 12	...	F. 9
T. 1	T. 30	T. 37	T. 6	...	...	T. 18	...	T. 9
M. 1	M. 13	M. 22	M. 3	...	...	M. 10	...	M. 2
...	F. 17	F. 15	F. 3	...	...	F. 8	...	F. 7
T. 19	*T. 107*	*T. 60*	*T. 35*	...	*T. 8*	*T. 41*	...	*T. 28*
M. 9	*M. 56*	*M. 32*	*M. 18*	...	*M. 3*	*M. 21*	...	*M. 12*
F. 10	*F. 51*	*F. 28*	*F. 17*	...	*F. 5*	*F. 20*	...	*F. 16*
...	...	T. 124	T. 5	...	...	T. 3	...	...
...	...	M. 62	M. 1	...	...	M. 2	...	...
...	...	F. 62	F. 4	...	...	F. 1	...	...
...	T. 49	...	T. 75	...	...	...	...	...
...	M. 24	...	M. 34	...	...	...	...	...
...	F. 25	...	F. 41	...	...	...	...	...
...	...	T. 136	...	T. 1	...	...	...	...
...	...	M. 61	...	M. 1	...	...	...	...
...	...	F. 75	...	...	...	...	...	...
T. 5,602	T. 677	T. 2,309	T. 960	T. 1	T. 2,789	T. 2,158	T. 2,832	T. 60
M. 2,846	M. 346	M. 1,200	M. 475	M. 1	M. 1,396	M. 1,081	M. 1,436	M. 34
F. 2,756	F. 331	F. 1,109	F. 485	...	F. 1,393	F. 1,077	F. 1,396	F. 26
...	...	T. 21	...	...	...	...	...	...
...	...	M. 9	...	...	...	...	...	...
...	...	F. 12	...	...	...	...	...	...
T. 4	...	T. 2	...	...	T. 1	...	T. 23	...
M. 4	...	M. 1	...	...	M. 1	...	M. 20	...
...	...	F. 1	...	...	...	...	F. 3	...
T. 1	...	...	...	...	...	...	...	...
M. 1	...	...	...	...	...	...	...	...
...	...	...	...	...	...	...	...	...
...	...	T. 6	...	...	...	...	...	...
...	...	M. 2	...	...	...	...	...	...
...	...	F. 4	...	...	...	...	...	...
T. 12	T. 43	T. 60	T. 6	...	T. 369	T. 35	T. 176	...
M. 10	M. 22	M. 31	M. 5	...	M. 201	M. 24	M. 85	...
F. 2	F. 21	F. 29	F. 1	...	F. 168	F. 11	F. 91	...
...	...	...	...	...	...	...	...	...
...	...	...	...	...	...	...	...	...
...	...	...	...	...	...	...	...	...
...	...	T. 501	...	...	...	...	...	...
...	...	M. 241	...	...	...	...	...	...
...	...	F. 260	...	...	...	...	...	...
T. 19	T. 188	T. 3	T. 12	...	T. 114	T. 10	T. 17	T. 94
M. 17	M. 108	M. 2	M. 12	...	M. 57	M. 7	M. 10	M. 43
F. 2	F. 80	F. 1	...	...	F. 57	F. 3	F. 7	F. 51
...	...	T. 2	...	...	...	...	...	...
...	...	M. 1	...	...	...	...	...	...
...	...	F. 1	...	...	...	...	...	...
...	T. 3	...	...	...	...	T. 2	...	...
...	M. 2	...	...	...	...	M. 1	...	...
...	F. 1	...	...	...	...	F. 1	...	...
...	...	T. 1	T. 6	...	...	...	...	...
...	...	M. 1	M. 4	...	...	...	...	...
...	...	...	F. 2	...	...	...	...	...
...	...	...	...	...	...	T. 1	...	...
...	...	...	...	...	...	M. 1	...	...
...	...	...	...	...	...	...	...	...
T. 7	...	T. 1	...	...	T. 13	T. 2	T. 1	...
M. 6	...	M. 1	...	...	M. 8	M. 2	M. 1	...
F. 1	...	...	...	...	F. 5	...	...	...

TABLE XVI.—Castes, Tribes, and Races, by

Class.	Group.	Caste.	Religion.	DISTRICT AKOLA. Akola. Total, Males, and Females.	Akot. Total, Males, and Females.	Balapur. Total, Males, and Females.	Jalgaon. Total, Males, and Females.	Khamgaon. Total, Males, and Females.	DISTRICT Ellichpur. Total, Males, and Females.
17	18	19	20	21	22	23	24	25	26
A.—AGRICULTURAL.	1.—Military and Dominant.	Multáni	Musalman	... ...	... ...	... ...	... ...	... ...	... ...
		Sikh	Hindu	T. 5 M. 3 F. 2	... ...	... ...	T. 9 M. 6 F. 3	... ...	T. 4 M. 2 F. 2
		Do.	Sikh	T. 4 M. 4 ...	... ...	... ...	T. 2 M. 1 F. 1	T. 7 M. 4 F. 3	... ...
			Total Group 1	*T. 9* *M. 7* *F. 2*	... ...	... ...	*T. 11* *M. 7* *F. 4*	*T. 7* *M. 4* *F. 8*	*T. 4* *M. 2* *F. 2*
	2.—Other Agricultural— (a) Cultivators.	Ayáwár	Hindu	... ...	... ...	... ...	... ...	... ...	... ...
		Bágwán	Musalman	... ...	... ...	... ...	... ...	... ...	... ...
		Barai	Hindu	T. 5 M. 4 F. 1	... ...	... ...	... ...	... ...	... ...
		Bári	Do.	T. 229 M. 124 F. 105	T. 2,611 M. 1,354 F. 1,257	T. 277 M. 128 F. 149	T. 5,188 M. 2,650 F. 2,538	T. 227 M. 119 F. 108	T. 3,148 M. 1,624 F. 1,524
		Bhanári	Do.	... ...	... ...	... ...	... ...	... ...	... ...
		Bhoyer	Do.	... ...	... ...	... ...	... ...	... ...	T. 3 M. 3 ...
		Bhute	Do.	... ...	... ...	... ...	... ...	... ...	... ...
		Bhuvésh	Do.	... ...	... ...	... ...	... ...	... ...	... ...
		Gujar	Do.	T. 31 M. 15 F. 16	T. 163 M. 86 F. 77	T. 1 M. 1 ...	T. 3 M. 1 F. 2	T. 82 M. 41 F. 41	T. 7 M. 7 ...
		Do.	Jain	... ...	... ...	T. 9 M. 4 F. 5	... ...	... ...	... ...
		Gurud Kápuwár	Hindu	... ...	... ...	... ...	... ...	... ...	... ...
		Ját	Do.	T. 10 M. 8 F. 2	T. 16 M. 11 F. 5	T. 5 M. 4 F. 1	T. 4 M. 3 F. 1	T. 21 M. 10 F. 11	T. 8 M. 8 ...
		Do.	Musalman	... ...	... ...	... ...	... ...	... ...	... ...
		Do.	Jain	... ...	... ...	... ...	... ...	... ...	... ...
		Do.	Sikh	... ...	... ...	... ...	... ...	... ...	... ...
		Kachhwáhá	Hindu	... ...	... ...	... ...	... ...	... ...	... ...
		Káchi	Do.	T. 2 M. 2 ...	T. 2 M. 2 ...	... ...	... ...	... ...	... ...

Nationality or traditional Occupation.

ELLICHPUR.		DISTRICT BULDANA.			DISTRICT WUN.				DISTRICT BASIM.		
DARYAPUR.	MELGHAT.	CHIKHLI.	MALKAPUR.	MEHKAR.	YEOTMAL.	DARWHA.	KELAPUR.	WUN.	BASIM.	MANGRUL.	PUSAD.
Total, Males, and Females.	Total, Males, and Females.	Total, Males, and Females.	Total, Males, and Females.	Total, Males, and Females.	Total, Males, and Females.	Total, Males, and Females.	Total, Males, and Females.	Total, Males, and Females.	Total, Males, and Females.	Total, Males, and Females.	Total, Males, and Females.
27	28	29	30	31	32	33	34	35	36	37	38
...	T. 7	...	...	...	...	...	...	...	...	...	T. 2
...	M. 3	...	...	...	...	...	...	...	...	...	M. 1
...	F. 4	...	...	...	...	...	...	...	...	...	F. 1
...	T. 7	T. 13	T. 29	T. 35	T. 5	T. 2	T. 16	...	T. 11	...	T. 16
...	M. 3	M. 9	M. 15	M. 19	M. 2	M. 1	M. 7	...	M. 9	...	M. 5
...	F. 4	F. 4	F. 14	F. 10	F. 3	F. 1	F. 9	...	F. 2	...	F. 11
T. 1	...	T. 1	...	T. 29	T. 1	...	T. 36	...	...	...	T. 6
M. 1	...	...	...	M. 13	M. 1	...	M. 21	...	...	...	M. 3
...	...	F. 1	...	F. 16	...	...	F. 15	...	...	...	F. 3
T. 1	*T. 14*	*T. 14*	*T. 29*	*T. 64*	*T. 6*	*T. 2*	*T. 52*	...	*T. 11*	...	*T. 24*
M. 1	*M. 6*	*M. 9*	*M. 15*	*M. 32*	*M. 3*	*M. 1*	*M. 28*	...	*M. 9*	...	*M. 9*
...	*F. 8*	*F. 5*	*F. 14*	*F. 32*	*F. 3*	*F. 1*	*F. 24*	...	*F. 2*	...	*F. 15*
...	...	...	...	...	...	T. 18	T. 66	T. 40	T. 1	...	T. 4
...	...	...	...	...	...	M. 11	M. 29	M. 22	M. 1	...	...
...	...	...	...	...	...	F. 7	F. 37	F. 18	...	...	F. 4
...	...	T. 25	T. 24	...	...	...	...	...	T. 68	...	T. 7
...	...	M. 13	M. 11	...	...	...	...	...	M. 30	...	M. 4
...	...	F. 12	F. 13	...	...	...	...	...	F. 38	...	F. 3
...	...	...	...	...	...	...	T. 124	T. 12	...	...	...
...	...	...	...	...	...	...	M. 53	M. 8	...	...	...
...	...	...	...	...	...	...	F. 71	F. 4	...	...	...
T. 2,446	T. 8	T. 283	T. 382	T. 12	T. 236	T. 1,933	T. 82	T. 58	T. 7	T. 44	T. 909
M. 1,216	M. 6	M. 145	M. 195	M. 6	M. 130	M. 998	M. 40	M. 32	M. 3	M. 21	M. 451
F. 1,230	F. 2	F. 138	F. 187	F. 6	F. 106	F. 935	F. 42	F. 26	F. 4	F. 23	F. 458
...	...	...	...	...	...	...	...	T. 21	...	...	...
...	...	...	...	...	...	...	...	M. 9	...	...	...
...	...	...	...	...	...	...	...	F. 12	...	...	...
...	T. 1	...	...	...	T. 2	...	...	...	...	...	...
...	M. 1	...	...	...	M. 1	...	...	...	...	...	...
...	...	...	...	...	F. 1	...	...	...	...	...	...
...	T. 1	...	...	...	...	...	...	...	...	...	...
...	M. 1	...	...	...	...	...	...	...	...	...	...
...	...	...	...	...	...	...	...	...	...	...	...
...	...	...	...	...	T. 6	...	...	...	...	...	...
...	...	...	...	...	M. 2	...	...	...	...	...	...
...	...	...	...	...	F. 4	...	...	...	...	...	...
T. 3	T. 2	T. 35	T. 6	T. 2	...	T. 33	T. 27	...	T. 4	T. 2	...
M. 1	M. 2	M. 14	M. 6	M. 2	...	M. 16	M. 15	...	M. 3	M. 2	...
F. 2	...	F. 21	...	...	...	F. 17	F. 12	...	F. 1	...	...
...	...	...	...	...	...	...	...	...	...	...	...
...	...	...	...	...	...	...	...	...	...	...	...
...	...	...	...	...	...	...	...	...	...	...	...
...	...	...	...	...	...	...	T. 418	T. 83	...	...	...
...	...	...	...	...	...	...	M. 201	M. 40	...	...	...
...	...	...	...	...	...	...	F. 217	F. 43	...	...	...
T. 4	T. 7	T. 1	T. 6	T. 181	T. 2	...	...	T. 1	T. 12	...	...
M. 3	M. 6	M. 1	M. 5	M. 102	M. 2	...	...	...	M. 12	...	...
F. 1	F. 1	...	F. 1	F. 79	...	...	...	F. 1	...	...	...
...	...	...	...	...	...	T. 2	...	...	...	...	...
...	...	...	...	...	...	M. 1	...	...	...	...	...
...	...	...	...	...	...	F. 1	...	...	...	...	...
...	...	...	...	T. 3	...	...	...	...	...	...	...
...	...	...	...	M. 2	...	...	...	...	...	...	...
...	...	...	...	F. 1	...	...	...	...	...	...	...
...	...	...	...	...	...	T. 1	...	...	...	...	T. 6
...	...	...	...	...	...	M. 1	...	...	...	...	M. 4
...	...	...	...	...	...	...	...	...	...	...	F. 2
...	...	...	...	...	...	...	...	...	...	...	...
...	...	...	...	...	...	...	...	...	...	...	...
...	...	...	...	...	...	...	...	...	...	...	...
T. 5	T. 2	...	...	...	T. 1	...	...	...	...	...	...
M. 4	M. 2	...	...	...	M. 1	...	...	...	...	...	...
F. 1	...	...	...	...	...	...	...	...	...	...	...

TABLE XVI.—Castes, Tribes, and Races, by

Name and Classification.				Provincial Total.	Distribution	
					Amraoti.	Akola.
Class.	Group.	Caste.	Religion.	Total, Males, and Females.	Total, Males, and Females.	Total, Males, and Females.
1	2	3	4	5	6	7
A.—AGRICULTURAL—*contd.*	2.—Other Agricultural—*contd.* 2(a).—Cultivators—*contd.*	Kakar	Hindu	T. 102 M. 56 F. 46	T. 50 M. 29 F. 21	... ...
		Kápuwáru	Do.	T. 82 M. 45 F. 37	T. 4 M. 1 F. 3	... ...
		Khichar	Do.	T. 1 M. 1 ...	T. 1 M. 1 ...	... ...
		Kunbi	Do.	T. 834,419 M. 426,429 F. 407,990	T. 167,029 M. 85,890 F. 81,139	T. 186,968 M. 95,316 F. 91,652
		Do.	Jain	T. 13 M. 7 F. 6	... ...	T. 1 M. 1 ...
		Lodhi	Hindu	T. 1,915 M. 1,147 F. 768	T. 674 M. 417 F. 257	T. 348 M. 209 F. 139
		Do.	Musalman	T. 5 M. 2 F. 3	... ...	T. 5 M. 2 F. 3
		Londhári	Hindu	T. 23 M. 13 F. 10	... ...	... ...
		Máli	Do.	T. 202,488 M. 102,717 F. 99,771	T. 61,383 M. 31,366 F. 30,017	T. 50,907 M. 25,686 F. 25,221
		Do.	Jain	T. 10 M. 10 ...	... ...	T. 10 M. 10 ...
		Máná	Hindu	T. 217 M. 114 F. 103	T. 44 M. 24 F. 20	... ...
		Máwhár	Do.	T. 1 M. 1 ...	T. 1 M. 1 ...	... ...
		Mudliár	Do.	T. 66 M. 29 F. 37	T. 20 M. 10 F. 10	T. 20 M. 9 F. 11
		Munarwár	Do.	T. 2,120 M. 1,092 F. 1,028	T. 25 M. 13 F. 12	T. 9 M. 4 F. 5
		Muráde	Do.	T. 1 M. 1 ...	T. 1 M. 1 ...	... ...
		Murái	Do.	T. 119 M. 93 F. 26	T. 40 M. 30 F. 10	T. 22 M. 19 F. 3
		Náyer	Do.	T. 14 M. 10 F. 4	T. 5 M. 4 F. 1	T. 9 M. 6 F. 3
		Paháp	Do.	T. 836 M. 437 F. 399	T. 280 M. 132 F. 148	T. 121 M. 46 F. 75
		Pataliyá	Do.	T. 2 M. 1 F. 1	T. 2 M. 1 F. 1	... ...
		Phanádi	Do.	T. 102 M. 58 F. 44	... ...	T. 2 M. 2 ...
		Phulári	Do.	T. 29 M. 19 F. 10	T. 27 M. 17 F. 10	... ...

Nationality or traditional Occupation—*contd.*

BY DISTRICT.				RAILWAY PASSENGERS, ETC.	DISTRICT AMRAOTI.			
ELLICHPUR.	BULDANA.	WUN.	BASIM.		AMRAOTI.	CHANDUR.	MORSI.	MURTAZAPUR.
Total, Males, and Females.	Total, Males, and Females.	Total, Males, and Females.	Total, Males, and Females.	Total, Males, and Females.	Total, Males, and Females.	Total, Males, and Females.	Total, Males, and Females.	Total, Males, and Females.
8	9	10	11	12	13	14	15	16
T. 1	...	T. 51	...	...	T. 7	...	T. 43	...
M. 1	...	M. 26	...	...	M. 4	...	M. 25	...
...	...	F. 25	...	...	F. 3	...	F. 18	...
...	...	T. 78	...	...	...	...	T. 4	...
...	...	M. 44	...	...	...	...	M. 1	...
...	...	F. 34	...	...	...	...	F. 3	...
...	...	...	...	...	T. 1	...	...	...
...	...	...	...	...	M. 1	...	...	...
...	...	...	...	...	...	...	...	...
T. 75,413	T. 177,410	T. 106,424	T. 121,137	T. 38	T. 37,897	T. 50,254	T. 42,839	T. 36,039
M. 38,371	M. 90,190	M. 54,633	M. 61,999	M. 30	M. 19,452	M. 25,752	M. 22,037	M. 18,649
F. 37,042	F. 87,220	F. 51,791	F. 59,138	F. 8	F. 18,445	F. 24,502	F. 20,802	F. 17,390
...	...	T. 12	...	...	...	...	...	...
...	...	M. 6	...	...	...	...	...	...
...	...	F. 6	...	...	...	...	...	...
T. 652	T. 79	T. 130	T. 32	...	T. 283	T. 291	T. 27	T. 73
M. 371	M. 52	M. 80	M. 18	...	M. 185	M. 166	M. 19	M. 47
F. 281	F. 27	F. 50	F. 14	...	F. 98	F. 125	F. 8	F. 26
...	...	...	...	...	...	...	...	...
...	...	...	...	...	...	...	...	...
...	...	...	...	...	...	...	...	...
T. 20	T. 3	...	...	...	...	...	...	...
M. 10	M. 3	...	...	...	...	...	...	...
F. 10	...	...	...	...	...	...	...	...
T. 27,063	T. 30,621	T. 19,545	T. 12,967	T. 2	T. 12,372	T. 18,289	T. 22,318	T. 8,404
M. 13,658	M. 15,429	M. 9,963	M. 6,613	M. 2	M. 6,317	M. 9,352	M. 11,377	M. 4,320
F. 13,405	F. 15,192	F. 9,582	F. 6,354	...	F. 6,055	F. 8,937	F. 10,941	F. 4,084
...	...	...	...	...	...	...	...	...
...	...	...	...	...	...	...	...	...
...	...	...	...	...	...	...	...	...
...	...	T. 173	...	...	T. 1	T. 42	...	T. 1
...	...	M. 90	...	...	M. 1	M. 22	...	M. 1
...	...	F. 83	...	...	...	F. 20	...	...
...	...	...	...	...	...	T. 1	...	...
...	...	...	...	...	...	M. 1	...	...
...	...	...	...	...	...	...	...	...
T. 11	...	T. 15	...	...	T. 9	T. 3	...	T. 8
M. 3	...	M. 7	...	...	M. 5	M. 1	...	M. 4
F. 8	...	F. 8	...	...	F. 4	F. 2	...	F. 4
T. 27	...	T. 2,010	T. 49	...	T. 13	T. 4	T. 8	...
M. 14	...	M. 1,039	M. 22	...	M. 7	M. 3	M. 3	...
F. 13	...	F. 971	F. 27	...	F. 6	F. 1	F. 5	...
...	...	...	...	...	...	T. 1	...	...
...	...	...	...	...	...	M. 1	...	...
...	...	...	...	...	...	...	...	...
T. 32	...	T. 13	T. 12	...	T. 27	T. 2	T. 4	T. 7
M. 25	...	M. 10	M. 9	...	M. 19	M. 2	M. 3	M. 6
F. 7	...	F. 3	F. 3	...	F. 8	...	F. 1	F. 1
...	...	...	...	...	T. 5	...	...	...
...	...	...	...	...	M. 4	...	...	...
...	...	...	...	...	F. 1	...	...	...
T. 146	...	T. 279	T. 10	...	T. 116	T. 31	T. 8	T. 125
M. 88	...	M. 166	M. 5	...	M. 56	M. 16	M. 5	M. 55
F. 58	...	F. 113	F. 5	...	F. 60	F. 15	F. 3	F. 70
...	...	...	...	...	...	T. 2	...	...
...	...	...	...	...	...	M. 1	...	...
...	...	...	...	...	...	F. 1	...	...
...	...	...	T. 100	...	...	...	...	...
...	...	...	M. 56	...	...	...	...	...
...	...	...	F. 44	...	...	...	...	...
T. 2	...	...	...	...	...	T. 2	...	T. 25
M. 2	...	...	...	...	...	M. 1	...	M. 16
...	...	...	...	...	...	F. 1	...	F. 9

TABLE XVI.—Castes, Tribes, and Races, by

Name and Classification.				District Akola.					District
				Akola.	Akot.	Balapur.	Jalgaon.	Khamgaon.	Ellichpur.
Class.	Group.	Caste.	Religion.	Total, Males, and Females.	Total, Males, and Females.	Total, Males, and Females.	Total, Males, and Females.	Total, Males, and Females.	Total, Males, and Females.
17	18	19	20	21	22	23	24	25	26
A.—AGRICULTURAL—*contd.*	2.—Other Agricultural—*contd.* 2(*a*).—Cultivators—*contd.*	Kakar	Hindu	... ...	... ...	... ...	... ...	... ...	... ...
		Kápuwáru	Do.	... ...	... ...	... ...	... ...	... ...	... ...
		Khichar	Do.	... ...	... ...	... ...	... ...	... ...	... ...
		Kunbi	Do.	T. 43,296 M. 22,249 F. 21,047	T. 46,830 M. 23,500 F. 23,330	T. 30,326 M. 15,522 F. 14,804	T. 28,966 M. 14,669 F. 14,297	T. 37,550 M. 19,376 F. 18,174	T. 35,682 M. 18,170 F. 17,512
		Do.	Jain	... ...	T. 1 M. 1 ...	... ...	... ...	... ...	... ...
		Lodhi	Hindu	T. 84 M. 54 F. 30	T. 143 M. 88 F. 55	T. 9 M. 5 F. 4	T. 108 M. 59 F. 49	T. 4 M. 3 F. 1	T. 481 M. 261 F. 220
		Do.	Musalman	... ...	T. 5 M. 2 F. 3	... ...	... ...	... ...	... ...
		Londhári	Hindu	... ...	... ...	... ...	... ...	... ...	... ...
		Máli	Do.	T. 7,355 M. 3,811 F. 3,544	T. 11,607 M. 5,771 F. 5,836	T. 10,713 M. 5,381 F. 5,332	T. 11,528 M. 5,752 F. 5,776	T. 9,704 M. 4,971 F. 4,733	T. 17,556 M. 8,851 F. 8,705
		Do.	Jain	... ...	T. 2 M. 2 ...	... ...	... ...	T. 8 M. 8 ...	... ...
		Máná	Hindu	... ...	... ...	... ...	... ...	... ...	... ...
		Máwhár	Do.	... ...	... ...	... ...	... ...	... ...	... ...
		Mudliár	Do.	T. 11 M. 5 F. 6	... ...	... ...	... ...	T. 9 M. 4 F. 5	T. 11 M. 3 F. 8
		Munarwár	Do.	T. 9 M. 4 F. 5	... ...	... ...	... ...	... ...	T. 22 M. 12 F. 10
		Muráde	Do.	... ...	... ...	... ...	... ...	... ...	... ...
		Murái	Do.	T. 4 M. 4 ...	T. 3 M. 3 ...	T. 6 M. 5 F. 1	T. 2 M. 2 ...	T. 7 M. 5 F. 2	T. 28 M. 21 F. 7
		Náyer	Do.	T. 9 M. 6 F. 3	... ...	... ...	... ...	... ...	... ...
		Pahád	Do.	T. 17 M. 11 F. 6	T. 15 M. 7 F. 8	T. 80 M. 23 F. 57	... ...	T. 9 M. 5 F. 4	T. 48 M. 29 F. 19
		Pataliyá	Do.	... ...	... ...	... ...	... ...	... ...	... ...
		Phanádi	Do.	... ...	... ...	T. 2 M. 2 ...	... ...	... ...	... ...
		Phulári	Do.	... ...	... ...	... ...	... ...	... ...	T. 2 M. 2 ...

Nationality or traditional Occupation—*contd.*

ELLICHPUR.		DISTRICT BULDANA.			DISTRICT WUN.				DISTRICT BASIM.		
DARYAPUR.	MELGHAT.	CHIKHLI.	MALKAPUR.	MEHKAR.	YEOTMAL.	DARWHA.	KELAPUR.	WUN.	BASIM.	MANGRUL.	PUSAD.
Total, Males, and Females.	Total, Males, and Females.	Total, Males, and Females.	Total, Males, and Females.	Total, Males, and Females.	Total, Males, and Females.	Total, Males, and Females.	Total, Males, and Females.	Total, Males, and Females.	Total, Males, and Females.	Total, Males, and Females.	Total, Males, and Females.
27	28	29	30	31	32	33	4	35	36	37	38
T. 1 M. 1 ...	... ...	... ...	... ...	... ...	... ...	... ...	T. 51 M. 26 F. 25	... ...	... ...	... ...	... ...
... ...	... ...	... ...	... ...	... ...	... ...	... ...	T. 78 M. 44 F. 34	... ...	... ...	... ...	... ...
... ...	... ...	... ...	... ...	... ...	... ...	... ...	... ...	... ...	... ...	... ...	... ...
T. 39,523 M. 20,062 F. 19,461	T. 208 M. 139 F. 69	T. 60,989 M. 31,011 F. 29,978	T. 65,855 M. 33,396 F. 32,459	T. 50,566 M. 25,783 F. 24,783	T. 24,586 M. 12,602 F. 11,984	T. 28,211 M. 14,647 F. 13,564	T. 20,275 M. 10,355 F. 9,920	T. 33,352 M. 17,029 F. 16,323	T. 64,394 M. 33,065 F. 31,329	T. 26,010 M. 13,473 F. 12,537	T. 30,733 M. 15,461 F. 15,272
... ...	... ...	... ...	... ...	... ...	... ...	T. 12 M. 6 F. 6	... ...	... ...	... ...	... ...	... ...
T. 136 M. 88 F. 48	T. 35 M. 22 F. 13	T. 6 M. 5 F. 1	T. 73 M. 47 F. 26	... ...	T. 11 M. 9 F. 2	T. 26 M. 22 F. 4	T. 2 M. 2 ...	T. 91 M. 47 F. 44	T. 17 M. 6 F. 11	T. 9 M. 6 F. 3	T. 6 M. 6 ...
... ...	... ...	... ...	... ...	... ...	... ...	... ...	... ...	... ...	... ...	... ...	... ...
T. 20 M. 10 F. 10	... ...	T. 3 M. 3 ...	... ...	... ...	... ...	... ...	... ...	... ...	... ...	... ...	... ...
T. 9,417 M. 4,751 F. 4,666	T. 90 M. 56 F. 34	T. 5,541 M. 2,786 F. 2,755	T. 14,899 M. 7,547 F. 7,352	T. 10,181 M. 5,096 F. 5,085	T. 6,630 M. 3,419 F. 3,211	T. 8,254 M. 4,217 F. 4,037	T. 3,440 M. 1,737 F. 1,703	T. 1,221 M. 590 F. 631	T. 6,090 M. 3,077 F. 3,013	T. 3,773 M. 1,969 F. 1,804	T. 3,104 M. 1,567 F. 1,537
... ...	... ...	... ...	... ...	... ...	... ...	... ...	... ...	... ...	... ...	... ...	... ...
... ...	... ...	... ...	... ...	... ...	T. 6 M. 3 F. 3	... ...	T. 88 M. 48 F. 40	T. 79 M. 39 F. 40	... ...	... ...	... ...
... ...	... ...	... ...	... ...	... ...	... ...	... ...	... ...	... ...	... ...	... ...	... ...
... ...	... ...	... ...	... ...	... ...	T. 14 M. 7 F. 7	... ...	... ...	T. 1 ... F. 1	... ...	... ...	... ...
T. 5 M. 2 F. 3	... ...	... ...	... ...	... ...	T. 23 M. 15 F. 8	T. 273 M. 136 F. 137	T. 1,175 M. 601 F. 574	T. 539 M. 287 F. 252	... ...	... ...	T. 49 M. 22 F. 27
... ...	... ...	... ...	... ...	... ...	... ...	... ...	... ...	... ...	... ...	... ...	... ...
T. 3 M. 3 ...	T. 1 M. 1 ...	... ...	... ...	... ...	T. 8 M. 6 F. 2	T. 2 M. 2 ...	T. 3 M. 2 F. 1	... ...	T. 11 M. 8 F. 3	T. 1 M. 1 ...	... ...
... ...	... ...	... ...	... ...	... ...	... ...	... ...	... ...	... ...	... ...	... ...	... ...
T. 95 M. 56 F. 39	T. 3 M. 3 ...	... ...	... ...	... ...	T. 157 M. 92 F. 65	T. 43 M. 24 F. 19	T. 59 M. 35 F. 24	T. 20 M. 15 F. 5	... ...	T. 10 M. 5 F. 5	... ...
... ...	... ...	... ...	... ...	... ...	... ...	... ...	... ...	... ...	... ...	... ...	... ...
... ...	... ...	... ...	... ...	... ...	... ...	... ...	... ...	... ...	... ...	... ...	T. 100 M. 56 F. 44
... ...	... ...	... ...	... ...	... ...	... ...	... ...	... ...	... ...	... ...	... ...	... ...

TABLE XVI.—Castes, Tribes, and Races, by

Class.	Group.	Caste.	Religion.	PROVINCIAL TOTAL. Total, Males, and Females.	DISTRIBUTION: AMRAOTI. Total, Males, and Females.	AKOLA. Total, Males, and Females.
1	2	3	4	5	6	7
A.—AGRICULTURAL—*contd.*	2.—OTHER AGRICULTURAL—*concld.* 2(*a*).—CULTIVATORS—*concld.*	RAJPUT	Hindu	T. 50,916	T. 12,755	T. 12,623
				M. 26,850	M. 6,832	M. 6,622
				F. 24,066	F. 5,923	F. 6,001
		Do.	Sikh	T. 14	...	T. 14
				M. 8	...	M. 8
				F. 6	...	F. 6
		REDDI	Hindu	T. 1	T. 1	...
				M. 1	M. 1	...
				...	...	...
		REDDI KÁPUWÁR	Do.	T. 9	...	...
				M. 5	...	...
				F. 4	...	...
		TIRMALE	Do.	T. 449	T. 167	T. 17
				M. 208	M. 76	M. 6
				F. 241	F. 91	F. 11
		VELLÁLÁR	Do.	T. 17	...	T. 17
				M. 9	...	M. 9
				F. 8	...	F. 8
		WALHER	Do.	T. 4	...	...
				M. 2	...	...
				F. 2	...	...
		YELAMÁ	Do.	T. 495	...	...
				M. 246	...	...
				F. 249	...	...
			Total Group 2(*a*)	*T. 1,122,893*	*T. 251,209*	*T. 259,979*
				M. 574,119	*M. 129,256*	*M. 132,522*
				F. 548,774	*F. 121,953*	*F. 127,457*
	2(*b*).—CATTLE BREEDERS AND GRAZIERS.	GAHLÁN	Hindu	T. 1	...	...
				M. 1	...	...
				...	...	...
		GAOLI (AHIR, GAOLÁN AND GAWÁRI)	Do.	T. 35,680	T. 11,760	T. 3,109
				M. 19,087	M. 6,468	M. 1,725
				F. 16,593	F. 5,292	F. 1,384
		Do. (AHIR AND GAWÁRI)	Musalman	T. 815	T. 617	T. 67
				M. 418	M. 316	M. 32
				F. 397	F. 301	F. 35
		Do.	Jain	T. 1	T. 1	...
				M. 1	M. 1	...
				...	...	...
		GAOLÁN (GAWÁRI)	Animistic	T. 771	T. 179	...
				M. 382	M. 88	...
				F. 389	F. 91	...
		GOLKAR	Hindu	T. 2,454	T. 1	T. 2
				M. 1,231	M. 1	M. 2
				F. 1,223	...	...
		KÁNADI	Do.	T. 1,447	T. 463	T. 138
				M. 727	M. 224	M. 73
				F. 720	F. 239	F. 65
			Total Group 2(*b*)	*T. 41,169*	*T. 13,021*	*T. 3,316*
				M. 21,847	*M. 7,098*	*M. 1,832*
				F. 19,322	*F. 5,923*	*F. 1,484*
	2(*c*).—FIELD LABOURERS.	DÁSARI	Hindu	T. 64	...	...
				M. 26	...	...
				F. 38	...	...
		KABIR	Do.	T. 5	T. 5	...
				M. 2	M. 2	...
				F. 3	F. 3	...
		KÁTEKAR	Do.	T. 1	...	...
				M. 1	...	...
				...	...	...
		KOL	Do.	T. 11	T. 10	...
				M. 5	M. 4	...
				F. 6	F. 6	...

Nationality or traditional Occupation—*contd.*

BY DISTRICT.				RAILWAY PASSENGERS, ETC.	DISTRICT AMRAOTI.			
ELLICHPUR.	BULDANA.	WUN.	BASIM.		AMRAOTI.	CHANDUR.	MORSI.	MURTAZAPUR.
Total, Males, and Females.	Total, Males, and Females.	Total, Males, and Females.	Total, Males, and Females.	Total, Males, and Females.	Total, Males, and Females.	Total, Males, and Females.	Total, Males, and Females.	Total, Males, and Females.
8	9	10	11	12	13	14	15	16
T. 5,141 M. 2,877 F. 2,264	T. 13,999 M. 7,115 F. 6,884	T. 3,141 M. 1,676 F. 1,465	T. 3,256 M. 1,727 F. 1,529	T. 1 M. 1 ...	T. 3,948 M. 2,182 F. 1,766	T. 5,013 M. 2,621 F. 2,392	T. 2,195 M. 1,155 F. 1,040	T. 1,599 M. 874 F. 725
... ...	... ...	... ...	... ...	... ...	... ...	... ...	... ...	... ...
... ...	... ...	... ...	... ...	... ...	T. 1 M. 1 ...	... ...	... ...	... ...
... ...	... ...	T. 9 M. 5 F. 4	... ...	... ...	... ...	... ...	... ...	... ...
... ...	T. 8 M. 2 F. 6	T. 253 M. 122 F. 131	T. 4 M. 2 F. 2	... ...	... ...	T. 72 M. 36 F. 36	... ...	T. 95 M. 40 F. 55
... ...	... ...	... ...	... ...	... ...	... ...	... ...	... ...	... ...
... ...	... ...	... ...	T. 4 M. 2 F. 2	... ...	... ...	... ...	... ...	... ...
... ...	... ...	T. 400 M. 194 F. 206	T. 95 M. 52 F. 43	... ...	... ...	... ...	... ...	... ...
T. 114,153 *M. 58,304* *F. 55,849*	*T. 223,080* *M. 113,293* *F. 109,787*	*T. 135,699* *M. 69,673* *F. 66,026*	*T. 138,730* *M. 71,036* *F. 67,694*	*T. 43* *M. 35* *F. 8*	*T. 57,966* *M. 29,897* *F. 28,069*	*T. 76,218* *M. 39,093* *F. 37,125*	*T. 70,495* *M. 36,177* *F. 34,318*	*T. 46,530* *M. 24,089* *F. 22,441*
T. 1 M. 1 ...	... ...	... ...	... ...	... ...	... ...	... ...	... ...	... ...
T. 4,490 M. 2,442 F. 2,048	T. 1,185 M. 598 F. 587	T. 11,817 M. 6,138 F. 5,679	T. 3,277 M. 1,690 F. 1,587	T. 42 M. 26 F. 16	T. 2,912 M. 1,662 F. 1,250	T. 5,217 M. 2,838 F. 2,379	T. 2,966 M. 1,558 F. 1,408	T. 665 M. 410 F. 255
T. 19 M. 8 F. 11	T. 72 M. 39 F. 33	... ...	T. 40 M. 23 F. 17	... ...	T. 11 M. 8 F. 3	... ...	... ...	T. 606 M. 308 F. 298
... ...	... ...	... ...	... ...	... ...	T. 1 M. 1 ...	... ...	... ...	... ...
T. 516 M. 256 F. 260	... ...	T. 76 M. 38 F. 38	... ...	... ...	T. 22 M. 11 F. 11	T. 22 M. 9 F. 13	T. 135 M. 68 F. 67	... ...
... ...	... ...	T. 2,405 M. 1,208 F. 1,197	T. 46 M. 20 F. 26	... ...	... ...	... ...	T. 1 M. 1 ...	... ...
T. 7 M. 4 F. 3	T. 10 M. 8 F. 2	T. 49 M. 24 F. 25	T. 780 M. 394 F. 386	... ...	T. 76 M. 35 F. 41	... ...	T. 4 M. 3 F. 1	T. 383 M. 186 F. 197
T. 5,033 *M. 2,711* *F. 2,322*	*T. 1,267* *M. 645* *F. 622*	*T. 14,347* *M. 7,408* *F. 6,939*	*T. 4,143* *M. 2,127* *F. 2,016*	*T. 42* *M. 26* *F. 16*	*T. 3,022* *M. 1,717* *F. 1,305*	*T. 5,239* *M. 2,847* *F. 2,392*	*T. 3,106* *M. 1,630* *F. 1,476*	*T. 1,654* *M. 904* *F. 750*
... ...	... ...	T. 14 M. 5 F. 9	T. 50 M. 21 F. 29	... ...	... ...	... ...	... ...	... ...
... ...	... ...	... ...	... ...	... ...	... ...	... ...	... ...	T. 5 M. 2 F. 3
T. 1 M. 1 ...	... ...	... ...	... ...	... ...	... ...	... ...	... ...	... ...
... ...	... ...	T. 1 M. 1 ...	... ...	... ...	... ...	... ...	T. 10 M. 4 F. 6	... ...

TABLE XVI.—Castes, Tribes, and Races, by

Name and Classification.				District Akola.					District
				Akola.	Akot.	Balapur.	Jalgaon.	Khamgaon.	Ellichpur.
Class.	Group.	Caste.	Religion.	Total, Males, and Females.	Total, Males, and Females.	Total, Males, and Females.	Total, Males, and Females.	Total, Males, and Females.	Total, Males, and Females.
17	18	19	20	21	22	23	24	25	26
A.—AGRICULTURAL—*contd.*	2.—Other Agricultural—*concld.*	Rajput	Hindu	T. 2,434 M. 1,298 F. 1,136	T. 2,302 M. 1,270 F. 1,032	T. 1,855 M. 943 F. 912	T. 2,906 M. 1,454 F. 1,452	T. 3,126 M. 1,657 F. 1,469	T. 2,716 M. 1,521 F. 1,195
	2(*a*).—Cultivators—*concld.*	Do.	Sikh	T. 14 M. 8 F. 6	...	...	...	...	...
		Reddi	Hindu	...	...	...	...	...	...
		Reedi Kápuwár	Do.	...	...	...	...	...	...
		Tirmale	Do.	...	...	...	...	T. 17 M. 6 F. 11	...
		Vellálár	Do.	T. 4 M. 3 F. 1	...	...	...	T. 13 M. 6 F. 7	...
		Walher	Do.	...	...	...	...	...	...
		Velamá	Do.	...	...	...	...	...	...
			Total Group 2(*a*)	*T. 53,514* *M. 27,606* *F. 25,908*	*T. 63,700* *M. 32,097* *F. 31,603*	*T. 43,283* *M. 22,018* *F. 21,265*	*T. 48,705* *M. 24,590* *F. 24,115*	*T. 50,777* *M. 26,211* *F. 24,566*	*T. 59,712* *M. 30,512* *F. 29,200*
	2(*b*).—Cattle Breeders and Graziers.	Gahlán	Hindu	...	...	...	...	...	...
		Gaoli (Ahir Gaolán and Gawári).	Do.	T. 1,457 M. 786 F. 671	T. 584 M. 344 F. 240	T. 696 M. 364 F. 332	T. 132 M. 86 F. 46	T. 240 M. 145 F. 95	T. 1,773 M. 1,014 F. 759
		Do. (Ahir and Gawári)	Musalman	T. 57 M. 30 F. 27	...	T. 1 ... F. 1	...	T. 9 M. 2 F. 7	T. 19 M. 8 F. 11
		Do.	Jain	...	...	...	...	...	...
		Gaolán (Gawári)	Animistic	...	...	...	...	...	T. 30 M. 15 F. 15
		Golkar	Hindu	T. 2 M. 2 ...	...	...	...	...	...
		Kánadi	Do.	...	T. 71 M. 38 F. 33	T. 37 M. 22 F. 15	T. 29 M. 12 F. 17	T. 1 M. 1 ...	...
			Total Group 2(*b*)	*T. 1,516* *M. 818* *F. 698*	*T. 655* *M. 382* *F. 273*	*T. 734* *M. 386* *F. 348*	*T. 161* *M. 98* *F. 63*	*T. 260* *M. 148* *F. 102*	*T. 1,822* *M. 1,037* *F. 785*
	2(*c*).—Field Labourers.	Dásari	Hindu	...	...	...	...	...	...
		Kabir	Do.	...	...	...	...	...	...
		Kátekar	Do.	...	...	...	...	...	...
		Kol	Do.	...	...	...	...	...	...

Nationality or traditional Occupation—*contd.*

ELLICHPUR.		DISTRICT BULDANA.			DISTRICT WUN.				DISTRICT BASIM.		
DARYAPUR.	MELGHAT.	CHIKHLI.	MALKAPUR.	MEHKAR.	YEOTMAL.	DARWHA.	KELAPUR.	WUN.	BASIM.	MANGRUL.	PUSAD.
Total, Males, and Females.	Total, Males, and Females.	Total, Males, and Females.	Total, Males, and Females.	Total, Males, and Females.	Total, Males, and Females.	Total, Males, and Females.	Total, Males, and Females.	Total, Males, and Females.	Total, Males, and Females.	Total, Males, and Females.	Total, Males, and Females.
27	28	29	30	31	32	33	34	35	36	37	38
T. 1,689 M. 956 F. 733	T. 736 M. 400 F. 336	T. 6,042 M. 3,056 F. 2,986	T. 6,622 M. 3,366 F. 3,256	T. 1,335 M. 693 F. 642	T. 955 M. 526 F. 429	T. 1,706 M. 891 F. 815	T. 312 M. 174 F. 138	T. 168 M. 85 F. 83	T. 1,714 M. 896 F. 818	T. 799 M. 429 F. 370	T. 743 M. 402 F. 341
... ...	... ...	... ...	... ...	... ...	... ...	... ...	... ...	... ...	... ...	... ...	... ...
... ...	... ...	... ...	... ...	... ...	... ...	... ...	... ...	... ...	... ...	... ...	... ...
... ...	... ...	... ...	... ...	... ...	... ...	... ...	T. 9 M. 5 F. 4	... ...	... ...	... ...	... ...
... ...	... ...	... ...	T. 2 M. 2 ...	T. 6 ... F. 6	T. 15 M. 6 F. 9	T. 238 M. 116 F. 122	... ...	... ...	T. 2 ... F. 2	T. 2 M. 2 ...	... ...
... ...	... ...	... ...	... ...	... ...	... ...	... ...	... ...	... ...	... ...	... ...	... ...
... ...	... ...	... ...	... ...	... ...	... ...	... ...	... ...	... ...	... ...	... ...	T. 4 M. 2 F. 2
... ...	... ...	... ...	... ...	... ...	... ...	... ...	T. 379 M. 186 F. 193	T. 21 M. 8 F. 13	... ...	... ...	T. 95 M. 52 F. 43
T. [illegible]347 M. 21,153 F. 26,194	T. 1,094 M. 639 F. 455	T. 72,925 M. 37,034 F. 35,891	T. 87,869 M. 44,575 F. 43,294	T. 62,286 M. 31,684 F. 30,602	T. 32,652 M. 16,821 F. 15,831	T. 40,752 M. 21,088 F. 19,664	T. 26,588 M. 13,553 F. 13,035	T. 35,707 M. 18,211 F. 17,496	T. 72,320 M. 37,101 F. 35,219	T. 30,650 M. 15,908 F. 14,742	T. 35,760 M. 18,027 F. 17,733
... ...	T. 1 M. 1 ...	... ...	... ...	... ...	... ...	... ...	... ...	... ...	... ...	... ...	... ...
T. 533 M. 342 F. 191	T. 2,184 M. 1,086 F. 1,098	T. 235 M. 123 F. 112	T. 902 M. 444 F. 458	T. 48 M. 31 F. 17	T. 6,193 M. 3,200 F. 2,993	T. 1,556 M. 848 F. 708	T. 3,143 M. 1,612 F. 1,531	T. 925 M. 478 F. 447	T. 248 M. 130 F. 118	T. 84 M. 56 F. 28	T. 2,945 M. 1,504 F. 1,441
... ...	... ...	... ...	T. 1 ... F. 1	T. 71 M. 39 F. 32	... ...	... ...	... ...	... ...	T. 1 M. 1 ...	T. 39 M. 22 F. 17	... ...
... ...	... ...	... ...	... ...	... ...	... ...	... ...	... ...	... ...	... ...	... ...	... ...
T. 1 ... F. 1	T. 485 M. 241 F. 244	... ...	... ...	... ...	T. 35 M. 18 F. 17	T. 1 M. 1 ...	T. 40 M. 19 F. 21	... ...	... ...	... ...	... ...
... ...	... ...	... ...	... ...	... ...	T. 8 M. 5 F. 3	T. 22 M. 12 F. 10	T. 1,931 M. 960 F. 971	T. 444 M. 231 F. 213	... ...	... ...	T. 46 M. 20 F. 26
T. 7 M. 4 F. 3	... ...	... ...	... ...	T. 10 M. 8 F. 2	T. 30 M. 15 F. 15	T. 19 M. 9 F. 10	... ...	... ...	T. 665 M. 334 F. 331	T. 115 M. 60 F. 55	... ...
T. 541 M. 346 F. 195	T. 2,670 M. 1,328 F. 1,342	T. 235 M. 123 F. 112	T. 903 M. 444 F. 459	T. 129 M. 78 F. 51	T. 6,266 M. 3,238 F. 3,028	T. 1,598 M. 870 F. 728	T. 5,114 M. 2,591 F. 2,523	T. 1,369 M. 709 F. 660	T. 914 M. 465 F. 449	T. 238 M. 138 F. 100	T. 2,991 M. 1,524 F. 1,467
... ...	... ...	... ...	... ...	... ...	... ...	... ...	... ...	T. 14 M. 5 F. 9	... ...	... ...	T. 50 M. 21 F. 29
... ...	... ...	... ...	... ...	... ...	... ...	... ...	... ...	... ...	... ...	... ...	... ...
... ...	T. 1 M 1 ...	... ...	... ...	... ...	... ...	... ...	... ...	... ...	... ...	... ...	... ...
... ...	... ...	... ...	... ...	... ...	... ...	... ...	T. 1 M. 1 ...	... ...	... ...	... ...	... ...

TABLE XVI.—Castes, Tribes, and Races, by

Name and Classification.				Provincial Total.	Distribution.	
					Amraoti.	Akola.
Class.	Group.	Caste.	Religion.	Total, Males, and Females.	Total, Males, and Females.	Total, Males, and Females.
1	2	3	4	5	6	7
A.—AGRICULTURAL—*contd.*	2(*c*).—Field Labourers—*contd.*	Lugáwár	Hindu	T. 5 M. 4 F. 1	T. 5 M. 4 F. 1	... ...
		Pube	Do.	T. 2 M. 2 ...	... ...	... ...
			Total Group 2(*c*)	*T.* *88* *M.* *40* *F.* *48*	*T.* *20* *M.* *10* *F.* *10*	... ...
	4.—Forest and Hill Tribes.	Andh	Hindu	T. 43,297 M. 21,671 F. 21,626	T. 113 M. 55 F. 58	T. 3,518 M. 1,728 F. 1,790
		Do.	Animistic	T. 305 M. 165 F. 140	... ...	... ...
		Arakh	Hindu	T. 235 M. 128 F. 107	T. 209 M. 109 F. 100	T. 21 M. 17 F. 4
		Do.	Animistic	T. 18 M. 9 F. 9	T. 18 M. 9 F. 9	... ...
		Bhil	Hindu	T. 3,483 M. 1,735 F. 1,748	T. 6 M. 3 F. 3	T. 178 M. 92 F. 86
		Do.	Musalman	T. 1,928 M. 950 F. 978	T. 1 M. 1 ...	T. 952 M. 458 F. 494
		Do.	Animistic	T. 783 M. 405 F. 378	T. 10 M. 4 F. 6	T. 23 M. 16 F. 7
		Bijhad	Hindu	T. 5 M. 2 F. 3	T. 5 M. 2 F. 3	... ...
		Bopchi	Do.	T. 613 M. 318 F. 295	M. 613 M. 318 F. 295	... ...
		Gond	Do.	T. 9,058 M. 4,850 F. 4,208	T. 2,746 M. 1,456 F. 1,290	T. 1,448 M. 802 F. 646
		Do.	Animistic	T. 71,869 M. 35,918 F. 35,951	T. 16,108 M. 8,078 F. 8,030	T. 252 M. 142 F. 110
		Gorwán	Hindu	T. 13 M. 11 F. 2	... ...	... ...
		Do.	Animistic	T. 148 M. 73 F. 75	... ...	... ...
		Kolám	Hindu	T. 954 M. 498 F. 456	T. 1 M. 1 ...	... ...
		Do.	Animistic	T. 16,460 M. 8,268 F. 8,192	T. 97 M. 56 F. 41	... ...
		Korku	Hindu	T. 379 M. 193 F. 186	T. 40 M. 21 F. 19	T. 278 M. 141 F. 137
		Do.	Animistic	T. 34,602 M. 17,522 F. 17,080	T. 594 M. 294 F. 300	T. 1,076 M. 553 F. 523
		Koyelá Bhute	Do.	T. 10 M. 5 F. 5	... ...	... ...

Nationality or traditional Occupation—*contd.*

BY DISTRICT.				RAILWAY PASSENGERS, ETC.	DISTRICT AMRAOTI.			
ELLICHPUR.	BULDANA.	WUN.	BASIM.		AMRAOTI.	CHANDUR.	MORSI.	MURTAZAPUR.
Total, Males, and Females.	Total, Males, and Females.	Total, Males, and Females.	Total, Males, and Females.	Total, Males, and Females.	Total, Males, and Females.	Total, Males, and Females.	Total, Males, and Females.	Total, Males, and Females.
8	9	10	11	12	13	14	15	16
...	...	...	...	...	...	...	...	T. 5 M. 4 F. 1
T. 2 M. 2	...	...	...	...	...	...	...	...
T. 3 *M.* 3	...	*T.* 15 *M.* 6 *F.* 9	*T.* 50 *M.* 21 *F.* 29	...	...	...	*T.* 10 *M.* 4 *F.* 6	*T.* 10 *M.* 6 *F.* 4
T. 1 F. 1	T. 4,053 M. 1,993 F. 2,060	T. 12,517 M. 6,175 F. 6,342	T. 23,095 M. 11,720 F. 11,375	...	T. 1 M. 1	T. 8 M. 6 F. 2	...	T. 104 M. 48 F. 56
...	...	T. 117 M. 64 F. 53	T. 188 M. 101 F. 87	...	...	...	...	...
T. 5 M. 2 F. 3	...	...	...	...	T. 43 M. 23 F. 20	...	T. 165 M. 85 F. 80	T. 1 M. 1
...	...	...	...	...	...	...	T. 18 M. 9 F. 9	...
T. 10 M. 6 F. 4	T. 774 M. 387 F. 387	T. 599 M. 298 F. 301	T. 1,916 M. 949 F. 967	...	...	T. 1 F. 1	...	T. 5 M. 3 F. 2
T. 818 *M.* 409 *F.* 409	T. 157 M. 82 F. 75	...	...	...	T. 1 M. 1	...	...	...
T. 42 M. 22 F. 20	T. 6 M. 4 F. 2	T. 589 M. 306 F. 283	T. 113 M. 53 F. 60	...	...	T. 10 M. 4 F. 6	...	...
...	...	...	...	...	...	T. 5 M. 2 F. 3	...	...
...	...	...	...	...	T. 2 M. 1 F. 1	T. 5 M. 4 F. 1	T. 606 M. 313 F. 293	...
T. 1,044 M. 608 F. 436	T. 256 M. 128 F. 128	T. 2,734 M. 1,424 F. 1,310	T. 829 M. 431 F. 398	T. 1 M. 1	T. 798 M. 426 F. 372	T. 982 M. 525 F. 457	T. 282 M. 144 F. 138	T. 684 M. 361 F. 323
T. 3,247 M. 1,637 F. 1,610	T. 1 F. 1	T. 52,150 M. 26,010 F. 26,140	T. 108 M. 51 F. 57	T. 3 F. 3	T. 1,512 M. 749 F. 763	T. 6,527 M. 3,291 F. 3,236	T. 7,771 M. 3,878 F. 3,893	T. 298 M. 160 F. 138
T. 13 M. 11 F. 2	...	...	...	...	...	...	...	...
T. 142 M. 70 F. 72	...	T. 6 M. 3 F. 3	...	...	...	...	...	...
...	...	T. 953 M. 497 F. 456	...	...	...	T. 1 M. 1	...	...
T. 467 M. 234 F. 233	...	T. 15,896 M. 7,978 F. 7,918	...	...	T. 1 M. 1	T. 96 M. 55 F. 41	...	...
T. 58 M. 30 F. 28	T. 2 M. 1 F. 1	T. 1 F. 1	...	...	T. 8 M. 3 F. 5	...	T. 32 M. 18 F. 14	...
T. 32,803 M. 16,610 F. 16,193	...	T. 129 M. 65 F. 64	...	...	T. 221 M. 109 F. 112	T. 101 M. 44 F. 57	T. 272 M. 141 F. 131	...
...	...	T. 10 M. 5 F. 5	...	...	...	...	...	...

TABLE XVI—Castes, Tribes, and Races, by

Name and Classification.				District Akola.					District
				Akola.	Akot.	Balapur.	Jalgaon.	Khamgaon.	Ellichpur.
Class.	Group.	Caste.	Religion.	Total, Males, and Females.	Total, Males, and Females.	Total, Males, and Females.	Total, Males, and Females.	Total, Males, and Females.	Total, Males, and Females,
17	18	19	20	21	22	23	24	15	26
A.—Agricultural—*contd.*	2(*c*).—Field Labourers—*contd.*	Lugáwár	Hindu	...	...	...	...	...	...
		Pube	Do.	...	...	...	...	...	...
			Total Group 2(*c*).	...	...	...	...	...	...
	4.—Forest and Hill Tribes.	Andh	Hindu	T. 1,075 M. 543 F. 532	...	T. 2,440 M. 1,182 F. 1,258	T. 1 M. 1 ...	T. 2 M. 2 ...	...
		Do.	Animistic	...	...	...	...	...	...
		Arakh	Hindu	T. 1 M. 1 ...	T. 19 M. 15 F. 4	...	T. 1 M. 1 ...	...	T. 4 M. 1 F. 3
		Do.	Animistic	...	...	...	...	...	...
		Bhil	Hindu	T. 5 M. 4 F. 1	T. 13 M. 10 F. 3	T. 43 M. 18 F. 25	T. 80 M. 39 F. 41	T. 37 M. 21 F. 16	T. 1 ... F. 1
		Do.	Musalman	...	T. 138 M. 62 F. 76	...	T. 814 M. 396 F. 418	...	T. 81 M. 41 F. 40
		Do.	Animistic	T. 9 M. 9 ...	T. 11 M. 6 F. 5	...	T. 3 M. 1 F. 2	...	...
		Bijhad	Hindu	...	...	...	...	...	...
		Borchi	Do.	...	...	...	...	...	...
		Gond	Do.	T. 387 M. 214 F. 173	T. 443 M. 251 F. 192	T. 204 M. 108 F. 96	T. 389 M. 214 F. 175	T. 25 M. 15 F. 10	T. 614 M. 378 F. 236
		Do.	Animistic	T. 134 M. 71 F. 63	T. 82 M. 46 F. 36	T. 8 M. 3 F. 5	T. 8 M. 6 F. 2	T. 20 M. 16 F. 4	T. 943 M. 464 F. 479
		Gorwán	Hindu	...	...	...	...	...	...
		Do.	Animistic	...	...	...	...	...	...
		Kolám	Hindu	...	...	...	...	...	...
		Do.	Animistic	...	...	...	...	...	...
		Korku	Hindu	...	T. 4 M. 4 ...	...	T. 274 M. 137 F. 137	...	T. 9 M. 3 F. 6
		Do.	Animistic	...	T. 618 M. 322 F. 296	...	T. 458 M. 231 F. 227	...	T. 1,233 M. 651 F. 582
		Koyelá Bhute	Do.	...	...	...	...	...	...

Nationality or traditional Occupation—*contd.*

ELLICHPUR.		DISTRICT BULDANA.			DISTRICT WUN.				DISTRICT BASIM.		
DARYAPUR.	MELGHAT.	CHIKHLI.	MALKAPUR.	MEHKAR.	YEOTMAL.	DARWHA.	KELAPUR.	WUN.	BASIM.	MANGRUL.	PUSAD.
Total, Males, and Females.	Total, Males, and Females.	Total, Males, and Females.	Total, Males, and Females.	Total, Males, and Females.	Total, Males, and Females.	Total, Males, and Females.	Total, Males, and Females.	Total, Males, and Females.	Total, Males, and Females.	Total, Males, and Females.	Total, Males, and Females.
27	28	29	30	31	32	33	34	35	36	37	38
...	...	...	...	...	...	...	...	...	...	...	...
...	T. 2 M. 2	...	...	...	...	...	...	...	...	...	...
...	*T. 3* *M. 3*	...	...	...	...	...	*T. 1* *M. 1*	*T. 14* *M. 5* *F. 9*	...	...	*T. 50* *M. 21* *F. 29*
T. 1 F. 1	...	T. 642 M. 306 F. 336	...	T. 3,411 M. 1,687 F. 1,724	T. 2,634 M. 1,326 F. 1,308	T. 9,741 M. 4,780 F. 4,961	T. 142 M. 69 F. 73	...	T. 6,746 M. 3,384 F. 3,362	T. 5,015 M. 2,532 F. 2,483	T. 11,334 M. 5,804 F. 5,530
...	...	...	...	...	T. 117 M. 64 F. 53	...	...	...	...	...	T. 188 M. 101 F. 87
T. 1 M. 1	...	...	...	...	...	...	...	...	...	...	...
...	...	...	...	...	...	...	...	...	...	...	...
T. 1 M. 1	T. 8 M. 5 F. 3	T. 494 M. 251 F. 243	T. 245 M. 119 F. 126	T. 35 M. 17 F. 18	...	T. 494 M. 248 F. 246	T. 105 M. 50 F. 55	...	T. 34 M. 13 F. 21	T. 133 M. 67 F. 66	T. 1,749 M. 869 F. 880
T. 50 *M. 23* *F. 27*	T. 687 M. 345 F. 342	T. 102 M. 54 F. 48	T. 54 M. 27 F. 27	T. 1 M. 1	...	...	...	...	...	...	...
T. 10 M. 5 F. 5	T. 32 M. 17 F. 15	T. 6 M. 4 F. 2	...	...	T. 1 M. 1	T. 588 M. 305 F. 283	...	...	...	...	T. 113 M. 53 F. 60
...	...	...	...	...	...	...	...	...	...	...	...
...	...	...	...	...	...	...	...	...	...	...	...
T. 218 M. 109 F. 109	T. 212 M. 121 F. 91	T. 73 M. 35 F. 38	T. 9 M. 5 F. 4	T. 174 M. 88 F. 86	T. 568 M. 302 F. 266	T. 840 M. 444 F. 396	T. 1,015 M. 513 F. 502	T. 311 M. 165 F. 146	T. 66 M. 38 F. 28	T. 348 M. 183 F. 165	T. 415 M. 210 F. 205
T. 196 M. 100 F. 96	T. 2,108 M. 1,073 F. 1,035	T. 1 F. 1	...	...	T. 13,958 M. 6,964 F. 6,994	T. 7,274 M. 3,655 F. 3,619	T. 20,501 M. 10,208 F. 10,293	T. 10,417 M. 5,183 F. 5,234	...	T. 39 M. 17 F. 22	T. 69 M. 34 F. 35
...	T. 13 M. 11 F. 2	...	...	...	...	...	...	...	...	...	...
...	T. 142 M. 70 F. 72	...	...	...	...	...	T. 6 M. 3 F. 3	...	...	...	...
...	...	...	...	...	T. 113 M. 62 F. 51	T. 707 M. 364 F. 343	T. 132 M. 70 F. 62	T. 1 M. 1	...	...	...
...	T. 467 M. 234 F. 233	...	...	...	T. 8,467 M. 4,290 F. 4,177	T. 231 M. 126 F. 105	T. 4,523 M. 2,243 F. 2,280	T. 2,675 M. 1,319 F. 1,356	...	...	...
T. 1 M. 1	T. 48 M. 26 F. 22	T. 2 M. 1 F. 1	...	...	T. 1 F. 1	...	...	...	...	...	...
T. 7 M. 5 F. 2	T. 31,563 M. 15,954 F. 15,609	...	...	...	T. 1 M. 1	T. 1 F. 1	T. 72 M. 33 F. 39	T. 55 M. 31 F. 24	...	...	...
...	...	...	...	...	T. 10 M. 5 F. 5	...	...	...	...	...	...

TABLE XVI.—Castes, Tribes, and Races, by

Name and Classification.				Provincial Total.	Distribution	
					Amraoti.	Akola.
Class.	Group.	Caste.	Religion.	Total, Males, and Females.	Total, Males, and Females.	Total, Males, and Females.
1	2	3	4	5	6	7
A.—Agricultural—*contd.*	4.—Forest and Hill Tribes—*contd.*	Lajjhad	Hindu	T. 1,763 M. 851 F. 912	T. 1,241 M. 605 F. 636	T. 9 M. 7 F. 2
		Do.	Animistic	T. 97 M. 54 F. 43	T. 34 M. 19 F. 15	... ...
		Marāl	Hindu	T. 410 M. 213 F. 197	T. 9 M. 7 F. 2	... ...
		Minā	Do.	T. 12 M. 5 F. 7	... ...	T. 2 M. 1 F. 1
		Moghe	Hindu	T. 2 M. 2 ...	T. 1 M. 1 ...	... ...
		Do.	Animistic	T. 217 M. 124 F. 93	... ...	... ...
		Nihāl	Hindu	T. 104 M. 51 F. 53	T. 2 M. 1 F. 1	T. 40 M. 16 F. 24
		Do.	Animistic	T. 2,201 M. 1,101 F. 1,100	... ...	T. 194 M. 102 F. 92
		Pankā	Hindu	T. 1 M. 1 ...	... ...	... ...
		Pardhān	Hindu	T. 3,766 M. 1,899 F. 1,867	T. 611 M. 305 F. 306	T. 438 M. 235 F. 203
		Do.	Animistic	T. 9,170 M. 4,614 F. 4,556	T. 271 M. 140 F. 131	... ...
			Total Group 4	*T. 201,903* *M. 101,636* *F. 100,267*	*T. 22,730* *M. 11,485* *F. 11,245*	*T. 8,429* *M. 4,310* *F. 4,119*
B.—Professional.	5.—Priests	Brāhman	Hindu	T. 71,272 M. 41,772 F. 29,500	T. 18,522 M. 10,979 F 7,543	T. 18,741 M. 11,071 F. 7,670
		Do.	Jain	T. 36 M. 24 F. 12	T. 11 M. 8 F. 3	T. 2 M. 2 ...
		Jangam	Hindu	T. 1,882 M. 988 F. 894	T. 531 M. 285 F. 246	T. 147 M. 76 F. 71
		Jati	Jain	T. 17 M. 17 ...	... ...	T. 12 M. 12 ...
		Do.	Hindu	T. 6 M. 6 ...	T. 5 M. 5 ...	T. 1 M 1 ...
		Mullā	Musalman	T. 1 M. 1 ...	T. 1 M. 1 ...	... ...
		Pirzāde	Do.	T. 6 M. 5 F. 1	... ...	... ...
			Total Group 5	*T. 73,220* *M. 42,813* *F. 30,407*	*T. 19,070* *M. 11,278* *F. 7,792*	*T. 18,908* *M. 11,162* *F. 7,741*
	6.—Devotees	Aghori	Hindu	T. 10 M. 6 F. 4	T. 6 M. 3 F. 3	... ...

Nationality or traditional Occupation—*contd.*

BY DISTRICT.				RAILWAY PASSENGERS, ETC.	DISTRICT AMRAOTI.			
ELLICHPUR.	BULDANA.	WUN.	BASIM.		AMRAOTI.	CHANDUR.	MORSI.	MURTAZAPUR.
Total, Males, and Females.	Total, Males, and Females.	Total, Males, and Females.	Total, Males, and Females.	Total, Males, and Females.	Total, Males, and Females.	Total, Males, and Females.	Total, Males, and Females.	Total, Males, and Females.
8	9	10	11	12	13	14	15	16
T. 443 M. 208 F. 235	... ...	T. 18 M. 5 F. 13	T. 52 M. 26 F. 26	... ...	T. 17 M. 10 F. 7	T. 150 M. 70 F. 80	T. 1,046 M. 509 F. 537	T. 28 M. 16 F. 12
T. 55 M. 31 F. 24	... ...	T. 8 M. 4 F. 4	... ...	... ...	... ...	... ...	T. 34 M. 19 F. 15	... ...
... ...	... ...	T. 394 M. 201 F. 193	T. 7 M. 5 F. 2	... ...	T. 7 M. 5 F. 2	T. 1 M. 1 ...	T. 1 M. 1 ...	... ...
... ...	T. 10 M. 4 F. 6	... ...	... ...	... ...	... ...	... ...	... ...	... ...
T. 1 M. 1 ...	... ...	... ...	... ...	... ...	T. 1 M. 1 ...	... ...	... ...	... ...
T. 217 M. 124 F. 93	... ...	... ...	... ...	... ...	... ...	... ...	... ...	... ...
T. 62 M. 34 F. 28	... ...	... ...	... ...	... ...	... ...	... ...	T. 2 M. 1 F. 1	... ...
T. 2,007 M. 999 F. 1,008	... ...	... ...	... ...	... ...	... ...	... ...	... ...	... ...
... ...	... ...	T. 1 M. 1 ...	... ...	... ...	... ...	... ...	... ...	... ...
T. 20 M. 10 F. 10	... ...	T. 2,665 M. 1,331 F. 1,334	T. 32 M. 18 F. 14	... ...	T. 3 M. 2 F. 1	T. 607 M. 302 F. 305	T. 1 M. 1 ...	... ...
T. 98 M. 47 F. 51	... ...	T. 8,761 M. 4,407 F. 4,354	T. 40 M. 20 F. 20	... ...	... ...	T. 144 M. 78 F. 66	T. 127 M. 62 F. 65	... ...
T. 41,553 *M. 21,093* *F. 20,460*	*T. 5,259* *M. 2,599* *F. 2,660*	*T. 97,548* *M. 48,774* *F. 48,774*	*T. 26,380* *M. 13,374* *F. 13,006*	*T. 4* *M. 1* *F. 3*	*T. 2,615* *M. 1,332* *F. 1,283*	*T. 8,638* *M. 4,383* *F. 4,255*	*T. 10,357* *M. 5,181* *F. 5,176*	*T. 1,120* *M. 589* *F. 531*
T. 7,900 M. 4,855 F. 3,045	T. 11,645 M. 6,417 F. 5,228	T. 6,536 M. 3,913 F. 2,623	T. 7,876 M. 4,493 F. 3,383	T. 52 M. 44 F. 8	T. 7,584 M. 4,477 F. 3,107	T. 4,365 M. 2,676 F. 1,689	T. 2,946 M. 1,664 F. 1,282	T. 3,627 M. 2,162 F. 1,465
T. 2 M. 1 F. 1	T. 18 M. 10 F. 8	T. 3 M. 3 ...	... ...	... ...	... ...	T. 7 M. 4 F. 3	T. 4 M. 4 ...	... ...
T. 30 M. 14 F. 16	T. 183 M. 102 F. 81	T. 373 M. 184 F. 189	T. 618 M. 327 F. 291	... ...	T. 137 M. 86 F. 51	T. 173 M. 85 F. 88	T. 144 M. 75 F. 69	T. 77 M. 39 F. 38
T. 1 M. 1 ...	T. 3 M. 3 ...	... ...	T. 1 M. 1 ...	... ...	... ...	... ...	... ...	... ...
... ...	... ...	... ...	... ...	... ...	T. 4 M. 4 ...	... ...	T. 1 M. 1 ...	... ...
... ...	... ...	... ...	... ...	... ...	... ...	... ...	... ...	T. 1 M. 1 ...
T. 6 M. 5 F. 1	... ...	... ...	... ...	... ...	... ...	... ...	... ...	... ...
T. 7,989 *M. 4,876* *F. 3,063*	*T. 11,849* *M. 6,532* *F. 5,317*	*T. 6,912* *M. 4,100* *F. 2,812*	*T. 8,495* *M. 4,821* *F. 3,674*	*T. 52* *M. 44* *F. 8*	*T. 7,725* *M. 4,567* *F. 3,158*	*T. 4,545* *M. 2,765* *F. 1,780*	*T. 3,095* *M. 1,744* *F. 1,351*	*T. 3,705* *M. 2,202* *F. 1,503*
... ...	... ...	T. 4 M. 3 F. 1	... ...	... ...	... ...	T. 6 M. 3 F. 3	... ...	... ...

TABLE XVI.—Castes, Tribes, and Races, by

Name and Classification.				District Akola.					District
				Akola.	Akot.	Balapur.	Jalgaon.	Khamgaon.	Ellichpur.
Class.	Group.	Caste.	Religion.	Total, Males, and Females.	Total, Males, and Females.	Total, Males, and Females.	Total, Males, and Females.	Total, Males, and Females.	Total, Males, and Females.
17	18	19	20	21	22	23	24	25	26
A.—Agricultural—*contd.*	4.—Forest and Hill Tribes—*contd.*	Lajjhad	Hindu	... ...	T. 9 M. 7 F. 2	... ...	... ...	... ...	T. 329 M. 148 F. 181
		Do.	Animistic	... ...	... ...	... ...	... ...	... ...	... ...
		Marál	Hindu	... ...	... ...	... ...	... ...	... ...	... ...
		Miná	Do.	... ...	... ...	... ...	... ...	T. 2 M. 1 F. 1	... ...
		Moghe	Hindu	... ...	... ...	... ...	... ...	... ...	... ...
		Do.	Animistic	... ...	... ...	... ...	... ...	... ...	... ...
		Nihál	Hindu	... ...	... ...	... ...	T. 40 M. 16 F. 24	... ...	T. 9 M. 3 F. 6
		Do.	Animistic	... ...	T. 74 M. 41 F. 33	... ...	T. 120 M. 61 F. 59	... ...	... ...
		Panká	Hindu	... ...	... ...	... ...	... ...	... ...	... ...
		Pardhán	Do.	T. 5 M. 4 F. 1	T. 433 M. 231 F. 202	... ...	... ...	... ...	T. 6 M. 2 F. 4
		Do.	Animistic	... ...	... ...	... ...	... ...	... ...	T. 7 M. 3 F. 4
			Total Group 4	*T. 1,616* *M. 846* *F. 770*	*T. 1,844* *M. 995* *F. 849*	*T. 2,695* *M. 1,311* *F. 1,384*	*T. 2,188* *M. 1,103* *F. 1,085*	*T. 86* *M. 55* *T. 31*	*T. 3,236* *M. 1,694* *F. 1,542*
B.—Professional	5.—Priests	Bráhman	Hindu	T. 4,550 M. 2,690 F. 1,860	T. 4,963 M. 2,937 F. 2,026	T. 2,300 M. 1,297 F. 1,003	T. 3,106 M. 1,764 F. 1,342	T. 3,822 M. 2,383 F. 1,439	T. 4,811 M. 2,929 F. 1,882
		Do.	Jain	... ...	T. 1 M. 1 ...	... ...	... ...	T. 1 M. 1 ...	T. 2 M. 1 F. 1
		Jangam	Hindu	T. 19 M. 13 F. 6	T. 31 M. 14 F. 17	T. 40 M. 21 F. 19	T. 24 M. 11 F. 13	T. 33 M. 17 F. 16	T. 22 M. 11 F. 11
		Jati	Jain	... ...	... ...	T. 11 M. 11 ...	... ...	T. 1 M. 1 ...	T. 1 M. 1 ...
		Do.	Hindu	... ...	... ...	T. 1 M. 1 ...	... ...	... ...	... ...
		Mullá	Musalman	... ...	... ...	... ...	... ...	... ...	... ...
		Pirzáde	Do.	... ...	... ...	... ...	... ...	... ...	T. 6 M. 5 F. 1
			Total Group 5	*T. 4,569* *M. 2,703* *F. 1,866*	*T. 4,995* *M. 2,952* *F. 2,043*	*T. 2,352* *M. 1,330* *F. 1,022*	*T. 3,130* *M. 1,775* *F. 1,355*	*T. 3,857* *M. 2,402* *F. 1,455*	*T. 4,842* *M. 2,947* *F. 1,895*
	6.—Devotees	Aghori	Hindu	... ...	... ...	... ...	... ...	... ...	... ...

Nationality or traditional Occupation—*contd.*

ELLICHPUR.		DISTRICT BULDANA.			DISTRICT WUN.				DISTRICT BASIM.		
DARYAPUR.	MELGHAT.	CHIKHLI.	MALKAPUR.	MEHKAR.	YEOTMAL.	DARWHA.	KELAPUR.	WUN.	BASIM.	MANGRUL.	PUSAD.
Total, Males, and Females.	Total, Males, and Females.	Total, Males, and Females.	Total, Males, and Females.	Total, Males, and Females.	Total, Males, and Females.	Total, Males, and Females.	Total, Males, and Females.	Total, Males, and Females.	Total, Males, and Females.	Total, Males, and Females.	Total, Males, and Females.
27	28	29	30	31	32	33	34	35	36	37	38
T. 3 M. 2 F. 1	T. 111 M. 58 F. 53	... ...	... ...	... ...	T. 3 M. 1 F. 2	T. 6 M. 2 F. 4	T. 9 M. 2 F. 7	... ...	... ...	T. 52 M. 26 F. 26	... ...
... ...	T. 55 M. 31 F. 24	... ...	... ...	... ...	T. 8 M. 4 F. 4	... ...	... ...	... ...	... ...	... ...	... ...
... ...	... ...	... ...	... ...	... ...	... ...	T. 18 M. 11 F. 7	T. 17 M. 10 F. 7	T. 359 M. 180 F. 179	T. 2 M. 2 ...	... ...	T. 5 M. 3 F. 2
... ...	... ...	T. 10 M. 4 F. 6	... ...	... ...	... ...	... ...	... ...	... ...	... ...	... ...	... ...
... ...	T. 1 M. 1 ...	... ...	... ...	... ...	... ...	... ...	... ...	... ...	... ...	... ...	... ...
... ...	T. 217 M. 124 F. 93	... ...	... ...	... ...	... ...	... ...	... ...	... ...	... ...	... ...	... ...
... ...	T. 53 M. 31 F. 22	... ...	... ...	... ...	... ...	... ...	... ...	... ...	... ...	... ...	... ...
... ...	T. 2,007 M. 999 F. 1,008	... ...	... ...	... ...	... ...	... ...	... ...	... ...	... ...	... ...	... ...
... ...	... ...	... ...	... ...	... ...	... ...	T. 1 M. 1 ...	... ...	... ...	... ...	... ...	... ...
... ...	T. 14 M. 8 F. 6	... ...	... ...	... ...	T. 479 M. 236 F. 243	T. 303 M. 146 F. 157	T. 1,722 M. 871 F. 851	T. 161 M. 78 F. 83	... ...	... ...	T. 32 M. 18 F. 14
... ...	T. 91 M. 44 F. 47	... ...	... ...	... ...	T. 1,734 M. 875 F. 859	T. 755 M. 376 F. 379	T. 2,608 M. 1,317 F. 1,291	T. 3,664 M. 1,839 F. 1,825	... ...	... ...	T. 40 M. 20 F. 20
T. 488 *M. 247* *F. 241*	*T. 37,829* *M. 19,152* *F. 18,677*	*T. 1,330* *M. 655* *F. 675*	*T. 308* *M. 151* *F. 157*	*T. 3,621* *M. 1,793* *F. 1,828*	*T. 28,094* *M. 14,131* *F. 13,963*	*T. 20,959* *M. 10,458* *F. 10,501*	*T. 30,852* *M. 15,389* *F. 15,463*	*T. 17,643* *M. 8,796* *F. 8,847*	*T. 6,848* *M. 3,437* *F. 3,411*	*T. 5,587* *M. 2,825* *F. 2,762*	*T. 13,945* *M. 7,112* *F. 6,833*
T. 2,809 M. 1,683 F. 1,126	T. 280 M. 243 F. 37	T. 4,326 M. 2,309 F. 2,017	T. 3,839 M. 2,143 F. 1,696	T. 3,480 M. 1,965 F. 1,515	T. 2,194 M. 1,395 F. 799	T. 2,122 M. 1,270 F. 852	T. 1,101 M. 670 F. 431	T. 1,119 M. 578 F. 541	T. 3,917 M. 2,258 F. 1,659	T. 1,121 M. 669 F. 452	T. 2,838 M. 1,566 F. 1,272
... ...	... ...	... ...	T. 2 M. 2 ...	T. 16 M. 8 F. 8	T. 3 M. 3 ...	... ...	... ...	... ...	... ...	... ...	... ...
T. 8 M. 3 F. 5	... ...	T. 49 M. 24 F. 25	T. 14 M. 8 F. 6	T. 120 M. 70 F. 50	T. 63 M. 36 F. 27	T. 121 M. 57 F. 64	T. 88 M. 44 F. 44	T. 101 M. 47 F. 54	T. 188 M. 96 F. 92	T. 32 M. 17 F. 15	T. 398 M. 214 F. 184
... ...	... ...	... ...	... ...	T. 3 M. 3 ...	... ...	... ...	... ...	... ...	T. 1 M. 1 ...	... ...	... ...
... ...	... ...	... ...	... ...	... ...	... ...	... ...	... ...	... ...	... ...	... ...	... ...
... ...	... ...	... ...	... ...	... ...	... ...	... ...	... ...	... ...	... ...	... ...	... ...
... ...	... ...	... ...	... ...	... ...	... ...	... ...	... ...	... ...	... ...	... ...	... ...
T. 2,817 *M. 1,686* *F. 1,131*	*T. 280* *M. 243* *F. 37*	*T. 4,375* *M. 2,333* *F. 2,042*	*T. 3,855* *M. 2,153* *F. 1,702*	*T. 3,619* *M. 2,046* *F. 1,573*	*T. 2,260* *M. 1,434* *F. 826*	*T. 2,243* *M. 1,327* *F. 916*	*T. 1,189* *M. 714* *F. 475*	*T. 1,220* *M. 625* *F. 595*	*T. 4,106* *M. 2,355* *F. 1,751*	*T. 1,153* *M. 686* *F. 467*	*T. 3,236* *M. 1,780* *F. 1,456*
... ...	... ...	... ...	... ...	... ...	... ...	T. 2 M. 2 ...	T. 2 M. 1 F. 1	... ...	... ...	... ...	... ...

TABLE XVI.—Castes, Tribes, and Races, by

Name and Classification.				Provincial Total.	Distribution: Amraoti.	Distribution: Akola.
Class.	Group.	Caste.	Religion.	Total, Males, and Females.	Total, Males, and Females.	Total, Males, and Females.
1	2	3	4	5	6	7
B.—PROFESSIONAL—*contd.*	6.—Devotees—*contd.*	Aughad	Hindu	T. 5	...	...
				M. 2	...	...
				F. 3	...	...
		Báragi	Do.	T. 1,436	T. 477	T. 209
				M. 858	M. 267	M. 147
				F. 578	F. 210	F. 62
		Bharádi	Do.	T. 1,452	T. 640	T. 96
				M. 742	M. 333	M. 45
				T. 710	F. 307	F. 51
		Fakir	Musalman	T. 7,190	T. 1,594	T. 1,880
				M. 3,779	M. 846	M. 989
				F. 3,411	F. 748	F. 891
		Gosáwi	Hindu	T. 12,152	T. 3,239	T. 2,257
				M. 6,890	M. 1,832	M. 1,342
				F. 5,262	F. 1,407	F. 915
		Jogi	Do.	T. 2,177	T. 200	T. 63
				M. 1,068	M. 94	M. 39
				F. 1,109	F. 106	F. 24
		Mánbháo	Do.	T. 3,559	T. 1,095	T. 850
				M. 1,904	M. 590	M. 462
				F. 1,655	F. 505	F. 388
		Nának Shái	Do.	T. 22	T. 13	T. 6
				M. 15	M. 9	M. 3
				F. 7	F. 4	F. 3
		Náth	Do.	T. 2,973	T. 611	T. 1,290
				M. 1,532	M. 324	M. 662
				F. 1,441	F. 287	F. 628
		Sádhu	Do.	T. 27	T. 1	T. 2
				M. 16	M. 1	M. 2
				F. 11	...	...
		Sanyáshi	Do.	T. 28	T. 8	T. 4
				M. 21	M. 8	M. 4
				F. 7	...	...
		Swámi	Do.	T. 3	T. 1	T. 2
				M. 2	M. 1	M. 1
				F. 1	...	F. 1
		Udási	Do.	T. 109	T. 39	T. 17
				M. 75	M. 25	M. 14
				F. 34	F. 14	F. 3
		Do.	Sikh	T. 2	...	T. 2
				M. 1	...	M. 1
				F. 1	...	F. 1
		Virbhadra	Hindu	T. 44	...	...
				M. 23	...	...
				F. 21	...	...
		Wásudeo	Do.	T. 314	...	...
				M. 160	...	...
				F. 154	...	...
			Total Group 6	*T. 31,503*	*T. 7,924*	*T. 6,678*
				M. 17,094	*M. 4,333*	*M. 3,711*
				F. 14,409	*F. 3,591*	*F. 2,967*
	7.—Temple Servants.	Gurao	Do.	T. 9,229	T. 3,707	T. 1,616
				M. 4,655	M. 1,861	M. 796
				F. 4,574	F. 1,846	F. 820
		Do.	Jain	T. 1	...	...
				M. 1	...	...
				...	...	...
			Total Group 7	*T. 9,230*	*T. 3,707*	*T. 1,616*
				M. 4,656	*M. 1,861*	*M. 796*
				F. 4,574	*F. 1,846*	*F. 820*
	8.—Genealogists	Bhát	Hindu	T. 3,065	T. 1,378	T. 276
				M. 1,630	M. 712	M. 158
				F. 1,435	F. 666	F. 118

Nationality or traditional Occupation—*contd.*

BY DISTRICT.				RAILWAY PASSENGERS, ETC.	DISTRICT AMRAOTI.			
Ellichpur.	Buldana.	Wun.	Basim.		Amraoti.	Chandur.	Morsi.	Murtazapur.
Total, Males, and Females.	Total, Males, and Females.	Total, Males, and Females.	Total, Males, and Females.	Total, Males, and Females.	Total, Males, and Females.	Total, Males, and Females.	Total, Males, and Females.	Total, Males, and Females.
8	9	10	11	12	13	14	15	16
... ...	... ...	... ...	T. 5 M. 2 F. 3	... ...	... ...	... ...	... ...	... ...
T. 195 M. 103 F. 92	T. 344 M. 209 F. 135	T. 62 M. 43 F. 19	T. 148 M. 88 F. 60	T. 1 M. 1 ...	T. 146 M. 86 F. 60	T. 153 M. 84 F. 69	T. 162 M. 86 F. 76	T. 16 M. 11 F. 5
T. 77 M. 39 F. 38	T. 411 M. 209 F. 202	T. 222 M. 113 F. 109	T. 6 M. 3 F. 3	... ...	T. 117 M. 61 F. 56	T. 156 M. 83 F. 73	T. 122 M. 67 F. 55	T. 245 M. 122 F. 123
T. 1,046 M. 500 F. 546	T. 1,200 M. 644 F. 556	T. 735 M. 394 F. 341	T. 735 M. 400 F. 329	... ...	T. 553 M. 289 F. 264	T. 268 M. 147 F. 121	T. 240 M. 123 F. 117	T. 533 M. 287 F. 246
T. 928 M. 574 F. 354	T. 1,785 M. 979 F. 806	T. 1,724 M. 902 F. 822	T. 2,218 M. 1,260 F. 958	T. 1 M. 1 ...	T. 836 M. 485 F. 351	T. 1,128 M. 610 F. 518	T. 566 M. 331 F. 235	T. 709 M. 406 F. 303
T. 34 M. 20 F. 14	T. 526 M. 256 F. 270	T. 526 M. 256 F. 270	T. 828 M. 403 F. 425	... ...	T. 45 M. 24 F. 21	T. 50 M. 25 F. 25	T. 1 M. 1 ...	T. 104 M. 44 F. 60
T. 635 M. 317 F. 318	T. 432 M. 223 F. 209	T. 235 M. 149 F. 86	T. 312 M. 163 F. 149	... ...	T. 249 M. 144 F. 105	T. 199 M. 111 F. 88	T. 554 M. 285 F. 269	T. 93 M. 50 F. 43
T. 2 M. 2 ...	T. 1 M. 1 ...	... ...	... ...	... ...	T. 3 M. 2 F. 1	... ...	T. 3 M. 3 ...	T. 7 M. 4 F. 3
T. 269 M. 136 F. 133	T. 615 M. 318 F. 297	T. 49 M. 29 F. 20	T. 139 M. 63 F. 76	... ...	T. 285 M. 152 F. 133	T. 45 M. 24 F. 21	T. 172 M. 88 F. 84	T. 109 M. 60 F. 49
... ...	T. 23 M. 12 F. 11	... ...	T. 1 M. 1 ...	... ...	... ...	... ...	... ...	T. 1 M. 1 ...
T. 15 M. 8 F. 7	... ...	... ...	T. 1 M. 1 ...	... ...	T. 1 M. 1 ...	T. 3 M. 3 ...	T. 3 M. 3 ...	T. 1 M. 1 ...
... ...	... ...	... ...	... ...	... ...	T. 1 M. 1 ...	... ...	... ...	... ...
T. 15 M. 12 F. 3	T. 30 M. 17 F. 13	T. 3 M. 3 ...	T. 5 M. 4 F. 1	... ...	T. 20 M. 10 F. 10	T. 3 M. 3 ...	T. 16 M. 12 F. 4	... ...
... ...	... ...	... ...	... ...	... ...	... ...	... ...	... ...	... ...
... ...	... ...	T. 44 M. 23 F. 21	... ...	... ...	... ...	... ...	... ...	... ...
... ...	T. 33 M. 22 F. 11	T. 38 M. 29 F. 9	T. 243 M. 109 F. 134	... ...	... ...	... ...	... ...	... ...
T. 3,216 *M. 1,711* *F. 1,505*	*T. 5,400* *M. 2,890* *F. 2,510*	*T. 3,642* *M. 1,944* *F. 1,698*	*T. 4,641* *M. 2,503* *F. 2,138*	*T. 2* *M. 2* ...	*T. 2,256* *M. 1,255* *F. 1,001*	*T. 2,011* *M. 1,093* *F. 918*	*T. 1,839* *M. 999* *F. 840*	*T. 1,818* *M. 986* *F. 832*
T. 522 M. 273 F. 249	T. 1,486 M. 722 F. 764	T. 794 M. 419 F. 375	T. 1,103 M. 583 F. 520	T. 1 M. 1 ...	T. 1,280 M. 630 F. 650	T. 1,435 M. 739 F. 696	T. 574 M. 279 F. 295	T. 418 M. 213 F. 205
... ...	... ...	... ...	T. 1 M. 1	... ...	... ...	... ...	... ...	... ...
T. 522 *M. 273* *F. 249*	*T. 1,486* *M. 722* *F. 764*	*T. 794* *M. 419* *F. 375*	*T. 1,104* *M. 584* *F. 520*	*T. 1* *M. 1* ...	*T. 1,280* *M. 630* *F. 650*	*T. 1,435* *M. 739* *F. 696*	*T. 574* *M. 279* *F. 295*	*T. 418* *M. 213* *F. 205*
T. 488 M. 270 F. 218	T. 269 M. 139 F. 130	T. 537 M. 287 F. 250	T. 117 M. 64 F. 53	... ...	T. 531 M. 271 F. 260	T. 343 M. 171 F. 172	T. 399 M. 203 F. 196	T. 105 M. 67 F. 38

TABLE XVI.—Castes, Tribes, and Races, by

Class.	Group.	Caste.	Religion.	DISTRICT AKOLA. Akola. Total, Males, and Females.	Akot. Total, Males, and Females.	Balapur. Total, Males, and Females.	Jalgaon. Total, Males, and Females.	Khamgaon. Total, Males, and Females.	DISTRICT Ellichpur. Total, Males, and Females.
17	18	19	20	21	22	23	24	25	26
B.—PROFESSIONAL—*contd.*	6.—Devotees —*contd.*	Aughad	Hindu	... ...	... ...	... ...	... ...	... ...	... ...
		Béragi	Do.	T. 38 M. 26 F. 12	T. 47 M. 34 F. 13	T. 19 M. 16 F. 3	T. 69 M. 45 F. 24	T. 36 M. 26 F. 10	T. 165 M. 80 F. 85
		Bharádi	Do.	T. 32 M. 12 F. 20	T. 42 M. 21 F. 21	... ...	T. 22 M. 12 F. 10	... ...	... ...
		Fakir	Musalman	T. 428 M. 234 F. 194	T. 852 M. 443 F. 409	T. 254 M. 119 F. 135	T. 191 M. 107 F. 84	T. 155 M. 86 F. 69	T. 562 M. 246 F. 316
		Gosáwi	Hindu	T. 695 M. 390 F. 305	T. 497 M. 308 F. 189	T. 436 M. 268 F. 168	T. 359 M. 200 F. 159	T. 270 M. 176 F. 94	T. 298 M. 187 F. 111
		Jogi	Do	T. 55 M. 34 F. 21	... ...	... ...	T. 8 M. 5 F. 3	... ...	T. 24 M. 16 F. 8
		Mánbháo	Do.	T. 277 M. 161 F. 116	T. 141 M. 76 F. 65	T. 243 M. 135 F. 108	T. 50 M. 20 F. 30	T. 139 M. 70 F. 69	T. 406 M. 204 F. 202
		Nának Shái	Do.	... ...	... ...	T. 4 M. 2 F. 2	... ...	T. 2 M. 1 F. 1	T. 2 M. 2 ...
		Náth	Do.	T. 374 M. 192 F. 182	T. 332 M. 170 F. 162	T. 342 M. 177 F. 165	T. 126 M. 68 F. 58	T. 116 M. 55 F. 61	T. 35 M. 18 F. 17
		Sádhv	Do.	T. 1 M. 1 ...	... ...	... ...	... ...	T. 1 M. 1 ...	... ...
		Sanyáshi	Do.	... ...	... ...	T. 1 M. 1 ...	T. 2 M. 2 ...	T. 1 M. 1 ...	T. 13 M. 6 F. 7
		Swámi	Do.	T. 2 M. 1 F. 1	... ...	... ...	... ...	... ...	... ...
		Udási	Do.	T. 2 M. 2 ...	T. 4 M. 3 F. 1	T. 5 M. 4 F. 1	... ...	T. 6 M. 5 F. 1	T. 4 M. 4 ...
		Do.	Sikh	... ...	... ...	... ...	T. 2 M. 1 F. 1	... ...	... ...
		Virbhadra	Hindu	... ...	... ...	... ...	... ...	... ...	... ...
		Wásudeo	Do.	... ...	... ...	... ...	... ...	... ...	... ...
			Total Group 6	*T. 1,904* *M. 1,053* *F. 851*	*T. 1,916* *M. 1,056* *F. 860*	*T. 1,304* *M. 722* *F. 582*	*T. 829* *M. 460* *F. 369*	*T. 726* *M. 421* *F. 305*	*T. 1,509* *M. 763* *F. 746*
	7.—Temple Servants.	Gurao	Do.	T. 432 M. 200 F. 232	T. 325 M. 154 F. 171	T. 156 M. 76 F. 80	T. 374 M. 203 F. 171	T. 329 M. 163 F. 166	T. 246 M. 131 F. 115
		Do.	Jain	... ...	... ...	... ...	... ...	... ...	... ...
			Total Group 7	*T. 432* *M. 200* *F. 232*	*T. 325* *M. 154* *F. 171*	*T. 156* *M. 76* *F. 80*	*T. 374* *M. 203* *F. 171*	*T. 329* *M. 163* *F. 166*	*T. 246* *M. 131* *F. 115*
	8.—Genealogists.	Bhát	Hindu	T. 98 M. 55 F. 43	T. 92 M. 50 F. 42	T. 15 M. 8 F. 7	T. 51 M. 31 F. 20	T. 20 M. 14 F. 6	T. 225 M. 121 F. 104

Nationality or traditional Occupation—*contd.*

LLICHPUR.		DISTRICT BULDANA.			DISTRICT WUN.				DISTRICT BASIM.		
DARYAPUR.	MELGHAT.	CHIKHLI.	MALKAPUR.	MEHKAR.	YEOTMAL.	DARWHA.	KELAPUR.	WUN.	BASIM.	MANGRUL.	PUSAD.
Total, Males, and Females.	Total, Males, and Females.	Total, Males, and Females.	Total, Males, and Females.	Total, Males, and Females.	Total, Males, and Females.	Total, Males, and Females.	Total, Males, and Females.	Total, Males, and Females.	Total, Males, and Females.	Total, Males, and Females.	Total, Males, and Females.
27	28	29	30	31	32	33	34	35	36	37	38
...	...	...	...	...	...	...	...	...	T. 5 M. 2 F. 3	...	...
T. 25 M. 18 F. 7	T. 5 M. 5 ...	T. 127 M. 68 F. 59	T. 161 M. 98 F. 63	T. 56 M. 43 F. 13	T. 14 M. 14 ...	T. 18 M. 14 F. 4	T. 6 M. 4 F. 2	T. 24 M. 11 F. 13	T. 103 M. 60 F. 43	T. 34 M. 20 F. 14	T. 11 M. 8 F. 3
T. 77 M. 39 F. 38	...	T. 92 M. 45 F. 47	T. 220 M. 115 F. 105	T. 99 M. 49 F. 50	T. 84 M. 44 F. 40	T. 80 M. 38 F. 42	T. 46 M. 23 F. 23	T. 12 M. 8 F. 4	...	T. 6 M. 3 F. 3	...
T. 471 M. 247 F. 224	T. 13 M. 7 F. 6	T. 584 M. 316 F. 268	T. 395 M. 212 F. 183	T. 221 M. 116 F. 105	T. 226 M. 124 F. 102	T. 306 M. 168 F. 138	T. 146 M. 72 F. 74	T. 57 M. 30 F. 27	T. 270 M. 158 F. 112	T. 262 M. 139 F. 123	T. 203 M. 109 F. 94
T. 549 M. 342 F. 207	T. 81 M. 45 F. 36	T. 588 M. 318 F. 270	T. 593 M. 323 F. 270	T. 604 M. 338 F. 266	T. 659 M. 311 F. 348	T. 710 M. 402 F. 308	T. 251 M. 131 F. 120	T. 104 M. 58 F. 46	T. 1,125 M. 648 F. 477	T. 418 M. 223 F. 195	T. 675 M. 389 F. 286
T. 10 M. 4 F. 6	...	T. 73 M. 33 F. 40	T. 224 M. 114 F. 110	T. 229 M. 109 F. 120	T. 93 M. 50 F. 43	T. 262 M. 113 F. 149	T. 158 M. 87 F. 71	T. 13 M. 6 F. 7	T. 369 M. 175 F. 194	T. 315 M. 155 F. 160	T. 144 M. 73 F. 71
T. 228 M. 112 F. 116	T. 1 M. 1 ...	T. 140 M. 76 F. 64	T. 166 M. 86 F. 80	T. 126 M. 61 F. 65	T. 37 M. 18 F. 19	T. 190 M. 125 F. 65	T. 8 M. 6 F. 2	...	T. 118 M. 57 F. 61	T. 85 M. 46 F. 39	T. 109 M. 60 F. 49
...	...	T. 1 M. 1 ...	...	...	...	...	...	...	...	...	...
T. 234 M. 118 F. 116	...	T. 131 M. 69 F. 62	T. 157 M. 85 F. 72	T. 327 M. 164 F. 163	T. 4 M. 3 F. 1	T. 20 M. 9 F. 11	T. 9 M. 6 F. 3	T. 16 M. 11 F. 5	T. 68 M. 30 F. 38	T. 71 M. 33 F. 38	...
...	...	T. 22 M. 11 F. 11	T. 1 M. 1 ...	...	...	...	...	...	...	...	T. 1 M. 1 ...
T. 2 M. 2 ...	...	...	...	...	...	...	...	...	T. 1 M. 1 ...	...	...
...	...	...	...	...	...	...	...	...	...	...	...
T. 11 M. 8 F. 3	...	T. 17 M. 8 F. 9	T. 10 M. 7 F. 3	T. 3 M. 2 F. 1	T. 1 M. 1 ...	...	T. 1 M. 1 ...	T. 1 M. 1 ...	T. 3 M. 2 F. 1	...	T. 2 M. 2 ...
...	...	...	...	...	...	...	...	...	...	...	...
...	...	...	...	...	T. 2 M. 2 ...	...	T. 16 M. 9 F. 7	T. 26 M. 12 F. 14	...	...	...
...	...	T. 3 M. 2 F. 1	T. 5 M. 5 ...	T. 25 M. 15 F. 10	T. 5 M. 3 F. 2	T. 33 M. 26 F. 7	...	...	T. 5 M. 4 F. 1	T. 8 M. 5 F. 3	T. 230 M. 100 F. 130
T. 1,607 *M. 890* *F. 717*	*T. 100* *M. 58* *F. 42*	*T. 1,778* *M. 947* *F. 831*	*T. 1,932* *M. 1,046* *F. 886*	*T. 1,690* *M. 897* *F. 793*	*T. 1,125* *M. 570* *F. 555*	*T. 1,621* *M. 897* *F. 724*	*T. 643* *M. 340* *F. 303*	*T. 253* *M. 137* *F. 116*	*T. 2,067* *M. 1,137* *F. 930*	*T. 1,199* *M. 624* *F. 575*	*T. 1,375* *M. 742* *F. 633*
T. 274 M. 140 F. 134	T. 2 M. 2 ...	T. 560 M. 282 F. 278	T. 700 M. 322 F. 378	T. 226 M. 118 F. 108	T. 147 M. 79 F. 68	T. 212 M. 114 F. 98	T. 87 M. 49 F. 38	T. 348 M. 177 F. 171	T. 700 M. 372 F. 328	T. 113 M. 58 F. 55	T. 290 M. 153 F. 137
...	...	...	...	...	...	...	...	...	...	T. 1 M. 1 ...	...
T. 274 *M. 140* *F. 134*	*T. 2* *M. 2* ...	*T. 560* *M. 282* *F. 278*	*T. 700* *M. 322* *F. 378*	*T. 226* *M. 118* *F. 108*	*T. 147* *M. 79* *F. 68*	*T. 212* *M. 114* *F. 98*	*T. 87* *M. 49* *F. 38*	*T. 348* *M. 177* *F. 171*	*T. 700* *M. 372* *F. 328*	*T. 114* *M. 59* *F. 55*	*T. 290* *M. 153* *F. 137*
T. 260 M. 146 F. 114	T. 3 M. 3 ...	T. 16 M. 9 F. 7	T. 185 M. 93 F. 92	T. 68 M. 37 F. 31	T. 101 M. 49 F. 52	T. 166 M. 90 F. 76	T. 42 M. 25 F. 17	T. 228 M. 123 F. 105	T. 83 M. 44 F. 39	T. 3 M. 3 ...	T. 31 M. 17 F. 14

TABLE XVI.—Castes, Tribes, and Races, by

Name and Classification.				Provincial Total.	Distribution	
					Amraoti.	Akola.
Class.	Group.	Caste.	Religion.	Total, Males, and Females.	Total, Males, and Females.	Total, Males, and Females.
1	2	3	4	5	6	7
B.—PROFESSIONAL—*contd.*	8.—Genealogists—*contd.*	Bhát	Animistic	T. 47 M. 21 F. 26	T. 47 M. 21 F. 26	... ...
		Do.	Musalman	T. 45 M. 25 F. 20	T. 22 M. 12 F. 10	T. 6 M. 4 F. 2
		Thákur	Hindu	T. 5,099 M. 2,750 F. 2,349	T. 891 M. 545 F. 346	T. 1,480 M. 760 F. 720
			Total Group 8	*T.* *8,256* *M.* *4,426* *F.* *3,830*	*T.* *2,338* *M.* *1,290* *F.* *1,048*	*T.* *1,762* *M.* *922* *F.* *840*
	9.—Writers	Boral	Hindu	T. 25 M. 13 F. 12	T. 2 M. 1 F. 1	... ...
		Golak	Do.	T. 146 M. 73 F. 73	T. 8 M. 7 F. 1	T. 66 M. 28 F. 38
		Kást	Do.	T. 259 M. 131 F. 128	T. 103 M. 51 F. 52	T. 61 M. 31 F. 30
		Káyet	Do.	T. 974 M. 570 F. 404	T. 211 M. 136 F. 75	T. 301 M. 176 F. 125
		Parbhu	Do.	T. 632 M. 352 F. 280	T. 212 M. 131 F. 81	T. 128 M. 65 F. 63
		Purbhaiye	Do.	T. 94 M. 67 F. 27	T. 4 M. 4 ...	T. 20 M. 16 F. 4
			Total Group 9	*T.* *2,130* *M.* *1,206* *F.* *924*	*T.* *540* *M.* *330* *F.* *210*	*T.* *576* *M.* *316* *F.* *260*
	10.—Astrologers	Gárpagári	Hindu	T. 3,041 M. 1,564 F. 1,477	T. 1,124 M. 590 F. 534	T. 522 M. 261 F. 261
		Joshi	Do.	T. 419 M. 249 F. 170	T. 8 M. 4 F. 4	T. 36 M. 25 F. 11
		Do.	Jain	T. 5 M. 3 F. 2	T. 5 M. 3 F. 2	... ...
		Sarode	Hindu	T. 1,330 M. 675 F. 655	T. 202 M. 121 F. 81	T. 18 M. 15 F. 3
			Total Group 10	*T.* *4,795* *M.* *2,491* *F.* *2,304*	*T.* *1,339* *M.* *718* *F.* *621*	*T.* *576* *M.* *301* *F.* *275*
	11.—Musicians	Devalwár	Hindu	T. 103 M. 45 F. 58	... ...	... ...
		Gondhali	Do.	T. 3,033 M. 1,511 F. 1,522	T. 470 M. 269 F. 201	T. 1,255 M. 596 F. 659
		Mirási	Do.	T. 5 M. 2 F. 3	... ...	... ...
			Total Group 11	*T.* *3,141* *M.* *1,558* *F.* *1,583*	*T.* *470* *M.* *269* *F.* *201*	*T.* *1,255* *M.* *596* *F.* *659*

Nationality or traditional Occupation—*contd.*

	BY DISTRICT.					DISTRICT AMRAOTI.			
	ELLICHPUR.	BULDANA.	WUN.	BASIM.	RAILWAY PASSENGERS, ETC.	AMRAOTI.	CHANDUR.	MORSI.	MURTAZAPUR.
	Total, Males, and Females.	Total, Males, and Females.	Total, Males, and Females.	Total, Males, and Females.	Total, Males, and Females.	Total, Males, and Females.	Total, Males, and Females.	Total, Males, and Females.	Total, Males, and Females.
	8	9	10	11	12	13	14	15	16
T.	...	...	...	...	...	...	47	...	...
M.	...	...	...	...	...	...	21	...	...
F.	...	...	...	...	...	...	26	...	...
T.	...	...	17	...	...	22	...	...	...
M.	...	...	9	...	...	12	...	...	...
F.	...	...	8	...	...	10	...	...	...
T.	589	705	650	983	1	295	163	153	280
M.	242	353	353	496	1	189	101	87	168
F.	147	352	297	487	...	106	62	66	112
T.	*877*	*974*	*1,204*	*1,100*	*1*	*848*	*553*	*552*	*385*
M.	*512*	*492*	*649*	*560*	*1*	*472*	*293*	*290*	*235*
F.	*365*	*482*	*555*	*540*	...	*376*	*260*	*262*	*150*
T.	...	22	...	1	...	...	...	...	2
M.	...	11	...	1	...	...	...	...	1
F.	...	11	...	...	...	...	...	...	1
T.	7	60	2	3	...	...	...	4	4
M.	4	31	1	2	...	...	...	4	3
F.	3	29	1	1	...	...	...	...	1
T.	26	55	10	4	...	18	4	...	81
M.	9	31	0	3	...	10	2	...	39
F.	17	24	4	1	...	8	2	...	42
T.	265	60	68	68	1	105	34	15	57
M.	148	30	42	37	1	71	24	8	33
F.	117	30	26	31	...	34	10	7	24
T.	123	22	99	48	...	171	6	24	11
M.	63	13	51	29	...	105	3	17	6
F.	60	9	48	19	...	66	3	7	5
T.	3	56	1	10	...	2	1	1	...
M.	3	33	1	10	...	2	1	1	...
F.	...	23	...	...	...	...	...	...	...
T.	*424*	*275*	*180*	*134*	*1*	*296*	*45*	*44*	*155*
M.	*227*	*149*	*101*	*82*	*1*	*188*	*30*	*30*	*82*
F.	*197*	*126*	*79*	*52*	...	*108*	*15*	*14*	*73*
T.	645	225	310	215	...	345	250	262	267
M.	335	116	155	107	...	180	123	142	145
F.	310	109	155	108	...	165	127	120	122
T.	...	150	...	225	...	...	8	...	...
M.	...	82	...	138	...	...	4	...	...
F.	...	68	...	87	...	...	4	...	...
T.	...	...	...	...	...	...	5	...	...
M.	...	...	...	...	...	...	3	...	...
F.	...	...	...	...	...	...	2	...	...
T.	205	33	850	22	...	98	34	66	4
M.	108	19	403	9	...	56	27	34	4
F.	97	14	447	13	...	42	7	32	...
T.	*850*	*408*	*1,160*	*462*	...	*443*	*297*	*328*	*271*
M.	*443*	*217*	*558*	*254*	...	*236*	*157*	*176*	*149*
F.	*407*	*191*	*602*	*208*	...	*207*	*140*	*152*	*122*
T.	...	...	103	...	...	...	...	...	...
M.	...	...	45	...	...	...	...	...	...
F.	...	...	58	...	...	...	...	...	...
T.	192	424	318	374	...	140	95	40	195
M.	97	214	158	177	...	84	60	29	96
F.	95	210	160	197	...	56	35	11	99
T.	...	5	...	...	...	...	...	...	...
M.	...	2	...	...	...	...	...	...	...
F.	...	3	...	...	...	...	...	...	...
T.	*192*	*429*	*421*	*374*	...	*140*	*95*	*40*	*195*
M.	*97*	*216*	*208*	*177*	...	*84*	*60*	*29*	*98*
F.	*95*	*213*	*218*	*197*	...	*56*	*35*	*11*	*99*

TABLE XVI.—Castes, Tribes, and Races, by

Name and Classification.				District Akola.					District
				Akola.	Akot.	Balapur.	Jalgaon.	Khamgaon.	Ellichpur.
Class.	Group.	Caste.	Religion.	Total, Males, and Females.	Total, Males, and Females.	Total, Males, and Females.	Total, Males, and Females.	Total, Males, and Females.	Total, Males, and Females.
17	18	19	20	21	22	23	24	25	26
B.—PROFESSIONAL—contd.	8.—Genealogists—contd.	Bhát	Animistic	...	...	...	...	...	...
				...	...	...	...	...	...
				...	...	...	...	...	...
		Do.	Musalman	...	T. 2	...	...	T. 4	...
				...	M. 2	...	...	M. 2	...
				...	...	...	...	F. 2	...
		Thákur	Hindu	T. 423	T. 377	T. 163	T. 257	T. 260	T. 117
				M. 218	M. 190	M. 89	M. 128	M. 135	M. 82
				F. 205	F. 187	F. 74	F. 129	F. 125	F. 35
			Total Group 8	*T. 521*	*T. 471*	*T. 178*	*T. 308*	*T. 284*	*T. 342*
				M. 273	*M. 242*	*M. 97*	*M. 159*	*M. 151*	*M. 203*
				F. 248	*F. 229*	*F. 81*	*F. 149*	*F. 133*	*F. 139*
	9.—Writers	Boral	Hindu	...	...	...	...	...	...
				...	...	...	...	...	...
				...	...	...	...	...	...
		Golak	Do.	T. 2	T. 6	T. 56	T. 1	T. 1	T. 3
				M. 1	M. 2	M. 23	M. 1	M. 1	M. 3
				F. 1	F. 4	F. 33	...	...	...
		Kást	Do.	T. 30	T. 26	T. 5	...	...	T. 12
				M. 19	M. 11	M. 1	...	...	M. 4
				F. 11	F. 15	F. 4	...	...	F. 8
		Káyet	Do.	T. 33	T. 128	T. 20	T. 104	T. 16	T. 127
				M. 17	M. 77	M. 12	M. 58	M. 12	M. 69
				F. 16	F. 51	F. 8	F. 46	F. 4	F. 58
		Parbhu	Do.	T. 62	T. 44	T. 9	...	T. 13	T. 92
				M. 35	M. 18	M. 5	...	M. 7	M. 48
				F. 27	F. 26	F. 4	...	F. 6	F. 44
		Purbhaiye	Do.	T. 10	T. 2	T. 3	T. 4	T. 1	...
				M. 7	M. 2	M. 3	M. 3	M. 1	...
				F. 3	...	...	F. 1	...	...
			Total Group 9	*T. 137*	*T. 206*	*T. 93*	*T. 109*	*T. 31*	*T. 234*
				M. 79	*M. 110*	*M. 44*	*M. 62*	*M. 21*	*M. 124*
				F. 58	*F. 96*	*F. 49*	*F. 47*	*F. 10*	*F. 110*
	10.—Astrologers.	Gárpagári	Hindu	T. 159	T. 122	T. 87	T. 45	T. 109	T. 310
				M. 72	M. 67	M. 39	M. 24	M. 59	M. 166
				F. 87	F. 55	F. 48	F. 21	F. 50	F. 144
		Joshi	Do.	T. 2	...	...	T. 2	T. 32	...
				M. 2	...	...	M. 2	M. 21	...
				...	...	...	...	F. 11	...
		Do.	Jain	...	...	...	...	...	...
				...	...	...	...	...	...
				...	...	...	...	...	...
		Sarode	Hindu	T. 3	...	...	T. 2	T. 13	T. 194
				M. 2	...	...	M. 1	M. 12	M. 101
				F. 1	...	...	F. 1	F. 1	F. 93
			Total Group 10	*T. 164*	*T. 122*	*T. 87*	*T. 49*	*T. 154*	*T. 504*
				M. 76	*M. 67*	*M. 39*	*M. 27*	*M. 92*	*M. 267*
				F. 88	*F. 55*	*F. 48*	*F. 22*	*F. 62*	*F. 237*
	11.—Musicians	Devalwár	Hindu	...	...	...	...	...	...
				...	...	...	...	...	...
				...	...	...	...	...	...
		Gondhali	Do.	T. 491	T. 139	T. 251	T. 130	T. 244	T. 49
				M. 213	M. 78	M. 111	M. 71	M. 123	M. 25
				F. 278	F. 61	F. 140	F. 59	F. 121	F. 24
		Mirási	Do.	...	...	...	...	...	...
				...	...	...	...	...	...
				...	...	...	...	...	...
			Total Group 11	*T. 491*	*T. 139*	*T. 251*	*T. 130*	*T. 244*	*T. 49*
				M. 213	*M. 78*	*M. 111*	*M. 71*	*M. 123*	*M. 25*
				F. 278	*F. 61*	*F. 140*	*F. 59*	*F. 121*	*F. 24*

Nationality or traditional Occupation—*contd.*

ELLICHPUR.		DISTRICT BULDANA.			DISTRICT WUN.				DISTRICT BASIM.		
DARYAPUR.	MELGHAT.	CHIKHLI.	MALKAPUR.	MEHKAR.	YEOTMAL.	DARWHA.	KELAPUR.	WUN.	BASIM.	MANGRUL.	PUSAD.
Total, Males, and Females.	Total, Males, and Females	Total, Males, and Females.	Total, Males, and Females.	Total, Males, and Females.	Total, Males, and Females.	Total, Males, and Females.	Total, Males, and Females.	Total, Males, and Females.	Total, Males, and Females.	Total, Males, and Females.	Total, Males, and Females.
27	28	29	30	31	32	33	34	35	36	37	38
... ...	... ...	... ...	... ...	... ...	... ...	... ...	... ...	... ...	... ...	... ...	... ...
... ...	... ...	... ...	... ...	... ...	... ...	T. 14 M. 6 F. 8	T. 3 M. 3 ...	... ...	... ...	... ...	... ...
T. 250 M. 141 F. 109	T. 22 M. 19 F. 3	T. 144 M. 76 F. 68	T. 384 M. 191 F. 193	T. 177 M. 86 F. 91	T. 181 M. 100 F. 81	T. 390 M. 208 F. 182	T. 34 M. 21 F. 13	T. 45 M. 24 F. 21	T. 494 M. 251 F. 243	T. 193 M. 100 F. 93	T. 296 M. 145 F. 151
T. 510 *M. 287* *F. 228*	*T. 25* *M. 22* *F. 3*	*T. 160* *M. 85* *F. 75*	*T. 569* *M. 284* *F. 285*	*T. 245* *M. 123* *F. 122*	*T. 282* *M. 149* *F. 133*	*T. 570* *M. 304* *F. 266*	*T. 79* *M. 49* *F. 30*	*T. 273* *M. 147* *F. 126*	*T. 577* *M. 295* *F. 282*	*T. 196* *M. 103* *F. 93*	*T. 327* *M. 162* *F. 165*
... ...	... ...	T. 22 M. 11 F. 11	... ...	... ...	... ...	... ...	... ...	... ...	... ...	T. 1 M. 1 ...	... ...
T. 4 M. 1 F. 3	... ...	T. 52 M. 26 F. 26	T. 5 M. 3 F. 2	T. 3 M. 2 F. 1	... ...	T. 2 M. 1 F. 1	... ...	... ...	T. 3 M. 2 F. 1	... ...	... ...
T. 14 M. 5 F. 9	... ...	T. 25 M. 13 F. 12	T. 8 M. 5 F. 3	T 22 M. 13 F. 9	T. 2 M. 2 ...	T. 8 M. 4 F. 4	... ...	... ...	T. 2 M. 1 F. 1	T. 1 M. 1 ...	T. 1 M. 1 ...
T. 117 M. 60 F. 57	T. 21 M. 19 F. 2	T. 5 M. 4 F. 1	T. 53 M. 25 F. 28	T. 2 M. 1 F. 1	T. 16 M. 9 F. 7	T. 29 M. 20 F. 9	T. 19 M. 10 F. 9	T. 4 M. 3 F. 1	T. 23 M. 15 F. 8	T. 28 M. 16 F. 12	T. 17 M. 6 F. 11
T. 28 M. 12 F. 16	T. 3 M. 3 ...	T. 16 M. 9 F. 7	T. 6 M. 4 F. 2	... ...	T. 61 M. 35 F. 26	T. 6 M. 1 F. 5	T. 9 M. 6 F. 3	T. 23 M. 9 F. 14	T. 21 M. 13 F. 8	T. 1 M. 1 ...	T. 26 M. 15 F. 11
T. 3 M. 3 ...	... ...	T. 40 M. 22 F. 18	T. 15 M. 10 F. 5	T. 1 M. 1 ...	... ...	... ...	T. 1 M. 1 ...	... ...	T. 8 M. 8 ...	T. 1 M. 1 ...	T. 1 M. 1 ...
T. 166 *M. 81* *F. 85*	*T. 24* *M. 22* *F. 2*	*T. 160* *M. 85* *F. 75*	*T. 87* *M. 47* *F. 40*	*T. 28* *M. 17* *F. 11*	*T. 79* *M. 46* *F. 33*	*T. 45* *M. 26* *F. 19*	*T. 29* *M. 17* *F. 12*	*T. 27* *M. 12* *F. 15*	*T. 57* *M. 39* *F. 18*	*T. 32* *M. 20* *F. 12*	*T. 45* *M. 23* *F. 22*
T. 335 M. 169 F. 166	... ...	T. 77 M. 43 F. 34	T. 32 M. 17 F. 15	T. 116 M. 56 F. 60	T. 123 M. 64 F. 59	T. 108 M. 52 F. 56	T. 52 M. 24 F. 28	T. 27 M. 15 F. 12	T. 153 M. 72 F. 81	T. 61 M. 34 F. 27	T. 1 M. 1 ...
... ...	... ...	T. 29 M. 15 F. 14	T. 50 M. 32 F. 18	T. 71 M. 35 F. 36	... ...	... ...	... ...	... ...	T. 201 M. 124 F. 77	T. 13 M. 8 F. 5	T. 11 M. 6 F. 5
... ...	... ...	... ...	... ...	... ...	... ...	... ...	... ...	... ...	... ...	... ...	... ...
T. 2 M. 2 ...	T. 9 M. 5 F. 4	... ...	T. 25 M. 13 F. 12	T. 8 M. 6 F. 2	T. 270 M 116 F. 154	T. 161 M. 83 F. 78	T. 346 M. 160 F. 186	T. 73 M. 44 F. 29	... ...	T. 22 M. 9 F. 13	... ...
T. 337 *M. 171* *F. 166*	*T. 9* *M. 5* *F. 4*	*T. 106* *M. 58* *F. 48*	*T. 107* *M. 62* *F. 45*	*T. 195* *M. 97* *F. 98*	*T. 393* *M. 180* *F. 213*	*T. 269* *M. 135* *F. 134*	*T. 398* *M. 184* *F. 214*	*T. 100* *M. 59* *F. 41*	*T. 354* *M. 196* *F. 158*	*T. 96* *M. 51* *F. 45*	*T. 12* *M. 7* *F. 5*
... ...	... ...	... ...	... ...	... ...	... ...	... ...	T. 101 M. 45 F. 56	T. 2 ... F. 2	... ...	... ...	... ...
T. 143 M. 72 F. 71	... ...	T. 104 M. 51 F. 53	T. 148 M. 79 F. 69	T. 172 M. 84 F. 88	T. 59 M. 36 F. 23	T. 211 M. 88 F. 123	T. 48 M. 34 F. 14	... ...	T. 214 M. 102 F. 112	T. 69 M. 32 F. 37	T. 91 M. 43 F. 48
... ...	... ...	T. 5 M. 2 F. 3	... ...	... ...	... ...	... ...	... ...	... ...	... ...	... ...	... ...
T. 143 *M. 72* *F. 71*	... ...	*T. 109* *M. 53* *F. 56*	*T. 148* *M. 79* *F. 69*	*T. 172* *M. 84* *F. 88*	*T. 59* *M. 36* *F. 23*	*T. 211* *M. 88* *F. 123*	*T. 149* *M. 79* *F. 70*	*T. 2* ... *F. 2*	*T. 214* *M. 102* *F. 112*	*T. 69* *M. 32* *F. 37*	*T. 91* *M. 43* *F. 48*

TABLE XVI.—Castes, Tribes, and Races, by

Name and Classification.				Provincial Total.	Distribution	
					Amraoti.	Akola.
Class.	Group.	Caste.	Religion.	Total, Males, and Females.	Total, Males, and Females.	Total, Males, and Females.
1	2	3	4	5	6	7
B.—PROFESSIONAL,—*concld.*	12.—Dancers and Singers.	Dhádi	Musalman	T. 5 M. 3 F. 2	T. 5 M. 3 F. 2	... ...
		Kalwant	Hindu	T. 94 M. 28 F. 66	T. 3 M. 1 F. 2	... ...
		Wághe	Do.	T. 47 M. 23 F. 24	T. 8 M. 3 F. 5	T. 3 M. 1 F. 2
			Total Group 12	*T. 146* *M. 54* *F. 92*	*T. 16* *M. 7* *F. 9*	*T. 3* *M. 1* *F. 2*
	12A.—Minor Professions.	Chitári	Hindu	T. 76 M. 38 F. 38	T. 30 M. 15 F. 15	T. 1 M. 1 ...
	13.—Actors and Mimes.	Bahurupi	Do.	T. 157 M. 78 F. 79	T. 51 M. 27 F. 24	T. 5 M. 3 F. 2
		Do. (Ráerang)	Musalman	T. 6 M. 2 F. 4	... ...	... ...
		Bhánd	Do.	T. 2 ... F. 2	T. 2 ... F. 2	... ...
			Total Group 13	*T. 165* *M. 80* *F. 85*	*T. 53* *M. 27* *F. 26*	*T. 5* *M. 3* *F. 2*
C.—COMMERCIAL.	14.—Traders	Bháttiá	Hindu	T. 104 M. 75 F. 29	T. 20 M. 16 F. 4	T. 69 M. 49 F. 20
		Do.	Jain	T. 55 M. 27 F. 28	T. 7 M. 4 F. 3	T. 48 M. 23 F. 25
		Bohari	Musalman	T. 479 M. 335 F. 144	T. 214 M. 143 F. 71	T. 171 M. 114 F. 57
		Kachhi	Do.	T. 175 M. 154 F. 21	T. 77 M. 66 F. 11	T. 26 M. 21 F. 5
		Khojá	Do.	T. 27 M. 13 F. 14	... ...	... ...
		Komti	Hindu	T. 2,750 M. 1,362 F. 1,388	T. 126 M. 60 F. 66	T. 115 M. 52 F. 63
		Lád	Hindu	T. 1,371 M. 717 F. 654	T. 210 M. 105 F. 105	T. 118 M. 68 F. 50
		Do.	Jain	T. 1,454 M. 733 F. 721	T. 165 M. 85 F. 80	T. 99 M. 47 F. 52
		Mantri	Hindu	T. 1 M. 1 ...	... ...	... ...
		Náidu	Do.	T. 52 M. 26 F. 26	T. 31 M. 16 F. 15	T. 3 M. 2 F. 1
		Sárlan	Do.	T. 2 M. 2 ...	... ...	... ...
		Shelki	Do.	T. 1 ... F. 1	... ...	... ...

Nationality or traditional Occupation—*contd.*

BY DISTRICT.					DISTRICT AMRAOTI.			
ELLICHPUR.	BULDANA.	WUN.	BASIM.	RAILWAY PASSENGERS, ETC.	AMRAOTI.	CHANDUR.	MORSI.	MURTAZAPUR.
Total, Males, and Females.	Total, Males, and Females.	Total, Males, and Females.	Total, Males, and Females.	Total, Males, and Females.	Total, Males, and Females.	Total, Males, and Females.	Total, Males, and Females.	Total, Males, and Females.
8	9	10	11	12	13	14	15	16
...	...	...	...	...	T. 5 M. 3 F. 2	...	...	...
...	T. 3 F. 3	T. 44 M. 15 F. 29	T. 44 M. 12 F. 32	...	T. 3 M. 1 F. 2	...	...	...
T. 5 M. 2 F. 3	T. 6 M. 5 F. 1	T. 1 M. 1	T. 24 M. 11 F. 13	...	T. 4 M. 1 F. 3	...	T. 4 M. 2 F. 2	...
T. 5 *M. 2* *F. 3*	*T. 9* *M. 5* *F. 4*	*T. 45* *M. 16* *F. 29*	*T. 68* *M. 23* *F. 45*	...	*T. 12* *M. 5* *F. 7*	...	*T. 4* *M. 2* *F. 2*	...
T. 21 M. 10 F. 11	...	T. 24 M. 12 F. 12	...	...	T. 1 M. 1	T. 18 M. 10 F. 8	T. 11 M. 4 F. 7	...
T. 2 M. 1 F. 1	T. 18 M. 9 F. 9	T. 53 M. 25 F. 28	T. 28 M. 13 F. 15	...	...	T. 6 M. 3 F. 3	...	T. 45 M. 24 F. 21
...	T. 6 M. 2 F. 4	...	...	...	...	...	...	...
...	...	...	...	...	...	...	...	T. 2 F. 2
T. 2 *M. 1* *F. 1*	*T. 24* *M. 11* *F. 13*	*T. 53* *M. 25* *F. 28*	*T. 28* *M. 13* *F. 15*	...	...	*T. 6* *M. 3* *F. 3*	...	*T. 47* *M. 24* *F. 23*
...	T. 3 M. 2 F. 1	T. 9 M. 5 F. 4	T. 3 M. 3	...	T. 4 M. 4	...	...	T. 16 M. 12 F. 4
...	...	...	...	...	T. 6 M. 3 F. 3	...	...	T. 1 M. 1
T. 55 M. 46 F. 9	T. 13 M. 8 F. 5	T. 11 M. 11	T. 12 M. 11 F. 1	T. 3 M. 2 F. 1	T. 149 M. 98 F. 51	T. 31 M. 26 F. 5	T. 14 M. 8 F. 6	T. 20 M. 11 F. 9
...	T. 21 M. 21	T. 25 M. 21 F. 4	T. 26 M. 25 F. 1	...	T. 52 M. 41 F. 11	T. 18 M. 18	T. 3 M. 3	T. 4 M. 4
...	...	T. 27 M. 13 F. 14	...	...	...	...	...	...
T. 21 M. 8 F. 13	T. 45 M. 19 F. 26	T. 2,035 M. 1,018 F. 1,017	T. 399 M. 201 F. 198	T. 9 M. 4 F. 5	T. 38 M. 20 F. 18	T. 31 M. 11 F. 20	T. 48 M. 21 F. 27	T. 9 M. 8 F. 1
T. 11 M. 4 F. 7	T. 774 M. 383 F. 391	T. 23 M. 12 F. 11	T. 234 M. 144 F. 90	T. 1 M. 1	T. 177 M. 86 F. 91	T. 2 M. 2	T. 2 M. 2	T. 29 M. 15 F. 14
T. 157 M. 74 F. 83	T. 146 M. 63 F. 83	T. 3 M. 3	T. 884 M. 461 F. 423	...	T. 91 M. 43 F. 48	T. 9 M. 7 F. 2	T. 1 M. 1	T. 64 M. 34 F. 30
...	...	...	T. 1 M. 1	...	...	...	...	...
T. 17 M. 8 F. 9	...	...	T. 1 F. 1	...	T. 22 M. 12 F. 10	...	T. 9 M. 4 F. 5	...
...	...	...	T. 2 M. 2	...	...	...	...	...
...	T. 1 F. 1	...	...	...	...	...	...	...

TABLE XVI.—Castes, Tribes, and Races, by

Name and Classification.				District Akola.					District
				Akola.	Akot.	Balapur.	Jalgaon.	Khamgaon.	Ellichpur.
Class.	Group.	Caste.	Religion.	Total, Males, and Females.	Total, Males, and Females.	Total, Males, and Females.	Total, Males, and Females.	Total, Males, and Females.	Total, Males, and Females.
17	18	19	20	21	22	23	24	25	26
B.—Professional—*concld.*	12.—Dancers and Singers.	Dhádi	Musalman	...	...	...	...	...	...
		Kalwant	Hindu	...	...	...	...	...	...
		Wághe	Do.	T. 1 M. 1 ...	...	...	...	T. 2 ... F. 2	T. 5 M. 2 F. 3
			Total Group 12	*T. 1* *M. 1* ...	...	...	...	*T. 2* ... *F. 2*	*T. 5* *M. 2* *F. 3*
	12*A*.—Minor Professions.	Chitári	Hindu	...	...	T. 1 M. 1 ...	...	...	T. 21 M. 10 F. 11
	13.—Actors and Mimes.	Bahurupi	Do.	...	...	T. 5 M. 3 F. 2	...	...	...
		Do. (Rábrang)	Musalman	...	...	...	...	...	...
		Bhánd	Do.	...	...	...	...	...	...
			Total Group 13	...	...	*T. 6* *M. 3* *F. 2*	...	...	...
C.—Commercial.	14.—Traders	Bhattiá	Hindu	T. 8 M. 8 ...	T. 4 M. 4 ...	...	T. 1 M. 1 ...	T. 56 M. 36 F. 20	...
		Do.	Jain	T. 48 M. 23 F. 25	...	...	...	...	...
		Bohari	Musalman	T. 52 M. 37 F. 15	T. 22 M. 15 F. 7	...	T. 5 M. 4 F. 1	T. 92 M. 58 F. 34	T. 16 M. 13 F. 3
		Kachhi	Do.	T. 6 M. 2 F. 4	T. 16 M. 15 F. 1	T. 1 M. 1 ...	T. 3 M. 3 ...	...	...
		Khojá	Do.	...	...	...	...	...	...
		Komti	Hindu	T. 45 M. 22 F. 23	T. 10 M. 5 F. 5	T. 4 M. 2 F. 2	T. 28 M. 10 F 18	T. 28 M. 13 F. 15	T. 4 M. 2 F. 2
		Lád	Hindu	T. 75 M. 44 F. 31	...	T. 11 M. 6 F. 5	T. 15 M. 8 F. 7	T. 17 M. 10 F. 7	T. 11 M. 4 F. 7
		Do.	Jain	...	...	T. 97 M. 47 F. 50	T. 2 ... F. 2	...	T. 15 M. 9 F. 6
		Mantri	Hindu	...	...	...	...	...	...
		Náidu	Do.	...	...	...	...	T. 3 M. 2 F. 1	T. 17 M. 8 F. 9
		Sárlan	Do.	...	...	...	...	...	...
		Shelki	Do.	...	...	...	...	...	...

Nationality or traditional Occupation—*contd.*

Ellichpur.		District Buldana.			District Wun.				District Basim.		
Daryapur.	Melghat.	Chikhli.	Malkapur.	Mehkar.	Yeotmal.	Darwha.	Kelapur.	Wun.	Basim.	Mangrul.	Pusad.
Total, Males, and Females.	Total, Males, and Females.	Total, Males, and Females.	Total, Males, and Females.	Total, Males, and Females.	Total, Males, and Females.	Total, Males, and Females.	Total, Males, and Females.	Total, Males, and Females.	Total, Males, and Females.	Total, Males, and Females.	Total, Males, and Females.
27	28	29	30	31	32	33	34	35	36	37	38
...	...	...	...	...	...	...	...	...	...	...	...
...	...	...	...	T. 3 ... F. 3	T. 3 M. 1 F. 2	T. 9 M. 4 F. 5	T. 20 M. 9 F. 11	T. 12 M. 1 F. 11	T. 11 M. 3 F. 8	T. 3 M. 1 F. 2	T. 30 M. 8 F. 22
...	...	...	T. 5 M. 5 ...	T. 1 ... F. 1	...	T. 1 M. 1 ...	...	...	T. 24 M. 11 F. 13	...	...
...	...	...	*T. 6* *M. 6* ...	*T. 4* ... *F. 4*	*T. 3* *M. 1* *F. 2*	*T. 10* *M. 5* *F. 5*	*T. 20* *M. 9* *F. 11*	*T. 12* *M. 1* *F. 11*	*T. 35* *M. 14* *F. 21*	*T. 3* *M. 1* *F. 2*	*T. 30* *M. 8* *F. 22*
...	...	...	...	...	T. 24 M. 12 F. 12	...	...	...	...	...	...
T. 2 M. 1 F. 1	...	...	T. 7 M. 4 F. 3	T. 11 M. 5 F. 6	T. 3 M. 2 F. 1	T. 14 M. 5 F. 9	T. 36 M. 18 F. 18	...	T. 7 M. 5 F. 2	T. 18 M. 7 F. 11	T. 3 M. 1 F. 2
...	...	...	T. 6 M. 2 F. 4	...	...	...	...	...	...	...	...
...	...	...	...	...	...	...	...	...	...	...	...
T. 2 *M. 1* *F. 1*	...	...	*T. 13* *M. 6* *F. 7*	*T. 11* *M. 5* *F. 6*	*T. 3* *M. 2* *F. 1*	*T. 14* *M. 5* *F. 9*	*T. 36* *M. 18* *F. 18*	...	*T. 7* *M. 5* *F. 2*	*T. 18* *M. 7* *F. 11*	*T. 3* *M. 1* *F. 2*
...	...	T. 3 M. 2 F. 1	...	...	T. 1 M. 1 ...	T. 8 M. 4 F. 4	...	...	T. 2 M. 2 ...	T. 1 M. 1 ...	...
...	...	...	...	...	...	...	...	...	...	...	...
T. 2 M. 2 ...	T. 37 M. 31 F. 6	T. 5 M. 5 ...	T. 8 M. 3 F. 5	...	T. 11 M. 11 ...	...	...	...	T. 12 M. 11 F. 1	...	...
...	...	T. 6 M. 6 ...	T 12 M. 12 ...	T. 3 M. 3 ...	T. 15 M. 13 F. 2	T. 2 M. 2 ...	T. 7 M. 5 F. 2	T. 1 M. 1 ...	T. 14 M. 14 ...	T. 12 M. 11 F. 1	...
...	...	...	...	...	T. 4 M. 2 F. 2	...	T. 23 M. 11 F. 12	...	...	...	...
T. 17 M. 6 F. 11	...	T. 23 M. 12 F. 11	T. 13 M. 3 F. 10	T. 9 M. 4 F. 5	T. 473 M. 226 F. 247	T. 346 M. 182 F. 164	T. 930 M. 402 F. 468	T. 286 M. 148 F. 138	T. 36 M. 18 F. 18	T. 106 M. 54 F. 52	T. 257 M. 129 F. 128
...	...	T. 252 M. 134 F. 118	T. 104 M. 45 F. 59	T. 418 M. 204 F. 214	T. 11 M. 6 F. 5	T. 8 M. 5 F. 3	T. 4 M. 1 F. 3	...	T. 161 M. 102 F. 59	T. 64 M. 36 F. 28	T. 9 M. 6 F. 3
T. 142 M. 65 F. 77	...	T. 61 M. 28 F. 33	T. 7 M. 4 F. 3	T. 78 M. 31 F. 47	...	T. 2 M. 2 ...	...	T. 1 M. 1 ...	T. 803 M. 420 F. 383	T. 17 M. 10 F. 7	T. 64 M. 31 F. 33
...	...	...	...	...	...	...	...	...	T. 1 M. 1 ...	...	...
...	...	...	...	...	...	...	...	...	...	...	T. 1 ... F. 1
...	...	...	...	...	...	...	...	...	...	T. 2 M. 2 ...	...
...	...	...	...	T. 1 ... F. 1	...	...	...	...	...	...	...

TABLE XVI.—Castes, Tribes, and Races, by

Class.	Group.	Caste.	Religion.	PROVINCIAL TOTAL. Total, Males, and Females.	DISTRIBUTION — Amraoti. Total, Males, and Females.	Akola. Total, Males, and Females.
1	2	3	4	5	6	7
C.—COMMERCIAL—*contd.*	14.—TRADERS—*contd.*	WÁNI (BANIÁ AND MÁRWÁDI)	Hindu	T. 50,270 M. 27,456 F. 22,814	T. 10,659 M. 5,881 F. 4,778	T. 11,618 M. 6,571 F. 5,047
		Do. Do.	Jain	T. 13,260 M. 7,172 F. 6,088	T. 4,895 M. 2,593 F. 2,302	T. 2,283 M. 1,256 F. 1,027
		Do. Do.	Sikh	T. 3 M. 3 ...	... ...	T. 3 M. 3 ...
			Total Group 14	*T. 70,004* *M. 38,076* *F. 31,928*	*T. 16,404* *M. 8,969* *F. 7,435*	*T. 14,553* *M. 8,206* *F. 6,347*
	15.—PEDLARS	GÁZULÁBALIJÁ	Hindu	T. 2 M. 1 F. 1	... ...	... ...
		MANIHÁR	Musalman	T. 15 M. 9 F. 6	... ...	T. 4 M. 3 F. 1
		MEMAN	Do.	T. 7 M. 7 ...	... ...	T. 3 M. 3 ...
		PERKI	Hindu	T. 1,499 M. 761 F. 738	T. 15 M. 6 F. 9	... ...
			Total Group 15	*T. 1,528* *M. 778* *F. 745*	*T. 15* *M. 6* *F. 9*	*T. 7* *M. 6* *F. 1*
	16.—CARRIERS	BANJÁRI	Do.	T. 52,470 M. 27,983 F. 24,487	T. 2,906 M. 1,558 F. 1,348	T. 1,375 M. 814 F. 561
		Do.	Musalman	T. 120 M. 71 F. 49	... ...	... ...
		Do.	Jain	T. 29 M. 17 F. 12	... ...	... ...
		HAMÁL	Hindu	T. 99 M. 59 F. 40	T. 88 M. 54 F. 34	... ...
		LABHÁNI	Do.	T. 25,525 M. 13,365 F. 12,160	T. 1,501 M. 772 F. 729	T. 1,588 M. 909 F. 679
		Do.	Musalman	T. 56 M. 29 F. 27	... ...	... ...
		Do.	Jain	T. 6 M. 5 F. 1	... ...	... ...
		WANJÁRI	Hindu	T. 31,802 M. 16,341 F. 15,461	T. 1,492 M. 786 F. 706	T. 3,683 M. 1,911 F. 1,772
			Total Group 16	*T. 110,107* *M. 57,870* *F. 52,237*	*T. 5,987* *M. 3,170* *F. 2,817*	*T. 6,646* *M. 3,634* *F. 3,012*
	17.—GOLDSMITHS	JOHARI	Hindu	T. 161 M. 87 F. 74	T. 74 M. 36 F. 38	T. 68 M. 34 F. 34
		SONÁR	Do.	T. 29,217 M. 15,130 F. 14,087	T. 7,731 M. 4,072 F. 3,659	T. 6,592 M. 3,414 F. 3,178

Nationality or traditional Occupation—*contd.*

BY DISTRICT.				RAILWAY PASSENGERS, ETC.	DISTRICT AMRAOTI.			
ELLICHPUR.	BULDANA.	WUN.	BASIM.		AMRAOTI.	CHANDUR.	MORSI.	MURTAZAPUR.
Total, Males, and Females.	Total, Males, and Females.	Total, Males, and Females.	Total, Males, and Females.	Total, Males, and Females.	Total, Males, and Females.	Total, Males, and Females.	Total, Males, and Females.	Total, Males, and Females.
8	9	10	11	12	13	14	15	16
T. 3,959 M. 2,184 F. 1,775	T. 8,046 M. 4,328 F. 3,718	T. 6,093 M. 3,174 F. 2,919	T. 9,871 M. 5,298 F. 4,573	T. 24 M. 20 F. 4	T. 4,686 M. 2,566 F. 2,120	T. 2,125 M. 1,208 F. 917	T. 1,881 M. 1,049 F. 832	T. 1,967 M. 1,058 F. 909
T. 999 M. 533 F. 466	T. 2,241 M. 1,240 F. 1,001	T. 1,439 M. 796 F. 643	T. 1,403 M. 754 F. 649	... ...	T. 1,037 M. 604 F. 433	T. 1,400 M. 750 F. 650	T. 907 M. 437 F. 470	T. 1,551 M. 802 F. 749
... ...	... ...	... ...	... ...	... ...	... ...	... ...	... ...	... ...
T. 5,219 M. 2,857 F. 2,362	T. 11,290 M. 6,064 F. 5,226	T. 9,665 M. 5,053 F. 4,612	T. 12,836 M. 6,900 F. 5,936	T. 37 M. 27 F. 10	T. 6,262 M. 3,477 F. 2,785	T. 3,616 M. 2,022 F. 1,594	T. 2,865 M. 1,525 F. 1,340	T. 3,661 M. 1,945 F. 1,716
T. 2 M. 1 F. 1	... ...	... ...	... ...	... ...	... ...	... ...	... ...	... ...
... ...	T. 11 M. 6 F. 5	... ...	... ...	... ...	... ...	... ...	... ...	... ...
T. 1 M. 1 ...	T. 3 M. 3 ...	... ...	... ...	... ...	... ...	... ...	... ...	... ...
... ...	... ...	T. 1,484 M. 755 F. 729	... ...	... ...	T. 8 M. 3 F. 5	T. 6 M. 2 F. 4	T. 1 M. 1 ...	... ...
T. 3 M. 2 F. 1	T. 14 M. 9 F. 5	T. 1,484 M. 755 F. 729	... ...	... ...	T. 8 M. 3 F. 5	T. 6 M. 2 F. 4	T. 1 M. 1 ...	... ...
T. 601 M. 371 F. 230	T. 4,011 M. 2,095 F. 1,916	T. 24,732 M. 13,005 F. 11,727	T. 18,845 M. 10,140 F. 8,705	... ...	T. 512 M. 272 F. 240	T. 1,027 M. 558 F. 469	T. 64 M. 36 F. 28	T. 1,303 M. 692 F. 611
... ...	... ...	T. 96 M. 58 F. 38	T. 24 M. 13 F. 11	... ...	... ...	... ...	... ...	... ...
... ...	... ...	T. 29 M. 17 F. 12	... ...	... ...	... ...	... ...	... ...	... ...
T. 11 M. 5 F. 6	... ...	... ...	... ...	... ...	T. 80 M. 49 F. 31	... ...	... ...	T. 8 M. 5 F. 3
T. 16 M. 14 F. 2	T. 4,695 M. 2,483 F. 2,212	T. 5,456 M. 2,828 F. 2,628	T. 12,269 M. 6,359 F. 5,910	... ...	T. 139 M. 71 F. 68	T. 491 M. 267 F. 224	T. 15 M. 13 F. 2	T. 856 M. 421 F. 435
T. 6 M. 3 F. 3	T. 11 M. 7 F. 4	T. 13 M. 5 F. 8	T. 26 M. 14 F. 12	... ...	... ...	... ...	... ...	... ...
... ...	... ...	T. 6 M. 5 F. 1	... ...	... ...	... ...	... ...	... ...	... ...
T. 322 M. 165 F. 157	T. 17,879 M. 9,137 F. 8,742	T. 1,406 M. 752 F. 654	T. 7,015 M. 3,586 F. 3,429	T. 5 M. 4 F. ...	T. 27 M. 24 F. 3	T. 665 M. 341 F. 324	... ...	T. 800 M. 421 F. 379
T. 956 M. 558 F. 398	T. 26,596 M. 13,722 F. 12,874	T. 31,738 M. 16,670 F. 15,068	T. 38,179 M. 20,112 F. 18,067	T. 5 M. 4 F. 1	T. 758 M. 416 F. 342	T. 2,183 M. 1,166 F. 1,017	T. 79 M. 49 F. 30	T. 2,967 M. 1,539 F. 1,428
T. 3 M. 2 F. 1	T. 2 M. 1 F. 1	T. 11 M. 11 ...	T. 3 M. 3 ...	... ...	T. 26 M. 13 F. 13	T. 11 M. 7 F. 4	T. 37 M. 16 F. 21	... ...
T. 3,478 M. 1,816 F. 1,662	T. 4,966 M. 2,502 F. 2,464	T. 3,408 M. 1,774 F. 1,634	T. 3,042 M. 1,552 F. 1,490	... ...	T. 2,090 M. 1,137 F. 953	T. 2,260 M. 1,184 F. 1,076	T. 1,837 M. 960 F. 877	T. 1,544 M. 791 F. 753

TABLE XVI.—Castes, Tribes, and Races, by

Class.	Group.	Caste.	Religion.	DISTRICT AKOLA. Akola. Total, Males, and Females.	DISTRICT AKOLA. Akot. Total, Males, and Females.	DISTRICT AKOLA. Balapur. Total, Males, and Females.	DISTRICT AKOLA. Jalgaon. Total, Males, and Females.	DISTRICT AKOLA. Khamgaon. Total, Males, and Females.	DISTRICT Ellichpur. Total, Males, and Females.
17	18	19	20	21	22	23	24	25	26
C.—COMMERCIAL—contd.		Wáni (Baniá and Márwádi)	Hindu	T. 2,441 M. 1,457 F. 984	T. 2,839 M. 1,594 F. 1,245	T. 1,689 M. 906 F. 783	T. 1,977 M. 1,086 F. 891	T. 2,672 M. 1,528 F. 1,144	T. 2,105 M. 1,151 F. 954
		Do.	Jain	T. 727 M. 387 F. 340	T. 434 M. 227 F. 207	T. 408 M. 219 F. 189	T. 132 M. 85 F. 47	T. 582 M. 338 F. 244	T. 723 M. 369 F. 354
		Do.	Sikh	... ...	T. 3 M. 3 ...	... ...	... ...	... ...	... ...
			Total Group 14	*T. 3,402* *M. 1,980* *F. 1,422*	*T. 3,328* *M. 1,863* *F. 1,465*	*T. 2,210* *M. 1,181* *F. 1,029*	*T. 2,163* *M. 1,197* *F. 966*	*T. 3,460* *M. 1,985* *F. 1,465*	*T. 2,891* *M. 1,556* *F. 1,335*
	15.—Pedlars	Gázulábalijá	Hindu	... ...	... ...	... ...	... ...	... ...	... ...
		Manihár	Musalman	... ...	... ...	... ...	... ...	T. 4 M. 3 F. 1	... ...
		Meman	Do.	... ...	... ...	... ...	... ...	T. 3 M. 3 ...	... ...
		Perki	Hindu	... ...	... ...	... ...	... ...	... ...	... ...
			Total Group 15	... ...	... ...	... ...	... ...	*T. 7* *M. 6* *F. 1*	... ...
	16.—Carriers	Banjári	Do.	T. 505 M. 301 F. 204	T. 370 M. 213 F. 157	T. 295 M. 184 F. 111	T. 40 M. 24 F. 16	T. 165 M. 92 F. 73	T. 204 M. 119 F. 85
		Do.	Musalman	... ...	... ...	... ...	... ...	... ...	... ...
		Do.	Jain	... ...	... ...	... ...	... ...	... ...	... ...
		Hamál	Hindu	... ...	... ...	... ...	... ...	... ...	T. 8 M. 4 F. 4
		Labháni	Do.	T. 1,249 M. 706 F. 543	T. 1 M. 1 ...	T. 337 M. 201 F. 136	... ...	T. 1 M. 1 ...	... ...
		Do.	Musalman	... ...	... ...	... ...	... ...	... ...	T. 6 M. 3 F. 3
		Do.	Jain	... ...	... ...	... ...	... ...	... ...	... ...
		Wanjári	Hindu	T. 1,858 M. 983 F. 875	T. 824 M. 404 F. 420	T. 668 M. 330 F. 338	T. 17 M. 15 F. 2	T. 316 M. 179 F. 137	T. 13 M. 7 F. 6
			Total Group 16	*T. 3,612* *M. 1,990* *F. 1,622*	*T. 1,195* *M. 618* *F. 577*	*T. 1,300* *M. 715* *F. 585*	*T. 57* *M. 39* *F. 18*	*T. 482* *M. 272* *F. 210*	*T. 231* *M. 133* *F. 98*
	17.—Goldsmiths	Johari	Hindu	T. 66 M. 33 F. 33	T. 1 M. 1 ...	T. 1 ... F. 1	... ...	... ...	... ...
		Sonár	Do.	T. 1,423 M. 760 F. 663	T. 2,108 M. 1,085 F. 1,023	T. 896 M. 467 F. 429	T. 971 M. 511 F. 460	T. 1,194 M. 591 F. 603	T. 1,898 M. 972 F. 926

Nationality or traditional Occupation—*contd.*

ELLICHPUR.		DISTRICT BULDANA.			DISTRICT WUN.				DISTRICT BASIM.		
DARYAPUR.	MELGHAT.	CHIKHLI.	MALKAPUR.	MEHKAR.	YEOTMAL.	DARWHA.	KELAPUR.	WUN.	BASIM.	MANGRUL.	PUSAD.
Total, Males, and Females.	Total, Males, and Females.	Total, Males, and Females.	Total, Males, and Females.	Total, Males, and Females.	Total, Males, and Females.	Total, Males, and Females.	Total, Males, and Females.	Total, Males, and Females.	Total, Males, and Females.	Total, Males, and Females.	Total, Males, and Females.
27	28	29	30	31	32	33	34	35	36	37	38
T. 1,762 M. 977 F. 785	T. 92 M. 56 F. 36	T. 2,209 M. 1,203 F. 1,006	T. 2,709 M. 1,464 F. 1,245	T. 3,128 M. 1,661 F. 1,467	T. 1,330 M. 726 F. 604	T. 3,071 M. 1,575 F. 1,496	T. 1,067 M. 565 F. 502	T. 625 M. 308 F. 317	T. 3,930 M. 2,164 F. 1,766	F. 1,481 M. 784 F. 697	T. 4,460 M. 2,350 F. 2,110
T. 274 M. 162 F. 112	T. 2 M. 2 ...	T. 706 M. 386 F. 320	T. 700 M. 396 F. 304	T. 835 M. 458 F. 377	T. 645 M. 346 F. 299	T. 556 M. 314 F. 242	T. 217 M. 122 F. 95	T. 21 M. 14 F. 7	T. 578 M. 313 F. 265	T. 248 M. 131 F. 117	T. 577 M. 310 F. 267
... ...	... ...	... ...	... ...	... ...	... ...	... ...	... ...	... ...	... ...	... ...	... ...
T. 2,197 M. 1,212 F. 985	*T. 131 M. 89 F. 42*	*T. 3,265 M. 1,776 F. 1,489*	*T. 3,553 M. 1,927 F. 1,626*	*T. 4,472 M. 2,361 F. 2,111*	*T. 2,490 M. 1,331 F. 1,159*	*T. 3,993 M. 2,084 F. 1,909*	*T. 2,248 M. 1,166 F. 1,082*	*T. 934 M. 472 F. 462*	*T. 5,537 M. 3,045 F. 2,492*	*T. 1,931 M. 1,029 F. 902*	*T. 5,368 M. 2,826 F. 2,542*
... ...	T. 2 M. 1 F. 1	... ...	... ...	... ...	... ...	... ...	... ...	... ...	... ...	... ...	... ...
... ...	... ...	... ...	T. 11 M. 6 F. 5	... ...	... ...	... ...	... ...	... ...	... ...	... ...	... ...
T. 1 M. 1 ...	... ...	... ...	T. 3 M. 3 ...	... ...	... ...	... ...	... ...	... ...	... ...	... ...	... ...
... ...	... ...	... ...	... ...	... ...	T. 120 M. 62 F. 58	... ...	T. 987 M. 503 F. 484	T. 377 M. 190 F. 187	... ...	... ...	... ...
T. 1 M. 1 ...	*T. 2 M. 1 F. 1*	... ...	*T. 14 M. 8 F. 6*	... ...	*T. 120 M. 62 F. 58*	... ...	*T. 987 M. 503 F. 484*	*T. 377 M. 190 F. 187*	... ...	... ...	... ...
T. 30 M. 21 F. 9	T. 367 M. 231 F. 136	T. 616 M. 326 F. 290	T. 106 M. 63 F. 43	T. 3,289 M. 1,706 F. 1,583	T. 3,554 M. 1,883 F. 1,671	T. 17,586 M. 9,262 F. 8,324	T. 3,308 M. 1,720 F. 1,588	T. 284 M. 140 F. 144	T. 3,287 M. 1,648 F. 1,639	T. 5,085 M. 2,810 F. 2,275	T. 10.473 M. 5,682 F. 4,791
... ...	... ...	... ...	... ...	... ...	... ...	T. 58 M. 37 F. 21	T. 38 M. 21 F. 17	... ...	... ...	T. 24 M. 13 F. 11	... ...
... ...	... ...	... ...	... ...	... ...	T. 29 M. 17 F. 12	... ...	... ...	... ...	... ...	... ...	... ...
T. 3 M. 1 F. 2	... ...	... ...	... ...	... ...	... ...	... ...	... ...	... ...	... ...	... ...	... ...
T. 12 M. 12 ...	T. 4 M. 2 F. 2	T. 423 M. 249 F. 174	... ...	T. 4,272 M. 2,234 F. 2,038	T. 1,092 M. 564 F. 528	T. 1,856 M. 986 F. 870	T. 2,223 M. 1,121 F. 1,102	T. 285 M. 157 F. 128	T. 5,674 M. 2,794 F. 2,880	T. 2,207 M. 1,210 F. 997	T. 4,388 M. 2,355 F. 2,033
... ...	... ...	... ...	... ...	T. 11 M. 7 F. 4	... ...	T. 13 M. 5 F. 8	... ...	... ...	... ...	T. 26 M. 14 F. 12	... ...
... ...	... ...	... ...	... ...	... ...	T. 6 M. 5 F. 1	... ...	... ...	... ...	... ...	... ...	... ...
T. 287 M. 148 F. 139	T. 22 M. 10 F. 12	T. 3,795 M. 1,958 F. 1,837	T. 701 M. 371 F. 330	T. 13,383 M. 6,808 F. 6,575	T. 80 M. 47 F. 33	T. 637 M. 345 F. 292	T. 602 M. 320 F. 282	T. 87 M. 40 F. 47	T 5,385 M. 2,705 F. 2,680	T. 581 M. 295 F. 286	T. 1,049 M. 586 F. 463
T. 332 M. 182 F. 150	*T. 398 M. 248 F. 150*	*T. 4,834 M. 2,533 F. 2,301*	*T. 807 M. 434 F. 373*	*T. 20,965 M. 10,765 F. 10,200*	*T. 4,761 M. 2,516 F. 2,245*	*T. 20,150 M. 10,635 F. 9,515*	*T. 6,171 M. 3,182 F. 2,989*	*T. 656 M. 337 F. 319*	*T. 14,346 M. 7,147 F. 7,199*	*T. 7,923 M. 4,342 F. 3,581*	*T. 15,910 M. 8,623 F, 7,287*
T. 1 M. 1 ...	T. 2 M. 1 F. 1	T. 2 M. 1 F. 1	... ...	... ...	... ...	T. 4 M. 4 ...	T. 6 M. 6 ...	T. 1 M. 1 ...	... ...	... ...	T. 3 M. 3 ...
T. [illegible],546 M. 817 F. 729	T. 34 M. 27 F. 7	T. 1,567 M. 812 F. 755	T. 2,036 M. 1,014 F. 1,022	T 1,363 M. 676 F. 687	T. 956 M. 497 F. 459	T. 1,478 M. 781 F. 697	T. 531 M. 275 F. 256	T. 443 M. 221 F. 222	T. 1,266 M. 651 F. 615	T. 743 M. 375 F. 368	T. 1,033 M. 526 F. 507

TABLE XVI.—Castes, Tribes, and Races, by

Name and Classification.				Provincial Total.	Distribution	
					Amraoti.	Akola.
Class.	Group.	Caste.	Religion.	Total, Males, and Females.	Total, Males, and Females.	Total, Males, and Females.
1	2	3	4	5	6	7
C.—Commercial—*contd.*	17.—Goldsmiths—*contd.*	Sonár	Jain	T. 2	T. 2	...
				M. 1	M. 1	...
				F. 1	F. 1	...
		Tarkihár	Hindu	T. 1	...	T. 1
				M. 1	...	M. 1
				...	...	...
			Total Group 17	*T. 29,381*	*T. 7,807*	*T. 6,661*
				M. 15,219	*M. 4,109*	*M. 3,449*
				F. 14,162	*F. 3,698*	*F. 3,212*
	18.—Barbers	Mháli (Hajjám, Nhávi and Wárik)	Hindu	T. 35,225	T. 8,455	T. 7,848
				M. 18,231	M. 4,461	M. 4,070
				F. 16,994	F. 3,994	F. 3,778
		Do. do.	Musalman	T. 17	T. 4	...
				M. 11	M. 3	...
				F. 6	F. 1	...
		Do. do.	Jain	T. 3	T. 1	...
				M. 3	M. 1	...
				...	...	...
			Total Group 18	*T. 35,245*	*T. 8,460*	*T. 7,848*
				M. 18,245	*M. 4,465*	*M. 4,070*
				F. 17,000	*F. 3,995*	*F. 3,778*
D.—Artisan and Village Menial.	19.—Blacksmiths	Dángare	Hindu	T. 188	T. 136	...
				M. 97	M. 70	...
				F. 91	F. 66	...
		Ghisádi	Do.	T. 708	T. 5	T. 4
				M. 368	M. 2	M. 4
				F. 340	F. 3	...
		Do.	Musalman	T. 11	...	...
				M. 6	...	...
				F. 5	...	...
		Jiráyat	Hindu	T. 312	T. 39	T. 131
				M. 160	M. 19	M. 72
				F. 152	F. 20	F. 59
		Kathilkár	Do.	T. 20	T. 2	T. 3
				M. 10	...	M. 1
				F. 10	F. 2	F. 2
		Lohár (Kháti)	Do.	T. 15,889	T. 4,171	T. 2,304
				M. 8,351	M. 2,193	M. 1,232
				F. 7,538	F. 1,978	F. 1,072
		Do.	Animistic	T. 18	T. 18	...
				M. 7	M. 7	...
				F. 11	F. 11	...
		Nálband	Hindu	T. 13	T. 13	...
				M. 6	M. 6	...
				F. 7	F. 7	...
		Panchál (Panchál Lohár)	Do.	T. 1,876	T. 345	T. 219
				M. 968	M. 189	M. 119
				F. 908	F. 156	F. 100
		Do. do.	Musalman	T. 9	T. 1	...
				M. 5	M. 1	...
				F. 4	...	...
			Total Group 19	*T. 19,044*	*T. 4,730*	*T. 2,661*
				M. 9,978	*M. 2,487*	*M. 1,428*
				F. 9,066.	*F. 2,243*	*F. 1,233*
	20.—Carpenters, Turners and Masons.	Gaondi (Rái)	Hindu	T. 639	T. 148	T. 50
				M. 335	M. 80	M. 32
				F. 304	F. 68	F. 18
		Gosangi	Do.	T. 6	...	T. 6
				M. 4	...	M. 4
				F. 2	...	F. 2

Nationality or traditional Occupation—*contd.*

	BY DISTRICT.					DISTRICT AMRAOTI.			
	ELLICHPUR.	BULDANA.	WUN.	BASIM.	RAILWAY PASSENGERS, ETC.	AMRAOTI.	CHANDUR.	MORSI.	MURTAZAPUR.
	Total, Males, and Females.	Total, Males, and Females.	Total, Males, and Females.	Total, Males, and Females.	Total, Males, and Females.	Total, Males, and Females.	Total, Males, and Females.	Total, Males, and Females.	Total, Males, and Females.
	8	9	10	11	12	13	14	15	16
T.	...	...	...	...	...	2	...	...	...
M.	...	...	...	...	...	1	...	...	...
F.	...	...	...	...	...	1	...	...	...
T.	...	...	...	...	...	...	...	...	...
M.	...	...	...	...	...	...	...	...	...
F.	...	...	...	...	...	...	...	...	...
T.	*3,481*	*4,968*	*3,419*	*3,045*	...	*2,118*	*2,271*	*1,874*	*1,544*
M.	*1,818*	*2,503*	*1,785*	*1,555*	...	*1,151*	*1,191*	*976*	*791*
F.	*1,663*	*2,465*	*1,634*	*1,490*	...	*967*	*1,080*	*898*	*753*
T.	3,644	5,521	5,489	4,267	1	2,320	2,622	2,036	1,477
M.	1,875	2,839	2,820	2,165	1	1,257	1,409	1,027	768
F.	1,769	2,682	2,669	2,102	...	1,063	1,213	1,009	709
T.	...	6	6	1	...	4	...	...	...
M.	...	4	3	1	...	3	...	...	...
F.	...	2	3	...	...	1	...	...	...
T.	...	2	...	...	...	...	...	...	1
M.	...	2	...	...	...	...	...	...	1
F.	...	...	...	...	...	...	...	...	...
T.	*3,644*	*5,529*	*5,495*	*4,268*	*1*	*2,324*	*2,622*	*2,036*	*1,478*
M.	*1,876*	*2,845*	*2,823*	*2,166*	*1*	*1,260*	*1,409*	*1,027*	*769*
F.	*1,769*	*2,684*	*2,672*	*2,102*	...	*1,064*	*1,213*	*1,009*	*709*
T.	...	4	48	...	...	...	136	...	...
M.	...	2	25	...	...	...	70	...	...
F.	...	2	23	...	...	...	66	...	...
T.	...	342	63	294	...	...	5	...	...
M.	...	190	30	142	...	...	2	...	...
F.	...	152	33	152	...	...	3	...	...
T.	...	11	...	...	...	...	...	...	...
M.	...	6	...	...	...	...	...	...	...
F.	...	5	...	...	...	...	...	...	...
T.	10	108	...	24	...	5	2	...	32
M.	3	54	...	12	...	4	2	...	13
F.	7	54	...	12	...	1	...	...	19
T.	9	6	...	...	...	...	...	2	...
M.	5	4	...	...	...	...	...	...	...
F.	4	2	...	...	...	...	...	2	...
T.	1,538	1,869	4,479	1,526	2	994	1,606	888	683
M.	870	961	2,272	821	2	536	824	475	358
F.	668	908	2,207	705	...	458	782	413	325
T.	...	...	...	...	...	...	...	18	...
M.	...	...	...	...	...	...	...	7	...
F.	...	...	...	...	...	...	...	11	...
T.	...	...	...	...	...	...	13	...	...
M.	...	...	...	...	...	...	6	...	...
F.	...	...	...	...	...	...	7	...	...
T.	162	299	703	144	4	76	103	69	97
M.	75	146	359	76	4	43	63	33	50
F.	87	153	344	68	...	33	40	36	47
T.	...	...	8	...	...	1	...	...	...
M.	...	...	4	...	...	1	...	...	...
F.	...	...	4	...	...	...	...	...	...
T.	*1,719*	*2,639*	*5,301*	*1,988*	*6*	*1,076*	*1,865*	*977*	*812*
M.	*953*	*1,363*	*2,690*	*1,051*	*6*	*584*	*967*	*515*	*421*
F.	*766*	*1,276*	*2,611*	*937*	...	*492*	*898*	*462*	*391*
T.	32	125	16	267	1	45	7	6	90
M.	16	65	9	132	1	26	3	4	47
F.	16	60	7	135	...	19	4	2	43
T.	...	...	...	...	...	...	...	...	...
M.	...	...	...	...	...	...	...	...	...
F.	...	...	...	...	...	...	...	...	...

TABLE XVI—Castes, Tribes, and Races, by

Class.	Group.	Caste.	Religion.	DISTRICT AKOLA. Akola. Total, Males, and Females.	Akot. Total, Males, and Females.	Balapur. Total, Males, and Females.	Jalgaon. Total, Males, and Females.	Khamgaon. Total, Males, and Females.	DISTRICT Ellichpur. Total, Males, and Females.
17	18	19	20	21	22	23	24	25	26
C.—COMMERCIAL—*concld.*	17.—Goldsmiths—*contd.*	Sonár	Jain	...	...	...	...	...	...
		Tarkihár	Hindu	...	T. 1 M. 1 ...	...	...	...	...
			Total Group 17	*T. 1,489* *M. 793* *F. 696*	*T. 2,110* *M. 1,087* *F. 1,023*	*T. 897* *M. 467* *F. 430*	*T. 971* *M. 511* *F. 460*	*T. 1,194* *M. 591* *F. 603*	*T. 1,898* *M. 972* *F. 926*
	18.—Barbers	Mháli (Hajjám, Nhávi and Wárik).	Hindu	T. 1,907 M. 974 F. 933	T. 1,970 M. 1,019 F. 951	T. 1,356 M. 694 F. 662	T. 1,273 M. 651 F. 622	T. 1,342 M. 732 F. 610	T. 1,960 M. 1,015 F. 945
		Do. do.	Musalman	...	...	...	...	...	...
		Do. do.	Jain	...	...	...	...	...	...
			Total Group 18	*T. 1,907* *M. 974* *F. 933*	*T. 1,970* *M. 1,019* *F. 951*	*T. 1,356* *M. 694* *F. 662*	*T. 1,273* *M. 651* *F. 622*	*T. 1,342* *M. 732* *F. 610*	*T. 1,960* *M. 1,015* *F. 945*
D.—ARTISAN AND VILLAGE MENIAL.	19.—Blacksmiths.	Dángare	Hindu	...	...	...	...	...	...
		Ghisádi	Do.	...	...	...	...	T. 4 M. 4 ...	...
		Do.	Musalman	...	...	...	...	...	...
		Jiráyat	Hindu	T. 1 ... F. 1	T. 14 M. 9 F. 5	T. 2 M. 1 F. 1	T. 76 M. 41 F. 35	T. 38 M. 21 F. 17	T. 3 M. 1 F. 2
		Kathilkár	Do.	...	...	T. 3 M. 1 F. 2	...	...	T. 9 M. 5 F. 4
		Lohár (Kháti)	Do.	T. 495 M. 271 F. 224	T. 577 M. 324 F. 253	T. 351 M. 186 F. 165	T. 513 M. 254 F. 259	T. 368 M. 197 F. 171	T. 743 M. 422 F. 321
		Do.	Animistic	...	...	...	...	...	...
		Nálband	Hindu	...	...	...	...	...	...
		(PancháL Lohár)	Do.	T. 49 M. 29 F. 20	T. 15 M. 11 F. 4	T. 70 M. 33 F. 37	T. 45 M. 25 F. 20	T. 40 M 21 F. 19	T. 150 M. 69 F. 81
		Do. do.	Musalman	...	...	...	...	...	...
			Total Group 19	*T. 545* *M. 300* *F. 245*	*T. 606* *M. 344* *F. 262*	*T. 426* *M. 221* *F. 205*	*T. 634* *M. 320* *F. 314*	*T. 450* *M. 243* *F. 207*	*T. 905* *M. 497* *F. 408*
	20.—Carpenters, Turners and Masons.	Gaondi (Ráj)	Hindu	T. 18 M. 10 F. 8	T. 14 M. 13 F. 1	T. 18 M. 9 F. 9	...	...	T. 31 M. 15 F. 16
		Gosangi	Do.	...	...	...	T. 6 M. 4 F. 2	...	...

Nationality or traditional Occupation—*contd.*

ELLICHPUR.		DISTRICT BULDANA.			DISTRICT WUN.				DISTRICT BASIM.		
DARYAPUR.	MELGHAT.	CHIKHLI.	MALKAPUR.	MEHKAR.	YEOTMAL.	DARWHA.	KELAPUR.	WUN.	BASIM.	MANGRUL.	PUSAD.
Total, Males, and Females.	Total, Males, and Females.	Total, Males, and Females.	Total, Males, and Females.	Total, Males, and Females.	Total, Males, and Females.	Total, Males, and Females.	Total, Males, and Females.	Total, Males, and Females.	Total, Males, and Females.	Total, Males, and Females.	Total, Males, and Females.
27	28	29	30	31	32	33	34	35	36	37	38
...	...	...	...	...	...	...	...	...	...	...	...
...	...	...	...	...	...	...	...	...	...	...	...
T. 1,547 M. 818 F. 729	*T. 36 M 28 F. 8*	*T. 1,569 M. 813 F. 756*	*T. 2,036 M. 1,014 F. 1,022*	*T. 1,363 M. 676 F. 687*	*T. 956 M. 497 F. 459*	*T. 1,482 M. 785 F. 697*	*T. 537 M. 281 F. 256*	*T. 444 M. 222 F. 222*	*T. 1,266 M. 651 F. 615*	*T. 748 M. 375 F. 368*	*T. 1,036 M. 529 F. 507*
T. 1,642 M. 827 F. 815	T. 42 M. 33 F. 9	T. 1,647 M. 827 F. 820	T. 2,334 M. 1,188 F. 1,146	T. 1,540 M. 824 F. 716	T. 1,360 M. 721 F. 639	T. 1,612 M. 829 F. 783	T. 1,274 M. 656 F. 618	T. 1,243 M. 614 F. 629	T. 1,903 M. 977 F. 926	T. 966 M. 479 F. 487	T. 1,398 M. 709 F. 689
...	...	T. 6 M. 4 F. 2	...	...	T. 6 M. 3 F. 3	...	...	...	T. 1 M. 1 ...	...	...
...	...	...	...	T. 2 M. 2 ...	...	...	...	...	...	...	...
T. 1,642 M. 827 F. 815	*T. 42 M. 33 F. 9*	*T. 1,653 M. 831 F. 822*	*T. 2,334 M. 1,188 F. 1,146*	*T. 1,542 M. 826 F. 716*	*T. 1,366 M. 724 F. 642*	*T. 1,612 M. 829 F. 783*	*T. 1,274 M. 656 F. 618*	*T. 1,243 M. 614 F. 629*	*T. 1,904 M. 978 F. 926*	*T. 966 M. 479 F. 487*	*T. 1,398 M. 709 F. 689*
...	...	T. 4 M. 2 F. 2	...	...	T. 16 M. 8 F. 8	T. 1 M. 1 ...	T. 31 M. 16 F. 15	...	...	...	...
...	...	T. 124 M. 68 F. 56	...	T. 218 M. 122 F. 96	T. 9 M. 4 F. 5	T. 54 M. 26 F. 28	...	...	T. 126 M. 66 F. 60	T. 12 M. 4 F. 8	T. 156 M. 72 F. 84
...	...	...	...	T. 11 M. 6 F. 5	...	...	...	...	...	...	...
T. 7 M. 2 B. 5	...	T. 43 M. 19 F. 24	T. 45 M. 24 F. 21	T. 20 M. 11 F. 9	...	...	...	...	T. 24 M. 12 F. 12	...	...
...	...	T. 6 M. 4 F. 2	...	...	...	...	...	...	...	...	...
T. 417 M. 239 F. 178	T. 378 M. 209 F. 169	T. 731 M. 365 F. 366	T. 693 M. 355 F. 338	T. 445 M. 241 F. 204	T. 1,113 M. 576 F. 537	T. 1,015 M. 519 F. 496	T. 1,111 M. 532 F. 579	T. 1,240 M. 645 F. 595	T. 663 M. 368 F. 295	T. 423 M. 225 F. 198	T. 440 M. 228 F. 212
...	...	...	...	...	...	...	...	...	...	...	...
...	...	...	...	...	...	...	...	...	...	...	...
T. 12 M. 6 F. 6	...	T. 37 M. 19 F. 18	T. 135 M. 64 F. 71	T. 127 M. 63 F. 64	T. 41 M. 22 F. 19	T. 121 M. 66 F. 55	T. 247 M. 127 F. 120	T. 294 M. 144 F. 150	T. 34 M. 16 F. 18	T. 108 M. 58 F. 50	T. 2 M. 2 ...
...	...	...	...	...	T. 8 M. 4 F. 4	...	...	...	...	...	...
T. 436 M. 247 F. 189	*T. 378 M. 209 F. 169*	*T. 946 M. 477 F. 468*	*T. 873 M. 443 F. 430*	*T. 821 M. 443 F. 378*	*T. 1,187 M. 614 F. 573*	*T. 1,191 M. 612 F. 579*	*T. 1,389 M. 675 F. 714*	*T. 1,534 M. 789 F. 745*	*T. 847 M. 462 F. 385*	*T. 543 M. 287 F. 256*	*T. 598 M. 302 F. 296*
T. 1 M. 1 ...	...	T. 45 M. 24 F. 21	T. 4 M. 1 F. 3	T. 76 M. 40 F. 36	T. 8 M. 5 F. 3	T. 1 M. 1 ...	T. 7 M. 3 F. 4	...	T. 3 M. 3 ...	T. 14 M. 9 F. 5	T. 250 M. 120 F. 130
...	...	...	...	...	...	...	...	...	...	...	...

TABLE XVI.—Castes, Tribes, and Races, by

Name and Classification.				Provincial Total.	Distribution	
					Amraoti.	Akola.
Class.	Group.	Caste.	Religion.	Total, Males, and Females.	Total, Males, and Females.	Total, Males, and Females.
1	2	3	4	5	6	7
D.—ARTISAN AND VILLAGE MENIAL—*contd.*	20.—Carpenters, Turners and Masons—*contd.*	Sutár (Badhai and Wádhi)	Hindu	T. 32,478 M. 17,440 F 15,038	T. 8,827 M. 4,722 F. 4,105	T. 6,324 M. 3,513 F. 2,811
		Do.	Jain	T. 13 M. 13 ...	... ...	... ...
			Total Group 20	*T. 33,136* *M. 17,792* *F. 15,344*	*T. 8,975* *M. 4,802* *F. 4,173*	*T. 6,380* *M. 3,549* *F. 2,831*
	21.—Brass and Copper Smiths.	Kásár	Hindu	T. 7,558 M. 3,929 F. 3,629	T. 1,844 M. 960 F. 884	T. 1,641 M. 914 F. 727
		Do.	Jain	T. 196 M. 109 F. 87	... ...	T. 5 M. 2 F. 3
		Otári (Watankár)	Hindu	T. 1,477 M. 772 F. 705	T. 289 M. 157 F. 132	T. 463 M. 249 F. 214
		Do.	Musalman	T. 1 M. 1 ...	... ...	... ...
		Do.	Animistic	T. 6 M. 4 F. 2	... ...	... ...
		Támbatkár	Hindu	T. 590 M. 304 F. 286	T. 102 M. 55 F. 47	T. 262 M. 145 F. 117
			Total Group 21	*T. 9,828* *M. 5,119* *F. 4,709*	*T. 2,235* *M. 1,172* *F. 1,063*	*T. 2,371* *M. 1,310* *F. 1,061*
	22.—Tailors	Simpi (Darzi)	Hindu	T. 13,725 M. 7,232 F. 6,493	T. 3,247 M. 1,690 F. 1,557	T. 4,638 M. 2,474 F. 2,164
		Do.	Musalman	T. 14 M. 8 F. 6	T. 2 M. 1 F. 1	... ...
		Do.	Jain	T. 2,626 M. 1,294 F. 1,332	T. 149 M. 75 F. 74	T. 557 M. 293 F. 264
			Total Group 22	*T. 16,365* *M. 8,534* *F. 7,831*	*T. 3,398* *M. 1,766* *F. 1,632*	*T. 5,195* *M. 2,767* *F. 2,428*
	22A.—Gram Parchers and Confectioners.	Bharad-bhunjá	Hindu	T. 601 M. 413 F. 188	T. 175 M. 118 F. 57	T. 115 M. 95 F. 20
		Dáliye	Do.	T. 1 M. 1 ...	... ...	... ...
		Halwái	Do.	T. 237 M. 140 F. 97	T. 89 M. 62 F. 27	T. 26 M. 12 F. 14
		Do.	Jain	T. 1 ... F. 1	... ...	T. 1 ... F. 1
			Total Group 22A	*T. 840* *M. 554* *F. 286*	*T. 264* *M. 180* *F. 84*	*T. 143* *M. 107* *F. 36*
	22B.—Perfume and Drug Preparers and Sellers and Betel Leaf Dealers.	Gandhi (Sugandhi)	Hindu	T. 92 M. 47 F. 45	T. 1 M. 1 ...	T. 44 M. 25 F. 19

Nationality or traditional Occupation—*contd.*

BY DISTRICT.				RAILWAY PASSENGERS, ETC.	DISTRICT AMRAOTI.			
ELLICHPUR.	BULDANA.	WUN.	BASIM.		AMRAOTI.	CHANDUR.	MORSI.	MURTAZAPUR.
Total, Males, and Females.	Total, Males, and Females.	Total, Males, and Females.	Total, Males, and Females.	Total, Males, and Females.	Total, Males, and Females.	Total, Males, and Females.	Total, Males, and Females.	Total, Males, and Females.
8	9	10	11	12	13	14	15	16
T. 3,028 M. 1,652 F. 1,376	T. 4,727 M 2,499 F. 2,228	T. 5,517 M. 2,802 F. 2,715	T. 4,050 M. 2,247 F. 1,803	T. 5 M. 5 ...	T. 2,228 M. 1,186 F. 1,042	T. 2,970 M. 1,600 F. 1,370	T. 2,264 M. 1,182 F. 1,082	T. 1,365 M. 754 F. 611
... ...	T. 12 M. 12 ...	T. 1 M. 1 ...	... ...	... ...	... ...	... ...	... ...	... ...
T. 3,080 *M. 1,668* *F. 1,392*	*T. 4,864* *M. 2,576* *F. 2,288*	*T. 5,534* *M. 2,812* *F. 2,722*	*T. 4,317* *M. 2,379* *F. 1,938*	*T. 6* *M. 6* ...	*T. 2,273* *M. 1,212* *F. 1,061*	*T. 2,977* *M. 1,603* *F. 1,374*	*T. 2,270* *M. 1,186* *F. 1,084*	*T. 1,455* *M. 801* *F. 654*
T. 724 M. 333 F. 391	T. 1,598 M. 785 F. 813	T. 657 M. 359 F. 298	T. 1,094 M. 578 F. 516	... ...	T. 297 M. 148 F. 149	T. 572 M. 329 F. 243	T. 456 M. 229 F. 227	T. 519 M. 254 F. 265
T. 38 M. 36 F. 2	T. 15 M. 8 F. 7	... ...	T. 138 M. 63 F. 75	... ...	... ...	... ...	... ...	... ...
T. 190 M. 95 F. 95	T. 145 M. 73 F. 72	T. 139 M. 76 F. 63	T. 251 M. 122 F. 129	... ...	T. 104 M. 50 F. 54	T. 41 M. 26 F. 15	T. 94 M. 50 F. 44	T. 50 M. 31 F. 19
... ...	... ...	... ...	T. 1 M. 1 ...	... ...	... ...	... ...	... ...	... ...
... ...	... ...	T. 6 M. 4 F. 2	... ...	... ...	... ...	... ...	... ...	... ...
T. 139 M. 56 F. 83	T. 40 M. 25 F. 15	T. 6 M. 2 F. 4	T. 41 M. 21 F. 20	... ...	T. 68 M. 31 F. 37	T. 18 M. 13 F. 5	T. 2 M. 1 F. 1	T. 14 M. 10 F. 4
T. 1,091 *M. 520* *F. 571*	*T. 1,798* *M. 891* *F. 907*	*T. 808* *M. 441* *F. 367*	*T. 1,525* *M. 785* *F. 740*	... ...	*T. 469* *M. 229* *F. 240*	*T. 631* *M. 368* *F. 263*	*T. 552* *M. 280* *F. 272*	*T. 583* *M. 295* *F. 288*
T. 1,461 M. 759 F. 702	T. 1,674 M. 851 F. 823	T. 2,157 M. 1,133 F. 1,024	T. 546 M. 323 F. 223	T. 2 M. 2 ...	T. 997 M. 518 F. 479	T. 1,182 M. 592 F. 590	T. 706 M. 372 F. 334	T. 362 M. 208 F. 154
... ...	T. 12 M. 7 F. 5	... ...	... ...	... ...	... ...	T. 2 M. 1 F. 1	... ...	... ...
T. 62 M. 34 F. 28	T. 1,215 M. 576 F 639	T. 20 M. 12 F. 8	T. 623 M. 304 F. 319	... ...	T. 1 M. 1 ...	T. 11 M. 9 F. 2	... ...	T. 137 M. 65 F. 72
T. 1,523 *M. 793* *F. 730*	*T. 2,901* *M. 1,434* F. *1,467*	*T. 2,177* *M. 1,145* *F. 1,032*	*T. 1,169* *M. 627* *F. 542*	*T. 2* *M. 2* ...	*T. 998* *M. 519* *F. 479*	*T. 1,195* *M. 602* *F. 593*	*T. 706* *M. 372* *F. 334*	*T. 499* *M. 273* *F. 226*
T. 185 M. 111 F. 74	T. 27 M. 18 F. 9	T. 66 M. 46 F. 20	T. 32 M. 25 F. 7	T. 1 ... F. 1	T. 70 M. 51 F. 19	T. 55 M. 41 F. 14	T. 37 M. 15 F. 22	T. 13 M. 11 F. 2
T. 1 M. 1 ...	... ...	... ...	... ...	... ...	... ...	... ...	... ...	... ...
T. 27 M. 15 F. 12	T. 73 M 36 F. 37	T. 17 M. 11 F. 6	T. 5 M. 4 F. 1	... ...	T. 25 M. 19 F. 6	T. 11 M. 7 F. 4	T. 16 M. 9 F. 7	T. 37 M. 27 F. 10
... ...	... ...	... ...	... ...	... ...	... ...	... ...	... ...	... ...
T. 213 *M. 127* *F. 86*	*T. 100* *M. 54* *F. 46*	*T. 83* *M. 57* *F. 26*	*T. 37* *M. 29* *F. 8*	*T. 1* ... *F. 1*	*T. 95* *M. 70* *F. 25*	*T. 66* *M. 48* *F. 18*	*T. 53* *M. 24* *F. 29*	*T. 50* *M. 38* *F. 12*
T. 39 M. 16 F. 23	T. 5 M. 2 F. 3	T. 1 M. 1 ...	T. 2 M. 2 ...	... ...	... ...	... ...	... ...	T. 1 M. 1 ...

TABLE XVI—Castes, Tribes, and Races, by

Name and Classification.				District Akola.					District
				Akola.	Akot.	Balapur.	Jalgaon.	Khamgaon.	Ellichpur.
Class.	Group.	Caste.	Religion.	Total, Males, and Females.	Total, Males, and Females.	Total, Males, and Females.	Total, Males, and Females.	Total, Males, and Females.	Total, Males, and Females.
17	18	19	20	21	22	23	24	25	26
D.—ARTISAN AND VILLAGE MENIAL—*contd.*	20.—Carpenters, Turners and Masons—*contd.*	Sutár (Badhai and Wádhi).	Hindu	T. 1,494 M. 825 F. 669	T. 1,468 M. 856 F. 612	T. 1,205 M. 640 F. 565	T. 1,026 M. 569 F. 457	T. 1,131 M. 623 F. 508	T. 1,623 M. 886 F. 737
		Do.	Jain	... ...	... ...	... ...	... ...	... ...	... ...
			Total Group 20	*T. 1,512* *M. 835* *F. 677*	*T. 1,482* *M. 869* *F. 613*	*T. 1,223* *M. 649* *F. 574*	*T. 1,032* *M. 573* *F. 459*	*T. 1,131* *M. 623* *F. 508*	*T. 654* *M. 801* *F. 753*
	21.—Brass and Copper Smiths.	Kásár	Hindu	T. 412 M. 204 F. 208	T. 317 M. 167 F. 150	T. 242 M. 145 F. 97	T. 418 M. 292 F. 126	T. 252 M. 106 F. 146	T. 413 M. 174 F. 239
		Do.	Jain	... ...	T. 5 M. 2 F. 3	... ...	... ...	... ...	T. 38 M. 36 F. 2
		Otári (Watankár)	Hindu	T. 54 M. 25 F. 29	T. 167 M. 86 F. 81	T. 52 M. 24 F. 28	T. 122 M. 80 F. 42	T. 68 M. 34 F. 34	T. 73 M. 37 F. 36
		Do.	Musalman	... ...	... ...	... ...	... ...	... ...	... ...
		Do.	Animistic	... ...	... ...	... ...	... ...	... ...	... ...
		Támbatkár	Hindu	T. 149 M. 82 F. 67	T. 16 M. 9 F. 7	T. 16 M. 10 F. 6	T. 45 M. 23 F. 22	T. 36 M. 21 F. 15	T. 135 M. 55 F. 80
			Total Group 21	*T. 615* *M. 311* *F. 304*	*T. 505* *M. 264* *F. 241*	*T. 310* *M. 179* *F. 131*	*T. 585* *M. 395* *F. 190*	*T. 356* *M. 161* *F. 195*	*T. 659* *M. 302* *F. 357*
	22.—Tailors	Simpi (Darzi)	Hindu	T. 544 M. 298 F. 246	T. 1,128 M. 578 F. 550	T. 449 M. 230 F. 213	T 1,982 M. 1,081 F. 901	T. 535 M. 281 F. 254	T. 719 M. 370 F. 349
		Do.	Musalman	... ...	... ...	... ...	... ...	... ...	... ...
		Do.	Jain	T. 190 M. 93 F. 97	T. 100 M. 56 F. 44	T. 96 M. 57 F. 39	T. 10 M. 9 F. 1	T. 161 M. 78 F. 83	T. 11 M. 6 F. 5
			Total Group 22	*T. 734* *M. 391* *F. 343*	*T 1,228* *M. 634* *F. 594*	*T. 545* *M. 293* *F. 252*	*T. 1,992* *M. 1,090* *F. 902*	*T. 696* *M. 359* *F. 337*	*T. 730* *M. 376* *F. 354*
	22A.—Gram Parchers and Confectioners.	Bharad-bhunjá	Hindu	T. 11 M. 9 F. 2	T. 52 M. 44 F. 8	T. 3 M. 2 F. 1	T. 22 M. 20 F. 2	T. 27 M. 20 F. 7	T. 148 M. 82 F. 66
		Dálite	Do.	... ...	... ...	... ...	... ...	... ...	... ...
		Halwái	Do.	T. 3 M. 2 F. 1	T. 18 M. 8 F. 10	... ...	... ...	T. 5 M. 2 F. 3	T. 12 M. 7 F. 5
		Do.	Jain	T. 1 ... F. 1	... ...	... ...	... ...	... ...	... ...
			Total Group 22A	*T. 15* *M. 11* *F. 4*	*T. 70* *M. 52* *F. 18*	*T. 3* *M. 2* *F. 1*	*T. 22* *M. 20* *F. 2*	*T. 32* *M. 22* *F. 10*	*T. 160* *M. 89* *F. 71*
	22B.—Perfume and Drug Preparers and Sellers and Betel Leaf Dealers.	Gandhi (Sugandhi)	Hindu	T. 1 M. 1 ...	T. 21 M. 10 F. 11	T. 7 M. 3 F. 4	T. 9 M. 6 F. 3	T. 6 M. 5 F. 1	T. 38 M. 15 F. 23

Nationality or traditional Occupation—*contd.*

ELLICHPUR.		DISTRICT BULDANA.			DISTRICT WUN.				DISTRICT BASIM.		
DARYAPUR.	MELGHAT.	CHIKHLI.	MALKAPUR.	MEHKAR.	YEOTMAL.	DARWHA.	KELAPUR.	WUN.	BASIM.	MANGRUL.	PUSAD.
Total, Males, and Females.	Total, Males, and Females.	Total, Males, and Females.	Total, Males, and Females.	Total, Males, and Females.	Total, Males, and Females.	Total, Males, and Females.	Total, Males, and Females.	Total, Males, and Females.	Total, Males, and Females.	Total, Males, and Females.	Total, Males, and Females.
27	28	29	30	31	32	33	34	35	36	37	38
T. 1,389 M. 751 F. 638	T. 16 M. 15 F. 1	T. 1,468 M. 779 F. 689	T. 1,951 M. 988 F. 963	T. 1,308 M. 732 F. 576	T. 1,472 M. 738 F. 734	T. 1,448 M. 762 F. 686	T. 1,274 M. 641 F. 633	T. 1,323 M. 661 F. 662	T. 1,881 M. 1,062 F. 819	T. 929 M. 510 F. 419	T. 1,240 M. 675 F. 565
... ...	... ...	T. 3 M. 3 ...	... ...	T. 9 M. 9 ...	T. 1 M. 1 ...	... ...	... ...	... ...	... ...	... ...	... ...
T. 1,390 *M. 762* *F. 638*	*T. 16* *M. 15* *F. 1*	*T. 1,516* *M. 806* *F. 710*	*T. 1,955* *M. 989* *F. 966*	*T. 1,393* *M. 781* *F. 612*	*T. 1,481* *M. 744* *F. 737*	*T. 1,449* *M. 763* *F. 686*	*T. 1,281* *M. 644* *F. 637*	*T. 1,323* *M. 661* *F. 662*	*T. 1,884* *M. 1,065* *F. 819*	*T. 948* *M. 519* *F. 424*	*T. 1,490* *M. 795* *F. 695*
T. 307 M. 156 F. 151	T. 4 M. 3 F. 1	T. 536 M. 282 F. 254	T. 578 M. 258 F. 320	T. 484 M. 245 F. 239	T. 106 M. 64 F. 42	T. 372 M. 198 F. 174	T. 162 M. 87 F. 75	T. 17 M. 10 F. 7	T. 733 M. 376 F. 357	T. 110 M. 59 F. 51	T. 251 M. 143 F. 108
... ...	... ...	... ...	T. 4 M. 2 F. 2	T. 11 M. 6 F. 5	... ...	... ...	... ...	... ...	T. 11 M. 7 F. 4	... ...	T. 127 M. 56 F. 71
T. 101 M. 52 F. 49	T. 16 M. 6 F. 10	T. 49 M. 27 F. 22	T. 47 M. 20 F. 27	T. 49 M. 20 F. 23	T. 46 M. 28 F. 18	T. 84 M. 42 E. 42	... ...	T. 9 M. 6 F. 3	T. 99 M. 50 F. 49	T. 31 M. 13 F. 18	T. 121 M. 59 F. 62
... ...	... ...	... ...	... ...	... ...	... ...	... ...	... ...	... ...	T. 1 M. 1 ...	... ...	... ...
... ...	... ...	... ...	... ...	... ...	... ...	T. 6 M. 4 F. 2	... ...	... ...	... ...	... ...	... ...
T. 4 M. 1 F. 3	... ...	T. 17 M. 12 F. 5	... ...	T. 23 M. 13 F. 10	T. 6 M. 2 F. 4	... ...	... ...	... ...	T. 38 M. 19 F. 19	T. 1 ... F. 1	T. 2 M. 2 ...
T. 412 *M. 209* *F. 203*	*T. 20* *M. 9* *F. 11*	*T. 602* *M. 321* *F. 281*	*T. 629* *M. 280* *F. 349*	*T. 667* *M. 290* *F. 277*	*T. 158* *M. 94* *F. 64*	*T. 462* *M. 244* *F. 218*	*T. 162* *M. 87* *F. 75*	*T. 26* *M. 16* *F. 10*	*T. 882* *M. 453* *F. 429*	*T. 142* *M. 72* *F. 70*	*T. 501* *M. 260* *F. 241*
T. 734 M. 383 F. 351	T. 8 M. 6 F. 2	T. 196 M. 96 F. 100	T. 1,277 M. 623 F. 654	T. 201 M. 132 F. 69	T. 742 M. 383 F. 359	T. 417 M. 231 F. 186	T. 580 M. 308 F. 272	T. 418 M. 211 F. 207	T. 257 M. 159 F. 98	T. 92 M. 53 F. 39	T. 197 M. 111 F. 86
... ...	... ...	T. 2 M. 2 ...	T. 1 M. 1 ...	T. 9 M. 4 F. 5	... ...	... ...	... ...	... ...	... ...	... ...	... ...
T. 51 M. 28 T. 23	... ...	T. 510 M. 238 F. 272	T. 505 M. 238 F. 267	T. 200 M. 100 F. 100	... ...	T. 20 M. 12 F. 8	... ...	... ...	T. 468 M. 228 F. 240	T. 55 M. 30 F. 25	T. 100 M. 46 F. 54
T. 785 *M. 411* *F. 374*	*T. 8* *M. 6* *F. 2*	*T. 708* *M. 336* *F. 372*	*T. 1,783* *M. 862* *F. 921*	*T. 410* *M. 236* *F. 174*	*T. 742* *M. 383* *F. 359*	*T. 437* *M. 243* *F. 194*	*T. 680* *M. 308* *F. 272*	*T. 418* *M. 211* *F. 207*	*T. 725* *M. 387* *F. 338*	*T. 147* *M. 83* *F. 64*	*T. 297* *M. 157* *F. 140*
T. 26 M. 20 F. 6	T. 11 M. 9 F. 2	T. 5 M. 4 F. 1	T. 20 M. 12 F. 8	T. 2 M. 2 ...	T. 45 M. 30 F. 15	T. 15 M. 13 F. 2	T. 6 M. 3 F. 3	... ...	T. 12 M. 9 F. 3	T. 6 M. 6 ...	T. 14 M. 10 F. 4
... ...	T. 1 M. 1 ...	... ...	... ...	... ...	... ...	... ...	... ...	... ...	... ...	... ...	... ...
T. 11 M. 7 F. 4	T. 4 M. 1 F. 3	T. 53 M. 22 F. 31	T. 19 M. 13 F. 6	T. 1 M. 1 ...	T. 15 M. 9 F. 6	T. 1 M. 1 ...	T. 1 M. 1 ...	... ...	T. 5 M. 4 F. 1	... ...	... ...
... ...	... ...	... ...	... ...	... ...	... ...	... ...	... ...	... ...	... ...	... ...	... ...
T. 37 *M. 27* *F. 10*	*T. 16* *M. 11* *F. 5*	*T. 58* *M. 26* *F. 32*	*T. 39* *M. 25* *F. 14*	*T. 3* *M. 3* ...	*T. 60* *M. 39* *F. 21*	*T. 16* *M. 14* *F. 2*	*T. 7* *M. 4* *F. 3*	... ...	*T. 17* *M. 13* *F. 4*	*T. 6* *M. 6* ...	*T. 14* *M. 10* *F. 4*
T. 1 M. 1 ...	... ...	... ...	T. 5 M. 2 F. 3	... ...	... ...	... ...	T. 1 M. 1 ...	... ...	T. 2 M. 2 ...	... ...	... ...

TABLE XVI.—Castes, Tribes, and Races, by

Name and Classification.				Provincial Total.	Distribution	
					Amraoti.	Akola.
Class.	Group.	Caste.	Religion.	Total, Males, and Females.	Total, Males, and Females.	Total, Males, and Females.
1	2	3	4	5	6	7
D.—Artisan and Village Menial—*contd.*	22B.—Perfume and Drug Preparers and Sellers and Betel Leaf Dealers—*contd.*	Gandhi (Sugandhi)	Jain	T. 9 M. 5 F. 4	T. 8 M. 4 F. 4	T. 1 M. 1 ...
		Támboli	Hindu	T. 754 M. 407 F. 347	T. 208 M. 114 F. 94	T. 41 M. 22 F. 19
		Do.	Musalman	T. 11 M. 6 F. 5	... ...	... ...
			Total Group 22B	*T. 866* *M. 465* *F. 401*	*T. 217* *M. 119* *F. 98*	*T. 88* *M. 48* *F. 38*
	23.—Weavers, Calenderers and Dyers.	Álkari	Hindu	T. 7 M. 2 F. 5	T. 4 M. 1 F. 3	T. 3 M. 1 F. 2
		Atári	Do.	T. 32 M. 14 F. 18	T. 19 M. 12 F. 7	T. 10 M. 2 F. 8
		Do.	Musalman	T. 60 M. 26 F. 34	T. 24 M. 8 F. 16	T. 10 M. 5 F. 5
		Bunkar	Hindu	T. 99 M. 50 F. 49	... ...	T. 4 M. 3 F. 1
		Chenwár	Do.	T. 203 M. 108 F. 95	... ...	... ...
		Chhipá	Do.	T. 1 M. 1 ...	... ...	... ...
		Hálbi	Do.	T. 2,841 M. 1,492 F. 1,349	T. 473 M. 258 F. 215	T. 201 M. 106 F. 95
		Hátgár	Do.	T. 6,599 M. 3,352 F. 3,247	T. 166 M. 80 F. 86	T. 1,234 M. 636 F. 598
		Inkar	Do.	T. 5 M. 2 F. 3	... ...	... ...
		Katiá	Do.	T. 2 M. 2 ...	T. 2 M. 2 ...	... ...
		Khatri	Do.	T. 1,710 M. 885 F. 825	T. 526 M. 269 F. 257	T. 393 M. 202 F. 191
		Do.	Sikh	T. 4 M. 3 F. 1	... ...	T. 4 M. 3 F. 1
		Kori	Hindu	T. 435 M. 319 F. 116	T. 177 M. 125 F. 52	T. 81 M. 64 F. 17
		Koshti	Do.	T. 14,549 M. 7,576 F. 6,973	T. 5,550 M. 2,943 F. 2,607	T. 363 M. 206 F. 157
		Do.	Jain	T. 269 M. 129 F. 140	T. 257 M. 124 F. 133	... ...
		Momin	Musalman	T. 290 M. 161 F. 129	T. 73 M. 42 F. 31	T. 18 M. 13 F. 5
		Nirâli	Hindu	T. 61 M. 28 F. 33	T. 20 M. 10 F. 10	T. 10 M. 5 F. 5

Nationality or traditional Occupation—*contd.*

BY DISTRICT.					DISTRICT AMRAOTI.			
ELLICHPUR.	BULDANA.	WUN.	BASIM.	RAILWAY PASSENGERS, ETC.	AMRAOTI.	CHANDUR.	MORSI.	MURTAZAPUR.
Total, Males, and Females.	Total, Males, and Females.	Total, Males, and Females.	Total, Males, and Females.	Total, Males, and Females.	Total, Males, and Females.	Total, Males, and Females.	Total, Males, and Females.	Total, Males, and Females.
8	9	10	11	12	13	14	15	16
...	...	...	...	...	T. 1	T. 1	...	T. 6
...	...	...	...	...	M. 1	M 1	...	M. 2
...	...	...	...	...	...	...	...	F. 4
T. 149	T. 5	T. 3	T. 348	...	T. 108	T. 19	T. 14	T. 67
M. 87	M. 5	M. 2	M. 177	...	M. 54	M. 11	M. 9	M. 40
F. 62	...	F. 1	F. 171	...	F. 54	F. 8	F. 5	F. 27
...	T. 11	...	...	...	...	...	...	...
...	M. 6	...	...	...	...	...	...	...
...	F. 5	...	...	...	...	...	...	...
T. 188	*T. 21*	*T. 4*	*T. 350*	...	*T. 109*	*T. 20*	*T. 14*	*T. 74*
M. 108	*M. 13*	*M. 3*	*M. 179*	...	*M. 55*	*M. 12*	*M. 9*	*M. 43*
F. 85	*F. 8*	*F. 1*	*F. 171*	...	*F. 54*	*F. 8*	*F. 5*	*F. 31*
...	...	...	...	...	T. 4	...	...	...
...	...	...	...	...	M. 1	...	...	...
...	...	...	...	...	F. 3	...	...	...
T. 1	...	T. 2	...	...	T. 19	...	...	...
...	...	...	...	...	M. 12	...	...	...
F. 1	...	F. 2	...	...	F. 7	...	...	...
...	...	T. 1	T. 25	...	T. 7	...	...	T. 17
...	...	...	M. 13	...	M. 2	...	...	M. 6
...	...	F. 1	F. 12	...	F. 5	...	...	F. 11
T. 71	T. 24	...	...	...	...	...	...	...
M. 34	M. 13	...	...	...	...	...	...	...
F. 37	F. 11	...	...	...	...	...	...	...
...	...	...	T. 203	...	...	...	...	...
...	...	...	M. 108	...	...	...	...	...
...	...	...	F. 95	...	...	...	...	...
T. 1	...	...	...	...	...	...	...	...
M. 1	...	...	...	...	...	...	...	...
...	...	...	...	...	...	...	...	...
T. 1,639	T. 6	T. 261	T. 261	...	T. 90	T. 292	T. 61	T. 30
M. 862	M. 2	M. 132	M. 132	...	M. 56	M. 154	M. 33	M. 15
F. 777	F. 4	F 129	F. 129	...	F. 34	F. 138	F. 28	F. 15
T. 395	T. 1,207	T. 2,249	T. 1,348	...	...	T. 81	T. 1	T. 84
M. 202	M. 621	M. 1,123	M. 690	...	...	M. 39	M. 1	M. 40
F. 193	F. 586	F. 1,126	F. 658	...	...	F. 42	...	F. 44
...	...	...	T. 5	...	...	...	...	...
...	...	...	M. 2	...	...	...	...	...
...	...	...	F. 3	...	...	...	...	...
...	...	...	...	...	...	...	T. 2	...
...	...	...	...	...	...	...	M. 2	...
...	...	...	...	...	...	...	...	...
T. 367	T. 362	T. 54	T. 8	...	T. 441	T. 26	T. 47	T. 12
M. 190	M. 182	M. 29	M. 4	...	M. 224	M. 15	M. 22	M. 8
F. 168	F. 180	F. 25	F. 4	...	F. 217	F. 11	F. 25	F. 4
...	...	...	...	...	...	...	...	...
...	...	...	...	...	...	...	...	...
...	...	...	...	...	...	...	...	...
T. 128	T. 4	T 29	T. 16	...	T. 143	T. 14	T. 5	T. 15
M. 97	M. 3	M. 21	M. 9	...	M. 98	M. 10	M. 5	M. 12
F. 31	F. 1	F. 8	F. 7	...	F. 45	F. 4	...	F. 3
T. 3,979	T. 651	T. 2,543	T. 1,461	T. 2	T. 828	T. 1,245	T. 2,688	T. 789
M. 2,022	M. 337	M. 1,318	M. 748	M. 2	M. 445	M. 675	M. 1,406	M. 417
F. 1,957	F. 314	F. 1,225	F. 713	...	F. 383	F. 570	F. 1,282	F. 372
...	...	...	T. 12	...	T. 4	T. 114	T. 139	...
...	...	...	M. 5	...	M. 2	M. 55	M. 67	...
...	...	...	F. 7	...	F. 2	F. 59	F. 72	...
T. 2	T. 178	...	T. 19	...	T. 73	...	...	...
M. 2	M. 91	...	M. 13	...	M. 42	...	...	...
...	F. 87	...	F, 6	...	F, 31	...	...	...
T. 29	...	...	T. 2	...	T. 20	...	...	...
M. 12	...	...	M. 1	...	M. 10	...	...	...
F. 17	...	...	F. 1	...	F. 10	...	...	...

TABLE XVI.—Castes, Tribes, and Races, by

Name and Classification.				DISTRICT AKOLA.					DISTRICT
				Akola.	Akot.	Balapur.	Jalgaon.	Khamgaon.	Ellichpur.
Class.	Group.	Caste.	Religion.	Total, Males, and Females.	Total, Males, and Females.	Total, Males, and Females.	Total, Males, and Females.	Total, Males, and Females.	Total, Males, and Females.
17	18	19	20	21	22	23	24	25	26
D.—ARTISAN AND VILLAGE MENIAL—*contd.*	22B.—Perfume and Drug preparers and Sellers and betel leaf dealers—*contd.*	Gandhi (Sugandhi)	Jain	T. 1 M. 1 ...	... ...	... ...	... ...	... ...	... ...
		Támboli	Hindu	T. 29 M. 14 F. 15	T. 7 M. 6 F. 1	T. 4 M. 1 F. 3	... ...	T. 1 M. 1 ...	T. 119 M. 68 F. 51
		Do.	Musalman	... ...	... ...	... ...	... ...	... ...	... ...
			Total Group 22B	*T. 31* *M. 16* *F. 15*	*T. 28* *M. 16* *F. 12*	*T. 11* *M. 4* *F. 7*	*T. 9* *M. 6* *F. 3*	*T. 7* *M. 6* *F. 1*	*T. 157* *M. 83* *F. 74*
	23.—Weavers, Calenderers and Dyers.	Álkari	Hindu	... ...	... ...	... ...	T. 3 M. 1 F. 2	... ...	... ...
		Atári	Do.	... ...	... ...	T. 4 M. 1 F. 3	... ...	T. 6 M. 1 F. 5	T. 1 ... F. 1
		Do.	Musalman	T. 4 M. 2 F. 2	... ...	... ...	... ...	T. 6 M. 3 F. 3	... ...
		Bunkar	Hindu	... ...	... ...	... ...	T. 4 M. 3 F. 1	... ...	T. 59 M. 27 F. 32
		Chenwár	Do.	... ...	... ...	... ...	... ...	... ...	... ...
		Chhipá	Do.	... ...	... ...	... ...	... ...	... ...	... ...
		Hálbi	Do.	T. 25 M. 14 F. 11	T. 111 M. 57 F. 54	... ...	T. 65 M. 35 F. 30	... ...	T. 1,404 M. 738 F. 666
		Hátgar	Do.	T. 235 M. 112 F. 123	T. 285 M. 146 F. 139	T. 509 M. 267 F. 242	T. 116 M. 66 F. 50	T. 89 M. 45 F. 44	T. 120 M. 64 F. 56
		Inkar	Do.	... ...	... ...	... ...	... ...	... ...	... ...
		Katiá	Do.	... ...	... ...	... ...	... ...	... ...	... ...
		Khatri	Do.	T. 33 M. 18 F. 15	T. 107 M. 55 F. 52	T. 131 M. 64 F. 67	T. 8 M. 6 F. 2	T. 114 M. 59 F. 55	T. 67 M. 40 F. 27
		Do.	Sikh	... ...	T. 4 M. 3 F. 1	... ...	... ...	... ...	... ...
		Kori	Hindu	T. 25 M. 22 F. 3	T. 42 M. 28 F. 14	T. 3 M. 3 ...	T. 1 M. 1 ...	T. 10 M. 10 ...	T. 41 M. 30 F. 11
		Koshti	Do.	T. 78 M. 41 F. 37	T. 56 M. 41 F. 15	T. 144 M. 75 F. 69	T. 53 M. 31 F. 22	T. 32 M. 18 F. 14	T. 2,399 M 1,202 F. 1,197
		Do.	Jain	... ...	... ...	... ...	... ...	... ...	... ...
		Momin	Musalman	... ...	... ...	T. 17 M. 12 F. 5	... ...	T. 1 M. 1 ...	... ...
		Nirâli	Hindu	T. 10 M. 5 F. 5	... ...	... ...	... ...	... ...	T. 29 M. 12 F. 17

Nationality or traditional Occupation.—*contd.*

ELLICHPUR.		DISTRICT BULDANA.			DISTRICT WUN.				DISTRICT BASIM.		
DARYAPUR.	MELGHAT.	CHIKHLI.	MALKAPUR.	MEHKAR.	YEOTMAL.	DARWHA.	KELAPUR.	WUN.	BASIM.	MANGRUL.	PUSAD.
Total, Males, and Females.	Total, Males, and Females.	Total, Males, and Females.	Total, Males, and Females.	Total, Males, and Females.	Total, Males, and Females.	Total, Males, and Females.	Total, Males, and Females.	Total, Males, and Females.	Total, Males, and Females.	Total, Males, and Females.	Total, Males, and Females.
27	28	29	30	31	32	33	34	35	36	37	38
...	...	...	...	...	...	...	...	...	...	...	...
T. 29 M. 18 F. 11	T. 1 M. 1 ...	T. 1 M. 1 ...	T. 2 M. 2 ...	T. 2 M. 2 ...	...	...	...	T. 3 M. 2 F. 1	T. 2 M. 2 ...	...	T. 346 M. 175 F. 171
...	T. 1 M. 1 ...	T. 4 M. 3 F. 1	...	T. 7 M. 3 F. 4	...	...	...	...	...	...	...
T. 30 *M. 19* *F. 11*	*T. 1* *M. 1* ...	*T. 5* *M. 4* *F. 1*	*T. 7* *M. 4* *F. 3*	*T. 9* *M. 5* *F. 4*	...	...	*T. 1* *M. 1* ...	*T. 3* *M. 2* *F. 1*	*T. 4* *M. 4* ...	...	*T. 346* *M. 175* *F. 171*
...	...	...	...	...	...	...	...	...	...	...	...
...	...	...	...	...	T. 1 ... F. 1	T. 1 ... F. 1	...	...	...	...	...
...	...	...	...	...	...	T. 1 ... F. 1	...	...	T. 19 M. 11 F. 8	T. 2 M. 1 F. 1	T. 4 M. 1 F. 3
T. 1 M. 1 ...	T. 11 M. 6 F. 5	T. 24 M. 13 F. 11	...	...	...	...	...	...	...	...	...
...	...	...	...	...	...	...	...	...	...	...	T. 203 M. 108 F. 95
...	T. 1 M. 1 ...	...	...	...	...	...	...	...	...	...	...
T. 170 M. 89 F. 81	T. 65 M. 35 F. 30	...	...	T. 6 M. 2 F. 4	T. 90 M. 47 F. 43	T. 149 M. 71 F. 78	T. 22 M. 14 F. 8	...	T. 1 M. 1 ...	...	T. 260 M. 131 F. 129
T. 275 M. 138 F. 137	...	T. 400 M. 206 F. 194	T. 482 M. 241 F. 241	T. 325 M. 174 F. 151	T. 464 M. 243 F. 221	T. 1,155 M. 570 F. 585	T. 541 M. 207 F. 274	T. 89 M. 43 F. 46	T. 503 M. 255 F. 248	T. 112 M. 61 F. 51	T. 733 M. 374 F. 359
...	...	...	...	...	...	...	...	...	...	...	T. 5 M. 2 F. 3
...	...	...	...	...	...	...	...	...	...	...	...
T. 299 M. 158 F. 141	T. 1 M. 1 ...	T. 231 M. 118 F. 113	T. 128 M. 63 F. 65	T. 3 M. 1 F. 2	T. 7 M. 5 F. 2	T. 47 M. 24 F. 23	...	...	T. 5 M. 2 F. 3	...	T. 3 M. 2 F. 1
...	...	...	...	...	...	...	...	...	...	...	...
T. 23 M. 17 F. 6	T. 64 M. 50 F. 14	T. 4 M. 3 F. 1	...	...	T. 15 M. 11 F. 4	T. 1 M. 1 ...	...	T. 13 M. 9 F. 4	T. 9 M. 4 F. 5	T. 3 M. 3 ...	T. 4 M. 2 F. 2
T. 1,570 M. 810 F. 760	T. 10 M. 10 ...	T. 472 M. 239 F. 233	T. 156 M. 84 F. 72	T. 23 M. 14 F. 9	T. 660 M. 352 F. 308	T. 1,439 M. 731 F. 708	T. 328 M. 179 F. 149	T. 116 M. 56 F. 60	T. 410 M. 217 F. 193	T. 310 M. 158 F. 152	T. 741 M. 373 F. 368
...	...	...	...	...	...	...	...	...	...	T. 12 M. 5 F. 7	...
T. 2 M. 2 ...	...	T. 2 M. 1 F. 1	T. 168 M. 86 F. 82	T. 8 M. 4 F. 4	...	...	...	...	T. 2 M. 2 ...	T. 12 M. 6 F. 6	T. 5 M. 5 ...
...	...	...	...	...	...	...	...	...	T. 2 M. 1 F. 1	...	...

TABLE XVI.—Castes, Tribes, and Races, by

Name and Classification.				Provincial Total.	Distribution	
					Amraoti.	Akola.
Class.	Group.	Caste.	Religion.	Total, Males, and Females.	Total, Males, and Females.	Total, Males, and Females.
1	2	3	4	5	6	7
D.—Artisan and Village Menial—*contd.*	23.—Weavers, Calenderers and Dyers—*contd.*	Patuál	Hindu	T. 20 M. 10 F. 10	... ...	T. 20 M. 10 F. 10
		Patwi (Patwekar)	Do.	T. 466 M. 249 F. 217	T. 168 M. 81 F. 87	T. 79 M. 44 F. 35
		Do.	Jain	T. 58 M. 32 F. 26	T. 4 M. 3 F. 1	T. 3 M. 2 F. 1
		Rangári	Hindu	T. 11,865 M. 6,053 F. 5,812	T. 1,842 M. 968 F. 874	T. 2,704 M. 1,399 F. 1,305
		Do.	Jain	T. 325 M. 150 F. 175	T. 5 M. 2 F. 3	T. 23 M. 13 F. 10
		Sálewár	Hindu	T. 1,103 M. 539 F. 564	... ...	... ...
		Sáli	Do.	T. 7,985 M. 4,095 F. 3,890	T. 2,367 M. 1,207 F. 1,160	T. 823 M. 438 F. 385
		Do.	Jain	T. 12 M. 5 F. 7	... ...	T. 5 M. 5 ...
		Sálve	Hindu	T. 5 M. 3 F. 2	... ...	... ...
			Total Group 23	*T. 49,006* *M. 25,286* *F. 23,720*	*T. 11,677* *M. 6,135* *F. 5,542*	*T. 5,988* *M. 3,157* *F. 2,831*
	24.—Washermen	Dhobi	Musalman	T. 9 M. 4 F. 5	... ...	T. 9 M. 4 F. 5
		Warthi (Dhobi and Parit)	Hindu	T. 23,075 M. 11,749 F. 11,326	T. 5,573 M. 2,848 F. 2,725	T. 5,777 M. 2,958 F. 2,819
			Total Group 24	*T. 23,084* *M. 11,753* *F. 11,331*	*T. 5,573* *M. 2,848* *F. 2,725*	*T. 5,786* *M. 2,962* *F. 2,824*
	25.—Cotton Cleaners.	Pinjári	Hindu	T. 67 M. 34 F. 33	T. 2 M. 1 F. 1	... ...
		Do.	Musalman	T. 1,085 M. 548 F. 537	T. 386 M. 196 F. 190	T. 60 M. 34 F. 26
			Total Group 25	*T. 1,152* *M. 582* *F. 570*	*T. 388* *M. 197* *F. 191*	*T. 60* *M. 34* *F. 26*
	26.—Shepherds and Wool-weavers.	Dhangar	Hindu	T. 81,027 M. 41,589 F. 39,438	T. 15,734 M. 8,088 F. 7,646	T. 17,823 M. 9,211 F. 8,612
		Gadariyá	Do.	T. 49 M. 43 F. 6	T. 9 M. 6 F. 3	T. 8 M. 6 F. 2
		Kuramwár	...	T. 3 M. 1 F. 2	... ...	... — ...
			Total Group 26	*T. 81,079* *M. 41,633* *F. 39,446*	*T. 15,743* *M. 8,094* *F. 7,649*	*T. 17,831* *M. 9,217* *F. 8,614*

Nationality or traditional Occupation—*contd.*

	BY DISTRICT.				RAILWAY PASSENGERS, ETC.	DISTRICT AMRAOTI.			
	ELLICHPUR.	BULDANA.	WUN.	BASIM.		AMRAOTI.	CHANDUR.	MORSI.	MURTAZAPUR.
	Total, Males, and Females.	Total, Males, and Females.	Total, Males, and Females.	Total, Males, and Females.	Total, Males, and Females.	Total, Males, and Females.	Total, Males, and Females.	Total, Males, and Females.	Total, Males, and Females.
	8	9	10	11	12	13	14	15	16
	... ...	... ...	... ...	... ...	... ...	... ...	... ...	... ...	... ...
	T. 144 M. 87 F. 57	T. 61 M. 31 F. 30	... ...	T. 14 M. 6 F. 8	... ...	T. 104 M. 50 F. 54	T. 9 M. 5 F. 4	T. 25 M. 14 F. 11	T. 30 M. 12 F. 18
	... ...	T. 51 M. 27 F. 24	... ...	... ...	... ...	T. 3 M. 2 F. 1	T. 1 M. 1 ...	... ...	... ...
	T. 1,878 M. 949 F. 929	T. 2,314 M. 1,125 F. 1,189	T. 1,911 M. 992 F. 919	T. 1,216 M. 620 F. 596	... ...	T. 418 M. 226 F. 192	T. 503 M. 257 F. 246	T. 349 M. 205 F. 144	T. 572 M. 280 F. 292
	... ...	T. 176 M. 79 F. 97	T. 116 M. 54 F. 62	T. 5 M. 2 F. 3	... ...	... ...	... ...	... ...	T. 5 M. 2 F. 3
	... ...	... ...	T. 1,103 M. 539 F. 564	... ...	... ...	... ...	... ...	... ...	... ...
	T. 2,091 M. 1,080 F. 1,011	T. 1,580 M. 806 F. 774	T. 236 M. 120 F. 116	T. 888 M. 444 F. 444	... ...	T. 548 M. 292 F. 256	T. 824 M. 415 F. 409	T. 183 M. 96 F. 87	T. 812 M. 404 F. 408
	... ...	... ...	... ...	T. 7 ... F. 7	... ...	... ...	... ...	... ...	... ...
	T. 5 M. 3 F. 2	... ...	... ...	... ...	... ...	... ...	... ...	... ...	... ...
	T. 10,730 *M. 5,550* *F. 5,180*	*T. 6,614* *M. 3,317* *F. 3,297*	*T. 8,505* *M. 4,328* *F. 4,177*	*T. 5,490* *M. 2,797* *F. 2,693*	*T. 2* *M. 2* ...	*T. 2,702* *M. 1,462* *F. 1,240*	*T. 3,109* *M. 1,626* *F. 1,483*	*T. 3,500* *M. 1,851* *F. 1,649*	*T. 2,366* *M. 1,196* *F. 1,170*
	... ...	... ...	... ...	... ...	... ...	... ...	... ...	... ...	... ...
	T. 3,116 M. 1,619 F. 1,497	T. 2,781 M. 1,373 F. 1,408	T. 4,120 M. 2,050 F. 2,070	T. 1,706 M. 899 F. 807	T. 2 M. 2 ...	T. 1,743 M. 900 F. 843	T. 1,555 M. 783 F. 772	T. 1,158 M. 583 F. 575	T. 1,117 M. 582 F. 535
	T. 3,116 *M. 1,619* *F. 1,497*	*T. 2,781* *M. 1,373* *F. 1,408*	*T. 4,120* *M. 2,050* *F. 2,070*	*T. 1,706* *M. 899* *F. 807*	*T. 2* *M. 2* ...	*T. 1,743* *M. 900* *F. 843*	*T. 1,555* *M. 783* *F. 772*	*T. 1,158* *M. 583* *F. 575*	*T. 1,117* *M. 582* *F. 535*
	T. 2 ... F. 2	T. 34 M. 18 F. 16	T. 29 M. 15 F. 14	... ...	... ...	... ...	... ...	T. 2 M. 1 F. 1	... ...
	T. 183 M. 71 F. 62	T. 82 M. 36 F. 46	T. 414 M. 206 F. 208	T. 10 M. 5 F. 5	... ...	T. 199 M. 113 F. 86	T. 102 M. 42 F. 60	T. 83 M. 39 F. 44	T. 2 M. 2 ...
	T. 185 *M. 71* *F. 64*	*T. 116* *M. 54* *F. 62*	*T. 443* *M. 221* *F. 222*	*T. 10* *M. 5* *F. 5*	... ...	*T. 199* *M. 113* *F. 86*	*T. 102* *M. 42* *F. 60*	*T. 85* *M. 40* *F. 45*	*T. 2* *M. 2* ...
	T. 6,486 M. 3,386 F. 3,100	T. 12,316 M. 6,222 F. 6,094	T. 11,440 M. 5,842 F. 5,598	T. 17,211 M. 8,831 F. 8,380	T. 17 M. 9 F. 8	T. 3,859 M. 1,989 F. 1,870	T. 5,198 M. 2,624 F. 2,574	F. 3,174 M. 1,607 F. 1,567	T. 3,503 M. 1,868 F. 1,635
	T. 23 M. 22 F. 1	T. 6 M. 6 ...	T. 2 M. 2 ...	T. 1 M. 1 ...	... ...	T. 2 M. 2 ...	... ...	T. 7 M. 4 F. 3	... ...
	... ...	... ...	T. 3 M. 1 F. 2	... ...	... ...	... ...	... ...	... ...	... ...
	T. 6,509 *M. 3,408* *F. 3,101*	*T. 12,322* *M. 6,228* *F. 6,094*	*T. 11,445* *M. 5,845* *F. 5,600*	*T. 17,212* *M. 8,832* *F. 8,380*	*T. 17* *M. 9* *F. 8*	*T. 3,861* *M. 1,991* *F. 1,870*	*T. 5,198* *M. 2,624* *F. 2,574*	*T. 3,181* *M. 1,611* *F. 1,570*	*T. 3,503* *M. 1,868* *F. 1,635*

TABLE XVI.—Castes, Tribes, and Races, by

Class.	Group.	Caste.	Religion.	DISTRICT AKOLA. Akola. Total, Males, and Females.	Akot. Total, Males, and Females.	Balapur. Total, Males, and Females.	Jalgaon. Total, Males, and Females.	Khamgaon. Total, Males, and Females.	DISTRICT Ellichpur. Total, Males, and Females.
17	18	19	20	21	22	23	24	25	26
D.—ARTISAN AND VILLAGE MENIAL—*contd.*	23.—Weavers, Calenderers and Dyers—*contd.*	Patuál	Hindu	... ...	T. 20 M. 10 F. 10	... ...	... ...	... ...	... ...
		Patwi (Patwekar)	Do.	T. 36 M. 20 F. 16	T. 19 M. 11 F. 8	T. 19 M. 8 F. 11	... ...	T. 5 M. 5 ...	T. 122 M. 75 F. 47
		Do.	Jain	... ...	T. 1 M. 1 ...	T. 2 M. 1 F. 1	... ...	... ...	... ...
		Rangári	Hindu	T. 472 M. 238 F. 234	T. 251 M. 135 F. 116	T. 582 M 276 F. 306	T. 1,020 M. 531 F. 489	T. 379 M. 219 F. 160	T. 1,290 M. 631 F. 659
		Do.	Jain	... ...	T. 23 M. 13 F. 10	... ...	... ...	... ...	... ...
		Sálewár	Hindu	... ...	... ...	... ...	... ...	... ...	... ...
		Sáli	Do.	T. 334 M. 179 F. 155	T. 162 M. 78 F. 84	T. 236 M. 133 F. 103	T. 70 M. 35 F. 35	T. 21 M. 13 F. 8	T. 1,127 M. 578 F. 549
		Do.	Jain	... ...	... ...	... ...	T. 5 M. 5 ...	... ...	... ...
		Sálve	Hindu	... ...	... ...	... ...	... ...	... ...	T. 5 M. 3 F. 2
			Total Group 23	*T. 1,252 M. 651 F. 601*	*T. 1,081 M. 578 F. 503*	*T. 1,647 M. 840 F. 807*	*T. 1,345 M. 714 F. 631*	*T. 663 M. 374 F. 289*	*T. 6,664 M. 3,400 F. 3,264*
	24.—Washermen.	Dhobi	Musalman	... ...	T. 9 M. 4 F. 5	... ...	... ...	... ...	... ...
		Warthi (Dhobi and Parit).	Hindu	T. 1,580 M. 814 F. 766	T. 1,422 M. 718 F. 704	T. 1,225 M. 624 F. 601	T. 791 M. 414 F. 377	T. 759 M. 388 F. 371	T. 1,578 M. 818 F. 760
			Total Group 24	*T. 1,580 M. 814 F. 766*	*T. 1,431 M. 722 F. 709*	*T. 1,225 M. 624 F. 601*	*T. 791 M. 414 F. 377*	*T. 759 M. 388 F. 371*	*T. 1,578 M. 818 F. 760*
	25.—Cotton Cleaners.	Pinjári	Hindu	... ...	... ...	... ...	... ...	... ...	... ...
		Do.	Musalman	... ...	T. 30 M. 16 F. 14	T. 20 M. 11 F. 9	T. 10 M. 7 F. 3	... ...	T. 78 M. 43 F. 35
			Total Group 25	... ...	*T. 30 M. 16 F. 14*	*T. 20 M. 11 F. 9*	*T. 10 M. 7 F. 3*	... ...	*T. 78 M. 43 F. 35*
	26.—Shepherds and Wool-weavers.	Dhangar	Hindu	T. 4,186 M. 2,192 F. 1,994	T. 3,684 M. 1,875 F. 1,809	T. 3,658 M. 1,899 F. 1,759	T. 3,196 M. 1,624 F. 1,572	T. 3,099 M. 1,621 F. 1,478	T. 2,331 M. 1,219 F. 1,112
		Gadariyá	Do.	T. 8 M. 6 F. 2	... ...	... ...	... ...	... ...	T. 11 M. 10 F. 1
		Kuramwár	Do.	... ...	... ...	... ...	... ...	... ...	... ...
			Total Group 26	*T. 4,194 M. 2,198 F. 1,996*	*T. 3,684 M. 1,875 F. 1,809*	*T. 3,658 M. 1,899 F. 1,759*	*T. 3,196 M. 1,624 F. 1,572*	*T. 3,099 M. 1,621 F. 1,478*	*T. 2,342 M. 1,229 F. 1,113*

Nationality or traditional Occupation—*contd.*

ELLICHPUR.		DISTRICT BULDANA.			DISTRICT WUN.				DISTRICT BASIM.		
Daryapur.	Melghat.	Chikhli.	Malkapur.	Mehkar.	Yeotmal.	Darwha.	Kelapur.	Wun.	Basim.	Mangrul.	Pusad.
Total, Males, and Females.	Total, Males, and Females.	Total, Males, and Females.	Total, Males, and Females.	Total, Males, and Females.	Total, Males, and Females.	Total, Males, and Females.	Total, Males, and Females.	Total, Males, and Females.	Total, Males, and Females.	Total, Males, and Females.	Total, Males, and Females.
27	28	29	30	31	32	33	34	35	36	37	38
... ...	... ...	... ...	... ...	... ...	... ...	... ...	... ...	... ...	... ...	... ...	... ...
T. 22 M. 12 F. 10	... ...	T. 52 M. 24 F. 28	T. 1 M. 1 ...	T. 8 M. 6 F. 2	... ...	... ...	... ...	... ...	T. 14 M. 6 F. 8	... ...	... ...
... ...	... ...	T. 51 M. 27 F. 24	... ...	... ...	... ...	... ...	... ...	... ...	... ...	... ...	... ...
T. 523 M. 281 F. 242	T. 65 M. 37 F. 28	T. 273 M. 138 F. 135	T. 1,788 M. 860 F. 928	T. 253 M. 127 F. 126	T. 90 M. 65 F. 25	T. 1,291 M. 663 F. 628	T. 98 M. 54 F. 44	T. 432 M. 210 F. 222	T. 346 M. 190 F. 156	T. 174 M. 86 F. 88	T. 696 M. 344 F. 352
... ...	... ...	... ...	T. 176 M. 79 F. 97	... ...	... ...	T. 116 M. 54 F. 62	... ...	... ...	T. 3 M. 1 F. 2	... ...	T. 2 M. 1 F. 1
... ...	... ...	... ...	... ...	... ...	T. 4 M. 2 F. 2	... ...	T. 708 M. 346 F. 362	T. 391 M. 191 F. 200	... ...	... ...	... ...
T. 964 M. 502 F. 462	... ...	T. 1,268 M. 648 F. 620	T. 174 M. 94 F. 80	T. 138 M. 64 F. 74	T. 99 M. 51 F. 48	T. 137 M. 69 F. 68	... ...	... ...	T. 414 M. 204 F. 210	T. 3 ... F. 3	T. 471 M. 240 F. 231
... ...	... ...	... ...	... ...	... ...	... ...	... ...	... ...	... ...	... ...	... ...	T. 7 ... F. 7
... ...	... ...	... ...	... ...	... ...	... ...	... ...	... ...	... ...	... ...	... ...	... ...
T. 3,849 M. 2,010 F. 1,839	*T. 217 M. 140 F. 77*	*T. 2,777 M. 1,417 F. 1,360*	*T. 3,073 M. 1,508 F. 1,565*	*T. 764 M. 392 F. 372*	*T. 1,430 M. 776 F. 654*	*T. 4,337 M. 2,183 F. 2,154*	*T. 1,697 M. 860 F. 837*	*T. 1,041 M. 509 F. 532*	*T. 1,728 M. 894 F. 834*	*T. 628 M. 320 F. 308*	*T. 3,134 M. 1,583 F. 1,551*
... ...	... ...	... ...	... ...	... ...	... ...	... ...	... ...	... ...	... ...	... ...	... ...
T. 1,514 M. 785 F. 729	T. 24 M. 16 F. 8	T. 663 M. 322 F. 341	T. 1,540 M. 773 F. 767	T. 578 M. 278 F. 300	T. 913 M. 459 F. 454	T. 1,054 M. 542 F. 512	T. 1,039 M. 512 F. 527	T. 1,114 M. 537 F. 577	T. 667 M. 358 F. 309	T. 485 M. 252 F. 233	T. 554 M. 289 F. 265
T. 1,514 M. 785 F. 729	*T. 24 M. 16 F. 8*	*T. 663 M. 322 F. 341*	*T. 1,540 M. 773 F. 767*	*T. 578 M. 278 F. 300*	*T. 913 M. 459 F. 454*	*T. 1,054 M. 542 F. 512*	*T. 1,039 M. 512 F. 527*	*T. 1,114 M. 537 F. 577*	*T. 667 M. 358 F. 309*	*T. 485 M. 252 F. 233*	*T. 554 M. 289 F. 265*
... ...	T. 2 ... F. 2	... ...	T. 34 M. 18 F. 16	... ...	... ...	T. 29 M. 15 F. 14	... ...	... ...	... ...	... ...	... ...
T. 55 M. 28 F. 27	... ...	... ...	T. 82 M. 36 F. 46	... ...	T. 75 M. 41 F. 34	T. 104 M. 52 F. 52	T. 102 M. 56 F. 46	T. 133 M. 57 F. 76	... ...	T. 4 M. 3 F. 1	T. 6 M. 2 F. 4
T. 55 M. 28 F. 27	*T. 2 ... F. 2*	... ...	*T. 116 M. 54 F. 62*	... ...	*T. 75 M. 41 F. 34*	*T. 133 M. 67 F. 66*	*T. 102 M. 56 F. 46*	*T. 133 M. 57 F. 76*	... ...	*T. 4 M. 3 F. 1*	*T. 6 M. 2 F. 4*
T. 4,125 M. 2,144 F. 1,981	T. 30 M. 23 F. 7	T. 3,149 M. 1,618 F. 1,531	T. 5,509 F. 2,790 M. 2,719	T. 3,658 M. 1,814 F. 1,844	T. 3,052 M. 1,530 F. 1,522	T. 4,153 M. 2,137 F. 2,016	T. 1,672 M. 867 F. 805	T. 2,563 M. 1,308 F. 1,255	T. 4,316 M. 2,238 F. 2,078	T. 3,182 M. 1,677 F. 1,505	T. 9,713 M. 4,916 F. 4,797
T. 1 M. 1 ...	T. 11 M. 11 ...	... ...	T. 6 M. 6 ...	... ...	T. 1 M. 1 ...	T. 1 M. 1 ...	... ...	... ...	T. 1 M. 1 ...	... ...	... ...
... ...	... ...	... ...	... ...	... ...	... ...	... ...	... ...	T. 3 M. 1 F. 2	... ...	... ...	... ...
T. 4,126 M. 2,145 F. 1,981	*T. 41 M. 34 F. 7*	*T. 3,149 M. 1,618 F. 1,531*	*T. 5,515 M. 2,796 F. 2,719*	*T. 3,658 M. 1,814 F. 1,844*	*T. 3,053 M. 1,531 F. 1,522*	*T. 4,154 M. 2,138 F. 2,016*	*T. 1,672 M. 867 F. 805*	*T. 2,566 M. 1,309 F. 1,257*	*T. 4,317 M. 2,239 F. 2,078*	*T. 3,182 M. 1,677 F. 1,505*	*T. 9,713 M. 4,916 F. 4,797*

TABLE XVI.—Castes, Tribes, and Races, by

Name and Classification.				Provincial Total.	Distribution. Amraoti.	Akola.
Class.	Group.	Caste.	Religion.	Total, Males, and Females.	Total, Males, and Females.	Total, Males, and Females.
1	2	3	4	5	6	7
D.—Artisan and Village Menial—*contd.*	27.—Oil-pressers	Kásid	Hindu	T. 12 M. 7 F. 5	... ...	... ...
		Teli	Do.	T. 82,069 M. 42,114 F. 39,955	T. 27,955 M. 14,456 F. 13,499	T. 12,530 M. 6,459 F. 6,071
		Do.	Animistic	T. 8 M. 6 F. 2	T. 5 M. 4 F. 1	... ...
		Do.	Musalman	T. 17 M. 13 F. 4	T. 1 M. 1 ...	... ...
		Do.	Sikh	T. 1 M. 1 ...	... ...	T. 1 M. 1 ...
			Total Group 27	*T. 82,107* *M. 42,141* *F. 39,966*	*T. 27,961* *M. 14,461* *F. 13,500*	*T. 12,531* *M. 6,460* *F. 6,071*
	28.—Potters	Arvi	Hindu	T. 11 M. 4 F. 7	T. 5 M. 1 F. 4	... ...
		Kumbhár	Do.	T. 22,465 M. 12,558 F. 9,907	T. 6,665 M. 4,036 F. 2,629	T. 4,497 M. 2,440 F. 2,057
			Total Group 28	*T. 22,476* *M. 12,562* *F. 9,914*	*T. 6,670* *M. 4,037* *F. 2,633*	*T. 4,497* *M. 2,440* *F. 2,057*
	29.—Glass-workers	Kachár	Hindu	T. 564 M. 283 F. 281	T. 72 M. 40 F. 32	T. 88 M. 45 F. 43
	29*A*.—Lac bangle-makers.	Lakhári	Do.	T. 126 M. 67 F. 59	T. 90 M. 46 F. 44	T. 4 M. 1 F. 3
	30.—Salt, &c., workers.	Lonári (Luniyá)	Do.	T. 1,096 M. 538 F. 558	T. 132 M. 68 F. 64	T. 715 M. 343 F. 372
	33.—Gold washers	Jhárekari	Musalman	T. 1 M. 1 ...	... ...	... ...
	35.—Fishermen, Boatmen, Palki-bearers, Cooks, etc.	Bhatiárá	Do.	T. 2 M. 1 F. 1	... ...	... ...
		Bhisti	Do.	T. 5 M. 2 F. 3	T. 5 M. 2 F. 3	... ...
		Bhoi (Windhewár)	Hindu	T. 27,415 M. 14,253 F. 13,162	T. 8,297 M. 4,384 F. 3,913	T. 5,326 M. 2,741 F. 2,585
		Injhwár	Do.	T. 221 M. 118 F. 103	T. 81 M. 44 F. 37	... ...
		Jhingábhoi	Do.	T. 75 M. 38 F. 37	... ...	T. 60 M. 30 F. 30
		Káhár	Do.	T. 359 M. 232 F. 127	T. 89 M. 69 F. 20	T. 42 M. 34 F. 8
		Kevati	Do.	T. 76 M. 59 F. 17	T. 42 M. 34 F. 8	T. 13 M. 11 F. 2
		Koli	Do.	T. 32,628 M. 16,497 F. 16,131	T. 5,728 M. 2,893 F. 2,835	T. 10,243 M. 5,225 5,018

Nationality or traditional Occupation—*contd.*

BY DISTRICT.				RAILWAY PASSENGERS, ETC.	DISTRICT AMRAOTI.			
ELLICHPUR.	BULDANA.	WUN.	BASIM.		AMRAOTI.	CHANDUR.	MORSI.	MURTAZAPUR.
Total, Males, and Females.	Total, Males, and Females.	Total, Males, and Females.	Total, Males, and Females.	Total, Males, and Females.	Total, Males, and Females.	Total, Males, and Females.	Total, Males, and Females.	Total, Males, and Females.
8	9	10	11	12	13	14	15	16
... ...	... ...	T. 8 M. 3 F. 5	T. 4 M. 4 ...	... ...	... ...	... ...	... ...	... ...
T. 6,667 M. 3,362 F. 3,305	T. 10,645 M. 5,383 F. 5,262	T. 15,184 M. 7,816 F. 7,368	T. 9,081 M. 4,631 F. 4,450	T. 7 M. 7 ...	T. 7,828 M. 4,049 F. 3,779	T. 12,182 M. 6,278 F. 5,904	T. 4,494 M. 2,365 F. 2,129	T. 3,451 M. 1,764 F. 1,687
T. 3 M. 2 F. 1	... ...	... ...	... ...	... ...	... ...	T. 5 M. 4 F. 1	... ...	... ...
... ...	... ...	T. 16 M. 12 F. 4	... ...	... ...	T. 1 M. 1 ...	... ...	... ...	... ...
... ...	... ...	... ...	... ...	... ...	... ...	... ...	... ...	... ...
T. 6,670 *M. 3,364* *F. 3,306*	*T. 10,645* *M. 5,383* *F. 5,262*	*T. 15,208* *M. 7,831* *F. 7,377*	*T. 9,085* *M. 4,635* *F. 4,450*	*T. 7* *M. 7* ...	*T. 7,829* *M. 4,050* *F. 3,779*	*T. 12,187* *M. 6,282* *F. 5,905*	*T. 4,494* *M. 2,365* *F. 2,129*	*T. 3,451* *M. 1,764* *F. 1,687*
... ...	T. 6 M. 3 F. 3	... ...	... ...	... ...	T. 5 M. 1 F. 4	... ...	... ...	... ...
T. 2,546 M. 1,439 F. 1,107	T. 3,244 M. 1,649 F. 1,595	T. 2,681 M. 1,531 F. 1,150	T. 2,832 M. 1,463 F. 1,369	... ...	T. 2,246 M. 1,297 F. 949	T. 2,046 M. 1,313 F. 733	T. 1,201 M. 741 F. 460	T. 1,172 M. 685 F. 487
T. 2,546 *M. 1,439* *F. 1,107*	*T. 3,250* *M. 1,652* *F. 1,598*	*T. 2,681* *M. 1,531* *F. 1,150*	*T. 2,832* *M. 1,463* *F. 1,369*	... ...	*T. 2,251* *M. 1,298* *F. 953*	*T. 2,046* *M. 1,313* *F. 733*	*T. 1,201* *M. 741* *F. 460*	*T. 1,172* *M. 685* *F. 487*
T. 34 M. 15 F. 19	T. 183 M. 89 F. 94	T. 143 M. 72 F. 71	T. 44 M. 22 F. 22	... ...	T. 3 M. 3 ...	T. 68 M. 36 F. 32	T. 1 M. 1 ...	... ...
T. 8 M. 7 F. 1	... ...	T. 14 M. 4 F. 10	T. 10 M. 9 F. 1	... ...	T. 54 M. 27 F. 27	T. 1 M. 1 ...	T. 10 M. 4 F. 6	T. 25 M. 14 F. 11
T. 91 M. 48 F. 43	T. 122 M. 63 F. 59	T. 24 M. 11 F. 13	T. 12 M. 5 F. 7	... ...	T. 36 M. 16 F. 20	T. 42 M. 23 F. 19	T. 27 M. 14 F. 13	T. 27 M. 15 F. 12
T. 1 M. 1 ...	... ...	... ...	... ...	... ...	... ...	... ...	... ...	... ...
... ...	T. 2 M. 1 F. 1	... ...	... ...	... ...	... ...	... ...	... ...	... ...
... ...	... ...	... ...	... ...	... ...	T. 5 M. 2 F. 3	... ...	... ...	... ...
T. 3,678 M. 1,988 F. 1,690	T. 1,401 M. 718 F. 683	T. 7,213 M. 3,674 F. 3,539	T. 1,495 M. 745 F. 750	T. 5 M. 3 F. 2	T. 2,200 M. 1,173 F. 1,027	T. 2,936 M. 1,548 F. 1,388	T. 1,813 M. 962 F. 851	T. 1,348 M. 701 F. 647
T. 138 M. 72 F. 66	... ...	T. 2 M. 2 ...	... ...	... ...	T. 29 M. 15 F. 14	T. 52 M. 29 F. 23	... ...	... ...
T. 7 M. 3 F. 4	T. 8 M. 5 F. 3	... ...	... ...	... ...	... ...	... ...	... ...	... ...
T. 111 M. 70 F. 41	T. 95 M. 40 F. 55	T. 18 M. 15 F. 3	T. 4 M. 4 ...	... ...	T. 61 M. 50 F. 11	T. 20 M. 12 F. 8	T. 2 M. 2 ...	T. 6 M. 5 F. 1
T. 7 M. 4 F. 3	T. 7 M. 3 F. 4	T. 6 M. 6 ...	T. 1 M. 1 ...	... ...	T. 29 M. 22 F. 7	T. 7 M. 6 F. 1	T. 2 M. 2 ...	T. 4 M. 4 ...
T. 2,737 M. 1,446 F. 1,291	T. 8,345 M. 4,148 F. 4,197	T. 2,309 M. 1,141 F. 1,168	T. 3,264 M. 1,642 F. 1,622	T. 2 M. 2 ...	T. 4,829 M. 2,431 F. 2,398	T. 162 M. 89 F. 73	T. 42 M. 24 F. 18	T. 695 M. 349 F. 346

TABLE XVI.—Castes, Tribes, and Races, by

Name and Classification.				District Akola.					District
				Akola.	Akot.	Balapur.	Jalgaon.	Khamgaon.	Ellichpur.
Class.	Group.	Caste.	Religion.	Total, Males, and Females.	Total, Males, and Females.	Total, Males, and Females.	Total, Males, and Females.	Total, Males, and Females.	Total, Males, and Females.
17	18	19	20	21	22	23	24	25	26
D.—ARTISAN AND VILLAGE MENIAL—*contd.*	27.—Oil presses	Kásid	Hindu	... ...	... ...	... ...	... ...	... ...	... ...
		Teli	Do.	T. 3,197 M. 1,663 F. 1,534	T. 2,865 M. 1,470 F. 1,395	T. 2,181 M. 1,107 F. 1,074	T. 2,272 M. 1,150 F. 1,122	T. 2,015 M. 1,069 F. 946	T. 3,825 M. 1,882 F. 1,943
		Do.	Animistic	... ...	... ...	... ...	... ...	... ...	... ...
		Do.	Musalman	... ...	... ...	... ...	... ...	... ...	... ...
		Do.	Sikh	T. 1 M. 1 ...	... ...	... ...	... ...	... ...	... ...
			Total Group 27	*T. 3,198 M. 1,664 F. 1,534*	*T. 2,865 M. 1,470 F. 1,395*	*T. 2,181 M. 1,107 F. 1,074*	*T. 2,272 M. 1,150 F. 1,122*	*T. 2,015 M. 1,069 F. 946*	*T. 3,825 M. 1,882 F. 1,943*
	28.—Potters	Arvi	Hindu	... ...	... ...	... ...	... ...	... ...	... ...
		Kumbhár	Do.	T. 1,067 M. 586 F. 481	T. 1,334 M. 720 F. 614	T. 639 M. 337 F. 302	T. 799 M. 440 F. 359	T. 658 M. 357 F. 301	T. 1,232 M. 667 F. 565
			Total Group 28	*T. 1,067 M. 586 F. 481*	*T. 1,334 M 720 F. 614*	*T. 639 M. 337 F. 302*	*T. 799 M. 440 F. 359*	*T. 658 M. 357 F. 301*	*T. 1,232 M. 667 F. 565*
	29.—Glass-workers.	Kachár	Hindu	T. 2 M. 2 ...	T. 1 M. 1 ...	T. 79 M. 38 F. 41	... ...	T. 6 M. 4 F. 2	T. 2 ... F. 2
	29*A*.—Lac Bangle-makers.	Lakhári	Do.	... ...	T. 1 M. 1 ...	... ...	... ...	T. 3 ... F. 3	T. 1 M. 1 ...
	30.—Salt, &c., workers.	Lonári (Luniya)	Do.	T. 23 M. 13 F. 10	T. 223 M. 104 F. 119	T. 136 M. 59 F. 77	T. 178 M. 94 F. 84	T. 155 M. 73 F. 82	T. 25 M. 12 F. 13
	33.—Gold-washers.	Jhárekari	Musalman	... ...	... ...	... ...	... ...	... ...	... ...
	35.—Fishermen, Boatmen Palki Bearers, Cooks, etc.	Bhatiárá	Do.	... ...	... ...	... ...	... ...	... ...	... ...
		Bhisti	Do.	... ...	... ...	... ...	... ...	... ...	... ... —
		Bhoi (Windhewár)	Hindu	T. 1,042 M. 511 F. 531	T. 1,533 M. 806 F. 727	T. 1,012 M. 509 F. 503	T. 1,098 M. 579 F. 519	T. 641 M. 336 F. 305	T. 2,136 M. 1,118 F. 1,018
		Injhwár	Do.	... ...	... ...	... ...	... ...	... ...	T. 94 M. 52 F. 42
		Jhingábhoi	Do.	... ...	T. 24 M. 10 F. 14	T. 36 M. 20 F. 16	... ...	... ...	T. 7 M. 3 F. 4
		Káhár	Do.	T. 14 M. 12 F. 2	T. 15 M. 10 F. 5	T. 6 M. 5 F. 1	T. 2 M. 2 ...	T. 5 M. 5 ...	T. 33 M. 26 F. 7
		Kevati	Do.	T. 2 M. 2 ...	T. 6 M. 6 ...	T. 1 M. 1 ...	... ...	T. 4 M. 2 F. 2	... ...
		Koli	Do.	T. 2,865 M. 1,445 F. 1,420	T. 3,585 M. 1,817 F. 1,768	T. 568 M. 291 F. 277	T. 2,269 M. 1,143 F. 1,126	T. 956 M. 529 F. 427	T. 217 M. 124 F. 93

Nationality or traditional Occupation—*contd.*

ELLICHPUR.		DISTRICT BULDANA.			DISTRICT WUN.				DISTRICT BASIM.		
DARYAPUR.	MELGHAT.	CHIKHLI.	MALKAPUR.	MEHKAR.	YEOTMAL.	DARWHA.	KELAPUR.	WUN.	BASIM.	MANGRUL.	PUSAD.
Total, Males, and Females.	Total, Males, and Females.	Total, Males, and Females.	Total, Males, and Females.	Total, Males, and Females.	Total, Males, and Females.	Total, Males, and Females.	Total, Males, and Females.	Total, Males, and Females.	Total, Males, and Females.	Total, Males, and Females.	Total, Males, and Females.
27	28	29	30	31	32	33	34	35	36	37	38
...	...	...	...	...	...	T. 8 M. 3 F. 5	...	...	...	...	T. 4 M. 4 ...
T. 2,594 M. 1,345 F. 1,249	T. 248 M. 135 F. 113	T. 3,340 M. 1,662 F. 1,678	T. 4,725 M. 2,426 F. 2,299	T. 2,580 M. 1,295 F. 1,285	T. 6,005 M. 3,098 F. 2,907	T. 5,341 M. 2,724 F. 2,617	T. 2,604 M. 1,356 F. 1,248	T. 1,234 M. 638 F. 596	T. 3,682 M. 1,912 F. 1,770	T. 2,274 M. 1,146 F. 1,128	T. 3,125 M. 1,573 F. 1,552
...	T. 3 M. 2 F. 1	...	...	...	...	...	...	...	...	...	...
...	...	...	...	...	T. 16 M. 12 F. 4	...	...	...	...	...	...
...	...	...	...	...	...	...	...	...	...	...	...
T. 2,594 M. 1,345 F. 1,249	*T. 251 M. 137 F. 114*	*T. 3,340 M. 1,662 F. 1,678*	*T. 4,725 M. 2,426 F. 2,299*	*T. 2,580 M. 1,295 F. 1,285*	*T. 6,021 M. 3,110 F. 2,911*	*T. 5,349 M. 2,727 F. 2,622*	*T. 2,604 M. 1,356 F. 1,248*	*T. 1,234 M. 638 F. 596*	*T. 3,682 M. 1,912 F. 1,770*	*T. 2,274 M. 1,146 F. 1,128*	*T. 3,129 M. 1,577 F. 1,552*
...	...	T. 6 M. 3 F. 3	...	...	...	...	...	...	...	...	...
T. 1,287 M. 756 F. 531	T. 27 M. 16 F. 11	T. 914 M. 464 F. 450	T. 1,068 M. 546 F. 522	T. 1,262 M. 639 F. 623	T. 776 M. 457 F. 319	T. 1,100 M. 646 F. 454	T. 539 M. 297 F. 242	T. 266 M. 131 F. 135	T. 1,471 M. 768 F. 703	T. 562 M. 301 F. 261	T. 799 M. 394 F. 405
T. 1,287 M. 756 F. 531	*T. 27 M. 16 F. 11*	*T. 920 M. 467 F. 453*	*T. 1,068 M. 546 F. 522*	*T. 1,262 M. 639 F. 623*	*T. 776 M. 457 F. 319*	*T. 1,100 M. 646 F. 454*	*T. 539 M. 297 F. 242*	*T. 266 M. 131 F. 135*	*T. 1,471 M. 768 F. 703*	*T. 562 M. 301 F. 261*	*T. 799 M. 394 F. 405*
T. 32 M. 15 F. 17	...	T. 135 M. 67 F. 68	...	T. 48 M. 22 F. 26	T. 18 M. 12 F. 6	T. 125 M. 60 F. 65	...	...	T. 4 M. 4 ...	T. 40 M. 18 F. 22	...
T. 3 M. 2 F. 1	T. 4 M. 4 ...	...	...	...	T. 7 M. 4 F. 3	T. 7 ... F. 7	...	...	T. 6 M. 5 F. 1	T. 2 M. 2 ...	T. 2 M. 2 ...
T. 53 M. 23 F. 30	T. 13 M. 13 ...	T. 15 M. 4 F. 11	T. 74 M. 39 F. 35	T. 33 M. 20 F. 13	...	T. 24 M. 11 F. 13	...	...	T. 4 M. 1 F. 3	...	T. 8 M. 4 F. 4
T. 1 M. 1 ...	...	...	...	...	...	...	...	...	...	...	...
...	...	T. 2 M. 1 F. 1	...	...	...	...	...	...	...	...	...
...	...	...	...	...	...	...	...	...	...	...	...
T. 1,218 M. 643 F. 575	T. 324 M. 227 F. 97	T. 363 M. 180 F. 183	T. 812 M. 419 F. 393	T. 226 M. 119 F. 107	T. 1,695 M. 893 F. 802	T. 1,143 M. 574 F. 569	T. 2,249 M. 1,129 F. 1,120	T. 2,126 M. 1,078 F. 1,048	T. 270 M. 131 F. 139	T. 219 M. 121 F. 98	T. 1,006 M. 493 F. 513
T. 43 M. 19 F. 24	T. 1 M. 1 ...	...	...	...	T. 1 M. 1 ...	T. 1 M. 1 ...	...	...	...	...	...
...	...	...	T. 8 M. 5 F. 3	...	...	...	...	...	...	...	...
T. 8 M. 7 F. 1	T. 70 M. 37 F. 33	T. 19 M. 7 F. 12	T. 76 M. 33 F. 43	...	T. 14 M. 11 F. 3	T. 3 M. 3 ...	...	T. 1 M. 1 ...	T. 2 M. 2 ...	T. 1 M. 1 ...	T. 1 M. 1 ...
T. 3 M. 3 ...	T. 4 M. 1 F. 3	T. 7 M. 3 F. 4	...	...	T. 4 M. 4 ...	T. 1 M. 1 ...	...	T. 1 M. 1 ...	T. 1 M. 1 ...	...	...
T. 2,514 M. 1,319 F. 1,195	T. 6 M. 3 F. 3	T. 1,839 M. 918 F. 921	T. 5,812 M. 2,890 F. 2,922	T. 694 M. 340 F. 354	T. 296 M. 148 F. 148	T. 875 M. 440 F. 435	T. 832 M. 412 F. 420	T. 306 M. 141 F. 165	T. 1,503 M. 786 F. 717	T. 388 M. 192 F. 196	T. 1,373 M. 664 F. 709

TABLE XVI.—Castes, Tribes, and Races, by

NAME AND CLASSIFICATION.				PROVINCIAL TOTAL.	DISTRIBUTION	
					AMRAOTI.	AKOLA.
Class.	Group.	Caste.	Religion.	Total, Males, and Females.	Total, Males, and Females.	Total, Males, and Females.
1	2	3	4	5	6	7
D.—ARTISAN AND VILLAGE MENIAL—*contd.*	35.—FISHERMEN, BOATMEN, PALKI-BEARERS, COOKS, ETC.	MALLA	Hindu	T. 4 M. 2 F. 2	... ...	... ...
		PAKHÁLI	Do.	T. 99 M. 51 F. 48	T. 18 M. 9 F. 9	T. 4 M. 3 F. 1
		SHIKHARPÁNIWÁLE	Do.	T. 3 M. 2 F. 1	T. 3 M. 2 F. 1	... ...
		WÁGHÁDE	Do.	T. 2 M. 2 ...	T. 2 M. 2 ...	... ...
			Total Group 35	*T. 60,889* *M. 31,257* *F. 29,632*	*T. 14,265* *M. 7,439* *F. 6,826*	*T. 15,688* *M. 8,044* *F. 7,644*
	35A.—SERVANT CASTE.	KHAWÁS	Hindu	T. 8 M. 5 F. 3	... ...	... ...
		THÁKNAK	Do.	T. 1 M. 1 ...	T. 1 M. 1 ...	... ...
			Total Group 35A	*T. 9* *M. 6* *F. 3*	*T. 1* *M. 1* ...	... ...
	36.—DISTILLERS AND TODDY-DRAWERS.	BANKAR	Hindu	T. 1 M. 1 ...	T. 1 M. 1 ...	... ...
		BHANDÁRI	Do.	T. 2 M. 1 F. 1	... ...	T. 2 M. 1 F. 1
		KALÁL	Do.	T. 16,035 M. 8,390 F. 7,645	T. 5,646 M. 2,946 F. 2,700	T. 2,077 M. 1,084 F. 993
		Do.	Musalman	T. 11 M. 5 F. 6	... ...	T. 1 M. 1 ...
		Do.	Jain	T. 186 M. 98 F. 88	T. 114 M. 59 F. 55	... ...
		Do.	Animistic	T. 2 M. 1 F. 1	T. 2 M. 1 F. 1	... ...
		KALWÁR	Hindu	T. 49 M. 16 F. 33	T. 29 M. 16 F. 13	... ...
		PÁSI	Do.	T. 467 M. 304 F. 163	T. 219 M. 142 F. 77	T. 48 M. 36 F. 12
			Total Group 36	*T. 16,753* *M. 8,816* *F. 7,937*	*T. 6,011* *M. 3,165* *F. 2,846*	*T. 2,128* *M. 1,122* *F. 1,006*
	37.—BUTCHERS.	KASAI (BAKAR KASAI AND KHÁTIK).	Hindu	T. 4,959 M. 2,553 F. 2,406	T. 2,401 M. 1,236 F. 1,165	T. 549 M. 287 F. 262
		Do.	Musalman	T. 384 M. 194 F. 190	T. 47 M. 22 F. 25	T. 47 M. 27 F. 20
			Total Group 37	*T. 5,343* *M. 2,747* *F. 2,596*	*T. 2,448* *M. 1,258* *F. 1,190*	*T. 596* *M. 314* *F. 282*

Nationality or traditional Occupation—*contd.*

BY DISTRICT.				RAILWAY PASSENGERS, ETC.	DISTRICT AMRAOTI.			
ELLICHPUR.	BULDANA.	WUN.	BASIM.		AMRAOTI.	CHANDUR.	MORSI.	MURTAZAPUR.
Total, Males, and Females.	Total, Males, and Females.	Total, Males, and Females.	Total, Males, and Females.	Total, Males, and Females.	Total, Males, and Females.	Total, Males, and Females.	Total, Males, and Females.	Total, Males, and Females.
8	9	10	11	12	13	14	15	16
T. 3 M. 1 F. 2	...	T. 1 M. 1	...	...	...	...	...	...
T. 77 M. 39 F. 38	...	...	...	...	T. 18 M. 9 F. 9	...	...	...
...	...	...	...	...	T. 3 M. 2 F. 1	...	...	...
...	...	...	...	...	T. 2 M. 2	...	...	...
T. 6,758 M. 3,623 F. 3,135	*T. 9,858 M. 4,915 F. 4,943*	*T. 9,549 M. 4,839 F. 4,710*	*T. 4,764 M. 2,392 F. 2,372*	*T. 7 M. 5 F. 2*	*T. 7,176 M. 3,706 F. 3,470*	*T. 3,177 M. 1,684 F. 1,493*	*T. 1,859 M. 990 F. 869*	*T. 2,053 M. 1,059 F. 994*
...	T. 8 M. 5 F. 3	...	...	...	...	...	...	...
...	...	...	...	...	...	...	T. 1 M. 1	...
...	*T. 8 M. 5 F. 3*	...	...	...	...	...	*T. 1 M. 1*	...
...	...	...	...	...	...	T. 1 M. 1	...	...
...	...	...	...	...	...	...	...	...
T. 2,154 M. 1,123 F. 1,031	T. 1,006 M. 536 F. 470	T. 3,910 M. 2,049 F. 1,861	T. 1,241 M. 651 F. 590	T. 1 M. 1	T. 1,226 M. 626 F. 600	T. 2,458 M. 1,294 F. 1,164	T. 1,002 M. 510 F. 492	T. 960 M. 516 F. 444
...	T. 10 M. 4 F. 6	...	...	...	...	...	...	...
...	...	T. 72 M. 39 F. 33	...	...	T. 58 M. 23 F. 35	T. 42 M. 29 F. 13	...	T. 14 M. 7 F. 7
...	...	...	...	...	...	T. 2 M. 1 F. 1	...	...
...	...	T. 20 F. 20	...	...	...	T. 4 M. 4	T. 25 M. 12 F. 13	...
T. 121 M. 81 F. 40	T. 2 M. 2	T. 44 M. 20 F. 24	T. 16 M. 11 F. 5	T. 17 M. 12 F. 5	T. 93 M. 62 F. 31	T. 26 M. 16 F. 10	T. 12 M. 7 F. 5	T. 88 M. 57 F. 31
T. 2,275 M. 1,204 F. 1,071	*T. 1,018 M. 542 F. 476*	*T. 4,046 M. 2,108 F. 1,938*	*T. 1,257 M. 662 F. 595*	*T. 18 M. 13 F. 5*	*T. 1,377 M. 711 F. 666*	*T. 2,533 M. 1,345 F. 1,188*	*T. 1,039 M. 529 F. 510*	*T. 1,062 M. 580 F. 482*
T. 1,331 M. 677 F. 654	T. 235 M. 107 F. 128	T. 346 M. 188 F. 158	T. 97 M. 58 F. 39	...	T. 1,138 M. 588 F. 550	T. 442 M. 216 F. 226	T. 520 M. 281 F. 239	T. 301 M. 151 F. 150
T. 25 M. 16 F. 9	T. 206 M. 99 F. 107	T. 17 M. 10 F. 7	T. 42 M. 20 F. 22	...	T. 34 M. 14 F. 20	T. 3 M. 3	T. 3 M. 1 F. 2	T. 7 M. 4 F. 3
T. 1,356 M. 693 F. 663	*T. 441 M. 206 F. 235*	*T. 363 M. 198 F. 165*	*T. 139 M. 78 F. 61*	...	*T. 1,172 M. 602 F. 570*	*T. 445 M. 219 F. 226*	*T. 523 M. 282 F. 241*	*T. 308 M. 155 F. 153*

TABLE XVI.—Castes, Tribes, and Races, by

Name and Classification.				District Akola.					District
				Akola.	Akot.	Balapur.	Jalgaon.	Khamgaon.	Ellichpur.
Class.	Group.	Caste.	Religion.	Total, Males, and Females.	Total, Males, and Females.	Total, Males, and Females.	Total, Males, and Females.	Total, Males, and Females.	Total, Males, and Females.
17	18	19	20	21	22	23	24	25	26
D.—ARTISAN AND VILLAGE MENIAL—*contd.*	35.—Fishermen, Boatmen, Palki-bearers, Cooks, etc.	Malla	Hindu	... ...	... ...	... ...	... ...	... ...	T. 3 M. 1 F. 2
		Pakhāli	Do.	... ...	... ...	... ...	... ...	T. 4 M. 3 F. 1	T. 4 M. 2 F. 2
		Shikharpāniwāle	Do.	... ...	... ...	... ...	... ...	... ...	... ...
		Wāghāde	Do.	... ...	... ...	... ...	... ...	... ...	... ...
			Total Group 35	*T. 3,923 M. 1,970 F. 1,953*	*T. 5,163 M. 2,649 F. 2,514*	*T. 1,623 M. 826 F. 797*	*T. 3,369 M. 1,724 F. 1,645*	*T. 1,610 M. 875 F. 735*	*T. 2,494 M. 1,326 F. 1,168*
	35A.—Servant Caste.	Khawās	Hindu	... ...	... ...	... ...	... ...	... ...	... ...
		Thārnak	Do.	... ...	... ...	... ...	... ...	... ...	... ...
			Total Group 35A	... ...	... ...	... ...	... ...	... ...	... ...
	36.—Distillers and Toddy-drawers.	Bavkar	Hindu	... ...	... ...	... ...	... ...	... ...	... ...
		Bhandāri	Do.	... ...	... ...	... ...	... ...	T. 2 M. 1 F. 1	... ...
		Kalāl	Do.	T. 660 M. 347 F. 313	T. 578 M. 291 F. 287	T. 377 M. 192 F. 185	T. 342 M. 185 F. 157	T. 120 M. 69 F. 51	T. 821 M. 434 F. 387
		Do.	Musalman	... ...	... ...	T. 1 M. 1 ...	... ...	... ...	... ...
		Do.	Jain	... ...	... ...	... ...	... ...	... ...	... ...
		Do.	Animistic	... ...	... ...	... ...	... ...	... ...	... ...
		Kalwār	Hindu	... ...	... ...	... ...	... ...	... ...	... ...
		Pāsi	Do.	T. 17 M. 14 F. 3	T. 21 M. 16 F. 5	T. 4 M. 4 ...	T. 1 M. 1 ...	T. 5 M. 1 F. 4	T. 65 M. 47 F. 18
			Total Group 36	*T. 677 M. 361 F. 316*	*T. 599 M. 307 F. 292*	*T. 382 M. 197 F. 185*	*T. 343 M. 186 F. 157*	*T. 127 M. 71 F. 56*	*T. 886 M. 481 F. 405*
	37.—Butchers.	Kasai (Bakar Kasai and Khātik)	Hindu	T. 91 M. 45 F. 46	T. 151 M. 78 F. 73	T. 84 M. 43 F. 41	T. 181 M. 97 F. 84	T. 42 M. 24 F. 18	T. 718 M. 371 F. 347
		Do.	Musalman	T. 8 M. 6 F. 2	T. 32 M. 16 F. 16	T. 7 M. 5 F. 2	... ...	... ...	T. 25 M. 16 F. 9
			Total Group 37	*T. 99 M. 51 F. 48*	*T. 183 M. 94 F. 89*	*T. 91 M. 48 F. 43*	*T. 181 M. 97 F. 84*	*T. 42 M. 24 F. 18*	*T. 743 M. 387 F. 356*

Nationality or traditional Occupation—*contd.*

ELLICHPUR.		DISTRICT BULDANA.			DISTRICT WUN.				DISTRICT BASIM.		
DARYAPUR.	MELGHAT.	CHIKHLI.	MALKAPUR.	MEHKAR.	YEOTMAL.	DARWHA.	KELAPUR.	WUN.	BASIM.	MANGRUL.	PUSAD.
Total, Males, and Females.	Total, Males, and Females.	Total, Males, and Females.	Total, Males, and Females.	Total, Males, and Females.	Total, Males, and Females.	Total, Males, and Females.	Total, Males, and Females.	Total, Males, and Females.	Total, Males, and Females.	Total, Males, and Females.	Total, Males, and Females.
27	28	29	30	31	32	33	34	35	36	37	38
...	...	...	...	...	T. 1 M. 1 ...	...	...	...	...	...	...
T. 73 M. 37 F. 36	...	...	...	...	...	...	...	...	...	...	...
...	...	...	...	...	...	...	...	...	...	...	...
...	...	...	...	...	...	...	...	...	...	...	...
T. 3,859 M. 2,028 F. 1,831	*T. 405 M. 269 F. 136*	*T. 2,230 M. 1,109 F. 1,121*	*T. 6,708 M. 3,347 F. 3,361*	*T. 920 M. 459 F. 461*	*T. 2,011 M. 1,058 F. 953*	*T. 2,023 M. 1,019 F. 1,004*	*T. 3,081 M. 1,541 F. 1,540*	*T. 2,434 M. 1,221 F. 1,213*	*T. 1,776 M. 920 F. 856*	*T. 608 M. 314 F. 294*	*T. 2,380 M. 1,158 F. 1,222*
...	...	T. 8 M. 5 F. 3	...	...	...	...	...	...	...	...	...
...	...	...	...	...	...	...	...	...	...	...	...
...	...	*T. 8 M. 5 F. 3*	...	...	...	...	...	...	...	...	...
...	...	...	...	...	...	...	...	...	...	...	...
...	...	...	...	...	...	...	...	...	...	...	...
T. 973 M. 501 F. 472	T. 360 M. 188 F. 172	T. 203 M. 108 F. 95	T. 607 M. 333 F. 274	T. 196 M. 95 F. 101	T. 1,394 M. 737 F. 657	T. 1,052 M. 538 F. 514	T. 1,021 M. 549 F. 472	T. 443 M. 225 F. 218	T. 434 M. 238 F. 196	T. 398 M. 209 F. 189	T. 409 M. 204 F. 205
...	...	T. 10 M. 4 F. 6	...	...	...	...	...	...	...	...	...
...	...	...	...	...	T. 37 M. 20 F. 17	T. 7 M. 5 F. 2	T. 2 M. 1 F. 1	T. 26 M. 13 F. 13	...	...	...
...	...	...	...	...	...	...	...	...	...	...	...
...	...	...	...	...	...	...	T. 20 ... F. 20	...	...	...	...
T. 28 M. 17 F. 11	T. 28 M. 17 F. 11	T. 1 M. 1 ...	...	T. 1 M. 1 ...	T. 5 M. 4 F. 1	T. 38 M. 15 F. 23	T. 1 M. 1 ...	...	T. 8 M. 6 F. 2	T. 1 M. 1 ...	T. 7 M. 4 F. 3
T. 1,001 M. 518 F. 483	*T. 388 M. 205 F. 183*	*T. 214 M. 113 F. 101*	*T. 607 M. 333 F. 274*	*T. 197 M. 96 F. 101*	*T. 1,436 M. 761 F. 675*	*T. 1,097 M. 558 F. 539*	*T. 1,044 M. 551 F. 493*	*T. 469 M. 238 F. 231*	*T. 442 M. 244 F. 198*	*T. 399 M. 210 F. 189*	*T. 416 M. 208 F. 208*
T. 595 M. 294 F. 301	T. 18 M. 12 F. 6	T. 6 M. 3 F. 3	T. 199 M. 90 F. 109	T. 30 M. 14 F. 16	T. 120 M. 66 F. 54	T. 178 M. 95 F. 83	T. 48 M. 27 F. 21	...	T. 13 M. 11 F. 2	T. 82 M. 46 F. 36	T. 2 M. 1 F. 1
...	...	T. 143 M. 69 F. 74	T. 55 M. 28 F. 27	T. 8 M. 2 F. 6	T. 15 M. 9 F. 6	T. 2 M. 1 F. 1	...	...	T. 23 M. 12 F. 11	T. 19 M. 8 F. 11	...
T. 595 M. 294 F. 301	*T. 18 M. 12 F. 6*	*T. 149 M. 72 F. 77*	*T. 254 M. 118 F. 136*	*T. 38 M. 16 F. 22*	*T. 135 M. 75 F. 60*	*T. 180 M. 96 F. 84*	*T. 48 M. 27 F. 21*	...	*T. 36 M. 23 F. 13*	*T. 101 M. 54 F. 47*	*T. 2 M. 1 F. 1*

TABLE XVI.—Castes, Tribes, and Races, by

Name and Classification.				Provincial Total.	Distribution	
					Amraoti.	Akola.
Class.	Group.	Caste.	Religion.	Total, Males, and Females.	Total, Males, and Females.	Total, Males, and Females.
1	2	3	4	5	6	7
D.—Artisan and Village Menial—*contd.*	38.—Leather-workers.	Chámbhár (Mochi)	Hindu	T. 29,174 M. 15,150 F. 14,024	T. 5,471 M. 2,792 F. 2,679	T. 8,027 M. 4,158 F. 3,869
		Dabgar	Do.	T. 56 M. 27 F. 29	... ...	T. 56 M. 27 F. 29
		Dohor	Do.	T. 5,082 M. 2,629 F. 2,453	T. 767 M. 395 F. 372	T. 917 M. 475 F. 442
		Mádgi	Do.	T. 2,670 M. 1,317 F. 1,353	... ...	T. 1 M. 1 ...
		Do.	Animistic	T. 7 M. 4 F. 3	... ...	... ...
		Zingar	Hindu	T. 1,313 M. 664 F. 649	T. 348 M. 172 F. 170	T. 429 M. 216 F. 213
			Total Group 38	*T. 38,302* *M. 19,791* *F. 18,511*	*T. 6,580* *M. 3,359* *F. 3,221*	*T. 9,430* *M. 4,877* *F. 4,553*
	38A.—Village Watchmen, etc.	Baláhi	Hindu	T. 249 M. 118 F. 131	... ...	... ...
		Do.	Animistic	T. 78 M. 38 F. 40	... ...	... ...
		Bhumak	Hindu	T. 11 M. 5 F. 6	T. 11 M. 5 F. 6	... ...
		Khángar	Do.	T. 229 M. 106 F. 123	T. 56 M. 29 F. 27	T. 86 M. 39 F. 47
		Mahár (Dher and Kotwál)	Do.	T. 354,997 M. 177,675 F. 177,322	T. 100,685 M. 50,397 F. 50,288	T. 68,400 M. 34,149 F. 34,251
		Do.	Animistic	T. 8 M. 6 F. 2	T. 8 M. 6 F. 2	... ...
		Pahelwán	Hindu	T. 3 M. 2 F. 1	T. 3 M. 2 F. 1	... ...
		Rámoshi	Do.	T. 91 M. 51 F. 40	T. 3 M. 2 F. 1	T. 38 M. 20 F. 18
			Total Group 38A	*T. 355,666* *M. 178,001* *F. 177,665*	*T. 100,766* *M. 50,441* *F. 50,325*	*T. 68,524* *M. 34,208* *F. 34,316*
	39.—Scavengers	Bhangi (Hálálkhor, Khákrob and Mehtar.)	Hindu	T. 1,303 M. 775 F. 528	T. 434 M. 247 T. 187	T. 499 M. 314 F. 185
		Do.	Musalman	T. 180 M. 97 F. 83	T. 55 M. 27 F. 28	T. 33 M. 21 F. 12
		Máng	Hindu	T. 52,150 M. 25,974 F. 26,176	T. 10,338 M. 5,206 F. 5,132	T. 9,684 M. 4,842 F. 4,842
		Do.	Animistic	T. 1 ... F. 1	... ...	... ...
		Máng Gárodi	Hindu	T. 161 M. 87 F. 74	... ...	... ...

Nationality or traditional Occupation—*contd.*

BY DISTRICT.				RAILWAY PASSENGERS, ETC.	DISTRICT AMRAOTI.			
ELLICHPUR.	BULDANA.	WUN.	BASIM.		AMRAOTI.	CHANDUR.	MORSI.	MURTAZAPUR.
Total, Males, and Females.	Total, Males, and Females.	Total, Males, and Females.	Total, Males, and Females.	Total, Males, and Females.	Total, Males, and Females.	Total, Males, and Females.	Total, Males, and Females.	Total, Males, and Females.
8	9	10	11	12	13	14	15	16
T. 3,181 M. 1,669 F. 1,512	T. 5,780 M. 3,002 F. 2,778	T. 2,689 M. 1,448 F. 1,241	T. 4,009 M. 2,070 F. 1,939	T. 17 M. 11 F. 6	T. 1,958 M. 989 F. 969	T. 1,045 M. 531 F. 514	T. 1,161 M. 607 F. 554	T. 1,307 M. 665 F. 642
... ...	... ...	... ...	... ...	... ...	... ...	... ...	... ...	... ...
T. 817 M. 434 F. 383	T. 2,201 M. 1,120 F. 1,081	T. 12 M. 9 F. 3	T. 368 M. 196 F. 172	... ...	T. 307 M. 148 F. 159	T. 209 M. 108 F. 101	T. 193 M. 111 F. 82	T. 58 M. 28 F. 30
... ...	... ...	T. 2,669 M. 1,316 F. 1,353	... ...	... ...	... ...	... ...	... ...	... ...
... ...	... ...	T. 7 M. 4 F. 3	... ...	... ...	... ...	... ...	... ...	... ...
T. 154 M. 75 F. 79	T. 169 M. 86 F. 83	T. 72 M. 39 F. 33	T. 147 M. 76 F. 71	... ...	T. 121 M. 58 F. 63	T. 31 M. 19 F. 12	T. 92 M. 41 F. 51	T. 98 M. 54 F. 44
T. 4,152 *M. 2,178* *F. 1,974*	*T. 8,150* *M. 4,208* *F. 3,942*	*T. 6,449* *M. 2,816* *F. 2,633*	*T. 4,524* *M. 2,342* *F. 2,182*	*T. 17* *M. 11* *F. 6*	*T. 2,386* *M. 1,195* *F. 1,191*	*T. 1,285* *M. 658* *F. 627*	*T. 1,446* *M. 759* *F. 687*	*T. 1,463* *M. 747* *F. 716*
T. 249 M. 118 F. 131	... ...	... ...	... ...	... ...	... ...	... ...	... ...	... ...
T. 78 M. 38 F. 40	... ...	... ...	... ...	... ...	... ...	... ...	... ...	... ...
... ...	... ...	... ...	... ...	... ...	... ...	... ...	T. 11 M. 5 F. 6	... ...
T. 87 M. 38 F. 49	... ...	... ...	... ...	... ...	T. 25 M. 15 F. 10	T. 25 M. 11 F. 14	... ...	T. 6 M. 3 F. 3
T. 36,160 M. 18,116 F. 18,044	T. 55,943 M. 27,972 F. 27,971	T. 41,102 M. 20,828 F. 20,274	T. 52,631 M. 26,174 F. 26,457	T. 76 M. 39 F. 37	T. 31,420 M. 15,512 F. 15,908	T. 31,217 M. 15,754 F. 15,463	T. 18,969 M. 9,514 F. 9,455	T. 19,079 M. 9,617 F. 9,462
... ...	... ...	... ...	... ...	... ...	... ...	... ...	T. 8 M. 6 F. 2	... ...
... ...	... ...	... ...	... ...	... ...	... ...	T. 3 M. 2 F. 1	... ...	... ...
T. 1 M. 1 ...	T. 10 M. 5 F. 5	T. 29 M 17 F. 12	T. 8 M. 5 F. 3	T. 2 M. 1 F. 1	... ...	... ...	... ...	T. 3 M. 2 F. 1
T. 36,575 *M. 18,311* *F. 18,264*	*T. 55,953* *M. 27,977* *F. 27,976*	*T. 41,131* *M. 20,845* *F. 20,286*	*T. 52,639* *M. 26,179* *F. 26,460*	*T. 78* *M. 40* *F. 38*	*T. 31,445* *M. 15,527* *F. 15,918*	*T. 31,245* *M. 15,767* *F. 15,478*	*T. 18,988* *M. 9,525* *F. 9,463*	*T. 19,088* *M. 9,622* *F. 9,466*
T. 106 M. 60 F. 46	T. 112 M. 60 F. 52	T. 92 M. 57 F. 35	T. 60 M. 37 F. 23	... ...	T. 310 M. 171 F. 139	T. 31 M. 18 F. 13	T. 33 M. 20 F. 13	T. 60 M. 38 F. 22
T. 34 M. 19 F. 15	T. 26 M. 13 F. 13	T. 16 M. 8 F. 8	T. 16 M. 9 F. 7	... ...	T. 24 M. 12 F. 12	T. 9 M. 4 F. 5	T. 14 M. 7 F. 7	T. 8 M. 4 F. 4
T. 4,683 M. 2,330 F. 2,353	T. 10,123 M. 4,987 F. 5,136	T. 5,317 M. 2,625 F. 2,692	T. 12,003 M. 5,983 F. 6,020	T. 2 M. 1 F. 1	T. 3,504 M. 1,729 F. 1,775	T. 3,028 M. 1,559 F. 1,469	T. 1,463 M. 753 F. 710	T. 2,343 M. 1,165 F. 1,178
... ...	... ...	T. 1 ... F. 1	... ...	... ...	... ...	... ...	... ...	... ...
... ...	... ...	T. 161 M. 87 F. 74	... ...	... ...	... ...	... ...	... ...	... ...

TABLE XVI.—Castes, Tribes, and Races, by

				DISTRICT AKOLA.					DISTRICT
NAME AND CLASSIFICATION.				AKOLA.	AKOT.	BALAPUR.	JALGAON.	KHAMGAON.	ELLICHPUR.
Class.	Group.	Caste.	Religion.	Total, Males, and Females.	Total, Males, and Females.	Total, Males, and Females.	Total, Males, and Females.	Total, Males, and Females.	Total, Males, and Females.
17	18	19	20	21	22	23	24	25	26
D.—ARTISAN AND VILLAGE MENIAL—*contd.*	38.—LEATHER-WORKERS.	CHÁMBHÁR (MOCHI)	Hindu	T. 1,872 M. 985 F. 887	T. 1,801 M. 914 F. 887	T. 1,156 M. 602 F. 554	T. 1,556 M. 804 F. 752	T. 1,642 M. 853 F. 789	T. 1,479 M. 789 F. 690
	...	DABGAR	Do.	... ...	... ...	T. 56 M. 27 F. 29	... ...	... ...	... ...
		DOHOR	Do.	T. 310 M. 145 F. 165	T. 214 M. 112 F. 102	T. 252 M. 130 F. 122	T. 87 M. 47 F. 40	T. 54 M. 41 T. 13	T. 607 M. 323 F. 284
	...	MÁDGI	Do.	T. 1 M. 1 ...	... ...	... ...	... ...	... ...	... ...
	...	Do.	Animistic	... ...	... ...	... ...	... ...	... ...	... ...
		ZINGAR	Hindu	T. 31 M. 15 F. 16	T. 190 M. 96 F. 94	T. 73 M. 34 F. 39	T. 73 M. 45 F. 28	T. 62 M. 26 F. 36	T. 88 M. 42 F. 46
			Total Group 38	*T. 2,214* *M. 1,146* *F. 1,068*	*T. 2,205* *M. 1,122* *F. 1,083*	*T. 1,537* *M. 793* *F. 744*	*T. 1,716* *M. 896* *F. 820*	*T. 1,758* *M. 920* *F. 838*	*T. 2,174* *M. 1,164* *F. 1,020*
	38A.—VILLAGE WATCHMEN, ETC.	BALÁHI	Hindu	... ...	... ...	... ...	... ...	... ...	... ...
	...	Do.	Animistic	... ...	... ...	... ...	... ...	... ...	... ...
		BHUMAK	Hindu	... ...	... ...	... ...	... ...	... ...	... ...
	...	KHÁNGAR	Do.	T. 80 M. 35 F. 45	... ...	T. 5 M. 3 F. 2	... ...	T. 1 M. 1 ...	T. 87 M. 38 F. 49
		MAHÁR (DHER AND KOTWÁL.)	Do.	T. 20,639 M. 10,284 F. 10,355	T. 14,297 M. 7,046 F. 7,251	T. 13,139 M. 6,667 F. 6,472	T. 9,148 M. 4,582 F. 4,566	T. 11,177 M. 5,570 F. 15,607	T. 17,661 M. 8,832 F. 8,829
		Do.	Animistic	... ...	... ...	... ...	... ...	... ...	... ...
		PAHELWÁN	Hindu	... ...	... ...	... ...	... ...	... ...	... ...
		RÁMOSHI	Do	T. 1 M. 1 ...	... ...	T. 32 M. 17 F. 15	... ...	T. 5 M. 2 F. 3	... ...
			Total Group 38A	*T. 20,720* *M. 10,320* *F. 10,400*	*T. 14,297* *M. 7,046* *F. 7,251*	*T. 13,176* *M. 6,687* *F. 6,489*	*T. 9,148* *M. 4,582* *F. 4,566*	*T. 11,183* *M. 5,573* *F. 5,610*	*T. 17,748* *M. 8,870* *F. 8,878*
	39.—SCAVENGERS.	BHANGI (HÁLÁLKHOR, KHÁKROB AND MEHTAR.)	Hindu	T. 152 M. 86 F. 66	T. 145 M. 90 F. 55	T. 4 M. 1 F. 3	T. 38 M. 27 F. 11	T. 160 M. 110 F. 50	T. 79 M. 46 F. 33
		Do.	Musalman	T. 15 M. 9 F. 6	T. 8 M. 4 F. 4	T. 3 M. 3 ...	T. 3 M. 2 F. 1	T. 4 M. 3 F. 1	T. 29 M. 15 F. 14
		MÁNG	Hindu	T. 2,843 M. 1,435 F. 1,408	T. 2,431 M. 1,212 F. 1,219	T. 1,530 M 749 F. 781	T. 1,411 M. 699 F. 712	T. 1,469 M. 747 F. 722	T. 1,999 M. 1,003 F. 996
	...	Do.	Animistic	... ...	... ...	... ...	... ...	... ...	... ...
		MÁNG GÁRODI	Hindu	... ...	... ...	... ...	... ...	... ...	... ...

Nationality or traditional Occupation—*contd.*

ELLICHPUR.		DISTRICT BULDANA.			DISTRICT WUN.				DISTRICT BASIM.		
DARYAPUR.	MELGHAT.	CHIKHLI.	MALKAPUR.	MEHKAR.	YEOTMAL.	DARWHA.	KELAPUR.	WUN.	BASIM.	MANGRUL.	PUSAD.
Total, Males, and Females.	Total, Males, and Females.	Total, Males, and Females.	Total, Males, and Females.	Total, Males, and Females.	Total, Males, and Females.	Total, Males, and Females.	Total, Males, and Females.	Total, Males, and Females.	Total, Males, and Females.	Total, Males, and Females.	Total, Males, and Females.
27	28	29	30	31	32	33	34	35	36	37	38
T. 1,577 M. 802 F. 775	T. 125 M. 78 F. 47	T. 1,283 M. 690 F. 593	T. 2,892 M. 1,485 F. 1,407	T. 1,605 M. 827 F. 778	T. 810 M. 457 F. 353	T. 1,088 M. 556 F. 532	T. 345 M. 196 F. 149	T. 446 M. 239 F. 207	T. 1,788 M. 925 F. 863	T. 827 M. 452 F, 375	T. 1,394 M. 693 F. 701
... ...	... ...	... ...	... ...	... ...	... ...	... ...	... ...	... ...	... ...	... ...	... ...
T. 210 M. 111 F. 99	... ...	T. 980 M. 499 F. 481	T. 216 M. 113 F. 103	T. 1,005 M. 508 F. 497	T. 1 M. 1 ...	T. 11 M. 8 F. 3	... ...	... ...	T. 294 M. 158 F. 136	T. 30 M. 15 F. 15	T. 44 M. 23 F. 21
... ...	... ...	... ...	... ...	... ...	T. 97 M. 50 F. 47	T. 138 M. 63 F. 75	T. 1,509 M. 743 F. 766	T. 925 M. 460 F. 465	... ...	... ...	... ...
... ...	... ...	... ...	... ...	... ...	... ...	... ...	T. 7 M. 4 F. 3	... ...	... ...	... ...	... ...
T. 66 M. 33 F. 33	... ...	T. 83 M. 41 F. 42	T. 56 M. 27 F. 29	T. 30 M. 18 F. 12	T. 7 M. 3 F. 4	T. 47 M. 27 F. 20	T. 17 M. 8 F. 9	T. 1 M. 1 ...	T. 45 M. 24 F. 21	T. 21 M. 11 F. 10	T. 81 M. 41 F. 40
T. 1,858 *M. 946* *F. 907*	*T. 125* *M. 78* *F. 47*	*T. 2,348* *M. 1,230* *F. 1,116*	*T. 3,164* *M. 1,625* *F. 1,539*	*T. 2,640* *M. 1,353* *F. 1,287*	*T. 915* *M. 511* *F. 404*	*T. 1,284* *M. 654* *F. 630*	*T. 1,878* *M. 951* *F. 927*	*T. 1,372* *M. 700* *F. 672*	*T. 2,127* *M. 1,107* *F. 1,020*	*T. 878* *M. 478* *F. 400*	*T. 1,519* *M. 757* *F. 762*
... ...	T. 249 M. 118 F. 131	... ...	... ...	... ...	... ...	... ...	... ...	... ...	... ...	... ...	... ...
... ...	T. 78 M. 38 F. 40	... ...	... ...	... ...	... ...	... ...	... ...	... ...	... ...	... ...	... ...
... ...	... ...	... ...	... ...	... ...	... ...	... ...	... ...	... ...	... ...	... ...	... ...
... ...	... ...	... ...	... ...	... ...	... ...	... ...	... ...	... ...	... ...	... ...	... ...
T. 17,353 M. 8,690 F. 8,663	T. 1,146 M. 594 F. 552	T. 18,437 M. 9,324 F. 9,113	T. 19,027 M. 9,497 F. 9,530	T. 18,479 M. 9,151 F. 9,328	T. 11,762 M. 5,975 F. 5,787	T. 17,842 M. 8,984 F, 8,858	T. 6,365 M. 3,288 F. 3,077	T. 5,133 M. 2,581 F. 2,552	T. 23,768 M. 11,889 F. 11,879	T. 12,189 M. 6,035 F. 6,154	T. 16,674 M. 8,250 F. 8,424
... ...	... ...	... ...	... ...	... ...	... ...	... ...	... ...	... ...	... ...	... ...	... ...
... ...	... ...	... ...	... ...	... ...	... ...	... ...	... ...	... ...	... ...	... ...	... ...
... ...	T. 1 M. 1 ...	... ...	T. 10 M. 5 F. 5	... ...	... ...	T. 29 M. 17 F. 12	... ...	... ...	T. 8 M. 5 F. 3	... ...	... ...
T. 17,853 *M. 8,690* *F. 8,663*	*T. 1,474* *M. 751* *F. 723*	*T. 18,437* *M. 9,324* *F. 9,113*	*T. 19,037* *M. 9,502* *F. 9,535*	*T. 18,479* *M. 9,151* *F. 9,328*	*T. 11,762* *M. 5,975* *F. 5,787*	*T. 17,871* *M. 9,001* *F. 8,870*	*T. 6,365* *M. 3,288* *F. 3,077*	*T. 5,133* *M. 2,581* *F. 2,552*	*T. 23,776* *M. 11,894* *F. 11,882*	*T. 12,189* *M. 6,035* *F. 6,154*	*T. 16,674* *M. 8,250* *F. 8,424*
T. 19 M. 11 F. 8	T. 8 M. 3 F. 5	T. 50 M. 26 F. 24	T. 32 M. 15 F. 17	T. 30 M. 19 F. 11	T. 65 M. 40 F. 25	T. 4 M. 3 F. 1	T. 8 M. 5 F. 3	T. 15 M. 9 F. 6	T. 41 M. 23 F. 18	T. 11 M. 9 F. 2	T. 8 M. 5 F. 3
T. 5 M. 4 F. 1	... ...	T. 19 M. 9 F. 10	T. 2 M. 1 F. 1	T. 5 M. 3 F. 2	T. 9 M. 4 F. 5	T. 7 M. 4 F. 3	... ...	... ...	T. 13 M. 7 F. 6	... ...	T. 3 M. 2 F. 1
T. 2,641 M. 1,302 F. 1,339	T. 43 M. 25 F. 18	T. 3,326 M. 1,637 F. 1,689	T. 2,929 M. 1,438 F. 1,491	T. 3,868 M. 1,912 F. 1,956	T. 1,297 M. 649 F. 648	T. 3,561 M. 1,762 F. 1,799	T. 302 M. 150 F. 152	T. 157 M. 64 F. 93	T. 6,697 M. 3,358 F. 3,339	T. 2,008 M. 903 F. 1,015	T. 3,298 M. 1,632 F. 1,666
... ...	... ...	... ...	... ...	... ...	... ...	... ...	T. 1 ... F. 1	... ...	... ...	... ...	... ...
... ...	... ...	... ...	... ...	... ...	... ...	... ...	T. 32 M. 21 F. 11	T. 129 M. 66 F. 63	... ...	... ...	... ...

TABLE XVI.—Castes, Tribes, and Races, by

Class.	Group.	Caste.	Religion.	PROVINCIAL TOTAL. Total, Males, and Females.	DISTRIBUTION Amraoti. Total, Males, and Females.	Akola. Total, Males, and Females.
1	2	3	4	5	6	7
D.—ARTISAN AND VILLAGE MENIAL—*concld.*	39.—SCAVENGERS —*contd.*	MEHTAR	Sikh	T. 32 M. 17 F. 15	T. 2 M. 1 F. 1	T. 30 M. 16 F. 14
		Do.	Animistic	T. 2 M. 1 F. 1	... ...	... ...
		TÁGWÁLE	Hindu	T. 113 M. 56 F. 57	... ...	... ...
			Total Group 39	*T. 53,942* *M. 27,007* *F. 26,935*	*T. 10,829* *M. 5,481* *F. 5,348*	*T. 10,246* *M. 5,193* *F. 5,053*
	40.—GRIND-STONE-MAKERS AND STONE-QUARRIERS.	GOTEPOD (FATARPOD)	Hindu	T. 132 M. 71 F. 61	T. 3 M. 1 F. 2	... ...
		PÁTHRAT (PÁTHARKAR AND PÁTHAR).	Do.	T. 877 M. 422 F. 455	T. 137 M. 63 F. 74	T. 391 M. 195 F. 196
		TÁKANKÁR (TAKÁRI)	Do.	T. 5,414 M. 2,791 F. 2,623	T. 1,843 M. 924 F. 919	T. 2,323 M. 1,217 F. 1,106
			Total Group 40	*T. 6,423* *M. 3,284* *F. 3,139*	*T. 1,983* *M. 988* *F. 995*	*T. 2,714* *M. 1,412* *F. 1,302*
E.—VAGRANT, MINOR ARTISANS AND PERFORMERS, ETC.	41.—EARTHWORKERS AND STONE-DRESSERS.	BÁGARI	Hindu	T. 1 M. 1 ...	... ...	T. 1 M. 1 ...
		BELDÁR	Do.	T. 12,217 M. 6,163 F. 6,054	T. 2,499 M. 1,264 F. 1,235	T. 3,002 M. 1,492 F. 1,510
		Do.	Musalman	T. 11 M. 7 F. 4	T. 11 M. 7 F. 4	... ...
		GOCHKÍ	Hindu	T. 94 M. 47 F. 47	... ...	... ...
		MANEWÁD	Do.	T. 54 M. 25 F. 29	T. 20 M. 11 F. 9	T. 8 M. 3 F. 5
		SAGUR	Do.	T. 63 M. 32 F. 31	T. 6 M. 2 F. 4	... ...
		SILÁWAT	Do.	T. 6 M. 3 F. 3	... ...	... ...
		WADDAR	Do.	T. 6,116 M. 3,101 F. 3,015	T. 832 M. 411 F. 421	T. 289 M. 151 F. 138
			Total Group 41	*T. 18,562* *M. 9,379* *F. 9,183*	*T. 3,368* *M. 1,695* *F. 1,673*	*T. 3,300* *M. 1,647* *F. 1,653*
	42.—KNIFE-GRINDERS.	SIKLIKAR	Hindu	T. 36 M. 19 F. 17	T. 8 M. 4 F. 4	... ...
		Do.	Musalman	T. 37 M. 16 F. 21	... ...	... ...
			Total Group 42	*T. 73* *M. 35* *F. 38*	*T. 8* *M. 4* *F. 4*	... ...

Nationality or traditional Occupation—*contd.*

BY DISTRICT.				RAILWAY PASSENGERS, ETC.	DISTRICT AMRAOTI.			
ELLICHPUR.	BULDANA.	WUN.	BASIM.		AMRAOTI.	CHANDUR.	MORSI.	MURTAZAPUR.
Total, Males, and Females.	Total, Males, and Females.	Total, Males, and Females.	Total, Males, and Females.	Total, Males, and Females.	Total, Males, and Females.	Total, Males, and Females.	Total, Males, and Females.	Total, Males, and Females.
8	9	10	11	12	13	14	15	16
...	...	...	...	...	T. 2	...	...	...
...	...	...	...	...	M. 1	...	...	...
...	...	...	...	...	F. 1	...	...	...
...	...	T. 2	...	...	...	...	...	...
...	...	M. 1	...	...	...	...	...	...
...	...	F. 1	...	...	...	...	...	...
...	T. 113	...	...	...	...	...	...	...
...	M. 56	...	...	...	...	...	...	...
...	F. 57	...	...	...	...	...	...	...
T. 4,823	*T. 10,874*	*T. 5,589*	*T. 12,079*	*T. 2*	*T. 3,840*	*T. 3,068*	*T. 1,510*	*T. 2,411*
M. 2,409	*M. 5,116*	*M. 2,778*	*M. 6,029*	*M. 1*	*M. 1,913*	*M. 1,581*	*M. 780*	*M. 1,207*
F. 2,414	*F. 5,258*	*F. 2,811*	*F. 6,050*	*F. 1*	*F. 1,927*	*F. 1,487*	*F. 730*	*F. 1,204*
...	T. 38	T. 64	T. 27	...	...	T. 2	T. 1	...
...	M. 19	M. 35	M. 10	...	...	M. 1	...	...
...	F. 19	F. 29	F. 11	...	...	F. 1	F. 1	...
...	T. 167	T. 115	T. 67	...	...	...	...	T. 137
...	M. 69	M. 64	M. 31	...	...	...	...	M. 63
...	F. 98	F. 51	F. 36	...	...	...	...	F. 74
T. 863	T. 106	T. 222	T. 57	...	T. 675	T. 384	T. 140	T. 644
M. 450	M. 58	M. 110	M. 32	...	M. 345	M. 187	M. 74	M. 318
F. 413	F. 48	F. 112	F. 25	...	F. 330	F. 197	F. 66	F. 326
T. 863	*T. 311*	*T. 401*	*T. 151*	...	*T. 675*	*T. 386*	*T. 141*	*T. 781*
M. 450	*M. 146*	*M. 209*	*M. 79*	...	*M. 345*	*M. 188*	*M. 74*	*M. 381*
F. 413	*F. 165*	*F. 192*	*F. 72*	...	*F. 330*	*F. 198*	*F. 67*	*F. 400*
...	...	...	...	...	...	...	...	...
...	...	...	...	...	...	...	...	...
...	...	...	...	...	...	...	...	...
T. 346	T. 2,364	T. 2,792	T. 1,214	...	T. 603	T. 1,355	T. 91	T. 450
M. 175	M. 1,188	M. 1,409	M. 635	...	M. 305	M. 688	M. 36	M. 235
F. 171	F. 1,176	F. 1,383	F. 579	...	F. 298	F. 667	F. 55	F. 215
...	...	...	...	...	...	...	T. 9	T. 2
...	...	...	...	...	...	...	M. 5	M. 2
...	...	...	...	...	...	...	F. 4	...
...	...	T. 94	...	...	...	...	...	...
...	...	M. 47	...	...	...	...	...	...
...	...	F. 47	...	...	...	...	...	...
T. 7	...	T. 19	...	...	T. 17	...	T. 3	...
M. 1	...	M. 10	...	...	M. 9	...	M. 2	...
F. 6	...	F. 9	...	...	F. 8	...	F. 1	...
...	T. 57	...	...	...	...	...	T. 6	...
...	M. 30	...	...	...	...	...	M. 2	...
...	F. 27	...	...	...	...	...	F. 4	...
...	T. 6	...	...	...	...	...	...	...
...	M. 3	...	...	...	...	...	...	...
...	F. 3	...	...	...	...	...	...	...
T. 43	T. 1,976	T. 1,055	T. 1,921	...	T. 422	T. 240	T. 52	T. 118
M. 23	M. 977	M. 551	M. 988	...	M. 210	M. 111	M. 30	M. 60
F. 20	F. 999	F. 504	F. 933	...	F. 212	F. 129	F. 22	F. 58
T. 396	*T. 4,403*	*T. 3,960*	*T. 3,135*	...	*T. 1,042*	*T. 1,595*	*T. 161*	*T. 570*
M. 199	*M. 2,198*	*M. 2,017*	*M. 1,623*	...	*M. 524*	*M. 799*	*M. 75*	*M. 297*
F. 197	*F. 2,205*	*F. 1,943*	*F. 1,512*	...	*F. 518*	*F. 796*	*F. 86*	*F. 273*
...	T. 28	...	...	...	...	...	T. 8	...
...	M. 15	...	...	...	...	...	M. 4	...
...	F. 13	...	...	...	...	...	F. 4	...
...	T. 7	T. 20	T. 10	...	...	...	...	...
...	M. 2	M. 9	M. 5	...	...	...	...	...
...	F. 5	F. 11	F. 5	...	...	...	...	...
...	*T. 35*	*T. 20*	*T. 10*	...	...	...	*T. 8*	...
...	*M. 17*	*M. 9*	*M. 5*	...	...	...	*M. 4*	...
...	*F. 18*	*F. 11*	*F. 5*	...	...	...	*F. 4*	...

TABLE XVI.—Castes, Tribes, and Races, by

Name and Classification.				District Akola.					District
				Akola.	Akot.	Balapur.	Jalgaon	Khamgaon.	Ellichpur.
Class.	Group.	Caste.	Religion.	Total, Males, and Females.	Total, Males, and Females.	Total, Males, and Females.	Total, Males, and Females.	Total, Males, and Females.	Total, Males, and Females.
17	18	19	20	21	22	23	24	25	26
D.—Artisan and Village Menial—*concld.*	39.—Scavengers —*contd.*	Mehtar	Sikh	T. 30 M. 16 F. 14	... ...	... ...	... ...	... ...	... ...
		Do.	Animistic	... ...	... ...	... ...	... ...	... ...	... ...
		Tágwále	Hindu	... ...	... ...	... ...	... ...	... ...	... ...
			Total Group 39	*T.* 3,040 *M.* 1,546 *F.* 1,494	*T.* 2,584 *M.* 1,306 *F.* 1,278	*T.* 1,537 *M.* 753 *F.* 784	*T.* 1,452 *M.* 728 *F.* 724	*T.* 1,633 *M.* 860 *F.* 773	*T.* 2,107 *M.* 1,064 *F.* 1,043
	40.—Grind-stone-makers and Stone-quarriers.	Gotepod (Fatarod)	Hindu	... ...	... ...	... ...	... ...	... ...	... ...
		Páthrat (Pátharkar and Páthar).	Do.	T. 62 M. 31 F. 31	T. 26 M. 13 F. 13	T. 216 M. 92 F. 124	T. 87 M. 59 F. 28	... ...	... ...
		Tákankár (Takári)	Do.	T. 671 M. 367 F. 304	T. 875 M. 448 F. 427	T. 260 M. 133 F. 127	T. 341 M. 170 F. 171	T. 176 M. 99 F. 77	T. 224 M. 128 F. 96
			Total Group 40	*T.* 733 *M.* 398 *F.* 335	*T.* 901 *M.* 461 *F.* 440	*T.* 476 *M.* 225 *F.* 251	*T.* 428 *M.* 229 *F.* 199	*T.* 176 *M.* 99 *F.* 77	*T.* 224 *M.* 128 *F.* 96
E.—Vagrant, Minor Artisans and Performers, Etc.	41.—Earthworkers and Stone-dressers.	Bágari	Hindu	... ...	T. 1 M. 1 ...	... ...	... ...	... ...	... ...
		Beldár	Do.	T. 938 M. 483 F. 455	T. 373 M. 180 F. 193	T. 534 M. 257 F. 277	T. 527 M. 259 F. 268	T. 630 M. 313 F. 317	T. 85 M. 47 F. 38
		Do.	Musalman	... ...	... ...	... ...	... ...	... ...	... ...
		Gochki	Hindu	... ...	... ...	... ...	... ...	... ...	... ...
		Manewád	Do.	T. 8 M. 3 F. 5	... ...	... ...	... ...	... ...	T. 7 M. 1 F. 6
		Sagur	Do.	... ...	... ...	... ...	... ...	... ...	... ...
		Siláwat	Do.	... ...	... ...	... ...	... ...	... ...	... ...
		Waddar	Do.	T. 72 M. 41 F. 31	T. 9 M. 5 F. 4	T. 59 M. 29 F. 30	T. 26 M. 17 F. 9	T. 123 M. 59 F. 64	T. 5 M. 3 F. 2
			Total Group 41	*T.* 1,018 *M.* 527 *F.* 491	*T.* 383 *M.* 186 *F.* 197	*T.* 573 *M.* 286 *F.* 287	*T.* 553 *M.* 276 *F.* 277	*T.* 753 *M.* 372 *F.* 381	*T.* 97 *M.* 51 *F.* 46
	42.—Knife-grinders.	Siklikar	Hindu	... ...	... ...	... ...	... ...	... ...	... ...
		Do.	Musalman	... ...	... ...	... ...	... ...	... ...	... ...
			Total Group 42	... ...	... ...	... ...	... ...	... ...	... ...

Nationality or traditional Occupation—*contd.*

ELLICHPUR.		DISTRICT BULDANA.			DISTRICT WUN.				DISTRICT BASIM.		
DARYAPUR.	MELGHAT.	CHIKHLI.	MALKAPUR.	MEHKAR.	YEOTMAL.	DARWHA.	KELAPUR.	WUN.	BASIM.	MANGRUL.	PUSAD.
Total, Males, and Females.	Total, Males, and Females.	Total, Males, and Females.	Total, Males, and Females.	Total, Males, and Females.	Total, Males, and Females.	Total, Males, and Females.	Total, Males, and Females.	Total, Males, and Females.	Total, Males, and Females.	Total, Males, and Females.	Total, Males, and Females.
27	28	29	30	31	32	33	34	35	36	37	38
... ...	... ...	... ...	... ...	... ...	... ...	... ...	... ...	... ...	... ...	... ...	... ...
... ...	... ...	... ...	... ...	... ...	... ...	... ...	T. 2 M. 1 F. 1	... ...	... ...	... ...	... ...
... ...	... ...	T. 81 M. 41 F. 40	... ...	T. 32 M. 15 F. 17	... ...	... ...	... ...	... ...	... ...	... ...	... ...
T. 2,665 M. 1,317 F. 1,348	*T. 51 M. 28 F. 23*	*T. 3,476 M. 1,713 F. 1,763*	*T. 2,963 M. 1,454 F. 1,509*	*T. 3,935 M. 1,949 F. 1,986*	*T. 1,371 M. 693 F. 678*	*T. 3,572 M. 1,769 F. 1,803*	*T. 345 M. 177 F. 168*	*T. 301 M. 139 F. 162*	*T. 6,751 M. 3,388 F. 3,363*	*T. 2,019 M. 1,002 F. 1,017*	*T. 3,309 M. 1,639 F. 1,670*
... ...	... ...	... ...	T. 6 M. 2 F. 4	T. 32 M. 17 F. 15	T. 26 M. 14 F. 12	T. 38 M. 21 F. 17	... ...	... ...	T. 27 M. 10 F. 11	... ...	... ...
... ...	... ...	T. 108 M. 41 F. 67	T. 11 M. 7 F. 4	T. 48 M. 21 F. 27	... ...	T. 115 M. 64 F. 51	... ...	... ...	T. 54 M. 25 F. 29	... ...	T. 13 M. 6 F. 7
T. 638 M. 321 F. 317	T. 1 M. 1 ...	... ...	T. 105 M. 57 F. 48	T. 1 M. 1 ...	T. 49 M. 26 F. 23	T. 173 M. 84 F. 89	... ...	... ...	T. 17 M. 13 F. 4	T. 40 M. 19 F. 21	... ...
T. 638 M. 321 F. 317	*T. 1 M. 1 ..*	*T. 108 M. 41 F. 67*	*T. 122 M. 66 F. 56*	*T. 81 M. 39 F. 42*	*T. 75 M. 40 F. 35*	*T. 326 M. 169 F. 157*	... ...	... ...	*T. 98 M. 54 F. 44*	*T. 40 M. 19 F. 21*	*T. 13 M. 6 F. 7*
... ...	... ...	... ...	... ...	... ...	... ...	... ...	... ...	... ...	... ...	... ...	... ...
T. 209 M. [illegible]02 F. [illegible]07	T. 52 M. 26 F. 26	T. 474 M. 252 F. 222	T. 980 M. 477 F. 503	T. 910 M. 459 F. 451	T. 646 M. 342 F. 304	T. 1,550 M. 757 F. 793	T. 465 M. 241 F. 224	T. 131 M. 69 F. 62	T. 835 M. 435 F. 400	T. 181 M. 108 F. 73	T. 198 M. 92 F. 106
... ...	... ...	... ...	... ...	... ...	... ...	... ...	... ...	... ...	... ...	... ...	... ...
... ...	... ...	... ...	... ...	... ...	... ...	... ...	... ...	T. 94 M. 47 F. 47	... ...	... ...	... ...
... ...	... ...	... ...	... ...	... ...	T. 19 M. 10 F. 9	... ...	... ...	... ...	... ...	... ...	... ...
... ...	... ...	... ...	... ...	T. 57 M. 30 F. 27	... ...	... ...	... ...	... ...	... ...	... ...	... ...
... ...	... ...	... ...	T. 6 M. 3 F. 3	... ...	... ...	... ...	... ...	... ...	... ...	... ...	... ...
... ...	T. 38 M. 20 F. 18	T. 563 M. 258 F. 305	T. 316 M. 161 F. 155	T. 1,097 M. 558 F. 539	T. 415 M. 224 F. 191	T. 363 M. 190 F. 173	T. 208 M. 98 F. 110	T. 69 M. 39 F. 30	T. 568 M. 299 F. 269	T. 364 M. 190 F. 174	T. 989 M. 499 F. 490
T. 209 M. 102 F. 107	*T. 90 M. 46 F. 44*	*T. 1,037 M. 510 F. 527*	*T. 1,302 M. 641 F. 661*	*T. 2,064 M. 1,047 F. 1,017*	*T. 1,080 M. 576 F. 504*	*T. 1,913 M. 947 F. 966*	*T. 673 M. 339 F. 334*	*T. 294 M. 155 F. 139*	*T. 1,403 M. 734 F. 669*	*T. 545 M. 298 F. 247*	*T. 1,187 M. 591 F. 596*
... ...	... ...	... ...	... ...	T. 28 M. 15 F. 13	... ...	... ...	... ...	... ...	... ...	... ...	... ...
... ...	... ...	T. 7 M. 2 F. 5	... ...	... ...	... ...	T. 20 M. 9 F. 11	... ...	... ...	... ...	T. 10 M. 5 F. 5	... ...
... ...	... ...	*T. 7 M. 2 F. 5*	... ...	*T. 28 M. 15 F. 13*	... ...	*T. 20 M. 9 F. 11*	... ...	... ...	... ...	*T. 10 M. 5 F. 5*	... ...

TABLE XVI.—Castes, Tribes, and Races, by

Class.	Group.	Caste.	Religion.	PROVINCIAL TOTAL. Total, Males, and Females.	DISTRIBUTION: Amraoti. Total, Males, and Females.	Akola. Total, Males, and Females.
1	2	3	4	5	6	7
E.—VAGRANT, MINOR ARTISANS AND PERFORMERS, ETC.—contd.	43.—MAT-MAKERS, CANE-SPLITTERS AND GRASS-CUTTERS.	BÁNSFOD	Hindu	T. 26 M. 11 F. 15	T. 23 M. 10 F. 13	T. 1 ... F. 1
		BASOD	Do.	T. 191 M. 94 F. 97	T. 152 M. 73 F. 79	... ...
		Do.	Animistic	T. 70 M. 31 F. 39	... ...	... ...
		BOREKAR	Hindu	T. 120 M. 58 F. 68	... ...	T. 118 M. 57 F. 61
		BURUD	Do.	T. 1,247 M. 618 F. 629	T. 344 M. 171 F. 173	T. 197 M. 98 F. 99
		Do.	Animistic	T. 22 M. 10 F. 12	... ...	... ...
		KÁNGAR	Hindu	T. 35 M. 22 F. 13	T. 27 M. 15 F. 12	... ...
		Do.	Musalman	T. 2 M. 1 F. 1	T. 2 M. 1 F. 1	... ...
		KEKÁDI	Hindu	T. 2,024 M. 1,004 F. 1,020	T. 339 M. 175 F. 164	T. 399 M. 205 F. 194
		THOTI	Hindu	T. 43 M. 20 F. 23	... ...	... ...
		Do.	Animistic	T. 183 M. 76 F. 107	... ...	... ...
			Total Group 43	*T. 3,963* *M. 1,945* *F. 2,018*	*T. 887* *M. 445* *F. 442*	*T. 716* *M. 360* *F. 355*
	44.—HUNTERS, FOWLERS, ETC.	BAHELIYÁ	Hindu	T. 61 M. 52 F. 9	T. 21 M. 20 F. 1	T. 7 M. 7 ...
		BEDAR	Do.	T. 3,041 M. 1,515 F. 1,526	T. 162 M. 93 F. 69	T. 1,859 M. 882 F. 977
		BERAD	Do.	T. 163 M. 86 F. 77	T. 3 M. 2 F. 1	... ...
		MUTRÁSI	Do.	T. 29 M. 20 F. 9	... ...	... ...
		PÁRDHI	Do.	T. 6,894 M. 3,537 F. 3,357	T. 1,166 M. 582 F. 584	T. 1,635 M. 874 F. 761
		Do.	Animistic	T. 5 M. 2 F. 3	... ...	... ...
			Total Group 44	*T. 10,163* *M. 5,212* *F. 4,951*	*T. 1,352* *M. 697* *F. 655*	*T. 3,501* *M. 1,763* *F. 1,738*
	45.—MISCELLANEOUS AND DISREPUTABLE LIVERS (BEGGARS AND PROSTITUTES.)	ARIDRA	Hindu	T. 4 M. 1 F. 3	... ...	... ...

Nationality or traditional Occupation—*contd.*

	BY DISTRICT.				RAILWAY PASSENGERS, ETC.	DISTRICT AMRAOTI.			
	ELLICHPUR.	BULDANA.	WUN.	BASIM.		AMRAOTI.	CHANDUR.	MORSI.	MURTAZAPUR.
	Total, Males, and Females.	Total, Males, and Females.	Total, Males, and Females.	Total, Males, and Females.	Total, Males, and Females.	Total, Males, and Females.	Total, Males, and Females.	Total, Males, and Females.	Total, Males, and Females.
	8	9	10	11	12	13	14	15	16
T.	2	...	...	...	...	...	4	19	...
M.	1	...	...	...	...	...	2	8	...
F.	1	...	...	...	...	...	2	11	...
T.	38	...	1	...	...	25	...	127	...
M.	20	...	1	...	...	13	...	60	...
F.	18	...	...	...	...	12	...	67	...
T.	70	...	...	...	...	...	...	...	...
M.	31	...	...	...	...	...	...	...	...
F.	39	...	...	...	...	...	...	...	...
T.	2	...	...	...	...	...	...	...	...
M.	1	...	...	...	...	...	...	...	...
F.	1	...	...	...	...	...	...	...	...
T.	235	15	268	188	...	131	116	55	42
M.	124	7	128	90	...	67	60	27	17
F.	111	8	140	98	...	64	56	28	25
T.	...	...	22	...	...	...	...	...	...
M.	...	...	10	...	...	...	...	...	...
F.	...	...	12	...	...	...	...	...	...
T.	2	...	6	...	...	23	...	...	4
M.	1	...	6	...	...	13	...	...	2
F.	1	...	...	...	...	10	...	...	2
T.	...	...	...	...	...	2	...	...	...
M.	...	...	...	...	...	1	...	...	...
F.	...	...	...	...	...	1	...	...	...
T.	234	646	104	302	...	129	34	47	129
M.	112	323	45	144	...	64	16	18	77
F.	122	323	59	158	...	65	18	29	52
T.	...	...	43	...	...	...	...	...	...
M.	...	...	20	...	...	...	...	...	...
F.	...	...	23	...	...	...	...	...	...
T.	...	...	183	...	...	...	...	...	...
M.	...	...	76	...	...	...	...	...	...
F.	...	...	107	...	...	...	...	...	...
T.	*583*	*661*	*627*	*490*	...	*310*	*154*	*248*	*175*
M.	*290*	*330*	*286*	*234*	...	*158*	*78*	*113*	*96*
F.	*293*	*331*	*341*	*256*	...	*152*	*76*	*135*	*79*
T.	29	...	2	2	...	16	3	1	1
M.	21	...	2	2	...	16	3	...	1
F.	8	...	...	...	...	...	...	1	...
T.	264	303	235	218	...	142	12	6	2
M.	144	167	113	116	...	78	8	5	2
F.	120	136	122	102	...	64	4	1	...
T.	...	17	143	...	...	1	...	...	2
M.	...	10	74	...	...	1	...	...	1
F.	...	7	69	...	...	...	...	...	1
T.	29	...	...	...	...	...	...	...	...
M.	20	...	...	...	...	...	...	...	...
F.	9	...	...	...	...	...	...	...	...
T.	1,145	1,680	1,079	189	...	797	69	66	234
M.	570	838	562	111	...	405	29	31	117
F.	575	842	517	78	...	392	40	35	117
T.	...	...	5	...	...	...	...	...	...
M.	...	...	2	...	...	...	...	...	...
F.	...	...	3	...	...	...	...	...	...
T.	*1,467*	*2,000*	*1,464*	*409*	...	*956*	*84*	*73*	*239*
M.	*755*	*1,015*	*753*	*229*	...	*500*	*40*	*36*	*121*
F.	*712*	*985*	*711*	*180*	...	*456*	*44*	*37*	*118*
T.	...	...	4	...	...	...	...	...	...
M.	...	...	1	...	...	...	...	...	...
F.	...	...	3	...	...	...	...	...	...

TABLE XVI.—Castes, Tribes, and Races, by

Name and Classification.				District Akola.					District
				Akola.	Akot.	Balapur.	Jalgaon.	Khamgaon.	Ellichpur.
Class.	Group.	Caste.	Religion.	Total, Males, and Females.	Total, Males, and Females.	Total, Males, and Females.	Total, Males, and Females.	Total, Males, and Females.	Total, Males, and Females.
17	18	19	20	21	22	23	24	25	26
E.—Vagrant, Minor Artisans and Performers, Etc.—*contd.*	43.—Mat-makers, Cane-splitters and Grass-cutters.	Bánspod	Hindu	... ...	... ...	T. 1 ... F. 1	... ...	... ...	T. 1 ... F. 1
		Basod	Do.	... ...	... ...	... ...	... ...	... ...	... ...
		Do.	Animistic	... ...	... ...	... ...	... ...	... ...	... ...
		Borekar	Hindu	... ...	T. 75 M. 41 F. 34	... ...	T. 14 M. 8 F. 6	T. 29 M. 8 F. 21	... ...
		Burud	Do.	T. 38 M. 15 F. 23	T. 19 M. 8 F. 11	T. 29 M. 15 F. 14	T. 8 M. 3 F. 5	T. 103 M. 57 F. 46	T. 176 M. 93 F. 83
		Do.	Animistic	... ...	... ...	... ...	... ...	... ...	... ...
		Kángar	Hindu	... ...	... ...	... ...	... ...	... ...	T. 2 M. 1 F. 1
		Do.	Musalman	... ...	... ...	... ...	... ...	... ...	... ...
		Kekádi	Hindu	T. 118 M. 58 F. 60	T. 39 M. 22 F. 17	T. 93 M. 48 F. 45	T. 52 M. 27 F. 25	T. 97 M. 50 F. 47	T. 114 M. 58 F. 56
		Thoti	Do.	... ...	... ...	... ...	... ...	... ...	... ...
		Do.	Animistic	... ...	... ...	... ...	... ...	... ...	... ...
			Total Group 43	*T. 156* *M. 73* *F. 83*	*T. 133* *M. 71* *F. 62*	*T. 123* *M. 63* *F. 60*	*T. 74* *M. 38* *F. 36*	*T. 229* *M. 115* *F. 114*	*T. 293* *M. 152* *F. 141*
	44.—Hunters, Fowlers, etc.	Baheliyá	Hindu	... ...	T. 3 M. 3 ...	... ...	... ...	T. 4 M. 4 ...	T. 25 M. 18 F. 7
		Bedar	Do.	T. 1,492 M. 682 F. 810	T. 28 M. 23 F. 5	T. 42 M. 31 F. 11	T. 30 M. 17 F. 13	T. 267 M. 129 F. 138	T. 213 M. 110 F. 103
		Berad	Do.	... ...	... ...	... ...	... ...	... ...	... ...
		Mutrási	Do.	... ...	... ...	... ...	... ...	... ...	T. 29 M. 20 F. 9
		Párdhi	Do.	T. 257 M. 150 F. 107	T. 221 M. 121 F. 100	T. 263 M. 144 F. 119	T. 405 M. 207 F. 198	T. 489 M. 252 F. 237	T. 403 M. 204 F. 199
		Do.	Animistic	... ...	... ...	... ...	... ...	... ...	... ...
			Total Group 44	*T. 1,749* *M. 832* *F. 917*	*T. 252* *M. 147* *F. 105*	*T. 305* *M. 175* *F. 130*	*T. 435* *M. 224* *F. 211*	*T. 760* *M. 885* *F. 875*	*T. 670* *M. 352* *F. 318*
	45.—Miscellaneous and disreputable livers (Beggars and Prostitutes.)	Aridra	Hindu	... ...	... ...	... ...	... ...	... ...	... ...

Nationality or traditional Occupation—*contd.*

Ellichpur.		District Buldana.			District Wun.				District Basim.		
Daryapur.	Melghat.	Chikhli.	Malkapur.	Mehkar.	Yeotmal.	Darwha.	Kelapur.	Wun.	Basim.	Mangrul.	Pusad.
Total, Males, and Females.	Total, Males, and Females.	Total, Males, and Fmales.	Total, Males, and Females.	Total, Males, and Females.	Total, Males, and Females.	Total, Males, and Females.	Total, Males, and Females.	Total, Males, and Females.	Total, Males, and Females.	Total, Males, and Females.	Total, Males, and Females.
27	28	29	30	31	32	33	34	35	36	37	38
T. 1 M. 1 ...	...	...	...	...	...	...	...	...	...	...	...
...	T. 38 M. 20 F. 18	...	...	...	...	...	...	T. 1 M. 1 ...	...	...	...
...	T. 70 M. 31 F. 39	...	...	...	...	...	...	...	...	...	...
T. 2 M. 1 F. 1	...	...	...	...	...	...	...	...	...	...	...
T. 59 M. 31 F. 28	...	T. 5 M. 2 F. 3	...	T. 10 M. 5 F. 5	T. 68 M. 35 F. 33	T. 10 M. 6 F. 4	T. 129 M. 59 F. 70	T. 61 M. 28 F. 33	T. 85 M. 36 F. 49	T. 32 M. 19 F. 13	T. 71 M. 35 F. 36
...	...	...	...	...	T. 3 M. 1 F. 2	...	...	T. 19 M. 9 F. 10	...	...	...
...	...	...	...	...	...	T. 6 M. 6 ...	...	...	...	...	...
...	...	...	...	...	...	...	...	...	...	...	...
T. 120 M. 54 F. 66	...	T. 331 M. 180 F. 151	T. 74 M. 31 F. 43	T. 241 M. 112 F. 129	T. 7 M. 3 F. 4	T. 94 M. 39 F. 55	...	T. 3 M. 3 ...	T. 140 M. 72 F. 68	T. 145 M. 65 F. 80	T. 17 M. 7 F. 10
...	...	...	...	...	T. 2 ... F. 2	T. 5 M. 4 F. 1	T. 36 M. 16 F. 20	...	...	...	...
...	...	...	...	...	...	T. 31 M. 15 F. 16	T. 76 M. 33 F. 43	T. 76 M. 28 F. 48	...	...	...
T. 182 *M. 87* *F. 95*	*T. 108* *M. 51* *F. 57*	*T. 336* *M. 182* *F. 154*	*T. 74* *M. 31* *F. 43*	*T. 251* *M. 117* *F. 134*	*T. 80* *M. 39* *F. 41*	*T. 146* *M. 70* *F. 76*	*T. 241* *M. 108* *F. 133*	*T. 160* *M. 69* *F. 91*	*T. 225* *M. 108* *F. 117*	*T. 177* *M. 84* *F. 93*	*T. 88* *M. 42* *F. 46*
...	T. 4 M. 3 F. 1	...	...	...	T. 1 M. 1 ...	...	T. 1 M. 1 ...	...	...	T. 2 M 2 ...	...
T. 29 M. 18 F. 11	T. 22 M. 16 F. 6	T. 239 M. 128 F. 111	T. 35 M. 21 F. 14	T. 29 M. 18 F. 11	T. 103 M. 48 F. 55	...	T. 49 M. 29 F. 20	T. 83 M. 36 F. 47	T. 186 M. 97 F. 89	T. 19 M. 12 F. 7	T. 13 M. 7 F. 6
...	...	...	...	T. 17 M. 10 F. 7	...	T. 143 M. 74 F. 69	...	...	...	...	...
...	...	...	...	...	...	...	...	...	...	...	...
T. 742 M. 366 F. 376	...	T. 125 M. 63 F. 62	T. 1,479 M. 735 F. 744	T. 76 M. 40 F. 36	T. 302 M. 158 F. 144	T. 269 M. 138 F. 131	T. 360 M. 186 F. 174	T. 148 M. 80 F. 68	T. 90 M. 45 F. 45	T. 88 M. 61 F. 27	T. 11 M. 5 F. 6
...	...	...	...	...	...	...	...	T. 5 M. 2 F. 3	...	...	...
T. 771 *M. 384* *F. 387*	*T. 26* *M. 19* *F. 7*	*T. 364* *M. 191* *F. 173*	*T. 1,514* *M. 756* *F. 758*	*T. 122* *M. 68* *F. 54*	*T. 406* *M. 207* *F. 199*	*T. 412* *M. 212* *F. 200*	*T. 410* *M. 216* *F. 194*	*T. 236* *M. 118* *F. 118*	*T. 276* *M. 142* *F. 134*	*T. 109* *M. 75* *F. 34*	*T. 24* *M. 12* *F. 12*
...	...	...	...	...	...	...	T. 4 M. 1 F. 3	...	...	...	...

TABLE XVI.—Castes, Tribes, and Races by

Class.	Group.	Caste.	Religion.	PROVINCIAL TOTAL. Total, Males, and Females.	DISTRIBUTION — Amraoti. Total, Males, and Females.	Akola. Total, Males, and Females.
1	2	3	4	5	6	7
E.—VAGRANT, MINOR ARTISANS AND PERFORMERS, ETC.—*contd.*	45.—MISCELLANEOUS AND DISREPUTABLE LIVERS (BEGGARS AND PROSTITUTES)—*contd.*	BÁLSANTO	Hindu	T. 4	...	...
				M. 2	...	...
				F. 2	...	...
		BHÁMTI	Do.	T. 1,774	T. 477	T. 462
				M. 838	M. 214	M. 217
				F. 936	F. 263	F. 245
		BHUTTÁWÁD	Do.	T. 8	...	...
				M. 4	...	...
				F. 4	...	...
		DAKALWÁD	Do.	T. 30	T. 9	...
				M. 15	M. 7	...
				F. 15	F. 2	...
		DÁNGAT	Do.	T. 486	...	T. 21
				M. 244	...	M. 9
				F. 242	...	F. 12
		DUSÁDH	Do.	T. 5	T. 3	...
				M. 5	M. 3	...
				...	...	...
		GUJRÁTHI	Do.	T. 1,098	T. 143	T. 366
				M. 611	M. 88	M. 210
				F. 487	F. 55	F. 156
		Do.	Jain	T. 347	T. 30	T. 306
				M. 179	M. 19	M. 154
				F. 168	F. 11	F. 152
		HINDUSTÁNI	Hindu	T. 32	T. 5	T. 9
				M. 28	M. 5	M. 8
				F. 4	...	F. 1
		HIRMUSTHI	Do.	T. 4	...	...
				M. 3	...	...
				F. 1	...	...
		KÁMÁTHI	Do.	T. 22	T. 2	T. 18
				M. 12	M. 1	M. 9
				F. 10	F. 1	F. 9
		KASBAN (KASBI)	Do.	T. 14	T. 5	...
				M. 4	...	...
				F. 10	F. 5	...
		KASBAN (KASBI NAIKAN)	Musalman	T. 15	T. 3	T. 6
				M. 2	...	...
				F. 13	F. 3	F. 6
		KUNJDÁ	Do.	T. 1	...	...
				M. 1	...	...
				...	...	...
		MADRÁSI	Hindu	T. 16	T. 5	T. 1
				M. 10	M. 4	...
				F. 6	F. 1	F. 1
		MARÁTHE	Do.	T. 19,038	T. 6,000	T. 1,941
				M. 9,551	M. 3,046	M. 914
				F. 9,487	F. 2,954	F. 1,027
		MUSALMAN	Musalman	T. 1,992	T. 556	T. 218
				M. 1,110	M. 314	M. 126
				F. 882	F. 242	F. 92
		PÁDHAR	Do.	T. 9	...	T. 9
				...	...	...
				F. 9	...	F. 9
		PARDESHI	Hindu	T. 639	T. 195	T. 64
				M. 440	M. 151	M. 51
				F. 199	F. 44	F. 13
		RÁMJÁNI	Do.	T. 4	...	T. 4
				M. 2	...	M. 2
				F. 2	...	F. 2
		TÁLKUTE	Do.	T. 18	...	T. 2
				M. 11	...	M. 1
				F. 7	...	F. 1

Nationality or traditional Occupation—*contd.*

BY DISTRICT.					DISTRICT AMRAOTI.			
ELLICHPUR.	BULDANA.	WUN.	BASIM.	RAILWAY PASSENGERS, ETC.	AMRAOTI.	CHANDUR.	MORSI.	MURTAZAPUR.
Total, Males, and Females.	Total, Males, and Females.	Total, Males, and Females.	Total, Males, and Females.	Total, Males, and Females.	Total, Males, and Females.	Total, Males, and Females.	Total, Males, and Females.	Total, Males, and Females.
8	9	10	11	12	13	14	15	16
... ...	... ...	T. 4 M. 2 F. 2	... ...	... ...	... ...	... ...	... ...	... ...
T. 167 M. 76 F. 91	T. 7 M. 3 F. 4	T. 658 M. 327 F. 331	T. 3 M. 1 F. 2	... ...	T. 127 M. 52 F. 75	T. 350 M. 162 F. 188	... ...	... ...
... ...	... ...	T. 8 M. 4 F. 4	... ...	... ...	... ...	... ...	... ...	... ...
T. 6 M. 3 F. 3	... ...	T. 4 ... F. 4	T. 11 M. 5 F. 6	... ...	... ...	T. 9 M. 7 F. 2	... ...	... ...
... ...	T. 345 M. 178 F. 107	T. 16 M. 8 F. 8	T. 104 M. 49 F. 55	... ...	... ...	... ...	... ...	... ...
T. 2 M. 2 ...	... ...	... ...	... ...	... ...	T. 3 M. 3 ...	... ...	... ...	... ...
T. 327 M. 180 F. 147	T. 211 M. 105 F. 106	T. 37 M. 20 F. 17	T. 11 M. 5 F. 6	T. 3 M. 3 ...	T. 123 M. 72 F. 51	T. 12 M. 10 F. 2	... ...	T. 8 M. 6 F. 2
T. 10 M. 5 F. 5	T. 1 M. 1 ...	... ...	... ...	... ...	T. 18 M. 11 F. 7	... ...	... ...	T. 12 M. 8 F. 4
... ...	T. 1 M. 1 ...	T. 7 M. 4 F. 3	T. 10 M. 10 ...	... ...	T. 1 M. 1 ...	T. 1 M. 1 ...	... ...	T. 3 M. 3 ...
... ...	... ...	... ...	T. 4 M. 3 F. 1	... ...	... ...	... ...	... ...	... ...
... ...	T. 2 M. 2 ...	... ...	... ...	... ...	... ...	T. 2 M. 1 F. 1	... ...	... ...
... ...	... ...	T. 8 M. 4 F. 4	T. 1 ... F. 1	... ...	... ...	... ...	T. 5 ... F. 5	... ...
... ...	T. 2 ... F. 2	T. 2 M. 1 F. 1	T. 2 M. 1 F. 1	... ...	T. 3 ... F. 3	... ...	... ...	... ...
T. 1 M. 1 ...	... ...	... ...	... ...	... ...	... ...	... ...	... ...	... ...
... ...	T. 1 M. 1 ...	T. 8 M. 4 F. 4	... ...	T. 1 M. 1 ...	T. 5 M. 4 F. 1	... ...	... ...	... ...
T. 703 M. 352 F. 351	T. 3,992 M. 2,002 F. 1,990	T. 3,438 M. 1,718 F. 1,720	T. 2,958 M. 1,513 F. 1,445	T. 6 M. 6 ...	T. 1,771 M. 877 F. 894	T. 2,433 M. 1,269 F. 1,164	T. 900 M. 458 F. 442	T. 896 M. 442 F. 454
T. 69 M. 47 F. 22	T. 375 M. 199 F. 176	T. 159 M. 100 F. 59	T. 602 M. 313 F. 289	T. 13 M. 11 F. 2	T. 221 M. 135 F. 86	T. 43 M. 29 F. 14	T. 254 M. 127 F. 127	T. 38 M. 23 F. 15
... ...	... ...	... ...	... ...	... ...	... ...	... ...	... ...	... ...
T. 42 M. 30 F. 12	T. 249 M. 136 F. 113	T. 56 M. 45 F. 11	T. 33 M. 27 F. 6	... ...	T. 80 M. 67 F. 13	T. 29 M. 19 F. 10	T. 61 M. 42 F. 19	T. 25 M. 23 F. 2
... ...	... ...	... ...	... ...	... ...	... ...	... ...	... ...	... ...
... ...	... ...	... ...	T. 16 M. 10 F. 6	... ...	... ...	... ...	... ...	... ...

TABLE XVI.—Castes, Tribes, and Races, by

Name and Classification.				District Akola.					District
				Akola.	Akot.	Balapur.	Jalgaon.	Khamgaon.	Ellichpur.
Class.	Group.	Caste.	Religion.	Total, Males, and Females.	Total, Males, and Females.	Total, Males, and Females.	Total, Males, and Females.	Total, Males, and Females.	Total, Males, and Females.
17	18	19	20	21	22	23	24	25	26
E.—Vagrant, Minor Artisans and Performers, Etc.—*contd.*	45.—Miscellaneous and Disreputable Livers (Beggars and Prostitutes)—*contd.*	Bálsanto	Hindu	...	...	...	...	...	...
		Bhámti	Do.	T. 36 M. 16 F. 20	T. 1 M. 1 ...	T. 425 M. 200 F. 225	...	...	T. 152 M. 69 F. 83
		Bhuttáwád	Do.	...	...	...	...	...	...
		Dakalwád	Do.	...	...	...	...	...	...
		Dángat	Do.	T. 1 ... F. 1	T. 2 M. 1 F. 1	T. 6 M. 2 F. 4	...	T. 12 M. 6 F. 6	...
		Dusádh	Do.	...	...	...	...	...	T. 2 M. 2 ...
		Gujráthi	Do.	T. 141 M. 76 F. 65	T. 28 M. 19 F. 9	T. 146 M. 86 F. 60	T. 27 M. 15 F. 12	T. 24 M. 14 F. 10	T. 38 M. 14 F. 24
		Do.	Jain	T. 4 M. 3 F. 1	T. 7 M. 5 F. 2	T. 291 M. 142 F. 149	T. 2 M. 2 ...	T. 2 M. 2 ...	T. 10 M 5 F. 5
		Hindustáni	Hindu	T. 1 M. 1 ...	...	...	...	T. 8 M. 7 F. 1	...
		Hirmusthi	Do.	...	...	...	...	...	...
		Kámáthi	Hindu	T. 14 M. 7 F. 7	...	...	...	T. 4 M. 2 F. 2	...
		Kasban (Kasbi)	Do.	...	...	...	...	...	...
		Kasban (Kasbi Naikan)	Musalman	...	T. 5 ... F. 5	...	...	T. 1 ... F. 1	...
		Kunjdá	Do.	...	...	...	...	...	...
		Madrási	Hindu	...	...	...	...	T. 1 ... F. 1	...
		Maráthe	Do.	T. 295 M. 147 F. 148	T. 458 M. 238 F. 220	T. 601 M. 277 F. 324	T. 78 M. 35 F. 43	T. 509 M. 217 F. 292	T. 186 M. 97 F. 89
		Musalman	Musalman	T. 32 M. 21 F. 11	T. 37 M. 19 F. 18	T. 129 M. 73 F. 56	T. 2 M. 1 F. 1	T. 18 M. 12 F. 6	T. 41 M. 25 F. 16
		Pádhar	Do.	...	T. 2 ... F. 2	...	...	T. 7 ... F. 7	...
		Pardeshi	Hindu	T. 23 M. 19 F. 4	T. 25 M. 18 F. 7	T. 10 M. 9 F. 1	T. 1 M. 1 ...	T. 5 M. 4 F. 1	T. 32 M. 21 F. 11
		Rámjáni	Do.	...	T. 4 M. 2 F. 2	...	...	...	...
		Tálkute	Do.	T. 2 M. 1 F. 1	...	...	...	...	...

Nationality or traditional Occupation—*contd.*

Ellichpur.		District Buldana.			District Wun.				District Basim.		
Daryapur.	Melghat.	Chikhli.	Malkapur.	Mehkar.	Yeotmal.	Darwha.	Kelapur.	Wun.	Basim.	Mangrul.	Pusad.
Total, Males, and Females.	Total, Males, and Females.	Total, Males, and Females.	Total, Males, and Females.	Total, Males, and Females.	Total, Males, and Females.	Total, Males, and Females.	Total, Males, and Females.	Total, Males, and Females.	Total, Males, and Females.	Total, Males, and Females.	Total, Males, and Females.
27	28	29	30	31	32	33	34	35	36	37	38
...	...	...	...	...	...	...	T. 4 M. 2 F. 2	...	...	...	...
T. 15 M. 7 F. 8	...	...	...	T. 7 M. 3 F. 4	T. 454 M. 233 F. 221	T. 192 M. 88 F. 104	T. 2 ... F. 2	T. 10 M. 6 F. 4	T. 3 M. 1 F. 2	...	...
...	...	...	...	...	...	...	T. 8 M. 4 F. 4	...	...	...	...
T. 6 M. 3 F. 3	...	...	...	...	...	...	...	T. 4 ... F. 4	T. 11 M. 5 F. 6	...	...
...	...	...	T. 345 M. 178 F. 167	...	...	T. 16 M. 8 F. 8	...	...	T. 51 M. 17 F. 34	...	T. 53 M. 32 F. 21
...	...	...	...	...	...	...	...	...	...	...	...
T. 285 M. 162 F. 123	T. 4 M. 4 ...	T. 154 M. 70 F. 84	T. 55 M. 33 F. 22	T. 2 M. 2 ...	T. 4 M. 2 F. 2	T. 28 M. 15 F. 13	T. 1 M. 1 ...	T. 4 M. 2 F. 2	T. 10 M. 4 F. 6	...	T. 1 M. 1 ...
...	...	...	...	T. 1 M. 1 ...	...	...	...	...	...	...	...
...	...	...	...	T. 1 M. 1 ...	...	T. 6 M. 3 F. 3	T. 1 M. 1 ...	...	T. 8 M. 8 ...	...	T. 2 M. 2 ...
...	...	...	...	...	...	...	...	...	...	...	T. 4 M. 3 F. 1
...	...	T. 2 M. 2 ...	...	...	...	...	...	...	...	...	...
...	...	...	...	...	T. 8 M. 4 F. 4	...	...	...	...	...	T. 1 ... F. 1
...	...	T. 1 ... F. 1	...	T. 1 ... M. 1	T. 2 M. 1 F. 1	...	...	...	T. 2 M. 1 F. 1	...	...
...	T. 1 M. 1 ...	...	...	...	...	...	...	...	...	...	...
...	...	T. 1 M. 1 ...	...	...	T. 7 M. 3 F. 4	...	T. 1 M. 1 ...	...	...	...	...
T. 500 M. 242 F. 258	T. 17 M. 13 F. 4	T. 1,153 M. 591 F. 562	T. 979 M. 483 F. 496	T. 1,860 M. 928 F. 932	T. 1,363 M. 668 F. 695	T. 1,045 M. 514 F. 531	T. 527 M. 272 F. 255	T. 503 M. 264 F. 239	T. 1,313 M. 653 F. 660	T. 717 M. 364 F. 353	T. 928 M. 496 F. 432
T. 18 M. 13 F. 5	T. 10 M. 9 F. 1	T. 227 M. 114 F. 113	T. 73 M. 39 F. 34	T. 75 M. 46 F. 29	T. 46 M. 21 F. 25	T. 55 M. 43 F. 12	T. 35 M. 20 F. 15	T. 23 M. 16 F. 7	T. 204 M. 112 F. 92	T. 352 M. 172 F. 180	T. 46 M. 29 F. 17
...	...	...	...	...	...	...	...	...	...	...	...
T. 6 M. 5 F. 1	T. 4 M. 4 ...	T. 135 M. 71 F. 64	T. 40 M. 25 F. 15	T. 74 M. 40 F. 34	T. 24 M. 19 F. 5	T. 6 M. 5 F. 1	T. 20 M. 15 F. 5	T. 6 M. 6 ...	T. 21 M. 18 F. 3	T. 4 M. 3 F. 1	T. 8 M. 6 F. 2
...	...	...	...	...	...	...	...	...	...	...	...
...	...	...	...	...	...	...	...	...	T. 16 M. 10 F. 6	...	...

TABLE XVI.—Castes, Tribes, and Races, by

Name and Classification.				Provincial Total.	Distribution	
					Amraoti.	Akola.
Class.	Group.	Caste.	Religion.	Total, Males, and Females.	Total, Males, and Females.	Total, Males, and Females.
1	2	3	4	5	6	7
E.—VAGRANT, MINOR ARTISANS AND PERFORMERS—*contd.*	45.—Miscellaneous and disreputable livers (Beggars and Prostitutes)—*contd.*	Telangá	Hindu	T. 2,081 M. 1,076 F. 1,005	T. 103 M. 52 F. 51	T. 98 M. 55 F. 43
		Vidur (Krishnapakshi)	Do.	T. 10,691 M. 5,314 F. 5,377	T. 3,850 M. 1,942 F. 1,908	T. 1,819 M. 899 F. 920
		Do.	Jain	T. 4 M. 1 F. 3	T. 4 M. 1 F. 3	... ...
			Total Group 45	*T. 38,336* *M. 19,464* *F. 18,872*	*T. 11,390* *M. 6,847* *F. 6,543*	*T. 5,344* *M. 2,655* *F. 2,689*
	46.—Tumblers and Acrobats.	Gopál	Hindu	T. 3,419 M. 1,725 F. 1,694	T. 111 M. 56 F. 55	T. 262 M. 121 F. 141
		Kanjhár	Do.	T. 1 M. 1 ...	T. 1 M. 1 ...	... ...
		Kolháti	Do.	T. 1,248 M. 502 F. 746	T. 81 M. 32 F. 49	T. 640 M. 261 F. 379
		Do.	Musalman	T. 9 M. 3 F. 6	... ...	... ...
		Pángul	Hindu	T. 2,085 M. 1,020 F. 1,065	T. 336 M. 163 F. 173	T. 42 M. 25 F. 17
			Total Group 46	*T. 6,762* *M. 3,251* *F. 3,511*	*T. 529* *M. 252* *F. 277*	*T. 944* *M. 407* *F. 537*
	47.—Jugglers, Snake Charmers, and Animal Exhibitors.	Chitrakathi	Hindu	T. 1,612 M. 799 F. 813	T. 1,143 M. 571 F. 572	T. 199 M. 99 F. 100
		Kalsutri	Do.	T. 1 M. 1 ...	... ...	T. 1 M. 1 ...
			Total Group 47	*T. 1,613* *M. 800* *F. 813*	*T. 1,141* *M. 571* *F. 572*	*T. 200* *M. 100* *F. 100*
F.—RACES AND NATIONALITIES.	48.—Non-Indian Asiatic Races.	Apridi	Musalman	T. 4 M. 2 F. 2	T. 4 M. 2 F. 2	... ...
		Arab	Do.	T. 84 M. 44 F. 40	T. 60 M. 31 F. 29	T. 17 M. 8 F. 9
		Chinese	Hindu	T. 1 M. 1 ...	T. 1 M. 1 ...	... ...
		Do.	Buddhist	T. 4 M. 2 F. 2	... ...	T. 4 M. 2 F. 2
		Isabzai	Musalman	T. 12 M. 9 F. 3	... ...	T. 7 M. 5 F. 2
		Jew	Jew	T. 2 M. 2 ...	T. 1 M. 1 ...	T. 1 M. 1 ...
		Kákezai	Musalman	T. 1 M. 1 ...	... ...	T. 1 M. 1 ...

Nationality or traditional Occupation—*contd.*

BY DISTRICT.				RAILWAY PASSENGERS, ETC.	DISTRICT AMRAOTI.			
ELLICHPUR.	BULDANA.	WUN.	BASIM.		AMRAOTI.	CHANDUR.	MORSI.	MURTAZAPUR.
Total, Males, and Females.	Total, Males, and Females.	Total, Males, and Females.	Total, Males, and Females.	Total, Males, and Females.	Total, Males, and Females.	Total, Males, and Females.	Total, Males, and Females.	Total, Males, and Females.
8	9	10	11	12	13	14	15	16
T. 50 M. 28 F. 22	T. 173 M. 95 F. 78	T. 1,534 M. 775 F. 759	T. 123 M. 71 F. 52	... ...	T. 44 M. 22 F. 22	T. 19 M. 12 F. 7	T. 15 M. 9 F. 6	T. 25 M. 9 F. 16
T. 637 M. 337 F. 300	T. 1,408 M. 693 F. 715	T. 2,114 M. 1,020 F. 1,094	T. 858 M. 420 F. 438	T. 5 M. 3 F. 2	T. 1,048 M. 509 F. 539	T. 1,398 M. 717 F. 681	T. 922 M. 467 F. 455	T. 482 M. 249 F. 233
... ...	... ...	... ...	... ...	... ...	... ...	T. 4 M. 1 F. 3	... ...	... ...
T. 2,014 *M. 1,061* *F. 958*	*T. 6,767* *M. 3,416* *F. 3,351*	*T. 8,067* *M. 4,033* *F. 4,024*	*T. 4,736* *M. 2,428* *F. 2,308*	*T. 28* *M. 24* *F. 4*	*T. 3,444* *M. 1,753* *F. 1,691*	*T. 4,300* *M. 2,228* *F. 2,072*	*T. 2,157* *M. 1,103* *F. 1,054*	*T. 1,489* *M. 763* *F. 726*
... ...	T. 1,376 F. 694 F. 682	T. 65 M. 44 F. 21	T. 1,605 M. 810 F. 795	... ...	T. 2 M. 2 ...	T. 21 M. 16 F. 5	T. 29 M. 11 F. 18	T. 59 M. 27 F. 32
... ...	... ...	... ...	... ...	... ...	T. 1 M. 1 ...	... ...	... ...	... ...
T. 162 M. 65 F. 97	T. 286 M. 107 F. 179	T. 60 M. 27 F. 33	T. 19 M. 10 F. 9	... ...	T. 35 M. 13 F. 22	T. 25 M. 8 F. 17	T. 9 M. 4 F. 5	T. 12 M. 7 F. 5
... ...	T. 9 M. 3 F. 6	... ...	... ...	... ...	... ...	... ...	... ...	... ...
T. 35 M. 20 F. 15	T. 1 ... F. 1	T. 884 M. 421 F. 463	T. 787 M. 391 F. 396	... ...	... ...	T. 107 M. 44 F. 63	... ...	T. 229 M. 119 F. 110
T. 197 *M. 85* *F. 112*	*T. 1,672* *M. 804* *F. 868*	*T. 1,009* *M. 492* *F. 517*	*T. 2,411* *M. 1,211* *F. 1,200*	... ...	*T. 38* *M. 16* *F. 22*	*T. 153* *M. 68* *F. 85*	*T. 38* *M. 15* *F. 23*	*T. 300* *M. 153* *F. 147*
T. 12 M. 7 F. 5	T. 2 M. 1 F. 1	T. 184 M. 83 F. 101	T. 72 M. 38 F. 34	... ...	T. 10 ... F. 10	T. 150 M. 64 F. 86	T. 34 M. 24 F. 10	T. 949 M. 483 F. 466
... ...	... ...	... ...	... ...	... ...	... ...	... ...	... ...	... ...
T. 12 *M. 7* *F. 5*	*T. 2* *M. 1* *F. 1*	*T. 184* *M. 83* *F. 101*	*T. 72* *M. 38* *F. 34*	... ...	*T. 10* ... *F. 10*	*T. 150* *M. 64* *F. 86*	*T. 34* *M. 24* *F. 10*	*T. 949* *M. 483* *F. 466*
... ...	... ...	... ...	... ...	... ...	... ...	... ...	T. 4 M. 2 F. 2	... ...
T. 1 M. 1 ...	T. 5 M. 3 F. 2	... ...	T. 1 M. 1 ...	... ...	T. 25 M. 14 T. 11	T. 11 M. 5 F. 6	... ...	T. 24 M. 12 F. 12
... ...	... ...	... ...	... ...	... ...	T. 1 M. 1 ...	... ...	... ...	... ...
... ...	... ...	... ...	... ...	... ...	... ...	... ...	... ...	... ...
T. 2 M. 2 ...	... ...	T. 1 M. 1 ...	T. 2 M. 1 F. 1	... ...	... ...	... ...	... ...	... ...
... ...	... ...	... ...	... ...	... ...	T. 1 M. 1 ...	... ...	... ...	... ...
... ...	... ...	... ...	... ...	... ...	... ...	... ...	... ...	... ...

TABLE XVI.—Castes, Tribes, and Races, by

Name and Classification.				District Akola.					District
				Akola.	Akot.	Balapur.	Jalgaon.	Khamgaon.	Ellichpur.
Class.	Group.	Caste.	Religion.	Total, Males, and Females.	Total, Males, and Females.	Total, Males, and Females.	Total, Males, and Females.	Total, Males, and Females.	Total, Males, and Females.
17	18	19	20	21	22	23	24	25	26
E.—Vagrant, Minor Artisans and Performers—*contd.*	45.—Miscellaneous and Disreputable Livers (Beggars and Prostitutes)—*contd.*	Telangá	Hindu	T. 68 M. 37 F. 31	T. 9 M. 5 F. 4	T. 16 M. 10 F. 6	T. 1 M. 1 ...	T. 4 M. 2 F. 2	T. 45 M. 24 F. 21
		Vidur (Krishnapakshi)	Do.	T. 493 M. 258 F. 235	T. 482 M. 227 F. 255	T. 168 M. 74 F. 94	T. 310 M. 152 F. 158	T. 366 M. 188 F. 178	T. 432 M. 214 F. 218
		Do.	Jain	... ...	... ...	... ...	... ...	... ...	... ...
			Total Group 45	*T. 1,110* *M. 586* *F. 524*	*T. 1,060* *M. 535* *F. 525*	*T. 1,792* *M. 873* *F. 919*	*T. 421* *M. 207* *F. 214*	*T. 961* *M. 454* *F. 507*	*T. 958* *M. 471* *F. 487*
	46.—Tumblers and Acrobats.	Gopál	Hindu	T. 49 M. 24 F. 25	T. 20 M. 9 F. 11	T. 5 M. 2 F. 3	T. 154 M. 70 F. 84	T. 34 M. 16 F. 18	... ...
		Kanjhár	Do.	... ...	... ...	... ...	... ...	... ...	... ...
		Kolháti	Do.	T. 116 M. 45 F. 71	T. 173 M. 72 F. 101	T. 74 M. 28 F. 46	T. 111 M. 42 F. 69	T. 166 M. 74 F. 92	T. 38 M. 18 F. 20
		Do.	Musalman	... ...	... ...	... ...	... ...	... ...	... ...
		Pángul	Hindu	T. 9 M. 4 F. 5	T. 33 M. 21 F. 12	... ...	... ...	... ...	... ...
			Total Group 46	*T. 174* *M. 73* *F. 101*	*T. 226* *M. 102* *F. 124*	*T. 79* *M. 30* *F. 49*	*T. 265* *M. 112* *F. 153*	*T. 200* *M. 90* *F. 110*	*T. 38* *M. 18* *F. 20*
	47.—Jugglers, Snake Charmers and Animal Exhibitors.	Chitrakathi	Hindu	T. 195 M. 97 F. 98	... ...	... ...	... ...	T. 4 M. 2 F. 2	... ...
		Kalsutri	Do.	T. 1 M. 1 ...	... ...	... ...	... ...	... ...	... ...
			Total Group 47	*T. 196* *M. 98* *F. 98*	... ...	... ...	... ...	*T. 4* *M. 2* *F. 2*	... ...
F.—Races and Nationalities.	48.—Non-Indian Asiatic Races.	Afridi	Musalman	... ...	... ...	... ...	... ...	... ...	... ...
		Arab	Do.	... ...	T. 17 M. 8 F. 9	... ...	... ...	... ...	... ...
		Chinese	Hindu	... ...	... ...	... ...	... ...	... ...	... ...
		Do.	Buddhist	T. 4 M. 2 F. 2	... ... —	... ...	... ...	... ...	... ...
		Isabzai	Musalman	T. 5 M. 3 F. 2	... ...	... ...	... ...	T. 2 M. 2 ...	T. 2 M. 2 —
		Jew	Jew	... ...	... ...	... ...	... ...	T. 1 M. 1 ...	... ...
		Kákezai	Musalman	T. 1 M. 1 ...	... ...	... ...	... ...	... ...	... ...

Nationality or traditional Occupation—*contd.*

ELLICHPUR.		DISTRICT BULDANA.			DISTRICT WUN.				DISTRICT BASIM.		
DARYAPUR.	MELGHAT.	CHIKHLI.	MALKAPUR.	MEHKAR.	YEOTMAL.	DARWHA.	KELAPUR.	WUN.	BASIM.	MANGRUL.	PUSAD.
Total, Males, and Females.	Total, Males, and Females.	Total, Males, and Females.	Total, Males, and Females.	Total, Males, and Females.	Total, Males, and Females.	Total, Males, and Females.	Total, Males, and Females.	Total, Males, and Females.	Total, Males, and Females.	Total, Males, and Females.	Total, Males, and Females.
27	28	29	30	31	32	33	34	35	36	37	38
...	T. 5 M. 4 F. 1	T. 92 M. 47 F. 45	T. 5 M. 5 ...	T. 76 M. 43 F. 33	T. 4 M. 2 F. 2	T. 65 M. 40 F. 25	T. 421 M. 194 F. 227	T. 1,044 M. 539 F. 505	T. 67 M. 41 F. 26	T. 13 M. 8 F. 5	T. 43 M. 22 F. 21
T. 197 M. 117 F. 80	T. 8 M. 6 F. 2	T. 760 M. 364 F. 396	T. 194 M. 97 F. 97	T. 454 M. 232 F. 222	T. 693 M. 341 F. 352	T. 513 M. 251 F. 262	T. 575 M. 275 F. 300	T. 333 M. 153 F. 180	T. 401 M. 193 F. 208	T. 192 M. 101 F. 91	T. 265 M. 120 F. 139
...	...	...	...	...	...	...	...	...	...	...	...
T. 1,027 *M. 549* *F. 478*	*T. 49* *M. 41* *F. 8*	*T. 2,525* *M. 1,260* *F. 1,265*	*T. 1,691* *M. 860* *F. 831*	*T. 2,551* *M. 1,296* *F. 1,255*	*T. 2,605* *M. 1,294* *F. 1,311*	*T. 1,926* *M. 967* *F. 959*	*T. 1,599* *M. 786* *F. 813*	*T. 1,927* *M. 986* *F. 941*	*T. 2,107* *M. 1,063* *F. 1,044*	*T. 1,278* *M. 648* *F. 630*	*T. 1,351* *M. 717* *F. 634*
...	...	T. 149 M. 80 F. 69	T. 7 M. 3 F. 4	T. 1,220 M. 611 F. 609	T. 25 M. 19 F. 6	T. 31 M. 17 F. 14	T. 7 M. 7 ...	T. 2 M. 1 F. 1	T. 1,422 M. 720 F. 702	T. 31 M. 17 F. 14	T. 152 M. 73 F. 79
...	...	...	...	...	...	...	...	...	...	...	...
T. 124 M. 47 F. 77	...	T. 9 M. 2 F. 7	T. 241 M. 90 F. 151	T. 36 M. 15 F. 21	T. 13 M. 9 F. 4	T. 46 M. 17 F. 29	T. 1 M. 1 ...	...	T. 9 M. 2 F. 7	T. 2 M. 1 F. 1	T. 8 M. 7 F. 1
...	...	T. 7 M. 3 F. 4	T. 2 ... F. 2	...	...	...	...	...	...	...	...
T. 35 M. 20 F. 15	...	...	...	T. 1 ... F. 1	T. 1 M. 1 ...	T. 883 M. 420 F. 463	...	...	T. 514 M. 255 F. 259	T. 148 M. 71 F. 77	T. 125 M. 65 F. 60
T. 159 *M. 67* *F. 92*	...	*T. 165* *M. 85* *F. 80*	*T. 250* *M. 93* *F. 157*	*T. 1,257* *M. 626* *F. 631*	*T. 39* *M. 29* *F. 10*	*T. 960* *M. 454* *F. 506*	*T. 8* *M. 8* ...	*T. 2* *M. 1* *F. 1*	*T. 1,945* *M. 977* *F. 968*	*T. 181* *M. 89* *F. 92*	*T. 285* *M. 145* *F. 140*
T. 12 M. 7 F. 5	...	T. 1 ... F. 1	T. 1 M. 1 ...	...	T. 142 M. 62 F. 80	T. 42 M. 21 F. 21	...	...	T. 1 ... F. 1	T. 71 M. 38 F. 33	...
...	...	...	...	...	...	...	...	...	...	...	...
T. 12 *M. 7* *F. 5*	...	*T. 1* ... *F. 1*	*T. 1* *M. 1* ...	...	*T. 142* *M. 62* *F. 80*	*T. 42* *M. 21* *F. 21*	...	...	*T. 1* ... *F. 1*	*T. 71* *M. 38* *F. 33*	...
...	...	...	...	...	...	...	...	...	...	...	...
T. 1 M. 1 ...	...	T. 2 M. 1 F. 1	...	T. 3 M. 2 F. 1	...	...	...	...	...	T. 1 M. 1 ...	...
...	...	...	...	...	...	...	...	...	...	...	...
...	...	...	...	...	...	...	...	...	...	...	...
...	...	...	...	...	T. 1 M. 1 ...	...	...	...	T. 2 M. 1 F. 1	...	...
...	...	...	...	...	...	...	...	...	...	...	...
...	...	...	...	...	...	...	...	...	...	...	...

TABLE XVI.—Castes, Tribes, and Races, by

Class.	Group.	Caste.	Religion.	PROVINCIAL TOTAL. Total, Males, and Females.	DISTRIBUTION — Amraoti. Total, Males, and Females.	DISTRIBUTION — Akola. Total, Males, and Females.
1	2	3	4	5	6	7
F.—RACES AND NATIONALITIES—*contd.*	48.—Non-Indian Asiatic Races—*contd.*	Khán	Musalman	T. 11	T. 3	T. 5
				M. 5	...	M. 2
				F. 6	F. 3	F. 3
		Khánzádá	Do.	T. 1	...	T. 1
				M. 1	...	M. 1
				...	...	...
		Khorásáni	Do.	T. 5	T. 5	...
				M. 2	M. 2	...
				F. 3	F. 3	...
		Moghal	Do.	T. 4,437	T. 1,146	T. 910
				M. 2,278	M. 618	M. 453
				F. 2,159	F. 528	F. 457
		Naumuslim	Do.	T. 1	T. 1	...
				M. 1	M. 1	...
				...	...	...
		Parsi	Parsi	T. 412	T. 235	T. 145
				M. 271	M. 132	M. 111
				F. 141	F. 103	F. 34
		Do.	Hindu	T. 5	T. 3	...
				M. 5	M. 3	...
				...	...	...
		Pathán	Musalman	T. 48,393	T. 10,711	T. 11,636
				M. 25,190	M. 5,618	M. 5,986
				F. 23,203	F. 5,093	F. 5,650
		Rohilla	Do.	T. 174	T. 64	T. 31
				M. 140	M. 39	M. 27
				F. 34	F. 25	F. 4
		Shekh	Do.	T. 124,232	T. 28,503	T. 31,349
				M. 64,297	M. 14,871	M. 16,382
				F. 59,935	F. 13,632	F. 14,967
		Syed	Do.	T. 15,107	T. 3,314	T. 3,818
				M. 7,959	M. 1,732	M. 1,093
				F. 7,148	F. 1,582	F. 1,925
			Total Group 48	*T. 192,886*	*T. 44,051*	*T. 47,926*
				M. 100,210	*M. 28,051*	*M. 24,972*
				F. 92,676	*F. 21,000*	*F. 22,953*
	50.—Non-Asiatic Races.	Armenian	Christian	T. 1	...	T. 1
				M. 1	...	M. 1
				...	...	...
		European	Do.	T. 329	T. 156	T. 64
				M. 186	M. 81	M. 40
				F. 143	F. 75	F. 24
		Do.	Others	T. 4	...	T. 2
				M. 4	...	M. 2
				...	...	...
			Total Group 50	*T. 334*	*T. 156*	*T. 67*
				M. 191	*M. 81*	*M. 48*
				F. 143	*F. 75*	*F. 24*
	51.—Eurasians	Eurasian (Anglo-Indian, East Indian, and Indo-Briton.)	Christian	T. 318	T. 177	T. 48
				M. 158	M. 82	M. 28
				F. 160	F. 95	F. 20
	52.—Christian Converts.	Goanese	Do.	T. 172	T. 84	T. 56
				M. 117	M. 54	M. 44
				F. 55	F. 30	F. 12
		Singhálese	Do.	T. 5	...	...
				M. 1	...	...
				F. 4	...	...
		Native Christian	Do.	T. 534	T. 212	T. 136
				M. 275	M. 100	M. 70
				F. 259	F. 112	F. 66
			Total Group 52	*T. 711*	*T. 296*	*T. 192*
				M. 393	*M. 154*	*M. 114*
				F. 318	*F. 142*	*F. 78*

Nationality or traditional Occupation—*contd.*

BY DISTRICT.				RAILWAY PASSENGERS, ETC.	DISTRICT AMRAOTI.			
ELLICHPUR.	BULDANA.	WUN.	BASIM.		AMRAOTI.	CHANDUR.	MORSI.	MURTAZAPUR.
Total, Males, and Females.	Total, Males, and Females.	Total, Males, and Females.	Total, Males, and Females.	Total, Males, and Females.	Total, Males, and Females.	Total, Males, and Females.	Total, Males, and Females.	Total, Males, and Females.
8	9	10	11	12	13	14	15	16
T. 2 M. 2 ...	... ...	T. 1 M. 1 ...	... ...	... ...	... ...	... ...	... ...	T. 3 ... F. 3
... ...	... ...	... ...	... ...	... ...	... ...	... ...	... ...	... ...
... ...	... ...	... ...	... ...	... ...	... ...	... ...	T. 5 M. 2 F. 3	... ...
T. 799 M. 403 F. 396	T. 668 M. 328 F. 340	T. 493 M. 248 F. 245	T. 421 M. 228 F. 193	... ...	T. 411 M. 219 F. 192	T. 165 M. 89 F. 76	T. 217 M. 127 F. 90	T. 353 M. 183 F. 170
... ...	... ...	... ...	... ...	... ...	... ...	... ...	... ...	T. 1 M. 1 ...
T. 22 M. 20 F. 2	T. 5 M. 4 F. 1	T. 5 M. 4 F. 1	... ...	M	T. 220 M. 120 F. 100	... ...	T. 2 M. 2 ...	T. 13 M. 10 F. 3
... ...	... ...	... ...	T. 2 M. 2 ...	... ...	... ...	... ...	... ...	T. 3 M. 3 ...
T. 7,115 M. 3,653 F. 3,462	T. 8,518 M. 4,405 F. 4,113	T. 5,214 M. 2,763 F. 2,451	T. 5,283 M 2,752 F. 2,431	T. 16 M. 13 F. 3	T. 4,083 M. 2,146 F. 1,937	T. 2,034 M. 1,070 F. 964	T. 2,353 M. 1,230 F. 1,123	T. 2,241 M. 1,172 F. 1,069
T. 9 M. 9 ...	T. 34 M. 30 F. 4	T. 10 M. 10 ...	T. 26 M. 25 F. 1	... ...	T. 50 M. 27 F. 23	T. 6 M. 5 F. 1	T. 7 M. 7 ...	T. 1 ... F. 1
T. 18,151 M. 9,255 F. 8,896	T. 20,449 M. 10,419 F. 10,030	T. 11,917 M. 6,219 F. 5,698	T. 13,837 M. 7,127 F. 6,710	T. 26 M. 24 F. 2	T. 11,317 M. 5,937 F. 5,380	T. 5,589 M. 2,940 F. 2,649	T. 5,450 M. 2,748 F. 2,702	T. 6,147 M. 3,246 F. 2,901
T. 2,343 M. 1,214 F. 1,129	T. 2,245 M. 1,184 F. 1,061	T. 1,506 M. 825 F. 681	T. 1,879 M. 1,009 F. 870	T. 2 M. 2 ...	T. 1,131 M. 591 F. 540	T. 779 M. 415 F. 364	T. 561 M. 296 F. 265	T. 843 M. 430 F. 413
T. 28,444 *M. 14,559* *F. 13,885*	*T. 31,924* *M. 16,373* *F. 15,551*	*T. 19,147* *M. 10,071* *F. 9,076*	*T. 21,351* *M. 11,145* *F. 10,206*	*T. 44* *M. 39* *F. 5*	*T. 17,239* *M. 9,056* *F. 8,183*	*T. 8,584* *M. 4,524* *F. 4,060*	*T. 8,599* *M. 4,414* *F. 4,185*	*T. 9,629* *M. 5,057* *F. 4,572*
... ...	... ...	... ...	... ...	... ...	... ...	... ...	... ...	... ...
T. 35 M. 19 F. 16	T. 18 M. 12 F. 6	T. 24 M. 15 F. 9	T. 17 M. 11 F. 6	T. 15 M. 8 F. 7	T. 141 M. 67 F. 74	T. 8 M. 8 ...	... ...	T. 7 M. 6 F. 1
T. 1 M. 1 ...	... ...	... ...	T. 1 M. 1 ...	... ...	... ...	... ...	... ...	... ...
T. 36 *M. 20* *F. 16*	*T. 18* *M. 12* *F. 6*	*T. 24* *M. 15* *F. 9*	*T. 18* *M. 12* *F. 6*	*T. 15* *M. 8* *F. 7*	*T. 141* *M. 67* *F. 74*	*T. 8* *M. 8* ...	... ...	*T. 7* *M. 6* *F. 1*
T. 31 M. 18 F. 13	T. 16 M. 8 F. 8	T. 21 M. 9 F. 12	T. 20 M. 10 F. 10	T. 5 M. 3 F. 2	T. 168 M. 76 F. 92	T. 1 M. 1 ...	... ...	T. 8 M. 5 F. 3
T. 14 M. 7 F. 7	T. 5 M. 4 F. 1	T. 10 M. 5 F. 5	T. 1 M. 1 ...	T. 2 M. 2 ...	T. 83 M. 53 F. 30	... ...	... ...	T. 1 M. 1 ...
... ...	T. 5 M. 1 F. 4	... ...	... ...	... ...	... ...	... ...	... ...	... ...
T. 43 M. 24 F. 19	T. 59 M. 35 F. 24	T. 34 M. 20 F. 14	T. 50 M. 26 F. 24	... ...	T. 200 M. 91 F. 109	T. 6 M. 4 F. 2	T. 5 M. 4 F. 1	T. 1 M. 1 ...
T. 57 *M. 31* *F. 26*	*T. 69* *M. 40* *F. 29*	*T. 44* *M. 25* *F. 19*	*T. 51* *M. 27* *F. 24*	*T. 2* *M. 2* ...	*T. 283* *M. 144* *F. 139*	*T. 6* *M. 4* *F. 2*	*T. 5* *M. 4* *F. 1*	*T. 2* *M. 2* ...

TABLE XVI.—Castes, Tribes, and Races, by

Name and Classification.				District Akola.					District
				Akola.	Akot.	Balapur.	Jalgaon.	Khamgaon.	Ellichpur.
Class.	Group.	Caste.	Religion.	Total, Males, and Females.	Total, Males, and Females.	Total, Males, and Females.	Total, Males, and Females.	Total, Males, and Females.	Total, Males, and Females.
17	18	19	20	21	22	23	24	25	26
F.—Races and Nationalities—contd.	48.—Non-Indian Asiatic Races—contd.	Khán	Musalman	...	...	T. 5	...	...	T. 2
				...	...	M. 2	...	...	M. 2
				...	...	F. 3	...	...	...
		Khánzádá	Do.	T. 1	...	...	...	...	...
				M. 1	...	...	...	...	...
				...	...	...	...	...	...
		Khorásáni	Do.	...	...	...	...	...	...
				...	...	...	...	...	...
				...	...	...	...	...	...
		Moghal	Do.	T. 187	T. 279	T. 121	T. 177	T. 146	T. 558
				M. 91	M. 133	M. 61	M. 94	M. 74	M. 271
				F. 96	F. 146	F. 60	F. 83	F. 72	F. 287
		Naumuslim	Do.	...	...	...	...	...	...
				...	...	...	...	...	...
				...	...	...	...	...	...
		Parsi	Parsi	T. 68	T. 8	T. 4	...	T. 65	T. 11
				M. 46	M. 5	M. 4	...	M. 56	M. 11
				F. 22	F. 3	...	...	F. 9	...
		Do.	Hindu	...	...	...	...	...	...
				...	...	...	...	...	...
				...	...	...	...	...	...
		Pathán	Musalman	T. 3,757	T. 2,936	T. 1,986	T. 1,391	T. 1,566	T. 4,810
				M. 1,834	M. 1,510	M. 1,051	M. 752	M. 839	M. 2,380
				F. 1,923	F. 1,426	F. 935	F. 639	F. 727	F. 2,430
		Rohilla	Do.	T. 22	T. 5	T. 4	...	...	...
				M. 18	M. 5	M. 4	...	...	...
				F. 4	...	...	...	...	...
		Shekh	Do.	T. 6,846	T. 7,991	T. 8,041	T. 3,725	T. 4,746	T. 11,327
				M. 3,675	M. 4,079	M. 4,017	M. 2,044	M. 2,567	M. 5,645
				F. 3,171	F. 3,912	F. 4,024	F. 1,681	F. 2,179	F. 5,682
		Syed	Do.	T. 1,041	T. 943	T. 750	T. 612	T. 472	T. 1,458
				M. 580	M. 470	M. 362	M. 332	M. 249	M. 749
				F. 461	F. 473	F. 388	F. 280	F. 223	F. 709
			Total Group 48	*T. 11,932*	*T. 12,179*	*T. 10,911*	*T. 5,905*	*T. 6,998*	*T. 18,168*
				M. 6,251	*M. 6,210*	*M. 5,501*	*M. 3,222*	*M. 3,788*	*M. 9,060*
				F. 5,681	*F. 5,969*	*F. 5,410*	*F. 2,683*	*F. 3,210*	*F. 9,108*
	50.—Non-Asiatic Races.	Armenian	Christian	T. 1	...	...	...	...	...
				M. 1	...	...	...	...	...
				...	...	...	...	...	...
		European	Do.	T. 31	T. 3	T. 1	T. 1	T. 28	T. 28
				M. 16	M. 2	M. 1	M. 1	M. 20	M. 15
				F. 15	F. 1	...	...	F. 8	F. 13
		Do.	Others	T. 1	...	...	...	T. 1	T. 1
				M. 1	...	...	...	M. 1	M. 1
				...	...	...	...	...	...
			Total Group 50	*T. 33*	*T. 3*	*T. 1*	*T. 1*	*T. 29*	*T. 29*
				M. 18	*M. 2*	*M. 1*	*M. 1*	*M. 21*	*M. 16*
				F. 15	*F. 1*	...	...	*F. 8*	*F. 13*
	51.—Eurasians	Eurasian (Anglo-Indian, East-Indian, and Indo-Briton.)	Christian	T. 31	...	...	T. 1	T. 16	T. 31
				M. 17	...	...	M. 1	M. 10	M. 18
				F. 14	...	...	...	F. 6	F. 13
	52.—Christian Converts.	Goanese	Do.	T. 24	T. 3	...	...	T. 29	T. 14
				M. 16	M. 3	...	...	M. 25	M. 7
				F. 8	...	...	...	F. 4	F. 7
		Singhálese	Do.	...	...	...	...	...	...
				...	...	...	...	...	...
				...	...	...	...	...	...
		Native Christian	Do.	T. 104	...	T. 7	...	T. 25	T. 38
				M. 54	...	M. 4	...	M. 12	M. 21
				F. 50	...	F. 3	...	F. 13	F. 17
			Total Group 52	*T. 128*	*T. 3*	*T. 7*	...	*T. 54*	*T. 52*
				M. 70	*M. 3*	*M. 4*	...	*M. 37*	*M. 28*
				F. 58	...	*F. 3*	...	*F. 17*	*F. 24*

Nationality or traditional Occupation—*contd.*

ELLICHPUR.		DISTRICT BULDANA.			DISTRICT WUN.				DISTRICT BASIM.		
DARYAPUR.	MELGHAT.	CHIKHLI.	MALKAPUR.	MEHKAR.	YEOTMAL.	DARWHA.	KELAPUR.	WUN.	BASIM.	MANGRUL.	PUSAD.
Total, Males, and Females.	Total, Males, and Females.	Total, Males, and Females.	Total, Males, and Females.	Total, Males, and Females.	Total, Males, and Females.	Total, Males, and Females.	Total, Males, and Females.	Total, Males, and Females.	Total, Males, and Females.	Total, Males, and Females.	Total, Males, and Females.
27	28	29	30	31	32	33	34	35	36	37	38
... ...	... ...	... ...	... ...	... ...	... ...	T. 1 M. 1 ...	... ...	... ...	... ...	... ...	... ...
... ...	... ...	... ...	... ...	... ...	... ...	... ...	... ...	... ...	... ...	... ...	... ...
... ...	... ...	... ...	... ...	... ...	... ...	... ...	... ...	... ...	... ...	... ...	... ...
T. 230 M. 125 F. 105	T. 11 M. 7 F. 4	T. 155 M. 72 F. 83	T. 369 M. 192 F. 177	T. 144 M. 64 F. 80	T. 157 M. 82 F. 75	T. 263 M. 130 F. 133	T. 36 M. 12 F. 24	T. 37 M. 24 F. 13	T. 157 M. 86 F. 71	T. 111 M. 57 F. 54	T. 153 M. 85 F. 68
... ...	... ...	... ...	... ...	... ...	... ...	... ...	... ...	... ...	... ...	... ...	... ...
T. 11 M. 9 F. 2	... ...	T. 1 M. 1 ...	T. 4 M. 3 F. 1	... ...	T. 5 M. 4 F. 1	... ...	... ...	... ...	... ...	... ...	... ...
... ...	... ...	... ...	... ...	... ...	... ...	... ...	... ...	... ...	T. 2 M. 2 ...	... ...	... ...
T. 2,118 M. 1,164 F. 954	T. 187 M. 109 F. 78	T. 2,485 M. 1,280 F. 1,205	T. 4,125 M. 2,098 F. 2,027	T. 1,908 M. 1,027 F. 881	T. 1,469 M. 805 F. 664	T. 2,756 M. 1,437 F. 1,319	T. 598 M. 323 F. 275	T. 391 M. 198 F. 193	T. 2,021 M. 1,078 F. 943	T. 1,088 M. 573 F. 515	T. 2,074 M. 1,101 F. 973
T. 9 M. 9 ...	... ...	T. 19 M. 15 F. 4	T. 4 M. 4 ...	T. 11 M. 11 ...	T. 8 M. 8 ...	... ...	T. 2 M. 2 ...	... ...	... ...	T. 21 M. 21 ...	T. 5 M. 4 F. 1
T. 6,460 M. 3,381 F. 3,079	T. 364 M. 229 F. 135	T. 7,310 M. 3,739 F. 3,571	T. 8,067 M. 4,082 F. 3,985	T. 5,072 M. 2,598 F. 2,474	T. 3,161 M. 1,649 F. 1,512	T. 5,469 M. 2,942 F. 2,527	T. 1,829 M. 907 F. 922	T. 1,458 M. 721 F. 737	T. 5,770 M. 3,017 F. 2,753	T. 2,505 M. 1,278 F. 1,227	T. 5,562 M. 2,832 F. 2,730
T. 840 M. 438 F. 402	T. 45 M. 27 F. 18	T. 730 M. 399 F. 331	T. 928 M. 489 F. 439	T. 587 M. 296 F. 291	T. 366 M. 216 F. 150	T. 724 M. 381 F. 343	T. 233 M. 132 F. 101	T. 183 M. 96 F. 87	T. 730 M. 391 F. 339	T. 230 M. 126 F. 104	T. 919 M. 492 F. 427
T. 9,669 *M. 5,127* *F. 4,542*	*T. 607* *M. 872* *F. 235*	*T. 10,702* *M. 5,507* *F. 5,195*	*T. 13,497* *M. 6,868* *F. 6,629*	*T. 7,725* *M. 3,998* *F. 3,727*	*T. 5,167* *M. 2,765* *F. 2,402*	*T. 9,213* *M. 4,891* *F. 4,322*	*T. 2,698* *M. 1,876* *F. 1,822*	*T. 2,069* *M. 1,039* *F. 1,030*	*T. 8,682* *M. 4,575* *F. 4,107*	*T. 3,956* *M. 2,056* *F. 1,900*	*T. 8,713* *M. 4,514* *F. 4,199*
... ...	... ...	... ...	... ...	... ...	... ...	... ...	... ...	... ...	... ...	... ...	... ...
... ...	T. 7 M. 4 F. 3	T. 16 M. 11 F. 5	T. 2 M. 1 F. 1	... ...	T. 24 M. 15 F. 9	... ...	... ...	... ...	T. 17 M. 11 F. 6	... ...	... ...
... ...	... ...	... ...	... ...	... ...	... ...	... ...	... ...	... ...	T. 1 M. 1 ...	... ...	... ...
... ...	*T. 7* *M. 4* *F. 3*	*T. 16* *M. 11* *F. 5*	*T. 2* *M. 1* *F. 1*	... ...	*T. 24* *M. 15* *F. 9*	... ...	... ...	... ...	*T. 18* *M. 12* *F. 6*	... ...	... ...
... ...	... ...	T. 14 M. 6 F. 8	T. 2 M. 2 ...	... ...	T. 21 M. 9 F. 12	... ...	... ...	... ...	T. 20 M. 10 F. 10	... ...	... ...
... ...	... ...	T. 5 M. 4 F. 1	... ...	... ...	T. 10 M. 5 F. 5	... ...	... ...	... ...	... ...	T. 1 M. 1 ...	... ...
... ...	... ...	... ...	T. 5 M. 1 F. 4	... ...	... ...	... ...	... ...	... ...	... ...	... ...	... ...
T. 1 ... F. 1	T. 4 M. 3 F. 1	T. 42 M. 26 F. 16	T. 11 M. 7 F. 4	T. 6 M. 2 F. 4	T. 34 M. 20 F. 14	... ...	... ...	... ...	T. 48 M. 25 F. 23	... ...	T. 2 M. 1 F. 1
T. 1 ... *F. 1*	*T. 4* *M. 8* *F. 1*	*T. 47* *M. 80* *F. 17*	*T. 16* *M. 8* *F. 8*	*T. 6* *M. 2* *F. 4*	*T. 44* *M. 26* *F. 19*	... ...	... ...	... ...	*T. 48* *M. 26* *F. 28*	*T. 1* *M. 1* ...	*T. 2* *M. 1* *F. 1*

TABLE XVI.—Castes, Tribes, and Races, by

Name and Classification.				Provincial Total.	Distribution	
					Amraoti.	Akola.
Class.	Group.	Caste.	Religion.	Total, Males, and Females.	Total, Males, and Females.	Total, Males, and Females.
1	2	3	4	5	6	7
	Unrecognizable.	Dandigán	Christian	T. 184 M. 78 F. 106	T. 27 M. 12 F. 15	... ...
		Naghát	Hindu	T. 5 M. 1 F. 4	... ...	... ...
		Shekdáu	Do.	T. 1 M. 1 ...	... ...	... ...
		Soliá	Do.	T. 1 M. 1 ...	... ...	... ...
		Unspecified	Do.	T. 140 M. 87 F. 53	T. 36 M. 28 F. 8	T. 42 M. 26 F. 16
		Do.	Musalman	T. 11 M. 7 F. 4	... ...	... ...
		Do.	Unspecified	T. 1 M. 1 ...	... ...	T. 2 M. 2 ...

Nationality or traditional Occupation—*concld.*

BY DISTRICTS.				RAILWAY PASSENGERS, ETC.	DISTRICT AMRAOTI.			
ELLICHPUR.	BULDANA.	WUN.	BASIM.		AMRAOTI.	CHANDUR.	MORSI.	MURTAZAPUR.
Total, Males, and Females.	Total, Males, and Females.	Total, Males, and Females.	Total, Males, and Females.	Total, Males, and Females.	Total, Males, and Females.	Total, Males, and Females.	Total, Males, and Females.	Total, Males, and Females.
8	9	10	11	12	13	14	15	16
...	...	T. 112	T. 45	...	...	T. 27	...	...
...	...	M. 48	M. 18	...	...	M. 12	...	...
...	...	F. 64	F. 27	...	...	F. 15	...	...
...	...	...	T. 5	...	...	...	...	...
...	...	...	M. 1	...	...	...	...	...
...	...	...	F. 4	...	...	...	...	...
T. 1	...	...	...	...	...	...	...	...
M. 1	...	...	...	...	...	...	...	...
...	...	...	...	...	...	...	...	...
T. 1	...	...	...	...	...	...	...	...
M. 1	...	...	...	...	...	...	...	...
...	...	...	...	...	...	...	...	...
T. 11	T. 15	T. 20	T. 13	T. 3	T. 26	T. 4	T. 5	T. 1
M. 6	M. 7	M. 6	M. 11	M. 3	M. 20	M. 3	M. 4	M. 1
F. 5	F. 8	F. 14	F. 2	...	F. 6	F. 1	F. 1	...
...	...	...	T. 3	...	...	...	...	...
...	...	...	M. 2	...	...	...	...	...
...	...	...	F. 1	...	...	...	...	...
...	T. 6	...	T. 1	...	...	...	...	...
...	M. 3	...	M. 1	...	...	...	...	...
...	F. 3	...	...	...	...	...	...	...

TABLE XVI —Castes, Tribes, and Races, by

Name and Classification.				District Akola.					District
				Akola.	Akot.	Balapur.	Jalgaon.	Khamgaon.	Ellichpur.
Class.	Group.	Caste.	Religion.	Total, Males, and Females.	Total, Males, and Females.	Total, Males, and Females.	Total, Males, and Females.	Total, Males, and Females.	Total, Males, and Females.
17	18	19	20	21	22	23	24	25	26
	Unrecognizable.	Dandigán	Christian	... ...	... ...	... ...	... ...	... ...	... ...
		Naghát	Hindu	... ...	... ...	... ...	... ...	... ...	... ...
		Shekdáu	Do.	... ...	... ...	... ...	... ...	... ...	... ...
		Soliá	Do.	... ...	... ...	... ...	... ...	... ...	... ...
		Unspecified	Do.	T. 2 M. 2 ...	T. 4 M. 3 F. 1	T. 35 M. 21 F. 14	T. 1 ... F. 1	... ...	T. 5 M. 2 F. 3
		Do.	Musalman	... ...	... ...	... ...	... ...	... ...	... ...
		Do.	Unspecified	T. 1 M. 1 ...	T. 1 M. 1 ...	... ...	... ...	... ...	... ...

Nationality or traditional Occupation—*concld.*

ELLICHPUR.		DISTRICT BULDANA.			DISTRICT WUN.				DISTRICT BASIM.		
DARYAPUR.	MELGHAT.	CHIKHLI.	MALKAPUR.	MEHKAR.	YEOTMAL.	DARWHA.	KELAPUR.	WUN.	BASIM.	MANGRUL.	PUSAD.
Total, Males, and Females.	Total, Males, and Females.	Total, Males, and Females.	Total, Males, and Females.	Total, Males, and Females.	Total, Males, and Females.	Total, Males, and Females.	Total, Males, and Females.	Total, Males, and Females.	Total, Males, and Females.	Total, Males, and Females.	Total, Males, and Females.
27	28	29	30	31	32	33	34	35	36	37	38
...	...	...	...	...	T. 98	T. 14	...	...	...	T. 9	T. 36
...	...	...	...	...	M. 40	M. 8	...	...	...	M. 3	M. 15
...	...	...	...	...	F. 58	F. 6	...	...	...	F. 6	F. 21
...	...	...	...	...	...	...	...	...	T. 5	...	...
...	...	...	...	...	...	...	...	...	M. 1	...	...
...	...	...	...	...	...	...	...	...	F. 4	...	...
T. 1	...	...	...	...	...	...	...	...	...	...	...
M. 1	...	...	...	...	...	...	...	...	...	...	...
...	...	...	...	...	...	...	...	...	...	...	...
T. 1	...	...	...	...	...	...	...	...	...	...	...
M. 1	...	...	...	...	...	...	...	...	...	...	...
...	...	...	...	...	...	...	...	...	...	...	...
...	T. 6	T. 10	T. 2	T. 3	T. 10	...	T. 9	T. 1	T. 10	...	T. 3
...	M. 4	M. 5	M. 1	M. 1	M. 4	...	M. 1	M. 1	M. 8	...	M. 3
...	F. 2	F. 5	F. 1	F. 2	F. 6	...	F. 8	...	F. 2	...	...
...	...	...	...	...	...	...	...	...	...	...	...
...	...	...	...	...	...	...	...	...	...	...	...
...	...	...	...	...	...	...	...	...	...	...	...
...	...	...	T. 5	T. 1	...	...	...	...	T. 3	...	T. 1
...	...	...	M. 2	M. 1	...	...	...	...	M. 2	...	M. 1
...	...	...	F. 3	...	...	...	...	...	F. 1	...	...

TABLE XVII.

Occupations, by Age.

Part A.—PROVINCIAL SUMMARY.

TABLE XVII.—Occupations, by Age.—

Class.	Order.	Sub-order and Group.	Occupation.	PROVINCIAL — Total. — Total.	Total. — 0—4	Total. — 5—14	Total. — 15—	Males. — Total.	Males. — 0—4
1	2	3	4	5	6	7	8	9	10
CLASS A.—GOVERNMENT.	ORDER I.—ADMINISTRATION.	1.—Service of the Imperial and Provincial Governments.	1. The Viceroy, Governors, Lieutenant-Governors, and Chief Commissioners and their families.	...	...	...	...	...	...
			2. Officers	265	30	62	173	150	14
			3. Office Superintendents and clerical establishments, Police and Excise Inspectors, Sub-Registrars, etc.	2,840	361	646	1,833	1,596	190
			4. Messengers, bailiffs, warders, menials, etc.	12,313	1,690	2,627	7,996	6,682	811
			4a. Police, rank and file	5,176	544	879	3,753	3,234	279
			Total Sub-order 1	20,594	2,625	4,214	13,755	11,662	1,294
		2.—Service of Local and Municipal Bodies.	5. Inspecting and supervising officials	23	2	7	14	9	...
			6. Clerical establishments	84	13	18	53	58	6
			7. Menials	1,452	190	292	970	942	94
			Total Sub-order 2	1,559	205	317	1,037	1,009	100
		3.—Village Service.	8. Headmen, when not agriculturists	5,998	793	1,386	3,819	3,030	361
			9. Accountants	6,919	831	1,378	4,710	3,847	423
			11. Watchmen and other menials	51,394	9,838	12,106	29,450	32,949	5,106
			Total Sub-order 3	64,311	11,462	14,870	37,979	39,826	5,890
			Total Order I	**86,464**	**14,292**	**19,401**	**52,771**	**52,497**	**7,284**
	ORDER II.—DEFENCE.	4.—Army	12. Officers	168	27	42	99	75	9
			13. Non-commissioned officers and privates	1,618	208	271	1,139	1,101	115
			14. Followers	165	13	27	125	106	5
			15. Administrative establishments	8	2	3	3	3	1
			Total Sub-order 4	1,959	250	343	1,366	1,285	130
		5.—Navy and Marine	16. Officers	...	...	...	...	...	...
			17. Engineers, warrant officers, and seamen	...	...	...	...	...	...
			18. Administrative staff	...	...	...	...	...	...
			Total Sub-order 5	...	...	...	...	...	...
			Total Order II	**1,959**	**250**	**343**	**1,366**	**1,285**	**130**
	ORDER III.—FOREIGN AND FEUDATORY STATE SERVICE.	6.—Administrative Service.	19. Chiefs, Consuls, and Officers	9	3	1	5	4	2
			20. Clerical establishments	...	...	...	...	...	...
			21. Menials, etc.	5	...	...	5	2	...
			Total Sub-order	14	3	1	10	6	2
		7.—Army and Marine	22. Officers	...	...	...	...	...	...
			23. Privates and seamen, etc.	6	1	...	5	4	...
			Total Sub-order 7	6	1	...	5	4	...
			Total Order III	**20**	**4**	**1**	**15**	**10**	**2**
			Total Class A.	**88,443**	**14,546**	**19,745**	**54,152**	**53,792**	**7,416**
CLASS B.—PASTURE AND AGRICULTURE.	ORDER IV.—LIVE STOCK.	8.—Stock breeding and dealing. (a)—Horses and horned cattle.	24. Horse breeders and dealers	44	4	6	34	35	3
			25. Cattle breeders and dealers and Commissariat farm establishments.	1,331	125	322	884	1,066	86
			26. Herdsmen	25,508	2,815	11,680	11,013	20,521	1,578
			27. Buffalo breeders and dealers	221	35	64	122	184	12
		(b)—Other draught, etc., animals.	28. Elephant catchers and breeders	...	...	...	...	...	...
			29. Camel breeders and dealers	44	5	7	32	39	5
			30. Ass and mule breeders and dealers	129	17	51	61	110	13
		(c)—Small stock	31. Sheep and goat breeders and dealers	1,328	184	352	792	873	112
			31a. Shepherds	6,344	791	1,802	3,751	4,539	457
			32. Pig breeders and dealers	8	...	2	6	6	...
			Total Sub-order 8	34,957	3,976	14,286	16,695	27,313	2,236
		9.—Subsidiary Services to Stock. (a)—Training and doctoring live-stock.	33. Veterinary Surgeons and assistants	5	...	...	5	3	...
			34. Farriers and gelders	52	3	12	37	29	2
			35. Horse and elephant breakers and trainers, etc.	64	10	11	43	36	4
		(b)—Vermin destroying.	36. Rat, monkey, jackal, crocodile, etc., catchers	...	...	...	...	...	...
			Total Sub-order 9	121	13	23	85	68	6
			Total Order IV	**35,078**	**3,989**	**14,309**	**16,780**	**27,381**	**2,242**

Part A.—PROVINCIAL SUMMARY.

TOTAL. Males. 5—14	Males. 15—	Females. Total.	Females. 0—4	Females. 5—14	Females. 15—	Sub-order and Group.	Occupation.	Order.	Class.
11	12	13	14	15	16				
...	...	...	...	...	...	1. The Viceroy, Governors, Lieutenant-Governors, and Chief Commissioners and their families.	1.—Service of the Imperial and Provincial Governments.	Order I.—Administration.	Class A.—Government.
34	102	115	16	28	71	2. Officers			
329	1,077	1,244	171	317	756	3. Office Superintendents and clerical establishments, Police and Excise Inspectors, Sub-Registrars, etc.			
1,357	4,514	5,631	879	1,270	3,482	4. Messengers, bailiffs, warders, menials, etc.			
459	2,496	1,942	265	420	1,257	4a. Police, rank and file			
2,179	8,189	8,932	1,331	2,035	5,566	Total Sub-order 1			
2	7	14	2	5	7	5. Inspecting and supervising officials	2.—Service of Local and Municipal Bodies.		
15	37	26	7	3	16	6. Clerical establishments			
160	688	510	96	132	282	7. Menials			
177	732	550	105	140	305	Total Sub-order 2			
661	2,008	2,968	432	725	1,811	8. Headmen, when not agriculturists	3.—Village Service		
696	2,728	3,072	408	682	1,982	9. Accountants			
6,658	21,185	18,445	4,732	5,448	8,265	11. Watchmen and other menials			
8,015	25,921	24,485	5,572	6,855	12,058	Total Sub-order 3			
10,371	34,842	33,967	7,008	9,030	17,929	**Total Order I.**			
12	54	93	18	30	45	12. Officers	4.—Army	Order II.—Defence.	
150	836	517	93	121	303	13. Non-commissioned officers and privates			
11	90	59	8	16	35	14. Followers			
1	1	5	1	2	2	15. Administrative establishments			
174	981	674	120	169	385	Total Sub-order 4			
...	...	...	...	...	...	16. Officers	5.—Navy and Marine		
...	...	...	...	...	...	17. Engineers, warrant officers and seamen			
...	...	...	...	...	...	18. Administrative Staff			
...	...	...	...	...	...	Total Sub-order 5			
174	981	674	120	169	385	**Total Order II**			
...	2	5	1	1	3	19. Chiefs, Consuls and officers	6.—Administrative Service.	Order III.—Foreign and Feudatory State Service.	
...	...	...	...	...	...	20. Clerical establishments			
...	2	3	...	...	3	21. Menials, etc.			
...	4	8	1	1	6	Total Sub-order 6			
...	...	...	...	...	...	22. Officers	7.—Army and Marine		
...	4	2	1	...	1	23. Privates and seamen, etc.			
...	4	2	1	...	1	Total Sub-order 7			
...	8	10	2	1	7	**Total Order III**			
10,545	35,831	34,651	7,130	9,200	18,321	**Total Class A**			
3	29	9	1	3	5	24. Horse breeders and dealers	8. Stock breeding and dealing. (a).—Horses and horned cattle.	Order IV.—Live Stock.	Class B.—Pasture and Agriculture.
258	722	265	39	64	162	25. Cattle breeders and dealers and Commissariat farm establishments.			
9,954	8,989	4,987	1,237	1,726	2,024	26. Herdsmen			
35	77	97	23	29	45	27. Buffalo breeders and dealers			
...	...	...	...	...	...	28. Elephant catchers and breeders	(b).—Other draught, etc animals.		
6	28	5	...	1	4	29. Camel breeders and dealers			
46	51	19	4	5	10	30. Ass and mule breeders and dealers			
237	524	455	72	115	268	31. Sheep and goat breeders and dealers	(c).—Small stock		
1,288	2,824	1,805	364	514	927	31a. Shepherds			
2	4	2	...	...	2	32. Pig breeders and dealers			
11,829	13,248	7,644	1,740	2,457	3,447	Total Sub-order 8			
...	3	2	...	...	2	33. Veterinary Surgeons and assistants	9. Subsidiary Services to Stock. (a).—Training and doctoring live stock.		
7	20	23	1	5	17	34. Farriers and gelders			
4	28	26	6	7	15	35. Horse and elephant breakers and trainers, etc.			
...	...	...	...	...	...	36. Rat, monkey, jackal, crocodile, etc. catchers	(b).—Vermin-destroying.		
11	51	53	7	12	34	Total Sub-order 9			
11,840	13,299	7,697	1,747	2,469	3,481	**Total Order IV**			

TABLE XVII.—Occupations, by Age.—

Class.	Order.	Sub-order and Group.	Occupation.	TOWN. Total. Total.	0—4	5—14	15—	Males. Total.	0—4	5—14	15—	Females. Total.	0—4	5—14	15—
				17	18	19	20	21	22	23	24	25	26	27	28
CLASS A.—GOVERNMENT.	ORDER I.—ADMINISTRATION.	1.—Service of the Imperial and Provincial Governments.	1. The Viceroy, Governors, Lieutenant-Governors, and Chief Commissioners, and their families.	...	...	...	...	...	...	...	...	...	...	...	...
			2. Officers	188	22	48	118	105	10	28	67	83	12	20	51
			3. Office Superintendents and clerical establishments, Police and Excise Inspectors, Sub-Registrars, etc.	2,149	277	507	1,365	1,193	144	257	792	956	133	250	573
			4. Messengers, bailiffs, warders, menials, etc.	6,619	899	1,450	4,260	3,481	428	777	2,276	3,138	471	683	1,984
			4a. Police, rank and file	2,903	318	507	2,078	1,731	162	270	1,299	1,172	156	237	779
			Total sub-order 1	11,859	1,516	2,522	7,821	6,510	744	1,332	4,434	5,349	772	1,190	3,387
		2.—Service of Local and Municipal Bodies.	5. Inspecting and supervising officials.	15	1	3	11	5	...	...	5	10	1	3	6
			6. Clerical establishments	53	7	12	34	40	5	10	25	13	2	2	9
			7. Menials	877	109	177	591	543	50	100	393	334	59	77	198
			Total Sub-order 2	945	117	192	636	588	55	110	423	357	62	82	213
		3.—Village Service	8. Headmen, when not agriculturists.	332	32	65	235	156	12	35	109	176	20	30	126
			9. Accountants	1,426	170	314	952	770	90	169	511	656	80	145	431
			11. Watchmen and other menials	3,300	557	770	1,973	1,994	297	406	1,291	1,306	260	364	682
			Total Sub-order 3	5,058	759	1,149	3,150	2,920	379	610	1,911	2,138	386	539	[illegible]
			Total Order I	**17,862**	**2,392**	**3,863**	**11,607**	**10,018**	**1,198**	**2,052**	**6,768**	**7,844**	**1,194**	**1,811**	**4,839**
	ORDER II.—DEFENCE.	4.—Army	12. Officers	164	27	42	95	73	9	12	52	91	18	30	43
			13. Non-commissioned officers and privates.	1,570	203	264	1,103	1,073	113	145	815	497	90	119	288
			14. Followers	164	13	27	124	105	5	11	89	59	8	16	35
			15. Administrative establishments	8	2	3	3	3	1	1	1	5	1	2	1
			Total Sub-order 4	1,906	245	336	1,325	1,254	128	169	957	652	117	167	368
		5.—Navy and Marine	16. Officers	...	...	...	...	...	...	...	...	...	...	...	...
			17. Engineers, warrant officers and seamen.	...	...	...	...	...	...	...	...	...	...	...	...
			18. Administrative staff	...	...	...	...	...	...	...	...	...	...	...	...
			Total Sub-order 5	...	...	...	...	...	...	...	...	...	...	...	...
			Total Order II	**1,906**	**245**	**336**	**1,325**	**1,254**	**128**	**169**	**957**	**652**	**117**	**167**	**368**
	ORDER III.—FOREIGN AND FEUDATORY STATE SERVICE.	6.—Administrative Service.	19. Chiefs, Consuls, and Officers	...	...	...	...	...	...	...	...	...	...	...	...
			20. Clerical establishments	...	...	...	...	...	...	...	...	...	...	...	...
			21. Menials, etc.	1	...	...	1	1	...	...	1	...	...	...	...
			Total Sub-order 6	1	...	...	1	1	...	...	1	...	...	...	...
		7.—Army and Marine	22. Officers	...	...	...	...	...	...	...	...	...	...	...	...
			23. Privates and seamen, etc.	3	...	...	3	3	...	...	3	...	...	...	...
			Total Sub-order 7	3	...	...	3	3	...	...	3	...	...	...	...
			Total Order III	**4**	...	...	**4**	**4**	...	...	**4**	...	...	...	...
			Total Class A	**19,772**	**2,637**	**4,199**	**12,936**	**11,276**	**1,326**	**2,221**	**7,729**	**8,496**	**1,311**	**1,978**	**5,207**
CLASS B.—PASTURE AND AGRICULTURE.	ORDER IV.—LIVE STOCK.	8.—Stock breeding and dealing. (a).—Horses and horned cattle.	24. Horse breeders and dealers	15	2	3	10	9	1	1	7	6	1	2	3
			25. Cattle breeders and dealers and Commissariat farm establishments.	269	30	57	182	164	17	38	109	105	13	19	73
			26. Herdsmen	1,728	176	632	920	1,316	105	507	704	412	71	125	216
			27. Buffalo breeders and dealers	8	1	3	4	6	1	2	3	2	...	1	1
		(b).—Other draught, etc., animals.	28. Elephant catchers and breeders	...	...	...	...	...	...	...	...	...	...	...	...
			29. Camel breeders and dealers	21	3	2	16	17	3	2	12	4	...	...	4
			30. Ass and mule breeders and dealers.	46	8	9	29	44	8	9	27	2	...	...	2
		(c).—Small stock.	31. Sheep and goat breeders and dealers.	126	19	30	77	80	10	21	49	46	9	9	28
			31a. Shepherds	401	42	127	232	284	22	95	167	117	20	32	65
			32. Pig breeders and dealers	...	...	...	...	...	...	...	...	...	...	...	...
			Total Sub-order 8	2,614	281	863	1,470	1,920	167	675	1,078	694	114	188	392
		9.—Subsidiary services to stock. (a).—Training and doctoring live-stock.	33. Veterinary Surgeons and assistants.	3	...	...	3	1	...	...	1	2	...	...	2
			34. Farriers and gelders	50	3	12	35	27	2	7	18	23	1	5	17
			35. Horse and elephant breakers and trainers, etc.	11	1	...	10	7	...	...	7	4	1	...	3
		(b).—Vermin destroying.	36. Rat, monkey, jackal, crocodile, etc., catchers.	...	...	...	...	...	...	...	...	...	...	...	...
			Total Sub-order 9	64	4	12	48	35	2	7	26	29	2	5	22
			Total Order IV	**2,678**	**285**	**875**	**1,518**	**1,955**	**169**	**682**	**1,104**	**723**	**116**	**198**	**414**

Part A.—PROVINCIAL SUMMARY—*contd.*

COUNTRY.												Occupation.	Sub-order and Group.	Order.	Class.
Total.				Males.				Females.							
Total.	0—4	5—14	15—	Total.	0—4	5—14	15—	Total.	0—4	5—14	15—				
29	30	31	32	33	34	35	36	37	38	39	40				
...	...	...	...	...	...	...	...	...	...	...	...	1. The Viceroy, Governors, Lieutenant Governors, and Chief Commissioners, and their families.	1.—Service of the Imperial and Provincial Governments.	Order I.—Administration.	Class A.—Government.
77	8	14	55	45	4	6	35	32	4	8	20	2. Officers			
691	84	139	458	403	46	72	285	288	38	67	183	3. Office Superintendents and clerical establishments. Police and Excise Inspectors, Sub-Registrars, etc.			
5,694	791	1,167	3,736	3,201	383	580	2,238	2,493	408	587	1,498	4. Messengers, bailiffs, warders, menials, etc.			
2,273	226	372	1,675	1,503	117	189	1,197	770	109	183	478	4a. Police, rank and file.			
8,735	1,109	1,692	5,934	5,152	550	847	3,755	3,583	559	845	2,179	Total sub-order 1			
8	1	4	3	4	...	2	2	4	1	2	1	5. Inspecting and Supervising officials.	2.—Service of Local and Municipal Bodies.		
31	6	6	19	18	1	5	12	13	5	1	7	6. Clerical establishments			
575	81	115	379	399	44	60	295	176	37	55	84	7. Menials			
614	88	125	401	421	45	67	309	193	43	58	92	Total Sub-order 2			
5,666	761	1,321	3,584	2,874	349	626	1,899	2,792	412	695	1,685	8. Headmen, when not agriculturists	3.—Village Service.		
5,493	661	1,064	3,768	3,077	333	527	2,217	2,416	328	537	1,551	9. Accountants			
46,094	9,281	11,336	27,477	30,955	4,809	6,252	19,894	17,139	4,472	5,084	7,583	11. Watchmen and other menials.			
59,253	10,703	13,721	34,829	36,906	5,491	7,405	24,010	22,347	5,212	6,316	10,819	Total Sub-order 3			
68,602	**11,900**	**15,538**	**41,164**	**42,479**	**6,086**	**8,319**	**28,074**	**26,123**	**5,814**	**7,219**	**13,090**	**Total Order I**			
4	...	...	4	2	...	...	2	2	...	...	2	12. Officers	4.—Army	Order II.—Defence.	
48	5	7	36	28	2	5	21	20	3	2	15	13. Non-commissioned officers and privates.			
1	...	...	1	1	...	...	1	...	...	...	...	14. Followers			
—	...	...	...	...	...	...	...	...	...	...	...	15. Administrative establishments.			
53	5	7	41	31	2	5	24	22	3	2	17	Total Sub-order 4			
—	...	...	...	...	...	...	...	...	...	...	...	16. Officers	5.—Navy and Marine		
...	...	...	...	...	...	...	...	...	...	...	...	17. Engineers, warrant officers and seamen.			
...	...	...	...	...	...	...	...	...	...	...	...	18. Administrative Staff			
...	...	...	...	...	...	...	...	...	...	...	...	Total Sub-order 5			
53	**5**	**7**	**41**	**31**	**2**	**5**	**24**	**22**	**3**	**2**	**17**	**Total Order II**			
9	3	1	5	4	2	...	2	5	1	1	3	19. Chiefs, Consuls, and Officers	6.—Administrative Service.	Order III.—Foreign and Feudatory State Service.	
—	...	...	...	...	...	...	...	...	...	...	...	20. Clerical establishments			
4	...	...	4	1	...	...	1	3	...	...	3	21. Menials, etc.			
13	3	1	9	5	2	...	3	8	1	1	6	Total Sub-order 6			
...	...	...	...	...	...	...	...	...	...	...	...	22. Officers	7.—Army and Marine		
2	1	...	2	1	...	...	1	2	1	...	1	23. Privates and seamen, etc.			
3	1	...	2	1	...	...	1	2	1	...	1	Total Sub-order 7			
16	**4**	**1**	**11**	**6**	**2**	...	**4**	**10**	**2**	**1**	**7**	**Total Order III**			
68,671	**11,909**	**15,546**	**41,216**	**42,516**	**6,090**	**8,324**	**28,102**	**26,155**	**5,819**	**7,222**	**13,114**	**Total Class A.**			
													8.—Stock breeding and dealing.	Order IV.—Live Stock.	Class B.—Pasture and Agriculture.
29	2	3	24	26	2	2	22	3	...	1	2	24. Horse breeders and dealers	(a).—Horses and horned cattle.		
1,062	95	265	702	902	69	220	613	160	26	45	89	25. Cattle breeders and dealers and Commissariat farm establishments.			
23,760	2,639	11,048	10,073	19,205	1,473	9,447	8,285	4,575	1,166	1,601	1,808	26. Herdsmen			
213	34	61	118	118	11	33	74	95	23	28	44	27. Buffalo breeders and dealers			
...	...	...	...	...	...	...	...	...	...	...	...	28. Elephant catchers and breeders.	(b).—Other draught, etc., animals.		
23	2	5	16	22	2	4	16	1	...	1	...	29. Camel breeders and dealers			
83	9	42	32	66	5	37	24	17	4	5	8	30. Ass and mule breeders and dealers.			
1,202	165	322	715	793	102	216	475	409	63	106	240	31. Sheep and goat breeders and dealers.	(c).—Small stock		
5,943	749	1,675	3,519	4,255	405	1,193	2,657	1,688	344	482	862	31a. Shepherds			
8	...	2	6	6	...	2	4	2	...	...	2	32. Pig breeders and dealers			
32,343	3,695	13,423	15,225	25,393	2,069	11,154	12,170	6,950	1,626	2,269	3,055	Total Sub-order			
2	...	...	2	2	...	...	2	...	...	...	...	33. Veterinary Surgeons and assistants.	9. Subsidiary Services to Stock. (a).—Training and doctoring live stock		
2	...	...	2	2	...	...	2	...	...	...	...	34. Farriers and gelders			
53	9	11	33	29	4	4	21	24	5	7	12	35. Horse and elephant breakers and trainers, etc.			
...	...	...	...	...	...	...	...	...	...	...	...	36. Rat, monkey, jackal, crocodile, etc., catchers.	(b).—Vermin destroying.		
57	9	11	37	33	4	4	25	24	5	7	12	Total Sub-order 9			
32,400	**3,704**	**13,434**	**15,262**	**25,426**	**2,073**	**11,158**	**12,195**	**6,974**	**1,631**	**2,276**	**3,067**	**Total Order IV**			

TABLE XVII.—Occupations, by Age.—

PROVINCIAL

Class.	Order.	Sub-order and Group.	Occupation.	Total. Total.	Total. 0—4	Total. 5—14	Total. 15—	Males. Total.	Males. 0—4
1	2	3	4	5	6	7	8	9	10
CLASS B.—PASTURE AND AGRICULTURE—*contd.*	ORDER V.—AGRICULTURE.	10.—Interest in land	37. Land occupants, not cultivating	10,967	1,477	2,628	6,862	5,659	789
			38. Land occupants, cultivating	642,689	101,043	161,606	380,040	338,658	49,602
			39. Lessees of villages, etc.	51	12	7	32	25	6
			40. Tenants, not cultivating	...	...	...	...	...	...
			41. Tenants and sharers, cultivating	343,895	56,140	80,310	207,445	194,061	27,758
			Total Sub-order 10	997,602	158,672	244,551	594,379	538,403	78,125
		11.—Agricultural labourers.	42. Farm servants	108,594	14,934	25,625	68,035	82,503	8,280
			43. Field labourers and crop watchers	878,050	104,182	217,029	556,839	371,391	47,798
			Total Sub-order 11	986,644	119,116	242,654	624,874	453,894	56,078
		12.—Growers of special products and trees.	44. Tea, coffee and cinchona planters, managers, and assistants.	...	...	...	...	...	...
			45. Cocoanut growers	...	...	...	...	...	...
			46. Betel-vine and areca-nut growers	466	45	106	315	213	15
			47. Waternut growers	6	2	...	4	3	2
			48. Cardamom and pepper growers	...	...	...	...	...	...
			49. Indigo planters, managers, etc.	...	...	...	...	...	...
			50. Fruit growers	326	34	89	193	184	16
			51. Market gardeners (vegetable growers)	19	3	5	11	10	1
			52. Gardeners, seedsmen, etc.	787	104	169	514	472	50
			53. Manure preparers and sellers	4	2	1	1	...	...
			54. Forest Officers	18	3	3	12	10	1
			55. Forest rangers, guards, and peons	401	32	46	323	287	17
			Total Sub-order 12	2,027	225	429	1,373	1,179	111
		13.—Agricultural training and supervision.	56. Directors of Agriculture and their assistants	1	...	...	1	1	...
			57. Model-farm managers, etc.	...	...	...	...	...	...
			58. Agents and managers of landed estates (not planters).	1	...	...	1	1	...
			Total Sub-order 13	2	...	...	2	2	...
			Total Order V	**1,986,265**	**278,013**	**487,624**	**1,220,628**	**993,478**	**134,814**
			Total Class B.	**2,021,343**	**282,002**	**501,933**	**1,237,408**	**1,020,859**	**136,556**
CLASS C.—PERSONAL SERVICES.	ORDER VI.—PERSONAL AND HOUSEHOLD SERVICES.	14.—Personal and domestic services.	59. Barbers	21,283	3,034	4,639	13,610	13,233	1,540
			60. Ear-pickers	8	2	1	5	3	1
			61. Tattooers	10	...	4	6	8	...
			62. Caste-mark appliers	...	...	...	...	...	...
			63. Washermen	14,051	1,949	3,338	8,764	7,018	967
			64. Water-carriers	1,359	128	233	998	875	63
			65. Cooks	1,257	82	143	1,032	802	34
			66. In-door servants	30,817	3,956	6,869	19,992	14,677	1,545
			67. Grooms, coachmen and dog-boys, etc.	1,333	127	225	981	946	67
			68. Door-keepers	...	...	...	...	...	...
			Total Sub-order 14	70,118	9,278	15,452	45,388	37,962	4,217
		15.—Non-domestic establishment.	69. Hotel, lodging and boarding house, bar and refreshment-room keepers.	55	6	11	38	35	3
			70. Rest-house, serai, bath-house, etc., owners and managers.	40	3	4	33	29	1
			71. Club secretaries, managers, stewards, etc.	...	...	...	...	...	...
			Total Sub-order 15	95	9	15	71	64	4
		16.—Sanitation	72. Sanitary officers of Government	5	1	...	4	3	1
			73. Sanitary inspectors, etc., local and municipal	13	4	...	9	8	...
			74. Sweepers and scavengers	2,065	246	464	1,355	1,213	129
			75. Dust and sweeping contractors	5	...	...	5	5	...
			Total Sub-order 16	2,088	251	464	1,373	1,223	130
			Total Order VI.	**72,301**	**9,538**	**15,931**	**46,832**	**38,849**	**4,351**
			Total Class C.	**72,301**	**9,538**	**15,931**	**46,832**	**38,849**	**4,351**
CLASS D.—PREPARATION AND SUPPLY OF MATERIAL SUBSTANCES	ORDER VII.—FOOD AND DRINK.	17.—Animal food	76. Cow and buffalo keepers and milk and butter sellers.	4,478	593	1,019	2,866	1,935	276
			77. Ghee preparers and sellers	670	84	151	435	368	58
			78. Cheese makers and sellers	...	...	...	...	...	...
			79. Butchers	6,746	1,102	1,778	3,866	3,558	520
			80. Fowl and egg dealers	26	5	3	18	18	1
			81. Fishermen and fish curers	13,363	2,527	3,577	7,259	8,215	1,136
			82. Fish dealers	12	...	5	7	7	...
			Total Sub-order 17	25,295	4,321	6,533	14,451	14,095	2,069

Part A.—PROVINCIAL SUMMARY—*contd.*

TOTAL. Males. 5—14	Males. 15—	Females. Total.	Females. 0—4	Females. 5—14	Females. 15—	Sub-order and Group.	Occupation.	Order.	Class.
11	12	13	14	15	16				
1,348	3,552	5,308	718	1,280	3,310	37. Land occupants, not cultivating	10.—Interest in land.	Order V.—Agriculture.	Class B.—Pasture and Agriculture—*contd.*
83,279	205,777	304,031	51,441	78,327	174,263	38. Land occupants, cultivating			
2	17	26	6	5	15	39. Lessees of villages, etc.			
...	...	...	...	...	...	40. Tenants, not cultivating			
42,011	123,392	149,834	28,382	37,399	84,053	41. Tenants and sharers, cultivating			
127,540	332,738	459,199	80,547	117,011	261,641	Total Sub-order 10			
18,202	56,021	26,091	6,654	7,423	12,014	42. Farm servants	11.—Agricultural labourers.		
102,205	221,388	506,659	56,384	114,824	335,451	43. Field labourers and crop watchers			
120,407	277,409	532,750	63,038	122,247	347,465	Total Sub-order 11			
...	...	...	...	...	...	44. Tea, coffee and cinchona planters, managers, and assistants.	12.—Growers of special products and trees.		
...	...	...	...	...	...	45. Cocoanut growers			
51	137	253	20	55	178	46. Betel-vine and areca-nut growers			
...	2	3	1	...	2	47. Water-nut growers			
...	...	...	...	...	...	48. Cardamom and pepper growers			
...	...	...	...	...	...	49. Indigo planters, managers, etc.			
58	110	132	18	31	83	50. Fruit growers			
2	7	9	2	3	4	51. Market gardeners (vegetable growers)			
82	340	315	54	87	174	52. Gardeners, seedsmen, etc.			
...	...	4	2	1	1	53. Manure preparers and sellers			
3	6	8	2	...	6	54. Forest officers			
21	249	114	15	25	74	55. Forest rangers, guards, and peons			
217	851	838	114	202	522	Total Sub-order 12			
...	1	...	...	...	...	56. Directors of Agriculture and their assistants	13.—Agricultural training and supervision.		
...	...	...	...	...	...	57. Model-farm managers, etc.			
...	1	...	...	...	...	58. Agents and managers of landed estates (not planters).			
...	2	...	...	...	...	Total Sub-order 13			
248,164	**611,000**	**992,787**	**143,699**	**239,460**	**609,628**	**Total Order V**			
260,004	**624,299**	**1,000,484**	**145,446**	**241,929**	**613,109**	**Total Class B**			
2,641	9,052	8,050	1,494	1,998	4,558	59. Barbers	14.—Personal and domestic services.	Order VI.—Personal and Household Services.	Class C.—Personal Services.
...	2	5	1	1	3	60. Ear-pickers			
4	4	2	...	...	2	61. Tattooers			
...	...	...	...	...	...	62. Caste-marks appliers			
1,671	4,380	7,033	982	1,667	4,384	63. Washermen			
127	685	484	65	106	313	64. Water-carriers			
74	694	455	48	69	338	65 Cooks			
3,137	9,995	16,140	2,411	3,732	9,997	66. Indoor servants			
135	744	387	60	90	237	67. Grooms, coachmen, and dog boys, etc.			
...	...	...	...	...	...	68. Door-keepers, etc.			
7,789	25,556	32,556	5,061	7,663	19,832	Total Sub-order 14			
9	23	20	3	2	15	69. Hotel, lodging and boarding house, bar and refreshment-room keepers.	15.—Non-domestic establishment.		
3	25	11	2	1	8	70. Rest-house, serai, bath-house, etc., owners and managers.			
...	...	...	...	...	...	71. Club secretaries, managers, stewards, etc.			
12	48	31	5	3	23	Total Sub-order 15			
...	2	2	...	...	2	72. Sanitary officers of Government	16.—Sanitation.		
...	2	11	4	...	7	73. Sanitary Inspectors, etc., local and municipal.			
247	837	852	117	217	518	74. Sweepers and scavengers			
...	5	...	...	...	...	75. Dust and sweeping contractors			
247	846	865	121	217	527	Total Sub-order 16			
8,048	**26,450**	**33,452**	**5,187**	**7,883**	**20,382**	**Total Order VI**			
8,048	**26,450**	**33,452**	**5,187**	**7,883**	**20,382**	**Total Class C**			
501	1,158	2,543	317	518	1,708	76. Cow and buffalo keepers and milk and butter sellers	17.—Animal food.	Order VII.—Food and Drink.	Class D.—Preparation and Supply of Material Substances.
76	256	302	48	75	179	77. Ghee preparers and sellers			
...	...	...	...	...	...	78. Cheese makers and sellers			
950	2,088	3,188	582	828	1,778	79. Butchers			
2	9	14	4	1	9	80. Fowl and egg dealers			
2,047	4,932	5,148	1,291	1,530	2,327	81. Fishermen and fish curers			
3	4	5	...	2	3	82. Fish dealers			
3,579	8,447	11,200	2,248	2,954	6,004	Total Sub-order 17			

TABLE XVII.—Occupations, by Age.—

Class.	Order.	Sub-order and Group.	Occupation.	TOWN. Total. Total.	Total. 0—4	Total. 5—14	Total. 15—	Males. Total.	Males. 0—4	Males. 5—14	Males. 15—	Females. Total.	Females. 0—4	Females. 5—14	Females. 15—
				17	18	19	20	21	22	23	24	25	26	27	28
CLASS B.—PASTURE AND AGRICULTURE—contd.	ORDER V.—AGRICULTURE.	10.—Interest in land.	37. Land occupants, not cultivating	1,776	200	413	1,163	833	96	196	541	943	104	217	622
			38. Land occupants, cultivating	47,402	6,763	11,228	29,411	24,877	3,376	5,930	15,571	22,525	3,387	5,298	13,840
			39. Lessees of villages, etc.	1	...	...	1	...	...	...	...	1	...	...	1
			40. Tenants, not cultivating	...	...	...	...	...	...	...	...	...	...	...	...
			41. Tenants and sharers, cultivating	14,554	2,189	3,108	9,257	8,044	1,063	1,625	5,356	6,510	1,126	1,483	3,901
			Total Sub-order 10	63,733	9,152	14,749	39,832	33,754	4,535	7,751	21,468	29,979	4,617	6,998	18,364
		11.—Agricultural labourers.	42. Farm servants	4,015	565	1,045	3,305	3,739	304	709	2,726	1,276	261	336	679
			43. Field labourers and crop watchers	56,421	6,197	12,535	37,679	25,393	2,966	6,316	16,111	31,028	3,231	6,219	21,578
			Total Sub-order 11	61,326	6,762	13,580	40,984	29,132	3,270	7,025	18,837	32,194	3,492	6,555	22,147
		12.—Growers of special products and trees.	44. Tea, coffee and cinchona planters, managers, and assistants.	...	...	...	...	...	...	...	...	...	...	...	...
			45. Cocoanut growers	...	...	...	...	...	...	...	...	...	...	...	...
			46. Betel-vine and areca-nut growers.	216	14	30	172	75	8	17	50	141	6	13	122
			47. Water-nut growers	...	...	...	...	...	...	...	...	...	...	...	...
			48. Cardamom and pepper growers	...	...	...	...	...	...	...	...	...	...	...	...
			49. Indigo planters, managers, etc.	...	...	...	...	...	...	...	...	...	...	...	...
			50. Fruit growers	118	16	34	68	68	8	22	38	50	8	12	30
			51. Market gardeners (vegetable growers).	6	...	3	3	2	...	...	2	4	...	3	1
			52. Gardeners, seedsmen, etc.	449	59	97	293	252	26	44	182	197	33	53	111
			53. Manure preparers and sellers	...	...	...	...	...	...	...	...	...	...	...	...
			54. Forest officers	15	3	3	9	8	1	3	4	7	2	...	5
			55. Forest rangers, guards, and peons	96	8	21	67	66	5	13	48	30	3	8	19
			Total Sub-order 12	900	100	188	612	471	48	99	324	429	52	89	288
		13.—Agricultural training and supervision.	56. Directors of agriculture and their assistants.	1	...	...	1	1	...	...	1	...	...	...	...
			57. Model-farm managers, etc.	...	...	...	...	...	...	...	...	...	...	...	...
			58. Agents and managers of landed estates (not planters).	...	...	...	...	...	...	...	...	...	...	...	...
			Total Sub-order 13	1	...	...	1	1	...	...	1	...	...	...	...
			Total Order V.	125,960	16,014	28,517	81,429	63,358	7,853	14,875	40,630	62,602	8,161	13,642	40,799
			Total Class B.	128,638	16,299	29,392	82,947	65,313	8,022	15,557	41,734	63,325	8,277	13,835	41,213
CLASS C.—PERSONAL SERVICES.	ORDER VI.—PERSONAL AND HOUSEHOLD SERVICES.	14.—Personal and domestic services.	59. Barbers	3,497	413	694	2,390	2,107	212	368	1,527	1,390	201	326	863
			60. Ear-pickers	2	...	...	2	1	...	...	1	1	...	...	1
			61. Tattooers	3	...	1	2	3	...	1	2	...	...	...	...
			62. Caste-mark appliers	...	...	...	...	...	...	...	...	...	...	...	...
			63. Washermen	2,511	333	618	1,560	1,251	170	313	768	1,260	163	305	792
			64. Water-carriers	801	68	139	594	505	31	72	402	296	37	69	191
			65. Cooks	740	57	85	598	467	23	51	393	273	34	34	205
			66. In-door servants	7,598	905	1,611	5,082	3,853	371	788	2,694	3,745	534	823	2,388
			67. Grooms, coachmen, and dog-boys, etc.	924	98	160	666	606	52	90	464	318	46	70	202
			68. Door-keepers, etc.	...	...	...	...	...	...	...	...	...	...	...	...
			Total Sub-order 14	16,076	1,874	3,308	10,894	8,793	859	1,683	6,251	7,283	1,015	1,625	4,643
		15.—Non-domestic establishment.	69. Hotel, lodging and boarding house, bar and refreshment-room keepers.	53	6	11	36	33	3	9	21	20	3	2	15
			70. Rest-house, serai, bath-house, etc., owners and managers.	15	2	3	10	8	...	2	6	7	2	1	4
			71. Club secretaries, managers, stewards, etc.	...	...	...	...	...	...	...	...	...	...	...	...
			Total Sub-order 15	68	8	14	46	41	3	11	27	27	5	3	19
		16.—Sanitation	72. Sanitary officers of Government	5	1	...	4	3	1	...	2	2	...	...	2
			73. Sanitary inspectors, etc., local and municipal.	13	4	...	9	2	...	...	2	11	4	...	7
			74. Sweepers and scavengers	1,350	172	325	853	779	92	181	506	571	80	144	347
			75. Dust and sweeping contractors	...	...	...	...	...	...	...	...	...	...	...	...
			Total Sub-order 16	1,368	177	325	866	784	93	181	510	584	84	144	356
			Total Order VI.	17,512	2,059	3,647	11,806	9,618	955	1,875	6,788	7,894	1,104	1,772	5,018
			Total Class C.	17,512	2,059	3,647	11,806	9,618	955	1,875	6,788	7,894	1,104	1,772	5,018
CLASS D.—PREPARATION AND SUPPLY OF MATERIAL SUBSTANCES.	ORDER VII.—FOOD AND DRINK.	17.—Animal food	76. Cow and buffalo keepers and milk and butter sellers.	1,860	285	437	1,138	843	128	241	474	1,017	157	196	664
			77. Ghee preparers and sellers	238	24	56	158	130	13	28	89	108	11	28	69
			78. Cheese makers and sellers	...	...	...	...	...	...	...	...	...	...	...	...
			79. Butchers	3,140	509	857	1,783	1,571	223	454	894	1,569	286	409	889
			80. Fowl and egg dealers	15	3	1	11	5	...	...	5	10	3	1	6
			81. Fishermen and fish curers	1,700	327	462	911	1,099	173	262	664	601	154	200	247
			82. Fish dealers	3	...	1	2	1	...	...	1	2	...	1	1
			Total Sub-order 17	6,965	1,148	1,814	4,003	3,649	537	985	2,127	3,316	611	829	1,876

Part A.—PROVINCIAL SUMMARY—*contd.*

COUNTRY.												Occupation.	Sub-order and Group.	Group.	Class.
Total.				Males.				Females.							
Total	0—4	5—14	15—	Total.	0—4	5—14	15—	Total.	0—4	5—14	15—				
29	30	31	32	33	34	35	36	37	38	39	40				
9,191	1,277	2,215	5,699	4,826	663	1,152	3,011	4,365	614	1,063	2,688	37. Land occupants, not-cultivating	10.—Interest in land.	ORDER V.—AGRICULTURE.	CLASS B.—PASTURE AND AGRICULTURE—*contd.*
595,287	94,280	150,378	350,629	313,781	46,226	77,349	190,206	281,506	48,054	73,029	160,423	38. Land occupants, cultivating			
50	12	7	31	25	6	2	17	25	6	5	14	39. Lessees of villages, etc			
...	...	...	...	...	...	...	...	...	...	...	...	40. Tenants, not cultivating			
329,341	53,951	77,202	198,188	186,017	26,695	41,286	118,036	143,324	27,256	35,916	80,152	41. Tenants and sharers, cultivating			
933,869	149,580	229,802	554,547	504,649	73,590	119,789	311,270	429,220	75,930	110,013	243,277	Total Sub-order 10			
103,679	14,369	24,580	64,730	78,764	7,976	17,403	53,295	24,915	6,393	7,087	11,435	42. Farm servants	11.—Agricultural labourers.		
821,639	97,985	204,494	519,160	345,998	44,832	95,889	205,277	475,641	53,153	108,605	313,883	43. Field labourers and crop watchers			
925,318	112,354	229,074	583,890	424,762	52,808	113,382	258,572	500,556	59,546	115,692	325,318	Total Sub-order 11			
...	...	...	...	...	...	...	...	...	...	...	...	44. Tea, coffee and cinchona planters, managers and assistants.	12.—Growers of special products and trees.		
...	...	...	...	...	...	...	...	...	...	...	...	45. Cocoanut growers			
250	31	76	143	138	17	34	87	112	14	42	56	46. Betel-vine and areca-nut growers.			
6	2	...	4	3	1	...	2	3	1	...	2	47. Water-nut growers			
...	...	...	...	...	...	...	...	...	...	...	...	48. Cardamom and pepper growers			
...	...	...	...	...	...	...	...	...	...	...	...	49. Indigo planters, managers, etc.			
198	18	55	125	116	8	36	72	82	10	19	53	50. Fruit growers			
13	3	2	8	8	1	2	5	5	2	...	3	51. Market gardeners (vegetable growers)			
339	45	72	221	220	24	38	158	118	21	34	63	52. Gardeners, seedsmen, etc.			
4	2	1	1	...	...	...	...	4	2	1	1	53. Manure preparers and sellers			
3	...	...	3	2	...	...	2	1	...	...	1	54. Forest officers			
305	24	25	256	221	12	8	201	84	12	17	55	55. Forest rangers, guards, and peons.			
1,117	125	231	761	708	63	118	527	409	62	113	234	Total Sub-order 12			
...		...	...	...	...	...	...	...	...	...	...	56. Directors of Agriculture and their assistants	13.—Agricultural training and supervision.		
...	...	...	...	...	...	...	...	...	...	...	...	57. Model-farm managers, etc.			
1	...	...	1	1	...	...	1	...	...	...	...	58. Agents and managers of landed estates (not planters).			
1	...	...	1	1	...	...	1	...	...	...	...	Total Sub-order 13			
[illegible]	261,999	459,107	1,139,199	930,120	126,461	233,289	570,370	930,185	135,538	225,818	568,829	Total Order V			
1,892,705	265,703	472,541	1,154,461	955,546	128,534	244,447	582,565	937,159	137,169	228,094	571,896	Total Class B			
17,786	2,522	3,945	11,320	11,126	1,328	2,273	7,525	6,660	1,293	1,672	3,695	59. Barbers	14.—Personal and domestic services.	ORDER VI.—PERSONAL AND HOUSEHOLD SERVICES.	CLASS C.—PERSONAL SERVICES.
6	2	1	3	2	1	...	1	4	1	1	2	60. Ear-pickers			
7	...	3	4	5	...	3	2	2	...	...	2	61. Tattooers			
...	...	...	...	...	...	...	...	...	...	...	...	62. Caste-mark appliers			
11,540	1,616	2,720	7,204	5,767	797	1,358	3,612	5,773	819	1,362	3,592	63. Washermen			
558	60	94	404	370	32	55	283	188	28	39	121	64. Water-carriers			
517	25	58	434	335	11	23	301	182	14	35	133	65. Cooks			
23,219	3,051	5,258	14,910	10,824	1,174	2,349	7,301	12,395	1,877	2,909	7,609	66. In-door servants			
409	29	65	315	340	15	45	280	69	14	20	35	67. Grooms, coachmen, and dog-boys, etc.			
...	...	...	...	...	...	...	...	...	...	...	...	68. Door-keepers, etc.			
54,042	7,404	12,144	34,494	28,769	3,358	6,106	19,305	25,273	4,046	6,038	15,189	Total Sub-order 14			
2	...	...	2	2	...	...	2	...	...	...	...	69. Hotel, lodging and boarding house, bar and refreshment-room keepers.	15.—Non-domestic establishment.		
25	1	1	23	21	1	1	19	4	...	...	4	70. Rest-house, serai, bath-house, etc., owners and managers.			
...	...	...	...	...	...	...	...	...	...	...	...	71. Club secretaries, managers, stewards, etc.			
27	1	1	25	23	1	1	21	4	...	...	4	Total Sub-order 15			
...	...	...	...	...	...	...	...	...	...	...	...	72. Sanitary officers of Government	16.—Sanitation.		
...	...	...	...	...	...	...	...	...	...	...	...	73. Sanitary inspectors, etc., local and municipal.			
715	74	159	502	434	37	65	331	281	37	73	171	74. Sweepers and scavengers			
5	...	...	5	5	...	...	5	...	...	...	...	75. Dust and sweeping contractors			
720	74	139	507	439	37	66	336	281	37	73	171	Total Sub-order 16			
54,789	7,479	12,284	35,026	29,231	3,396	6,173	19,662	25,558	4,083	6,111	15,364	Total Order VI			
54,789	7,479	12,284	35,026	29,231	3,396	6,173	19,662	25,558	4,083	6,111	15,364	Total Class C			
2,618	308	582	1,728	1,092	148	260	684	1,526	160	322	1,044	76. Cow and buffalo keepers and milk and butter sellers.	17.—Animal food.	ORDER VII.—FOOD AND DRINK.	CLASS D.—PREPARATION AND SUPPLY OF MATERIAL SUBSTANCES.
432	60	95	277	238	23	48	167	194	37	47	110	77. Ghee preparers and sellers			
...	...	...	...	...	...	...	...	...	...	...	...	78. Cheese makers and sellers			
3,597	503	921	2,083	1,987	297	496	1,194	1,610	206	425	889	79. Butchers			
11	2	2	7	7	1	2	4	4	1	...	3	80. Fowl and egg dealers			
11,663	2,200	3,115	6,348	7,116	1,063	1,785	4,268	4,547	1,137	1,330	2,080	81. Fishermen and fish curers			
9	...	4	5	6	...	3	3	3	...	1	2	82. Fish dealers			
18,330	3,163	4,729	10,448	10,446	1,532	2,594	6,320	7,884	1,631	2,125	4,128	Total Sub-order 17			

TABLE XVII.—Occupations, by Age.—

PROVINCIAL

Class.	Order.	Sub-order and Group.	Occupation.	Total. Total.	Total. 0—4	Total. 5—14	Total. 15—	Males. Total.	Males. 0—4
1	2	3	4	5	6	7	8	9	10
CLASS D.—PREPARATION AND SUPPLY OF MATERIAL SUBSTANCES—contd.	ORDER VII.—FOOD AND DRINK—contd.	18.—Vegetable Food	83. Grain dealers	8,920	1,087	1,900	5,933	5,182	544
			84. Grain parchers	2,959	371	626	1,962	1,234	177
			85. Pulse and flour preparers and sellers	1,513	149	301	1,063	873	71
			86. Flour-mill service and management	4	...	...	4	2	...
			87. Bakers	116	6	19	91	62	2
			88. Bran sellers	...	...	...	...	...	...
			89. Vegetable sellers	2,256	248	400	1,608	1,005	118
			90. Fruit and sugarcane sellers	1,387	169	311	907	780	89
			91. Cocoanut dealers	24	3	7	14	6	...
			91a. Cotton-seed dealers	154	14	33	107	99	12
			92. Confectioners and sweetmeat makers and sellers.	2,327	239	390	1,698	1,426	103
			93. Sweetmeat pedlars	32	2	4	26	25	...
			Total Sub-order 18	19,692	2,288	3,991	13,413	10,694	1,126
		19.—Drink, Condiments and Narcotics.	94. Ice manufacturers and sellers	...	...	...	...	...	...
			94a. Water sellers	29	5	6	18	18	4
			95. Soda-water, lemonade, etc., manufacturers and sellers.	1	...	...	1	1	...
			96. Sharbat preparers and sellers	...	...	...	...	...	...
			97 Country spirits distillers and sellers	6,160	750	1,232	4,178	3,739	361
			98. Toddy drawers and sellers	844	140	190	514	566	74
			99. Foreign wine and spirit dealers	15	1	2	12	10	1
			100. Brewers	...	...	...	...	...	...
			101. Tea sellers and tasters (not planters)	1	...	...	1	...	...
			102. Coffee preparers and sellers (not planters)	...	...	...	...	...	...
			103 Sugar manufacturers and sellers	...	...	...	...	...	...
			104. Molasses (jaggery, gur, etc.,) makers and sellers.	1,410	183	312	915	805	95
			105. Salt preparers and sellers	615	61	135	419	291	20
			106. Assafœtida, turmeric, etc., sellers	238	30	55	153	133	11
			107. Vinegar manufacturers and sellers	...	...	...	...	...	...
			108. Pickle makers and sellers	21	2	6	13	...	...
			109. Grocers and general condiment dealers	19,852	2,344	4,076	13,432	11,628	1,189
			110. Cardamom-preparers and dealers	...	...	...	...	...	...
			111. Betel-leaf and areca-nut sellers	6,285	648	1,147	4,490	2,204	181
			112. Tobacco and snuff manufacturers and sellers.	2,626	337	529	1,760	1,536	158
			113. Prepared hukka pedlars	6	1	...	5	5	1
			114. Opium, etc., manufacturers, and sellers	886	92	162	632	500	48
			115. Bhang, ganja, etc., preparers and sellers	26	5	7	14	2	...
			Total Sub-order 19	39,015	4,599	7,859	26,557	21,528	2,044
			Total Order VII	**84,002**	**11,198**	**18,383**	**54,421**	**46,317**	**5,429**
	ORDER VIII.—LIGHT, FIRING AND FORAGE.	20.—Lighting	116. Oil pressers and sellers	16,311	2,148	3,639	10,524	8,346	1,019
			117. Oil and salt sellers	16	1	4	11	1	...
			118. Oil-cake dealers	8	1	3	4	4	...
			119. Candle makers and sellers	...	...	...	...	...	...
			120. Torch makers and sellers	...	...	...	...	...	...
			121. Kerosine oil dealers	169	20	38	111	93	15
			122. Match makers and sellers	104	6	23	75	89	4
			123. Lamp and lantern makers and sellers	12	2	5	5	6	1
			124. Gas workers, Gas Company Managers, etc.	...	...	...	...	...	...
			Total Sub-order 20	16,620	2,178	3,722	10,720	8,539	1,439
		21.—Fuel and Forage	125. Firewood and grass gatherers and sellers	19,903	2,610	5,028	12,265	8,622	1,115
			126. Firewood contractors and dealers	2,400	346	602	1,452	977	131
			127. Coal miners, etc.	...	...	...	...	...	...
			128. Coal dealers, brokers, Coal Company Managers, etc.	1	...	...	1	1	...
			129. Charcoal burners and dealers	505	59	118	328	296	25
			130. Cowdung-fuel preparers and sellers	1,118	99	287	732	357	44
			131. Hay, etc., contractors and dealers	4,144	560	955	2,629	1,800	251
			Total Sub-order 21	28,071	3,674	6,990	17,407	12,053	1,666
			Total Order VIII	**44,691**	**5,852**	**10,702**	**28,137**	**20,592**	**2,705**
	ORDER IX.—BUILDINGS.	22.—Building materials.	132. Brick and tile burners and sellers	5,709	499	775	4,435	4,171	251
			133. Lime, chunam and shell burners and sellers	898	96	224	578	498	48
			134. Stone-quarry owners, contractors, and marble dealers, etc.	27	5	4	18	18	3
			135. Thatch-dealers and thatchers	67	13	10	44	39	5
			Total Sub-order 22	6,701	613	1,013	5,075	4,726	307
		23.—Artificers in Building.	136. Building contractors	4	...	...	4	3	...
			137. Stone and marble workers	476	83	109	284	239	35
			138. Masons	5,839	861	1,282	3,696	3,375	430
			139. Builders and joiners	263	24	61	178	249	8
			140. Plasterers and house painters	116	9	34	73	57	6
			141. Mud-wall and roof builders	4,702	722	1,085	2,895	2,904	359
			142. Plumbers and glaziers	...	...	...	...	...	...
			143. Tilers and tile-turners	...	...	...	...	...	...
			Total Sub-order 23	11,400	1,699	2,571	7,130	6,727	839
			Total Order IX	**18,101**	**2,312**	**3,584**	**12,205**	**11,453**	**1,188**

Part A.—PROVINCIAL SUMMARY—*contd.*

TOTAL: Males 5—14	TOTAL: Males 15—	Females: Total	Females: 0—4	Females: 5—14	Females: 15—	Occupation.	Sub-Order and Group.	Order.	Class.
11	12	13	14	15	16				
1,057	3,581	3,738	543	843	2,352	83. Grain dealers	18.—Vegetable food	Order VII.—Food and Drink—*contd.*	Class D.—Preparation and Supply of Material Substances—*contd.*
269	788	1,725	191	357	1,174	84. Grain parchers			
163	639	640	78	138	424	85. Pulse and flour preparers and sellers			
...	2	2	...	...	2	86. Flour-mill service and management			
8	52	54	4	11	39	87. Bakers			
...	...	...	...	...	...	88. Bran sellers			
200	687	1,251	130	200	921	89. Vegetable sellers			
175	516	607	80	136	391	90. Fruit and sugarcane sellers			
2	4	18	3	5	10	91. Cocoanut dealers			
18	69	55	2	15	38	91a. Cotton-seed dealers			
213	1,310	902	136	177	588	92. Confectioners and sweetmeat makers and sellers.			
2	23	7	2	2	3	93. Sweetmeat pedlars			
2,107	7,471	8,998	1,172	1,884	5,942	Total Sub-order 18			
...	...	...	...	...	...	94. Ice manufacturers and sellers	19.—Drink, condiments and narcotics.		
5	9	11	1	1	9	94a. Water sellers			
...	1	...	...	...	...	95. Soda-water, lemonade, etc., manufacturers and sellers.			
...	...	...	...	...	...	96. Sharbat preparers and sellers			
660	2,718	2,421	380	572	1,460	97. Country spirits distillers and sellers			
102	390	278	66	88	124	98. Toddy drawers and sellers			
2	7	5	...	...	5	99. Foreign wine and spirit dealers			
...	...	...	...	...	...	100. Brewers			
...	...	1	...	...	1	101. Tea sellers and tasters (not planters)			
...	...	...	...	...	...	102. Coffee preparers and sellers (not planters)			
...	...	...	...	...	...	103. Sugar manufacturers and sellers			
170	540	605	88	142	375	104. Molasses (jaggery, gur, etc.) makers and sellers.			
63	208	324	41	72	211	105. Salt preparers and sellers			
31	90	105	18	24	63	106. Assafœtida, turmeric, etc., sellers			
...	...	...	...	...	...	107. Vinegar manufacturers and sellers			
...	...	21	2	6	13	108. Pickle makers and sellers			
2,276	8,163	8,224	1,155	1,800	5,269	109. Grocers and general condiment dealers			
...	...	...	...	...	...	110. Cardamom preparers and dealers			
505	1,417	4,081	366	642	3,073	111. Betel-leaf and areca-nut sellers			
284	1,095	1,090	180	245	665	112. Tobacco and snuff manufacturers and sellers.			
...	4	1	...	...	1	113. Prepared hukka pedlars			
102	440	296	44	60	192	114. Opium, etc., manufacturers and sellers			
...	2	24	5	7	12	115. Bhang, ganja, etc., preparers and sellers			
4,200	15,024	17,487	2,355	3,659	11,473	Total Sub-order 19			
9,886	**31,002**	**37,685**	**5,769**	**8,497**	**23,419**	**Total Order VII**			
1,835	5,492	7,965	1,129	1,804	5,032	116. Oil pressers and sellers	20.—Lighting	Order VIII.—Light, Firing and Forage.	
...	1	15	1	4	10	117. Oil and salt sellers			
2	2	4	1	1	2	118. Oil cake dealers			
...	...	...	...	...	...	119. Candle-makers and sellers			
...	...	...	...	...	...	120. Torch-makers and sellers			
15	63	76	5	23	48	121. Kerosine oil dealers			
18	67	15	2	5	8	122. Match makers and sellers			
1	4	6	1	4	1	123. Lamp and lantern makers and sellers			
...	...	...	...	...	...	124. Gas workers, Gas Company Managers, &c.			
1,871	5,629	8,081	1,139	1,841	5,101	Total Sub-order 20			
2,305	5,102	11,281	1,395	2,723	7,163	125. Firewood and grass gatherers and sellers	21.—Fuel and Forage		
252	594	1,423	215	350	858	126. Firewood contractors and dealers			
...	...	...	...	...	...	127. Coal miners, etc.			
...	1	...	...	...	...	128. Coal dealers, brokers, Coal Company Managers, etc.			
59	212	209	34	59	116	129. Charcoal burners and dealers			
122	191	761	55	165	541	130. Cowdung-fuel preparers and sellers			
450	1,099	2,344	309	505	1,530	131. Hay, etc., Contractors and dealers			
3,188	7,199	16,018	2,008	3,802	10,208	Total Sub-order 21			
5,059	**12,828**	**24,099**	**3,147**	**5,643**	**15,309**	**Total Order VIII**			
426	3,494	1,538	248	349	941	132. Brick and tile burners and sellers	22.—Building materials.	Order IX.—Buildings.	
125	325	400	48	99	253	133. Lime, chunam and shell burners and sellers			
1	14	9	2	3	4	134. Stone-quarry owners, contractors, and marble dealers, etc.			
7	27	28	8	3	17	135. Thatch-dealers and thatchers			
559	3,860	1,975	306	454	1,215	Total Sub-order 22			
...	3	1	...	...	1	136. Building contractors	23.—Artificers in building.		
55	149	237	48	54	135	137. Stone and marble workers			
659	2,286	2,464	431	623	1,410	138. Masons			
30	111	114	16	31	67	139. Builders and joiners			
14	37	59	3	20	35	140. Plasterers and house painters			
615	1,939	1,798	372	470	956	141. Mud-wall and roof builders			
...	...	...	...	...	...	142. Plumbers and glaziers			
...	...	...	...	...	...	143. Tilers and tile-turners			
1,372	4,525	4,673	870	1,298	2,605	Total Sub-order 23			
1,932	**8,385**	**6,648**	**1,176**	**1,652**	**3,820**	**Total Order IX**			

TABLE XVII.—Occupations, by Age.—

Class.	Order.	Occupation.	Sub-order and Group.	Town. Total. Total.	Total. 0—4	Total. 5—14	Total. 15—	Males. Total.	Males. 0—4	Males. 5—14	Males. 15—	Females. Total.	Females. 0—4	Females. 5—14	Females. 15—
				17	18	19	20	21	22	23	24	25	26	27	28
CLASS D.—PREPARATION AND SUPPLY OF MATERIAL SUBSTANCES—contd.	ORDER VII.—FOOD AND DRINK—contd.	18.—Vegetable food	83. Grain dealers	4,052	487	865	2,700	2,192	212	464	1,516	1,860	275	401	1,184
			84. Grain parchers	1,001	130	202	669	451	61	84	306	550	69	218	263
			85. Pulse and flour preparers and sellers.	791	73	165	553	456	36	91	329	335	37	74	224
			86. Flour-mill service and management.	4	...	...	4	2	...	...	2	2	...	...	2
			87. Bakers	98	6	16	76	54	2	8	44	44	4	8	32
			88. Bran sellers	...	...	...	...	...	...	...	...	...	...	...	...
			89. Vegetable sellers	1,062	105	198	759	485	46	94	345	577	59	104	414
			90. Fruit and sugarcane sellers	796	105	171	520	411	54	84	273	385	51	87	247
			91. Cocoanut dealers	7	...	4	3	3	...	2	1	4	...	2	2
			91a. Cotton-seed dealers	130	12	29	89	79	10	15	54	51	2	14	35
			92. Confectioners and sweetmeat makers and sellers.	1,179	132	190	857	700	62	106	532	479	70	84	325
			93. Sweetmeat pedlars	25	2	2	21	9	...	1	8	6	2	1	3
			Total Sub-order 18	9,135	1,052	1,842	6,241	4,842	483	949	3,410	4,293	569	892	2,831
		19.—Drink, condiments and narcotics.	94. Ice manufacturers and sellers	...	...	...	...	...	...	...	...	...	...	...	...
			94a. Water sellers	24	5	5	14	15	4	4	7	9	1	1	7
			95. Soda-water, lemonade, etc., manufacturers and sellers.	1	...	...	1	1	...	...	1	...	...	...	...
			96. Sharbat preparers and sellers	...	...	...	...	...	...	...	...	...	...	...	...
			97. Country spirits distillers and sellers.	583	60	119	404	250	29	64	157	333	31	55	247
			98. Toddy drawers and sellers	160	15	47	88	78	11	24	43	82	24	23	45
			99. Foreign wine and spirit dealers	6	...	1	5	5	...	1	4	1	...	...	1
			100. Brewers	...	...	...	...	...	...	...	...	...	...	...	...
			101. Tea sellers and tasters (not planters).	1	...	...	1	...	...	...	...	1	...	...	1
			102. Coffee preparers and sellers (not planters).	...	...	...	...	...	...	...	...	...	...	...	...
			103. Sugar manufacturers and sellers.	...	...	...	...	...	...	...	...	...	...	...	...
			104. Molasses (jaggery, gur, etc.) makers and sellers.	370	43	78	249	225	25	48	152	145	18	30	97
			105. Salt preparers and sellers	178	18	31	129	89	7	15	67	89	11	16	62
			106. Assafœtida, turmeric, etc., sellers.	40	5	13	22	25	3	10	12	15	2	8	10
			107. Vinegar manufacturers and sellers.	...	...	...	...	...	...	...	...	...	...	...	...
			108. Pickle makers and sellers	2	...	...	2	...	...	...	...	2	...	...	2
			109. Grocers and general condiment dealers.	5,033	557	1,032	3,444	2,844	296	562	1,986	2,189	261	470	1,458
			110. Cardamom preparers and dealers.	...	...	...	...	...	...	...	...	...	...	...	...
			111. Betel-leaf and areca-nut sellers	1,946	188	328	1,430	594	80	142	372	1,352	108	186	1,058
			112. Tobacco and snuff manufacturers and sellers.	1,105	141	230	734	615	73	114	428	490	68	116	306
			113. Prepared hukka pedlars	3	1	...	2	2	1	...	1	1	...	...	1
			114. Opium, etc., manufacturers and sellers.	196	18	38	140	113	7	22	84	83	11	16	56
			115. Bhang, ganja, etc., preparers and sellers.	3	...	...	3	1	...	...	1	2	...	...	2
			Total Sub-order 19	9,651	1,061	1,922	6,668	4,957	526	1,006	3,425	4,694	535	916	3,243
			Total Order VII	**25,751**	**3,261**	**5,578**	**16,912**	**13,448**	**1,558**	**2,940**	**8,952**	**12,303**	**1,705**	**2,838**	**7,760**
	ORDER VIII.—LIGHT, FIRING AND FORAGE.	20.—Lighting	116. Oil pressers and sellers	4,859	663	1,020	3,236	2,422	277	526	1,619	2,437	326	494	1,617
			117. Oil and salt sellers	1	...	...	1	1	...	...	1	...	...	...	...
			118. Oil-cake dealers	8	1	3	4	4	...	2	2	4	1	1	2
			119. Candle makers and sellers	...	...	...	...	...	...	...	...	...	...	...	...
			120. Torch makers and sellers	...	...	...	...	...	...	...	...	...	...	...	...
			121. Kerosine oil dealers	76	7	16	53	33	5	2	25	43	2	14	27
			122. Match makers and sellers	43	2	15	26	24	1	13	10	9	1	2	6
			123. Lamp and lantern makers and sellers.	11	2	5	4	5	1	1	3	6	1	4	1
			124. Gas workers, Gas Company Managers, etc.	...	...	...	...	...	...	...	...	...	...	...	...
			Total Sub-order 20	4,998	615	1,059	3,324	2,499	284	544	1,671	2,499	331	515	1,653
		21.—Fuel and Forage.	125. Firewood and grass-gatherers and sellers.	5,831	784	1,440	3,607	2,826	401	738	1,687	3,005	383	702	1,920
			126. Firewood contractors and dealers.	423	66	102	255	93	11	27	55	330	55	75	200
			127. Coal miners, etc.	...	...	...	...	...	...	...	...	...	...	...	...
			128. Coal dealers, brokers, Coal Company Managers, etc.	...	...	...	...	...	...	...	...	...	...	...	...
			129. Charcoal burners and dealers	49	3	10	36	30	1	6	23	19	2	4	13
			130. Cowdung-fuel preparers and sellers.	418	38	111	269	132	18	52	62	286	20	59	207
			131. Hay, etc., contractors and dealers.	2,676	375	644	1,657	1,305	186	327	792	1,371	189	317	865
			Total Sub-order 21	9,397	1,266	2,207	5,824	4,386	617	1,150	2,619	5,011	649	1,057	3,305
			Total Order VIII	**14,395**	**1,881**	**3,266**	**9,148**	**6,885**	**901**	**1,694**	**4,290**	**7,510**	**980**	**1,572**	**4,958**
	ORDER IX.—BUILDINGS.	22.—Building materials.	132. Brick and tile burners and sellers.	882	109	172	601	511	59	90	362	371	50	82	239
			133. Lime, chunam and shell burners and sellers.	493	48	125	320	249	23	62	164	244	25	63	156
			134. Stone-quarry owners, contractors, and marble dealers, etc.	15	4	4	7	9	3	1	5	6	1	3	2
			135. Thatch-dealers and thatchers	53	13	7	33	28	8	2	18	25	5	5	15
			Total Sub-order 22	1,443	174	308	961	797	90	158	549	646	84	150	412
		23.—Artificers in Building.	136. Building contractors	...	...	...	...	...	...	...	...	...	...	...	...
			137. Stone and marble workers	80	15	18	47	44	7	10	27	36	8	8	20
			138. Masons	2,592	400	600	1,592	1,268	208	216	844	1,324	192	384	748
			139. Builders and joiners	102	12	26	64	46	5	6	31	56	7	16	33
			140. Plasterers and house painters	75	9	21	45	38	6	10	22	37	3	11	23
			141. Mud-wall and roof builders	348	26	59	163	254	17	35	102	94	9	24	61
			142. Plumbers and glaziers	...	...	...	...	...	...	...	...	...	...	...	...
			143. Tilers and tile-turners	...	...	...	...	...	...	...	...	...	...	...	...
			Total Sub-order 23	3,094	462	721	1,911	1,649	243	280	1,026	1,445	219	2	[illegible]
			Total Order IX	**4,537**	**636**	**1,029**	**2,872**	**2,446**	**333**	**388**	**1,575**	**2,091**	**303**	**491**	**1,297**

Part A.—PROVINCIAL SUMMARY—*contd.*

COUNTRY.															
TOTAL.				MALES.				FEMALES.				OCCUPATION.	Sub-order and Group.	Order.	Class.
Total.	0—4	5—14	15—	Total.	0—4	5—14	15—	Total.	0—4	5—14	15—				
29	30	31	32	33	34	35	36	37	38	39	40				
4,868	600	1,035	3,233	2,990	332	593	2,065	1,878	268	442	1,168	83. Grain dealers	18.—VEGETABLE FOOD	ORDER VII.—FOOD AND DRINK—contd.	CLASS D.—PREPARATION AND SUPPLY OF MATERIAL SUBSTANCES—contd.
1,958	241	424	1,293	783	116	185	482	1,175	125	239	811	84. Grain parchers			
722	76	136	510	417	35	72	310	305	41	64	200	85. Pulse and flour preparers and sellers.			
...	...	...	...	...	...	...	...	...	...	...	...	86. Flour-mill service and management.			
18	...	3	15	8	...	...	8	10	...	3	7	87. Bakers			
...	...	...	...	...	...	...	...	...	...	...	...	88. Bran sellers			
1,194	143	202	849	520	72	106	342	674	71	96	507	89. Vegetable sellers			
591	64	140	387	369	35	91	243	222	29	49	144	90. Fruit and sugarcane sellers			
17	3	3	11	3	...	...	3	14	3	3	8	91. Cocoanut dealers			
24	2	4	18	20	2	3	15	4	...	1	3	91a. Cotton-seed dealers			
1,148	107	200	841	726	41	107	578	422	66	93	263	92. Confectioners and sweetmeat makers and sellers.			
17	...	2	15	16	...	1	15	1	...	1	...	93. Sweetmeat pedlars			
10,557	1,236	2,149	7,172	5,852	632	1,158	4,061	4,705	603	991	3,111	TOTAL SUB-ORDER 18			
...	...	...	...	...	...	...	...	...	...	...	...	94. Ice manufacturers and sellers	19.—DRINK CONDIMENTS AND NARCOTICS.		
2	...	...	2	...	...	...	...	2	...	...	2	94a. Water sellers			
3	...	1	2	3	...	1	2	...	...	...	...	95. Soda-water, lemonade, etc. manufacturers and sellers.			
...	...	...	...	...	...	...	...	...	...	...	...	96. Sharbat preparers and sellers			
5,577	690	1,113	3,774	3,389	332	596	2,461	2,188	358	517	1,313	97. Country spirits distillers and sellers.			
684	115	143	426	488	63	78	347	196	52	65	79	98. Toddy drawers and sellers			
9	1	1	7	5	1	1	3	4	...	...	4	99. Foreign wine and spirit dealers.			
...	...	...	...	...	...	...	...	...	...	...	...	100. Brewers			
...	...	...	...	...	...	...	...	...	...	...	...	101. Tea sellers and tasters (not planters.)			
...	...	...	...	...	...	...	...	...	...	...	...	102. Coffee preparers and sellers (not planters.)			
...	...	...	...	...	...	...	...	...	...	...	...	103. Sugar manufacturers and sellers.			
1,040	140	234	666	580	70	122	388	460	70	112	278	104. Molasses (jaggery, gur, etc.) makers and sellers.			
437	43	104	290	202	13	48	141	235	30	56	149	105. Salt preparers and sellers			
198	25	42	131	108	9	21	78	90	16	21	53	106. Assafœtida, turmeric, etc., sellers.			
...	...	...	...	...	...	...	...	...	...	...	...	107. Vinegar manufacturers and sellers.			
19	2	6	11	...	...	...	...	19	2	6	11	108. Pickle makers and sellers			
14,819	1,787	3,044	9,988	8,784	893	1,714	6,177	6,035	894	1,330	3,811	109. Grocers and general condiment dealers.			
...	...	...	...	...	...	...	...	...	...	...	...	110. Cardamom preparers and dealers.			
4,339	460	819	3,060	1,610	202	363	1,045	2,729	258	456	2,015	111. Betel-leaf and areca-nut sellers			
1,521	196	299	1,026	921	84	170	667	600	112	129	359	112. Tobacco and snuff manufacturers and sellers.			
3	...	...	3	3	...	...	3	...	...	...	...	113. Prepared hukka pedlars			
690	74	124	492	477	41	80	356	213	33	44	136	114. Opium, etc., manufacturers and sellers.			
23	5	7	11	1	...	...	1	22	5	7	10	115. Bhang, ganja, etc., preparers and sellers.			
29,364	3,538	5,937	19,889	16,571	1,708	3,194	11,669	12,793	1,830	2,743	8,220	TOTAL SUB-ORDER 19			
58,251	7,987	12,805	37,509	32,869	3,873	6,946	22,050	25,382	4,064	5,859	15,459	**Total Order VII**			
11,452	1,545	2,619	7,288	5,924	742	1,309	3,873	5,528	803	1,310	3,415	116. Oil pressers and sellers	20.—LIGHTING	ORDER VIII.—LIGHT, FIRING AND FORAGE.	
15	1	4	10	...	...	...	...	15	1	4	10	117. Oil and salt sellers			
...	...	...	...	...	...	...	...	...	...	...	...	118. Oil-cake dealers			
...	...	...	...	...	...	...	...	...	...	...	...	119. Candle makers and sellers			
...	...	...	...	...	...	...	...	...	...	...	...	120. Torch makers and sellers			
93	13	22	58	60	10	13	37	33	3	9	21	121. Kerosine oil dealers			
61	4	8	49	55	3	5	47	6	1	3	2	122. Match makers and sellers			
1	...	...	1	1	...	...	1	...	...	...	...	123. Lamp and lantern makers and sellers.			
...	...	...	...	...	...	...	...	...	...	...	...	124. Gas workers, Gas Company Managers, etc.			
11,622	1,563	2,653	7,406	6,040	755	1,327	3,958	5,582	808	1,326	3,448	TOTAL SUB-ORDER 20			
14,072	1,826	3,588	8,658	5,796	814	1,567	3,415	8,276	1,012	2,021	5,243	125. Fire wood and grass gatherers and sellers.	21.—FUEL AND FORAGE		
1,977	280	500	1,197	884	120	225	539	1,093	160	275	658	126. Fire wood contractors and dealers.			
...	...	...	...	...	...	...	...	...	...	...	...	127. Coal miners, etc.			
1	...	...	1	1	...	...	1	...	...	...	...	128. Coal dealers, brokers, Coal Company Managers, etc.			
456	56	108	292	266	24	53	189	190	32	55	103	129. Charcoal burners and dealers			
700	61	176	463	225	26	70	129	475	35	106	334	130. Cowdung-fuel preparers and sellers.			
1,468	185	311	972	495	65	123	307	973	120	188	665	131. Hay, etc., contractors and dealers.			
18,674	2,408	4,683	11,583	7,667	1,049	2,038	4,580	11,007	1,359	2,645	7,003	TOTAL SUB-ORDER 21			
30,296	3,971	7,336	18,989	13,707	1,804	3,365	8,538	16,589	2,167	3,971	10,451	**Total Order VIII**			
4,827	290	603	3,834	3,660	192	336	3,132	1,167	198	267	702	132. Brick and tile burners and sellers.	22.—BUILDING MATERIALS.	ORDER IX.—BUILDINGS.	
405	48	99	258	249	25	63	161	156	23	36	97	133. Lime, chunam and shell burners and sellers.			
12	1	...	11	9	...	...	9	3	1	...	2	134. Stone-quarry owners, contractors, and marble dealers, etc.			
14	...	3	11	11	...	2	9	3	...	1	2	135. Thatch-dealers and thatchers.			
5,258	439	705	4,114	3,929	217	401	3,311	1,329	222	304	803	TOTAL SUB-ORDER 22			
4	...	...	4	3	...	...	3	1	...	...	1	136. Building contractors	23.—ARTIFICERS IN BUILDING.		
396	68	91	237	195	28	45	122	201	40	46	115	137. Stone and marble workers			
3,247	461	682	2,104	2,007	222	343	1,442	1,240	239	339	662	138. Masons			
162	12	36	114	104	3	21	80	58	9	15	34	139. Builders and joiners			
41	...	13	28	19	...	4	15	22	...	9	13	140. Plasterers and house painters			
4,456	696	1,028	2,732	2,750	333	580	1,837	1,706	363	448	895	141. Mud-wall and roof builders			
...	...	...	...	...	...	...	...	...	...	...	...	142. Plumbers and glaziers			
...	...	...	...	...	...	...	...	...	...	...	...	143. Tilers and tile-turners			
8,306	1,237	1,850	5,219	5,078	586	993	3,499	3,228	651	857	1,720	TOTAL SUB-ORDER 23			
13,564	1,676	2,555	9,333	9,007	803	1,394	6,810	4,557	873	1,161	2,523	**Total Order IX**			

TABLE XVII.—Occupations, by Age.—

Class.	Order.	Sub-order and Group.	Occupation.	Provincial: Total: Total.	Total: 0—4	Total: 5—14	Total: 15—	Males: Total.	Males: 0—4
1	2	3	4	5	6	7	8	9	10
CLASS D.—PREPARATION AND SUPPLY OF MATERIAL SUBSTANCES—contd.	ORDER X.—VEHICLES AND VESSELS.	24.—Railway plant	144. Railway mechanics (fitters, painters, boiler-makers, rivetters, etc.)	108	17	19	72	61	12
			145. Railway permanent-way foremen, plate-layers, inspectors, etc.	30	5	3	22	18	4
			Total Sub-order 24	138	22	22	94	79	16
		25.—Carts, carriages, etc.	146. Cart makers, carriage makers and sellers	154	11	27	116	127	7
			147. Palki, dandi, rick-shaw, etc., makers and sellers.	...	...	...	...	...	...
			Total Sub-order 25	154	11	27	116	127	7
		26.—Ships and Boats	148. Shipwrights, boat-builders, etc.	...	...	...	...	...	...
			149. Boat and ship painters, tarrers, etc.	...	...	...	...	...	...
			150. Sail-makers	...	...	...	...	...	...
			151. Wicker-boat-makers, canoe diggers, etc.	...	...	...	...	...	...
			152. Ship chandlers and marine store dealers	...	...	...	...	...	...
			Total Sub-order 26	...	...	...	...	...	...
			Total Order X	**292**	**33**	**49**	**210**	**206**	**23**
	ORDER XI.—SUPPLEMENTARY REQUIREMENTS.	27.—Paper, etc.	153. Paper makers and sellers, and palm-leaf-binders.	111	22	32	57	55	12
			154. Stationers	125	14	29	82	71	7
			155. Waste paper and rag dealers	...	...	...	...	...	...
			156. Waxed cloth preparers and sellers	...	...	...	...	...	...
			Total Sub-order 27	236	36	61	139	126	19
		28.—Books and prints, etc.	157. Press proprietors, lithographers and printers.	56	1	9	46	40	...
			158. Book-binders	53	16	10	27	23	3
			159. Book-sellers and publishers	154	22	34	98	65	5
			160. Newspaper proprietors and managers	10	2	1	7	4	...
			161. News agents, book agents and newspaper sellers, etc.	...	...	...	...	...	...
			162. Print and picture dealers	41	4	8	29	29	2
			Total Sub-order 28	314	45	62	207	161	10
		29.—Watches, clocks and scientific instruments.	163. Watch and clock makers and sellers	32	4	8	20	17	2
			164. Opticians	...	...	...	...	...	...
			165. Surgical instrument makers and sellers	...	...	...	...	...	...
			166. Photographic apparatus dealers	...	...	...	...	...	...
			167. Other scientific instrument makers, menders and sellers.	...	...	...	...	...	...
			168. Scale makers and sellers	1	...	...	1	1	...
			Total Sub-order 29	33	4	8	21	18	2
		30.—Carving, engraving, etc.	169. Wood and ebony carvers	6	1	2	3	4	1
			170. Ivory carvers	...	...	...	...	...	...
			171. Cotton-stamp makers and sellers	...	...	...	...	...	...
			172. Turners and lacquerers	99	9	17	73	44	4
			173. Die-sinkers and seal, etc., engravers	...	...	...	...	...	...
			174. Type-founders	...	...	...	...	...	...
			175. Mica, flint and talc workers and sellers	3	1	...	2	3	1
			175a. Granitic stone workers	52	10	12	30	23	4
			176. Mosaic and alabaster workers and sellers	...	...	...	...	...	...
			Total Sub-order 30	160	21	31	108	74	10
		31.—Toys, curiosities, etc.	177. Toy, kite, and cage makers and sellers, bird stuffers.	379	63	78	238	164	27
			178. Hukka-stem makers and sellers	...	...	...	...	...	...
			179. Papier-maché workers and sellers	...	...	...	...	...	...
			180. Card makers and sellers	...	...	...	...	...	...
			181. Tabut and tazia makers and sellers	7	1	2	4	6	...
			182. Curiosity dealers	...	...	...	...	...	...
			Total Sub-order 31	386	64	80	242	170	27
		32.—Music and musical instruments.	183 Music and musical instrument dealers	27	2	1	24	20	1
			184. Conch dealers, drum and horn makers, etc.	11	1	2	8	7	1
			Total Sub-order 32	38	3	3	32	27	2

Part A.—PROVINCIAL SUMMARY—*contd.*

TOTAL.

Males. 5–14	Males. 15–	Females. Total.	Females. 0–4	Females. 5–14	Females. 15–	Occupation.	Sub-order and Group.	Order.	Class.
11	12	13	14	15	16				
11	38	47	5	8	34	144. Railway mechanics (fitters, painters, boiler-makers, rivetters, etc.)	24.—Railway plant	Order X.—Vehicles and Vessels.	Class D.—Preparation and Supply of Material Substances—*contd.*
2	12	12	1	1	10	145. Railway permanent-way foremen, plate-layers, inspectors, etc.			
13	50	59	6	9	44	Total Sub-order 24			
19	101	27	4	8	15	146. Cart makers, carriage makers and sellers	25.—Carts, carriages, etc.		
...	...	...	...	...	...	147. Palki, dandi, rick-shaw, etc., makers and sellers.			
19	101	27	4	8	15	Total Sub-order 25			
...	...	...	...	...	...	148. Shipwrights, boat-builders, etc.	26.—Ships and Boats		
...	...	...	...	...	...	149. Boat and ship painters, tarrers, etc.			
...	...	...	...	...	...	150. Sail-makers			
...	...	...	...	...	...	151. Wicker-boat-makers, canoe diggers, etc.			
...	...	...	...	...	...	152. Ship chandlers and marine store dealers			
...	...	...	...	...	...	Total Sub-order 26			
32	**151**	**86**	**10**	**17**	**59**	**Total Order X**			
14	29	56	10	18	28	153. Paper makers and sellers, and palm-leaf-binders.	27.—Paper, etc.	XI.—Supplementary Requirements.	
11	53	54	7	18	29	154. Stationers			
...	...	...	...	...	...	155. Waste paper and rag dealers			
...	...	...	...	...	...	156. Waxed cloth preparers and sellers			
25	82	110	17	36	57	Total Sub-order 27			
5	35	16	1	4	11	157. Press proprietors, lithographers and printers.	28.—Books and Prints, etc.		
3	17	30	13	7	10	158. Book-binders			
11	49	89	17	23	49	159. Book-sellers and publishers			
1	3	6	2	...	4	160. Newspaper proprietors and managers			
...	...	...	...	...	...	161. News agents, book agents and newspaper sellers, etc.			
5	22	12	2	3	7	162. Print and picture dealers			
25	126	153	35	37	81	Total Sub-order 28			
4	11	15	2	4	9	163. Watch and clock makers and sellers	29.—Watches, clocks and scientific instruments.		
...	...	...	...	...	...	164. Opticians			
...	...	...	...	...	...	165. Surgical instrument makers and sellers			
...	...	...	...	...	...	166. Photographic apparatus dealers			
...	...	...	...	...	...	167. Other scientific instrument makers, menders and sellers.			
...	1	...	...	...	...	168. Scale makers and sellers			
4	12	15	2	4	9	Total Sub-order 29			
1	2	2	...	1	1	169. Wood and ebony carvers	30.—Carving, engraving, etc.		
...	...	...	...	...	...	170. Ivory carvers			
...	...	...	...	...	...	171. Cotton-stamp makers and sellers			
10	30	55	5	7	43	172. Turners and lacquerers			
...	...	...	...	...	...	173. Die-sinkers and seal, etc., engravers			
...	...	...	...	...	...	174. Type-founders			
...	2	...	...	...	...	175. Mica, flint and talc workers and sellers			
4	15	29	6	8	15	175a. Granitic stone workers			
...	...	...	...	...	...	176. Mosaic and alabaster workers and sellers			
15	49	86	11	16	59	Total Sub-order 30			
35	102	215	36	43	136	177. Toy, kite and cage makers and sellers, bird stuffers.	31.—Toys, Curiosities, etc.		
...	...	...	...	...	...	178. Hukka-stem makers and sellers			
...	...	...	...	...	...	179. Papier-maché workers and sellers			
...	...	...	...	...	...	180. Card makers and sellers			
2	4	1	1	...	...	181. Tabut and tazia makers and sellers			
...	...	...	...	...	...	182. Curiosity dealers			
37	106	216	37	43	136	Total Sub-order 31			
1	18	7	1	...	6	183. Music and musical instrument dealers	32.—Music and Musical instruments.		
1	5	4	...	1	3	184. Couch dealers, drum and horn makers, etc.			
2	23	11	1	1	9	Total Sub-order 32			

TABLE XVII.—Occupations, by Age.—

Class.	Order.	Sub-order and Group.	Occupation.	Town. Total. Total.	Total. 0—4	Total. 5—14	Total. 15—	Males. Total.	Males. 0—4	Males. 5—14	Males. 15—	Females. Total.	Females. 0—4	Females. 5—14	Females. 15—
				17	18	19	20	21	22	23	24	25	26	27	28
CLASS D.—PREPARATION AND SUPPLY OF MATERIAL SUBSTANCES—contd.	ORDER X.—VEHICLES AND VESSELS.	24.—Railway plant	144. Railway mechanics (fitters, painters, boiler-makers, rivetters, etc.)	102	17	18	67	58	12	11	35	44	5	7	32
			145. Railway permanent-way foremen, plate-layers, inspectors, etc.	30	5	3	22	18	4	2	12	12	1	1	10
			Total Sub-order 24	132	22	21	89	76	16	13	47	56	6	8	42
		25.—Carts, carriages, etc.	146. Cart makers, carriage makers and sellers.	18	2	3	13	15	2	3	10	3	...	...	3
			147. Palki, dandi, rick-shaw, etc., makers and sellers.	...	...	...	...	...	...	...	...	...	...	...	...
			Total Sub-order 25	18	2	3	13	15	2	3	10	3	...	...	3
		26.—Ships and boats.	148. Shipwrights, boat-builders, etc.	...	...	...	...	...	...	...	...	...	...	...	...
			149. Boat and ship painters, tarters, etc.	...	...	...	...	...	...	...	...	...	...	...	...
			150. Sail makers	...	...	...	...	...	...	...	...	...	...	...	...
			151. Wicker-boat-makers, canoe diggers, etc.	...	...	...	...	...	...	...	...	...	...	...	...
			152. Ship chandlers and marine store dealers.	...	...	...	...	...	...	...	...	...	...	...	...
			Total Sub-order 26	...	...	...	...	...	...	...	...	...	...	...	...
			Total Order X	**150**	**24**	**24**	**102**		**18**		**57**	**59**	**6**	**8**	**45**
	ORDER XI.—SUPPLEMENTARY REQUIREMENTS.	27.—Paper, etc.	153. Paper makers and sellers and palm-leaf-binders.	107	21	31	55	53	12	13	28	54	9	18	27
			154. Stationers	98	12	22	64	56	6	9	41	42	6	13	23
			155. Waste paper and rag dealers	...	...	...	...	...	...	...	...	...	...	...	...
			156. Waxed cloth preparers and sellers.	...	...	...	...	...	...	...	...	...	...	...	...
			Total Sub-order 27	205	33	53	119	109	18	22	69	96	15	31	50
		28.—Books and prints, etc.	157. Press proprietors, lithographers and printers.	52	1	9	42	37	...	5	32	15	1	4	10
			158. Book-binders	53	16	10	27	23	3	3	17	30	13	7	10
			159. Book-sellers and publishers	59	12	11	36	18	3	3	12	41	9	8	24
			160. Newspaper proprietors and managers.	10	2	1	7	4	...	1	3	6	2	...	4
			161. News agents, book agents and newspaper sellers, etc.	...	...	...	...	...	...	...	...	...	...	...	...
			162. Print and picture dealers	16	1	6	9	10	...	5	5	6	1	1	4
			Total Sub-order 28	190	32	27	131	92	6	17	69	98	26	20	52
		29.—Watches, clocks and scientific instruments.	163. Watch and clock makers and sellers.	32	4	8	20	17	2	4	11	15	2	4	9
			164. Opticians	...	...	...	...	...	...	...	...	...	...	...	...
			165. Surgical instrument makers and sellers.	...	...	...	...	...	...	...	...	...	...	...	...
			166. Photographic apparatus dealers	...	...	...	...	...	...	...	...	...	...	...	...
			167. Other scientific instrument makers, menders and sellers.	...	...	...	...	...	...	...	...	...	...	...	...
			168. Scale makers and sellers	...	...	...	...	...	...	...	...	...	...	...	...
			Total Sub-order 29	32	4	8	20	17	2	4	11	15	2	4	9
		30.—Carving, engraving, etc.	169. Wood and ebony carvers	...	...	...	...	...	...	...	...	...	...	...	...
			170. Ivory carvers	...	...	...	...	...	...	...	...	...	...	...	...
			171. Cotton-stamp makers and sellers.	...	...	...	...	...	...	...	...	...	...	...	...
			172. Turners and lacquerers	24	2	5	17	16	2	2	12	8	...	3	5
			173. Die-sinkers and seal, etc., engravers.	...	...	...	...	...	...	...	...	...	...	...	...
			174. Type-founders	...	...	...	...	...	...	...	...	...	...	...	...
			175. Mica, flint and talc workers and sellers.	2	1	...	1	2	1	...	1	...	...	...	...
			175a. Granitic stone workers	...	...	...	...	...	...	...	...	...	...	...	...
			176. Mosaic and alabaster workers and sellers.	...	...	...	...	...	...	...	...	...	...	...	...
			Total Sub-order 30	26	3	5	18	18	3	2	13	8	...	3	5
		31.—Toys, curiosities, etc.	177. Toy, kite and cage makers and sellers, bird stuffers.	223	46	48	129	87	16	26	45	136	30	22	84
			178. Hukka-stem makers and sellers	...	...	...	...	...	...	...	...	...	...	...	...
			179. Papier-maché workers and sellers.	...	...	...	...	...	...	...	...	...	...	...	...
			180. Card makers and sellers	...	...	...	...	...	...	...	...	...	...	...	...
			181. Tabut and tazia makers and sellers.	6	1	2	3	5	...	2	3	1	1	...	...
			182. Curiosity dealers	...	...	...	...	...	...	...	...	...	...	...	...
			Total Sub-order 31	229	47	50	132	92	16	28	48	137	31	22	84
		32.—Music and musical instruments.	183. Music and musical instrument dealers.	18	1	1	16	14	1	1	12	4	...	...	4
			184. Conch dealers, drum and horn makers, etc.	2	...	...	2	1	...	...	1	1	...	...	1
			Total Sub-order 32	20	1	1	18	15	1	1	13	5	...	...	5

Part A.—PROVINCIAL SUMMARY—*contd.*

COUNTRY.															
TOTAL.				MALES.				FEMALES.				OCCUPATION.	Sub-order and Group.	Order.	Class.
TOTAL.	0–4	5–14	15–	TOTAL.	0–4	5–14	15–	TOTAL.	0–4	5–14	15–				
29	30	31	32	33	34	35	36	37	38	39	40				
6	...	1	5	3	...	...	3	3	...	1	2	144. Railway mechanics (fitters, painters, boiler-makers, rivetters, etc.)	24.—RAILWAY PLANT	ORDER X.—VEHICLES AND VESSELS.	
...	...	...	...	...	...	...	...	...	...	...	...	145. Railway permanent-way foremen, plate-layers, inspectors, etc.			
6	...	1	5	3	...	...	3	3	...	1	2	TOTAL SUB-ORDER 24			
136	9	24	103	112	5	16	91	24	4	8	12	146. Cart makers, carriage makers and sellers.	25.—CARTS, CARRIAGES, ETC.		
...	...	...	...	...	...	...	...	...	...	...	...	147. Palki, dandi, rick-shaw, etc., makers and sellers.			
136	9	24	103	112	5	16	91	24	4	8	12	TOTAL SUB-ORDER 25			
...	...	...	...	...	...	...	...	...	...	...	...	148. Shipwrights, boat-builders, etc.	26.—SHIPS AND BOATS		
...	...	...	...	...	...	...	...	...	...	...	...	149. Boat and ship painters, tarrers, etc.			
...	...	...	...	...	...	...	...	...	...	...	...	150. Sail-makers			
...	...	...	...	...	...	...	...	...	...	...	...	151. Wicker-boat-makers, canoe diggers, etc.			
...	...	...	...	...	...	...	...	...	...	...	...	152. Ship chandlers and marine store dealers.			
...	...	...	...	...	...	...	...	...	...	...	...	TOTAL SUB-ORDER 26			
142	**9**	**25**	**108**	**115**	**5**	**16**	**94**	**27**	**4**	**9**	**14**	**Total Order X**			
4	1	1	2	2	...	1	1	2	1	...	1	153. Paper makers and sellers, and palm-leaf-binders.	27.—PAPER, ETC.	ORDER XI.—SUPPLEMENTARY REQUIREMENTS.	CLASS D.—PREPARATION AND SUPPLY OF MATERIAL SUBSTANCES—*contd.*
27	2	7	18	15	1	2	12	12	1	5	6	154. Stationers			
...	...	...	...	...	...	...	...	...	...	...	...	155. Waste paper and rag dealers			
...	...	...	...	...	...	...	...	...	...	...	...	156. Waxed cloth preparers and sellers.			
31	3	8	20	17	1	3	13	14	2	5	7	TOTAL SUB-ORDER 27			
4	...	...	4	3	...	...	3	1	...	...	1	157. Press proprietors, lithographers, and printers.	28.—BOOKS AND PRINTS, ETC.		
...	...	...	...	...	...	...	...	...	...	...	...	158. Book-binders			
95	10	23	62	47	2	8	37	48	8	15	25	159. Book-sellers and publishers			
...	...	...	...	...	...	...	...	...	...	...	...	160. Newspaper proprietors and managers.			
...	...	...	...	...	...	...	...	...	...	...	...	161. News agents, book agents and newspaper sellers, etc.			
25	3	2	20	19	2	...	17	6	1	2	3	162. Print and picture dealers			
124	13	25	86	69	4	8	57	55	9	17	29	TOTAL SUB-ORDER 28			
...	...	...	...	...	...	...	...	...	...	...	...	163. Watch and clock makers and sellers.	29.—WATCHES, CLOCKS AND SCIENTIFIC INSTRUMENTS.		
...	...	...	...	...	...	...	...	...	...	...	...	164. Opticians			
...	...	...	...	...	...	...	...	...	...	...	...	165. Surgical instrument makers and sellers.			
...	...	...	...	...	...	...	...	...	...	...	...	166. Photographic apparatus dealers.			
...	...	...	...	...	...	...	...	...	...	...	...	167. Other scientific instrument makers, menders and sellers			
1	...	...	1	1	...	...	1	...	...	...	...	168. Scale makers and sellers			
1	...	...	1	1	...	...	1	...	...	...	...	TOTAL SUB-ORDER 29			
6	1	2	3	4	1	1	2	2	...	1	1	169. Wood and ebony carvers	30.—CARVING, ENGRAVING, ETC.		
...	...	...	...	...	...	...	...	...	...	...	...	170. Ivory carvers			
...	...	...	...	...	...	...	...	...	...	...	...	171. Cotton-stamp makers and sellers.			
75	7	12	56	28	2	8	18	47	5	4	38	172. Turners and lacquerers			
...	...	...	...	...	...	...	...	...	...	...	...	173. Die-sinkers and seal, etc., engravers.			
...	...	...	...	...	...	...	...	...	...	...	...	174. Type-founders			
1	...	...	1	1	...	...	1	...	...	...	...	175. Mica, flint and talc workers and sellers.			
52	10	12	30	23	4	4	15	29	6	8	15	175a. Granitic stone workers			
...	...	...	...	...	...	...	...	...	...	...	...	176. Mosaic and alabaster workers and sellers.			
134	18	26	90	56	7	13	36	78	11	13	54	TOTAL SUB-ODER 30			
156	17	30	109	77	11	9	57	79	6	21	52	177. Toy, kite and cage makers and sellers, bird stuffers.	31.—TOYS, CURIOSITIES, ETC.		
...	...	...	...	...	...	...	...	...	...	...	...	178. Hukka-stem makers and sellers.			
...	...	...	...	...	...	...	...	...	...	...	...	179. Papier-maché workers and sellers.			
...	...	...	...	...	...	...	...	...	...	...	...	180. Card makers and sellers			
1	...	...	1	1	...	...	1	...	...	...	...	181. Tabut and tazia makers and sellers.			
...	...	...	...	...	...	...	...	...	...	...	...	182. Curiosity dealers			
157	17	30	110	78	11	9	58	79	6	21	52	TOTAL SUB-ORDER 31			
9	1	...	8	6	...	...	6	3	1	...	2	183. Music and musical instrument dealers.	32.—MUSIC AND MUSICAL INSTRUMENTS.		
9	1	2	6	6	1	1	4	3	...	1	2	184. Conch dealers, drum and horn makers, etc.			
18	2	2	14	12	1	1	10	6	1	1	4	TOTAL SUB-ORDER 32			

TABLE XVII.—Occupations, by Age.—

Class.	Order.	Sub-order and Group.	Occupation.	PROVINCIAL — Total. — Total.	Total. — 0—4	Total. — 5—14	Total. — 15—	Males. — Total.	Males. — 0—4
1	2	3	4	5	6	7	8	9	10
CLASS D.—PREPARATION AND SUPPLY OF MATERIAL SUBSTANCES—*contd.*	ORDER XI.—SUPPLEMENTARY REQUIREMENTS—*continued.*	33.—Necklaces, bracelets, beads, sacred threads, etc.	185. Bangle makers and sellers in lac	674	78	136	460	366	30
			186. Bangle makers and sellers in stone	...	...	...	...	...	...
			187. Bangle makers and sellers in wood and bone	22	...	4	18	11	...
			188. Bangle makers and sellers in clay	...	...	...	...	...	...
			189. Bangle makers and sellers in glass	586	71	112	403	326	30
			189a. Bangle makers and sellers unspecified	4,771	618	1,065	3,088	2,586	308
			190. Bangle fitters	305	55	73	177	118	18
			191. Imitation and pewter jewelry makers and sellers.	498	64	101	333	289	38
			192. Bead makers and sellers	26	4	6	16	21	3
			193. Rosary and necklace makers and sellers	8	2	2	4	...	...
			194. Flower garland makers and sellers	464	61	89	314	230	38
			195. Artificial flower and caste-mark spangle makers and sellers.	5	1	2	2	5	1
			196. Sacred-thread makers and sellers	24	2	8	14	11	2
			Total Sub-order 33	7,383	956	1,598	4,829	3,963	468
		34.—Furniture	197. Upholsterers	...	...	...	...	...	...
			198. Furniture makers	19	3	4	12	18	3
			199. Frame makers	5	1	1	3	3	...
			200. Looking-glass makers and sellers	...	...	...	...	...	...
			Total Sub-order 34	24	4	5	15	21	3
		35.—Harness	201. Saddlery and harness makers and sellers	430	54	99	277	243	29
			202. Saddle-cloth makers, embroiderers and sellers.	50	10	13	27	22	4
			203. Whip, goad, etc., makers	4	...	1	3	2	...
			Total Sub-order 35	484	64	113	307	267	33
		36.—Tools and machinery.	204. Knife and tool makers and sellers	66	7	17	42	38	1
			204a. Agricultural implement makers, etc.	183	19	53	111	120	8
			205. Knife and tool grinders	470	74	112	284	265	49
			206. Looms and loom-comb makers and sellers	19	...	5	14	12	...
			207. Mechanics (not railway)	137	14	17	106	79	8
			208. Machinery dealers, etc.	...	...	...	...	...	...
			Total Sub-order 36	875	114	204	557	514	66
		37.—Arms and ammunition.	209. Gun makers, menders and sellers	42	6	16	20	19	2
			210. Ammanition and cap dealers	7	1	1	5	1	...
			211. Gunpowder-makers and sellers	136	20	31	85	63	11
			212. Firework makers and sellers	42	7	5	30	25	2
			213. Sword and scabbard makers and sellers	20	3	4	13	11	1
			214. Spear-head, shield, etc., makers and sellers.	...	...	...	...	...	...
			215. Bow and arrow makers and sellers	...	...	...	...	...	...
			216. Cudgel (lathi) makers and sellers	3	2	...	1	1	1
			Total Sub-order 37	250	39	57	154	120	17
			Total Order XI	**10,183**	**1,350**	**2,222**	**6,611**	**5,461**	**657**
	ORDER XII.—TEXTILE FABRICS AND DRESS.	38.—Wool and Fur	217. Carpet weavers and sellers	...	...	...	...	...	...
			218. Shawl ditto	2	...	...	2	2	...
			219. Felt and pashm workers and sellers	...	...	...	...	...	...
			220. Blanket weavers and sellers	4,827	803	1,153	2,871	2,796	403
			221. Woollen cloth manufacturers and dealers	65	8	15	42	29	3
			222. Do. yarn spinners and sellers	272	16	40	216	25	2
			223. Wool carders	9	1	2	6	3	...
			224. Do. dyers	...	...	...	...	...	...
			225. Fur dealers	112	16	28	68	50	8
			Total Sub-order 38	5,287	844	1,238	3,205	2,905	426
		39.—Silk	226. Silkworm rearers and cocoon gatherers	...	...	...	...	...	...
			227. Silk carders and spinners	1,387	133	273	981	625	60
			228. Silk weavers and dealers	481	55	104	321	309	30
			229. Silk printers and dyers	10	2	1	7	4	1
			230. Braid and ribbon makers and sellers	13	...	3	10	6	...
			Total Sub-order 39	1,891	191	381	1,319	944	91
		40.—Cotton	231. Cotton cleaners, pressers and ginners	14,103	1,362	2,513	10,228	3,911	554
			231a. Raw cotton dealers	7,731	1,014	1,639	5,078	4,496	503
			232. Cotton carpet and rug makers and sellers	1,900	275	433	1,192	1,097	132
			233. Cotton spinners, sizers and yarn beaters	8,342	562	1,245	6,535	986	151
			234. Do. weavers, mill-owners and managers	27,212	3,996	6,200	17,016	15,473	1,981
			234a. Do. factory engineers	207	32	32	143	121	16
			235. Do. factory hands (undefined)	4,883	512	923	3,448	2,983	262
			236. Calenderers, fullers and printers	7	...	1	6	5	...
			237. Cotton dyers	7,424	978	1,675	4,771	3,865	455
			238. Tape-makers and sellers	96	8	30	58	60	4
			239. Tent manufacturers and sellers	...	...	...	...	...	...
			Total Sub-order 40	71,905	8,739	14,691	48,475	32,997	4,059

Part A.—PROVINCIAL SUMMARY—*contd.*

TOTAL. Males. 5–14	Males. 15–	Females. Total.	Females. 0–4	Females. 5–14	Females. 15–	Occupation.	Sub-order and Group.	Order.	Class.
11	12	13	14	15	16				
75	261	308	48	61	199	185. Bangle makers and sellers in lac	33.—Necklaces, bracelets, beads, sacred threads, etc.	ORDER XI.—SUPPLEMENTARY REQUIREMENTS—*contd.*	CLASS D.—PREPARATION AND SUPPLY OF MATERIAL SUBSTANCES—*contd.*
...	...	...	...	...	...	186. Bangle makers and sellers in stone			
2	9	11	...	2	9	187. Bangle makers and sellers in wood and bone			
...	...	...	...	...	...	188. Bangle makers and sellers in clay			
62	234	260	41	50	169	189. Bangle makers and sellers in glass			
553	1,725	2,185	310	512	1,363	189*a*. Bangle makers and sellers unspecified			
33	67	187	37	40	110	190 Bangle fitters			
56	195	209	26	45	138	191. Imitation and pewter jewelry makers and sellers.			
6	12	5	1	...	4	192. Bead makers and sellers			
...	...	8	2	2	4	193. Rosary and necklace makers and sellers			
30	153	234	23	50	161	194. Flower garland makers and sellers			
2	2	...	...	...	...	195. Artificial flower and caste-mark spangle makers and sellers.			
3	6	13	...	5	8	196. Sacred thread makers and sellers			
831	2,664	3,420	488	767	2,165	TOTAL SUB-ORDER 33			
...	...	...	...	...	...	197. Upholsterers	34.—Furniture		
4	11	1	...	...	1	198. Furniture makers			
1	2	2	1	...	1	199. Frame makers			
...	...	...	...	...	...	200. Looking-glass makers and sellers			
5	13	3	1	...	2	TOTAL SUB-ORDER 34			
53	161	187	25	46	116	201. Saddlery and harness makers and sellers	35.—Harness		
6	12	28	6	7	15	202. Saddle-cloth makers, embroiderers and sellers.			
...	2	2	...	1	1	203. Whip, goad, etc., makers			
59	175	217	31	54	132	TOTAL SUB-ORDER 35			
11	26	28	6	6	16	204. Knife and tool makers and sellers	36.—Tools and machinery.		
35	77	63	11	18	34	204*a*. Agricultural implement makers, etc.			
63	153	205	25	49	131	205. Knife and tool grinders			
2	10	7	...	3	4	206. Looms and loom-comb makers and sellers			
9	62	58	6	8	44	207. Mechanics (not railway)			
...	...	...	...	...	...	208. Machinery dealers, etc.			
120	328	361	48	84	229	TOTAL SUB-ORDER 36			
7	10	23	4	9	10	209. Gun makers, menders and sellers	37.—Arms and ammunition.		
...	1	6	1	1	4	210. Ammunition and cap dealers			
12	40	73	9	19	45	211. Gunpowder makers and sellers			
4	19	17	5	1	11	212. Firework makers and sellers			
...	10	9	2	4	3	213. Sword and scabbard makers and sellers			
...	...	...	...	...	...	214. Spear-head, shield, etc., makers and sellers			
...	...	...	...	...	...	215. Bow and arrow makers and sellers			
...	...	2	1	...	1	216. Cudgel (lathi) makers and sellers			
23	80	130	22	34	74	TOTAL SUB-ORDER 37			
1,146	3,658	4,722	693	1,076	2,953	**Total Order XI**			
...	...	...	...	...	...	217. Carpet weavers and sellers	38.—Wool and Fur	ORDER XII.—TEXTILE FABRICS AND DRESS.	
...	2	...	...	...	...	218. Shawl ditto			
...	...	...	...	...	...	219. Felt and pashm workers and sellers			
620	1,773	2,031	400	533	1,098	220. Blanket weavers and sellers			
5	21	36	5	10	21	221. Woollen cloth manufacturers and dealers			
8	15	247	14	32	201	222. Do. yarn spinners and sellers			
...	3	6	1	2	3	223. Wool carders			
...	...	...	...	...	...	224. Do. dyers			
12	30	62	8	16	38	225. Fur dealers			
645	1,844	2,382	428	593	1,361	TOTAL SUB-ORDER 38			
...	...	...	...	...	...	226. Silkworm rearers and cocoon gatherers	39.—Silk		
144	421	762	73	129	560	227. Silk carders and spinners			
60	219	172	26	44	102	228. Silk weavers and dealers			
...	3	6	1	1	4	229. Silk printers and dyers			
...	6	7	...	3	4	230. Braid and ribbon makers and sellers			
204	649	947	100	177	670	TOTAL SUB-ORDER 39			
912	2,445	10,192	808	1,601	7,783	231. Cotton cleaners, pressers and ginners	40.—Cotton		
891	3,102	3,235	511	748	1,976	231*a*. Raw cotton dealers			
228	737	803	143	205	455	232. Cotton carpet and rug makers and sellers			
279	555	7,356	410	966	5,980	233. Cotton spinners, sizers and yarn beaters			
3,379	10,113	11,739	2,015	2,821	6,903	234. Do. weavers, mill-owners and managers			
16	89	86	16	16	54	234*a*. Do. factory engineers			
527	2,194	1,900	250	395	1,254	235. Do. factory hands (undefined)			
...	5	2	...	1	1	236. Calenderers, fullers and printers			
850	2,560	3,559	523	825	2,211	237. Cotton dyers			
22	34	36	4	8	24	238. Tape makers and sellers			
...	...	...	...	...	...	239. Tent manufacturers and sellers			
7,104	21,834	38,908	4,680	7,587	26,641	TOTAL SUB-ORDER 40			

TABLE XVII.—Occupations, by Age.—

Class.	Order.	Sub-order and Group.	Occupation.	Town. Total. Total.	Town. Total. 0—4	Town. Total. 5—14	Town. Total. 15—	Town. Males. Total.	Town. Males. 0—4	Town. Males. 5—14	Town. Males. 15—	Town. Females. Total.	Town. Females. 0—4	Town. Females. 5—14	Town. Females. 15—
				17	18	19	20	21	22	23	24	25	26	27	28
CLASS D—PREPARATION AND SUPPLY OF MATERIAL SUBSTANCES—contd.	ORDER XI.—SUPPLEMENTARY REQUIREMENTS—contd.	33.—Necklaces, bracelets, beads, sacred threads, etc.	185. Bangle makers and sellers in lac.	401	48	86	267	208	17	49	142	193	31	37	115
			186. Bangle makers and sellers in stone.	...	...	...	...	...	...	...	...	...	...	...	...
			187. Bangle makers and sellers in wood and bone.	1	...	...	1	1	...	...	1	...	...	...	...
			188. Bangle makers and sellers in clay.	...	...	...	...	...	...	...	...	...	...	...	...
			189. Bangle makers and sellers in glass.	33	6	2	25	25	4	1	20	8	2	1	5
			189a. Bangle makers and sellers unspecified.	1,074	141	275	658	498	69	136	293	576	72	139	365
			190. Bangle fitters	65	12	17	36	11	1	7	3	54	11	10	33
			191. Imitation and pewter jewelry makers and sellers.	106	13	31	62	61	10	19	32	45	3	12	30
			192. Bead makers and sellers	19	3	6	10	17	3	6	8	2	...	...	2
			103. Rosary and necklace makers and sellers.	...	...	...	...	...	...	...	...	...	...	...	...
			194. Flower garland makers and sellers.	266	41	50	175	134	26	23	85	132	15	27	90
			195. Artificial flower and caste-mark spangle makers and sellers.	...	...	...	...	...	...	...	...	...	...	...	...
			196. Sacred thread makers and sellers.	13	1	4	8	7	1	3	3	6	...	1	5
			Total Sub-order 33	1,978	265	471	1,242	962	131	244	587	1,016	134	227	655
		34.—Furniture	197. Upholsterers	...	...	...	...	...	...	...	...	...	...	...	...
			198. Furniture makers	15	3	3	9	14	3	3	8	1	...	...	1
			199. Frame makers	5	1	1	3	3	...	1	2	2	1	...	1
			200. Looking-glass makers and sellers.	...	...	...	...	...	...	...	...	...	...	...	...
			Total Sub-order 34	20	4	4	12	17	3	4	10	3	1	...	2
		35.—Harness	201. Saddlery and harness makers and sellers.	229	32	56	141	120	14	27	79	109	18	29	62
			202. Saddle-cloth makers, embroiderers and sellers.	26	6	8	12	11	3	3	5	15	3	5	7
			203. Whip, goad, etc., makers	4	...	1	3	2	...	...	2	2	...	1	1
			Total Sub-order 35	259	38	65	156	133	17	30	86	126	21	35	70
		36.—Tools and Machinery.	204. Knife and tool makers and sellers.	22	3	5	14	10	...	4	6	12	3	1	8
			204a. Agricultural implements makers, etc.	24	2	7	15	16	1	4	11	8	1	3	4
			205. Knife and tool grinders	156	24	40	92	73	12	19	42	83	12	21	50
			206. Looms and loom-comb makers and sellers.	14	...	4	10	8	...	1	7	6	...	3	3
			207. Mechanics (not railway)	98	9	11	78	64	7	7	50	34	2	4	28
			208. Machinery dealers, etc.	...	...	...	...	...	...	...	...	...	...	...	...
			Total Sub-order 36	314	38	67	209	171	20	35	116	143	18	32	93
		37.—Arms and Ammunition.	209. Gun makers, menders and sellers.	26	4	11	11	9	...	5	4	17	4	6	7
			210. Ammunition and cap dealers	1	...	...	1	1	...	...	1	...	...	...	...
			211. Gunpowder makers and sellers.	80	13	14	53	40	7	5	28	40	6	9	25
			212. Firework makers and sellers	32	4	3	25	20	2	2	16	12	2	1	9
			213. Sword and scabbard makers and sellers.	10	...	3	7	5	...	...	5	5	...	3	2
			214. Spear-head, shield, etc., makers and sellers.	...	...	...	...	...	...	...	...	...	...	...	...
			215. Bow and arrow makers and sellers.	...	...	...	...	...	...	...	...	...	...	...	...
			216. Cudgel (lathi) makers and sellers.	...	...	...	...	...	...	...	...	...	...	...	...
			Total Sub-order 37	149	21	31	97	75	9	12	54	74	12	19	43
			Total Order XI	**3,422**	**486**	**792**	**2,144**	**1,701**	**226**	**399**	**1,076**	**1,721**	**260**	**393**	**1,068**
	ORDER XII.—TEXTILE FABRICS AND DRESS.	38.—Wool and Fur.	217. Carpet weavers and sellers	...	...	...	...	...	...	...	...	...	...	...	...
			218. Shawl ditto	1	...	...	1	1	...	...	1	...	...	...	...
			219. Felt and pashm workers and sellers.	...	...	...	...	...	...	...	...	...	...	...	...
			220. Blanket weavers and sellers	420	72	87	261	210	25	49	136	210	47	38	125
			221. Woollen cloth manufacturers and dealers.	5	...	...	5	5	...	...	5	...	...	...	...
			222. Woolen yarn spinners and sellers.	10	...	3	7	5	...	2	3	5	...	1	4
			223. Wool carders	...	...	...	...	...	...	...	...	...	...	...	...
			224. Wool dyers	...	...	...	...	...	...	...	...	...	...	...	...
			225. Fur dealers	3	...	...	3	1	...	...	1	2	...	...	2
			Total Sub-order 38	439	72	90	277	222	25	51	146	217	47	39	131
		39.—Silk	226. Silk worm rearers and cocoon gatherers.	...	...	...	...	...	...	...	...	...	...	...	...
			227. Silk carders and spinners	832	66	144	622	349	32	74	243	483	34	70	379
			228. Silk weavers and dealers	413	47	91	275	277	37	55	195	136	20	36	80
			229. Silk printers and dyers	9	2	1	6	3	1	...	2	6	1	1	4
			230. Braid and ribbon makers and sellers.	8	...	2	6	4	...	...	4	4	...	2	2
			Total Sub-order 39	1,262	115	238	909	633	60	129	444	629	55	109	465
		40.—Cotton	231. Cotton cleaners, dressers and ginners.	4,901	444	824	3,633	1,215	177	287	751	3,686	267	537	2,882
			231a. Raw cotton dealers	2,841	377	625	1,839	1,604	217	345	1,042	1,237	160	280	797
			232. Cotton carpet and rug makers and sellers.	821	99	199	523	445	47	103	295	376	52	96	228
			233. Cotton spinners, sizers and yarn beaters.	2,041	146	358	1,537	220	20	77	123	1,821	126	281	1,414
			234. Cotton weavers, mill-owners and managers.	12,148	1,560	2,655	7,933	6,793	804	1,472	4,517	5,355	756	1,183	3,416
			234a. Cotton factory engineers	143	27	20	96	95	16	13	66	48	11	7	30
			235. Cotton factoryhands (undefined)	4,067	437	766	2,864	2,460	223	429	1,808	1,607	214	337	1,056
			236. Calenderers, fullers and printers	3	...	...	3	3	...	...	3	...	...	...	...
			237. Cotton dyers	2,966	384	656	1,926	1,465	192	304	969	1,501	192	352	957
			238. Tape makers and sellers	17	2	6	9	5	1	2	2	12	1	4	7
			239. Tent manufacturers and sellers	...	...	...	...	...	...	...	...	...	...	...	...
			Total Sub-order 40	29,948	3,476	6,109	20,363	14,305	1,697	3,032	9,576	15,643	1,779	3,077	10,787

Part A.—PROVINCIAL SUMMARY—*contd.*

COUNTRY.												Occupation.	Sub-order and Group.	Order.	Class.
Total.				Males.				Females.							
Total.	0—4	5—14	15—	Total.	0—4	5—14	15—	Total.	0—4	5—14	15—				
29	30	31	32	33	34	35	36	37	38	39	40				
273	30	50	193	158	13	26	119	115	17	24	74	185. Bangle makers and sellers in lac.	33.—Necklaces, bracelets, beads, sacred threads, etc.	Order XI.—Supplementary Requirements—contd.	Class D.—Preparation and Supply of Material Substances—contd.
...	...	...	...	...	...	...	...	...	...	...	...	186. Bangle makers and sellers in stone.			
21	...	4	17	10	...	2	8	11	...	2	9	187. Bangle makers and sellers in wood and bone.			
...	...	...	...	...	...	...	...	...	...	...	...	188. Bangle makers and sellers in clay.			
553	65	110	378	301	26	61	214	252	39	49	164	189. Bangle makers and sellers in glass.			
3,697	477	790	2,430	2,088	239	417	1,432	1,609	238	373	998	189a. Bangle makers and sellers unspecified.			
240	43	56	141	107	17	26	64	133	25	30	77	190. Bangle fitters			
392	51	70	271	228	28	37	163	164	23	33	108	191. Imitation and pewter jewelry makers and sellers.			
7	1	...	6	4	...	...	4	3	1	...	2	192. Bead makers and sellers			
8	2	2	4	...	...	...	...	8	2	2	4	193. Rosary and necklace makers and sellers.			
198	20	39	139	96	12	16	68	102	8	23	71	194. Flower garland makers and sellers.			
5	1	2	2	5	1	2	2	...	...	...	...	195. Artificial flower and caste-mark spangle makers and sellers.			
11	1	4	6	4	1	...	3	7	...	4	3	196. Sacred thread makers and sellers.			
5,405	691	1,127	3,587	3,001	337	587	2,077	2,404	354	540	1,510	Total Sub-order 33			
...	...	...	...	...	...	...	...	...	...	...	...	197. Upholsterers	34.—Furniture		
4	...	1	3	4	...	1	3	...	...	...	...	198. Furniture makers			
...	...	...	...	...	...	...	...	...	...	...	...	199. Frame makers			
...	...	...	...	...	...	...	...	...	...	...	...	200 Looking-glass makers and sellers.			
4	...	1	3	4	...	1	3	...	...	...	...	Total Sub-order 34			
201	22	43	136	123	15	26	82	78	7	17	54	201. Saddlery and harness makers and sellers.	35.—Harness		
24	4	5	15	11	1	3	7	13	3	2	8	202. Saddle-cloth makers, embroiderers and sellers.			
...	...	...	...	...	...	...	...	...	...	...	...	203. Whip, goad, etc., makers			
225	26	48	151	134	16	29	89	91	10	19	62	Total Sub-order 35			
44	4	12	28	28	1	7	20	16	3	5	8	204. Knife and tool makers and sellers.	36.—Tools and Machinery.		
159	17	46	96	104	7	31	66	55	10	15	30	204a. Agricultural implements makers, etc.			
314	50	72	192	192	37	44	111	122	13	28	81	205. Knife and tool grinders			
5	...	1	4	4	...	1	3	1	...	...	1	206. Looms and loom-comb makers and sellers.			
39	5	6	28	15	1	2	12	24	4	4	16	207. Mechanics (not railway)			
...	...	...	...	...	...	...	...	...	...	...	...	208. Machinery dealers, etc.			
561	76	137	348	343	46	85	212	218	30	52	136	Total Sub-order 36			
16	2	5	9	10	2	2	6	6	...	3	3	209. Gun makers, menders and sellers.	37.—Arms and Ammunition.		
6	1	1	4	...	...	...	...	6	1	1	4	210. Ammunition and cap dealers			
56	7	17	32	23	4	7	12	33	3	10	20	211. Gunpowder makers and sellers.			
10	3	2	5	5	...	2	3	5	3	...	2	212. Firework makers and sellers			
10	3	1	6	6	1	...	5	4	2	1	1	213. Sword and scabbard makers and sellers.			
...	...	...	...	...	...	...	...	...	...	...	...	214. Spear-head, shield, etc., makers and sellers.			
...	...	...	...	...	...	...	...	...	...	...	...	215. Bow and arrow makers and sellers.			
3	2	...	1	2	1	...	...	2	1	...	1	216. Cudgel (lathi) makers and sellers.			
101	18	26	57	45	8	11	26	56	10	15	31	Total Sub-order 37			
6,761	**864**	**1,430**	**4,467**	**3,760**	**431**	**747**	**2,582**	**3,001**	**433**	**683**	**1,885**	**Total Order XI**			
...	...	...	...	...	...	...	...	...	...	...	...	217. Carpet weavers and sellers	38.—Wool and Fur	Order XII.—Textile Fabrics and Dress.	
1	...	...	1	1	...	...	1	...	...	...	...	218. Shawl ditto			
...	...	...	...	...	...	...	...	...	...	...	...	219. Felt and pashm workers and sellers.			
4,407	731	1,066	2,610	2,586	378	571	1,637	1,821	353	495	973	220. Blanket weavers and sellers			
60	8	15	37	24	3	5	16	36	5	10	21	221. Woollen cloth manufacturers and dealers			
262	16	37	209	20	2	6	12	242	14	31	197	222. Woollen yarn spinners and sellers.			
9	1	2	6	3	...	...	3	6	1	2	3	223. Wool carders			
...	...	...	...	...	...	...	...	...	...	...	...	224. Wool dyers			
109	16	28	65	49	8	12	29	60	8	16	36	225. Fur dealers			
4,848	772	1,148	2,928	2,683	391	594	1,698	2,165	381	554	1,230	Total Sub-order 38			
...	...	...	...	...	...	...	...	...	...	...	...	226. Silkworm rearers and cocoon gatherers.	39.—Silk		
565	67	139	359	276	28	70	178	279	39	59	181	227. Silk carders and spinners			
68	9	13	46	32	3	5	24	36	6	8	22	228. Silk weavers and dealers			
1	...	...	1	1	...	...	1	...	...	...	...	229. Silk printers and dyers			
5	...	1	4	2	...	...	2	3	...	1	2	230. Braid and ribbon makers and sellers			
639	76	143	410	311	31	75	205	318	45	68	205	Total Sub-order 39			
9,202	918	1,689	6,595	2,696	377	625	1,694	6,506	541	1,064	4,901	231. Cotton cleaners, pressers and ginners.	40.—Cotton		
4,890	637	1,014	3,239	2,892	286	546	2,060	1,998	351	468	1,179	231a. Raw cotton dealers			
1,079	176	234	669	652	85	125	442	427	91	109	227	232. Cotton carpet and rug makers and sellers.			
6,301	416	887	4,998	766	132	202	432	5,535	284	685	4,566	233. Cotton spinners, sizers and yarn beaters.			
15,064	2,436	3,545	9,083	8,680	1,177	1,907	5,596	6,384	1,259	1,638	3,487	234. Cotton weavers, mill-owners and managers.			
64	5	12	47	26	...	3	23	38	5	9	24	234a. Cotton factory Engineers			
816	73	157	584	523	39	93	386	293	35	59	198	235. Do. factory hands (undefined)			
4	...	1	3	2	...	...	2	2	...	1	1	236. Calenderers, fullers and printers			
4,458	594	1,019	2,845	2,400	263	546	1,591	2,058	331	473	1,254	237. Cotton dyers			
79	6	24	49	55	3	20	32	24	3	4	17	238. Tape makers and sellers			
...	...	...	...	...	...	...	...	...	...	...	...	239. Tent manufacturers and sellers			
41,957	5,263	8,582	28,112	18,692	2,362	4,072	12,258	23,265	2,901	4,510	15,854	Total Sub-order 40			

TABLE XVII.—Occupations, by Age.—

PROVINCIAL

Class.	Order.	Sub-order and Group.	Occupation.	Total. Total.	Total. 0—4	Total. 5—14	Total. 15—	Males. Total.	Males. 0—4
1	2	3	4	5	6	7	8	9	10
CLASS D.—PREPARATION AND SUPPLY OF MATERIAL SUBSTANCES—contd.	ORDER XII.—TEXTILE FABRICS AND DRESS—contd.	41.—Jute, Flax, Coir, etc.	240. Flax-spinners, weavers and sellers	...	...	...	...	...	...
			241. Hemp rope makers and sellers	851	101	203	547	434	46
			242. Jute manufacturers, managers and agents	...	...	...	...	...	...
			243. Sacking, tarpaulin and gunny makers and sellers.	1,587	212	378	997	923	96
			244. Net makers and sellers	47	4	15	28	22	1
			245. Fancy work dealers	...	...	...	...	...	...
			246. Coir preparers, manufacturers and sellers	...	...	...	...	...	...
			Total Sub-order 41	2,485	327	596	1,572	1,379	144
		42.—Dress	247. Tailors and darners	12,189	1,436	2,407	8,346	6,066	700
			248. Milliners and dress makers	...	...	...	...	...	...
			249. Out-fitters, and clothes and quilt dealers	1,914	214	375	1,325	1,103	109
			250. Hosiers and haberdashers	...	...	...	...	...	...
			251. Hat, cap and turban makers and sellers	11	...	1	10	5	...
			252. Turban binders	3	...	...	3	3	...
			253. Umbrella makers and sellers	2	...	...	2	...	...
			254. Embroiderers and lace and muslin makers	482	57	88	337	30	9
			255. Button makers and sellers	...	...	...	...	...	...
			256. False-plait makers and sellers	...	...	...	...	...	...
			257. Piece-goods dealers	15,973	2,060	3,356	10,557	9,579	1,035
			Total Sub-order 42	30,574	3,767	6,227	20,580	16,786	1,853
			Total Order XII	**112,142**	**13,858**	**23,133**	**75,151**	**58,011**	**6,563**
	ORDER XIII.—METALS AND PRECIOUS STONES.	43.—Gold, Silver, and Precious Stones	258. Gold and silver dealers	394	46	92	256	252	29
			259. Gold and silver assayers	3	...	2	1	3	...
			260. Gold and silver workers	20,180	2,779	4,550	12,851	11,301	1,396
			261. Gold beaters	...	...	...	...	...	...
			262. Goldsmith's dust washers	269	25	54	190	150	12
			263. Gold miners, managers, agents	...	...	...	...	...	...
			264. Enamellers	...	...	...	...	...	...
			265. Electro-platers	15	...	...	15	12	...
			266. Gold and silver wire drawers and braid makers.	39	3	2	34	33	1
			267. Plate and plated ware dealers	19	3	5	11	12	1
			268. Diamond polishers and dealers	...	...	...	...	...	...
			269. Diamond diggers, washers, etc.	...	...	...	...	...	...
			270. Ruby workers	...	...	...	...	...	...
			271. Ruby and emerald, etc., dealers	...	...	...	...	...	...
			272. Pearl divers	...	...	...	...	...	...
			273. Pearl and other precious stone (unspecified) dealers.	326	40	59	227	188	16
			274. Coral dealers	15	3	2	10	8	1
			275. Cornelian and agate cutters and sellers	...	...	...	...	...	...
			Total Sub-order 43	21,260	2,899	4,766	13,595	11,959	1,456
		44. Brass, Copper and Bell-metal.	276. Brass workers and sellers	110	13	17	80	50	7
			277. Brass pot makers and sellers	343	44	65	234	201	20
			278. Brass image casters and sellers	1	...	1	...	1	...
			279. Copper workers and sellers	125	25	21	79	65	13
			280. Brass and copper wire drawers and sellers	20	...	1	19	19	...
			281. Bell-metal workers and sellers	559	73	127	359	281	31
			282. General workers in brass, copper and bell-metal.	319	76	94	149	166	38
			283. Brass and copper dealers	1,622	183	334	1,105	1,096	96
			Total Sub-order 44	3,099	424	660	2,025	1,839	201
		45. Tin, Zinc, Mercury and Lead.	284. Tin workers and sellers	849	105	181	563	468	53
			285. Tin foil makers and sellers	...	...	...	...	...	...
			286. Zinc workers and sellers	16	1	4	11	11	1
			287. Lead and quicksilver workers and sellers	2	...	...	2	1	...
			288. General workers in tin, lead and zinc	79	10	28	41	44	5
			Total Sub-order 45	946	116	213	617	524	59
		46. Iron and Steel	289. Iron and steel founders, smelters and sellers	23	5	8	10	2	...
			290. Blacksmiths	12,510	1,790	3,018	7,702	6,954	887
			291. Iron hardware dealers	247	25	37	185	157	14
			292. Nail makers and sellers	...	...	...	...	...	...
			293. Lock makers, menders and sellers	41	2	15	24	23	1
			294. Weight makers and stampers	3	...	3	...	2	...
			Total Sub-order 46	12,824	1,822	3,081	7,921	7,137	902
			Total Order XIII	**38,129**	**5,251**	**8,720**	**24,158**	**21,459**	**2,616**
	ORDER XIV.—GLASS, POTTERY AND STONE-WARE.	47.—Glass and China-ware.	295. Glass-blowers, window glass makers, etc.	...	...	...	...	...	...
			296. Bottle dealers	9	...	2	7	9	...
			297. Glass and Chinaware dealers	21	3	1	17	6	...
			Total Sub-order 47	30	3	2	24	15	...

Part A.—PROVINCIAL SUMMARY—*contd.*

TOTAL.									
Males.		Females.				Occupation.	Sub-order and Group.	Order.	Class.
5—14	15—	Total	0—4	5—14	15—				
11	12	13	14	15	16				
...	...	...	...	...	...	240. Flax-spinner, weavers and sellers	41. Jute, Flax, Coir, etc.	ORDER XII.—TEXTILE FABRICS AND DRESS—contd.	CLASS D.—PREPARATION AND SUPPLY OF MATERIAL SUBSTANCES—contd.
94	294	417	55	109	253	241. Hemp rope makers and sellers			
...	...	...	...	...	...	242. Jute manufacturers, managers and agents			
207	620	664	116	171	377	243. Sacking, tarpaulin and gunny makers and sellers			
3	17	25	2	12	11	244. Net makers and sellers			
...	...	...	...	...	...	245. Fancy work dealers			
...	...	...	...	...	...	246. Coir preparers, manufacturers and sellers			
304	931	1,106	173	292	641	Total Sub-order 41			
1,199	4,167	6,123	735	1,208	4,179	247. Tailors and darners	42.—Dress		
...	...	...	...	...	...	248 Milliners and dress-makers			
191	803	811	105	184	522	249. Out-fitters, and clothes and quilt dealers			
...	...	...	...	...	...	250. Hosiers and haberdashers			
...	5	6	...	1	5	251. Hat, cap and turban makers and sellers			
...	3	...	...	...	...	252. Turban binders			
...	...	2	...	...	2	253. Umbrella makers and sellers			
8	13	452	48	80	324	254. Embroiderers and lace and muslin makers			
...	...	...	...	...	...	255. Button makers and sellers			
...	...	...	...	...	...	256. False-plait makers and sellers			
1,851	6,693	6,394	1,025	1,505	3,864	257. Piece-goods dealers			
3,249	11,684	13,782	1,914	2,978	8,896	Total Sub-order 42			
11,506	**36,942**	**57,131**	**7,295**	**11,627**	**38,209**	**Total Order XII**			
53	170	142	17	39	86	258. Gold and silver dealers	43.—Gold, Silver, and Precious Stones.	ORDER XIII.—METALS AND PRECIOUS STONES.	
2	1	...	...	...	...	259. Gold and silver assayers			
2,411	7,494	8,879	1,383	2,139	5,357	260. Gold and silver workers			
...	...	...	...	...	...	261. Gold beaters			
30	108	119	13	24	82	262. Goldsmith's dust washers			
...	...	...	...	...	...	263. Gold miners, managers, agents			
...	...	...	...	...	...	264. Enamellers			
...	12	3	...	...	3	265. Electro-platers			
...	32	6	2	2	2	266. Gold and silver wire drawers and braid makers			
4	7	7	2	1	4	267. Plate and plated ware dealers			
...	...	...	...	...	...	268. Diamond polishers and dealers			
...	...	...	...	...	...	269. Diamond diggers, washers, etc.			
...	...	...	...	...	...	270. Ruby workers			
...	...	...	...	...	...	271. Ruby and emerald, etc., dealers			
...	...	...	...	...	...	272. Pearl divers			
32	140	138	24	27	87	273. Pearl and other precious stone (unspecified) dealers,			
2	5	7	2	...	5	274. Coral dealers			
...	...	...	...	...	...	275. Cornelian and agate cutters and sellers			
2,534	7,969	9,301	1,443	2,232	5,626	Total Sub-order 43			
7	36	60	6	10	44	276. Brass workers and sellers	44. Brass, Copper and Bell-metal.		
36	145	142	24	29	89	277. Brass pot makers and sellers			
1	...	...	...	...	...	278. Brass image casters and sellers			
9	43	60	12	12	36	279. Copper workers and sellers			
1	18	1	...	...	1	280. Brass and copper wire drawers and sellers			
58	190	278	40	69	169	281. Bell-metal workers and sellers			
47	81	153	38	47	68	282. General workers in brass, copper and bell-metal.			
197	769	566	93	137	336	283. Brass and copper dealers			
356	1,282	1,260	213	304	743	Total Sub-order 44			
94	321	381	52	87	242	284. Tin workers and sellers	45. Tin, Zinc, Mercury and Lead.		
...	...	...	...	...	...	285. Tin foil makers and sellers			
3	7	5	...	1	4	286. Zinc workers and sellers			
...	1	1	...	...	1	287. Lead and quicksilver workers and sellers			
19	20	35	5	9	21	288. General workers in tin, lead and zinc			
116	349	422	57	97	268	Total Sub-order 45			
...	1	22	5	8	9	289. Iron and steel founders, smelters and sellers	46. Iron and Steel		
1,625	4,442	5,556	903	1,393	3,260	290. Blacksmiths			
24	119	90	11	13	66	291. Iron and hardware dealers			
...	...	...	...	...	...	292. Nail makers and sellers			
7	15	18	1	8	9	293. Lock makers, menders and sellers			
2	...	1	...	1	...	294. Weight makers and stampers			
1,658	4,577	5,687	920	1,423	3,344	Total Sub-order 46			
4,664	**14,177**	**16,670**	**2,633**	**4,056**	**9,981**	**Total Order XIII**			
...	...	...	...	...	...	295. Glass-blowers, window glass makers, etc.	47.—Glass and China-ware.	ORDER XIV.—GLASS, POTTERY AND STONEWARE.	
2	7	...	...	...	...	296. Bottle dealers			
1	5	15	3	...	12	297. Glass and Chinaware dealers			
3	12	15	3	...	12	Total Sub-order 47			

TABLE XVII.—Occupations, by Age.—

Class.	Order.	Sub-order and Group.	Occupation.	TOWN. Total. Total.	Total. 0—4	Total. 5—14	Total. 15—	Males. Total.	Males. 0—4	Males. 5—14	Males. 15—	Females. Total.	Females. 0—4	Females. 5—14	Females. 15—
				17	18	19	20	21	22	23	24	25	26	27	28
CLASS D.—PREPARATION AND SUPPLY OF MATERIAL SUBSTANCES—*contd.*	ORDER XII.—TEXTILE FABRICS AND DRESS—*contd.*	41.—Jute, Flax, Coir, etc.	240. Flax-spinners, weavers and sellers.	...	...	...	...	...	...	...	...	...	...	...	...
			241. Hemp rope makers and sellers	420	58	111	251	205	26	50	129	215	32	61	122
			242. Jute manufacturers, managers and agents.	...	...	...	...	...	...	...	...	...	...	...	...
			243. Sacking, tarpaulin and gunny makers and sellers.	643	73	119	451	410	31	67	312	233	42	52	139
			244. Net makers and sellers	9	...	4	5	...	...	...	...	9	...	4	5
			245. Fancy work dealers	...	...	...	...	...	...	...	...	...	...	...	...
			246. Coir preparers, manufacturers and sellers.	...	...	...	...	...	...	...	...	...	...	...	...
			TOTAL SUB-ORDER 41	1,072	131	234	707	615	57	117	441	457	74	127	256
		42.—Dress	247. Tailors and darners	3,391	396	663	2,332	1,753	188	351	1,214	1,638	208	312	1,118
			248. Milliners and dress makers	...	...	...	...	...	...	...	...	...	...	...	...
			249. Out-fitters, and clothes and quilt dealers.	1,056	139	214	703	505	66	91	348	551	73	123	355
			250. Hosiers and haberdashers	...	...	...	...	...	...	...	...	...	...	...	...
			251. Hat, cap and turban makers and sellers.	7	...	1	6	1	...	...	1	6	...	1	5
			252. Turban binders	2	...	...	2	2	...	...	2	...	...	...	...
			253. Umbrella makers and sellers	...	...	...	...	...	...	...	...	...	...	...	...
			254. Embroiderers and lace and muslin makers.	96	6	11	79	3	1	1	1	93	5	10	78
			255. Button makers and sellers	...	...	...	...	...	...	...	...	...	...	...	...
			256. False-plait makers and sellers	...	...	...	...	...	...	...	...	...	...	...	...
			257. Piece-goods dealers	6,467	827	1,373	4,267	3,602	416	743	2,443	2,865	411	630	1,824
			TOTAL SUB-ORDER 42	11,019	1,368	2,262	7,389	5,866	671	1,186	4,009	5,153	697	1,076	3,380
			Total Order XII	**43,740**	**5,162**	**8,933**	**29,645**	**21,641**	**2,510**	**4,515**	**14,616**	**22,099**	**2,652**	**4,418**	**15,029**
	ORDER XIII.—METALS AND PRECIOUS STONES.	43.—Gold, Silver and Precious Stones.	258. Gold and silver dealers	138	14	35	89	88	9	19	60	50	5	16	29
			259. Gold and silver assayers	...	...	...	...	...	...	...	...	...	...	...	...
			260. Gold and silver workers	4,540	561	938	3,041	2,470	276	504	1,690	2,070	285	434	1,351
			261. Gold beaters	...	...	...	...	...	...	...	...	...	...	...	...
			262. Goldsmith's dust washers	195	21	39	135	98	12	20	66	97	9	19	69
			263. Gold miners, managers and agents.	...	...	...	...	...	...	...	...	...	...	...	...
			264. Enamellers	...	...	...	...	...	...	...	...	...	...	...	...
			265. Electro-platers	1	...	...	1	1	...	...	1	...	...	...	...
			266. Gold and silver wire drawers and braid makers.	20	...	...	20	20	...	...	20	...	...	...	...
			267. Plate and plated ware dealers	6	1	3	2	3	...	2	1	3	1	1	1
			268. Diamond polishers and dealers	...	...	...	...	...	...	...	...	...	...	...	...
			269. Diamond diggers, washers, etc.	...	...	...	...	...	...	...	...	...	...	...	...
			270. Ruby workers	...	...	...	...	...	...	...	...	...	...	...	...
			271. Ruby and emerald, etc., dealers	...	...	...	...	...	...	...	...	...	...	...	...
			272. Pearl divers	...	...	...	...	...	...	...	...	...	...	...	...
			273. Pearl and other precious stone (unspecified) dealers.	158	19	29	110	77	8	15	54	81	11	14	56
			274. Coral dealers	...	...	...	...	...	...	...	...	...	...	...	...
			275. Cornelian and agate cutters and sellers.	...	...	...	...	...	...	...	...	...	...	...	...
			TOTAL SUB-ORDER 43	5,058	616	1,044	3,398	2,757	305	560	1,892	2,301	311	484	1,506
		44.—Brass, Copper and Bell-metal.	276. Brass workers and sellers	87	11	14	62	41	5	7	29	46	6	7	33
			277. Brass pot makers and sellers	49	3	12	34	29	3	4	22	20	...	8	12
			278. Brass image casters and sellers	...	...	...	...	...	...	...	...	...	...	...	...
			279. Copper workers and sellers	12	2	3	7	6	1	1	4	6	1	2	3
			280. Brass and copper wire drawers and sellers.	...	...	...	...	...	...	...	...	...	...	...	...
			281. Bell-metal workers and sellers.	98	14	21	63	39	5	7	27	59	9	14	36
			282. General workers in brass, copper and bell-metal.	102	15	15	72	50	6	6	38	52	9	9	34
			283. Brass and copper dealers	423	63	103	257	213	27	58	128	210	36	45	129
			TOTAL SUB-ORDER 44	771	108	168	495	378	47	83	248	393	61	85	247
		45.—Tin, Zinc, Mercury and Lead.	284. Tin workers and sellers	402	59	87	256	201	27	44	130	201	32	43	126
			285. Tin foil makers and sellers	...	...	...	...	...	...	...	...	...	...	...	...
			286. Zinc workers and sellers	14	1	4	9	10	1	3	6	4	...	1	3
			287. Lead and quicksilver workers and sellers.	1	...	...	1	...	...	...	...	1	...	...	1
			288. General workers in tin, lead and zinc.	...	...	...	...	...	...	...	...	...	...	...	...
			TOTAL SUB-ORDER 45	417	60	91	266	211	28	47	136	206	32	44	130
		46.—Iron and Steel	289. Iron and steel founders, smelters and sellers.	...	...	...	...	...	...	...	...	...	...	...	...
			290. Blacksmiths	1,949	252	449	1,248	1,089	128	270	691	860	124	179	557
			291. Iron and hardware dealers	80	7	12	61	51	5	6	40	29	2	6	21
			292. Nail makers and sellers	...	...	...	...	...	...	...	...	...	...	...	...
			293. Lock makers, menders and sellers.	30	1	10	19	16	1	4	11	14	...	6	8
			294. Weight makers and stampers.	...	...	...	...	...	...	...	...	...	...	...	...
			TOTAL SUB-ORDER 46	2,059	260	471	1,328	1,156	134	280	742	903	126	191	586
			Total Order XIII	**8,305**	**1,044**	**1,774**	**5,487**	**4,502**	**514**	**970**	**3,018**	**3,803**	**530**	**804**	**2,469**
	ORDER XIV.—GLASS, POTTERY AND STONEWARE.	47.—Glass and Chinaware.	295. Glass-blowers, window glass makers, etc.	...	...	...	...	...	...	...	...	...	...	...	...
			296. Bottle dealers	8	...	2	6	8	...	2	6	...	...	...	...
			297. Glass and Chinaware dealers	3	...	...	3	1	...	...	1	2	...	...	2
			TOTAL SUB-ORDER 47	11	...	2	9	9	...	2	7	2	...	...	2

Part A.—PROVINCIAL SUMMARY—*contd.*

COUNTRY.												Occupation.	Sub-order and Group.	Order.	Class.
Total.				Males.				Females.							
Total.	0—4	5—14	15—	Total.	0—4	5—14	15—	Total.	0—4	5—14	15—				
29	30	31	32	33	34	35	36	37	38	39	40				
...	...	...	...	...	...	...	...	...	...	...	...	240. Flax-spinners, weavers and sellers	41.—Jute, Flax, Coir, etc.	ORDER XII.—TEXTILE FABRICS AND DRESS—*contd.*	CLASS D.—PREPARATION AND SUPPLY OF MATERIAL SUBSTANCES—*contd.*
431	43	92	296	229	20	44	165	202	23	48	131	241. Hemp rope makers and sellers			
...	...	...	...	...	...	...	...	...	...	...	...	242. Jute manufacturers, managers and agents			
944	139	259	546	513	65	140	308	431	74	119	238	243. Sacking tarpaulin and gunny makers and sellers			
38	4	11	23	22	2	3	17	16	2	8	6	244. Net makers and sellers			
...	...	...	...	...	...	...	...	...	...	...	...	245. Fancy work dealers			
...	...	...	...	...	...	...	...	...	...	...	...	246. Coir preparers, manufacturers and sellers			
1,413	186	362	865	764	87	187	490	649	99	175	375	Total Sub-order 41			
6,798	1,040	1,744	6,014	4,313	512	848	2,953	4,485	528	896	3,061	247. Tailors and darners	42.—Dress		
...	...	...	...	...	...	...	...	...	...	...	...	248. Milliners and dress-makers			
858	75	161	622	598	43	100	455	260	32	61	167	249. Out-fitters, and clothes and quilt dealers			
...	...	...	...	...	...	...	...	...	...	...	...	250. Hosiers and haberdashers			
4	...	...	4	4	...	...	4	...	...	...	...	251. Hat, cap and turban makers and sellers			
1	...	...	1	1	...	...	1	...	...	...	...	252. Turban binders			
2	...	...	2	...	...	...	...	2	...	...	2	253. Umbrella makers and sellers			
386	51	77	258	27	8	7	12	359	43	70	246	254. Embroiderers and lace and muslin makers			
...	...	...	...	...	...	...	...	...	...	...	...	255. Button makers and sellers			
...	...	...	...	...	...	...	...	...	...	...	...	256. False-plait makers and sellers			
9,506	1,233	1,983	6,290	5,977	619	1,108	4,250	3,529	614	875	2,040	257. Piece-goods dealers			
19,555	2,399	3,965	13,191	10,920	1,182	2,063	7,675	8,635	1,217	1,902	5,516	Total Sub-order 42			
68,402	**8,696**	**14,200**	**45,506**	**33,370**	**4,058**	**6,991**	**22,326**	**35,032**	**4,643**	**7,209**	**23,180**	**Total Order XII**			
256	32	57	167	164	20	34	110	92	12	23	57	258. Gold and silver dealers	43.—Gold, Silver and Precious Stones.	ORDER XIII.—METALS AND PRECIOUS STONES.	
3	...	2	1	3	...	2	1	...	...	...	...	259. Gold and silver assayers			
15,640	2,218	3,612	9,810	8,831	1,120	1,907	5,804	6,809	1,098	1,705	4,006	260. Gold and silver workers			
...	...	...	...	...	...	...	...	...	...	...	...	261. Gold beaters			
74	4	15	55	52	...	10	42	22	4	5	13	262. Goldsmith's dust washers			
...	...	...	...	...	...	...	...	...	...	...	...	263. Gold miners, managers, agents			
...	...	...	...	...	...	...	...	...	...	...	...	264. Enamellers			
14	...	...	14	11	...	...	11	3	...	...	3	265. Electro-platers			
29	3	2	24	23	1	...	22	6	2	2	2	266. Gold and silver wire drawers and braid makers			
13	2	2	9	9	1	2	6	4	1	...	3	267. Plate and plated ware dealers			
...	...	...	...	...	...	...	...	...	...	...	...	268. Diamond polishers and dealers			
...	...	...	...	...	...	...	...	...	...	...	...	269. Diamond diggers, washers, etc.			
...	...	...	...	...	...	...	...	...	...	...	...	270. Ruby workers			
...	...	...	...	...	...	...	...	...	...	...	...	271. Ruby and emerald, etc., dealers			
...	...	...	...	...	...	...	...	...	...	...	...	272. Pearl divers			
168	31	30	117	111	8	17	86	57	13	13	31	273. Pearl and other precious stone (unspecified) dealers.			
15	3	2	10	8	1	2	5	7	2	...	5	274. Coral dealers			
...	...	...	...	...	...	...	...	...	...	...	...	275. Cornelian and agate cutters and sellers.			
16,202	2,283	3,722	10,197	9,202	1,151	1,974	6,077	7,000	1,132	1,748	4,120	Total Sub-order 43			
23	2	3	18	9	2	...	7	14	...	3	11	276. Brass workers and sellers	44.—Brass, Copper and Bell-metal.		
294	41	53	200	172	17	32	123	122	24	21	77	277. Brass pot makers and sellers			
1	...	1	...	1	...	1	...	...	...	...	...	278. Brass image casters and sellers.			
113	23	18	72	59	12	8	39	54	11	10	33	279. Copper workers and sellers			
20	...	1	19	19	...	1	18	1	...	...	1	280. Brass and copper wire drawers and sellers.			
461	59	106	296	242	28	51	163	219	31	55	133	281. Bell-metal workers and sellers			
217	61	79	77	116	32	41	43	101	29	38	34	282. General workers in brass, copper and bell-metal.			
1,199	120	231	848	843	63	139	641	356	57	92	207	283. Brass and copper dealers			
2,328	306	492	1,530	1,461	254	273	1,034	867	152	219	496	Total Sub-order 44			
447	46	94	307	267	26	50	191	180	20	44	116	284. Tin workers and sellers	45.—Tin, Zinc, Mercury and Lead.		
...	...	...	...	...	...	...	...	...	...	...	...	285. Tin foil makers and sellers			
2	...	...	2	1	...	...	1	1	...	...	1	286. Zinc workers and sellers			
1	...	...	1	1	...	...	1	...	...	...	...	287. Lead and quicksilver workers and sellers.			
79	10	28	41	44	5	19	20	35	5	9	21	288. General workers in tin, lead, and zinc.			
529	56	122	351	313	31	69	213	216	25	53	138	Total Sub-order 45			
23	5	8	10	1	...	...	1	22	5	8	9	289. Iron and steel founders, smelters and sellers.	46.—Iron and Steel.		
10,561	1,538	2,569	6,454	5,865	759	1,355	3,751	4,696	779	1,214	2,703	290. Blacksmiths			
167	18	25	124	106	9	18	79	61	9	7	45	291. Iron and hardware dealers			
...	...	...	...	...	...	...	...	...	...	...	...	292. Nail makers and sellers			
11	1	5	5	7	...	3	4	4	1	2	1	293. Lock makers, menders and sellers.			
3	...	3	...	2	...	2	...	1	...	1	...	294. Weight makers and stampers			
10,765	1,562	2,610	6,593	5,981	768	1,378	3,835	4,784	794	1,232	2,758	Total Sub-order 46			
29,824	**4,207**	**6,946**	**18,671**	**16,957**	**2,104**	**3,694**	**11,159**	**12,867**	**2,103**	**3,252**	**7,512**	**Total Order XIII**			
...	...	...	...	...	...	...	...	...	...	...	...	295. Glass-blowers, window glass makers, etc.	47.—Glass and Chinaware.	ORDER XIV.—GLASS, POTTERY AND STONEWARE.	
1	...	...	1	1	...	...	1	...	...	...	...	296. Bottle dealers			
18	3	1	14	5	...	1	4	13	3	...	10	297. Glass and China ware dealers			
19	3	1	15	6	...	1	5	13	3	...	10	Total Sub-order 47			

TABLE XVII.—Occupations, by Age.—

Class.	Order.	Sub-order and Group.	Occupation.	PROVINCIAL Total. Total.	Total. 0—4	Total. 5—14	Total. 15—	Males. Total.	Males. 0—4
1	2	3	4	5	6	7	8	9	10
CLASS D.—PREPARATION AND SUPPLY OF MATERIAL SUBSTANCES—*contd.*	ORDER XIV.—GLASS, POTTERY AND STONE-WARE—*contd.*	48. Earthen and Stoneware.	298. Putters and pot and pipe-bowl makers and sellers.	15,921	2,244	3,746	9,931	8,371	1,100
			299. Grind stone and millstone makers, menders and sellers.	2,890	463	705	1,722	1,588	131
			300. Pestle and mortar and stone idol makers and sellers.	43	3	11	29	24	1
			301. Quartz and soap-stone powder preparers and sellers.	...	...	...	...	...	...
			Total Sub-order 48	18,854	2,710	4,462	11,682	9,983	1,331
			Total Order XIV	**18,884**	**2,713**	**4,465**	**11,706**	**9,998**	**1,332**
	ORDER XV.—WOOD, CANE AND LEAVES, ETC.	49.—Timber and Wood.	302. Timber and bamboo agents and dealers	2,819	405	664	1,750	1,634	207
			303. Wood cutters and sawyers	2,531	378	450	1,703	1,765	201
			304. Carpenters	28,942	3,946	5,951	19,045	17,427	1,939
			305. Coopers and box makers	73	4	14	55	68	3
			Total Sub-order 49	34,365	4,733	7,079	22,553	20,894	2,351
		50.—Canework, Matting and Leaves, etc.	306. Bamboo and rattan splitters, workers and sellers.	889	139	220	530	391	64
			307. Basket weavers and winnowing-pan makers and sellers.	6,573	1,068	1,619	3,886	3,285	531
			308. Mat makers and sellers	917	131	235	551	429	51
			309. Screen (chik) makers and sellers	...	...	...	...	...	...
			310. Leaf-plate makers and sellers	452	59	101	292	252	33
			311. Tooth-stick sellers	46	6	12	28	20	1
			312. Leaf-fan makers and sellers	4	...	...	4	4	...
			313. Brush and comb makers and sellers	108	15	28	65	56	9
			314. Broom makers and sellers	4,795	766	1,245	2,784	2,108	329
			315. Pith and bark collectors, workers and sellers	...	...	...	...	...	...
			Total Sub-order 50	13,784	2,184	3,460	8,140	6,535	1,018
			Total Order XV	**48,149**	**6,917**	**10,539**	**30,693**	**27,429**	**3,359**
	ORDER XVI.—DRUGS, GUMS, DYES, ETC.	51.—Gums, Wax and similar Forest Produce.	316. India-rubber collectors and sellers	...	...	...	...	...	...
			317. Camphor and gum collectors and sellers	31	4	6	21	5	...
			318. Gallnut (myrabolam) collectors and sellers	...	...	...	...	...	...
			319. Catechu preparers and sellers	2	...	...	2	2	...
			320. Lac collectors and sellers	...	...	...	...	...	...
			321. Sealing-wax makers and sellers	4	2	...	2	4	2
			322. Tar preparers and sellers	2	...	...	2	...	...
			323. Wax, honey and general minor forest produce collectors and sellers.	629	82	137	410	336	44
			Total Sub-order 51	668	88	143	437	347	46
		52.—Drugs, Dyes, Pigments, etc.	324. Chemists and druggists	772	104	225	443	431	53
			325. Borax workers and sellers	9	3	...	6	8	3
			326. Saltpetre workers and sellers	3	...	...	3	2	...
			327. Alum, soda, etc., workers and sellers	99	17	28	54	55	8
			328. Soap makers and sellers	...	...	...	...	...	...
			329. Sulphur workers and sellers	2	...	1	1	...	...
			330. Indigo workers and dealers (not planters)	103	13	21	69	62	6
			331. Madder and logwood and kusumb dye workers and dealers.	19	1	3	15	3	...
			332. Ink makers and sellers	23	4	5	14	14	2
			333. Antimony preparers and sellers	19	1	3	15	7	...
			334. Henna preparers and sellers	...	...	...	...	...	...
			335. Carmine preparers and sellers	...	...	...	...	...	...
			336. Kanku (red powder) preparers and sellers	1,356	161	297	898	657	73
			337. Perfume preparers and sellers	672	104	145	423	386	56
			Total Sub-order 52	3,077	408	728	1,941	1,625	201
			Total Order XVI	**3,745**	**496**	**871**	**2,378**	**1,972**	**247**
	ORDER XVII.—LEATHER, HORNS, BONES AND GREASE.	53. Leather, etc.	338. Tanners, curriers and hide sellers	228	39	56	133	138	22
			339. Shoe, sandals, boot-makers and sellers	20,839	3,420	5,187	12,232	12,265	1,678
			340. Leather dyers	986	174	239	573	560	85
			341. Water-bag, well-bag, bucket and ghee-pot makers and sellers.	679	121	170	388	382	59
			342. Hide, horns, and bone dealers	1,113	202	270	641	657	88
			343. Catgut preparers and sellers	38	5	13	20	23	3
			344. Glue makers and sellers	...	...	...	...	...	...
			345. Grease preparers and sellers	...	...	...	...	...	...
			Total Sub-order 53	23,883	3,961	5,935	13,987	14,025	1,935
			Total Order XVII	**23,883**	**3,961**	**5,935**	**13,987**	**14,025**	**1,935**
			Total Class D	**402,201**	**53,941**	**88,603**	**259,657**	**213,923**	**26,006**

Part A.—PROVINCIAL SUMMARY—*contd.*

TOTAL.

Males. 5—14	Males. 15—	Females. Total.	Females. 0—4	Females. 5—14	Females. 15—	Occupation.	Sub-order and Group.	Order.	Class.
11	12	13	14	15	16				
2,008	5,263	7,550	1,144	1,738	4,668	298. Potters and pot and pipe-bowl makers and sellers.	48.—Earthen and Stoneware.	Order XIV.—Glass, Pottery and Stoneware—*contd.*	Class D.—Preparation and Supply of Material Substances—*contd.*
362	995	1,302	232	343	727	299. Grind stone and mill stone makers, menders and sellers.			
5	18	19	2	6	11	300. Pestle and mortar and stone idol makers and sellers.			
...	...	...	...	...	...	301. Quartz and soap-stone powder preparers and sellers.			
2,375	6,276	8,871	1,378	2,087	5,406	Total Sub-order 48			
2,378	**6,288**	**8,886**	**1,381**	**2,087**	**5,418**	**Total Order XIV**			
365	1,062	1,185	198	299	688	302. Timber and bamboo agents and dealers	49.—Timber and Wood.	Order XV.—Wood, Cane and Leaves, etc.	
361	1,302	766	176	189	401	303. Wood cutters and sawyers			
3,157	12,331	11,515	2,007	2,794	6,714	304. Carpenters			
13	52	5	1	1	3	305. Coopers and box makers			
3,796	14,747	13,471	2,382	3,283	7,806	Total Sub-order 49			
95	232	498	75	125	298	306. Bamboo and rattan splitters, workers and sellers.	50.—Canework, Matting and Leaves, etc.		
842	1,922	3,288	547	777	1,964	307. Basket weavers and winnowing-pan makers and sellers.			
111	267	488	80	124	284	308. Mat makers and sellers			
...	...	...	...	...	...	309. Screen (chik) makers and sellers			
55	164	200	26	46	128	310. Leaf-plate makers and sellers			
2	7	36	5	10	21	311. Tooth-stick sellers			
...	4	...	...	...	...	312. Leaf-fan makers and sellers			
19	28	52	6	9	37	313. Brush and comb makers and sellers			
591	1,188	2,687	437	654	1,596	314. Broom makers and sellers			
...	...	...	...	...	...	315. Pith and bark collectors, workers and sellers			
1,715	3,812	7,249	1,176	1,745	4,328	Total Sub-order 50			
5,611	**18,559**	**20,720**	**3,558**	**5,028**	**12,134**	**Total Order XV**			
...	...	...	...	...	...	316. India-rubber collectors and sellers	51.—Gums, Wax and similar Forest Produce.	Order XVI.—Drugs, Gums, Dyes, etc.	
...	5	26	4	6	16	317. Camphor and gum collectors and sellers			
...	...	...	...	...	...	318. Gallnut (myrabolam) collectors and sellers			
...	2	...	...	...	...	319. Catechu preparers and sellers			
...	...	...	...	...	...	320. Lac collectors and sellers			
...	2	...	...	...	...	321. Sealing-wax makers and sellers			
...	...	2	...	...	2	322. Tar preparers and sellers			
77	215	293	38	60	195	323. Wax, honey and general minor forest produce collectors and sellers.			
77	224	321	42	66	213	Total Sub-order 51			
117	261	341	51	108	182	324. Chemists and druggists	52.—Drugs, Dyes, Pigments, etc.		
...	5	1	...	...	1	325. Borax workers and sellers			
...	2	1	...	...	1	326. Saltpetre workers and sellers			
14	33	44	9	14	21	327. Alum, soda, etc., workers and sellers			
...	...	...	...	...	...	328. Soap makers and sellers			
...	...	2	...	1	1	329. Sulphur workers and sellers			
10	46	41	7	11	23	330. Indigo workers and dealers (not planters)			
2	1	16	1	1	14	331. Madder and logwood and kusumb dye workers and dealers.			
3	9	9	2	2	5	332. Ink makers and sellers			
1	6	12	1	2	9	333. Antimony preparers and sellers			
...	...	...	...	...	...	334. Henna preparers and sellers			
...	...	...	...	...	...	335. Carmine preparers and sellers			
258	486	690	88	130	472	336. Kanku (red powder) preparers and sellers			
69	261	286	48	76	162	337. Perfume preparers and sellers			
374	1,050	1,452	207	354	891	Total Sub-order 52			
451	**1,274**	**1,773**	**249**	**420**	**1,104**	**Total Order XVI**			
34	82	90	17	22	51	338. Tanners, curriers and hide sellers	53.—Leather, etc.	Order XVII.—Leather, Horns, Bones and Grease.	
2,938	7,649	8,574	1,742	2,249	4,583	339. Shoe, sandals, boot-makers and sellers			
130	345	426	89	109	228	340. Leather dyers			
80	234	297	62	81	154	341. Water-bag, well-bag, bucket and ghee-pot makers and sellers.			
143	426	456	114	127	215	342. Hide, horns and bone dealers			
7	13	15	2	6	7	343. Catgut preparers and sellers			
...	...	...	...	...	...	344. Glue makers and sellers			
...	...	...	...	...	...	345. Grease preparers and sellers			
3,341	8,749	9,858	2,026	2,594	5,238	Total Sub-order 53			
3,341	**8,749**	**9,858**	**2,026**	**2,594**	**5,238**	**Total Order XVII**			
45,908	**142,013**	**188,278**	**27,937**	**42,697**	**117,644**	**Total Class D**			

TABLE XVII.—Occupations, by Age.—

Class.	Order.	Sub-order and Group.	Occupation.	TOWN. Total. Total.	Total. 0—4	Total. 5—14	Total. 15—	Males. Total.	Males. 0—4	Males. 5—14	Males. 15—	Females. Total.	Females. 0—4	Females. 5—14	Females. 15—
				17	18	19	20	21	22	23	24	25	26	27	28
CLASS D.—PREPARATION AND SUPPLY OF MATERIAL SUBSTANCES—contd.	ORDER XIV.—GLASS, POTTERY AND STONE-WARE—contd.	48.—Earthen and Stoneware.	298. Potters and pot and pipe-bowl makers and sellers.	2,102	292	511	1,299	1,075	137	277	661	1,027	155	234	638
			299. Grindstone and millstone makers, menders and sellers.	230	20	62	148	138	13	29	96	92	7	33	52
			300. Pestle and mortar and stone idol makers and sellers.	1	...	...	1	...	...	...	...	1	...	...	1
			301. Quartz and soap-stone powder preparers and sellers.	...	...	...	...	...	...	...	...	...	...	...	...
			Total Sub-order 48	2,333	312	573	1,448	1,213	150	306	757	1,120	162	267	691
			Total Order XIV	**2,344**	**312**	**575**	**1,457**	**1,222**	**150**	**308**	**764**	**1,122**	**162**	**267**	**693**
	ORDER XV.—WOOD, CANE AND LEAVES, ETC.	49.—Timber and Wood.	302. Timber and bamboo agents and dealers.	332	48	82	202	174	30	43	101	158	18	39	101
			303. Wood cutters and sawyers	952	167	210	575	608	92	119	397	344	75	91	178
			304. Carpenters	3,816	446	719	2,651	2,278	223	393	1,662	1,538	223	326	989
			305. Coopers and box makers	5	...	...	5	4	...	...	4	1	...	...	1
			Total Sub-order 49	5,105	661	1,011	3,433	3,064	345	555	2,164	2,041	316	456	1,269
		50.—Canework, Matting and Leaves, etc.	306. Bamboo and rattan splitters, workers and sellers.	102	15	21	66	54	8	11	35	48	7	10	31
			307. Basket weavers and winnowing-pan makers and sellers.	1,374	198	335	841	653	89	168	396	721	109	167	445
			308. Mat makers and sellers	22	5	3	14	14	3	1	10	8	2	2	4
			309. Screen (chik) makers and sellers.	...	...	...	...	...	...	...	...	...	...	...	...
			310. Leaf-plate makers and sellers	61	7	11	43	28	3	5	20	33	4	6	23
			311. Tooth-stick sellers	19	2	3	14	1	...	...	1	18	2	3	13
			312. Leaf-fan makers and sellers	...	...	...	...	...	...	...	...	...	...	...	...
			313. Brush and comb makers and sellers.	82	11	24	47	41	5	17	19	41	6	7	28
			314. Broom makers and sellers	599	86	155	358	188	37	50	101	411	49	105	257
			315. Pith and bark collectors, workers and sellers.	...	...	...	...	...	...	...	...	...	...	...	...
			Total Sub-order 50	2,259	324	552	1,383	979	145	252	582	1,280	179	300	801
			Total Order XV	**7,364**	**985**	**1,563**	**4,816**	**4,043**	**490**	**807**	**2,746**	**3,321**	**495**	**756**	**2,070**
	ORDER XVI.—DRUGS, GUMS, DYES, ETC.	51.—Gums, Wax and similar Forest Produce.	316. India-rubber collectors and sellers.	...	...	...	...	...	...	...	...	...	...	...	...
			317. Camphor and gum collectors and sellers.	...	...	...	...	...	...	...	...	...	...	...	...
			318. Gallnut (myrabolam) collectors and sellers.	...	...	...	...	...	...	...	...	...	...	...	...
			319. Catechu preparers and sellers	...	...	...	...	...	...	...	...	...	...	...	...
			320. Lac collectors and sellers	...	...	...	...	...	...	...	...	...	...	...	...
			321. Sealing-wax makers and sellers	...	...	...	...	...	...	...	...	...	...	...	...
			322. Tar preparers and sellers	2	...	...	2	...	...	...	...	2	...	...	2
			323. Wax, honey and general minor forest produce collectors and sellers.	166	17	40	109	99	12	27	60	67	5	13	49
			Total Sub-order 51	168	17	40	111	99	12	27	60	69	5	13	51
		52.—Drugs, Dyes, Pigments, etc.	324. Chemists and druggists	144	21	34	89	71	12	14	45	73	9	20	44
			325. Borax workers and sellers	...	...	...	...	...	...	...	...	...	...	...	...
			326. Saltpetre workers and sellers	...	...	...	...	...	...	...	...	...	...	...	...
			327. Alum, soda, etc., workers and sellers.	...	...	...	...	...	...	...	...	...	...	...	...
			328. Soap makers and sellers	...	...	...	...	...	...	...	...	...	...	...	...
			329. Sulphur workers and sellers	2	...	1	1	...	...	...	...	2	...	1	1
			330. Indigo workers and dealers (not planters).	74	10	16	48	45	5	9	31	29	5	7	17
			331. Madder and logwood and kusumb dye workers & dealers	19	1	3	15	3	...	2	1	16	1	1	14
			332. Ink makers and sellers	11	1	2	8	8	1	1	6	3	...	1	2
			333. Antimony preparers and sellers	18	1	3	14	7	...	1	6	11	1	2	8
			334. Henna preparers and sellers	...	...	...	...	...	...	...	...	...	...	...	...
			335. Carmine preparers and sellers	...	...	...	...	...	...	...	...	...	...	...	...
			336. Kanku (red powder) preparers and sellers.	504	70	115	319	224	37	59	128	280	33	56	191
			337. Perfume preparers and sellers	269	35	56	178	146	16	29	101	123	19	27	77
			Total Sub-order 52	1,041	139	230	672	504	71	115	318	537	68	115	354
			Total Order, XVI	**1,209**	**156**	**270**	**783**	**603**	**83**	**142**	**378**	**606**	**73**	**128**	**405**
	ORDER XVII.—LEATHER, HORNS, BONES AND GREASE.	53.—Leather, etc.	338. Tanners, curriers and hide sellers.	60	13	17	30	34	9	9	16	26	4	8	14
			339. Shoe, sandals, boot-makers and sellers.	3,801	586	896	2,319	2,227	296	501	1,430	1,574	290	395	889
			340. Leather dyers	462	80	103	279	264	44	61	159	198	36	42	120
			341. Water-bag, well-bag, bucket and ghee-pot makers and sellers.	131	24	34	73	57	11	18	28	74	13	16	45
			342. Hide, horns and bone dealers	469	76	104	289	284	33	60	191	185	43	44	98
			343. Catgut preparers and sellers	4	1	1	2	1	1	...	...	3	...	1	2
			344. Glue makers and sellers	...	...	...	...	...	...	...	...	...	...	...	...
			345. Grease preparers and sellers	...	...	...	...	...	...	...	...	...	...	...	...
			Total Sub-order 53	4,927	780	1,155	2,992	2,867	394	649	1,824	2,060	386	506	1,168
			Total Order XVII	**4,927**	**780**	**1,155**	**2,992**	**2,867**	**394**	**649**	**1,824**	**2,060**	**386**	**506**	**1,168**
			Total Class D	**116,144**	**14,727**	**25,059**	**76,358**	**59,449**	**7,175**	**12,978**	**39,296**	**56,695**	**7,552**	**12,081**	**37,062**

Part A.—PROVINCIAL SUMMARY—*contd.*

COUNTRY.												Occupation.	Sub-order and Group.	Order.	Class.
Total.				Males.				Females.							
Total.	0—4	5—14	15—	Total.	0—4	5—14	15—	Total.	0—4	5—14	15—				
29	30	31	32	33	34	35	36	37	38	39	40				
13,829	1,952	3,235	8,632	7,296	963	1,731	4,602	6,533	989	1,504	4,030	298. Potters and pot and pipe-bowl makers and sellers.	48.—Earthen and Stoneware.	ORDER XIV.—GLASS, POTTERY AND STONE-WARE—*contd.*	CLASS D.—PREPARATION AND SUPPLY OF MATERIAL SUBSTANCES—*contd.*
2,660	443	643	1,574	1,450	218	333	899	1,210	225	310	675	299. Grind stone and mill stone makers, menders and sellers.			
42	3	11	28	24	1	5	18	18	2	6	10	300. Pestle and mortar and stone idol makers and sellers.			
...	...	...	...	...	...	...	...	...	...	...	...	301. Quartz and soap-stone powder preparers and sellers.			
16,521	2,398	3,889	10,234	8,770	1,182	2,069	5,519	7,751	1,216	1,820	4,715	Total Sub-order 48			
16,540	**2,401**	**3,890**	**10,249**	**8,776**	**1,182**	**2,070**	**5,524**	**7,764**	**1,219**	**1,820**	**4,725**	**Total Order XIV**			
2,487	357	582	1,548	1,460	177	322	961	1,027	180	260	587	302. Timber and bamboo agents and dealers.	49.—Timber and Wood.	ORDER XV.—WOOD, CANE AND LEAVES, ETC.	
1,579	211	240	1,128	1,157	110	142	905	422	101	98	223	303. Wood cutters and sawyers			
25,117	3,500	5,232	16,394	15,140	1,716	2,764	10,669	9,977	1,784	2,468	5,725	304. Carpenters			
68	4	14	50	64	3	13	48	4	1	1	2	305. Coopers and box makers			
29,260	4,072	6,068	19,120	17,830	2,006	3,241	12,583	11,430	2,066	2,827	6,537	Total Sub-order 49			
787	124	199	464	337	56	84	197	450	68	115	267	306. Bamboo and rattan splitters, workers and sellers.	50.—Canework, Matting and Leaves, etc.		
5,199	870	1,284	3,045	2,632	432	674	1,526	2,567	438	610	1,519	307. Basket weavers and winnowing-pan makers and sellers.			
895	126	232	537	415	48	110	257	480	78	122	280	308. Mat makers and sellers			
—	...	...	...	...	...	...	...	...	...	...	...	309. Screen (chik) makers and sellers.			
391	52	90	249	224	30	50	144	167	22	40	105	310. Leaf-plate makers and sellers			
27	4	9	14	9	1	2	6	18	3	7	8	311. Tooth-stick sellers			
4	...	...	4	4	...	...	4	...	...	...	...	312. Leaf-fan makers and sellers			
26	4	4	18	15	4	2	9	11	...	2	9	313. Brush and comb makers and sellers.			
4,196	680	1,090	2,426	1,920	292	541	1,087	2,276	388	549	1,339	314. Broom makers and sellers			
—	...	...	...	...	...	...	...	...	...	...	...	315. Pith and bark collectors, workers and sellers.			
11,525	1,860	2,908	6,757	5,556	863	1,463	3,230	5,969	997	1,445	3,527	Total Sub-order 50			
40,785	**5,932**	**8,976**	**25,877**	**23,386**	**2,869**	**4,704**	**15,813**	**17,399**	**3,063**	**4,272**	**10,064**	**Total Order XV**			
—	...	...	...	...	...	...	...	...	...	...	...	316. India-rubber collectors and sellers.	51.—Gums, Wax and similar Forest Produce.	ORDER XVI.—DRUGS, GUMS, DYES, ETC.	
31	4	6	21	5	...	...	5	26	4	6	16	317. Camphor and gum collectors and sellers.			
—	...	...	...	...	...	...	...	...	...	...	...	318. Gallnut (myrabolam) collectors and sellers.			
2	...	...	2	2	...	...	2	...	...	...	...	319. Catechu preparers and sellers			
—	...	...	...	...	...	...	...	...	...	...	...	320. Lac-collectors and sellers			
4	2	...	2	4	2	...	2	...	...	...	...	321. Sealing-wax makers and sellers			
...	...	...	...	...	...	...	...	...	...	...	...	322. Tar preparers and sellers			
463	65	97	301	237	32	50	155	226	33	47	146	323. Wax, honey and general minor forest produce collectors and sellers.			
900	71	103	326	248	34	50	164	252	37	53	162	Total Sub-order 51			
628	83	191	354	360	41	103	216	268	42	88	138	324. Chemists and druggists	52.—Drugs, Dyes, Pigments, etc.		
9	3	...	6	8	3	...	5	1	...	...	1	325. Borax workers and sellers			
3	...	...	3	2	...	...	2	1	...	...	1	326. Saltpetre workers and sellers			
99	17	28	54	55	8	14	33	44	9	14	21	327. Alum, soda, etc., workers and sellers.			
—	...	...	...	...	...	...	...	...	...	...	...	328. Soap makers and sellers			
—	...	...	...	...	...	...	...	...	...	...	...	329. Sulphur workers and sellers			
29	3	5	21	17	1	1	15	12	2	4	6	330. Indigo workers and dealers (not planters).			
—	...	...	...	...	...	...	...	...	...	...	...	331. Madder and logwood and kusumb dye workers and dealers.			
12	3	3	6	6	1	2	3	6	2	1	3	332. Ink-makers and sellers			
1	...	...	1	...	...	...	...	1	...	...	1	333. Antimony preparers and sellers			
...	...	...	...	...	...	...	...	...	...	...	...	334. Henna preparers and sellers			
—	...	...	...	...	...	...	...	...	...	...	...	335. Carmine preparers and sellers			
852	91	182	579	433	36	99	298	419	55	83	281	336. Kaaku (red powder) preparers and sellers.			
403	69	89	245	240	40	40	160	163	29	49	85	337. Perfume preparers and sellers.			
2,036	269	498	1,269	1,121	130	259	732	915	139	239	537	Total Sub-order 52			
2,536	**340**	**601**	**1,595**	**1,369**	**164**	**309**	**896**	**1,167**	**176**	**292**	**699**	**Total Order XVI**			
168	26	39	103	104	13	25	66	64	13	14	37	338. Tanners, curriers and hide sellers.	53. Leather, etc.	ORDER XVII.—LEATHER, HORNS, BONES AND GREASE.	
17,038	2,834	4,291	9,913	10,038	1,382	2,437	6,219	7,000	1,452	1,854	3,694	339. Shoe, sandals, boot-makers and sellers.			
524	94	135	294	296	41	69	186	228	53	67	108	340. Leather dyers			
548	97	136	315	325	48	71	206	223	49	65	109	341. Water-bag, well-bag, bucket and ghee-pot makers and sellers.			
644	126	166	352	373	55	83	235	271	71	83	117	342. Hide, horns, and bone dealers			
34	4	12	18	22	2	7	13	12	2	5	5	343. Catgut preparers and sellers			
...	...	...	...	...	...	...	...	...	...	...	...	344. Glue makers and sellers			
...	...	...	...	...	...	...	...	...	...	...	...	345. Grease preparers and sellers			
18,956	2,181	4,780	10,995	11,158	1,541	2,692	6,925	7,798	1,640	2,088	4,070	Total Sub-order 53			
18,956	**2,181**	**4,780**	**10,995**	**11,158**	**1,541**	**2,692**	**6,925**	**7,798**	**1,640**	**2,088**	**4,070**	**Total Order XVII**			
286,057	39,214	63,544	18,3299	154,474	18,829	32,928	102,717	131,583	20,385	30,616	80,582	**Total Class D**			

TABLE XVII.—Occupations, by Age.—

PROVINCIAL

Class.	Order.	Sub-order and Group.	Occupation.	Total. Total.	Total. 0—4	Total. 5—14	Total. 15—	Males. Total.	Males. 0—4
1	2	3	4	5	6	7	8	9	10
CLASS E.—COMMERCE, TRANSPORT AND STORAGE.	ORDER XVIII.—COMMERCE.	54.—Dealers in Money and Securities.	345. Bankers and bank-managers	4	...	...	4	4	...
			347. Money-lenders and pawn-brokers	19,282	2,078	4,095	13,109	11,185	1,010
			348. Bill discounters, etc.	1	...	1	...	...	...
			349. Insurance agents and under-writers	...	...	...	...	...	...
			350. Money changers and testers	1,041	97	214	730	584	52
			351. Bank clerks, cashiers, bill-collectors, accountants, etc.	23	4	5	14	12	1
			Total Sub-order 54	20,351	2,179	4,315	13,857	11,785	1,063
		55.—General Merchandise.	352. General merchants	1,618	239	390	989	734	58
			353. Merchants' Managers, accountants, clerks, assistants, etc.	3,546	375	639	2,532	2,306	135
			Total Sub-order 55	5,164	614	1,029	3,521	3,030	193
		56.—Dealing unspecified.	354 Shop-keepers' clerks, salesmen, etc.	624	69	101	454	296	43
			355. Shopkeepers' and money-lenders' servants	12,910	1,383	2,277	9,250	8,302	702
			356. Shopkeepers, otherwise unspecified	5,764	761	1,301	3,702	2,627	327
			357. Pedlars, hawkers, etc.	1,923	196	392	1,325	1,193	91
			Total Sub-order 56	21,221	2,409	4,071	14,731	12,518	1,163
		57.—Middlemen, etc. (a) Brokers, etc.	358. Brokers, agents, dubash	2,919	282	567	2,070	1,731	144
			359. Auctioneers, auditors, actuaries, notaries public, appraisers, house agents, etc.	29	7	6	16	8	1
		(b) Contractors and farmers.	360. Farmers of tolls, ferries	12	2	1	9	9	3
			361. Farmers of liquor, opium, etc.	1,134	139	256	739	693	75
			362. Lessees and superintendents of markets, stalls, etc.	90	17	21	52	46	9
			363. Contractors, otherwise unspecified	1,667	306	408	953	647	111
			364. Contractors for labour, emigration agents, etc.	94	10	22	62	54	4
			Total Sub-order 57	5,945	763	1,281	3,901	3,188	347
			Total Order XVIII	**52,671**	**5,965**	**10,698**	**36,010**	**30,530**	**2,866**
	ORDER XIX.—TRANSPORT AND STORAGE.	58.—Railway. (a) Administration.	365. Agents, directors, managers and their assistants.	...	...	...	...	...	...
			366. Traffic managers, superintendents and assistants.	...	...	...	...	...	...
			367. Locomotive superintendents and assistants.	...	...	...	...	...	...
			368. Auditors, accountants, etc.	...	...	...	...	...	...
			369. Engineers (when not returned under general heading).	24	...	...	24	23	...
			370. Clerical staff in railway establishment	225	44	39	142	118	10
		(b) Working staff	371. Station-masters and assistants, inspectors, overseers, etc.	194	36	50	108	91	15
			372. Guards, drivers, firemen, etc.	283	51	45	187	155	11
			373. Pointsmen, shunters, porters, signallers, etc.	634	91	90	453	448	48
			373a. Railway servants (indefinite)	2,050	300	416	1,334	1,247	145
			Total Sub-order 58	3,410	522	640	2,248	2,076	249
		59.—Road. (a) Cart, carriage, and tram-way, owners and drivers.	374. Tramway, mail carriage, etc., companies, contractors, etc.	...	...	...	...	...	...
			375. Cart-owners and drivers, and carting agents, etc.	14,738	1,809	2,928	9,911	9,615	941
			376. Livery stable-keepers, etc.	...	...	...	...	...	...
			377. Drivers, stable-boys, etc. (not private servants).	14	2	...	12	2	...
		(b) Carriers by pack animals.	378. Palki, etc., owners, bearers, etc.	37	3	5	29	28	...
			379. Pack bullock owners, drivers, etc.	1,917	299	491	1,127	1,152	132
			380. Pack camel, elephant, mule, etc., owners and drivers.	317	32	60	225	220	17
			Total Sub-order 59	17,083	2,235	3,484	11,304	11,017	1,090
		60.—Water. (a) Owners, etc., of vessels.	381. Ship owners, Companies, agents	...	...	...	...	...	...
			382. Shipping clerks, supercargoes, and stevedores.	...	...	...	...	...	...
			383. Boat and barge owners, etc.	...	...	...	...	...	...
		(b) Working Staff of vessels.	384. Ships officers, engineers, mariners, and firemen	...	...	...	...	...	...
			385. Boat and barge men	5	1	...	4	2	...
			386. Pilots	...	...	...	...	...	...
			387. Lock-keepers, etc., and canal service	...	...	...	...	...	...
			388. Dock and harbour service	...	...	...	...	...	...
			389. Divers (not for pearls).	7	1	2	4	5	1
			Total Sub-order 60	12	2	2	8	7	1

Part A.—PROVINCIAL SUMMARY —*contd.*

TOTAL.

Males.		Females.				Occupation.	Sub-order and Group.	Order.	Class.
5—14	15—	Total.	0—4	5—14	15—				
11	12	13	14	15	16				
...	4	...	...	...	...	346. Bankers and bank-managers	54.—Dealers in Money and Securities.	ORDER XVIII.—COMMERCE.	CLASS E.—COMMERCE, TRANSPORT, AND STORAGE.
2,255	7,920	8,097	1,068	1,840	5,189	347. Money-lenders and pawn-brokers			
...	...	1	...	1	...	348. Bill discounters, etc.			
...	...	...	...	...	...	349. Insurance agents and under-writers			
104	428	457	45	110	302	350. Money-changers and testers			
3	8	11	3	1	6	351. Bank clerks, cashiers, bill-collectors, accountants, etc.			
2,362	8,360	8,566	1,116	1,953	5,497	Total Sub-order 54			
171	465	884	141	219	524	352. General merchants	55.—General Merchandise.		
379	1,731	1,241	180	260	801	353. Merchants' managers, accountants, clerks, assistants, etc.			
550	2,196	2,125	321	479	1,325	Total Sub-order 55			
53	300	228	26	48	154	354. Shop-keepers' clerks, salesmen, etc.	56.—Dealing unspecified.		
1,221	6,379	4,608	681	1,056	2,871	355. Shop-keepers' and money lenders' servants			
582	1,718	3,137	434	719	1,984	356. Shop-keepers, otherwise unspecified			
221	881	720	105	171	444	357. Pedlars, hawkers, etc.			
2,077	9,278	8,693	1,246	1,994	5,453	Total Sub-order 56			
308	1,279	1,188	138	259	791	358. Brokers, agents, dubash	57.—Middlemen, etc. (a) Brokers, etc.		
3	3	22	5	3	13	359. Auctioneers, auditors, actuaries, notaries public, appraisers, house-agents, etc.			
...	7	3	...	1	2	360. Farmers of tolls, ferries	(b) Contractors and farmers.		
141	477	441	64	115	262	361. Farmers of liquor, opium, etc.			
10	27	44	8	11	25	362. Lessees and superintendents of markets, stalls, etc.			
141	395	1,020	195	267	558	363. Contractors, otherwise unspecified			
11	39	40	6	11	23	364. Contractors for labour, emigration agents, etc.			
624	2,227	2,757	416	667	1,674	Total Sub-order 57			
5,603	**22,061**	**22,141**	**3,099**	**5,093**	**13,949**	**Total Order XVIII**			
...	...	...	...	...	...	365. Agents, directors, managers and their Assistants.	58.—Railway. (a) Administration.	ORDER XIX.—TRANSPORT AND STORAGE.	
...	...	...	...	...	...	366. Traffic managers, superintendents and assistants.			
...	...	...	...	...	...	367. Locomotive superintendents and assistants.			
...	...	...	...	...	...	368. Auditors, accountants, etc.			
...	23	1	...	...	1	369. Engineers (when not returned under general heading).			
21	77	107	24	18	65	370. Clerical Staff in Railway establishment			
21	55	103	21	29	53	371. Station-masters and assistants, inspectors, overseers	(b) Working staff.		
20	114	128	30	25	73	372. Guards, drivers, firemen, etc.			
54	340	192	43	36	113	373. Pointsmen, shunters, porters, signallers, etc.			
230	872	803	155	186	462	373a. Railway servants (indefinite)			
346	1,481	1,334	273	294	767	Total Sub-order 58			
...	...	...	...	...	...	374. Tramway, mail carriage, etc., companies, contractors, etc.	59.—Road. (a) Cart, carriage and tramway owners and drivers.		
1,661	7,013	5,123	958	1,267	2,898	375. Cart owners and drivers, and carting agents, etc.			
...	...	...	...	...	...	376. Livery stable-keepers, etc.			
...	2	12	2	...	10	377. Drivers, stable-boys, etc. (not private servants).			
4	24	9	3	1	5	378. Palki, etc., owners, bearers, etc.	(b) Carriers by pack animals.		
275	745	765	167	216	382	379. Pack bullock owners, drivers, etc.			
34	169	97	15	26	56	380. Pack camel, elephant, mule, etc., owners and drivers			
1,974	7,953	6,006	1,145	1,510	3,352	Total Sub-order 59			
...	...	...	...	...	...	381. Ship owners, companies, agents	60.—Water. (a) Owners, etc., of vessels.		
...	...	...	...	...	...	382. Shipping clerks, supercargoes and stevedores.			
...	...	...	...	...	...	383. Boat and barge owners, etc.			
...	...	...	...	...	...	384. Ship's officers, engineers, mariners, and firemen.	(b)—Working Staff of vessels.		
...	2	3	1	...	2	385. Boat and barge men			
...	...	...	...	...	...	386. Pilots			
...	...	...	...	...	...	387. Lock-keepers, etc., and canal service			
...	...	...	...	...	...	388. Dock and harbour service			
2	2	2	...	...	2	389. Divers (not for pearls)			
2	4	5	1	...	4	Total Sub-order 60			

TABLE XVII.—Occupations, by Age.—

Class.	Order.	Sub-order and Group.	Occupation.	TOWN. Total. Total.	Total. 0—4	Total. 5—14	Total. 15—	Males. Total.	Males. 0—4	Males. 5—14	Males. 15—	Females. Total.	Females. 0—4	Females. 5—14	Females. 15—
				17	18	19	20	21	22	23	24	25	26	27	28
CLASS E.—COMMERCE, TRANSPORT AND STORAGE.	ORDER XVIII.—COMMERCE.	54.—Dealers in Money and Securities.	346. Bankers and bank-managers	4	...	...	4	4	...	...	4	...	...	...	...
			347. Money-lenders and pawn-brokers.	4,452	412	936	3,104	2,489	206	536	1,747	1,963	206	400	1,357
			348. Bill discounters, etc.	...	...	...	...	...	...	...	...	...	...	...	...
			349. Insurance agents and under-writers.	...	...	...	...	...	...	...	...	...	...	...	...
			350. Money changers and testers	601	51	125	425	323	27	64	232	278	24	61	193
			351. Bank clerks, cashiers, bill-collectors, accountants, etc.	21	4	5	12	11	1	3	7	10	3	2	5
			Total Sub-order 54	5,078	467	1,066	3,545	2,827	234	603	1,990	2,251	233	463	1,555
		55.—General Merchandise.	352. General merchants	361	44	81	236	163	17	35	111	198	27	46	125
			353. Merchants' managers, accountants, clerks, assistants, etc.	1,629	171	309	1,149	981	82	174	725	648	89	135	424
			Total Sub-order 55	1,990	215	390	1,385	1,144	99	209	836	846	116	181	549
		56.—Dealing unspecified.	354. Shop-keepers' clerks, salesmen, etc.	376	41	63	272	226	25	31	170	150	16	32	102
			355. Shop-keepers' and money-lenders' servants.	6,226	686	1,191	4,349	3,649	324	635	2,690	2,577	362	556	1,659
			356. Shop-keepers, otherwise unspecified.	1,309	198	312	819	602	82	148	372	707	96	164	447
			357. Pedlars, hawkers, etc.	856	111	185	560	433	47	96	290	423	64	89	270
			Total Sub-order 56	8,767	1,016	1,751	6,000	4,910	478	920	3,522	3,857	538	841	2,478
		57.—Middlemen, etc. (a) Brokers, etc.	358. Brokers, agents, dubash	2,244	193	440	1,611	1,316	97	240	979	928	96	200	632
			359. Auctioneers, auditors, actuaries, notaries-public, appraisers, house-agents, etc.	3	...	1	2	1	...	...	1	2	...	1	1
		(b) Contractors, and farmers.	360. Farmers of tolls, ferries	11	2	1	9	9	2	...	7	3	...	1	2
			361. Farmers of liquor, opium, etc.	174	17	38	119	86	10	19	57	88	7	19	62
			362. Lessees and superintendents of markets, stalls, etc.	43	9	13	21	23	5	7	11	20	4	6	10
			363. Contractors, otherwise unspecified.	430	52	100	278	206	31	52	123	224	21	48	155
			364. Contractors for labour, emigration agents, etc.	60	6	15	39	27	2	6	19	33	4	9	20
			Total Sub-order 57	2,956	279	608	2,079	1,668	147	324	1,197	1,298	132	284	882
			Total Order XVIII	**18,801**	**1,977**	**3,815**	**13,009**	**10,549**	**958**	**2,046**	**7,545**	**8,252**	**1,019**	**1,769**	**5,484**
	ORDER XIX.—TRANSPORT AND STORAGE.	58.—Railway. (a) Administration.	365. Agents, directors, managers and their assistants.	...	...	...	...	...	...	...	...	...	...	...	...
			366. Traffic managers, superintendents and assistants.	...	...	...	...	...	...	...	...	...	...	...	...
			367. Locomotive superintendents and assistants.	...	...	...	...	...	...	...	...	...	...	...	...
			368. Auditors, accountants, etc.	...	...	...	...	...	...	...	...	...	...	...	...
			369. Engineers (when not returned under general heading).	23	...	...	23	22	...	...	22	1	...	...	1
			370. Clerical staff in railway establishment.	163	26	29	108	100	15	18	67	63	11	11	41
		(b) Working staff	371. Station-masters and assistants, inspectors, overseers, etc.	91	14	21	56	43	5	9	29	48	9	12	27
			372. Guards, drivers, firemen, etc.	269	50	41	178	152	31	20	111	117	19	21	67
			373. Pointsmen, shunters, porters, signallers, etc.	342	48	52	242	227	25	27	175	115	23	25	67
			373a. Railway servants (indefinite)	774	113	169	492	426	64	86	276	348	49	83	216
			Total Sub-order 58	1,562	251	312	1,099	970	130	160	680	592	121	152	419
		59.—Road. (a) Cart, carriage, and tramway owners and drivers.	374. Tramway, mail carriage, etc., companies, contractors, etc.	...	...	...	...	...	...	...	...	...	...	...	...
			375. Cart-owners and drivers and carting agents, etc.	5,247	671	1,037	3,539	3,251	317	581	2,353	1,996	354	456	1,186
			376. Livery stable-keepers, etc.	...	...	...	...	...	...	...	...	...	...	...	...
			377. Drivers, stable-boys, etc. (not private servants).	14	2	...	12	2	...	...	2	12	2	...	10
			378. Palki, etc., owners, bearers, etc.	10	...	...	10	9	...	...	9	1	...	...	1
		(b) Carriers by pack animals.	379. Pack bullock owners, drivers, etc.	108	20	20	68	72	12	10	50	36	8	10	18
			380. Pack camel, elephant, mule, etc., owners and drivers.	221	18	47	146	135	10	24	101	76	8	23	45
			Total Sub-order 59	5,590	711	1,104	3,775	3,469	339	615	2,515	2,121	372	489	1,260
		60.—Water. (a) Owners, etc., of vessels.	381. Ship-owners, companies and agents.	...	...	...	...	...	...	...	...	...	...	...	...
			382. Shipping clerks, supercargoes and stevedores.	...	...	...	...	...	...	...	...	...	...	...	...
			383. Boat and barge owners, etc.	...	...	...	...	...	...	...	...	...	...	...	...
		(b) Working staff of vessels.	384. Ship's officers, engineers, mariners, and firemen.	...	...	...	...	...	...	...	...	...	...	...	...
			385. Boat and barge men	...	...	...	...	...	...	...	...	...	...	...	...
			386. Pilots	...	...	...	...	...	...	...	...	...	...	...	...
			387. Lock-keepers, etc., and canal service.	...	...	...	...	...	...	...	...	...	...	...	...
			388. Dock and Harbour Service	...	...	...	...	...	...	...	...	...	...	...	...
			389. Divers (not for pearls)	7	1	2	4	5	1	2	2	2	...	...	1
			Total Sub-order 60	7	1	2	4	5	1	2	2	2	...	...	2

Part A.—PROVINCIAL SUMMARY—*contd.*

COUNTRY.												Occupation.	Sub-order and Group.	Order.	Class.
Total.				Males.				Females.							
Total.	0—4	5—14	15—	Total.	0—4	5—14	15—	Total.	0—4	5—14	15—				
29	30	31	32	33	34	35	36	37	38	39	40				
...	...	...	...	...	...	...	...	...	...	...	...	346. Bankers and bank-managers	54.—Dealers in Money and Securities.	ORDER XVIII.—COMMERCE.	CLASS E.—COMMERCE, TRANSPORT AND STORAGE.
14,830	1,686	3,159	10,005	8,696	804	1,719	6,173	6,134	862	1,440	3,832	347. Money-lenders and pawn-brokers.			
1	...	1	...	...	...	...	...	1	...	1	...	348. Bill discounters, etc.			
...	...	...	...	...	...	...	...	...	...	...	...	349. Insurance agents and under-writers.			
440	46	89	305	261	25	40	196	179	21	49	109	350. Money changers and testers			
2	...	...	2	1	...	...	1	1	...	...	1	351. Bank clerks, cashiers, bill-collectors, accountants, assistants, etc.			
15,273	1,712	3,249	10,312	8,958	829	1,759	6,370	6,315	883	1,490	3,942	Total Sub-order 54			
1,157	195	209	753	571	81	135	354	686	114	173	379	352. General merchants	55.—General Merchandise.		
1,917	204	330	1,383	1,324	113	205	1,006	593	91	125	377	353. Merchants' managers, accountants, clerks, assistants, etc.			
3,074	399	639	2,136	1,895	194	341	1,360	1,279	205	298	776	Total Sub-order 55			
248	28	38	182	170	18	22	130	78	10	16	52	354. Shop-keepers' clerks, salesmen, etc.	56.—Dealing unspecified.		
6,684	697	1,086	4,901	4,653	378	586	3,689	2,031	319	500	1,212	355. Shop-keepers' and money-lenders' servants.			
4,455	583	989	2,883	2,025	245	434	1,345	2,430	338	555	1,537	356. Shop-keepers, otherwise unspecified.			
1,057	85	207	765	760	44	125	591	297	41	82	174	357. Pedlars, hawkers, etc.			
12,444	1,393	2,320	8,731	7,608	685	1,167	5,756	4,836	708	1,153	2,975	Total Sub-order 56			
675	89	127	459	415	47	68	300	260	42	59	159	358. Brokers, agents, dubash	57.—Middlemen, etc. (a) Brokers, etc.		
26	7	5	14	7	2	3	2	19	5	2	12	359. Auctioneers, auditors, actuaries, notaries public, appraisers, house-agents, etc.			
...	...	...	...	...	...	...	...	...	...	...	...	360. Farmers of tolls, ferries	(b) Contractors and farmers.		
960	122	218	620	607	65	122	420	353	57	96	200	361. Farmers of liquor, opium, etc.			
47	8	8	31	23	4	3	16	24	4	5	15	362. Lessees and superintendents of markets, stalls, etc.			
1,237	254	308	675	441	80	89	272	796	174	219	403	363. Contractors, otherwise unspecified.			
34	4	7	23	27	2	5	20	7	2	2	3	364. Contractors for labour, emigration agents, etc.			
2,979	484	673	1,822	1,520	200	290	1,030	1,459	284	383	792	Total Sub-order 57			
33,870	**3,988**	**6,881**	**23,001**	**19,981**	**1,908**	**3,557**	**14,516**	**13,889**	**2,080**	**3,324**	**8,485**	**Total Order XVIII**			
...	...	...	...	...	...	...	...	...	...	...	...	365. Agents, directors, managers and their assistants.	58.—Railway. (a) Administration.	ORDER XIX.—TRANSPORT AND STORAGE.	
...	...	...	...	...	...	...	...	...	...	...	...	366. Traffic managers, superintendents and assistants.			
...	...	...	...	...	...	...	...	...	...	...	...	367. Locomotive superintendents and assistants.			
...	...	...	...	...	...	...	...	...	...	...	...	368. Auditors, accountants, etc.			
1	...	...	1	1	...	...	1	...	...	...	...	369. Engineers (when not returned under general heading).			
62	18	10	34	18	5	3	10	44	23	7	24	370. Clerical staff in railway establishment.			
103	22	29	52	48	10	12	26	55	12	17	26	371 Station-masters and assistants, inspectors, overseers, etc.	(b) Working staff.		
14	1	4	9	3	...	...	3	11	1	4	6	372. Guards, drivers, firemen, etc.			
292	43	38	211	215	23	27	165	77	20	11	46	373. Pointsmen, shunters, porters, signallers, etc.			
1,276	187	247	842	821	81	144	596	455	106	103	246	373a. Railway servants (indefinite)			
1,748	271	328	1,149	1,106	119	186	801	642	152	142	348	Total Sub-order 58			
...	...	...	...	...	...	...	...	...	...	...	...	374. Tramway, mail carriage, etc., companies, contractors, etc.	59.—Road. (a) Cart, carriage and tramway owners and drivers.		
9,491	1,228	1,891	6,372	6,364	624	1,080	4,660	3,127	604	811	1,712	375. Cart-owners and drivers and carting agents, etc.			
...	...	...	...	...	...	...	...	...	...	...	...	376. Livery stable-keepers, etc.			
...	...	...	...	...	...	...	...	...	...	...	...	377. Drivers, stable-boys, etc. (not private servants).			
27	3	5	19	19	...	4	15	8	3	1	4	378. Palki, etc., owners, bearers, etc.			
1,809	279	471	1,059	1,080	120	265	695	729	159	206	364	379. Pack bullock owners, drivers, etc.	(b) Carriers by pack animals.		
106	14	13	79	85	7	10	68	21	7	3	11	380. Pack camel, elephant, mule, etc., owners and drivers.			
11,433	1,524	2,380	7,529	7,548	751	1,359	5,438	3,885	773	1,021	2,091	Total Sub-order 59			
...	...	...	...	...	...	...	...	...	...	...	...	381. Ship owners, companies, agents.	60.—Water. (a) Owners, etc., of vessels.		
...	...	...	...	...	...	...	...	...	...	...	...	382. Shipping clerks, supercargoes, and stevedores.			
...	...	...	...	...	...	...	...	...	...	...	...	383. Boat and barge owners, etc.			
...	...	...	...	...	...	...	...	...	...	...	...	384. Ship's officers, engineers, mariners and firemen	(b) Working Staff of vessels.		
5	1	...	4	2	...	...	2	3	1	...	2	385. Boat and bargemen			
...	...	...	...	...	...	...	...	...	...	...	...	386. Pilots			
...	...	...	...	...	...	...	...	...	...	...	...	387. Lock-keepers, etc., and canal service			
...	...	...	...	...	...	...	...	...	...	...	...	388. Dock and harbour service			
...	...	...	...	...	...	...	...	...	...	...	...	389. Divers (not for pearls)			
5	1	...	4	2	...	...	2	3	1	...	2	Total Sub-order 60			

TABLE XVII.—Occupations, by Age.—

PROVINCIAL

Class.	Order.	Sub-order and Group.	Occupation.	Total. Total.	Total. 0—4	Total. 5—14	Total. 15—	Males. Total.	Males. 0—4
1	2	3	4	5	6	7	8	9	10
CLASS E.—COMMERCE, TRADE AXD STORAGE —contd.	ORDER XIX.—TRANSPORT AND STORAGE —contd.	61.—Messages— (a) Post, etc.	390. Postal Directors, Post masters and clerks	222	23	47	152	114	9
			391. Do. messengers, runners, etc.	718	84	117	517	498	51
			392. Messengers (unspecified)	2,725	317	463	1,945	1,757	170
		(b) Telegraph and Telephone.	393. Telegraph officers (Government and Railway and others), and clerical and accounts establishment.	53	2	8	43	31	...
			394. Signallers and messengers	16	4	2	10	9	1
			395. Telephone Company's service	...	...	...	...	...	...
			Total Sub-order 61	3,734	430	637	2,667	2,403	231
		62.—Storage and Weighing.	396. Warehouse owners, keepers, etc.	12	3	1	8	3	...
			397. Warehouse service	436	51	95	290	248	29
			398. Porters (general)	4,094	588	762	2,744	2,618	303
			399. Weighmen and measurers	786	108	156	522	435	51
			400. Watchmen (not village)	180	13	25	142	122	5
			Total Sub-order 62	5,508	763	1,039	3,706	3,426	388
			Total Order XIX	**29,687**	**3,952**	**5,802**	**19,933**	**18,929**	**1,959**
			Total Class E.	**82,358**	**9,917**	**16,498**	**55,943**	**49,459**	**4,825**
CLASS F.—PROFESSIONS.	ORDER XX.—LEARNED AND ARTISTIC PROFESSIONS.	63.—Religion— (a) Priests, Ministers, etc.	401. Priests, ministers, preachers, missionaries, etc.	2,504	288	548	1,668	1,384	139
			402. Catechists, readers, zanana mission service, etc.	179	19	30	130	127	12
			403. Exercists, hail-averters, amulettiers, etc.	155	23	35	97	83	12
		(b) Subsidiary religious services.	404. Religious mendicants, inmates of monasteries, convents, etc.	15,077	1,552	3,026	10,499	9,327	790
			405. Church, temple, masjid, pagoda, ghât, burial or burning ground service, pilgrim conductors and undertakers.	935	76	178	681	550	33
			Total Sub-order 63	18,850	1,958	3,817	13,075	11,471	986
		64.—Education	406. Administrative and inspecting officials	38	1	10	27	22	...
			407. Principals, professors, and teachers, in colleges and schools, etc.	4,807	588	814	3,405	3,072	300
			408. Clerks, etc., on establishments of educational institutions.	122	16	18	88	68	9
			Total Sub-order 64	4,967	605	842	3,520	3,162	309
		65.—Literature	409. Authors, editors, journalists, ballad-makers	39	4	12	23	24	4
			410. Reporters, short-hand writers, book copyists	...	...	...	...	...	...
			411. Private secretartes and clerks	472	54	108	310	251	33
			412. Public scribes and copyists	...	...	...	...	...	...
			413. Service in libraries and literary institutions	18	...	1	17	11	...
			Total Sub-order 65	529	58	121	350	286	37
		66.—Law	414. Barristers, advocates and pleaders	676	80	260	436	352	36
			415. Solicitors and attorneys	...	...	...	...	...	...
			415a. Kazis	241	26	63	152	139	11
			416. Law agents, mukhtears, etc.	26	2	2	22	17	1
			417. Articled clerks and other lawyers' clerks	148	14	40	94	80	8
			418. Stamp-vendors	395	37	62	296	241	21
			419. Petition-writers	417	43	67	307	241	13
			Total Sub-order 66	1,903	202	394	1,307	1,070	100
		67.—Medicine— (a) Practitioners	420. Administrative and inspecting staff (when not returned under general head).	...	...	...	...	...	...
			421. Practitioners by diploma	148	16	25	107	83	10
			422. Practitioners without diploma (baid, hakim, kobiraj, etc.)	1,458	184	332	942	867	97
			423. Dentists	...	...	...	...	...	...
			424. Oculists	...	...	...	...	...	...
			425. Vaccinators	143	23	26	94	75	11
			426. Midwifery	869	60	109	700	115	19
		(b) Subsidiary medical services.	427. Hospital and asylum matrons, assistants and apothecaries.	53	9	11	33	28	7
			428. Compounders, nurses, and hospital, asylum and dispensary service.	82	10	17	55	49	2
			Total Sub-order 67	2,753	302	520	1,931	1,217	146

Part A.—PROVINCIAL SUMMARY—*contd.*

TOTAL.

Males.		Females.				Occupation.	Sub-order and Group.	Order.	Class.
5—14	15—	Total.	0—4	5—14	15—				
11	12	13	14	15	16				
19	86	108	14	48	66	390. Postal Directors, Postmasters and clerks	61.—Messages— (a) Post, etc.	ORDER XIX.—TRANSPORT AND STORAGE—*contd.*	CLASS E.—COMMERCE, TRANSPORT AND STORAGE—*contd.*
71	370	226	33	46	147	391. Do. messengers, runners, etc.			
239	1,348	968	147	224	597	392. Messengers (unspecified)			
5	26	22	2	3	17	393. Telegraph officers (Government, Railway and others), and clerical and accounts establishment.	(b) Telegraph and Telephone.		
2	6	7	3	...	4	394. Signallers and messengers			
...	...	...	...	...	...	395. Telephone Company's service			
336	1,836	1,331	299	301	831	Total Sub-order 61			
1	2	9	3	...	6	396. Warehouse owners, keepers, etc.	62.—Storage and Weighing.		
41	178	188	22	54	112	397. Warehouse service			
411	1,904	1,476	285	351	840	398. Porters (general)			
81	303	351	57	75	219	399. Weighmen and measurers			
11	106	58	8	14	36	400. Watchmen (not village)			
545	2,403	2,082	375	494	1,213	Total Sub-order 62			
3,203	13,767	10,758	1,993	2,599	6,166	**Total Order XIX**			
8,806	35,828	32,899	5,092	7,692	20,115	**Total Class E**			
291	954	1,120	149	257	714	401. Priests, ministers, preachers, missionaries, etc.	63.—Religion— (a) Priests, Ministers, etc.	ORDER XX.—LEARNED AND ARTISTIC PROFESSIONS.	CLASS F.—PROFESSIONS.
18	97	52	7	12	33	402. Catechists, readers, zanana mission service, etc.			
18	53	72	11	17	44	403. Exorcists, hail-averters, amulettiers, etc.	(b) Subsidiary religious services.		
1,766	6,771	5,750	762	1,260	3,728	404. Religious mendicants, inmates of monasteries, convents, etc.			
93	424	385	43	85	257	405. Church, temple, masjid, pagoda, ghât, burial or burning ground service, pilgrim conductors, and undertakers.			
2,186	8,299	7,379	972	1,631	4,776	Total Sub-order 63			
7	15	16	1	3	12	406. Administrative and inspecting officials	64.—Education		
466	2,306	1,735	288	348	1,099	407. Principals, professors and teachers in colleges and schools, etc.			
9	50	54	7	9	38	408. Clerks, etc., on establishments of educational institutions.			
482	2,371	1,805	296	360	1,149	Total Sub-order 64			
6	14	15	...	6	9	409. Authors, editors, journalists, ballad-makers	65.—Literature		
...	...	...	...	...	...	410. Reporters, short-hand writers, book copyists			
46	172	222	21	62	138	411. Private secretaries and clerks			
...	...	...	...	...	...	412. Public scribes and copyists			
...	11	7	...	1	6	413. Service in libraries and literary institutions			
52	197	243	22	69	153	Total Sub-order 65			
87	229	324	44	73	207	414. Barristers, advocates and pleaders	66.—Law		
...	...	...	...	...	...	415. Solicitors and attorneys			
37	91	102	15	26	61	415a. Kazis			
2	14	9	1	...	8	416. Law agents, mukhtears, etc.			
18	54	68	6	32	40	417. Articled clerks and other lawyers' clerks			
34	186	154	16	28	110	418. Stamp-vendors			
36	182	176	20	31	125	419. Petition-writers			
214	756	833	108	180	551	Total Sub-order 66			
...	...	...	...	...	...	420. Administrative and inspecting staff (when not returned under general head.)	67.—Medicine—		
13	60	65	6	12	47	421. Practitioners by diploma	(a) Practitioners		
198	873	591	87	134	370	422. Practitioners without diploma (baid, hakim, kobiraj, etc.)			
...	...	...	...	...	...	423. Dentists			
...	...	...	...	...	...	424. Oculists			
13	51	68	13	13	43	425. Vaccinators			
49	47	754	41	60	653	426. Midwifery			
8	16	25	2	6	17	427. Hospital and asylum matrons, assistants and apothecaries.	(b) Subsidiary medical services.		
8	39	33	8	9	16	428. Compounders, nurses, and hospital, asylum and dispensary service.			
286	784	1,536	156	234	1,146	Total Sub-order 67			

TABLE XVII.—Occupations, by Age.—

Class.	Order.	Sub-order and Group.	Occupation.	Town: Total: Total.	Total: 0–4	Total: 5–14	Total: 15–	Males: Total.	Males: 0–4	Males: 5–14	Males: 15–	Females: Total.	Females: 0–4	Females: 5–14	Females: 15–
				17	18	19	20	21	22	23	24	25	26	27	28
CLASS E.—COMMERCE, TRANSPORT AND STORAGE—*contd.*	ORDER XIX.—TRANSPORT AND STORAGE—*contd.*	61.—Messages—													
		(a) Post, etc.	390. Postal Directors, Postmasters and clerks.	131	11	33	87	69	4	17	48	62	7	16	39
			391. Postal messengers, runners, etc.	332	37	50	245	238	24	36	178	94	13	14	67
			392. Messengers (unspecified)	1,394	171	234	989	841	91	111	639	553	80	123	350
		(b) Telegraph and Telepone.	393. Telegraph officers (Government; Railway and others), and clerical and accounts establishment.	46	2	7	37	26	...	5	21	20	2	2	16
			394. Signallers and messengers	14	4	1	9	7	1	1	5	7	3	...	4
			395. Telephone Company's service	...	...	...	...	...	...	...	...	...	...	...	...
			Total Sub-order 61	1,917	225	325	1,367	1,181	120	170	891	736	105	155	476
		62.—Storage and Weighing.	396. Warehouse owners, keepers, etc.	12	3	1	8	3	...	1	2	9	3	...	6
			397. Warehouse service	385	45	85	255	220	27	37	156	165	18	48	99
			398. Porters (general)	3,239	465	611	2,163	2,109	243	325	1,541	1,130	222	286	622
			399. Weighmen and measurers	582	77	116	389	323	34	63	226	259	43	53	163
			400. Watchmen (not village)	104	4	14	86	79	2	7	70	25	2	7	16
			Total Sub-order 62	4,322	594	827	2,901	2,734	306	433	1,995	1,588	288	394	906
			Total Order XIX	**13,498**	**1,782**	**2,570**	**9,146**	**8,359**	**896**	**1,380**	**6,083**	**5,139**	**886**	**1,190**	**3,063**
			Total Class E	**32,299**	**3,759**	**6,385**	**22,155**	**18,908**	**1,854**	**3,426**	**13,628**	**13,391**	**1,905**	**2,959**	**8,527**
CLASS F.—PROFESSIONS.	ORDER XX.—LEARNED AND ARTISTIC PROFESSIONS.	63.—Religion—													
		(a) Priests, Ministers, etc.	401. Priests, ministers, preachers, missionaries, etc.	658	81	148	429	325	41	77	207	333	40	71	222
			402. Catechists, readers, zanana mission service, etc.	96	16	23	57	56	11	11	34	40	5	12	23
			403. Exorcists, hail-averters, amulettiers, etc.	31	4	7	20	14	1	2	11	17	3	5	9
		(b) Subsidiary religious services.	404. Religious mendicants, inmates of monasteries, convents, etc.	4,604	438	881	3,285	2,806	223	497	2,086	1,798	215	384	1,199
			405. Church, temple, masjid, pagoda, ghat, burial or burning ground service, pilgrim conductors and undertakers.	426	31	77	318	252	13	41	198	174	18	36	120
			Total Sub-order 63	5,815	570	1,136	4,109	3,453	289	628	2,536	2,362	281	508	1,573
		64.—Education	406. Administrative and inspecting officials.	28	1	8	19	16	...	6	10	12	1	2	9
			407. Principals, professors and teachers, in colleges and schools, etc.	1,422	166	280	976	842	82	163	597	580	84	117	379
			408. Clerks, etc., on establishments of educational institutions.	79	9	11	59	40	3	5	32	39	6	6	27
			Total Sub-order 64	1,529	176	299	1,054	898	85	174	639	631	91	125	415
		65.—Literature	409. Authors, editors, journalists, ballad-makers.	34	2	11	21	20	2	5	13	14	...	6	8
			410. Reporters, short-hand writers, book-copyists.	...	...	...	...	...	...	...	...	...	...	...	...
			411. Private secretaries and clerks.	268	33	67	168	112	17	17	78	156	16	50	90
			412. Public scribes and copyists	...	...	...	...	...	...	...	...	...	...	...	...
			413. Service in libraries and literary institutions.	15	...	1	14	9	...	...	9	6	...	1	5
			Total Sub-order 65	317	35	79	203	141	19	22	100	176	16	57	103
		66.—Law	414. Barristers, advocates and pleaders.	601	73	145	383	319	34	81	204	282	39	64	179
			415. Solicitors and attorneys	...	...	...	...	...	...	...	...	...	...	...	...
			415a. Kazis	116	17	29	70	65	7	17	41	51	10	12	29
			416. Law Agents, mukhtears, etc.	9	...	1	8	7	...	1	6	2	...	...	2
			417. Articled clerks and other lawyers' clerks.	95	8	22	65	58	4	10	44	37	4	12	21
			418. Stamp-vendors	193	20	30	143	118	14	16	88	75	6	14	55
			419. Petition-writers	269	27	42	200	146	13	22	111	123	14	20	89
			Total Sub-order 66	1,283	145	269	869	713	72	147	494	570	73	122	375
		67.—Medicine—													
		(a) Practitioners	420. Administrative and inspecting staff (when not returned under general head.)	...	...	...	...	...	...	...	...	...	...	...	...
			421. Practitioners by diploma.	117	11	19	87	67	7	11	49	50	4	8	38
			422. Practitioners without diploma (baid, hakim, kobiraj, etc.)	574	71	124	370	342	39	71	232	232	32	53	147
			423. Dentists	...	...	...	...	...	...	...	...	...	...	...	...
			424. Oculists	...	...	...	...	...	...	...	...	...	...	...	...
			425. Vaccinators	74	14	16	44	35	7	8	20	39	7	8	24
			426. Midwifery	204	13	29	162	16	4	7	5	188	9	22	157
		(b) Subsidiary medical services.	427. Hospital and asylum matrons, assistants and apothecaries.	42	6	9	27	23	5	5	13	19	1	4	14
			428. Compounders, nurses, and hospital, asylum and dispensary service.	63	10	15	38	33	2	6	25	30	8	9	13
			Total Sub-order 67	1,074	125	212	737	516	64	108	344	558	61	104	393

Part A.—PROVINCIAL SUMMARY—*contd.*

COUNTRY.												Occupation.	Sub-order and Group.	Order.	Class.
Total.				Males.				Females.							
Total.	0—4	5—14	15—	Total.	0—4	5—14	15—	Total.	0—4	5—14	15—				
29	30	31	32	33	34	35	36	37	38	39	40				
91	12	14	65	45	5	2	38	46	7	12	27	390. Postal Directors, Postmasters and clerks.	61.—Messages— (a) Post, etc.	ORDER XIX.—TRANSPORT AND STORAGE—contd.	CLASS E.—COMMERCE, TRANSPORT AND STORAGE—contd.
386	47	67	272	254	27	35	192	132	20	32	80	391. Postal messengers, runners, etc.			
1,331	146	229	956	916	79	128	709	425	67	101	247	392. Messengers (unspecified).			
7	...	1	6	5	—	...	5	2	...	1	1	393. Telegraph officers (Government, Railway and others), and clerical and accounts establishment.	(b) Telegraph and Telephone.		
2	...	1	1	2	-	1	1	...	...	...	...	394. Signallers and messengers			
...	...	...	...	...	...	...	...	...	...	...	...	395. Telephone Company's service			
1,817	205	312	1,300	1,222	111	166	945	595	94	146	355	Total Sub-order 61			
...	...	...	...	...	...	...	...	...	...	..	...	396. Warehouse owners, keepers, etc.	62.—Storage and Weighing.		
52	6	10	35	28	2	4	22	23	4	6	13	397. Warehouse service			
855	123	151	581	509	60	86	353	346	63	65	218	398. Porters (general)			
204	31	40	133	112	17	18	77	92	14	22	56	399. Weighmen and measurers			
76	9	11	56	43	3	4	36	33	6	7	20	400. Watchmen (not village)			
1,186	169	212	805	692	82	112	498	494	87	100	307	Total Sub-order 62			
16,189	2,170	3,232	10,787	10,570	1,063	1,823	7,684	5,619	1,107	1,409	3,103	**Total Order XIX**			
50,059	6,158	10,113	33,788	30,551	2,971	5,380	22,200	19,508	3,187	4,733	11,588	**Total Class E**			
1,846	207	400	1,239	1,059	98	214	747	787	109	186	492	401. Priests, ministers, preachers, missionaries, etc.	63.—Religion— (a) Priests, Ministers, etc.	ORDER XX.—LEARNED AND ARTISTIC PROFESSIONS.	CLASS F.—PROFESSIONS.
83	3	7	73	71	1	7	63	12	2	...	10	402. Catechists, readers, zanana mission service, etc.			
124	19	28	77	69	11	16	42	55	8	12	35	403. Exorcists, hail-averters, amulet-tiers, etc.			
10,473	1,114	2,145	7,214	6,521	567	1,269	4,685	3,952	547	876	2,529	404. Religious mendicants, inmates of monasteries, convents, etc.	(b) Subsidiary religious services.		
509	45	101	363	298	20	52	226	211	25	49	137	405. Church, temple, masjid, pagoda, ghât, burial or burning ground service, pilgrim conductors and undertakers.			
13,035	1,388	2,681	8,966	8,018	697	1,558	5,763	5,017	691	1,123	3,203	Total Sub-order 63			
10	...	2	8	6	...	1	5	4	...	1	3	406. Administrative and inspecting officials.	64.—Education		
2,385	422	534	1,429	1,230	218	303	1,709	1,155	204	231	720	407. Principals, professors and teachers in colleges and schools, etc.			
43	7	7	29	28	6	4	18	15	1	3	11	408. Clerks, etc., on establishments of educational institutions.			
2,438	429	543	1,466	1,264	224	308	1,732	1,174	205	235	734	Total Sub-order 64			
5	2	1	2	4	2	1	1	1	...	...	1	409. Authors, editors, journalists, ballad-makers.	65.—Literature		
...	...	...	...	...	...	...	...	...	...	...	...	410. Reporters, short-hand writers, book-copyists.			
204	21	41	142	139	16	29	94	65	5	12	48	411. Private secretaries and clerks			
—	...	...	...	...	...	...	...	...	...	...	...	412. Public scribes and copyists			
3	...	...	3	2	...	...	2	1	...	...	1	413. Service in libraries and literary institutions.			
212	23	42	147	145	18	30	97	67	5	12	50	Total Sub-order 65			
75	7	15	53	33	2	6	25	42	5	9	28	414. Barristers, advocates and pleaders.	66.—Law		
...	...	...	—	...	...	...	...	...	...	...	...	415. Solicitors and attorneys			
125	9	34	82	74	4	20	50	51	5	14	32	415a. Kazis			
17	2	1	14	10	1	1	8	7	1	...	6	416. Law agents, mukhtears, etc.			
53	6	18	29	22	4	8	10	31	2	10	19	417. Articled clerks and other lawyers' clerks.			
202	17	32	153	123	7	18	98	79	10	14	55	418. Stamp-vendors			
148	16	25	107	95	10	14	71	53	6	11	36	419. Petition-writers			
620	57	125	438	357	28	67	262	263	29	58	176	Total Sub-order 66			
...	...	...	...	...	...	...	...	...	...	...	...	420. Administrative and inspecting staff (when not returned under general head.)	67.—Medicine— (a) Practitioners		
31	5	6	20	16	3	2	11	15	2	4	9	421. Practitioners by diploma			
884	113	208	563	525	58	127	340	359	55	81	223	422. Practitioners without diploma (baid, hakim, kobiraj, etc.)			
...	...	...	...	...	...	...	...	...	...	...	...	423. Dentists			
...	...	...	...	...	...	...	...	...	...	...	...	424. Oculists			
69	9	10	50	40	4	5	31	29	5	5	19	425. Vaccinators			
665	47	80	538	99	15	42	42	566	32	38	496	426. Midwifery			
11	3	2	6	5	2	...	3	6	1	2	3	427. Hospital and asylum matrons, assistants and apothecaries.	(b) Subsidiary medical services.		
19	...	2	17	16	...	2	14	3	...	...	3	428. Compounders, nurses, and hospital, asylum and dispensary service.			
1,679	177	308	1,194	701	82	178	441	978	95	130	752	Total Sub-order 67			

TABLE XVII.—Occupations, by Age.—

Class.	Order.	Sub-order and Group.	Occupation.	PROVINCIAL — Total. — Total.	Total. — 0–4	Total. — 5–14	Total. — 15–	Males. — Total.	Males. — 0–4
1	2	3	4	5	6	7	8	9	10
CLASS F.—PROFESSIONS—*contd.*	ORDER XX.—LEARNED AND ARTISTIC PROFESSIONS—*contd.*	68.—Engineering and Surveying. (a) Engineers, Architects and Surveyors.	429. Administrative and inspecting staff	...	...	...	...	...	...
			430. Civil engineers and architects	59	8	16	35	51	6
			431. Topographical, archæological and revenue surveyors.	21	2	6	13	14	1
		(b) Subsidiary Staff	432. Draughtsmen and operators in survey offices, overseers, etc.	215	20	37	158	117	10
			433. Clerks, etc., in offices of the above	163	24	39	100	111	15
			Total Sub-order 68	458	54	98	306	293	32
		69.—Other Sciences (a) Astronomy, etc.	434. Astronomers and meteorologists and establishments.	...	...	...	...	...	...
			435. Botanists, naturalists and officers of scientific institutions.	...	...	...	...	...	...
			436. Metallurgists	...	...	...	...	...	...
		(b) Minor Sciences	437. Astrologers, genealogists and horoscope-casters.	34	6	4	24	25	3
			438. Almanack makers and sellers	...	...	...	...	...	...
			439. Diviners (selectors of wells and house-sites, etc.)	...	...	...	...	...	...
			Total Sub-order 69	34	6	4	24	25	3
		70. Pictorial Art and Sculpture.	440. Painters, superintendents of schools of art, etc.	49	5	8	36	23	1
			441. Sculptors	...	...	...	...	...	...
			442. Photographers	17	1	8	8	12	1
			Total Sub-order 70	66	6	16	44	35	2
		71.—Music, Acting, Dancing.	443. Music composers and teachers	6	...	...	6	3	...
			444. Band-masters and players (not military)	5,669	1,020	1,336	3,313	2,943	539
			445. Piano-tuners	...	...	...	...	...	...
			446. Actors, singers and dancers and their accompanists.	1,203	87	201	915	692	33
			Total Sub-order 71	6,878	1,107	1,537	4,234	4,638	572
			Total Order XX	**36,438**	**4,298**	**7,349**	**24,791**	**22,197**	**2,188**
	ORDER XXI.—SPORT AND AMUSEMENTS.	72.—Sport	447. Race-course service, book-makers, jockeys, etc.	...	...	...	...	...	...
			448. Shikaris, falconers and bird-catchers	1,366	243	435	688	795	115
			449. Huntsmen, whippers-in	...	...	...	...	...	...
			Total Sub-order 72	1,366	243	435	688	795	115
		73.—Exhibition and Games. (a) Catching, training and exhibiting animals.	450. Exhibitors of trained animals (bulls, bears, snakes, monkeys, etc.)	474	67	127	280	277	18
			451. Circus owners, managers, etc.	...	...	...	...	...	...
			452. Cock and pigeon fanciers	...	...	...	...	...	...
		(b) Conjuring, fortune-telling and other exhibitions.	453. Buffoons	...	...	...	...	...	...
			454. Story and ballad reciters	263	39	60	164	164	14
			455. Exhibitors of puppets and pictures	492	42	116	333	307	13
			456. Conjurors and fortune-tellers	10	...	1	9	10	...
		(c) Acrobatics and athletics.	457. Tumblers, acrobats, wrestlers, professional cricketers, etc.	839	126	255	458	589	85
		(d) Service of places of entertainment.	458. Swing and merry-go-round keepers	32	4	8	19	23	3
			459. Tennis and racket court, gymkhana and boat club service.	...	...	...	...	...	...
			460. Billiard-room and theatre ownership, managership and service.	16	4	3	9	9	1
			Total Sub-order 73	2,124	282	570	1,272	1,459	159
			Total Order XXI	**3,490**	**525**	**1,005**	**1,960**	**2,254**	**274**
			Total Class F.	**39,928**	**4,823**	**8,354**	**26,751**	**24,451**	**2,462**
CLASS G.—INDEFINITE AND INDEPENDENT.	ORDER XXII.—COMPLEX OCCUPATIONS.	......	461. Village, etc., combined functions	...	...	...	...	...	...
			Total Order XXII	...	...	...	...	...	...

TOTAL. Males. 5—14	Males. 15—	Females. Total.	Females. 0—4	Females. 5—14	Females. 15—	Occupation.	Sub-order and Group.	Order.	Class.
11	12	13	14	15	16				
							68. Engineering and Surveying.	ORDER XX.—LEARNED AND ARTISTIC PROFESSIONS—*contd.*	CLASS F.—PROFESSIONS—*contd.*
...	...	...	...	...	...	429. Administrative and inspecting staff	(a) Engineers, Architects and Surveyors.		
13	32	8	2	3	3	430. Civil engineers and architects			
4	8	7	...	2	5	431. Topographical, archæological and revenue surveyors.			
18	89	98	10	19	69	432. Draughtsmen and operators in survey offices, overseers, etc.	(b) Subsidiary Staff.		
28	68	52	9	11	32	433. Clerks, etc., in offices of the above			
63	197	165	21	35	109	Total Sub-order 68			
							69.—Other Sciences.		
...	...	...	...	...	...	434. Astronomers and meteorologists and establishments.	(a) Astronomy, etc.		
...	...	...	...	...	...	435. Botanists, naturalists, and officers of scientific institutions.			
...	...	...	...	...	...	436. Metallurgists			
3	19	9	3	1	5	437. Astrologers, genealogists and horoscope-casters.	(b) Minor Sciences.		
...	...	...	...	...	...	438. Almanack-makers and sellers			
...	...	...	...	...	...	439. Diviners (selectors of well and house-sites, etc.)			
3	19	9	3	1	5	Total Sub-order 69			
3	19	26	4	5	17	440. Painters, superintendents of schools of art, etc.	70.—Pictorial Art and Sculpture.		
...	...	...	...	...	...	441. Sculptors			
5	6	5	...	3	2	442. Photographers			
8	25	31	4	8	19	Total Sub-order 70			
...	3	3	...	...	3	443. Music composers and teachers	71.—Music, Acting, Dancing.		
825	2,579	1,726	481	511	734	444. Band-masters and players (not military)			
...	...	...	...	...	...	445. Piano-tuners			
107	552	511	54	94	363	446. Actors, singers and dancers and their accompanists.			
932	3,134	2,240	535	605	1,100	Total Sub-order 71			
4,226	**15,783**	**14,241**	**2,110**	**3,123**	**9,008**	**Total Order XX**			
...	...	...	...	...	...	447. Race-course service, book-makers, jockeys, etc.	72.—Sport	ORDER XXI.—SPORT AND AMUSEMENTS.	
250	430	571	128	185	258	448. Shikaris, falconers and bird-catchers			
...	...	...	...	...	...	449. Huntsmen, whippers-in			
250	430	571	128	185	258	Total Sub-order 72			
							73.—Exhibition and Games.		
75	174	197	39	52	106	450. Exhibitors of trained animals (bulls, bears, snakes, monkeys, etc.)	(a) Catching, training and exhibiting animals.		
...	...	...	...	...	...	451. Circus owners, managers, etc.			
...	...	...	...	...	...	452. Cock and pigeon fanciers			
...	...	...	...	...	...	453. Buffoons	(b) Conjuring, fortune-telling and other exhibitions.		
33	117	99	25	27	47	454. Story and ballad reciters			
79	285	104	19	37	48	455. Exhibitors of puppets and pictures			
1	9	...	...	...	...	456. Conjurors and fortune-tellers			
181	319	250	37	74	139	457. Tumblers, acrobats, wrestlers, professional cricketers, etc.	(c) Acrobatics and athletics.		
6	14	8	1	2	5	458. Swing and merry-go-round keepers	(d) Services of places of entertainment.		
...	...	...	...	...	...	459. Tennis and racket court, gymkhana and boat club service.			
2	5	7	2	1	4	460. Billiard-room and theatre ownership, managership and service.			
377	923	665	123	193	349	Total Sub-order 73			
627	**1,353**	**1,236**	**251**	**378**	**607**	**Total Order XXI**			
4,853	**17,136**	**15,477**	**2,361**	**3,501**	**9,615**	**Total Class F**			
...	...	...	...	...	...	461. Village, etc., combined functions		ORDER XXII.—COMPLEX OCCUPATIONS.	CLASS G.—INDEFINITE AND INDEPENDENT.
...	...	...	...	...	...	**Total Order XXII**			

TABLE XVII.—Occupations, by Age.—

Class.	Order.	Sub-order and Group.	Occupation.	TOWN. Total. Total.				Males. Total.				Females. Total.			
				Total.	0—4	5—14	15—	Total.	0—4	5—14	15—	Total.	0—4	5—14	15—
				17	18	19	20	21	22	23	24	25	26	27	28
CLASS F.—PROFESSIONS—contd.	ORDER XX.—LEARNED AND ARTISTIC PROFESSIONS—contd.	68.—Engineering and Surveying— (a) Engineers, Architects and Surveyors.	429. Administrative and inspecting staff.	...	...	...	...	...	...	...	...	...	...	...	...
			430. Civil Engineers and architects	53	6	13	34	47	5	11	31	6	1	2	3
			431. Topographical, archæological and revenue surveyors.	9	2	2	5	8	2	2	4	1	...	...	1
		(b) Subsidiary staff.	432. Draughtsmen and operators in survey offices, overseers, etc.	152	15	26	111	74	8	11	55	78	7	15	56
			433. Clerks, etc., in offices of the above.	122	15	34	73	83	10	24	49	39	5	10	24
			Total Sub-order 68	336	38	75	223	212	25	48	139	124	13	27	84
		69.—Other Sciences— (a) Astronomy, etc.	434. Astronomers and meteorologists, and establishments.	...	...	...	...	...	...	...	...	...	...	...	...
			435. Botanists, naturalists, and officers of scientific institutions.	...	...	...	...	...	...	...	...	...	...	...	...
			436. Metallurgists	...	...	...	...	...	...	...	...	...	...	...	...
		(b) Minor sciences.	437. Astrologers, genealogists and horoscope-casters.	8	2	...	6	4	1	...	3	4	1	...	3
			438. Almanack-makers and sellers	...	...	...	...	...	...	...	...	...	...	...	...
			439. Diviners (selectors of well and house sites, etc.)	...	...	...	...	...	...	...	...	...	...	...	...
			Total Sub-order 69	8	2	...	6	4	1	...	3	4	1	...	3
		70.—Pictorial Art and Sculpture.	440. Painters, superintendents of schools of art, etc.	37	5	6	26	14	1	2	11	23	4	4	15
			441. Sculptors	...	...	...	...	...	...	...	...	...	...	...	...
			442. Photographers	17	1	8	8	12	1	5	6	5	...	3	2
			Total Sub-order 70	54	6	14	34	26	2	7	17	28	4	7	17
		71.—Music, Acting, Dancing.	443. Music composers and teachers	3	...	...	3	3	...	...	3	...	...	...	...
			444. Band masters and players (not military).	1,829	303	425	1,101	1,268	177	257	834	561	126	168	267
			445. Piano-tuners	...	...	...	...	...	...	...	...	...	...	...	...
			446. Actors, singers and dancers and their accompanists.	343	38	51	254	163	16	21	126	180	22	30	128
			Total Sub-order 71	2,175	341	476	1,358	1,434	193	278	963	741	148	198	395
			Total Order XX	**12,591**	**1,438**	**2,560**	**8,593**	**7,397**	**750**	**1,412**	**5,235**	**5,194**	**688**	**1,148**	**3,358**
	ORDER XXI.—SPORT AND AMUSEMENTS.	72.—Sport	447. Race-course service, book makers, jockeys, etc.	...	...	...	...	...	...	...	...	...	...	...	...
			448. Shikaris, falconers and bird catchers.	53	20	16	17	31	10	6	15	22	10	10	2
			449. Huntsmen, whippers-in	...	...	...	...	...	...	...	...	...	...	...	...
			Total Sub-order 72	53	20	16	17	31	10	6	15	22	10	10	2
		73.—Exhibition and Games— (a) Catching, training and exhibiting animals.	450. Exhibitors of trained animals (bulls, bears, snakes, monkeys, etc.)	33	2	3	28	30	1	3	26	3	1	...	2
			451. Circus owners, managers, etc.	...	...	...	...	...	...	...	...	...	...	...	...
			452. Cock and pigeon fanciers	...	...	...	...	...	...	...	...	...	...	...	...
		(b) Conjuring, fortune-telling and other exhibitions.	453. Buffoons	...	...	...	...	...	...	...	...	...	...	...	...
			454. Story and ballad reciters	35	3	10	22	25	2	8	15	10	1	2	7
			455. Exhibitors of puppets and pictures.	9	...	1	8	8	...	1	7	1	...	...	1
			456. Conjurors and fortune-tellers	...	...	...	...	...	...	...	...	...	...	...	...
		(c) Acrobatics and athletics.	457. Tumblers, acrobats, wrestlers, professional cricketers, etc.	51	10	14	27	51	10	14	27	...	...	...	...
		(d) Service of places of entertainment.	458. Swing and merry-go-round keepers.	10	2	2	6	3	1	...	2	7	1	2	4
			459. Tennis and racket court, gymkhana and boat club service.	...	...	...	...	...	...	...	...	...	...	...	...
			460. Billiard room and theatre ownership, managership and service.	16	4	3	9	9	2	2	5	7	2	1	4
			Total Sub-order 73	154	21	33	100	126	16	28	82	28	5	5	18
			Total Order XXI	**207**	**41**	**49**	**117**	**157**	**26**	**34**	**97**	**50**	**15**	**15**	**20**
			Total Class F	**12,798**	**1,479**	**2,609**	**8,710**	**7,554**	**776**	**1,446**	**5,332**	**5,244**	**703**	**1,163**	**3,378**
CLASS G.—INDEFINITE AND INDEPENDENT.	ORDER XXII.—COMPLEX OCCUPATIONS.		461. Village, etc., combined functions.	...	...	...	...	...	...	...	...	...	...	...	...
			Total Order XXII	...	...	...	...	...	...	...	...	...	...	...	...

Part A.—PROVINCIAL SUMMARY—*contd.*

COUNTRY.												Occupation.	Sub-order and Group.	Order.	Class.
Total.				Males.				Females.							
Total.	0—4	5—14	15—	Total.	0—4	5—14	15—	Total.	0—4	5—14	15—				
29	30	31	32	33	34	35	36	37	38	39	40				
													68.—Engineering and Surveying—	ORDER XX.—LEARNED AND ARTISTIC PROFESSIONS—*contd.*	CLASS F.—PROFESSIONS—*contd.*
...	...	...	...	...	...	...	...	...	...	...	...	429. Administrative and inspecting staff.	(a) Engineers, Architects and Surveyors.		
6	2	3	1	4	1	2	1	2	1	1	...	430. Civil Engineers and architects			
12	...	4	8	6	...	2	4	6	...	2	4	431. Topographical, archæological and revenue surveyors.			
63	5	11	47	43	2	7	34	20	3	4	13	432. Draughtsmen and operators in survey offices, overseers, etc.	(b) Subsidiary Staff.		
41	9	5	27	28	5	4	19	13	4	1	8	433. Clerks, etc., in offices of the above.			
122	16	23	83	81	8	15	58	41	8	8	25	Total Sub-order 68			
													69.—Other Sciences.		
...	...	...	...	...	...	...	...	...	...	...	...	434. Astronomers and meteorologists, and establishments.	(a) Astronomy, etc.		
...	...	...	...	...	...	...	...	...	...	...	...	435. Botanists, naturalists, and officers of scientific institutions.			
...	...	...	...	...	...	...	...	...	...	...	...	436. Meteorologists			
26	4	4	18	21	2	3	16	5	2	1	2	437. Astrologers, genealogists and horoscope-casters.	(b) Minor sciences.		
...	...	...	...	...	...	...	...	...	...	...	...	438. Almanack-makers and sellers.			
...	...	...	...	...	...	...	...	...	...	...	...	439. Diviners (selectors of well and house sites, etc.)			
26	4	4	18	21	2	3	16	5	2	1	2	Total Sub-order 69			
12	...	2	10	9	...	1	8	3	...	1	2	440. Painters, superintendents of schools of Art, etc.	70.—Pictorial Art and Sculpture.		
...	...	...	...	...	...	...	...	...	...	...	...	441. Sculptors			
...	...	...	...	...	...	...	...	...	...	...	...	442. Photographers			
12	...	2	10	9	...	1	8	3	...	1	2	Total Sub-order 70			
3	...	...	3	...	...	...	...	3	...	...	3	443. Music composers and teachers	71.—Music, Acting, Dancing.		
3,840	717	911	2,212	2,675	362	568	1,745	1,165	355	343	467	444. Band masters and players (not military).			
...	...	...	...	...	...	...	...	...	...	...	...	445. Piano-tuners			
860	49	150	661	529	17	86	426	331	32	64	235	446. Actors, singers and dancers and their accompanists.			
4,703	766	1,061	2,876	3,204	379	654	2,171	1,499	387	407	705	Total Sub-order 71			
23,847	**2,860**	**4,789**	**16,198**	**14,800**	**1,438**	**2,814**	**10,548**	**9,047**	**1,422**	**1,975**	**5,650**	**Total Order XX**			
...	...	...	...	...	...	...	...	...	...	...	...	447. Race-course service, book makers, jockeys, etc.	72.—Sport	ORDER XXI.—SPORT AND AMUSEMENTS.	
1,313	223	419	671	764	105	244	415	549	118	175	256	448. Shikaris, falconers and bird catchers.			
...	...	...	...	...	...	...	...	...	...	...	...	449. Huntsmen, whippers-in			
1,313	223	419	671	764	105	244	415	549	118	175	256	Total Sub-order 72			
													73.—Exhibition and Games—		
441	65	124	252	247	27	72	148	194	38	52	104	450. Exhibitors of trained animals (bulls, bears, snakes, monkeys, etc.)	(a) Catching, training and exhibiting animals.		
...	...	...	...	...	...	...	...	...	...	...	...	451. Circus owners, managers, etc.			
...	...	...	...	...	...	...	...	...	...	...	...	452. Cock and pigeon fanciers			
...	...	...	...	...	...	...	...	...	...	...	...	453. Buffoons	(b) Conjuring, fortune-telling and other exhibitions.		
228	36	50	142	139	12	25	102	89	24	25	40	454. Story and ballad reciters			
482	42	115	325	379	23	78	278	103	19	37	47	455. Exhibitors of puppets and pictures.			
10	...	1	9	10	...	1	9	...	...	...	...	456. Conjurors and fortune-tellers			
788	116	241	431	538	79	167	292	250	37	74	139	457. Tumblers, acrobats, wrestlers, professional cricketers, etc.	(c) Acrobatics and Athletics.		
21	2	6	13	20	2	6	12	1	...	...	1	458. Swing and merry-go-round keepers.	(d) Service of places of entertainment.		
...	...	...	...	...	...	...	...	...	...	...	...	459. Tennis and racket court, gymkhana and boat club service.			
...	...	...	...	...	...	...	...	...	...	...		460. Billiard room and theatre ownership, management and service.			
1,970	261	537	1,172	1,333	143	349	841	637	118	188	331	Total Sub-order 73			
3,283	**484**	**956**	**1,843**	**2,097**	**248**	**593**	**1,256**	**1,186**	**236**	**363**	**587**	**Total Order XXI**			
27,130	**3,344**	**5,745**	**18,041**	**16,897**	**1,686**	**3,407**	**11,804**	**10,233**	**1,658**	**2,338**	**6,237**	**Total Class F**			
...	...	...	...	...	...	...	...	...	...	...	...	461. Village, etc., combined functions.		ORDER XXII.—COMPLEX OCCUPATIONS.	CLASS G.—INDEFINITE AND INDEPENDENT.
...	...	...	...	...	...	...	...	...	...	...	...	**Total Order XXII.**			

TABLE XVII.—Occupations, by Age—

PROVINCIAL

Class.	Order.	Sub-order and Group.	Occupation.	Total: Total.	Total: 0—4	Total: 5—14	Total: 15—	Males: Total.	Males: 0—4
1	2	3	4	5	6	7	8	9	10
CLASS G.—INDEFINITE AND INDEPENDENT—*contd.*	ORDER XXIII.—INDEFINITE.	74.—Unskilled Labour.							
		(a) Special branches	461. Well-sinkers	98	8	21	69	72	1
			462. Tank diggers and excavators	29	...	6	23	10	—
			463. Road, canal and railway labourers	17,035	2,295	3,916	10,824	9,751	1,161
			464. Quarrymen (stone-splitters, etc.)	3,888	600	1,024	2,264	2,182	278
			465. Miners (unspecified)	69	7	23	39	31	4
			466. Rice-pounders and huskers	8,130	534	1,271	6,325	1,178	216
		(b) General	467. General labour	103,383	19,038	28,688	55,657	44,527	8,567
			Total Sub-order 74	132,632	22,482	34,949	75,201	57,750	[illegible]
		75.—Undefined, etc.	468. Undefined and disreputable means of livelihood. a. Disreputable	2,347	184	368	1,795	345	81
			b. Undefined	2,573	752	644	1,177	1,265	381
			c. Dependent	1,242	357	328	557	503	170
			Total Sub-order 75	6,162	1,293	1,340	3,529	2,113	[illegible]
			Total Order XXIII	**138,794**	**23,775**	**36,289**	**78,730**	**59,863**	**10,847**
	ORDER XXIV.—INDEPENDENT OF WORK.	76.—Property and Alms.							
		(a) Property and allowances.	469. House-rent, shares and other property not being land.	2,069	314	528	1,227	1,008	144
			470. Allowances from patrons or relatives	65	25	17	23	29	11
		(b) Charity and endowment.	471. Educational or other endowments, scholarships, etc.	225	10	78	137	204	6
			472. Mendicancy (not being affiliated to a religious order).	46,927	5,567	9,892	31,468	27,485	2,684
			Total Sub-order 76	49,286	5,916	10,515	32,855	28,726	2,846
		77.—Supported at the public charge.							
		(a) Pension	473. Pension, civil services	125	15	30	80	68	11
			474. Pension, military services	226	23	67	136	126	13
			474a. Pension, unspecified	1,592	149	351	1,092	842	75
		(b) Prisoners	475. Inmates of asylums, etc.	...	...	...	...	...	...
			476. Prisoners, under trial	74	...	1	73	73	...
			477. Prisoners, for debt	5	...	...	5	5	...
			478. Prisoners, convicted or in reformatories, etc.	815	3	4	808	790	1
			Total Sub-order 77	2,837	190	453	2,194	1,904	100
			Total Order XXIV	**52,123**	**6,106**	**10,968**	**35,049**	**30,630**	**2,946**
			Total Class G	**190,917**	**29,881**	**47,257**	**113,779**	**90,493**	**13,793**

Part A.—PROVINCIAL SUMMARY—*concld.*

TOTAL.									
Males.		Females.				Occupation.	Sub-order and Group.	Order.	Class.
5—14	15—	Total.	0—4	5—14	15—				
11	12	13	14	15	16				
							74.—Unskilled Labour.	ORDER XXIII.—INDEFINITE.	CLASS G.—INDEFINITE AND INDEPENDENT—*contd.*
11	52	27	...	10	17	461. Well-sinkers	(a) Special branches		
2	8	29	...	4	15	462. Tank diggers and excavators			
2,044	6,543	7,284	1,131	1,872	4,281	463. Road, canal and railway labourers			
562	1,342	1,706	322	462	922	464. Quarrymen (stone-splitters, etc.)			
8	19	38	3	15	20	465. Miners (unspecified)			
517	455	6,952	328	754	5,870	466. Rice-pounders and huskers			
13,622	22,338	58,856	10,471	15,066	33,319	467. General labour	(b) General		
16,766	30,757	74,882	12,255	18,183	44,444	Total Sub-order 74			
110	151	2,002	100	258	1,644	468. Undefined and disreputable means of livelihood. a. Disreputable	75.—Undefined, etc.		
318	581	1,308	386	326	596	b. Undefined			
160	173	739	187	168	384	c. Dependent			
588	905	4,049	673	752	2,624	Total Sub-order 75			
17,354	**31,662**	**78,931**	**12,928**	**18,935**	**47,068**	**Total Order XXIII**			
							76.—Property and Alms.	ORDER XXIV.—INDEPENDENT OF WORK.	
286	578	1,061	170	242	649	469. House-rent, shares and other property not being land.	(a) Property and allowances.		
9	8	36	13	8	15	470. Allowances from patrons or relatives			
74	124	21	4	4	13	471. Educational or other endowments, scholarships, etc.	(b) Charity and endowment.		
5,469	19,332	19,442	2,883	4,423	12,136	472. Mendicancy not being affiliated to a religious order.			
5,838	20,042	20,560	2,070	4,677	12,813	Total Sub-order 76			
							77.—Supported at the public charge.		
15	42	57	4	15	38	473. Pension, civil services	(a) Pension.		
35	79	100	11	32	57	474. Pension, military services			
186	581	750	74	165	511	474a. Pension, unspecified			
...	...	...	...	...	...	475. Inmates of asylums, etc.	(b) Prisoners.		
1	72	1	...	...	1	476. Prisoners under trial			
...	5	...	...	...	...	477. Prisoners for debt			
3	785	25	1	1	23	478. Prisoners convicted or in reformatories, etc.			
240	1,564	933	90	213	630	Total Sub-order 77			
6,078	21,606	21,493	3,160	4,890	13,443	**Total Order XXIV**			
23,432	52,268	100,424	16,088	23,825	60,511	**Total Class G**			

TABLE XVII.—Occupations, by Age.—

Class.	Order.	Sub-order and Group.	Occupation.	Town: Total: Total.	Total: 0–4	Total: 5–14	Total: 15–	Males: Total.	Males: 0–4	Males: 5–14	Males: 15–	Females: Total.	Females: 0–4	Females: 5–14	Females: 15–
				17	18	19	20	21	22	23	24	25	26	27	28
CLASS G.—INDEFINITE AND INDEPENDENT,—contd.	ORDER XXIII.—INDEFINITE.	74.—Unskilled labour.													
		(a) Special branches.	461. Well-sinkers	1	...	...	1	...	...	...	...	1	...	...	1
			462. Tank diggers and excavators	2	...	...	2	2	...	...	2	...	...	...	...
			463. Road, canal and railway labourers.	3,582	426	780	2,376	2,003	232	421	1,350	1,579	194	359	1,026
			464. Quarrymen (stone-splitters, etc.)	639	102	179	358	367	59	112	196	272	43	67	161
			465. Miners (unspecified)	...	...	...	...	...	...	...	...	...	...	...	...
			466. Rice-pounders and huskers	3,351	215	538	2,598	438	84	246	108	2,913	131	292	2,490
		(b) General.	467. General labour	12,651	1,922	3,113	7,616	5,707	904	1,562	3,241	6,944	1,018	1,551	4,375
			Total Sub-order 74	20,226	2,665	4,610	12,951	8,517	1,279	2,341	4,897	11,709	1,386	2,269	8,054
		75.—Undefined, etc.	468. Undefined and disreputable means of livelihood. a. Disreputable.	1,033	62	154	817	120	28	40	52	913	34	114	765
			b. Undefined	356	66	99	191	171	38	55	78	185	28	44	113
			c. Dependent	301	42	71	188	110	18	25	67	191	24	46	121
			Total Sub-order 75	1,690	170	324	1,196	401	84	120	197	1,289	86	204	999
			Total Order XXIII	**21,916**	**2,835**	**4,934**	**14,147**	**8,918**	**1,363**	**2,461**	**5,094**	**12,998**	**1,472**	**2,473**	**9,053**
	ORDER XXIV.—INDEPENDENT OF WORK.	76.—Property and Alms.													
		(a) Property and allowances.	469. House-rent, shares and other property not being land.	513	37	106	370	236	16	57	163	277	21	49	207
			470. Allowances from patrons or relatives.	8	...	1	7	4	...	1	3	4	...	...	4
		(b) Charity and endowment.	471. Educational or other endowments, scholarship, etc.	143	3	26	114	134	3	25	106	9	...	1	8
			472. Mendicancy (not being affiliated to a religious order).	8,705	897	1,670	6,138	4,995	419	933	3,643	3,710	478	737	2,495
			Total Sub-order 76	9,369	937	1,803	6,629	5,369	438	1,016	3,915	4,000	499	787	2,714
		77.—Supported at the public charge.													
		(a) Pension	473. Pension, civil services	114	14	28	72	63	10	15	38	51	4	13	34
			474. Pension, military services	170	19	48	103	93	10	25	58	77	9	23	45
			474a. Pension unspecified	1,168	105	264	799	618	51	147	420	550	54	117	379
		(b) Prisoners.	475. Inmates of asylums, etc.	...	...	...	...	...	...	...	...	...	...	...	...
			476. Prisoners, under trial	52	...	1	51	51	...	1	50	1	...	...	1
			477. Prisoners for debt	5	...	...	5	5	...	...	5	...	...	...	...
			478. Prisoners, convicted or in reformatories &c.	754	3	4	747	730	2	3	725	24	1	1	22
			Total Sub-order 77	2,263	141	345	1,777	1,560	73	191	1,296	703	68	154	481
			Total Order XXIV	**11,632**	**1,078**	**2,148**	**8,406**	**6,929**	**511**	**1,207**	**5,211**	**4,703**	**567**	**941**	**3,195**
			Total Class G	**33,548**	**3,913**	**7,082**	**22,553**	**15,847**	**1,874**	**3,668**	**10,305**	**17,701**	**2,039**	**3,414**	**12,248**

Part A.—PROVINCIAL SUMMARY—*concld.*

COUNTRY.												Occupation.	Sub-order and Group.	Order.	Class.
Total.				Males.				Females.							
Total.	0—4	5—14	15—	Total.	0—4	5—14	15—	Total.	0—4	5—14	15—				
29	30	31	32	33	34	35	36	37	38	39	40				
													74.—Unskilled labour.	ORDER XXIII.—INDEFINITE.	CLASS G.—INDEFINITE AND INDEPENDENT—*contd.*
97	8	21	68	71	8	11	52	26	...	10	16	461. Well sinkers	(a) Special branches.		
27	...	6	21	8	...	2	6	19	...	4	15	462. Tank diggers and excavators			
13,453	1,869	3,136	8,448	7,748	932	1,623	5,193	5,705	937	1,513	3,255	463. Road, canal, and railway labourers.			
3,249	498	845	1,906	1,815	219	450	1,146	1,434	279	395	760	464. Quarrymen (stone-splitters, etc.)			
69	7	23	39	31	4	8	19	38	3	15	20	465. Miners (unspecified)			
4,779	319	733	3,727	740	122	271	347	4,039	197	462	3,380	466. Rice-pounders and huskers			
90,732	17,116	25,575	48,041	38,820	7,663	12,060	19,097	51,912	9,453	13,515	28,944	467. General labour	(b) General		
112,406	19,817	30,339	62,250	49,233	8,948	14,425	25,860	63,173	10,869	15,914	36,390	Total Sub-order 74			
1,324	122	214	978	235	56	70	99	1,089	66	144	879	468. Undefined and disreputable means of livelihood. a. Disreputable.	75.—Undefined, etc.		
2,217	686	545	985	1,094	328	263	503	1,123	358	282	483	b. Undefined.			
941	315	257	369	393	152	135	106	548	163	122	263	c. Dependent.			
4,472	1,123	1,016	2,333	1,712	536	468	708	2,760	587	548	1,625	Total Sub-order 75			
116,878	20,940	31,355	64,583	50,945	9,484	14,893	26,568	65,933	11,456	16,462	38,015	**Total Order XXIII.**			
													76.—Property and Alms.	ORDER XXIV.—INDEPENDENT OF WORK.	
1,556	277	422	857	772	128	229	415	784	149	193	442	469. House-rent, shares and other property not being land.	(a) Property and allowances.		
57	25	16	16	25	12	8	5	32	13	8	11	470. Allowances from patrons or relatives.			
82	7	52	23	70	3	49	18	12	4	3	5	471. Educational or other endowments, scholarships, etc.	(b) Charity and endowment.		
38,222	4,670	8,222	25,330	22,490	2,265	4,536	15,689	15,732	2,405	3,686	9,641	472. Mendicancy (not being affiliated to a religious order).			
39,917	4,979	8,712	26,226	23,357	2,408	4,822	16,127	16,560	2,571	3,890	10,099	Total Sub-order 76			
													77.—Supported at the public charge.		
11	1	2	8	5	1	...	4	6	...	2	4	473. Pension, civil services	(a) Pension		
56	4	19	33	33	2	10	21	23	2	9	12	474. Pension, military services			
424	44	87	293	224	24	39	161	200	20	48	132	474a. Pension, unspecified			
...	...	...	...	...	...	...	...	...	...	...	...	475. Inmates of asylums, etc.	(b) Prisoners.		
22	...	...	22	22	...	...	22	...	...	...	...	476. Prisoners under trial			
...	...	...	...	...	...	...	...	...	...	...	...	477. Prisoners for debt			
61	...	...	61	60	...	...	60	1	...	...	1	478. Prisoners convicted or in reformatories, etc.			
574	49	108	417	344	27	49	268	230	22	59	149	Total Sub-order 77			
40,491	5,028	8,820	26,643	23,701	2,435	4,871	16,395	16,790	2,593	3,949	10,248	**Total Order XXIV**			
157,369	25,968	40,175	91,226	74,646	11,919	19,764	42,963	82,723	14,049	20,411	48,263	**Total Class G**			

TABLE XVII.—Part B.

Occupations, by Districts.

TABLE XVII.—Part B.—

Class.	Order.	Sub-order, Group and Occupation.	District Amraoti.			District Akola.		
			Total.	Males.	Females.	Total.	Males.	Females.
1	2	3	4	5	6	7	8	9
Class A.—Government.	Order I.—Administration.	1. The Viceroy, Governors, etc.	...	...	...	...	...	...
		2. Officers	100	51	49	53	37	16
		3. Office Superintendents and clerks, etc.	935	542	393	795	414	381
		4. Messengers, bailiffs, etc.	2,039	1,085	954	2,811	1,573	1,238
		4A. Police, rank and file	1,254	809	445	1,058	587	471
		Total Sub-order 1.—Service of the Imperial and Provincial Governments	4,328	2,487	1,841	4,717	2,611	2,106
		5. Inspecting and supervising officials	1	1	...	3	1	2
		6. Clerical establishments	36	23	13	33	25	8
		7. Menials	459	301	158	472	289	183
		Total Sub-order 2.—Service of Local and Municipal Bodies	496	325	171	508	315	193
		8. Headmen, etc.	941	475	466	1,423	714	709
		9. Accountants	1,477	845	632	1,743	955	788
		11. Watchmen, etc.	8,431	5,750	2,681	9,684	6,438	3,246
		Total Sub-order 3.—Village Service	10,849	7,070	3,779	12,850	8,107	4,743
		Total Order I.—Administration	**15,678**	**9,882**	**5,791**	**18,075**	**11,033**	**7,042**
	Order II.—Defence.	12. Officers	3	1	2	2	1	1
		13. Non-commissioned officers	52	34	18	31	21	10
		14. Followers	155	101	54	...	...	...
		15. Administrative establishments	...	...	...	...	...	...
		Total Sub-order 4.—Army	210	136	74	33	22	11
		16. Officers	...	...	...	...	...	...
		17. Engineers, etc.	...	...	...	...	...	...
		18. Administrative staff	...	...	...	...	...	...
		Total Sub-order 5.—Navy and Marine	...	...	...	...	...	...
		Total Order II.—Defence	**210**	**136**	**74**	**33**	**22**	**11**
	Order III.—Foreign and Feudatory State Service.	19. Chiefs, consuls, etc.	...	...	...	...	...	...
		20. Clerical establishments	...	...	...	...	...	...
		21. Menials, etc.	...	...	...	...	...	...
		Total Sub-order 6.—Administrative Service	...	...	...	...	...	...
		22. Officers	...	...	...	...	...	...
		23. Privates and seamen, etc.	3	3	...	...	...	...
		Total Sub-order 7.—Army and Marine	3	3	...	...	...	...
		Total Order III.—Foreign and Feudatory State Service	**3**	**3**	...	...	...	...
		Total Class A	**15,886**	**10,021**	**5,865**	**18,108**	**11,055**	**7,053**
Class B.—Pasture and Agriculture.	Order IV.—Live Stock.	24. Horse breeders, etc.	16	14	2	9	8	1
		25. Cattle breeders, etc.	622	554	68	107	83	24
		26. Herdsmen	4,860	4,043	817	3,373	2,870	503
		27. Buffalo breeders, etc.	7	6	1	2	2	...
		28. Elephant catchers, etc.	...	...	...	...	...	...
		29. Camel breeders, etc.	9	5	4	13	13	...
		30. Ass and mule breeders, etc.	19	16	3	20	18	2
		31. Sheep and goat breeders, etc.	211	168	43	460	257	203
		31A. Shepherds	929	753	176	1,099	791	308
		32. Pig breeders, etc.	8	6	2	...	...	...
		Total Sub-order 8.—Stock breeding and dealing	6,681	5,565	1,116	5,083	4,042	1,041

Occupations, by Districts.

DISTRICT ELLICHPUR.			DISTRICT BULDANA.			DISTRICT WUN.			DISTRICT BASIM.			RAILWAY PASSENGERS.		
TOTAL.	Males.	Females.	TOTAL.	Males.	Females.	TOTAL.	Males.	Females.	TOTAL.	Males.	Females.	TOTAL.	Males.	Females.
10	11	12	13	14	15	16	17	18	19	20	21	22	23	24
...	...	...	...	...	...	...	...	...	...	...	...	...	...	...
23	13	10	12	9	3	46	21	25	31	19	12	...	...	...
273	167	106	300	158	142	277	172	105	246	136	110	14	7	7
1,766	914	852	2,167	1,190	977	1,492	805	687	2,037	1,114	923	1	1	...
624	405	219	795	498	297	837	538	299	601	392	209	7	5	2
2,686	1,499	1,187	3,274	1,855	1,419	2,652	1,536	1,116	2,915	1,661	1,254	22	13	9
11	3	8	8	4	4	...	...	...	...	...	...	...	...	...
10	6	4	4	3	1	1	1	...	...	...	...	...	...	...
201	137	64	145	108	37	98	60	38	77	47	30	...	...	...
222	146	76	157	115	42	99	61	38	77	47	30	...	...	...
664	311	353	1,130	582	548	1,080	577	503	759	370	389	1	1	...
791	435	356	1,463	824	639	585	330	255	860	458	402	...	...	...
5,821	3,869	1,952	11,809	7,253	4,556	7,347	4,528	2,819	8,301	5,110	3,191	1	1	...
7,276	4,615	2,661	14,402	8,659	5,743	9,012	5,435	3,577	9,920	5,938	3,982	2	2	...
10,184	6,260	3,924	17,833	10,629	7,204	11,763	7,032	4,731	12,912	7,646	5,266	24	15	9
162	72	90	...	...	...	1	1	...	...	...	...	...	...	...
1,499	1,029	470	1	1	...	3	2	1	32	14	18	...	...	...
6	5	1	...	...	...	...	...	...	4	...	4	...	...	...
8	3	5	...	...	...	...	...	...	...	...	...	...	...	...
1,675	1,109	566	1	1	...	4	3	1	36	14	22	...	...	...
...	...	...	...	...	...	...	...	...	...	...	...	...	...	...
...	...	...	...	...	...	...	...	...	...	...	...	...	...	...
...	...	...	...	...	...	...	...	...	...	...	...	...	...	...
...	...	...	...	...	...	...	...	...	...	...	...	...	...	...
1,675	1,109	566	1	1	...	4	3	1	36	14	22	...	...	...
...	...	...	...	...	...	...	...	...	...	...	...	...	...	...
...	...	...	...	...	...	...	...	...	9	4	5	...	...	...
...	...	...	3	1	2	...	...	...	2	1	1	...	...	...
...	...	...	3	1	2	...	...	...	11	5	6	...	...	...
...	...	...	...	...	...	...	...	...	...	...	...	...	...	...
...	...	...	...	...	...	3	1	2	...	...	...	...	...	...
...	...	...	...	...	...	3	1	2	...	...	...	...	...	...
...	...	...	3	1	2	3	1	2	11	5	6	...	...	...
11,859	7,369	4,490	17,837	10,631	7,206	11,770	7,036	4,734	12,959	7,665	5,294	24	15	9
5	3	2	2	2	...	...	...	...	12	8	4	...	...	...
103	72	31	253	146	107	154	138	16	92	73	19	...	...	...
3,586	2,770	816	2,915	2,443	472	8,176	6,264	1,912	2,598	2,131	467	...	...	...
2	1	1	203	108	95	5	5	...	2	2	...	...	...	...
...	...	...	...	...	...	...	...	...	...	...	...	...	...	...
4	4	...	7	6	1	11	11	...	...	...	...	...	...	...
54	52	2	8	6	2	8	6	2	20	12	8	...	...	...
131	92	39	329	222	107	122	91	31	75	43	32	...	...	...
413	334	79	1,990	1,304	686	1,121	791	330	7[illegible]2	566	226	...	...	...
...	...	...	...	...	...	...	...	...	...	...	...	...	...	...
4,298	3,328	970	5,707	4,237	1,470	9,597	7,306	2,291	3,591	2,835	756	...	...	...

TABLE XVII.—PART B.—

Class.	Order.	Sub-order, Group and Occupation.	District Amraoti. Total.	Males.	Females.	District Akola. Total.	Males.	Females.
1	2	3	4	5	6	7	8	9
Class B.—Pasture and Agriculture—*continued*.	Order IV.—Live Stock—*contd.*	33. Veterinary surgeons, etc.	...	...	...	3	1	2
		34. Farriers and gelders	7	4	3	24	13	11
		35. Horse and elephant breakers, etc.	15	10	5	6	3	3
		36. Rat, monkey-catchers, etc.	...	...	...	...	...	...
		Total Sub-order 9.—Subsidiary Services to Stock	22	14	8	33	17	16
		Total Order IV.—Live Stock	**6,703**	**5,579**	**1,124**	**5,116**	**4,059**	**1,067**
	Order V.—Agriculture.	37. Land occupants, not cultivating	3,994	1,903	2,091	2,360	1,204	1,156
		38. Land occupants, cultivating	132,924	70,369	62,555	145,124	75,757	69,367
		39. Lessees of villages, etc.	51	25	26	...	...	...
		40. Tenants, not cultivating	...	...	...	...	...	...
		41. Tenants, etc., cultivating	41,808	24,966	16,842	60,009	33,741	26,268
		Total Sub-order 10.—Interest in land	178,777	97,263	81,514	207,493	110,702	96,791
		42. Farm servants	27,027	21,381	5,646	10,775	8,548	2,227
		43. Field labourers, etc.	246,505	106,747	139,758	169,010	75,113	93,897
		Total Sub-order 11.—Agricultural labourers	273,532	128,128	145,404	179,785	83,661	96,124
		44. Tea, coffee, and cinchona planters, etc.	...	...	...	...	...	...
		45. Cocoanut growers	...	...	...	...	...	...
		46. Betel-vine, etc., growers	351	145	206	36	29	7
		47. Waternut growers	...	...	...	6	3	3
		48. Cardamom, etc., growers	...	...	...	...	...	...
		49. Indigo planters, etc.	...	...	...	...	...	...
		50. Fruit growers	29	14	15	89	52	37
		51. Market gardeners, etc.	18	10	8	1	...	1
		52. Gardeners, seedsmen, etc.	227	120	107	225	154	71
		53. Manure preparers and sellers	...	...	...	...	...	...
		54. Forest officers	8	4	4	...	...	...
		55. Forest rangers, etc.	70	47	23	60	41	19
		Total Sub-order 12.—Growers of Special Products and Trees	703	340	363	417	279	138
		56. Directors of agriculture, etc.	...	...	...	...	...	...
		57. Model-farm managers, etc.	...	...	...	...	...	...
		58. Agents and managers of land, estates, etc.	...	...	...	...	...	...
		Total Sub-order 13.—Agricultural training and supervision	...	...	...	...	...	...
		Total Order V.—Agriculture	**453,012**	**225,731**	**227,281**	**387,695**	**194,642**	**193,053**
		Total Class B	**459,715**	**231,310**	**228,405**	**392,811**	**198,701**	**194,110**
Class C.—Personal Services.	Order VI.—Personal and Household Services.	59. Barbers	4,951	3,231	1,720	4,610	2,923	1,687
		60. Ear-pickers	6	2	4	...	...	...
		61. Tattooers	3	3	...	6	5	1
		62. Caste mark appliers	...	...	...	...	...	...
		63. Washermen	3,281	1,613	1,668	3,358	1,698	1,660
		64. Water-carriers	413	264	149	366	247	119
		65. Cooks	470	290	180	406	298	108
		66. Indoor servants	6,562	3,138	3,424	5,241	2,830	2,411
		67. Grooms, coachmen, etc.	353	255	98	301	227	74
		68. Door-keepers, etc.	...	...	...	...	...	...
		Total Sub-order 14.—Personal and Domestic Services	16,039	8,796	7,243	14,288	8,228	6,060
		69. Hotel and refreshment-room keepers	22	13	9	27	19	8
		70. Rest-house, serai owners and managers, etc.	2	2	...	18	11	7
		71. Club secretaries, etc.	...	...	...	...	...	...
		Total Sub-order 15.—Non-domestic Establishment	24	15	9	45	30	15
		72. Sanitary officers, etc.	5	3	2	...	...	...
		73. Sanitary inspectors, etc.	13	2	11	...	...	...
		74. Sweepers and scavengers, etc.	448	248	200	672	435	237
		75. Dust and sweepings contractors	1	1	...	...	...	...
		Total Sub-order 16.—Sanitation	467	254	213	672	435	237
		Total Order VI.—Personal and household services	**16,580**	**9,065**	**7,465**	**15,005**	**8,693**	**6,312**
		Total Class C	**16,580**	**9,065**	**7,465**	**15,005**	**8,693**	**6,312**

Occupations, by Districts—*contd.*

DISTRICT ELLICHPUR.			DISTRICT BULDANA.			DISTRICT WUN.			DISTRICT BASIM.			RAILWAY PASSENGERS.		
TOTAL.	Males.	Females.	TOTAL.	Males.	Females.	TOTAL.	Males.	Females.	TOTAL.	Males.	Females.	TOTAL.	Males.	Female.
10	11	12	13	14	15	16	17	18	19	20	21	22	23	24
...	...	...	2	2	...	...	...	...	...	...	...	...	...	...
19	10	9	2	2	...	...	...	...	...	...	...	...	...	...
5	1	4	12	7	5	19	12	7	7	3	4	...	...	...
...	...	...	...	...	...	...	...	...	...	...	...	...	...	...
24	11	13	16	11	5	19	12	7	7	3	4	...	...	...
4,322	3,339	983	5,723	4,248	1,475	9,616	7,318	2,298	3,598	2,838	760	...	...	...
1,348	753	595	476	254	222	2,021	1,139	882	768	406	362	...	...	...
68,366	35,268	33,098	129,650	67,520	62,130	75,046	41,030	34,016	91,575	48,710	42,865	4	4	...
...	...	...	...	...	...	...	...	...	...	...	...	...	...	...
...	...	...	...	...	...	...	...	...	...	...	...	...	...	...
25,294	14,522	10,772	74,885	39,613	35,272	64,642	39,199	25,443	77,227	42,003	35,224	30	17	13
95,008	50,543	44,465	205,011	107,387	97,624	141,709	81,368	60,341	169,570	91,119	78,451	34	21	13
8,817	6,515	2,302	8,103	6,309	1,794	46,497	34,321	12,176	7,374	5,428	1,946	1	1	...
95,723	42,738	52,985	112,315	49,149	63,166	154,846	54,588	100,258	99,641	43,049	56,592	10	7	3
104,540	49,253	55,287	120,418	55,458	64,960	201,343	88,909	112,434	107,015	48,477	58,538	11	8	3
...	...	...	...	...	...	...	...	...	...	...	...	...	...	...
...	...	...	...	...	...	...	...	...	...	...	...	...	...	...
72	35	37	...	...	...	1	...	1	6	4	2	...	...	...
...	...	...	...	...	...	...	...	...	...	...	...	...	...	...
...	...	...	...	...	...	...	...	...	...	...	...	...	...	...
...	...	...	...	...	...	...	...	...	...	...	...	...	...	...
9	4	5	118	69	49	20	12	8	51	33	18	...	...	...
...	...	...	...	...	...	...	...	...	...	...	...	...	...	...
66	38	28	91	53	38	109	79	30	69	28	41	...	...	...
...	...	...	...	...	...	4	...	4	...	...	...	...	...	...
1	1	...	2	1	1	3	1	2	4	3	1	...	...	...
92	72	20	49	30	19	82	64	18	48	33	15	...	...	...
240	150	90	260	153	107	219	156	63	178	101	77	...	...	...
...	...	...	...	...	...	1	1	...	...	...	...	...	...	...
...	...	...	...	...	...	...	...	...	...	...	...	...	...	...
...	...	...	...	...	...	1	1	...	...	...	...	...	...	...
...	...	...	...	...	...	2	2	...	...	...	...	...	...	...
199,788	99,946	99,842	325,689	162,998	162,691	343,273	170,435	172,838	276,763	139,697	137,066	45	29	16
204,110	103,285	100,825	331,412	167,246	164,166	352,889	177,753	175,136	280,361	142,535	137,826	45	29	16
2,215	1,407	808	3,331	1,929	1,402	3,474	2,213	1,261	2,701	1,529	1,172	1	1	...
2	1	1	...	...	...	...	...	...	...	...	...	...	...	...
...	...	...	...	...	...	1	...	1	...	...	...	...	...	...
...	...	...	...	...	...	...	...	...	...	...	...	...	...	...
2,271	1,133	1,138	1,552	749	803	2,705	1,368	1,337	882	455	427	2	2	...
196	122	74	142	79	63	85	62	23	157	101	56	...	...	...
104	71	33	174	71	103	37	27	10	65	44	21	1	1	...
3,527	1,947	1,580	5,020	2,035	2,985	6,150	2,975	3,175	4,298	1,738	2,560	19	14	5
318	193	125	96	61	35	193	156	37	72	54	18	...	...	...
...	...	...	...	...	...	...	...	...	...	...	...	...	...	...
8,633	4,874	3,759	10,315	4,924	5,391	12,645	6,801	5,844	8,175	3,921	4,254	23	18	5
1	...	1	...	...	...	1	1	...	4	2	2	...	...	...
2	2	...	2	2	...	13	10	3	3	2	1	...	...	...
...	...	...	...	...	...	...	...	...	...	...	...	...	...	...
3	2	1	2	2	...	14	11	3	7	4	3	...	...	...
...	...	...	...	...	...	...	...	...	...	...	...	...	...	...
...	...	...	...	...	...	...	...	...	...	...	...	...	...	...
391	226	165	254	133	121	218	125	93	82	46	36	...	...	...
3	3	...	1	1	...	...	...	...	...	...	...	...	...	...
394	229	165	255	134	121	218	125	93	82	46	36	...	...	...
9,080	5,105	3,925	10,572	5,060	5,512	12,877	6,937	5,940	8,264	3,971	4,293	28	18	5
9,080	5,105	3,925	10,572	5,060	5,512	12,877	6,937	5,940	8,264	3,971	4,293	28	18	5

TABLE XVII.—Part B.—

Class.	Order.	Sub-order, Group and Occupation.	District Amraoti. Total.	District Amraoti. Males.	District Amraoti. Females.	District Akola. Total.	District Akola. Males.	District Akola. Females.
1	2	3	4	5	6	7	8	9
Class D.—Preparation and Supply of Material Substances.	Order VII.—Food and Drink.	76. Cow and buffalo keepers, etc.	1,359	576	783	742	331	14
		77. Ghee preparers and sellers	202	109	93	204	132	72
		78. Cheese makers and sellers	...	...	...	...	...	...
		79. Butchers	1,789	1,034	755	1,842	883	959
		80. Fowl and egg dealers	5	2	3	8	3	5
		81. Fishermen, etc.	3,670	2,314	1,356	1,886	1,250	636
		82. Fish dealers	1	1	...	6	1	5
		Total Sub-order 17.—Animal Food	7,026	4,036	2,990	4,688	2,600	2,088
		83. Grain dealers	2,075	1,225	850	2,500	1,411	1,089
		84. Grain parchers	420	223	197	1,038	399	639
		85. Pulse and flour preparers and sellers	577	326	251	381	247	134
		86. Flour-mill service, etc.	...	...	...	4	2	2
		87. Bakers	36	18	18	62	33	29
		88. Bran sellers	...	...	...	...	...	...
		89. Vegetables sellers	480	237	243	601	298	303
		90. Fruit, etc., sellers	234	122	112	252	151	101
		91. Cocoanut dealers	8	2	6	13	1	12
		91A. Cotton seed dealers	31	19	12	79	50	29
		92. Confectioners, etc., makers and sellers	732	457	275	677	442	235
		93. Sweetmeat pedlars	18	15	3	10	7	3
		Total Sub-order 18.—Vegetable Food	4,611	2,644	1,967	5,617	3,041	2,576
		94. Ice manufacturers and sellers	...	...	...	...	...	...
		94A. Water sellers	...	...	...	...	...	...
		95. Soda-water, lemonade, etc., manufacturers and sellers	...	...	...	1	1	...
		96. Sherbat preparers and sellers	...	...	...	...	...	...
		97. Country spirits distillers and sellers	1,264	835	429	855	487	368
		98. Toddy drawers and sellers	347	264	83	18	16	2
		99. Foreign wine, etc., dealers	8	6	2	4	3	1
		100. Brewers	...	...	...	...	...	...
		101. Tea sellers and tasters, etc.	1	...	1	...	...	...
		102. Coffee preparers and sellers	...	...	...	...	...	...
		103. Sugar manufacturers and sellers	...	...	...	...	...	...
		104. Molasses, etc., makers and sellers	322	207	115	255	148	107
		105. Salt preparers and sellers	189	75	114	64	37	27
		106. Assafœtida, etc., sellers	48	37	11	36	19	17
		107. Vinegar manufacturers and sellers	...	...	...	...	...	...
		108. Pickle makers and sellers	12	...	12	1	...	1
		109. Grocers, etc.	4,972	2,883	2,089	3,535	2,133	1,402
		110. Cardamom preparers and dealers	...	...	...	...	...	...
		111. Betel-leaf, etc., sellers	1,732	526	1,206	1,408	488	920
		112. Tobacco, etc., manufacturers and sellers	605	364	241	647	381	266
		113. Prepared hukka pedlars	3	2	1	2	2	...
		114. Opium, etc., manufacturers and sellers	220	140	80	151	88	63
		115. Bhang, Ganja, etc., preparers and sellers	4	2	2	...	...	...
		Total Sub-order 19.—Drink, Condiments and Narcotics	9,727	5,341	4,386	6,977	3,803	3,174
		Total Order VII.—Food and Drink	**21,364**	**12,021**	**9,343**	**17,282**	**9,444**	**7,838**
	Order VIII.—Light, Firing and Forage.	116. Oil pressers and sellers	3,770	1,921	1,849	2,513	1,277	1,236
		117. Oil and salt sellers	1	1	...	...	...	...
		118. Oil-cake dealers	8	4	4	...	...	...
		119. Candle makers and sellers	...	...	...	...	...	...
		120. Torch makers and sellers	...	...	...	...	...	...
		121. Kerosine oil dealers	33	19	14	75	35	40
		122. Matches, makers and sellers	46	35	11	22	19	3
		123. Lamp, etc., makers and sellers	11	5	6	1	1	...
		124. Gas workers, etc.	...	...	...	...	...	...
		Total Sub-order 20.—Lighting	3,869	1,985	1,884	2,611	1,332	1,279
		125. Firewood, etc., gatherers and sellers	3,243	1,649	1,594	3,654	1,576	2,078
		126. Firewood contractors and dealers	485	21	464	270	118	152
		127. Coal miners, etc.	...	...	...	...	...	...
		128. Coal dealers, brokers, etc.	1	1	...	...	...	...
		129. Charcoal burners and dealers	55	33	22	197	108	89
		130. Cowdung-fuel preparers and sellers	333	133	200	226	57	169
		131. Hay, etc., contractors	1,530	714	816	819	396	423
		Total Sub-order 21.—Fuel and Forage	5,647	2,551	3,096	5,166	2,255	2,911
		Total Order VIII.—Light, Firing and Forage	**9,516**	**4,536**	**4,980**	**7,777**	**3,587**	**4,190**

Occupations, by Districts—*contd.*

DISTRICT ELLICHPUR.			DISTRICT BULDANA.			DISTRICT WUN.			DISTRICT BASIM.			RAILWAY PASSENGERS.		
TOTAL.	Males.	Females.	TOTAL.	Males.	Females.	TOTAL.	Males.	Females.	TOTAL.	Males.	Females.	TOTAL.	Males.	Females.
10	11	12	13	14	15	16	17	18	19	20	21	22	23	24
1,011	413	598	367	206	161	767	298	469	232	111	121	...	...	...
186	82	104	19	13	6	46	25	21	13	7	6	...	...	...
...	...	...	...	...	...	...	...	...	...	...	...	...	...	...
1,100	578	522	997	522	475	451	251	200	566	289	277	1	1	...
4	1	3	7	6	1	2	...	2	...	...	...	...	...	...
2,044	1,255	789	514	294	220	4,762	2,759	2,003	483	341	142	4	2	2
...	...	...	...	...	...	...	...	...	5	5	...	...	...	...
4,345	2,329	2,016	1,504	1,041	863	6,028	3,333	2,695	1,299	753	546	5	3	2
1,256	730	526	1,341	784	557	952	593	359	796	439	357	...	...	...
190	106	84	622	278	344	300	86	214	389	142	247	...	...	...
158	91	67	78	41	37	167	81	86	152	87	65	...	...	...
...	...	...	...	...	...	...	...	...	...	...	...	...	...	...
6	4	2	3	2	1	3	3	...	6	2	4	...	...	...
...	...	...	...	...	...	...	...	...	...	...	...	...	...	...
458	194	264	321	87	234	105	48	57	291	141	150	...	...	...
401	230	171	251	136	115	18	11	7	231	130	101	...	...	...
...	...	...	...	...	...	...	...	...	3	3	...	...	...	...
6	3	3	23	16	7	6	6	...	9	5	4	...	...	...
374	214	160	241	124	117	168	101	67	134	87	47	1	1	...
1	...	1	1	1	...	2	2	...	...	...	...	...	...	...
2,850	1,572	1,278	2,881	1,469	1,412	1,721	931	790	2,011	1,036	975	1	1	...
...	...	...	...	...	...	...	...	...	...	...	...	...	...	...
29	18	11	...	...	...	...	...	...	...	...	...	...	...	...
...	...	...	...	...	...	...	...	...	...	...	...	...	...	...
...	...	...	...	...	...	...	...	...	...	...	...	...	...	...
841	506	335	703	371	332	1,669	1,023	646	827	516	311	1	1	...
12	6	6	11	10	1	121	81	40	335	189	146	...	...	...
...	...	...	2	...	2	1	1	...	...	...	...	...	...	...
...	...	...	...	...	...	...	...	...	...	...	...	...	...	...
...	...	...	...	...	...	...	...	...	...	...	...	...	...	...
...	...	...	...	...	...	...	...	...	...	...	...	...	...	...
...	...	...	...	...	...	...	...	...	...	...	...	...	...	...
166	100	66	94	53	41	548	274	274	25	23	2	...	...	...
63	26	37	39	27	12	243	118	125	17	8	9	...	...	...
5	2	3	10	5	5	138	69	69	1	1	...	...	...	...
...	...	...	...	...	...	...	...	...	...	...	...	...	...	...
1	...	1	...	...	...	...	...	...	7	...	7	...	...	...
1,434	853	581	3,540	2,013	1,527	3,004	1,819	1,185	3,367	1,927	1,440	...	...	...
...	...	...	...	...	...	...	...	...	...	...	...	...	...	...
1,157	300	857	711	331	380	706	290	416	571	269	302	...	...	...
370	220	150	285	170	115	509	287	222	210	114	96	...	...	...
1	1	...	...	...	...	...	...	...	...	...	...	...	...	...
47	37	10	122	84	38	307	213	94	39	28	11	...	...	...
...	...	...	...	...	...	22	...	22	...	...	...	...	...	...
4,126	2,069	2,057	5,517	3,064	2,453	7,268	4,175	3,093	5,399	3,075	2,324	1	1	...
11,321	**5,970**	**5,351**	**10,302**	**5,574**	**4,728**	**15,017**	**8,489**	**6,578**	**8,709**	**4,864**	**3,845**	**7**	**5**	**2**
2,472	1,243	1,229	2,710	1,364	1,316	2,770	1,446	1,324	2,075	1,094	981	1	1	...
5	...	5	...	...	...	...	...	...	10	...	10	...	...	...
...	...	...	...	...	...	...	...	...	...	...	...	...	...	...
...	...	...	...	...	...	...	...	...	...	...	...	...	...	...
...	...	...	...	...	...	...	...	...	...	...	...	...	...	...
10	6	4	19	11	8	31	22	9	1	...	1	...	...	...
18	17	1	1	1	...	14	14	...	3	3	...	...	...	...
...	...	...	...	...	...	...	...	...	...	...	...	...	...	...
...	...	...	...	...	...	...	...	...	...	...	...	...	...	...
2,505	1,266	1,239	2,730	1,376	1,354	2,815	1,482	1,333	2,089	1,097	992	1	1	...
7,390	3,292	4,098	1,935	788	1,147	2,142	646	1,496	1,538	671	867	1	...	1
1,461	770	691	96	47	49	76	17	59	12	4	8	...	...	...
...	...	...	...	...	...	...	...	...	...	...	...	...	...	...
...	...	...	...	...	...	...	...	...	...	...	...	...	...	...
225	135	90	26	19	7	1	...	1	1	1	...	...	...	...
325	97	228	110	32	78	52	6	46	72	32	40	...	...	...
546	206	340	313	139	174	692	210	482	244	135	109	...	...	...
9,947	4,500	5,447	2,480	1,025	1,455	2,963	879	2,084	1,867	843	1,024	1	...	1
12,452	**5,766**	**6,686**	**5,210**	**2,401**	**2,809**	**5,778**	**2,361**	**3,417**	**3,956**	**1,940**	**2,016**	**2**	**1**	**1**

TABLE XVII.—Part B.—

Class.	Order.	Sub-order, Group and Occupation.	District Amraoti. Total.*	District Amraoti. Males.	District Amraoti. Females.	District Akola. Total.	District Akola. Males.	District Akola. Females.
1	2	3	4	5	6	7	8	9
Class D.—Preparation and Supply of Material Substances—*continued.*	Order IX.—Buildings.	132. Brick and tile burners, etc.	2,604	2,062	542	731	487	244
		133. Lime, etc., burners and sellers	272	148	124	285	148	137
		134. Stone-quarry owners, etc.	21	15	6	...	...	...
		135. Thatch dealers and thatchers	27	13	14	20	12	8
		Total Sub-order 22.—Building Materials	2,924	2,238	686	1,036	647	389
		136. Building contractors	1	1	...	2	1	1
		137. Stone, etc., workers	35	22	13	64	40	24
		138. Masons	1,473	842	631	1,536	877	659
		139. Builders and joiners	131	74	57	14	13	1
		140. Plasterers and house painters	38	21	17	22	11	11
		141. Mud wall and roof builders	834	552	282	525	350	175
		142. Plumbers and glaziers	...	...	...	...	...	...
		143. Tilers and tile turners	...	...	...	...	...	...
		Total Sub-order 23.—Artificers in Building	2,512	1,512	1,000	2,163	1,292	871
		Total Order IX.—Buildings	**5,436**	**3,750**	**1,686**	**3,199**	**1,939**	**1,260**
	Order X.—Vehicles and Vessels.	144. Railway mechanics, (fitters, painters, etc.)	92	49	43	13	9	4
		145. Railway permanent-way fore-men, etc.	12	5	7	18	13	5
		Total Sub-order 24.—Railway Plant	104	54	50	31	22	9
		146. Cart makers and sellers	123	105	18	14	9	5
		147. Palki, etc., makers and sellers	...	...	...	...	...	...
		Total Sub-order 25.—Carts, Carriages, etc.	123	105	18	14	9	5
		148. Shipwrights, boat-builders, etc.	...	...	...	...	...	...
		149. Boat, etc., painters and tarrers	...	...	...	...	...	...
		150. Sail makers	...	...	...	...	...	...
		151. Wicker-boat makers, etc.	...	...	...	...	...	...
		152. Ship chandlers, etc.	...	...	...	...	...	...
		Total Sub-order 26.—Ships and Boats	...	...	...	...	...	...
		Total Order X.—Vehicles and Vessels	**227**	**159**	**68**	**45**	**31**	**14**
	Order XI.—Supplementary requirements.	153. Paper makers and sellers, etc.	...	...	...	107	53	54
		154. Stationers	63	25	38	36	26	10
		155. Waste-paper, etc., dealers	...	...	...	...	...	...
		156. Waxed-cloth preparers and sellers	...	...	...	...	...	...
		Total Sub-order 27.—Paper, etc.	63	25	38	143	79	64
		157. Press proprietors, etc.	23	15	8	29	21	8
		158. Book-binders	19	8	11	6	3	3
		159. Book-sellers and publishers	52	17	35	23	17	6
		160. Newspaper proprietors, etc.	...	...	...	10	4	6
		161. News agents and newspaper sellers, etc.	...	...	...	...	...	...
		162. Print and picture dealers	22	14	8	10	10	...
		Total Sub-order 28.—Books and Prints, etc.	116	54	62	78	55	23
		163. Watch, etc., makers and sellers	28	14	14	4	3	1
		164. Opticians	...	...	...	...	...	...
		165. Surgical instrument makers and sellers	...	...	...	...	...	...
		166. Photographic apparatus dealers	...	...	...	...	...	...
		167. Other scientific instrument makers, etc.	...	...	...	...	...	...
		168. Scale makers and sellers	...	...	...	...	...	...
		Total Sub-order 29.—Watches, Clocks and Scientific Instruments	28	14	14	4	3	1
		169. Wood and ebony carvers	...	...	...	...	...	...
		170. Ivory carvers	...	...	...	...	...	...
		171. Cotton-stamp makers and sellers	...	...	...	...	...	...
		172. Turners and lacquerers	22	...	22	7	6	1
		173. Die-sinkers and seal, etc., engravers	...	...	...	...	...	...
		174. Type-founders	...	...	...	...	...	...
		175. Mica, etc., workers and sellers	...	...	...	3	3	...
		175A. Granitic stone workers and dealers	...	...	...	36	17	19
		176. Mosaic, etc., workers and sellers	...	...	...	...	...	...
		Total Sub-order 30.—Carving, Engraving, etc.	22	...	22	46	26	20

Occupations, by Districts—*contd.*

DISTRICT ELLICHPUR.			DISTRICT BULDANA.			DISTRICT WUN.			DISTRICT BASIM.			RAILWAY PASSENGERS.		
TOTAL.	Males.	Females.	TOTAL.	Males.	Females.	TOTAL.	Males.	Females.	TOTAL.	Males.	Females.	TOTAL.	Males.	Females.
10	11	12	13	14	15	16	17	18	19	20	21	22	23	24
950	712	238	340	200	140	737	509	228	347	201	146	...	...	...
172	102	70	113	63	50	24	12	12	32	25	7	...	...	...
...	...	...	...	...	...	...	...	...	6	3	3	...	...	...
15	10	5	3	3	...	...	...	...	2	1	1	...	...	...
1,137	824	313	456	266	190	761	521	240	387	230	157	...	...	...
...	...	...	1	1	...	...	...	...	...	...	...	...	...	...
12	6	6	156	85	71	114	25	89	95	61	34	...	...	...
537	367	170	1,131	634	497	471	295	176	685	357	328	6	3	3
45	20	25	49	27	22	12	11	1	12	4	8	...	...	...
39	24	15	16	...	16	...	...	...	1	1	...	...	...	...
78	59	19	1,501	860	641	705	427	278	1,059	655	403	...	...	...
...	...	...	...	...	...	...	...	...	...	...	...	...	...	...
...	...	...	...	...	...	...	...	...	...	...	...	...	...	...
711	476	235	2,854	1,607	1,247	1,302	758	544	1,852	1,079	773	6	3	3
1,848	**1,300**	**548**	**8,310**	**1,878**	**1,487**	**2,068**	**1,279**	**784**	**2,239**	**1,809**	**980**	**6**	**8**	**8**
...	...	...	...	...	...	...	...	...	...	...	...	3	3	...
...	...	...	...	...	...	...	...	...	...	...	...	...	...	...
...	...	...	...	...	...	...	...	...	...	...	...	3	3	...
...	...	...	3	2	1	14	11	3	...	...	...	...	...	...
...	...	...	...	...	...	...	...	...	...	...	...	...	...	...
...	...	...	3	2	1	14	11	3	...	...	...	...	...	...
...	...	...	...	...	...	...	...	...	...	...	...	...	...	...
...	...	...	...	...	...	...	...	...	...	...	...	...	...	...
...	...	...	...	...	...	...	...	...	...	...	...	...	...	...
...	...	...	...	...	...	...	...	...	...	...	...	...	...	...
...	...	...	...	...	...	...	...	...	...	...	...	...	...	...
...	...	...	...	...	...	...	...	...	...	...	...	...	...	...
...	**...**	**...**	**8**	**2**	**1**	**14**	**11**	**8**	**...**	**...**	**...**	**8**	**8**	**...**
...	...	...	...	...	...	...	...	...	4	2	2	...	...	...
3	2	1	...	...	...	11	11	...	12	7	5	...	...	...
...	...	...	...	...	...	...	...	...	...	...	...	...	...	...
...	...	...	...	...	...	...	...	...	...	...	...	...	...	...
3	2	1	...	...	...	11	11	...	16	9	7	...	...	...
2	2	...	2	2	...	...	...	...	...	...	...	...	...	...
14	6	8	...	...	...	8	4	4	6	2	4	...	...	...
78	30	48	1	1	...	...	...	...	...	...	...	...	...	...
...	...	...	...	...	...	...	...	...	...	...	...	...	...	...
...	...	...	...	...	...	...	...	...	...	...	...	...	...	...
6	4	2	3	1	2	...	...	...	...	...	...	...	...	...
100	42	58	6	4	2	8	4	4	6	2	4	...	...	...
...	...	...	...	...	...	...	...	...	...	...	...	...	...	...
...	...	...	...	...	...	...	...	...	...	...	...	...	...	...
...	...	...	...	...	...	...	...	...	...	...	...	...	...	...
...	...	...	...	...	...	...	...	...	...	...	...	...	...	...
...	...	...	...	...	...	...	...	...	...	...	...	...	...	...
...	...	...	1	1	...	...	...	...	...	...	...	...	...	...
...	...	...	1	1	...	...	...	...	...	...	...	...	...	...
...	...	...	6	4	2	...	...	...	...	...	...	...	...	...
...	...	...	...	...	...	...	...	...	...	...	...	...	...	...
...	...	...	...	...	...	...	...	...	...	...	...	...	...	...
15	8	7	14	7	7	39	22	17	2	1	1	...	...	...
...	...	...	...	...	...	...	...	...	...	...	...	...	...	...
...	...	...	...	...	...	...	...	...	...	...	...	...	...	...
...	...	...	...	...	...	...	...	...	...	...	...	...	...	...
3	2	1	...	...	...	7	2	5	6	2	4	...	...	...
...	...	...	...	...	...	...	...	...	...	...	...	...	...	...
18	10	8	20	11	9	46	24	22	8	3	5	...	...	...

TABLE XVII.—Part B.—

Class.	Order.	Sub-order, Group and Occupation.	District Amraoti. Total.	District Amraoti. Males.	District Amraoti. Females.	District Akola. Total.	District Akola. Males.	District Akola. Females.
1	2	3	4	5	6	7	8	9
Class D.—Preparation and Supply of Material Substances—*continued.*	Order XI.—Supplementary requirements.—*continued.*	177. Toy, kite, etc., makers and sellers	107	44	63	167	65	102
		178. Hukka-stem makers and sellers	...	...	...	...	...	...
		179. Papier maché workers and sellers	...	...	...	...	...	...
		180. Card makers and sellers	...	...	...	...	...	...
		181. Tabut, etc., makers and sellers	1	1	...	...	...	...
		182. Curiosity dealers	...	...	...	...	...	...
		Total Sub-order 31.—Toys, Curiosities, etc.	108	45	63	167	65	102
		183. Music and musical instrument dealers	13	9	4	3	3	...
		184. Conch dealers, etc.	10	6	4	1	1	...
		Total Sub-order 32.—Music and Musical Instruments	23	15	8	4	4	...
		185. Bangle makers and sellers in lac	251	129	122	191	105	86
		186. Bangle makers and sellers in stone	...	...	...	...	...	...
		187. Bangle makers and sellers in wood	1	...	1	2	1	1
		188. Bangle makers and sellers in clay	...	...	...	...	...	...
		189. Bangle makers and sellers in glass	51	36	15	107	81	26
		189A. Bangle makers and sellers, unspecified	998	498	500	972	555	417
		190. Bangle fitters	37	11	26	53	28	25
		191. Imitation jewellery, etc., makers and sellers	74	46	28	192	116	76
		192. Bead makers and sellers	14	14	...	1	1	...
		193. Rosary, etc., makers and sellers	...	...	...	...	...	...
		194. Flower garland makers and sellers	117	59	58	80	38	42
		195. Artificial flower, etc., makers and sellers	...	...	...	...	...	...
		196. Sacred-thread makers and sellers	19	8	11	...	...	...
		Total Sub-order 33.—Necklaces, Bracelets, Sacred Threads, etc.	1,562	801	761	1,598	925	673
		197. Upholsterers	...	...	...	...	...	...
		198. Furniture makers	...	...	...	5	4	1
		199. Frame makers	...	...	...	...	...	...
		200. Looking-glass makers and sellers	...	...	...	...	...	...
		Total Sub-order 34.—Furniture	...	...	...	5	4	1
		201. Saddlery, etc., makers and sellers	62	37	25	197	111	86
		202. Saddle cloth makers, etc.	29	12	17	1	1	...
		203. Whip, etc., makers	...	...	...	...	...	...
		Total Sub-order 35.—Harness	91	49	42	198	112	86
		204. Knife, etc., makers and sellers	27	16	11	25	14	11
		204A. Agricultural implements makers and sellers	99	76	23	19	9	10
		205. Knife and tool grinders	70	33	37	155	81	74
		206. Looms, etc., makers and sellers	3	2	1	3	2	1
		207. Mechanics (not Railway)	53	28	25	70	40	30
		208. Machinery dealers, etc.	...	...	...	...	—	...
		Total Sub-order 36.—Tools and Machinery	252	155	97	272	146	126
		209. Gun, etc., makers and sellers	7	4	3	...	...	...
		210. Ammunition, etc., dealers	...	...	...	7	1	6
		211. Gunpowder makers and sellers	66	31	35	27	11	16
		212. Firework makers and sellers	13	10	3	7	4	3
		213. Sword, etc., makers and sellers	10	6	4	...	...	...
		214. Spear-head, etc., makers and sellers	...	...	...	...	...	...
		215. Bow, etc., makers and sellers	...	...	...	...	...	...
		216. Cudgel, etc., makers and sellers	...	...	...	3	1	2
		Total Sub-order 37.—Arms and Ammunition	96	51	45	44	17	27
		Total Order XI.—Supplementary requirements.	**2,361**	**1,209**	**1,152**	**2,559**	**1,486**	**1,128**
	Order XII.—Textile Fabrics and Dress.	217. Carpet, etc., sellers	...	...	...	...	...	...
		218. Shawl, etc., sellers	...	...	...	1	1	...
		219. Felt, etc., workers and sellers	...	...	...	...	...	...
		220. Blanket, etc., sellers	697	497	200	542	299	243
		221. Woollen cloth, etc., dealers	11	11	...	7	3	4
		222. Woollen yarn, etc., sellers	33	1	32	18	7	11
		223. Wool carders	...	...	...	6	3	3
		224. Wool dyers	...	...	...	...	...	...
		225. Fur dealers	22	11	11	2	...	2
		Total Sub-order 38.—Wool and Fur	763	520	243	576	313	263

Occupations, by Districts—*contd.*

DISTRICT ELLICHPUR.			DISTRICT BULDANA.			DISTRICT WUN.			DISTRICT BASIM.			RAILWAY PASSENGERS.		
TOTAL.	Males.	Females.	TOTAL.	Males.	Females.	TOTAL.	Males.	Females.	TOTAL.	Males.	Females.	TOTAL.	Males.	Females.
10	11	12	13	14	15	16	17	18	19	20	21	22	23	24
44	21	23	45	22	23	4	3	1	12	9	3	...	...	...
...	...	...	...	...	...	...	...	...	...	...	...	...	...	...
...	...	...	...	...	...	...	...	...	...	...	...	...	...	...
...	...	...	...	...	...	...	...	...	...	...	...	...	...	...
6	5	1	...	...	...	...	...	...	...	...	...	...	...	...
...	...	...	...	...	...	...	...	...	...	...	...	...	...	...
50	26	24	45	22	23	4	3	1	12	9	3	...	...	...
7	4	3	4	4	...	...	...	...	...	...	...	...	...	...
...	...	...	...	...	...	...	...	...	...	...	...	...	...	...
7	4	3	4	4	...	...	...	...	...	...	...	...	...	...
142	79	63	19	7	12	15	10	5	56	36	20	...	...	...
...	...	...	...	...	...	...	...	...	...	...	...	...	...	...
5	5	...	...	...	...	...	...	...	14	5	9	...	...	...
...	...	...	...	...	...	...	...	...	...	...	...	...	...	...
235	119	116	125	48	77	31	16	15	37	26	11	...	...	...
378	202	176	1,050	577	473	463	271	192	910	483	427	...	...	...
12	1	11	122	42	80	54	20	34	27	16	11	...	...	...
84	48	36	83	41	42	26	14	12	39	24	15	...	...	...
...	...	...	...	...	...	...	...	...	11	6	5	...	...	...
...	...	...	...	...	...	8	...	8	...	...	...	...	...	...
159	72	87	25	6	19	26	12	14	57	43	14	...	...	...
5	5	...	...	...	...	...	...	...	...	...	...	...	...	...
...	...	...	3	1	2	2	2	...	...	...	...	...	...	...
1,020	531	489	1,427	722	705	625	345	280	1,151	639	512	...	...	...
...	...	...	...	...	...	...	...	...	...	...	...	...	...	...
10	10	...	...	...	...	2	2	...	2	2	...	...	...	...
5	3	2	...	...	...	...	...	...	...	...	...	...	...	...
...	...	...	...	...	...	...	...	...	...	...	...	...	...	...
15	13	2	...	...	...	2	2	...	2	2	...	...	...	...
39	24	15	76	37	39	24	13	11	32	21	11	...	...	...
2	...	2	18	9	9	...	...	...	...	...	...	...	...	...
4	2	2	...	...	...	...	...	...	...	...	...	...	...	...
45	26	19	94	46	48	24	13	11	32	21	11	...	...	...
3	3	...	11	5	6	...	...	...	...	...	...	...	...	...
31	20	11	15	8	7	1	1	...	9	6	3	...	...	...
49	23	26	68	44	24	26	17	9	111	67	44	...	...	...
3	2	1	10	6	4	...	...	...	...	...	...	...	...	...
5	4	1	4	4	...	5	3	2	...	...	...	...	...	...
...	...	...	...	...	...	...	...	...	...	...	...	...	...	...
91	52	39	108	67	41	32	21	11	120	73	47	...	...	...
...	...	...	3	3	...	...	...	...	32	12	20	...	...	...
...	...	...	...	...	...	...	...	...	...	...	...	...	...	...
12	5	7	24	14	10	7	2	5	...	...	...	...	...	...
15	8	7	7	3	4	...	...	...	...	...	...	...	...	...
...	...	...	6	3	3	...	...	...	4	2	2	...	...	...
...	...	...	...	...	...	...	...	...	...	...	...	...	...	...
...	...	...	...	...	...	...	...	...	...	...	...	...	...	...
...	...	...	...	...	...	...	...	...	...	...	...	...	...	...
27	13	14	40	23	17	7	2	5	36	14	22	...	...	...
1,376	719	657	1,745	900	845	759	425	334	1,383	772	611	...	...	...
...	...	...	...	...	...	...	...	...	...	...	...	...	...	...
...	...	...	...	...	...	1	1	...	...	...	...	...	...	...
...	...	...	...	...	...	...	...	...	...	...	...	...	...	...
190	117	73	2,048	1,113	935	483	282	201	867	488	379	...	...	...
...	...	...	12	...	12	4	2	2	31	13	18	...	...	...
6	...	6	148	11	137	10	1	9	57	5	52	...	...	...
...	...	...	3	...	3	...	...	...	...	...	...	...	...	...
...	...	...	...	...	...	...	...	...	...	...	...	...	...	...
...	...	...	15	4	11	1	...	1	72	35	37	...	...	...
196	117	79	2,226	1,128	1,098	499	286	213	1,027	541	486	...	...	...

TABLE XVII.—Part B.—

Class.	Order.	Sub-order, Group and Occupation.	District Amraoti. Total.	District Amraoti. Males.	District Amraoti. Females.	District Akola. Total.	District Akola. Males.	District Akola. Females.
1	2	3	4	5	6	7	8	9
CLASS D.—PREPARATION AND SUPPLY OF MATERIAL SUBSTANCES—*continued*.	ORDER XII.—TEXTILE FABRICS AND DRESS—*contd.*	226. Silk worm, etc., gatherers	...	...	...	...	...	...
		227. Silk carders and spinners	394	143	251	229	107	122
		228. Silk weavers and dealers	254	184	70	73	40	33
		229. Silk printers, etc.	...	...	...	...	...	...
		230. Braid, etc., makers and sellers	1	1	...	10	5	5
		TOTAL SUB-ORDER 39.—SILK	649	328	321	312	152	160
		231. Cotton cleaners, etc.	5,427	1,860	3,567	4,022	652	3,370
		231A. Raw cotton dealers	1,988	1,169	819	1,928	1,077	851
		232. Cotton carpet, etc., makers and sellers	287	178	109	729	382	347
		233. Cotton spinners, etc.	2,193	235	1,958	1,410	105	1,305
		234. Cotton weavers, etc.	5,523	3,441	2,082	3,430	1,848	1,582
		234A. Cotton factory engineers	77	50	27	108	55	53
		235. Cotton factory hands (undefined)	2,574	1,514	1,060	1,933	1,183	750
		236. Calenderers, etc.	...	...	...	2	2	...
		237. Cotton dyers	1,333	685	648	921	504	417
		238. Tape makers and sellers	23	8	15	32	20	12
		239. Tent manufacturers, etc.	...	...	...	...	...	...
		TOTAL SUB-ORDER 40.—COTTON	19,425	9,140	10,285	14,515	5,828	8,687
		240. Flax-spinners, etc.	...	...	...	...	...	...
		241. Hemp rope makers, etc.	284	136	148	128	92	36
		242. Jute manufacturers, etc.	...	...	...	...	...	...
		243. Sacking, etc., makers and sellers	470	258	212	332	245	87
		244. Net makers and sellers	18	14	4	19	6	13
		245. Fancy work dealers	...	...	...	...	...	...
		246. Coir preparers, etc.	...	...	...	...	...	...
		TOTAL SUB-ORDER 41.—JUTE, FLAX, COIR, ETC.	772	408	364	479	343	136
		247. Tailors and darners	3,214	1,602	1,612	2,805	1,418	1,387
		248. Milliners, etc.	...	...	...	...	...	...
		249. Outfitters, etc.	481	294	187	386	275	111
		250. Hosiers, etc.	...	...	...	...	...	...
		251. Hat, etc., makers and sellers	3	1	2	4	4	...
		252. Turban binders	2	2	...	1	1	...
		253. Umbrella makers, etc.	...	...	...	...	...	...
		254. Embroiderers etc.,	151	2	149	137	16	121
		255. Button makers and sellers	...	...	...	...	...	...
		256. False plait makers, etc.	...	...	...	...	...	...
		257. Piece goods dealers	3,497	2,201	1,256	3,205	1,832	1,373
		TOTAL SUB-ORDER 42.—DRESS	7,348	4,102	3,246	6,538	3,546	2,992
		Total Order XII.—Textile Fabrics and Dress	**28,957**	**14,498**	**14,459**	**22,420**	**10,182**	**12,238**
	ORDER XIII.—METALS AND PRECIOUS STONES.	258. Gold and silver dealers	130	83	47	81	67	14
		259. Gold and silver assayers	...	...	...	...	...	...
		260. Gold and silver workers	4,992	2,875	2,117	4,333	2,404	1,929
		261. Gold beaters	...	...	...	...	...	...
		262. Goldsmith's dust washers	61	35	26	94	58	36
		263. Gold miners, etc.	...	...	...	...	...	...
		264. Enamellers	...	...	...	...	...	...
		265. Electro-platers	14	11	3	...	...	...
		266. Gold and silver wire drawers, etc.	9	9	...	12	11	1
		267. Plate and platedware dealers	6	3	3	2	2	...
		268. Diamond polishers, etc.	...	...	...	...	...	...
		269. Diamond diggers, etc.	...	...	...	...	...	...
		270. Ruby workers	...	...	...	...	...	...
		271. Ruby, etc., dealers	...	...	...	...	...	...
		272. Pearl divers	—	...	...	...	..	...
		273. Pearl, etc., dealers	158	84	74	85	59	26
		274. Coral dealers	6	3	3	...	...	...
		275. Cornelian, etc., sellers	...	...	...	...	...	...
		TOTAL SUB-ORDER 43.—GOLD, SILVER AND PRECIOUS STONES	5,376	3,103	2,273	4,607	2,601	2,006
		276. Brass workers and sellers	16	8	8	...	...	...
		277. Brass pot makers and sellers	90	56	34	204	121	83
		278. Brass image casters, etc.	...	...	...	1	1	...
		279. Copper workers and sellers	28	15	13	30	18	12
		280. Brass, etc., drawers and sellers	1	1	...	1	...	1
		281. Bell metal workers, etc.	102	54	48	91	47	44
		282. General workers in brass, etc.	131	75	56	4	4	...
		283. Brass, etc., dealers	303	231	72	429	316	113
		TOTAL SUB-ORDER 44.—BRASS, COPPER AND BELL METAL	671	440	231	760	507	253

Occupations, by Districts—*contd.*

DISTRICT ELLICHPUR.			DISTRICT BULDANA.			DISTRICT WUN.			DISTRICT BASIM.			RAILWAY PASSENGERS.		
TOTAL.	Males.	Females.	TOTAL.	Males.	Females.	TOTAL.	Males.	Females.	TOTAL.	Males.	Females.	TOTAL.	Males.	Females.
10	11	12	13	14	15	16	17	18	19	20	21	22	23	24
...	...	...	...	...	...	...	...	...	...	...	...	...	...	...
303	108	195	228	110	118	55	28	27	178	129	49	...	...	...
81	55	26	63	26	37	4	2	2	6	2	4	...	...	...
5	3	2	4	...	4	...	...	...	1	1	...	...	...	...
...	...	...	...	...	...	2	...	2	...	...	...	...	...	...
389	166	223	295	136	159	61	30	31	185	132	53	...	...	...
2,086	621	1,465	1,390	279	1,111	832	371	461	345	127	218	...	...	...
1,474	815	659	824	505	319	851	534	317	666	396	270	1	1	...
684	405	279	120	62	58	52	51	1	28	19	9	...	...	...
1,516	136	1,380	792	103	689	1,525	351	1,174	906	56	850	...	...	...
6,658	3,741	2,917	4,010	2,082	1,928	4,851	2,904	1,947	2,739	1,456	1,283	1	1	...
17	12	5	2	1	1	3	3	...	...	...	...	...	...	...
208	155	53	37	23	14	55	42	13	76	66	10	...	...	...
1	1	...	4	2	2	...	...	...	...	...	...	...	...	...
1,209	639	570	1,612	789	823	1,345	737	608	1,003	510	493	1	1	...
9	6	3	20	17	3	2	1	1	10	8	2	...	...	...
...	...	...	...	...	...	...	...	...	...	...	...	...	...	...
13,862	6,531	7,331	8,811	3,863	4,948	9,516	4,994	4,522	5,773	2,638	3,135	3	3	...
...	...	...	...	...	...	...	...	...	...	...	...	...	...	...
133	78	55	45	26	19	195	79	116	66	23	43	...	...	...
...	...	...	...	...	...	...	...	...	...	...	...	...	...	...
12	7	5	330	189	141	71	21	50	372	203	169	...	...	...
...	...	...	10	2	8	...	...	...	...	...	...	...	...	...
...	...	...	...	...	...	...	...	...	...	...	...	...	...	...
...	...	...	...	...	...	...	...	...	...	...	...	...	...	...
145	85	60	385	217	168	266	100	166	438	226	212	...	...	...
1,377	673	704	1,737	806	931	1,954	959	995	1,099	605	494	3	3	...
...	...	...	...	...	...	...	...	...	...	...	...	...	...	...
866	415	451	90	63	27	83	53	30	8	3	5	...	...	...
...	...	...	...	...	...	...	...	...	...	...	...	...	...	...
4	...	4	...	...	...	...	...	...	...	...	...	...	...	...
...	...	...	...	...	...	...	...	...	...	...	...	...	...	...
...	...	...	2	...	2	...	...	...	...	...	...	...	...	...
59	3	56	55	...	55	17	1	16	63	8	55	...	...	...
...	...	...	...	...	...	...	...	...	...	...	...	...	...	...
...	...	...	...	...	...	...	...	...	...	...	...	...	...	...
2,094	1,306	788	2,618	1,532	1,086	2,355	1,464	891	2,204	1,244	960	...	...	...
4,400	2,397	2,003	4,502	2,401	2,101	4,409	2,477	1,932	3,374	1,860	1,514	3	3	...
18,992	9,296	9,696	16,219	7,745	8,474	14,751	7,887	6,864	10,797	5,397	5,400	6	6	...
31	20	11	41	12	29	55	29	26	56	41	15	...	...	...
3	3	...	...	...	...	...	...	...	...	...	...	...	...	...
2,317	1,307	1,010	3,246	1,774	1,472	2,875	1,630	1,245	2,414	1,308	1,106	3	3	...
...	...	...	...	...	...	...	...	...	...	...	...	...	...	...
73	38	35	23	9	14	12	7	5	6	3	3	...	...	...
...	...	...	...	...	...	...	...	...	...	...	...	...	...	...
...	...	...	...	...	...	...	...	...	...	...	...	...	...	...
...	...	...	...	...	...	...	...	...	1	1	...	...	...	...
3	3	...	1	1	...	14	9	5	...	...	...	...	...	...
2	2	...	...	...	...	9	5	4	...	...	...	...	...	...
...	...	...	...	...	...	...	...	...	...	...	...	...	...	...
...	...	...	...	...	...	...	...	...	...	...	...	...	...	...
...	...	...	...	...	...	...	...	...	...	...	...	...	...	...
...	...	...	...	...	...	...	...	...	...	...	...	...	...	...
...	...	...	...	...	...	...	...	...	...	...	...	...	...	...
7	5	2	16	12	4	25	17	8	35	11	24	...	...	...
...	...	...	1	...	1	8	5	3	...	...	...	...	...	...
...	...	...	...	...	...	...	...	...	...	...	...	...	...	...
2,436	1,378	1,058	3,328	1,808	1,520	2,998	1,702	1,296	2,512	1,364	1,148	3	3	...
86	41	45	...	...	...	2	1	1	6	...	6	...	...	...
12	3	9	3	3	...	9	6	3	25	12	13	...	...	...
...	...	...	...	...	...	...	...	...	...	...	...	...	...	...
20	10	10	18	12	6	10	5	5	19	5	14	...	...	...
...	...	...	...	...	...	18	18	...	...	...	...	...	...	...
43	22	21	26	16	10	146	86	60	151	56	95	...	...	...
16	4	12	8	1	7	20	13	7	140	69	71	...	...	...
256	157	99	266	129	137	143	91	52	224	131	93	1	1	...
433	237	196	321	161	160	348	220	128	565	273	292	1	1	...

TABLE XVII.—Part B.—

Class.	Order.	Sub-order, Group and Occupation.	District Amraoti. Total.	District Amraoti. Males.	District Amraoti. Females.	District Akola. Total.	District Akola. Males.	District Akola. Females.
1	2	3	4	5	6	7	8	9
CLASS D.—PREPARATION AND SUPPLY OF MATERIAL SUBSTANCES—*contd.*	ORDER XIII.—METALS AND PRECIOUS STONES—*contd.*	284. Tin workers, etc.	319	184	135	161	91	70
		285. Tinfoil makers, etc.	...	...	...	...	...	...
		286. Zinc workers, etc.	8	7	1	7	4	3
		287. Lead, etc., workers and sellers	1	...	1	...	...	...
		288. General workers in tin, etc.	...	...	...	...	...	...
		TOTAL SUB-ORDER 45.—TIN, ZINC, MERCURY AND LEAD	328	191	137	168	95	73
		289. Iron, etc., smelters and sellers	...	...	...	...	...	...
		290. Blacksmiths	2,930	1,652	1,278	1,980	1,091	889
		291. Iron, etc., dealers	105	75	30	76	39	37
		292. Nail makers, etc.	...	...	...	...	...	...
		293. Lock makers, etc.	12	6	6	19	13	6
		294. Weight makers, etc.	...	...	...	1	...	1
		TOTAL SUB-ORDER 46.—IRON AND STEEL	3,047	1,733	1,314	2,076	1,143	933
		Total Order XIII.—Metals and Precious Stones	**9,422**	**5,467**	**3,955**	**7,611**	**4,346**	**3,265**
	ORDER XIV.—GLASS, POTTERY AND STONE-WARE.	295. Glass-blowers, etc.	...	...	...	...	...	...
		296. Bottle dealers	7	7	...	2	2	...
		297. Glass, etc., dealers	...	...	...	8	6	2
		TOTAL SUB-ORDER 47.—GLASS AND CHINAWARE	7	7	...	10	8	2
		298. Potters, etc.	3,680	1,965	1,715	3,537	1,868	1,669
		299. Grindstone, etc., makers and sellers	300	164	136	978	577	401
		300. Pestle, etc., makers and sellers	2	...	2	25	10	15
		301. Quartz, etc., preparers and sellers	...	...	...	...	...	...
		TOTAL SUB-ORDER 48.—EARTHEN AND STONE-WARE	3,982	2,129	1,853	4,540	2,455	2,085
		Total Order XIV.—Glass, Pottery and Stone-ware	**3,989**	**2,136**	**1,853**	**4,550**	**2,463**	**2,087**
	ORDER XV.—WOOD, CANE AND LEAVES, ETC.	302. Timber, etc., dealers	181	116	65	803	464	339
		303. Wood-cutters and sawyers	815	572	243	744	498	246
		304. Carpenters	6,745	4,173	2,572	5,476	3,343	2,133
		305. Coopers and box makers	20	17	3	4	4	...
		TOTAL SUB-ORDER 49.—TIMBER AND WOOD	7,761	4,878	2,883	7,027	4,309	2,718
		306. Bamboo, etc., workers and sellers	78	47	31	367	127	240
		307. Basket, etc., makers and sellers	986	519	467	2,573	1,296	1,277
		308. Mat makers and sellers	123	39	84	392	195	197
		309. Screen, etc., makers and sellers	...	...	...	...	...	...
		310. Leaf-plate makers and sellers	59	26	33	10	8	2
		311. Toothstick sellers	2	...	2	18	3	15
		312. Leaf-fan makers and sellers	...	...	...	...	...	...
		313. Brush, etc., makers and sellers	8	7	1	...	...	...
		314. Broom makers and sellers	484	153	331	1,161	530	631
		315. Pith, etc., workers and sellers	...	...	...	...	...	...
		TOTAL SUB-ORDER 50.—CANEWORK, MATTING AND LEAVES, ETC.	1,740	791	949	4,521	2,159	2,362
		Total Order XV.—Wood, Cane and Leaves, etc.	**9,501**	**5,669**	**3,832**	**11,548**	**6,468**	**5,080**
	ORDER XVI.—DRUGS, GUMS, DYES, ETC.	316. India-rubber collectors and sellers	...	...	...	...	...	...
		317. Camphor, etc., collectors and sellers	...	...	...	...	...	...
		318. Gallnut, etc., collectors and sellers	...	...	...	...	...	...
		319. Catechu preparers and sellers	...	...	...	...	...	...
		320. Lac collectors and sellers	...	...	...	...	...	...
		321. Sealing-wax makers and sellers	...	...	...	...	...	...
		322. Tar preparers and sellers	...	...	...	...	...	...
		323. Wax, etc., collectors and sellers	53	26	27	58	24	34
		TOTAL SUB-ORDER 51.—GUMS, WAX AND SIMILAR FOREST PRODUCE	53	26	27	58	24	34

Occupations, by Districts—*contd.*

DISTRICT ELLICHPUR.			DISTRICT BULDANA.			DISTRICT WUN.			DISTRICT BASIM.			RAILWAY PASSENGERS.		
TOTAL.	Males.	Females.	TOTAL.	Males.	Females.	TOTAL.	Males.	Females.	TOTAL.	Males.	Females.	TOTAL.	Males.	Females.
10	11	12	13	14	15	16	17	18	19	20	21	22	23	24
60	31	29	90	50	40	183	98	85	36	14	22	...	...	...
...	...	...	...	...	...	...	...	...	...	...	...	...	...	...
1	1	...	...	...	...	1	...	1	...	...	...	...	...	...
...	...	...	...	...	...	79	44	35	...	...	...	...	...	...
61	32	29	90	50	40	263	142	121	36	14	22	...	...	...
1	1	...	...	...	...	22	...	22	...	...	...	...	...	...
1,202	667	535	2,082	1,082	1,000	2,935	1,725	1,210	1,373	729	644	8	8	...
30	18	12	3	1	2	...	...	...	33	24	9	...	...	...
...	...	...	...	...	...	...	...	...	...	...	...	...	...	...
10	4	6	...	...	...	...	...	...	...	...	...	...	...	...
2	2	...	...	...	...	...	...	...	...	...	...	...	...	...
1,245	692	553	2,085	1,083	1,002	2,957	1,725	1,232	1,406	753	653	8	8	...
4,175	2,339	1,836	5,824	3,102	2,722	6,566	3,789	2,777	4,519	2,404	2,115	12	12	...
...	...	...	...	...	...	...	...	...	...	...	...	...	...	...
...	...	...	...	...	...	...	...	...	...	...	...	...	...	...
...	...	...	7	...	7	...	...	...	6	...	6	...	...	...
...	...	...	7	...	7	...	...	...	6	...	6	...	...	...
1,797	905	892	2,570	1,341	1,229	2,113	1,162	951	2,224	1,130	1,094	...	...	...
146	91	55	673	349	324	288	157	131	505	250	255	...	...	...
...	...	...	10	8	2	...	...	...	6	6	...	...	...	...
...	...	...	...	...	...	...	...	...	...	...	...	...	...	...
1,943	996	947	3,253	1,698	1,555	2,401	1,319	1,082	2,735	1,386	1,349	...	...	...
1,943	996	947	3,260	1,698	1,562	2,401	1,319	1,082	2,741	1,386	1,355	...	...	...
1,732	992	740	19	11	8	20	15	5	64	36	28	...	...	...
181	140	41	358	243	115	166	127	39	267	185	82	...	...	...
2,833	1,773	1,060	4,722	2,707	2,015	5,192	3,069	2,123	3,969	2,357	1,612	5	5	...
3	1	2	2	2	...	...	...	...	44	44	...	...	...	...
4,749	2,906	1,843	5,101	2,963	2,138	5,378	3,211	2,167	4,344	2,622	1,722	5	5	...
212	109	103	74	33	41	157	75	82	1	...	1	...	...	...
665	304	361	1,349	687	662	399	179	220	601	300	301	...	...	...
120	60	60	...	...	...	9	4	5	273	131	142	...	...	...
...	...	...	...	...	...	...	...	...	...	...	...	...	...	...
6	2	4	17	8	9	313	182	131	47	26	21	...	...	...
3	1	2	3	1	2	4	2	2	16	3	13	...	...	...
4	4	...	...	...	...	...	...	...	...	...	...	...	...	...
81	38	43	16	8	8	3	3	...	...	...	...	...	...	...
176	76	100	1,863	858	1,005	167	64	103	944	427	517	...	...	...
...	...	...	...	...	...	...	...	...	...	...	...	...	...	...
1,267	594	673	3,322	1,595	1,727	1,052	509	543	1,882	887	995	...	...	...
6,016	3,500	2,516	8,423	4,558	3,865	6,430	3,720	2,710	6,226	3,509	2,717	5	5	...
8	3	5	...	...	...	19	...	19	4	2	2	...	...	...
...	...	...	...	...	...	...	...	...	...	...	...	...	...	...
...	...	...	2	2	...	...	...	...	...	...	...	...	...	...
...	...	...	...	...	...	...	...	...	...	...	...	...	...	...
...	...	...	...	...	...	...	...	...	...	...	...	...	...	...
4	4	...	...	...	...	...	...	...	...	...	...	...	...	...
2	...	2	...	...	...	...	...	...	...	...	...	...	...	...
41	20	21	205	126	79	42	22	20	230	118	112	...	...	...
55	27	28	207	128	79	61	22	39	234	120	114	...	...	...

TABLE XVII.—Part B.—

Class.	Order.	Sub-order, Group and Occupation.	District Amraoti. Total.	Males.	Females.	District Akola. Total.	Males.	Females.
1	2	3	4	5	6	7	8	9
Class D.—Preparation and Supply, etc.—*concld.*	Order XVI.—Drugs, Gums, Dyes, etc.—*contd.*	324. Chemists and druggists	248	146	102	199	109	90
		325. Borax workers and sellers	...	...	...	4	4	...
		326. Saltpetre workers and sellers	...	...	...	2	2	...
		327. Alum, etc., workers and sellers	73	40	33	7	5	2
		328. Soap makers and sellers	...	...	...	...	...	...
		329. Sulphur workers and sellers	2	...	2	...	...	...
		330. Indigo workers and dealers (not planters)	7	2	5	2	2	...
		331. Madder, etc., workers and sellers	...	...	...	...	...	...
		332. Ink makers and sellers	4	1	3	...	...	...
		333. Antimony preparers and sellers	4	...	4	5	3	2
		334. Henna preparers and sellers	...	...	...	...	...	...
		335. Carmine preparers and sellers	...	...	...	...	...	...
		336. Kanku, etc., preparers and sellers	481	239	242	288	126	162
		337. Perfume preparers and sellers	135	81	54	125	79	46
		Total Sub-order 52.—Drugs, Dyes, Pigments, etc.	954	509	445	632	330	302
		Total Order XVI.—Drugs, Gums, Dyes, etc.	**1,007**	**585**	**472**	**690**	**354**	**336**
	Order XVII.—Leather, Horns, Bones and Grease.	338. Tanners, etc.	105	67	38	18	15	3
		339. Shoe, etc., makers and sellers	3,261	2,037	1,224	4,457	2,692	1,765
		340. Leather dyers	88	64	24	223	135	88
		341. Water bag, etc., makers and sellers	196	110	86	97	43	54
		342. Hide, etc., dealers	224	119	105	178	101	77
		343. Catgut preparers and sellers	...	...	...	4	1	3
		344. Glue makers and sellers	...	...	...	...	...	...
		345. Grease preparers and sellers	...	...	...	...	...	...
		Total Sub-order 53.—Leather, etc.	3,874	2,397	1,477	4,977	2,987	1,990
		Total Order XVII.—Leather, Horns, Bones and Grease	**3,874**	**2,397**	**1,477**	**4,977**	**2,987**	**1,990**
		Total Class D	**95,654**	**52,377**	**48,277**	**82,658**	**48,237**	**39,421**
Class E.—Commerce, Transport, Storage.	Order XVIII.—Commerce.	346. Bankers and bank managers	1	1	...	...	...	...
		347. Money lenders, etc.	4,811	2,713	2,098	4,880	2,978	1,902
		348. Bill-discounters, etc.	...	...	...	...	...	...
		349. Insurance agents, etc.	...	...	...	...	...	...
		350. Money changers and testers	195	101	94	348	209	139
		351. Bank clerks, etc.	13	6	7	8	5	3
		Total Sub-order 54.—Dealers in Money and Securities	5,020	2,821	2,199	5,236	3,192	2,044
		352. General merchants	334	144	190	396	183	213
		353. Merchants' managers, etc.	1,043	665	378	1,071	694	377
		Total Sub-order 55.—General Merchandise	1,377	809	568	1,467	877	590
		354. Shop-keepers' clerks, etc.	311	196	115	180	107	73
		355. Shop-keepers and money-lenders' servants	3,711	2,415	1,296	2,518	1,591	927
		356. Shop-keepers, etc., unspecified	1,074	426	648	686	321	365
		357. Pedlars, etc.	554	343	211	595	369	226
		Total Sub-order 56.—Dealing unspecified	5,650	3,380	2,270	3,979	2,388	1,591
		358. Brokers, etc.	1,426	833	593	894	539	355
		359. Auctioneers, etc.	6	4	2	...	...	...
		360. Farmers of tolls, etc.	12	9	3	...	...	...
		361. Farmers of liquor, etc.	219	151	68	303	179	124
		362. Lessees and superintendents of markets, etc.	35	20	15	24	12	12
		363. Contractors, etc., unspecified	380	167	213	183	100	83
		364. Contractors for labour, etc.	3	...	3	34	23	11
		Total Sub-order 57.—Middlemen, etc.	2,081	1,184	897	1,438	853	585
		Total Order XVIII.—Commerce, etc.	**14,128**	**8,194**	**5,934**	**12,120**	**7,810**	**4,810**
	Order XIX.—Transport and Storage.	365. Agents, directors, etc.	...	...	...	...	...	...
		366. Traffic managers, etc.	...	...	...	...	...	...
		367. Locomotive superintendents, etc.	...	...	...	...	...	...
		368. Auditors, accountants, etc.	...	...	...	...	...	...
		369. Engineers, etc.	1	1	...	22	21	1
		370. Clerical staff in Railway establishment	125	71	54	89	45	44
		371. Station masters, etc.	99	48	51	70	34	36
		372. Guards, drivers, etc.	224	113	111	55	38	17
		373. Pointsmen, etc.	294	214	80	254	173	81
		373A. Railway servants, etc.	758	461	297	678	394	284
		Total Sub-order 58.—Railway	1,501	908	593	1,168	705	463

Occupations, by Districts—*contd.*

DISTRICT ELLICHPUR.			DISTRICT BULDANA.			DISTRICT WUN.			DISTRICT BASIM.			RAILWAY PASSENGERS.		
TOTAL.	Males.	Females.	TOTAL.	Males.	Females.	TOTAL.	Males.	Females.	TOTAL.	Males.	Females.	TOTAL.	Males.	Females.
10	11	12	13	14	15	16	17	18	19	20	21	22	23	24
11	5	6	240	125	115	19	11	8	55	35	20	...	...	...
...	...	...	...	...	...	5	4	1	...	...	...	...	...	...
...	...	...	...	...	...	1	...	1	...	...	...	...	...	...
...	...	...	10	6	4	...	...	...	9	4	5	...	...	...
...	...	...	...	...	...	...	...	...	...	...	...	...	...	...
...	...	...	...	...	...	...	...	...	...	...	...	...	...	...
88	56	32	...	...	...	4	2	2	2	...	2	...	...	...
19	3	16	...	...	...	...	...	...	...	...	...	...	...	...
14	9	5	3	3	...	2	1	1	...	...	...	...	...	...
...	...	...	10	4	6	...	...	...	...	...	...	...	...	...
...	...	...	...	...	...	...	...	...	...	...	...	...	...	...
...	...	...	...	...	...	...	...	...	...	...	...	...	...	...
163	80	83	145	60	85	207	112	95	72	40	32	...	...	...
58	28	30	75	46	29	127	72	55	152	80	72	...	...	...
353	181	172	483	244	239	365	202	163	290	159	131	...	...	...
408	**208**	**200**	**690**	**372**	**318**	**426**	**224**	**202**	**524**	**279**	**245**	...	...	...
41	22	19	51	26	25	...	...	...	12	7	5	1	1	...
1,877	1,133	744	4,638	2,666	1,972	3,480	2,042	1,438	3,118	1,687	1,431	8	8	...
270	133	137	356	196	160	29	18	11	20	14	6	...	...	...
95	49	46	126	79	47	134	85	49	31	16	15	...	...	...
148	98	50	238	117	121	152	107	45	173	115	58	...	...	...
...	..	...	12	8	4	15	8	7	7	6	1	...	...	...
...	...	...	...	...	...	...	...	...	...	...	...	...	...	...
...	...	...	...	...	...	...	...	...	...	...	...	...	...	...
2,431	1,435	996	5,421	3,092	2,329	3,810	2,260	1,550	3,361	1,845	1,516	9	9	...
2,431	**1,435**	**996**	**5,421**	**3,092**	**2,329**	**3,810**	**2,260**	**1,550**	**3,361**	**1,845**	**1,516**	**9**	**9**	..
60,962	**31,529**	**29,433**	**60,407**	**31,317**	**29,090**	**58,015**	**31,714**	**26,301**	**44,455**	**23,705**	**20,750**	**50**	**44**	**6**
...	...	...	3	3	...	...	...	...	...	...	...	...	...	...
2,053	1,191	862	3,972	2,234	1,738	1,358	780	578	2,206	1,287	919	2	2	...
...	...	...	...	...	...	1	...	1	...	...	...	...	...	...
...	...	...	...	...	...	...	...	...	...	...	...	...	...	...
129	74	55	154	80	74	59	31	28	156	89	67	...	...	...
2	1	1	...	...	...	...	...	...	...	...	...	...	...	...
2,184	1,266	918	4,129	2,317	1,812	1,418	811	607	2,362	1,376	986	2	2	...
104	26	78	422	194	228	132	57	75	189	93	96	41	37	4
455	286	169	368	254	114	388	259	129	219	145	74	2	2	...
559	312	247	790	448	342	520	316	204	408	238	170	43	39	4
64	40	24	36	33	3	17	13	4	16	7	9	...	...	...
1,595	1,001	594	1,905	1,242	663	1,354	877	477	1,818	1,169	649	9	7	2
335	142	193	1,351	615	736	925	433	492	1,393	690	703	...	...	...
279	163	116	183	105	78	99	56	43	203	157	46	...	...	...
2,273	1,346	927	3,475	1,995	1,480	2,395	1,379	1,016	3,430	2,023	1,407	9	7	2
217	115	102	29	47	22	219	150	69	94	47	47	...	...	...
...	...	...	63	4	19	...	...	...	...	...	...	...	...	...
...	...	...	...	...	...	...	...	...	...	...	...	...	...	...
133	80	53	161	103	58	235	129	106	83	51	32	...	...	...
7	3	4	2	2	...	12	3	9	10	6	4	...	...	...
127	74	53	103	48	55	777	210	567	95	46	49	2	2	...
24	11	13	21	9	12	11	11	...	1	...	1	...	...	...
508	283	225	379	213	166	1,254	503	751	283	150	133	2	2	...
5,524	**3,207**	**2,317**	**8,773**	**4,978**	**3,800**	**5,587**	**3,009**	**2,578**	**6,483**	**3,787**	**2,696**	**56**	**50**	**6**
...	...	...	...	...	...	...	...	...	...	...	...	...	...	...
...	...	...	...	...	...	...	...	...	...	...	...	...	...	...
...	...	...	...	...	...	...	...	...	...	...	...	...	...	...
...	...	...	...	...	...	...	...	...	...	...	...	...	...	...
...	...	...	...	...	...	...	...	...	...	...	...	1	1	...
...	...	...	9	2	7	...	...	...	2	...	2	...	...	...
...	...	...	25	9	16	...	...	...	...	...	...	...	...	...
...	...	...	2	2	...	...	...	...	...	...	...	2	2	...
...	...	...	82	51	31	...	...	...	...	...	...	4	4	...
1	...	1	427	268	159	8	6	2	3	2	1	175	116	59
1	...	1	545	332	213	8	6	2	5	2	3	182	123	59

TABLE XVII.—Part B.—

Class.	Order.	Sub-order, Group and Occupation.	District Amraoti. Total.	Males.	Females.	District Akola. Total.	Males.	Females.
1	2	3	4	5	6	7	8	9
Class E.—Commerce, Transport, Storage—*contd.*	Order XIX.—Transport and Storage—*contd.*	374. Tramway, etc.	...	...	...	...	...	...
		375. Cart owners, etc.	3,378	2,263	1,115	2,756	1,902	854
		376. Livery stable-keepers, etc.	...	...	...	...	...	...
		377. Drivers, stable-boys, etc.	14	2	12	...	...	...
		378. Palki owners, etc.	15	9	6	13	10	3
		379. Pack bullock owners, etc.	42	29	13	115	69	46
		380. Pack camel owners, etc.	91	56	35	68	40	28
		Total Sub-order 59.—Road	3,540	2,359	1,181	2,952	2,021	931
		381. Ship owners, etc.	...	...	...	...	...	...
		382. Shipping clerks, etc.	...	...	...	...	...	...
		383. Boat and barge owners, etc.	...	...	...	...	...	...
		384. Ship's officers, etc	...	...	...	...	...	...
		385. Boat and barge men	...	...	...	...	...	...
		386. Pilots	...	...	...	...	...	...
		387. Lock-keepers, etc.	...	...	...	...	...	...
		388. Dock and harbour service	...	...	...	...	...	...
		389. Divers (not for pearls)	7	5	2	...	...	...
		Total Sub-orer 60.—Water	7	5	2	...	...	...
		390. Postal directors, etc.	54	23	31	81	39	42
		391. Postal messengers, etc.	220	146	74	190	119	71
		392. Messengers (unspecified)	884	576	308	781	519	262
		393. Telegraph officers, etc.	20	14	6	20	8	12
		394. Signallers, etc.	12	7	5	4	2	2
		395. Telephone Company's service	...	...	...	...	...	...
		Total Sub-order 61.—Messengers	1,190	766	424	1,076	687	389
		396. Warehouse owners, etc.	3	3	...	...	...	...
		397. Warehouse service	340	190	150	84	47	37
		398. Porters (general)	1,676	1,031	645	1,910	1,245	665
		399. Weighmen, etc.	222	112	110	410	232	178
		400. Watchmen (not village)	116	75	41	27	17	10
		Total Sub-order 62.—Storage and Weighing	2,357	1,411	946	2,431	1,541	890
		Total Order XIX.—Transport and Storage	**8,595**	**5,449**	**3,146**	**7,627**	**4,954**	**2,673**
		Toalt Class E	**22,723**	**13,643**	**9,080**	**19,747**	**12,264**	**7,483**
Class F.—Professions.	Order XX.—Learned and Artistic Professions.	401. Priests, etc.	698	378	320	498	270	228
		402. Catechists, etc.	56	38	18	47	25	22
		403. Exorcists, etc.	84	48	36	2	...	2
		404. Religious mendicants, etc.	4,491	2,804	1,687	3,189	2,075	1,114
		405. Church, temple, etc., service	250	175	75	236	138	98
		Total Sub-order 63.—Religion	5,579	3,443	2,136	3,972	2,508	1,464
		406. Administrative and inspecting officials	6	3	3	18	12	6
		407. Principals, etc., in schools	1,261	799	462	1,214	770	444
		408. Clerks, etc.	39	26	13	64	26	38
		Total Sub-order 64.—Education	1,306	828	478	1,296	808	488
		409. Authors, etc.	17	8	9	21	15	6
		410. Reporters, etc.	...	...	...	...	...	...
		411. Private secretaries, etc.	99	39	60	106	41	65
		412. Public scribes, etc.	...	...	...	...	...	...
		413. Service in libraries, etc.	6	3	3	6	5	1
		Total Sub-order 65.—Literature	122	50	72	133	61	72
		414. Barristers, etc.	246	131	115	170	91	79
		415. Solicitors, etc.	...	...	...	...	...	...
		415A. Kazis	34	19	15	51	27	24
		416. Law-agents, etc.	5	5	...	15	8	7
		417. Articled clerks, etc.	38	25	13	25	15	10
		418. Stamp vendors	89	54	35	125	64	61
		419. Petition-writers	157	95	62	114	68	46
		Total Sub-order 66.—Law	569	329	240	500	273	227

Occupations, by Districts—*contd.*

DISTRICT ELLICHPUR.			DISTRICT BULDANA.			DISTRICT WUN.			DISTRICT BASIM.			RAILWAY PASSENGERS.		
TOTAL.	Males.	Females.	TOTAL.	Males.	Females.	TOTAL.	Males.	Females.	TOTAL.	Males.	Females.	TOTAL.	Males.	Females.
10	11	12	13	14	15	16	17	18	19	20	21	22	23	24
...	...	...	..	...	...	...	...	...	...	...	...	...	...	...
1,423	927	496	1,966	1,230	736	1,051	710	341	4,162	2,581	1,581	2	2	...
...	...	...	...	...	...	...	...	...	...	...	...	...	...	...
...	...	...	...	...	...	...	...	...	...	...	...	...	...	...
3	3	...	...	...	...	...	...	...	6	6	...	...	...	...
58	34	24	604	410	194	28	19	9	1,070	591	479	...	...	...
47	33	14	49	33	16	29	29	...	33	29	4	...	...	...
1,531	997	534	2,619	1,673	946	1,108	758	350	5,271	3,207	2,064	2	2	...
...	...	...	...	...	...	...	...	...	...	...	...	...	...	...
...	...	...	...	...	...	...	...	...	...	...	...	...	...	...
...	...	...	...	...	...	...	...	...	...	...	...	...	...	...
...	...	...	...	...	...	...	...	...	...	...	...	...	...	...
...	...	...	...	...	...	5	2	3	...	...	...	...	...	...
...	...	...	...	...	...	...	...	...	...	...	...	...	...	...
...	...	...	...	...	...	...	...	...	...	...	...	...	...	...
...	...	...	...	...	...	...	...	...	...	...	...	...	...	...
...	...	...	...	...	...	...	...	...	...	...	...	...	...	...
...	...	...	...	...	...	5	2	3	...	...	..	...	...	...
23	17	6	24	14	10	15	10	5	25	11	14	...	...	...
77	51	26	72	55	17	79	54	25	80	67	13	...	...	...
420	226	194	256	173	83	235	172	63	147	89	58	2	2	...
1	1	...	4	3	1	...	...	...	8	5	3	...	...	...
...	...	...	...	...	...	...	...	...	...	...	...	...	...	...
...	...	...	...	...	...	...	...	...	...	...	...	...	...	...
521	295	226	356	245	111	329	236	93	260	172	88	2	2	...
9	...	9	...	...	...	...	...	...	...	...	...	...	...	...
6	5	1	2	2	...	...	...	...	4	4	...	...	...	...
207	144	63	248	156	92	37	27	10	9	9	...	7	6	1
47	34	13	45	21	24	22	9	13	40	27	13	...	...	...
13	11	2	6	6	...	13	9	4	3	2	1	2	2	...
282	194	88	301	185	116	72	45	27	56	42	14	9	8	1
2,335	1,486	849	3,821	2,485	1,336	1,522	1,047	475	5,592	3,423	2,169	195	135	60
7,859	4,693	3,166	12,594	7,408	5,186	7,109	4,056	3,053	12,075	7,210	4,865	251	185	66
299	193	106	363	187	176	300	171	129	346	185	161	...	...	...
15	13	2	28	25	3	1	1	...	32	25	7	...	...	...
34	16	18	6	3	3	22	10	12	7	6	1	...	...	...
2,145	1,305	840	2,260	1,355	905	1,335	823	512	1,657	965	692	...	...	...
112	59	53	149	65	84	76	41	35	112	72	40	...	...	...
2,605	1,586	1,019	2,806	1,635	1,171	1,734	1,046	688	2,154	1,253	901	...	...	...
1	1	...	5	2	3	2	1	1	6	3	3	...	...	...
572	380	192	907	564	343	470	314	156	382	244	138	1	1	...
6	5	1	4	4	...	4	4	...	5	3	2	...	...	...
579	386	193	916	570	346	476	319	157	393	250	143	1	1	...
1	1	...	...	...	...	...	...	...	...	...	...	...	...	...
...	...	...	...	...	...	...	...	...	...	...	...	...	...	...
68	35	33	58	38	20	97	74	23	42	22	20	2	2	...
...	...	...	...	...	...	...	...	...	...	...	...	...	...	...
2	1	1	...	...	...	4	2	2	...	...	...	...	...	...
71	37	34	58	38	20	101	76	25	42	22	20	2	2	...
98	48	50	76	39	37	14	7	7	72	36	36	...	...	...
...	...	...	...	...	...	...	...	...	...	...	...	...	...	...
35	22	13	36	30	6	54	30	24	31	11	20	...	...	...
...	...	...	...	...	...	2	1	1	4	3	1	...	...	...
15	5	10	26	12	14	35	14	21	9	9	...	...	...	...
36	23	13	65	47	18	29	21	8	51	32	19	...	...	...
22	15	7	79	39	40	24	14	10	21	10	11	...	...	...
206	113	93	282	167	115	158	87	71	188	101	87	...	...	...

TABLE XVII.—Part B.—

Class.	Order.	Sub-order, Group and Occupation.	District Amraoti. Total.	District Amraoti. Males.	District Amraoti. Females.	District Akola. Total.	District Akola. Males.	District Akola. Females.
1	2	3	4	5	6	7	8	9
CLASS F.—PROFESSIONS—*contd.*	ORDER XX.—LEARNED AND ARTISTIC PROFESSIONS—*cont.*	420. Administrative and inspecting staff, etc.	...	...	...	...	...	...
		421. Practitioners by diploma	38	20	18	50	28	22
		422. Practitioners without diploma	508	286	222	283	167	116
		423. Dentists	...	...	...	...	...	...
		424. Oculists	...	...	...	...	...	...
		425. Vaccinators	24	15	9	26	12	14
		426. Midwifery	333	22	311	172	9	163
		427. Hospital and asylum matrons, etc.	19	11	8	10	5	5
		428. Compounders, etc.	31	17	14	21	11	10
		TOTAL SUB-ORDER 67.—MEDICINE	953	371	582	562	232	330
		429. Administrative and inspecting staff	...	...	...	...	...	...
		430. Civil engineers, etc.	39	36	3	1	1	...
		431. Topographical surveyors, etc.	7	4	3	3	3	...
		432. Draughtsmen, etc.	95	49	46	46	22	24
		433. Clerks, etc., in offices of the above	42	31	11	74	48	26
		TOTAL SUB-ORDER 68.—ENGINEERING AND SURVEYING	183	120	63	124	74	50
		434. Astronomers, etc.	...	...	...	...	...	...
		435. Botanists, etc.	...	...	...	...	...	...
		436. Metallurgists	...	...	...	...	...	...
		437. Astrologers, etc.	24	18	6	2	2	...
		438. Almanac makers, etc.	...	...	...	...	...	...
		439. Diviners, etc.	...	...	...	...	...	...
		TOTAL SUB-ORDER 69.—OTHER SCIENCES	24	18	6	2	2	...
		440. Painters, etc.	20	11	9	2	2	...
		441. Sculptors	...	...	...	...	...	...
		442. Photographers	9	4	5	1	1	...
		TOTAL SUB-ORDER 70.—PICTORIAL ART AND SCULPTURE	29	15	14	3	3	...
		443. Music composers, etc.	1	1	...	2	2	...
		444. Bandmasters, etc.	1,867	1,396	471	955	686	269
		445. Piano-tuners	...	...	...	...	...	...
		446. Actors, etc.	321	196	125	263	157	106
		TOTAL SUB-ORDER 71.—MUSIC, ACTING, DANCING	2,189	1,593	596	1,220	845	375
		Total Order XX.—Learned and Artistic Professions.	**10,954**	**6,767**	**4,187**	**7,812**	**4,806**	**3,006**
	ORDER XXI.—SPORT AND AMUSEMENTS.	447. Race-course service	...	...	...	...	...	...
		448. Shikaris, etc.	201	122	79	42	29	13
		449. Huntsmen, etc.	...	...	...	...	...	...
		TOTAL SUB-ORDER 72.—SPORT	201	122	79	42	29	13
		450. Exhibitors of trained animals, etc.	72	47	25	82	59	23
		451. Circus owners, etc.	...	...	...	...	...	...
		452. Cock and pigeon fanciers	...	...	...	...	...	...
		453. Buffoons	...	...	...	...	...	...
		454. Story and ballad recitors	42	28	14	27	18	9
		455. Exhibitors of puppets	126	95	31	99	88	11
		456. Conjurors, etc.	...	...	...	...	...	...
		457. Tumblers, etc.	105	63	42	124	13	111
		458. Swing and merry-go-round keepers	4	2	2	9	3	6
		459. Tennis and racquet court service, etc.	...	...	...	...	...	...
		460. Billiard-room service, etc.	3	1	2	13	8	5
		TOTAL SUB-ORDER 73.—EXHIBITION AND GAMES	352	236	116	354	189	165
		Total Order XXI.—Sport and Amusements	**558**	**358**	**195**	**396**	**218**	**178**
		Total Class F	**11,507**	**7,125**	**4,382**	**8,208**	**5,024**	**3,184**
CLASS G.—INDEFINITE AND INDEPENDENT.	ORDER XXII.—COMPLEX OCCUPATIONS.	Village, etc., combined functions	...	...	...	...	...	...
		Total Order XXII.—Complex Occupations	...	...	...	...	...	...

Occupations, by Districts—*contd.*

DISTRICT ELLICHPUR.			DISTRICT BULDANA.			DISTRICT WUN.			DISTRICT BASIM.			RAILWAY PASSENGERS.		
TOTAL.	Males.	Females.	TOTAL.	Males.	Females.	TOTAL.	Males.	Females.	TOTAL.	Males.	Females.	TOTAL.	Males.	Females
10	11	12	13	14	15	16	17	18	19	20	21	22	23	24
...	...	...	...	...	...	...	...	...	...	...	...	...	...	...
13	8	5	12	7	5	13	7	6	22	13	9	...	...	...
100	63	37	297	193	104	187	111	76	83	47	36	...	...	...
...	...	...	...	...	...	...	...	...	...	...	...	...	...	...
...	...	...	...	...	...	...	...	...	...	...	...	...	...	...
19	8	11	43	19	24	27	19	8	4	2	2	...	...	...
141	2	139	49	5	44	154	75	79	20	2	18	...	...	...
22	10	12	1	1	...	1	1	...	...	...	...	...	...	...
13	10	3	4	3	1	3	3	...	10	5	5	...	...	...
308	101	207	406	228	178	385	216	169	139	69	70	...	...	...
...	...	...	...	...	...	...	...	...	...	...	...	...	...	...
3	...	3	4	2	2	2	2	...	10	10	...	...	...	...
...	...	...	3	2	1	3	3	...	5	2	3	...	...	...
24	18	6	18	12	6	22	11	11	10	5	5	...	...	...
14	11	3	4	4	...	29	17	12	...	...	...	...	...	...
41	29	12	29	20	9	56	33	23	25	17	8	...	...	...
...	...	...	...	...	...	...	...	...	...	...	...	...	...	...
...	...	...	...	...	...	...	...	...	...	...	...	...	...	...
...	...	...	...	...	...	...	...	...	...	...	...	...	...	...
3	1	2	5	4	1	...	...	...	...	...	...	...	...	...
...	...	...	...	...	...	...	...	...	...	...	...	...	...	...
...	...	...	...	...	...	...	...	...	...	...	...	...	...	...
3	1	2	5	4	1	...	...	...	...	...	...	...	...	...
3	...	3	4	4	...	2	1	1	18	5	13	...	...	...
...	...	...	...	...	...	...	...	...	...	...	...	...	...	...
...	...	...	...	...	...	...	...	...	7	7	...	...	...	...
3	...	3	4	4	...	2	1	1	25	12	13	...	...	...
...	...	...	...	...	...	3	...	3	...	...	...	...	...	...
613	425	188	797	488	309	434	329	105	1,003	619	384	...	...	...
...	...	...	...	...	...	...	...	...	...	...	...	...	...	...
115	68	47	221	139	82	88	56	32	195	76	119	...	...	...
728	493	235	1,018	627	391	525	385	140	1,198	695	503	...	...	...
4,544	**2,746**	**1,798**	**5,524**	**3,293**	**2,231**	**3,487**	**2,163**	**1,274**	**4,164**	**2,419**	**1,745**	**8**	**8**	...
...	...	...	...	...	...	...	...	...	...	...	...	...	...	...
...	...	...	86	42	44	899	502	397	138	100	38	...	...	...
...	...	...	...	...	...	...	...	...	...	...	...	...	...	...
...	...	...	86	42	44	899	502	397	138	100	38	...	...	...
4	4	...	98	57	41	170	83	87	48	27	21	...	...	...
...	...	...	...	...	...	...	...	...	...	...	...	...	...	...
...	...	...	...	...	...	...	...	...	...	...	...	...	...	...
...	...	...	...	...	...	...	...	...	...	...	...	...	...	...
2	2	...	97	53	44	45	29	16	50	34	16	...	...	...
28	26	2	51	30	21	118	95	23	69	53	16	...	...	...
...	...	...	7	7	...	...	...	...	3	3	...	...	...	...
31	20	11	184	170	14	202	165	37	193	158	35	...	...	...
...	...	...	...	...	...	18	18	...	...	...	...	...	...	...
...	...	...	...	...	...	...	...	...	...	...	...	...	...	...
...	...	...	...	...	...	...	...	...	...	...	...	...	...	...
65	52	13	437	317	120	553	390	163	363	275	88	...	...	...
65	**52**	**13**	**523**	**359**	**164**	**1,452**	**892**	**560**	**501**	**875**	**126**	...	...	...
4,[illegible]09	**2,798**	**1,811**	**6,047**	**3,652**	**2,395**	**4,889**	**3,055**	**1,834**	**4,665**	**2,794**	**1,871**	**8**	**8**	...
...	...	...	...	...	...	...	...	...	...	...	...	...	...	...
...	...	...	...	...	...	...	...	...	...	...	...	...	...	...

TABLE XVII.—Part B.—

Class.	Order.	Sub-order, Group and Occupation.	District Amraoti. Total.	Males.	Females.	District Akola. Total.	Males.	Females.
1	2	3	4	5	6	7	8	9
CLASS G.—INDEFINITE AND INDEPENDENT—*contd.*	Order XXIII.—Indefinite.	461. Well sinkers	13	8	5	6	6	–
		462. Tank diggers, etc.	12	8	4	2	2	...
		463. Road, canal, and Railway labourers	3,424	2,068	1,356	3,037	1,718	1,319
		464. Quarry men, etc.	898	516	382	491	273	218
		465. Miners, etc.	...	...	...	9	9	...
		466. Rice-pounders, etc.	1,822	211	1,611	2,143	510	1,633
		467. General labour	14,720	6,661	8,059	20,534	8,720	11,814
		Total Sub-Order 74.—Unskilled Labour	20,889	9,472	11,417	26,222	11,238	14,984
		468. Undefined and disreputable means of livelihood. *a.* Disreputable	548	59	489	586	88	498
		b. Undefined	386	193	193	493	247	246
		c. Dependent	373	170	203	338	93	245
		Total Sub-Order 75.—Undefined, etc.	1,307	422	885	1,417	428	989
		Total Order XXIII.—Indefinite	**22,196**	**9,894**	**12,302**	**27,639**	**11,666**	**15,973**
	Order XXIV.—Independent of Work.	469. House-rent, etc.	635	302	333	283	140	143
		470. Allowances from patrons or relatives	3	1	2	60	27	33
		471. Educational or other endowments, etc.	44	42	2	124	120	4
		472. Mendicancy, etc.	10,123	5,996	4,127	9,226	5,430	3,796
		Total Sub-order 76.—Property and Alms	10,805	6,341	4,464	9,693	5,717	3,976
		473. Pension, civil services	83	42	41	5	2	3
		474. Pension, military services	13	7	6	32	11	21
		474A. Pensioners undefined	259	146	113	480	251	229
		475. Inmates of asylums, etc.	...	...	...	...	...	...
		476. Prisoners under trial	16	15	1	24	24	...
		477. Prisoners for debt	4	4	...	1	1	...
		478. Prisoners convicted or in reformatories, etc.	254	245	9	371	365	6
		Total Sub-order 77.—Supported at the public charge	629	459	170	913	654	259
		Total Order XXIV.—Independent of work	**11,434**	**6,800**	**4,634**	**10,606**	**6,371**	**4,285**
		Total Class G	**33,630**	**16,694**	**16,936**	**38,245**	**18,087**	**20,208**

Occupations, by Districts—*concld.*

District Ellichpur.			District Buldana.			District Wun.			District Basim.			Railway Passengers.		
Total.	Males.	Females.	Total.	Males.	Females.	Total.	Males.	Females.	Total.	Males.	Females.	Total.	Males.	Females.
10	11	12	13	14	15	16	17	18	19	20	21	22	23	24
...	...	...	26	21	5	25	14	11	28	22	6	...	...	...
1	...	1	14	...	14	...	...	...	...	...	...	...	...	...
3,265	1,928	1,337	2,698	1,428	1,270	1,981	1,155	826	2,630	1,454	1,176	...	...	...
98	62	36	994	533	461	313	201	112	1,094	597	497	...	...	...
...	...	...	...	...	...	60	22	38	...	...	...	...	...	...
1,529	168	1,361	1,235	135	1,100	592	72	520	809	82	727	...	...	...
6,626	2,755	3,871	26,757	11,657	15,100	12,260	4,656	7,604	22,460	10,059	12,401	26	19	7
11,519	4,913	6,606	31,724	13,774	17,950	15,231	6,120	9,111	27,021	12,214	14,807	26	19	7
402	38	364	382	85	297	185	31	154	244	44	200	...	...	...
162	62	100	713	337	376	380	210	170	437	214	223	2	2	...
120	65	55	262	108	154	26	8	18	105	56	49	18	3	15
684	165	519	1,357	530	827	591	249	342	786	314	472	20	5	15
12,203	**5,078**	**7,125**	**33,081**	**14,304**	**18,777**	**15,822**	**6,369**	**9,453**	**27,807**	**12,528**	**15,279**	**46**	**24**	**22**
160	79	81	609	288	321	211	121	90	171	78	93	...	...	...
2	1	1	...	...	...	...	...	...	...	...	...	...	...	...
12	12	...	18	12	6	11	5	6	16	13	3	...	...	...
4,387	2,693	1,694	8,185	4,698	3,487	7,826	4,534	3,292	7,171	4,126	3,045	9	8	1
4,561	2,785	1,776	8,812	4,998	3,814	8,048	4,660	3,388	7,358	4,217	3,141	9	8	1
7	6	1	7	5	2	23	13	10	...	...	...	...	...	...
119	73	46	34	19	15	14	10	4	14	6	8	...	...	...
452	223	229	162	104	58	122	50	72	117	68	49	...	...	...
...	...	...	...	...	...	...	...	...	...	...	...	...	...	...
1	1	...	7	7	...	1	1	...	25	25	...	...	...	...
...	...	...	...	...	...	...	...	...	...	...	...	...	...	...
26	24	2	49	48	1	34	34	...	81	74	7	...	...	...
605	327	278	259	183	76	194	108	86	237	173	64	...	...	...
5,166	**3,112**	**2,054**	**9,071**	**5,181**	**3,890**	**8,242**	**4,768**	**3,474**	**7,595**	**4,390**	**3,205**	**9**	**8**	**1**
17,369	**8,190**	**9,179**	**42,152**	**19,485**	**22,667**	**24,064**	**11,137**	**12,927**	**35,402**	**16,918**	**18,484**	**55**	**32**	**23**

TABLE XVII.

Part C.—Occupations combined with Agriculture (Both Sexes).

TABLE XVII—Part C.—Occupations combined with Agriculture (Both Sexes).

Sub-order.	OCCUPATION, ETC.	Total persons returned under each, in Table XVII—A, including those combining it with Agriculture.	PERSONS RETURNED AS COMBINING THE OCCUPATION WITH AGRICULTURE. Total persons.	CONNECTION WITH THE LAND. (a) Owners or Occupants.	(b) Tenants.	(c) Farm servants or field labourers.
1	2	3	4	5	6	7
1	TOTAL SUB-ORDER	20,594	152	140	12	...
	2. Officers	265	3	3	...	...
	3. Office Clerks, etc.	2,840	9	5	4	...
	4. Messengers, etc.	12,313	136	131	5	...
	4a. Police rank and file	5,176	4	1	3	...
2	TOTAL SUB-ORDER	1,559	14	14	...	...
	7. Menials	1,452	14	14	...	...
	Others	107	...	...	...	...
3	TOTAL SUB-ORDER	64,311	2,404	1,898	110	396
	9. Accountants	6,919	1,166	1,166	...	...
	11. Watchmen, etc.	51,394	1,238	732	110	396
	Others	5,998	...	...	...	...
	Total Order I	**86,464**	**2,570**	**2,052**	**122**	**396**
4	TOTAL SUB-ORDER	1,959	1	...	1	...
	13. Non-Commissioned Officers, etc.	1,618	1	...	1	...
	Others	341	...	...	...	...
	Total Order II	**1,959**	**1**	**...**	**1**	**...**
8	TOTAL SUB-ORDER	34,957	330	193	62	75
	25. Cattle breeders, etc.	1,331	7	6	...	1
	26. Herdsmen	25,508	162	72	26	64
	31. Sheep breeders, etc.	1,328	81	70	11	...
	31a. Shepherds	6,344	80	45	25	10
	Others	446	...	...	...	...
9	TOTAL SUB-ORDER	121	1	1	...	...
	35. Horse breeders, etc.	64	1	1	...	...
	Others	57	...	...	...	...
	Total Order IV	**35,078**	**331**	**194**	**62**	**75**
12	TOTAL SUB-ORDER	2,017	14	7	6	1
	52. Gardeners, etc.	787	7	...	6	1
	55. Forest Rangers, etc.	401	7	7	...	...
	Others	829	...	...	...	...
	Total from Order V	**2,017**	**14**	**7**	**6**	**1**
14	TOTAL SUB-ORDER	70,118	1,916	1,241	497	178
	59. Barbers	21,283	1,057	720	326	11
	63. Washermen	14,051	490	235	171	84
	66. In-door servants	30,817	333	259	...	74
	Others	3,967	36	27	...	9

TABLE XVII—Part C.—Occupations combined with Agriculture (Both Sexes)—*contd.*

Sub-order.	Occupation, etc.	Total persons returned under each, in Table XVII—A, including those combining it with Agriculture.	Persons returned as combining the occupation with agriculture.			
			Total persons.	Connection with the land. (a) Owners or Occupants.	(b) Tenants.	(c) Farm servants or field labourers.
1	2	3	4	5	6	7
16	Total Sub-order	2,088	5	4	...	1
	74. Sweepers, etc.	2,065	5	4	...	1
	Others	23	...	...	...	...
	Total from Order VI	**72,206**	**1,921**	**1,245**	**497**	**179**
17	Total Sub-order	25,295	231	106	38	87
	76. Cow-keepers, etc.	4,478	52	35	14	3
	77. Ghee preparers	670	7	...	4	3
	79. Butchers	6,746	89	68	20	1
	81. Fishermen, etc.	13,363	83	3	...	80
	Others	38	...	...	...	...
18	Total Sub-order	19,692	298	223	64	11
	83. Grain dealers	8,920	186	136	47	3
	85. Pulse sellers, etc.	1,513	24	19	5	...
	89. Vegetable sellers	2,256	64	58	4	2
	Others	7,003	24	10	8	6
19	Total Sub-order	39,015	1,127	876	200	51
	97. Country spirits distillers, etc.	6,160	199	191	7	1
	109. Grocers, etc.	19,852	623	496	127	...
	111. Betel-leaf sellers	6,285	211	130	36	45
	112. Tobacco sellers, etc.	2,626	63	34	25	4
	Others	4,092	31	25	5	1
	Total Order VII	**84,002**	**1,656**	**1,205**	**302**	**149**
20	Total Sub-order	16,620	815	514	281	20
	116. Oil-pressers, etc.	16,311	812	513	281	18
	Others	309	3	1	...	2
21	Total Sub-order	28,071	964	217	3	744
	125. Firewood gatherers, etc.	19,903	698	131	3	564
	129. Charcoal burners, etc.	505	97	79	...	18
	131. Hay, etc., dealers, etc.	4,144	154	...	...	154
	Others	3,519	15	7	...	8
	Total Order VIII	**44,691**	**1,779**	**731**	**284**	**764**
22	Total Sub-order	6,701	45	38	5	2
	132. Brick burners, etc.	5,709	21	17	2	2
	133. Lime burners, etc.	898	24	21	3	...
	Others	94	...	...	...	...
23	Total Sub-order	11,400	155	103	6	46
	138. Masons	5,839	31	25	...	6
	141. Mud wall builders	4,702	124	78	6	40
	Others	859	...	...	...	...
	Total Order IX	**18,101**	**200**	**141**	**11**	**48**

TABLE XVII—Part C.—Occupations combined with Agriculture (Both Sexes)—*contd.*

Sub-order.	Occupation, etc.	Total persons returned under each, in Table XVII—A, including those combining it with Agriculture.	Persons returned as combining the occupation with agriculture. — Total persons.	Connection with the land. — (a) Owners or Occupants.	(b) Tenants.	(c) Farm servants or field labourers.
1	2	3	4	5	6	7
25	Total Sub-order	154	1	1	...	...
	146. Cart makers, etc.	154	1	1	...	...
	Total from Order X	154	1	1	...	...
28	Total, Sub-order	314	1	1	...	...
	159. Book-sellers	154	1	1	...	...
	Others	160	...	...	...	...
31	Total Sub-order	386	2	2	...	...
	177. Toy makers, etc.	379	2	2	...	...
	Others	7	...	...	...	...
33	Total Sub-order	7,383	73	24	36	13
	189*a*. Bangle makers	4,771	44	7	24	13
	Others	2,612	29	17	12	...
35	Total Sub-order	484	6	2	4	...
	201. Harness makers, etc.	430	6	2	4	...
	Others	54	...	...	...	...
36	Total Sub-order	875	34	17	17	...
	204*a*. Agricultural implements makers	183	6	6	...	...
	205. Knife grinders, etc.	470	28	11	17	...
	Others	222	...	...	...	...
37	Total Sub-order	250	8	8	...	...
	211. Gunpowder makers	136	1	1	...	...
	212. Fire-work makers	42	7	7	...	...
	Others	72	...	...	...	...
	Total from Order XI	9,692	124	54	57	13
38	Total Sub-order	5,287	91	29	59	3
	220. Blanket weavers	4,827	89	29	59	1
	222. Woollen yarn spinners	272	2	...	...	2
	Others	188	...	...	...	...
39	Total Sub-order	1,891	10	8	2	...
	227. Silk carders, etc.	1,387	10	8	2	...
	Others	504	...	...	...	...

TABLE XVII—Part C.—Occupations combined with Agriculture (both Sexes)—*contd.*

Sub-order.	Occupation, etc.	Total persons returned under each, in Table XVII—A, including those combining it with Agriculture.	Persons returned as combining the occupation with agriculture.			
			Total persons.	Connection with the land.		
				(a) Owners or Occupants.	(b) Tenants.	(c) Farm servants or field labourers.
1	2	3	4	5	6	7
40	Total Sub-order	71,905	1,482	771	413	298
	231. Cotton cleaners, etc.	14,103	310	153	40	117
	231a. Raw cotton dealers	7,731	719	461	256	2
	233. Cotton spinners, etc.	8,342	158	13	45	100
	234. Cotton weavers, etc.	27,212	135	52	12	71
	Others	14,517	160	92	60	8
41	Total Sub-order	2,485	51	...	37	14
	241. Hemp rope makers	851	24	...	24	...
	243. Sacking, etc., makers	1,587	27	...	13	14
	Others	47	...	...	...	...
42	Total Sub-order	30,574	797	338	132	327
	247. Tailors	12,189	405	126	46	233
	257. Piece-goods dealers	15,973	338	186	86	66
	Others	2,412	54	26	...	28
	Total Order XII	**112,142**	**2,431**	**1,146**	**643**	**642**
43	Total Sub-order	21,260	781	622	159	...
	260. Goldsmiths, etc.	20,180	774	615	159	...
	Others	1,080	7	7	...	...
44	Total Sub-order	3,099	88	86	2	...
	283. Brass and copper dealers	1,622	72	70	2	...
	Others	1,477	16	16	...	...
46	Total Sub-order	12,824	186	154	23	9
	290. Blacksmiths	12,510	184	152	23	9
	293. Lock makers, etc.	41	2	2	...	...
	Others	273	...	...	...	...
	Total from Order XIII	**37,183**	**1,055**	**862**	**184**	**9**
48	Total Sub-order	18,854	311	179	105	27
	298. Potters, etc.	15,921	202	160	39	3
	299. Grindstone makers, etc.	2,890	109	19	66	24
	Others	43	...	...	...	...
	Total from Order XIV	**18,854**	**311**	**179**	**105**	**27**
49	Total Sub-order	34,365	1,185	890	169	126
	302. Timber agents, etc.	2,819	34	15	19	...
	303. Wood cutters	2,531	313	279	...	34
	304. Carpenters	28,942	838	596	150	92
	Others	73	...	...	...	...
50	Total Sub-order	13,784	126	18	8	100
	307. Basket weavers	6,573	45	3	4	38
	314. Broom makers	4,795	61	6	...	55
	Others	2,416	20	9	4	7
	Total Order XV	**48,149**	**1,311**	**908**	**177**	**226**

TABLE XVII—Part C.—Occupations combined with Agriculture (Both Sexes)—*contd.*

Sub-order.	Occupation, etc.	Total persons returned under each, in Table XVII—A, including those combining it with Agriculture.	Persons returned as combining the occupation with agriculture. Total persons.	Connection with the land. (a) Owners or Occupants.	(b) Tenants.	(c) Farm servants or field labourers.
1	2	3	4	5	6	7
51	TOTAL SUB-ORDER	668	11	4	6	1
	317. Camphor collectors, etc.	31	4	...	4	...
	323. Wax collectors, etc.	629	7	4	2	1
	Others	8	...	...	...	...
52	TOTAL SUB-ORDER	3,077	5	2	...	3
	336. Kanku preparers, etc.	1,356	4	1	...	3
	337. Perfume preparers	672	1	1	...	...
	Others	1,049	...	...	...	...
	Total Order XVI	**3,745**	**16**	**6**	**6**	**4**
53	TOTAL SUB-ORDER	23,883	315	104	90	121
	339. Shoe-makers, etc.	20,839	289	88	90	111
	Others	3,044	26	16	...	10
	Total Order XVII	**23,883**	**315**	**104**	**90**	**121**
54	TOTAL SUB-ORDER	20,351	4,724	4,492	228	4
	347. Money-lenders	19,282	4,684	4,454	226	4
	350. Money-changers	1,041	40	38	2	...
	Others	28	...	...	...	...
55	TOTAL SUB-ORDER	5,164	190	159	30	1
	352. General merchants	1618	87	86	...	1
	353. Merchants' managers, etc.	3,546	103	73	30	...
56	TOTAL SUB-ORDER	21,211	373	249	121	3
	355. Shop-keepers' servants	12,910	173	113	57	3
	356. Shop-keepers (unspecified)	5,764	157	111	46	...
	Others	2,537	43	25	18	...
57	TOTAL SUB-ORDER	5,945	128	105	19	4
	358. Brokers, etc.	2,919	68	52	16	...
	361. Farmers of liquor, etc.	1,134	38	38	...	...
	Others	1,892	22	15	3	4
	Total Order XVIII	**52,671**	**5,415**	**5,005**	**398**	**12**
58	TOTAL SUB-ORDER	3,410	16	2	14	...
	373. Pointsmen, etc.	634	2	2	...	...
	373a. Railway servants (undefined)	2,050	14	...	14	...
	Others	726	...	...	...	...
59	TOTAL SUB-ORDER	17,023	297	165	47	85
	375. Cart owners, etc.	14,738	220	165	33	22
	379. Pack bullock owners, etc.	1,917	77	...	14	63
	Others	368	...	...	...	...

TABLE XVII—Part C.—Occupations combined with Agriculture (Both Sexes)—*contd.*

Sub-order.	Occupation, etc.	Total persons returned under each, in Table XVII—A, including those combining it with Agriculture.	Persons returned as combining the occupation with agriculture.			
			Total persons.	Connection with the land.		
				(*a*) Owners or Occupants.	(*b*) Tenants.	(*c*) Farm servants or field labourers.
1	2	3	4	5	6	7
61	Total Sub-order	3,734	30	27	3	...
	391. Postal messengers, etc.	718	1	1	...	...
	392. Messengers (unspecified)	2,725	29	26	3	...
	Others	291	...	...	...	...
62	Total Sub-order	5,508	49	21	17	11
	398. Porters (general)	4,094	38	12	17	9
	399. Weighmen, etc.	786	11	9	...	2
	Others	628	...	...	...	...
	Total from Order XIX	**29,675**	**392**	**215**	**81**	**96**
63	Total Sub-order	18,850	986	837	148	1
	401. Priests, etc.	2,504	232	209	23	...
	404. Religious mendicants, etc.	15,077	690	568	122	...
	Others	1,269	64	60	3	1
64	Total Sub-order	4,967	73	56	17	...
	407. Principals, teachers, etc.	4,807	62	54	8	...
	408. Clerks, etc.	122	11	2	9	...
	Others	38	...	...	...	...
65	Total Sub-order	529	1	1	...	...
	411. Private Secretaries, etc.	472	1	1	...	...
	Others	57	...	...	...	...
66	Total Sub-order	1,903	66	62	4	...
	414. Barristers, pleaders, etc.	676	26	26	...	...
	415*a*. Kazis	241	12	12	...	...
	418. Stamp vendors	395	13	10	3	..
	Others	591	15	14	1	...
67	Total Sub-order	2,753	38	15	4	19
	422. Practitioners without diploma	1,458	16	15	...	1
	426. Midwifery	869	22	...	4	18
	Others	426	...	...	...	...
68	Total Sub-order	458	1	1	...	...
	432. Draughtsmen, etc.	215	1	1	...	...
	Others	243	...	...	...	...
71	Total Sub-order	6,878	213	30	15	168
	444. Band Masters, etc. (not Military)	5,669	204	27	15	162
	446. Actors, dancers, etc.	1,203	9	3	...	6
	Others	6	...	...	...	...
	Total from Order XX	**36,838**	**1,878**	**1,002**	**188**	**188**
72	Total Sub-order	1,366	10	4	...	6
	448. Shikaris, etc.	1,366	10	4	...	6

TABLE XVII—Part C.—Occupations combined with Agriculture (Both Sexes)—*concld.*

Sub-order.	Occupation, etc.	Total persons returned under each, in Table XVII—A, including those combining it with Agriculture.	Persons returned as combining the occupation with agriculture.	Connection with the land.		
			Total persons.	(a) Owners or Occupants.	(b) Tenants.	(c) Farm servants or field labourers.
1	2	3	4	5	6	7
73	TOTAL SUB-ORDER	2,124	3	1	2	...
	455. Exhibitors of puppets, etc.	491	3	1	2	...
	Others	1,633	...	...	...	...
	Total Order XXI	**3,490**	**13**	**5**	**2**	**6**
74	TOTAL SUB-ORDER	132,632	330	98	27	205
	466. Rice pounders, etc.	8,130	117	1	...	116
	467. General labourer	103,383	114	62	2	50
	Others	21,119	99	35	25	39
75	TOTAL SUB-ORDER	6,162	85	73	3	9
	468*a*. Disreputable	2,347	38	28	1	9
	468*c*. Dependent	1,242	47	45	2	...
	Others	2,573	...	...	...	...
	Total Order XXIII	**138,794**	**415**	**171**	**30**	**214**
76	TOTAL SUB-ORDER	49,286	1,301	1,075	150	76
	469. House-rent, etc.	2,069	425	337	54	34
	472. Mendicancy	46,927	876	738	96	42
	Others	290	...	...	...	...
77	TOTAL SUB-ORDER	2,837	171	129	39	3
	474. Pension (Military)	226	17	...	17	...
	474*a*. Pension (unspecified)	1,592	145	120	22	3
	478. Prisoners (convicted)	815	9	9	...	...
	Others	204	...	...	...	...
	Total Order XXIV	**52,123**	**1,472**	**1,204**	**189**	**79**
	Grand Total	**911,411**	**23,121**	**16,487**	**3,435**	**3,249**

TABLE A.

Christians.

TABLE A.—Christians by

DISTRICT.	TOTAL CHRISTIANS.			DISTRIBUTION															
				CHURCH OF ENGLAND.								ROMAN CATHOLIC.							
				TOTAL.		Foreign.		Eurasian.		Native.		TOTAL.		Foreign.		Eurasian.		Native.	
	TOTAL.	Males.	Females.	Males.	Females.	Males.	Females.	Males.	Females.	Males.	Females.	Males.	Females.	Males.	Females.	Males.	Females.	Males.	Females.
1	2	3	4	5	6	7	8	9	10	11	12	13	14	15	16	17	18	19	20
Amraoti . . .	*629*	317	312	131	127	52	40	61	73	18	14	143	144	17	23	19	21	107	100
Akola . . .	*305*	183	122	59	46	23	16	18	15	18	15	83	43	5	4	7	4	71	35
Ellichpur . . .	*123*	68	55	28	22	14	10	13	10	1	2	35	26	2	...	5	3	28	23
Buldana . . .	*103*	60	43	36	20	10	5	6	4	20	11	13	9	1	...	1	3	11	6
Wun . . .	*89*	49	40	28	25	12	9	9	12	7	4	14	12	2	...	...	...	12	12
Basim . . .	*88*	48	40	16	4	8	4	2	...	6	...	10	7	1	1	3	3	6	3
Railway Passengers, etc. . . .	*22*	13	9	11	9	8	7	3	2	...	...	2	...	...	...	...	...	2	...
Total . . .	*1,359*	738	621	309	253	127	91	112	116	70	46	300	241	28	23	35	34	237	179

DISTRICT.	DISTRIBUTION																							
	METHODIST.								CONGREGATIONALIST.								WESLEYAN.							
	TOTAL.		Foreign.		Eurasian.		Native.		TOTAL.		Foreign.		Eurasian.		Native.		TOTAL.		Foreign.		Eurasian.		Native.	
	Males.	Females.	Males.	Females.	Males.	Females.	Males.	Females.	Males.	Females.	Males.	Females.	Males.	Females.	Males.	Female.	Males.	Females.	Males.	Females.	Males.	Females.	Males.	Females.
	45	46	47	48	49	50	51	52	53	54	55	56	57	58	59	60	61	62	63	64	65	66	67	68
Amraoti . .	2	...	1	...	1	...	...	...	...	...	...	...	...	...	...	...	2	3	2	3	...	...	...	...
Akola . . .	1	1	1	...	...	1	...	...	10	9	3	...	...	...	7	9	...	...	...	...	...	...	...	...
Ellichpur . .	1	3	1	3	...	...	...	...	...	2	...	2	...	...	...	...	...	...	...	...	...	...	...	...
Buldana . .	1	1	...	1	1	...	...	...	...	...	...	...	...	...	...	...	...	...	...	...	...	...	...	...
Wun . . .	...	...	...	...	...	...	...	...	...	...	...	...	...	...	...	...	...	...	...	...	...	...	...	...
Basim . . .	1	...	...	...	1	...	...	...	3	...	...	...	...	...	3	...	...	...	...	...	...	...	...	...
Railway Passengers, etc.	...	...	...	...	...	...	...	...	...	...	...	...	...	...	...	...	...	...	...	...	...	...	...	...
Total .	6	5	3	4	3	1	...	...	13	11	3	2	...	...	10	9	2	3	2	3	...	...	...	...

Sect and Race.—Part I.—Sects.

BY SECT.

Church of Scotland.								Presbyterian.								Baptist.								DISTRICT.
Total.		Foreign.		Eurasian.		Native.		Total.		Foreign.		Eurasian.		Native.		Total.		Foreign.		Eurasian.		Native.		
Males.	Females.	Males.	Females.	Males.	Females.	Males.	Females.	Males.	Females.	Males.	Females.	Males.	Females.	Males.	Females.	Males.	Females.	Males.	Females.	Males.	Females.	Males.	Females.	
21	22	23	24	25	26	27	28	29	30	31	32	33	34	35	36	37	38	39	40	41	42	43	44	
2	...	2	...	...	...	...	...	4	5	3	3	...	...	1	2	3	2	...	...	...	...	3	2	Amraoti.
...	...	...	...	...	...	...	...	6	3	4	3	...	...	2	...	...	1	...	1	...	...	...	...	Akola.
...	...	...	...	...	...	...	...	...	...	...	...	...	...	...	...	...	...	...	...	...	...	...	...	Ellichpur.
...	1	...	...	...	1	...	...	...	...	...	...	...	...	...	...	...	...	...	...	...	...	...	...	Buldana.
...	...	...	...	...	...	...	...	3	3	...	...	...	...	3	3	...	...	...	...	...	...	...	...	Wun.
...	...	...	...	...	...	...	...	...	...	...	...	...	...	...	...	...	...	...	...	...	...	...	...	Basim.
...	...	...	...	...	...	...	...	...	...	...	...	...	...	...	...	...	...	...	...	...	...	...	...	Railway Passengers, etc.
2	1	2	...	...	1	...	...	18	11	7	6	...	...	6	5	3	3	...	1	...	...	3	2	Total.

BY SECT.

Free Church (Church Mission).								Unsectarian and Unspecified.								Greek Church.								DISTRICT.
Total.		Foreign.		Eurasian.		Native.		Total.		Foreign.		Eurasian.		Native.		Total.		Foreign.		Eurasian.		Native.		
Males.	Females.	Males.	Females.	Males.	Females.	Males.	Females.	Males.	Females.	Males.	Females.	Males.	Females.	Males.	Females.	Males.	Females.	Males.	Females.	Males.	Females.	Males.	Females.	
69	70	71	72	73	74	75	76	77	78	79	80	81	82	83	84	85	86	87	88	89	90	91	92	
18	24	...	...	...	...	18	24	11	7	3	6	1	1	7	...	1	...	1	...	...	...	...	...	Amraoti.
11	8	...	...	...	...	11	8	11	11	3	...	3	...	5	11	2	...	2	...	...	...	...	...	Akola.
...	...	...	...	...	...	...	...	4	2	2	1	...	...	2	1	...	...	...	...	...	...	...	...	Ellichpur.
4	8	...	...	...	...	4	8	5	4	...	...	...	...	5	4	1	...	1	...	...	...	...	...	Buldana.
...	...	...	...	...	...	...	...	4	...	1	...	...	...	3	...	...	...	...	...	...	...	...	...	Wun.
1	...	...	...	...	...	1	...	17	29	2	1	4	7	11	21	...	...	...	...	...	...	...	...	Basim.
...	...	...	...	...	...	...	...	...	...	...	...	...	...	...	...	...	...	...	...	...	...	...	...	Railway Passengers, etc.
34	40	...	...	...	...	34	40	52	53	11	8	8	8	33	37	4	...	4	...	...	...	...	...	Total.

TABLE A.—PART II.—Races.

DISTRICT.	TOTAL CHRISTIANS.			DISTRIBUTION BY RACE. — FOREIGN.																							
				Total.			Church of England.		Roman Catholic.		Church of Scotland.		Presbyterian.		Baptist.		Methodist.		Congregationalist.		Wesleyan.		Unsectarian and Unspecified.		Greek Church.	
	Total.	Males.	Females.	Total.	Males.	Females.	Males.	Females.	Males.	Females.	Males.	Females.	Males.	Females.	Males.	Females.	Males.	Females.	Males.	Females.	Males.	Females.	Males.	Females.	Males.	Females.
1	2	3	4	5	6	7	8	9	10	11	12	13	14	15	16	17	18	19	20	21	22	23	24	25	26	27
Amraoti	629	317	312	156	81	75	52	40	17	23	2	...	3	3	...	...	1	...	...	...	2	3	3	6	1	...
Akola	305	183	122	65	41	24	23	16	5	4	...	...	4	3	...	1	1	...	3	...	...	...	3	...	2	...
Ellichpur	123	68	55	35	19	16	14	10	2	...	...	...	...	...	...	...	1	3	...	2	...	...	2	1	...	...
Buldana	103	60	43	18	12	6	10	5	1	...	...	...	...	...	...	...	...	1	...	...	...	...	...	...	1	...
Wun	89	49	40	24	15	9	12	9	2	...	...	...	...	...	...	...	...	...	...	...	...	...	1	...	...	...
Basim	88	48	40	17	11	6	8	4	1	1	...	...	...	...	...	...	...	...	...	...	...	...	2	1	...	...
Railway Passengers, etc.	22	13	9	15	8	7	8	7	...	...	...	...	...	...	...	...	...	...	...	...	...	...	...	...	...	...
Total	1,359	738	621	330	187	143	127	91	28	28	2	...	7	6	...	1	3	4	3	2	2	3	11	8	4	...

DISTRICT.	EURASIAN.													NATIVE.																
	Total.			Church of England.		Roman Catholic.		Church of Scotland.		Methodist.		Unsectarian and Unspecified.		Total.			Church of England.		Roman Catholic.		Presbyterian.		Baptist.		Congregationalist.		Free Church (Church mission.)		Unsectarian and Unspecified.	
	Total.	Males.	Females.	Males.	Females.	Males.	Females.	Males.	Females.	Males.	Females.	Males.	Females.	Total.	Males.	Females.	Males.	Females.	Males.	Females.	Males.	Females.	Males.	Females.	Males.	Females.	Males.	Females.	Males.	Females.
28	29	30	31	32	33	34	35	36	37	38	39	40	41	42	43	44	45	46	47	48	49	50	51	52	53	54	55	56	57	58
Amraoti	177	82	95	61	73	19	21	...	...	1	...	1	1	296	154	142	18	14	107	100	1	2	3	2	...	...	18	24	7	...
Akola	48	28	20	18	15	7	4	...	...	...	1	3	...	192	114	78	18	15	71	35	2	...	...	...	7	9	11	8	5	11
Ellichpur	31	18	13	13	10	5	3	...	...	...	...	...	...	57	31	26	1	2	28	23	...	...	...	...	...	...	...	...	2	1
Buldana	16	8	8	6	4	1	3	...	1	1	...	...	...	69	40	29	20	11	11	6	...	...	...	...	...	...	4	8	5	4
Wun	21	9	12	9	12	...	...	...	...	...	...	...	...	44	25	19	7	4	12	12	3	3	...	...	...	...	...	...	3	...
Basim	20	10	10	2	...	3	3	...	...	1	...	4	7	51	27	24	6	...	6	3	...	...	...	...	3	...	1	...	11	21
Railway Passengers, etc.	5	3	2	3	2	...	...	...	...	...	...	...	...	2	2	...	...	...	2	...	...	...	...	...	...	...	...	...	...	...
Total	318	158	160	112	116	35	34	...	1	3	1	8	8	711	393	318	70	46	237	179	6	5	3	2	10	9	34	40	33	37

TABLE B.

Europeans, Eurasians, and Armenians, by Race and Age.

TABLE B.—Europeans, Eurasians, and Armenians, by Race and Age.

DISTRICT.	TOTAL.			EUROPEANS.										EURASIANS.										ARMENIANS.									
				Males.					Females.					Males.					Females.					Males.					Females.				
	Total.	Males.	Females.	Total.	0—14	15—34	35—49	50 and over.	Total	0—14	15—34	35—49	50 and over.	Total	0—14	15—34	35—49	50 and over.	Total	0—14	15—34	35—49	50 and over.	Total	0—14	15—34	35—49	50 and over.	Total	0—14	15—34	35—49	50 and over.
1	2	3	4	5	6	7	8	9	10	11	12	13	14	15	16	17	18	19	20	21	22	23	24	25	26	27	28	29	30	31	32	33	34
Amraoti	333	163	170	81	21	24	31	5	75	24	36	13	2	82	22	28	24	8	95	40	35	13	7	...	...	...	...	...	...	...	...	...	...
Akola	114	70	44	41	3	23	8	7	24	4	11	6	3	28	7	8	12	1	20	9	9	2	...	1	...	1	...	...	...	...	...	...	...
Do. Military	1	1	...	1	...	1	...	...	...	...	...	...	...	...	...	...	...	...	...	...	...	...	...	...	...	...	...	...	...	...	...	...	...
Ellichpur	32	17	15	11	2	1	5	3	9	3	5	1	...	6	2	1	3	...	6	4	1	...	1	...	...	...	...	...	...	...	...	...	...
Do. Military	35	21	14	9	...	8	1	...	7	1	4	1	1	12	8	1	3	...	7	3	3	1	...	...	...	...	...	...	...	...	...	...	...
Buldana	34	20	14	12	2	6	4	...	6	3	2	1	...	8	2	3	2	1	8	5	2	1	...	...	...	...	...	...	...	...	...	...	...
Wun	45	24	21	15	...	7	7	1	9	2	5	1	1	9	5	...	2	2	12	3	7	2	...	...	...	...	...	...	...	...	...	...	...
Basim	38	22	16	12	2	3	6	1	6	...	4	2	...	10	5	4	1	...	10	8	2	...	...	...	...	...	...	...	...	...	...	...	...
Railway Passengers	20	11	9	8	3	3	1	1	7	5	2	...	...	3	...	3	...	...	2	1	...	1	...	...	...	...	...	...	...	...	...	...	...
Total	652	349	303	190	33	76	63	18	143	42	69	25	7	158	51	48	47	12	160	73	59	20	8	1	...	1	...	...	...	...	...	...	...

TABLE D.

Castes by Education.

NOTE.—Table C is combined with Table D.

TABLE D.—Castes by Education.

Class.	Group.	Caste.	Religion.	Total Strength — Males — Total Males.	Males — Pupils.	Males — Literate — Total Literate.	Males — Literate — Knowing English.	Males — Illiterate.	Females — Total Females.	Females — Pupils.	Females — Literate — Total Literate.	Females — Literate — Knowing English.	Females — Illiterate.	Territorial Distribution, District Amraoti — Males — Total.	Males — Pupils.	Males — Literate — Total Literate.	Males — Literate — Knowing English.	Males — Illiterate.	Females — Total.	Females — Pupils.	Females — Literate — Total Literate.	Females — Literate — Knowing English.	Females — Illiterate.
1	2	3	4	5	6	7	8	9	10	11	12	13	14	15	16	17	18	19	20	21	22	23	24
A.—AGRICULTURAL.	1.—MILITARY AND DOMINANT.	MULTÁNI	Musalman	4	...	...	...	4	5	...	...	...	5	...	...	...	...	...	...	...	...	...	...
		SIKH	Hindu	105	5	20	...	80	97	...	1	...	96	24	1	2	...	21	26	...	...	...	26
		Do.	Sikh	60	1	8	...	51	54	...	1	...	53	12	1	2	...	9	15	...	...	...	15
			Total Group 1	*169*	*6*	*28*	...	*135*	*156*	...	*2*	...	*164*	*86*	*2*	*4*	...	*80*	*41*	...	...	...	*41*
	2.—OTHER AGRICULTURAL (a) CULTIVATORS	AYÁWÁR	Hindu	65	5	20	...	40	67	...	...	...	67	2	1	...	...	1	1	...	...	...	1
		BÁGWÁN	Musalman	58	1	1	...	56	66	...	...	...	66	...	...	...	...	...	...	...	...	...	...
		BARAI	Hindu	66	3	9	...	54	76	...	...	...	76	...	...	...	...	...	...	...	...	...	...
		BÁRI	Do.	13,190	171	204	*1*	12,815	12,730	2	...	...	12,728	3,947	36	55	...	3,856	3,892	...	...	...	3,892
		BHANÁRI	Do.	9	...	...	...	9	12	...	...	...	12	...	...	...	...	...	...	...	...	...	...
		BHOYER	Do.	26	...	1	...	25	4	...	...	...	4	21	...	1	...	20	3	...	...	...	3
		BHUTE	Do.	1	...	...	...	1	...	...	...	...	...	...	...	...	...	...	...	...	...	...	...
		BHUVÉSH	Do.	2	...	2	...	...	4	2	...	...	2	...	...	...	...	...	...	...	...	...	...
		GUJAR	Do.	522	31	60	...	431	459	1	...	...	458	310	19	28	...	263	270	1	...	...	269
		Do.	Jain	4	1	2	...	1	5	...	...	...	5	...	...	...	...	...	...	...	...	...	...
		GURUD KÁPUWÁR	Hindu	241	...	2	...	239	260	...	...	...	260	...	...	...	...	...	...	...	...	...	...
		JÁT	Do.	292	6	16	...	270	221	1	...	...	220	117	4	9	...	104	118	1	...	...	117
		Do.	Musalman	1	...	...	...	1	1	...	...	...	1	...	...	...	...	...	...	...	...	...	...
		Do.	Jain	3	...	...	...	3	2	...	...	...	2	1	...	...	...	1	1	...	...	...	1
		Do.	Sikh	5	2	1	...	2	2	...	...	...	2	...	...	...	...	...	...	...	...	...	...
		KACHHWÁHÁ	Hindu	1	...	...	...	1	...	...	...	...	...	1	...	...	...	1	...	...	...	...	...
		KÁCHI	Do.	22	...	...	...	22	6	...	...	...	6	11	...	...	...	11	5	...	...	...	5
		KAKAR	Do.	56	1	1	...	54	46	...	1	...	45	29	1	...	...	28	21	...	...	...	21
		KÁPUWÁRU	Do.	45	5	2	...	38	37	...	...	...	37	1	...	...	...	1	3	...	...	...	3
		KHICHAR	Do.	1	...	...	...	1	...	...	...	...	...	1	...	...	...	1	...	...	...	...	...
		KUNBI	Do.	426,429	11,059	15,751	*127*	399,619	407,990	101	172	*1*	407,717	85,890	2,720	4,247	*32*	78,923	81,139	19	33	...	81,087
		Do.	Jain	7	...	...	...	7	6	...	...	...	6	...	...	...	...	...	...	...	...	...	...
		LODHI	Hindu	1,147	12	33	*1*	1,102	768	...	...	...	768	417	2	4	...	411	257	...	...	...	257
		Do.	Musalman	2	...	...	...	2	3	...	...	...	3	...	...	...	...	...	...	...	...	...	...
		LONDHÁRI	Hindu	13	1	4	...	8	10	...	...	...	10	...	...	...	...	...	...	...	...	...	...
		MÁLI	Do.	102,717	1,606	2,213	*85*	98,898	99,771	16	12	...	99,743	31,366	454	633	*61*	30,279	30,017	4	2	...	30,011
		Do.	Jain	10	...	7	...	3	...	...	...	...	...	...	...	...	...	...	...	...	...	...	...
		MÁNÁ	Hindu	114	...	...	...	114	103	...	...	...	103	24	...	...	...	24	20	...	...	...	20
		MÁWHÁR	Do.	1	...	...	...	1	...	...	...	...	...	1	...	...	...	1	...	...	...	...	...
		MUDLIÁR	Do.	29	6	14	*13*	9	37	...	5	...	32	10	4	5	*5*	1	10	...	...	...	10
		MUNARWÁR	Do.	1,092	9	12	...	1,071	1,028	1	...		1,027	13	1	1	...	11	12	...	...	...	12
		MURÁDE	Do.	1	...	...	...	1	...	...	...	...	...	1	...	...	...	1	...	...	...	...	...
		MURÁI	Do.	93	2	14	...	77	26	...	...	...	26	30	...	2	...	28	10	...	...	...	10
		NÁYER	Do.	10	5	2	...	3	4	...	...	...	4	4	2	2	...	...	1	...	...	...	1
		PAHÁD	Do.	437	13	11	...	413	399	3	...	...	396	132	2	7	...	123	148	...	...	...	148
		PATALIYÁ	Do.	1	...	...	...	1	1	...	...	...	1	1	...	...	...	1	1	...	...	...	1
		PHANÁDI	Do.	58	...	...	...	58	44	...	...	...	44	...	...	...	...	...	...	...	...	...	...
		PHULÁRI	Do.	19	...	1	...	18	10	...	...	...	10	17	...	1	...	16	10	...	...	...	10

Table D.—[Castes by Education].

Class.	Group.	Caste.	Religion.	Akola Males Total.	Akola Males Pupils.	Akola Males Literate Total Literate.	Akola Males Literate Knowing English.	Akola Males Illiterate.	Akola Females Total.	Akola Females Pupils.	Akola Females Literate Total Literate.	Akola Females Literate Knowing English.	Akola Females Illiterate.	Ellichpur Males Total.	Ellichpur Males Pupils.	Ellichpur Males Literate Total Literate.	Ellichpur Males Literate Knowing English.	Ellichpur Males Illiterate.	Ellichpur Females Total.	Ellichpur Females Pupils.	Ellichpur Females Literate Total Literate.	Ellichpur Females Literate Knowing English.	Ellichpur Females Illiterate.
25	26	27	28	29	30	31	32	33	34	35	36	37	38	39	40	41	42	43	44	45	46	47	48
A.—AGRICULTURAL.	1.—MILITARY AND DOMINANT.	MULTÁNI	Musalman	...	...	...	...	...	...	...	...	...	...	3	...	...	...	3	4	...	...	...	4
		SIKH	Hindu	9	1	...	...	8	5	...	...	...	5	5	...	...	...	5	6	...	...	...	6
		Do.	Sikh	9	...	2	...	7	4	...	1	...	3	1	...	...	...	1	...	...	...	...	...
			Total Group 1	*18*	*1*	*2*	...	*15*	*9*	...	*1*	...	*8*	*9*	...	...	...	*9*	*10*	...	...	...	*10*
	2.—OTHER AGRICULTURAL (a) CULTIVATORS	AYÁWÁR	Hindu	...	...	...	...	...	...	...	...	...	...	...	...	...	...	...	...	...	...	...	...
		BÁGWÁN	Musalman	...	...	...	...	...	...	...	...	...	...	...	...	...	...	...	...	...	...	...	...
		BARAI	Hindu	4	...	3	...	1	1	...	...	...	1	...	...	...	...	...	...	...	...	...	...
		BÁRI	Do.	4,375	58	52	*1*	4,265	4,157	1	...	...	4,156	2,846	36	48	...	2,762	2,756	...	...	...	2,756
		BHANÁRI	Do.	...	...	...	...	...	...	...	...	...	...	...	...	...	...	...	...	...	...	...	...
		BHOYER	Do.	...	...	...	...	...	...	...	...	...	...	4	...	...	...	4	...	...	...	...	...
		BHUTE	Do.	...	...	...	...	...	...	...	...	...	...	1	...	...	...	1	...	...	...	...	...
		BHUVÉSH	Do.	...	...	...	...	...	...	...	...	...	...	...	...	...	...	...	...	...	...	...	...
		GUJAR	Do.	144	10	20	...	114	136	...	...	...	136	10	1	1	...	8	2	...	...	...	2
		Do.	Jain	4	1	2	...	1	5	...	...	...	5	...	...	...	...	...	...	...	...	...	...
		GURUD KÁPUWÁR	Hindu	...	...	...	...	...	...	...	...	...	...	...	...	...	...	...	...	...	...	...	...
		JÁT	Do.	36	1	4	...	31	20	...	...	...	20	17	1	1	...	15	2	...	...	...	2
		Do.	Musalman	...	...	...	...	...	...	...	...	...	...	...	...	...	...	...	...	...	...	...	...
		Do.	Jain	...	...	...	...	...	...	...	...	...	...	...	...	...	...	...	...	...	...	...	...
		Do.	Sikh	...	...	...	...	...	...	...	...	...	...	...	...	...	...	...	...	...	...	...	...
		KACHHWÁRÁ	Hindu	...	...	...	...	...	...	...	...	...	...	...	...	...	...	...	...	...	...	...	...
		KÁCHI	Do.	4	...	...	...	4	...	...	...	...	...	6	...	...	...	6	1	...	...	...	1
		KAKAR	Do.	...	...	...	...	...	...	...	...	...	...	1	...	...	...	1	...	...	...	...	...
		KÁPUWÁRU	Do.	...	...	...	...	...	...	...	...	...	...	...	...	...	...	...	...	...	...	...	...
		KHICHAR	Do.	...	...	...	...	...	...	...	...	...	...	...	...	...	...	...	...	...	...	...	...
		KUNBI	Do.	95,316	3,117	3,896	*29*	88,303	91,652	38	66	...	91,548	38,371	1,808	2,701	27	33,862	37,042	8	9	*1*	37,025
		Do.	Jain	1	...	...	...	1	...	...	...	...	...	...	...	...	...	...	...	...	...	...	...
		LODHI	Hindu	209	5	6	...	198	139	...	...	...	139	371	4	19	*1*	348	281	...	...	...	281
		Do.	Musalman	2	...	...	...	2	3	...	...	...	3	...	...	...	...	...	...	...	...	...	...
		LONDHÁRI	Hindu	...	...	...	...	...	...	...	...	...	...	10	1	4	...	5	10	...	...	...	10
		MÁLI	Do.	25,686	416	629	*10*	24,641	25,221	8	5	...	25,208	13,658	318	424	*8*	12,916	13,405	1	3	...	13,401
		Do.	Jain	10	...	7	...	3	...	...	...	...	...	...	...	...	...	...	...	...	...	...	...
		MÁNÁ	Hindu	...	...	...	...	...	...	...	...	...	...	...	...	...	...	...	...	...	...	...	...
		MÁWHÁR	Do.	...	...	...	...	...	...	...	...	...	...	...	...	...	...	...	...	...	...	...	...
		MUDLIÁR	Do.	9	1	4	*4*	4	11	...	2	...	9	3	1	2	*2*	...	8	...	3	...	5
		MUNARWÁR	Do.	4	...	...	...	4	5	...	...	...	5	14	1	7	...	6	13	...	...	...	13
		MURÁDE	Do.	...	...	...	...	...	...	...	...	...	...	...	...	...	...	...	...	...	...	...	...
		MURÁI	Do.	19	...	1	...	18	3	...	...	...	3	25	1	6	...	18	7	...	...	...	7
		NÁYER	Do.	6	3	...	...	3	3	...	...	...	3	...	...	...	...	...	...	...	...	...	...
		PAHÁD	Do.	46	2	1	...	43	75	1	...	...	74	88	...	...	...	88	58	...	...	...	58
		PATALIYÁ	Do.	...	...	...	...	...	...	...	...	...	...	...	...	...	...	...	...	...	...	...	...
		PHANÁDI	Do.	2	...	...	...	2	...	...	...	...	...	...	...	...	...	...	...	...	...	...	...
		PHULÁRI	Do.	...	...	...	...	...	...	...	...	...	...	2	...	...	...	2	...	...	...	...	...

TABLE D.—Castes by Education.

Caste and Religion.				Territorial Distribution.																			
				District Buldana.										District Wun.									
				Males.					Females.					Males.					Females.				
						Literate.					Literate.					Literate.					Literate.		
Class.	Group.	Caste.	Religion.	Total.	Pupils.	Total Literate.	Knowing English.	Illiterate.	Total.	Pupils.	Total Literate.	Knowing English.	Illiterate.	Total.	Pupils.	Total Literate.	Knowing English.	Illiterate.	Total.	Pupils.	Total Literate.	Knowing English.	Illiterate.
49	50	51	52	53	54	55	56	57	58	59	60	61	62	63	64	65	66	67	68	69	70	71	72
A.—Agricultural.	1.—Military and Dominant.	Multáni	Musalman	...	...	...	...	...	...	...	...	...	...	...	...	...	...	...	...	...	...	...	...
		Sikh	Hindu	43	2	12	...	29	34	...	1	...	33	10	...	...	...	10	13	...	...	...	13
		Do.	Sikh	18	...	2	...	11	17	...	...	...	17	22	...	...	...	22	15	...	...	...	15
			Total Group 1	*58*	*2*	*14*	...	*40*	*51*	...	*1*	...	*60*	*82*	...	...	...	*82*	*28*	...	...	...	*28*
	2.—Other Agricultural (a) Cultivators	Ayáwár	Hindu	...	...	...	...	...	...	...	...	...	...	62	4	20	...	38	62	...	...	...	62
		Bágwán	Musalman	24	...	...	...	24	25	...	...	...	25	...	...	...	...	...	...	...	...	...	...
		Barai	Hindu	...	...	...	...	...	...	...	...	...	...	61	3	6	...	52	75	...	...	...	75
		Bári	Do.	346	10	16	...	320	331	...	...	...	331	1,200	31	30	...	1,139	1,109	1	...	...	1,108
		Bhanári	Do.	...	...	...	...	...	...	...	...	...	...	9	...	...	...	9	12	...	...	...	12
		Bhoyer	Do.	...	...	...	...	...	...	...	...	...	...	1	...	...	...	1	1	...	...	...	1
		Bhute	Do.	...	...	...	...	...	...	...	...	...	...	...	...	...	...	...	...	...	...	...	...
		Bhuvesh	Do.	...	...	...	...	...	...	...	...	...	...	2	...	2	...	...	4	2	...	...	2
		Gujar	Do.	22	...	11	...	11	21	...	...	...	21	31	...	...	...	31	29	...	...	...	29
		Do.	Jain	...	...	...	...	...	...	...	...	...	...	...	...	...	...	...	...	...	...	...	...
		Gurud Kápuwár	Hindu	...	...	...	...	...	...	...	...	...	...	241	...	2	...	239	260	...	...	...	260
		Ját	Do.	108	...	2	...	106	80	...	...	...	80	2	...	...	...	2	1	...	...	...	1
		Do.	Musalman	...	...	...	...	...	...	...	...	...	...	1	...	...	...	1	1	...	...	...	1
		Do.	Jain	2	...	...	...	2	1	...	...	...	1	...	...	...	...	...	...	...	...	...	...
		Do.	Sikh	...	...	...	...	...	...	...	...	...	...	1	...	...	...	1	...	...	...	...	...
		Kachhwáhá	Hindu	...	...	...	...	...	...	...	...	...	...	...	...	...	...	...	...	...	...	...	...
		Káchi	Do.	...	...	...	...	...	...	...	...	...	...	1	...	...	...	1	...	...	...	...	...
		Kakar	Do.	...	...	...	...	...	...	...	...	...	...	26	...	1	...	25	25	...	1	...	24
		Kápuwáru	Do.	...	...	...	...	...	...	...	...	...	...	44	5	2	...	37	34	...	...	...	34
		Khichar	Do.	...	...	...	...	...	...	...	...	...	...	...	...	...	...	...	...	...	...	...	...
		Kunbi	Do.	90,190	1,850	2,600	*11*	85,740	87,220	20	37	...	87,163	54,633	849	1,334	*18*	52,450	51,791	10	19	...	51,762
		Do.	Jain	...	...	...	...	...	...	...	...	...	...	6	...	...	...	6	6	...	...	...	6
		Lodhi	Hindu	52	...	2	...	50	27	...	...	...	27	80	1	2	...	77	50	...	...	...	50
		Do.	Musalman	...	...	...	...	...	...	...	...	...	...	...	...	...	...	...	...	...	...	...	...
		Londhári	Hindu	3	...	...	...	3	...	...	...	...	...	...	...	...	...	...	...	...	...	...	...
		Máli	Do.	15,429	223	264	*1*	14,942	15,192	1	1	...	15,190	9,963	142	179	*1*	9,642	9,582	1	...	...	9,581
		Do.	Jain	...	...	...	...	...	...	...	...	...	...	...	...	...	...	...	...	...	...	...	...
		Máná	Hindu	...	...	...	...	...	...	...	...	...	...	90	...	...	...	90	83	...	...	...	83
		Máwhár	Do.	...	...	...	...	...	...	...	...	...	...	...	...	...	...	...	...	...	...	...	...
		Mudliár	Do.	...	...	...	...	...	...	...	...	...	...	7	...	3	*2*	4	8	...	...	...	8
		Munarwár	Do.	...	...	...	...	...	...	...	...	...	...	1,039	7	3	...	1,029	971	1	...	...	970
		Muráde	Do.	...	...	...	...	...	...	...	...	...	...	...	...	...	...	...	...	...	...	...	...
		Murái	Do.	...	...	...	...	...	...	...	...	...	...	10	...	3	...	7	3	...	...	...	3
		Náyer	Do.	...	...	...	...	...	...	...	...	...	...	...	...	...	...	...	...	...	...	...	...
		Pahád	Do.	...	...	...	...	...	...	...	...	...	...	166	9	3	...	154	113	2	...	...	111
		Pataliyá	Do.	...	...	...	...	...	...	...	...	...	...	...	...	...	...	...	...	...	...	...	...
		Phanádi	Do.	...	...	...	...	...	...	...	...	...	...	...	...	...	...	...	...	...	...	...	...
		Phulári	Do.	...	...	...	...	...	...	...	...	...	...	...	...	...	...	...	...	...	...	...	...

Caste and Religion.				Territorial Distribution.																			
				District Basim.										Railway Passengers.									
				Males.					Females.					Males.					Females.				
						Literate.					Literate.					Literate.					Literate.		
Class.	Group.	Caste.	Religion.	Total.	Pupils.	Total Literate.	Knowing English.	Illiterate.	Total.	Pupils.	Total Literate.	Knowing English.	Illiterate.	Total.	Pupils.	Total Literate.	Knowing English.	Illiterate.	Total.	Pupils.	Total Literate.	Knowing English.	Illiterate.
73	74	75	76	77	78	79	80	81	82	83	84	85	86	87	88	89	90	91	92	93	94	95	96
A.—Agricultural.	1.—Military and Dominant.	Multáni	Musalman	1	...	...	...	1	1	...	...	...	1	...	...	...	...	...	...	...	...	...	...
		Sikh	Hindu	14	1	6	...	7	13	...	...	...	13	...	...	...	...	...	...	...	...	...	...
		Do.	Sikh	3	...	2	...	1	3	...	...	...	3	...	...	...	...	...	...	...	...	...	...
			Total Group 1	18	1	8	...	9	17	...	...	...	17		...	...	...	...	...	...	...	...	...
	2.—Other Agricultural (a) Cultivators	Anáwár	Hindu	1	...	...	...	1	4	...	...	...	4	...	...	...	...	...	...	...	...	...	...
		Bágwán	Musalman	34	1	1	...	32	41	...	...	...	41	...	...	...	...	...	...	...	...	...	...
		Barai	Hindu	...	...	...	...	...	...	...	...	...	...	1	...	...	...	1	...	...	...	...	...
		Bári	Do.	475	...	2	...	473	485	...	...	...	485	1	...	1	...	...	...	...	...	...	...
		Bhanári	Do.	...	...	...	...	...	...	...	...	...	...	...	...	...	...	...	...	...	...	...	...
		Bhoyer	Do.	...	...	...	...	...	...	...	...	...	...	...	...	...	...	...	...	...	...	...	...
		Bhute	Do.	...	...	...	...	...	...	...	...	...	...	...	...	...	...	...	...	...	...	...	...
		Bhuvésh	Do.	...	...	...	...	...	...	...	...	...	...	...	...	...	...	...	...	...	...	...	...
		Gujar	Do.	5	1	...	...	4	1	...	...	...	1	...	...	...	...	...	...	...	...	...	...
		Do.	Jain	...	...	...	...	...	...	...	...	...	...	...	...	...	...	...	...	...	...	...	...
		Gurud Kápuwár	Hindu	...	...	...	...	...	...	...	...	...	...	...	...	...	...	...	...	...	...	...	...
		Ját	Do.	12	...	...	...	12	...	...	...	...	...	...	...	...	...	...	...	...	...	...	...
		Do.	Musalman	...	...	...	...	...	...	...	...	...	...	...	...	...	...	...	...	...	...	...	...
		Do.	Jain	...	...	...	...	...	...	...	...	...	...	...	...	...	...	...	...	...	...	...	...
		Do.	Sikh	4	2	1	...	1	2	...	...	...	2	...	...	...	...	...	...	...	...	...	...
		Kachhwáhá	Hindu	...	...	...	...	...	...	...	...	...	...	...	...	...	...	...	...	...	...	...	...
		Káchi	Do.	...	...	...	...	...	...	...	...	...	...	...	...	...	...	...	...	...	...	...	...
		Kakar	Do.	...	...	...	...	...	...	...	...	...	...	...	...	...	...	...	...	...	...	...	...
		Kápuwáru	Do.	...	...	...	...	...	...	...	...	...	...	...	...	...	...	...	...	...	...	...	...
		Khichar	Do.	...	...	...	...	...	...	...	...	...	...	...	...	...	...	...	...	...	...	...	...
		Kunbi	Do.	61,999	715	969	10	60,315	59,138	6	8	...	59,124	30	...	4	...	26	8	...	...	...	8
		Do.	Jain	...	...	...	...	...	...	...	...	...	...	...	...	...	...	...	...	...	...	...	...
		Lodhi	Hindu	18	...	...	...	18	14	...	...	...	14	...	...	...	...	...	...	...	...	...	...
		Do.	Musalman	...	...	...	...	...	...	...	...	...	...	...	...	...	...	...	...	...	...	...	...
		Londhári	Hindu	...	...	...	...	...	...	...	...	...	...	...	...	...	...	...	...	...	...	...	...
		Máli	Do.	6,613	53	83	4	6,477	6,354	1	1	...	6,352	2	...	1	...	1	...	...	...	...	...
		Do.	Jain	...	...	...	...	...	...	...	...	...	...	...	...	...	...	...	...	...	...	...	...
		Máná	Hindu	...	...	...	...	...	...	...	...	...	...	...	...	...	...	...	...	...	...	...	...
		Máwhár	Do.	...	...	...	...	...	...	...	...	...	...	...	...	...	...	...	...	...	...	...	...
		Mudliár	Do.	...	...	...	...	...	...	...	...	...	...	...	...	...	...	...	...	...	...	...	...
		Munarwár	Do.	22	...	1	...	21	27	...	...	...	27	...	...	...	...	...	...	...	...	...	...
		Murádе	Do.	...	...	...	...	...	...	...	...	...	...	...	...	...	...	...	...	...	...	...	...
		Murái	Do.	9	1	2	...	6	3	...	...	...	3	...	...	...	...	...	...	...	...	...	...
		Náyer	Do.	...	...	...	...	...	...	...	...	...	...	...	...	...	...	...	...	...	...	...	...
		Pahád	Do.	5	...	...	...	5	5	...	...	...	5	...	...	...	...	...	...	...	...	...	...
		Pataliyá	Do.	...	...	...	...	...	...	...	...	...	...	...	...	...	...	...	...	...	...	...	...
		Phanádi	Do.	56	...	...	...	56	44	...	...	...	44	...	...	...	...	...	...	...	...	...	...
		Phulári	Do.	...	...	...	...	...	...	...	...	...	...	...	...	...	...	...	...	...	...	...	...

TABLE D.—Castes, by Education—*contd.*

Class.	Group.	Caste.	Religion.	Total Strength: Males: Total Males.	Total Strength: Males: Pupils.	Total Strength: Males: Literate: Total Literate.	Total Strength: Males: Literate: Knowing English.	Total Strength: Males: Illiterate.	Total Strength: Females: Total Females.	Total Strength: Females: Pupils.	Total Strength: Females: Literate: Total Literate.	Total Strength: Females: Literate: Knowing English.	Total Strength: Females: Illiterate.	District Amraoti: Males: Total.	District Amraoti: Males: Pupils.	District Amraoti: Males: Literate: Total Literate.	District Amraoti: Males: Literate: Knowing English.	District Amraoti: Males: Illiterate.	District Amraoti: Females: Total.	District Amraoti: Females: Pupils.	District Amraoti: Females: Literate: Total Literate.	District Amraoti: Females: Literate: Knowing English.	District Amraoti: Females: Illiterate.
1	2	3	4	5	6	7	8	9	10	11	12	13	14	15	16	17	18	19	20	21	22	23	24
A.—AGRICULTURAL—*contd.*	2.—OTHER AGRICULTURAL (*a*) CULTIVATORS—*contd.*	RAJPUT	Hindu	26,850	1,495	3,355	59	22,000	24,066	30	41	...	23,995	6,832	425	968	18	5,439	5,923	2	16	...	5,905
		Do.	Sikh	8	2	6	...	...	6	...	1	...	5	...	...	...	...	...	...	...	...	...	...
		REDDI	Hindu	1	...	...	...	1	...	...	...	...	...	1	...	...	...	1	...	...	...	...	...
		REDDIKÁPUWÁR	Do.	5	...	...	...	5	4	...	...	...	4	...	...	...	...	...	...	...	...	...	...
		TIRMALE	Do.	208	1	...	...	207	241	...	...	...	241	76	...	...	...	76	91	...	...	...	91
		VELLÁLÁR	Do.	9	4	2	2	3	8	...	1	...	7	...	...	...	...	...	...	...	...	...	...
		WALHER	Do.	2	...	...	...	2	2	...	...	...	2	...	...	...	...	...	...	...	...	...	...
		YELAMÁ	Do.	246	13	11	...	222	249	...	...	...	249	...	...	...	...	...	...	...	...	...	...
			Total Group 2A	*574,119*	*14,464*	*21,757*	*288*	*537,908*	*548,774*	*157*	*233*	*1*	*548,384*	*129,256*	*8,671*	*5,968*	*116*	*119,622*	*121,953*	*27*	*51*	...	*121,875*
	(*b*) CATTLE-BREEDERS AND GRAZIERS.	GAHLÁN	Hindu	1	...	...	...	1	...	...	...	...	...	...	...	...	...	...	...	...	...	...	...
		GAOLI (ÁHIR, GAULÁN AND GAWÁRI)	Do.	19,087	121	208	3	18,758	16,593	...	2	...	16,591	6,468	39	55	...	6,374	5,292	...	...	...	5,292
		GAOLI (ÁHIR AND GAWÁRI)	Musalman	418	...	...	...	418	397	...	...	...	397	316	...	...	...	316	301	...	...	...	301
		Do.	Jain	1	...	...	...	1	...	...	...	...	...	1	...	...	...	1	...	...	...	...	...
		GAULÁN (GAWÁRI)	Animistic	382	...	1	...	381	389	...	...	...	389	88	...	...	...	88	91	...	...	...	91
		GOLKAR	Hindu	1,231	2	1	...	1,228	1,223	...	...	...	1,223	1	...	...	...	1	..	...	...	...	...
		KÁNADI	Do.	727	17	33	...	677	720	...	...	...	720	224	5	12	...	207	239	...	...	...	239
			Total Group 2B	*21,847*	*140*	*243*	*3*	*21,464*	*19,322*	...	*2*	...	*19,320*	*7,098*	*'44*	*67*	...	*6,987*	*5,928*	...	...	...	*5,923*
	(*c*) FIELD LABOURERS	DÁSARI	Hindu	26	...	1	...	25	38	...	...	...	38	...	...	...	...	...	...	...	...	...	...
		KABIR	Do.	2	...	...	...	2	3	...	...	...	3	2	...	...	...	2	3	...	...	...	3
		KATEKAR	Do.	1	...	...	...	1	...	...	...	...	...	...	...	...	...	...	...	...	...	...	...
		KOL	Do.	5	...	...	...	5	6	...	...	...	6	4	...	...	...	4	6	...	...	...	6
		LUGÁWÁR	Do.	4	...	...	...	4	1	...	...	...	1	4	...	...	...	4	1	...	...	...	1
		PUBE	Do.	2	...	...	...	2	...	...	...	...	...	...	...	...	...	...	...	...	...	...	...
			Total Group 2C	*40*	...	*1*	...	*39*	*48*	...	...	...	*48*	*10*	...	...	...	*10*	*10*	...	...	...	*10*
	4.—FOREST AND HILL TRIBES	ÁNDH	Hindu	21,671	28	27	...	21,616	21,626	...	...	...	21,626	55	...	...	...	55	58	...	...	...	58
		Do.	Animistic	165	...	...	...	165	140	...	...	...	140	...	...	...	...	...	...	...	...	...	...
		ARAKH	Hindu	128	...	...	...	128	107	...	...	...	107	109	...	...	...	109	100	...	...	...	100
		Do.	Animistic	9	...	...	...	9	9	...	...	...	9	9	...	...	...	9	9	...	...	...	9
		BHIL	Hindu	1,735	2	10	...	1,723	1,748	...	...	...	1,748	3	...	...	...	3	3	...	...	...	3
		Do.	Musalman	950	2	3	...	945	978	...	...	...	978	1	1	...	...	...	...	...	...	...	...
		Do.	Animistic	405	...	2	...	403	378	...	...	...	378	4	...	...	...	4	6	...	...	...	6
		BIJHAD	Hindu	2	...	...	...	2	3	...	...	...	3	2	...	...	...	2	3	...	...	...	3
		BOPCHI	Do.	318	...	...	...	318	295	...	...	...	295	318	...	...	...	318	295	...	...	...	295
		GOND	Do.	4,850	14	18	...	4,818	4,208	...	...	...	4,208	1,456	4	2	...	1,450	1,290	...	...	...	1,290
		Do.	Animistic	35,918	58	44	2	35,816	35,951	...	...	...	35,951	8,078	19	10	...	8,049	8,030	...	...	...	8,030

Table D.—[Castes, by Education].

Class.	Group.	Caste.	Religion.	District Akola. Males. Total.	Pupils.	Literate. Total Literate.	Knowing English.	Illiterate.	Females. Total.	Pupils.	Literate. Total Literate.	Knowing English.	Illiterate.	District Ellichpur. Males. Total.	Pupils.	Literate. Total Literate.	Knowing English.	Illiterate.	Females. Total.	Pupils.	Literate. Total Literate.	Knowing English.	Illiterate.
25	26	27	28	29	30	31	32	33	34	35	36	37	38	39	40	41	42	43	44	45	46	47	48
A.—AGRICULTURAL—*contd.*	2.—Other Agricultural (a) Cultivators—*contd.*	Rajput	Hindu	6,622	453	963	*11*	5,206	6,001	18	10	...	5,973	2,877	153	485	*16*	2,239	2,264	2	2	...	2,260
		Do.	Sikh	8	2	6	...	...	6	...	1	...	5	...	...	...	...	...	...	...	...	...	...
		Reddí	Hindu	...	...	...	...	...	...	...	...	...	...	...	...	...	...	...	...	...	...	...	...
		Reddikápuwár	Do.	...	...	...	...	...	...	...	...	...	...	...	...	...	...	...	...	...	...	...	...
		Tirmale	Do.	6	1	...	...	5	11	...	...	...	11	...	...	...	...	...	...	...	...	...	...
		Vellálár	Do.	9	4	2	2	3	8	...	1	...	7	...	...	...	...	...	...	...	...	...	...
		Walher	Do.	...	...	...	...	...	...	...	...	...	...	...	...	...	...	...	...	...	...	...	...
		Yelamá	Do.	...	...	...	...	...	...	...	...	...	...	...	...	...	...	...	...	...	...	...	...
			Total Group 2A	*132,522*	*4,074*	*5,596*	*57*	*122,852*	*127,457*	*66*	*85*	...	*127,306*	*58,304*	*2,826*	*3,698*	*54*	*52,281*	*55,849*	*11*	*17*	*1*	*55,821*
	(b) Cattle-breeders and Graziers.	Gahlán	Hindu	...	...	...	...	...	...	...	...	...	...	1	...	...	...	1	...	...	...	...	...
		Gaoli (Áhir, Gaulán and Gawári)	Do.	1,725	29	52	...	1,644	1,384	...	1	...	1,383	2,442	16	50	*3*	2,376	2,048	...	...	...	2,048
		Gaoli (Áhir and Gawári)	Musalman	32	...	...	...	32	35	...	...	...	35	8	...	...	...	8	11	...	...	...	11
		Do.	Jain	...	...	...	...	...	...	...	...	...	...	...	...	...	...	...	...	...	...	...	...
		Gawlán (Gawári)	Animistic	...	...	...	...	...	...	...	...	...	...	256	...	1	...	255	260	...	...	...	260
		Golkar	Hindu	2	...	...	...	2	...	...	...	...	...	...	...	...	...	...	...	...	...	...	...
		Kándi	Do.	73	4	6	...	63	65	...	...	...	65	4	...	...	...	4	3	...	...	...	3
			Total Group 2B	*1,832*	*83*	*58*	...	*1,741*	*1,484*	...	*1*	...	*1,488*	*2,711*	*16*	*51*	*8*	*2,644*	*2,322*	...	...	...	*2,822*
	(c) Field Labourers	Dásari	Hindu	...	...	...	...	...	...	...	...	...	...	...	...	...	...	...	...	...	...	...	...
		Kabir	Do.	...	...	...	...	...	...	...	...	...	...	...	...	...	...	...	...	...	...	...	...
		Kátekar	Do.	...	...	...	...	...	...	...	...	...	...	1	...	...	...	1	...	...	...	...	...
		Kol	Do.	...	...	...	...	...	...	...	...	...	...	...	...	...	...	...	...	...	...	...	...
		Lugáwár	Do.	...	...	...	...	...	...	...	...	...	...	...	...	...	...	...	...	...	...	...	...
		Pube	Do.	...	...	...	...	...	...	...	...	...	...	2	...	...	...	2	...	...	...	...	...
			Total Group 2C	...	...	...	...	...	...	...	...	...	...	*8*	...	...	...	*8*	...	...	...	...	...
	4.—Forest and Hill Tribes.	Ándh	Hindu	1,728	3	4	...	1,721	1,790	...	...	...	1,790	...	...	...	...	...	1	...	...	...	1
		Do.	Animistic	...	...	...	...	...	...	...	...	...	...	...	...	...	...	...	...	...	...	...	...
		Arakh	Hindu	17	...	...	...	17	4	...	...	...	4	2	...	...	...	2	3	...	...	...	3
		Do.	Animistic	...	...	...	...	...	...	...	...	...	...	...	...	...	...	...	...	...	...	...	...
		Bhil	Hindu	92	...	1	...	91	86	...	...	...	86	6	...	...	...	6	4	...	...	...	4
		Do.	Musalman	458	1	3	...	454	494	...	...	...	494	409	...	...	...	409	409	...	...	...	409
		Do.	Animistic	16	...	...	...	16	7	...	...	...	7	22	...	...	...	22	20	...	...	...	20
		Bijhad	Hindu	...	...	...	...	...	...	...	...	...	...	...	...	...	...	...	...	...	...	...	...
		Bopchi	Do.	...	...	...	...	...	...	...	...	...	...	...	...	...	...	...	...	...	...	...	...
		Gond	Do.	802	4	3	...	795	646	...	...	...	646	608	2	4	...	602	436	...	...	...	436
		Do.	Animistic	142	2	...	...	140	110	...	...	...	110	1,637	1	2	...	1,634	1,610	...	...	...	1,610

TABLE D.—Castes, by Education—*contd.*

Class.	Group.	Caste.	Religion.	Buldana Males Total.	Buldana Males Pupils.	Buldana Males Literate Total Literate.	Buldana Males Literate Knowing English.	Buldana Males Illiterate.	Buldana Females Total.	Buldana Females Pupils.	Buldana Females Literate Total Literate.	Buldana Females Literate Knowing English.	Buldana Females Illiterate.	Wun Males Total.	Wun Males Pupils.	Wun Males Literate Total Literate.	Wun Males Literate Knowing English.	Wun Males Illiterate.	Wun Females Total.	Wun Females Pupils.	Wun Females Literate Total Literate.	Wun Females Literate Knowing English.	Wun Females Illiterate.
				TERRITORIAL DISTRIBUTION.																			
49	50	51	52	53	54	55	56	57	58	59	60	61	62	63	64	65	66	67	68	69	70	71	72
A.—AGRICULTURAL—*contd.*	2.—Other Agricultural (*a*) Cultivators—*contd.*	Rajput	Hindu	7,115	286	478	5	6,351	6,884	6	5	...	6,873	1,676	97	244	6	1,335	1,465	1	5	...	1,459
		Do.	Sikh	...	...	...	...	...	...	...	...	...	...	...	...	...	...	...	...		...		...
		Reddí	Hindu	...	...	...	...	...	...	...	...	...	...	...	...	...	...	...	...	...	...	...	...
		Reddikápuwár	Do.	...	...	...	...	...	...	...	...	...	...	5	...	...	...	5	4	...	...	...	4
		Tirmale	Do.	2	...	...	...	2	6	...	...	...	6	122	...	...	...	122	131	...	...	...	131
		Vellálár	Do.	...	...	...	...	...	...	...	...	...	...	...	...	...	...	...	...	...	...	...	...
		Walher	Do.	...	...	...	...	...	...	...	...	...	...	...	...	...	...	...	...	...	...	...	...
		Yelamá	Do.	...	...	...	...	...	...	...	...	...	...	194	13	11	...	170	206	...	...	...	206
			Total Group 2A	*113,293*	*2,369*	*3,873*	*17*	*107,551*	*109,787*	*27*	*43*	...	*109,717*	*69,678*	*1,161*	*1,846*	*27*	*66,667*	*66,026*	*18*	*25*	...	*65,983*
	(*b*) Cattle-breeders and Graziers	Gahlán	Hindu	...	...	...	...	...	...	...	...	...	...	...	...	...	...	...	...	...	...	...	...
		Gaoli (Áhir, Gaulán and Gawári)	Do.	598	13	19	...	566	587	...	...	...	587	6,138	14	16	...	6,108	5,679	...	1	...	5,678
		Gaoli (Áhir, Gawári)	Musalman	39	...	...	...	39	33	...	...	...	33	...	...	...	...	...	...	...	...	...	...
		Do.	Jain	...	...	...	...	...	...	...	...	...	...	...	...	...	...	...	...	...	...	...	...
		Gaulán (Gawári)	Animistic	...	...	...	...	...	...	...	...	...	...	38	...	...	...	38	38	...	...	...	38
		Golkar	Hindu	...	...	...	...	...	...	...	...	...	...	1,208	2	1	...	1,205	1,197	...	...	...	1,197
		Kándi	Do.	8	...	1	...	7	2	...	...	...	2	24	...	1	...	23	25	...	...	...	25
			Total Group 2B	*645*	*13*	*20*	...	*612*	*622*	...	...	...	*622*	*7,408*	*16*	*18*	...	*7,374*	*6,939*	...	*1*	...	*6,938*
	(*c*) Field Labourers	Dásari	Hindu	...	...	...	...	...	...	...	...	...	...	5	...	...	...	5	9	...	...	...	9
		Kabir	Do.	...	...	...	...	...	...	...	...	...	...	...	...	...	...	...	...	...	...	...	...
		Kátekar	Do.	...	...	...	...	...	...	...	...	...	...	...	...	...	...	...	...	...	...	...	...
		Kol	Do.	...	...	...	...	...	...	...	...	...	...	1	...	...	...	1	...	...	...	...	...
		Lugáwár	Do.	...	...	...	...	...	...	...	...	...	...	...	...	...	...	...	...	...	...	...	...
		Pubb	Do.	...	...	...	...	...	...	...	...	...	...	...	...	...	...	...	...	...	...	...	...
			Total Group 2C	...	...	...	...	...	...	...	...	...	...	*6*	...	...	...	*6*	*9*	...	...	...	*9*
	4.—Forest and Hill Tribes	Ándh	Hindu	1,993	8	4	...	1,981	2,060	...	...	...	2,060	6,175	13	19	...	6,152	6,342	...	...	...	6,342
		Do.	Animistic	...	...	...	...	...	...	...	...	...	...	64	...	...	...	64	53	...	...	...	53
		Arakh	Hindu	...	...	...	...	...	...	...	...	...	...	...	...	...	...	...	...	...	...	...	...
		Do.	Animistic	...	...	...	...	...	...	...	...	...	...	...	...	...	...	...	...	...	...	...	...
		Bhil	Hindu	387	1	7	...	379	387	...	...	...	387	298	1	...	...	297	301	...	...	...	301
		Do.	Musalman	82	...	...	...	82	75	...	...	...	75	...	...	...	...	...	...	...	...	...	...
		Do.	Animistic	4	...	...	...	4	2	...	...	...	2	306	...	2	...	304	283	...	...	...	283
		Bíjhad	Hindu	...	...	...	...	...	...	...	...	...	...	...	...	...	...	...	...	...	...	...	...
		Bopchi	Do.	...	...	...	...	...	...	...	...	...	...	...	...	...	...	...	...	...	...	...	...
		Gond	Do.	128	...	3	...	125	128	...	...	...	128	1,424	2	4	...	1,418	1,310	...	...	...	1,310
		Do.	Animistic	...	...	...	...	...	1	...	...	...	1	26,010	36	32	2	25,942	26,140	...	...	...	26,140

Class.	Group.	Caste.	Religion.	District Basim. Males. Total.	Pupils.	Literate. Total Literate.	Knowing English.	Illiterate.	Females. Total.	Pupils.	Literate. Total Literate.	Knowing English.	Illiterate.	Railway Passengers. Males. Total.	Pupils.	Literate. Total Literate.	Knowing English.	Illiterate.	Females. Total.	Pupils.	Literate. Total Literate.	Knowing English.	Illiterate.
73	74	75	76	77	78	79	80	81	82	83	84	85	86	87	88	89	90	91	92	93	94	95	96
A.—AGRICULTURAL—contd.	2.—Other Agricultural (a) Cultivators—contd.	Rajput	Hindu	1,727	81	217	3	1,429	1,529	1	3	...	1,525	1	...	...	...	1	...	...	...	...	...
		Do.	Sikh	...	...	...	...	...	...	...	...	...	...	...	...	...	...	...	...	...	...	...	...
		Reddí	Hindu	...	...	...	...	...	...	...	...	...	...	...	...	...	...	...	...	...	...	...	...
		Reddikápuwár	Do.	...	...	...	...	...	...	...	...	...	...	...	...	...	...	...	...	...	...	...	...
		Tirmale	Do.	2	...	...	...	2	2	...	...	...	2	...	...	...	...	...	...	...	...	...	...
		Vellálár	Do.	...	...	...	...	...	...	...	...	...	...	...	...	...	...	...	...	...	...	...	...
		Walner	Do.	2	...	...	...	2	2	...	...	...	2	...	...	...	...	...	...	...	...	...	...
		Yelamá	Do.	52	...	...	...	52	43	...	...	...	43	...	...	...	...	...	...	...	...	...	...
			Total Group 2A	71,038	854	1,276	17	68,906	67,694	8	12	...	67,874	35	...	6	...	29	8	...	...	...	8
	(b) Cattle-breeders and Graziers	Gahlán	Hindu	...	...	...	...	...	...	...	...	...	...	...	...	...	...	...	...	...	...	...	...
		Gaoli (Ahir, Gaulán and Gawári)	Do.	1,690	10	15	...	1,665	1,587	...	...	...	1,587	26	...	1	...	25	16	...	...	...	16
		Gaoli (Ahir, Gawári)	Musalman	23	...	...	...	23	17	...	...	...	17	...	...	...	...	...	...	...	...	...	...
		Do.	Jain	...	...	...	...	...	...	...	...	...	...	...	...	...	...	...	...	...	...	...	...
		Gaulán (Gawári)	Animistic	...	...	...	...	...	...	...	...	...	...	...	...	...	...	...	...	...	...	...	...
		Golkar	Hindu	20	...	...	...	20	26	...	...	...	26	...	...	...	...	...	...	...	...	...	...
		Kándi	Do.	394	8	13	...	373	386	...	...	...	386	...	...	...	...	...	...	...	...	...	...
			Total Group 2B	2,127	18	28	...	2,081	2,016	...	...	...	2,016	26	...	1	...	25	16	...	...	...	16
	(c) Field Labourers	Dásari	Hindu	21	...	1	...	20	29	...	...	...	29	...	...	...	...	...	...	...	...	...	...
		Kabir	Do.	...	...	...	...	...	...	...	...	...	...	...	...	...	...	...	...	...	...	...	...
		Kátekar	Do.	...	...	...	...	...	...	...	...	...	...	...	...	...	...	...	...	...	...	...	...
		Kol	Do.	...	...	...	...	...	...	...	...	...	...	...	...	...	...	...	...	...	...	...	...
		Lugáwár	Do.	...	...	...	...	...	...	...	...	...	...	...	...	...	...	...	...	...	...	...	...
		Pube	Do.	...	...	...	...	...	...	...	...	...	...	...	...	...	...	...	...	...	...	...	...
			Total Group 2C	21	...	1	...	20	29	...	...	...	29	...	...	...	...	...	...	...	...	...	...
	4.—Forest and Hill Tribes	Ándh	Hindu	11,720	4	9	...	11,707	11,375	...	...	...	11,375	...	...	...	...	...	...	...	...	...	...
		Do.	Animistic	101	...	...	...	101	87	...	...	...	87	...	...	...	...	...	...	...	...	...	...
		Arakh	Hindu	...	...	...	...	...	...	...	...	...	...	...	...	...	...	...	...	...	...	...	...
		Do.	Animistic	...	...	...	...	...	...	...	...	...	...	...	...	...	...	...	...	...	...	...	...
		Bhil	Hindu	949	...	2	...	947	967	...	...	...	967	...	...	...	...	...	...	...	...	...	...
		Do.	Musalman	...	...	...	...	...	...	...	...	...	...	...	...	...	...	...	...	...	...	...	...
		Do.	Animistic	53	...	...	...	53	60	...	...	...	60	...	...	...	...	...	...	...	...	...	...
		Bijhad	Hindu	...	...	...	...	...	...	...	...	...	...	...	...	...	...	...	...	...	...	...	...
		Bopchi	Do.	...	...	...	...	...	...	...	...	...	...	...	...	...	...	...	...	...	...	...	...
		Gond	Do.	431	2	2	...	427	398	...	...	...	398	1	...	...	...	1	...	...	...	...	...
		Do.	Animistic	51	...	...	...	51	57	...	...	...	57	...	...	...	...	...	3	...	...	...	3

TABLE D.—Castes, by Education—*contd.*

Class.	Group.	Caste.	Religion.	Total Strength. Males. Total Males.	Total Strength. Males. Pupils.	Total Strength. Males. Literate. Total Literate.	Total Strength. Males. Literate. Knowing English.	Total Strength. Males. Illiterate.	Total Strength. Females. Total Females.	Total Strength. Females. Pupils.	Total Strength. Females. Literate. Total Literate.	Total Strength. Females. Literate. Knowing English.	Total Strength. Females. Illiterate.	Territorial Distribution. District Amraoti. Males. Total.	District Amraoti. Males. Pupils.	District Amraoti. Males. Literate. Total Literate.	District Amraoti. Males. Literate. Knowing English.	District Amraoti. Males. Illiterate.	District Amraoti. Females. Total.	District Amraoti. Females. Pupils.	District Amraoti. Females. Literate. Total Literate.	District Amraoti. Females. Literate. Knowing English.	District Amraoti. Females. Illiterate.
1	2	3	4	5	6	7	8	9	10	11	12	13	14	15	16	17	18	19	20	21	22	23	24
A.—AGRICULTURAL—*concld.*	4.—FOREST AND HILL TRIBES—*contd.*	GORWÁN	Hindu	11	...	...	...	11	2	...	...	...	2	...	...	...	...	...	...	...	...	...	...
		Do.	Animistic	73	...	...	...	73	75	...	...	...	75	...	...	...	...	...	...	...	...	...	...
		KOLÁM	Hindu	498	...	...	...	498	456	...	...	...	456	1	...	...	...	1	...	...	...	...	...
		Do.	Animistic	8,268	1	1	...	8,266	8,192	...	...	...	8,192	56	1	...	...	55	41	...	...	...	41
		KORKU	Hindu	193	...	1	...	192	186	...	...	...	186	21	...	...	...	21	19	...	...	...	19
		Do.	Animistic	17,522	7	8	...	17,507	17,080	...	...	...	17,080	294	1	...	...	293	300	...	...	...	300
		KOYELA-BHUTE	Do.	5	...	...	...	5	5	...	...	...	5	...	...	...	...	...	...	...	...	...	...
		LAJJHAD	Hindu	851	2	1	...	848	912	...	...	...	912	605	1	...	...	604	636	...	...	...	636
		Do.	Animistic	54	...	...	...	54	43	...	...	...	43	19	...	...	...	19	15	...	...	...	15
		MARÁL	Hindu	213	...	...	...	213	197	...	...	...	197	7	...	...	...	7	2	...	...	...	2
		MINÁ	Do.	5	...	1	...	4	7	...	...	...	7	...	...	...	...	...	...	...	...	...	...
		MOGHE	Do.	2	...	...	...	2	...	...	...	...	...	1	...	...	...	1	...	...	...	...	...
		Do.	Animistic	124	...	...	...	124	93	...	...	...	93	...	...	...	...	...	...	...	...	...	...
		NIHÁL	Hindu	51	...	...	...	51	53	...	...	...	53	1	...	...	...	1	1	...	...	...	1
		Do.	Animistic	1,101	...	...	...	1,101	1,100	...	...	...	1,100	...	...	...	...	...	...	...	...	...	...
		PANKÁ	Hindu	1	...	...	...	1	...	...	...	...	...	...	...	...	...	...	...	...	...	...	...
		PARDHÁN	Do.	1,899	5	4	...	1,890	1,867	...	...	...	1,867	305	...	...	...	305	306	...	...	...	306
		Do.	Animistic	4,614	2	4	...	4,608	4,556	...	...	...	4,556	140	...	...	...	140	131	...	...	...	131
			Total Group 4	*101,636*	*121*	*124*	*2*	*101,391*	*100,267*	...	...	...	*100,267*	*11,485*	*27*	*12*	...	*11,446*	*11,245*	...	...	...	*11,245*
B.—PROFESSIONAL.	5.—PRIESTS	BRÁHMAN	Hindu	41,772	5,938	20,704	*1,219*	15,130	29,500	221	388	*1*	28,891	10,979	1,473	5,248	*381*	4,258	7,543	56	155	*1*	7,332
		Do.	Jain	24	...	9	...	15	12	...	1	...	11	8	...	...	...	8	3	...	...	...	3
		JANGAM	Hindu	988	63	209	...	716	894	3	...	...	891	285	21	72	...	192	246	1	...	...	245
		JATI	Jain	17	...	6	...	11	...	...	...	...	...	...	...	...	...	...	...	...	...	...	...
		Do.	Hindu	6	...	4	...	2	...	...	...	...	...	5	...	4	...	1	...	...	...	...	...
		MULLA	Musalman	1	...	...	...	1	...	...	...	...	...	1	...	...	...	1	...	...	...	...	...
		PIRZÁDE	Do.	5	2	2	...	1	1	...	...	...	1	...	...	...	...	...	...	...	...	...	...
			Total Group 5	*42,813*	*6,008*	*20,984*	*1,219*	*15,876*	*30,407*	*224*	*389*	*1*	*29,794*	*11,278*	*1,494*	*5,824*	*381*	*4,460*	*7,792*	*57*	*155*	*1*	*7,580*
	6.—DEVOTEES	AGHORI	Hindu	6	...	...	...	6	4	...	...	...	4	3	...	...	...	3	3	...	...	...	3
		AUGHAD	Do.	2	...	...	...	2	3	...	...	...	3	...	...	...	...	...	...	...	...	...	...
		BÉRÁGI	Do.	858	24	133	...	701	578	...	2	...	576	267	4	42	...	221	210	...	...	...	210
		BHARÁDI	Do.	742	1	6	...	735	710	...	...	...	710	333	...	1	...	332	307	...	...	...	307
		FAKIR	Musalman	3,779	89	139	...	3,551	3,411	...	5	...	3,406	846	18	35	...	793	748	...	1	...	747
		GOSÁWI	Hindu	6,890	214	643	*7*	6,033	5,262	2	11	...	5,249	1,832	63	167	*4*	1,602	1,407	...	7	...	1,400
		JOGI	Do.	1,068	15	20	...	1,033	1,109	2	...	...	1,107	94	...	...	...	94	106	...	...	...	106
		MÁNBHÁO	Do.	1,904	130	563	*1*	1,211	1,655	39	102	...	1,514	590	16	173	...	401	505	5	17	...	483
		NÁNAKSHÁI	Do.	15	...	2	...	13	7	...	...	...	7	9	...	1	...	8	4	...	...	...	4
		NÁTH	Do.	1,532	32	77	...	1,423	1,441	1	...	...	1,440	324	1	10	...	313	287	...	...	...	287
		SÁDHU	Do.	16	...	3	...	13	11	...	...	...	11	1	...	...	...	1	...	...	...	...	...
		SANYÁSHI	Do.	21	...	9	...	12	7	...	...	...	7	8	...	6	...	2	...	...	...	...	...

Table D.—[Castes, by Education].

Class.	Group.	Caste.	Religion.	Akola Males Total.	Akola Males Pupils.	Akola Males Literate Total Literate.	Akola Males Literate Knowing English.	Akola Males Illiterate.	Akola Females Total.	Akola Females Pupils.	Akola Females Literate Total Literate.	Akola Females Literate Knowing English.	Akola Females Illiterate.	Ellichpur Males Total.	Ellichpur Males Pupils.	Ellichpur Males Literate Total Literate.	Ellichpur Males Literate Knowing English.	Ellichpur Males Illiterate.	Ellichpur Females Total.	Ellichpur Females Pupils.	Ellichpur Females Literate Total Literate.	Ellichpur Females Literate Knowing English.	Ellichpur Females Illiterate.
25	26	27	28	29	30	31	32	33	34	35	36	37	38	39	40	41	42	43	44	45	46	47	48
A.—AGRICULTURAL.	4.—FOREST AND HILL TRIBES *concld*	GORWÁN	Hindu	...	...	...	...	...	...	...	...	...	...	11	...	...	...	11	2	...	...	...	2
		Do.	Animistic	...	...	...	...	...	...	...	...	...	...	70	...	...	...	70	72	...	...	...	72
		KOLÁM	Hindu	...	...	...	...	...	...	...	...	...	...	...	...	...	...	...	...	...	...	...	...
		Do.	Animistic	...	...	...	...	...	...	...	...	...	...	...	...	...	...	...	...	...	...	...	...
		KORKU	Hindu	141	...	...	...	141	137	...	...	...	137	234	...	...	...	234	233	...	...	...	233
		Do.	Animistic	553	...	...	...	553	523	...	...	...	523	30	...	...	...	30	28	...	...	...	28
		KOYELA-BHUTE	Do.	...	...	...	...	...	...	...	...	...	...	16,610	6	8	...	16,596	16,193	...	...	...	16,193
		LAJJHAD	Hindu	7	...	...	...	7	2	...	...	...	2	...	...	...	...	...	...	...	...	...	...
		Do.	Animistic	...	...	...	...	...	...	...	...	...	...	208	...	...	...	208	235	...	...	...	235
		MARÁL	Hindu	...	...	...	...	...	...	...	...	...	...	31	...	...	...	31	24	...	...	...	24
		MINÁ	Hindu	1	...	1	...	...	1	...	...	...	1	...	...	...	...	...	...	...	...	...	...
		MOGHE	Do.	...	...	...	...	...	...	...	...	...	...	...	...	...	...	...	...	...	...	...	...
		Do.	Animistic	...	...	...	...	...	...	...	...	...	...	1	...	...	...	1	...	...	...	...	...
		NIHÁL	Hindu	16	...	...	...	16	24	...	...	...	24	124	...	...	...	124	93	...	...	...	93
		Do.	Animistic	102	...	...	...	102	92	...	...	...	92	34	...	...	...	34	28	...	...	...	28
		PANKÁ	Do.	...	...	...	...	...	...	...	...	...	...	999	...	...	...	999	1,008	...	...	...	1,008
		PARDHÁN	Do.	235	2	...	...	233	203	...	...	...	203	10	...	1	...	9	10	...	...	...	10
		Do.	Animistic	...	...	...	...	...	...	...	...	...	...	47	...	...	...	47	51	...	...	...	51
			Total Group 4	*4,310*	*12*	*12*	...	*4,286*	*4,119*	...	...	...	*4,119*	*21,093*	*9*	*16*	...	*21,069*	*20,480*	...	...	...	*20,480*
B.—PROFESSIONAL.	5.—PRIESTS	BRÁHMAN	Hindu	11,071	1,714	5,274	349	4,083	7,670	78	94	...	7,498	4,855	522	2,098	121	2,235	3,045	13	20	...	3,012
		Do.	Jain	2	...	2	...	...	...	...	...	...	...	1	...	1	...	...	1	...	1	...	...
		JANGAM	Hindu	76	7	21	...	48	71	...	...	...	71	14	...	6	...	8	16	...	...	...	16
		JATI	Jain	12	...	1	...	11	...	...	...	...	...	1	...	1	...	...	...	...	...	...	...
		Do.	Hindu	1	...	...	...	1	...	...	...	...	...	...	...	...	...	...	...	...	...	...	...
		MULLA	Musalman	...	...	...	...	...	...	...	...	...	...	...	...	...	...	...	...	...	...	...	...
		PIRZÁDE	Do.	...	...	...	...	...	...	...	...	...	...	5	2	2	...	1	1	...	...	...	1
			Total Group 5	*11,162*	*1,721*	*5,298*	*349*	*4,143*	*7,741*	*78*	*94*	...	*7,569*	*4,876*	*624*	*2,108*	*121*	*2,244*	*3,063*	*13*	*21*	...	*3,029*
	6.—DEVOTEES	AGHORI	Hindu	...	...	...	...	...	...	...	...	...	...	...	...	...	...	...	...	...	...	...	...
		AUGHAD	Do.	...	...	...	...	...	...	...	...	...	...	...	...	...	...	...	...	...	...	...	...
		BÉRÁGI	Do.	147	8	33	...	106	62	...	2	...	60	103	2	12	...	89	92	...	...	...	92
		BHARÁDI	Do.	45	...	1	...	44	51	...	...	...	51	39	...	...	...	39	38	...	...	...	38
		FAKIR	Musalman	989	27	33	...	929	891	...	4	...	887	500	13	18	...	469	546	...	...	...	546
		GOSÁWI	Hindu	1,342	57	145	3	1,140	915	1	2	...	912	574	18	77	...	479	354	...	...	...	354
		JOGI	Do.	39	...	...	...	39	24	...	...	...	24	20	...	2	...	18	14	...	...	...	14
		MÁNBHÁO	Do.	462	61	184	...	217	388	18	41	...	329	317	21	97	1	199	318	3	23	...	292
		NÁNAKSHÁI	Do.	3	...	1	...	2	3	...	...	...	3	2	...	...	...	2	...	...	...	...	...
		NÁTH	Do.	662	25	40	...	597	628	1	...	...	627	136	2	7	...	127	133	...	...	...	133
		SÁDHU	Do.	2	...	1	...	1	...	...	...	...	...	...	...	...	...	...	...	...	...	...	...
		SANYÁSHI	Do.	4	...	...	...	4	...	...	...	...	...	8	...	3	...	5	7	...	...	...	7

TABLE D.—Castes, by Education—*contd.*

Class.	Group.	Catse.	Religion.	District Búldana. Males. Total	Pupils.	Literate. Total Literate.	Literate. Knowing English.	Illiterate.	Females. Total.	Pupils.	Literate. Total Literate.	Literate. Knowing English.	Illiterate.	District Wun. Males. Total.	Pupils.	Literate. Total Literate.	Literate. Knowing English.	Illiterate.	Females. Total.	Pupils.	Literate. Total Literate.	Literate. Knowing English.	Illiterate.
49	50	51	52	53	54	55	56	57	58	59	60	61	62	63	64	65	66	67	68	69	70	71	72
A.—AGRICULTURAL.	4.—Forest and Hill Tribes—*contd.*	Gorwán	Hindu	...	...	...	...	...	...	...	...	...	...	...	...	...	...	...	...	...	...	...	...
		Do.	Animistic	..	...	...	...	...	...	...	...	...	...	3	...	...	...	3	3	...	...	...	3
		Kolám	Hindu	...	...	...	...	...	...	...	...	...	...	497	...	...	...	497	456	...	...	...	456
		Do.	Animistic	...	...	..	...	...	...	...	...	...	...	7,978	...	1	...	7,977	7,918	...	...	...	7,918
		Korku	Hindu	1	...	1	...	...	1	...	...	...	1	...	...	...	...	...	1	...	...	...	1
		Do.	Animistic	...	...	...	...	...	...	...	...	...	...	65	...	...	...	65	64	...	...	...	64
		Kovela-Bhute	Do.	...	...	...	...	...	...	...	...	...	...	5	...	...	...	5	5	...	...	...	5
		Lajjhad	Hindu	...	...	...	...	...	...	...	...	...	...	5	1	1	...	3	13	...	...	...	13
		Do.	Animistic	...	...	...	...	...	...	...	...	...	...	4	...	...	...	4	4	...	...	...	4
		Marál	Hindu	...	...	...	...	...	...	...	...	...	...	201	...	...	...	201	193	...	...	...	193
		Miná	Do.	4	...	...	...	4	6	...	...	...	6	...	...	...	...	...	...	...	...	...	...
		Moghe	Do.	...	...	...	...	...	...	...	...	...	...	...	...	...	...	...	...	...	...	...	...
		Do.	Animistic	...	...	...	...	...	...	...	...	...	...	...	...	...	...	...	...	...	...	...	...
		Nihál	Hindu	...	...	..	...	...	...	...	...	...	...	...	...	...	...	...	...	...	...	...	...
		Do.	Animistic	...	...	...	...	...	...	...	...	...	...	...	...	...	...	...	...	...	...	...	...
		Panká	Hindu	...	...	...	...	...	...	...	...	...	...	1	...	...	...	1	...	...	...	...	...
		Pardhán	Do.	...	...	...	...	...	...	...	...	...	...	1,331	3	3	...	1,325	1,334	...	...	...	1,334
		Do.	Animistic.	...	...	...	...	...	...	...	...	...	...	4,407	2	4	...	4,401	4354	...	...	...	4,354
			Total Group 4	*2,699*	*9*	*16*	...	*2,575*	*2,660*	...	...	...	*2,660*	*48,774*	*58*	*57*	*2*	*48,659*	*48,774*	...	...	...	*48,774*
B.—PROFESSIONAL.	5.—Priests	Bráhman	Hindu	6,417	1095	3,448	*149*	1,874	5,228	35	45	...	5,148	3,913	477	2,033	*109*	1,403	2,623	31	44	...	2,548
		Do.	Jain	10	...	3	...	7	8	...	...	...	8	3	...	3	...	...	...	...	...	...	...
		Jangam	Hindu	102	8	27	...	67	81	2	...	...	79	184	13	35	...	136	189	...	...	...	189
		Jati	Jain	3	...	3	...	...	...	...	...	...	...	...	...	...	...	...	...	...	...	...	...
		Do.	Hindu	...	...	...	...	...	...	...	...	...	...	...	...	...	..	...	...	...	...	...	...
		Mulia	Musalman	...	...	...	...	...	...	...	...	...	...	...	...	...	...	...	...	...	...	...	...
		Pirzáde	Do.	...	...	...	...	...	...	...	...	...	...	...	...	...	...	...	...	...	...	...	...
			Total Group 5	*6,532*	*1,103*	*3,481*	*149*	*1,948*	*5,317*	*37*	*45*	...	*5,235*	*4,100*	*490*	*2,071*	*109*	*1,539*	*2,812*	*81*	*44*	...	*2,787*
	6.—Devotees	Aghori	Hindu	...	...	...	...	...	...	...	...	...	...	3	...	...	...	3	1	...	...	...	1
		Aughad	Do.	...	...	...	...	...	...	...	...	...	...	...	...	...	...	...	...	...	...	...	...
		Béràgi	Do.	209	5	29	...	175	135	...	...	...	135	43	...	9	...	34	19	...	...	...	19
		Bharádi	Do.	209	1	4	...	204	202	...	...	...	202	113	...	...	...	113	109	...	...	...	109
		Fakir	Musalman	644	11	25	...	608	556	...	...	...	556	394	15	15	...	364	341	...	...	...	341
		Gosáwi	Hindu	979	23	91	...	865	806	1	2	...	803	902	29	68	...	805	822	...	...	...	822
		Jogi	Do.	256	10	6	...	240	270	2	...	...	268	256	1	2	...	253	270	...	...	...	270
		Mánbháo	Do.	223	5	45	...	173	209	...	15	...	194	149	21	46	...	82	86	12	5	...	69
		Nánakshái	Do.	1	...		...	1	...	...	...	...	...	...	...	...	...	...	...	...	...	...	...
		Náth	Do.	318	3	15	...	300	297	...	...	...	297	29	...	1	...	28	20	...	...	...	20
		Sádhu	Do.	12	...	2	...	10	11	...	...	...	11	...	...	...	...	...	...	...	...	...	...
		Sanyáshi	Do.	...	...	...	...	...	...	...	...	...	...	...	...	...	...	...	...	...	...	...	...

Caste and Religion.				Territorial Distribution.																			
				District Basim.										Railway Passengers.									
				Males.					Females.					Males.					Females.				
						Literate.					Literate.					Literate.					Literate.		
Class.	Group.	Caste.	Religion.	Total.	Pupils.	Total Literate.	Knowing English.	Illiterate.	Total.	Pupils.	Total Literate.	Knowing English.	Illiterate.	Total.	Pupils.	Total Literate.	Knowing English.	Illiterate.	Total.	Pupils.	Total Literate.	Knowing English.	Illiterate.
73	74	75	76	77	78	79	80	81	82	83	84	85	86	87	88	89	90	91	92	93	94	95	96
A.—AGRICULTURAL—*contd.*	4.—Forest and Hill Tribes—*contd.*	Gorwán	Hindu	...	...	...	...	...	...	...	...	...	...	...	...	...	...	...	...	...	...	...	...
		Do.	Animistic	...	...	...	...	...	...	...	...	...	...	...	...	...	...	...	...	...	...	...	...
		Kólám	Hindu	...	...	...	...	...	...	...	...	...	...	...	...	...	...	...	...	...	...	...	...
		Do.	Animistic	...	...	...	...	...	...	...	...	...	...	...	...	...	...	...	...	...	...	...	...
		Korku	Hindu	...	...	...	...	...	...	...	...	...	...	...	...	...	...	...	...	...	...	...	...
		Do.	Animistic	...	...	...	...	...	...	...	...	...	...	...	...	...	...	...	...	...	...	...	...
		Kovela-Bhute	Do.	...	...	...	...	...	...	...	...	...	...	...	...	...	...	...	...	...	...	...	...
		Lajjhad	Do.	26	...	...	...	26	26	...	...	...	26	...	...	...	...	...	...	...	...	...	...
		Do.	Animistic	...	...	...	...	...	...	...	...	...	...	...	...	...	...	...	...	...	...	...	...
		Marál	Hindu	5	...	...	...	5	2	...	...	...	2	...	...	...	...	...	...	...	...	...	...
		Miná	Hindu	...	...	...	...	...	...	...	...	...	...	...	...	...	...	...	...	...	...	...	...
		Moghe	Do.	...	...	...	...	...	...	...	...	...	...	...	...	...	...	...	...	...	...	...	...
		Do.	Animistic	...	...	...	...	...	...	...	...	...	...	...	...	...	...	...	...	...	...	...	...
		Nihál	Hindu	...	...	...	...	...	...	...	...	...	...	...	...	...	...	...	...	...	...	...	...
		Do.	Animistic	...	...	...	...	...	...	...	...	...	...	...	...	...	...	...	...	...	...	...	...
		Panká	Hindu	...	...	...	...	...	...	...	...	...	...	...	...	...	...	...	...	...	...	...	...
		Pardhán	Do.	18	...	...	...	18	14	...	...	...	14	...	...	...	...	...	...	...	...	...	...
		Do.	Animistic	20	...	...	...	20	20	...	...	...	20	...	...	...	...	...	...	...	...	...	...
			Total Group 4	*13,374*	*6*	*13*	...	*13,355*	*13,006*	...	...	...	*13,006*	*1*	...	...	...	*1*	*8*	...	...	...	*8*
B.—PROFESSIONAL.	5.—Priests	Bráhman	Hindu	4,493	657	2,588	109	1,248	3,383	8	30	...	3,345	44	...	15	1	29	8	...	...	...	8
		Do.	Jain	...	...	...	...	...	...	...	...	...	...	...	...	...	...	...	...	...	...	...	...
		Jangam	Hindu	327	14	48	...	265	291	...	...	...	291	...	...	...	...	...	...	...	...	...	...
		Játi	Jain	1	...	1	...	...	...	...	...	...	...	...	...	...	...	...	...	...	...	...	...
		Do.	Hindu	...	...	...	...	...	...	...	...	...	...	...	...	...	...	...	...	...	...	...	...
		Mulla	Musalman	...	...	...	...	...	...	...	...	...	...	...	...	...	...	...	...	...	...	...	...
		Pirzáde	Do.	...	...	...	...	...	...	...	...	...	...	...	...	...	...	...	...	...	...	...	...
			Total Group 5	*4,821*	*671*	*2,637*	*109*	*1,513*	*3,674*	*8*	*30*	...	*3,636*	*44*	...	*15*	*1*	*29*	*8*	...	...	...	*8*
	6.—Devotees	Aghori	Hindu	...	...	...	...	...	...	...	...	...	...	...	...	...	...	...	...	...	...	...	...
		Aughad	Do.	2	...	...	...	2	3	...	...	...	3	...	...	...	...	...	...	...	...	...	...
		Béragi	Do.	88	5	8	...	75	60	...	...	...	60	1	...	...	...	1	...	...	...	...	...
		Bharádi	Do.	3	...	...	...	3	3	...	...	...	3	...	...	...	...	...	...	...	...	...	...
		Fakir	Musalman	406	5	13	...	388	329	...	...	...	329	...	...	...	...	...	...	...	...	...	...
		Gosáwi	Hindu	1,260	24	94	...	1,142	958	...	...	...	958	1	...	1	...	...	...	...	...	...	...
		Jogi	Do.	403	4	10	...	389	425	...	...	...	425	...	...	...	...	...	...	...	...	...	...
		Mánbháo	Do.	163	6	18	...	139	149	1	1	...	147	...	...	...	...	...	...	...	...	...	...
		Nánakshái	Do.	...	...	...	...	...	...	...	...	...	...	...	...	...	...	...	...	...	...	...	...
		Náth	Do.	63	1	4	...	58	76	...	...	...	76	...	...	...	...	...	...	...	...	...	...
		Sádhu	Do.	1	...	...	...	1	...	...	...	...	...	...	...	...	...	...	...	...	...	...	...
		Sanyáshi	Do.	1	...	...	...	1	...	...	...	...	...	...	...	...	...	...	...	...	...	...	...

TABLE D.—Castes, by Education—*contd.*

Class.	Group.	Caste.	Religion.	Total Strength. Males. Total Males.	Males. Pupils.	Males. Literate. Total Literate.	Males. Literate. Knowing English.	Males. Illiterate.	Females. Total Females.	Females. Pupils.	Females. Literate. Total Literate.	Females. Literate. Knowing English.	Females. Illiterate.	Territorial Distribution. District Amraoti. Males. Total.	Males. Pupils.	Males. Literate. Total Literate.	Males. Literate. Knowing English.	Males. Illiterate.	Females. Total.	Females. Pupils.	Females. Literate. Total Literate.	Females. Literate. Knowing English.	Females. Illiterate.
1	2	3	4	5	6	7	8	9	10	11	12	13	14	15	16	17	18	19	20	21	22	23	24
B.—PROFESSIONAL—*contd.*	6.—DEVOTEES—*contd.*	SWÁMI	Hindu	2	...	...	...	2	1	...	...	...	1	1	...	...	...	1	...	...	...	...	...
		UDÁSI	Do.	75	2	24	...	49	34	...	1	...	33	25	2	5	...	18	14	...	...	...	14
		Do.	Sikh	1	...	1	...	...	1	...	...	...	1	...	...	...	...	...	...	...	...	...	...
		VIRBHADRA	Hindu	23	...	...	...	23	21	...	...	...	21	...	...	...	...	...	...	...	...	...	...
		WÁSUDEO	Do.	160	2	...	...	158	154	...	...	...	154	...	...	...	...	...	...	...	...	...	...
			Total Group 6	*17,094*	*509*	*1,620*	*8*	*14,965*	*14,409*	*44*	*121*	...	*14,244*	*4,338*	*104*	*440*	*4*	*3,789*	*3,591*	*5*	*26*	...	*3,561*
	7.—TEMPLE SERVANTS	GURAO	Hindu	4,655	318	741	10	3,596	4,574	6	8	...	4,560	1,861	149	375	5	1,337	1,846	3	3	...	1,840
		Do.	Jain	1	...	...	...	1	...	...	...	...	...	...	...	...	...	...	...	...	...	...	...
			Total Group 7	*4,656*	*318*	*741*	*10*	*3,597*	*4,574*	*6*	*8*	...	*4,560*	*1,861*	*149*	*375*	*5*	*1,337*	*1,846*	*3*	*3*	...	*1,840*
	8.—GENEALOGISTS	BHÁT	Hindu	1,630	66	231	1	1,333	1,435	...	3	...	1,432	712	31	90	1	591	666	...	...	...	666
		Do.	Animistic	21	...	...	...	21	26	...	...	...	26	21	...	...	...	21	26	...	...	...	26
		Do.	Musalman	25	...	3	...	22	20	...	...	...	20	12	...	...	...	12	10	...	...	...	10
		THÁKUR	Hindu	2,750	71	190	2	2,489	2,349	1	...	...	2,348	545	18	51	...	476	346	...	...	...	346
			Total Group 8	*4,426*	*137*	*424*	*3*	*3,865*	*3,830*	*1*	*3*	...	*3,826*	*1,290*	*49*	*141*	*1*	*1,100*	*1,048*	...	...	...	*1,048*
	9.—WRITERS	BORAL	Hindu	13	...	7	...	6	12	...	...	...	12	1	...	...	...	1	1	...	...	...	1
		GOLAK	Do.	73	16	34	...	23	73	1	3	...	69	7	...	1	...	6	1	...	...	...	1
		KÁST	Do.	131	12	61	4	58	128	...	1	...	127	51	3	22	3	26	52	...	...	...	52
		KÁYET	Do.	570	39	158	9	373	404	1	3	...	400	136	16	38	4	82	75	1	3	...	71
		PARBHU	Do.	352	105	164	53	83	280	18	27	...	235	131	48	54	16	29	81	4	6	...	71
		PURBHAIYE	Do.	67	4	7	...	56	27	...	...	...	27	4	...	...	...	4	...	...	...	...	...
			Total Group 9	*1,206*	*176*	*431*	*66*	*599*	*924*	*20*	*34*	...	*870*	*330*	*67*	*115*	*23*	*148*	*210*	*5*	*9*	...	*196*
	10.—ASTROLOGERS	GÁRPAGÁRI	Hindu	1,564	42	53	...	1,469	1,477	...	...	...	1,477	590	13	18	...	559	534	...	...	...	534
		JOSHI	Do.	249	...	10	...	239	170	...	...	...	170	4	...	...	...	4	4	...	...	...	4
		Do.	Jain	3	...	...	...	3	2	...	...	...	2	3	...	...	...	3	2	...	...	...	2
		SARODE	Hindu	675	1	5	...	669	655	...	...	...	655	121	1	...	...	120	81	...	...	...	81
			Total Group 10	*2,491*	*43*	*68*	...	*2,380*	*2,304*	...	...	...	*2,304*	*718*	*14*	*18*	...	*686*	*621*	...	...	...	*621*
	11.—MUSICIANS	DEWALWÁR	Hindu	45	2	2	...	41	58	...	...	...	58	...	...	...	...	...	...	...	...	...	...
		GONDHALI	Do.	1,511	20	39	...	1,452	1,522	...	...	...	1,522	269	3	7	...	259	201	...	...	...	201
		MIRÁSI	Do.	2	...	...	...	2	3	...	...	...	3	...	...	...	...	...	...	...	...	...	...
			Total Group 11	*1,558*	*22*	*41*	...	*1,495*	*1,583*	...	...	...	*1,583*	*269*	*3*	*7*	...	*259*	*201*	...	...	...	*201*

CASTE AND RELIGION.				TERRITORIAL DISTRIBUTION.																			
				DISTRICT AKOLA.										DISTRICT ELLICHPUR.									
				Males.					Females.					Males.					Females.				
						Literate.					Literate.					Literate.					Literate.		
Class.	Group.	Caste.	Religion.	Total.	Pupils.	Total Literate.	Knowing English.	Illiterate.	Total.	Pupils.	Total Literate.	Knowing English.	Illiterate.	Total.	Pupils.	Total Literate.	Knowing English.	Illiterate.	Total.	Pupils.	Total Literate.	Knowing English.	Illiterate.
25	26	27	28	29	30	31	32	33	34	35	36	37	38	39	40	41	42	43	44	45	46	47	48
B.—PROFESSIONAL—contd.	6.—DEVOTEES—contd.	SWÁMI	Hindu	1	...	...	...	1	1	...	...	...	1	...	...	...	...	...	...	...	...	...	...
		UDÁSI	Do.	14	...	8	...	6	3	...	...	...	3	12	...	3	...	9	3	...	...	...	3
		Do.	Sikh	1	...	1	...	...	1	...	...	...	1	...	...	...	...	...	...	...	...	...	...
		VIRBHADRA	Hindu	...	...	...	...	...	...	...	...	...	...	...	...	...	...	...	...	...	...	...	...
		WÁSUDEO	Do.	...	...	...	...	...	...	...	...	...	...	...	...	...	...	...	...	...	...	...	...
			Total Group 6	*3,711*	*178*	*447*	*3*	*3,086*	*2,967*	*20*	*49*	...	*2,898*	*1,711*	*56*	*219*	*1*	*1,436*	*1,505*	*3*	*23*	...	*1,479*
	7.—TEMPLE SERVANTS	GURAO	Hindu	796	52	150	3	594	820	2	2	...	816	273	34	50	...	189	249	...	1	...	248
		Do.	Jain	...	...	...	...	...	...	...	...	...	...	...	...	...	...	...	...	...	...	...	...
			Total Group 7	*796*	*52*	*150*	*3*	*594*	*820*	*2*	*2*	...	*816*	*273*	*34*	*50*	...	*189*	*249*	...	*1*	...	*248*
	8.—GENEALOGISTS	BHÁT	Hindu	158	10	31	...	117	118	...	3	...	115	270	11	45	...	214	218	...	...	...	218
		Do.	Animistic	...	...	...	...	...	...	...	...	...	...	...	...	...	...	...	...	...	...	...	...
		Do.	Musalman	4	...	3	...	1	2	...	...	...	2	...	...	...	...	...	...	...	...	...	...
		THÁKUR	Hindu	760	22	41	2	697	720	1	...	...	719	242	7	22	...	213	147	...	...	...	147
			Total Group 8	*922*	*32*	*75*	*2*	*815*	*840*	*1*	*3*	...	*836*	*512*	*18*	*67*	...	*427*	*365*	...	...	...	*365*
	9.—WRITERS	BORAL	Hindu	...	...	...	...	...	...	...	...	...	...	...	...	...	...	...	...	...	...	...	...
		GOLAK	Do.	28	9	13	...	6	38	...	...	...	38	4	2	...	...	2	3	...	...	...	3
		KÁST	Do.	31	6	18	...	7	30	...	...	...	30	9	1	5	...	3	17	...	1	...	16
		KÁYET	Do.	176	10	50	...	116	125	...	...	...	125	148	6	37	3	105	117	...	...	...	117
		PARBHU	Do.	65	18	32	10	15	63	7	8	...	48	63	20	30	10	13	60	3	5	...	52
		PURBHAIYE	Do.	16	...	2	...	14	4	...	...	...	4	3	...	...	...	3	...	...	...	...	...
			Total Group 9	*316*	*43*	*115*	*10*	*158*	*260*	*7*	*8*	...	*245*	*227*	*29*	*72*	*13*	*126*	*197*	*3*	*6*	...	*188*
	10.—ASTROLOGERS	GÁRPAGÁRI	Hindu	261	16	14	...	231	261	...	...	...	261	335	3	5	...	327	310	...	...	...	310
		JOSHI	Do.	25	...	3	...	22	11	...	...	...	11	...	...	...	...	...	...	...	...	...	...
		Do.	Jain	...	...	...	...	...	...	...	...	...	...	...	...	...	...	...	...	...	...	...	...
		SARODE	Hindu	15	...	3	...	12	3	...	...	...	3	108	...	...	...	108	97	...	...	...	97
			Total Group 10	*301*	*16*	*20*	...	*265*	*275*	...	...	...	*275*	*443*	*3*	*5*	...	*435*	*407*	...	...	...	*407*
	11.—MUSICIANS	DEWALWÁR	Hindu	...	...	...	...	...	...	...	...	...	...	...	...	...	...	...	...	...	...	...	...
		GONDHALI	Do.	596	7	18	...	571	659	...	...	...	659	97	3	...	...	94	95	...	...	...	95
		MIRÁSI	Do.	...	...	...	...	...	...	...	...	...	...	...	...	...	...	...	...	...	...	...	...
			Total Group 11	*596*	*7*	*18*	...	*571*	*659*	...	...	...	*659*	*97*	*3*	...	...	*94*	*95*	...	...	...	*95*

TABLE D.—Castes by Education—*contd.*

Caste and Religion.				Territorial Distribution.																			
				District Buldana.										District Wun.									
				Males.					Females.					Males.					Females.				
						Literate.					Literate.					Literate.					Literate.		
Class.	Group.	Caste.	Religion.	Total.	Pupils.	Total Literate.	Knowing English.	Illiterate.	Total.	Pupils.	Total Literate.	Knowing English.	Illiterate.	Total.	Pupils.	Total Literate.	Knowing English.	Illiterate.	Total.	Pupils.	Total Literate.	Knowing English.	Illiterate.
49	50	51	52	53	54	55	56	57	58	59	60	61	62	63	64	65	66	67	68	69	70	71	72
B.—Professional—*contd.*	6.—Devotees—*contd.*	Swámi	Hindu	...	...	...	...	...	...	...	...	...	...	...	...	...	...	...	...	...	...	...	...
		Udási	Do.	17	...	6	...	11	13	...	1	...	12	3	...	...	...	3	...	...	...	...	...
		Do.	Sikh	...	...	...	...	...	...	...	...	...	...	...	...	...	...	...	...	...	...	...	...
		Virbhadra	Hindu	...	...	...	...	...	...	...	...	...	...	23	...	...	...	23	21	...	...	...	21
		Wásudeo	Do.	22	...	...	...	22	11	...	...	...	11	29	...	...	...	29	9	...	...	...	9
			Total Group 6	*2,890*	*58*	*228*	...	*2,609*	*2,510*	*8*	*18*	...	*2,489*	*1,944*	*66*	*141*	...	*1,737*	*1,698*	*12*	*5*	...	*1,681*
	7.—Temple Servants	Gurao	Hindu	722	35	53	...	634	764	1	...	...	763	419	24	62	2	333	375	...	1	...	374
		Do.	Jain	...	...	...	...	...	...	...	...	...	...	...	...	...	...	...	...	...	...	...	...
			Total Group 7	*722*	*35*	*53*	...	*634*	*764*	*1*	...	...	*763*	*419*	*24*	*62*	*2*	*333*	*375*	...	*1*	...	*374*
	8.—Genealogists	Bhát	Hindu	139	2	39	...	98	130	...	...	...	130	287	11	22	...	254	250	...	...	...	250
		Do.	Animistic	...	...	...	...	...	...	...	...	...	...	...	...	...	...	...	...	...	...	...	...
		Do.	Musalman	...	...	...	...	...	...	...	...	...	...	9	...	...	...	9	8	...	...	...	8
		Thákur	Hindu	353	9	30	...	314	352	...	...	...	352	353	5	24	...	324	297	...	...	...	297
			Total Group 8	*492*	*11*	*69*	...	*412*	*482*	...	...	...	*482*	*649*	*16*	*46*	...	*587*	*555*	...	...	...	*555*
	9.—Writers	Boral	Hindu	11	...	6		5	11	...	...	...	11	...	...	...	...	...	...	...	...	...	...
		Golak	Do.	31	4	19	...	8	29	1	3	...	25	1	1	...	...	...	1	...	...	...	1
		Kást	Do.	31	2	11	...	18	24	...	...	...	24	6	...	4	1	2	4	...	...	...	4
		Káyet	Do.	30	4	13	2	13	30	...	...	...	30	42	...	8	...	34	26	...	...	...	26
		Parbhu	Do.	13	3	8	5	2	9	1	3	...	5	51	14	27	7	10	48	3	3	...	42
		Purbháiye	Do.	33	4	5	...	24	23	...	...	...	23	1	...	...	...	1	...	...	...	...	...
			Total Group 9	*149*	*17*	*62*	*7*	*70*	*126*	*2*	*6*	...	*118*	*101*	*15*	*39*	*8*	*47*	*79*	*3*	*3*	...	*73*
	10.—Astrologers	Gárpagári	Hindu	116	3	4	...	109	109	...	...	...	109	155	3	3	...	149	155	...	...	...	155
		Joshi	Do.	82	...	3	...	79	68	...	...	...	68	...	...	...	...	...	...	...	...	...	...
		Do.	Jain	...	...	...	...	...	...	...	...	...	...	...	...	...	...	...	...	...	...	...	...
		Sarode	Hindu	19	...	...	...	19	14	...	...	...	14	403	...	2	...	401	447	...	...	...	447
			Total Group 10	*217*	*3*	*7*	...	*207*	*191*	...	...	...	*191*	*558*	*3*	*5*	...	*550*	*602*	...	...	...	*602*
	11.—Musicians	Dewalwár	Hindu	...	...	...	...	...	...	...	...	...	...	45	2	2	...	41	58	...	...	...	58
		Gondhali	Do.	214	5	9	...	200	210	...	...	...	210	158	1	1	...	156	160	...	...	...	160
		Mirási	Do.	2	...	...	...	2	3	...	...	...	3	...	...	...	...	...	...	...	...	...	...
			Total Group 11	*216*	*5*	*9*	...	*202*	*218*	...	...	...	*218*	*208*	*3*	*3*	...	*197*	*218*	...	...	...	*218*

Table D.—[Castes by Education].

Class.	Group.	Caste.	Religion.	District Basim. Males. Total.	Pupils.	Literate. Total Literate.	Literate. Knowing English.	Illiterate.	Females. Total.	Pupils.	Literate. Total Literate.	Literate. Knowing English.	Illiterate.	Railway Passengers. Males. Total.	Pupils.	Literate. Total Literate.	Literate. Knowing English.	Illiterate.	Females. Total.	Pupils.	Literate. Total Literate.	Literate. Knowing English.	Illiterate.
73	74	75	76	77	78	79	80	81	82	83	84	85	86	87	88	89	90	91	92	93	94	95	96
B.—PROFESSIONAL—*contd.*	6.—DEVOTEES—*contd.*	SWÁMI	Hindu	...	...	...	...	...	...	...	...	...	...	...	...	...	...	...	...	...	...	...	...
		UDÁSI	Do.	4	...	2	...	2	1	...	...	...	1	...	...	...	...	...	...	...	...	...	...
		Do.	Sikh	...	...	...	...	...	...	...	...	...	...	...	...	...	...	...	...	...	...	...	...
		VIRBHADRA	Hindu	...	...	...	...	...	...	...	...	...	...	...	...	...	...	...	...	...	...	...	...
		WÁSUDEO	Do.	109	2	...	...	107	134	...	...	...	134	...	...	...	...	...	...	...	...	...	...
			Total Group 6	*2,508*	*47*	*149*	...	*2,307*	*2,138*	*1*	*1*	...	*2,136*	*2*	...	*1*	...	*1*	...	...	...	...	...
	7.—TEMPLE SERVANTS	GURAO	Hindu	583	24	51	...	508	520	...	1	...	519	1	...	...	...	1	...	...	...	...	...
		Do.	Jain	1	...	...	...	1	...	...	...	...	...	...	...	...	...	...	...	...	...	...	...
			Total Group 7	*584*	*24*	*51*	...	*509*	*520*	...	*1*	...	*519*	*1*	...	...	...	*1*	...	...	...	...	...
	8.—GENEALOGISTS	BHÁT	Hindu	64	1	4	...	59	53	...	...	...	53	...	...	...	...	...	...	...	...	...	...
		Do.	Animistic	...	...	...	...	...	...	...	...	...	...	...	...	...	...	...	...	...	...	...	...
		Do.	Musalman	...	...	...	...	...	...	...	...	...	...	...	...	...	...	...	...	...	...	...	...
		THÁKUR	Hindu	496	10	22	...	464	487	...	...	...	487	1	...	...	...	1	...	...	...	...	...
			Total Group 8	*560*	*11*	*26*	...	*523*	*540*	...	...	...	*540*	*1*	...	...	...	*1*	...	...	...	...	...
	9.—WRITERS	BORÁL	Hindu	1	...	1	...	...	...	...	...	...	...	...	...	...	...	...	...	...	...	...	...
		GOLAK	Do.	2	...	1	...	1	1	...	...	...	1	...	...	...	...	...	...	...	...	...	...
		KÁST	Do.	3	...	1	...	2	1	...	...	...	1	...	...	...	...	...	...	...	...	...	...
		KÁYET	Do.	37	3	11	...	23	31	...	...	...	31	1	...	1	...	...	...	...	...	...	...
		PARBHU	Do.	29	2	13	5	14	19	...	2	...	17	...	...	...	...	...	...	...	...	...	...
		PURBHAIYE	Do.	10	...	...	...	10	...	...	...	...	...	...	...	...	...	...	...	...	...	...	...
			Total Group 9	*82*	*5*	*27*	*5*	*50*	*52*	...	*2*	...	*50*	*1*	...	*1*	...	...	...	...	...	...	...
	10.—ASTROLOGERS	GÁRPAGÁRI	Hindu	107	4	9	...	94	108	...	...	...	108	...	...	...	...	...	...	...	...	...	...
		JOSHI	Do.	138	...	4	...	134	87	...	...	...	87	...	...	...	...	...	...	...	...	...	...
		Do.	Jain	...	...	...	...	...	...	...	...	...	...	...	...	...	...	...	...	...	...	...	...
		SARODE	Hindu	9	...	...	...	9	13	...	...	...	13	...	...	...	...	...	...	...	...	...	...
			Total Group 10	*254*	*4*	*13*	...	*237*	*208*	...	...	...	*208*	...	...	...	...	...	...	...	...	...	...
	11.—MUSICIANS	DEWALWÁR	Hindu	...	...	...	...	...	...	...	...	...	...	...	...	...	...	...	...	...	...	...	...
		GONDHALI	Do.	177	1	4	...	172	197	...	...	...	197	...	...	...	...	...	...	...	...	...	...
		MIRÁSI	Do.	...	...	...	...	...	...	...	...	...	...	...	...	...	...	...	...	...	...	...	...
			Total Group 11	*177*	*1*	*4*	...	*172*	*197*	...	...	...	*197*	...	...	...	...	...	...	...	...	...	...

TABLE D.—Castes by Education—*contd.*

Class.	Group.	Caste.	Religion.	Total Strength: Males: Total Males.	Total Strength: Males: Pupils.	Total Strength: Males: Literate: Total Literate.	Total Strength: Males: Literate: Knowing English.	Total Strength: Males: Illiterate.	Total Strength: Females: Total Females.	Total Strength: Females: Pupils.	Total Strength: Females: Literate: Total Literate.	Total Strength: Females: Literate: Knowing English.	Total Strength: Females: Illiterate.	Territorial Distribution, District Amraoti: Males: Total.	Males: Pupils.	Males: Literate: Total Literate.	Males: Literate: Knowing English.	Males: Illiterate.	Females: Total.	Females: Pupils.	Females: Literate: Total Literate.	Females: Literate: Knowing English.	Females: Illiterate.
1	2	3	4	5	6	7	8	9	10	11	12	13	14	15	16	17	18	19	20	21	22	23	24
B.—PROFESSIONAL—*contd.*	12.—Dancers and Singers	Dhádi	Musalman	3	...	...	...	3	2	...	...	...	2	3	...	...	...	3	2	...	...	...	2
		Kalwant	Hindu	28	4	2	...	22	66	1	2	...	63	1	...	...	...	1	2	...	...	...	2
		Wághe	Do.	23	1	2	...	20	24	...	...	...	24	3	...	1	...	2	5	...	...	...	5
			Total Group 12	*54*	*6*	*4*	...	*45*	*92*	*1*	*2*	...	*89*	*7*	...	*1*	...	*6*	*9*	...	...	...	*9*
	12A.—Minor Professions	Chitári	Hindu	38	...	1	...	37	38	...	...	...	38	15	...	1	...	14	15	...	...	...	15
	13.—Actors and Mimes	Bahurupi (Rárang)	Do.	78	...	1	...	77	79	...	...	...	79	27	...	...	...	27	24	...	...	...	24
		Do.	Musalman	2	...	...	...	2	4	...	...	...	4	...	...	...	...	...	...	...	...	...	...
		Bhánd	Do.	...	...	...	...	...	2	...	...	...	2	...	...	...	...	...	2	...	...	...	2
			Total Group 13	*80*	...	*1*	...	*79*	*85*	...	...	...	*85*	*27*	...	...	...	*27*	*26*	...	...	...	*26*
C.—COMMERCIAL.	14.—Traders	Bháttiá	Hindu	75	7	33	*1*	35	29	...	...	...	29	16	2	13	...	1	4	...	...	...	4
		Do.	Jain	27	2	18	...	7	28	...	...	...	28	4	...	3	...	1	3	...	...	...	3
		Bohari	Musalman	335	46	186	*4*	103	144	5	17	...	122	143	31	69	*1*	43	71	2	13	...	56
		Kachhi	Do.	154	4	94	*1*	56	21	...	...	...	21	66	4	40		22	11	...	...	...	11
		Khoja	Do.	13	...	9	...	4	14	...	...	...	14	...	...	...	...	...	...	...	...	...	...
		Komti	Hindu	1,362	88	387	*1*	887	1,388	...	2	...	1,386	60	1	17	*1*	42	66	...	...	...	66
		Lád	Do.	717	91	328	*10*	298	654	2	3	...	649	105	9	52	*2*	44	105	2	...	...	103
		Do.	Jain	733	93	272	*1*	368	721	4	...	...	717	85	6	44		35	80	...	...	...	80
		Mantri	Hindu	1	...	...	...	1	...	...	...	...	...	...	...	...	...	...	...	...	...	...	...
		Náidu	Do.	26	5	17	*11*	4	26	...	7	...	19	16	3	11	*5*	2	15	...	4	...	11
		Sárlan	Do.	2	...	...	...	2	...	...	...	...	...	...	...	...	...	...	...	...	...	...	...
		Shelki	Do.	...	...	...	...	...	1	...	...	...	1	...	...	...	...	...	...	...	...	...	...
		Wáni (Baniá and Márwádi)	Do.	27,456	2,440	10,725	*46*	14,291	22,814	43	51	...	22,720	5,881	565	2,558	*8*	2,758	4,778	6	9	...	4,763
		Do.	Jain	7,172	744	2,994	*13*	3,434	6,088	15	23	...	6,050	2,593	241	994	..	1,358	2,302	3	10	...	2,289
		Do.	Sikh	3	...	1	...	2	...	...	...	...	...	...	...	...	...	...	...	...	...	...	...
			Total Group 14	*38,076*	*3,520*	*15,064*	*88*	*19,492*	*31,928*	*69*	*103*	...	*31,756*	*8,969*	*862*	*3,801*	*17*	*4,306*	*7,435*	*13*	*36*	...	*7,386*
	15.—Pedlars	Gázulábalijá	Hindu	1	...	1	*1*	...	1	...	...	...	1	...	...	...	...	...	...	...	...	...	...
		Manihár	Musalman	9	...	...	...	9	6	...	...	...	6	...	...	...	...	...	...	...	...	...	...
		Memon	Do.	7	...	6	...	1	...	...	...	...	...	...	...	...	...	...	...	...	...	...	...
		Perki	Hindu	761	9	10	...	742	738	...	...	...	738	6	...	...	...	6	9	...	...	...	9
			Total Group 15	*778*	*9*	*17*	*1*	*752*	*746*	...	...	...	*746*	*6*	...	...	...	*6*	*9*	...	...	...	*9*

Table D.—[Castes by Education].

Class.	Group.	Caste.	Religion.	Akola Males Total.	Akola Males Pupils.	Akola Males Literate Total Literate.	Akola Males Literate Knowing English.	Akola Males Illiterate.	Akola Females Total.	Akola Females Pupils.	Akola Females Literate Total Literate.	Akola Females Literate Knowing English.	Akola Females Illiterate.	Ellichpur Males Total.	Ellichpur Males Pupils.	Ellichpur Males Literate Total Literate.	Ellichpur Males Literate Knowing English.	Ellichpur Males Illiterate.	Ellichpur Females Total.	Ellichpur Females Pupils.	Ellichpur Females Literate Total Literate.	Ellichpur Females Literate Knowing English.	Ellichpur Females Illiterate.
25	26	27	28	29	30	31	32	33	34	35	36	37	38	39	40	41	42	43	44	45	46	47	48
B.—PROFESSIONAL—*contd.*	12.—Dancers and Singers	Dhâdi	Musalman	...	...	...	...	...	...	...	...	...	...	...	...	...	...	...	...	...		...	...
		Kalwant	Hindu	...	...	...	...	...	...	...	...	...	...	...	...	...	...	...	...	...	...	...	...
		Wághe	Do.	1	...	...	...	1	2	...	...	...	2	2	...	...	...	2	3	...	...	...	3
			Total Group 12	*1*	...	...	...	*1*	*2*	...	...	...	*2*	*2*	...	...	...	*2*	*3*	...	...	...	*3*
	12A.—Minor Professions	Chitári	Hindu	1	...	...	...	1	...	...	...	...	...	10	...	...	...	10	11	...	...	...	11
	13.—Actors and Mimes	Bahurupi (Rárang)	Do.	3	...	...	...	3	2	...	...	...	2	1	...	...	...	1	1	...	...	...	1
		Do.	Musalman	...	...	...	...	...	...	...	...	...	...	...	...	...	...	...	...	...	...	...	...
		Bhánd	Do.	...	...	...	...	...	...	...	...	...	...	...	...	...	...	...	...	...	...	...	...
			Total Group 13	*3*	...	...	...	*3*	*2*	...	...	...	*2*	*1*	...	...	...	*1*	*1*	...	...	...	*1*
C.—COMMERCIAL	14.—Traders	Bháttiá	Hindu	49	5	15	*1*	29	20	...	...	...	20	...	...	...	...	...	...	...	...	...	...
		Do.	Jain	23	2	15	...	6	25	...	...	...	25	...	...	...	...	...	...	...	...	...	...
		Bohari	Musalman	114	10	66	*2*	38	57	2	3	...	52	46	5	32	*1*	9	9	1	1	...	7
		Kachhi	Do.	21	...	18	*1*	3	5	...	...	...	5	...	...	...	...	...	...	...	...	...	...
		Khoja	Do.	...	...	...	...	...	...	...	...	...	...	...	...	...	...	...	...	...	...	...	...
		Komti	Hindu	52	...	8	...	44	63	...	1	...	62	8	...	1	...	7	13	...	...	...	13
		Lâd	Do.	68	10	21	*1*	37	50	...	...	...	50	4	...	3	...	1	7	...	...	...	7
		Do.	Jain	47	6	14	...	27	52	4	...	...	48	74	13	40	...	21	83	...	...	...	83
		Mantri	Hindu	...	...	...	...	...	...	...	...	...	...	...	...	...	...	...	...	...	...	...	...
		Náidu	Do.	2	...	1	*1*	1	1	...	1	...	...	8	2	5	5	1	9	...	2	...	7
		Sárlan	Do.	...	...	...	...	...	...	...	...	...	...	...	...	...	...	...	...	...	...	...	...
		Shelki	Do.	...	...	...	...	...	...	...	...	...	...	...	...	...	...	...	...	...	...	...	...
		Wáni (Baniá and Márwádi	Do.	6,571	621	3,075	*11*	2,875	5,047	26	22	...	4,999	2,184	201	1,004	*16*	979	1,775	2	5	...	1,768
		Do.	Jain	1,256	118	636	*8*	502	1,027	10	2	...	1,015	533	59	167	...	307	466	1	2	...	463
		Do.	Sikh	3	...	1	...	2	...	...	...	...	...	...	...	...	...	...	...	...	...	...	...
			Total Group 14	*8,206*	*772*	*3,870*	*25*	*3,564*	*6,347*	*42*	*29*	...	*6,276*	*2,857*	*280*	*1,252*	*22*	*1,325*	*2,382*	*4*	*10*	...	*2,348*
	15.—Pedlars	Gázulábalijá	Hindu	...	...	...	...	...	...	...	...	...	...	1	...	1	*1*	...	1	...	...	...	1
		Manihár	Musalman	3	...	...	...	3	1	...	...	...	1	...	...	...	...	...	...	...	...	...	...
		Memon	Do.	3	...	3	...	...	...	...	...	...	...	1	...	...	...	1	...	...	...	...	...
		Perki	Hindu	...	...	...	...	...	...	...	...	...	...	...	...	...	...	...	...	...	...	...	...
			Total Group 15	*6*	...	*3*	...	*3*	*1*	...	...	...	*1*	*2*	...	*1*	*1*	*1*	*1*	...	...	...	*1*

TABLE D.—Castes by Education—*contd.*

Table D.—[Castes by Education].

Class.	Group.	Caste.	Religion.	District Buldana. Males. Total.	Males. Pupils.	Males. Literate. Total Literate.	Males. Literate. Knowing English.	Males. Illiterate.	Females. Total.	Females. Pupils.	Females. Literate. Total Literate.	Females. Literate. Knowing English.	Females. Illiterate.	District Wun. Males. Total.	Males. Pupils.	Males. Literate. Total Literate.	Males. Literate. Knowing English.	Males. Illiterate.	Females. Total.	Females. Pupils.	Females. Literate. Total Literate.	Females. Literate. Knowing English.	Females. Illiterate.
49	50	51	52	53	54	55	56	57	58	59	60	61	62	63	64	65	66	67	68	69	70	71	72
B.—PROFESSIONAL—*contd.*	12.—DANCERS AND SINGERS	DHÁDI	Musalman	...	...	...	...	...	...	...	...	...	...	...	...	...	...	...	...	...	...	...	...
		KALWANT	Hindu	...	...	...	...	...	3	...	...	...	3	15	2	2	...	11	29	...	1	...	28
		WÁGHE	Do.	5	...	...	...	5	1	...	...	...	1	1	...	...	...	1	...	...	...	...	...
			Total Group 12	*5*	...	...	...	*5*	*4*	...	...	...	*4*	*16*	*2*	*2*	...	*12*	*29*	...	*1*	...	*28*
	12A.—MINOR PROFESSIONS	CHITÁRI	Hindu	...	...	...	...	...	...	...	...	...	...	12	...	...	...	12	12	...	...	...	12
	13.—ACTORS AND MIMES	BAHURUPI (RÁERANG)	Do.	9	...	...	...	9	9	...	...	...	9	25	...	1	...	24	28	...	...	...	28
		Do.	Musalman	2	...	...	...	2	4	...	...	...	4	...	...	...	...	...	...	...	...	...	...
		BHÁND	Do.	...	...	...	...	...	...	...	...	...	...	...	...	...	...	...	...	...	...	...	...
			Total Group 13	*11*	...	...	...	*11*	*13*	...	...	...	*13*	*25*	...	*1*	...	*24*	*28*	...	...	...	*28*
C.—COMMERCIAL.	14.—TRADERS	BHÁTTIÁ	Hindu	2	...	1	...	1	1	...	...	...	1	5	...	1	...	4	4	...	...	...	4
		Do.	Jain	...	...	...	...	...	...	...	...	...	...	...	...	...	...	...	...	...	...	...	...
		BOHARI	Musalman	8	...	...	...	8	5	...	...	...	5	11	...	9	...	2	...	...	...	...	...
		KACHHI	Do.	21	...	10	...	11	...	...	...	...	...	21	...	12	...	9	4	...	...	...	4
		KHOJÁ	Do.	...	...	...	...	...	...	...	...	...	...	13	...	9	...	4	14	...	...	...	14
		KOMTI	Hindu	19	1	4	...	14	26	...	...	...	26	1,018	79	283	...	656	1,017	...	1	...	1,016
		LÂD	Do.	383	68	207	6	108	391	...	1	...	390	12	...	7	1	5	11	...	2	...	9
		Do.	Jain	63	10	23	...	30	83	...	...	...	83	3	...	2	...	1	...	...	...	...	...
		MANTRI	Hindu	...	...	...	...	...	...	...	...	...	...	...	...	...	...	...	...	...	...	...	...
		NÁIDU	Do.	...	...	...	...	...	...	...	...	...	...	...	...	...	...	...	...	...	...	...	...
		SÁRLAN	Do.	...	...	...	...	...	...	...	...	...	...	...	...	...	...	...	...	...	...	...	...
		SHELKI	Do.	...	...	...	...	...	1	...	...	...	1	...	...	...	...	...	...	...	...	...	...
		WÁNI (BANIÁ AND MÁRWÁDI)	Do.	4,328	394	1,650	3	2,284	3,718	7	7	...	3,704	3,174	291	875	5	2,008	2,919	1	2	...	2,916
		Do.	Jain	1,240	164	608	2	468	1,001	1	2	...	998	796	71	341	3	384	643	...	3	...	640
		Do.	Sikh	...	...	...	...	...	...	...	...	...	...	...	...	...	...	...	...	...	...	...	...
			Total Group 14	*6,064*	*637*	*2,508*	*11*	*2,924*	*5,226*	*8*	*10*	...	*5,208*	*5,053*	*441*	*1,539*	*9*	*3,073*	*4,612*	*1*	*8*	...	*4,608*
	15.—PEDLARS	GÁZULÁBALIJÁ	Hindu	...	...	...	...	...	...	...	...	...	...	...	...	...	...	...	...	...	...	...	...
		MANIHÁR	Musalman	6	...	...	...	6	5	...	...	...	5	...	...	...	...	...	...	...	...	...	...
		MEMON	Do.	3	...	3	...	...	...	...	...	...	...	...	...	...	...	...	...	...	...	...	...
		PERKI	Hindu	...	...	...	...	...	...	...	...	...	...	755	9	10	...	736	729	...	...	...	729
			Total Group 15	*9*	...	*3*	...	*6*	*5*	...	...	...	*5*	*755*	*9*	*10*	...	*736*	*729*	...	...	...	*729*

Table D.—[Castes by Education].

Caste and Religion.				Territorial Distribution.																			
				District Basim.										Railway Passengers.									
				Males.					Females.					Males.					Females.				
						Literate.					Literate.					Literate.					Literate.		
Class.	Group.	Caste.	Religion.	Total.	Pupils.	Total Literate.	Knowing English.	Illiterate.	Total.	Pupils.	Total Literate.	Knowing English.	Illiterate.	Total.	Pupils.	Total Literate.	Knowing English.	Illiterate.	Total.	Pupils.	Total Literate.	Knowing English.	Illiterate.
73	74	75	76	77	78	79	80	81	82	83	84	85	86	87	88	89	90	91	92	93	94	95	96
B.—PROFESSIONAL—*contd.*	12.—Dancers and Singers	Dhádi	Musalman	...	...	...	...	...	...	...	...	...	...	...	...	...	...	...	...	...	...	...	...
		Kalwant	Hindu	12	2	...	...	10	32	1	1	...	30	...	...	...	...	...	...	...	...	...	...
		Waghé	Do.	11	1	1	...	9	13	...	...	...	13	...	...	...	...	...	...	...	...	...	...
			Total Group 12	*23*	*8*	*1*	...	*19*	*45*	*1*	*1*	...	*43*	...	...	...	...	...	...	...	...	...	...
	12a.—Minor Professions	Chitári	Hindu	...	...	...	...	...	...	...	...	...	...	...	...	...	...	...	...	...	...	...	...
	13.—Actors and Mimes	Bahurupi (Rávrang)	Do.	13	...	...	...	13	15	...	...	...	15	...	...	...	...	...	...	...	...	...	...
		Do.	Musalman	...	...	...	...	...	...	...	...	...	...	...	...	...	...	...	...	...	...	...	...
		Bhánd	Do.	...	...	...	...	...	...	...	...	...	...	...	...	...	...	...	...	...	...	...	...
			Total Group 13	*13*	...	...	...	*13*	*15*	...	...	...	*15*	...	...	...	...	...	...	...	...	...	...
C.—COMMERCIAL.	14.—Traders	Bhátiá	Hindu	3	...	3	...	...	...	...	...	...	...	...	...	...	...	...	...	...	...	...	...
		Do.	Jain	...	...	...	...	...	...	...	...	...	...	...	...	...	...	...	...	...	...	...	...
		Bohari	Musalman	11	...	9	...	2	1	...	...	...	1	2	...	1	...	1	1	...	...	...	1
		Kachhi	Do.	25	...	14	...	11	1	...	...	...	1	...	...	...	...	...	...	...	...	...	...
		Khojá	Do.	...	...	...	...	...	...	...	...	...	...	...	...	...	...	...	...	...	...	...	...
		Komti	Hindu	201	7	72	...	122	198	...	...	...	198	4	...	2	...	2	5	...	...	...	5
		Lád	Do.	144	4	37	...	103	90	...	...	...	90	1	...	1	...	...	...	...	...	...	...
		Do.	Jain	461	58	149	*1*	254	423	...	...	...	423	...	...	...	...	...	...	...	...	...	...
		Mantri	Hindu	1	...	...	...	1	...	...	...	...	...	...	...	...	...	...	...	...	...	...	...
		Náidu	Do.	...	...	...	...	...	1	...	...	...	1	...	...	...	...	...	...	...	...	...	...
		Sárlan	Do.	2	...	...	...	2	...	...	...	...	...	...	...	...	...	...	...	...	...	...	...
		Shelki	Do.	...	...	...	...	...	...	...	...	...	...	...	...	...	...	...	...	...	...	...	...
		Wâni (Baniá and Márwádi)	Do.	5,298	368	1,552	*3*	3,378	4,573	1	6	...	4,566	20	...	11	...	9	4	...	...	...	4
		Do.	Jain	754	91	248	...	415	649	...	4	...	645	...	...	...	...	...	...	...	...	...	...
		Do.	Sikh	...	...	...	...	...	...	...	...	...	...	...	...	...	...	...	...	...	...	...	...
			Total Group 14	*6,800*	*528*	*2,084*	*4*	*4,288*	*5,936*	*1*	*10*	...	*5,926*	*27*	...	*15*	...	*12*	*10*	...	...	...	*10*
	15.—Pedlars	Gázulábalijá	Hindu	...	...	...	...	...	...	...	...	...	...	...	...	...	...	...	...	...	...	...	...
		Manihár	Musalman	...	...	...	...	...	...	...	...	...	...	...	...	...	...	...	...	...	...	...	...
		Memon	Do.	...	...	...	...	...	...	...	...	...	...	...	...	...	...	...	...	...	...	...	...
		Perki	Hindu	...	...	...	...	...	...	...	...	...	...	...	...	...	...	...	...	...	...	...	...
			Total Group 15	...	...	...	...	...	...	...	...	...	...	...	...	...	...	...	...	...	...	...	...

TABLE D.—Castes by Education—*contd.*

Class.	Group.	Caste.	Religion.	Total Strength. Males. Total Males.	Total Strength. Males. Pupils.	Total Strength. Males. Literate. Total Literate.	Total Strength. Males. Literate. Knowing English.	Total Strength. Males. Illiterate.	Total Strength. Females. Total Females.	Total Strength. Females. Pupils.	Total Strength. Females. Literate. Total Literate.	Total Strength. Females. Literate. Knowing English.	Total Strength. Females. Illiterate.	Territorial Distribution. District Amraoti. Males. Total.	District Amraoti. Males. Pupils.	District Amraoti. Males. Literate. Total Literate.	District Amraoti. Males. Literate. Knowing English.	District Amraoti. Males. Illiterate.	District Amraoti. Females. Total.	District Amraoti. Females. Pupils.	District Amraoti. Females. Literate. Total Literate.	District Amraoti. Females. Literate. Knowing English.	District Amraoti. Females. Illiterate.
1	2	3	4	5	6	7	8	9	10	11	12	13	14	15	16	17	18	19	20	21	22	23	24
C.—COMMERCIAL—*contd.*	16.—CARRIERS	BANJÁRI	Hindu	27,583	33	58	*1*	27,892	24,487	...	...	...	24,487	1,558	7	7	...	1,514	1,348	...	...	...	1,348
		Do.	Musalman	71	...	...	...	71	49	...	...	...	49	...	...	...	...	...	...	...	...	...	...
		Do.	Jain	17	...	...	...	17	12	...	...	...	12	...	...	...	...	...	...	...	...	...	...
		HAMÁL	Hindu	59	2	...	...	57	40	...	...	...	40	54	1	...	...	53	34	...	...	...	34
		LABHÁNI	Do.	13,365	2	28	*1*	13,335	12,160	...	...	...	12,160	772	1	5	...	766	729	...	...	...	729
		Do.	Musalman	29	...	...	...	29	27	...	...	...	27	...	...	...	...	...	...	...	...	...	...
		Do.	Jain	5	...	...	...	5	1	...	...	...	1	...	...	...	...	...	...	...	...	...	...
		WANJÁRI	Hindu	16,341	180	236	*1*	15,925	15,461	2	2	...	15,457	786	13	12	*1*	761	706	...	..	...	706
			Total Group 16	*57,870*	*217*	*322*	*3*	*57,331*	*52,237*	*2*	*2*	...	*52,233*	*3,170*	*22*	*24*	*1*	*3,124*	*2,817*	...	...	...	*2,817*
	17.—GOLDSMITHS	JOHARI	Hindu	87	7	7	...	73	74	...	...	...	74	36	1	1	...	34	38	...	...	...	38
		SONÁR	Do.	15,130	1,135	2,602	*25*	11,393	14,087	15	17	...	14,055	4,072	310	800	*11*	2,962	3,659	...	6	...	3,653
		Do.	Jain	1	...	1	...	...	1	...	...	...	1	1	...	1	...	...	1	...	...	...	1
		TARKIHÁR	Hindu	1	...	...	...	1	...	...	...	...	...	...	...	...	...	...	...	...	...	...	...
			Total Group 17	*15,219*	*1,142*	*2,610*	*25*	*11,467*	*14,162*	*15*	*17*	...	*14,130*	*4,109*	*311*	*802*	*11*	*2,996*	*3,698*	...	*6*	...	*3,692*
D.—ARTISAN AND VILLAGE MENIAL.	18.—BARBERS	MHÁLI (HAJJÁM, NHÁVI, WÁRIK)	Hindu	18,231	382	447	*5*	17,402	16,994	6	2	1	16,986	4,461	100	135	*1*	4,226	3,594	2	2	*1*	3,990
		Do.	Musalman	11	...	...	...	11	6	...	...	...	6	3	...	...	...	3	1	...	...	...	1
		Do.	Jain	3	...	...	...	3	...	...	...	...	...	1	...	...	...	1	...	...	...	...	...
			Total Group 18	*18,245*	*382*	*447*	*5*	*17,416*	*17,000*	*6*	*2*	*1*	*16,992*	*4,465*	*100*	*135*	*1*	*4,230*	*3,995*	*2*	*2*	*1*	*3,991*
	19.—BLACKSMITHS	DÁNGARE	Hindu	97	1	...	...	96	91	...	...	...	91	70	1	...	..	69	66	...	...	...	66
		GHISÁDI	Do.	368	...	1	...	367	340	...	...	...	340	2	...	...	...	2	3	...	...	...	3
		Do.	Musalman	6	...	...	...	6	5	...	...	...	5	...	...	...	...	...	...	...	...	...	...
		JIRÁYET	Hindu	160	11	16	...	133	152	...	...	...	152	19	...	...	...	19	20	...	...	...	20
		KATHILKÁR	Do.	10	...	1	...	9	10	...	...	...	10	...	...	...	...	...	2	...	...	...	2
		LOHÁR (KHÁTI)	Do.	8,351	156	290	*8*	7,905	7,538	4	5	...	7,529	2,193	46	86	*1*	2,061	1,978	2	...	...	1,976
		Do.	Animistic	7	...	...	...	7	11	...	...	...	11	7	...	...	...	7	11	...	...	...	11
		NÁLBAND	Hindu	6	...	...	...	6	7	...	...	...	7	6	...	...	...	6	7	...	...	...	7
		PANCHÁL (PANCHÁL LOHÁR)	Do.	968	11	43	...	914	908	...	...	...	908	189	6	12	...	171	156	...	...	...	156
		Do.	Musalman	5	...	...	...	5	4	...	...	...	4	1	...	...	...	1	...	...	...	...	...
			Total Group 19	*9,978*	*179*	*351*	*8*	*9,448*	*9,066*	*4*	*5*	...	*9,057*	*2,487*	*58*	*98*	*1*	*2,386*	*2,243*	*2*	...	...	*2,241*

Table D.—[Castes by Education].

Caste and Religion.				Territorial Distribution.																			
				District Akola.										District Ellichpur.									
				Males.					Females.					Males.					Females.				
						Literate.					Literate.					Literate.					Literate.		
Class.	Group.	Caste.	Religion.	Total.	Pupils.	Total Literate.	Knowing English.	Illiterate.	Total.	Pupils.	Total Literate.	Knowing English.	Illiterate.	Total.	Pupils.	Total Literate.	Knowing English.	Illiterate.	Total.	Pupils.	Total Literate.	Knowing English.	Illiterate.
25	26	27	28	29	30	31	32	33	34	35	36	37	38	39	40	41	42	43	44	45	46	47	48
C.—COMMERCIAL—*contd.*	16.—CARRIERS	BANJÁRI	Hindu	814	9	13	1	792	561	...	...	...	561	371	3	2	...	366	230	...	...	...	230
		Do.	Musalman	...	...	...	...	...	...	...	...	...	...	...	...	...	...	...	...	...	...	...	...
		Do.	Jain	...	...	...	...	...	...	...	...	...	...	...	...	...	...	...	...	...	...	...	...
		HAMÁL	Hindu	...	...	...	...	...	...	...	...	...	...	5	1	...	...	4	6	...	...	...	6
		LABHANI	Do.	909	...	3	1	906	679	...	...	...	679	14	...	4	...	10	2	...	...	...	2
		Do.	Musalman	...	...	...	...	...	...	...	...	...	...	3	...	...	...	3	3	...	...	...	3
		Do.	Jain	...	...	...	...	...	...	...	...	...	...	...	...	...	...	...	...	...	...	...	...
		WANJÁRI	Hindu	1,911	66	78	...	1,767	1,772	2	1	...	1,769	165	4	6	...	155	157	...	...	...	157
			Total Group 16	*3,634*	*75*	*94*	*2*	*3,465*	*3,012*	*2*	*1*	...	*3,009*	*558*	*8*	*12*	...	*538*	*398*	...	...	...	*398*
	17.—GOLDSMITHS	JOHÁRI	Hindu	34	6	4	...	24	34	...	...	...	34	2	...	1	...	1	1	...	...	...	1
		SONÁR	Do.	3,414	284	586	4	2,544	3,178	8	4	...	3,166	1,816	140	267	2	1,409	1,662	2	1	...	1,659
		Do.	Jain	...	...	...	...	...	...	...	...	...	...	...	...	...	...	...	...	...	...	...	...
		TARKIHÁR	Hindu	1	...	...	...	1	...	...	...	...	...	...	...	...	...	...	...	...	...	...	...
			Total Group 17	*3,449*	*290*	*590*	*4*	*2,569*	*3,212*	*8*	*4*	...	*3,200*	*1,818*	*140*	*268*	*2*	*1,410*	*1,663*	*2*	*1*	...	*1,660*
D.—ARTISAN AND VILLAGE MENIAL.	18.—BARBERS	MHÁLI (HAJJÁM, NHÁVI, WÁRIK)	Hindu	4,070	98	110	...	3,862	3,778	1	...	...	3,777	1,875	48	53	2	1,774	1,769	2	...	...	1,767
		Do.	Musalman	...	...	...	...	...	...	...	...	...	...	...	...	...	...	...	...	...	...	...	...
		Do.	Jain	...	...	...	...	...	...	...	...	...	...	...	...	...	...	...	...	...	...	...	...
			Total Group 18	*4,070*	*98*	*110*	...	*3,862*	*3,778*	*1*	...	...	*3,777*	*1,875*	*48*	*53*	*2*	*1,774*	*1,769*	*2*	...	...	*1,767*
	19.—BLACKSMITHS	DÁNGARE	Hindu	...	...	...	...	...	...	...	...	...	...	...	...	...	...	...	...	...	...	...	...
		GHISÁDI	Do.	4	...	...	...	4	...	...	...	...	...	...	...	...	...	...	...	...	...	...	...
		Do.	Musalman	...	...	...	...	...	...	...	...	...	...	...	...	...	...	...	...	...	...	...	...
		JIRÁYET	Hindu	72	4	7	...	61	59	...	...	...	59	3	...	1	...	2	7	...	...	...	7
		KATHILKAR	Do.	1	...	...	...	1	2	...	...	...	2	5	...	1	...	4	4	...	...	...	4
		LOHÁR (KHÁTI)	Do.	1,232	40	64	1	1,128	1,072	...	2	...	1,070	870	8	34	4	828	668	1	2	...	665
		Do.	Animistic	...	...	...	...	...	...	...	...	...	...	...	...	...	...	...	...	...	...	...	...
		NÁLBAND	Hindu	...	...	...	...	...	...	...	...	...	...	...	...	...	...	...	...	...	...	...	...
		PANCHÁL (PANCHÁL LOHÁR)	Do.	119	...	2	...	117	100	...	...	...	100	75	...	5	...	70	87	...	...	...	87
		Do.	Musalman	...	...	...	...	...	...	...	...	...	...	...	...	...	...	...	...	...	...	...	...
			Total Group 19	*1,428*	*44*	*73*	*1*	*1,311*	*1,233*	...	*2*	...	*1,231*	*953*	*8*	*41*	*4*	*804*	*766*	*1*	*2*	...	*763*

TABLE D.—Castes by Education—*contd.*

Caste and Religion.				Territorial Distribution.																			
				District Buldana.										District Wun.									
				Males.					Females.					Males.					Females.				
						Literate.					Literate.					Literate.					Literate.		
Class.	Group.	Caste.	Religion.	Total.	Pupils.	Total Literate.	Knowing English.	Illiterate.	Total.	Pupils.	Total Literate.	Knowing English.	Illiterate.	Total.	Pupils.	Total Literate.	Knowing English.	Illiterate.	Total.	Pupils.	Total Literate.	Knowing English.	Illiterate.
49	50	51	52	53	54	55	56	57	58	59	60	61	62	63	64	65	66	67	68	69	70	71	72
C.—COMMERCIAL—*contd.*	16.—Carriers	Banjári	Hindu	2,095	1	9	...	2,085	1,916	...	...	...	1,916	13,005	9	18	...	12,978	11,727	...	...	...	11,727
		Do.	Musalman	...	...	...	...	...	...	...	...	...	...	58	...	...	...	58	38	...	...	...	38
		Do.	Jain	...	...	...	...	...	...	...	...	...	...	17	...	...	...	17	12	...	...	...	12
		Hamál	Hindu	...	...	...	...	...	...	...	...	...	...	...	...	...	...	...	...	...	...	...	...
		Labháni	Do.	2,483	1	1	...	2,481	2,212	...	...	...	2,212	2,828	...	14	...	2,814	2,628	...	...	...	2,628
		Do.	Musalman	7	...	...	...	7	4	...	...	...	4	5	...	...	...	5	8	...	...	...	8
		Do.	Jain	...	...	...	...	...	...	...	...	...	...	5	...	...	...	5	1	...	...	...	1
		Wanjári	Hindu	9,137	41	61	...	9,035	8,742	...	1	...	8,741	752	2	12	...	738	654	...	...	...	654
			Total Group 16.	*13,722*	*43*	*71*	...	*13,608*	*12,874*	...	*1*	...	*12,873*	*16,670*	*11*	*44*	...	*16,616*	*15,068*	...	...	...	*15,068*
	17.—Goldsmiths	Johari	Hindu	1	...	...	...	1	1	...	...	...	1	11	...	1	...	10	...	...	...	...	...
		Sonár	Do.	2,502	171	382	3	1,949	2,464	1	2	...	2,461	1,774	136	291	2	1,347	1,634	4	4	...	1,626
		Do.	Jain	...	...	...	...	...	...	...	...	...	...	...	...	...	...	...	...	...	...	...	...
		Tarkihár	Hindu	...	...	...	...	...	...	...	...	...	...	...	...	...	...	...	...	...	...	...	...
			Total Group 17.	*2,508*	*171*	*382*	*3*	*1,950*	*2,465*	*1*	*2*	...	*2,462*	*1,785*	*136*	*292*	*2*	*1,357*	*1,634*	*4*	*4*	...	*1,626*
D.—ARTISAN AND VILLAGE MENIAL.	18.—Barbers	Mháli (Hajjám, Nhávi, Wárik)	Hindu	2,839	53	56	1	2,730	2,682	1	...	...	2,681	2,820	55	46	...	2,719	2,669	...	...	...	2,669
		Do.	Musalman	4	...	...	...	4	2	...	...	...	2	3	...	...	...	3	3	...	...	...	3
		Do.	Jain	2	...	...	...	2	...	...	...	...	...	...	...	...	...	...	...	...	...	...	...
			Total Group 18.	*2,845*	*53*	*56*	*1*	*2,736*	*2,684*	*1*	...	...	*2,683*	*2,823*	*55*	*46*	...	*2,722*	*2,672*	...	...	...	*2,672*
	19.—Blacksmiths	Dângare	Hindu	2	...	...	...	2	2	...	...	...	2	25	...	...	...	25	23	...	...	...	23
		Ghisâdi	Do.	190	...	1	...	189	152	...	...	...	152	30	...	...	...	30	33	...	...	...	33
		Do.	Musalman	6	...	...	...	6	5	...	...	...	5	...	...	...	...	...	...	...	...	...	...
		Jiráyet	Hindu	54	7	8	...	39	54	...	...	...	54	...	...	...	...	...	...	...	...	...	...
		Kathilkar	Do.	4	...	...	...	4	2	...	...	...	2	...	...	...	...	...	...	...	...	...	...
		Lohár (Kháti)	Do.	961	23	46	2	892	908	...	1	...	907	2,272	19	32	...	2,221	2,207	...	...	...	2,207
		Do.	Animistic	...	...	...	...	...	...	...	...	...	...	...	...	...	...	...	...	...	...	...	...
		Nálband	Hindu	...	...	...	...	...	...	...	...	...	...	...	...	...	...	...	...	...	...	...	...
		Panchál (Panchál lohár)	Do.	146	5	2	...	139	153	...	...	...	153	359	...	21	...	338	344	...	...	...	344
		Do.	Musalman	...	...	...	...	...	...	...	...	...	...	4	...	...	...	4	4	...	...	...	4
			Total Group 19.	*1,363*	*35*	*57*	*2*	*1,271*	*1,276*	...	*1*	...	*1,275*	*2,690*	*19*	*53*	...	*2,618*	*2,611*	...	...	...	*2,611*

Class.	Group.	Caste.	Religion.	District Basim. Males. Total.	Males. Pupils.	Males. Literate. Total Literate.	Males. Literate. Knowing English.	Males. Illiterate.	Females. Total.	Females. Pupils.	Females. Literate. Total Literate.	Females. Literate. Knowing English.	Females. Illiterate.	Railway Passengers. Males. Total.	Males. Pupils.	Males. Literate. Total Literate.	Males. Literate. Knowing English.	Males. Illiterate.	Females. Total.	Females. Pupils.	Females. Literate. Total Literate.	Females. Literate. Knowing English.	Females. Illiterate.
73	74	75	76	77	78	79	80	81	82	83	84	85	86	87	88	89	90	91	92	93	94	95	96
C.—COMMERCIAL—*contd.*	16.—CARRIERS	BANJÁRI	Hindu	10,140	4	9	...	10,127	8,705	...	...	...	8,705	...	...	...	...	...	...	...	...	...	...
		Do.	Musalman	13	...	...	...	13	11	...	...	...	11	...	...	...	...	...	...	...	...	...	...
		Do.	Jain	...	...	...	...	...	...	...	...	...	...	...	...	...	...	...	...	...	...	...	...
		HAMÁL	Hindu	...	...	...	...	...	...	...	...	...	...	...	...	...	...	...	...	...	...	...	...
		LABHÁNI	Do.	6,359	...	1	...	6,358	5,910	...	...	...	5,910	...	...	...	...	...	...	...	...	...	...
		Do.	Musalman	14	...	...	...	14	12	...	...	...	12	...	...	...	...	...	...	...	...	...	...
		Do.	Jain	...	...	...	...	...	...	...	...	...	...	...	...	...	...	...	...	...	...	...	...
		WANJÁRI	Hindu	3,586	53	67	...	3,466	3,429	...	...	...	3,429	4	1	...	...	3	1	...	...	...	1
			Total Group 16	*20,112*	*57*	*77*	...	*19,978*	*18,087*	...	...	...	*18,087*	*4*	*1*	...	...	*8*	*1*	...	...	...	*1*
D.—ARTISAN AND VILLAGE MENIAL.	17.—GOLDSMITHS	JOHORI	Hindu	3	...	...	...	3	...	...	...	...	...	...	...	...	...	...	...	...	...	...	...
		SONÁR	Do.	1,552	94	276	3	1,182	1,490	...	...	...	1,490	...	...	...	...	...	...	...	...	...	...
		Do.	Jain	...	...	...	...	...	...	...	...	...	...	...	...	...	...	...	...	...	...	...	...
		TARKIHÁR	Hindu	...	...	...	...	...	...	...	...	...	...	...	...	...	...	...	...	...	...	...	...
			Total Group 17	*1,555*	*94*	*276*	*3*	*1,185*	*1,490*	...	...	...	*1,490*	...	...	...	...	...	...	...	...	...	...
	18.—BARBERS	MHÁLI (HAJJÁM, NHÁVI, WÁRIK)	Hindu	2,165	28	47	1	2,090	2,102	...	...	...	2,102	1	...	...	...	1	...	...	...	...	...
		Do.	Musalman	1	...	...	...	1	...	...	...	...	...	...	...	...	...	...	...	...	...	...	...
		Do.	Jain	...	...	...	...	...	...	...	...	...	...	...	...	...	...	...	...	...	...	...	...
			Total Group 18	*2,166*	*28*	*47*	*1*	*2,091*	*2,102*	...	...	...	*2,102*	*1*	...	...	...	*1*	...	...	...	...	...
	19.—BLACKSMITHS	DÂNGARE	Hindu	...	...	...	...	...	...	...	...	...	...	...	...	...	...	...	...	...	...	...	...
		GHISÂDI	Do.	142	...	...	...	142	152	...	...	...	152	...	...	...	...	...	...	...	...	...	...
		Do.	Musalman	...	...	...	...	...	...	...	...	...	...	...	...	...	...	...	...	...	...	...	...
		JIRÁYET	Hindu	12	...	...	...	12	12	...	...	...	12	...	...	...	...	...	...	...	...	...	...
		KATHIL KAR	Do.	...	...	...	...	...	...	...	...	...	...	...	...	...	...	...	...	...	...	...	...
		LOHÁR (KHÁTI)	Do.	821	20	27	...	774	705	1	...	...	704	2	...	1	...	1	...	...	...	...	...
		Do.	Animistic	...	...	...	...	...	...	...	...	...	...	...	...	...	...	...	...	...	...	...	...
		NÁLBAND	Hindu	...	...	...	...	...	...	...	...	...	...	...	...	...	...	...	...	...	...	...	...
		PANCHÁL (PANCHÁL LOHÁR)	Do.	76	...	1	...	75	68	...	...	...	68	4	...	...	...	4	...	...	...	...	...
		Do.	Musalman	...	...	...	...	...	...	...	...	...	...	...	...	...	...	...	...	...	...	...	...
			Total Group 19	*1,051*	*20*	*28*	...	*1,003*	*937*	*1*	...	...	*1936*	*6*	...	*1*	...	*6*	...	...	...	...	...

TABLE D.—Castes by Education—*contd.*

Class	Group.	Caste.	Religion.	Total Strength — Males — Total Males.	Males — Pupils.	Males — Literate — Total Literate.	Males — Literate — Knowing English.	Males — Illiterate.	Females — Total Females.	Females — Pupils.	Females — Literate — Total Literate.	Females — Literate — Knowing English.	Females — Illiterate.	Territorial Distribution — District Amraoti — Males — Total.	Males — Pupils.	Males — Literate — Total Literate.	Males — Literate — Knowing English.	Males — Illiterate.	Females — Total.	Females — Pupils.	Females — Literate — Total Literate.	Females — Literate — Knowing English.	Females — Illiterate.
1	2	3	4	5	6	7	8	9	10	11	12	13	14	15	16	17	18	19	20	21	22	23	24
	20.—Carpenters, Turners, and Masons	Gaondi (Ráj)	Hindu	335	14	16	...	305	304	1	...	...	303	80	6	5	...	69	68	1	...	...	67
		Gosangi	Do.	4	...	...	...	4	2	...	...	...	2	...	...	...	...	...	...	...	...	...	...
		Sutár (Badhai and Wádhi)	Do.	17,440	482	795	2	16,163	15,038	5	4	...	15,029	4,722	121	187	1	4,414	4,105	1	2	...	4,102
		Do.	Jain	13	...	...	...	13	...	...	...	...	...	...	...	...	...	...	...	...	...	...	...
			Total Group 20	*17,792*	*496*	*811*	*2*	*16,485*	*15,344*	*6*	*4*	...	*15,334*	*4,802*	*127*	*192*	*1*	*4,483*	*4,173*	*2*	*2*	...	*4,169*
	21.—Brass and Coppersmiths	Kásár	Hindu	3,929	356	854	11	2,719	3,629	10	8	...	3,611	960	73	242	1	645	884	6	3	...	875
		Do.	Jain	109	4	8	...	97	87	...	...	...	87	...	...	...	...	...	...	...	...	...	...
		Otári (Watankár)	Hindu	772	10	26	...	736	705	...	1	...	704	157	4	4	...	149	132	...	...	...	132
		Do.	Musalman	1	...	...	...	1	...	...	...	...	...	...	...	...	...	...	...	...	...	...	...
		Do.	Animistic	4	...	...	...	4	2	...	...	...	2	...	...	...	...	...	...	...	...	...	...
		Támbatkár	Hindu	304	19	34	...	251	286	...	1	...	285	55	4	2	...	49	47	...	...	...	47
			Total Group 21	*5,119*	*389*	*922*	*11*	*3,808*	*4,709*	*10*	*10*	...	*4,689*	*1,172*	*81*	*248*	*1*	*843*	*1,063*	*6*	*3*	...	*1,054*
	22.—Tailors	Simpi (Darzi)	Hindu	7,232	418	1,048	22	5,766	6,493	17	5	...	6,471	1,690	76	206	3	1,408	1,557	...	2	...	1,555
		Do.	Musalman	8	1	2	...	5	6	...	...	...	6	1	...	...	...	1	1	...	...	...	1
		Do.	Jain	1,294	123	365	1	806	1,332	1	...	...	1,331	75	4	11	...	60	74	...	...	...	74
			Total Group 22	*8,534*	*542*	*1,415*	*23*	*6,577*	*7,831*	*18*	*5*	...	*7,808*	*1,766*	*80*	*217*	*3*	*1,469*	*1,632*	...	*2*	...	*1,630*
	22A.—Gram-Parchers and Confectioners	Bharad-Bhunjá	Hindu	413	14	33	...	366	188	...	...	...	188	118	5	6	...	107	57	...	...	...	57
		Dálive	Do.	1	...	...	...	1	...	...	...	...	...	...	...	...	...	...	...	...	...	...	...
		Halwái	Do.	140	8	27	...	105	97	...	...	...	97	62	3	12	...	47	27	...	...	...	27
		Do.	Jain	...	...	...	...	...	1	...	...	...	1	...	...	...	...	...	...	...	...	...	...
			Total Group 22A	*554*	*22*	*60*	...	*472*	*286*	...	...	...	*286*	*180*	*8*	*18*	...	*154*	*84*	...	...	...	*84*
	22B.—Perfume and Drug Preparers and Sellers and Betel-leaf Dealers	Gandhi (Sugandhi)	Hindu	47	3	11	...	33	45	...	...	...	45	1	...	...	...	1	...	...	...	...	...
		Do.	Jain	5	...	1	...	4	4	...	...	...	4	4	...	1	...	3	4	...	...	...	4
		Támboli	Hindu	407	16	50	1	341	347	...	...	...	347	114	3	23	...	88	94	...	...	...	94
		Do.	Musalman	6	...	...	...	6	5	...	...	...	5	...	...	...	...	...	...	...	...	...	...
			Total Group 22B	*465*	*19*	*62*	*1*	*384*	*401*	...	...	...	*401*	*119*	*3*	*24*	...	*92*	*98*	...	...	...	*98*
	23.—Weavers, Calenderers and Dyers	Álkari	Hindu	2	...	...	...	2	5	...	...	...	5	1	...	...	...	1	3	...	...	...	3
		Átári	Do.	14	...	...	...	14	18	...	...	...	18	12	...	...	...	12	7	...	...	...	7
		Do.	Musalman	26	...	...	...	26	34	...	...	...	34	8	...	...	...	8	16	...	...	...	16
		Bunkar	Hindu	50	1	...	...	49	49	...	...	...	49	...	...	...	...	...	...	...	...	...	...
		Chenwár	Do.	108	...	...	...	108	95	...	...	...	95	...	...	...	...	...	...	...	...	...	...
		Chhipá	Do.	1	...	...	...	1	...	...	...	...	...	...	...	...	...	...	...	...	...	...	...
		Hálbi	Do.	1,492	80	66	...	1,406	1,349	...	...	...	1,349	258	1	2	...	255	215	...	...	...	215

Class.	Group.	Caste.	Religion.	District Akola. Males. Total.	Pupils.	Literate. Total Literate.	Knowing English.	Illiterate.	Females. Total.	Pupils.	Literate. Total Literate.	Knowing English.	Illiterate.	District Ellichpur. Males. Total.	Pupils.	Literate. Total Literate.	Knowing English.	Illiterate.	Females. Total.	Pupils.	Literate. Total Literate.	Knowing English.	Illiterate.
25	26	27	28	29	30	31	32	33	34	35	36	37	38	39	40	41	42	43	44	45	46	47	48
D.—ARTISAN AND VILLAGE MENIAL—contd.	20.—CARPENTERS, TURNERS, AND MASONS	GAONDI (RÁJ)	Hindu	32	2	1	...	29	18	...	...	...	18	16	...	1	...	15	16	...	...	...	16
		GOSANGI	Do.	4	...	...	...	4	2	...	...	...	2	...	...	...	...	...	...	...	...	...	...
		SUTÁR (BADHAI AND WÁDHI)	Do.	3,513	117	200	1	3,196	2,811	2	2	...	2,807	1,652	60	94	...	1,498	1,376	...	...	...	1,376
		Do.	Jain	...	...	...	...	...	...	...	...	...	...	...	...	...	...	...	...	...	...	...	...
			Total Group 20	*3,549*	*119*	*201*	*1*	*3,229*	*2,831*	*2*	*2*	...	*2,827*	*1,668*	*60*	*95*	...	*1,513*	*1,392*	...	...	...	*1,392*
	21.—BRASS AND COPPERSMITHS	KÁSÁR	Hindu	914	96	209	4	609	727	2	2	...	723	333	36	62	2	235	391	1	2	...	388
		Do.	Jain	2	...	...	...	2	3	...	...	...	3	36	1	4	...	31	2	...	...	...	2
		OTÁRI (WATANKÁR)	Hindu	249	3	12	...	234	214	...	1	...	213	95	1	1	...	93	95	...	...	...	95
		Do.	Musalman	...	...	...	...	...	...	...	...	...	...	...	...	...	...	...	...	...	...	...	...
		Do.	Animistic	...	...	...	...	...	...	...	...	...	...	...	...	...	...	...	...	...	...	...	...
		TÁMBATKÁR	Hindu	145	12	24	...	109	117	...	1	...	116	56	2	3	...	51	83	...	...	...	83
			Total Group 21	*1,310*	*111*	*245*	*4*	*954*	*1,061*	*2*	*4*	...	*1,055*	*520*	*40*	*70*	*2*	*410*	*571*	*1*	*2*	...	*568*
	22.—TAILORS	SIMPI (DARZI)	Hindu	2,474	200	462	13	1,812	2,164	15	1	...	2,148	759	47	90	1	622	702	...	...	...	702
		Do.	Musalman	...	...	...	...	...	...	...	...	...	...	...	...	...	...	...	...	...	...	...	...
		Do.	Jain	293	28	63	...	202	264	...	...	...	264	34	2	6	...	26	28	...	...	...	28
			Total Group 22	*2,767*	*228*	*525*	*13*	*2,014*	*2,428*	*15*	*1*	...	*2,412*	*793*	*49*	*96*	*1*	*648*	*730*	...	...	...	*730*
	22A.—GRAM-PARCHERS AND CONFECTIONERS.	BHARAD-BHUNJÁ	Hindu	95	2	12	...	81	20	...	...	...	20	111	5	10	...	96	74	...	...	...	74
		DÁLIYE	Do.	...	...	...	...	...	...	...	...	...	...	1	...	...	...	1	...	...	...	...	...
		HALWÁI	Do.	12	...	3	...	9	14	...	...	...	14	15	...	4	...	11	12	...	...	...	12
		Do.	Jain	...	...	...	...	...	1	...	...	...	1	...	...	...	...	...	...	...	...	...	...
			Total Group 22A	*107*	*2*	*15*	...	*90*	*35*	...	...	...	*35*	*127*	*5*	*14*	...	*108*	*86*	...	...	...	*86*
	22B.—PERFUME AND DRUG PREPARERS AND SELLERS AND BETEL-LEAF DEALERS.	GANDHI (SUGANDHI)	Hindu	25	3	6	...	16	19	...	...	...	19	16	...	5	...	11	23	...	...	...	23
		Do.	Jain	1	...	...	...	1	...	...	...	...	...	...	...	...	...	...	...	...	...	...	...
		TÁMBOLI	Hindu	22	2	1	...	19	19	...	...	...	19	87	11	23	1	53	62	...	...	...	62
		Do.	Musalman	...	...	...	...	...	...	...	...	...	...	...	...	...	...	...	...	...	...	...	...
			Total Group 22B	*48*	*5*	*7*	...	*36*	*38*	...	...	...	*38*	*103*	*11*	*28*	*1*	*64*	*85*	...	...	...	*85*
	23.—WEAVERS, CALENDERERS AND DYERS	ÁLKARI	Hindu	1	...	...	...	1	2	...	...	...	2	...	...	...	...	...	...	...	...	...	...
		ÁTÁRI	Do.	2	...	...	...	2	8	...	...	...	8	...	...	...	...	...	1	...	...	...	1
		Do.	Musalman	5	...	...	...	5	5	...	...	...	5	...	...	...	...	...	...	...	...	...	...
		BUNKAR	Hindu	3	...	...	...	3	1	...	...	...	1	34	...	...	...	34	37	...	...	...	37
		CHENWÁR	Do.	...	...	...	...	...	...	...	...	...	...	...	...	...	...	...	...	...	...	...	...
		CHHIPÁ	Do.	...	...	...	...	...	...	...	...	...	...	1	...	...	...	1	...	...	...	...	...
		HÁLBI	Do.	106	...	1	...	105	95	...	...	...	95	862	14	50	...	798	777	...	...	...	777

TABLE D.—Castes by Education—*contd.*

Class.	Group.	Caste.	Religion.	Buldana Males Total.	Buldana Males Pupils.	Buldana Males Literate Total Literate.	Buldana Males Literate Knowing English.	Buldana Males Illiterate.	Buldana Females Total.	Buldana Females Pupils.	Buldana Females Literate Total Literate.	Buldana Females Literate Knowing English.	Buldana Females Illiterate.	Wun Males Total.	Wun Males Pupils.	Wun Males Literate Total Literate.	Wun Males Literate Knowing English.	Wun Males Illiterate.	Wun Females Total.	Wun Females Pupils.	Wun Females Literate Total Literate.	Wun Females Literate Knowing English.	Wun Females Illiterate.
49	50	51	52	53	54	55	56	57	58	59	60	61	62	63	64	65	66	67	68	69	70	71	72
D.—ARTISAN AND VILLAGE MENIAL—*contd.*	20.—CARPENTERS, TURNERS, AND MASONS	GAONDI (RÁJ)	Hindu	65	5	8	...	52	60	...	...	...	60	9	1	...	...	8	7	...	...	...	7
		GOSANGI	Do.	...	...	...	...	...	...	...	...	...	...	...	...	...	...	...	...	...	...	...	...
		SUTÁR (BADHAI AND WÁDHI)	Do.	2,499	93	129	...	2,277	2,228	...	...	...	2,228	2,802	36	74	...	2,692	2,715	2	...	...	2,713
		Do.	Jain	12	...	...	...	12	...	...	...	...	...	1	...	...	...	1	...	...	...	...	...
			Total Group 20	*2,576*	*98*	*137*	...	*2,341*	*2,288*	...	...	...	*2,288*	*2,812*	*37*	*74*	...	*2,701*	*2,722*	*2*	...	...	*2,720*
	21.—BRASS AND COPPERSMITHS	KÁSÁR	Hindu	785	82	177	1	526	813	...	1	...	812	359	28	66	3	265	298	...	...	...	298
		Do.	Jain	8	...	...	...	8	7	...	...	...	7	...	...	...	...	...	...	...	...	...	...
		OTÁRI (WATANKÁR)	Hindu	73	1	1	...	71	72	...	...	...	72	76	1	...	...	75	63	...	...	...	63
		Do.	Musalman	...	...	...	...	...	...	...	...	...	...	...	...	...	...	...	...	...	...	...	...
		Do.	Animistic	...	...	...	...	...	...	...	...	...	...	4	...	...	...	4	2	...	...	...	2
		TÁMBATKÁR	Hindu	25	...	4	...	21	15	...	...	...	15	2	1	...	...	1	4	...	...	...	4
			Total Group 21	*891*	*83*	*182*	*1*	*626*	*907*	...	*1*	...	*906*	*441*	*30*	*66*	*3*	*345*	*367*	...	...	...	*367*
	22.—TAILORS	SIMPI (DARZI)	Hindu	851	52	169	3	630	823	2	1	...	820	1,133	35	62	1	1,036	1,024	...	1	...	1,023
		Do.	Musalman	7	1	2	...	4	5	...	...	...	5	...	...	...	...	...	...	...	...	...	...
		Do.	Jain	576	57	166	...	353	639	1	...	...	638	12	1	1	...	10	8	...	...	...	8
			Total Group 22	*1,434*	*110*	*337*	*3*	*987*	*1,467*	*3*	*1*	...	*1,463*	*1,145*	*36*	*63*	*1*	*1,046*	*1,032*	...	*1*	...	*1,031*
	22A.—GRAM-PARCHERS AND CONFECTIONERS	BHARAD-BHUNJÁ	Hindu	18	...	...	...	18	9	...	...	...	9	46	1	1	...	44	20	...	...	...	20
		DÁLIYE	Do.	...	...	...	...	...	...	...	...	...	...	...	...	...	...	...	...	...	...	...	...
		HALWÁI	Do.	36	4	6	...	26	37	...	...	...	37	11	1	1	...	9	6	...	...	...	6
		Do.	Jain	...	...	...	...	...	...	...	...	...	...	...	...	...	...	...	...	...	...	...	...
			Total Group 22A	*54*	*4*	*6*	...	*44*	*46*	...	...	...	*46*	*57*	*2*	*2*	...	*53*	*26*	...	...	...	*26*
	22B.—PERFUME AND DRUG PREPARERS AND SELLERS AND BETEL-LEAF DEALERS.	GANDHI (SUGANDHI)	Hindu	2	...	...	...	2	3	...	...	...	3	1	...	...	...	1	...	...	...	...	...
		Do.	Jain	...	...	...	...	...	...	...	...	...	...	...	...	...	...	...	...	...	...	...	...
		TÁMBOLI	Hindu	5	...	...	...	5	...	...	...	...	...	2	...	1	...	1	1	...	...	...	1
		Do.	Musalman	6	...	...	...	6	5	...	...	...	5	...	...	...	...	...	...	...	...	...	...
			Total Group 22B	*13*	...	...	...	*13*	*8*	...	...	...	*8*	*3*	...	*1*	...	*2*	*1*	...	...	...	*1*
	23.—WEAVERS, CALENDERERS AND DYERS.	ÁLKARI	Hindu	...	...	...	...	...	...	...	...	...	...	...	...	...	...	...	...	...	...	...	...
		ÁTÁRI	Do.	...	...	...	...	...	...	...	...	...	...	...	...	...	...	...	2	...	...	...	2
		Do.	Musalman	...	...	...	...	...	...	...	...	...	...	...	...	...	...	...	1	...	...	...	1
		BUNKAR	Hindu	13	1	...	...	12	11	...	...	...	11	...	...	...	...	...	...	...	...	...	...
		CHENWÁR	Do.	...	...	...	...	...	...	...	...	...	...	...	...	...	...	...	...	...	...	...	...
		CHHIPÁ	Do.	...	...	...	...	...	...	...	...	...	...	...	...	...	...	...	...	...	...	...	...
		HÁLBI	Do.	2	...	...	...	2	4	...	...	...	4	132	2	6	...	124	129	...	...	...	129

Table—D. [Castes by Education].

Class.	Group.	Caste.	Religion.	District Basin. Males. Total.	Males. Pupils.	Males. Literate. Total Literate.	Males. Literate. Knowing English.	Males. Illiterate.	Females. Total.	Females. Pupils.	Females. Literate. Total Literate.	Females. Literate. Knowing English.	Females. Illiterate.	Railway Passengers. Males. Total.	Males. Pupils.	Males. Literate. Total Literate.	Males. Literate. Knowing English.	Males. Illiterate.	Females. Total.	Females. Pupils.	Females. Literate. Total Literate.	Females. Literate. Knowing English.	Females. Illiterate.
73	74	75	76	77	78	79	80	81	82	83	84	85	86	87	88	89	90	91	92	93	94	95	96
D.—ARTISAN AND VILLAGE MENIAL—*contd.*	20.—CARPENTERS TURNERS, AND MASONS	GAONDI (RÁJ)	Hindu	132	...	...	...	132	135	...	...	...	135	1	...	1	...	...	...	...	...	...	...
		GOSANGI	Do.	...	...	...	...	...	...	...	...	...	...	...	...	...	...	...	...	...	...	...	...
		SUTÁR (BADHAI AND WÁDHI)	Do.	2,247	55	110	...	2,082	1,803	...	...	...	1,803	5	...	1	...	4	...	...	...	...	...
		Do.	Jain	...	...	...	...	...	...	...	...	...	...	...	...	...	...	...	...	...	...	...	...
			Total Group 20	*2,879*	*55*	*110*	...	*2,214*	*1,938*	...	...	...	*1,938*	*6*	...	*2*	...	*4*	...	...	...	...	...
	21.—BRASS AND COPPERSMITHS	KÁSÁR	Hindu	578	41	98	...	439	516	1	...	...	515	...	...	...	...	...	...	...	...	...	...
		Do.	Jain	63	3	4	...	56	75	...	...	...	75	...	...	...	...	...	...	...	...	...	...
		OTÁRI (WÁTANKÁR)	Hindu	122	...	8	...	114	129	...	...	...	129	...	...	...	...	...	...	...	...	...	...
		Do.	Musalman	1	...	...	...	1	...	...	...	...	...	...	...	...	...	...	...	...	...	...	...
		Do.	Animistic	...	...	...	...	...	...	...	...	...	...	...	...	...	...	...	...	...	...	...	...
		TÁMBATKÁR	Hindu	21	...	1	...	20	20	...	...	...	20	...	...	...	...	...	...	...	...	...	...
			Total Group 21	*786*	*44*	*111*	...	*630*	*740*	*1*	...	...	*739*	...	...	...	...	...	...	...	...	...	...
	22.—TAILORS	SIMPI (DARZI)	Hindu	323	8	59	*1*	256	223	...	...	...	223	2	...	...	...	2	...	...	...	...	...
		Do.	Musalman	...	...	...	...	...	...	...	...	...	...	...	...	...	...	...	...	...	...	...	...
		Do.	Jain	304	31	118	*1*	155	319	...	...	...	319	...	...	...	...	...	...	...	...	...	...
			Total Group 22	*627*	*39*	*177*	*2*	*411*	*542*	...	...	...	*542*	*2*	...	...	...	*2*	...	...	...	...	...
	22A.—GRAM-PARCHERS AND CONFECTIONERS.	BHARÁD-BHUNJÁ	Hindu	25	1	4	...	20	7	...	...	...	7	...	...	...	...	...	1	...	...	...	1
		DÁLIYE	Do.	...	...	...	...	...	...	...	...	...	...	...	...	...	...	...	...	...	...	...	...
		HALWÁI	Do.	4	...	1	...	3	1	...	...	...	1	...	...	...	...	...	...	...	...	...	...
		Do.	Jain	...	...	...	...	...	...	...	...	...	...	...	...	...	...	...	...	...	...	...	...
			Total Group 22A	*29*	*1*	*5*	...	*23*	*8*	...	...	...	*8*	...	...	...	...	...	*1*	...	...	...	*1*
	22B.—PERFUME AND DRUG PREPARERS AND SELLERS AND BETEL-LEAF DEALERS.	GANDHI (SUGANDHI)	Hindu	2	...	...	...	2	...	...	...	...	...	...	...	...	...	...	...	...	...	...	...
		Do.	Jain	...	...	...	...	...	...	...	...	...	...	...	...	...	...	...	...	...	...	...	...
		TÁMBOLI	Hindu	177	...	2	...	175	171	...	...	...	171	...	...	...	...	...	...	...	...	...	...
		Do.	Musalman	...	...	...	...	...	...	...	...	...	...	...	...	...	...	...	...	...	...	...	...
			Total Group 22B	*179*	...	*2*	...	*177*	*171*	...	...	...	*171*	...	...	...	...	...	...	...	...	...	...
	23.—WEAVERS, CALENDERERS AND DYERS.	ÁLKARI	Hindu	...	...	...	...	...	...	...	...	...	...	...	...	...	...	...	...	...	...	...	...
		ÁTÁRI	Do.	...	...	...	...	...	...	...	...	...	...	...	...	...	...	...	...	...	...	...	...
		Do.	Musalman	13	...	...	...	13	12	...	...	...	12	...	...	...	...	...	...	...	...	...	...
		BUNKAR	Hindu	...	...	...	...	...	...	...	...	...	...	...	...	...	...	...	...	...	...	...	...
		CHENWÁR	Do.	108	...	...	...	108	95	...	...	...	95	...	...	...	...	...	...	...	...	...	...
		CHHIPÁ	Do.	...	...	...	...	...	...	...	...	...	...	...	...	...	...	...	...	...	...	...	...
		HÁLBI	Do.	132	3	7	...	122	129	...	...	...	129	...	...	...	...	...	...	...	...	...	...

TABLE D.—Castes by Education—*contd.*

Class.	Group.	Caste.	Religion.	Total Strength. Males. Total Males.	Pupils.	Literate. Total Literate.	Literate. Knowing English.	Illiterate.	Total Strength. Females. Total Females.	Pupils.	Literate. Total Literate.	Literate. Knowing English.	Illiterate.	Territorial Distribution. District Amraoti. Males. Total.	Pupils.	Literate. Total Literate.	Literate. Knowing English.	Illiterate.	Females. Total.	Pupils.	Literate. Total Literate.	Literate. Knowing English.	Illiterate.
1	2	3	4	5	6	7	8	9	10	11	12	13	14	15	16	17	18	19	20	21	22	23	24
	23.—WEAVERS, CALENDERERS AND DYERS—*contd.*	HÁTGAR	Hindu	3,352	68	140	...	3,144	3,247	...	2	...	3,245	80	2	1	...	77	86	...	...	...	86
		INKAR	Do.	2	...	...	...	2	3	...	...	...	3	...	...	...	...	...	...	...	...	...	...
		KATIÁ	Do.	2	...	...	...	2	...	...	...	...	...	2	...	...	...	2	...	...	...	...	...
		KHATRI	Do.	885	64	206	9	615	825	3	4	...	818	269	17	48	4	204	257	...	...	...	257
		Do.	Sikh	3	1	2	...	...	1	...	...	...	1	...	...	...	...	...	...	...	...	...	...
		KORI	Hindu	319	1	10	...	308	116	...	1	...	115	125	...	7	...	118	52	...	1	...	51
		KOSHTI	Do.	7,576	225	466	1	6,885	6,973	3	5	...	6,965	2,943	73	155	1	2,715	2,607	1	2	...	2,604
		Do.	Jain	129	2	15	...	112	140	...	...	...	140	124	2	15	...	107	133	...	...	...	133
		MOMIN	Musalman	161	7	14	...	140	129	...	...	...	129	42	...	...	...	42	31	...	...	...	31
		NIRÁLI	Hindu	28	2	1	...	25	33	...	...	...	33	10	1	...	...	9	10	...	...	...	10
		PATUÁL	Do.	10	...	...	...	10	10	...	...	...	10	...	...	...	...	...	...	...	...	...	...
		PATWI (PATWEKAR)	Do.	249	12	19	...	218	217	...	...	...	217	81	5	11	...	65	87	...	...	...	87
		Do.	Jain	32	2	10	...	20	26	...	...	...	26	3	...	1	...	2	1	...	...	...	1
		RANGÁRI	Hindu	6,053	454	1,142	13	4,457	5,812	17	10	...	5,785	968	70	195	4	703	874	4	1	...	869
		Do.	Jain	150	17	28	...	105	175	2	1	...	172	2	...	1	...	1	3	...	...	...	3
		SÁLEWÁR	Hindu	539	3	5	...	531	564	...	...	...	564	...	...	...	...	...	...	...	...	...	...
		SÁLI	Do.	4,095	156	376	2	3,563	3,890	6	5	...	3,879	1,207	40	112	...	1,055	1,160	...	...	...	1,160
		Do.	Jain	5	...	4	...	1	7	...	...	...	7	...	...	...	...	...	...	...	...	...	...
		SÁLVE	Hindu	3	...	...	...	3	2	...	...	...	2	...	...	...	...	...	...	...	...	...	...
			Total Group 23	*26,286*	*1,036*	*2,504*	*26*	*21,747*	*23,720*	*31*	*28*	...	*23,661*	*6,186*	*211*	*548*	*9*	*5,376*	*5,542*	*5*	*4*	...	*5,538*
	24.—WASHERMEN	DHOBI	Musalman	4	...	...	...	4	5	...	...	...	5	...	...	...	...	...	...	...	...	...	...
		WARTHI (DHOBI and PARIT)	Hindu	11,749	121	99	4	11,529	11,326	2	3	...	11,321	2,848	32	22	3	2,794	2,725	...	2	...	2,723
			Total Group 24	*11,753*	*127*	*99*	*4*	*11,533*	*11,331*	*2*	*3*	...	*11,326*	*2,848*	*32*	*22*	*3*	*2,794*	*2,725*	...	*2*	...	*2,723*
	25.—COTTON CLEANERS	PINJÁRI	Hindu	34	...	...	...	34	33	...	...	...	33	1	...	...	...	1	1	...	...	...	1
		Do.	Musalman	548	7	17	...	524	537	...	...	...	537	196	1	5	...	190	190	...	...	...	190
			Total Group 25	*582*	*7*	*17*	...	*558*	*570*	...	...	...	*570*	*197*	*1*	*5*	...	*191*	*191*	...	...	...	*191*
	26.—SHEPHERDS AND WOOL WEAVERS	DHANGAR	Hindu	41,589	303	306	4	40,980	39,438	1	1	...	39,436	8,088	67	97	3	7,924	7,646	1	...	...	7,645
		GADARIYÁ	Do.	43	1	3	...	39	6	...	...	...	6	6	1	...	...	5	3	...	...	...	3
		KURAMWÁR	Do.	1	...	...	...	1	2	...	...	...	2	...	...	...	...	...	...	...	...	...	...
			Total Group 26	*41,633*	*304*	*309*	*4*	*41,020*	*39,446*	*1*	*1*	...	*39,444*	*8,094*	*68*	*97*	*3*	*7,929*	*7,649*	*1*	...	...	*7,648*

Class.	Group.	Caste.	Religion.	Akola Males Total.	Akola Males Pupils.	Akola Males Literate Total Literate.	Akola Males Literate Knowing English.	Akola Males Illiterate.	Akola Females Total.	Akola Females Pupils.	Akola Females Literate Total Literate.	Akola Females Literate Knowing English.	Akola Females Illiterate.	Ellichpur Males Total.	Ellichpur Males Pupils.	Ellichpur Males Literate Total Literate.	Ellichpur Males Literate Knowing English.	Ellichpur Males Illiterate.	Ellichpur Females Total.	Ellichpur Females Pupils.	Ellichpur Females Literate Total Literate.	Ellichpur Females Literate Knowing English.	Ellichpur Females Illiterate.
25	26	27	28	29	30	31	32	33	34	35	36	37	38	39	40	41	42	43	44	45	46	47	48
D.—ARTISAN AND VILLAGE MENIAL—contd.	23.—WEAVERS, CALENDERERS AND DYERS—contd.	HÁTGAR	Hindu	636	26	37	...	573	598	...	...	...	598	202	5	14	...	183	193	...	2	...	191
		INKAR	Do.	...	...	...	...	...	...	...	...	...	...	...	...	...	...	...	...	...	...	...	...
		KATIÁ	Do.	...	...	...	...	...	...	...	...	...	...	...	...	...	...	...	...	...	...	...	...
		KHATRI	Do.	202	20	57	3	125	191	...	1	...	190	199	11	27	...	161	168	1	...	...	167
		Do.	Sikh	3	1	2	...	...	1	...	...	...	1	...	...	...	...	...	...	...	...	...	...
		KORI	Hindu	64	1	1	...	62	17	...	...	...	17	57	...	1	...	96	31	...	...	...	31
		KOSHTI	Do.	206	5	9	...	192	157	...	...	...	157	2,022	58	128	...	1,836	1,957	...	1	...	1,956
		Do.	Jain	...	...	...	...	...	...	...	...	...	...	...	...	...	...	...	...	...	...	...	...
		MOMIN	Musalman	13	2	3	...	8	5	...	...	...	5	2	...	1	...	1	...	...	...	...	...
		NIRÁLI	Hindu	5	...	...	...	5	5	...	...	...	5	12	1	1	...	10	17	...	...	...	17
		PATUÁL	Do.	10	...	...	...	10	10	...	...	...	10	...	...	...	...	...	...	...	...	...	...
		PATWI (PATWEKAR)	Do.	44	2	2	...	40	35	...	...	...	35	87	3	1	...	83	57	...	...	...	57
		Do.	Jain	2	...	2	...	...	1	...	...	...	1	...	...	...	...	...	...	...	...	...	...
		RANGÁRI	Hindu	1,359	108	300	3	991	1,305	11	4	...	1,290	949	74	166	2	709	929	...	1	...	928
		Do.	Jain	13	...	1	...	12	10	...	...	...	10	...	...	...	...	...	...	...	...	...	...
		SÁLEWÁR	Hindu	...	...	...	...	...	...	...	...	...	...	...	...	...	...	...	...	...	...	...	...
		SÁLI	Do.	438	17	36	...	385	385	1	2	...	382	1,080	51	112	...	917	1,011	3	1	...	1,007
		Do.	Jain	5	...	4	...	1	...	...	...	...	...	...	...	...	...	...	...	...	...	...	...
		SÁLVE	Hindu	...	...	...	...	...	...	...	...	...	...	3	...	...	...	3	2	...	...	...	2
			Total Group 23	3,157	182	465	6	2,520	2,831	12	7	...	2,812	5,550	217	501	2	4,832	5,180	4	5	...	5,171
	24.—WASHERMEN	DHOBI	Musalman	4	...	...	...	4	5	...	...	...	5	...	...	...	...	...	...	...	...	...	...
		WARTHI (DHOBI and PARIT)	Hindu	2,958	40	29	...	2,889	2,819	2	...	...	2,817	1,619	12	14	1	1,593	1,497	...	...	...	1,497
			Total Group 24	2,962	40	29	...	2,893	2,824	2	...	...	2,822	1,619	12	14	1	1,593	1,497	...	...	...	1,497
	25.—COTTON CLEANERS	PINJÁRI	Hindu	...	...	...	...	...	...	...	...	...	...	...	...	...	...	...	2	...	...	...	2
		Do.	Musalman	34	1	...	...	33	26	...	...	...	26	71	3	4	...	64	62	...	...	...	62
			Total Group 25	34	1	...	...	33	26	...	...	...	26	71	3	4	...	64	64	...	...	...	64
	26.—SHEPHERDS AND WOOL WEAVERS.	DHANGAR	Hindu	9,211	61	37	...	9,113	8,612	...	1	...	8,611	3,386	24	36	...	3,326	3,100	...	...	...	3,100
		GADARIYÁ	Do.	6	...	1	...	5	2	...	...	...	2	22	...	2	...	20	1	...	...	...	1
		KURAMWÁR	Do.	...	...	...	...	...	...	...	...	...	...	...	...	...	...	...	...	...	...	...	...
			Total Group 26	9,217	61	38	...	9,118	8,614	...	1	...	8,613	3,408	24	38	...	3,346	3,101	...	...	...	3,101

TABLE D.—Castes by Education—*contd.*

Caste and Religion.				Territorial Distribution.																			
				District Buldana.										District Wun.									
				Males.					Females.					Males.					Females.				
						Literate.					Literate.					Literate.					Literate.		
Class.	Group.	Caste.	Religion.	Total.	Pupils.	Total Literate.	Knowing English.	Illiterate.	Total.	Pupils.	Total Literate.	Knowing English.	Illiterate.	Total.	Pupils.	Total Literate.	Knowing English.	Illiterate.	Total.	Pupils.	Total Literate.	Knowing English.	Illiterate.
49	50	51	52	53	54	55	56	57	58	59	60	61	62	63	64	65	66	67	68	69	70	71	72
D.—Artisan and Village Menial—*contd.*	23.—Weavers, Calenderers and Dyers—*contd.*	Hátgar	Hindu	621	17	96	...	568	586	...	...	...	586	1,123	14	33	...	1,076	1,126	...	...	...	1,126
		Inkar	Do.	...	...	...	...	...	...	...	...	...	...	...	...	...	...	...	...	...	...	...	...
		Katiá	Do.	...	...	...	...	...	...	...	...	...	...	...	...	...	...	...	...	...	...	...	...
		Khatri	Do.	182	16	67	1	99	180	2	2	...	176	29	...	7	1	22	25	...	1	...	24
		Do.	Sikh	...	...	...	...	...	...	...	...	...	...	...	...	...	...	...	...	...	...	...	...
		Kori	Hindu	3	...	...	...	3	1	...	...	...	1	21	...	1	...	20	8	...	...	...	8
		Koshti	Do.	337	13	11	...	313	314	1	2	...	311	1,318	56	97	...	1,165	1,225	...	...	...	1,225
		Do.	Jain	...	...	...	...	...	...	...	...	...	...	...	...	...	...	...	...	...	...	...	...
		Momin	Musalman	91	5	7	...	79	87	...	...	...	87	...	...	...	...	...	...	...	...	...	...
		Nirálі	Hindu	...	...	...	...	...	...	...	...	...	...	...	...	...	...	...	...	...	...	...	...
		Patuál	Do.	...	...	...	...	...	...	...	...	...	...	...	...	...	...	...	...	...	...	...	...
		Patwi (Patwekar)	Do.	31	2	5	...	24	30	...	...	...	30	...	...	...	...	...	...	...	...	...	...
		Do.	Jain	27	2	7	...	18	24	...	...	...	24	...	...	...	...	...	...	...	...	...	...
		Rangári	Hindu	1,125	82	186	1	857	1,189	1	2	...	1,186	992	64	158	1	770	919	...	1	...	918
		Do.	Jain	79	7	10	...	62	97	...	...	...	97	54	9	16	...	29	62	2	1	...	59
		Sálewár	Hindu	...	...	...	...	...	...	...	...	...	...	539	3	5	...	531	564	...	...	...	564
		Sáli	Do.	806	19	62	1	725	774	2	2	...	770	120	6	7	...	107	116	...	...	...	116
		Do.	Jain	...	...	...	...	...	...	...	...	...	...	...	...	...	...	...	...	...	...	...	...
		Sálve	Hindu	...	...	...	...	...	...	...	...	...	...	...	...	...	...	...	...	...	...	...	...
			Total Group 23	*3,817*	*164*	*391*	*3*	*2,762*	*3,297*	*6*	*8*	...	*3,283*	*4,328*	*164*	*330*	*2*	*3,844*	*4,177*	*2*	*3*	...	*4,172*
	24.—Washermen	Dhobi	Musalman	...	...	...	...	...	...	...	...	...	...	...	...	...	...	...	...	...	...	...	...
		Warthi (Dhobi and Parit)	Hindu	1,373	24	19	...	1,330	1,408	...	...	...	1,408	2,050	7	11	...	2,032	2,070	...	1	...	2,069
			Total Group 24	*1,373*	*24*	*19*	...	*1,330*	*1,408*	...	...	...	*1,408*	*2,050*	*7*	*11*	...	*2,032*	*2,070*	...	*1*	...	*2,069*
	25.—Cotton cleaners	Pinjári	Hindu	18	...	...	...	18	16	...	...	...	16	15	...	...	...	15	14	...	...	...	14
		Do.	Musalman	36	1	1	...	34	46	...	...	...	46	206	1	7	...	198	208	...	...	...	208
			Total Group 25	*54*	*1*	*1*	...	*52*	*62*	...	...	...	*62*	*221*	*1*	*7*	...	*213*	*222*	...	...	...	*222*
	26.—Shepherds and wool weavers	Dhangar	Hindu	6,222	29	26	...	6,167	6,094	...	...	...	6,094	5,842	37	46	...	5,759	5,598	...	...	...	5,598
		Gadariyá	Do.	6	...	...	...	6	...	...	...	...	...	2	...	...	...	2	...	...	...	...	...
		Kukamwár	Do.	...	...	...	...	...	...	...	...	...	...	1	...	...	...	1	2	...	...	...	2
			Total Group 26	*6,228*	*29*	*26*	...	*6,173*	*6,094*	...	...	...	*6,094*	*5,845*	*37*	*46*	...	*5,762*	*5,600*	...	...	...	*5,600*

D.—ARTISAN AND VILLAGE MENIAL—*contd.*

Class.	Group.	Caste.	Religion.	District Basin. Males. Total.	District Basin. Males. Pupils.	District Basin. Males. Literate. Total Literate.	District Basin. Males. Literate. Knowing English.	District Basin. Males. Illiterate.	District Basin. Females. Total.	District Basin. Females. Pupils.	District Basin. Females. Literate. Total Literate.	District Basin. Females. Literate. Knowing English.	District Basin. Females. Illiterate.	Railway Passengers. Males. Total.	Railway Passengers. Males. Pupils.	Railway Passengers. Males. Literate. Total Literate.	Railway Passengers. Males. Literate. Knowing English.	Railway Passengers. Males. Illiterate.	Railway Passengers. Females. Total.	Railway Passengers. Females. Pupils.	Railway Passengers. Females. Literate. Total Literate.	Railway Passengers. Females. Literate. Knowing English.	Railway Passengers. Females. Illiterate.
73	74	75	76	77	78	79	80	81	82	83	84	85	86	87	88	89	90	91	92	93	94	95	96
	23.—WEAVERS, CALENDERERS AND DYERS—*contd.*	HÁTGAR	Hindu	690	4	19	...	667	658	...	...	...	658	...	...	...	...	...	...	...	...	...	...
		INKAR	Do.	2	...	...	...	2	3	...	...	...	3	...	...	...	...	...	...	...	...	...	...
		KATIÁ	Do.	...	...	...	...	...	...	...	...	...	...	...	...	...	...	...	...	...	...	...	...
		KHATRI	Do.	4	...	...	...	4	4	...	...	...	4	...	...	...	...	...	...	...	...	...	...
		Do.	Sikh	...	...	...	...	...	...	...	...	...	...	...	...	...	...	...	...	...	...	...	...
		KORI	Hindu	9	...	...	...	9	7	...	...	...	7	...	...	...	...	...	...	...	...	...	...
		KOSHTI	Do.	748	20	66	...	662	713	1	...	...	712	2	...	...	...	2	...	...	...	...	...
		Do.	Jain	5	...	...	...	5	7	...	...	...	7	...	...	...	...	...	...	...	...	...	...
		MOMIN	Musalman	13	...	3	...	10	6	...	...	...	6	...	...	...	...	...	...	...	...	...	...
		NIRÁLI	Hindu	1	...	...	...	1	1	...	...	...	1	...	...	...	...	...	...	...	...	...	...
		PATUÁL	Do.	...	...	...	...	...	...	...	...	...	...	...	...	...	...	...	...	...	...	...	...
		PATWI (PATWEKAR)	Do.	6	...	...	...	6	8	...	...	...	8	...	...	...	...	...	...	...	...	...	...
		Do.	Jain	...	...	...	...	...	...	...	...	...	...	...	...	...	...	...	...	...	...	...	...
		RANGÁRI	Hindu	620	56	137	2	427	596	1	1	...	594	...	...	...	...	...	...	...	...	...	...
		Do.	Jain	2	1	...	...	1	3	...	...	...	3	...	...	...	...	...	...	...	...	...	...
		SÁLEWÁR	Hindu	...	...	...	...	...	...	...	...	...	...	...	...	...	...	...	...	...	...	...	...
		SÁLI	Do.	444	23	47	1	374	444	...	...	...	444	...	...	...	...	...	...	...	...	...	...
		Do.	Jain	...	...	...	...	...	7	...	...	...	7	...	...	...	...	...	...	...	...	...	...
		SÁLVE	Hindu	...	...	...	...	...	...	...	...	...	...	...	...	...	...	...	...	...	...	...	...
			Total Group 23	*2,797*	*107*	*279*	*8*	*2,411*	*2,693*	*2*	*1*	...	*2,690*	*2*	...	...	...	*2*	...	...	...	...	...
	24.—WASHERMEN	DHOBI	Musalman	...	...	...	...	...	...	...	...	...	...	...	...	...	...	...	...	...	...	...	...
		WARTHI (DHOBI and PARIT)	Hindu	899	6	4	...	889	807	...	...	...	807	2	...	...	...	2	...	...	...	...	...
			Total Group 24	*899*	*6*	*4*	...	*889*	*807*	...	...	...	*807*	*2*	...	...	...	*2*	...	...	...	...	...
	25.—COTTON CLEANERS	PINJÁRI	Hindu	...	...	...	...	...	...	...	...	...	...	...	...	...	...	...	...	...	...	...	...
		Do.	Musalman	5	...	...	...	5	5	...	...	...	5	...	...	...	...	...	...	...	...	...	...
			Total Group 25	*5*	...	...	...	*5*	*5*	...	...	...	*5*	...	...	...	...	...	...	...	...	...	...
	26.—SHEPHERDS AND WOOL WEAVERS	DHANGAR	Hindu	8,831	85	64	1	8,682	8,380	...	...	...	8,380	9	...	...	...	9	8	...	...	...	8
		GADARIYÁ	Do.	1	...	...	...	1	...	...	...	...	...	...	...	...	...	...	...	...	...	...	...
		KURAMWÁR	Do.	...	...	...	...	...	...	...	...	...	...	...	...	...	...	...	...	...	...	...	...
			Total Group 26	*8,832*	*85*	*64*	*1*	*8,683*	*8,380*	...	...	...	*8,380*	*9*	...	...	...	*9*	*8*	...	...	...	*8*

TABLE D.—Castes by Education—*contd.*

Class.	Group.	Caste.	Religion.	Total Strength. Males. Total Males.	Total Strength. Males. Pupils.	Total Strength. Males. Literate. Total Literate.	Total Strength. Males. Literate. Knowing English.	Total Strength. Males. Illiterate.	Total Strength. Females. Total Females.	Total Strength. Females. Pupils.	Total Strength. Females. Literate. Total Literate.	Total Strength. Females. Literate. Knowing English.	Total Strength. Females. Illiterate.	District Amraoti. Males. Total.	District Amraoti. Males. Pupils.	District Amraoti. Males. Literate. Total Literate.	District Amraoti. Males. Literate. Knowing English.	District Amraoti. Males. Illiterate.	District Amraoti. Females. Total.	District Amraoti. Females. Pupils.	District Amraoti. Females. Literate. Total Literate.	District Amraoti. Females. Literate. Knowing English.	District Amraoti. Females. Illiterate.
1	2	3	4	5	6	7	8	9	10	11	12	13	14	15	16	17	18	19	20	21	22	23	24
D.—Artisan and Village Menial—*contd.*	27.—Oil Pressers	Kásid	Hindu	7	...	...	...	7	5	...	...	...	5	...	...	...	...	...	...	...	...	...	...
		Teli	Do.	42,114	1,098	1,674	4	39,342	39,955	11	14	...	39,930	14,456	301	537	1	13,618	13,459	2	4	...	13,493
		Do.	Animistic	6	...	...	...	6	2	...	...	...	2	4	...	...	...	4	1	...	...	...	1
		Do.	Musalman	13	...	...	...	13	4	...	...	...	4	1	...	...	...	1	...	...	...	...	...
		Do.	Sikh	1	...	...	...	1	...	...	...	...	...	...	...	...	...	...	...	...	...	...	...
			Total Group 27	*42,141*	*1,098*	*1,674*	*4*	*39,369*	*39,966*	*11*	*14*	...	*39,941*	*14,461*	*301*	*537*	*1*	*13,623*	*13,500*	*2*	*4*	...	*13,494*
	28.—Potters	Arvi	Hindu	4	...	3	...	1	7	...	...	...	7	1	...	...	...	1	4	...	...	...	4
		Kumbhár	Do.	12,558	135	119	1	12,304	9,907	2	2	...	9,903	4,036	44	46	...	3,946	2,629	...	1	...	2,628
			Total Group 28	*12,562*	*135*	*122*	*1*	*12,305*	*9,914*	*2*	*2*	...	*9,910*	*4,037*	*44*	*46*	...	*3,947*	*2,633*	...	*1*	...	*2,632*
	29.—Glass workers	Kachár	Hindu	283	14	20	1	249	281	...	...	...	281	40	3	3	...	34	32	...	...	...	32
	29A.—Lac Bangle makers.	Lakhári	Do.	67	2	8	...	57	59	...	...	...	59	46	2	6	...	38	44	...	...	...	44
	30.—Salt, etc., workers	Lonári (Luṅiyá)	Do.	538	11	9	...	518	558	...	...	...	558	68	2	4	...	62	64	...	...	...	64
	33.—Gold washers	Jhárekari	Musalman	1	...	1	...	...	...	...	...	...	...	...	...	...	...	...	...	...	...	...	...
	35.—Fishermen, boatmen, palki-bearers, cooks, etc.	Bhatiárá	Do.	1	...	...	...	1	1	...	...	...	1	...	...	...	...	...	...	...	...	...	...
		Bhisti	Do.	2	...	...	...	2	3	...	...	...	3	2	...	...	...	2	3	...	...	...	3
		Bhoi (Vindhewár)	Hindu	14,253	45	58	1	14,150	13,162	...	...	...	13,162	4,384	10	19	...	4,355	3,913	...	...	...	3,913
		Injhwár	Do.	118	...	1	...	117	103	...	...	...	103	44	...	...	...	44	37	...	...	...	37
		Jhingábhoi	Do.	38	...	...	...	38	37	...	...	...	37	...	...	...	...	...	...	...	...	...	...
		Káhár	Do.	232	5	24	...	203	127	...	...	...	127	69	...	2	...	67	20	...	...	...	20
		Kevati	Do.	59	...	4	...	55	17	...	...	...	17	34	...	1	...	33	8	...	...	...	8
		Koli	Do.	16,497	286	292	1	15,919	16,131	4	4	...	16,123	2,893	55	66	1	2,772	2,835	1	...	...	2,834
		Mallá	Do.	2	...	...	...	2	2	...	...	...	2	...	...	...	...	...	...	...	...	...	...
		Pakháli	Do.	51	2	...	...	49	48	...	...	...	48	9	1	...	...	8	9	...	...	...	9
		Shikharpániwále	Do.	2	...	...	...	2	1	...	...	...	1	2	...	...	...	2	1	...	...	...	1
		Wágháde	Do.	2	...	...	...	2	...	...	...	...	...	2	...	...	...	2	...	...	...	...	...
			Total Group 35	*31,257*	*338*	*379*	*2*	*30,540*	*29,632*	*4*	*4*	...	*29,624*	*7,439*	*66*	*88*	*1*	*7,285*	*6,826*	*1*	...	...	*6,825*
	35 A.—Servant Caste.	Khawás	Hindu	5	1	3	1	1	3	...	...	...	3	...	...	...	...	...	...	...	...	...	...
		Thárnak	Do.	1	...	...	...	1	...	...	...	...	...	1	...	...	...	1	...	...	...	...	...
			Total Group 35A	*6*	*1*	*3*	*1*	*2*	*3*	...	...	...	*3*	*1*	...	...	...	*1*	...	...	...	...	...

Table D.—[Castes by Education].

Class.	Group.	Caste.	Religion.	Akola Males Total.	Akola Males Pupils.	Akola Males Literate Total Literate.	Akola Males Literate Knowing English.	Akola Males Illiterate.	Akola Females Total.	Akola Females Pupils.	Akola Females Literate Total Literate.	Akola Females Literate Knowing English.	Akola Females Illiterate.	Ellichpur Males Total.	Ellichpur Males Pupils.	Ellichpur Males Literate Total Literate.	Ellichpur Males Literate Knowing English.	Ellichpur Males Illiterate.	Ellichpur Females Total.	Ellichpur Females Pupils.	Ellichpur Females Literate Total Literate.	Ellichpur Females Literate Knowing English.	Ellichpur Females Illiterate.
25	26	27	28	29	30	31	32	33	34	35	36	37	38	39	40	41	42	43	44	45	46	47	48
D.—ARTISAN AND VILLAGE MENIAL—contd.	27.—Oil Pressers	Kásid	Hindu	...	...	...	...	...	...	...	...	...	...	...	...	...	...	...	...	...	...	...	...
		Teli	Do.	6,459	212	281	...	5,966	6,071	6	3	...	6,062	3,362	104	188	1	3,070	3,305	...	2	...	3,303
		Do.	Animistic	...	...	...	...	...	...	...	...	...	...	2	...	...	...	2	1	...	...	...	1
		Do.	Musalman	...	...	...	...	...	...	...	...	...	...	...	...	...	...	...	...	...	...	...	...
		Do.	Sikh	1	...	...	...	1	...	...	...	...	...	...	...	...	...	...	...	...	...	...	...
			Total Group 27	6,460	212	281	...	5,967	6,071	6	3	...	6,062	3,364	104	188	1	3,072	3,306	...	2	...	3,304
	28.—Potters	Arvi	Hindu	...	...	...	...	...	...	...	...	...	...	...	...	...	...	...	...	...	...	...	...
		Kumbhár	Do.	2,440	43	29	1	2,368	2,057	2	1	...	2,054	1,439	17	15	...	1,407	1,107	...	...	...	1,107
			Total Group 28	2,440	43	29	1	2,368	2,057	2	1	...	2,054	1,439	17	15	...	1,407	1,107	...	...	...	1,107
	29.—Glass workers	Kachár	Hindu	45	1	5	1	39	43	...	...	...	43	15	...	...	...	15	19	...	...	...	19
	29A.—Lac bangle makers.	Lakhári	Do.	1	...	...	...	1	3	...	...	...	3	7	...	...	...	7	1	...	...	...	1
	30.—Salt, etc., workers	Lonári (Luniyá)	Do.	343	8	3	...	332	372	...	...	...	372	48	...	1	...	47	43	...	...	...	43
	33.—Gold washers	Jhárekari	Musalman	...	...	...	...	...	...	...	...	...	...	1	...	1	...	...	...	...	...	...	...
	35.—Fishermen, boatmen, palki-bearers, cooks, etc.	Bhatiárá	Do.	...	...	...	...	...	...	...	...	...	...	...	...	...	...	...	...	...	...	...	...
		Bhisti	Do.	...	...	...	...	...	...	...	...	...	...	...	...	...	...	...	...	...	...	...	...
		Bhoi (Vindhewár)	Hindu	2,741	15	19	1	2,707	2,585	...	...	...	2,585	1,988	5	10	...	1,973	1,690	...	...	...	1,690
		Injhwár	Do.	...	...	...	...	...	...	...	...	...	...	72	...	1	...	71	66	...	...	...	66
		Jhingábhoi	Do.	30	...	...	...	30	30	...	...	...	30	3	...	...	...	3	4	...	...	...	4
		Káhár	Do.	34	2	4	...	28	8	...	...	...	8	70	...	5	...	65	41	...	...	...	41
		Kevati	Do.	11	...	3	...	8	2	...	...	...	2	4	...	...	...	4	3	...	...	...	3
		Koli	Do.	5,225	140	116	...	4,969	5,018	3	1	...	5,014	1,446	24	29	...	1,393	1,291	...	...	...	1,291
		Mallá	Do.	...	...	...	...	...	...	...	...	...	...	1	...	...	...	1	2	...	...	...	2
		Pakháli	Do.	3	...	...	...	3	1	...	...	...	1	39	1	...	...	38	38	...	...	...	38
		Shikharpániwále	Do.	...	...	...	...	...	...	...	...	...	...	...	...	...	...	...	...	...	...	...	...
		Wágháde	Do.	...	...	...	...	...	...	...	...	...	...	...	...	...	...	...	...	...	...	...	...
			Total Group 35	8,044	157	142	1	7,745	7,644	3	1	...	7,640	3,623	30	45	...	3,548	3,135	...	...	...	3,135
	35 A.—Servant Caste	Khawás	Hindu	...	...	...	...	...	...	...	...	...	...	...	...	...	...	...	...	...	...	...	...
		Tháenak	Do.	...	...	...	...	...	...	...	...	...	...	...	...	...	...	...	...	...	...	...	...
			Total Group 35A	...	...	...	...	...	...	...	...	...	...	...	...	...	...	...	...	...	...	...	...

TABLE D.—Castes by Education—*contd.*

Class.	Group.	Caste.	Religion.	District Buldana. Males. Total.	Males. Pupils.	Males. Literate. Total Literate.	Males. Literate. Knowing English.	Males. Illiterate.	Females. Total.	Females. Pupils.	Females. Literate. Total Literate.	Females. Literate. Knowing English.	Females. Illiterate.	District Wun. Males. Total.	Males. Pupils.	Males. Literate. Total Literate.	Males. Literate. Knowing English.	Males. Illiterate.	Females. Total.	Females. Pupils.	Females. Literate. Total Literate.	Females. Literate. Knowing English.	Females. Illiterate.
49	50	51	52	53	54	55	56	57	58	59	60	61	62	63	64	65	66	67	68	69	70	71	72
D.—ARTISAN AND VILLAGE MENIAL—*contd.*	27.—Oil Pressers	Kásid	Hindu	...	...	...	...	...	...	...	...	...	...	3	...	...	...	3	5	...	...	...	5
		Teli	Do.	5,383	200	316	2	4,867	5,262	3	4	...	5,255	7,816	168	203	...	7,445	7,368	...	...	...	7,368
		Do.	Animistic	...	...	...	...	...	...	...	...	...	...	...	...	...	...	...	...	...	...	...	...
		Do.	Musalman	...	...	...	...	...	...	...	...	...	...	12	...	...	...	12	4	...	...	...	4
		Do.	Sikh	...	...	...	...	...	...	...	...	...	...	...	...	...	...	...	...	...	...	...	...
			Total Group 27.	*5,383*	*200*	*316*	*2*	*4,867*	*5,262*	*3*	*4*	...	*5,255*	*7,831*	*168*	*203*	...	*7,460*	*7,377*	...	...	...	*7,377*
	28.—Potters	Árvi	Hindu	3	...	3	...	...	3	...	...	...	3	...	...	...	...	...	...	...	...	...	...
		Kumbhár	Do.	1,649	8	10	...	1,631	1,595	...	...	...	1,595	1,531	16	12	...	1,503	1,150	...	...	...	1,150
			Total Group 28.	*1,652*	*8*	*13*	...	*1,631*	*1,598*	...	...	...	*1,598*	*1,581*	*16*	*12*	...	*1,503*	*1,150*	...	...	...	*1,150*
	29.—Glass workers	Kachár	Hindu	89	7	8	...	74	94	...	...	...	94	72	2	1	...	69	71	...	...	...	71
	29A.—Lac bangle makers.	Lakhárí	Do.	...	...	...	...	...	...	...	...	...	...	4	...	1	...	3	10	...	...	...	10
	30.—Salt, etc., workers	Lonári (Luniyá)	Do.	63	1	...	...	62	59	...	...	...	59	11	...	...	...	11	13	...	...	...	13
	33.—Gold washers	Jhárekari	Musalman	...	...	...	...	...	...	...	...	...	...	...	...	...	...	...	...	...	...	...	...
	35.—Fishermen, boatmen, palki-bearers, cooks, etc.	Bhatiárá	Do.	1	...	...	...	1	1	...	...	...	1	...	...	...	...	...	...	...	...	...	...
		Bhisti	Do.	...	...	...	...	...	...	...	...	...	...	...	...	...	...	...	...	...	...	...	...
		Bhoi (Vindhewár)	Hindu	718	3	3	...	712	683	...	...	...	683	3,674	10	7	...	3,657	3,539	...	...	...	3,539
		Injhwár	Do.	...	...	...	...	...	...	...	...	...	...	2	...	...	...	2	...	...	...	...	...
		Jhingábhoi	Do.	5	...	...	...	5	3	...	...	...	3	...	...	...	...	...	...	...	...	...	...
		Káhár	Do.	40	3	11	...	26	55	...	...	...	55	15	...	...	...	15	3	...	...	...	3
		Kevati	Do.	3	...	...	...	3	4	...	...	...	4	6	...	...	...	6	...	...	...	...	...
		Koli	Do.	4,148	53	58	...	4,037	4,197	...	...	...	4,197	1,141	12	18	...	1,111	1,168	...	2	...	1,166
		Mallá	Hindu	...	...	...	...	...	...	...	...	...	...	1	...	...	...	1	...	...	...	...	...
		Pakháli	Do.	...	...	...	...	...	...	...	...	...	...	...	...	...	...	...	...	...	...	...	...
		Shikharpániwále	Do.	...	...	...	...	...	...	...	...	...	...	...	...	...	...	...	...	...	...	...	...
		Wághádе	Do.	...	...	...	...	...	...	...	...	...	...	...	...	...	...	...	...	...	...	...	...
			Total Group 35.	*4,915*	*59*	*72*	...	*4,784*	*4,943*	...	...	...	*4,943*	*4,839*	*22*	*25*	...	*4,792*	*4,710*	...	*2*	...	*4,708*
	35A.—Servant Caste	Khawás	Hindu	5	1	3	1	1	3	...	...	...	3	...	...	...	...	...	...	...	...	...	...
		Thárnak	Do.	...	...	...	...	...	...	...	...	...	...	...	...	...	...	...	...	...	...	...	...
			Total Group 35A	*5*	*1*	*3*	*1*	*1*	*3*	...	...	...	*3*	...	...	...	...	...	...	...	...	...	...

D.—ARTISAN AND VILLAGE MENIAL—contd.

Class.	Group.	Caste.	Religion.	District Basim. Males. Total.	Males. Pupils.	Males. Literate. Total Literate.	Males. Literate. Knowing English.	Males. Illiterate.	Females. Total.	Females. Pupils.	Females. Literate. Total Literate.	Females. Literate. Knowing English.	Females. Illiterate.	Railway Passengers. Males. Total.	Males. Pupils.	Males. Literate. Total Literate.	Males. Literate. Knowing English.	Males. Illiterate.	Females. Total.	Females. Pupils.	Females. Literate. Total Literate.	Females. Literate. Knowing English.	Females. Illiterate.
73	74	75	76	77	78	79	80	81	82	83	84	85	86	87	88	89	90	91	92	93	94	95	96
	27.—Oil Pressers	Kásid	Hindu	4	...	...	...	4	...	...	...	...	...	...	...	...	...	...	...	...	...	...	...
		Teli	Do.	4,631	113	149	...	4,369	4,450	...	1	...	4,449	7	...	...	...	7	...	...	...	...	...
		Do.	Animistic	...	...	...	...	...	...	...	...	...	...	...	...	...	...	...	...	...	...	...	...
		Do.	Musalman	...	...	...	...	...	...	...	...	...	...	...	...	...	...	...	...	...	...	...	...
		Do.	Sikh	...	...	...	...	...	...	...	...	...	...	...	...	...	...	...	...	...	...	...	...
			Total Group 27	*4,636*	*113*	*149*	...	*4,378*	*4,450*	...	*1*	...	*4,449*	*7*	...	...	...	*7*	...	...	...	...	...
	28.—Potters	Árvi	Hindu	...	...	...	...	...	...	...	...	...	...	...	...	...	...	...	...	...	...	...	...
		Kumbhár	Do.	1,463	7	7	...	1,449	1,369	...	...	...	1,369	...	...	...	...	...	...	...	...	...	...
			Total Group 28	*1,463*	*7*	*7*	...	*1,449*	*1,369*	...	...	...	*1,369*	...	...	...	...	...	...	...	...	...	...
	29.—Glass workers	Kachár	Hindu	22	1	3	...	18	22	...	...	...	22	...	...	...	...	...	...	...	...	...	...
	29A.—Lac bangle makers	Lakhári	Do.	9	...	1	...	8	1	...	...	...	1	...	...	...	...	...	...	...	...	...	...
	30.—Salt, etc., workers	Lonári (Luniyá)	Do.	5	...	1	...	4	7	...	...	...	7	...	...	...	...	...	...	...	...	...	...
	33.—Gold washers	Jhárekari	Musalman	...	...	...	...	...	...	...	...	...	...	...	...	...	...	...	...	...	...	...	...
	35.—Fishermen, boatmen, palki-bearers, cooks, etc.	Bhatiárá	Do.	...	...	...	...	...	...	...	...	...	...	...	...	...	...	...	...	...	...	...	...
		Bhisti	Do.	...	...	...	...	...	...	...	...	...	...	...	...	...	...	...	...	...	...	...	...
		Bhoi (Vindhewár)	Hindu	745	2	...	...	743	750	...	...	...	750	3	...	...	...	3	2	...	...	...	2
		Injhwár	Do.	...	...	...	...	...	...	...	...	...	...	...	...	...	...	...	...	...	...	...	...
		Jhingábhoi	Do.	...	...	...	...	...	...	...	...	...	...	...	...	...	...	...	...	...	...	...	...
		Káhár	Do.	4	...	2	...	2	...	...	...	...	...	...	...	...	...	...	...	...	...	...	...
		Kevati	Do.	1	...	...	...	1	...	...	...	...	...	...	...	...	...	...	...	...	...	...	...
		Koli	Do.	1,642	2	5	...	1,635	1,622	...	1	...	1,621	2	...	...	...	2	...	...	...	...	...
		Mallá	Do.	...	...	...	...	...	...	...	...	...	...	...	...	...	...	...	...	...	...	...	...
		Pakháli	Do.	...	...	...	...	...	...	...	...	...	...	...	...	...	...	...	...	...	...	...	...
		Shikharpániwále	Do.	...	...	...	...	...	...	...	...	...	...	...	...	...	...	...	...	...	...	...	...
		Wágháde	Do.	...	...	...	...	...	...	...	...	...	...	...	...	...	...	...	...	...	...	...	...
			Total Group 35	*2,392*	*4*	*7*	...	*2,381*	*2,372*	...	*1*	...	*2,371*	*5*	...	...	...	*5*	*2*	...	...	...	*2*
	35A.—Servant Caste	Khawás	Hindu	...	...	...	...	...	...	...	...	...	...	...	...	...	...	...	...	...	...	...	...
		Thárnak	Do.	...	...	...	...	...	...	...	...	...	...	...	...	...	...	...	...	...	...	...	...
			Total Group 35A	...	...	...	...	...	...	...	...	...	...	...	...	...	...	...	...	...	...	...	...

TABLE D.—Castes by Education —*contd.*

Class.	Group.	Caste.	Religion.	Total Strength. Males. Total Males.	Pupils.	Literate. Total Literate.	Knowing English.	Illiterate.	Females. Total Females.	Pupils.	Literate. Total Literate.	Knowing English.	Illiterate.	Territorial Distribution. District Amraoti. Males. Total.	Pupils.	Literate. Total Literate.	Knowing English.	Illiterate.	Females. Total.	Pupils.	Literate. Total Literate.	Knowing English.	Illiterate.
1	2	3	4	5	6	7	8	9	10	11	12	13	14	15	16	17	18	19	20	21	22	23	24
D.—ARTISAN AND VILLAGE MENIAL—*concld.*	36.—DISTILLERS AND TODDY DRAWERS.	BANKAR	Hindu	1	...	...	...	1	...	...	...	...	...	1	...	...	...	1	...	...	...	...	...
		BHANDÁRI	Do.	1	...	1	...	...	1	...	...	...	1	...	...	...	...	...	...	...	...	...	...
		KALÁL	Do.	8,390	330	1,152	3	6,908	7,645	4	8	...	7,633	2,946	99	357	1	2,490	2,700	1	2	...	2,697
		Do.	Musalman	5	...	...	...	5	6	...	...	...	6	...	...	...	...	...	...	...	...	...	...
		Do.	Jain	58	2	6	...	90	88	...	...	...	88	59	...	6	...	53	55	...	...	...	55
		Do.	Animistic	1	...	...	...	1	1	...	...	...	1	1	...	...	...	1	1	...	...	...	1
		KALWÁR	Hindu	16	4	3	...	9	33	...	...	...	33	16	4	3	...	9	13	...	...	...	13
		PÁSI	Do.	304	5	16	3	283	163	...	...	...	163	142	2	7	2	133	77	...	...	...	77
			Total Group 36	*8,816*	*841*	*1,178*	*8*	*7,297*	*7,937*	*4*	*8*	...	*7,925*	*3,165*	*105*	*373*	*8*	*2,687*	*2,846*	*1*	*2*	...	*2,843*
	37.—BUTCHERS	KASÁI (BAKAR-KASÁI, KHÁTIK)	Hindu	2,553	22	19	...	2,512	2,406	...	...	...	2,406	1,236	6	6	...	1,224	1,165	...	...	...	1,165
		Do.	Musalman	194	2	1	...	191	190	...	1	...	1 9	22	1	...	...	21	25	...	...	...	25
			Total Group 37	*2,747*	*24*	*20*	...	*2,703*	*2,596*	...	*1*	...	*2,595*	*1,258*	*7*	*6*	...	*1,245*	*1,190*	...	...	...	*1,190*
	38.—LEATHER WORKERS.	CHÁMBHÁR (MOCHI)	Hindu	15,150	56	56	...	15,038	14,024	...	...	...	14,024	2,792	4	9	...	2,779	2,679	...	...	...	2,679
		DABGAR	Do.	27	...	...	...	27	29	...	...	...	29	...	...	...	...	...	...	...	...	...	...
		DOHOR	Do.	2,629	4	7	...	2,618	2,453	...	...	...	2,453	395	...	1	...	394	372	...	...	...	372
		MÁDGI	Do.	1,317	...	3	...	1,314	1,353	...	...	...	1,353	...	...	...	...	...	...	...	...	...	...
		Do.	Animistic	4	...	...	...	4	3	...	...	...	3	...	...	...	...	...	...	...	...	...	...
		ZINGAR	Hindu	664	25	45	3	594	649	...	...	...	649	172	3	10	...	159	170	...	...	...	170
			Total Group 38	*19,791*	*85*	*111*	*3*	*19,595*	*18,511*	...	...	...	*18,511*	*3,369*	*7*	*20*	...	*3,332*	*3,221*	...	...	...	*3,221*
	38A.—VILLAGE WATCHMEN, ETC.	BALÁHI	Hindu	118	...	...	...	118	131	...	...	...	131	...	...	...	...	...	...	...	...	...	...
		Do.	Animistic	38	...	...	...	38	40	...	...	...	40	...	...	...	...	...	...	...	...	...	...
		BHUMAK	Hindu	5	...	...	...	5	6	...	...	...	6	5	...	...	...	5	6	...	...	...	6
		KHANGAR	Do.	106	4	3	...	99	123	...	...	...	123	29	...	1	...	28	27	...	...	...	27
		MAHÁR (DHER and KOTWÁL)	Do.	177,675	631	904	14	176,140	177,322	6	12	...	177,304	50,397	148	299	7	49,950	50,288	1	4	...	50,283
		Do.	Animistic	6	...	...	...	6	2	...	...	...	2	6	...	...	...	6	2	...	...	...	2
		PAHELWÁN	Hindu	2	...	...	...	2	1	...	...	...	1	2	...	...	...	2	1	...	...	...	1
		RÁMOSHI	Do.	51	...	...	...	51	40	...	...	...	40	2	...	...	...	2	1	...	...	...	1
			Total Group 38A	*178,001*	*635*	*907*	*14*	*176,459*	*177,665*	*6*	*12*	...	*177,647*	*50,441*	*148*	*300*	*7*	*49,998*	*50,325*	*1*	*4*	...	*50,32[illegible]*
	39.—SCAVENGERS.	BHANGI (HÁLÁLKHOR, KHÁKROB and MEHTAR).	Hindu	775	2	18	...	755	528	...	...	...	528	247	...	7	...	240	187	...	...	...	187
		Do.	Musalman	97	3	2	...	92	83	...	1	...	82	27	...	...	...	27	28	...	...	...	28
		MÁNG	Hindu	25,974	49	88	3	25,837	26,176	2	13	...	26,161	20 6	3	14	...	5,189	5,132	1	...	...	5,131
		Do.	Animistic	...	...	...	...	...	1	...	...	...	1	...	...	...	...	...	...	...	...	...	...

Class.	Group.	Caste.	Religion.	Akola Males Total.	Akola Males Pupils.	Akola Males Literate Total Literate.	Akola Males Literate Knowing English.	Akola Males Illiterate.	Akola Females Total.	Akola Females Pupils.	Akola Females Literate Total Literate.	Akola Females Literate Knowing English.	Akola Females Illiterate.	Ellichpur Males Total.	Ellichpur Males Pupils.	Ellichpur Males Literate Total Literate.	Ellichpur Males Literate Knowing English.	Ellichpur Males Illiterate.	Ellichpur Females Total.	Ellichpur Females Pupils.	Ellichpur Females Literate Total Literate.	Ellichpur Females Literate Knowing English.	Ellichpur Females Illiterate.
25	26	27	28	29	30	31	32	33	34	35	36	37	38	39	40	41	42	43	44	45	46	47	48
D.—ARTISAN AND VILLAGE MENIAL—contd.	36.—Distillers and toddy drawers	Bankar	Hindu	...	...	...	...	...	...	...	...	...	...	...	...	...	...	...	...	...	...	...	...
		Bhandári	Do.	1	...	1	...	...	1	...	...	...	1	...	...	...	...	...	...	...	...	...	...
		Kalál	Do.	1,084	71	209	...	804	993	2	2	...	989	1,123	38	146	...	939	1,031	...	2	...	1,029
		Do.	Musalman	1	...	...	...	1	...	...	...	...	...	...	...	...	...	...	...	...	...	...	...
		Do.	Jain	...	...	...	...	...	...	...	...	...	...	...	...	...	...	...	...	...	...	...	...
		Do.	Animistic	...	...	...	...	...	...	...	...	...	...	...	...	...	...	...	...	...	...	...	...
		Kalwár	Hindu	...	...	...	...	...	...	...	...	...	...	...	...	...	...	...	...	...	...	...	...
		Pási	Do.	36	...	7	...	29	12	...	...	...	12	81	3	1	1	77	40	...	...	...	40
			Total Group 36	*1,122*	*71*	*217*	...	*884*	*1,006*	*2*	*2*	...	*1,002*	*1,204*	*41*	*147*	*1*	*1,018*	*1,071*	...	*2*	...	*1,069*
	37.—Butchers	Kasái (Bakar-Kasái, Khátik)	Hindu	287	3	2	...	282	262	...	...	...	262	677	7	6	...	664	654	...	...	...	654
		Do.	Musalman	27	1	...	...	26	20	...	1	...	19	16	...	...	...	16	9	...	...	...	9
			Total Group 37	*314*	*4*	*2*	...	*308*	*282*	...	*1*	...	*281*	*693*	*7*	*6*	...	*680*	*663*	...	...	...	*663*
	38.—Leather workers	Chámbhár (Mochi)	Hindu	4,158	31	13	...	4,114	3,869	...	...	...	3,869	1,669	12	14	...	1,643	1,512	...	...	...	1,512
		Dabgar	Do.	27	...	...	...	27	29	...	...	...	29	...	...	...	...	...	...	...	...	...	...
		Dohor	Do.	475	1	2	...	472	442	...	...	...	442	434	3	1	...	430	383	...	...	...	383
		Mádgi	Do.	1	...	...	...	1	...	...	...	...	...	...	...	...	...	...	...	...	...	...	...
		Do.	Animistic	...	...	...	...	...	...	...	...	...	...	...	...	...	...	...	...	...	...	...	...
		Zingar	Hindu	216	13	21	3	182	213	...	...	...	213	75	2	2	...	71	79	...	...	...	79
			Total Group 38	*4,877*	*45*	*36*	*3*	*4,796*	*4,553*	...	...	...	*4,553*	*2,178*	*17*	*17*	...	*2,144*	*1,974*	...	...	...	*1,974*
	38A.—Village watchmen, etc.	Baláhi	Hindu	...	...	...	...	...	...	...	...	...	...	118	...	...	...	118	131	...	...	...	131
		Do.	Animistic	...	...	...	...	...	...	...	...	...	...	38	...	...	...	38	40	...	...	...	40
		Bhumak	Hindu	...	...	...	...	...	...	...	...	...	...	...	...	...	...	...	...	...	...	...	...
		Khángar	Do.	39	2	...	...	37	47	...	...	...	47	38	2	2	...	34	49	...	...	...	49
		Mahár (Dher and Kotwál)	Do.	34,149	262	216	4	33,671	34,251	5	2	...	34,244	18,116	90	133	2	17,893	18,044	...	3	...	18,041
		Do.	Animistic	...	...	...	...	...	...	...	...	...	...	...	...	...	...	...	...	...	...	...	...
		Pahelwán	Hindu	...	...	...	...	...	...	...	...	...	...	...	...	...	...	...	...	...	...	...	...
		Rámoshi	Do.	20	...	...	...	20	18	...	...	...	18	1	...	...	...	1	...	...	...	...	...
			Total Group 38A	*34,208*	*264*	*216*	*4*	*33,728*	*34,316*	*5*	*2*	...	*34,309*	*18,311*	*92*	*135*	*2*	*18,084*	*18,264*	...	*3*	...	*18,261*
	39.—Scavengers	Bhangi (Hálálkhor, Khákrob and Mehtar)	Hindu	314	2	7	...	305	185	...	...	...	185	60	...	3	...	57	46	...	...	...	46
		Do.	Musalman	21	...	1	...	20	12	...	...	...	12	19	3	1	...	15	15	...	1	...	14
		Máng	Hindu	4,842	22	13	1	4,807	4,842	...	...	...	4,842	2,330	10	40	2	2,280	2,353	...	13	...	2,340
		Do.	Animistic	...	...	...	...	...	...	...	...	...	...	...	...	...	...	...	...	...	...	...	...

TABLE D.—Castes by Education—*contd.*

Class.	Group.	Caste.	Religion.	District Buldana. Males. Total.	Pupils.	Literate. Total Literate.	Knowing English.	Illiterate.	Females. Total.	Pupils.	Literate. Total Literate.	Knowing English.	Illiterate.	District Wun. Males. Total.	Pupils.	Literate. Total Literate.	Knowing English.	Illiterate.	Females. Total.	Pupils.	Literate. Total Literate.	Knowing English.	Illiterate.
49	50	51	52	53	54	55	56	57	58	59	60	61	62	63	64	65	66	67	68	69	70	71	72
D.—ARTISAN AND VILLAGE MENIAL—*contd.*	36.—DISTILLERS AND TODDY DRAWERS.	BANKAR	Hindu	...	...	...	...	...	...	...	...	...	...	...	...	...	...	...	...	...	...	...	...
		BHANDÁRI	Do.	...	...	...	...	...	...	...	...	...	...	...	...	...	...	...	...	...	...	...	...
		KALÁL	Do.	536	34	90		412	470	...	...	...	470	2,049	61	240	2	1,748	1,861	...	...	...	1,861
		Do.	Musalman	4	...	...	...	4	6	...	...	...	6	...	...	...	...	...	...	...	...	...	...
		Do.	Jain	...	...	...	...	...	...	...	...	...	...	...	...	...	...	...	...	...	...	...	...
		Do.	Animistic	...	...	...	...	...	...	...	...	...	...	39	2	...	...	37	33	...	...	...	33
		KALWÁR	Hindu	...	...	...	...	...	...	...	...	...	...	...	...	...	...	...	20	...	...	...	20
		PÁSI	Do.	2	...	...	...	2	...	...	...	...	...	20	...	...	...	20	24	...	...	...	24
			Total Group 36	*542*	*34*	*90*	...	*418*	*476*	...	...	...	*476*	*2,108*	*63*	*240*	*2*	*1,805*	*1,938*	...	...	...	*1,938*
	37.—BUTCHERS	KASÁI (BAKAR-KASÁI, KHÁTIK)	Hindu	107	...	...	...	107	128	...	...	...	128	188	3	2	...	183	158	...	...	...	158
		Do.	Musalman	99	...	1	...	98	107	...	...	...	107	10	...	...	...	10	7	...	...	...	7
			Total Group 37	*206*	...	*1*	...	*205*	*235*	...	...	...	*235*	*198*	*3*	*2*	...	*193*	*165*	...	...	...	*165*
	38.—LEATHER WORKERS	CHÁMBHÁR (MOCHI)	Hindu	3,002	4	8	...	2,990	2,778	...	...	...	2,778	1,448	1	7	...	1,440	1,241	...	...	...	1,241
		DABGAR	Do.	...	...	...	...	...	...	...	...	...	...	...	...	...	...	...	...	...	...	...	...
		DOHOR	Do.	1,120	...	3	...	1,117	1,081	...	...	...	1,081	9	...	...	...	9	3	...	...	...	3
		MÁDGI	Do.	...	...	...	...	...	...	...	...	...	...	1,316	...	3	...	1,313	1,353	...	...	...	1,353
		Do.	Animistic	...	...	...	...	...	...	...	...	...	...	4	...	...	...	4	3	...	...	...	3
		ZINGAR	Hindu	86	4	6	...	76	83	...	...	...	83	39	2	1	...	36	33	...	...	...	33
			Total Group 38	*4,208*	*8*	*17*	...	*4,183*	*3,942*	...	...	...	*3,942*	*2,816*	*3*	*11*	...	*2,802*	*2,633*	...	...	...	*2,633*
	38A.—VILLAGE WATCHMEN, ETC.	BALÁHI	Hindu	...	...	...	...	...	...	...	...	...	...	...	...	...	...	...	...	...	...	...	...
		Do.	Animistic	...	...	...	...	...	...	...	...	...	...	...	...	...	...	...	...	...	...	...	...
		BHUMAK	Hindu	...	...	...	...	...	...	...	...	...	...	...	...	...	...	...	...	...	...	...	...
		KHÁNGAR	Do.	...	...	...	...	...	...	...	...	...	...	...	...	...	...	...	...	...	...	...	...
		MAHÁR (DHER and KOTWÁL).	Do.	27,972	55	87	...	27,830	27,971	...	1	...	27,970	20,828	44	118	...	20,666	20,274	...	1	...	20,273
		Do.	Animistic	...	...	...	...	...	...	...	...	...	...	...	...	...	...	...	...	...	...	...	...
		PAHELWÁN	Hindu	...	...	...	...	...	...	...	...	...	...	...	...	...	...	...	...	...	...	...	...
		RÁMOSHI	Do.	5	...	...	...	5	5	...	...	...	5	17	...	...	...	17	12	...	...	...	12
			Total Group 38A	*27,977*	*55*	*87*	...	*27,835*	*27,976*	...	*1*	...	*27,975*	*20,845*	*44*	*118*	...	*20,683*	*20,286*	...	*1*	...	*20,285*
	39.—SCAVENGERS	BHANGI (HÁLÁLKHOR, KHAKROB and MEHTAR).	Hindu	60	...	...	...	60	52	...	...	...	52	57	...	...	...	57	35	...	...	...	35
		Do.	Musalman	13	...	...	...	13	13	...	...	...	13	8	...	...	...	8	8	...	...	...	8
		MÁNG	Hindu	4,987	11	19	...	4,957	5,136	...	...	...	5,136	2,625	1	...	...	2,624	2,692	...	...	...	2,692
		Do.	Animistic	...	...	...	...	...	...	...	...	...	...	...	...	...	...	...	1	...	...	...	1

Class.	Group.	Caste.	Religion.	District Basim. Males. Total.	District Basim. Males. Pupils.	District Basim. Males. Literate. Total Literate.	District Basim. Males. Literate. Knowing English.	District Basim. Males. Illiterate.	District Basim. Females. Total.	District Basim. Females. Pupils.	District Basim. Females. Literate. Total Literate.	District Basim. Females. Literate. Knowing English.	District Basim. Females. Illiterate.	Railway Passengers. Males. Total.	Railway Passengers. Males. Pupils.	Railway Passengers. Males. Literate. Total Literate.	Railway Passengers. Males. Literate. Knowing English.	Railway Passengers. Males. Illiterate.	Railway Passengers. Females. Total.	Railway Passengers. Females. Pupils.	Railway Passengers. Females. Literate. Total Literate.	Railway Passengers. Females. Literate. Knowing English.	Railway Passengers. Females. Illiterate.
73	74	75	76	77	78	79	80	81	82	83	84	85	86	87	88	89	90	91	92	93	94	95	96
D.—ARTISAN AND VILLAGE MENIAL—concld.	36.—DISTILLERS AND TODDY DRAWERS.	BANKAR	Hindu	...	...	...	...	...	...	...	...	...	...	...	...	...	...	...	...	...	...	...	...
		BHANDÁRI	Do.	...	...	...	...	...	...	...	...	...	...	...	...	...	...	...	...	...	...	...	...
		KALÁL	Do.	651	27	110	...	514	590	1	2	...	587	1	...	...	...	1	...	...	...	...	...
		Do.	Musalman	...	...	...	...	...	...	...	...	...	...	...	...	...	...	...	...	...	...	...	...
		Do.	Jain	...	...	...	...	...	...	...	...	...	...	...	...	...	...	...	...	...	...	...	...
		Do.	Animistic	...	...	...	...	...	...	...	...	...	...	...	...	...	...	...	...	...	...	...	...
		KALWÁR	Hindu	...	...	...	...	...	...	...	...	...	...	...	...	...	...	...	...	...	...	...	...
		PÁSI	Do.	11	...	1	...	10	5	...	...	...	5	12	...	...	...	12	5	...	...	...	5
			Total Group 36	*662*	*27*	*111*	...	*524*	*595*	*1*	*2*	...	*592*	*13*	...	...	...	*13*	*5*	...	...	...	*5*
	37.—BUTCHERS	KASÁI (BAKAR-KASÁI, KHÁTIK)	Hindu	58	3	3	...	52	39	...	...	...	39	...	...	...	...	...	...	...	...	...	...
		Do.	Musalman	20	...	...	...	20	22	...	...	...	22	...	...	...	...	...	...	...	...	...	...
			Total Group 37	*78*	*3*	*3*	...	*72*	*61*	...	...	...	*61*	...	...	...	...	...	...	...	...	...	...
	38.—LEATHER WORKERS.	CHÁMBHÁR (MOCHI)	Hindu	2,070	4	5	...	2,061	1,939	...	...	...	1,939	11	...	...	...	11	6	...	...	...	6
		DABGAR	Do.	...	...	...	...	...	...	...	...	...	...	...	...	...	...	...	...	...	...	...	...
		DOHOR	Do.	196	...	...	...	196	172	...	...	...	172	...	...	...	...	...	...	...	...	...	...
		MÁDGI	Do.	...	...	...	...	...	...	...	...	...	...	...	...	...	...	...	...	...	...	...	...
		Do.	Animistic	...	...	...	...	...	...	...	...	...	...	...	...	...	...	...	...	...	...	...	...
		ZINGAR	Hindu	76	1	5	...	70	71	...	...	...	71	...	...	...	...	...	...	...	...	...	...
			Total Group 38	*2,342*	*5*	*10*	...	*2,327*	*2,182*	...	...	...	*2,182*	*11*	...	...	...	*11*	*6*	...	...	...	*6*
	38A.—VILLAGE WATCHMEN, ETC.	BALÁHI	Hindu	...	...	...	...	...	...	...	...	...	...	...	...	...	...	...	...	...	...	...	...
		Do.	Animistic	...	...	...	...	...	...	...	...	...	...	...	...	...	...	...	...	...	...	...	...
		BHUMAK	Hindu	...	...	...	...	...	...	...	...	...	...	...	...	...	...	...	...	...	...	...	...
		KHÁNGAR	Do.	...	...	...	...	...	...	...	...	...	...	...	...	...	...	...	...	...	...	...	...
		MAHÁR (DHER and KOTWÁL).	Do.	26,174	30	48	1	26,096	26,457	...	1	...	26,456	39	2	3	...	34	37	...	...	...	37
		Do.	Animistic	...	...	...	...	...	...	...	...	...	...	...	...	...	...	...	...	...	...	...	...
		PAHELWÁN	Hindu	...	...	...	...	...	...	...	...	...	...	...	...	...	...	...	...	...	...	...	...
		RÁMOSHI	Do.	5	...	...	...	5	3	...	...	...	3	1	...	...	...	1	1	...	...	...	1
			Total Group 38A	*26,179*	*30*	*48*	*1*	*26,101*	*26,460*	...	*1*	...	*26,459*	*40*	*2*	*3*	...	*35*	*38*	...	...	...	*38*
	39.—SCAVENGERS.	BHANGI (HÁLÁLKHOR, KHÁKROB and MEHTAR).	Hindu	37	...	1	...	36	23	...	...	...	23	...	...	...	...	...	...	...	...	...	...
		Do.	Musalman	9	...	...	...	9	7	...	...	...	7	...	...	...	...	...	...	...	...	...	...
		MÁNG	Hindu	5,983	2	2	...	5,979	6,020	1	...	...	6,019	1	...	...	...	1	1	...	...	...	1
		Do.	Animistic	...	...	...	...	...	...	...	...	...	...	...	...	...	...	...	...	...	...	...	...

TABLE D.—Castes by Education—*contd.*

Class.	Group.	Caste.	Religion.	Total Strength. Males. Total.	Males. Pupils.	Males. Literate. Total Literate.	Males. Literate. Knowing English.	Males. Illiterate.	Females. Total.	Females. Pupils.	Females. Literate. Total Literate.	Females. Literate. Knowing English.	Females. Illiterate.	Territorial Distribution. District Amraoti. Males. Total.	Males. Pupils.	Males. Literate. Total Literate.	Males. Literate. Knowing English.	Males. Illiterate.	Females. Total.	Females. Pupils.	Females. Literate. Total Literate.	Females. Literate. Knowing English.	Females. Illiterate.
1	2	3	4	5	6	7	8	9	10	11	12	13	14	15	16	17	18	19	20	21	22	23	24
E.—VAGRANT MINOR ARTISANS AND PERFORMERS, &c.	39.—SCAVENGERS—*contd.*	MĀNG GĀRODI	Hindu	87	...	...	...	87	74	...	...	...	74	...	...	...	...	...	...	...	...	...	...
		MEHTAR	Sikh	17	...	1	..	16	15	..	...	...	15	1	...	...	...	1	1	...	...	...	1
		Do.	Animistic	1	...	...	...	1	1	...	...	...	1	...	...	...	...	...	...	...	...	...	...
		TĀGWĀLE	Hindu	56	...	...	...	56	57	...	...	...	57	...	...	...	...	...	...	...	...	...	...
			Total Group 39	*27,007*	*54*	*109*	*8*	*26,844*	*26,936*	*2*	*14*	...	*26,919*	*5,481*	*3*	*21*	...	*5,457*	*5,348*	*1*	...	...	*5,347*
	40.—GRINDSTONE MAKERS AND STONE-QUARRIERS.	GOTEFOD (FATARFOD)	Hindu	71	...	...	...	71	61	...	...	...	61	1	...	...	...	1	2	...	...	...	2
		PĀTHRAT (PĀTHARKAR AND PĀTHAR)	Do.	422	2	3	...	417	455	...	...	...	455	63	2	3	...	58	74	...	...	...	74
		TĀKANKĀR (TAKĀRI)	Do.	2,791	13	21	...	2,757	2,623	...	...	...	2,623	924	3	1	...	920	919	...	...	...	919
			Total Group 40	*3,284*	*15*	*24*	..	*3,245*	*3,139*	...	...	...	*3,139*	*988*	*5*	*4*	...	*979*	*995*	...	...	...	*995*
	41.—EARTH WORKERS AND STONE DRESSERS.	BĀGARI	Hindu	1	...	...	...	1	...	...	...	...	...	...	...	...	...	...	...	...	...	...	...
		BELDĀR	Do.	6,163	37	43	...	6,083	6,054	...	1	...	6,053	1,264	19	11	...	1,234	1,235	...	...	...	1,235
		Do.	Musalman	7	...	...	...	7	4	...	...	...	4	7	...	...	...	7	4	...	...	...	4
		GOCHKI	Hindu	47	...	...	...	47	47	...	...	...	47	...	...	...	...	...	...	...	...	...	...
		MĀNEWĀD	Do.	25	...	11	2	14	29	...	...	...	29	11	...	9	2	2	9	...	...	...	4
		SAGUR	Do.	32	...	2	...	30	31	...	...	...	31	2	...	...	...	2	4	...	...	...	9
		SILĀWAT	Do.	3	...	...	...	3	3	...	...	...	3	...	...	...	...	...	...	...	...	...	...
		WADDAR	Do.	3,101	6	6	...	3,089	3,015	...	...	...	3,015	411	2	1	...	408	421	...	...	...	421
			Total Group 41	*9,379*	*48*	*62*	*2*	*9,274*	*9,188*	...	*1*	...	*9,182*	*1,696*	*21*	*21*	*2*	*1,653*	*1,673*	...	...	...	*1,678*
	42.—KNIFE GRINDERS	SIKLIKAR	Hindu	19	...	...	...	19	17	...	...	...	17	4	...	...	...	4	4	...	...	...	4
		Do.	Musalman	16	...	...	...	16	21	...	...	...	21	...	...	...	...	...	...	...	...	...	...
			Total Group 42	*35*	...	...	...	*35*	*38*	...	...	...	*38*	*4*	...	...	...	*4*	*4*	...	...	...	*4*
	43.—MAT MAKERS, CANE SPLITTERS AND GRASS-CUTTERS.	BĀNSFOD	Hindu	11	...	...	...	11	15	...	...	...	15	10	...	...	...	10	13	...	...	...	13
		BASOD	Do.	94	...	...	...	94	97	...	...	...	97	73	...	...	...	73	79	...	...	...	79
		Do.	Animistic	31	...	...	...	31	39	...	...	...	39	...	...	...	...	...	...	...	...	...	...
		BOREKAR	Hindu	58	...	...	...	58	62	...	...	...	62	...	...	...	...	...	...	...	...	...	...
		BURUD	Do.	618	8	24	...	586	629	...	...	...	629	171	...	6	...	165	173	...	...	...	173
		Do.	Animistic	10	...	...	...	10	12	...	...	...	12	...	...	...	...	...	...	...	...	...	...
		KĀNGAR	Hindu	22	2	...	...	20	13	...	...	...	13	15	1	...	...	14	12	...	...	...	12
		Do.	Musalman	1	...	...	...	1	1	...	...	...	1	1	...	...	...	1	1	...	...	...	1
		KEKĀDI	Hindu	1,004	2	6	...	996	1,020	...	...	...	1,020	175	...	1	...	174	164	...	...	...	164
		THOTI	Do.	20	...	...	...	20	23	...	...	...	23	...	...	...	...	...	...	...	...	...	...
		Do.	Animistic	76	...	...	...	76	107	...	...	...	107	...	...	...	...	...	...	...	...	...	...
			Total Group 43	*1,946*	*12*	*80*	...	*1,908*	*2,018*	...	...	...	*2,018*	*446*	*1*	*7*	...	*437*	*442*	...	...	...	*442*

Class.	Group.	Caste.	Religion.	District Akola. Males. Total.	Males. Pupils.	Males. Literate. Total Literate.	Males. Literate. Knowing English.	Males. Illiterate.	Females. Total.	Females. Pupils.	Females. Literate. Total Literate.	Females. Literate. Knowing English.	Females. Illiterate.	District Ellichpur. Males. Total.	Males. Pupils.	Males. Literate. Total Literate.	Males. Literate. Knowing English.	Males. Illiterate.	Females. Total.	Females. Pupils.	Females. Literate. Total Literate.	Females. Literate. Knowing English.	Females. Illiterate.
25	26	27	28	29	30	31	32	33	34	35	36	37	38	39	40	41	42	43	44	45	46	47	48
E.—VAGRANT MINOR ARTISANS AND PERFORMERS, &c.	39.—SCAVENGERS—contd.	MÁNG GÁRODI	Hindu	...	...	...	...	...	...	...	...	...	...	...	...	...	...	...	...	...	...	...	...
		MEHTAR	Sikh	16	...	1	...	15	14	...	...	...	14	...	...	...	...	...	...	...	...	...	...
		Do.	Animistic	...	...	...	...	...	...	...	...	...	...	...	...	...	...	...	...	...	...	...	...
		TÁGWÁLE	Hindu	...	...	...	...	...	...	...	...	...	...	...	...	...	...	...	...	...	...	...	...
			Total Group 39*	5,198	24	22	1	5,147	5,053	...	...	...	5,053	2,409	13	44	2	2,352	2,414	...	14	...	2,400
	40.—GRINDSTONE MAKERS AND STONE-QUARRIERS.	GOTEPOD (FATARPOD)	Hindu	...	...	...	...	...	...	...	...	...	...	...	...	...	...	...	...	...	...	...	...
		PÁTHRAT (PÁTHARKAR AND PÁTHAR)	Do.	195	...	...	...	195	196	...	...	...	196	...	...	...	...	...	...	...	...	...	...
		TÁKANKÁR (TAKÁRI)	Do.	1,217	6	4	...	1,207	1,106	...	...	...	1,106	450	2	...	...	448	413	...	...	...	413
			Total Group 40	1,412	6	4	...	1,402	1,302	...	...	...	1,302	450	2	...	...	448	413	...	...	...	413
	41.—EARTH WORKERS AND STONE DRESSERS.	BÁGARI	Hindu	1	...	...	...	1	...	...	...	...	...	...	...	...	...	...	...	...	...	...	...
		BELDÁR	Do.	1,492	5	6	...	1,481	1,510	...	...	...	1,510	175	1	1	...	173	171	...	...	...	171
		Do.	Musalman	...	...	...	...	...	...	...	...	...	...	...	...	...	...	...	...	...	...	...	...
		GOCHKI	Hindu	...	...	...	...	...	...	...	...	...	...	...	...	...	...	...	...	...	...	...	...
		MÁNEWÁD	Do.	3	...	1	...	2	5	...	...	...	5	1	...	...	...	1	6	...	...	...	6
		SAGUR	Do.	...	...	...	...	...	...	...	...	...	...	...	...	...	...	...	...	...	...	...	...
		SILÁWAT	Do.	...	...	...	...	...	...	...	...	...	...	...	...	...	...	...	...	...	...	...	...
		WADDAR	Do.	151	2	1	...	148	138	...	...	...	138	23	1	...	...	22	20	...	...	...	20
			Total Group 41	1,647	7	8	...	1,632	1,653	...	...	...	1,653	199	2	1	...	196	197	...	...	...	197
	42.—KNIFE GRINDERS	SIKLIKAR	Hindu	...	...	...	...	...	...	...	...	...	...	...	...	...	...	...	...	...	...	...	...
		Do.	Musalman	...	...	...	...	...	...	...	...	...	...	...	...	...	...	...	...	...	...	...	...
	43.—MAT MAKERS, CANE SPLITTERS AND GRASS-CUTTERS	BÁNSFOD	Hindu	...	...	...	...	...	1	...	...	...	1	1	...	...	...	1	1	...	...	...	1
		BASOD	Do.	...	...	...	...	...	...	...	...	...	...	20	...	...	...	20	18	...	...	...	18
		Do.	Animistic	...	...	...	...	...	...	...	...	...	...	31	...	...	...	31	39	...	...	...	39
		BOREKAR	Hindu	57	...	...	...	57	61	...	...	...	61	1	...	...	...	1	1	...	...	...	1
		BURUD	Do.	98	1	6	...	91	99	...	...	...	99	124	2	5	...	117	111	...	...	...	111
		Do.	Animistic	...	...	...	...	...	...	...	...	...	...	...	...	...	...	...	...	...	...	...	...
		KÁNGAR	Hindu	...	...	...	...	...	...	...	...	...	...	1	1	...	...	...	1	...	...	...	1
		Do.	Musalman	...	...	...	...	...	...	...	...	...	...	...	...	...	...	...	...	...	...	...	...
		KEKÁDI	Hindu	205	1	2	...	202	194	...	...	...	194	112	1	...	...	111	122	...	...	...	122
		THOTI	Do.	...	...	...	...	...	...	...	...	...	...	...	...	...	...	...	...	...	...	...	...
		Do.	Animistic	...	...	...	...	...	...	...	...	...	...	...	...	...	...	...	...	...	...	...	...
			Total Group 43	360	2	8	...	350	355	...	...	...	355	290	4	5	...	281	293	...	...	...	293

TABLE D.—astes by Education—*contd.*

Class.	Group.	Caste.	Religion.	Buldana Males Total.	Buldana Males Pupils.	Buldana Males Literate Total Literate.	Buldana Males Literate Knowing English.	Buldana Males Illiterate.	Buldana Females Total.	Buldana Females Pupils.	Buldana Females Literate Total Literate.	Buldana Females Literate Knowing English.	Buldana Females Illiterate.	Wun Males Total.	Wun Males Pupils.	Wun Males Literate Total Literate.	Wun Males Literate Knowing English.	Wun Males Illiterate.	Wun Females Total.	Wun Females Pupils.	Wun Females Literate Total Literate.	Wun Females Literate Knowing English.	Wun Females Illiterate.
49	50	51	52	53	54	55	56	57	58	59	60	61	62	63	64	65	66	67	68	69	70	71	72
E.—VAGRANT MINOR ARTISANS AND PERFORMERS, &c.	39.—SCAVENGERS—*contd.*	MÁNG GÁRODI	Hindu	...	...	...	...	...	...	...	...	...	...	87	...	...	...	87	74	...	...	...	74
		MEHTAR	Sikh	...	...	...	...	...	...	...	...	...	...	...	...	...	...	...	...	...	...	...	...
		Do.	Animistic	...	...	...	...	...	...	...	...	...	...	1	...	...	...	1	1	...	...	...	1
		TÁGWÁLE	Hindu	56	...	...	...	56	57	...	...	...	57	...	...	...	...	...	...	...	...	...	...
			Total Group 39	*5,116*	*11*	*19*	...	*5,086*	*5,268*	...	...	...	*5,268*	*2,778*	*1*	...	...	*2,777*	*2,811*	...	...	...	*2,811*
	40.—GRINDSTONE MAKERS AND STONE-QUARRIERS.	GOTEFOD (FATARFOD)	Hindu	19	...	...	...	19	19	...	...	...	19	35	...	...	...	35	29	...	...	...	29
		PÁTHRAT (PÁTHARKAR AND PÁTHAR).	Do.	69	...	...	...	69	98	...	...	...	98	64	...	...	...	64	51	...	...	...	51
		TÁKANKÁR (TAKÁRI)	Do.	58	...	1	...	57	48	...	...	...	48	110	2	15	...	93	112	...	...	...	112
			Total Group 40	*146*	...	*1*	...	*145*	*165*	...	...	...	*165*	*209*	*2*	*16*	...	*192*	*192*	...	...	...	*192*
	41.—EARTH WORKERS AND STONE DRESSERS.	BÁGARI	Hindu	...	...	...	...	...	...	...	...	...	...	...	...	...	...	...	...	...	...	...	...
		BELDÁR	Do.	1,188	6	9	...	1,173	1,176	...	...	...	1,176	1,409	5	15	...	1,389	1,383	...	1	...	1,382
		Do.	Musalman	...	...	...	...	...	...	...	...	...	...	...	...	...	...	...	...	...	...	...	...
		GOCHKI	Hindu	...	...	...	...	...	...	...	...	...	...	47	...	...	...	47	47	...	...	...	47
		MÁNEWÁD	Do.	...	...	...	...	...	...	...	...	...	...	10	...	1	...	9	9	...	...	...	9
		SAGUR	Do.	30	...	2	...	28	27	...	...	...	27	...	...	...	...	...	...	...	...	...	...
		SILÁWAT	Do.	3	...	...	...	3	3	...	...	...	3	...	...	...	...	...	...	...	...	...	...
		WADDAR	Do.	977	1	3	...	973	999	...	...	...	999	551	...	...	...	551	504	...	...	...	504
			Total Group 41	*2,198*	*7*	*14*	...	*2,177*	*2,206*	...	...	...	*2,206*	*2,017*	*5*	*16*	...	*1,996*	*1,943*	...	*1*	...	*1,942*
	42.—KNIFE GRINDERS	SIKLIKAR	Hindu	15	...	...	...	15	13	...	...	...	13	...	...	...	...	...	...	...	...	...	...
		Do.	Musalman	2	...	...	...	2	5	...	...	...	5	9	...	...	...	9	11	...	...	...	11
			Total Group 42	*17*	...	...	...	*17*	*18*	...	...	...	*18*	*9*	...	...	...	*9*	*11*	...	...	...	*11*
	43.—MAT MAKERS, CANE SPLITTERS AND GRASS-CUTTERS.	BÁNSFOD	Hindu	...	...	...	...	...	...	...	...	...	...	...	...	...	...	...	...	...	...	...	...
		BASOD	Do.	...	...	...	...	...	...	...	...	...	...	1	...	...	...	1	...	...	...	...	...
		Do.	Animistic	...	...	...	...	...	...	...	...	...	...	...	...	...	...	...	...	...	...	...	...
		BOREKAR	Hindu	...	...	...	...	...	...	...	...	...	...	...	...	...	...	...	...	...	...	...	...
		BURUD	Do.	7	...	...	...	7	8	...	...	...	8	128	2	5	...	121	140	...	...	...	140
		Do.	Animistic	...	...	...	...	...	...	...	...	...	...	10	...	...	...	10	12	...	...	...	12
		KÁNGAR	Hindu	...	...	...	...	...	...	...	...	...	...	6	...	...	...	6	...	...	...	...	...
		Do.	Musalman	...	...	...	...	...	...	...	...	...	...	...	...	...	...	...	...	...	...	...	...
		KEKÁDI	Hindu	323	...	2	...	321	323	...	...	...	323	45	...	...	...	45	59	...	...	...	59
		THOTI	Do.	...	...	...	...	...	...	...	...	...	...	20	...	...	...	20	23	...	...	...	23
		Do.	Animistic	...	...	...	...	...	...	...	...	...	...	76	...	...	...	76	107	...	...	...	107
			Total Group 43	*330*	...	*2*	...	*328*	*331*	...	...	...	*331*	*286*	*2*	*6*	...	*279*	*341*	...	...	...	*341*

Class.	Group.	Caste.	Religion.	District Basim. Males. Total.	Males. Pupils.	Males. Literate. Total Literate.	Males. Literate. Knowing English.	Males. Illiterate.	Females. Total.	Females. Pupils.	Females. Literate. Total Literate.	Females. Literate. Knowing English.	Females. Illiterate.	Railway Passengers. Males. Total.	Males. Pupils.	Males. Literate. Total Literate.	Males. Literate. Knowing English.	Males. Illiterate.	Females. Total.	Females. Pupils.	Females. Literate. Total Literate.	Females. Literate. Knowing English.	Females. Illiterate.
73	74	75	76	77	78	79	80	81	82	83	84	85	86	87	88	89	90	91	92	93	94	95	96
E.—Vagrant Minor Artisans and Performers, &c.	39.—Scavengers—*contd.*	Máng Gárodi	Hindu	...	...	...	...	...	...	...	...	...	...	...	...	...	...	...	...	...	...	...	...
		Mehtar	Sikh	...	...	...	...	...	...	...	...	...	...	...	...	...	...	...	...	...	...	...	...
		Do.	Animistic	...	...	...	...	...	...	...	...	...	...	...	...	...	...	...	...	...	...	...	...
		Tágwále	Hindu	...	...	...	...	...	...	...	...	...	...	...	...	...	...	...	...	...	...	...	...
			Total Group 39	6,029	2	3	...	6,024	6,050	1	...	...	6,049	1	...	...	...	1	1	...	...	...	1
	40.—Grindstone makers and stone-quarriers.	Gotefod (Fatarfod)	Hindu	16	...	...	...	16	11	...	...	...	11	...	...	...	...	...	...	...	...	...	...
		Páthrat (Pátharkar and Páthar).	Do.	31	...	...	...	31	36	...	...	...	36	...	...	...	...	...	...	...	...	...	...
		Tákankár (Takári)	Do.	32	...	...	...	32	25	...	...	...	25	...	...	...	...	...	...	...	...	...	...
			Total Group 40	79	...	...	...	79	72	...	...	...	72	...	...	...	...	...	...	...	...	...	...
	41.—Earth workers and stone dressers.	Bágari	Hindu	...	...	...	...	...	...	...	...	...	...	...	...	...	...	...	...	...	...	...	...
		Beldár	Do.	635	1	1	...	633	579	...	...	...	579	...	...	...	...	...	...	...	...	...	...
		Do.	Musalman	...	...	...	...	...	...	...	...	...	...	...	...	...	...	...	...	...	...	...	...
		Gochki	Hindu	...	...	...	...	...	...	...	...	...	...	...	...	...	...	...	...	...	...	...	...
		Mánewád	Do.	...	...	...	...	...	...	...	...	...	...	...	...	...	...	...	...	...	...	...	...
		Sagur	Do.	...	...	...	...	...	...	...	...	...	...	...	...	...	...	...	...	...	...	...	...
		Siláwat	Do.	...	...	...	...	...	...	...	...	...	...	...	...	...	...	...	...	...	...	...	...
		Waddar	Do.	988	...	1	...	987	933	...	...	...	933	...	...	...	...	...	...	...	...	...	...
			Total Group 41	1,628	1	2	...	1,620	1,612	...	...	...	1,612	...	...	...	...	...	...	...	...	...	...
	42.—Knife grinders	Siklikar	Hindu	...	...	...	...	...	...	...	...	...	...	...	...	...	...	...	...	...	...	...	...
		Do.	Musalman	5	...	...	...	5	5	...	...	...	5	...	...	...	...	...	...	...	...	...	...
			Total Group 42	6	...	...	...	6	6	...	...	...	6	...	...	...	...	...	...	...	...	...	...
	43.—Mat makers, cane splitters and grass-cutters.	Bánsfod	Hindu	...	...	...	...	...	...	...	...	...	...	...	...	...	...	...	...	...	...	...	...
		Basod	Do.	...	...	...	...	...	...	...	...	...	...	...	...	...	...	...	...	...	...	...	...
		Do.	Animistic	...	...	...	...	...	...	...	...	...	...	...	...	...	...	...	...	...	...	...	...
		Borekar	Hindu	...	...	...	...	...	...	...	...	...	...	...	...	...	...	...	...	...	...	...	...
		Burud	Do.	90	3	2	...	85	98	...	...	...	98	...	...	...	...	...	...	...	...	...	...
		Do.	Animistic	...	...	...	...	...	...	...	...	...	...	...	...	...	...	...	...	...	...	...	...
		Kángar	Hindu	...	...	...	...	...	...	...	...	...	...	...	...	...	...	...	...	...	...	...	...
		Do.	Musalman	...	...	...	...	...	...	...	...	...	...	...	...	...	...	...	...	...	...	...	...
		Kekádi	Do.	144	...	1	...	143	158	...	...	...	158	...	...	...	...	...	...	...	...	...	...
		Thoti	Do.	...	...	...	...	...	...	...	...	...	...	...	...	...	...	...	...	...	...	...	...
		Do.	Animistic	...	...	...	...	...	...	...	...	...	...	...	...	...	...	...	...	...	...	...	...
			Total Group 43	234	3	3	...	228	258	...	...	...	258	...	...	...	...	...	...	...	...	...	...

TABLE D.—Castes by Education —*contd.*

Class.	Group.	Caste.	Religion.	Total Strength: Males: Total.	Males: Pupils.	Males: Literate: Total Literate.	Males: Literate: Knowing English.	Males: Illiterate.	Females: Total.	Females: Pupils.	Females: Literate: Total Literate.	Females: Literate: Knowing English.	Females: Illiterate.	Territorial Distribution, District Amraoti: Males: Total.	Males: Pupils.	Males: Literate: Total Literate.	Males: Literate: Knowing English.	Males: Illiterate.	Females: Total.	Females: Pupils.	Females: Literate: Total Literate.	Females: Literate: Knowing English.	Females: Illiterate.
1	2	3	4	5	6	7	8	9	10	11	12	13	14	15	16	17	18	19	20	21	22	23	24
B.—VAGRANT MINOR ARTISANS AND PERFORMERS, &c.—*contd.*	44.—HUNTERS, FOWLERS, ETC.	BAHELIYÁ	Hindu	52	...	2	...	50	9	...	...	...	9	20	...	...	...	20	1	...	...	...	1
		BEDAR	Do.	1,515	97	249	*19*	1,169	1,526	4	4	...	1,518	93	4	25	...	64	69	...	...	...	69
		BERAD	Do.	86	10	30	...	46	77	...	...	...	77	2	...	1	...	1	1	...	...	...	1
		MUTRÁSI	Do.	20	6	4	...	10	9	...	1	...	8	...	...	...	...	...	...	...	...	...	...
		PÁRDHI	Do.	3,537	16	13	...	3,508	3,357	...	...	...	3,357	582	3	1	...	578	584	...	...	...	584
		Do.	Animistic	2	...	...	...	2	3	...	...	...	3	...	...	...	...	...	...	...	...	...	...
			Total Group 44	*5,212*	*129*	*298*	*19*	*4,786*	*4,981*	*4*	*5*	...	*4,972*	*697*	*7*	*27*	...	*663*	*655*	...	...	...	*655*
	45.—MISCELLANEOUS AND DISREPUTABLE LIVERS (BEGGARS AND PROSTITUTES).	ARIDRA	Hindu	1	...	1	...	...	3	...	...	...	3	...	...	...	...	...	...	...	...	...	...
		BÁLSANTO	Do.	2	...	...	...	2	2	...	...	...	2	...	...	...	...	...	...	...	...	...	...
		BHÁMTI	Do.	838	9	10	...	819	936	...	1	...	935	214	...	4	...	210	263	...	...	...	263
		BHATTÁWÁD	Do.	4	...	1	...	3	4	...	...	...	4	...	...	...	...	...	...	...	...	...	...
		DAKALWÁD	Do.	15	...	...	...	15	15	...	...	...	15	7	...	...	...	7	2	...	...	...	2
		DÁNGAT	Do.	244	3	2	...	239	242	...	...	...	242	...	...	...	...	...	...	...	...	...	...
		DUSÁDH	Do.	5	...	1	...	4	...	...	...	...	...	3	...	1	...	2	...	...	...	...	...
		GUJRÁTHI	Do.	611	43	121	*1*	447	487	...	...	...	487	88	2	16	...	70	55	...	...	...	55
		Do.	Jain	179	22	90	...	67	168	3	...	...	165	19	1	6	...	12	11	...	...	...	11
		HINDUSTÁNI	Hindu	28	1	5	...	22	4	...	...	...	4	5	...	...	...	5	...	...	...	...	...
		HIRMUSTHI	Do.	3	...	...	...	3	1	...	...	...	1	...	...	...	...	...	...	...	...	...	...
		KÁMÁTHI	Do.	12	2	5	*3*	5	10	...	...	...	10	1	...	1	...	...	1	...	...	...	1
		KASBAN (KASBI)	Do.	4	...	...	...	4	10	...	...	...	10	...	...	...	...	...	5	...	...	...	5
		Do. (KÁSBI AND NÁIKAN)	Musalman	2	...	...	...	2	13	...	1	...	12	...	...	...	...	...	3	...	1	...	2
		KUNJDÁ	Do.	1	...	...	...	1	...	...	...	...	...	...	...	...	...	...	...	...	...	...	...
		MADRÁSI	Hindu	10	...	5	...	5	6	...	...	...	6	4	...	3	...	1	1	...	...	...	1
		MARÁTHE	Do.	9,551	322	613	*16*	8,616	9,487	5	6	...	9,476	3,046	73	149	*7*	2,824	2,954	1	1	...	2,952
		MUSALMAN	Musalman	1,110	39	87	*2*	984	882	5	3	...	874	314	13	33	*2*	268	242	2	3	...	237
		PÁDHAR	Do.	...	...	...	...	...	9	...	...	...	9	...	...	...	...	...	...	...	...	...	...
		PARDESHI	Hindu	440	17	46	...	377	199	...	1	...	198	151	11	18	...	122	44	...	1	...	43
		RÁMJÁNI	Do.	2	...	...	...	2	2	...	...	...	2	...	...	...	...	...	...	...	...	...	...
		TÁLKUTE	Do.	11	...	...	...	11	7	...	...	...	7	...	...	...	...	...	...	...	...	...	...
		TELANGÁ	Do.	1,076	10	47	*1*	1,019	1,005	...	3	*1*	1,002	52	1	5	...	46	51	...	...	...	51
		VIDUR (KRIHNAPAKSHI)	Do.	5,314	548	1,410	*19*	3,356	5,377	10	10	...	5,357	1,942	195	530	*4*	1,217	1,908	3	6	...	1,899
		Do.	Jain	1	...	1	...	...	3	...	...	...	3	1	...	1	...	...	3	...	...	...	3
			Total Group 45	*19,484*	*1,016*	*2,445*	*42*	*16,008*	*18,872*	*28*	*25*	*1*	*18,824*	*5,847*	*296*	*767*	*18*	*4,784*	*5,548*	*6*	*12*	...	*5,526*
	46.—TUMBLERS AND ACROBATS.	GOPÁL	Hindu	1,725	2	...	...	1,723	1,694	...	...	...	1,694	56	2	...	...	54	55	...	...	...	55
		KANJHÁR	Do.	1	...	...	...	1	...	...	...	...	...	1	...	...	...	1	...	...	...	...	...

Table D.—[Castes by Education.]

E.—VAGRANT MINOR ARTISANS AND PERFORMERS, ETC.—*contd.*

Class.	Group.	Caste.	Religion.	District Akola. Males. Total.	Males. Pupils.	Males. Literate. Total Literate.	Males. Literate. Knowing English.	Males. Illiterate.	Females. Total.	Females. Pupils.	Females. Literate. Total Literate.	Females. Literate. Knowing English.	Females. Illiterate.	District Ellichpur. Males. Total.	Males. Pupils.	Males. Literate. Total Literate.	Males. Literate. Knowing English.	Males. Illiterate.	Females. Total.	Females. Pupils.	Females. Literate. Total Literate.	Females. Literate. Knowing English.	Females. Illiterate.
25	26	27	28	29	30	31	32	33	34	35	36	37	38	39	40	41	42	43	44	45	46	47	48
	44.—Hunters, fowlers, etc.	Bahaliyá	Hindu	7	...	1	...	6	...	...	...	...	...	21	...	1	...	20	8	...	...	...	8
		Bedar	Do.	882	67	152	14	663	977	3	3	...	971	144	11	23	...	110	120	...	...	...	120
		Berad	Do.	...	...	...	...	...	...	...	...	...	...	...	...	...	...	...	...	...	...	...	...
		Mutrási	Do.	...	...	...	...	...	...	...	...	...	...	20	6	4	...	10	9	...	1	...	8
		Párdhi	Do.	874	6	9	...	859	761	...	...	...	761	570	...	...	...	570	575	...	...	...	575
		Do.	Animistic	...	...	...	...	...	...	...	...	...	...	...	...	...	...	...	...	...	...	...	...
			Total Group 44	*1,768*	*73*	*182*	*14*	*1,528*	*1,738*	*3*	*3*	...	*1,732*	*755*	*17*	*28*	...	*710*	*712*	...	*1*	...	*711*
	45.—Miscellaneous and disreputable livers (Beggars and Prostitutes).	Aridra	Hindu	...	...	...	...	...	...	...	...	...	...	...	...	...	...	...	...	...	...	...	...
		Bálsanto	Do.	...	...	...	...	...	...	...	...	...	...	...	...	...	...	...	...	...	...	...	...
		Bhámtí	Do.	217	6	1	...	210	245	...	1	...	244	76	1	2	...	73	91	...	...	...	91
		Bhattáwád	Do.	...	...	...	...	...	...	...	...	...	...	...	...	...	...	...	...	...	...	...	...
		Dakalwád	Do.	...	...	...	...	...	...	...	...	...	...	3	...	...	...	3	3	...	...	...	3
		Dángat	Do.	9	...	...	...	9	12	...	...	...	12	...	...	...	...	...	...	...	...	...	...
		Dusádh	Do.	...	...	...	...	...	...	...	...	...	...	2	...	...	...	2	...	...	...	...	...
		Gujráthi	Do.	210	17	73	...	120	156	...	...	...	156	180	22	20	...	138	147	...	...	...	147
		Do.	Jain	154	21	81	...	52	152	3	...	...	149	5	...	2	...	3	5	...	...	...	5
		Hindustáni	Hindu	8	1	1	...	6	1	...	...	...	1	...	...	...	...	...	...	...	...	...	...
		Hirmusthi	Do.	...	...	...	...	...	...	...	...	...	...	...	...	...	...	...	...	...	...	...	...
		Kámáthi	Do.	9	2	3	3	4	9	...	...	...	9	...	...	...	...	...	...	...	...	...	...
		Kasbañ (Kasbi)	Do.	...	...	...	...	...	...	...	...	...	...	...	...	...	...	...	...	...	...	...	...
		Do. (Kasbi and Náikan)	Musalman	...	...	...	...	...	6	...	...	...	6	...	...	...	...	...	...	...	...	...	...
		Kunjdá	Do.	...	...	...	...	...	...	...	...	...	...	1	...	...	...	1	...	...	...	...	...
		Madrási	Hindu	...	...	...	...	...	1	...	...	...	1	...	...	...	...	...	...	...	...	...	...
		Maráthe	Do.	914	51	123	*3*	740	1,027	...	1	...	1,026	352	23	32	*1*	297	351	...	...	...	351
		Musalman	Musalman	126	4	10	...	112	92	...	...	...	92	47	2	12	...	33	22	...	...	...	22
		Pádhar	Do.	...	...	...	...	...	9	...	...	...	9	...	...	...	...	...	...	...	...	...	...
		Pardeshi	Hindu	51	...	8	...	43	13	...	...	...	13	30	...	1	...	29	12	...	...	...	12
		Rámjáni	Do.	2	...	...	...	2	2	...	...	...	2	...	...	...	...	...	...	...	...	...	...
		Tálkute	Do.	1	...	...	...	1	1	...	...	...	1	...	...	...	...	...	...	...	...	...	...
		Telangá	Do.	55	...	6	...	49	43	...	2	*1*	41	28	1	10	*1*	17	22	...	1	...	21
		Vidur (Krishnapakshi)	Do.	899	121	261	*3*	517	920	4	2	...	914	337	48	106	*4*	183	300	...	...	...	300
		Do.	Jain	...	...	...	...	...	...	...	...	...	...	...	...	...	...	...	...	...	...	...	...
			Total Group 45	*2,655*	*228*	*587*	*9*	*1,865*	*2,689*	*7*	*6*	*1*	*2,676*	*1,061*	*97*	*185*	*6*	*779*	*953*	...	*1*	...	*952*
	46.—Tumblers and Acrobats.	Gopál	Hindu	121	...	...	...	121	141	...	...	...	141	...	...	...	...	...	...	...	...	...	...
		Kanjhár	Do.	...	...	...	...	...	...	...	...	...	...	...	...	...	...	...	...	...	...	...	...

TABLE D.—Castes by Education—*contd.*

E.—VAGRANT MINOR ARTISANS AND PERFORMERS, ETC.—*contd.*

Class.	Group.	Caste.	Religion.	District Buldana. Males. Total.	Pupils.	Literate. Total Literate.	Literate. Knowing English.	Illiterate.	District Buldana. Females. Total.	Pupils.	Literate. Total Literate.	Literate. Knowing English.	Illiterate.	District Wun. Males. Total.	Pupils.	Literate. Total Literate.	Literate. Knowing English.	Illiterate.	District Wun. Females. Total.	Pupils.	Literate. Total Literate.	Literate. Knowing English.	Illiterate.
49	50	51	52	53	54	55	56	57	58	59	60	61	62	63	64	65	66	67	68	69	70	71	72
	44.—Hunters, fowlers, etc.	Baheliyá	Hindu	...	...	...	...	...	...	...	...	...	...	2	...	...	...	2	...	...	...	...	...
		Bedar	Do.	167	7	25	3	135	136	1	1	...	134	113	8	11	2	94	122	...	...	...	122
		Berad	Do.	10	...	3	...	7	7	...	...	...	7	74	10	26	...	38	69	...	...	...	69
		Mutrási	Do.	...	...	...	...	...	...	...	...	...	...	...	...	...	...	...	...	...	...	...	...
		Párdhi	Do.	838	7	3	...	828	842	...	...	...	842	562	...	...	...	562	517	...	...	...	517
		Do.	Animistic	...	...	...	...	...	...	...	...	...	...	2	...	...	...	2	3	...	...	...	3
			Total Group 44	*1,015*	*14*	*31*	*3*	*970*	*985*	*1*	*1*	...	*983*	*753*	*18*	*37*	*2*	*698*	*711*	...	...	...	*711*
	45.—Miscellaneous and disreputable livers (Beggars and Prostitutes).	Aridra	Hindu	...	...	...	...	...	...	...	...	...	...	1	...	1	...	...	3	...	...	...	3
		Bálsanto	Do.	...	...	...	...	...	...	...	...	...	...	2	...	...	...	2	2	...	...	...	2
		Bhámtí	Do.	3	...	...	...	3	4	...	...	...	4	327	2	3	...	322	331	...	...	...	331
		Bhattáwád	Do.	...	...	...	...	...	...	...	...	...	...	4	...	1	...	3	4	...	...	...	4
		Dakalwád	Do.	...	...	...	...	...	...	...	...	...	...	...	...	...	...	...	4	...	...	...	4
		Dángat	Do.	178	3	1	...	174	167	...	...	...	167	8	...	...	...	8	8	...	...	...	8
		Dusádh	Do.	...	...	...	...	...	...	...	...	...	...	...	...	...	...	...	...	...	...	...	...
		Gujráthi	Do.	105	1	10	*1*	94	106	...	...	...	106	20	1	2	...	17	17	...	...	...	17
		Do.	Jain	1	...	1	...	...	...	...	...	...	...	...	...	...	...	...	...	...	...	...	...
		Hindustáni	Hindu	1	...	...	...	1	...	...	...	...	...	4	...	2	...	2	3	...	...	...	3
		Hirmusthi	Do.	...	...	...	...	...	...	...	...	...	...	...	...	...	...	...	...	...	...	...	...
		Kámáthi	Do.	2	...	1	...	1	...	...	...	...	...	...	...	...	...	...	...	...	...	...	...
		Kasban (Kasbi)	Do.	...	...	...	...	...	...	...	...	...	...	4	...	...	...	4	4	...	...	...	4
		Do. (Kasbi and Náikan)	Musalman	...	...	...	...	...	2	...	...	...	2	1	...	...	...	1	1	...	...	...	1
		Kunjdá	Do.	...	...	...	...	...	...	...	...	...	...	...	...	...	...	...	...	...	...	...	...
		Madrási	Hindu	1	...	...	...	1	...	...	...	...	...	4	...	1	...	3	4	...	...	...	4
		Maráthe	Do.	2,002	104	170	2	1,728	1,990	3	3	...	1,984	1,718	38	78	2	1,602	1,720	1	...	...	1,719
		Musalman	Musalman	199	5	12	...	182	176	...	...	...	176	100	1	5	...	94	59	...	...	...	59
		Pádhar	Do.	...	...	...	...	...	...	...	...	...	...	...	...	...	...	...	...	...	...	...	...
		Pardeshi	Hindu	136	4	10	...	122	113	...	...	...	113	45	...	4	...	41	11	...	...	...	11
		Rámjáni	Do.	...	...	...	...	...	...	...	...	...	...	...	...	...	...	...	...	...	...	...	...
		Tálkute	Do.	...	...	...	...	...	...	...	...	...	...	...	...	...	...	...	...	...	...	...	...
		Telangá	Do.	95	1	12	...	82	78	...	...	...	78	775	2	11	...	762	759	...	...	...	759
		Vidur (Krishnapakshi)	Do.	693	53	154	2	486	715	...	...	...	715	1,020	91	242	2	687	1,094	3	1	...	1,090
		Do.	Jain	...	...	...	...	...	...	...	...	...	...	...	...	...	...	...	...	...	...	...	...
			Total Group 45	*3,416*	*171*	*371*	*5*	*2,874*	*3,351*	*3*	*3*	...	*3,345*	*4,033*	*135*	*350*	*4*	*3,548*	*4,024*	*4*	*1*	...	*4,019*
	46.—Tumblers and Acrobats.	Gopál	Hindu	694	...	...	...	694	682	...	...	...	682	44	...	...	...	44	21	...	...	...	21
		Kanjhár	Do.	...	...	...	...	...	...	...	...	...	...	...	...	...	...	...	...	...	...	...	...

Table D.—[Castes by Education.]

E.—VAGRANT MINOR ARTISANS AND PERFORMERS, ETC.—*contd.*

Class.	Group.	Caste.	Religion.	District Basim. Males. Total.	Pupils.	Literate. Total Literate.	Knowing English.	Illiterate.	Females. Total.	Pupils.	Literate. Total Literate.	Knowing English.	Illiterate.	Railway Passengers. Males. Total.	Pupils.	Literate. Total Literate.	Knowing English.	Illiterate.	Females. Total.	Pupils.	Literate. Total Literate.	Knowing English.	Illiterate.
73	74	75	76	77	78	79	80	81	82	83	84	85	86	87	88	89	90	91	92	93	94	95	96
	44.—Hunters, fowlers, etc.	Bahbliyá	Hindu	2	...	...	...	2	...	...	...	...	...	...	...	...	...	...	...	...	...	...	...
		Bedar	Do.	116	...	13	...	103	102	...	...	...	102	...	...	...	...	...	...	...	...	...	...
		Berad	Do.	...	...	...	...	...	...	...	...	...	...	...	...	...	...	...	...	...	...	...	...
		Mutrási	Do.	...	...	...	...	...	...	...	...	...	...	...	...	...	...	...	...	...	...	...	...
		Párdhi	Do.	111	...	...	...	111	78	...	...	...	78	...	...	...	...	...	...	...	...	...	...
		Do.	Animistic	...	...	...	...	...	...	...	...	...	...	...	...	...	...	...	...	...	...	...	...
			Total Group 44	*229*	...	*13*	...	*216*	*180*	...	...	...	*180*	...	...	...	...	...	...	...	...	...	...
	45.—Miscellaneous and disreputable livers (Beggars and Prostitutes).	Aridra	Hindu	...	...	...	...	...	...	...	...	...	...	...	...	...	...	...	...	...	...	...	...
		Bálsanto	Do.	...	...	...	...	...	...	...	...	...	...	...	...	...	...	...	...	...	...	...	...
		Bhámti	Do.	1	...	...	...	1	2	...	...	...	2	...	...	...	...	...	...	...	...	...	...
		Bhattáwád	Do.	...	...	...	...	...	...	...	...	...	...	...	...	...	...	...	...	...	...	...	...
		Dakalwád	Do.	5	...	...	...	5	6	...	...	...	6	...	...	...	...	...	...	...	...	...	...
		Dángat	Do.	49	...	1	...	48	55	...	...	...	55	...	...	...	...	...	...	...	...	...	...
		Dusádh	Do.	...	...	...	...	...	...	...	...	...	...	...	...	...	...	...	...	...	...	...	...
		Gujráthi	Do.	5	...	...	...	5	6	...	...	...	6	3	...	...	...	3	...	...	...	...	...
		Do.	Jain	...	...	...	...	...	...	...	...	...	...	...	...	...	...	...	...	...	...	...	...
		Hindustáni	Hindu	10	...	2	...	8	...	...	...	...	...	...	...	...	...	...	...	...	...	...	...
		Hirmusthi	Do.	3	...	...	...	3	1	...	...	...	1	...	...	...	...	...	...	...	...	...	...
		Kámathi	Do.	...	...	...	...	...	...	...	...	...	...	...	...	...	...	...	...	...	...	...	...
		Kasban (Kasbi)	Do.	...	...	...	...	...	1	...	...	...	1	...	...	...	...	...	...	...	...	...	...
		Do. (Kasbi and Náikan)	Musalman	1	...	...	...	1	1	...	...	...	1	...	...	...	...	...	...	...	...	...	...
		Kunjdá	Do.	...	...	...	...	...	...	...	...	...	...	...	...	...	...	...	...	...	...	...	...
		Madrási	Hindu	...	...	...	...	...	...	...	...	...	...	1	...	1	...	...	...	...	...	...	...
		Maráthe	Do.	1,513	33	61	1	1,419	1,445	...	1	...	1,444	6	...	...	...	6	...	...	...	...	...
		Musalman	Musalman	313	14	14	...	285	289	3	...	...	286	11	...	1	...	10	2	...	...	...	2
		Pádhar	Do.	...	...	...	...	...	...	...	...	...	...	...	...	...	...	...	...	...	...	...	...
		Pardeshi	Hindu	27	2	5	...	20	6	...	...	...	6	...	...	...	...	...	...	...	...	...	...
		Rámjáni	Do.	...	...	...	...	...	...	...	...	...	...	...	...	...	...	...	...	...	...	...	...
		Tálkute	Do.	10	...	...	...	10	6	...	...	...	6	...	...	...	...	...	...	...	...	...	...
		Telangá	Do.	71	5	3	...	63	52	...	...	...	52	...	...	...	...	...	...	...	...	...	...
		Vidur (Krishnapakshi)	Do.	420	39	116	4	265	438	...	1	...	437	3	1	1	...	1	2	...	...	...	2
		Do.	Jain	...	...	...	...	...	...	...	...	...	...	...	...	...	...	...	...	...	...	...	...
			Total Group 45	*2,428*	*93*	*202*	*6*	*2,133*	*2,308*	*3*	*2*	...	*2,303*	*24*	*1*	*3*	...	*20*	*4*	...	...	...	*4*
	46.—Tumblers and Acrobats.	Gopál	Hindu	810	...	...	...	810	795	...	...	...	795	...	...	...	...	...	...	...	...	...	...
		Kanjhár	Do.	...	...	...	...	...	...	...	...	...	...	...	...	...	...	...	...	...	...	...	...

TABLE D.—Castes by Education—*contd.*

Class.	Group.	Caste.	Religion.	Total Strength. Males. Total Males.	Males. Pupils.	Males. Literate. Total Literate.	Males. Literate. Knowing English.	Males. Illiterate.	Females. Total Females.	Females. Pupils.	Females. Literate. Total Literate.	Females. Literate. Knowing English.	Females. Illiterate.	Territorial Distribution. District Amraoti. Males. Total.	Males. Pupils.	Males. Literate. Total Literate.	Males. Literate. Knowing English.	Males. Illiterate.	Females. Total.	Females. Pupils.	Females. Literate. Total Literate.	Females. Literate. Knowing English.	Females. Illiterate.
1	2	3	4	5	6	7	8	9	10	11	12	13	14	15	16	17	18	19	20	21	22	23	24
E.—VAGRANT MINOR ARTISANS, ETC.—*concld.*	46.—Tumblers and Acrobats—*contd.*	Kolhâti	Hindu	502	7	10	...	485	746	4	1	...	741	32	...	...	...	32	49	...	...	...	49
		Do.	Musalman	3	...	...	...	3	6	...	...	...	6	...	...	...	...	...	...	...	...	...	...
		Pângul	Hindu	1,020	4	2	...	1,014	1,065	...	...	...	1,065	163	...	...	...	163	173	...	...	...	173
			Total Group 46	*3,251*	*13*	*12*	...	*3,226*	*3,611*	*4*	*1*	...	*3,606*	*252*	*2*	...	...	*250*	*277*	...	...	...	*277*
	47.—Jugglers, Snake Charmers and Animal Exhibitors.	Chitrakathi	Hindu	799	3	2	...	794	813	...	...	...	813	571	...	2	...	569	572	...	...	...	572
		Kalsutri	Do.	1	...	...	...	1	...	...	...	...	...	...	...	...	...	...	...	...	...	...	...
			Total Group 47	*800*	*3*	*2*	...	*795*	*813*	...	...	...	*813*	*571*	...	*2*	...	*569*	*572*	...	...	...	*572*
F.—RACES AND NATIONALITIES.	48.—Non-Indian Asiatic Races.	Afridi	Musalman	2	...	...	...	2	2	...	...	...	2	2	...	...	...	2	2	...	...	...	2
		Arab	Do.	44	2	6	...	36	40	1	...	...	39	31	1	4	...	26	29	1	...	...	28
		Chinese	Hindu	1	...	1	...	...	...	...	...	...	...	1	...	1	...	...	...	...	...	...	...
		Do.	Buddhist	2	...	...	...	2	2	...	...	...	2	...	...	...	...	...	...	...	...	...	...
		Isabzai	Musalman	9	...	1	...	8	3	...	...	...	3	...	...	...	...	...	...	...	...	...	...
		Jew	Jew	2	...	...	...	2	...	...	...	...	...	1	...	...	...	1	...	...	...	...	...
		Kákezai	Musalman	1	...	1	*1*	...	...	...	...	...	...	...	...	...	...	...	...	...	...	...	...
		Khán	Do.	5	...	...	...	5	6	...	...	...	6	...	...	...	...	...	3	...	...	...	3
		Khánzádá	Do.	1	...	...	...	1	...	...	...	...	...	...	...	...	...	...	...	...	...	...	...
		Khorásáni	Do.	2	...	...	...	2	3	...	...	...	3	2	...	...	...	2	3	...	...	...	3
		Moghal	Do.	2,278	95	196	*1*	1,987	2,159	7	6	...	2,146	618	26	55	...	537	528	2	1	...	525
		Naumuslim	Do.	1	...	...	...	1	...	...	...	...	...	1	...	...	...	1	...	...	...	...	...
		Pársi	Pársi	271	37	190	*125*	44	141	14	70	*5*	57	132	24	78	*60*	30	103	9	51	*4*	43
		Do.	Hindu	5	...	5	*4*	...	...	...	...	...	...	3	...	3	*3*	...	...	...	...	...	...
		Pathán	Musalman	25,190	1,070	1,763	*38*	22,357	23,203	47	83	...	23,073	5,618	231	414	*12*	4,973	5,093	17	30	...	5,046
		Rohilla	Do.	140	...	13	...	127	34	...	...	...	34	39	...	3	...	36	25	...	...	...	25
		Shekh	Do.	64,297	2,534	4,856	*81*	56,907	59,935	145	144	*1*	59,646	14,871	598	1,086	*28*	13,187	13,632	36	35	*1*	13,561
		Syed	Do.	7,959	400	801	*26*	6,758	7,148	27	57	...	7,064	1,732	111	199	*4*	1,422	1,582	4	16	...	1,562
			Total Group 48	*100,210*	*4,138*	*7,838*	*276*	*88,239*	*92,676*	*241*	*360*	*6*	*92,075*	*28,061*	*981*	*1,843*	*107*	*20,217*	*21,000*	*69*	*138*	*5*	*20,798*
	50.—Non-Asiatic-Races	Armenian	Christian	1	...	1	...	...	...	...	...	...	...	...	...	...	...	...	...	...	...	...	...
		European	Do.	186	15	150	*138*	21	143	12	116	*103*	15	81	13	60	*48*	8	75	11	57	*44*	7
		Do.	Others	4	...	4	*4*	...	...	...	...	...	...	...	...	...	...	...	...	...	...	...	...
			Total Group 50	*191*	*15*	*155*	*142*	*21*	*143*	*12*	*116*	*108*	*15*	*81*	*13*	*60*	*48*	*8*	*75*	*11*	*57*	*44*	*7*
	51.—Eurasians	Eurasian (Anglo-Indian, East-Indian and Indo-Briton)	Christian	158	13	109	*82*	36	160	21	99	*85*	40	82	7	61	*38*	14	95	11	63	*54*	21

Class.	Group.	Caste.	Religion.	District Akola. Males. Total.	Pupils.	Literate. Total Literate.	Literate. Knowing English.	Illiterate.	Females. Total.	Pupils.	Literate. Total Literate.	Literate. Knowing English.	Illiterate.	District Ellichpur. Males. Total.	Pupils.	Literate. Total Literate.	Literate. Knowing English.	Illiterate.	Females. Total.	Pupils.	Literate. Total Literate.	Literate. Knowing English.	Illiterate.
25	26	27	28	29	30	31	32	33	34	35	36	37	38	39	40	41	42	43	44	45	46	47	48
E.—VAGRANT MINOR ARTISANS, ETC.—concld.	46.—TUMBLERS AND ACROBATS—contd	KOLHÁTI	Hindu	261	6	4	...	251	379	3	...	..	376	65	...	1	...	64	97	...	...	...	97
		Do.	Musalman	...	...	...	...	...	...	...	...	...	..	...	...	...	...	...	...	...	...	...	...
		PÁNGUL	Hindu	25	...	...	...	25	17	...	...	...	17	20	...	...	...	20	15	...	...	...	15
			Total Group 46	407	6	4	...	397	537	3	...	...	534	85	...	1	...	84	112	...	...	...	112
	47.—JUGGLERS, SNAKE CHARMERS AND ANIMAL EXHIBITORS.	CHITRAKATHI	Hindu	99	...	...	...	99	100	...	...	...	100	7	...	...	...	7	5	...	...	...	5
		KALSUTRI	Do.	1	...	...	...	1	...	...	...	...	...	...	...	...	...	...	...	...	...	...	...
			Total Group 47	100	...	...	...	100	100	...	...	...	100	7	...	...	...	7	5	...	...	...	5
F.—RACES AND NATIONALITIES.	48.—NON-INDIAN ASIATIC RACES.	AFRIDI	Musalman	...	...	...	...	...	...	...	...	...	...	...	...	...	...	...	...	...	...	...	...
		ARAB	Do.	8	1	1	...	6	9	...	...	...	9	1	...	...	...	1	...	...	...	...	...
		CHINESE	Hindu	...	...	...	...	...	...	...	...	...	...	...	...	...	...	...	...	...	...	...	...
		Do.	Buddhist	2	...	...	...	2	2	...	...	...	2	...	...	...	...	...	...	...	...	...	...
		ISABZAI	Musalman	5	...	1	...	4	2	...	...	...	2	2	...	...	...	2	...	...	...	...	...
		JEW	Jew	1	...	...	...	1	...	...	...	...	...	...	...	...	...	...	...	...	...	...	...
		KÁKEZAI	Musalman	1	...	1	1	...	...	...	...	...	...	...	...	...	...	...	...	...	...	...	...
		KHÁN	Do.	2	...	...	...	2	3	...	...	...	3	2	...	...	...	2	...	...	...	...	...
		KHÁNZÁDÁ	Do.	1	...	...	...	1	...	...	...	...	...	...	...	...	...	...	...	...	...	...	...
		KHORÁSÁNI	Do.	...	...	...	...	...	...	...	...	...	...	...	...	...	...	...	...	...	...	...	...
		MOGHAL	Do.	453	22	40	...	391	457	1	...	...	456	403	8	18	...	377	356	3	...	...	393
		NAUMUSLIM	Do.	...	...	...	...	...	...	...	...	...	...	...	...	...	...	...	...	...	...	...	...
		PÁRSI	Pársi	111	13	84	56	14	34	5	17	1	12	20	...	20	6	...	2	...	1	...	1
		Do.	Hindu	...	...	...	...	...	...	...	...	...	...	...	...	...	...	...	...	...	...	...	...
		PATHÁN	Musalman	5,986	258	440	8	5 288	5,650	6	24	...	5,620	3,653	155	279	8	3,219	3,462	6	8	...	3,448
		ROHILLA	Do.	27	...	2	...	25	4	...	...	...	4	9	...	..	...	9	...	...	...	...	...
		SHEKH	Do.	16,380	644	1,324	11	14,414	14,967	37	30	...	14,900	9,255	403	785	28	8,067	8,896	22	27	...	8,847
		SYED	Do.	1,993	102	235	6	1,656	1,825	8	8	...	1,809	1,214	43	127	5	1,044	1,129	2	6	...	1,121
			Total Group 48	24,972	1,040	2,128	82	21,804	22,953	57	79	1	22,817	14,559	609	1,229	47	12,721	13,885	33	42	...	13,810
	50.—NON-ASIATIC RACES	ARMENIAN	Christian	1	...	1	...	...	...	...	...	...	...	...	...	...	...	...	...	...	...	...	...
		EUROPEAN	Do.	40	2	33	33	5	24	...	22	22	2	19	...	17	17	2	16	...	14	14	2
		Do.	Others	2	...	2	2	...	...	...	...	...	...	1	...	1	1	...	...	...	...	...	...
			Total Group 50	43	2	36	35	5	24	...	22	22	2	20	...	18	18	2	16	...	14	14	2
	51.—EURASIANS	EURASIAN (ANGO-INDIAN, EAST-INDIAN AND INDO-BRITON)	Christian	28	6	19	17	3	20	5	12	9	3	18	...	9	8	9	13	2	8	8	3

TABLE D.—Castes by Education—*contd.*

Class.	Group.	Caste.	Religion.	Buldana Males Total.	Buldana Males Pupils.	Buldana Males Literate: Total Literate.	Buldana Males Literate: Knowing English.	Buldana Males Illiterate.	Buldana Females Total.	Buldana Females Pupils.	Buldana Females Literate: Total Literate.	Buldana Females Literate: Knowing English.	Buldana Females Illiterate.	Wun Males Total.	Wun Males Pupils.	Wun Males Literate: Total Literate.	Wun Males Literate: Knowing English.	Wun Males Illiterate.	Wun Females Total.	Wun Females Pupils.	Wun Females Literate: Total Literate.	Wun Females Literate: Knowing English.	Wun Females Illiterate.
49	50	51	52	53	54	55	56	57	58	59	60	61	62	63	64	65	66	67	68	69	70	71	72
E.—VAGRANT MINOR ARTISANS, ETC.—*concld.*	46.—TUMBLERS AND ACROBATS—*contd.*	KOLHÁTI	Hindu	107	1	...	...	106	179	1	...	...	178	27	...	3	...	24	33	...	...	...	33
		Do.	Musalman	3	...	...	...	3	6	...	...	...	6	...	...	...	...	...	...	...	...	...	...
		PÁNGUL	Hindu	...	...	...	...	...	1	...	...	...	1	421	3	...	...	418	463	...	...	...	463
			Total Group 46	*804*	*1*	...	...	*803*	*868*	*1*	...	...	*867*	*492*	*3*	*3*	...	*486*	*517*	...	...	...	*517*
	47.—JUGGLERS, SNAKE CHARMERS AND ANIMAL EXHIBITORS.	CHITRAKATHI	Hindu	1	...	...	...	1	1	...	...	...	1	83	...	...	...	83	101	...	...	...	101
		KALSUTRI	Do.	...	...	...	...	...	...	...	...	...	...	...	...	...	...	...	...	...	...	...	...
			Total Group 47	*1*	...	...	...	*1*	*1*	...	...	...	*1*	*88*	...	...	...	*83*	*101*	...	...	...	*101*
F.—RACES AND NATIONALITIES.	48.—NON-INDIAN ASIATIC RACES.	AFRIDI	Musalman	...	...	...	...	...	...	...	...	...	...	...	...	...	...	...	...	...	...	...	...
		ARAB	Do.	3	...	...	...	3	2	...	...	...	2	...	...	...	...	...	...	...	...	...	...
		CHINESE	Hindu	...	...	...	...	...	...	...	...	...	...	...	...	...	...	...	...	...	...	...	...
		Do.	Buddhist	...	...	...	...	...	...	...	...	...	...	...	...	...	...	...	...	...	...	...	...
		ISABZAI	Musalman	...	...	...	...	...	...	...	...	...	...	1	...	...	...	1	...	...	...	...	...
		JEW	Jew	...	...	...	...	...	...	...	...	...	...	...	...	...	...	...	...	...	...	...	...
		KÁKEZAI	Musalman	...	...	...	...	...	...	...	...	...	...	...	...	...	...	...	...	...	...	...	...
		KHÁN	Do.	...	...	...	...	...	...	...	...	...	...	1	...	...	...	1	...	...	...	...	...
		KHÁNZÁDÁ	Do.	...	...	...	...	...	...	...	...	...	...	...	...	...	...	...	...	...	...	...	...
		KHORÁSÁNI	Do.	...	...	...	...	...	...	...	...	...	...	...	...	...	...	...	...	...	...	...	...
		MOGHAL	Do.	328	10	33	*1*	285	340	...	...	...	340	248	14	26	...	208	245	1	5	...	239
		NAUMUSLIM	Do.	...	...	...	...	...	...	...	...	...	...	...	...	...	...	...	...	...	...	...	...
		PÁRSI	Pársi	4	...	4	2	...	1	...	1	...	...	4	...	4	*1*	...	1	...	...	...	1
		Do.	Hindu	...	...	...	...	...	...	...	...	...	...	...	...	...	...	...	...	...	...	...	...
		PATHÁN	Musalman	4,405	194	272	*6*	3,939	4,113	8	6	...	4,099	2,763	120	171	*3*	2,472	2,451	1	3	...	2,447
		ROHILLA	Do.	30	...	5	...	25	4	...	...	...	4	10	...	2	...	8	...	...	...	...	...
		SHEKH	Do.	10,419	423	691	*4*	9,305	10,030	12	22	...	9,996	6,219	261	512	*3*	5,446	5,698	10	16	...	5,672
		SYED	Do.	1,184	60	99	*5*	1,025	1,061	6	13	...	1,042	825	47	70	2	708	681	4	7	...	670
			Total Group 48	*16,373*	*687*	*1,104*	*18*	*14,682*	*15,551*	*28*	*42*	...	*15,483*	*10,071*	*442*	*785*	*9*	*8,844*	*9,076*	*16*	*31*	...	*9,029*
	50.—NON-ASIATIC RACES.	ARMENIAN	Christian	...	...	...	...	...	...	...	...	...	...	...	...	...	...	...	...	...	...	...	...
		EUROPEAN	Do.	12	...	10	*10*	2	6	1	4	*4*	1	15	...	15	*15*	...	9	...	9	*9*	...
		Do.	Others	...	...	...	...	...	...	...	...	...	...	...	...	...	...	...	...	...	...	...	...
			Total Group 50	*12*	...	*10*	*10*	*2*	*6*	*1*	*4*	*4*	*1*	*15*	...	*15*	*15*	...	*9*	...	*9*	*9*	...
	51.—EURASIANS	EURASIAN (ANGLO-INDIAN, EAST-INDIAN AND INDO-BRITON)	Christian	8	...	6	*5*	2	8	1	3	*3*	4	9	...	6	*6*	3	12	...	9	*9*	3

Table D.—[Castes by Education.]

Class.	Group.	Caste.	Religion.	District Basim. Males. Total.	Males. Pupils.	Males. Literate. Total Literate.	Males. Literate. Knowing English.	Males. Illiterate.	Females. Total.	Females. Pupils.	Females. Literate. Total Literate.	Females. Literate. Knowing English.	Females. Illiterate.	Railway Passengers. Males. Total.	Males. Pupils.	Males. Literate. Total Literate.	Males. Literate. Knowing English.	Males. Illiterate.	Females. Total.	Females. Pupils.	Females. Literate. Total Literate.	Females. Literate. Knowing English.	Females. Illiterate.
73	74	75	76	77	78	79	80	81	82	83	84	85	86	87	88	89	90	91	92	93	94	95	96
E.—VAGRANT MINOR ARTISANS, ETC.—*concld.*	46.—TUMBLERS AND ACROBATS—*contd.*	KOLHÁTI	Hindu	10	...	2	...	8	9	...	1	...	8	...	...	...	...	...	...	...	...	...	...
		Do.	Musalman	...	...	...	...	...	...	...	...	...	...	...	...	...	...	...	...	...	...	...	...
		PÁNGUL	Hindu	391	1	2	...	388	396	...	...	...	396	...	...	...	...	...	...	...	...	...	...
			Total Group 46	*1,211*	*1*	*4*	...	*1,208*	*1,200*	...	*1*	...	*1,199*	...	...	...	...	...	...	...	...	...	...
	47.—JUGGLERS, SNAKE CHARMERS AND ANIMAL EXHIBITORS.	CHITRAKATHI	Hindu	38	3	...	...	35	34	...	...	...	34	...	...	...	...	...	...	...	...	...	...
		KALSUTRI	Do.	...	...	...	...	...	...	...	...	...	...	...	...	...	...	...	...	...	...	...	...
			Total Group 47	*38*	*3*	...	...	*35*	*34*	...	...	...	*34*	...	...	...	...	...	...	...	...	...	...
F.—RACES AND NATIONALITIES.	48.—NON-INDIAN ASIATIC RACES	AFRIDI	Musalman	...	...	...	...	...	...	...	...	...	...	...	...	...	...	...	...	...	...	...	...
		ARAB	Do.	1	...	1	...	...	...	...	...	...	...	...	...	...	...	...	...	...	...	...	...
		CHINESE	Hindu	...	...	...	...	...	...	...	...	...	...	...	...	...	...	...	...	...	...	...	...
		Do.	Buddhist	...	...	...	...	...	...	...	...	...	...	...	...	...	...	...	...	...	...	...	...
		ISABZAI	Musalman	1	...	...	...	1	1	...	...	...	1	...	...	...	...	...	...	...	...	...	...
		JEW	Jew	...	...	...	...	...	...	...	...	...	...	...	...	...	...	...	...	...	...	...	...
		KÁKEZAI	Musalman	...	...	...	...	...	...	...	...	...	...	...	...	...	...	...	...	...	...	...	...
		KHÁN	Do.	...	...	...	...	...	...	...	...	...	...	...	...	...	...	...	...	...	...	...	...
		KHÁNZÁDÁ	Do.	...	...	...	...	...	...	...	...	...	...	...	...	...	...	...	...	...	...	...	...
		KHORÁSÁNI	Do.	...	...	...	...	...	...	...	...	...	...	...	...	...	...	...	...	...	...	...	...
		MOGHAL	Do.	228	15	24	...	189	193	...	...	...	193	...	...	...	...	...	...	...	...	...	...
		NAUMUSLIM	Do.	...	...	...	...	...	...	...	...	...	...	...	...	...	...	...	...	...	...	...	...
		PÁRSI	Pársi	...	...	...	...	...	...	...	...	...	...	...	...	...	...	...	...	...	...	...	...
		Do.	Hindu	2	...	2	1	...	...	...	...	...	...	...	...	...	...	...	...	...	...	...	...
		PATHÁN	Musalman	2,752	110	182	1	2,460	2,431	9	12	...	2,410	13	2	5	...	6	3	...	...	...	3
		ROHILLA	Do.	25	...	1	...	24	1	...	...	...	1	...	...	...	...	...	...	...	...	...	...
		SHEKH	Do.	7,127	205	455	7	6,467	6,710	98	14	...	6,668	24	...	3	...	21	2	...	...	...	2
		SYED	Do.	1,009	37	70	4	902	870	3	7	...	860	2	...	1	...	1	...	...	...	...	...
			Total Group 48	*11,145*	*367*	*735*	*13*	*10,043*	*10,206*	*40*	*33*	...	*10,133*	*39*	*2*	*9*	...	*28*	*5*	...	...	...	*5*
	50.—NON-ASIATIC RACES	ARMENIAN	Christian	...	...	...	...	...	...	...	...	...	...	...	...	...	...	...	...	...	...	...	...
		EUROPEAN	Do.	11	...	9	9	2	6	...	6	6	...	8	...	6	6	2	7	...	4	4	3
		Do.	Others	1	...	1	1	...	...	...	...	...	...	...	...	...	...	...	...	...	...	...	...
			Total Group 50	*12*	...	*10*	*10*	*2*	*6*	...	*6*	*6*	...	*8*	...	*6*	*6*	*2*	*7*	...	*4*	*4*	*3*
	51.—EURASIANS.	EURASIAN (ANGLO-INDIAN, EAST-INDIAN AND INDO-BRITON)	Christian	10	...	5	5	5	10	2	2	...	6	3	...	3	3	...	2	...	2	2	...

TABLE D.—Castes by Education—*concld.*

Caste and Religion.				Total Strength.										Territorial Distribution. District Amraoti.									
				Males.					Females.					Males.					Females.				
						Literate.					Literate.					Literate.					Literate.		
Class.	Group.	Caste.	Religion.	Total Males.	Pupils.	Total Literate.	Knowing English.	Illiterate.	Total Females.	Pupils.	Total Literate.	Knowing English.	Illiterate.	Total.	Pupils.	Total Literate.	Knowing English.	Illiterate.	Total.	Pupils.	Total Literate.	Knowing English.	Illiterate.
1	2	3	4	5	6	7	8	9	10	11	12	13	14	15	16	17	18	19	20	21	22	23	24
F.—Races and Nationalities—*contd.*	52.—Christian Converts.	Goanese	Christian	117	20	63	46	34	55	...	15	6	40	54	11	27	22	16	30	...	7	...	23
		Singhalese	Do.	1	...	1	1	...	4	...	1	1	3	...	...	...	...	...	...	...	...	...	...
		Native Christian	Do.	275	28	119	60	128	259	24	69	20	166	100	2	53	23	45	112	9	28	8	75
			Total Group 52	*393*	*48*	*183*	*97*	*162*	*318*	*24*	*85*	*27*	*209*	*154*	*13*	*80*	*45*	*61*	*142*	*9*	*35*	*8*	*98*
	Unrecognizable.	Dandigán	Hindu	78	...	...	...	78	106	...	...	...	106	12	...	...	...	12	15	...	...	...	15
		Naghát	Do.	1	...	...	...	1	4	...	...	...	4	...	...	...	...	...	...	...	...	...	...
		Shekdau	Do.	1	...	...	...	1	...	...	...	...	...	...	...	...	...	...	...	...	...	...	...
		Soliá	Do.	1	...	...	...	1	...	...	...	...	...	...	...	...	...	...	...	...	...	...	...
		Unspecified	Do.	87	1	6	...	80	53	1	1	...	51	28	...	1	...	27	8	...	...	...	8
		Do.	Musalman	7	...	...	...	7	4	...	...	...	4	...	...	...	...	...	...	...	...	...	...
		Do.	Unspecified	1	...	...	...	1	...	...	...	...	...	...	...	...	...	...	...	...	...	...	...
			GRAND TOTAL	1,491,826	38,502	87,128	*2,493*	1,366,196	1,405,665	976	1,722	*225*	1,402,967	840,235	9,627	22,976	*846*	307,632	315,410	240	611	*113*	314,559

Caste and Religion.				Territorial Distribution. District Akola. Males.					Females.				
Class.	Group.	Caste.	Religion.	Total.	Pupils.	Literate. Total Literate.	Literate. Knowing English.	Illiterate.	Total.	Pupils.	Literate. Total Literate.	Literate. Knowing English.	Illiterate.
25	26	27	28	29	30	31	32	33	34	35	36	37	38
F.—Races and Nationalities—*contd.*	52.—Christian Converts.	Goanese	Christian	44	9	19	12	16	12	...	3	2	9
		Singhalese	Do.	...	...	...	...	...	...	...	...	...	...
		Native Christian	Do.	70	13	28	10	29	66	12	16	3	38
			Total Group 52	114	22	47	22	45	78	12	19	5	47
	Unrecognizable.	Dandigán	Hindu	...	...	...	...	...	...	...	...	...	...
		Naghát	Do.	...	...	...	...	...	...	...	...	...	...
		Shekdau	Do.	...	...	...	...	...	...	...	...	...	...
		Soliá	Do.	...	...	...	...	...	...	...	...	...	...
		Unspecified	Do.	26	1	2	...	23	16	...	...	...	16
		Do.	Musalman	2	...	...	...	2	...	...	...	...	...
		Do.	Unspecified	...	...	...	...	...	...	...	...	...	...
			GRAND TOTAL	297,011	10,414	21,984	669	264,613	277,771	365	445	38	276,961

Caste and Religion.				Territorial Distribution. District Ellichpur. Males.					Females.				
Class.	Group.	Caste.	Religion.	Total.	Pupils.	Literate. Total Literate.	Literate. Knowing English.	Illiterate.	Total.	Pupils.	Literate. Total Literate.	Literate. Knowing English.	Illiterate.
25	26	27	28	39	40	41	42	43	44	45	46	47	48
F.—Races and Nationalities—*contd.*	52.—Christian Converts.	Goanese	Christian	7	...	7	7	...	7	...	4	4	3
		Singhalese	Do.	...	...	...	...	...	...	...	...	...	...
		Native Christian	Do.	24	2	11	8	11	19	...	6	6	13
			Total Group 52	31	2	18	16	11	28	...	10	10	16
	Unrecognizable.	Dandigán	Hindu	...	...	...	...	...	...	...	...	...	...
		Naghát	Do.	...	...	...	...	...	...	...	...	...	...
		Shekdau	Do.	1	...	...	...	1	...	...	...	...	...
		Soliá	Do.	1	...	...	...	1	...	...	...	...	...
		Unspecified	Do.	6	...	1	...	5	5	1	...	...	4
		Do.	Musalman	...	...	...	...	...	...	...	...	...	...
		Do.	Unspecified	...	...	...	...	...	...	...	...	...	...
			GRAND TOTAL	162,969	4,976	10,866	330	147,127	152,829	80	185	83	152,564

TABLE D.—Castes by Education—*concld.*

Class.	Caste and Religion. Group.	Caste.	Religion.	Territorial Distribution. District Buldana. Males. Total.	Males. Pupils.	Males. Literate. Total Literate.	Males. Literate. Knowing English.	Males. Illiterate.	Females. Total.	Females. Pupils.	Females. Literate. Total Literate.	Females. Literate. Knowing English.	Females. Illiterate.	District Wun. Males. Total.	Males. Pupils.	Males. Literate. Total Literate.	Males. Literate. Knowing English.	Males. Illiterate.	Females. Total.	Females. Pupils.	Females. Literate. Total Literate.	Females. Literate. Knowing English.	Females. Illiterate.
49	50	51	52	53	54	55	56	57	58	59	60	61	62	63	64	65	66	67	68	69	70	71	72
F.—RACES AND NATIONALITIES—*contd.*	52.—CHRISTIAN CONVERTS.	GOANESE	Christian	4	...	2	1	2	1	...	1	...	...	5	...	5	2	...	5	...	...	...	5
		SINGHALESE	Do.	1	...	1	1	...	4	...	1	1	3	...	...		...	...	...	...	...	...	...
		NATIVE CHRISTIAN	Do.	35	6	8	3	21	24	2	3	...	19	20	4	7	2	9	14	...	2	1	12
			Total Group 52	40	6	11	5	23	29	2	5	1	22	26	4	12	4	9	19	...	2	1	17
	UNRECOGNIZABLE.	DANDIGÁN	Hindu	...	...	...	...	...	...	...	...	...	...	48	...	...	...	48	64	...	...	...	64
		NAGHÁT	Do.	...	...	...	...	...	...	...	...	...	...	...	...	...	...	...	...	...	...	...	...
		SHEKDAU	Do.	...	...	...	...	...	...	...	...	...	...	...	...	...	...	...	...	...	...	...	...
		SOLIÁ	Do.	...	...	...	...	...	...	...	...	...	...	...	...	...	...	...	...	...	...	...	...
		UNSPECIFIED	Do.	7	...	...	...	7	8	...	...	...	8	6	...	1	...	5	14	...	1	...	13
		Do.	Musalman	3	...	...	...	3	3	...	...	...	3	...	...	...	...	...	...	...	...	...	...
		Do.	Unspecified	...	...	...	...	...	...	...	...	...	...	...	...	...	...	...	...	...	...	...	...
			GRAND TOTAL	244,799	6,347	13,673	246	224,779	286,222	127	200	8	235,895	241,688	3,762	8,732	207	229,194	229,925	93	154	19	229,678

Class.	Group.	Caste.	Religion.	District Basim. Males. Total.	District Basim. Males. Pupils.	District Basim. Males. Literate. Total Literate.	District Basim. Males. Literate. Knowing English.	District Basim. Males. Illiterate.	District Basim. Females. Total.	District Basim. Females. Pupils.	District Basim. Females. Literate. Total Literate.	District Basim. Females. Literate. Knowing English.	District Basim. Females. Illiterate.	Railway Passengers. Males. Total.	Railway Passengers. Males. Pupils.	Railway Passengers. Males. Literate. Total Literate.	Railway Passengers. Males. Literate. Knowing English.	Railway Passengers. Males. Illiterate.	Railway Passengers. Females. Total.	Railway Passengers. Females. Pupils.	Railway Passengers. Females. Literate. Total Literate.	Railway Passengers. Females. Literate. Knowing English.	Railway Passengers. Females. Illiterate.
73	74	75	76	77	78	79	80	81	82	83	84	85	86	87	88	89	90	91	92	93	94	95	96
F.—RACES AND NATIONALITIES—contd.	52.—CHRISTIAN CONVERTS.	GOANESE	Christian	1	...	1	...	...	...	...	...	...	...	2	...	2	2	...	...	...	...	...	...
		SINGHALESE	Do.	...	...	...	...	...	...	...	...	...	...	...	...	...	...	...	...	...	...	...	...
		NATIVE CHRISTIAN	Do.	26	1	12	4	13	24	1	14	2	9	...	...	...	...	...	...	...	...	...	...
			Total Group 52	27	1	13	4	13	24	1	14	2	9	2	...	2	2	...	...	...	...	...	...
	UNRECOGNIZABLE.	DANDIGÁN	Hindu	18	...	...	...	18	27	...	...	...	27	...	...	...	...	...	...	...	...	...	...
		NAGHÁT	Do.	1	...	...	...	1	4	...	...	...	4	...	...	...	...	...	...	...	...	...	...
		SHEKDAU	Do.	...	...	...	...	...	...	...	...	...	...	...	...	...	...	...	...	...	...	...	...
		SOLIÁ	Do.	...	...	...	...	...	...	...	...	...	...	...	...	...	...	...	...	...	...	...	...
		UNSPECIFIED	Do.	11	...	1	...	10	2	...	...	...	2	3	...	...	...	3	...	...	...	...	...
		Do.	Musalman	2	...	...	...	2	1	...	...	...	1	...	...	...	...	...	...	...	...	...	...
		Do.	Unspecified	1	...	...	...	1	...	...	...	...	...	...	...	...	...	...	...	...	...	...	...
			GRAND TOTAL	204,798	3,370	8,829	183	192,599	198,383	71	121	8	193,191	326	6	68	12	252	125	...	6	6	119

TABLE E.

Castes by Civil Condition and Age.

TABLE E.—Castes by Civil Condition and Age.

Class.	Group.	Caste.	Religion.	All ages. Total Males.	All ages. Single.	All ages. Married.	All ages. Widowed.	0—9 Total.	0—9 Single.	0—9 Married.	0—9 Widowed.	10—14 Total.	10—14 Single.	10—14 Married.	10—14 Widowed.	15—39 Total.	15—39 Single.	15—39 Married.	15—39 Widowed.	40 and over Total.	40 and over Single.	40 and over Married.	40 and over Widowed.
1	2	3	4	5	6	7	8	9	10	11	12	13	14	15	16	17	18	19	20	21	22	23	24
A—AGRICULTURAL.	2.—OTHER AGRICULTURAL. 2 (a).—CULTIVATORS	KUNBI	Hindu	426,429	137,960	260,080	28,389	106,336	101,013	5,120	203	47,031	25,068	21,267	696	164,239	10,545	144,938	8,756	1,08,823	1,334	88,755	18,734
		Do.	Jain	7	2	5	...	2	2	...	...	...	...	...	...	3	...	3	...	2	...	2	...
		MÁLI	Hindu	102,717	29,057	66,923	6,737	25,632	23,834	1,753	45	10,976	3,693	7,124	159	38,984	1,323	35,710	1,951	27,125	207	22,336	4,582
		Do.	Jain	10	3	6	1	...	...	...	...	1	1	...	.	6	2	4	...	3	...	2	1
		RAJPUT	Hindu	26,850	11,429	13,549	1,872	5,952	5,871	77	4	2,816	2,427	368	21	10,961	2,646	7,847	468	7,121	485	5,257	1,379
		Do.	Sikh	8	3	5	...	1	1	...	...	1	1	...	...	2	...	2	...	4	1	3	...
	2(b).—CATTLE BREEDERS AND GRAZIERS.	GAOLI (AHIR GAWÁRI, GAVLÁN).	Hindu	19,087	7,582	10,138	1,267	4,856	4,756	98	2	1,956	1,532	406	18	7,294	1,239	5,646	409	4,981	155	3,988	838
		Do.	Jain	1	...	...	1	...	...	...	...	...	...	...	...	..	...	...	...	1	...	...	1
		Do.	Animistic	382	178	186	18	97	97	...	...	46	41	5	...	147	39	105	3	92	1	76	15
		Do.	Musalman	418	209	173	36	132	132	...	...	57	55	1	1	131	21	100	10	98	1	72	25
	4.—FOREST AND HILL TRIBES.	ANDH	Hindu	21,671	10,048	10,967	656	7,625	7,359	255	11	2,624	1,893	708	23	7,335	766	6,384	185	4,087	30	3,620	437
		Do.	Animistic	165	69	84	12	49	43	6	...	20	14	6	...	61	11	46	4	35	1	26	8
		BHIL	Hindu	1,735	841	833	61	559	552	7	...	198	174	24	...	611	110	484	17	367	5	318	44
		Do.	Animistic	405	198	192	15	146	142	2	2	48	41	7	...	137	14	115	8	74	1	68	5
		Do.	Musalman	950	498	411	41	293	292	1	...	103	101	2	...	361	101	250	10	193	4	158	31
		GOND	Hindu	4,850	2,165	2,343	342	1,223	1,201	20	2	487	442	41	4	1,775	463	1,204	108	1,365	59	1,078	228
		Do.	Animistic	35,918	16,412	17,822	1,684	10,333	10,063	267	3	4,064	3,591	462	11	12,431	2,516	9,490	425	9,090	242	7,603	1,245
		KORKU	Hindu	193	98	89	6	56	55	...	1	27	27	...	...	71	15	55	1	39	1	34	4
		Do.	Animistic	17,522	9,492	7,553	477	5,756	5,680	76	...	2,204	2,108	94	2	6,335	1,65[illegible]	4,537	146	3,227	52	2,846	329
		PARDHÁN	Hindu	1,899	939	897	63	598	589	9	...	221	199	22	...	690	148	520	22	390	3	346	41
		Do.	Animistic	4,614	2,304	2,163	147	1,547	1,515	31	1	576	502	74	...	1,567	279	1,245	43	924	8	813	103
B.-PROFESSIONAL.	5.—PRIESTS	BRÁHMAN	Hindu	41,772	17,296	20,622	3,854	6,917	6,830	83	4	3,760	3,275	476	9	19,265	5,899	12,467	899	11,830	1,292	7,596	2,942
		Do.	Jain	24	11	11	2	5	5	...	...	3	2	1	...	10	3	7	...	6	1	3	2
C.—COMMERCIAL.	14.—TRADERS	WÁNI (MÁRWÁDI AND BANIÁ)	Hindu	27,456	11,117	14,230	2,109	5,553	5,395	150	8	2,902	2,238	634	30	12,051	2,969	8,492	590	6,950	515	4,954	1,481
		Do.	Jain	7,172	2,908	3,713	551	1,494	1,472	21	1	801	634	159	8	3,074	706	2,220	148	1,803	96	1,313	394
		Do.	Sikh	3	2	1	...	...	...	...	...	...	...	...	...	2	2	...	...	1	...	1	...
	16.—CARRIERS	BANJÁRI	Hindu	27,983	15,609	11,215	1,159	9,259	9,141	112	6	3,551	3,211	332	8	9,867	3,063	6,526	278	5,306	194	4,245	867
		Do.	Musalman	71	47	18	6	34	34	...	...	8	7	1	...	13	6	6	1	16	...	11	5
		Do.	Jain	17	15	2	...	5	5	...	...	5	5	...	...	6	5	1	...	1	...	1	...
		WANJÁRI	Hindu	16,341	5,465	10,026	850	4,522	4,162	342	18	1,944	871	1,018	55	6,411	409	5,717	285	3,464	23	2,949	492

Table E.—Castes by Civil Condition and Age.

Table E.—Castes by Civil Condition and Age.

Class	Group	Caste	Religion	All ages: Total Females	All ages: Single	All ages: Married	All ages: Widowed	0—9: Total	0—9: Single	0—9: Married	0—9: Widowed	10—14: Total	10—14: Single	10—14: Married	10—14: Widowed	15—39: Total	15—39: Single	15—39: Married	15—39: Widowed	40 and over: Total	40 and over: Single	40 and over: Married	40 and over: Widowed
				25	26	27	28	29	30	31	32	33	34	35	36	37	38	39	40	41	42	43	44
A.—Agricultural.	2.—Other Agricultural.																						
	2 (a).—Cultivators	Kunbi	Hindu	407,590	82,870	257,284	67,836	111,940	79,303	32,079	558	39,165	2,348	35,784	1,033	161,464	935	148,043	12,486	95,421	284	41,378	53,759
		Do.	Jain	6	1	5	...	2	1	1	...	...	...	...	...	3	...	3	...	1	...	1	...
		Máli	Hindu	99,771	17,692	66,194	15,885	27,131	17,167	9,789	175	9,369	318	8,831	220	39,482	152	36,824	2,506	23,789	55	10,750	12,984
		Do.	Jain	...	...	...	...	...	...	...	...	...	...	...	...	...	...	...	...	...	...	...	...
		Rajput	Hindu	24,066	5,996	12,511	5,559	5,967	5,322	624	21	2,242	553	1,636	53	9,889	91	8,329	1,469	5,968	30	1,922	4,016
		Do.	Sikh	6	...	4	2	...	...	...	...	...	...	...	...	3	...	2	1	3	...	2	1
	2(b).—Cattle Breeders and Graziers.	Gaoli (Ahir Gawári, Gaulán.)	Hindu	16,593	5,214	9,112	2,267	5,067	4,500	553	14	1,643	607	1,004	32	6,515	98	5,985	432	3,368	9	1,570	1,789
		Do.	Jain	...	...	...	...	...	...	...	...	...	...	...	...	...	...	...	...	...	...	...	...
		Do.	Animistic	389	150	197	42	122	112	10	...	31	27	4	...	164	9	147	8	72	2	36	34
		Do.	Musalman	397	158	185	54	143	139	4	...	33	13	19	1	147	6	130	11	74	...	32	42
	4.—Forest and Hill Tribes.	Andh	Hindu	21,626	7,892	11,077	2,657	8,068	7,176	873	19	2,009	576	1,383	50	7,829	116	7,134	579	3,720	24	1,687	2,009
		Do.	Animistic	140	49	81	10	47	36	10	1	17	12	5	...	58	1	56	1	18	...	10	8
		Bhil	Hindu	1,748	656	870	222	605	561	44	...	154	69	83	2	662	26	585	51	227	...	158	169
		Do.	Animistic	378	128	197	53	123	111	11	1	26	12	14	...	146	4	134	8	83	1	38	44
		Do.	Musalman	978	392	446	140	320	315	5	...	93	71	21	1	392	4	354	34	173	2	66	105
		Gond	Hindu	4,208	1,490	2,177	541	1,205	1,150	50	5	402	242	151	9	1,720	87	1,532	101	881	11	444	426
		Do.	Animistic	35,951	13,421	18,160	4,370	11,243	10,611	623	9	3,480	2,021	1,427	32	13,746	668	12,361	717	7,482	121	3,749	3,612
		Korku	Hindu	186	92	81	13	69	69	...	...	26	20	6	...	69	3	64	2	22	...	11	11
		Do.	Animistic	17,080	8,036	7,660	1,384	5,880	5,785	91	4	1,920	1,582	334	4	6,677	634	5,780	263	2,603	35	1,455	1,113
		Pardhán	Hindu	1,867	751	899	217	651	624	26	1	176	101	74	1	702	22	617	43	338	4	162	172
		Do.	Animistic	4,556	1,868	2,226	462	1,638	1,567	67	4	485	251	231	3	1,634	46	1,511	77	759	4	417	378
B.—Professional.	5.—Priests	Bráhman	Hindu	29,500	6,787	15,198	7,515	7,012	6,372	625	15	2,630	333	2,219	78	12,043	64	9,815	2,164	7,815	18	2,539	5,258
		Do.	Jain	12	5	6	1	5	5	...	...	...	...	...	...	6	...	6	...	1	...	...	1
C.—Commercial.	14.—Traders	Wáni (Márwádi and Baniá).	Hindu	22,814	5,632	12,166	5,016	5,831	5,003	812	16	2,158	515	1,576	67	9,348	87	7,954	1,307	5,477	27	1,824	3,626
		Do.	Jain	6,088	1,382	3,454	1,252	1,501	1,262	232	7	563	104	449	10	2,535	14	2,241	280	1,489	2	532	955
		Do.	Sikh	...	...	...	...	...	...	...	...	...	...	...	...	...	...	...	...	...	...	...	...
	16.—Carriers	Banjári	Hindu	24,487	10,784	10,816	2,887	9,179	8,738	433	8	2,617	1,647	950	20	8,592	366	7,639	587	4,099	33	1,794	2,272
		Do.	Musalman	49	26	19	4	19	19	...	...	8	7	1	...	11	...	10	1	11	...	8	3
		Do.	Jain	12	7	3	2	4	4	...	...	1	1	...	...	6	2	3	1	1	...	...	1
		Wanjári	Hindu	15,461	3,309	9,858	2,294	4,687	3,149	1,506	32	1,581	105	1,376	40	6,058	45	5,582	431	3,195	10	1,394	1,791

TABLE E.—Castes by Civil Condition and Age.

Caste and Religion.				Total Strength. Males. All ages.				0–9				10–14				15–39				40 and over.			
Class.	Group.	Caste.	Religion.	Total Males.	Single.	Married.	Widowed.	Total.	Single.	Married.	Widowed.	Total.	Single.	Married.	Widowed.	Total.	Single.	Married.	Widowed.	Total.	Single.	Married.	Widowed.
1	2	3	4	5	6	7	8	9	10	11	12	13	14	15	16	17	18	19	20	21	22	23	24
D.—Artisan and Village Menial.	17.—Goldsmiths	Sonár	Hindu	15,130	5,683	8,408	1,039	3,648	3,562	77	9	1,716	1,217	472	27	6,034	802	4,957	275	3,732	102	2,902	728
		Do.	Jain	1	...	1	...	...	...	...	...	...	...	...	...	...	...	...	...	1	...	1	...
	18.—Barbers	Mháli (Hajám, Nhávi and Wárik).	Hindu	18,231	6,130	10,900	1,201	4,467	4,306	153	8	1,920	1,145	750	25	7,351	591	6,378	382	4,493	88	3,619	786
		Do.	Musalman	11	4	7	...	3	3	...	...	1	1	...	...	3	...	3	...	4	...	4	...
		Do.	Jain	3	...	...	3	...	...	...	...	...	...	...	...	...	...	...	...	3	...	...	3
	19.—Blacksmiths	Lohár (Kháti)	Hindu	8,351	3,031	4,852	468	2,011	1,940	68	3	882	665	215	2	3,397	386	2,844	167	2,061	40	1,725	296
		Do.	Animistic	7	3	4	...	2	2	...	...	...	...	...	...	2	1	1	...	3	...	3	...
	20.—Carpenters, Turners and Masons.	Sutár (Badhai and Wádhi).	Hindu	17,440	5 446	10,860	1,134	3,812	3,693	113	6	1,701	1,079	609	13	7,408	604	6,463	341	4,519	70	3,675	774
		Do.	Jain	13	3	10	...	...	...	...	...	1	...	1	...	11	3	8	...	1	...	1	...
	22.—Tailors	Simpi (Darzi)	Hindu	7,232	2,441	4,340	451	1,599	1,571	28	...	753	529	220	4	3,044	319	2,587	138	1,836	22	1,505	309
		Do.	Musalman	8	3	4	1	2	2	...	...	1	1	...	...	2	...	2	...	3	...	2	1
		Do.	Jain	1,294	430	772	92	307	299	8	...	144	89	55	...	519	38	449	32	324	4	260	60
	23.—Weavers, Calenderers, and Dyers.	Koshti	Hindu	7,576	2,699	4,305	572	1,630	1,583	43	4	746	572	160	14	3,025	496	2,360	169	2,175	48	1,742	385
		Do.	Jain	129	37	84	8	26	26	...	...	12	5	7	...	56	6	46	4	35	...	31	4
	24.—Washermen	Warthi (Parit)	Hindu	11,749	4,308	6,771	670	3,108	3,020	84	4	1,336	903	423	10	4,509	364	3,981	164	2,796	21	2,283	492
		Dhobi	Musalman	4	1	3	...	1	1	...	...	...	...	...	...	2	...	2	...	1	...	1	...
	26.—Shepherds and Wool weavers.	Dhangar	Hindu	41,589	14,098	25,192	2,299	11,227	10,643	570	14	4,837	2,504	2,257	76	15,997	877	14,456	664	9,528	74	7,909	1,545
	27.—Oil pressers	Teli	Do.	42,114	13,485	25,783	2,846	10,337	9,961	351	25	4,688	2,557	2,072	59	16,162	877	14,483	802	10,927	90	8,877	1,960
		Do.	Musalman	13	3	9	1	1	1	...	...	1	...	1	...	8	2	6	...	3	...	2	1
		Do.	Sikh	1	...	1	...	...	...	...	...	...	...	...	...	...	...	...	...	1	...	1	...
		Do.	Animistic	6	3	3	...	1	1	...	...	1	1	...	...	1	1	...	...	3	...	3	...
	28.—Potters	Kumbhar	Hindu	12,558	4,170	7,740	648	2,845	2,757	84	4	1,174	818	346	10	5,462	546	4,720	196	3,077	49	2,590	438
	35.—Fishermen, boatmen, Palki bearers and cooks, &c.	Bhoi (Windhewár).	Do.	14,253	6,599	6,952	702	4,152	4,039	105	8	1,586	1,363	216	7	5,329	1,118	4,024	187	3,186	79	2,607	500
		Koli	Do.	16,497	6,584	9,276	637	4,660	4,560	99	1	1,904	1,451	441	12	6,216	531	5,540	145	3,717	42	3,196	479
	36.—Distillers and Toddy drawers.	Kalál	Do.	8,390	3,358	4,481	551	1,988	1,963	23	2	907	743	160	4	3,433	596	2,660	177	2,062	56	1,638	368
		Do.	Jain	98	40	52	6	19	18	1	...	10	9	1	...	49	13	35	1	20	...	15	5
		Do	Musalman	5	1	2	2	1	1	...	...	...	...	...	...	2	...	1	1	2	...	1	1
		Do.	Animistic	1	...	...	1	...	...	...	...	...	...	...	...	...	...	...	...	1	...	...	1

Table E.—Castes by Civil Condition and Age.

Class.	Group.	Caste.	Religion.	All ages: Total Females.	All ages: Single.	All ages: Married.	All ages: Widowed.	0–9: Total.	0–9: Single.	0–9: Married.	0–9: Widowed.	10–14: Total.	10–14: Single.	10–14: Married.	10–14: Widowed.	15–39: Total.	15–39: Single.	15–39: Married.	15–39: Widowed.	40 and over: Total.	40 and over: Single.	40 and over: Married.	40 and over: Widowed.
				25	26	27	28	29	30	31	32	33	34	35	36	37	38	39	40	41	42	43	44
D.—ARTISAN AND VILLAGE MENIAL.	17.—Goldsmiths	Sonár	Hindu	14,087	3,188	8,241	2,658	3,771	3,009	740	22	1,375	117	1,219	39	5,678	39	5,051	588	3,263	23	1,231	2,009
		Do.	Jain	1	...	1	...	...	...	...	...	...	...	...	...	1	...	1	...	...	...	...	...
	18.—Barbers	Mhálí (Hajám, Nhávi and Wárik.)	Hindu	16,994	3,603	10,396	2,995	4,601	3,424	1,158	19	1,570	130	1,406	34	6,914	34	6,286	594	3,909	15	1,546	2,348
		Do.	Musalman	6	2	3	1	2	2	...	...	...	...	...	...	3	...	3	...	1	...	...	1
		Do.	Jain	...	...	...	...	...	...	...	...	...	...	...	...	...	...	...	...	...	...	...	...
	19.—Blacksmiths	Lohár (Khátí)	Hindu	7,538	1,885	4,409	1,244	2,090	1,732	343	15	682	111	551	20	3,025	32	2,760	233	1,741	10	755	976
		Do.	Animistic	11	3	6	2	3	3	...	...	...	...	...	...	3	...	2	1	5	...	4	1
	20.—Carpenters, Turners and Masons.	Sutár (Badhai and Wádhi)	Hindu	15,038	3,254	9,360	2,424	4,034	3,074	945	15	1,392	112	1,238	42	6,132	40	5,674	418	3,480	28	1,503	1,949
		Do.	Jain	...	...	...	...	...	...	...	...	...	...	...	...	...	...	...	...	...	...	...	...
	22.—Tailors	Simpi (Darzi)	Hindu	6,493	1,392	3,964	1,137	1,674	1,330	339	5	609	38	557	14	2,647	15	2,443	189	1,563	9	625	929
		Do.	Musalman	6	1	4	1	1	1	...	...	...	...	...	...	4	...	4	...	1	...	...	1
		Do.	Jain	1,332	300	782	250	373	288	84	1	138	8	125	5	500	3	450	47	321	1	123	197
	23.—Weavers, Calenderers, and Dyers.	Koshti	Hindu	6,973	1,575	4,122	1,276	1,705	1,422	272	11	609	124	472	13	2,780	22	2,559	199	1,879	7	819	1,053
		Do.	Jain	140	29	83	28	33	28	5	...	10	...	10	...	56	1	52	3	41	...	16	25
	24.—Washermen	Warthi (Parit)	Hindu	11,326	2,745	6,707	1,874	3,219	2,581	628	10	1,134	129	980	25	4,493	25	4,107	361	2,480	10	992	1,478
		Dhobi	Musalman	5	...	4	1	1	...	1	...	2	...	2	...	...	...	...	...	2	...	1	1
	26.—Shepherds and Wool weavers.	Dhangar	Hindu	39,438	9,022	24,511	5,905	11,749	8,649	3,038	62	4,006	252	3,640	114	15,519	100	14,321	1,098	8,164	21	3,512	4,631
	27.—Oil pressers	Teli	Do.	39,955	8,023	25,432	6,500	10,819	7,732	3,022	65	3,935	198	3,647	90	16,016	72	14,847	1,097	9,185	21	3,916	5,248
		Do.	Musalman	4	2	2	...	2	2	...	...	...	...	...	...	2	...	2	...	...	...	...	...
		Do.	Sikh	...	...	...	...	...	...	...	...	...	...	...	...	...	...	...	...	...	...	...	...
		Do.	Animistic	2	...	2	...	...	...	...	...	...	...	...	...	1	...	1	...	1	...	1	...
	328.—Potters	Kumbhár	Hindu	9,907	2,489	5,877	1,541	2,746	2,273	462	11	971	171	772	28	4,006	34	3,699	273	2,184	11	944	1,329
	5.—Fishermen, boatmen, Palki bearers and cooks, etc.	Bhoi (Windhewár)	Do.	13,162	4,782	6,492	1,888	4,336	4,030	298	8	1,286	638	637	11	4,985	102	4,477	406	2,555	12	1,080	1,463
		Koli	Do.	16,131	4,331	9,350	2,450	4,852	4,052	783	17	1,565	209	1,332	24	6,276	57	5,758	461	3,438	13	1,477	1,948
	36.—Distillers and Toddydrawers	Kalál	Do.	7,645	2,015	4,231	1,399	2,027	1,781	239	7	755	201	529	25	3,108	31	2,785	292	1,755	2	678	1,075
		Do.	Jain	88	19	49	20	25	19	6	...	6	...	6	...	33	...	32	1	24	...	5	19
		Do.	Musalman	6	1	4	1	1	1	...	...	2	...	2	...	2	...	2	...	1	...	...	1
		Do.	Animistic	1	1	...	...	1	1	...	...	...	...	...	...	...	...	...	...	...	...	...	...

TABLE E.—Castes by Civil Condition and Age.

TOTAL STRENGTH. — MALES.

Class	Group	Caste	Religion	All ages: Total Males	All ages: Single	All ages: Married	All ages: Widowed	0–9: Total	0–9: Single	0–9: Married	0–9: Widowed	10–14: Total	10–14: Single	10–14: Married	10–14: Widowed	15–39: Total	15–39: Single	15–39: Married	15–39: Widowed	40 and over: Total	40 and over: Single	40 and over: Married	40 and over: Widowed
1	2	3	4	5	6	7	8	9	10	11	12	13	14	15	16	17	18	19	20	21	22	23	24
D.—ARTISAN AND VILLAGE MENIAL.	38.—LEATHER WORKERS.	CHÁMBHÁR (MOCHI).	Hindu	15,150	5,524	8,916	710	4,210	4,004	196	10	1,706	1,008	673	25	5,851	486	5,179	186	3,383	26	2,868	489
	38 (a).—VILLAGE WATCHMEN, &c.	MAHÁR (DHER AND KOTWÁL).	Do.	177,675	74,368	97,433	5,874	56,097	54,296	1,765	36	20,732	13,962	6,657	113	63,842	5,737	56,582	1,523	37,004	373	32,429	4,202
		Do.	Animistic	6	4	2	...	2	2	...	...	...	...	...	...	1	1	...	...	3	1	2	...
	39.—SCAVENGERS	MÁNG	Hindu	25,974	11,123	13,979	872	8,456	8,160	279	17	2,997	2,011	961	25	9,433	893	8,275	265	5,088	59	4,464	565
		Do.	Animistic	...	...	...	...	...	...	...	...	...	...	...	...	...	...	...	...	...	...	...	...
F.—RACES AND NATIONALITIES.	48.—NON-INDIAN ASIATIC RACES.	PATHÁN	Musalman	25,190	12,674	11,259	1,257	6,352	6,284	66	2	2,743	2,636	98	9	9,865	3,461	6,076	328	6,230	293	5,019	918
		SHEKH	Do.	64,297	31,905	29,112	3,280	16,243	16,110	120	13	7,134	6,789	336	9	25,543	8,383	16,382	778	15,377	623	12,274	2,480
			TOTAL	1,317,666	496,215	745,770	75,681	846,189	333,049	12,663	477	146,063	94,211	50,363	1,489	506,397	62,084	422,621	21,692	319,017	6,871	260,123	52,023

TOTAL STRENGTH. — FEMALES.

Class	Group	Caste	Religion	All ages: Total Females	All ages: Single	All ages: Married	All ages: Widowed	0–9: Total	0–9: Single	0–9: Married	0–9: Widowed	10–14: Total	10–14: Single	10–14: Married	10–14: Widowed	15–39: Total	15–39: Single	15–39: Married	15–39: Widowed	40 and over: Total	40 and over: Single	40 and over: Married	40 and over: Widowed
				25	26	27	28	29	30	31	32	33	34	35	36	37	38	39	40	41	42	43	44
D.—ARTISAN AND VILLAGE MENIAL.	38.—LEATHER WORKERS.	CHÁMBHÁR (MOCHI).	Hindu	14,024	3,572	8,643	1,809	4,223	3,334	874	15	1,426	182	1,210	34	5,650	49	5,261	340	2,725	7	1,298	1,420
	38(a).—VILLAGE WATCHMEN, ETC.	MAHÁR (DHER AND KOTWÁL).	Do.	177,322	55,275	99,575	22,472	59,534	50,396	8,968	170	17,513	3,862	13,321	330	67,560	863	62,170	4,527	32,715	154	15,116	17,445
		Do.	Animistic	2	1	1	...	...	...	...	...	...	...	...	...	1	...	1	...	1	1	...	...
	39.—SCAVENGERS	MÁNG	Hindu	26,176	8,313	14,593	3,270	8,928	7,619	1,273	36	2,540	533	1,963	44	10,062	136	9,239	687	4,646	25	2,118	2,503
		Do.	Animistic	1	...	1	...	...	...	...	...	...	...	...	...	1	...	1	...	...	...	...	...
F.—RACES AND NATIONALITIES.	48.—NON-INDIAN ASIATIC RACES.	PATHÁN	Musalman	23,203	8,207	10,709	4,287	6,503	6,317	175	11	2,159	1,461	682	16	8,976	354	7,790	832	5,565	75	2,062	3,428
		SHEKH	Do.	59,935	21,837	27,207	10,891	17,095	16,638	425	32	5,662	3,846	1,738	28	23,346	1,114	20,025	2,207	13,832	239	4,969	8,624
			TOTAL	1,243,311	320,655	725,647	197,009	362,807	288,839	72,546	1,422	120,116	23,857	93,667	2,592	487,681	6,603	442,664	38,414	272,707	1,336	116,770	154,581